The Fall of Napoleon

Crushing defeats in Russia (1812) and Germany (1813) caused the collapse of Napoleon's empire and brought his enemies to the Rhine River at the close of 1813. With a depleted and exhausted army, Napoleon attempted to direct the defense of his frontier from the Alps to the North Sea while he mobilized France. From Paris, the new Prometheus watched helplessly as his marshals conducted a headlong retreat from the Rhine to the Marne in less than one month. The breakdown of the French command structure and overwhelming Allied superiority placed the French marshals charged with defending the Rhine in an impossible situation. Although Napoleon needed them to use their scant forces to make a desperate stand on the Rhine and away from the administrative apparatus that fed his war machine, the marshals believed they had to trade land for time – the exact opposite of what Napoleon needed to maintain his crown.

Dr. Michael V. Leggiere is an associate professor of history at Louisiana State University in Shreveport. He received his Ph.D. from Florida State University in April 1997 after studying at the Institute of the French Revolution and Napoleon under the direction of D. D. Howard. He is also an adjunct professor of strategy and policy for the United States Naval War College's distance education program, where he teaches strategy and policy during the French Revolutionary and Napoleonic eras. His book, *Napoleon and Berlin: The Franco-Prussian War in North Germany, 1813* (2002), won the Société Napoléonienne Internationale's 2002 Literary Award. Dr. Leggiere has published numerous essays on various aspects of Napoleonic history, Prussian military history, and the German Wars of Liberation. His article, "From Berlin to Leipzig: Napoleon's Gamble in North Germany, 1813," which appeared in the January 2003 volume of the *Journal of Military History*, won the Society for Military History's 2004 Moncado Prize for Excellence in the Writing of Military History. In 2005, he received la Société Napoléonienne Internationale Legion of Merit Award for Outstanding Contributions to Napoleonic Studies.

CAMBRIDGE MILITARY HISTORIES

Edited by

HEW STRACHAN   Chichele Professor of the History of War, University of
Oxford and Fellow of All Souls College, Oxford

GEOFFREY WAWRO   Major General Olinto Mark Barsanti Professor of
Military History and Director, Center for the Study of Military History,
University of North Texas

The aim of this new series is to publish outstanding works of research on warfare throughout the ages and throughout the world. Books in the series will
take a broad approach to military history, examining war in all its military,
strategic, political, and economic aspects. The series is intended to complement
Studies in the Social and Cultural History of Modern Warfare by focusing on
the "hard" military history of armies, tactics, strategy, and warfare. Books in
the series will consist mainly of single-author works – works that are academ-
ically vigorous and groundbreaking – that will be accessible to both academics
and the interested general reader.

TITLES IN THE SERIES INCLUDE:

E. Bruce Reynolds   *Thailand's Secret War: OSS, SOE, and the Free Thai
Underground During World War II*
Robert T. Foley   *German Strategy and the Path to Verdun: Erich von
Falkenhayn and the Development of Attrition, 1870–1916*
Elizabeth Greenhalgh   *Victory through Coalition: Britain and France
during the First World War*

The Fall of Napoleon

Volume 1

The Allied Invasion of France, 1813–1814

MICHAEL V. LEGGIERE

Louisiana State University in Shreveport

CAMBRIDGE
UNIVERSITY PRESS

CAMBRIDGE UNIVERSITY PRESS
Cambridge, New York, Melbourne, Madrid, Cape Town, Singapore, São Paulo, Delhi

Cambridge University Press
32 Avenue of the Americas, New York, NY 10013-2473, USA

www.cambridge.org
Information on this title: www.cambridge.org/9780521875424

First published 2007

Printed in the United States of America

A catalog record for this publication is available from the British Library.

Library of Congress Cataloging in Publication Data
Leggiere, Michael V., 1969–
The Fall of Napoleon / Michael V. Leggiere.
p.   cm. – (Cambridge military histories)
Includes bibliographical references and index.
ISBN   978-0-521-87542-4 (hardback)
1. France – History – Invasion of 1814.   2. Napoleonic Wars, 1800–1815 – Campaigns –
France.   3. Napoleon I, Emperor of the French, 1769–1821 – Military leadership.
I. Title.   II. Series.
DC238.L44   2007
940.2′742 – dc22   2007003607

ISBN   978-0-521-87542-4 hardback

For Michele, loving wife and devoted friend

Contents

Illustrations

FIGURES

MAPS

Preface

In October 1813, Emperor Napoleon I entrenched himself in the Saxon city of Leipzig and prepared for a showdown with his enemies for control of Germany. Four Allied armies eventually surrounded the French during the epic Battle of Nations. Napoleon held Leipzig for four days until exhausting his ammunition supply. He then exploited a gap in the Allied lines to lead 70,000 of his soldiers out of the beleaguered city. In the weeks that followed, the Allied armies failed to catch the French army as it retreated to the Rhine River. After Napoleon escaped across the Rhine in early November, the Allies held a great council of war at Frankfurt-am-Main. These deliberations ended with the decision to launch a comprehensive invasion of France from the North Sea to Switzerland.

In late November, 40,000 Prussian, British, and Russian troops invaded Holland. One month later, 200,000 Allied soldiers crossed the upper Rhine to invade Alsace, Switzerland, and Franche-Comté. Shortly after, on New Year's Day, an additional 75,000 men crossed the middle Rhine and drove through Lorraine toward the fortress of Metz. To stop the Allied masses, Napoleon spread approximately 56,000 tired troops in a thin cordon along the length of the Rhine River. Napoleon himself remained at Paris during the Allied invasion to direct a mobilization that he expected would produce a new army of almost 400,000 men. The emperor fully expected that the skeletons of his shattered corps would stop the Allies at the Rhine. After this proved impossible, he implored his marshals to hold the Allies in Alsace, Lorraine, and Holland. However, by the end of January, Holland and Belgium had fallen, and two Allied armies stood at the Marne and Aube Rivers ready to march on Paris. This circumstance forced Bonaparte to leave his capital and finally assume personal command of the army.

This work analyzes the invasion of France from both the French and Allied perspectives. In particular, the performance of the four French marshals who received the overwhelming task of guarding the "sacred territory" is scrutinized. Gone were the marshals who had helped Bonaparte build the Grand Empire almost a decade earlier. Jean Lannes was dead, a somewhat disgraced André Masséna was in retirement, Louis-Nicholas Davout was shot in Hamburg, and Joachim Murat was on the verge of defecting to the Allies to keep his Neapolitan crown. In their absence, the marshals who held commands on the eastern front had to perform under extremely trying circumstances. Ultimate blame for their failures falls squarely on Napoleon for violating some of the fundamental principles of war that he himself had made famous. Stung by his subordinates' abysmal record of independent command during the 1813 German campaign, Napoleon refused to appoint a commander in chief to coordinate operations along the eastern front, despite repeated pleas from the marshals themselves. Instead, he issued desperate calls from Paris for his marshals to coordinate their operations. The emperor should have learned the lesson provided by the Peninsular War, in which his subordinates repeatedly failed to support one another. Not only did the French marshals fail to cooperate, they resorted to blaming one another for a retreat that took them from the Rhine to the Marne in less than one month.

Although the lack of unity of command considerably undermined French operations on the eastern front, Napoleon's inability to provide his subordinates with a clear objective led to the loss of Holland, Belgium, Alsace, Lorraine, and Franche-Comté. The marshals thought they had to preserve their troops for the emperor's eventual use. Fed by the propaganda machine in Paris, they believed Napoleon soon would field a massive new army. His genius again would direct them and provide them with an escape from what appeared to be the curse of independent command. Thus, it appeared urgent to save every man possible, retreat to the interior, and unite with the emperor. What the marshals did not realize and what Napoleon failed to convey was that every administrative district that fell to the Allies deprived the emperor of the precious manpower and revenue needed to complete this very mobilization – not to mention the damage Allied occupation caused imperial prestige. Soldiers whose homes fell behind Allied lines thought only of deserting rather than marching to the French interior in freezing temperatures with empty bellies.

On the other side of the Rhine, the Allies assembled the most powerful coalition history would see until the world wars of the twentieth century. For the first time during the French Revolutionary and Napoleonic wars, Great Britain, Austria, Russia, and Prussia marshaled their resources for an epic showdown against Bonaparte. The victory at Leipzig ended French hegemony by shattering Napoleon's control of central Europe. Paradoxically, this victory did more to undermine the unity of the coalition than to cement Allied resolve. Austria and Russia emerged as rivals over the issue of invading France and the fate of the French crown. Between these two behemoths stood Prussia, whose king and chancellor secretly supported Austria but feared being cast adrift by their benefactor, the Russian tsar. Great Britain had its own unique objectives, which its government feared would be ignored by the continental powers. Consequently, two factions emerged in the Allied camp: one, led by Tsar Alexander I, wanted to invade France, the other, which was dominated by the great Austrian statesman Klemens Wenzel von Metternich, called for a negotiated peace with Bonaparte. The result was hardly a coalition of the willing. The decision was made to invade France, yet the statesmen and generals who belonged to the peace party worked diligently and successfully to direct the war according to their politics.

This work examines the invasion of France from the perspective of a coalition undertaking, in which politics influenced strategy and military operations affected diplomacy. It is also dedicated to the old military history. It is about generals – their thoughts, plans, hopes, and despair. It tells the story of commanders and their operations during one of the most intense periods of European history: the Allied invasion of France in the twilight of the Napoleonic epoch. Although the soldier's perspective certainly has a place in history, this work focuses on the command of armies at the strategic and operational levels. The principal purpose of this work is to fill a surprising gap in the literature concerning the final year of Napoleon's reign. Numerous volumes tell the story of French disasters in Spain and Portugal. Napoleon's catastrophic 1812 campaign in Russia, where as many as 500,000 soldiers may have perished, likewise is told in monumental detail. Yet only a handful of scholarly studies are devoted to the details of the invasion of greater France at the end of 1813 and beginning of 1814.

Between 1814 and 1914, German, French, Austrian, and Russian historians, both civilian and military, published studies that examine various aspects of the invasion of France from a nationalist perspective. The vast majority of works concerning the 1814 campaign begin with the emperor leaving Paris on 25 January to take command of his army, thus ignoring the first critical month of the Allied invasion, during which the French marshals abandoned all of "New France." Based on Austrian, German, French, Russian, and private archival documents, this book provides the first modern comprehensive study of the Allied invasion of France. No previous study presents such an inclusive examination of the military operations that took place from Holland to Switzerland. Against this backdrop, this book expands Gordon Craig's noteworthy treatise on the problems of coalition warfare. Moreover, it will serve as the military supplement to the great works on the diplomacy of the period by Wilhelm Oncken, August Fournier, Henry Kissinger, Harold Nicholson, and Paul Schroeder.

I wrote this book with a Michelin motoring atlas by my side. Although this resource greatly enhanced my understanding of the campaign, I keenly felt the need to provide the reader with excellent maps. With a few exceptions, every population center mentioned in the book can be found on the maps. I included roads where space permitted. As much as possible I used native, modern spellings of villages, towns, smaller cities, and geographic features. Larger cities, capitals, and rivers such as Antwerp, Geneva, the Rhine, and the Moselle are anglicized; the spelling of rivers is standardized from country to country. Names of persons are likewise native, except for monarchs, whose names are anglicized. To avoid confusion, all generals are referred to simply as "general."

This six-year odyssey could not have been completed without the generous assistance of several people and institutions. First and foremost I wish to express my sincerest gratitude to Dennis Showalter, whose vision and insight encouraged me to write the complete history of the Allied invasion of France. Next I must express my heartfelt appreciation to my editor, Frank Smith, whose patience and persistent support sustained me during this long project. Geoff Wawro and the superb manuscript reviewers provided valuable insight and constructive criticism; I owe much to their suggestions and corrections. I also especially wish to thank Maggie Meitzler, Elizabeth Budd, Simina Calin, and the countless others involved in the production of this work.

Regarding the many friends whose support sustained me over the years: Rick Schneid brought clarity to my first drafts and provided valuable assistance in sorting through the diplomatic history of the period. I also wish to thank my colleagues from graduate school, Llewellyn Cook and John Weinzierl, for generously sharing their archival research and for providing much moral support. Jack Gill's enthusiasm for the Napoleonic period and ability to hunt down biographical information seemingly within hours saved me from despair on many occasions. Alexander Mikaberidze likewise provided crucial information on the Russian officer corps. I also want to thank Michael Pavkovic, Lee Eysturlid, Harold Blanton, Sam Mustafa, Owen Connelly, Charles White, and Peter Hofschröer for their ceaseless assistance, support, and advice over the years. Last but by no means least, a special word of sincere appreciation for my mentor, Donald D. Howard, for years of guidance, inspiration, and friendship.

I am indebted to several friends and colleagues at the Louisiana State University in Shreveport. My former chairman and fellow Napoleonic historian, Milton Finley, provided years of support and advice. Jason Mackowiak offered crucial technical support to prepare the maps. Megan Conway, Cecilia Smith, and Wolfgang Hinck contributed invaluable assistance translating French and German colloquialisms and phrases. The staff of the Noel Library diligently obtained books for me on the shortest notice. John Vassar and Cheryl White provided great moral support. Finally, I want to acknowledge Merrell Knighten, former dean of the College of Liberal Arts, whose financial support made possible three research trips to Europe.

Several other friends and kind strangers on both sides of "the pond" facilitated research in Paris, Berlin, and Vienna. Special thanks to Nathalie Genet-Rouffiac and the staff of the Service historique de l'armée de terre at Vincennes for patiently handling my requests to exceed the daily limit of cartons. I wish to thank Sylvain Dray for navigating the bureaucracy at the Archives Nationales in Paris to obtain documents for me. I express my gratitude to the helpful staff of Germany's Geheimes Staatsarchiv Preußischer Kulturbesitz zu Berlin for producing repositorium from the former German General Staff archive previously thought to have been lost during the Second World War. The extremely friendly director of the Bayerisches Hauptstaatsarchiv's Kriegsarchiv, Auchin Fuchs, provided documents with amazing speed. I have nothing but wonderful memories of conducting research at the Österreichisches Staatsarchiv and wish to thank the director of the Kriegsarchiv, Christoph Tepperberg, and his highly efficient staff for making my time in Vienna well spent.

I have to thank the kind of friend that every European historian should have: Beatrice Watt. Not only did Beatrice help me wade through the more difficult French translations, she also mobilized her extended family to assist me in Europe. Her extremely kind aunt and uncle became my surrogate family in Austria: every day her uncle, Siguy Baumgartner, drove me to and from Klosterneuburg to downtown Vienna. In the evenings, his wife, Lili, prepared a wonderful dinner. As a rule the wine flowed, sacking my plans to catch up on some reading during the crisp December nights in the suburbs of Vienna. I am deeply indebted to the Baumgartners: their kindness to a complete stranger and their willingness to inconvenience themselves and open their home to me represents all that is good in this world. Moving from Vienna to Paris, I had the good fortune of being hosted by Beatrice's father, Jacques Durantet, and his companion, Florence. Once again, these kind folks did the utmost to assist me as well as to show me the side of Paris that few Americans ever see. In addition, I must thank the Fifth Count Bülow von Dennewitz, Joachim-Albrecht, as well as his son, Hasso. Count Bülow kindly gave me two privately printed volumes of his ancestor's unpublished correspondence. For several years, both he and Hasso have produced a constant stream of documents and information that have greatly broadened my knowledge of the Prussian army. Lastly, I thank Peter Harrington of the Anne S. K. Brown Military Collection at Brown University for locating the artwork that accompanies the text.

I dedicate this volume to my wife of eight years and companion of thirteen, who patiently endured my absence during numerous research trips to Europe, who coped with endless days of my short temper due to sleep deprivation, and who for years talked to the back of my head because I was facing the computer. While I was writing this book she experienced two pregnancies and gave birth to our beautiful children, Jordyn and Nicholas. Finally, I thank my parents, Rosalie and Tom, who have always been a source of solid support.

The New Charlemagne

Starting in 1797 with his first conquest of a great power, Austria, Napoleon Bonaparte built an empire greater than those of Caesar, Charlemagne, and Hitler. When he crowned himself emperor of the French in 1804, he was master of a France that dominated Italy, Switzerland, the left bank of the Rhine, and the Low Countries. Whether conquered by him or by the forces that Revolutionary France unleashed on Europe while Bonaparte was a mere junior officer, Napoleon presented himself to the French people as the guarantor of the gains of the Revolution, be it territory or equality before the law. By the beginning of 1806, he had defeated the European powers in no less than three coalition wars. His aggrandizement, partly the cause of these wars and partly the result of them, brought Napoleon new laurels. He was king of Italy, protector of the Confederation of the Rhine, and mediator of the Swiss. Ancient and historic cities such as Rome, Geneva, Brussels, Antwerp, and Amsterdam belonged to France proper, and Naples, Milan, Venice, Mainz, Frankfurt, and Hamburg were among those of the Grand Empire. Following another victorious war in 1806–7, Napoleon distributed the crowns of Europe to his siblings. Joseph became the king of Spain, Caroline the queen of Naples, Louis the king of Holland, and Jerome the king of Westphalia. By 1808, Napoleon was master of Europe.

Of his rivals, Bonaparte defeated Austria in 1797, 1801, and 1805 – worse was yet to come for Vienna in 1809 after a fourth war with France ended in failure. Prussia challenged the French emperor only once, lost, and was almost erased from the map of Europe. After feeling the bite of three failed wars against France, Russia also made peace with the self-proclaimed child of the Revolution. In July 1807, Napoleon met with Tsar Alexander I to negotiate an end to the War of the Fourth Coalition. During the many talks that produced the monumental Treaty of Tilsit, the two monarchs established a general entente, which to the rest of Europe appeared to be an unholy alliance.

Essentially, the two emperors agreed to divide Europe between Russia and France, and each pledged to help the other pursue foreign policy objectives. For Napoleon, this meant Russian assistance in his perpetual struggle with Great Britain.

Napoleon inherited an Anglo–French rivalry that had locked the two countries at war since early 1793. After a short truce in 1802, London continued its policy of financing Bonaparte's enemies to wage war against him. Seemingly, the British wanted to restore the balance of power in Europe by forcing France to surrender conquests such as the Low Countries. Yet London wanted a balance of power that left Great Britain master of the seas and with a clear monopoly on global trade. By destroying Bonaparte's fleet in October 1805, the British slammed the door on Napoleon's dreams of ever defeating the Royal Navy and invading Great Britain. Thus, Napoleon had to devise another strategy to defeat his great foe. By all accounts a genius, the French emperor understood the essence of his problem. He realized that as long as the British continued to buy allies on the Continent, he would be forced to fight enemy coalitions every few years. Although he could not defeat the British militarily, he planned to crush them financially. Waging economic warfare to destroy the British economy became his strategy in late 1806. If he could wreck British finances, London would be denied the funds to pay the Continental powers to wage war against France. Ideally, the British merchants would be so hurt they would demand a change from a pro-war, anti-French cabinet to a pro-peace government that might be willing to cut cards with Bonaparte. He thus formulated the Continental System – a mammoth plan and undertaking. Accordingly, all European ports would be closed to British goods in an economic boycott. Any British goods found on the Continent would be seized as contraband. To make this ambitious plan work, Napoleon needed tight control of Europe's ports. Pursuit of this objective led him down the path of committing his two greatest mistakes: the Peninsular War in Iberia and the invasion of Russia.

By 1808, only Portugal, a staunch British satellite, continued to trade with Great Britain. Despite numerous French threats, Portuguese ports remained open to British shipping. Napoleon responded by invading Portugal. After securing Spain's agreement to assist the French with the conquest of Portugal in return for a slice of the Atlantic state, Napoleon unleashed his legions. Early in the war, his generals reported that the Spaniards were not complying with their treaty obligations. No friend of the Bourbon dynasty, a branch of which still ruled Spain, Napoleon arranged for the arrest and forced abdication of Spain's royal family. In the aftermath of what amounted to abduction and highway robbery, Napoleon awarded the Spanish crown to his older brother, Joseph. The Spanish reacted violently not so much to the usurpation of their throne but to fears the French would place restrictions on the Catholic Church of Spain. Rioting that French troops failed to quell erupted in Madrid. Soon a guerilla war spread throughout the country. Meanwhile, the French army reached Portugal, marching into Lisbon just as the Portuguese royal family sailed away with the state's treasury.

Taken together, the invasion of Portugal and the suppression of Spain are known as the Peninsular War. A broad range of insurmountable problems confronted Napoleon during this bloody conflict, which consumed the flower of his Grande Armée between the years 1808 and 1814. First and foremost, the emperor could not conduct the war personally. Concern over central Europe kept Bonaparte at Paris for most of the first year of the war, but French reverses eventually forced him to venture across the Pyrenees. Second, he never fully grasped the brutal nature of the guerilla war in Spain, which he referred to as his "bleeding ulcer." Third, the British ultimately changed policy and committed their small but highly trained army to the Continent. Supported by the Royal Navy, British land forces established a foothold in Portugal, united with the Portuguese army, and eventually drove out the French. Under the command of Arthur Wellesley, the duke of Wellington, the Anglo–Portuguese army crossed the Spanish frontier to add to the French military's deplorable situation. Finally, French defeats in Spain and Portugal brought hope to the conquered peoples of central Europe. Napoleon's setbacks in Iberia eroded the belief of French invulnerability. Russia and Prussia remained neutral, but Austria made another attempt to restore its shattered power in the 1809 War of the Fifth Coalition. Although another French victory, the conflict proved Napoleon could not turn his back on the rest of Europe to wage war in Spain – his marshals and generals would have to get the job done.

As the war raged in Iberia, Franco–Russian relations steadily deteriorated. Before departing for Spain in the fall of 1808, Napoleon hosted the Erfurt Conference from 27 September to 14 October. He hoped to bolster the 1807 agreements made with his ally, Alexander, and gain the tsar's assurance that the Russian court would do everything in its power to maintain the status quo in central Europe. Alexander insincerely agreed. The Russians neither participated in the War of the Fifth Coalition as France's ally nor did they attempt to stop the Austrians through diplomacy. A few strong words to the Prussian court sufficed to keep Berlin from intervening, but that was the extent of Russia's involvement.

Other issues widened the rift between the emperors of the West and East. The Russian imperial family snubbed Napoleon when he came calling for a Romanov princess to be his second wife. Not forgetting the affront, he simply moved on to the Habsburgs, who gratefully offered Marie Louis, the daughter of Kaiser Francis I. Because of the Austrian marriage, it appeared Vienna would replace St. Petersburg in Bonaparte's power-sharing structure. Nagging complaints by the tsar over the mistreatment of relatives whom Napoleon had driven from the thrones of minor German states as well as insincere efforts on the part of the French to assist Russia in its perpetual war with the Ottoman

Empire kept the embers of Franco–Russian relations smoldering. The final issue came when Alexander announced that he would pull Russia out of the Continental System, which had become the bane of Europe. Although the economic warfare hurt the British, it ruined the economies of Napoleon's satellites and allies. Domestic unrest over its financial hardships prompted Alexander to open Russia's ports to British trade. Despite Napoleon's warning that this would constitute an act of war, the Russian tsar followed through with his plan. In 1811, both Napoleon and Alexander prepared for war.

On 24 June 1812, Napoleon invaded Russia with his multinational Grande Armée – almost 600,000 strong with contingents from every continental European state west of the Russian frontier, including Austria and Prussia. Bonaparte personally led the main force toward Moscow. One week after the badly mauled Russian army limped away from the fields of Borodino, French forces entered the Russian capital. Napoleon attempted to negotiate a peace, but Alexander ignored him. Faced with the onset of winter, Napoleon ordered the fateful retreat to begin on 19 October. His main army finally staggered toward the Prussian frontier with barely 7,000 men under arms; over two-thirds of the Grande Armée had perished in six months. The emperor left the army on 5 December and raced back to Paris to rebuild his decimated forces and rehabilitate his shattered prestige.

Tsar Alexander was committed to carrying the war into central Europe and building a Russian-dominated coalition to liberate Europe, reestablish the balance of power, and expand his own empire.[1] Ever since Napoleon created the Grand Duchy of Warsaw in 1807, the tsar had eyed the rump Polish state with covetous intentions. He secretly desired to annex the majority of Poland by way of a personal union with Russia. Napoleon's disaster provided the opportunity to pursue this dream. He acknowledged the tremendous ramifications these plans would have on Europe, especially because the other eastern powers would undoubtedly object and Napoleon would seek revenge. "Making public my intentions on Poland will certainly drive Austria and Prussia into the arms of France," he noted on 13 January 1813.[2] Consequently, Alexander needed to weaken Napoleon's influence as much as possible to eliminate French resistance to a Romanov Poland. His designs required Russia to wage war to reduce French power. Because of the losses his own army suffered, he needed allies: Prussia seemed the logical choice.

Although indecision seized the Prussian government, the army acted. General Hans David Ludwig von Yorck, the commander of the Prussian contingent of the Grande Armée, negotiated the Convention of Tauroggen on 30 December 1812 with the Russians. By doing so, Yorck neutralized his corps and personally took the first step in breaking Prussia's alliance with France. Moreover, the East Prussian frontier now lay open to the advancing Russian army. According to all serious accounts, Yorck proceeded without Berlin's authorization, and King Frederick William III was quick to renounce his general's rebellious act. Regardless of the royal repudiation, forces the Hohenzollern monarch could not control were at work. An East Prussian provincial assembly convened, declared war on France, and issued a call for recruits. Caught between France and Russia, Prussian State Chancellor Karl von Hardenberg engaged in damage control. Initially he hoped to negotiate with Napoleon to restore Prussia's independence, but Tauroggen and the events in East Prussia tied his hands. Not averse to war with Napoleon, Hardenberg first sought to place Prussia in the best possible situation before taking that fateful step. Uncertain of the tsar's intentions and apprehensive over the price the Russians would demand to liberate Prussia, Hardenberg feared Prussia would become a Russian satellite, merely exchanging one foreign overlord for another. As a result, he requested Austria join Prussia in an armed neutrality to mediate between France and Russia. Should the Austrians refuse, the Prussians wanted Austria's formal support of a Russo–Prussian alliance in a desperate attempt to somehow commit Vienna to Berlin. However, Austrian Foreign Minister Clemens von Metternich recognized that an Austro–Prussian bloc would frustrate his own plans to arbitrate between Napoleon and Alexander. Metternich rejected an Austro–Prussian partnership and merely encouraged a Russo–Prussian alliance without offering Austria's formal support. After this failure, Hardenberg turned to the Russians, hoping for fair alliance terms.[3]

Although the tsar needed a Continental ally, he held the advantage when direct negotiations opened with the Prussians. From the start, the Russians made it very clear that they would be the senior partner in any Russo–Prussian alliance. After Alexander divulged his intentions regarding Poland, the fate of Prussia's Polish provinces became a point of contention. Concessions from both sides finally cleared the way for the signing of the Treaty of Kalisch on 28 February 1813. According to the terms, Alexander vowed to restore Prussia's pre-1806 material strength, and Frederick William acknowledged he would cede much of his Polish territory to Russia in return for compensation in Germany. The British did their part to bolster the new alliance by promptly dispatching material aid.

Frederick William issued a formal declaration of war against France on 16 March 1813. Three days later, on 19 March 1813, the Russians and Prussians signed the Treaty of Breslau in which Alexander affirmed his agreement to restore Prussia to its pre-1806 status and renounced his plans to annex East Prussia as stated in the 1812 Russo–Swedish Convention of Abo. He also relinquished his dream of reuniting all of Poland under the Russian monarchy. As for now, the tsar promised Frederick William enough Polish territory to connect East Prussia with Silesia. Prussia would be compensated in Germany for the loss of other Polish territory: Saxony became the target.

As for the Austrians, Prince Karl Philip zu Schwarzenberg, the commander of the Austrian Auxiliary Corps attached to the Grande Armée during the Russian campaign, signed an agreement with the Russians on 30 January 1813. Similar to the Russo–Prussian Convention of Tauroggen, the pact neutralized Schwarzenberg's corps and allowed it to withdraw through the Grand Duchy of Warsaw to the Austrian province of Galicia. Schwarzenberg had opened negotiations with the Russians on 20 December, but, unlike the Prussians, Metternich directed the entire affair from Vienna. Both he and Schwarzenberg properly notified the French High Command that Austria was withdrawing from the war.[4] Although bitter, the French could do nothing, and the Austro–Russian agreement, although long in coming, was no surprise. For the moment, Austria stood as an armed neutral, endeavoring to mediate between Napoleon and Alexander. Metternich's complex national security objectives meant Austria remained a wildcard; neither side could count on Vienna's support. He initially wanted to keep war far from Austria's frontiers until the army completed an extensive rearmament. Austria's treaty with France, solidified by the marriage of the emperor's daughter to Napoleon, also influenced decision making in Vienna. Although not bound to Bonaparte because of the marriage, Metternich felt Austria had to pursue a peaceful resolution before breaking a treaty with France because, according to German historian Thomas Nipperdey, "Austria's whole existence rested on the 'sanctity' of treaties." Thus, Metternich carefully extricated the Austrian Auxiliary Corps from its treaty obligations with France. In addition, the popular undertones of the Prussian mobilization and nationalist agitation in Germany alarmed the foreign minister. As far as he was concerned, the war would not be a "people's war, not a revolutionary nationalist war of patriots and emancipators, and certainly not a crusade. It would be a war of states to restore the balance of power in Europe...a war fought by politicians and diplomats with rational and clearly limited goals." Any "revolutionary nationalist sentiments" had to be harnessed and directed to serve the purposes of a cabinet war. "Only this," concludes Nipperdey, "would serve the security and power interests of the dynastic, artificial state of Austria." Agreement over war aims and the future European order were more important to Metternich than throwing the resources of Austria behind either belligerent to achieve victory.[5]

Because of the dynastic ties between France and Austria, the French emperor hoped Vienna would remain neutral or even ally with him. A decisive French victory over the Russians and Prussians certainly would impress Kaiser Francis, whose multinational state had been ravished by Napoleon's treaties on four previous occasions. As for the Russians, their councils of war had been divided for some time. Although Alexander fashioned himself the liberator of Europe, many Russian commanders opposed carrying the war into central Europe and expressed concerns over their tenuous supply lines. Crushing the Russian army on the battlefield amid so much disagreement would have put them to flight, similar to the aftermath of Napoleon's great victory over them at Austerlitz in 1805. Little question surrounded Prussia's fate: Frederick William would lose his throne and perhaps see Prussia partitioned in the event of another disastrous war against Bonaparte.

To achieve this victory, Napoleon rapidly rebuilt his army. Of the 600,000 men and 1,300 guns of the Grande Armée of 1812, only 93,000 men and 250 pieces returned from Russia. With remarkable speed, Bonaparte fielded the 140,000-man Army of the Main. Together with the Army of the Elbe, French forces amounted to 202,000 combatants by the end of April 1813. Napoleon began his counteroffensive on 30 April by leading 120,000 men across the Saale River to confront the Allied army in Saxony, where he achieved victories on 2 May at Lützen and 22 May at Bautzen.

Austria finally acted in early June. Instead of entering the war, Vienna proposed an armistice, which the belligerents signed at Pläswitz on 4 June. Subsequent negotiations extended the cease-fire to 10 August with a further six-day suspension of hostilities. Napoleon hoped the respite would allow him to rebuild his cavalry and rest his exhausted army, whose sick list numbered 90,000 men. He also sought a diplomatic coup by either splitting the allies or convincing Kaiser Francis to support France. The Allies, too, needed time to rest, reorganize, secure more subsidies from London, and court the Austrians.

Diplomatically, the armistice proved disastrous for Napoleon. London used gold to cement a new coalition – the Sixth. British granted subsidies to the Prussians and Russians amounting to £7,000,000. In return, Alexander and Frederick William pledged not to sign a separate peace with Napoleon. To increase Allied combat power, the British also ratified a generous subsidy treaty with Sweden. For 30,000 Swedes to fight on the continent, London granted Sweden a £1,000,000 subsidy, naval support in Sweden's war against Denmark for possession of Norway, and held out the possibility of Stockholm's acquisition of Guadeloupe.

Although willing to negotiate with Napoleon, the Allies demanded harsh terms. On 16 May, Hardenberg and Russian Foreign Minister Karl Robert von Nesselrode had expanded the Kalisch–Breslau war aims to include the dissolution of the Confederation of the Rhine (known as the Rheinbund) and the liberation of Spain, Holland, and Italy. Metternich agreed in principle with these terms yet believed the Allies would have to offer a minimum program to attract Napoleon to the peace table. Moreover, he sought to undermine the cornerstone of the Russo–Prussian alliance – the exchange of Prussian Poland for Saxony – which challenged Austria's national security objectives of limiting Prussia's influence in Germany and restraining Russian expansion in central Europe. Although unaware of the details, the Austrians knew of the tsar's desire for Poland. Metternich feared the Russians planned to make extensive changes to the map of central Europe that would destroy the balance of power and threaten Austrian national security more than Napoleonic France. He suspected Alexander would offer Francis conquered French provinces in return for his Polish provinces: specifically, Alsace for Galicia, which the Austrians would not accept.

Metternich used this opportunity to push his own peace plan, which not only added perplexing questions concerning Italy and Illyria but jeopardized the compromise between Russia, Prussia, and Great Britain. His blueprint called for Russia and France to retire behind their respective frontiers of the Vistula and the Rhine Rivers and remain separated by an independent and strengthened central Europe. Metternich wanted to weaken Napoleon and force him to relinquish control of Italy and Germany. Conversely, the Austrian statesman would demand that Napoleon cede territory to restore Austria and Prussia to their respective 1805–6 material status. In this way, no provinces would remain to compensate either for the cession of their Polish provinces to Russia. In Metternich's opinion, France had to remain strong enough to counter Russian ambition. He did not think the twin goals of destroying the French Empire and preventing Russian hegemony could be achieved. As a result, Austrian politics during the War of the Sixth Coalition sought to reduce French predominance and prevent Russian preponderance. This produced friction between Russia and Austria throughout the war and determined the various factions within the Allied camp. Alexander emerged as the leader of the hawks, and Metternich stood as master of the bloc that favored peace.

Napoleon's victory at Bautzen strengthened the Austrian position. Over the next month, Metternich worked to convince the Allies to offer Bonaparte a program of minimum demands as the basis for opening peace negotiations. On 27 June, the Austrians, Prussians, and Russians signed the Convention of Reichenbach, which authorized the Austrian minister to present a minimum program to Napoleon as the conditions for a peace conference. The Reichenbach Protocol demanded the end of French control over the Grand Duchy of Warsaw and its partition, Prussia's expansion eastward, the return of the Adriatic coast (Illyria) to Austria, and the independence of the Hanseatic cities in North Germany. Should Napoleon refuse these terms, Austria would join the Sixth Coalition with at least 150,000 men and fight for the harsher, maximum program as formulated by Hardenberg and Nesselrode. In July, Metternich presented the Reichenbach Protocol to Napoleon, who refused to make any major concessions for peace after defeating the Russo–Prussian army twice. During the course of a nine-hour discussion, Napoleon confessed to Metternich that he, the self-proclaimed son of the Revolution and a nonlegitimate monarch, simply could not present himself to the French people as a defeated man. With the collapse of their self-serving diplomatic initiative, the Austrians joined the Sixth Coalition in August. For the first time in Napoleon's career, France faced the combined efforts of Europe's other great powers.[6]

Metternich secured the supreme command of all Allied forces for his compatriot, the forty-two-year-old Schwarzenberg. Besides serving as Allied commander in chief, Schwarzenberg also commanded the main Allied army: the 252,200 men of the Army of Bohemia. Jean-Baptiste Bernadotte, the former French marshal and adopted crown prince of Sweden, received command of the 150,000-man Army of North Germany. The Prussian Gebhard Leberecht von Blücher led the 87,000 soldiers of the Army of Silesia.[7] Subsequent negotiations produced the Trachenberg Plan. Accordingly, the three Allied armies would form a wide arc around French forces in Saxony and only engage detached enemy corps; pitched battles with Napoleon were to be avoided. Should the emperor concentrate against any one army, it would retreat while the other two converged on his flanks and communications. The plan sought to overcome Napoleon's advantage of interior lines by splitting and exhausting French forces. Initial agreements called for Schwarzenberg's army to concentrate in the Bohemian mountains and confront French forces in either Saxony or Silesia. Bernadotte's army would assemble south of Berlin, cross the Elbe River at the end of the armistice, and march on Leipzig; Blücher would lead his army from Silesia into Saxony.

With 77,000 soldiers garrisoned in fortresses on the Elbe, Oder, and Vistula Rivers, Napoleon still managed to field an army of 422,000 men to face 530,500 Allied soldiers. He planned to open the campaign with an operation against Berlin. Napoleon assigned the task of capturing the Prussian capital to Marshal Nicolas-Charles Oudinot, who received command of the 70,000-man Army of Berlin. To facilitate Oudinot's operations, the emperor placed 130,000 men under the command of Marshal Etienne-Jacques-Joseph-Alexandre Macdonald. Situated in two lines on the Katzbach and Bober Rivers, this force, later christened the Army of the Bober, shielded Oudinot's right flank. The emperor himself led his remaining forces east to destroy Blücher. Although anxious to grapple with Napoleon, Blücher honored the Trachenberg Plan and withdrew into Silesia. After the Silesian Army eluded him, the emperor learned Schwarzenberg was advancing on Dresden. He instructed Macdonald to hold the Silesian Army east of the Bober River and immediately departed for Dresden. Despite the emperor's orders, Macdonald continued the offensive. On 26 August, Blücher smashed the marshal's army as it attempted to cross the rain-swollen Katzbach. Macdonald lost 15,000 men, and his army collapsed in the aftermath.

Meanwhile, Oudinot's army advanced toward Berlin along three roads that prevented mutual support. Despite Bernadotte's willingness to sacrifice the city, his corps commanders stopped the French army on 23 August a few miles south of the Prussian capital. A disheartened Oudinot retreated fifty-five miles south to Wittenberg. His headlong retreat exposed Macdonald's communications and limited Napoleon's operations by uncovering the rear of the Grande Armée. A disgusted Napoleon commented that few could be as stupid as Oudinot; he relieved the luckless marshal and placed Marshal Michel Ney in command of the Army of Berlin.

Upon reaching Dresden, Napoleon found the entire Bohemian Army stretched before the Saxon capital. At Frederick William's urging, Schwarzenberg elected to accept battle rather than retreat. During two days of heavy fighting on 26 and 27 August, the emperor inflicted 35,000 casualties on the main Allied army. Schwarzenberg retreated into the mountains of Bohemia during the night of 30 August pursued by General Dominique-Joseph-René Vandamme's I Corps. As Vandamme engaged the Russians, General Friedrich Heinrich von Kleist's Prussian II Corps surprised the French at Kulm. Vandamme, himself taken prisoner, lost approximately 15,000 men.

East of Dresden, Blücher pursued Macdonald's beleaguered army. His pressure required Napoleon's personal intervention to save the marshal. Bonaparte repulsed the Silesian Army's advance guard on 4 September and monitored Blücher's movements throughout the next day. Realizing Napoleon himself commanded the attack on the 4th, Blücher again withdrew eastward. Sensing his adversary had escaped, Napoleon ordered the VI Infantry and I Cavalry Corps to begin the march to Berlin. Although he had hoped to unite with Ney and personally command the offensive against the Prussian capital, Napoleon was forced to abandon these plans after reports arrived of Schwarzenberg's renewed advance toward Dresden. Napoleon recalled the two corps and sped back to the Saxon capital; Ney continued the operation against Berlin. On 6 September, the fiery marshal attempted to smash through the Prussian III and IV Corps at Dennewitz, forty miles south of the Prussian capital. This battle proved to be a disaster for the Army of Berlin. Ney's losses amounted to 21,500 men. Although the Prussians lost 9,700, Ney's army collapsed during the ensuing retreat across the Elbe.

These Allied victories further cemented the alliance against France. On 7 September, the three eastern powers signed the Teplitz Accords. The general terms called for the material restoration of Austria and Prussia to their pre–1805–6 material status; the restoration of the states of northwestern Europe to their 1803 status; the dissolution of the Rheinbund; the independence of the German states between the Rhine and the western frontiers of Austria and Prussia; and the partition of the Grand Duchy of Warsaw along lines that would be determined later. All three governments vowed not to make a separate peace with Napoleon, and each agreed to keep an army in the field until the end of the war.[8]

Although something could be found in the Teplitz Accords that satisfied each eastern power, Metternich achieved another victory. The stated goal of the alliance was not the ultimate destruction of France. For Austria's geopolitical interests, Metternich needed to retain a powerful and preferably Napoleonic France to help contain Russia. The accords ignored Italy, Holland, and Spain; Metternich figured he could use these issues later to coerce the British into accepting his designs for central Europe. More important, the people's war now had become a cabinet war, a war of the great powers. "The aim of the war," contends Nipperdey, "was not emancipation, freedom, or even national unity; it was order and the restoration of a balance of power. This was possible, of course, because in the last analysis, Russia and Prussia were also antirevolutionary powers."⁹ Yet Teplitz was not a total victory for the Austrians, and Tsar Alexander recovered some of the diplomatic initiative he lost to Metternich during the armistice.¹⁰ Both Prussia and Austria remained dependent on Russia to secure their postwar objectives. For Prussia, Frederick William could take comfort in the fact that as long as he remained loyal to the tsar, Prussian influence in Germany would increase, despite the Austrians.

Due to the numerous Allied victories over his subordinates, Napoleon's situation became critical by late September. To the north, Ney failed to dislodge Bernadotte's army from its bridgeheads on the left bank of the Elbe. On the southern front, a force of 45,000 men under Napoleon's brother-in-law, King Joachim Murat of Naples, attempted to slow Schwarzenberg's march on Leipzig. Napoleon held his main force of 80,000 men between the approaching Allied armies – he had no information on the whereabouts of Blücher. The idea of abandoning Germany crossed his mind as early as 27 September, when he ordered the French fortresses on the Rhine River prepared for defense.

Blücher had in fact marched down the Elbe toward Wittenberg. Bernadotte pledged that if the Silesian Army crossed the Elbe, the Army of North Germany would follow. That was enough to satisfy the seventy-year-old Blücher. On 3 October, Yorck's Prussian I Corps led the Silesian Army across the Elbe; the Army of North Germany followed. Ney retreated south with his 25,000 survivors to reunite with Napoleon. News that Blücher and Bernadotte had crossed the Elbe reached the emperor on 5 October. From his central position at Leipzig, he hoped to destroy at least one of these Allied armies. Leaving Murat's 45,000 men to hold Schwarzenberg south of Leipzig, the emperor moved the remainder of the Grande Armée to Wittenberg to engage Blücher and Bernadotte before Schwarzenberg reached Leipzig. By 8 October, the emperor had 140,000 men concentrated just south of Blücher's position. Forewarned of Napoleon's advance, Blücher and Bernadotte surprised the emperor by withdrawing west to the left bank of the Saale River between 8 and 11 October. The decision to retreat proved momentous as the French spent the 10th and 11th searching for the enemy armies. At 3:00 A.M. on the 12th, Napoleon finally learned they had retreated to Halle two days earlier. He initially ordered a pursuit but then changed his mind after receiving the discouraging news that Schwarzenberg accelerated his march. The emperor decided to turn south, concentrate his army at Leipzig, and draw the Allies to him for an epic struggle: the Battle of Nations.

As Blücher's army approached Leipzig from the northwest and Schwarzenberg steadily advanced from the south, General Levin August Theophile von Bennigsen's 50,000-man Army of Poland closed in from the east. Napoleon concentrated 177,000 men around the Saxon city on the evening of 14 October. Both sides spent much of the 15th probing and planning for the next day's battle. While Napoleon intended to destroy Schwarzenberg's army between the Pleisse and the Parthe Rivers, the Allies decided Schwarzenberg would launch the main attack in this southern sector; Blücher's army would assault Leipzig from the northwest. Bernadotte also planned to concentrate his army northwest of Leipzig on the 16th, but his three corps did not arrive in time.

On 16 October, the Silesian and Bohemian Armies executed their operations and attacked as planned. Heavy combat ensued along the northern, western, and southern sectors of the front with struggles centering around the villages of Möckern, Lindenau, and Wachau. The confusion caused by Blücher's unexpected arrival robbed Napoleon of the forces he planned to use against Schwarzenberg. By nightfall, the French had repulsed Schwarzenberg's offensive in the Wachau area and held Lindenau in the western sector, but lost at Möckern, where Yorck's Prussians fought a savage battle. French losses for the day amounted to 25,000 men; Allied casualties numbered 30,000, including one-third of Yorck's corps.

Fighting was minimal on the 17th as both sides rested to renew the struggle on the following day. Bernadotte and Bennigsen moved their armies into positions north and east of Leipzig, respectively. On the morning of 18 October, 295,000 Allied soldiers supported by 1,466 cannon launched six massive attacks along the entire front. Bonaparte stood in the middle of this whirlwind with 160,000 men. The Allies probably sustained another 20,000 casualties, and the French lost approximately 10,000 killed and wounded. Yet Napoleon's dwindling ammunition and Allied numerical superiority decided the issue. At 2:00 A.M. on the 19th, the French army started withdrawing from Leipzig. A rearguard of 30,000 men remained behind to defend the city as the army escaped.

Allied forces drove the French from Leipzig's suburbs and into the inner city by 11:00 A.M. on the 19th. Within Leipzig, "the slaughter was so awful that in places the Pleisse River was choked by a gruesome dam of dead men and horses, across which their comrades found a means of escape to the gardens beyond, only to be surrounded there and forced to surrender."[11] The battle ended; staggering losses marked the four-day struggle. Napoleon lost around 73,000 men, including 30,000 prisoners, 5,000 German deserters, 325 guns, and 40,000 muskets. Of the marshals, Prince Josef Anton Poniatowski drowned in the Elster River just twelve hours after receiving his baton, and Ney, Macdonald, and Auguste-Frédéric-Louis Marmont were wounded. Coalition forces also captured thirty-six French generals. The Allies sustained an estimated 54,000 casualties.

Although Napoleon's decisive defeat ended French hegemony east of the Rhine, the Allies did not believe the war was over. All agreed to continue operations to destroy the French army before it reached the Rhine. Discussions over the next move occurred both before and after the storming of Leipzig. A council of war took place when Alexander met Schwarzenberg on the battlefield during the morning of the 19th. According to a British observer in Austrian headquarters, Robert Wilson, Alexander presented himself as the new Allied commander in chief, "but professing not to understand the *métier* sufficiently, he said he would have a council to direct him. Metternich frankly told him that he would never obtain the consent of Austria; moreover, he had declared himself unqualified; and that a council on the field of battle was a project that would never produce any result other than misfortune and disgrace."[12]

Despite the tsar's hubris, Alexander and Schwarzenberg made the preliminary arrangements for a pursuit, which called for the Silesian Army to move north of Leipzig and then turn west to harry Napoleon's right flank. Schwarzenberg's Bohemian Army would advance southwest of Leipzig in two massive columns. Bernadotte, with the combined North German and Polish Armies, would immediately follow Blücher and then slide between the Silesian and Bohemian Armies. In this way, the French would be herded toward an Austro–Bavarian army commanded by General Karl Philipp von Wrede. Thus caught between the Allied forces, the remnant of Napoleon's army would be destroyed before it could escape across the Rhine.

This plan achieved only partial success. Wrede managed to block Napoleon's line of retreat, but the emperor smashed through the Austro–Bavarian army at Hanau, a few miles east of Frankfurt-am-Main, on 30 October. Unfortunately for Wrede, Napoleon outsmarted Schwarzenberg. The Allied generalissimo assumed he would turn off the main highway that ran southwest from Fulda through Frankfurt to Mainz to avoid Wrede. Schwarzenberg believed the French army would proceed due west through Wetzlar to cross the Rhine at Koblenz, where Blücher's army would be waiting. Napoleon made no such adjustment. Although Wrede reported the march of a French column toward Frankfurt, Schwarzenberg assured him this was a flank column of no more than 20,000 men meant to cover Napoleon's left as he crossed the Rhine at Koblenz. Wrede planned to pounce on this French column at Hanau with his 43,000 men. Rather than a flank column, Wrede confronted the emperor himself. After shattering the smaller Allied force and inflicting 9,000 casualties, Napoleon commented that although he had made Wrede a count, he had failed to make him a general.[13]

The battle of Hanau cost Napoleon significantly fewer men than Wrede, but the disorganization of the French army reached deplorable levels in its aftermath. Between 28 and 31 October, the Allies captured as many as 10,000 stragglers.[14] "Troops as disorganized as those we commanded," explains Marmont, "as harassed, as exhausted by marching and fighting, by reverses and privations, soon surrendered to indiscipline. The inability to regularly provide sufficient rations provoked and justified their actions. Each man's primary concern was finding food; as all military discipline collapsed, an indescribable depression and disgust took its place." The marshal estimates that of the 60,000 to 70,000 soldiers who still remained, "20,000 formed themselves into bands of eight or ten, scouring the countryside and marching on the flanks. The army gave these soldiers a nickname, which has become historic and recalls their sole occupation: the search for the means to survive. They were called *fricoteurs* (marauders)."[15] On 1 November, the main body of the French army reached Frankfurt, less than twenty miles from the fortress of Mainz and the safety of the Rhine.

After receiving reports that Napoleon had not changed course to reach Koblenz but instead remained on the highway that ran through Frankfurt to the Rhine, Schwarzenberg ordered the Bohemian Army to pursue on the same road. Cold weather and supply shortages slowed the march of his usually torpid army. On 6 November Schwarzenberg's advance guard relieved the forward troops of Wrede's Austro–Bavarian army and drove the French from Hochheim, just east of Mainz.[16]

Napoleon harbored no illusions over the state of his army. Weakened physically, mentally, and materially, it could not confront the main Allied armies: the retreat continued across the Rhine. Daily desertions combined with attrition to rob Napoleon of precious combat power; at most, the emperor commanded 70,000 soldiers. According to Professor Heinrich Steffens, a propaganda specialist attached to Blücher's headquarters:

> The rapidity of their flight completely exhausted the greater part of the army. At first we saw single Frenchmen lying among the bushes; as we proceeded the number of the exhausted, dying sufferers increased, and we found large groups of dead and dying. It pained me to observe that they believed it was a great evil to be discovered by us. Although we offered them assistance, they preferred to be left alone to perish from hunger and exhaustion among the undergrowth. I confess I wished myself away from the horrid scene, it was more terrible to me than the violence of the fiercest battle.[17]

The last units of the French army crossed the Rhine but maintained positions on the right bank at Wesel and the bridgeheads at Kastel and Kehl, facing Mainz and Strasbourg, respectively.

With their armies at the Rhine, the Allied monarchs, generals, and statesmen had to decide their next step. Disagreements had been few during the fall campaign when the Coalition labored to drive the French from central Europe. Allied unity began to wane shortly after their armies converged on the Rhine. For some, reaching this historic landmark symbolized Germany's liberation from French rule; driving the French across the river signaled the end of the war. This was particularly the case with the Russian officers, some of whom had questioned the wisdom of pursuing the French beyond Russia's frontiers. Many felt they had done their part to avenge themselves on the

French and the time had come to turn their backs on the troubles of western Europe. Another bloc – Metternich's doves – saw the Rhine as a geographic objective, the attainment of which would lead to a negotiated peace. Such a peace would not only restore the balance of power, but, by maintaining a Napoleonic France, the plans of ambitious allies could be held in check. The main question for this faction was not how the war should be continued but whether the war should be continued at all. Still for others, reaching the Rhine did not mark the end of the war but merely the conclusion of one campaign and the start of another. The hawks insisted on immediately crossing the Rhine and launching a rapid, decisive campaign against Paris. Peace terms would be dictated in the French capital.

Blücher and his chief of staff, General August Wilhelm Anton von Gneisenau, harbored no doubts over the next step. Shortly after the battle of Leipzig, Gneisenau informed Carl von Clausewitz that "the enemy makes his way toward Erfurt. If the enemy escapes or is destroyed, we go to Kassel and, if one gives us a free hand, to the Lower Rhine" (Appendix A).[18] Shortly after, Gneisenau formally submitted his thoughts to King Frederick William. As the "simplest plan," he suggested having three armies cross the upper, middle, and lower Rhine, respectively, while a fourth moved into Holland. His letter outlined the operations plan he would submit at the upcoming council of war at Frankfurt. The most important aspects of Gneisenau's proposal included his firm belief that of the four proposed Allied armies, the Silesian army should cross the lower Rhine and proceed toward Maastricht. Accordingly, this movement would deny Napoleon the resources of Holland and threaten the fortresses of northern France. Regarding these fortresses, Gneisenau insisted that they were "definitely poorly equipped with those effects that cannot be lacking [for] a strong defense."

This point led to Gneisenau's second basic tenet: in Napoleon's current crisis, the emperor would not be able "to create new field armies and provide his numerous fortresses with garrisons and other means of defense." Should he form a field army only, his denuded fortresses would fall; conversely, should he garrison the fortresses, few troops would be available for mobile operations. "In a word, we wanted garrisons," agrees French historian Adolphe Thiers, "and it was to be feared that in forming them we might weaken the active army, already so much impoverished."[19] In his memo, Gneisenau explains that "the fortresses are so numerous that all conscripts which he [Napoleon] can raise will not suffice to form garrisons." He informed the ever-cautious Frederick William that despite what some may advise, the French fortresses should not be avoided. Instead, Gneisenau's third point called for the Allies to take a position that "can threaten as many fortresses as possible to force the enemy to have concern for all." A movement toward Maastricht would serve this purpose. He assured the king that such measures would facilitate the conquest of Holland and place the Silesian army in a position to build a solid operations base on the lower Rhine. Gneisenau concluded his report with a request to allow the Silesian Army to march to the lower Rhine, promising that Blücher would then "be in the position to attain in a decisive manner . . . an honorable and lasting peace."[20]

On the same day Gneisenau wrote the king, he submitted a detailed version of his plan to Charles Stewart, the British ambassador to the Prussian court and half-brother of Britain's foreign minister, Robert Stewart, Viscount Castlereagh. "France has between 120 and 130 fortresses," explains Gneisenau. "Bonaparte left most of these places without garrisons, which gave him the forces to build numerous armies. If we compel him to leave garrisons in a greater part of these fortresses, we will prevent him from fielding an army with sufficient strength to oppose us." Gneisenau argued that "the frontier fortresses in France lack everything that is needed for defense and we can probably take them at little cost." Later in his letter, he explains that "in the previous year [1812], the enemy lost an army of 400,000 and in the current campaign another 300,000 men." Thus, the Allies had to exploit Napoleon's obvious shortage of trained manpower.

Both supporters and opponents of Gneisenau's plan claimed the attrition of the Allied armies during the German campaign had been too great. Before crossing the Rhine, the Allied soldiers needed rest and recovery. In his letter to Stewart, Gneisenau responded to this criticism:

> You say that our army has suffered too much and our numbers have decreased? This is true. Of the 39,000 men of Yorck's corps who started the campaign, no more than 10,000–11,000 men remain. But we have received 3,000 reinforcements and the Russians 15,000. I will attempt to raise 20,000–30,000 new conscripts from our former provinces. . . . The Hessians will probably join us – as well as the Saxon army – because the Elector will entrust his troops to a Prussian general. All of this will make a formidable army, which can undertake the conquest of Holland.[21]

Stewart issued a prompt, yet cautious reply that foreshadowed the opposition Gneisenau would encounter during the upcoming council of war:

> It appears essential to me that the operations of each army continue through general communication and agreement. At the moment, everything appears to be in disarray and the armies operate according to the ideas of each commander. I already have told you: you will lead, but according to a plan. Everything you have said to me concerning Holland shows great genius, and I completely agree that a large army must go there . . . but would it not be better to first make your levée and rebuild your troops before you invade Holland or cross the Rhine?[22]

Although a close friend of Gneisenau, Clausewitz, in his 1835 critique of the 1814 campaign, rejects Gneisenau's idea regarding the dispersion of Allied forces in four armies. Clausewitz maintains that after Leipzig, the

Kulminationspunkte for total Allied victory was a second defeat of the French army or the capture of Paris. Both required the Allies to cross the Rhine immediately and en masse, and the latter would lead Coalition forces deep within France. Clausewitz estimates the Allied armies at Leipzig to number around 290,000 men. After adding Wrede's army and subtracting losses and Bernadotte's march to Hamburg, he figures the Allies reached the Rhine with 245,000. Detaching 65,000 men for the necessary sieges and observation of the Rhenish fortresses, 180,000 men would remain to cross the Rhine. "By using great economy of force, 150,000 of this number could have been available on the battlefield. It has been proven and it was foreseen with the highest certainty that Bonaparte, aside from what he could draw from the Italian and Spanish armies, could have opposed this force with at most 60,000–70,000 men in the beginning of December." Although it was widely known that Paris served as the central nervous system of the French army, Clausewitz justified making Paris the Allied objective on political grounds. "In general, the political factions that exist in great and extensive empires can be mastered only from the core, this was especially the case in France. By rule the capital is the square root of these factions and Paris more so than any other. Thus, the objective of the strategic attack must be the total defeat of the enemy's military forces and the conquest of the capital. One without the other would not suffice."[23]

Joseph Radetzky von Radetz, who served as both the Allied chief of staff and Chief of the General Staff of the Austrian Army, submitted his views to Schwarzenberg in a memorandum likewise dated 31 October (Appendix B). According to Radetzky, only two operations could be considered *if* the French continued their retreat across the Rhine. The first involved all three Allied armies taking winter quarters along the right bank of the Rhine from Basel to the mouth of the Ems River. He estimated 246,000 Allied troops would occupy this line during the winter months. His other suggestion called for the Silesian and Bohemian armies to take winter quarters, while the Army of North Germany conquered Holland, and a portion of the Austrian Reserve moved into Italy. For the operation against Holland, Radetzky claimed it would be necessary to reinforce Bernadotte with one of Blücher's corps. Nevertheless, the Austrian officer advised against an Allied operation in a region of the French Empire that would figure prominently in any political negotiations. Radetzky also touched on a subject that would soon cause a rupture in Austro–Russian relations. "The situation may arise," he wrote, "in which the forces on the Upper Rhine must operate there in order to support the political measures of the Swiss and enter Switzerland." His treatise attempted to preempt the revenge-minded Prussian generals by first securing Austrian objectives in Italy. Radetzky claimed that only the occupation of the region between the Adige and Mincio Rivers as well as the capture of the Italian fortresses of Peschiera, Mantua, and Ferrara would "ensure operations against Paris at the beginning of the new campaign."[24] Much to Gneisenau's chagrin, Austrian national interests became more pronounced in the weeks to come.

The ideas circulating in Schwarzenberg's headquarters did little to deter Blücher, who was anxious to stomp his boots on French soil. On 5 November, he received news that the French army teetered on the brink of collapse, despite Napoleon's victory at Hanau. "If we quickly set out for Holland and cross the Rhine with double strength," predicts Blücher's quartermaster-general, Friedreich Karl von Müffling, "the conquest of Holland will be completed in two months and a lasting peace concluded. *If we remain on this side and allow ourselves to be delayed by negotiations, I thus predict a bloody campaign in 1814.* Napoleon is in the most awful situation . . . I am most eager to see how his genius will extract himself."[25] Agreeing with his staff officers, Blücher submitted his thoughts to the king and requested permission to cross the Rhine:

> I will immediately march from here to Köln on the lower Rhine in order to cross as quickly as possible and support the conquest of Holland, which Your Royal Majesty, I suspect, will assign to a part of the Army of North Germany. I do not see anything that can prevent me from overrunning a part of the Netherlands and thus facilitating the conquest of Holland. As long as we remain on the right bank of the Rhine the enemy has no need to garrison his many fortresses, but if we force him to occupy them, he will be too weak to operate in the field against us; if he keeps his men in the field, he will thus lose the fortresses. I await your orders.[26]

None of the reports Blücher received indicated the concentration of French reserves at the frontier. Moreover, spies and sympathizers claimed the French had not armed, provisioned, nor adequately garrisoned the left bank fortresses. "Places indispensable to our home protection, Huningue, Strasbourg, Landau, Mainz, Metz, Mézières, Valenciennes, and Lille, were left utterly defenseless," laments Thiers. "The guns were not mounted; there was a shortage of tools, of wood for blinds, of bridges of communication between the works, of horses for transport, of smiths and carpenters. Provisions had yet to arrive, and money, which can provide for so many needs, was not forthcoming, and it was doubtful whether it could be sent in time and in sufficient quantities."[27]

Reports also indicated the crown prince of Sweden had reached Hanover, which led Blücher to conclude that the Army of North Germany would soon invade Holland. Blücher refused to ignore these favorable circumstances. He and his staff devised another plan, this time calling for the Silesian army to cross the middle Rhine and advance through Aachen and Liège toward Brussels. According to the Prussians, Schwarzenberg would cross the Rhine between Mannheim and Mainz. Paris would be the general goal of all operations.[28] The Prussians hoped to surprise the French and capture several key fortresses during the confusion caused by the Allied invasion.

By marching to Belgium, the Silesian army would deprive Napoleon of valuable resources, including the armament factories at Liège and Namur. Blücher believed he would be ready to cross the Rhine on 15 November and estimated reaching Brussels ten days later. On 7 November, an optimistic Gneisenau left for Frankfurt to seek approval of this plan. Without authorization, Blücher led his army northwest toward Köln that same day. It was all for naught. Four days later, he received explicit orders from Tsar Alexander to turn around and besiege Mainz.

In early November, the question that faced the Coalition was whether Allied forces should cross the Rhine and pursue Napoleon's weak army. "The moment is of the greatest importance," Schwarzenberg explains to his wife, Maria Anna, "now it comes down to the decisive question, should one begin a winter campaign?"[29] The exhausted state of their armies suggested the Allies needed to halt at the Rhine. Yet Müffling's prediction that delay would result in a bloody campaign in 1814 adequately summarized the thought process behind the planning at Silesian army headquarters. By immediately resuming the campaign, they were prepared to accept further losses and impose further hardships on the soldiers. The reason was not callous indifference to the suffering of their men nor bloodthirsty revenge as the Austrians suggested, but the simple belief that by exploiting Napoleon's weakness the struggle would end sooner with less loss than if they allowed the master of war to recover. While en route to the Rhine, the Allies discovered Napoleon had implemented measures to rebuild his army. In several German cities, they found French newspapers dated as early as 13 October that announced the emperor's decree to raise 280,000 conscripts.[30] Only two alternatives remained to the Coalition: continue the war, or negotiate with Bonaparte.

The operations of the Silesian and Bohemian armies halted in November for both practical and political reasons. Physical and material exhaustion required rest, reorganization, and replenishment. Revitalizing on the march in the midst of winter did not appear feasible. Regardless of the dilapidated state of his army, Blücher's plan to march to Belgium in early November probably would have succeeded without much detriment to his men. French forces were in no condition to resist, and the march route of the Silesian Army would have avoided the departments of "old France," where the hostility of the local population posed a threat to rear-area security. Once in Belgium, Blücher would have facilitated General Friedrich Wilhelm von Bülow's invasion of Holland with the Prussian III Corps, detached from Bernadotte's Army of North Germany. Blücher's operation would have enabled Bülow's corps as well as General Ferdinand Federovich von Wintzingerode's Russian army corps to unite with the Silesian army before the end of 1813. Thus reinforced, the Prussian commander could have invaded old France with an army of 125,000 men. Taking strategic consumption into consideration, this figure is still quadruple the actual size of the Silesian army when it reached the Marne River in late January 1814. Moreover, an invasion of "new" France could have commenced one full month before the Bohemian Army started the Allied invasion by crossing the upper Rhine at Basel, and six weeks before the Silesian Army finally received authorization to cross the Rhine near Mainz. The distance between Mainz and Paris was double the stretch that separated the French capital from Belgium's southern border. Had Blücher invaded new France and reached Belgium before the end of November, the war could have taken a completely different turn. With the Silesian army much closer to the French capital and with the mobilization of the French army still in its infant stage, Blücher may well have reached Paris before the end of the year.

Blücher's recall after he initiated the march to Belgium also reflected the politics of the Sixth Coalition. At the head of the peace party stood Metternich. His concern over Russia increased with every mile the Allies advanced after the victory at Leipzig. If only Napoleon's power could be reduced rather than destroyed, France could counter postwar Russian hegemony. Metternich opposed the complete destruction and overthrow of Napoleon out of fear the succeeding French ruler might be a Russian puppet. Conversely, in the back of every Allied monarch's mind remained the fear that a Jacobin government could seize power in France and resume the Revolution's crusade against thrones.

Although the German campaign had required true military and political cooperation, the Prussian generals enjoyed enough independence to wage a war of retribution against Napoleon. After the Allies liberated Germany and reached the Rhine, Metternich had to slow the pace of the war to restrain the Prussians, whose impetuosity threatened his ability to direct the conflict at its most crucial stage. For this task, he received the assistance of many. Metternich himself attempted to manipulate the perceptions of peace and victory in the minds of Alexander and Frederick William. Relics from the eighteenth-century school of warfare who served as advisors influenced strategy and persistently undermined Gneisenau. Metternich also used Schwarzenberg himself to ensure that Allied military strategy did not supersede Austrian political interests. The Russian generals yearned for peace – in part from war weariness, in part because Russia appeared to have no interests west of the Rhine. Nevertheless, like Napoleon, Blücher and Gneisenau still measured victory only in terms of success on the battlefield. For this reason, they wanted to lead the Silesian Army across the Rhine at the first opportunity and make for the heart of France. On the basis of this desire, they formed a natural partnership with the tsar. Yet despite the demands of the war party, the Allies lost precious time in long deliberations at Frankfurt rather than pursuing Napoleon's defeated army across the Rhine. Instead of achieving a quick, decisive end to the conflict in 1813, the war continued into 1814, another campaign was fought, and tens of thousands of unfortunate men, women, and children lost their lives.

2

Barbarians at the Gate

Metternich schemed to outmaneuver the tsar at every opportunity, even with the arrival of the Allied monarchs at Frankfurt. "I want to regulate with you the entrance of the Kaiser in Frankfurt, which I want to be solemn and in the middle of his troops," he wrote to Schwarzenberg. "I desire that the Kaiser arrive before the Tsar of Russia. The first to arrive has a step up."[1] Despite his machinations, Tsar Alexander paraded into Frankfurt at the head of the Russo–Prussian Guard on 5 November. The following day, "Red Breeches," the popular nickname for Kaiser Francis, entered the former imperial city where he had been crowned Holy Roman Emperor twenty-one years earlier. Frederick William was absent, having returned to Berlin following the battle of Leipzig. "We were well-received," claims Wilson, "although Bonaparte warned the inhabitants not to commit any follies, since he would reappear in the spring." Describing the kaiser's entry on 6 November, Wilson notes: "*Te Deum* followed his entry, and for two hours we froze in a cold church. The troops then filed by the sovereigns, and this ceremony was almost as chilling. We then went to dine with Mr. Bethmann, who gave a *grande fête*. Afterwards we passed to the opera, where *Titus* was performed before the emperors and an overflowing house by some very talented actors."[2]

With Schwarzenberg making Frankfurt the headquarters of the Bohemian Army as well, the city served as Grand Allied Headquarters. It also became the prelude to the Congress of Vienna as monarchs, ministers, and courtiers made their way to the old city. Moreover, the German princes who had voluntarily seceded from the Rheinbund or had been forced to make peace with the Allies also gravitated to Frankfurt. "The entry of the Kaiser in this old German city . . . was very moving and extremely solemn," wrote Schwarzenberg. "But now I want to leave these walls. Kings, princes, and representatives from all sides stream here, and the time hardly suffices to deal with the current business."[3] Aside from the military planning, the futures of Germany and

Figure 1. General August Wilhelm Anton von Gneisenau (1760–1831). Chief of the General Staff of the Prussian Army.

France, as well as the general security of Europe, emerged as key issues. In this atmosphere, intrigue rather than unity reigned supreme. With victory at hand, national self-interest moved to the fore.

A great council of war convened on 7 November. Count Karl Emil von Löwenhielm delivered the crown prince of Sweden's proposed plan of campaign. According to Bernadotte, the Bohemian Army should place its left wing on the Main River and extend its right to the confluence of the Sieg with the Rhine. The Silesian Army would form the center, placing its left on the Sieg and its right toward Düsseldorf. After eliminating Marshal Davout's force at Hamburg, Bernadotte's Army of North Germany would invade and liberate Holland. From their positions along the right bank of the Rhine, the Bohemian and Silesian Armies would rest and reorganize. Operations would commence on the left bank of the Rhine "at the earliest moment."[4]

Gneisenau opened his argument by first expressing opposition to any negotiations with the French emperor, maintaining that Napoleon "could only be defeated through war, war, and more war."[5] He pressed for an immediate invasion of France (Appendix C). Gneisenau again explained how Napoleon would be forced to divide his limited manpower between the frontier fortresses and a field army. After losing so much manpower, the emperor did not have the resources to occupy the fortresses and field a considerable army. Instead of skirting the fortresses, Gneisenau wanted the Allies to proceed right through their midst.[6] Napoleon would be compelled to either leave a portion of the fortresses unoccupied, thus conceding strongholds in his own territory, or occupy all of the fortresses, which would deny him manpower for a field army. The Prussian general argued that by crossing the lower Rhine on 15 November and invading Belgium, the Silesian Army could simultaneously detach Holland from French control, liberate the Dutch, and threaten the fortresses of northern France. Gneisenau also proposed that Bülow drive across the Ijssel River and into Holland, while Schwarzenberg's Bohemian army invade France between Mainz and Strasbourg. In addition, a small auxiliary corps would advance through Switzerland to occupy Franche-Comté. Gneisenau did not offer any details regarding objectives, but it was clear to all in attendance that the Prussians targeted Paris as their ultimate goal.[7]

Gneisenau's proposal enjoyed the council's support; only the Austrian generals suggested reducing the size of the army on the middle Rhine to increase the forces moving through Switzerland. In addition, the Austrians wanted to secure the Alpine state to prevent the enemy from threatening the communications of any Allied forces en route to the French interior. The sole voice of opposition came from Gneisenau's own countryman: General Karl Friedrich von dem Knesebeck. The king's military advisor, Knesebeck liked to claim that he adhered "little to the old principles of war" but instead had formed his own art of war or essentially had none: "rather each time I discern what the situation demands and I do it."[8] His counterproposal called for a part of the Army of North Germany, mainly Bülow's corps, to invade Holland, while the Silesian and Bohemian Armies moved into winter quarters on the Rhine to pin the French at Mainz.[9] Knesebeck's plan generated much discussion and the day ended before the Allies reached a decision.

On the following day, 8 November, Radetzky presented his own proposal, which agreed with Gneisenau's plan on two important points: the immediate resumption of Allied operations and the Silesian army's conquest of the Netherlands. Radetzky called for the Bohemian army to move up the Rhine to Switzerland, cross the river, and invade southern France. Blücher's army would then proceed to the Netherlands. The idea of advancing on widely separated wings exaggerated both the strength of the numerous fortresses on the French eastern frontier as well as the memory of the failed campaign of 1792, when the main Austro–Prussian army advanced from Koblenz to Paris along a single axis that offered no flank protection nor permitted much mutual support.[10] Both Radetzky and Schwarzenberg feared a prolonged delay of the invasion of France. Schwarzenberg based his concerns on the inability to feed the army in its current position, which made advancing or retreating the only options. Moreover, Radetzky did not want to grant Napoleon time to "convert 100,000 demoralized men into 300,000 soldiers. We shall rue the time we have allowed to pass unused."[11]

Radetzky's plan appeared risky to some of his own compatriots, who feared undertaking an operation before neutralizing the French fortresses that could threaten the flank and rear of the Bohemian army. The kaiser's childhood friend, Peter Duka von Kadar, who now served as the monarch's principal military advisor, insisted on taking winter quarters on the right bank of the Rhine to begin a methodical invasion by besieging the enemy's frontier fortresses in 1814. The Bavarian general, Wrede, opposed Duka by insisting that the Allies immediately launch surprise attacks on the French fortresses along the middle and upper Rhine, all of which were purportedly in an excessively weak state of defense.[12] Regardless, Francis supported Duka until Schwarzenberg countered that the army could not be fed in winter quarters.

Although the kaiser did not see the merits of Radetzky's plan, it did serve Austrian grand strategy. By advancing through Switzerland, the Austrians could impose a pro-Austrian government on the Swiss. Likewise, the Habsburgs hoped to regain their lost lands in Italy, and Austrian operations against the French army in Italy could be facilitated by controlling Switzerland. French historian Alphonse de Beauchamp offers an interesting interpretation of the Austrian plan, asserting that it "presented another important question: what point should be attacked? The Austrian cabinet, whose principal objective was the conquest of Italy, argued that the invasion must take place through Switzerland and the eastern frontier. In this scenario, the conquest of Lyon had to precede the movement on Paris, and the main Allied army had to cut France in half by linking its operations in the east with those of Lord Wellington." Although, as Beauchamp admits, "the Russian cabinet insisted on marching straight to Paris," the mixing of Austrian strategy and Russian pressure later resulted in the erratic and confused operations of Schwarzenberg's left wing in southern France.[13]

National self-interest combined with the views of the Austrian General Staff in Radetzky's proposal. Although Schwarzenberg completely dedicated himself to helping Metternich achieve his grand strategy, the Austrian General Staff's direct complicity with the diplomat's scheming remains unclear. In fact, John Fane, Lord Burghersh, the British attaché to the Austrian army, provides a logical explanation for Radetzky's proposal: "It was an evident advantage to the Austrians to place their army in a situation from where, even in case of defeat, they could pour their forces into Italy, overwhelming the troops of the enemy, and thus securing for themselves an extension of territory."[14] The other officers of the Austrian General Staff supported Radetzky's draft according to their strategic views. The plan itself appeared to offer the possibility of waging war in a grand perspective. With the actual offensive commencing from Geneva, the Allies could, as Radetzky claimed, either detach troops to threaten the rear of the French forces in Italy and with the remainder march directly on Paris, or they could cooperate with the duke of Wellington in southern France. In either case, the Austrians firmly believed Napoleon would make peace after the loss of his frontier provinces.[15]

For the moment, Alexander did not perceive the covert aspects of this plan and endorsed the suggestion. Gneisenau, too, did not object to Radetzky's modification, although it would prevent tactical cooperation between the Silesian and Bohemian armies. By invading France from Belgium and Switzerland, Blücher and Schwarzenberg would not be able to unite their forces. Gneisenau did object to the projected timetable: Radetzky suggested postponing the Rhine passage until 1 January 1814 to reorganize the Allied armies. On the first of the year, the invasion of France would begin with Blücher advancing from Belgium and Schwarzenberg leading his army through Switzerland.

When the debate continued on 8 November, Knesebeck emerged as a dangerous opponent to Gneisenau's plans. Similar to the opposition the Kaiser's military advisor, Duka, made to Radetzky, the Austrian General Staff Chief, Frederick William's strategic councilor now challenged the proposals made by Gneisenau, the Chief of the General Staff of the Prussian Army. Indicative of the sharp differences that divided not just allies, but officers within the same army, such disagreement reflects the rift between the officers steeped in the traditions of eighteenth-century warfare and those who adopted the modern, "Napoleonic" principles of war. Knesebeck amended his argument and endorsed the idea of having the Bohemian Army invade southern France through Switzerland because this region contained the least number of fortresses. To cover Schwarzenberg's exposed right flank, he suggested that the Silesian army forego Gneisenau's proposed operation in the Netherlands, temporarily besiege Mainz, and take winter quarters along the Rhine to present the threat of a sudden breakout. After the Bohemian army completed its wheeling movement, Blücher could then operate on the left bank of the Rhine according to circumstances. The conquest of Holland and Belgium would be left to the crown prince of Sweden.[16] "You may recall the fire of the discussion with which I fought for my plan in the presence of the tsar," Knesebeck later wrote to Gneisenau in an attempt to justify his actions, "and the patient persistence which I exhibited, when Englishman and Dutchman, monarch and minister, assailed me because the former believed Holland would again be lost – and the latter wanted to completely finish the enemy. I wanted the same as you...to remain strong and firm when other men of strength looked on as weaklings."[17] Gneisenau never accepted Knesebeck's explanation and certainly could not see how this plan would produce greater results than his own.

Gneisenau held his ground in the face of Knesebeck's charge and throughout the debate on 9 November. By the end of the day, he outmaneuvered Knesebeck to win the support of the tsar and the Austrian generals. Schwarzenberg and Radetzky opted for an immediate invasion of France while Napoleon was unprepared and his people demoralized. Gneisenau made common cause with the Austrians, whose fair plan attracted him despite the obvious influence of

Figure 2. General Karl Friedrich von dem Knesebeck (1768–1848). Chief military advisor to King Frederick William III of Prussia.

Austrian politics. According to the Austrian plan, the Bohemian army would drive through Switzerland into France; one corps would observe Mainz, and another at Koblenz would sever French communications; the Silesian army would advance through Brabant and Flanders; the Army of North Germany would liberate Holland. The generals submitted this plan to the tsar, who gave his consent after long deliberations. The Allies designated 15 November for the historic crossing of the Rhine.[18]

On the next day, 10 November, Schwarzenberg summoned Gneisenau to another council on the grounds that Knesebeck had raised important concerns. After Gneisenau arrived, Knesebeck read a written statement calling for the Bohemian army to wheel through Switzerland into southern France to unite with Field Marshal Johann von Hiller's Austrian army in Italy. After the Bohemian army entered France, Schwarzenberg would attempt to arrange an operation against Paris with Wellington's Anglo-Portuguese army, which was in the midst of crossing the Pyrenees. Knesebeck reiterated his belief that the Silesian army had to remain at Mainz to cover Schwarzenberg's flank and rear. Gneisenau again argued the importance of liberating the Low Countries. According to Knesebeck, this task would be left to the good will of the crown prince of Sweden. Knesebeck contended that even if Bernadotte concentrated his efforts in north Germany to secure Norway, Holland and Belgium were secondary objectives that could be obtained at the peace table. Frustrated by his Prussian rival, Gneisenau fervently protested against leaving Napoleon in possession of the Netherlands. He repeated his belief that the French emperor would be allowed to reinforce his field army significantly unless the Allies threatened the fortresses on his northern frontier. On a practical note, Gneisenau dismissed as unlikely the intended cooperation with the Austro–Italian and Anglo–Portuguese armies. Knesebeck's draft contained enough similarities to Radetzky's original plan to receive the approval of the majority of Austrian generals. Although the representatives of the House of Orange and the British – who naturally had great interest in the liberation of Holland – gave their full support to Gneisenau, the rest of the council favored Knesebeck's suggestions. Moreover, although they never really expected to execute a campaign against Paris, to entice Alexander the Austrians did not rule out its possibility. Like Gneisenau, the authors of this plan said nothing about what would come next; unlike Gneisenau, they had no intention of marching on Paris. In a vote, the Austrian generals approved Knesebeck's proposals and submitted the changes to the tsar for his approval. Captivated by the idea of cooperating with the Austro–Italian and Anglo–Portuguese armies and ignoring the prospects of French resistance in Italy and western France, Alexander endorsed this plan.[19]

Symbolic of the chaos that sometimes characterized Allied war planning, Alexander and Gneisenau drafted another operations plan on 10 November. According to this scheme, the crown prince of Sweden with 50,000 men would turn against Hamburg, while the other 80,000 men of his army – mainly the corps of Bülow and Wintzingerode – would cross the Rhine at Köln and detach Holland from France. Blücher with 52,000 men in his first line and 80,000 men (Russo–Prussian reinforcements, Hessians, Westphalians, Württembergers, Badeners, Darmstädters, and Kleist's II Corps) in his second would occupy Koblenz and cross the Rhine at Mannheim, cover the right-wing and communications of the Bohemian army, and conduct offensive operations according to circumstances. The Bohemian army's 200,000 men would besiege Breisach and Kehl and invade France from across the upper Rhine. An Austro–Italian army of 68,000 men would attempt to reach the Var River to establish communication with the armies of Schwarzenberg and Wellington.[20]

That same day, 10 November, Gneisenau forwarded the tsar's plan to Silesian army headquarters. In a cover letter to Müffling, he distinguished between fact and fiction. He doubted the tsar would be able to induce the crown prince of Sweden to detach such a large force, despite the former's promise to use "resolute language." "Herr Bernhard [Bernadotte] has a very miserable demeanor," wrote Gneisenau. "In everything we have had to drag him by the hair and in our important undertakings has he left us completely in the lurch. We have completed our business without him, but he is very detrimental to us, because he deprives us of our troops, which we could use much better elsewhere."[21] Should the crown prince refuse to support this operation, Gneisenau viewed the Coalition's inability to attack the Netherlands as "very unsatisfactory." He also revealed to Müffling that he continued to fail in his attempts to convince the tsar to allow the Silesian army to cross the Rhine immediately. Gneisenau did have success protesting Blücher's passive role, and Alexander agreed to an eventual offensive on the left bank of the Rhine for the Silesian army. Moreover, the Russian monarch assured Gneisenau that if the crown prince of Sweden refused to support the Silesian army, he would detach the Prussians and Russians from the Army of North Germany and place these units under Blücher's command. As for the supposed 80,000 men who would form the second line of the Silesian army, Gneisenau revealed the truth: "The Hessians have yet to organize. The Württembergers have returned to their country to complete the mobilization. The Badenese and Darmstädters are likewise in no condition to join us. Kleist shall move toward us only when Erfurt surrenders. The 20,000 recruits from Westphalia will never join us because the crown prince of Sweden has decided that Bülow will recruit there and the king wants these recruits for the regiments of the Mark. For the present, we must rely upon our own strength." He concludes by lamenting that "the headquarters of the court and of the [Bohemian] army will, I fear, remain here still longer."[22]

Two plans of operations now existed, the "original," as Radetzky called the Knesebeck–Austrian scheme, and the tsar's plan. At least the two plans contained enough similarities so that it is possible to say that the Allies finally reached a consensus on *how* to invade France. Nevertheless, the larger question remained: *Would* the Allies invade France? Numerous opponents still refused to cross the Rhine, yet Napoleon did not remain idle. As early as 11 November, Wilson recorded in his diary that "the enemy is also making gigantic efforts, and all the tales respecting the want of men in France now bear their just character of fallacy. Never will France have had such a force on foot, and it must be remembered that it will be, with very little exception, a French force."[23]

The Prussian king, who arrived in Frankfurt on 13 November, refused to support an invasion and personally opposed Gneisenau. "He is a mischievous, meddling being who requires constant surveillance," purportedly commented the king to Wilson. According to this British officer, Frederick William was not alone in his aversion to the Prussian chief of staff. Wilson claims that Alexander described Gneisenau "as a man with a wild, heated imagination, and the most intemperate. He has two or three times nearly ruined our affairs with the crown prince of Sweden. He is an agent of the Hanoverian interest. His connection with Count Münster ... shows that this agency exists. He requires watching, and it is most fortunate that he has a sovereign with judgement and circumspection enough to weigh well his character and observe his conduct." Count Ernst Friedrich zu Münster was King George III of England's voice in Hanover. Although the king himself was insane, his government absolutely wanted the French out of Holland, and the Hanoverians likewise would never feel secure with Holland remaining in French hands. These issues provided the connection between Münster and Gneisenau and certainly caused suspicion of the latter's motives and insistence on military operations to liberate the Low Countries. Even Radetzky, a fellow staff chief, also shared a low opinion over Gneisenau: "I have received such and such a plan, and have had such and such a conversation, but I have told the prince [Schwarzenberg] that this man is not counseling by his head, but by the necessities of his purse. He is, I am sure, a *mauvais sujet* in some foreign pay."[24]

Frederick William's cautious nature made him immune to the influences of Gneisenau and Blücher, who saw Napoleon's total defeat as the Coalition's task. The Prussian king simply wanted peace. According to Stewart: "after his misfortunes, public and private, the king preferred it [peace] to any war.... Instead, the amiable domestic habits of this monarch led him to seek a mournful consolation near the tomb of his departed queen in Charlottenburg."[25] Hardenberg likewise did not embrace the idea of invading France. The Prussian chancellor secretly harbored fears concerning Russian hegemony, and his solution complemented Metternich's plans: remaining on the Rhine would be the best means to limit Russian expansion in Poland.[26] Moreover, neither Frederick William nor Hardenberg wanted to jeopardize the gains that the Coalition had achieved thus far. The condition in which his troops reached the Rhine further persuaded the monarch that an invasion of France should be postponed until the soldiers recovered.

The Prussian king's fears of invading France were not assuaged by Bernadotte's unsolicited advice. From afar, the crown prince of Sweden warned against crossing the Rhine and emphasized the dangers of invading French soil: a *levée en masse* – popular resistance – and ultimately an Allied defeat.[27] He wanted the Allies to negotiate with Napoleon, and only when they could inform the French people that the emperor refused peace would the time be right to invade France. According to the crown prince, such a peace included the separation of Holland from France, but the French frontiers would be those of 1807. In addition, Bernadotte did not hide his growing interest in the future of the French government. "The crown prince," states a report to Frederick William from the Prussian envoy attached to Bernadotte's headquarters, Friedrich Wilhelm von Krusemark, "has just authorized me to inform Your Majesty, that since he believes neither you nor the Tsar of Russia will make claims on the French throne his elevation to this throne can be exchanged very advantageously with the Emperor Napoleon."[28]

Like the Prussians, disagreement also divided the Austrian camp. Kaiser Francis still agreed with Duka, who wanted to move into winter quarters and begin a spring campaign with the systematic siege of France's frontier fortresses. Duka and Radetzky chided each other in a meeting attended by Francis, Schwarzenberg, and Metternich. According to Radetzky: "Duka, who no longer knew how to reply to my reasons for crossing the Rhine and marching straight to Paris, was so angry that he pounded his fist on the table so hard that the ink splashed up, shouting: 'confound it. Are you trying to be more clever than Prince Eugene [of Savoy]'? 'Prince Eugene would have crossed the Rhine long ago,' was my reply." Radetzky finally won the Kaiser's support but not before wearing out his monarch's eyes and ears. "The emperor sent for me and said: 'Among other things, if you do not stop sending me your plans and if you can think of nothing more clever than your plan of operations, I shall have you imprisoned in the Spielberg or made a head shorter'." All of this bickering took a toll on Radetzky's health:

> By the time I reached Basel during the campaign of 1813 my health was so shattered that I could scarcely manage the exhausting work.... Several doctors explained that I should stay behind, but our senior staff physician, who appreciated how impossible this would be, advised me to drink a glass of mulled Bordeaux wine every day at noon. Tsar Alexander learned of this, and wherever I happened to be, whether in camp or facing the enemy, a Cossack who already knew me well and always found me, God knows how, brought me a bottle of Bordeaux every day.[29]

As for the tsar, such debates did not disturb his councils. Although his officers and men believed the war was over for them, they understood that thoughts of crossing the Rhine and invading France consumed their master. "The Russian army remained quiet," laments Metternich in his memoirs.[30] Victory in Germany did not satiate Alexander. His dreams combined fantastic ideas of benevolence with harsh thoughts of vengeance. He first wanted to liberate and then reconstitute Europe under his magnanimous domination. Conversely, he wanted to punish France and completely destroy Napoleon's power. It mattered little that his faithful ally, Frederick William, did not wish to continue the war: The king's doglike loyalty would not allow him to forsake his Russian benefactor, and Alexander knew it.

Meanwhile, the Austrian intention to march through Switzerland increased tensions in Allied headquarters. Switzerland's political situation became complicated because of the growing conflict between Austria and Russia over Allied strategy, as well as the fact that both wanted influence over the Swiss.[31] Alexander promised to respect Swiss neutrality and the Austrians assured him they would honor his pledge. Schwarzenberg's campaign plan, however, called for the Bohemian army to move through Switzerland. In a letter to his wife, the commander in chief offers a concise evaluation of the Alpine state's importance:

Figure 3. Field Marshal Prince Karl Philipp zu Schwarzenberg (1771–1820). Allied commander in chief and commander of the Army of Bohemia.

> Here the great question will now be decided: whether we will recognize the neutrality of Switzerland or not. My opinion is clear: no salvation for the Allied army without the possession of Switzerland. The relationship of this land with France is of the kind that neutrality, in regard to France, is only a word without meaning, for nothing can hinder them, as soon as they concentrate their forces... from invading Switzerland and too late we would then regret a military sin, which nothing less than the whole world will have to atone. By far the majority of the Swiss wish to shake off the French yoke, the minority I must reconcile. From Switzerland one can seriously threaten France; through the military possession of Switzerland we can take Italy in the rear. A half-measure here is inexcusable. We are at the point where no rest is allowed; as risky as each step is, we must nevertheless be strong and bold. Vacillation here could be high treason to the welfare of Europe.[32]

To get around Swiss neutrality, the Allies sought one of two possible scenarios: either the Swiss would join the Coalition or they would grant the Allies free passage. The Swiss government not only rejected the invitation to join the Coalition but on 18 November passed a declaration of strict neutrality that closed Switzerland's borders. Regardless of this technicality, many of the military minds in Allied headquarters recognized the strategic value of Switzerland. "With respect to Switzerland," explains Stewart, "although deputies had arrived to proclaim its neutrality and arrange a route into France that did not infringe on its territory... it was evidently too important a military feature, both for the safety of Germany and Italy, not to secure it against any attempt from France."[33] Moreover, the Austrians did not feel obligated to recognize the neutrality of a state whose constitution affirmed Napoleon's title of "Mediator." In addition, the Swiss were actively recruiting to honor the 1803 Franco-Swiss alliance that called for them to provide 16,000 men for the French army.

According to Metternich, the tsar sought to strike a compromise between the plans posed by the "Austrian and Prussian generals" to honor Swiss neutrality. In his memoirs, Metternich recalls that Swiss nationals such as the tsar's own childhood tutor "[Frederick] La Harpe, [Antoine] Jomini, and other Swiss revolutionaries vehemently urged Tsar Alexander to respect what they called Helvetian neutrality." A Swiss deputation arrived in Frankfurt to meet with the tsar, who provided them "with a confident hope that the neutrality of Switzerland would not be violated." In a meeting with Metternich and the Allied generals, Alexander explained that although he agreed with the strategic advantages offered by a movement through Switzerland, he could never agree to the violation of Swiss neutrality. The Russian sovereign did consent to a plan for the Allies to use the bridge at Basel on the condition that they first obtain Swiss permission. He declared that Allied forces could move to the border but not violate Swiss neutrality. Alexander believed Austrian arguments for occupying Switzerland had more to do with their desire to gain control of Switzerland and Italy rather than supporting his goal of defeating Napoleon. Learning of this "Austrian trickery" from La Harpe and Jomini, he refused to discuss the issue further. The stalemate over Switzerland thus produced an Austro–Russian dispute.[34] "I am furious with Tsar Alexander," fumed Metternich to Schwarzenberg. "He is more than ever against any operation in Switzerland. We will march there and we will be there – that is best!"[35]

Gneisenau took advantage of this unexpected dissension to open a second round of debates over Allied strategy. The Prussian officer drafted another plan to impress his views on the tsar. Once again he proposed a rapid resumption of offensive operations to surprise Napoleon before he completed his mobilization. Reminiscent of the 1792 invasion plan, Gneisenau called for a joint offensive by the Bohemian and Silesian armies through Metz to Paris. To the north, Bülow and Wintzingerode would conquer the Netherlands while Bernadotte pursued his war with the Danes. Gneisenau resorted to blatant flattery to entice Alexander. "Instead of being satisfied with chasing the enemy from the borders of your empire," he explained to the tsar, "Your Imperial Majesty saved Europe by carrying the war into the heart of Germany. You can rescue Europe once more . . . you are the soul of the union of all people who were oppressed or menaced by France. Your Majesty can still save Europe if you hasten the movement of the army assembled on the Rhine; and you will dictate the peace to your insolent enemy if you strike his forces at the present moment."

Gneisenau also pointed to the crucial issue of timing: "This campaign plan has the advantage of being able to execute it immediately." He assured the Russian monarch that "disorder reigns in the departments on the left bank of the Rhine; the people no longer obey, and the government no longer possesses the power to enforce obedience. The fortresses are denuded of everything. French families flee to Paris, the soldiers desert, and two-thirds of the army is without arms." He concluded that such chaos invited "an immediate invasion of the departments of the left bank of the Rhine and the use of the good will of its inhabitants. Moreover the ice, which will form on the Rhine in the beginning of winter, dictates that we must hasten our operations."[36]

This plan failed to convince its opponents despite the support of the former Prussian chancellor Heinrich Friedrich Karl vom Stein. Now the tsar's principal advisor on German affairs, Stein branded Napoleon "the enemy of the human race" and declared that the shame of the French yoke had to be "washed away in streams of French blood."[37] Although Stein added a powerful voice to the war party, his rants did not prevent Gneisenau's latest proposal from being victimized by the Austrians. Radetzky deemed the advance of such a huge force on a single axis to be impossible. He also judged an advance straight across the middle Rhine as dangerous for three reasons. First, the significant fortress of Mainz would remain in the rear and threaten all communications. Second, the Allied armies would be forced to cross the natural obstacles of the Vosges Mountains and the Moselle and Meuse Rivers. Third, passing through the triple row of Vauban fortresses, which Schwarzenberg's general-quartermaster, Karl Friedrich von Langenau, numbered at 103 between Dunkirk and Huningue, appeared daunting. The tsar likewise exaggerated the strength of the fortress belt that guarded France's eastern frontier and thus did not relish the idea of marching through its midst.[38] "It was reiterated in vain," explains Burghersh, "that the 140 fortresses that surrounded France and which in other times had been of essential service to her defense were a burden in the present reduced state of her military resources: she was utterly unable to garrison and provision them. Such arguments were made to no avail."[39]

After the provisional negotiations with the Swiss proved fruitless and Alexander rejected the Austrian suggestion to force a passage, Gneisenau addressed another memo to the tsar that contained nine key points regarding the necessity of invading the Low Countries (Appendix D). He sent his note first to Knesebeck for comment, with the request that he share its contents with the tsar's adjutant, General Peter Mikhailovich Volkonsky II. The tone of his cover letter to Knesebeck suggests mounting frustration:

According to the reports that arrived today, Holland, Brabant, and the entire left bank of the Rhine are rife with rebellion. One awaits the crossing of the Rhine with longing. Seven weeks will be lost before the campaign in southern

France can even start. How much one can accomplish in seven weeks to prepare a defensive you and all of us know from experience. I refer you to the Armistice of Pläswitz. We should immediately attack the Belgian and Batavian states, and designate the attack on southern France as the second act of this new campaign.[40]

Knesebeck did show the memo to Volkonsky but added no support because he disagreed with Gneisenau. Moreover, he returned the memo on 18 November and refused to make any attempt to show it to the tsar. Gneisenau was amazed by his countryman's actions, and the business at Frankfurt began to wear on his mental and physical well-being. "For my part, I live here very lonely and rant in written doctrines, which is not easy," he wrote his wife, Caroline. "At the conferences all scream over one another and things are decided which look good on paper, but for all intents and purposes are impracticable. I am already half-sick from the aggravation and the stuffy atmosphere."[41]

The issue over Switzerland remained and ushered in a third phase of military planning as Metternich sought to adjust Allied strategy Austrian national interests. The Knesebeck–Austrian plan called for the Bohemian Army to march through Switzerland, invade southern France, and conduct a general offensive in unison with Wellington and Hiller. This plan would have enabled Metternich to correlate his diplomatic objectives with limited military operations – as opposed to Gneisenau's general offensive – and would have served Austrian policy in regards to Switzerland and Italy. However, when this scheme appeared to lose support, Schwarzenberg scrapped the invasion of southern France. Despite the initial enthusiasm over the idea, the Austrian General Staff, like Gneisenau, questioned the likelihood of actually linking with Wellington's army. It also expressed displeasure with Hiller's unproductive offensive in Italy by replacing him with General Heinrich von Bellegarde and opening negotiations with Napoleon's brother-in-law, King Joachim Murat of Naples. Furthermore, the Austrian staff doubted that an invasion of France's southern departments would bring Napoleon to the peace table. As for Metternich, he measured every move within the parameters of his contest with Alexander. By opening the new campaign with an invasion of southern France, the Austrians would not be able to conceal their intentions to occupy all of Switzerland. After the tsar's vehement opposition to the suggested violation of Swiss neutrality, Metternich could expect him to veto any plan that called for the Allies to move through the length of the Alpine state.[42]

As the deadlock ensued, Frederick William made one last attempt to stop the Allies from crossing the Rhine and instead limit themselves to the liberation of Holland. He dictated his proposal to Knesebeck, who in turn drafted a memo to the tsar that contained his own thoughts as well as the king's. Knesebeck did not oppose crossing of the Rhine but feared the passage would be too risky without possession of Switzerland. As long as Switzerland remained neutral, he viewed a campaign in France as unfeasible. Instead, he suggested awaiting the outcome of negotiations before invading France, because an offensive across the Rhine would gain the French government the moral support of the people. Frederick William presented this memo to Alexander on 7 December, but nothing became of it; even Metternich was committed to resuming hostilities.[43]

On 7 December, Radetzky likewise submitted yet another plan of campaign. Accordingly, the majority of the Bohemian army would cross the upper Rhine to bypass the sources of the Moselle and the Meuse Rivers and advance between the Vosges and the Jura Mountains to the Plateau of Langres.[44] Bernadotte's army again received the task of liberating the Low Countries, but Blücher would cross the middle Rhine and proceed through Metz to attract the enemy's attention and thus facilitate Schwarzenberg's march. If it appeared that Schwarzenberg could envelop the enemy's main army, the Bohemian army would advance to Troyes. Furthermore, to prevent the resources of the southern departments from reaching Paris, he would detach a portion of his army to Orléans. Yet if Blücher could execute the envelopment with better results, he would summon Bülow and Wintzingerode from the Netherlands and launch a general advance on Paris through the Marne Valley. According to the projected time-tables, Schwarzenberg would reach Langres on 15 January – the same day that Blücher should arrive at Metz. All Cossacks and available Streifkorps would immediately cross the Rhine, hinder French mobilization, and interrupt communications. Paris became the goal of further operations that would be determined later. On the basis of this plan, the Allies would invade France across a front that stretched from the North Sea to Switzerland.

Langenau supported the change in strategy, claiming that the Plateau of Langres dominated France and would allow the Allies to take control of the entire country – Knesebeck agreed. The Meuse, the Marne, and the tributaries of the Seine all flowed from Langres to the North Sea, whereas the tributary of the Saône flowed from the plateau to the Mediterranean. An army that crossed the upper Rhine could skirt the Vosges and the Moselle and circumvent the Meuse and the Marne at their sources. By taking a position at Langres to threaten the French interior, the Austrians hoped to avoid a bloody battle and force Napoleon to negotiate seriously. Finally, with Langres as the objective, the Bohemian army needed only to proceed through northern Switzerland to reach the bridges that spanned the upper Rhine. The Austrians hoped this concession would satisfy the tsar.[45]

Schwarzenberg changed the goal of the advance from southern France to Langres, yet he remained committed to cooperating with Wellington and Bellegarde. Alexander's eager support of a union with the Anglo–Portuguese army prompted Schwarzenberg to maintain this element of the previous campaign plan, which gave "the appearance of a grand and sweeping war of annihilation."[46] At this point, however, the Allied generalissimo did not have a clear idea of how he would achieve his objectives. Upon reaching Langres, would he proceed toward Paris or attempt to unite with the British commander? Schwarzenberg's later halt at Langres indicates that he had not fully considered this question and most likely had proceeded in the hope that peace would be concluded before the Bohemian army reached Langres.

Although the Austrians appeared to forego the occupation of Switzerland in favor of passing through Basel to facilitate the Rhine passage, this was not the case. Radetzky had referred to the possession of Switzerland as "indispensable."[47] In late November, Schwarzenberg had authorized his subordinates to advance through Switzerland in mid-December. Alexander, however, persuaded Francis to honor his decision regarding the inviolability of Swiss neutrality and the kaiser directed Schwarzenberg to countermand his orders.[48] Schwarzenberg conceded for the moment, but when he left Frankfurt on 9 December for the upper Rhine, he was still determined to march through Switzerland.[49]

Alexander's entourage opposed the plan. In particular, Jomini drafted a long rebuttal of the proposed cooperation with Wellington and Bellegarde. "Thus I will summarize to the best of my ability," wrote the former French staff officer. "First, the armies of Italy and Wellington only can be regarded as divisions or secondary armies, and it is not necessary for them to operate simultaneously with us. Second, the armies on the Rhine cannot be used for an invasion of inner France because it is impossible for them to extend too far beyond their base of operations on the Rhine in the face of a captain as energetic and bold as Napoleon, having the fortresses that he does in his possession. Third, it is necessary to have at least 200,000 men for the campaign [in France] not including the corps of observation on the Rhine and those in Holland."[50]

Regarding Switzerland, Alexander recognized the advantages of invading France from this direction, but still refused to violate Swiss neutrality. He insisted that the Bohemian army advance to Langres by marching through Badenese territory to cross the Rhine downstream of Basel. Resorting to what the Russian historian Bogdanovich refers to as "trickery," Metternich generated support in Bern for Austrian intervention in Switzerland. He then convinced Francis to authorize Schwarzenberg to march through the Alpine state. Metternich explained to the kaiser that the majority of the Swiss wanted the Allies to occupy their state to protect them from Napoleon. The Austrians also insisted that the Allies needed Basel to secure their communications. Alexander finally sanctioned the use of Basel on the condition that Allied forces move no further into Swiss territory. This concession did not satisfy Metternich, who instructed Schwarzenberg to move the army to points of passage further upstream from Basel. From there, Schwarzenberg could unexpectedly march into Swiss territory upon the request of the pro-Austrian Swiss faction before the tsar could counter. Without the tsar's prior knowledge, Schwarzen-berg instructed the commander of his advance guard to open negotiations with Swiss military authorities.

According to the final version of the Allied invasion plan, the Bohemian army would advance from Basel to Langres. To the north, Bülow and Wintzingerode would invade the Netherlands. Blücher's army, reinforced by Kleist's corps, would operate between these two Allied forces. After Blücher left behind part of his army to besiege Mainz, he could either cross the Rhine at Kaub and advance through Trier and Saarlouis or cross the Rhine upstream of Mainz and advance through Kaiserslautern to cover Schwarzenberg's com-munications. Essentially this plan allowed the Bohemian army to avoid most of the French fortresses that guarded the Rhine. In addition, by making for the gap between the Jura and Vosges Mountains, the majority of the army would be spared from crossing difficult terrain in the midst of winter. By extending his left wing southward, Schwarzenberg would be able to sever French communication with Italy through the Simplon and Mount Cenis Passes. Such a threat could even induce the French to withdraw from Italy, thus allowing the Austrian army to cross the Alps, pacify southern France, and link Schwarzenberg's left with Wellington's right.[51]

To Gneisenau and his supporters, the fact that six or seven weeks would be lost while the Bohemian army maneuvered through Switzerland to the French frontier remained incomprehensible. "I am inconsolable over this inactivity," complains Stewart to Gneisenau, "your army must go to Flanders without further delay, while the Main [Bohemian] Army operates on the upper Rhine and the crown prince in Holland."[52] The Prussians felt that the outcome of the war depended on denying Napoleon the time to raise a new army and prepare his defenses (Appendix E). "We remained idle for seven costly weeks," Gneisenau later wrote. "My proposals were to deny the enemy rest, to immediately cross the Rhine, and to hinder all troop concentrations in France. Had one seized this decision, we would be in Paris today and dictating the peace. But there was a lack of decisiveness. The diplomats and many others loved Frankfurt, and this place almost became our Capula."[53] Clausewitz argues that the Allied armies should have rested on the Rhine for only eight days before crossing the river in mid-November. "Once one had decided not to cross the middle Rhine before January, the march through Breisgau and Switzerland was seen as nothing more than a waste of time and to an extent useless," notes the philosopher of war.[54] "Time, however, was of vital consequence in the proposed operations," notes British historian Frederick Maycock, "though Blücher and Gneisenau alone of the senior commanders seemed fully to recognize the fact, and the prolonged delay caused by the inability of the Allies to decide on a plan of campaign and by Schwarzenberg's unnecessary march, undoubtedly enabled Napoleon to offer a much more effective resistance than would otherwise have been possible."[55]

Gneisenau adequately summarized his frustration in a letter to Colonel Hermann von Boyen, chief of staff of the Prussian III Corps: "I studied these diplomats during my stay in Frankfurt. From my interactions with them I have once again learned [that] if the general does not sweep them away, they will make the most ludicrous moves. To go to Paris and dictate peace there, as we must, is hysterical audacity to them.... Not only diplomats, but generals and regents think this way as well."[56] He saved his most powerful argument for a 20 November note to the king:

> So far Your Majesty's arms and those of the Allies have been very fortunate, but we have now reached a point where the choice is between two evils. Should we remain on the Rhine, allow the troops time to recuperate, and await our needs and reinforcements? Or should we make yet another effort and allow the enemy no rest in order to secure the fruits of our victory and to dictate a durable peace? These are now the two most important questions. Should we do the first, we will provide time for the enemy to assemble recruits and to make these recruits combat-ready. A few months will pass and we will again see numerous armies appear, with whom our brave soldiers will have to battle again. The course of this campaign has taught us many times that we must atone with blood for what we neglect through oversight. This consideration establishes the present issue as a matter of conscience. On the other hand, should we continue to pursue our course of victory, we will thus inflict hardships on our respectable soldiers, who already have endured so much deprivation. *Nevertheless, the hope that through a campaign of perhaps two months time we will be spared two years of war, rivers of blood, and uncertain battles that can once again threaten Your Majesty's throne, allows me to look past this reproach regarding the hardships.*[57]

Both contemporaries and historians have passed judgment over the Allied invasion plan and the objective of Langres. According to Stewart, the colorful Bernadotte "said that if the plan was that of the tsar of Russia, or of any military man of great character, he would, bad as he thought it, be disposed to acquiesce; but he knew it was either the offspring of the ideas of those *Faircuis*, alluding, I apprehend, to the Russian General Staff, who had yet to be instructed in war as much as he was; or else a plan which Austria was anxious to grasp to recover her hereditary states in Italy, to liberate that country, and to forward her own objectives rather than the common cause, or else it would not have been adopted."[58] More serious and less self-absorbing is Clausewitz's assessment. He criticizes the plan by arguing that the point of attack should have been designated to correspond with the objective of the operation: the French army and Paris. Although the shortest route ran from Mainz through Metz and Châlons-en-Champagne to Paris, the combined Allied armies could not utilize one road. Therefore, three "great columns" should have been formed to cross the Rhine between Koblenz and Mannheim to strike the three shortest highways leading to Paris. According to Clausewitz, the first column would advance from Trier through Luxembourg, the second from Kaiserslautern upon Metz, and the third from Phalsbourg through Nancy. Surprisingly, he does claim that the "main characteristics" of the Allied operations plan were very similar to his own, but that "one did not need to cross the Rhine through Switzerland ... in order to establish his line of communication on the upper Rhine."[59] Maycock notes that the invasion plan "had several weak points." The offensive would take place along such an enormous front, and thus "a dangerous dispersion ... was inevitable and an accurately timed cooperation almost impossible. Hence Napoleon would almost certainly be afforded an opportunity to fall on some isolated portion of the force and defeat the Allies in detail."[60] According to French historian Ignace Campana, "this strange plan, which had the effect of dispersing the two armies along a front of several hundred kilometers, planted the seeds of the mistakes that Napoleon would forcibly exploit to defeat his adversaries, despite their formidable numbers."[61] Another French historian, General Guillaume Vaudoncourt, makes the weak claim that it was Napoleon's cordon system that ultimately dictated Allied operations and strategy. "It was according to these considerations that the Coalition established its plan of campaign. The direction of their columns were fixed by the disposition of the defensive system of the French frontiers." Vaudoncourt also states that "the plan of invasion contained one major strategic fault that cannot be excused and which was certainly caused by the Coalition's belief in the weakness of the means that France possessed to oppose it. There remained a huge gap between the two Allied armies, which initially was around twenty-five leagues."[62]

Writing on the eve of the First World War, the German General Staff historian Rudolf Friederich notes that "the military value of the Plateau of Langres marks the folly of the pre-Napoleonic military theories, and at the same time demonstrates how little had been learned from the events of the past decade."[63] His colleague in the historical section of the German General Staff, Janson, contends that the Austrians believed it would be easier to descend on and master the lowlands of France from Langres: "Without striking a blow the enemy would be forced to abandon all those river lines, which would be enveloped, in order to take positions further rearwards, where he would have to confront the Allies as they descended from their higher position, which is always a force multiplier; it was not possible to find a position whose front was more covered by significant rivers than this."[64] Janson also provides an interesting, yet typical Prusso–German view of the Austrians: "The politics fully corresponded to the tendency of the then Austrian way of war, which in the Napoleonic Wars had learned nothing and had forgotten nothing. So it was touch and go if warfare would take a step backwards and if one would move into winter quarters as during the Seven Years' War."[65] Commenting on the Austrians, the German historian Roloff maintains that "all still lived in the theories of the eighteenth century and sought the decision not so much in battle and the defeat of the enemy's forces as in maneuver and the occupation of a so-called master point. To them, such a master point was the Plateau of Langres in France."[66] A more recent assessment by the late Gunther Rothenberg states: "Altogether, the plan exemplified classic eighteenth century maneuver strategy designed to avoid bloody actions while exerting pressure on the enemy to come to terms. The plan was sound, and if Prussian historians have criticized it as 'timid, hesitant, and old-fashioned', it served the political ends of Austrian policy that neither desired to rout Napoleon totally nor to achieve needless and costly military triumphs."[67]

Regarding logistics, the troubling prospect of feeding 200,000 men in hostile territory during the winter influenced the campaign plan considerably. "It was emphasized," explains Burghersh, "that the weakest point of the French frontier always had been acknowledged to be on the side of Switzerland; that Austria had suffered too much in the first years of the Revolutionary War by operating from the Netherlands and the lower Rhine; that the natural line for her to adopt was the one proposed, receiving her supplies from her own provinces by the Danube, and the direct communications [with Austria] through Bavaria."[68]

With France defenseless, Napoleon would not have been able to stop the Coalition's superior forces. The Allies could have sent numerous columns marching on the highways that led directly to Paris. At most, the Allies needed 150,000 men to continue the pursuit across the Rhine in early November. After driving through the remnants of the French army, Paris would have fallen – and with it Napoleon's power and prestige. Instead, the Allies granted Napoleon two months – all of November and December – to prepare his defenses and mobilize new conscripts. Moreover, the tsar and Schwarzenberg chose a roundabout detour as the invasion route for Schwarzenberg's army rather than the closer roads that led from the middle Rhine to the heart of France. By exaggerating the threat posed by the French fortress chain, the Allies deprived themselves of surprise and mass. Because of their weak garrisons and dilapidated conditions, these fortresses hardly deserved such concern. The Austrians believed that upon reaching Langres, Napoleon would immediately conclude a peace. If not, they planned to conduct a war of attrition by once again implementing the Trachenberg Plan. Rather than confront the emperor in a decisive battle, his rear, flanks, communications, and detached subordinates would be targeted.

In the final analysis of the great council of war at Frankfurt, the opposition Gneisenau encountered was based on very human factors. Despite Napoleon's recent catastrophic setbacks, many of the Allied generals and statesmen still stood in awe of the French emperor, and many shuddered at the thought of invading France itself. "If the masses who are today under arms are commanded by a single general and are animated by a single sentiment," wrote Jomini to the tsar, "I believe this general should not hesitate to make a resolution. But as my opinion is based on the facts and the interests of a great monarch and prince are at stake, I must tremble at the consequences of an invasion with the elements that we have and those that we will have to fight. In this state of things I believe that a prudent combination of well-based offensive operations is preferable to that which could expose us to great hazards."[69] "We must further consider," explains the tsar's secretary, Alexander Mikhailovsky-Danilevsky, "that the Allied generals ... were in many respects inferior to him who was looked upon as the first captain of the age, and who was master of his actions and accountable to no one."[70] "The name of Bonaparte was still appalling," adds Burghersh, "and the idea of attacking France, defended by his talents, considerably staggered many of those who were about to be called upon to do so. There was general fear and hesitation at the prospect of attacking this nation, which had put forth such resources and which, for the defense of its own soil, appeared invincible in the early part of its revolutionary career."[71] "One also must not forget," warns Bogdanovich, "the misfortune earlier coalitions suffered by invading France; thus both the diplomats as well as the army commanders gazed with suspicion on any offensive operation; the unsuccessful campaign in Champagne [1792] and the entire string of victories that Napoleon achieved in the previous campaigns still stood before them as a bogey-man."[72]

3

The Frankfurt Proposals

Contention over military operations must be viewed within the larger context of Coalition politics, national self-interest, and the grand strategy of the three eastern powers. Before the battle of Leipzig, the general objective of the Alliance was to liberate central Europe from French control. Yet the attainment of this goal would provide only *one* essential component of each power's complex and unique grand strategy. Aside from Metternich's subtle undermining of the Kalisch–Breslau agreement, no serious dissension in Coalition politics could be perceived while the three continental powers cooperated to complete this core task. However, upon reaching the Rhine, they could not agree on their next and ultimate objective: should they continue the war to overthrow Napoleon or should they negotiate a peace with the French emperor? At this moment, the facade of the concert ended, and the masks were torn off. Liberating Germany provided only one step, albeit a monumental step, toward the achievement of greater national security objectives. Russian – and by extension Prussian – as well as Austrian grand strategy demanded more than reaching the Rhine could provide, although Metternich perceived he was much closer to the realization of his goals than Alexander. As a result, Coalition politics immediately eclipsed both military operations and military cooperation. Naturally, Metternich wanted the Alliance to follow a course that reflected Austria's grand strategy and was conducive to acquiring Austrian national security objectives. The same held true for the tsar. In a letter to Münster, Gneisenau describes the relationship between Allied politics, grand strategy, and military operations:

> I will describe for you briefly the political situation although none of the monarchs nor their ministers have expressed themselves publicly. Tsar Alexander will retain all of Poland and, out of revenge, the king of Saxony will give us all his land. The Austrians do not want this. This has yet to be declared openly

of course, but we can perceive this from many signs. Austria's intentions are thus: they expect to gain control of a large part of Italy. For this reason there will be an invasion of southern France from Switzerland, and thus little value has been placed on the conquest of Holland, which alone can secure North Germany.[1]

Theoretically, the three Allied monarchs were at the heart of the decision-making process. None of the three sovereigns served as commander in chief, which Metternich secured for his countryman, Schwarzenberg. Although his army and the headquarters of the monarchs separated many times, each sovereign attempted to influence operations either by assuming leadership in a certain matter or by direct influence on the units of his own national army. Of the three monarchs, Francis made himself least conspicuous, preferring to have Metternich press Austrian policy in Allied councils. Frederick William, who Metternich accused of being "susceptible to petty fears," labored under the anxiety that an Allied mistake, or worse, Allied failure, would result in the loss of his crown.[2] Consequently, he harbored little sympathy for the impetuosity of the war party, among whom Blücher and several Prussian officers were counted. Rather than invade France, the grand-nephew of Frederick the Great preferred to negotiate a peace. His closest adviser, Knesebeck, failed to provide a balance between the king's prudence and Blücher's impulsiveness. Frederick William endeavored to conserve the Prussian army, which he would need for leverage at the peace table – a view that would prove the king to be far more insightful than Blücher. Moreover, as crown prince of Prussia, he had participated in the campaigns of 1792 and 1793. These operations firmly impressed on him the idea that despite the appearance of weakness, France could prove unexpectedly formidable.

The intrepid tsar provided the antithesis to the Prussian king. "Tsar Alexander is always conciliatory, benevolent, and steadfast;" wrote Stein, "he inspires confidence and a sentiment of devotion in all those who approach him. The king [of Prussia] is somewhat crabby, more or less snubbing those who see him."[3] In the pursuit of his ultimate prize, the tsar did not refrain from interfering with Schwarzenberg's leadership. Alexander also managed to redress Frederick William's reiterated misgivings and convince him to voice support for Russian objectives.[4] Consequently, Metternich emerged as his archrival for control of the Coalition.

Alexander provided the driving force at Allied headquarters and found a natural connection with Blücher, even if the respective motives of each varied at times. "His decided opinion always favored pushing the war to the last extremity," explains Mikhailovsky-Danilevsky, "and he maintained it despite the general wish of the foreign cabinets. By rejecting peace, Alexander stood alone in the Allied camp, as did Napoleon in France."[5] Metternich would have easily outmaneuvered the "war party," represented by Blücher,

Gneisenau, Stein, and Münster if not for the tsar.[6] Unmitigated hatred of Napoleon and a boundless desire for revenge formed the bond between Alexander and the Prussians of Blücher's entourage. Thiers offers an interesting French perspective regarding this relationship:

> They [the Prussians] were not content with winning over their own king, they enticed Tsar Alexander with flattery, calling him the king of kings, the Supreme Chief of the Coalition, by attributing to him the great decisions of the war, by promising to conduct him to Paris; all of which excited the vanity of this prince to a delirious height. Alexander, complaisant by nature and by calculation, adding to his natural amiability a continual care to flatter the passions of all, cajoled the Prussians, whose courage and patriotism he did not cease to praise, in order to have them on his side against the Austrians, of whom he was jealous.[7]

At the heart of the competition between Alexander and Metternich festered long-standing rivalries, national security objectives, and the inherent difficulties of a multinational coalition. During the spring campaign of 1813, the three original members of the Sixth Coalition – Russia, Prussia, and Great Britain – forged their objectives into an alliance. Alexander desired to reconstitute Poland into a Romanov possession. Frederick William would surrender his Polish provinces to the Russians and be compensated with Saxony to reestablish Prussia's pre-1806 material strength. In return for allowing its allies a free hand in central Europe, London could do as it pleased with Spain, Portugal, Sicily, Belgium, and Holland. Regarding Great Britain's insistence on "maritime rights" and possession of the colonies snatched from France and its satellites, the two eastern powers had little interest and even less to say as long as France was rendered incapable of further aggression.[8]

Austria's accession to the Sixth Coalition in August 1813 upset this balance. Beyond providing a commander in chief and 300,000 troops for the Allied armies, Vienna introduced new and complex issues such as the fate of Italy and Illyria. Metternich initially alienated the British by attempting to detach their objectives from those of the Coalition. Furthermore, he pursued a twofold policy that contradicted Russo–Prussian war aims. On one hand, the Austrian foreign minister wanted to create a balance between the great powers by using France as a counterweight against Russia. On the other, he wanted to establish an equilibrium of power among all European states: the powerful and the weak, the victors and the vanquished.[9] To counter Russia, Metternich needed a strong, preferably Napoleonic, France. To establish an equilibrium, Metternich had to thwart Russo–Prussian designs on Poland and Saxony as well as any other plans of retribution Berlin entertained regarding the Third Germany.

Metternich started implementing this dual policy before the battle of Leipzig. September's Teplitz Accords undermined the Kalisch–Breslau

Figure 4. Prince Clemens Lothar Wensceslas von Metternich (1773–1859). Austrian foreign minister and chancellor.

agreements regarding Poland and Saxony by stating that Allied war aims included the "entire and absolute independence" of the German states.[10] One month later, he assumed control over Allied occupation policy in the former Rheinbund in order to lay the groundwork for a postwar Germany that reflected Austrian interests.[11] Despite a long history of opposition, the Austrians and Bavarians signed the Treaty of Ried on 8 October 1813.[12] Historian Paul Schroeder describes the treaty as Metternich's "greatest victory in this campaign," and Nipperdey adds that the treaty "was to be of the utmost significance for the future of Germany."[13] With the Habsburg emperor's guarantee of Bavaria's sovereignty, King Max-Joseph entered the war not as a member of the Sixth Coalition but as Austria's ally. In German matters, Bavaria would be Austria's partner to frustrate Prussian plans for redemption. This diplomatic coup established the pattern for Napoleon's remaining German satellites to defect. Some in the Allied camp recognized Metternich's self-serving motives. "The arrangements made with the Bavarians tie our hands and are harmful to the general measures to be taken," wrote Stein to Hardenberg.[14] Yet Metternich's German policy fell completely in line with his strategy. Preferring stability and legitimacy over revolution, chaos, and upheaval, the Austrian minister purposefully maintained Napoleon's territorial reorganization of Germany. He understood that any attempt to make considerable changes to the German status quo would destabilize the equilibrium of central Europe and upset the balance of power, possibly even leading to a war between the great powers.[15]

On 30 October, Stein wrote a memorandum calling for harsh measures against the German princes who remained loyal to Napoleon, yet the Rheinbund collapsed shortly after the Allies reached the Rhine.[16] Of its three kings, Max-Joseph of Bavaria already had allied with Austria and King Frederick August of Saxony was taken prisoner at Leipzig after the battle. King Frederick of Württemberg signed the Treaty of Fulda – a convention similar to the Treaty of Ried – on 2 November.[17] Throughout this month, Metternich used the Treaty of Ried as a model to entice other former Rheinbund states into the Austrian camp by concluding similar conventions with Würzburg, Saxe-Coburg, Hesse-Darmstadt, Baden, Nassau, and Hesse-Kassel. Promises of protection, the retention of royal titles, and guarantees of territorial integrity provided a strong motive for Napoleon's former allies to base their future on Austrian benevolence. In essence, the Confederation of the Rhine would not be conquered and the Napoleonic reorganization of Germany became part of the postwar European order. The guarantee of individual sovereignty and the recognition of the historic issue of states' rights earned Metternich the ire of nineteenth-century German nationalist historians, who viewed his policy as a major setback for German political development.[18]

Metternich's masterful comprehension of the political landscape earned him considerable advantages not only in laying the groundwork for a postwar Europe that satisfied Austrian national security objectives but also in the perpetual struggle to restrain his allies. Wilson recounts a dinner hosted by Metternich on the night of 5 November during which the British officer sat next to the Austrian minister and the two engaged in a "very interesting conversation. He [Metternich] said that if the Allies would be cordial as to their real objects and put confidence in him, he would engage to make a satisfactory peace or deprive Bonaparte of the support of France, which alone could enable him to make the necessary efforts." The British officer recalls that Metternich "adds to the talents of a minister all the accomplishments of a liberal host, a gallant gentleman, and a *bel esprit*; so his table and his soirees are very delightful points of rendezvous."[19]

Whereas Great Britain's objectives remained relatively consistent throughout 1813, success on the battlefield substantially inflated those of Prussia and Russia. According to historian Paul Sweet, Hardenberg appointed his chief assistant, Wilhelm von Humboldt, "to articulate and promote a policy on the future of Germany that would reflect Prussia's perception of its interests and role as a great power." Sweet asserts that Allied victories in Germany, "which the Prussian army ascribed largely to its own prowess, had given rise to the illusion that Prussia, as the paladin of nationalist hopes in Germany, could impose its will on the settlement to come."[20] However, Metternich's alliances with the former Rheinbund princes shrewdly prevented the Prussians from exacting revenge on the Third Germany by treating its states as occupied territories and dictating the future of their political existence. For example, Metternich's guarantee to Max-Joseph in the Treaty of Ried regarding the retention of the provinces of Ansbach and Bayreuth as well as Bavarian expansion north of the Main River constituted what historian Enno Kraehe describes as "a blow to Prussia's aspirations comparable to the threat to Austria inherent in the Saxon question. On these grounds alone Hardenberg had reason to feel cheated by the treaty." Hardenberg demanded the reduction of the German states enlarged by Napoleon "for the aggrandizement of Austria and Prussia and to facilitate the partitioning of Germany between the two powers." Whereas Stein attempted to minimize Allied aggrandizement in the Third Germany, Hardenberg supported Austrian hegemony in the south to gain support for Prussian preponderance in the north. He planned to annex Saxony, most of Berg, parts of Westphalia, and to create a Prussian-dominated federal union.

On 21 October 1813, Austria, Prussia, and Russia had signed agreements creating the Central Executive Department for German Territories. The Allies vested this agency with authority to raise funds, mobilize troops, and draw supplies. Named the director of this body, Stein also received the dual task of mobilizing the resources of the former Rheinbund states to assist the Allied war effort and of temporarily governing conquered German states that had no government or whose rulers had not yet joined the Coalition. In his vision of Germany's future, Stein sought a tripartite arrangement. Mecklenburg, Holstein, and Saxony would go to Prussia, while Austria would be restored to its 1805 status and given the province of Ansbach. For the remaining German states, Stein hoped to create a third entity that had its own central government "with power over war and peace, foreign and military affairs, coinage and tariffs." Kraehe explains that "there was to be a Habsburg emperor, but the connection with Austria would be that of a personal union only. The three parts – Austria, Prussia, and 'Germany' – each with a population of about ten million, were then to be bound together in a perpetual defensive alliance."[21]

Metternich extended his hand to the German states as part of his efforts to undermine the "rabid nationalism" of the German patriots led by Stein, to ensure further that the conflict with France did not become a peoples' war, and to undermine Russian influence in Germany. He feared the creation of a German national state that could contribute to the dissolution of the Habsburg supranational empire or the European balance of power. Indifferent to Hardenberg's suggestion that Vienna establish hegemony over south Germany, Metternich envisioned Austria becoming an European rather than a Germanic power in the postwar order.[22]

In addition, the Russian colossus always remained a concern. Kraehe notes that if Metternich "now sought to appease the Rheinbund sovereigns rather than punish them, the reason was not dread of revolution or German unity, but rather fear of the limitless ambitions of Russia."[23] Alexander's interest in liberating Germany manifested itself early in the war with the Proclamation of Kalisch. Issued by Russian High Command on 25 March 1813, it contained the Russian and Prussian pledged of support for a united Germany.[24] This document called on the princes and peoples of Germany to accept the tsar's protection and lead in creating a free and independent Germany. Thus the aim of the war was to dissolve the Confederation of the Rhine and restore a "rejuvenated united empire with a constitution 'based on the inherent spirit of the German people'."[25] It promised the destruction of Napoleon's German allies should they refuse. Although the Teplitz Accords eliminated the objective of creating a united Germany, Metternich viewed Alexander's German policy with extreme suspicion. Brendan Simms claims that "by 1811 dynastic and political links between the Tsar and the southern German states, especially with Württemberg, represented a kind of *Rheinbundist* insurance policy against the collapse of French power and the renewal of Austro–Prussian tutelage."[26] "With Bonaparte destroyed," continues Kraehe, "Alexander would be the sole mediator in a German Reich and could resume his former role as protector of uncles, cousins, and in-laws in the middle states. What was important was the recovery of his following in the Third Germany without the competition from Bonaparte and without driving Austria from the Coalition."[27]

The guarantee to respect the sovereignty of these states and to uphold the deeply rooted German tradition of states' rights enabled Metternich to thwart any attempt to submerge the former members of the Rheinbund into a federally unified Germany. Nor did he wish to resurrect the antediluvian Holy Roman Empire. Instead, he wanted to base German and thus central European security on what historian Robert Billinger refers to as a "confederation of German princes and free cities dedicated to the preservation of the security of the individual German states." Although a German imperial prince himself, Metternich placed Habsburg national security above any sentiments for the German fatherland. He saw that his main concern, the survival of the Habsburg empire, could be advanced by turning the German states into a "central European defense community [to serve] as a barrier against France and Russia and as the keystone of continental equilibrium."[28] By the end of the year, Metternich eliminated any prospect of creating a unified Germany, leaving Humboldt to lament: "For German matters Metternich has...little feeling. If it turns out as he wishes, there will be pieces of Germany without...any connection to each other, or at the most a very loose one.... In my view, this is pernicious to the highest degree, for I believe that there must be a closer bond linking them together. To tie this knot, I feel, is going to be difficult, and it will not hold together forever, but nevertheless it can to some extent keep alive the idea that Germans are one people."[29]

Any discussion of Russian war aims must begin with Tsar Alexander. Contemporaries and historians alike have left many colorful descriptions of this fascinating individual. Gordon Craig provides one of the most biting caricatures: "Alexander was neurotic and possibly schizophrenic. He went through life haunted by a sense of guilt incurred when he was elevated to the throne over the murdered corpse of his father, and his attempts to escape from this by posing alternately as the scourge and as the savior of Europe, by indulging in paroxysms of idealistic reform and frenzies of sexual excess, and, finally, by giving his support to experiments in religious mysticism, failed to ease his troubled spirit or to prevent his eventual collapse... into the depths of manic depression."[30] Henry Kissinger adds: "At the same time mystic and cunning, idealistic and calculating, he presented an ambivalent mixture of universal principles justifying specifically Russian gains, of high motives supporting aspirations considered selfish in lesser men."[31] "The tsar," explains historian Steven Ross, "a cunning mystic and a Machiavellian idealist, who was convinced that his goals were identical with universal justice and that universal justice was identical with Russian strategic and diplomatic interests, apparently was planning to organize what he regarded as inevitable victory in such a manner as to leave Russia the arbiter of Europe."[32] Schwarzenberg perhaps states it best in a letter to Metternich: "There is no doubt that the word enigma explains the pertinacity of our dear weak Alexander."[33] Metternich himself bluntly recorded in his dubious memoirs: "The tsar of Russia, prepossessed by revolutionary ideas... entertained plans that would have led the world to ruin."[34] Finally, Nipperdey concludes that "the tsar styled himself as a liberator. His actions were, of course, bound with the power interests of Russia. No politician could predict how Russian power interests and the Russian ideology of liberation – especially considering the Tsar's unpredictability – would develop."[35]

The tsar convinced himself that he would risk continuing the war without the Austrians. At that moment, the Russians and Prussians together possessed adequate combat power to invade France without the Austrians. Metternich undoubtedly realized this, and, once again, his political acumen led him to an accurate evaluation of the situation. Time became crucial to Metternich: peace with Napoleon had to be achieved before Alexander invaded France without Austrian participation. Persuading Napoleon to accept peace and restraining the tsar became Metternich's primary objectives in the winter of 1813–14.[36]

As for peace with Napoleon, the Allies initially ignored their first opportunity to open negotiations when he proposed an armistice to his father-in-law, Francis, on 17 October during the battle of Leipzig. In discussing the possibility of peace with the captured Austrian corps commander, General Maximilian von Merveldt, Napoleon appeared disposed to surrender control over all of Germany and perhaps Italy as well. Yet he insisted the British presented the true obstacles to peace. Bonaparte believed London would attempt to limit the French fleet to an unacceptable thirty ships of the line.[37]

Figure 5. Alexander I (1777–1825), tsar of Russia.

Less than two weeks later, on 27 October, Metternich met with the tsar and the British ambassador to Austria, George Hamilton Gordon, Lord Aberdeen. They agreed to reply to Napoleon's overtures by means of a captured French chargé d'affaires, Nicolas-Auguste St. Aignan. Metternich and Aberdeen negotiated the details with Russian Foreign Minister Nesselrode; the Prussians were not consulted. Humboldt, the Prussian ambassador to Vienna, attempted to participate, but Metternich informed him that Hardenberg, who had not yet reached Frankfurt, already had deferred to Austria's judgment in this matter. Yet after Hardenberg arrived, Metternich ignored him as well.

During these three-way talks, Aberdeen sided with Metternich to oppose Nesselrode's insistence on harsh peace terms. Furthermore, Aberdeen committed an unforgivable error in the eyes of the British cabinet by agreeing that London would negotiate maritime rights – a point British statesmen had steadfastly refused to discuss. Metternich instructed St. Aignan to convey an oral summary of an informal conversation between the Austrian and Russian ministers on the evening of 9 November; by design Aberdeen stumbled on the meeting and added Great Britain's supposed concessions.

To be sure, Aberdeen committed a gigantic faux pas of which many attempts have been made to explain both the cause and the effect. Regarding the former, British historian Charles Webster claims that Aberdeen "had been deeply moved by the terrible scenes that he had witnessed. The ride across the Leipzig battlefield, while the screams of the wounded lying amidst the masses of dead fell unheeded on the ears of the cavalcade, made an indelible impression on the sensitive nature of the young envoy and affected all his future life. He realized the horror of war as no other British minister has ever done, and was more than ready to listen to Metternich's proposals."[38] "For three or four miles the ground is covered with bodies of men and horses, many not dead," wrote Aberdeen himself after the battle of Leipzig. "Wounded wretches unable to crawl, crying for water amidst heaps of putrefying bodies. Their screams are heard at an immense distance, and still ring in my ears."[39]

Regarding the consequences of Aberdeen's agreement to negotiate maritime rights: "it was a question in which the mediation of any ally with Great Britain could not be accepted," explains Charles Stewart, "and it was still less a question which Great Britain would ever discuss at a general congress."[40] According to Kissinger: "In his eagerness to gain the glory of pacifying Europe, Aberdeen forgot that no power can agree to negotiate about what it considers the condition of its existence."[41] Rory Muir agrees, stating that "where Castlereagh was willing to make peace to satisfy the Allies, Aberdeen was positively eager: He was genuinely horrified by war, and he wanted to go home with all the *éclat* of having negotiated a peace settlement."[42] Nevertheless, disagreement exists over Aberdeen's complicity with Metternich. Schroeder contends that Aberdeen "expressly reserved Britain's position on the maritime code, but did not try to stop the mission."[43] "Aberdeen," adds Nicolson, "while making verbal reservations regarding this formula, did not reject it completely." Moreover, Nicolson claims that St. Aignan himself twisted the meaning of the offer to insinuate that the British would accept French claims regarding free trade and navigation.[44] Aside from the subsequent historiography, Foreign Minister Castlereagh made it perfectly clear to his young subordinate how the British government felt over the issue of maritime rights: "At all times, a maritime question touches us to the quick."[45]

St. Aignan left for Paris on the 10th and arrived four days later; Napoleon received him on the 15th. The Allies insisted that Napoleon withdraw behind France's "natural" frontiers prior to the commencement of negotiations. St. Aignan's report to Napoleon, which contains the details of the conversation he had with the Allied ministers, states: "The Coalition powers have unanimously agreed that France must retain its integrity and be contained within its natural boundaries, which are the Alps, the Rhine, and the Pyrenees." Moreover, the Bourbon dynasty had to be restored in Spain. Although Napoleon would be forced to surrender Holland, Germany, Italy, and Spain, he could retain Belgium, the left bank of the Rhine, and Savoy in northwestern Italy – the original conquests of the Revolution. Collectively known as the Frankfurt

Proposals, these terms offered France territory that generations of Frenchmen had died in vain attempting to secure.[46]

Austrian grand strategy pervades Metternich's offer. Containing Russia and preventing the tsar from demanding Galicia in return for Alsace required the preservation of France as a great power in the postwar equilibrium. According to Metternich's plan, a France with its natural frontiers would have sufficient resources to deter Russian aggrandizement in central Europe. At this stage of the war, Metternich's mastery of Coalition politics allowed him to make this proposal without raising suspicions of Austrian duplicity, war weariness, or pacifism. He insisted that operations continue during the course of any negotiations. This would prevent Napoleon from using the cover of negotiations to gain time to reorganize his army, as he did during the Armistice of Pläswitz. Should the French emperor reject the Frankfurt Proposals, he would risk alienating his war-weary subjects, whereas the Allies could portray themselves as conciliatory and moderate to those French factions ready for peace. Although designed to contain Russia, Metternich received full support from the unsuspecting tsar as well as the kaiser and Aberdeen for recognizing the Rhine, Alps, and Pyrenees as the borders of the French empire.

Whether Metternich genuinely believed peace could be concluded at this time remains unclear. To Aberdeen and Nesselrode, he remained optimistic over the chances Napoleon would accept the Proposals. Yet in his correspondence with Armand de Caulaincourt, Napoleon's representative at the Congress of Prague earlier that year and a well-known peace advocate, Metternich appears hopeless.[47] In his self-serving memoirs, Metternich admits that at the time he realized Napoleon "would never voluntarily" accept the Frankfurt Proposals.[48] Yet the Frankfurt Proposals reflect his plan to maintain a strong France by tethering his allies to peace terms that were as lenient as possible. Gneisenau, however, called for a general offensive to drive the French from their natural frontiers of the Rhine and the Alps. What would become of Metternich's plan if the war party won and Allied armies stormed across the Rhine, bringing Napoleon to his knees? As a means to prevent this scenario, Knesebeck's influence on Frederick William certainly pleased the Austrian minister. Knesebeck did not imminently embrace peace but supported operations that would neither lead to a decisive engagement nor threaten any preliminary agreement with Napoleon.[49] Consequently, on 10 November, the day St. Aignan left for Paris, Schwarzenberg reconvened the Allied council of war to discuss Knesebeck's concerns.

Metternich desired to accompany St. Aignan's mission with an Allied ultimatum stating that Napoleon must make peace according to the Frankfurt Proposals or the Allies would invade France and impose a peace. Such a declaration would prove to the French that the Allies were committed to granting France its natural frontiers in return for peace. Aberdeen and Nesselrode agreed with the proclamation, but objected to the timing of its publication. Aberdeen argued the proclamation would have the opposite affect on both the French emperor and his subjects. Napoleon would interpret the message as an attack on the very foundation of his popularity: his martial abilities. If Metternich issued his proclamation before Bonaparte responded to the Frankfurt Proposals, it could serve to discourage Napoleon's opposition in France and electrify the French nation rather than win the support of the people. The British and Russian diplomats persuaded Metternich to publish the proclamation only if Napoleon rejected the Frankfurt Proposals.[50]

Whereas Metternich schemed to conclude a peace settlement that considered Russia to be the future threat to Europe's equilibrium, others remained focused on containing France. Stewart, for example, recognized that the basis of a durable peace depended first on gaining sufficient territory from France for the formation of buffer states along the French frontier. This would require France to restore conquered territory as part of a general peace settlement. Furthermore, Austria and Prussia – the powers behind such buffer states – needed to be strengthened and consolidated as much as possible to support them. Accordingly, this supposition posed several unanswered questions that troubled Metternich. In what direction and at whose expense would Prussia expand? Would Alsace be offered to Austria, thus opening the door for the Russians to claim Galicia? Yet a France confined to its natural frontiers would retain Alsace with its powerful fortress belt that offered a perfect staging ground for French aggression in the Third Germany. Such a threat would require either the augmentation of the medium German states opposite the Upper Rhine or Prussian expansion along the middle Rhine. Should Alsace remain a French possession, Stewart suggested the destruction of all Rhenish fortresses as far as Landau. Moreover, Strasbourg should return to its status as a free city. Then, in Stewart's opinion, "the ancient frontier of France, from Landau to Dunkirk, would be the most perfect military line." The British envoy also suggested tying the fate of France's northern border to the French boundary along the upper Rhine. "It was to be considered whether, in uniting territories under pretense of a sufficient barrier for Holland, we did not leave to France a greater population and extent than under her kings; we might give her the frontier of the Rhine from Basel to Landau, and then take what we might consider an adequate security for Holland, or for the power that would be placed between France and the Rhine." Metternich needed more time to flesh out such weighty details.[51]

But time was not a luxury to be enjoyed by the Austrian minister. Eager to reach a settlement before the tsar led the Allied armies cross the Rhine or the offer of France's natural frontiers was taken off the table, Metternich secretly wrote Caulaincourt. He tasked St. Aignan, Caulaincourt's brother-in-law, with delivering the letter. The Austrian emphasized the real opportunity for peace that the Frankfurt Proposals offered. Metternich also informed

Caulaincourt that should Napoleon reject these proposals, the Allies would increase their demands and there would be "upheavals without point and without limit."[52] Vast armies would invade France: 400,000 Germans alone would be under arms in two months. Using forceful language, Metternich insisted that peace was in the best interest of both France and Austria. He fully expected Caulaincourt to reveal the contents of this letter to Bonaparte. The Austrian minister understood Napoleon's nature better than any other official in the Allied camp. Undoubtedly, the emperor would scornfully view any peace proposal as a sign of Allied weakness and thus reject it. For this reason, Metternich candidly informed Caulaincourt of the Coalition's intent to continue the war relentlessly unless Napoleon agreed to seriously negotiate.[53]

Caulaincourt exercised little influence over his master as Napoleon continued to deceive himself. Rather than accept this generous offer that could lead to a peace that would leave France much stronger than it was under the Bourbons, he sought only to rebuild his army. Spain and Germany were lost, but to surrender Holland and Italy, Napoleon demanded assurances of a "speedy and sincere peace" that spared France from invasion and guaranteed the natural frontiers. Napoleon later referred to the Frankfurt Proposals as a "mask" and believed it quite possible "that the Allies have other ideas."[54] "The offer of the Rhine boundary," concludes Kissinger, "was thus no longer a plea for self-limitation, but a definition of Napoleon's real, perhaps even of his maximum strength. It was an appeal to Napoleon to give up his delusions, not indeed because Metternich wanted to save Napoleon, but because he wanted to save Saxony and Poland. For this end, Metternich proposed to find out if it was possible for the Emperor of the French to become... King of France."[55]

Bonaparte labored under the firm belief that his fortunes were tied to the original conquests of the Revolution: Belgium, the left bank of the Rhine, and northwest Italy. Napoleon's own military exploits and the resulting diplomatic settlements had secured these conquests as France's official borders. His 1797 Treaty of Campo Formio with Austria won Belgium and the left bank of the Rhine for France and recognized the French puppet states of northern Italy. Napoleon's 1801 Treaty of Lunéville, likewise with Austria, reconfirmed these agreements. In his opinion, surrendering the natural frontiers would be tantamount to betraying the Revolution, invalidating his own achievements, and committing political suicide.[56] Although the Frankfurt Proposals would not have stripped France of all these conquests, the terms appeared unreasonable compared with those offered at Prague four months earlier. In addition, Napoleon's acceptance of the Proposals would not have spared France from invasion; Metternich made it clear that military operations would continue during the negotiations.[57]

Metternich understood Napoleon's motives, or at least claimed to understand them when he penned his memoirs: "Any peace with Napoleon that would have thrown him back to the old boundaries of France, and which would have deprived him of districts that had been conquered before he came to power, would only have been a ridiculous armistice, and would have been repelled by him."[58] In fact, Humboldt accused Metternich of attempting to mislead the French because the Rhine frontier was absolutely out of the question: The French would have to be satisfied with their ancient boundaries.[59] Napoleon himself wrote:

> Europe seems to offer peace, but she does not sincerely wish it. You believe that by humiliating ourselves we shall disarm her; you are mistaken. The more yielding we are, the more exacting she will become, and from demand to demand she will lead us on to terms of peace that we cannot accept. She offers the line of the Rhine and the Alps, and even some part of Piedmont. These certainly are favorable conditions; but if we appear willing to accept, she will soon propose the frontiers of 1790. Well, can I accept them – I, to whom the natural frontiers have been entrusted by the Republic?[60]

Napoleon failed to recognize the rivalry that existed in the Allied camp regarding issues such as Belgium, the left bank of the Rhine, Poland, and Saxony.[61] French historian Jean Thiry contends that Bonaparte should have done more to divide the Allies over the "eastern question." He particularly notes that Alexander's ambition to gain Galicia, Metternich's fear of Russian preponderance in Poland, and Prussia's willingness to negotiate with Austria over Saxony all could have been exploited by Napoleon.[62] Bonaparte was aware of these issues and knew more of Metternich's intimate thoughts than the Austrian minister would ever admit, yet for the time being the French emperor still preferred to gain his victories with the sword rather than the quill.[63]

Diplomatic posturing continued in Frankfurt while the Allies awaited Napoleon's reply. British Foreign Minister Castlereagh sought the formation of a Grand Alliance to solidify the Coalition as well as to lay the groundwork for postwar collective security. Bequeathed to him through William Pitt's 1805 strategy, Castlereagh's continental policy contained four essential points: first, Russia would be viewed as Great Britain's "partner"; Russian expansion was permissible, but Austria and Prussia had to be compensated. Second, Prussia's influence in northern and western Germany should be increased. Third, Austria should receive a free hand in northern Italy. Fourth, Great Britain would surrender some of the French, Dutch, and Spanish colonies taken since the start of the French wars. An initial difference between Castlereagh and Metternich can be viewed in these objectives: The former obsessed over Europe's current problems, whereas potential issues preoccupied the latter.

During the Armistice of Pläswitz, Castlereagh watched Metternich steer the Coalition in a direction that would leave many of Great Britain's war aims unfulfilled. Metternich harbored little concern for the issues that most concerned the British: maritime trading rights, the Low Countries, and Iberia. On the other hand, British interests in the Italian peninsular alarmed Vienna. As a result, the peace plan that Metternich produced during the armistice ignored maritime trading rights, the Low Countries, Iberia, and Sicily, prompting Castlereagh to accuse him of submitting to Napoleon. Purposefully disregarding British interests, Metternich concentrated on peace for eastern, central, and southern Europe. To achieve his goal, he sought to isolate London and exclude the British from negotiations. He believed that Austria's main goals – containing Russia and preventing future revolutions – could best be achieved by maintaining Napoleon on the French throne and limiting France to its natural frontiers. His attempts to form this triumvirate between Austria, Russia, and Prussia to dictate a policy that ignored British interests unsettled Castlereagh. The British cabinet knew Metternich feared the consequences of Napoleon's fall, preferred a negotiated peace, and sought to exclude Great Britain from the Coalition's decision-making process. For example, neither of the two British envoys at Allied headquarters were consulted about the signing of the Armistice of Pläswitz on 4 June 1813. Moreover, Metternich did not invite the British to participate in the discussions with Russia and Prussia that produced the Treaty of Reichenbach.[64] In July and August, Castlereagh failed in his attempts to win over Metternich and prevent him from negotiating a settlement with Alexander and Frederick William that ignored British interests. In September, the British pound managed to bring Austria and Great Britain closer together. Needing British financial assistance to wage war, the Austrians agreed not to make a separate peace with Napoleon in return for a £1,000,000 subsidy. Ironically, that same month Metternich orchestrated the Teplitz agreements with Prussia and Russia, which said nothing of waging war to secure British interests in Italy, Holland, and Spain.

This omission is partly due to Metternich's doubt that London would help him secure his postwar objectives concerning central Europe, primarily the containment of Russia. He figured that a strong Napoleonic France would be more willing than the British to assist with the containment of Russia. Finally, despite Castlereagh's apparent willingness to make colonial adjustments, any concessions made by the British would be done from London rather than at the peace table where the French could issue their own demands and the two sides could then negotiate a settlement. Recognizing that Napoleon would never accept London's intransigence on this matter, the Austrian minister worried that the British could ultimately frustrate his goal of negotiating a peace. "With a certain obtuseness born of being shielded by the Channel from the grossest facts of international life," explains Kraehe, "Castlereagh thought his country entitled to a major voice in continental affairs, while refusing others a corresponding voice in non-European matters. On the continent, balance of power; on the high seas, British hegemony."[65] Metternich diligently worked to bridge the divide between him and Castlereagh – his eventual success generated another diplomatic revolution in international affairs.

Although Castlereagh and Metternich appeared diametrically opposed to each other's programs, a rift in Anglo–Russian relations opened the door for an Anglo–Austrian entente. Castlereagh's proposal for a Grand Alliance – directed first at Russia as Britain's "partner" in the Pitt Plan – reached the Allies on 20 October. The British ambassador to Russia, Cathcart, received the task of convincing the tsar. Cathcart had to wait six days before Alexander, who claimed to be busy with the pursuit of Napoleon's army, would receive him. Interestingly, Castlereagh chose the Reichenbach Protocol as the war objectives for the proposed Grand Alliance as long as Holland received a barrier to protect it from France. These terms, which would allow Napoleon to retain the throne of a relatively powerful France, had formed the minimum peace program in July. With the Allied armies now at the Rhine, Alexander quite possibly viewed these dated objectives as an attempt to deny him the fruits of victory. He informed Cathcart that such aims no longer reflected the actual situation. The tsar had yet to reveal his full plans regarding Poland and so remained evasive. Alexander refused to sign a treaty that did not guarantee him this major objective, yet he could not openly reveal his objective for fear the Austrians might make a separate peace with Napoleon. That Castlereagh made no reference to the colonial situation and maritime rights further aggravated the tsar, who demanded to know the specific colonies London intended to relinquish. As part of his developing grand strategy, Alexander wanted the British to make colonial concessions to France, Spain, Portugal, Holland, and the United States to enable Russia to challenge British maritime supremacy. Ultimately, the tsar rebuffed the British.[66] "I have neither on this, nor on any former occasion," wrote Cathcart, "found the tsar so much averse to a general treaty of alliance, offensive and defensive."[67]

At the moment, this setback in Anglo–Russian relations did not threaten to destroy the Coalition. Nevertheless, it did set the stage for future clashes and Metternich cleverly exploited this window of opportunity. He took advantage of the tsar's recalcitrance by presenting himself to the British as a flexible proponent of an Anglo–Austrian entente. Although Metternich would first have to weather the storm that would be caused in London by his Frankfurt Proposals, he paved the way for Austria and Great Britain to assume their relationship as natural allies.

As for the Prussians, Hardenberg also sought a closer relationship with Great Britain. The chancellor's exclusion from the three-way discussions that produced the Frankfurt Proposals spoke volumes of how easily Prussia could be ignored in great power politics. Hardenberg's disillusionment is evident in his 9 November journal entry: "Proposals for peace via St. Aignan without my participation.... Crazy business." Humboldt also wrote his wife over the issue: "I disapproved of the entire St. Aignan move. I gave the chancellor a written memorandum about it. He himself is blameless in the matter since Metternich did not bring him into the conversation with St. Aignan."[68] Gneisenau likewise expressed disgust:

> There is much diplomatic activity that is sometimes repugnant or absurd. The Austrian and Russian diplomats, their number is legion, are very active. To them are joined the Rheinbund princes. Our chancellor and his assistants are practically isolated, without aid, and their strength, due to their small number, does not allow them to do anything more than observe and scrutinize. The three British envoys are at odds among themselves. Aberdeen has been mastered by the cunning Metternich and is completely biased toward Austrian views.... Nesselrode is a tool in Metternich's hands.... Only the Tsar of Russia debates with Metternich.[69]

Metternich's disregard for Berlin's interests stemmed from Prussia's obstinate attitude toward Saxony. "The question of Prussian aggrandizement," Metternich supposedly informed Aberdeen, "is viewed by the Austrian government with the utmost solicitude. Nothing will induce Austria to agree to the incorporation of Saxony in Prussia."[70] To rehabilitate his position and build closer ties with Great Britain, Hardenberg frequently met with Stewart. The British envoy felt "great satisfaction" in discovering that Hardenberg agreed "entirely with the views of His Majesty's government." Conversely, Hardenberg could take comfort in Stewart's argument in favor of Prussia's digestion of Saxony:

> As long as this power [Saxony] remains independent in the rear of Prussia, the latter cannot become a sufficient barrier to the north against Russian invasion. If the Prussian armies should be defeated on the Oder, and Saxony awed into neutrality or confederacy with Russia, Berlin and Pomerania will immediately fall. But should Prussia be put in possession of Saxony, were she beat upon her first line of the Oder, she could form again with renewed force and strength on the Elbe, and be enabled to collect all her resources and those of her allies before Russia could master her fortresses, which would not be the case if Russia, by the means of the treachery or imbecility of Saxony, were to lay hold of the Elbe. Add to this argument that Prussia should not be looked at as a barrier against Russia, or to be prepared to place herself, conjointly with Austria, in that position, unless means are supplied to Prussia by the powers of Europe for playing that game with security and with effect.[71]

Stewart viewed Aberdeen as a rival – especially after Aberdeen informed neither him nor Cathcart of his negotiations with Metternich and Nesselrode over the Frankfurt Proposals – and thus it is unlikely the latter presented this argument to the Austrian court. Moreover, Castlereagh's apparent willingness to go to war in early 1815 to stop the Russians and Prussians during the Polish–Saxon Crisis is proof enough that he rejected his half-brother's arguments concerning Prussia's need to take all of Saxony. Nevertheless, a few interesting points that raise a few equally interesting questions are contained in Stewart's treatise. The logic behind his advice to fortify Prussia to form a bulwark against Russia in the post-Napoleonic world parallels Metternich's own concerns over Romanov aggrandizement. In addition, Stewart's polemic provides insight over the uncertainty surrounding the details of the Polish–Saxon Question. No member of the Allied camp knew for sure exactly how much Polish territory Alexander would demand from his allies: the tsar himself probably did not know. By identifying the Oder River rather than the Vistula as Prussia's first line of defense in the event of Russian aggression, Stewart presupposes that East Prussia, which the Russians had claimed in the 1812 Russo–Swedish Convention of Abo, would be included in the new Romanov Poland. Although the Russians subsequently renounced their claims on East Prussia in the stipulations of the Breslau treaty earlier that year, Hardenberg may have doubted the tsar's sincerity. In his many talks with Stewart, the Prussian chancellor probably expressed this concern, as well as his ideas regarding further compensation for Prussia in North Germany in the event Alexander forced the cession of East Prussia. Consequently, what appeared to Metternich to be Prussian desire for retribution in the Third Germany may well have been the manifestation of Hardenberg's doubts over Alexander's integrity combined with a proactive plan to offset the state's possible loss of East Prussia by having a clear idea of where compensation would be found to return Prussia to its pre-1806 material status.

In the midst of this maneuvering, Napoleon's response to the Frankfurt Proposals reached Allied headquarters on 23 November in the form of an ambiguous letter from French Foreign Minister Hughes Maret. Dated 16 November, the note acknowledged receipt of the Frankfurt Proposals, suggested a conference at Mannheim, and expressed interest in London's willingness to discuss maritime rights.[72] Maret also made vague demands for the negotiations "to be based on the independence of all nations"; for all nations to be accorded their natural limits; and that the British make sacrifices equal to those of the French.[73] This blatant attempt to drive a wedge between the British and their allies failed.[74] "The object of his answer is evidently to throw on England the responsibility of the result if not peace," notes Wilson's diary.[75] Yet what answer other than a noncommittal counterproposal could be expected from the Emperor of the French in response to a "mere oral and unofficial proposition?"[76] Metternich responded two days later: peace talks would not begin until Napoleon accepted the Frankfurt Proposals.

The controversy caused by the Frankfurt Proposals provided an opportunity for Metternich to strengthen ties with the British. Rather than the Austrian minister, London blamed Aberdeen for the clauses in the Frankfurt Proposals that contradicted British policy. Castlereagh informed Aberdeen that "this nation is likely to view with disfavor any peace which does not confine France strictly within her ancient limits."[77] In addition, when the other two British envoys in Allied headquarters, Cathcart and Stewart, learned of Aberdeen's clandestine negotiations with Metternich, little hope remained that the British themselves could work together. These factors led to a joint Anglo–Russian request for London to send a fully authorized plenipotentiary to the continent. The outrage of both the British government and the British public over Aberdeen's complicity in the "St. Aignan Affair" prompted the government to take the unprecedented step of sending Foreign Minister Castlereagh to the continent to safeguard London's interests. This later proved an essential facilitator to Metternich's Anglo–Austrian entente to counter Russia.[78]

In the meantime, Napoleon dismissed the prowar Maret on 20 November According to the emperor's private secretary, Agathon-Jean-François Fain: "In certain Parisian salons, endeavors were made to cast all the blame on the duke de Bassano [Maret]. He was accused of transmitting too vague a reply to Frankfurt, and it was affirmed that no negotiations could be expected to succeed so long as this minister continued to lead foreign affairs. He [Napoleon] was well aware that the censure which seemed to be directed against his minister was in reality aimed at himself...he thought it advisable to yield, and made this concession for the return of confidence."[79] Thiers adds: "When an erroneous opinion takes possession of the public mind, and this opinion is sure to be implacable because it is erroneous, it demands a victim...it was known that now again the emperor had just received a very satisfactory proposition, and an antechamber rumor reported that he had not replied in a suitable manner; and for all these faults Bassano was blamed."Consequently, Napoleon sacrificed Maret "on the altar of public opinion."[80]

To succeed Maret, Napoleon appointed Caulaincourt. An advocate of a negotiated peace, the new minister achieved some success in persuading Napoleon to maintain dialogue with the Allies. Regardless, he failed to induce Napoleon to see the Frankfurt Proposals for what they were: an opportunity to retain his throne and a means to dissolve the Coalition. Instead, the emperor viewed the offer as an armistice that afforded him the opportunity to stall for time and finish mobilizing his new army. Writing to clear his name, Caulaincourt does sound a note of truth in his memoirs when he states: "The recollection of Prague was all I needed to warn me that where peace was concerned, the emperor's fairest promises meant nothing."[81]

On 1 December, Napoleon finally authorized Caulaincourt to accept the Frankfurt Proposals, but time had run out for Metternich.[82] Although it is not clear why Alexander approved the Frankfurt Proposals in the first place, he now reversed his position.[83] Regardless, an overjoyed Metternich informed Caulaincourt that Napoleon's acceptance of the Proposals would be communicated to the British government, which he firmly believed would agree to the commencement of negotiations. In a short time, the peace congress would begin; this would allow Metternich to renew his crusade to guarantee France its natural frontiers.

Before receiving notification of the French emperor's acceptance of the Proposals, Metternich decided to take advantage of Napoleon's initial rejection of the offer to issue a proclamation according to his agreement with Nesselrode and Aberdeen. Although drafted before St. Aignan had departed Frankfurt, Metternich had yet to submit the proclamation to the tsar for his endorsement. At that time, Metternich only needed Nesselrode's approval to publish the document, which he received. Nevertheless, the Austrian wanted Alexander's permission to publish the proclamation but delayed presenting the draft to the Russian monarch for several days. Metternich understood that should the tsar reject it, he could count on receiving alternatives that would reflect the war party's punitive aspirations such as the cession of Alsace and Lorraine. During this delay, Metternich altered his draft and removed the pledge to grant France its natural frontiers. Instead, the Allies would promise to leave France greater than it had been under the Bourbons. Little is known of Metternich's original draft. Only Aberdeen refers to the original in his report to Castlereagh, which suggests that Metternich discussed this issue with him. Evidently, Nesselrode did not inform the tsar of the inclusion of the pledge of natural frontiers in the proposed proclamation, meaning the tsar never knew Metternich's original proclamation included the guarantee of France's natural frontiers.

The significance of this change cannot be underestimated. Metternich's decision to concede to France its natural frontiers represented his desire to contain Alexander just as much as the offer was designed to attract Napoleon to the peace table. Because the minister directly tied France's natural frontiers to Austria's national security, the exchange of the concrete pledge of the Rhine, Alps, and Pyrenees for an ambiguous promise of material status is perplexing. Certainly this could provide an opportunity for the tsar to make excessive territorial demands. Several reasons could have induced the Austrian to alter his original draft. As with the Frankfurt Proposals, British opposition to the natural frontiers focused on the independence of Holland as well as the fate of Antwerp and the mouth of the Scheldt River. Moreover, French possession of Belgium in a postwar Europe would threaten Dutch national security and British interests along the Scheldt. Metternich may have changed the draft due to concerns expressed by Aberdeen. In addition, Bülow's successful operation in Holland and London's support of his campaign indicated that the Prussian corps commander would likely continue his offensive into Belgium, thus undermining the pledge of natural frontiers. In view of the Dutch campaign, Aberdeen likewise may have suggested the removal of the pledge of natural frontiers. Yet because of his influence over the British statesman, it is more likely that Metternich himself made the change in view of the Dutch campaign and the opposition he anticipated from London.

Aside from the British, the tsar remained Metternich's main concern. To make matters worse, he now needed Alexander's approval to publish the proclamation: This meant winning the support of the war party. Metternich had drafted the original proclamation before 10 November and before the issue over Swiss neutrality shook Austro–Russian relations. Before the Swiss Affair, he could have published the proclamation with the consent of Nesselrode only. In less than three weeks, however, the situation had changed, and the Swiss Affair made Alexander deeply suspicious of Metternich. Stein's presence in Frankfurt likewise did not aid Metternich's cause. As the tsar's advisor on all German affairs, Stein loudly demanded the liberation of the left bank of the Rhine. Unable to guarantee the natural frontiers without risking a new dispute with Alexander, Metternich accepted this setback and changed the wording of the proclamation.[84]

Dated 1 December and published in the *Frankfurt Gazette* on the 7th, thousands of copies of Metternich's "Frankfurt Declaration" soon spread across the Rhine (Appendix F). The document attempted to demonstrate to the French that their emperor posed the real obstacle to peace by criticizing Napoleon's war preparations and insisting that the Allies now offered a fair and just peace. The effect of such Allied propaganda proved just as detrimental to the morale of the French as a defeat on the battlefield. "The Allied proclamations are doing us more harm than their weapons," wrote Caulaincourt to Napoleon after the Allies crossed the Rhine in January.[85] According to French historian Henry Houssaye, the Allied propaganda "had the effect of not only reassuring and so disarming the rural districts, but also of helping traitors evoke a new and formidable feeling in the majority of the towns. The malcontents were quick to exploit the distinction made by the Allies between the country and the sovereign." Metternich's proclamation successfully planted the idea of "peace to France and war to Napoleon."[86] Finally, Beauchamp asserts that "one was not accustomed to this tone of dignity, of candor, and of moderation on the part of the potentates of power. The moral aim of the war was wholly in their favor and this became overwhelming for Napoleon."[87] In this way, the Coalition hoped to avoid a popular uprising in France. Despite French interpretations regarding the effect of the Frankfurt Declaration and subsequent Allied proclamations, war weariness rather than words prevented a repeat of the national mobilization that had led France to victory in 1793.

4

Napoleon and the French

On the French side of the Rhine, the exhausted state of the troops and the scant resources at their disposal gave rise to the idea of abandoning the left bank. Yet Napoleon refused to provide the Allies such blatant proof of his weakness and thus kept the army posted along the Rhine. He still believed the sight of the tricolor floating from steeples along the left bank would intimidate the Allies long enough to preserve what Fain refers to as "the protective illusions" of the sanctity of French territory.[1] "The Rhine, which we were going to put between ourselves and the enemy," rationalizes the distinguished artillery officer Colonel Charles-Pierre-Lubin Griois, "seemed to us an impassable obstacle; and while we deplored what we were abandoning and what we had already lost, France, such as it still remained, appeared to us beautiful and large enough, under a leader like Napoleon, to soothe many sorrows." Not all shared this optimism, and others regretted Napoleon's decisions: "We ran as far as Moscow," maintains the former administrator of the Grand Duchy of Berg, Jean-Claude Beugnot, "to draw forth the Cossacks and bring them to the banks of the Seine."[2] Writing in 1816, French historian and chevalier of the Legion of Honor Beauchamp adds: "Everywhere these same French legions, which had conquered two-thirds of Europe, sought their safety behind the Rhine, behind this river, an insurmountable barrier, if the ruler of France had not wanted to spread his system of enslavement beyond it."[3]

Upon reaching Mainz, the need to reorganize the army and form a cordon along the left bank of the Rhine became Napoleon's main concerns. On 1 November, the army started crossing the river at Mainz. General Henri François Charpentier's XI Corps moved to quarters at Bingen.[4] Marshal Claude Victor's II Corps likewise crossed the river and proceeded to Oppenheim. The provisional commander of the V Corps, General Joseph-Jean-Baptiste Albert, led his tired soldiers to a position between Bingen and Mainz. On the right bank, Marmont's VI Corps and Gen. Etienne-Pierre-Sylvestre

63

Ricard's III Corps reached Höchst, where also arrived the Imperial Guard and Napoleon's headquarters. Cavalry under Jean-Tousaint Arrighi, Etienne-Marie Nansouty, and Horace-François-Bastien Sébastiani took post to guard Höchst. The XVI Corps camped near Hochheim to block the highway from Frankfurt. In the rear of the army, General Henri-Gatien Bertrand's IV Corps occupied Frankfurt.[5]

The emperor made his way to Mainz on the 2nd, passing thousands of stragglers – the debris of the III, VI, and VIII Corps – on the road from Höchst to Kastel. Occasionally, he found small groups of organized soldiers plodding toward the bridge they hoped would deliver them to safety. At the entrance of the bridge across the Rhine, the imperial escort had to clear a path through the throng of refugees who had once formed the Grande Armée of 1813. Upon entering Mainz, the imperial cavalcade proceeded even slower as wagons, equipment, draft horses, and even bivouacs cluttered the streets. Napoleon watched the army dissolve before his eyes. The need for rest and reorganization was acute. Having the strong fortress of Mainz in its center, the Rhine offered a considerable shield that would allow him to undertake such a massive task. Mainz was situated on the left bank of the Rhine; on the right bank, the fortified suburb of Kastel as well as Forts Montebello and St. Hilaire guarded the approaches to the fortress. On the 3rd, Napoleon ordered the two forts occupied along with the isle of St. Pierre.[6] With the proper entrenchments and adequate artillery, even a weak rearguard could prevent the Allies from crossing the river for some time. Napoleon, ever the master of war because he was the consummate student of war, recalled Henri Turenne's maxim that the best defense of the left bank of the Rhine was to cross to the right bank.[7] For this reason, he wanted the bridgeheads at Kehl, Kastel, and Wesel maintained. Should the Allies attempt to pass the upper Rhine, Strasbourg and the fortresses of Alsace would impede their progress. On the lower Rhine, he hoped the fortress of Wesel and the Dutch forts on the Ijssel River could delay the Allies indefinitely.

Allied patrols appeared before the outposts of the French rearguard, signaling the approach of their columns. Napoleon could do nothing at the moment except keep the road to Mainz open for the estimated 25,000 stragglers who were struggling to reach the fortress. For this purpose, his extreme rearguard – Bertrand's IV Corps and Marshal Adolphe-Edouard-Casimir-Joseph Mortier's 2nd and 4th Young Guard Divisions – moved west through Frankfurt to the Nidda River and its sole bridge at Höchst. Between Höchst and Mainz stood the 1st and 3rd Young Guard Divisions. Napoleon spent the majority of the day reviewing reports from Paris. By nightfall on the 2nd the French army stretched along a front of approximately forty-five miles with its center at Mainz, the right at Worms, and the left at Bingen.[8]

As the army crossed the Rhine on the 3rd, Napoleon continued to disperse the corps to form a cordon along the left bank between Bingen and Worms.

Ricard led the III Corps to a position upstream at Bechtheim. Marmont's VI Corps likewise crossed the Rhine and marched south to quarters in and around Oppenheim – less than half way to Worms. Victor himself went to Strasbourg, while his II Corps began the march to Worms, twenty-six miles upstream from Mainz. General Jean-Pierre Doumerc's I Cavalry Corps rode thirty-three miles southwest of Mainz to Kreuznach. North of these units, the emperor extended the V Corps between Bingen and Mainz to observe the great curve of the Rhine. Sébastiani's II Cavalry Corps moved to Koblenz. Some of the field artillery continued to Metz, while the rest remained at Mainz. Finally, Jean-Henri Dombrowski began the long seventy-mile march west to Zweibrücken with the Poles of the VIII Corps accompanied by the IV Cavalry Corps.[9]

To form the cordon, the emperor divided his frontier from Switzerland to the North Sea into three sectors and placed a marshal in command of each.[10] He intended to use the Rhine as a shield to cover the mobilization of a new army. Rather than fall back and consolidate his forces, the emperor maintained the pretense of defending France's natural frontiers for public consumption as well as to soothe his own ego. The regions along France's eastern frontier comprised the 5th, 25th, and 26th Military Districts. The 5th contained the Departments of the Haut-Rhin and Bas-Rhin with *chef-lieux* (capitals) at Colmar and Strasbourg, respectively; the 25th included the Departments of the Bouches-du-Rhin, Meuse-Inférieure, l'Ourte, Sambre-et-Meuse, Roer, and Lippe, with *chef-lieux* at Hertogenbosch (Bois-le-Duc), Maastricht, Liège, Namur, Aachen, and Münster; the 26th Military District consisted of the Departments of Mont-Tonnerre, the Sarre, and Rhin-et-Moselle, with *chef-lieux* at Mainz, Koblenz, and Trier.

Napoleon assigned the 25th Military District, which stretched 185 miles from Koblenz to Zwolle in Holland, to Macdonald with the remains of the XI Corps.[11] Bonaparte placed Marmont in the middle sector, the 26th Military District: the 110 miles between Koblenz and Landau.[12] In case the Allies continued their offensive, the emperor allotted Marmont the bulk of the army's scant manpower: the II, III, IV, V, and VI Corps. For cavalry support, the marshal received overall command of the I, II, III, and V Cavalry Corps. Reserves in the form of the dragoons from the Army of the Pyrenees and two regiments of Honor Guard were also en route to bolster Marmont's cavalry. Victor established his headquarters in Strasbourg to oversee the 138 miles of the southern sector of the frontier, the 5th Military District, which extended from Landau to Huningue, just north of the bridge over the Rhine at Basel. Victor initially had nothing more than a handful of National Guardsmen and conscripts to defend the region where Schwarzenberg's 200,000 men would eventually cross the Rhine.[13]

One evening, Napoleon and his generals discussed the invasion routes open to the Allies. Marmont supposedly suggested that the Allies would march up the Rhine with the majority of their forces, violate Swiss neutrality, and cross the river at Basel. He based this assumption on their need to secure a bridge over a sector of the Rhine that would be spared from heavy flows of winter drift ice. According to Marmont, the emperor lost his patience and asked what the Allies would do after crossing the Rhine. "They will march against Paris," responded the marshal. An agitated Napoleon called the plan crazy. When the marshal pointed to the fact that nothing could stop the Allies from advancing in this direction, the emperor purportedly complained over the lack of enthusiasm displayed by the chiefs of his army. The total silence among those present appeared to support Marmont's view. Sensing that his opinion did not hold sway, Napoleon turned and thumped the chest of the ultra-loyal General Antoine Drouot, exclaiming that he needed 100 men like him. Marmont maintained that the "sensible and honest" Drouot saw through the emperor's attempt to curry favor with a compliment and answered with admirable tact: "You will need 100,000, Sire."[14] Napoleon's troop displacements in early November suggests he saw little threat from the upper Rhine and believed the Allies would continue their direct pursuit across the middle Rhine. In less than three weeks, however, events drew his attention to the Netherlands and the lower Rhine, where he directed many of his new divisions.

Napoleon remained in Mainz until 7 November to reorganize the army and make the necessary arrangements to guard the frontier. At the emperor's side day and night, Marmont describes him as "gloomy and silent." "The impression I gained [of Napoleon] was vivid, and so painful that it remains to this day," adds General Philippe de Ségur. "His second disaster was over. The way that everyone regarded him was no longer the same. Misfortune had struck him like any other man, and had bowed his grandeur, so one felt more on the same level with him. One needed to raise their eyes less far to look at him. Everything around him seemed to have changed, but nothing in Napoleon himself. Struck down twice already, he still held his head high, his voice was clipped and peremptory, his manner regal."[15]

Napoleon placed his hopes in the deadlines that he forwarded to the imperial administration in Paris and his belief that the Allies would not mount a winter offensive. Marmont alleges that Napoleon did admit the severity of his situation in private discussions, but when surrounded by his entourage, "his language about hope for the future became proud and strong." In the evenings, the emperor could be found with a small circle of intimates including his chief of staff, Marshal Louis-Alexandre Berthier, as well as Marmont, Caulaincourt, and Drouot. This group attempted to convince him that he could make an honorable peace based on the enemy's exhaustion as well as French control of the many fortresses in Germany and Poland. Napoleon "did not think like this," recalls Marmont, "and seemed, at least in his public speeches, to believe in the most futile hope."[16]

Figure 6. Emperor Napoleon I (1769–1821).

Napoleon's situation appeared insurmountable when he returned to Paris on 9 November 1813. By all accounts, an exhausted French nation wanted peace and blamed the emperor for not ending his wars. "The French could not forgive him for having neglected the favorable opportunities for concluding peace which the victories of Lützen and Bautzen afforded," wrote Thiers. "They regarded his ambition as extravagant, cruel to the masses of mankind, and fatal to France. After the disaster of 1813, added to that of 1812, the French people did not think they were in a position to resist the formidable Coalition." The heady days when the cannons roared in Paris to commemorate victories at Austerlitz, Jena, and Friedland seemed like distant memories of a forgotten age. Since Napoleon's last decisive victory at Wagram in 1809, war had raged across the Iberian Peninsular, devouring the French army. After losing the Grande Armée of 1812 in Russia the previous year, another 500,000 men were left behind dead, wounded, captured, or besieged in fortresses throughout central Europe. The government-controlled press blamed the Russian disaster on the winter, and the loss of Germany on the treachery of France's allies such as Prussia, Saxony, and Bavaria. Even Colonel Jacques Montfort, the officer whose negligence led to the premature destruction of the Elster Bridge as the army retreated from Leipzig, became the scapegoat for the army's condition when it reached the Rhine.[17] In early November, the remains of the Grande Armée of 1813 limped across the Rhine with perhaps 70,000 men; the entire French army posted along the eastern and northern frontiers numbered only 103,600 men by December.

Napoleon faced the difficult task of mobilizing another army while at the same time buttressing his frontier defenses to slow the impending Allied invasion. The emperor adequately summarized the situation in his opening remarks to the French Senate: "One year ago all of Europe was marching with us, now all of Europe is marching against us."[18] With the resources of the empire vanishing, the French had to shoulder the full burden of feeding Napoleon's war machine. This meant renewed conscription and a heavier tax burden. As for the former, Napoleon considered 500,000 recruits sufficient for the upcoming campaign.[19] He had started rebuilding his army in October 1813 – before the battle of Leipzig. Specifically, on 9 October the French Senate approved two levies proposed in the name of the emperor by his wife, Marie Louise. The first summoned 120,000 men from the 1808–1814 classes – classes that already had been summoned on 24 August to provide 30,000 men for the Army of the Pyrenees. The second levée sought 160,000 recruits from the class of 1815. Initial plans called for these 280,000 men to form reserve armies at Bordeaux, Turin, Metz, and Antwerp. In response to Bavaria's defection, another Senate Decree on 15 November called up 150,000 men from the 1803–14 classes, plus a further levée of 150,000 men as a last resort if the Allies crossed the eastern frontier. Four days later, Napoleon added an additional 40,000 to the quota for the 1808–14 classes. According to the rotation schedule, the conscripts from the October levée would report to the regimental depots during December. These recruits would join the troops already in the depots and all would depart for their respective regiments; the untrained conscripts would drill on the march. Next, the 150,000 men summoned on 15

November from the 1803–14 classes would report to the depots. The other 150,000 conscripts would arrive in the depots after the first 150,000 were trained and sent to the front. Between October and mid-January, Napoleon summoned 936,500 men to the colors – little more than one-third answered the call, and of that number, only 120,000 actually saw combat.[20]

For these measures to achieve fruition, Napoleon desperately needed time. Despite his great organizational abilities, the new army could not be combat-ready before March 1814. Typical of the manner in which the emperor deceived himself toward the end of his career, he believed the Allies would opt for winter quarters on the right bank of the Rhine and not resume operations until May – six months later![21] Napoleon based this assumption on Allied exhaustion, disagreements, and the time they needed to reconfigure their communications and incorporate the forces of the Rheinbund.[22] If the Allies allowed him just half of this time, Bonaparte deemed he could create a third Grande Armée from the resources of France. The sober reality was that regardless of his energy and restless activity, Napoleon ran out of time. "I needed two months," he later lamented, "if I had them, they never would have crossed the Rhine."[23]

Regardless of the numbing effects produced by war weariness, the names of 127,433 recruits from the 1808–14 classes filled the lists in compliance with the first decree of 9 October. Yet of this number, only 72,265 men reached their units by 23 December. Desertion rates ranged between one-third and one-half; in the German departments of the empire, the rate was even higher. Moreover, the second levée of that decree, the conscription of 160,000 men from the class of 1815, encountered considerable difficulties. Aside from the opposition that surfaced in western and northern France, the age of the recruits only averaged nineteen, well below the heartier age of twenty-five, which Napoleon regarded as better suited for the rigors of life in his army. Astonishingly, of the 280,000 recruits summoned by both decrees of 9 October, at most only 95,000 conscripts reported to their depots. Of this number, almost 80 percent of the men did not complete basic training before joining their regiments.

November's decree for 300,000 men faced even more impediments and illustrates the harsh realities of life in the empire. Men from the 1800–7 classes faced conscription for a second time; the years 1808, 1813, and 1814 a third; those of 1809–12 a fourth. As Henry Houssaye asserts, this represented "the wiping out of an entire generation." Unlike the October levée that drafted unmarried men, that of November conscripted husbands and breadwinners. Consequently, the November levée made little progress as many men preferred to flee to the forests rather than die for the emperor. Realizing that 300,000 was somewhat overambitious, Napoleon lowered the immediate quota to 178,000 men. Even after this reduction, only 28,838 men had joined their units by 31 January 1814, and an additional 34,206 were en route to their depots – a shortfall of 115,656 men![24]

Manpower woes plagued Napoleon before and after the Allied invasion commenced. Conscription shortfalls prompted him to form units consisting of forest rangers, police, customs officials, and sailors. As his hold on Holland and Belgium unraveled, desertions of these nationals accelerated. Finding junior officers and noncommissioned officers also proved problematic. On 10 January, Napoleon informed Minister of War Henry-Jacques-Guillaume Clarke that he needed 540 sergeants and 1,080 corporals just for the regiments of Young Guard that he planned to create. He hoped that 700 to 800 soldiers who were recovering from slight wounds in les Invalides could fill the deficit.[25] "Affairs had come to a sorry pass when the Imperial Guard had to rely on invalids and pensioners for a substantial number of its subordinate leaders," comments historian David Chandler.[26]

In an attempt to recover veteran units, the emperor authorized Marmont to open negotiations with Schwarzenberg over the surrender of the Vistula and Oder fortresses of Danzig, Modlin, Zamosc, Stettin, Küstrin, and Glogau. In return for evacuating these places, Napoleon wanted the Allies to transport the garrisons to France along with their arms and baggage.[27] In addition, the sick in the hospitals would be treated and returned to France upon recovery. He instructed Marmont to inform the Allies that Danzig, Glogau, and Küstrin could hold out for another year, and thus the terms he now offered were generous. Of course Napoleon also expected Marmont to use these negotiations as a means to gather intelligence.[28] Marmont's envoy, General Marie-Joseph Delort, submitted the propositions, which the Allies naturally declined. Events ultimately outpaced the emperor. Stettin and Zamosc capitulated on 21 and 22 November, respectively.[29] On the Elbe, Wittenberg and Torgau followed suit in January, together yielding more than 400 guns as well as considerable magazines of powder and grain.[30] In addition, General Jean Rapp surrendered Danzig and the 9,000 men of his X Corps to a Russo–Prussian siege corps under Duke Alexander of Württemberg on 30 November.

To make matters worse, the emperor learned that Marshal Laurent Gouvion St. Cyr, besieged in Dresden with the 35,000 seasoned troops of the I and XVI Corps, capitulated. On 11 November, the marshal surrendered on the condition that his garrison be granted free access to France.[31] General Johann von Klenau, the commander of the Austro–Russian siege corps, agreed. Regardless, the Allied monarchs rejected this condition and ordered Klenau to force St. Cyr to return to Dresden. After St. Cyr refused, he and his men were marched to Bohemia as prisoners of war, thus making Klenau's siege-corps available for front-line duty.

The French army in Spain provided another source of manpower that Napoleon could tap. Unfortunately for him, diplomatic efforts to end the Peninsular War by reinstating the Spanish Bourbons failed in December. As a result, Wellington continued his offensive with 125,000 men, thus preventing Marshals Nicolas-Jean Soult and Louis-Gabriel Suchet from leading their 100,000 battle-hardened veterans to the Rhine frontier. Napoleon suffered a personal blow when his sister Caroline and brother-in-law Murat, queen and king of Naples by his grace, defected to the Allies on 11 January. The emperor had hoped Murat's small Neapolitan army of 24,000 soldiers would unite with Eugene de Beauharnais's 50,000 men to drive across northern Italy and threaten Vienna. Instead, Murat's army augmented the 75,000 men of the Austro–Italian army that confronted Eugene. Napoleon also had counted on Italian recruits augmenting his forces on the Rhine. These drafts never materialized in part because of Murat's defection. Just three days after Murat's betrayal, Denmark also withdrew from the war, thus freeing the majority of Bernadotte's army from operations in North Germany. Regarding both Spain and Italy, even if Napoleon had renounced his claims to both, he would have been obligated to leave substantial forces in both theaters to observe Wellington and Bellegarde. Consequently, the troops he could have culled from these theaters would have been minimal.[32]

Another source of manpower was the National Guard, which Napoleon activated in the eastern departments on 21 October. This initial call-up amounted to 31,200 men, half of whom would report for duty by 25 December. On 17 November, another decree activated National Guard units in the departments of the Haut-Rhin, Bas-Rhin, Haute-Saône, Meurthe, and Vosges Departments (Burgundy and Franche-Compté) and ordered the formation of 457 cohorts for a total of 176,500 men. Two more decrees on 30 December and 6 January authorized the mobilization of an additional 140,000 National Guardsmen. Theoretically, the National Guard would serve as auxiliary units to support the army both directly on the field of battle as well as indirectly by guarding communications, securing rear areas, garrisoning fortresses, and defending cities. Mobilization of the National Guard encountered more obstacles than that of the army. Clothing and equipment for the Guard remained in short supply because the emperor preferred to allocate his diminishing resources to the army; most guardsmen used civilian clothing to augment the few accouterments they received.[33]

Just as the Prussians merged their militia with the regular army, French military authorities made the National Guard "indistinguishable" from the Line troops. "Take care of the National Guard under your orders," Napoleon instructed Marmont. "Review them and organize them the best way possible." He later wrote Clarke, that "these troops are no longer National Guard, but actual troops of the Line."[34] Therefore, a summons to serve in the National Guard was, according to Houssaye, "interpreted as another form of conscription that fell almost entirely on married men who had escaped the earlier drafts, and on men over thirty-three, who also, especially in the rural districts, were almost all married." Substitutes could be purchased, but this expedient usually surpassed the financial means of the typical family man. All forms of evasion from riots to men fleeing their home districts occurred, which forced the government to temporarily suspend the issue of passports. Aside from the permanent National Guard units in France's major cities, those formed for the 1814 campaign never exceeded 40,000 men – a far cry from the 120,000 Landwehr fielded by the Prussians in August 1813.[35] "Langres was chosen to commence the implementation of this barbarous system," maintains the highly critical Beauchamp; "the National Guard would be summoned and armed by the order of old Line officers, but during the actual campaign, the forces of inertia seemed insurmountable."[36]

Concern over the political reliability and military dependability of the National Guard haunted Napoleon's planning throughout the campaign in France, particularly regarding the defense of Paris. According to Étienne-Denis Pasquier, Napoleon's prefect of police, the emperor claimed on 3 January 1814 that he had only 40,000 men to oppose the Allied armies that recently crossed the Rhine. When Pasquier suggested organizing the Paris National Guard, the emperor stated that such a measure would provide only 20,000 to 40,000 men. Moreover, he questioned the mood of the Parisian guardsmen. "If that spirit is bad, I will find that I have left in my rear a parallel force. And then, with what will I arm them? I need my muskets for the conscripts who are arriving."[37] Concerning the National Guard, Thiers comments: "Napoleon was not much inclined to employ them. Of course he distrusted them, because they might be, in a very disagreeable manner, the reflex of the public mind."[38] Beauchamp gripes that "nevertheless, the courtiers assured that in magnanimous silence, Napoleon performed marvels of activity and vigilance, possibly more surprising than his most brilliant successes. They presented the organization of the Paris National Guard as one of those great ideas that bred confidence, while one generally knew that Napoleon had long resisted the arming of the Parisians. He regarded them [the Parisians] indeed as the secret enemies of his power, and thorough caution surrounded the training of these civic legions."[39]

One final recruiting effort targeted the sons of the affluent middle class as replacements for the experienced cavalry troopers lost in Russia. Needing to rebuild his cavalry arm virtually overnight, Napoleon wanted unmarried equestrians who could provide their own horses. Instituted on 5 April 1813, the Honor Guard recruited volunteers between the ages of nineteen and thirty who possessed the financial means to equip themselves. For the 1814 campaign, Napoleon formed four Honor Guard regiments, each numbering 2,500 men for a total of 10,000; the actual number that saw action was 9,129 men. Napoleon conceived this plan to rally the bourgeoisie – his loudest detractors after the Russian disaster – and to ensure the loyalty of the empire's new nobility. The bourgeoisie typically avoided military service by purchasing replacements. As a political expedient, historian Robert Pawley claims that these men could "be considered as hostages to ensure the continuing loyalty of those families who played a large part in the organization and administration of the empire."[40]

As the mobilization progressed, an astonished Napoleon learned that his arsenals were empty. Although well-stocked with powder, lead, iron, bayonets, and cannon, a critical shortage of muskets existed, which Thiers cites as "one of the principal causes" of Napoleon's ruin. Organizational breakdowns and material exhaustion represented another set of complex problems. "The administrative services, the recruiting offices, the clothing factories, and above all the arsenals, could not handle so many men at once," notes Houssaye.[41] Owing to the army's material shortages, French authorities had to appropriate weapons, horses, fodder, and corn in a haphazard manner reminiscent of the mobilization of 1793.[42] The emperor himself subscribed to a conspiracy theory, repeatedly asking: "Why has the condition of the arsenals been hidden from me?"[43] Ironically, vast amounts of military stores had been moved from France to the Vistula, Oder, and Elbe fortresses in 1811 prior to the Russian campaign. Now far beyond Napoleon's reach, these military supplies either had fallen into Allied hands or were stored in fortresses besieged by Coalition forces.

On 16 November, the government ordered all prefects to procure weapons from the citizens of their departments. These civilian functionaries managed to collect 75,000 firearms of all sorts by 1 December, yet only 25 percent were serviceable. After losing an estimated 700,000 muskets in Russia and Germany, this paltry number did little to alleviate the severe shortage of weapons in the French army. For example, the 5th Light Infantry Regiment distributed only 150 muskets to its 545 men; the 1,088 men of the 153rd Line Regiment possessed 142 muskets; and only 289 muskets could be issued to the 2,344 men of the 115th Line Regiment. Of those who did receive firearms, the majority carried muskets previously recalled from the National Guard because the weapons badly needed repair. Despite the severe shortage of arms, Napoleon sent 50,000 musket to his army in Italy. "When threatened by a foreign force," groans Thiers, "France had more difficulty procuring 300,000 muskets than 300,000 men to carry them!"[44]

Weapons and horses for the cavalry likewise remained in short supply. In the main cavalry depot at Versailles, only 6,284 horses could be provided for 9,786 men. Consequently, every mayoralty of the empire had to supply two horses each so that approximately 20,000 could be collected. The government eventually decreed spade labor to prohibit ploughing and force peasants to surrender their horses. The prefects of the frontier departments were authorized to seize all disposable horses under the pretext that France had to be defended from a Cossack invasion. In addition, the qualifications for the remounts of the horse artillery were reduced, and several cavalry regiments received horses that under normal conditions would have been considered undersized and rejected. Cavalry sabers proved equally hard to come by. For example, the 17th Dragoon Regiment armed only 187 of 349 men. Similar to Cossacks, some regiments only received a lance and were thus designated "éclaireurs." Equipment shortages prompted the emperor to employ all of the saddlers and coach-makers who could be found in the capital to make saddles and harnesses.[45]

Hardly better off was the National Guard, half of whom went to war with sporting weapons. Berthier rebuked Marmont for attempting to arm his National Guard units with new muskets. "I submitted your letter to the emperor in which you informed me why you decided to give the new weapons to the National Guard. I must let you in on a secret: we do not have enough weapons for the army; the new muskets must be reserved for the Line troops. We must save them and give the National Guard the repaired muskets and execute the dispositions made by the minister [Clarke] who knows the state of affairs as a whole. Moreover, many National Guardsmen are deserting and taking their muskets with them."[46] Like the Prussian militia in 1813, French National Guard units in 1814 often armed themselves with captured enemy weapons – sometimes on the battlefield itself.[47]

Using the historic yet inaccurate term of *levée-en-masse*, Napoleon implemented the tool of controlled popular insurrection to add another dimension to his combat forces after the Allied invasion commenced. According to instructions issued on 1 January 1814, military authorities would direct civilians in guerilla operations for local defense. One general and several "superior officers" would be placed in charge of the insurrection in one or more department. The commanding generals were to cooperate closely with the commanders of the mobile army corps. One-third of the males of each village in their respective district would be organized and formed into partisan companies, companies into battalions, and battalions into corps. The commanding general would appoint the battalion and corps commanders and possessed the authority to raise the alarm in the department. Starting with the commanding generals, Napoleon wanted the officers of the insurrection to be veterans held in high esteem by the local population.[48] General Sigismond-Fréderic de Berckheim was named commander of the insurrection in the Alsatian department of the Haut-Rhin on 1 January. Three days later, General Frédéric-Auguste de Beurmann assumed command of the insurrection in the Department of the Vosges, and General Jean-Gabriel Marchand received orders to lead the insurrection in the Isère Department. General Pierre-Louis-François Paultre de la Motte took command of the arming of the people in the Department of the Haut-Marne on 15 January. Napoleon thought better of summoning the insurrection in the German districts between the Moselle and the middle Rhine.[49]

Fear of the Cossacks was used to motivate the people. The following 3 January 1814 proclamation was posted in Metz by Senator Charles-Antoine Chasset, who returned to his home district in December 1813 to help organize the defense of Lorraine:

> Our territory is threatened! It is in great danger! Your homes may soon fall prey to devastation, pillage, to the fires already set on French territory. You know the fierceness of these irregular, unruly Cossacks. Left on their own without any means to subsist, they will commit all kinds of depredations. These are men unworthy of the noble name of soldiers who, not daring to challenge the slightest resistance, will come together in an instant at your peaceful home and commit all the horrors of destruction: they are so repugnant that they do the same in their own country.
>
> You have regular troops to defend you; several cohorts of National Guard also will share the glory; but after having furnished your contingent for both of these arms, your own interest demands that you arm as well, that you rise up. It is necessary that this be done not tumultuously, but according to an organized process, in which you set the terms, the nature, the duration, and the goal of the service that is intended, under chiefs from among you and chosen by you. These combatants will not only complement the National Guard, but will be used as armies to counter the burning and pillaging.[50]

A critical shortage of money presented larger problems for the imperial administration than shortfalls in manpower and material. On 11 November and 9 January, the emperor decreed two considerable increases in taxation. Three practical problems prevented these measures from being effective. First, the people could not pay. Napoleon's Continental System had devastated the French economy. "The fields were uncultivated, the factories closed, and business and public works at a standstill," comments Houssaye, "the deduction of twenty-five percent from all incomes derived from non-military sources, and the great increase of taxation, had brought scarcity to the rich and misery to the poor."[51] Second, the people would not pay. Government tax collectors encountered threats, ill treatment, and physical abuse. Reports indicate the beating and hanging of tax collectors. In some regions, the news that the government planned to expropriate silver and jewelry brought the population to the brink of revolt. Third, the Allied invasion restricted the areas of France where imperial tax collectors could operate – by 27 January Allied armies controlled one-third of France. The rapid Allied drive that brought both Schwarzenberg and Blücher to the Marne and Aube Rivers before the end of January combined with the liberation of the Low Countries to sharply reduce the amount of government revenue. Collection of direct taxes only produced

33,743,000 francs in the first quarter of 1814 compared with 75,500,000 francs in the same period four years earlier.[52]

Other sources of government income reflected the extent of the empire's economic crisis. Revenue from indirect taxes likewise became negligible.[53] Shares of government stock fell by 30 percent following the battle of Leipzig. Salaried government employees and pensioners who earned more than 2,000 francs annually found their incomes slashed by 25 percent. Government contractors received promissory notes as payment, thus making bankruptcies common. Cash became so scarce that the government had to lift the 6 percent ceiling on interest rates so that money was lent at any rate the borrower would pay. The hoarding of funds only added to the shortage of currency. Napoleon eventually had to transfer his private funds to the public chest. Without the resources of the conquered states of the empire, it became exceedingly difficult for Mars to make war; in 1814, Napoleon had to spend 63,000,000 francs of his personal fortune to defend his throne.[54]

As for the morale of the people, the vast majority desired peace. They viewed the government's conscription decrees as unconscionable. "'He wants to sacrifice our children to his wild ambition,' was the cry of every family from Paris to the extremity of the most remote provinces," claims Thiers. "The French people now felt at the prospect of war the same horror that the guillotine had formerly inspired. The universal topic of conversation was the battlefields of Spain and Germany, the millions of dying, of wounded, and of sick expiring without attendance on the fields of Leipzig and Vitoria."[55] Many Frenchmen were frustrated, believing Napoleon had squandered an opportunity to make peace during the negotiations in July 1813.[56] Men seeking to avoid conscription fled their homes, leaving behind women and children to toil in the fields, which the government encouraged. Army units and police continuously swept the forests in search of draft-dodgers.

From November 1813 to March 1814, Napoleon's popularity among the educated and monied classes steadily decreased, and no amount of propaganda could convince them that his star had not set. According to French historian Jean Thiry:

> The *Moniteur* described the enthusiasm of the young recruits, the excellent state of the fortresses, the ease and the rapidity of the requisitions. It claimed that the enemy's armies were ravaged by epizooty and diseases of all kinds. The paper said that but for the treason of the Saxons and Bavarians, Napoleon would have come back to the Rhine victorious after having secured peace. But in reality, the departure of the conscripts, the requisitions, the halt in manufacturing, the problems with commerce, the misery that reigned in the ports where shipping could not enter or exit, disheartened the population. Above all, the fear of invasion rapidly spread.[57]

"Lying bulletins," adds British historian Maycock, "no longer availed to minimize the consternation caused by the long series of disasters ... the inhabitants of the Rhine provinces had tangible evidence of the severity of the reverses and of the forlorn state of the army."[58] It soon became clear to the monied classes that Napoleon was not only losing the war but was rejecting Allied peace proposals as well.[59] "They portrayed Napoleon as a kind of war demon, thirsting for blood, and happy only when surrounded by desolation and death," explains Thiers. "France, formerly disgusted with liberty after ten years of revolution, was now disgusted with despotism after fifteen years of military rule, and the effusion of human blood from one end of Europe to the other."[60]

Years of economic turmoil caused by the Continental System left the bourgeoisie bitter and disillusioned; the investor class responded to the recession of France's military might. When news reached Paris on 26 December that Allied forces had reached Basel, government stocks fell from 54.60 to 50.75 francs. By 5:00 P.M. that same day, the money changers exhausted their gold supply as a result of the panicked exchange of thousand franc notes for the precious metal. Financial anxiety did not end with this report; the progress of the Allied invasion triggered further selling. Stocks fell from 50.50 on 8 January to 46.50 on the 19th. On the previous day, 18 January, the government decreed that no more than 500,000 francs worth of banknotes could be exchanged per day. On the 20th, frantic Parisians met this limit at the Banque de France.[61]

While Bonaparte faced growing opposition in Paris, the countryside generally remained loyal. His popularity among the peasantry continued to be strong, particularly because the alternative could be a return of the feudal Old Regime. Of course the peasants experienced both financial hardship and Napoleon's domestic version of the odious "blood tax" that resulted in a longing for peace, yet Houssaye maintains that the emperor's popularity did not suffer from the fact that his wars and ambitions caused their grief. Despite the growing antiwar sentiment, the commoners did not immediately identify the person of the emperor as the source of their misery. Even the increase in taxes appeared to be the work of greedy bureaucrats rather than Napoleon. According to Houssaye: "with the same breath the peasants cried 'Down with the Taxes,' and 'Long live the Emperor.'"[62] On the other hand, in early November Wilson discussed Napoleon's mobilization with one of Frankfurt's leading bankers who had recently returned from France: "[He] informed me that ... the men were to be had and would be produced; but that great discontent prevailed over this never-ending war and that the peasants were beginning to group together and ... express their ill-will and dislike of Bonaparte, to whose name they generally applied some disrespectful term."[63]

Napoleon's great hope and, conversely, the Coalition's great fear was that an invasion would spark a popular uprising and thus energize the country to mobilize for a total war similar to the extreme patriotism that seized Revolutionary France twenty years earlier. The emperor would be greatly disappointed. An apathetic population submissively watched the Allied armies cross the Rhine and reach the Marne in one month. Passive resistance to imperial decrees soon eclipsed popular indifference. Refusal to pay taxes, report for military duty, and obey requisition orders symbolized an exhausted nation's desperate cry for peace. Although the Coalition's propaganda influenced popular opinion concerning Napoleon's recalcitrance, the atrocities committed by the half-starved invading Allied soldiers eventually stirred the peasants of eastern France.[64] Rape, murder, extortion, and larceny forced the peasant to defend hearth and home. The popular resistance that did occur – and, in particular, the threat of it – certainly aided Napoleon's cause. Yet because of the weakness of leadership, the paralyzing effect of the swift invasion, the Allied propaganda that portrayed the struggle as a war against Napoleon rather than the French nation, and the deadly combination of exhaustion and despair, popular resistance failed to play a pivotal role during the invasion of France.

Napoleon's downfall or a change in the ruling dynasty initially germinated among the monied classes, the remains of the royal nobility, the Parisians, and the imperial bureaucracy that drove the emperor's war machine. As the Malet Conspiracy of 1812 proved, open opposition could be found in the heart of France.[65] "When Napoleon arrived in Paris," asserts Thiers, "he found the public plunged in the most profound dejection, in fact almost in despair, but at the same time strongly excited against him."[66] He made immediate attempts to raise the morale of the Parisians. On 14 November, the emperor orchestrated a spectacle to recapture the hearts of his people. That morning a military band and troop of Guard Cavalry escorted Minister of War Clarke through the city with the Austro–Bavarian standards captured at Hanau. They proceeded to the Tuileries and presented the trophies to Marie Louise. After the imperial reception, the cavalcade continued to les Invalides, where the flags joined countless others taken during the glory days of the empire. "The sight of the flags taken through vast crowds to les Invalides," states one report, "confounds the malevolence that doubts our victories and still seeks every means of undermining morale."[67]

Bourbon sympathizers and British agents covertly and overtly worked for a restoration.[68] Although few in number, the activists among the former Bourbon nobility had long dreamed of a restoration, despite Napoleon's attempts to co-opt them into the new France. In the provinces, they waged a constant propaganda war, which the imperial administration could no longer control. Posting placards in public squares simply to remind the French people of the Bourbon name became a popular tactic. "The mass of the people hailed the name of the Bourbons in order to stop the cry of war," continues Thiers, "which was devouring their children, increasing taxation, and paralyzing commerce."[69] After the Allied invasion began, proclamations from

Louis XVIII began to appear. "Receive these generous allies as friends," states one such declaration, "open the gates of your town to them, avoid the violence which a criminal and futile resistance will cause you, and welcome their entrance into France with joy."[70] Napoleon resorted to extreme measures such as dispatching senators to serve as "extraordinary-commissioners" in the departments to curb treasonous activity similar to the task of the representatives on mission of 1793–4. Although the extraordinary-commissioners were authorized with sweeping authority to revive the zeal of the civil authorities, accelerate the conscription, outfit the troops, organize the National Guard, provision the fortresses, and enact the *levée-en-masse*, they had little success.[71] According to historian Georges Lefebvre, "the royalists added the finishing touches to the disintegration" of the empire by spreading discouragement and preaching disobedience.[72] A placard at the base of the Vendôme column in Paris, which commemorated the feats of the Grande Armée, stating "pass by quickly, it's going to fall," adequately summarized the sedition that thrived in Paris.

On the other hand, fear of a Bourbon restoration made Bonaparte's despotism appear more appealing to the Jacobins. They proposed making Napoleon dictator and calling the people to arms in the spirit of the Revolution. "On hearing of the price they set on their services, he allegedly said: 'There can be nothing in common between the demagogic principles of 1793 and the Monarchy, between clubs of madmen and a regular Ministry, between a Committee of Public Safety and an Emperor. If fall I must, I will not bequeath France to the Revolution, from which I delivered her'."[73] "They were maniacs," deems Thiers, "dreaming of a past that could never be recalled. The movement of 1792 had been a burst of indignation on the part of France when unjustly assailed by all of Europe; but now the cases were reversed."[74] According to Napoleon's private secretary and mouthpiece, Claude François de Méneval: "Napoleon might have appealed against them [the Allies] by calling out a mass levée of the [entire] nation...France might still have been saved. But to reduce himself to play the part of an adventurer; to put his glory into the lists with evil passions; to resuscitate, by illegal and disturbing measures, the factions and the anarchy that he had destroyed; to organize, it might be, a civil war; these things Napoleon was not willing to do. He sacrificed to the fear of such great calamities his crown and the future of his son and of his family; he did not wish to appear in the eyes of posterity as a mere vulgar, ambitious man."[75] Writing in 1826, General Vaudoncourt made the opposite argument:

> In the present circumstance, the principal mistake Napoleon committed was to resort solely to military means, which are long and difficult to assemble; and to not oppose the Coalition with a national defense, which would have been nationalized by an Allied attack. This was a mistake that reduced him to having an overly weak army everywhere, and deprived him of the immense

resources the population of France could have offered him. These resources, well employed, were such that the invasion would not have taken place, or if the Allies wanted to attempt it, the results would have caused them disgust for a long time.[76]

Rather than Jacobinism, Napoleon resorted to Bonapartism. To win the support of working-class Parisians, he sought to distract the masses with work and entertainment. As for the latter, almost daily military parades ensued. The emperor of the French often joined his soldiers on the Carrousel to bask in the public's ephemeral affection. Surrounded by police agents and disguised gendarmes, he spent days touring public works projects underway in Paris such as at the Louvre, the Palais du Luxembourg, the Hôtel des Postes, and the Palais des Archives. These visits provided a dual benefit. First, he became a "man of the people" by allowing himself to come in direct contact with the workers – distributing "handfuls of gold to the scum of society, who appeared to repulse him," comments Beauchamp.[77] Second, as he inspected the works, he called for faster progress, which the anxious crowds that accompanied him interpreted as the employment of more laborers. Napoleon's well-timed propaganda tactics alleviated public suspicion, generated popular enthusiasm, and eased the enforcement of the conscription edicts in the capital itself.

Nevertheless, economic difficulties undermined his efforts to secure the loyalty of the working class. A worsening recession steadily increased the ranks of the unemployed and lengthened the lines at the soup kitchens in the suburb of St. Marcel. This disturbing development prompted the emperor to lower the price of bread by one sou on 13 December. Estimates claiming that 21,000 artisans could not find work in Paris prompted Napoleon to instruct his Minister of the Interior, Jean-Pierre Bachasson, comte de Montalivet, to find work for them, particularly to support the war effort.[78] "It is scarcely credible," wrote the emperor, "that in Paris 350 trimmers, 700 hatters, 1,200 locksmiths, 500 carpenters, 200 joiners, 2,000 cartwrights, 300 bootmakers...are workless when there are complaints of insufficient men for the war industry and administration....The cotton-spinners can be put to work making clothing, shirts, greatcoats, gaiters, etc."[79]

In an effort to stem the tide of defeatism and expedite conscription, the Paris Municipal Council issued the following proclamation on 22 January:

> Parisians, His Majesty the Emperor and King...called on the French of Paris, of Brittany, etc....to fly to the aid of our provinces that have been invaded. The city of Paris will not linger behind Normandy, Brittany, and the rest of France; it will not remain behind when devotion to the country and honor must be shown, together with the unshakeable loyalty of the French to the sovereign who reestablished the monarchy. The people of Paris, who have always set the example by being the first to provide their quota for the conscriptions, will

once again prove their attachment to the sovereign to whom both as Frenchmen and Parisians they owe everything. What Frenchman can remain deaf to the groans of the Francs-Comtois, the Lorrainers, and the voice of the Lyonnais [thus] threatened by the enemy? Who would not shed his blood to preserve inviolate the honor we hold from our ancestors and to keep France within her natural frontiers . . . ? May recognition of these great and cherished benefits lead those men able to fight . . . [and] to join the valorous ranks which will do battle under the eyes . . . of the world's greatest captain.[80]

Napoleon remained at St. Cloud until 20 November to ensure that the Senate passed his conscription decrees and then took residence in the Tuileries for the next two months. Despite the disintegration of the empire, court life remained the same: rigid – owing to the Habsburg influence introduced by the empress – yet majestic with splendid balls and fêtes as if Paris were still the center of Europe. Even the *Marseillaise*, although frowned on by the imperial regime but never formally banned, echoed through the palace halls.[81] The facade of court could not hide the fact that Bonaparte's star was setting. According to Laure-Adélaïde-Constance Junot, Parisian society sadly reflected the emperor's diminishing greatness: "grief and alarm now prevailed in those houses that recently had been the scenes of uninterrupted festivity. The numerous families arrayed in mourning cast a gloom over the streets and the public promenades, and it was particularly melancholy to observe the many young females who wore widow's weeds."[82]

Napoleon's increasingly bleak military situation also exposed his pretense of constitutional government and representative institutions as well as the growing political opposition. After adjourning the Legislative Corps from 2 to 19 December "in order to escape importunate discussions," a ten-day showdown ensued between the emperor and the deputies over his alleged indifference toward peace.[83] The crisis climaxed on 29 December when Deputy Etienne-Henri Lainé, the chairman of a committee appointed by Napoleon to report on the state of France, accused the emperor of insincere efforts to make peace with his enemies. With the support of the Legislative Corps, Lainé demanded guarantees of civil and political liberties if the emperor wished for a national mobilization.[84] This challenge moved Napoleon to dissolve the Legislative Corps; the upper house, the Senate, had found no wrongdoing in the emperor's attempts to end the war. "I called you together," rants Napoleon in his final address to the deputies, "for the purpose of assisting me, but you came to say and do all that was required to assist the foreign enemy. Instead of uniting us, you divide us. To attack me is to attack the nation. If abuses exist, is this the proper moment for remonstrance, when 200,000 Cossacks are passing our frontiers?"[85] This episode, exploited by the growing underground opposition press, served to exacerbate the opportunism of middle-class liberals who viewed Napoleon's reverses as the moment to demand that he end the oppressive aspects of his regime. Certainly Napoleon would not put aside his own genius in favor of parliamentary rule. It is at this point, claims Lefebvre, that Napoleon parted ways with the middle class.[86]

The crisis peaked during the New Year's Day festivities at the Tuileries. In the Salle du Trône, he delivered a blistering speech that vilified his political opponents in the Legislative Corps:

> I have suppressed your address – it was incendiary. I called you to me to do good: you have done ill. Eleven-twelfths of the Legislative Corps are, I know, composed of good and well-intentioned citizens, and I attach no blame to them, but the others, and especially Lainé, are factious intriguers, devoted to England, to all my enemies, and are corresponding with the Bourbons through the advocate Sèze, and your committee was selected from this group. I have proof of this fact. The committee's report has hurt me exceedingly. I would rather have lost two battles. Your object was to humiliate me! My life may be sacrificed, but never my honor. You call yourselves Representatives of the Nation. It is not true, you are only deputies of the departments; a small portion of the state, inferior to the Senate, inferior even to the Council of State. The Representatives of the People! I alone am the Representative of the People. Twice 24,000,000 French called me to this throne: who of you would undertake such a burden? It had already overwhelmed your assemblies, your conventions, your Vergniauds, and your Gaudets, your Jacobins, and your Girondins. They are all dead! What, who are you? Nothing–all authority is in the Throne; and what is the Throne? A few boards covered with velvet? No – I am the Throne! The vengeance of the enemy is directed against my person more than against the French people. But, for that reason, should I be justified in dismembering the state? Must I sacrifice my pride to obtain peace? I am proud, because I am brave. I am proud, because I have done great things for France. In a word, France has more need of me than I have need of her. In three months we shall have peace, or I shall be dead.[87]

Inefficient imperial officials perhaps caused the most damage to Napoleon's cause during the invasion of France. On the local level, reluctant mayors delayed the draft, while on the regional level some prefects did not enforce the October and November conscription decrees, prompting Napoleon to complain bitterly.[88] Worse behavior came from the officials who foresaw the collapse of the empire. "There is no doubt that government circles are not as active as they should be in keeping spirits high," notes a report of 16 November. "This may not be true of the Councillors of State, but it is a fact that the people have nicknamed them 'the tremblers' and accused or suspected them of being the first to unload their government stocks and bank shares, while their speeches fail to show the firmness of tone expected of them."[89] These opportunists sought to secure their future by cutting deals with either the royalists, the Allies, or both. Vice-Grand Elector and former Foreign

Minister Charles-Maurice de Tallyrand stood ready to bury the empire. "In his mansion in the Rue St. Florentin," notes Maurice Guerrini, "Tallyrand was at the heart of intrigues fostered by royalist agitators, the salons of the Faubourg St. Germain, the opponents of the regime, or the merely discontented."[90] Although the wily former Bishop of Autun had rebuffed Napoleon's request that he assume the reigns of the Foreign Ministry after the firing of Maret, the emperor unwisely allowed Tallyrand to continue serving as Vice-Grand Elector. The emperor's secret police exposed Tallyrand's duplicity, yet Napoleon believed it better to keep Tallyrand in Paris and under observation rather than allow him free run of the country. Not only did Tallyrand establish communication with the Bourbons, but his friendship with Caulaincourt ensured that he was fully informed of Napoleon's diplomatic position.[91]

As for the highest members of the imperial aristocracy, especially the marshals, many had grown weary in the service of the emperor or had proven so incompetent that Napoleon no longer had use for them. The former now wished to retire to their estates and enjoy the benefits of a comfortable pension; the idea that they had served France rather than Napoleon quickly gained ascendancy over their loyalty to the person of the emperor and made them particularly desirous to secure their futures with anyone willing to guarantee their privileged status within France, be it a kingdom or an empire.[92] Of the latter group, Napoleon's own brother Louis provides a glaring example of the emperor's lack of faith in his family. The former king of Holland and father of the future Emperor Napoleon III wrote the emperor to offer his services to quell the unrest in Holland. Claiming to have influence over his former subjects, Louis requested to be reinstated. A disgusted Napoleon showed the letter to Marmont while in Mainz, commenting: "I would rather return Holland to the prince of Orange than send my brother there!"[93] "Under these circumstances of distrust and intrigue," explains Chandler, "it was impossible for the emperor to quit Paris immediately. For the time being, therefore, the defense of the frontiers had to be left to the marshals."[94] As Thiers avows:

> Such were the numerous occupations and the severe mental conflicts in which Napoleon passed the end of November and the beginning of December. As for the rest, if from time to time he roared like a lion that receives from afar the arrows of the hunters ... he exhibited neither his anxiety nor his despair. Alternately animated by hope, or meditating vengeance, he was seen active, animated, with flashing eye ... uttering such phrases as: "Wait, wait, you shall soon see that my soldiers and I have not forgotten our trade. We have been conquered between the Elbe and the Rhine – conquered by being betrayed – but there will be no traitors between the Rhine and Paris, and you shall again behold the soldiers and the General of Italy. Those who have dared to violate our frontier shall soon repent of having placed a foot on French soil.[95]

5

The Left Bank

French spies claimed that the Coalition armies likewise needed time to recover from weeks of combat, fatigue, and privation. Many Allied soldiers contracted typhus after moving into billets recently occupied and infected by French troops. Most Allied commanders dismissed ideas of a winter offensive without first resting and reinforcing their armies. In addition, the French recognized the Coalition's diplomatic needs. The Allied sovereigns and ministers required time to deliberate over the events of 1813 – the destruction of the French Empire east of the Rhine and the resulting fate of millions could not be decided over night. This respite enabled the French to reorganize their forces by rallying stragglers, reequipping the soldiers, refitting the horses, and refurbishing the artillery. Marmont, Victor, and Macdonald anxiously awaited the arrival of conscripts to complete their battalions and squadrons. Regardless, the initiative clearly belonged to the Allies. The Coalition enjoyed vast numerical superiority; the great victory at Leipzig and the French evacuation of Germany provided momentum. Ultimately, this factor limited the freedom of action of the three French marshals – Macdonald, Marmont, and Victor – assigned to command the cordon along the lower, middle, and upper Rhine. A surprise attack at an unassuming point along the frontier remained ever present and dictated their actions. All decisions depended on their ability to interpret the enemy's intentions.[1]

Of the 70,000 French soldiers who crossed the Rhine in early November, only 40,000 carried weapons.[2] The disaster at Leipzig had not been foreseen, and thus the army found Mainz ill supplied and completely unprepared to refurbish the soldiers. On 18 August, Napoleon had ordered Clarke to restock France's eastern fortresses after most of the military supplies had been consumed rebuilding the Grand Armée of 1813. Clarke's inexplicable negligence regarding this charge proved extremely detrimental to Napoleon's cause when the army limped across the Rhine in late 1813.[3] Mainz soon became overcrowded with the Imperial Guard, Napoleon's headquarters, and the remains of the various army corps. The available supplies vanished in what Marmont refers to as a "huge consumption," thus preventing any regular distribution of food.[4] According to the marshal the situation at Mainz reflected badly on the army's high command; "needs of all kinds gave way to embarrassments of all kinds," he recalls. "An army in such great disorder, after having sustained such sufferings, carries with it the germ of the cruelest epidemics. When nothing is ready to fight these fatal predispositions, one is guaranteed to see the worst devastations."[5]

After the emperor's departure, Marmont exercised unrestricted authority along the middle Rhine as supreme commander from Landau to Koblenz. Napoleon placed the II, IV, V, VI Infantry and I, III, and V Cavalry Corps under his command. All generals commanding troops in the 26th Military District likewise reported to the marshal.[6] Marmont's career in the French army had started twenty-three years earlier when he joined the garrison of Chartres as a sublieutenant in July 1790. Two years later, he graduated from the artillery school at Châlons as a lieutenant and served in the French Army of the Alps. He rose through the ranks during the Revolution by serving with distinction in Italy, at the siege of Toulon, and on the Rhine before becoming Napoleon's aide-de-campe in 1796. He accompanied Bonaparte on the First Italian Campaign and then to Egypt. After capturing the standard of the Knights of St. John, Napoleon promoted him to general of brigade on 10 June 1798 – one month before his twenty-fourth birthday. Marmont served at the battle of the Pyramids that same year and then escaped the Middle East with Bonaparte in August 1799. As a reward for his support in the coup of Brumaire, new First Consul Bonaparte appointed him councilor of state.

Continuing his service in the army, Marmont saw action at Marengo in 1800 as the commander of Napoleon's artillery. In the years that followed, he held senior posts in that branch. Despite his personal friendship with Bonaparte, Marmont was excluded from the original marshalate Napoleon created in May 1804. Pursuit of the marshal's baton led Marmont to Dalmatia as governor general and commander in chief of the Army of Dalmatia in July 1806. By raising the siege of Ragusa and driving the Russians from Illyria, Marmont received the title "duke of Raguse" in 1808. He improved the lives of the people along the Balkan coastline, who had become subjects of the French Empire as a result of Austria's cession of Dalmatia to France following the 1805 War of the Third Coalition. Marmont established public schools, built roads, and enhanced the economy. The emperor's wars soon brought him back to central Europe to participate in the 1809 War of the Fifth Coalition. Conducting the pursuit of the defeated Austrians after the 5–6 July battle of Wagram, Marmont raced forward in the hope of winning his marshal's baton by crushing the Austrian rearguard. Fate appeared to betray him on 9–10 July when he narrowly escaped being defeated at Znaim; only the emperor's

Figure 7. Marshal Auguste Frederic Louis Viesse de Marmont (1774–1852). French commandant on the middle Rhine.

personal intervention saved Marmont from an embarrassing reverse. Nevertheless, the emperor hesitatingly awarded him the coveted baton on the 12th, claiming that the new marshal needed to acquire certain military qualities to truly deserve the title. Friendship more than merit persuaded Napoleon. Three years later as commander of the French Army of Portugal, Marmont seemingly justified the emperor's reservations. On 22 July 1812, Wellington defeated Marmont at the battle of Salamanca. Although seriously wounded before the climax of the struggle, Marmont's poor handling of his divisions provided Wellington an opportunity to inflict 14,000 casualties on the 58,000-man Army of Portugal. The defeat at Salamanca shattered French control of northern and central Spain. Convalescing during the Russian campaign, he received command of the VI Corps for the 1813 German campaign.[7]

Marmont's debacle at Salamanca exposed a shortcoming in Napoleon's military system that became apparent after 1808. With the exception of Marshals Massena and Davout, few of the marshals who commanded armies could match the emperor's ability to improvise, adapt to conditions, scramble, and exploit the enemy's mistakes. Supported by a General Staff system that functioned more like a secretariat, many French field commanders could not formulate strategy and conduct operations on par with their master. Napoleon's system of command excelled at training his marshals to be tacticians, but failed to prepare his officers for independent command. Napoleon was sovereign, commander in chief, and chief of staff; his subordinates viewed strategy as the emperor's domain. Pride and jealousy among the marshals also plagued the army's operations, particularly in Iberia and Russia. Although hundreds or even thousands of miles from the area of operations, Bonaparte issued detailed orders and instructions to his army commanders partly to redress these personality clashes. Napoleon's inability to prepare his marshals for independent command or support them with a competent General Staff contributed to the eventual breakdown of the French command structure. This deficiency became acute when the number of forces and theaters of war multiplied after 1808. According to contemporary Philippe de Ségur, Napoleon could not be replaced "either because his subordinates' pride forbids them to obey another, or because . . . he had formed only able lieutenants, but no leaders."[8]

To maintain an offensive posture, Napoleon ordered Marmont to secure Hochheim, directly facing the enemy. The marshal found this to be odd, especially considering his scant resources, but occupied the town with General Armand-Charles Guilleminot's 13th Division of the IV Corps.[9] Allied forces attacked Hochheim on 9 November as Marmont busied himself with the reorganization of the VI Corps at Oppenheim. A spirited assault by Ignaz von Gyulay's Austrian III Corps forced the French to withdraw after losing 1,500 men, four guns, and one eagle.[10] Marmont marched to the sound of the guns and although his tired men quickly covered the ten miles between Oppenheim and Hochheim, Guilleminot's men retreated faster. When the marshal informed imperial headquarters of the loss of Hochheim, Berthier called the situation "annoying," and Napoleon himself responded that he regretted losing this advantageous point "since it would be one more obstacle to have to contend with in the spring."[11]

In evaluating Macdonald's situation on the northeastern frontier of the empire, Napoleon did not deceived himself. He recognized that his brother Jerome's kingdom of Westphalia had collapsed; the king himself already reached Köln with a column of 2,000 to 3,000 men, and a second unit of 4,000 to 5,000 men under General Antoine Rigau evacuated Kassel on 28 October and headed for Düsseldorf. This in turn precipitated the evacuation of the 32nd Military District. The emperor speculated that the 4,500 men in this region under General Claude Carra St. Cyr would withdraw to the Ems River and defend this line, but foresaw that St. Cyr would be forced from this position as well, thus allowing Allied forces to reach the Rhine – Ijssel line. Consequently, Macdonald's task of defending the length of the frontier from Koblenz to the mouth of the Ijssel River far surpassed his resources. His first assignment according to the emperor's orders included removing all boats from the banks of the Rhine between Koblenz and Zwolle to deny the enemy means to cross the river. Second, he had to arm and provision the fortresses of Wesel, Venlo, Grave, Jülich, and Deventer. To increase Macdonald's manpower, Napoleon placed the troops of the 25th Military District at his disposal and ordered the organization of the National Guard in the

Roer and Rhin-et-Moselle Departments. Moreover, the generals commanding the 17th (Gabriel-Jean-Joseph Molitor), 25th (Pierre-Hugues-Victoire Merle), 31st (Jean-Jacques Ambert), and 32nd (Carra St. Cyr) Military Districts were directed to cooperate with the marshal to defend the Ijssel.[12]

Despite these reinforcements, Macdonald quickly became frustrated after he arrived in Köln on 6 November. The debris of the XI Corps remained eighty miles south of Köln at Bingen, where Charpentier labored to reorganize the regiments. According to the information Macdonald received, the Westphalian columns consisted of very disparate units, which he had to return to their corps of origin according to a 7 November order.[13] Carra St. Cyr's troops of the 32nd Military District appeared to be of suspect quality, consisting of 1,500 Swiss soldiers who were inclined to desert, the dismounted cavalry of the Osnabrück depot, gendarmes, infantry detachments belonging to the XIII Corps, and customs agents. Molitor's 14,428 men of the 17th Military District had to maintain order in Holland's cities – no easy task after eight battalions of the 3rd and 4th *régimens étrangers* and two Dutch battalions deserted.[14] Macdonald found the units stationed in the 25th Military district consisted only of a few brigades of gendarmes and customs agents supported by Coast Guard artillery and a handful of Swiss infantry companies.

On 25 October Napoleon had issued instructions to place the fortresses of the 25th Military District in a state of defense. Regardless, the garrisons suffered both quantitatively and qualitatively. Incomplete staffs composed of old or infirm officers commanded garrisons that mainly consisted of depot personnel, unreliable foreign units, and untrained conscripts who possessed poor uniforms and equipment; artillerists, sappers, and engineers remained few in number.[15] Although Wesel's garrison eventually numbered 8,000 men, these troops had to hold the key fortress and could not be used in the field. Lacking stores of both arms and equipment, the prefects of the Roer and Rhin-et-Moselle refused to summon the National Guard. The promised reinforcements could not reach the Rhine for at least one month. In Köln itself, an agitated public greeted French officers with shouts of *Vive Alexandre* and *Vive les Cassocks*.

Behind Macdonald, the cauldron of nationalistic unrest began to bubble in the German, Dutch, and Belgian departments of the empire. In this atmosphere insurgents, enemy spies, refractory priests, defiant nobles, and smugglers operated freely. With Coalition forces approaching from the east and an increasingly hostile population to the west, the marshal certainly could claim that Marmont and Victor had easier assignments. It did not help that the marshal resented his task; Napoleon rejected his request to return to France to rest and recover from the German campaign. When Napoleon sent Beugnot to assist Macdonald with acquiring supplies for his "army," the marshal exploded:

Figure 8. Marshal Jacques Etienne Joseph Alexandre Macdonald (1765–1840). French commandant on the Lower Rhine.

Would you like to inspect my *army*? It would not take long; in person it consists of me, who you already have before your eyes, and my chief of staff, Gen. [Louis-Sébastien] Grundler, who will come in; it consists so far of four straw chairs and a table. Everyday I write to Paris that it is a bad joke to call what you have seen 'the Army of Marshal Macdonald'. With a loud voice I demand a real army because I am far from the general opinion that the enemy will not cross the Rhine. If the emperor can only oppose him with armies the strength of my own, then he will bring the enemy to a halt no sooner than before Paris.[16]

The son of a Scottish Jacobite, Macdonald's military career started as a member of the Irish Legion in 1784. One year later, the native of Sedan served in a French unit in Holland before returning to France in 1786. Commissioned a sublieutenant in 1789, Macdonald quickly rose through the ranks during the Revolution, reaching general of brigade in 1793 and general of division the following year at age twenty-nine. Between 1795 and 1798, he campaigned in the Low Countries until being transferred to Italy, where Macdonald served as commander of the French troops stationed in the Republic of Rome and then as governor of Rome in 1798. In the following year, he assumed command of the French army of Naples. His performance as an independent commander proved less than spectacular. After evacuating the kingdom of Naples, Macdonald moved north to unite with the French army of Italy. He drove the Austrians from Modena on 12 June, receiving a saber wound to the head. Five days later, a combined Austro–Russian force commanded by the famed Russian General Aleksandr Vasilievich Suvorov crushed the Army of Naples in three days of fighting along the Trebbia River. Macdonald criticized one of his divisional commanders, General Victor, for the defeat, thus forever souring the relationship between the two future marshals. He returned to Paris where, allegedly, the conspirators who eventually hatched the coup of Brumaire with Bonaparte as their frontman first offered the role to Macdonald. Declining, he actively supported Napoleon on the day of the coup by closing the roads leading to St. Cloud, where the French legislature was meeting. In late 1800, First Consul Bonaparte rewarded Macdonald for his loyalty by naming him commander of the Army of the Grisons. Crossing the Alps into Italy, Macdonald's lackluster campaign in early 1801 ended after Austria signed the Peace of Lunéville on 8 February and withdrew from the War of the Second Coalition. Macdonald's next assignment took him to Denmark as French envoy to the Danish court. Uncomfortable in this position, the general begged for a military post. By the time his transfer arrived, a growing scandal threatened his relationship with Bonaparte. The First Consul accused two of Macdonald's mentors and former commanders, Generals Jean-Victor Moreau and Jean-Charles Pichegru, of treason. Macdonald found himself implicated. Although nothing could be proven, he retired to his estate until March 1809.

Macdonald languished while the Grande Armée peaked between 1805–7. With French armies committed in Iberia, Italy, and Germany, Napoleon's need of experienced commanders prompted him to recall Macdonald. After fighting in Italy, Macdonald arrived in the German theater in time to participate in the battle of Wagram. On the second and final day of the battle, 6 July 1809, Macdonald's corps crushed the Austrian center. This not only reconciled him with the emperor but earned Macdonald the marshal's baton as well. Five weeks later, Napoleon elevated him to nobility with the title duke of Taranto and an annual annuity of 60,000 francs. From April 1810 to July 1811, he waged another nondescript campaign as commander of the French Army of Catalonia in Spain. He returned to Paris to recover from a painful attack of gout and the following year received command of the X Corps of the Grande Armée of 1812. Fortunately for Macdonald, the X Corps did not accompany the emperor's army to Moscow. Instead, it covered the left or northern flank of Napoleon's operation. Macdonald spent the majority of the campaign conducting the unsuccessful siege of Riga. He suffered the embarrassment of seeing his Prussian contingent defect in late December. During the reorganization of the French army that followed the Russian catastrophe, he received command of the XI Corps. The marshal performed well fighting under Napoleon's supervision at Lützen and Bautzen. Left on his own as commander of the Army of the Bober, he was smashed by Blücher at the Katzbach River. Like many of the marshals, Macdonald's limited skills allowed him to command no more than 20,000 men under the emperor's supervision. Left on his own as an independent commander he offered little hope for success. "He was no great drinker or bragger or swearer," describes historian Alan Hankinson. "He fought no duels and disdained the tricks of the con-man. He lacked élan. He would not stoop to self-promotion. And though he admired the military abilities of some of his fellow marshals, there were many whose personal characteristics he despised.... Macdonald was a solid, even a stolid man, careful and decent and conscientious. The thing he prized above all else was his reputation as a man of integrity."[17]

Because of the dearth of line troops, Macdonald had to rely on gendarmes, customs agents, and foresters to guard his sector of the Rhine during the first half of November. Napoleon attempted to remedy Macdonald's manpower woes by transferring the 2,500 troopers of Sébastiani's II Cavalry Corps to his command. The emperor issued orders for Sébastiani to proceed to Köln and observe a fifty-mile stretch of the Rhine downstream to Wesel. For infantry support, Charpentier led the 2,400 men of the XI Corps to Köln. To ease the pressure on Macdonald, Napoleon also pushed Marmont's units down the Rhine. Arrighi's III Cavalry Corps (2,000 sabers) and the V Infantry Corps – the 3,000 men of Albert's 10th Division – likewise received instructions to move north to Koblenz in order to guard the thirty-five miles of the Koblenz–Bingen sector.[18] To adjust his front to these movements, Napoleon directed the I Cavalry Corps to patrol the Rhine between Bingen and Mainz. The emperor also dispatched one engineer and one artillery general to Köln to take command of their respective branches in the fortresses between Koblenz and Zwolle. General Jean-Barthélemot Sorbier, the commander of the Grande Armée's artillery, scrambled to fill the emperor's demand for the formation of one light battery each for the II and III Cavalry Corps and to reorganize the artillery of the XI Corps.[19] Despite these measures, the mobile line forces at Macdonald's immediate disposal to cover a front of almost 125 miles amounted to only 3,300 cavalry, 3,500 infantry, and forty guns.[20]

Macdonald allowed the fatigue, frustration, and bitterness that seemed rife among the marshalate and upper echelons of the imperial bureaucracy to get the better of his discretion. During the battle of Leipzig, he had lost all his baggage and equipment, including an estimated sum of 12,000 to 15,000 francs. On 8 November he submitted a request for reimbursement in the amount of 150,000 francs to cover the loss of horses, wagons, baggage, saddlery, harnesses, silverware, personal affects, uniforms, and livery; the emperor eventually sent him 30,000 francs. Making little effort to conceal his indignation, he openly criticized the war effort and permitted his staff officers to do the same. According to police commissioner Paulze d'Ivoy:

> I have heard him a number of times say in front of the administrators of Köln that our affairs are bad, that our soldiers no longer want to fight, that peace is absolutely necessary, that without it France is lost, that with his few troops he cannot defend France. This talk produces an evil effect and increases

discouragement. He remained in Köln for ten days without leaving his apartment and without establishing any military posts. We are certain that everywhere he proceeds with the same negligence. He is surrounded by a staff that flatters him in the most servile way; Grundler, claims one, is indiscreet. The marshal complains continuously and often in a very inconvenient manner, as does the servicemen who are under his orders.[21]

Troop shortages forced Napoleon to reorganize and consolidate. On 7 November, Berthier issued a new order of battle for the field army. Because combat losses and disease reduced the III and VI Corps to the size of divisions, the III became the 8th Division commanded by Ricard, and the VI was reorganized into General Joseph Lagrange's 20th Division. These two divisions were then united to form a new VI Corps under Marmont's command. Macdonald resumed command of the XI Corps, which contained Charpentier's 31st Division, joined by General Michael-Sylvestre Brayer's 35th Division. Napoleon combined the three weak divisions of the II Corps into one: the 4th. The V Corps technically had no chief until Sébastiani took command on 18 November. Sébastiani's health did not permit him to retain command of the II Cavalry Corps, and in his place Napoleon appointed General Etienne Bordessoulle.[22] General Charles-Antoine Morand, who replaced Bertrand as commander of the IV Corps, received the skeletal remains of four divisions: the 12th, 13th, 32nd, and 51st.[23] This prompted Napoleon to forward to him all disposable conscripts from the various regimental depots.[24] Four divisions made up the I Cavalry Corps, while the II, III, and V contained three each.[25] On 12 November, the emperor repeated his instructions for Marmont to transfer the V Infantry and III Cavalry Corps to Koblenz. To fill the gap caused by their departure, one Young Guard division quartered between Mainz and Trier; a second division billeted between Koblenz and Trier. Marmont posted the II, IV, and VI Corps close to Mainz.[26] Napoleon informed him on 16 November that Victor did not need the II Corps at Strasbourg because the National Guard units being levied in the Vosges region would suffice to defend against an attack from Switzerland.[27] One week later a disgruntled Victor reported that thus far only 1,200 National Guardsmen had reported for duty.[28]

Napoleon also moved the regimental depots located in the first-line fortresses to the second echelon of fortifications that guarded the approaches to the French interior. Thus the depots in Wesel, Köln, Mainz, Landau, and Strasbourg were transferred to Metz, Nancy, Thionville, Lille, and Mézières. The commanding generals of the cavalry corps, the artillery, and the engineers received orders to organize large depots at Kreuznach (I Cavalry Corps); Koblenz (II Cavalry Corps); Bacharach (III Cavalry Corps); Winnweiler (V Cavalry Corps); Mommernheim (artillery); and Zahlbach (engineers). For the corps defending the middle and upper Rhine, Napoleon established the army's administrative headquarters at Metz under Marshal François-Etienne

Kellermann, the hero of the battle of Valmy which saved the French Revolution from the Allied invasion of 1792. According to the emperor's rotation system, the trained recruits coming out of the regimental depots would be directed to Metz, from where they would be distributed to the regiments. Metz and Paris provided the artillery for the troops along the middle and upper Rhine; Antwerp for the northern theater of war, and Lyon in the south. French cavalry would be organized around Paris.[29]

Napoleon intended to form a strong reserve behind the weak corps positioned along the Rhine. He decided that the Imperial Guard – two divisions of Old Guard and six of Young Guard – would serve as the nucleus of this reserve.[30] These units crossed the Rhine with barely 8,000 infantry and 4,000 cavalry. "The important point," he wrote, "is that the [Guard] cavalry and infantry reorganize; for this to occur we need more room."[31] To facilitate the reorganization of the Old Guard, the cavalry extended its quarters from Kreuznach to Simmern and Trier, and the infantry camped around Kaiserslautern. The Young Guard cavalry was transferred from Mainz and Kreuznach to Kaiserslautern, Zweibrücken, and Sarreguemines; Metz housed the Guard's depots. In the course of two weeks, the Guard increased to 17,500 infantry and 5,000 cavalry; with artillery and sappers, it totaled 28,000 men. Napoleon named Mortier commander in chief of the Imperial Guard and authorized Drouot to increase the Guard to 102 battalions totaling 85,600 men.[32] Because numerous veterans could be found among the 28,000 men of the Guard, the emperor instructed Drouot to utilize these seasoned warriors to train the recruits. Assuming the Allies remained in winter quarters until spring, Napoleon hoped to mobilize a new army consisting of 288,000 men. Together with the Guard, he planned to field more than 375,000 men by 15 January 1814.[33]

Bonaparte also made preparations for his own drive across the Rhine in the spring. "At the moment we are not ready for anything, but by the second week of December we will be ready for much," he declared. "Our current task is the arming and provisioning of the fortresses."[34] He ordered the creation of magazines at Saarbrücken, Trier, and Saarlouis and outlined plans for the new army he expected to be ready by January. It would consist of six infantry corps – the I, II, IV, V, VI, and XI – each containing four divisions and over fifty battalions.[35] Napoleon planned for 500 men to leave each depot on 1 December to reinforce every regiment along the Rhine frontier. "Therefore, 50,000 reinforcements will bring the IV, V, VI, and XI Corps to their full strength," he concluded. "At the same time, one battalion from each depot will leave for the II Corps. These twelve battalions will unite in Strasbourg."[36]

At Mainz Marmont noted that the shortage of food and other privations generated a psychological effect among the men similar to extreme prolonged fear: It weakened their will to live, lowered their immune systems, and made them susceptible to contagions. Supply remained in a horrible state – the men received a daily ration consisting of one-quarter of a pound of meat and one and one-quarter pounds of bread. The exhausted French soldiers quickly fell prey to typhus, which spread from the unsanitary hospitals along the Elbe River to the Rhine.[37] An acute infectious disease caused by a rickettsia, typhus can be transmitted to humans by the bite of fleas and lice and is characterized by fever, headache, and red blotches on the skin. "A trail of infantry," wrote Ségur, "remnants of the retreat, passed through our cantonments and infected them. The plague descended on our villages. Born of destitution, it indiscriminately attacked civilians and soldiers, rich and poor, strong and weak alike. The disease spread at an alarming rate. The symptoms varied: some people, struck down suddenly, died in a state of deep despair; others were seized by a raging delirium. One saw men jump out of windows ... [and die] in horrible convulsions."[38]

By late 1813, an unyielding epidemic raged in Mainz, its surrounding region, and as far west as the Moselle River. Napoleon established special hospitals to handle the human disaster. He ordered the creation of hospitals with 8,000 beds each in Mainz and Strasbourg, and hospitals for 10,000 sick in each of the fortresses between these two cities.[39] In the meantime Mainz's customs office had to be used as a make-shift hospital to accommodate the growing number of sick. Overcrowding in the hospitals and the lack of care facilitated the disease's deadly results. With 300 soldiers dying each day, the doctors and hospital workers feared treating the sick men. To insure that the sick received care, Marmont visited the hospitals daily in order to remind the doctors of their obligations and to encourage his dying men. Marmont maintains that the psychological despondency caused by the horrors found in Mainz had a direct correlation with the deadly course of the disease. "The inhabitants of Mainz and the surrounding region," he notes, "who had not fled their homes and had not been exposed to privations, were struck by terror at the sight of this mortality, and thus also fell victim like the soldiers. [Conversely], the army officers, who did not share the fear of the inhabitants and did not suffer physically as much as the soldiers, were affected less by the disease." Seeing so much sickness concentrated in such a confined area led each soldier to expect to share the same sad fate as his dying comrades. For this reason, Marmont felt obligated to rally the courage of the men in the hospital just like on the battlefield.[40]

Despite French efforts to contain the disease, typhus claimed more than 15,000 soldiers of the IV Corps and a similar number of civilians in the last two months of 1813. "We have many sick men and the number is growing at an alarming pace," Marmont informed the emperor on 19 November.[41] Again on the 27th, he reported: "The number of sick is growing daily and the corps is visibly weakening."[42] From mid-November to mid-December the IV Corps received more than 18,000 recruits, yet its musters never exceeded 16,500 men. Marmont eventually established a system to evacuate the sick. "Yet these evacuations," he admits, "which pushed [the sick] so far away because each of us felt more comfortable by distancing the heart of the contagions, were fatal. Disregarding the interests of humanity, soldiers suffering from typhus were sent as far as Bourgogne. A portion died during the trip, and the remainder brought to Bourgogne the epidemic that they had spread on their way."[43] The removal of large numbers of sick to the interior by roads and waterways "involved fresh calamities," judges Thiers. "The public roads were now seen covered with carts, each bearing thirty of these unfortunate creatures, some dead, others dying beside dead bodies, from which they could not separate."[44]

Marmont also noticed that the feet of many of his men had frozen during the retreat, which he found unusual because the temperature had not fallen below freezing. "Toes were struck by death and succumbing to gangrene in the same manner as if a violent freeze had occurred," recounts the marshal. He likewise attributed this phenomenon to his soldiers' mental and physical exhaustion; utter fatigue had sapped the life from their extremities. Discouragement and discontent cast a malaise over the survivors of Napoleon's last Grande Armée. "Men with the most base intelligence," explains Marmont, "understood that the consumption of almost 1,000,000 men in such a short time, the disappearance of our power and prestige, the blatant mistakes of our country, the disorganization of the empire made apparent everywhere either by the revolts or the desertions, signaled the danger that now threatened the heart of the state . . . this all discouraged the most vigorous spirit and gave rise to the thought that we had not reached the end of our misfortunes."[45]

After inspecting his sector, Marmont grew concerned over the Neckar River. His men found few boats on this tributary of the Rhine, which led him to believe that the Allies had amassed the craft upstream to send raiding parties downstream and across the Rhine. He considered one battery of three to four guns facing the confluence of the Neckar with the Rhine sufficient to prevent any boats from crossing. Napoleon communicated his approval on 5 November, adding that the marshal should build a larger, stronger redoubt to house heavy artillery.[46] The emperor's foresight proved prophetic, for Blücher's army would have to cross the Rhine in the face of this battery.

Until the arrival of the reinforcements promised by Napoleon, Marmont's forces only sufficed to defend the left bank against raids. Thinly stretched along a line too extensive for them to be effective, his divisions could not prevent an enemy army from crossing the middle Rhine in force. Should the Allies attempt a winter drive across the Rhine, he planned to retreat and regroup. On 14 November, he suggested preparing a second line with magazines at Kaiserslautern and Saarbrücken as well as Trarbach on the Moselle to fall back on if the enemy forced the Rhine or Macdonald needed support.[47]

On the upper Rhine, Marshal Victor received the arduous task of organizing French defenses from Landau to Huningue. His zone did not contain a single fortress in an acceptable state of defense. After the War of the Second

Coalition (1798–1801), the French had little concern over an invasion across their eastern frontier. As Napoleon pushed the borders of the "Grande Empire" deep into central Europe between 1801 and 1809, French engineers attended to tasks well beyond the frontiers of "old France." With the exception of the fortresses on the stretch of the Moselle River that ran through Flanders, French engineers generally neglected the maintenance of France's eastern frontier fortresses.[48]

Victor left Mainz on 3 November and established his headquarters in Strasbourg two days later. A native of Lamarche in the Vosges Mountains, Victor was described by a contemporary as having "the face of a good peasant of Lorraine. He was a big, strong man with gray hair, around 50, and looked very solid for his age."[49] Born on 7 December 1764, he entered the artillery regiment of Grenoble as a drummer in 1781, two months short of his seventeenth birthday. He transferred to the infantry during the Revolution and served as a grenadier in the National Guard of Valence. After receiving a commission, Victor participated in the siege of Toulon in 1793. During the operations to regain the port, Victor met a young Bonaparte, who had recently assumed command of the army's artillery. A professional relationship based on mutual respect quickly formed. When Bonaparte devised a plan to drive the British from Ft. Le Petit Gibraltar, he chose Victor to command one of the assault columns. On 17 December 1793, Bonaparte observed Colonel Victor lead his men valiantly, being one of the first to scale the wall and dive on top of the British defenders in the redoubt. Both Victor and Napoleon were wounded during the successful assault that drove the British from Toulon; both Victor and Napoleon were promoted to general of brigade for their conduct. It took Victor just three years of service in France's Revolutionary army to rise from sergeant to general.

Upon recovering from his fairly serious wound – a musket ball to the lower abdomen – he took a post with the Army of the Eastern Pyrenees on 1 January 1794. After an initial stint as commander of the army's reserve, he assumed command of the 4th Brigade and saw combat for the rest of 1794. In August 1795, Victor was transferred to the Army of Italy to participate in Napoleon's famous First Italian Campaign. Two months later Victor found himself serving in a division commanded by Masséna, one of the best generals in the French army. Bouncing between divisions under Masséna, Augereau, and General Jean-Pierre-Antoine Rey, the brigadier ultimately took command of the reserve of the Army of Italy, which itself was now commanded by Bonaparte. In this capacity, he participated in Napoleon's victory at Rivoli on 14 January 1797. Victor distinguished himself during the pursuit, and Bonaparte rewarded him with a promotion to general of division and command of the 8th Division of the Army of Italy.

While his benefactor invaded Egypt, Victor first served in the Army of England before requesting a transfer to the Army of Italy. Back in Italy, he

Figure 9. Marshal Claude Victor-Perrin (1764–1841). French commandant on the upper Rhine.

took part in the occupation of Piedmont in December 1797. French aggression in Italy contributed to the formation of the formidable Second Coalition of Great Britain, Russia, and Austria. French forces desperately attempted to hold their gains in the Italian peninsular, but Victor and other future marshals such as Macdonald and St. Cyr slowly yielded. In the midst of French reverses, Napoleon returned from Egypt, overthrew the French government, and installed himself as an enlightened dictator under the title of first consul. Victor accompanied Napoleon over the Alps for the Second Italian Campaign. Leading a corps of two divisions, Victor distinguished himself in the decisive battle of the campaign: Marengo. On 14 June 1800, Victor commanded the French army's left wing. Although Napoleon took much of the credit for the victory, Victor received a sword of honor for his conduct.

This trinket proved to be the extent of Napoleon's gratitude. Over the next four years Victor received assignments in Belgium, Louisiana, and Holland. As historian James Arnold notes, his appointment as *capitaine-général* of Louisiana, a relatively backwater command that Victor never assumed, indicated that "Bonaparte felt his services were expendable." Napoleon's indifference toward Victor possibly stemmed from the latter's staunch republican loyalties. Regardless, Victor's second-class status appeared to be confirmed on 19 May 1804 when Napoleon, now emperor of the French, restored the rank of marshal and created the marshalate. Victor's name was not among the eighteen generals who the emperor elevated to this exalted position. Over the next three years, Victor struggled to earn his place in the sun. A diplomatic assignment to Denmark in 1805 did not help his cause. Although Napoleon awarded him the Grand Eagle of the Legion of Honor on 6 March 1805, he did not entrust Victor with a command when France confronted the Third Coalition later that year. Not until the War of the Fourth Coalition did Victor see service in the Grande Armée. On 6 October 1806, Napoleon named him chief of staff of Marshal Jean Lannes's V Corps. Finally, on 5 January 1807, Victor received command of a corps, the X. Fifteen days later Prussian Hussars captured the hapless general. Exchanged for Blücher on 8 March, he assumed command of the siege of Graudenz before taking over the I Corps in place of the disgraced Bernadotte. Eight days later, Victor made the most of his opportunity. During the battle of Friedland, Ney attempted to deliver the coup de grâce, but a Russian counterattack nearly crushed his corps. With Napoleon attentively watching, Victor plugged the gap and stabilized the French line. On 13 July 1807, Victor finally gained his marshal's baton, the first to be awarded since the original marshalate. He received his title of imperial peerage, "duke of Bellune," on 18 September 1808.

Like many of the French marshals, Victor displayed great talent as a divisional commander: tactical prowess in assault and defense, personal bravery, sangfroid in battle, and administrative competence. Napoleon never considered him among the best of his marshals, yet Victor proved to be a competent corps commander on several occasions, particularly during the Peninsular War and the retreat from Russia. Again, similar to many of his fellow marshals, Victor lacked the skills of independent command, which led to his disgrace in 1814. Although diligent, conscientious, and intelligent, he had a poor relationship with his fellow marshals, particularly Ney. Moreover, his ambition and pride never allowed him to forgive Napoleon for passing him over in 1804. Even Victor's imperial title, duke of Bellune, served as an irritant for the snubbed officer. While others received titles that reflected their moments of glory on the battlefield such as Davout's "duke of Auerstädt" and Ney's "prince of the Moskowa," Victor's patent of Napoleonic peerage arose from a play on words by one of the emperor's sisters. Because Victor's nickname, le Beau Soleil, reflected his open and friendly nature, she suggested he be called "Bellune." When Napoleon returned to France in 1815 after his first exile, Victor did not rally to his cause.[50]

The industrious marshal wasted little time acquainting himself with the situation of the 5th Military District, mainly comprising Alsace, which he now had to prepare for a possible enemy invasion. "The line from Huningue to Landau is far from being in a state of defense," he informed Berthier on 6 November. "It is guarded at this moment by 300 foresters and the same number of customs agents, whose duty is purely observation." To increase his manpower, he attempted to train and arm all National Guard legions in his sector and to employ them as Line troops.

To improve the fortresses, Victor required "workers and money; mainly money. We are completely lacking money. The garrisons are formed by regimental depots and refractory conscripts who will offer no means of resistance. Strasbourg, which has a foundry and large artillery workshop, has no supplies, no means to hold against a siege, and no defense other than the walls." Lacking the requisite funds, he nevertheless worked feverishly to reinforce, palisade, arm, and provision the Alsatian fortresses of Strasbourg, Belfort, Neuf-Brisach, Sélestat, Landau, Huningue, Lauterbourg, Wissembourg, Haguenau, Colmar, and Mulhouse. Victor also tackled ambitious tasks such as raising the height of the walls of the fortresses and arming the inhabitants. He imposed a ten-hour workday on the smiths in the foundries. Although Sélestat still had no artillery by 26 December, 146 workers including nine carpenters worked on its defenses for six weeks. Victor organized the defense of Huningue, where a workshop of thirty-five blacksmiths produced cartridges nonstop. Despite his request for funding to complete Belfort's citadel, the city had to employ its own resources to finish the work. After several weeks of painstaking work, Victor, supported by several civilian and military functionaries, managed to provision and equip the fortresses that were expected to take an active role in the defense of the frontier.[51]

The inactivity of the Allied armies allowed Napoleon to direct his gaze north. On 11 November, he attached the "greatest importance" to the Dutch fortress of Gorinchem and issued instructions for General Antoine-Guillaume Rampon, the commandant of the National Guard of the Antwerp district, to go there himself with 3,000 Guardsmen to place the fortress in a state of defense. To replace these men in Antwerp, Napoleon directed units from Havre and Cherbourg to the great port city. Regarding Macdonald, the emperor wanted him to "fix his attention on Deventer and Coevorden" and to occupy Deventer, Delfzijl, and the line of the Ijssel with the troops Carra St. Cyr evacuated from the 32nd Military District. "Tell him [Macdonald] that 600,000 conscripts," wrote the emperor, "almost all men thirty years of age, are in movement; numerous detachments already have arrived in the depots and the armies will be promptly formed."[52]

Before Macdonald received this propaganda, news arrived of growing unrest in the Dutch interior. In Holland the French occupation force under Molitor could neither man the Dutch forts nor quell the growing insurrection. Of Molitor's 14,428 men, 8,902 were French soldiers, and the other 5,526 were Dutch, Belgians, Germans, or deserters from other countries, especially Prussia, who became increasingly unreliable as Allied forces approached. Among the French were the 3rd and 4th Battalions of the war orphans of the Guard: around 1,272 adolescents between the ages of fourteen and seventeen whose fathers had served in the Imperial Guard. Contemporary François Koch claims that Molitor's men "were of wretched composition."[53]

In early November, popular revolt against French rule fomented in Holland's major cities as the cries *"Vive Orange"* and *"Orange boven"* spread from Amsterdam to The Haag, signaling insurrection against the French conquerors. Napoleon had established a Bonapartist monarchy under his brother Louis in May 1806. Forcing Louis to abdicate four years later for violating the Continental System and trading with the British, the emperor directly incorporated Holland into the French Empire on 9 July 1810. "At that time," maintains Thiers, "Napoleon was irresistible, and besides, many different interests had found momentary advantages in the union. Dutch revolutionaries, Catholics, and merchants had submitted to a revolution, which to one party represented the expulsion of the house of Orange, to another the repression of Protestantism, and to a third, commercial annexation with the greatest empire in the world."[54] Nevertheless, Dutch desire for independence festered following the state's submergence into the increasingly repressive French Empire. Particularly hurt by Napoleon's Continental System, the Dutch proved to be the least dependable of the many peoples who constituted the empire. Opposition to French rule steadily grew; the emperor's monumental defeats in 1812 and 1813 fueled subversive activity. Although Napoleon's dreaded "blood tax" had least affected Holland, which supplied France with only 17,300 troops between January 1811 and July 1813, the publishing of the Dutch casualty list from the Russian campaign convinced many that the time had come for action. Of the 500 Dutch soldiers attached to Napoleon's Imperial Guard, only forty returned from Russia. The mainly Dutch 126th Infantry Regiment crossed the Russian frontier with 1,887 men in June 1812; on 28 November the Russians took the 206 survivors prisoner.[55]

By November 1813, Holland's larger cities were restless and ripe for revolt; Amsterdam was the first to declare national independence. Gijsbert Karel van Hogendorp and A. van der Duyn van Maasdam summoned the Dutch to fight for their independence. They placed themselves at the head of a national movement and called for a restoration of the House of Orange. Hogendorp's followers took advantage of the absence of French forces to take control of Amsterdam. The arming of the people, the general enthusiasm, and open anti-French sentiment convinced the French garrison at The Haag to depart. On 17 November, Hogendorp proclaimed the Netherlands free and the prince of Orange the highest political authority in the land. Two days later Hogendorp and Maasdam formed a provisional government to govern the Netherlands until the prince arrived from Great Britain. Regardless, the insurrection spread slowly because French forces still occupied the Dutch interior.[56]

Wintzingerode detached a large Streifkorps of 3,500 men (1,600 Cossacks, 1,100 infantry, and 800 Hussars) under General Alexander Khristoforovich Benckendorff, which advanced through Ostfriesland to Deventer on the lower

Ijssel in early November. He was reinforced by eight Cossack regiments; five under Colonel Stepan Fedorovich Balabin II moved on his left toward Doesburg. On Benckendorff's right Colonel Levin Alexandrovich Naryshkin led the other three regiments to Zwolle. Finding Deventer too strong, Benckendorff united with Naryshkin at Zwolle. Purportedly garrisoned by "200–300 poorly equipped cavalry troopers, Zwolle fell to the Russians. Benckendorff immediately dispatched 200 Cossacks on the direct road to Amsterdam. Aided by Dutch insurgents and Belgian smugglers, Russian light troops escorted staff officers into central Holland and Belgium to evaluate the mood of the inhabitants and to ascertain the size of the French army.[57] According to Benkendorff's memoirs, he decided to attempt a coup de main in Holland and despatched a Dutch colonel in Russian service to Amsterdam to collect intelligence. Benckendorff reported his intentions to Bülow and sought Wintzingerode's permission to invade Holland proper.[58]

News that Russian forces had crossed the frontier sparked the revolt in Amsterdam on the night of 14–15 November. During the day of the 15th, French Consul Anne-Charles Lebrun in Amsterdam, General Joseph Bouvier des Eclaz at The Haag, and General Pierre-Marie-Bartholomé Férino at Rotterdam requested Molitor's support to disperse anti-French mobs. Lebrun decided to evacuate to France the supplies that could be saved and to destroy the rest. That evening, the 15th, the National Guard of Amsterdam made common cause with the people. Lebrun and his administration fled the city. Shortly after, the Orangists took control of Amsterdam, and the insurrection spread.

Although described as prudent and humane, Lebrun, a financial expert, failed to direct and organize the defense of Holland. Already disappointed by the poor results of his administration, Lebrun plunged into a severe bereavement over the loss of a son killed during the Russian campaign. No longer interested in Dutch affairs, his inertia paralyzed the efforts of upper-level French officials, encouraged the Orangists, and alienated the partisans of the empire.[59] A completely demoralized Lebrun arrived in Utrecht on the 16th and rejected Molitor's suggestion to march on Amsterdam with 1,000 men. Lebrun preferred to await the arrival of the reinforcements promised by the emperor. Molitor agreed in order to maintain his central position at Utrecht, the midpoint in the Naarden–Gorinchem line. He wanted to hold this line for as long as possible to finish arming the forts, withdraw his detachments from the Ijssel, and prevent the Russians from linking with the insurgents at The Haag and Amsterdam. Benckendorff, however, continued his drive in order to support the Orangists. Avoiding the French posts, he reached Amsterdam on 24 November.

"Since the month of November, Holland had no longer been ours," wrote Baron Fain. "The approach of the corps of Bülow and Wintzingerode, who, after occupying Hanover and Westphalia, had advanced on Münster, Wesel, and Düsseldorf, suddenly excited a revolution in Holland."[60] "During the week between November 8 and 15," adds historian Simon Schama, "authority fell away from the French empire like dead flesh from a skeleton."[61] A Dutch deputation arrived in London on 21 November and reported to Parliament that a counterrevolution had commenced in support of the exiled House of Orange. This sentiment spread throughout the land, and the insurgents established a provisional government in the name of Prince William of Orange. The delegation solicited arms and assurances of support from the British government. London promised to provide 25,000 muskets that had been prepared in anticipation of this request. Moreover, between 5,000 and 6,000 British troops under the command of General Thomas Graham would be sent to Holland.

Carra St. Cyr's retreat from the Ems to Wesel opened the line of the Ijssel, whose forts contained fewer than 1,000 men combined and exposed Holland to invasion. Cossacks swarmed through Westphalia to Holland. Two days before Benckendorff entered Amsterdam, the smaller Cossack Streifkorps saw action on the Ijssel: One took possession of Doesburg, and the other engaged the French at Deventer. Although well suited to harass the French, impede communications, and disperse posts, the Cossacks could not formally assault the Dutch forts. Wintzingerode's corps remained idle in North Germany, but Bülow's Prussian III Corps left Minden on 13 November and moved through Münster toward the Dutch frontier. General Adolf Friederich von Oppen led Bülow's advance guard to Deutikum, nine miles east of Doesburg, on the 22nd. From there, Oppen established communications with Major Friedrich August Peter von Colomb's Prussian Streifkorps, which had been prowling between Wesel and Kleve on the left bank of the Rhine since the 19th. Oppen decided to march through Doesburg and along the left bank of the Ijssel to Arnhem, while Colomb moved on Westervoort and seized the ferries on the Ijssel to prevent the French from crossing the river and severing the communications between Oppen and Bülow.[62]

Bülow's march toward the Dutch frontier particularly alarmed Macdonald. Revolts in Amsterdam and The Haag, as well as the desertion of Molitor's foreign battalions, left the French with little means to resist an Allied invasion. Under these circumstances, Macdonald only hoped to slow Allied progress in Holland. To do so, he had to find some way to reinforce Molitor's troops. With the XI Infantry and the II Cavalry Corps posted on the 100-mile stretch of the Rhine between Andernach and Wesel, he had at his disposal only Carra St. Cyr's 4,500 men. Conforming with Napoleon's orders to employ these troops on the Ijssel, he instructed Merle, the commandant of the 25th Military District, to organize at Wesel a mobile column (2,000 men) consisting of two infantry battalions, one battalion of customs agents, and one squadron of gendarmes. Commanded by François-Pierre-Joseph Amey, the column left Wesel on 14 November headed for Arnhem and Deventer. To observe the

Rhine between Wesel and Nijmegen, another column of 1,400 men moved seventy miles downstream the Rhine from Köln to Kleve.[63] With Bülow's corps at Münster, seventy-five miles from Nijmegen, Macdonald could only send these 3,400 men to Molitor's aide.

Macdonald had his own problems, yet Allied movements all along the entire right bank of the Rhine kept the French puzzled. On 10 November, Marmont reported the movement of the "Bavarian Army" to the upper Rhine. "It is said that Wrede's corps, which we defeated at Hanau, reinforced by Württembergers and Badenese, is marching to Kehl," responds Berthier on the 12th, "they are making requisitions; these rumors could very well point to their objective to form a division in that area. It is also said that the army of Prince Schwarzenberg has divided into two corps, one at Mainz and the other at Wesel; but all of these rumors are extremely vague."[64] Two days later, Marmont claimed that the tsar had gone to Mannheim. French patrols observed Russian and Prussian troops along the lower and middle Rhine, and apparently the Austrians moved further upriver.[65] Despite this speculation, the summary of the reports from the middle and lower Rhine until mid-November confirmed that the Coalition's principal forces would operate against Holland, while the Austrian army occupied the middle Rhine and the Russian army moved to the upper Rhine to establish a cordon as far as Switzerland. These reports, provided by both civilian and military sources, affirmed the emperor's belief that the Allies planned to mask the middle and upper Rhine to operate against Holland and Belgium. Accordingly, he focused his attention on Holland and the 25th Military District. "It appears that our movement must be made toward Holland," he wrote Marmont on 16 November, "and that the enemy has intentions in this direction."[66]

Napoleon's views regarding Holland and the reorganization of the Guard had an impact on Marmont on the middle Rhine, particularly when the emperor shuffled his front-line corps. With only the XI Infantry and II Cavalry Corps at his disposal, Macdonald could not defend a line that extended from Koblenz to the North Sea. In a letter to Marmont on 18 November, the emperor explained his plans to limit the reorganization of the army to six infantry corps: the I, II, IV, V, VI, and XI. An additional corps, the XIII, would be formed at Antwerp. He hoped to complete this mobilization by January.[67] In addition, he transferred command of the V Corps from Marmont to Macdonald. Macdonald received orders to transfer his headquarters north to Wesel and to slide the XI Infantry and II Cavalry Corps seventy miles down the Rhine from Köln to Kleve on the Dutch frontier; the V Corps would march fifty miles north from Koblenz to take post at Köln. Two days later, Napoleon directed Macdonald to concentrate the XI Infantry and II Cavalry Corps on the lower Rhine between Nijmegen and Wesel. By moving the marshal farther down the Rhine, Napoleon believed Macdonald could cover the Ijssel and slow the progress of the Dutch revolt.[68] To compensate

Marmont, the emperor promised to increase the IV Corps to a strength of 30,000 to 40,000 men; purportedly 11,500 conscripts were already en route to Mainz. "All of the army corps will receive their complements, and the detachments are all en route to join the battalions on the Rhine," he assured Marmont on the 18th. As a further concession, the emperor accepted Marmont's suggestion and authorized the formation of magazines at Saarbrücken and Saarlouis on the Saar River as well as Trier on the Moselle.[69]

Albert's V Corps did not begin the march to Köln until 23 November.[70] To replace this corps in the cordon, Marmont instructed Arrighi to establish the headquarters of his III Cavalry Corps in Bonn and extend his right to Koblenz and his left to Köln in order to link with the II Cavalry Corps.[71] More transfers followed as Napoleon's concern over Holland increased. On the same day that the V Corps departed, Marmont received instructions dated the 20th: the emperor turned over command of Arrighi's III Cavalry Corps to Macdonald and directed the remaining Guard cavalry division to Sarreguemines. According to Berthier, the V and XI Infantry and II and III Cavalry Corps now formed Macdonald's "army." Moreover, the emperor wanted even more combat power shifted toward Macdonald. He pulled back the Young Guard divisions from the Rhine to Kaiserslautern. On 25 November Napoleon directed the 12th and 13th Guard Voltigeur Regiments (1,600 men each) at Metz to depart for Brussels as soon as General Philibert-Jean-Baptiste-François Curial completed their organization, which included removing all native Belgian and Dutch soldiers. At Brussels the two regiments would unite with the 12th and 13th Guard Regiments to form General François Roguet's 3rd Young Guard Tirailleur Division, which Napoleon projected would consist of 6,000 infantry, 200 cavalry, and one battery of eight guns. He also ordered General Charles Lefebvre-Desnouettes' 2nd Guard Cavalry Division to depart immediately for Brussels. Clarke was instructed to ensure that a battery of horse artillery left Metz to join this division at Brussels.[72]

To replace Arrighi's III Cavalry Corps, Napoleon instructed Marmont to slide the entire VI Corps downstream from Mainz so the 8th Division linked with Macdonald's posts at Koblenz and the 20th Division occupied the sector between Koblenz and Mainz. In Mainz itself the IV Corps would anchor Marmont's center, while the single division of the II Corps and General Edouard-Jean-Baptiste Milhaud's V Cavalry Corps held the line from Mainz to Landau, where it would link with Victor's patrols.[73] For Marmont these changes meant further extending his stretched divisions. To replace the III Cavalry Corps, the marshal concentrated Ricard's 8th Division (6,338 bayonets) at Koblenz to hold a thirty-mile zone extending to Bingen. Doumerc's I Cavalry Corps (2,998 sabers) quartered along the Nahe River and provided the pickets for Ricard's posts. "I am leaving Ricard's division at Koblenz," explained Marmont to the emperor on the 27th, "to guard this line and defend the passage of the Rhine in case the enemy makes an attempt at this point. I am leaving the

I Cavalry Corps to support him. If the enemy forces him, he will withdraw through Simmern and Kirchberg; he will also support the I Cavalry Corps, which is defending the Nahe, with some infantry units from this division. If I am forced at Mannheim, the I Cavalry Corps, placed on the Nahe, will move in line with me and cover my communication with Ricard's troops."[74]

In Marmont's center, the IV Corps extended its posts to Bingen after the Young Guard departed in mid-November. To defend Mainz as well as Kastel and the outworks on the right bank, Morand had 16,090 men at his disposal. Because of concern over an Allied attempt to cross the Rhine at Mannheim, Marmont did not move the 20th Division of the VI Corps downstream of Mainz, despite Napoleon's directive. Instead, Lagrange established the headquarters of the 20th Division (6,134 men) at Worms upstream of Mainz to observe the twelve-mile stretch along the Eich–Bobenheim front. Between Bobenheim and Roxheim, the 20th Division linked with the II Corps (6,000 men), which held the line between Frankenthal and Speyer. Milhaud's V Cavalry Corps – 3,973 excellent, well-mounted troopers – billeted behind the 20th Division; the corps provided 300 troopers daily to observe the Rhine between Mainz and Worms.[75] The 10th Hussars quartered between Durkheim, Frankenthal, and Mutterstadt to recuperate after prolonged service along both banks of the river. The 1st and 2nd Honor Guard Regiments contributed an additional 2,500 troopers, who took post at Worms and Speyer, respectively. By 1 December, Marmont had 19,777 infantry, 10,129 cavalry, and sixty-six guns at his disposal. Unless reinforcements arrived quickly, this number could be expected to decline rapidly because of the army's horrible health. By early December the number of sick in the hospitals climbed to 17,058: 7,110 for the II and VI Corps, 775 for the cavalry, and 9,633 for the IV Corps.[76]

On the other hand, Victor had no mobile army corps at his disposal and few line troops; his headquarters remained in a virtual state of panic due to this shortage of manpower. On 11 November, he warned imperial headquarters of an enemy mass of 50,000 men moving toward Mannheim.[77] Napoleon, however, believed the Allied attack would come from the north across the lower Rhine and through the Low Countries. Regardless of the emperor's opinion, the Allied troops besieging Kehl, and the daily skirmishing around the bridgehead that had ensued since 3 November convinced Victor the Allies intended to cross the middle or upper Rhine.[78] Laboring under the belief that he would be attacked at any moment, the marshal looked for ways to prevent the Allies from crossing. For an old grenadier, this meant infantry. Aside from the needs of the fortresses, manpower shortage posed even greater problems for the marshal. With the II Infantry and V Cavalry Corps still positioned between Mainz and Worms, Victor did not possess a single battalion in combat readiness. For the moment, only the 3rd and 4th Honor Guard Regiments patrolled the left bank of the Rhine in his sector of the cordon.[79]

Overall manpower shortages had prompted the French government to decree the levée of the "urban cohorts" or Civic Guard of the 5th Military District as well as seven legions (regiments) of National Guard totaling 16,000 men in the Bas-Rhin, Haut-Rhin, Vosges, Meurthe, Moselle, Haut-Marne, and Haut-Saône Departments on 21 October. On 7 November, the government issued another levée of an additional 9,000 National Guardsmen for the Swiss frontier. On 18 November, Napoleon approved the levée of 21 October and decreed that the Civic Guard be organized in all fortresses along France's ancient frontier. Conversely, he rejected the levée of 7 November as "too considerable" and only approved the organization of the Civic Guard in Besançon, Auxonne, Belfort, and "in the small forts along the Swiss frontier." During the months of October and November, the prefects of the earlier-named departments worked to mobilize the National and Civic Guard in order to reinforce the garrisons of the Alsatian fortresses.[80] Unfortunately, many of the guardsmen lacked uniforms and weapons, and others had to be guarded out of fear they would desert.[81] In many cities, particularly Strasbourg, the Civic Guard consisted mainly of family men who thought only of holding their jobs to ensure the survival of their family. "It would be just as much justice as charity to send them home," comments Victor in a report to Napoleon.[82] On the other hand, Marmont informed the emperor that the National Guard units he received "have in their ranks very few married men, they consist of vigorous men, and these men are in good spirits. I am certain that with a little care we will receive better service from the National Guard than from the Line troops."[83]

On the middle Rhine, Marmont prepared the defense of Mainz for the inevitable Allied siege. Prudence demanded that he store provisions – no easy task because the city served as the army's main hub. The situation slowly improved after the emperor ordered the Guard and several infantry and cavalry depots to depart for the French interior.[84] By 27 November, Marmont reported that "the supplies in Mainz are in good shape.... The mills have reached their limit... there are 2,000 head of cattle."[85] He also started establishing magazines between the Rhine and the Vosges to support the front-line troops. Although he required the Mont-Tonnerre Department to provide him daily with 100 head of cattle, 2,000 kilograms of hay, and 3,000 kilograms of oats, the marshal could not fill the magazines before the Allied invasion began.[86] Napoleon also wanted Marmont to inspect Kaiserslautern and its communications with Saarlouis and Landau. If the Allies besieged Mainz, the IV Corps would form the garrison and Marmont would take a position at Kaiserslautern with his remaining corps to observe the Allied siege. The emperor also urged him to build another redoubt at the mouth of the Lahn River similar to the one seventy miles upstream at the mouth of the Neckar.[87] Marmont complied, starting work on the redoubt at the mouth of the Lahn and completing the fortifications at the mouth of the Neckar on 21 November.

On the Neckar, his engineers built a strong, closed redoubt large enough for 500 to 600 men, armed with four 7-pounders and two howitzers and surrounded by palisades and barricades. French engineers also remained busy fortifying the historic city of Worms.[88]

Schwarzenberg's march to the southern districts of the Grand Duchy of Baden did not go unnoticed by the French marshals. From the moment when the Bohemian Army commenced its maneuver, intelligence poured into Marmont's and Victor's headquarters. Both marshals received an overwhelming number of reports from civil and military officials that ranged from accurate to absurd. Rather than decipher the truth, the marshals forwarded the intelligence en masse to Paris, where the emperor and his staff had to separate fact from fiction. Marmont's reports prior to 15 November appeared to support the emperor's notions regarding the Allied threat to the lower Rhine. However, between 16 and 24 November, Napoleon received persuasive evidence from both marshals regarding the march of considerable Allied forces up the Rhine: in the opposite direction of the Low Countries. On the 18th, he read Marmont's 15 November report that should have altered his view of the situation. The brief contained critical news provided by French prisoners returning from Germany through Frankfurt.[89] "The general rumor in Frankfurt is that the Russians will ascend the Rhine to Basel and the tsar himself will go to this city," relates the marshal, "it appears that the troops are in full march toward this objective. In my opinion, if the enemy wants to cross the Rhine at this time of the year, the city of Basel appears to be of the greatest importance to him; regarding bridging the Rhine, nothing can be substituted since in one month's time the river will have drift ice and it will be impossible to assemble a pontoon bridge."[90]

On the 16th, Marmont noted the concentration of Allied forces on the Neckar as well as their preparations to cross the Rhine.[91] Three days later, his anxiety somewhat subsided; the situation appeared stable because spies claimed the main Allied army still remained billeted several miles east of the Rhine. The Prussians held the right bank between Koblenz and Bingen, followed upstream by the Russians, and then the Austrians. Yet Marmont's statements regarding an enemy corps of 15,000 to 20,000 men that passed Kehl and continued toward the upper Rhine did little to change the emperor's convictions.[92] "Yesterday's confirmed intelligence declares that the emperors of Russia and Austria and the king of Prussia are still in Frankfurt," Marmont added on the 20th, "and that Russians, who I believe are from Wittgenstein's corps, are still facing us in Hochheim. It is certain that the majority of the Austrian army is on the banks of the Main, and that a considerable Prussian corps of infantry, cavalry and artillery is near the mouth of the Lahn."[93] On 24 November, Marmont reiterated his belief that possession of the Basel Bridge appeared to be a principal Allied objective.[94] However minor, the contradictions in these reports probably led Napoleon to believe that confusion reigned in Marmont's headquarters. This made it easy for Napoleon to maintain his convictions regarding Allied intentions on the lower Rhine. "The enemy probably will not attempt to cross the Rhine," the emperor assured Marmont on 20 November, "therefore allow your troops some rest and do not torment yourself; if the enemy crosses the Rhine, he will cross the lower Rhine."[95]

In Victor's sector, the reports of Allied movements toward Switzerland were no less convincing. On 14 November, the commandant of the Bas-Rhin Department, General Jean-Adam Schramm, informed Victor that Bavarian troops from a corps of 20,000 men, which formed part of the Austro–Bavarian army, had occupied Plittersdorf on the right bank of the Rhine opposite Seltz. According to Schramm's intelligence, this corps had billeted in and around Rastatt on the 13th before continuing its march that morning on the road to Offenburg, where the surrounding hills offered a dominating position to observe Kehl or launch an operation against the French bridgehead. Another corps of similar size was expected to arrive that evening in Rastatt; bridging equipment would supposedly reach Rastatt around the 17th or 18th. Shramm expressed his belief that the Allies intended to cross the Rhine at Ft. Vauban. From Landau, Colonel Jean-François Verdun warned that enemy movements appeared to have Ft. Vauban as the immediate objective. Victor forwarded this information to the emperor, who received it on the afternoon of the 16th.[96]

Victor continued to receive numerous reports of Allied movements and intentions throughout the month of November. Since the 17th, spies had revealed preparations in and around Mannheim to accommodate a large troop mass as well as the headquarters of the Russian tsar. Construction of pontoon bridges on the Neckar River, which joined the Rhine at Mannheim, made it apparent that an Allied crossing would be attempted near that city. Other sources claimed the tsar would continue upstream from Mannheim to Karlsruhle and that a corps of approximately 40,000 men would assemble at Rastatt and attempt to cross the Rhine between Landau and Strasbourg. Moreover, it was no secret that the tsar of Russia, kaiser of Austria, king of Prussia, their ministers, and Schwarzenberg remained in Frankfurt; neither the Russo–Prussian Guard and Reserve nor the Austrian Reserve had moved. Newspapers from Basel appeared to answer why the Allied high command remained in Frankfurt. According to the media, Schwarzenberg's army would cross the Rhine at Oppenheim and attack Mainz along both banks of the Rhine while Blücher's army moved to Koblenz. The Austro–Bavarian army supported by 20,000 Cossacks would make a diversion in Upper Alsace.

By the end of November, enemy columns accompanied by siege and bridging equipment were on the main highway leading to the Swiss frontier. Bavarian infantry and cavalry supported by an Austrian Hussar regiment drove the French advance posts from the village of Sundheim to the edge of Kehl on 30 November. The Allies established a perimeter around Kehl within musket range of the French defenders. Under constant skirmishing, work on the siege trenches ensued.

The events at Kehl and the intelligence that poured into his headquarters allowed Victor to reach the correct conclusion. No letter from Paris could convince him that the main Coalition armies would invade the Low Countries.[97] Despite the marshal's requests for manpower, Napoleon insisted on employing the II Infantry and V Cavalry Corps on the middle Rhine. He reiterated his belief that Victor should be content with the National Guard to defend Alsace. "Unless it is absolutely necessary," he wrote Marmont, "the division of the II Corps must remain under your command. The duke of Bellune would like to have it for himself, but he has no reason to fear for Strasbourg. The enemy would be crazy if he attacked from this direction. It is more natural to think the enemy will turn at Köln, Wesel, and Koblenz." He also assured Marmont that the single division of the II Corps – the 4th – and Lagrange's 20th Division of the VI Corps appeared sufficient to hold Mannheim, thirty-seven miles upstream the Rhine from Mainz.[98]

Napoleon's insistence that the Allies would not cross the middle Rhine did not correspond with the intelligence Marmont received. He informed Napoleon that all reports "from the past twenty-four hours show an increase in enemy forces on the banks of the Neckar." In addition to a rapid buildup of troops, the Allies appeared to be constructing batteries on the right bank of the Rhine near Mannheim. Rumors among the inhabitants claimed the enemy intended to cross the Rhine in that area; Schwarzenberg himself left Frankfurt for Mannheim on the 24th. Marmont communicated his doubt regarding Allied intentions to cross the Rhine simultaneously at Köln and Mannheim. Instead, he concluded they would soon cross at the latter point, because the onset of winter would cause concern over drift ice. Downstream of Mannheim, the ice became more prevalent because of the influx of the Moselle, Lahn, Main, and Neckar. In addition, the nature of the terrain downstream of Mainz offered favorable points of passage only at Bacharach and Koblenz. On the other hand, upstream, between Mainz and Landau, the Allies could find "a multitude of favorable places to cross the Rhine." Marmont informed the emperor that he planned to leave Ricard's division, which now numbered almost 5,000 men, in Koblenz and Bacharach to guard that stretch of the Rhine. Lagrange's division would hold the stretch between Worms and Mainz. This arrangement served a twofold purpose. First, Marmont would be able to defend the Rhine. Second, if the Allies managed to cross the river, Marmont could fall back to Alzey, Bad Dürkheim, and Kirchheimbolanden to defend the roads to Kaiserslautern.[99]

Two days later on the 25th Marmont panicked. Common sense told him it was too late for a large army to cross the Rhine at Mannheim. Moreover, he knew that in ten days it would be impossible to use pontoon bridges on the Rhine. Nevertheless, he became obsessed with the idea that the Allies were preparing to cross the river. He informed Napoleon that the Austrians had moved all their artillery to the outskirts of Mannheim and that all workers in the region had been summoned for bridge building. According to reports, the Austro–Bavarian corps, which would be joined by a Russian corps, reached the Swiss border along the upper Rhine. The Austrian army, with Wittgenstein's Russian corps, had taken position on both banks of the Neckar, but mainly on the left; and the majority of the Silesian Army stood between Frankfurt and Mainz. Spies claimed that the Allied monarchs remained in Frankfurt, but Schwarzenberg moved his headquarters to Mannheim. Blücher was in Höchst, and the other Russian and Prussian generals in Frankfurt. A few days after Bülow had crossed the Dutch frontier, Marmont informed Napoleon that only the Army of North Germany would operate on the lower Rhine.

Based on this intelligence, Marmont decided to transfer his headquarters from Mainz to Worms "in order to observe the enemy's movements from close range, to defend the crossing as much as possible, and to assure the return of the troops in good shape." If the Allies did not attempt a passage, he planned to return to Mainz in seven or eight days. He left Ricard's division at Koblenz and Doumerc's I Cavalry Corps at the Nahe with orders to support each other. Should the enemy force a passage near Koblenz, Ricard would fall back to Simmern and Kirchberg. Conversely, should the enemy cross the Rhine at Mannheim, Marmont planned to retreat and maintain communication with Ricard through Doumerc. The marshal moved his headquarters upstream to Worms on the 28th to better observe the right bank of the Rhine, but the enemy did not appear.[100] His posts and the French spies probably misinterpreted Blücher's reconnaissance missions to find favorable crossing points for the Silesian Army's forthcoming passage of the Rhine.[101] Marmont left Worms on 2 December, inspected some of the units in the region, and returned to Mainz on the 7th.

Downstream of Marmont's sector, rumors reached Macdonald on 19 November that Allied forces had taken Zwolle and Kampen. Worse news arrived on the following day: Reports confirmed the imminence of an Allied invasion. A large body of Coalition forces reached Emmerich on the Rhine, less than twenty miles from Nijmegen and only seven miles northeast of Kleve. Farther north, enemy units had penetrated Dutch territory and reached both Doesburg and Zwolle on the Ijssel. Macdonald planned to reach Kleve by the 24th at the latest, but the process of replacing the posts of the XI Infantry and II Cavalry Corps with those of the V Infantry and III Cavalry Corps took much longer than he anticipated.[102] After several delays, the marshal established his headquarters in Kleve on the 28th and completed the realignment of his corps on 1 December. By this time, his army extended along the northern frontier in three groups. On the left, Charpentier's 31st Division, the II Cavalry Corps, and Amey's flying column – a total of 10,000 men – held the lines of the Ijssel, lower Rhine, Waal, and Meuse Rivers. Macdonald's center consisted of the 6,000 men of Brayer's 35th Division at Wesel. Around 7,500 men of the V Infantry and III Cavalry Corps held the right wing by guarding the frontier from Wesel to Andernach. As of 15 November, Macdonald's four corps totaled forty-nine battalions, fifty squadrons, and forty-six guns or 28,273 men. Despite Napoleon's promise of 600,000 conscripts, the marshal received neither man, horse, nor canon.[103] Macdonald could do little to change his situation, which became increasingly worse: Bülow's Prussian III Corps breached the Ijssel line and turned toward the lower Rhine.

Around the same time French intelligence confirmed Schwarzenberg's march up the Rhine toward the Swiss frontier. Upon learning that Clarke's aide-de-camp, Jacques-Henry Baltazar, was traveling from Worms to Paris, Victor requested that the colonel meet with him in Strasbourg. During their meeting, Baltazar informed Victor that according to a reliable spy, Schwarzenberg had left Mannheim on 1 December en route for Karlsruhe. From there the Austrian commander and the troops accompanying him would proceed to Freiburg-im-Breisgau. Meanwhile, on the other side of the Black Forest, large enemy columns were moving toward eastern Switzerland. Victor then met with Louis-Pierre-Édouard Bignon, the former French minister in Warsaw, who was returning to France with diplomatic immunity. Traveling between Rastatt and Kehl, Bignon observed seemingly endless columns of Austrian troops, artillery, and bridging equipment en route to Freiburg-im-Breisgau to join the Austro–Bavarian corps, whose forward units already reached Huningue.

The information provided by Baltazar and Bignon provided Victor with compelling evidence to present Napoleon. In a 5 December letter to the emperor, Victor claimed that strong Austrian columns were en route to Freiburg-im-Breisgau with bridging equipment to make an attempt to invade Upper Alsace by crossing the Rhine between Neuf-Brisach and Huningue. He also believed the Allies intended to violate Swiss territory to occupy Franche-Comté. Possession of Basel's stone bridge would be indispensable to the Allies because drift ice on the Rhine during the winter rendered pontoons unreliable and risky. The marshal again warned Napoleon that the Swiss would open their borders to the Allies and that he had no troops to spare to defend Switzerland. "They know the weakness of our resources," declares Victor, "and they do not expect to encounter any difficulties other than those presented by the river."[104] On the next day, the head of Napoleon's intelligence service, Élisabeth-Louis-François Lelorgne d'Ideville, forwarded to the emperor a summary of the reports from the Rhine frontier. According to Ideville, Austrian and Russian troops with contingents from Baden and Württemberg, preceded by thousands of Cossacks, continued to march toward Switzerland along the highway that ran parallel to the Black Forest. With all this information at his disposal, it is difficult to determine why the master of war ignored Allied preparations to invade France through Upper Alsace and Franche-Comté.[105]

On 9 December, Marmont reported that the general movement of the Allied army continued in the direction of the upper Rhine; Austrian troops no longer stood on the banks of the Neckar. He added that after leaving its positions before Kastel, General Fabian Gotlib von der Osten-Sacken's Russian corps had taken the road to Mannheim. General Louis Alexandre Arnault de Langeron, who Marmont assumed was near Koblenz eight days earlier, now stood before Kastel. "It seems that Prussian troops are also near Mannheim, but I do not know exactly where."[106] Unlike Victor, whose reports sounded the impending doom, Marmont apparently accepted the emperor's assumption that the Allies probably would not attempt to cross the Rhine.[107] After his summary report of the 14th, in which he noted the departure of a siege train destined for the Austrian army at Basel, the marshal showed little concern over the security of his own front. In fact, he no longer mentioned the forces before him and evidently did not know the Silesian Army had received considerable reinforcements. Marmont simply relaxed after his fears of an Allied invasion at Mannheim subsided. As the evidence of an Allied concentration on the upper Rhine mounted, he believed the danger to his sector had passed and forgot about the Silesian Army. This allowed Blücher to exploit completely the element of surprise on New Year's Day.[108]

On the other hand, Victor's three-page brief to Berthier on 9 December again emphasized the marshal's vexation over Switzerland. He commended the determination of a unit of Swiss border guards for allegedly repulsing a Cossack incursion, but feared the Swiss government lacked the will to resist the Allies. Victor complained that when the Swiss should have an army of 100,000 men to defend their neutrality "with energy," the government remained content with having 40,000 men under arms.[109] Also on this day Victor received a letter from the Prefect Auguste-Joseph de la Vieuville of the Haut-Rhin Department that contained several details. According to Vieuville, the Allies had received considerable reinforcements on the right bank including numerous pieces of artillery. Support personnel could be seen assembling bridging equipment at Muhlheim, opposite Chalampé, described by Vieuville as one of the easiest points of passage. "He has severely prohibited all communication between the inhabitants on the right bank with those on the left," wrote the prefect, "which makes one suppose that he is thinking of an attempt to cross. He has started establishing batteries all along the line.... The enemy troops are composed almost exclusively of Austrian infantry and Russian cavalry. This hostile demonstration spreads fear all along the left bank."[110]

On the 10th, Victor warned Berthier that the enemy appeared poised to immediately cross the Rhine between Neuf-Brisach and Huningue.[111] Two days later travelers arriving from Lörrach informed the marshal that the enemy army would cross the Rhine near Huningue, probably at Basel because the Allies "refuse to recognize Swiss neutrality." This news confirmed his suspicions. Further statements alerted him to the direction the Allied army intended to take after crossing the Rhine: the Allies planned to penetrate France via the gorge at Porrentruy. Victor informed the emperor that he had nothing to prevent the Allies from easily executing this plan.[112]

The marshal did not tire in his efforts to draw Napoleon's attention to the upper Rhine. Yet is report to Berthier on 13 December sounded a note of despair: "The news I have received today signals the concentration of a large enemy army on the upper Rhine and its plan to immediately cross this river, confirms all that I have reported up until now." The stories that reached Strasbourg on this day placed the Allied sovereigns at Rastatt awaiting the result of the passage of the Rhine, which would be "effected in a few days between Huningue and Basel." According to Victor, the 9 December newspapers from Karlsruhe indicated that a 60,000-man Russian Reserve Army started marching through Germany toward the Rhine five days earlier.[113] Although dated 21 December, both Schwarzenberg's "Declaration to the French" and the Allied monarchs' "Declaration" already had been printed and widely circulated in Alsace thanks to smugglers. "By 15 December," notes French historian Lefebvre de Béhaine, "no one in Alsace doubted the imminence of the invasion."[114]

In the days just prior to the invasion, Allied commanders attempted to induce the commandants of Huningue, Neuf-Brisach, and its outwork on the right bank of the Rhine, Ft. Mortier, to surrender.[115] The great French military architect Sébastien le Prestre de Vauban had built Neuf-Brisach (thirty miles in either direction to Strasbourg in the north and Huningue in the south) to serve as an ammunition depot between the Huningue and Sélestat. Situated in open country less than two miles from the left bank of the Rhine, Neuf-Brisach could not be reached by enemy artillery on the opposite bank.[116] Failing to bribe the French commandants with gold, commissions in the Coalition armies, and even Austrian decorations, a detachment of 500 to 600 men from Gyulay's III Corps crossed the Rhine on the night of 17–18 December to attempt a coup de main at Neuf-Brisach. Although a dense fog allowed the Austrians to surprise the French forward posts, they wasting time pillaging the suburb of Geiswasser, which allowed the alarm to spread to the fortress. Neuf-Brisach's commander, Colonel Jean-Baptiste Klinger, led an infantry detachment with two guns toward Geiswasser. After having lost the element of surprise, the Austrians did not wait to be attacked and recrossed the Rhine with their loot of linen, calves, and goats.[117] Klinger informed Victor that the Allies appeared to be making preparations opposite of Geiswasser to cross the Rhine.

On the same night of 17–18 December, the Austrians also attempted to surprise the battery on the isle of Cordononniers that faced Huningue by crossing the Rhine in barges. Another Vauban fortress, Huningue stood on the left bank of the Rhine one mile downstream of Basel. At thirty miles from Neuf-Brisach and thirty-seven miles from Belfort, the fortress served as the gateway and key to Upper Alsace.[118] The detachment guarding the isle belonged to the 675-man National Guard Legion of the lower Rhine. Described by a contemporary as "superb and animated by the best spirit," the guardsmen charged the Austrians before they could clamber out of their boats. After sustaining several casualties, the Austrians paddled away as fast as they could.[119] Despite the setbacks, the Allies continued pushing detachments across the Rhine between Neuf-Brisach and Huningue on the 19th. "It appears," speculates Victor in a report to Berthier, "that the only objective of these incursions is to reconnoiter the various passages of the river since the troops that conduct them prefer to return to the opposite bank.[120]

Events along the upper Rhine finally forced the emperor to direct his attention to the defense of Alsace. He realized Victor required more than National Guard units to defend his sector. Bonaparte transferred command of the II Corps, which only consisted of the 4th Division, from Marmont to Victor on 7 December.[121] So acute became the need to defend Alsace that the emperor asked Berthier to reiterate his instructions to Marmont regarding the II Corps on the 12th.[122] On 10 December, Marmont reported that the 4th Division had surrendered its posts to the 20th Division to concentrate at Speyer on the following day.[123] The twelve battalions of the 4th Division along with the artillery and baggage of the II Corps reached Strasbourg on the 15th. Victor unfortunately discovered that most of the conscripts had dysentery, and soon 600 men reported to Strasbourg's overcrowded hospital.[124]

Napoleon also issued orders to better conceal the movement of Victor's troops from the numerous Allied spies operating on the left bank.[125] Victor and Marmont received very precise instructions to prohibit any passage from one bank to the other. According to Lefebvre de Béhaine, this order applied especially to Kastel, "where the advance posts allowed suspicious people to cross under the pretense of selling poultry or for other motives all too unlikely."[126] "One must not allow anything to cross for one reason or the other," asserts Berthier, "this is very important; vigilance is the greatest necessity."[127] A decree on the following day closed the French frontier from Huningue to Willemstad in Holland.

Although Gneisenau complained of postponing the invasion for almost two months while the Bohemian crept toward the Swiss border, the Silesian Army profited from Napoleon's growing awareness of the threat to Alsace as well as Bülow's invasion of Holland. Less than one week after he returned the II Corps to Victor, the emperor likewise transferred command of Milhaud's V Cavalry Corps from Marmont to the duke of Bellune. Indicative of the extent to which Marmont's reports ignored Blücher, the emperor no longer considered the middle Rhine to be threatened. As a result, Marmont lost his best unit. The marshal received Berthier's letter on 15 December; on the following day Milhaud's three divisions departed for Strasbourg, where they arrived between the 20th and 22nd.[128]

Events in the Low Countries ultimately robbed Marmont of his reserve – a point that probably aggravated the marshal because his intelligence indicated that only Bülow's Prussian III Corps had reached the lower Rhine.[129] On 20 December, Marmont learned the emperor had ordered Mortier to transfer the 1st Old Guard Division, the Old Guard Cavalry Division, and the Reserve Artillery from Trier to Namur; the 2nd Old Guard Division and the 1st and 2nd Young Guard Divisions would also move deeper into the French interior.[130] "Execute this order with as much haste as possible," urges the emperor in his letter to Mortier. "Your presence in Belgium has become necessary. Brussels is surrounded by Russian Cossacks."[131] With the Guard's departure, no troops remained near the middle Rhine to support Marmont's forces in case of an invasion. By extending French forces to the upper and lower Rhine, Napoleon left Marmont with only the IV and VI Infantry and I Cavalry Corps to face Blücher's vastly superior army (Map 1).

Victor waited impatiently for Milhaud's V Cavalry Corps to arrive. According to circumstances, he planned to deploy all or part of the corps on the left bank to stop Allied raids. "Up until this moment, I have only weak guards to oppose them," he explains, "but the presence of the V Cavalry Corps, which I will established on the Rhine, undoubtedly will force the enemy to remain on his bank."[132] On 21 December, Victor's reports and incessant admonitions regarding the threat to Alsace produced more results in Paris; Napoleon finally conceded the real possibility that the Allies would attempt to cross the upper Rhine. Unaware that Schwarzenberg's army was in the midst of crossing the river that very day, Napoleon issued a long series of directives entitled "Orders," which can be viewed as preliminary measures for the *eventual* defense of Upper Alsace and Franche-Comté. He wanted Marmont to shift the VI Corps and I Cavalry Corps south to Landau, leaving the IV Corps to guard Mainz and his line of communications.[133] General Emmanuel Grouchy received orders to report to Strasbourg and assume command of the cavalry in Victor's sector under the title of "Commander of the Cavalry of the Army."[134] Berthier's task was to organize a reserve brigade of fifteen battalions at Geneva, which Napoleon considered the only important point along the Swiss frontier. He wanted the city guarded by Line troops and a permanent French garrison of 2,000 to 3,000 veterans.[135] The emperor assigned the defense of Huningue to his own aide-de-camp, General Pierre-François-Marie-Auguste Dejean. Instructing Dejean to depart that same day, Bonaparte directed him to place the fortress in a state of defense and to send agents into Switzerland to procure information on the enemy's movements. In addition, Napoleon reiterated his orders to Clarke to arm and provision Belfort and Besançon, as well as to summon the Civic Guard of the latter.[136] As early as 14 November he had instructed Clarke to arm Belfort and the

Swiss châteaux of Lausanne, Blâmont, and Ft. Joux, without expressing any urgency. "No, I am not wary of the Swiss," he wrote Clarke at that time, "but due to the actual situation of the empire, it must be armed on all sides."[137] Clarke himself attached little value to these isolated posts and took no measures for the formation and provisioning of garrisons. He left this task to the commanding generals of the 5th, 6th, and 7th Military Districts, who lacked troops, material, and money to achieve effective results.[138]

The majority of Napoleon's "Orders" of 21 December concerned the ongoing reorganization of the I, II, IV, V, VI, and XI Corps. Regarding Victor, the emperor insisted that he organize the II Corps into three divisions of fourteen battalions each by 1 January and to echelon these divisions between Strasbourg and Huningue. He redesignated Dufour's division as the 1st and named Gens. Jean-Louis Dubreton and Philibert-Guillaume Duhesme commanders of the 2nd and 3rd Divisions, respectively. Because of Dubreton's serious health problems, General Jean-Baptiste Jamin commanded in his place. Other than describing the formation of the II Corps as "indispensable," Napoleon offered nothing further that can be interpreted as a response to Victor's daily warnings of a massive Allied build-up along the upper Rhine.[139]

However, two days later and before he received Victor's report of the Allied movement across the Rhine, the emperor focused his attention on the possibility of military operations in Franche-Comté and Alsace. Writing to Clarke, he described the Swiss frontier as having Huningue on its left, Besançon in the center, and Geneva on its right. The Jura Mountains, which marched along the length of this frontier, offered only four debouches from Switzerland into France: the first from Huningue through Belfort, the second through Blamont to Besançon, the third through Jougne, and the fourth through Geneva. He designated Belfort as the point d'appui on the left, Besançon in the center, and Geneva on the right. Accordingly, the passes through the Juras had to be covered by detachments from the garrisons of these three posts. He wanted Huningue, Lausanne, Ft. Joux, and Geneva prepared to provide the first line of defense; Belfort, Blamont, Salins, and Ft. de l'Écluse would form the second line; Besançon and Pierre-Châtel (south of Grenoble) the third (see Map 8 in Chapter 9). Auxonne would become an important point "*if* the war takes place on this frontier," which he still questioned. Formerly fortified, Napoleon believed Auxonne could be easily returned to a state of defense to have a strong post on the Saône River. He requested that Clarke attach to his report on the Swiss frontier a map of the Vosges Mountains and the passes through this portion of the eastern frontier.

General Louis-François-Félix Musnier received orders to proceed immediately to the Swiss frontier accompanied by engineer and artillery officers. The emperor authorized him to inspect and provision the frontier fortresses as far as Geneva, organize the National Guard to form the garrisons, and detach posts to defend the points of passage into France. Upon his arrival in

Geneva, Musnier would take command of the reserve brigade to accelerate the formation of its battalions. After completing his inspection, Musnier was to establish his headquarters in Belfort, from where he would exercise imperial authority to pressure the prefects, mayors, and commissioners of the region to provision the fortresses and provide the funds to arm and place them in a state of defense.[140]

As for his cordon, Napoleon asked Berthier to formulate a plan to unite the II and VI Corps at Strasbourg, and the V and XI Corps on the Meuse River, which indicated he had decided to move Marmont further south and leave the defense of Mainz solely to the IV Corps. He also expressed to Berthier his intention to form a division of 3,000 to 4,000 men with two horse batteries from the four Honor Guard regiments. This division would be united with the V Cavalry Corps – also slated to receive two horse batteries – and placed under Grouchy's orders to form a mass of 7,000 to 8,000 troopers and twenty-four pieces of artillery. "Inform the duke of Bellune that it is of the greatest importance to expedite, by all possible means, the formation of the II Corps, which I desire to be formed into three divisions by 1 January," provides the extent of the emperor's concerns for the 5th Military District on 23 December.[141] These measures, particularly regarding Huningue, Lausanne, and Belfort, suggest Napoleon considered Upper Alsace as merely threatened. By fixing 1 January as the deadline for the completion of the II Corps, the emperor obviously felt he had time before the Allies acted – despite Victor's reports. This attitude spread to the War Ministry, where on 22 December Clarke issued orders to the regimental depots to send to Strasbourg *at least* one of the battalions they were assigned to provide the II Corps. Consequently, when the Allied invasion commenced, the divisions of the II Corps lacked their full complements of infantry. In addition, Clarke did not authorize the transport of dressings and ambulances from Paris to Metz until 30 December; on this day he finally asked the Minister of the Department of War Administration, Pierre-Antoine-Noël-Brunno Daru, to organize the medical services for the mobile corps.[142]

Although the threat to Alsace increased with each day, the emperor remained convinced that the Allies would not violate Swiss neutrality in order to cross the French frontier between Basel and Geneva. On the 21st – the day the Army of Bohemia started moving into Switzerland – he apparently accepted the idea that the Allies might *attempt* such an operation. Despite conceding his error by acknowledging the possibility, he still considered Upper Alsace, Franche-Comté, and the Juras to be a secondary theater, unsuited for the strategic and tactical operations of large armies. Moreover, he counted on Swiss resistance to provide time for him to organize his defenses.[143] This suggests that Napoleon planned to use the Swiss, natural obstacles, fortresses, and the National Guard to defend the upper Rhine and Franche-Comté. The remains of the Grande Armée of 1813 augmented by the new recruits that trickled through the regimental depots to the mobile corps would guard the middle Rhine. For the lower Rhine, Napoleon allocated his elite troops – the Imperial Guard. Political motivations abounded this decision to commit the finest soldiers of the French army to the Low Countries. Control of the mouth of the Scheldt allowed France to regulate the trade flowing to and from the greatest port on the continent. By annexing Holland and Belgium, the French theoretically added the colonial empires of these states to France's global possessions. The conquest of the Low Countries handed the French control of the Dutch and Belgian fleets – so necessary for France to challenge the Royal Navy. Finally, Holland and Belgium provided Napoleon with staging areas from which he could launch an invasion of Great Britain.

Such considerations, as weighty as they appear, no longer had any bearing on the state of affairs by the end of 1813. British naval supremacy, the failure of Napoleon's Continental System, and the destruction of imperial armies in 1812 and 1813 voided the grand strategic advantages of controlling the Low Countries. At most, the Low Countries represented the first conquests of the Revolution, and Napoleon thus felt the solemn obligation to conserve them for France. Besides, his megalomania and lack of diplomatic tact would not permit him to surrender any territory unless it was ripped from his empire. At most Napoleon sought to hold the Low Countries for as long possible to use them as bargaining chips in future negotiations. He also may have hoped for a rift to occur among the Allies as they debated the structure of postwar Europe and the details of France's boundaries. Militarily, the emperor possibly viewed the Low Countries as the soft underbelly of France and envisioned the same wheeling movements that the Germans executed in the First and Second World Wars. Above all, he feared that by separating the Dutch and Belgians from the empire, the Allies would trigger a chain reaction that would unravel his hold over the French. Consequently, he moved his best troops to Belgium, regardless of the reports that poured in from Alsace.

Few excuses can be contrived to absolve the French emperor's misjudgment of Allied intentions. In this case, his marshals are not to blame. Both Marmont and Victor provided enough information to orient Napoleon toward the true direction of the Allied invasion. They correctly assessed the value of Basel and warned the Allies would violate Swiss neutrality to gain its bridge. Both waged a letter campaign in an effort to demonstrate the danger to Alsace and Franche-Comté. By mid-November, exceptional French intelligence provided Bonaparte with the most essential information regarding the impending Allied invasion, but he did little to prepare the defense of the Rhine between Strasbourg and Geneva. South of Belfort, no French garrisons blocked the roads into France.

By the end of 1813, the effects of the demoralizing defeat at Leipzig, the endless retreat, and the spread of typhus had decimated the French army that now attempted to guard France's eastern and northern frontiers. Of the corps that made up the Grande Armée after the Armistice of Pläswitz, the I and XVI surrendered to the Allies at Dresden; the X capitulated at Danzig, the XIII was besieged in Hamburg; the III, VII, and VIII were dissolved, while the IX was providing cadres for a reserve army in Lyon.[144] Along the Rhine frontier, the marshals had to make do with field units that amounted to approximately 56,000 men. Approximately 36,000 additional troops held the fortresses along the Rhine and facing the Swiss frontier. Two divisions of Old Guard, six divisions of Young Guard, and three divisions of Guard Cavalry numbering 28,000 men were spread amongst Paris, Brussels, Liège, Luxembourg, and Thionville. An additional 20,000 men occupied the fortresses of Holland and Belgium, where French field units amounted to 14,000 men. Therefore, the strength of combat-ready French forces numbered approximately 154,000 men.[145]

The majority of this manpower consisted of exhausted veterans, green recruits, and National Guardsmen. Their musters finally increased in mid-December as reinforcements in the form of the young conscripts, nicknamed "Marie Louises," started to arrive. "One could recognize them during the campaign," recounts Marmont, "first by their ignorance of the basic elements of military service, and also by their clothes, because having only had time to receive a greatcoat, a police helmet, shoes, a cartridge pouch, and a musket, they always lacked uniforms. One could also recognize them by their calm and sublime courage, which seemed to be inherent."[146] Their number, however, did not suffice to fill the holes in the ranks nor replace the daily losses to typhus. Still, the Ministries of War and War Administration did their best to meet the army's needs. Most of the troops benefited from adequate lodging and the regular distribution of food, although some had to resort to ruthless pillaging to avoid starvation. The weapons were generally in good condition, but the quality of uniforms varied greatly from unit to unit.[147]

On the upper Rhine, Victor guarded the eastern passes of the Vosges mountains. For this task he spread the 5,615 men and fourteen guns of his II Corps, 2,000 Honor Guards, and 4,265 troopers and six guns of Milhaud's V Cavalry Corps across a front of seventy miles between Strasbourg and Basel. His skeletal divisions contained between five and six weak battalions instead of the normal twelve or fourteen because the 2nd and 4th Battalions of his regiments had yet to arrive from Nancy. Victor's line units would be supported by the 25,600 National Guards summoned from the departments under his authority, of which 10,000 arrived by 1 January to occupy the frontier fortresses. Some units, like the National Guard of the Haut-Rhin, were completely incapable of military service. For example, 1,200 men of the 2,000-man garrison of Sélestat had never fired a musket.[148]

Marmont, on the middle Rhine, had the difficult task of guarding the great river, securing the Moselle Valley and the debouches leading to it, as well as maintaining communication with Victor. He spread the 10,000 men and twenty-three guns of his VI Corps, the 3,000 troopers of Doumerc's

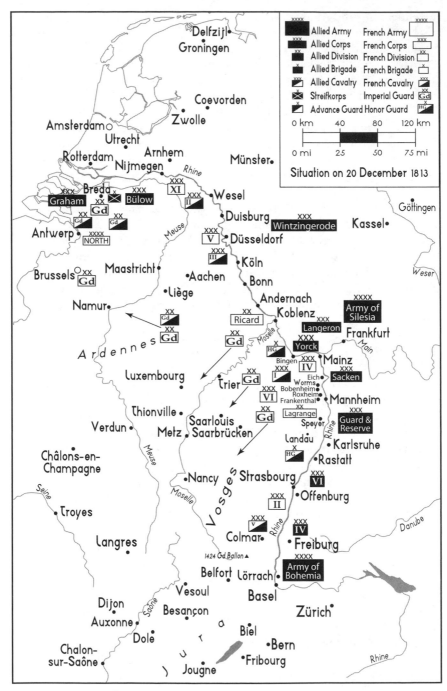

Map 1. Situation on 20 December 1813.

I Cavalry Corps, the 23rd Light Cavalry Brigade, and the 1,000 troopers of the 1st Honor Guard Regiment across a 100-mile front between Landau and Andernach. Morand's IV Corps which, despite being devastated by typhus, reached a strength of 16,460 men, held Mainz and guarded the Rhine to Bingen along with the 2nd Honor Guard Regiment. From Koblenz, Ricard's 1st Division anchored the line upstream to Bingen. South of Mainz, Lagrange's 3rd Division extended its posts to Worms.[149]

On the lower Rhine from Koblenz to Zwolle, an overextended Macdonald attempted to secure his sector. Sébastiani with the 3,000-man V Corps and the 1,533 troopers of Arrighi's III Cavalry Corps established posts along the 100-mile stretch between Köln and Wesel. Further north, Macdonald's XI Corps (11,742 men and eighteen guns) held Kleve, Nijmegen, Wesel, and Ft. St. Andries; the 2,768 troopers of the II Cavalry Corps also took positions at Nijmegen and Kleve. Both corps observed the Rhine and the Waal from Wesel to Ft. St. Andries.

Behind this thin cordon, the 1st and 2nd Old Guard Divisions and the Guard Cavalry reorganized at Trier, and the 1st and 2nd Young Divisions formed at Saarlouis and Thionville, respectively. Altogether, the five Guard divisions provided a reserve of 15,000 men. Moreover, the new "Army of the North" consisted of 1,400 troops of the 17th Military District and a few hundred men of the 31st Military District. Ambert, commandant of the 31st Military District, possessed no Line troops, except for the insufficient garrisons of Coevorden and Delfzijl. He managed to send 250 customs agents from the coast to the Ijssel fort of Deventer and had the departmental company of the Bouches-de-l'Yssel – incomplete and poorly disposed with neither the means nor the desire to make a serious resistance – guard the Ijssel crossings at Hattem and Kampen.[150] At Antwerp French authorities labored to organize the new I Corps from Imperial Guard units arriving from Brussels.[151]

The Allied invasion caught Napoleon woefully unprepared. "If the whole winter could have been used to form an army," claims Marmont, "in the spring we would have presented some strong forces to the enemy, at least numerically. But the events unfolded faster, and nothing was either prepared or organized when we were forced to enter into combat mode."[152] The small French army had to defend a 400-mile line from Switzerland to the North Sea. Behind this thin shield Napoleon desperately fought time and the despondent lethargy of his bureaucratic machine to create another army, but the conscripts and reserves assembling at Metz and on the Marne could not be combat-ready before the end of January. Soldiered by the youthful Marie Louises, men who had seen too many winters, invalids, and pensioners, all barely equipped and led by the tired marshalate, this last army of the French Empire had to face the seasoned veterans of the battle-hardened Allied armies. If the "great nation" had any strength left, it would need it during the upcoming invasion of France.

6

The Right Bank

All the roads leading from the Rhine to Paris traversed lofty mountains and the many rivers that irrigate France's eastern provinces. In the region of Belfort lies the Grande Ballon of Alsace, a broad, high summit that spawns three mountain chains. The first, the mainly granite Vosges, extends north between the Rhine and the Moselle. Its last heights branch in a northeastern direction past Kaiserslautern, where they take the name Mont-Tonnerre, to Bacharach on the Rhine to form a steep ridge called the Hunsrück. A second mountain chain, the Jura, marches south-southwest from the Grande Ballon to form a chain of sandstone summits and plateaus of considerable height. West of the Vosges, the third range – the mountains of Charolasi – run northwest from Alsace before turning south-southwest in the region of Mirecourt. At Montigny-le-Roi, this relatively flat chain climbs to significant heights until reaching the Plateau of Langres.

These ranges extend three arms that form hill chains: the first and steepest provides the watershed for the Seine and Loire Rivers by stretching northwest in the region of Arnay-le-Duc before knifing south at Saulieu and finally twisting for one last time to the northwest near Château-Chinon. The second hill chain, the Argonne, steps northward at Langres, follows the Meuse, and gradually gains elevation to form a significant ridge by the time it reaches Lorraine, where it culminates in the Argonne Forest. The third, the Ardennes, separates from the main mountain chain near the sources of the Madon, one of the tributaries of the Moselle, and forms a watershed between this river and the Meuse. Like the Plateau of Langres, the elevation of the Argonne and the Ardennes hill chains is not excessive, but both are protected by thick belts of forest that hindered the movement of troops.

Five highways ran from the Rhine to Paris (see Map 2). From Koblenz to Paris, 260 miles of road provided the first, which proceeded through Reims; the fortress of Luxembourg and the Meuse formed the main obstacles along

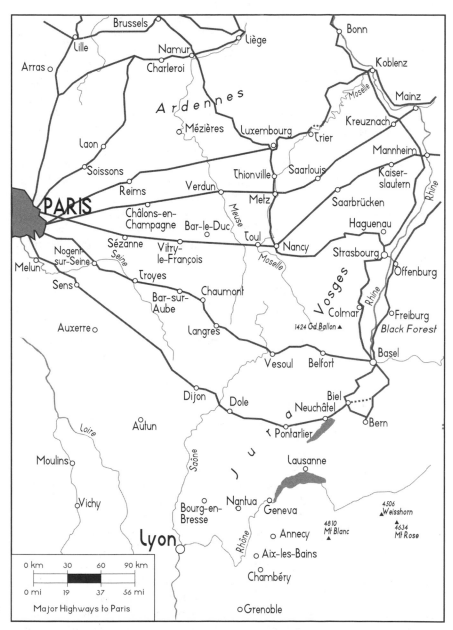

Map 2. Major Highways to Paris.

this route. The second, 300 miles long, ran from Mainz – the strongest of the fortresses and occupied by the most French troops – passed the large fortress of Metz on the Moselle, the small fortress of Verdun on the Meuse, and the fortified city of Châlons-en-Champagne on the Marne to Meaux. A third highway extended 295 miles from Mannheim through Saarbrücken, Nancy, Vitry-le-François on the Marne, and Sézanne. The fourth, which served as Schwarzenberg's main line of operations, ran 285 miles from Basel through the fortress of Belfort to Vesoul, Langres, Chaumont, Bar-sur-Aube, and Troyes to the bridges over the Seine at Nogent. After the Allies occupied Switzerland, they could advance 240 miles to Paris along the fifth route, which led from Neuchâtel through Pontarlier, Dole, Dijon, Joigny, Sens, and Melun. Powerful fortresses guarded the numerous junctions, intersections, and bridges that crossed these main highways. The fortresses of Saarlouis, Thionville, Luxembourg, Longwy, and Montmedey flanked the approaches to the French interior from Mainz. On the Mannheim–Paris highway, the Allies would be threatened by Landau, Strasbourg, Phalsbourg, Bitche, Lichtenberg, Lutzelbourg, and Ft. Vauban. Between the Mannheim–Paris and Basel–Paris routes were the fortresses of Neuf-Brisach and Huningue; south of the Basel–Paris road stood Besançon. The three principal lines that Blücher and Schwarzenberg eventually utilized to breech the fortress belts and reach the French interior ran from Mainz to Meaux; Mannheim to Sézanne; and the road leading from Basel between the Vosges and Jura through Vesoul and Langres to Troyes.[1]

Allied losses in the battle of Leipzig were considerable: 54,000 officers and men, including 15,000 Austrians, 16,000 Prussians, and 22,500 Russians. Combat losses, strategic consumption, and disease further eroded Allied strength during the pursuit to the Rhine. Coalition forces benefited from the pause in hostilities much the same way as they did during the Armistice of Pläswitz earlier that year. The Allies utilized the time not only to improve the uniforms and equipment of the troops but also to close the gaping holes in their ranks. All corps received significant reinforcements in the form of replacements, convalescents, and rearward units; newly formed contingents from the German states also joined the front-line armies as Allied diplomats worked to harness the resources of the former Rheinbund.[2] The Coalition imposed on the Rheinbund princes a contribution of 44,250,000 francs to be paid in twenty-four monthly installments. These funds would be used for the maintenance of the Coalition armies and were divided so that Prussia, Austria, and Russia each received five-seventeenths, and Sweden and Hanover received one-seventeenth each. In addition, the princes had to mobilize eight German army corps consisting of 145,060 men and a Landwehr of equal number for a grand total of 290,120 men – a strength that would never be reached. Line troops had to report for duty by 31 December; the Landwehr's deadline was set for 12 January. The ratification of the alliance treaties with each former

Rheinbund state would not occur until the stipulated troop contingent was combat-ready.[3]

Throughout late 1813 and early 1814, mobilizations occurred throughout the Third Germany with various degrees of enthusiasm and success. In Bavaria the crown prince and Wrede directed a thorough mobilization that fielded a corps of almost 40,000 men by the middle of December – no small task considering the Bavarian contingent of the Grande Armées of 1812 and 1813 were virtually wiped out in Russia and Germany. "The Bavarian Army," notes historian John Gill, "hastily cobbled together for this campaign, was an odd mixture of two-thirds line troops and one-third newly organized National Guard battalions known as the Mobile Legion." Wrede was intimately involved with the raising and training of his army throughout the summer. The general officers who commanded his divisions and brigades were relatively young yet experienced. Most of the Line officers likewise were veterans, but new recruits from Bavaria's third conscription in 1813 filled the ranks. On the other hand, a large percentage of the soldiers who served in the Mobile Legion battalions benefited from prior military service, "but the officers were frequently brand new or not entirely fit for active campaign duty," maintains Gill. Although defeated at Hanau in his first confrontation with the French, Wrede's familiarity with his army provided him a fairly accurate grasp of its capabilities and limitations.[4]

The Württembergers agreed to provide a corps of 12,250 Line infantry, 12,250 militia, 2,900 cavalry, and twenty-four guns. Similar to the Bavarians, the Württembergers faced a difficult task. Decimated in Russia and crippled by the fall campaign in Germany, the Württembergers essentially had to resurrect their army for a third time in less than one year. As early as the middle of October King Frederick formed a brigade, which departed Heilbronn on the 26th to support Wrede. Upon reaching the bridge over the Main River at Aschaffenburg three days later, the Württemberger brigadier received orders to hold the crossing against the French. Just two weeks had passed since Frederick wrote his last letter to Napoleon, and now his troops were preparing to fight his former liege.[5] On 6 November 1813, circumstances forced King Frederick to appeal to his people to support yet another war. Since 1793, Württemberger troops fought in each of the six coalition wars that engulfed Europe. Remarkably, the infantry regiments reached their full musters by the end of November as a result of aggressive recruiting. Kraehe's examination of the political intentions of King Frederick of Württemberg sheds light on the state's aggressive approach to meeting the new alliance obligations: "King Frederick was so determined to find favor with the tsar that he denounced Austria's hesitant military policy, and alone among the former wards of Napoleon zealously maintained a strenuous war effort. He fielded a contingent of double his assigned quota for Alexander, just as he had done in 1809 for Napoleon."[6] According to alliance agreements, the Württemberger corps would be part of

Schwarzenberg's army and commanded by its own generals. As Napoleon's allies during the German campaign, the Württembergers had served under French commanders. General Friedrich von Franquemont, the commander of the Württemberger division attached to the French IV Corps during the operations against Berlin in the fall campaign, had been highly critical of the French and in particular of having to serve under a French corps commander.[7]

A speedy mobilization of the Grand Duchy of Baden produced numerous Line regiments as well as a Landwehr of 10,000 men. The Grand Duchies of Nassau and Hesse raised volunteer jäger detachments on the Prussian model; the Elector of Hesse pushed his mobilization with such speed that by January his corps departed for France; in March an additional 12,000 men were combat-ready. The Hanoverians ordered the mobilization of thirty Landwehr battalions and several volunteer jäger cavalry regiments. Also the Saxons fielded a militia of 20,000 men and Line regiments of equal number.

However, the efforts of the former Rheinbund states did not satisfy all Allied observers. Stein appointed one of Blücher's staff officers, Prussian Lieutenant-Colonel Johann Jacob Otto August Rühle von Lilienstern, as his war minister to supervise the raising of German troops.[8] On 8 February 1814, Rühle von Lilienstern submitted this overly harsh and exaggerated report:

> The arming of the country proceeds slowly. It is acquiesced willingly by the people, but regarded by the governments with such indifference, not to say repugnance, that we may see the old spirit, which for centuries has forbidden our divided country to be great, grow worse rather than better as a result of what has happened. To begin, Württemberg has published an edict for a Landsturm of 100,000 men, which is a real mockery of the treaties and contemptuous of the Allies. As for Darmstadt, its edicts have the appearance of being intended to ridicule the conscription and all that concerns it through inadequacy in design and pitiable feebleness in execution. These petty governments will not do for the preservation of Germany what they never dared to refuse their master Napoleon. Most miserable of all seem to be the Hessians of the Electorate, dragging after the army without uniforms or coats – mere fodder for the hospitals.[9]

According to the agreements made in Frankfurt, Wrede's Bavarians and General Johann von Frimont's Austrian corps formed the 43,400-man German I Corps, which joined Schwarzenberg's army prior to crossing the Rhine and was designated the V Corps of the Bohemian Army. Troops from Hanover, Brunswick, Oldenburg, the Hanseatic cities, and Mecklenburg-Schwerin formed the 32,900 men of the German II Corps. Assigned to the Army of North Germany, only the 5,000 men and sixteen guns of the Brunswicker contingent arrived in time to participate in the war. The German III Corps, likewise designated for the Army of North Germany, consisted of troops from Saxony, Weimar, and Gotha; 14,000 men under Duke Carl

August of Weimar reached the Netherlands in early February, and thirteen battalions remained in Saxony as garrisons. Blücher received command of the German IV Corps – 12,000 Hessians commanded by Prince Ludwig of Hesse-Homburg – which assumed the investment of the Moselle fortresses at the end of January. Berg, Waldeck, Lippe, Nassau, Koburg, Meiningen, Hildburghausen, and Mecklenburg-Strelitz contributed 9,230 men to the German V Corps. Also assigned to the Silesian Army, the V Corps relieved the Russian troops besieging Mainz in February. Prince Philipp of Hesse-Homburg commanded the German VI Corps. Designated for Schwarzenberg's army, it contained 9,250 men from Würzburg, Darmstadt, Isenburg, Frankfurt, and Reuß. Crown Prince Frederick William of Württemberg's troops formed the German VII Corps. Baden, Hohenzollern, and Liechtenstein provided 10,330 men for the German VIII Corps, which Schwarzenberg assigned to the sieges of Kehl, Strasbourg, Landau, and Pfalzburg in January. Finally, one battalion of the Badenese guard joined the eight battalions of the Prussian Guard.[10]

In early December, Schwarzenberg and his staff completed the order of battle for the Army of Bohemia or "Hauptarmee." At the beginning of the fall campaign, the Austrian army was organized by divisions. When the Bohemian Army advanced into Saxony at the expiration of the armistice, Schwarzenberg divided the Austrian contingent into an advance guard, one flank corps, and a right and left wing. Because of command and control problems, the Austrians reinstated the corps system on 5 September 1813.[11] On the eve of the battle of Leipzig, the Austrian contingents of the Bohemian Army numbered 92,000 men.[12] In comparative terms, the Austrian corps suffered fewer casualties at Leipzig than the Russian and Prussian corps. Losses for Schwarzenberg's Austrian units between 14 and 19 October totaled 14,973 men.[13]

As a result of the reorganization and reinforcement of the units during the last two months of 1813, Bubna's 1st Light Division contained two brigades and three batteries of horse artillery for a total of 6,388 men and twenty-four guns. Liechtenstein's 2nd Light Division likewise included two brigades but only two horse batteries: 4,852 men and sixteen guns. The three divisions of Colloredo's I Corps totaled 15,708 men with sixty-four cannon. In place of the captured Merveldt, General Alois von Liechtenstein assumed command of the two divisions of the II Corps: 12,708 men likewise supported by sixty-four pieces of artillery. Gyulay's III Corps – three divisions – numbered 14,732 men and fifty-six guns. Because Klenau's IV Corps had assumed the siege of Dresden after the battle of Leipzig, Crown Prince Frederick William of Württemberg's German VII Corps (14,000 men and twenty-four guns) became the new IV Corps in Schwarzenberg's order of battle. Wrede's V Corps consisted of Frimont's two Austrian divisions (9,196 men with forty-eight guns) and 34,200 Bavarians with 124 guns dispersed among three divisions.

Wittgenstein's Russian army corps served as Schwarzenberg's VI Corps. On 9 August 1813 this corps had mustered 34,926 men and ninety-two guns;

by 29 October these numbers dropped to 10,735 men and fifty-eight guns. After suffering further attrition of manpower and material during the pursuit to the Rhine, reinforcements increased Wittgenstein's command to only 21,066 men and fifty-six guns on the eve of the invasion of France. The VI Corps contained two "infantry corps," the I and II, consisting of two divisions each, one cavalry division, and one Cossack division.

Prince Friedrich's Austrian Reserve Corps of two grenadier divisions and two cuirassier divisions provided an additional 18,500 men and 100 cannon for the Bohemian Army. An army itself, the Russo–Prussian Guard and Reserve, was formed by one Russian cavalry corps comprising one light and three cuirassier divisions supported by two horse batteries (8,409 men and sixteen guns), together with the Russian V Infantry Corps, which contained the 1st and 2nd Guard Divisions supported by the Guard Artillery Brigade (12,950 men and thirty-six guns). The Prussian Guard Cavalry and Guard Infantry Brigades offered an additional 7,127 men and sixteen cannons; this unit was later augmented by two Badenese units: the 706-man Guard Battalion and the 112 men who serviced the seven guns of the Guard Foot Battery. The Russian Reserve of two grenadier divisions yielded an additional 11,063 men and ninety pieces of artillery. In the history of the Napoleonic wars, no single enemy force had ever reached such massive proportions: Schwarzenberg's army totaled approximately 200,000 men and 690 guns at the outset of the invasion.[14]

Of the three major powers, the Russians found their army most disbursed among the forces of the Coalition. All three Allied field armies – the Bohemian, Silesian, and North German – contained Russian troops totaling 144,000 men and 524 guns. In addition, a 60,000-man reserve army under General Dmitri Ivanovich Lobanov-Rostovsky continued to assemble in Poland. General Mikhail Bogdanovich Barclay de Tolly technically held the title of Commander in Chief of the Russian Army, but in practice his authority extended only to the Russo–Prussian Guard and Reserve. His influence over the other Russian corps amounted to coordinating supply and overseeing the maintenance of equipment. This proved no simple task owing to the great distance between the Russians and their home base.

Among the tsar's entourage, the main figures responsible for army operations included General Aleksey Andreyevich Arakcheev, Volkonsky, and General Karl Fedorovich Toll. As head of the Imperial Field Chancellory, Arakcheev's principal task was to maintain the regiments and parks at full capacity. Constantly at Alexander's side as Chief of the General Staff of the Russian Army, Volkonsky issued the tsar's orders to both Russian and foreign generals. Volkonsky communicated with Toll, who was permanently attached to Schwarzenberg's headquarters. Toll provided regular reports to Volkonsky, who in turn submitted them to the tsar. Toll's other duties included forwarding Schwarzenberg's orders to Russian Streifkorps and, in times of great urgency, to Wittgenstein. "While the tsar confided his troops to the care of foreign commanders," notes Alexander's secretary, Mikhailovsky-Danilevsky, "he freely exercised a general influence over both military and diplomatic affairs and thus was in continual verbal and written communication with the leading commanders as well as with the ministers of the courts."[15] Much to his chagrin, Schwarzenberg, the nominal commander in chief, would agree with this appraisal.

Blücher also utilized the remainder of 1813 to refit and refurbish his men, horses, and equipment. Replacements from Silesia and Brandenburg arrived along with convalescents to rebuild Yorck's corps. Unfortunately for the Prussians, they inadvertently moved into quarters recently occupied by the French and infected with typhus. Dysentery also spread; some men became ill simply because their immune systems had gradually deteriorated from months of excessive strain; the sudden inactivity caused their ability to resist disease to collapse altogether. Between 5,000 to 6,000 men of the Prussian I Corps fell ill on the Rhine and had to be left behind when the invasion commenced. Despite these losses, around 9,932 combatants reinforced the I Corps and provided Yorck with four full brigades – the 1st, 2nd, 7th, and 8th – which corresponded to the corps's original order of battle. By 1 January 1814, the I Corps numbered 22,108 men and eighty-two guns.[16]

The two Russian corps of the Silesian Army also received considerable reinforcements in the month of December. Like the Prussians, General Fabian Vilgelmovich Sacken and General Louis Alexandre Arnault de Langeron used the respite to improve the material status of their units. Despite being at war since 1812 and on the verge of their fourth campaign, the Russian troops wore better uniforms than the Prussians. The Russian transport service also proved superior to that of the Prussian army. Although far from their own depots, supplies – especially ammunition – arrived in a prompt and orderly manner, notwithstanding the tremendous difficulties posed by time and space. "Such is the excellent organization of the Russian army and its perfect composition," noted Langeron in his journal, "that after the most horrible fatigues a short time sufficed to place it in a better state." Thanks in part to requisitions that Blücher allowed Langeron to make, the Russian soldiers received "the most necessary effects." "My brave soldiers," continues Langeron, "who during this short interval enjoyed a little repose after seventeen months of continuous marches in the most active and most bloody war...were ready to begin a new campaign." Although more than 5,000 men of Yorck's corps fell ill on the Rhine, the Russians sustained far fewer losses. According to Langeron: "The Russians soldier's aptitude for war, his physical strength, and the care of his officers protected my troops from the deadly diseases that followed the trail of the enemy to such an extent that many of the villages in Germany were infected. Almost one-quarter of the inhabitants of the towns and villages succumbed. At the beginning of the campaign of 1814 I had 800 sick and weak convalescents out of 43,000 men and I did not lose more than 100 men in the hospitals."[17]

Sacken has been described as: "bold, resolute, and energetic, he invariably carried out his orders to the letter, and was one of the hardest fighting generals in the Allied army. He was absolutely loyal to Blücher, to whom he was greatly attached, and throughout the campaign proved himself a thoroughly capable and reliable corps commander."[18] After suffering considerable losses during the German campaign, Sacken's corps reached the Rhine with a mere 10,000 men under arms. This prompted the Russians to transfer command of the VI Infantry Corps from Langeron to Sacken.[19] Within two months, reinforcements almost tripled the muster. Sacken's army corps consisted of two infantry corps, the VI and XI, one cavalry corps, and one Cossack corps for a total of 26,561 men and ninety-four guns.[20] The VI Infantry Corps, commanded by General Aleksey Grigorievich Sherbatov I, contained the 7th and 18th Divisions. Each division consisted of four Line and two jäger regiments. Furthermore, only one battalion of approximately 500 men comprised each regiment, making Russian after-action reports somewhat misleading. General Ivan Andreyevich Lieven III's XI Infantry Corps likewise consisted of two infantry divisions: the 10th and 27th. The XI Infantry Corps had the same order of battle as VI Corps with the exception of the Bialystock Regiment, which contained two battalions.

Langeron, on the other hand, was purportedly "a complete nonentity, who consistently mismanaged operations in which he took part, and was habitually inclined to thwart his leader's plans."[21] According to Langeron's journal, his musters totaled 30,000 men under arms on 8 November.[22] Langeron claims that the vast majority of his 18,000 casualties were killed or wounded, and that only "a small number" of sick had to be left behind in hospitals. His army corps contained three infantry corps, the VIII, IX, and X, one cavalry corps, one Ukrainian Cossack division, one Cossack corps and eventually totaled 43,000 men and 136 guns.[23] The 11th and 17th Infantry Divisions formed General Guillaume-Guignard St. Priest's VIII Infantry Corps; both divisions likewise contained four Line and two jäger regiments, but the regiments contained two battalions each for a total of 11,900 men. General Nikolay Dmitrevich Olsufiev III's IX Infantry Corps consisted of the 9th and 15th Infantry Divisions: 5,697 men. The 8th and 22nd Infantry Divisions formed General Petr Mikhailovich Kaptsevich's X Infantry Corps: sixteen battalions with 7,807 men. Langeron's regular cavalry consisted of 4,334 troopers grouped into four divisions.[24] "What especially earned Fieldmarshal Blücher's praise," boasts Langeron, "was when he saw the perfect state of my artillery at the end of December after the horses had suffered so terribly during the forced marches on frightful roads."[25]

As the month of January approached, the musters of the units along the Rhine steadily filled with the names of reinforcements. Allied forces immediately available for the invasion included the Bohemian Army's 201,900 men and 690 guns. The smaller Silesian Army contained 82,000 men and 312 guns. Of the Army of North Germany, the 30,000 men and ninety-six guns of Bülow's Prussian III Corps as well as a detachment of 4,500 men Russians from Wintzingerode's corps already crossed the Dutch frontier. A British auxiliary force of 9,000 men and twenty-four guns also landed in Holland. Thus, the Allies possessed approximately 327,000 men and 1,106 guns to begin the invasion of France.

Immediate reinforcements in the form of the 14,000 Württembergers of the German VII Corps joined Schwarzenberg's army, while the German VI Corps assembled at Frankfurt and departed in January for southern France with a strength of 13,000 men and sixteen guns. For the Silesian Army, the 16,000 men and seventy-two guns of Kleist's II Corps began its march from Erfurt to France on 6 January after being placed under Blücher's orders. From the Army of North Germany, Wintzingerode's corps of 9,500 infantry, 6,600 cavalry and sixty guns crossed the lower Rhine in early January. With these troops, Allied forces in France and the Netherlands reached 375,500 men.

The total strength of second-line Allied forces that reached the theater of war in February and March totaled 132,000 men with 198 guns. This number includes the 15,500 men of the German VIII Corps, the German IV Corps's 20,000 men and thirty-two guns, and the German V Corps's 24,500 men and twenty-four guns. The German III Corps reached the Netherlands in February with 8,700 men and twenty-four guns; one brigade from Thüringia-Anhalt arrived later with 12,300 men. On 12 and 25 March, two additional Saxon columns arrived in the Netherlands with a total of 12,000 men. The 31,000 men and sixty-two guns of Bernadotte's Swedish corps crossed the Dutch frontier in March. Wallmoden's corps, also from the Army of North Germany, reached the Netherlands at the end of March with a strength of 5,200 men and twenty-four guns. Finally, the German II Corps (5,000 men and sixteen guns) reached France before the end of the war.

An additional 267,500 men tied down French forces in secondary theaters. In Italy the Allies fielded the 91,500-man Austro–Italian army. These numbers increased when Murat defected to the Allies with the 24,000 men of the Neapolitan army. Wellington's Anglo–Portuguese army of 68,000 men was crossing the Pyrenees supported by a 60,000-man Spanish Army under the prince of Angola that likewise operated in the Pyrenees backed by a reserve of 48,000 troops. Behind the troops of the second line, the Allies had a reserve of around 300,000 men, which included the 100,000 Landwehr of the Rheinbund states; 20,000 Austrian reserves under Duke Ferdinand of Württemberg; 35,000 men of Bennigsen's Polish army; 50,000 men of the Prussian IV Corps; 20,000 men of the Prussian Reserve Corps; 15,000 men of the Russo–Prussian siege corps at Glogau; and 60,000 men of Lobanov-Rostovsky's Russian Reserve army.

Approximately 1,099,000 Allied soldiers were under arms by the beginning of January 1814. "Obviously the value of these troops varied considerably," comments Major Rudolf Friederich, an instructor at Berlin's Kriegsakademie and author of the German General Staff's official account of the fall campaign, "and the majority of them had absolutely no influence on the campaign of 1814 [in France], but these numbers provide a clear picture of the crushing superiority that the Allies had at their disposal in 1814 to face Napoleon's small forces."[26] For the moment, however, the fate of Europe hinged on the 327,000 men who invaded France between 23 November 1813 and 3 January 1814 as well as the ability of the Allies to maintain a semblance of unity in their operations. "We were indeed superior to the enemy in numbers," recalls Mikhailovsky-Danilevsky, "and to a certain extent in equipment; but with us there was not, and, from the very nature of a heterogeneous alliance, could not be, either unity of purpose or of will."[27]

At all costs the Allies had to prevent a popular insurrection from erupting in the French countryside. "We must carefully avoid driving a people to desperate resolves by insults to its honor," warned Bubna.[28] To prevent Napoleon from exploiting the loyalty of the French through a general call for insurrection, the Allies had to maintain strict military discipline and inflict as little hardship as possible on the French people. However, some Allied leaders made it clear that a "hearts and minds" campaign would not be a priority. On 9 January, just one week after crossing the Rhine, Gneisenau reminded Stein that "national revenge must be taken and we must repay the visits of the French to our cities with visits to theirs. If this does not happen, revenge and triumph are incomplete."[29] Such thoughts clearly indicate that some Prussians thirsted for revenge, yet the Allies officially frowned on a policy of rape, pillage, and plunder. The Coalition made careful preparations to ensure a smooth and uninterrupted flow of provisions. London continued to provide the Russians and Prussians with generous subsidies. Austria likewise became the grateful recipient of British loans.[30] The seven-week halt in operations meant that convoys delivered much needed supplies and equipment to the corps encamped on the Rhine. When the Coalition armies crossed the Rhine, they were neither ill fed nor ill clad. Moreover, their combat experience and growing confidence made them qualitatively superior to the Allied forces that had opened the fall campaign of 1813.

The Allies needed to launch a rapid, demoralizing invasion that would culminate with the capture of Paris to diminish the chances of a popular uprising. Blücher and Gneisenau remained convinced that the time had come either to destroy Napoleon or march straight to Paris. Gneisenau bitterly lamented to Clausewitz that had his plan been followed, "we would now be in Paris, judging from what we have learned in the last two months regarding the enemy's weakness and confusion."[31] Gneisenau insisted the Allies could end the war by taking Paris or achieving a decisive victory over Napoleon:

"The composition of the enemy's troops is poor. Our enemy's entire system is worm-ridden."[32] Intelligence indicated the emperor was losing popular support. In particular, Gneisenau pointed to the rupture between Napoleon and the Legislative Corps as an example of the emperor's growing domestic crisis: "According to our reports, confusion and discontent rule the French interior."[33]

Unlike the confidence that reigned in Blücher's headquarters, tension mounted in Schwarzenberg's immediately prior to the invasion. The commander in chief placed unbearable pressure on himself. While still in Frankfurt, he lamented to his wife that "the moment is of the greatest importance, the whole burden of the decision, and the responsibility linked with it, now rests on me again. The path upon which I tread is so narrow, that one false step will hurl me into an unfathomable abyss." Schwarzenberg remained skeptical of the likelihood of negotiating with Napoleon: "among us it is said that the Duke of Vicence [Caulaincourt] has made fairly acceptable proposals, which have been sent to England; the Prince Regent has moderate principles, therefore a peace is possible – but indeed one must not be lulled to sleep. After all, as long as the man [Napoleon] lives, peace is not to be considered." The change in the French Foreign Ministry did little to impress Schwarzenberg, as he explained to his wife: "I view it as a blatant deception, in which he [Napoleon] wants to prove to the people his wish for peace; I do not believe he actually thinks of peace after his great military misfortunes."[34]

Conversely, Schwarzenberg's opposite in the Silesian Army, the old warhorse Blücher, chomped at the bit for an opportunity to cross the Rhine. Blücher complained about his involuntary idleness. "Only God knows what they must be thinking by placing my army here, opposite Mainz," he wrote to a relative. "The role of a blockade or observation corps is hardly befitting for me, let alone my army. But all-corrupting envy has come into play. In the meantime, I will work to get free: cross the Rhine or die, that is my fate." Blücher declined an invitation from the people of Frankfurt to move his headquarters to the former imperial city. "The Frankfurters overwhelm me with friendliness ... [but] I still remain here on the Rhine. Had one listened to my suggestion, I would be in Brussels today. But Frankfurt was too seductive; all wanted to rest there and time was wasted." Wilson's journal entry for 11 November 1813 agrees with Blücher's views: "The days pass as if it were the 'piping time of peace.' Courts, galas, parades, banquets, etc., have succeeded the iron age."[35] "The Tsar of Russia is an excellent man," continues Blücher, "he will always judge for the best. But in Frankfurt is now an entire army of monarchs and princes, and this assembly makes a mess of everything, and will no longer conduct the war with energy, and I fear that we will dream away everything."[36]

Gneisenau also felt overwhelmed by his fruitless activities and complained bitterly in letter upon letter. "In Frankfurt intrigue is in full swing," he wrote

to General Wilhelm von Dörnberg. "Here abounds diplomats and industrious loafers, who eavesdrop and snoop and spread distrust. One conceals his
opinion from another and each seeks to win small advantages, while everything is supposed to gravitate toward a great purpose. Diplomacy now fetters
military operations."[37] "These people have learned how to gain a victory,"
Gneisenau comments to a friend, "without having any understanding of how
to use it."[38] "During the current standstill intriguing and peace-loving generals
have assembled in headquarters," he wails to Münster. "Treasonous influences
are found here. The natural jealousies of the diplomats find sustenance in this
environment; disagreements ensue and in the end tear one after the other
the threads that hold this coalition together. Thus, Frankfurt is a dangerous
sojourn and I will not cease to worry until this place is far behind us."[39]

   Whereas the staff chiefs of the two principal allied armies, Radetzky
and Gneisenau, shared some similarities in strategic thinking, Blücher and
Schwarzenberg represented polar opposites. Born in Mecklenburg in 1742,
the future Prussian field marshal enlisted in the Swedish Morner Cavalry
Regiment at age fourteen. He participated in three campaigns against Prussia
during the Seven Years' War before being captured in 1760. Blücher decided to
join the Prussian army and fought the remainder of the war as a cornet in the
8th Hussar Regiment. Like many of Frederick the Great's officers, Blücher
found peacetime garrison life extremely boring. Fond of heavy drinking and
gambling – hobbies befitting a hussar – the captain retired in 1773 on the verge
of being cashiered by Frederick for excessive behavior. Married that same year,
Blücher enjoyed prosperity managing his estate. Upon Frederick's death in
1786, new Prussian king Frederick William II accepted Blücher's request for
reinstatement. Seven years later, Major Blücher served in the War of the First
Coalition and gained a reputation as a fearless hussar. In mid-June 1794, he
was promoted to major general after his victory over the French at Landau.
The king's decision to sign a separate peace with France in 1795 and adopt an
official policy of neutrality vexed the "hussar general."

   For the next eleven years, Blücher's disdain for the French grew into a
burning hatred. Frustrated over his government's decision to sit out the Second and Third Coalition Wars, Blücher rejoiced when Frederick William III
issued the order for the army to mobilize in 1806. Failing to become Europe's
mediator, Prussia finally joined Russia and Great Britain in the War of the
Fourth Coalition against France. Blücher's dream of vanquishing Napoleon
and his Grande Armée turned into a nightmare on 14 October 1806. On that
day the main Prussian army (60,000 men) failed to defeat Davout's isolated
III Corps (27,000 men) at Auerstädt. With a massive superiority in cavalry,
Blücher easily drove the French cavalry from the field. He then led countless
attacks against Davout's solid infantry squares: all ended in failure and considerable Prussian losses. By nightfall the Prussians had lost 13,000 men and
115 guns; the king had seen enough and ordered a retreat. On the same day,
Napoleon defeated the other half of the Prussian army fifteen miles away at

Jena and unleashed one of the most effective pursuits in the annals of military history. Blücher commanded the Prussian rearguard as it retreated all the way to the Baltic. On 25 October, French forces occupied Berlin. Five days later on 30 October, the remnant of the Prussian army capitulated at Prenzlau. The surrender of another 10,000 Prussians under Blücher's command at Lübeck on 5 November made the collapse complete. The campaign ended with the fall of Magdeburg and its garrison of 22,000 Prussians on the next day. In a little over one month, the Prussian army lost 165,000 men killed, wounded, missing, and captured. A meager 20,000 men continued the struggle in East Prussia through the spring of 1807 until Tsar Alexander ended the war by opening negotiations with Napoleon.

The ensuing treaty of Tilsit reduced Prussia to a second-rate power and placed the state at Napoleon's mercy. Frederick William maintained a small army; the troops in Brandenburg-Pomerania under Blücher formed one of Prussia's three corps. Blücher, the newly appointed governor of Pomerania, had been ill for some time and in June 1808 his condition deteriorated. Relieving him of his command did not appear advisable, and replacing him was not easy. Friedrich Wilhelm assigned Bülow to be Blücher's adjutant and to assistant him in all military capacities and functions. Bülow witnessed the full effects of the older man's agony. Blücher suffered from mental and physical deterioration. An alcohol-induced schizophrenia caused wild and eccentric behavior. At times Blücher startled the household by shouting and smashing furniture as he engaged an invisible foe. He frequently begged his servants to smite his head with a hammer, claiming that it was made of stone. According to Hermann von Boyen: "He actually believed that he was pregnant with an elephant ... he imagined that his servants, bribed by France, had heated the floor of his room to burn his feet. Therefore, when sitting, he kept his legs raised above the floor or he would walk on the tips of his toes." Boyen attributed Blücher's condition to grief over Prussia's deplorable situation following the defeat as well as to Blücher's own vices.

Napoleon's 24 November 1808 demand for the dismissal of Stein, who at that time served as Prussian minister of the interior, and his subsequent proscription on 16 December also depressed Blücher. The old hussar battled insanity as well as venereal disease, alcoholism, and an ulcerated urethra. Bülow felt little compassion for his commander and viewed him as an insane hypochondriac whose excessive lifestyle caused his problems. When hostilities began between France and Austria on 9 April 1809 Blücher's health recovered with the prospect of war. Frederick William shattered his spirits by refusing to enter the conflict against France: Blücher's health plummeted. He recovered by the end of the summer and assumed full command of the corps for the next three years. In 1812, the king relieved Blücher as a result of French pressure during Napoleon's preparations for the invasion of Russia. The emperor's Russian debacle and Prussia's defection from the French alliance in March 1813 paved the way for Blücher to take command of the

Figure 10. Field Marshal Gebhard Leberecht von Blücher (1742–1819). Commander of the Army of Silesia.

Silesian corps in the spring campaign of 1813. After serving under Wittgenstein at Lützen and Bautzen, Blücher assumed command of the newly formed Army of Silesia during the Armistice of Pläswitz. Coupled with his aggressive chief of staff, Gneisenau, the two formed the best military marriage of commander and staff officer until Hindenburg and Ludendorff 100 years later. The two officers functioned as one: Gneisenau provided the intellect and Blücher the charisma. Although he drove his men forward with a fury, Blücher remained one of the most popular figures among the Allied troops of all nations.[40]

   Blücher is usually not counted among the upper echelon of Allied strategists. This omission is due more to his tactical shortcomings than his ignorance of operations and strategy, however. Although driven by hatred rather than intellect, Blücher understood the essence of Napoleonic warfare: the battle of annihilation. Rather than concern themselves with politics and postwar posturing, he and Gneisenau pursued the objective of winning the war on the battlefield in the same decisive manner as Napoleon. Unfortunately for them, their shoddy battlefield tactics sometimes undermined their ability to achieve a decisive victory. Moreover, in the case of Schwarzenberg in February 1814 and Wellington in June 1815, the Prussians did not receive the support they expected from these Allied commanders. At battles such as Dresden and Leipzig, Schwarzenberg demonstrated that he understood the importance of the decisive engagement in Napoleonic warfare, yet the primacy of Austrian politics prevented him from conducting operations in 1814 that would produce a battle of annihilation.

The essential difference in the spirit of Blücher and Schwarzenberg can be seen in the correspondence they exchanged. Blücher's terminology is generally confident, exact, and energetic. Indicative of his nickname, "Marshal Forwards," there is no hesitation and rarely any doubt. On the other hand, Schwarzenberg's terminology is fraught with caution and apprehension. His methodical and prudent nature caused him to squander countless opportunities during the 1814 campaign. The danger the Allies faced "was increased by the entirely opposite dispositions of the Allied commanders," judges British historian Maycock, "for while Blücher was certain to push forward with the utmost vigor, regardless of every obstacle, it was equally certain that Schwarzenberg would seize every conceivable opportunity to suspend his advance and, even if he encountered no opposition, would move forward with the utmost deliberation."[41] French historian Lefebvre de Béhaine states: "Formal and fossilized in the routine of the 18th century, the Austrians considered combat as a means to be employed in the last extreme, and sought to obtain geographic objectives through maneuver; the Prussians, more realistic, searched for battle to destroy the organized forces of the enemy."[42]

Blücher's junior by almost thirty years, Prince Karl zu Schwarzenberg's service in the Austrian cavalry began in 1788 at age seventeen. A native of Vienna descended from Franconian nobility, Schwarzenberg quickly ascended the ranks of the army after distinguishing himself in the 1787–91 Austro–Turkish War. Promoted to major in 1792, Schwarzenberg fought in the Austrian Netherlands during the War of the First Coalition. Two years later, the young officer received acclaim for leading a successful cavalry charge at Cateau-Cambrésis. Like Bonaparte, Schwarzenberg attained the rank of general at an uncommonly young age. His promotion to brigadier-general came in 1796 at age twenty-five as a result of his conduct at the combats of Amberg and Würzburg. Promoted to general of division four years later, Schwarzenberg saw action during the Austrian defeat at Hohenlinden on 3 December 1800 during the War of the Second Coalition.

At the outbreak of the War of the Third Coalition, Schwarzenberg's division formed part of the Austrian army that invaded Bavaria. In a brilliant envelopment that showcased the lightning speed of Napoleon's new system of warfare, the Grande Armée surprised, surrounded, and crushed the majority of this Austrian army around the Bavarian city of Ulm in October 1805. Schwarzenberg managed to extricate his division before the trap closed and then rallied stragglers during the retreat to Austria. After Austria's humbling defeat and the ensuing dissolution of the Holy Roman Empire in 1806, Schwarzenberg became active in diplomacy. For three years between 1806 and 1809, he represented his government as ambassador to Russia. He returned to Austria in time to participate in the battle of Wagram (5–6 July 1809) during the War of the Fifth Coalition. Following another defeat at the hands of Napoleon, Schwarzenberg took post in Paris as ambassador to France. He succeeded Metternich who, incidentally, became Austrian Foreign Minister in 1809 at age thirty-six. Schwarzenberg played a key role in negotiating the 1810 marriage between Napoleon and Kaiser Francis's daughter, Marie Louise. Napoleon also gained an affinity for the paunchy Austrian officer. His negotiations with Napoleon over Austria's participation in the French emperor's upcoming 1812 invasion of Russia secured favorable alliance terms for Vienna. As a result, the Austrian Auxiliary Corps of 30,000 men would operate with almost complete independence on the right wing of the Grande Armée. Preparations for the war itself prompted Schwarzenberg to leave the glitter of Paris and return to his native state to take command of this Austrian corps. Napoleon requested that the Kaiser's brother, Archduke Charles, command the Austrian contingent but, on Metternich's suggestion, Francis appointed Schwarzenberg. Fortunately for the Austrians, Schwarzenberg's corps did not accompany Bonaparte's main force to Moscow. As Napoleon's army retreated from the Russian capital, Schwarzenberg anchored himself at Warsaw and opened negotiations with the Russians. Directed from Vienna by Metternich, he passively allowed Russian forces to enter the Grand Duchy of Warsaw and then withdrew to Galicia.

Because of his lengthy diplomatic assignments, the general developed an intimate relationship with Metternich. Few Austrians had as much experience blending diplomacy and war as Schwarzenberg. For this reason and despite the tsar's preference for Archduke Charles, Metternich insisted on Schwarzenberg's appointment as Allied commander in chief. This choice caused controversy because Metternich disregarded several senior Austrian generals as well as Charles and the other Habsburg archdukes. Radetzky himself doubted the wisdom of placing such awesome responsibility in the hands of a man who appeared to be nothing more than a courtier. Relations between Schwarzenberg and Radetzky never resembled the military marriage of Blücher and Gneisenau, yet the two eventually formed an effective partnership. Described as able yet vain, ambitious, and much overrated, Schwarzenberg's other chief assistant, the Saxon Langenau, served as general quartermaster and head of the Bohemian Army's operations section. In 1812, the thirty-two-year-old impressed Schwarzenberg as chief of staff of the Saxon corps, which operated alongside the Austrian Auxiliary Corps during the Russian campaign. Resigning from the Saxon Army in 1813, Langenau began service with the Austrians that same year. With Saxony serving as the main theater of the German campaign, Schwarzenberg appointed him head of the operations section, hoping the native Saxon possessed unrivaled knowledge of his homeland's terrain. Committing several topographical errors during the battles of Dresden and Leipzig, Langenau proved to be a disappointment that Schwarzenberg did nothing about to conceal his own culpability. In addition, Langenau's arrogance and ambition became a source of friction with Radetzky.[43]

Regarding Schwarzenberg's abilities as a commander, strategist, and tactician, historians are mainly critical. "To be sure," concludes Kraehe, "it was Schwarzenberg who actually commanded the armies in the field, and it was Kaiser Francis who ultimately had to approve military and diplomatic decisions. But with the latter Metternich generally had his way . . . while with the general he enjoyed an efficacious relationship that owed much to Schwarzenberg's diplomatic service."[44] Maycock asserts that as a strategist, Schwarzenberg "was over-cautious and vacillating, belonging to the school . . . which considered that complicated maneuvers executed by a number of separate columns and elaborate turning movements, not decisive battles, were the main objects of campaign. As a tactician he had proved himself singularly incapable of handling large bodies of troops on the field of battle, both at Dresden and at Leipzig, where his faulty dispositions almost involved the Allies in disaster on the first day of the battle."[45] French historian Campana describes Schwarzenberg as "irresolute, circumspect, pusillanimous, and prone to delay."[46] The German General Staff historian, Janson, who wrote the official history of the 1814 campaign, provides a fairly accurate albeit negative assessment of Schwarzenberg:

> Political considerations came first and remained so during the entire campaign for Schwarzenberg, while strategy took a backseat. The political restraint was represented by Metternich, who found no counter-weight in the military element in the Austrian headquarters. Schwarzenberg himself was far from being a commander and thus hardly made the pretense to be one. He relied on the ideas of his general-quartermaster, Langenau, a man who was just as erudite as he was an impractical adherent of the old school, for which the experience of the Napoleonic Wars were ignored, and which looked at a battle as only a crude, dire expedient, unworthy of any educated field commander. The Austrian field commander had to subordinate his art of war to Austrian politics, which did not want Napoleon annihilated, and Schwarzenberg complied. Blücher and Gneisenau were opposed to such. The characters in the Austrian headquarters were otherwise. Obviously those men did their duty, and one can

completely assume that Radetzky had serious internal struggles in attempting
to persuade Langenau, who was a total theorist.[47]

Despite these critical judgments, Schwarzenberg possessed the necessary
talent, intelligence, and bravery to be a worthy army commander. Although
not on par with Napoleon, Wellington, or the Blücher/Gneisenau tandem,
Schwarzenberg's understanding of strategy and operations surpassed the
active French marshals as well as most of his contemporaries among Austria's allies. His task was neither easy nor enviable, yet he managed to limit
the problems posed by a heterogeneous coalition during the German campaign and quickly learned the art of managing his own multinational army
composed of Austrians, Russians, and Prussians. The Allied sovereigns with
their endless train of advisors and minions joined Schwarzenberg in the field.
All eagerly offered advice to the Austrian, complaining loudly when their
council did not appear to be favored and blaming him when their schemes
failed in execution. Their demand to be briefed on all proposed operations
led to continuous councils of war. No fewer than seventeen took place during
the German campaign, during which Schwarzenberg was outvoted on nine
occasions and complete agreement was achieved only six times.[48] "It really is
inhuman what I must tolerate and bear," wrote Schwarzenberg to his wife a
few days after his defeat at Dresden, "surrounded as I am by fools, eccentric
projectors, intriguers, asses, babblers, and niggling critics. Vermin in countless number gnaw at me and torment me to the very marrow of my bones."[49]
Moreover, his authority over his Allied subordinates such as Blücher and
Bernadotte remained illusory for much of the war. Regardless of the pres-
sures placed on him, his major shortcomings as Allied generalissimo surfaced
after the battle of Leipzig when his confidant, Metternich, conclusively influenced military operations. Placing Austrian national interests above those of
the Coalition remains the understandable yet inexcusable fault of the Allied
commander in chief.[50]

With the pieces rapidly aligning themselves on the great chessboard of
Europe, plans soon evolved into operations. On 12 December, Radetzky
submitted to Schwarzenberg his blueprint for the Bohemian Army to cross
the Rhine.[51] The next day, Schwarzenberg's army marched to the designated
points of passage between Schaffhausen and Basel.[52] After negotiating with
Bubna, the Swiss agreed to withdraw all troops from the Rhine and relinquish
the city of Basel and its surrounding districts to the Austrians.[53] On the following day, Schwarzenberg executed the operation. The left wing of the Bohemian
Army – under Schwarzenberg's immediate command and consisting solely
of Austrian troops – occupied northwestern Switzerland. Publicly, a bitter
Alexander could do nothing more than state his approval. However, he sent
a letter of protest to Schwarzenberg and, in a second note, professed that this
deed had grieved him like never before. Operationally, the maneuver allowed

the Bohemian Army to outflank the French fortresses on the upper Rhine. Diplomatically, the controversy caused by Switzerland almost destroyed the Sixth Coalition; the relationship between Alexander and Metternich reached a new low.[54]

The Allied generalissimo moved his headquarters to Freiburg on the 11th; Francis joined him on the 15th. Metternich attempted to detain the tsar in Frankfurt under the pretext that from there the Russian monarch could better direct the upcoming negotiations. This ploy to undermine Alexander's influence on the course of military operations did not deceive the tsar. He informed the Austrian minister that he considered military operations far more important than peace negotiations. Nevertheless, the tsar did not reach Freiburg until after Schwarzenberg's headquarters departed.

After Schwarzenberg conveyed the news of his army's successful passage of the Swiss frontier, Metternich had to plan his next move. "There still remained the difficulty of informing His Majesty the Tsar of Russia that the event really had been accomplished," he recalls. "Kaiser Francis instructed me to execute this commission on the following day, when the arrival of his ally was expected." Accompanied by Francis, Metternich rode out to meet Alexander on the 22nd. The tsar pressed him for tidings. Preferring to speak in private, the Austrian deferred to answer until they were alone. Later that evening, he broke the news: the Austrian army had crossed the Rhine at several points between Schaffhausen and Basel. "The Tsar was very much agitated by this news," recounts Metternich, and "when he collected himself, he asked how the army had been received. 'Amid cheers for the Coalition, Your Majesty'," responded Metternich. "I could easily read in the Tsar's features the conflicted feelings that this news evoked. After a longer pause, he took my hand and said: 'Success crowns the undertaking: it remains for success to justify what you have done. As one of the Allied monarchs I have nothing more to say to you; but as a man I declare that you have grieved me in a way that you can never repair.' I remained quiet, and replied to his Majesty that my conscience did not reproach me, because his glory was as dear to me as the great cause, which was his as well as that of all Europe. 'You do not know how you have grieved me,' said the Tsar hastily. 'You do not know the peculiar circumstances of my position.'"[55]

Despite the uneasiness of their relationship, Metternich made one more attempt to restrain the Russian sovereign. Napoleon's final acceptance of the Frankfurt Proposals meant that a peace congress would be held soon. The Austrian minister suggested that the Allied monarchs remain with their ministers in Freiburg and hold the conference in that city. Alexander, still smarting over the Swiss affair, vehemently rebuffed Metternich and departed the same day to join Schwarzenberg at Lörrach. Ultimately, the combination of Metternich's scheming and Alexander's own vanity prevented the Russian monarch from catching up with Schwarzenberg until the latter reached Langres.[56]

During this time, another affair added to the friction between the tsar and the Austrians. Apparently, Austrian intelligence identified a high-placed French spy in the Romanov palace. They claimed to have proof that a Madame de Merges, who was the former governess of Alexander's sister, the Grand-Duchess Marie, as well as a maid, were employed by a French spy. Metternich, however, linked this affair with the Swiss controversy: "A lady, formerly governess of the Grand-Duchess Marie of Weimar, a Vaudois who had been sent by the [Swiss] cantons to Frankfurt...had been listened to by the princess. Tsar Alexander, for his part, had promised his sister that he would never allow the Allied armies to enter Switzerland."[57] Regardless of the connections, the scandal first became known to Schwarzenberg, who brazenly confronted Alexander. "How can one involve women in the gravest affairs?" asks the Allied commander in a letter to Metternich. "He does not know how to respond to being compromised at this point by a governess and maid."[58] Of course Metternich stirred the pot, writing to Schwarzenberg: "If you again succeed in finding some small detail on this subject...to prove to the Tsar and his sister...that Madame de Merges is a scoundrel of the pawns of the French police, you will render an immense service to the Allies, because Tsar Alexander is madder than ever over this question in which he is found to be personally compromised."[59] The tsar in fact became so irate that he vented his anger at the Austrians – and specifically Schwarzenberg, as Metternich warns:

> You have received or will receive a response from Tsar Alexander to your letter that will prove to you he is offended. Do not reply to it, and place the thing *ad acta*. I was scolded for the way that you wrote. I explained to him that you have provided compelling proof of your desire to avoid becoming embroiled in questions that are relative to political principles – which are foreign to you – concerning the discovery that the governess of his sister has been linked to the French spy. He grimaced and was quiet. Everything is settled and the effect will not have been lost.[60]

Turning to military matters, Schwarzenberg's headquarters published bogus campaign plans in the German newspapers to deceive the French and divert attention from Upper Alsace and Franche-Comté. According to these stories, the main operation would take place in Italy: the left wing of the main Allied army would cross Switzerland, proceed through the Rhône Valley, and unite with the Austrian army in Italy as it advanced through Piedmont to sever communications between France and Italy. The "Austro–Bavarian army" would threaten Alsace, Schwarzenberg would cross the Rhine near Mannheim, and Blücher would pass the river downstream of Mainz. To the north, Bernadotte would operate on the Lower Rhine and invade Holland in conjunction with the British. In short, France soon would be attacked on all frontiers.[61]

According to Schwarzenberg's actual plans, the Austrian troops of the army's left wing would proceed to Lausanne and Geneva, while the commander in chief himself wheeled right at Bern with his center and maneuvered into Franche-Comté toward Besançon. On the right wing of the army, Wrede and Wittgenstein would besiege the fortress of Huningue and push toward Belfort and Strasbourg. According to Wilson's notes concerning a 19 December discussion between Schwarzenberg and himself, the Allied commander was already consumed by the fear of a French counteroffensive to sever his communications across the Rhine. Wilson claims Schwarzenberg "proposed to maneuver, not to make conquests; he thought the enemy would not have a disposable force of any great strength before February, when negotiations would be far advanced; but if the enemy crosses the Rhine at Kehl, he [Schwarzenberg] will return and recross the Rhine to oppose his progress on the right bank. The enemy, however, would have a good start and better communications to favor his operations."[62]

The intelligence that reached Schwarzenberg's headquarters on 18 December increased his anxiety. Wrede forwarded a report that 5,000 French reinforcements recently arrived at Strasbourg.[63] A detailed intelligence brief claimed Ney was guarding Strasbourg with 25,000 men and Marmont was at Mainz with 11,000 soldiers, although 50 to 100 were dying in the hospitals each day. Macdonald supposedly held the Rhine from Mainz to Strasbourg with an undisclosed number of troops. To support the marshals, the French had spread a force of 30,000 National Guards on the upper Rhine between Mainz and Strasbourg. The report further stated that Nansouty arrived at Nancy with 5,000 cavalry and Kellermann held Metz with 5,000 men.[64] Although none of these statements proved to be true, the prospects of crossing the Rhine with such a large enemy force to the immediate north provided cause for extreme caution.

On 20 December, Schwarzenberg issued orders for the advance of the Bohemian Army. Bubna commanded the vanguard, consisting of his own 1st Light Division and Alois von Liechtenstein's II Corps. The Allied generalissimo instructed him to cross the Rhine at Basel and Grenzach and lead the advance guard south toward Geneva on the extreme left of the army; Schwarzenberg expected the column to reach Fribourg on the 25th. En route to Fribourg, Liechtenstein would detach a strong advance guard to the crossroads at Solothurn. It would move west, skirt Lake Neuchâtel, and advance to the Pierre Pertuis Pass to observe the St. Imier Valley. This advance guard would then continue southwest to Neuchâtel to scour the roads to Pontarlier. Upon reaching Fribourg, Liechtenstein would separate from Bubna and follow his advance guard through Neuchâtel to Pontarlier.

Schwarzenberg wanted his second column – General Ludwig Karl von Crenneville's Light Division of Gyulay's III Corps temporarily reinforced by General Friedrich von Bianchi's grenadier division – to likewise cross the

Rhine at Basel and cover the right flank of the army. Crenneville's task was to blockade the French fortress of Huningue on the 21st. After being relieved by Wrede's Bavarians on the 22nd, this second column was to reach Biel by 26 December. Moritz von Liechtenstein's 2nd Light Division and Colloredo's I Corps formed the third column, which received orders to cross the Rhine upstream Basel at Laufenburg to be at Bern by the 26th.

Gyulay's III Corps constituted the fourth column; the Feldzeugmeister received orders to follow the second column across the Basel bridge, but then proceed to Aarberg, halfway between Biel and Bern, arriving by the 26th. A fifth column, Hesse-Homburg's Austrian Reserve Corps, would cross the Rhine at Schaffausen and advance through Zürich to reach Bern by 29 December. Wrede's V Corps formed the sixth column, which Schwarzenberg instructed to cross the Rhine at Basel on the 22nd, blockade the fortress of Huningue just north of Basel, and dispatch General Anton von Rechberg's Bavarian division west to establish posts around the fortress of Belfort. Schwarzenberg designated the IV Corps as the seventh column, which would follow the army to Lörrach and await further orders.[65]

As for the other units of the Bohemian Army, Wittgenstein's VI Corps did not enter Switzerland but instead blockaded Kehl and observed the Rhine from Strasbourg to Mannheim. The Russo–Prussian Guard and Reserve received instructions to reach Lörrach by 5 January.[66] Schwarzenberg ended the day of 20 December with a poetic letter to his wife that reveals his mood on the eve of his greatest military expedition: "I do not fight to seek glory or honorary columns, but a true peace. You know, Nani, my intent is clear . . . the desecrating spirit of vanity does not guide my footsteps. I rush to meet my fate."[67]

7

The Lower Rhine

Although the Bohemian and Silesian Armies halted at the Rhine, the Army of North Germany continued the campaign. Following the battle of Leipzig, the crown prince of Sweden directed his army to Göttingen. News that Marshal Davout had withdrew to Hamburg allayed Allied fears that he would seek to raise the sieges of Magdeburg and Torgau and then unite with Marshal St. Cyr to create a formidable French army between the Elbe's fortresses. Davout's retreat allowed the individual corps of the Army of North Germany to separate between 1 and 4 November. Bülow's Prussian III Corps moved toward Westphalia, and Wintzingerode's Russian corps continued toward the Weser River. Bernadotte maintained direct command over his Swedish corps and united with Wallmoden's corps, which had held the lower Elbe during the German campaign. In addition, Bernadotte retained General Mikhail Semenovich Vorontsov's infantry corps of Wintzingerode's army corps and received command of General Pavel Aleksandrovich Stroganov's Russian infantry corps from Bennigsen's Army of Poland. With this force of approximately 60,000 men, he advanced toward Hanover to confront Davout.[1] Nothing had changed for the crown prince of Sweden except the urgency of his mission. Since the resumption of hostilities in August, the issue between Sweden and Denmark over the fate of Norway was his main concern. Now that his army had saved Berlin on two occasions and he had assisted his allies with the liberation of Germany, he planned to use their troops to secure Norway.

Bülow's corps reached Münster on 16 November. As Berlin's new governor-general of Westphalia, he appointed officials to organize Landwehr and Line units in all former Prussian districts. Bülow worked quickly to fill the holes in his ranks. British aid again proved crucial to the cash-strapped Prussians. "Gen. Bülow recruited his army in His Prussian Majesty's ancient states," notes Stewart, "to the number it amounted to before the opening of the campaign. The generous and liberal aid of the prince-regent, in arms and clothing, was of invaluable importance to these brave Prussians at this moment: They were the means of re-equipping and arming the corps d'armée forthwith, nearly on their original establishment. It must be as gratifying to the English nation as credible to its government, to see how opportunely their aid was forthcoming."[2]

While tending to these duties, Bülow finalized plans to invade Holland. The Prussian general had been considering an operation in the Low Countries since October. After the battle of Leipzig, Bülow confidentially revealed to his chief of staff, Boyen, a plan to liberate the Low Countries. Bülow assured him that Hardenberg and Friedrich Wilhelm supported his plan and would issue orders for its execution.[3] It is possible that while in Leipzig Boyen discussed an invasion of Holland with his friend and superior, Gneisenau, who later demanded an operation in the Low Countries during the councils of war at Frankfurt. Regardless, Bülow's correspondence in November suggests that he decided to invade Holland on his own responsibility – before receiving authorization from the king, Hardenberg, Bernadotte, or Schwarzenberg.[4]

Rumors of Molitor's withdrawal to the Belgian frontier reached Bülow on 22 November. Ready to cross the Dutch border, he still had not received official permission. Schwarzenberg did not issue orders for a Dutch offensive, which in part reflected Austria's desire to check Prussian influence in northwest Germany and the Low Countries. However, orders did arrive for Bülow to dispatch the 10,000 men of General Karl Heinrich von Borstell's 5th Brigade to besiege Wesel; the Prussian corps commander reluctantly complied. On 27 November, Borstell's units reached Wesel and easily repulsed the French posts. The Prussians blockaded the fortress on the right bank of the Rhine but could not complete the investment without crossing to the left bank, which Borstell believed was too risky.[5]

On 19 November, Bernadotte authorized Bülow to continue his advance and to occupy the line of the Ijssel and Lower Rhine as soon as the investment of Wesel was complete.[6] Three days later, Frederick William finally answered Bülow's request for permission to invade Holland with words of caution but no definitive answer.[7] Although the political consequences – both positive and negative – of a Prussian military operation in the Low Countries very much concerned the king and Hardenberg, they understood the importance of this issue to the British, whose envoys in Frankfurt loudly demanded an Allied operation to detach Holland from France. As a result, the king granted Bülow the latitude to pursue the necessary diplomatic arrangements with the British and the exiled Dutch authorities in London. Consequently, Bülow dispatched his brother-in-law, Captain Louis von Auer, to London to secure support and approval from the prince-regent and William Frederick, the prince of Orange. Auer addressed Parliament to solicit weapons, supplies, and the support of British ground forces. The Prussian managed to secure approval of Bülow's plans as well as the promise of material support. News of the revolt in

Amsterdam and the growing Dutch insurrection also reached London. To facilitate the anti-French movement, the British reiterated their pledge to send Graham's auxiliary force as well as 25,000 muskets to the Dutch insurgents. London needed Prussian manpower to execute the invasion and liberation of the Low Countries, particularly because previous British expeditions to Holland had not faired well. Although the British wanted the French out of Holland, they refused to weaken Wellington to do so.[8]

To announce his invasion, Bülow issued a proclamation to the inhabitants of the United Provinces of the Netherlands on 20 November.[9] Thousands of copies circulated throughout the Dutch provinces (Appendix G). To impress the Dutch and gain their trust, he referred to the Army of North Germany as the successor to the great Swedish army of Gustavus Adolphus that liberated North Germany during the Thirty Years' War. Bülow summoned the Dutch to assist his efforts to liberate the country by appealing to their sense of honor. The French officer and contemporary Koch asserts that Bülow's advance toward the Dutch frontier "fermented the spirit of insurrection" and that this proclamation provided the signal for the Dutch to begin a general revolt in several of their cities.[10]

Prussian plans to liberate the Low Countries embraced a clear political agenda that emerged in part from Bülow's close relationship with Boyen. Bülow's personal distaste for Gneisenau did not affect his ability to work well with Boyen – one of Gneisenau's confidants. The frequent correspondence between Gneisenau and Boyen reveals the details of Prussian grand strategy and provided a vehicle for the Chief of the General Staff of the Prussian Army to implement his objectives within the context of a multinational coalition. In this way, Gneisenau directed Bülow to execute the same operations that Allied headquarters refused to allow Blücher to conduct. Furthermore, Bülow, much more than Blücher, considered Prussia's role in the post-Napoleonic balance of power. He and Boyen sought to expand Prussian influence by gaining the support of liberated peoples such as the Dutch and Belgians. Both Bülow and Boyen believed in the military and political advantages of liberating the Low Countries. In his correspondence with Hardenberg, Boyen emphasized Prussia's political interests and the significance that the liberation of Holland would afford Berlin during the eventual peace negotiations.[11] "It is essential," wrote Bülow on 23 November, "that the liberation of Holland be effected by our troops rather than by foreigners. . . . We must always seek to win the voice and support of the people."[12] By opening his campaign with an appeal to the Dutch people, Bülow attempted to secure for Berlin the support of a nation liberated mainly by Prussian arms. From afar Gneisenau expressed his concurrence in a letter to Boyen: "Use powerful language in your proclamations to the peoples who shall be liberated from the foreign yoke."[13]

After launching the propaganda campaign, Bülow completed his military preparations. He planned to take the French strongholds along the Ijssel

River, advance detachments between the Lower Rhine and the Waal, and move Oppen's vanguard against Utrecht. By taking Utrecht, he would gain a firm base of operations in the northern provinces. From Utrecht, he would drive south against the line of the Waal and the Meuse (Maas). Bülow counted on facing a weak and demoralized adversary; an energetic opponent could have easily prevented him from taking the numerous Dutch forts. His operation also depended on the active participation of the population, which he intended to arm with the British muskets and employ in the field as soon as possible.[14]

Two rows of fortified cities and fortresses protected the approaches to the Dutch interior (Map 3). The first line included Grave on the Meuse, with 2,000 inhabitants; Nijmegen on the Waal with approximately 15,000 inhabitants; Arnhem on the Lower Rhine with about 10,000 inhabitants; Doesburg, Zütphen, and Deventer on the Ijssel, with the last containing 10,000 inhabitants; Zwolle with a population of 12,000, likewise on the Ijssel; and Coevorden.[15] Behind these two belts Napoleon's northern frontier consisted of the six departments of the 25th Military District. A sufficient number of generally well-maintained roads ran between the cities of the district, connecting them with Belgium and France. Although the imperial highway that extended from Huningue to Nijmegen provided a crucial artery of transportation and communication along the left bank of the Rhine, from Koblenz to Köln it ran too close to the great river to prevent enemy spies on the opposite bank from observing troop movements. At some points, the road came within the range of artillery situated on the right bank. North of Neuss the highway curved away from the Rhine Valley and traversed the plateau between the Rhine and the Meuse through Krefeld, Geldern, and Kleve, where it reunited with the Rhine and followed the river to Nijmegen. Several forts covered the roads coming from Germany: Deventer on the Ijssel River; Arnhem at the junction of the Ijssel and the Rhine; Nijmegen on the Waal River; and Grave on the Meuse. Communications with "new France" (Alsace and Lorraine) ran from Koblenz to Strasbourg and Metz, and roads from Venlo, Roermond, and Maastricht meandered through "old France" to Paris; a third route to old France extended from Köln through Jülich, Aachen, and Liège to Mézières. Between these roads, geographic obstacles such as rivers and marshes provided natural barriers. North of the Antwerp–Maastricht road sprawled the Kempen, a region of poor and difficult terrain hardly suited for military operations that extended to the left bank of the Meuse. Flooding, strong currents, and drift ice made the Rhine, Waal, and Meuse almost impassible in winter. All three rivers carried much traffic, but only the Meuse had regular transports because the navigation on the others could be difficult. Dutch customs agents and gunboats observed the rivers, but their vigilance waned along with their loyalty.[16]

With Bülow's main body still three days behind, Oppen led the advance guard of four battalions, two dragoon regiments, one jäger company, and twelve guns (3,000 men total) across the Dutch frontier on 23 November. From Bocholt he advanced northwest to Doesburg with plans to proceed through the fort to reach the left bank of the Ijssel that same day. Amey, however, had chased the Cossacks from Doesburg during the night; he left behind a small garrison composed of customs agents, gendarmes, and infantry and returned to Arnhem. Oppen accelerated his march to prevent the French from preparing Doesburg's defenses. He ordered the Queen's Dragoon Regiment and a half-battery of horse artillery to attempt a coup de main. Around 3:00 P.M., the Prussians reached Doesburg and found the drawbridge raised. From the walls, French musket fire ruled out the chances of taking the fort by surprise.[17]

After failing to induce the commandant to surrender, Oppen reconnoitered the position and shelled the fort with his light artillery. He directed the jäger squadron of the Queen's Dragoons to dismount and skirmish with the enemy troops manning the walls. Around 4:00 that afternoon, Oppen's infantry arrived to press the attack. Prussian grape directed at the old ramparts sent the garrison running for cover. Joined by a company of Kolberg Fusiliers, the jäger waded across the moat hoisting a ladder above their heads. The Prussians scrambled up the ladder and cut the chain to drop the drawbridge. East Prussian infantry charged forward in an attack column.[18] With the Prussians in pursuit, the French withdrew to the pontoon that spanned the Ijssel. As they hurried to get across, the bridge came apart. Several French soldiers drowned or fell victim to Prussian marksmen. After the Prussians killed several, the remainder, including the commandant, surrendered. Oppen captured 4 officers and 108 men – not one soldier of the French garrison reached the left bank alive.

Although a small victory, the fall of Doesburg spread dismay throughout the region. Initial Dutch enthusiasm over being liberated turned to apathy and fear. Within twenty-four hours, Doesburg had been occupied by Russians, French, and now Prussians. Uncertainty over which faction would next control the town demoralized the Dutch. Fearing French vengeance, the townspeople did not offer any assistance. Expecting to be honored as a liberator, Oppen received little recognition and even less cooperation in repairing the Ijssel bridge. He finally declared that requisitions would be levied unless the inhabitants restored it by morning: the Prussians found the bridge operational by 8:00 A.M. on the 24th.[19]

On that day, the Prussians moved in force against Zutphen. Late in the afternoon, they prepared to assault the fort from both banks of the Ijssel. Observing that the enemy held both banks and completely encircled the fort, the French commandant offered to surrender on the condition that he and his men be granted free passage to France. With "insolent phrases," the Prussians rejected the offer and prepared to storm the fort. To avoid the bloodshed associated with the storming of any town or city, the inhabitants threatened to riot and open the gates to the Prussians. As a result, the French commandant agreed to yield the fort unconditionally, along with its garrison and several guns, before nightfall. The Prussians found a substantial amount of supplies, including a coveted tobacco magazine. During these events, Colomb demonstrated before Arnhem to prevent the French from sending reinforcements down the Ijssel. Sixty miles to the west, Benckendorff secured Amsterdam.[20]

According to reports, French forces had evacuated all of the primary strongholds in the southern Dutch provinces. Moreover, the forts still maintained by French troops were in disrepair and could barely be defended. By controlling all territory north of the Rhine and the Meuse, the Allies assured their communication with Germany and Great Britain. Yet with French forces still occupying Arnhem, Gorinchem, and Utrecht, they could threaten further Allied operations in the Low Countries. If French reinforcements arrived, Macdonald and Molitor would be able to launch a counteroffensive to drive the Russians and Prussians from Holland. Neither Molitor nor Benckendorff possessed sufficient troops in the region between Utrecht and Amsterdam to influence operations. Yet Macdonald and Bülow commanded sizable forces that could execute a campaign. Both commanders considered the possession of Arnhem as vital to their operations. Macdonald hoped to push back the Allies and restore his cordon along the Ijssel, whereas Bülow planned to take Arnhem and then Utrecht, from where he would drive deeper into Holland by pushing the French across the Rhine and the Waal.

With Molitor's 1,400 men of the 17th Military District holding Utrecht, Macdonald concentrated 11,500 bayonets between Grave and Nijmegen. His troops, almost all native French soldiers, lived in constant fear of the inhabitants and popular revolt. The marshal's scant intelligence estimated that a Russo–Prussian force of 12,000 men held all key points on the upper and middle Ijssel except Arnhem and perhaps Deventer. To make matters worse, German newspapers announced the approach of Bernadotte's army. According to the propaganda issued from the crown prince's headquarters, he would take Zwolle and proceed to Amsterdam. Because of the rapid spread of the Dutch insurrection north of the Waal River, Molitor prepared to evacuate Utrecht and retreat twelve miles south to Gorinchem. To protect his flank, Macdonald dispatched Amey's 2,000 men toward Deventer late on the 24th. At Deventer, Amey would unite with a hastily assembled force of customs officials and gendarmes under General Louis François Lauberdière. Amey's battalions never arrived.[21]

Bülow learned of a significant French force assembling at Nijmegen. To confirm these reports, he instructed Oppen to conduct reconnaissance between Arnhem and Nijmegen. The Prussian brigadier dispatched two squadrons from Doesburg on the morning of the 24th. At Velp, slightly northwest of Arnhem, the Prussian troopers encountered Amey's column.

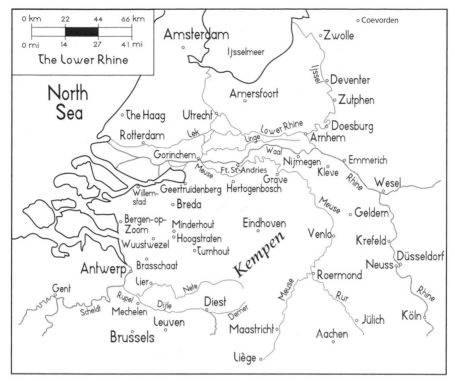

Map 3. The lower Rhine.

The Prussians withdrew to Middachten because of their small number (see Map 4). They observed the French and reported that an enemy force held the road to Arnhem. Bülow ordered Oppen to advance to Arnhem early on the 25th. The Prussian general arrived at Middachten and met Amey's battalions on the highway to Arnhem around noon. He enveloped both French flanks, and forced Amey to retreat. Prussian dragoons attempted to sever Amey's line of retreat near the forest of Rozendaal but arrived too late and only managed to take twenty prisoners. Steady rearguard action ensued as Oppen pursued the French through the wood of Rozendaal and Arnhem's Klarenbeek suburb to find Amey's men occupying an entrenched camp north of Arnhem that checked the Prussian advance.

Oppen led his main column on the highway through Velp to the Klarenbeek suburb. His infantry occupied the town and skirmishers probed the French entrenchments. He noted the weakness of the French forces occupying the redoubts. In addition, he could see that the Jans and Velp gates on Arnhem's northern side were barricaded and protected from artillery fire by bastions; the bridge over the moat had been destroyed. Oppen ordered the Kolberg Fusilier Battalion to charge the entrenched camp between the Klarenbeek suburb and Arnhem. Two cannon unlimbered to support the infantry, while the remaining pieces lobed shells into Arnhem. Skirmishing erupted on the northern and eastern sides of Arnhem as well. After a struggle that claimed several casualties, Oppen realized his three battalions could not achieve success. Rather than expend his ammunition in useless skirmishing, he sought to induce the French commander to surrender by offering free passage. Expecting reinforcements to arrive from Nijmegen at any moment, the French rejected the proposal. By the time the parley ended, the winter sun had set, and Oppen decided to withdraw. Leaving skirmishers in the Klarenbeek suburb as well as Lichtenbeek, a large estate near Arnhem, Oppen established pickets around the fort and moved his main body to Velp to await the arrival of General Karl August von Krafft's 6th Brigade, which was scheduled to reach Doesburg the following day.

A French counterattack on 26 November drove back the Prussian pickets to Velp before Oppen's main body could stabilize the situation. After causing much confusion, the French disengaged and returned to Arnhem. The only success Oppen enjoyed on this day came when an East Prussian jäger company supported by one Landwehr battalion fell on a small convoy of six guns escorted by French gendarmes. Later in the day, a detachment of three Landwehr cavalry regiments and two fusilier battalions under Lieutenant Colonel Hans Joachim von Sydow as well as Colomb's Streifkorps reached Arnhem, but Oppen needed more infantry to achieve success. He hoped the arrival of the 6th Brigade would allow him to storm Arnhem, but Krafft was twenty-four hours behind schedule. Krafft reached Doesburg on the 27th; his advance units joined Oppen the following day.

With twelve battalions and three batteries now at his disposal, Oppen planned to storm Arnhem on the 28th. After further contemplation, however, the Prussian commander hesitated to challenge the enemy position. Situated on the right bank of the lower Rhine, Arnhem at one time had been protected by extensive outworks and a covered way. All that remained of the original Dutch fortifications was the high main wall that enclosed the city and was buttressed by ten bastions. Not only did Arnhem intimidate the Prussian commander, but reports that French reinforcements had arrived added to his consternation. From a hill by the Klarenbeek suburb, the Prussians observed approximately 1,000 French cuirassiers and carabineers escort a large artillery train over the Rhine bridge into Arnhem. This led Oppen to believe that Macdonald's entire corps was approaching from Nijmegen, only ten miles to the south. In fact, the rumor spread that Macdonald himself had arrived. French engineers and artillery officers could be seen erecting batteries on the left bank of the lower Rhine to defend the approaches to Arnhem. The French garrison reportedly consisted of 3,000 to 4,000 men from Charpentier's division. Whether Macdonald had arrived or was approaching, the threat convinced

Oppen to withdraw his troops from the vicinity of Arnhem until additional Prussian troops could support his operation.

Macdonald left Kleve on 27 November to join the II Cavalry Corps and Charpentier's 31st Division at Nijmegen. The marshal thought he could salvage the far from satisfactory situation. For this he counted on Rampon's 3,000 National Guardsmen reaching Gorinchem from Antwerp. Macdonald judged that the combination of Rampon's units, Molitor's detachment, and his own troops could hold the Allies at the Ijssel. He decided to move to Arnhem on the 28th to reconnoiter and attack the enemy if an opportunity for success presented itself. During the day Macdonald and Charpentier reached Arnhem with the 2,500 men of General Jean-Baptiste-Simon-Firmin Marie's 2nd Brigade (six battalions) reinforced by the lead battalion of General Auguste-Julien Bigarré's 1st Brigade, the main body of which still had not arrived in Nijmegen. Although Macdonald knew of the presence of Prussian cavalry north of Arnhem, he declined to move the II Cavalry Corps north of the Waal. Altogether Charpentier commanded approximately 4,000 men for the defense of Arnhem. Before turning over the fort to the general, Macdonald inspected Arnhem and found the position untenable if attacked by superior forces. After ordering Charpentier to dispatch patrols to ascertain news of the enemy, he left for Nijmegen.

On 29 November, the French completed their measures and opened a strong cannonade from the left bank of the lower Rhine. French gunners fired on anything they could see moving along the right bank. Oppen, who did not remain idle, attacked the entrenched camp north of Arnhem. After hard fighting, the Prussians managed to break through the French defenses, but could not hold their ground. A French counterattack drove back Oppen's soldiers to Rozendaal and Velp. Lacking cavalry, Charpentier could not press his advantage but did prepare a sortie. After reinforcing the walls and redoubts with men and guns, Charpentier launched an extensive attack around noon that surprised the Prussian post at Lichtenbeek. The attack claimed fifty casualties before the Kolberg Fusilier Battalion supported by two guns finally forced the French to break off their assault. Oppen decided to postpone further operations for that day, the 29th, and instructed his troops to pass the night in Rozendaal and Velp. Colomb's Streifkorps observed Arnhem from Westervoort on the right bank of the Ijssel. Bülow arrived in Doesburg that evening and learned that Arnhem remained in French hands. Concerned that Macdonald would drive eastward and sever his communications, the Prussian corps commander immediately ordered Oppen to storm the fort on the next morning. That night four additional battalions from General Heinrich Ludwig von Thümen's 4th Brigade marched to participate in the attack.

Oppen's retreat after the surprise attack on the 29th allowed Amey to establish a strong perimeter outside the fort and along the right bank of the lower Rhine. To support Amey, Charpentier posted four battalions from

Marie's 2nd Brigade in the entrenched camp; the remaining battalions of the 31st Division served as Arnhem's garrison. Apparently Macdonald had returned to Arnhem on the 29th and observed Oppen's columns debouch on the road from Doesburg. Despite the success of his troops on this day, he correctly concluded that the Prussian force constituted the advance guard of a numerically superior army corps that could surround Arnhem and sever Charpentier's line of retreat. News of Molitor's difficulties also reached the marshal. On the 27th, Dutch insurgents and Russian Cossacks attempted to invest Utrecht. To avoid being trapped, Molitor withdrew to Gorinchem, where he hoped to unite with Rampon. For Macdonald, the imminent arrival of Bülow's corps and Molitor's retreat settled the issue over Arnhem. Because he could neither unite with Molitor at Utrecht nor march down the Ijssel through Doesburg to Deventer, Macdonald saw no justification for holding Arnhem. The marshal ordered Charpentier to evacuate the fort and retreat across the lower Rhine. He planned to post the 31st Division between the lower Rhine and the Waal in the region called the Betuwe. The lower Rhine and the Leck would form his first line of defense, the Waal his second, and the Meuse his third. From this position, he hoped to cover Belgium until the arrival of reinforcements. Rather than supervise Charpentier's withdrawal, Macdonald made the mistake of returning to Nijmegen.[22]

In one of many examples in which time has failed to uncover a plausible excuse, Charpentier did not follow Macdonald's orders. Rather than lead his 4,000 men to the safety of the Waal, he decided to maintain his positions on the 30th. Inconceivably, Charpentier neglected to post guards at Arnhem's gates and the access to the bridge. Heavy fog, typical in Holland at that time of year, delayed the Prussian assault for several hours. While the Prussians waited, they could hear cavalry and wagons crossing the bridge over the lower Rhine and apparently leaving Arnhem. This raised hopes that the French might capitulate. The Prussians later learned that the noise had been Macdonald departing.

Before dawn on 30 November, Bülow himself arrived to oversee the operation. After surveying the fort, he ordered a four-pronged assault. Of the four columns, the two on the left wing would be feints, and the main attack would come from the right because these columns would be closest to the bridge over the lower Rhine and in position to sever the enemy's line of retreat. Colomb's Streifkorps, reinforced by two battalions and two guns, formed a fifth column that would operate on the extreme left wing. Lieutenant Colonel Wilhelm Ernst von Zastrow commanded the two right wing columns. He placed the first under Major von Schmidt, who assembled his command at Oosterbeek to attack Arnhem's Rhine gate. Zastrow's second column, commanded by Major Karl Friedrich von Zglinitzki, formed in the Zijpe suburb. Zglinitzki received the task of attacking the redoubt on the windmill hill near the Rhine gate. He would then occupy the domineering outwork, position his artillery, and shell Arnhem. After Schmidt's column broke through the Rhine gate, Zglinitzki's men would occupy the defensive positions on the main wall and support Schmidt's drive to the Rhine bridge.

Oppen himself commanded the two left wing columns. His first would advance against the Jans gate while the second column assaulted the Velp gate. Colomb's detachment was to support these attacks by simultaneously advancing against Arnhem's main entrance: the Sabelpoort gate. Once an assault column breached its respective gate, it would leave a portion of its units at the gate in reserve and divide the remaining units into two groups. The first would proceed to the neighboring gate to support the assault there, while the second portion, led by the cavalry, would press to the inner city and pursue the French across the Rhine bridge. One or two pieces of artillery from the column's reserve should then move into the city. Two Landwehr cavalry regiments and the Leib Hussars remained ready to repulse any sortie.

Shortly before the attack commenced, Thümen's four battalions arrived to reinforce the columns. With the mist still lingering, Oppen gave the order for a simultaneous advance around 11:00 A.M. The Prussian artillery, which already had opened fire on Arnhem, moved with the infantry closer to the fort's outworks. At the entrenched camp, the Prussians penetrated but were repulsed. After renewing their assault, Bülow's troops drove Marie's four battalions from their entrenchments and into the fort. Charpentier barricaded Arnhem's gates and exhorted the garrison to defend the walls. Although his troop strength sufficed to hold Arnhem, Charpentier failed to determine the actual point of Bülow's assault, which unfolded on three roads. Prussian howitzers ignited a small blaze, thus adding to the garrison's confusion. As the Prussian columns approached the fort, indecision paralyzed the French. Oppen's feint attack on the left wing succeeded above all expectations. On the northeast side of Arnhem, Major Friedrich von Clausewitz, brother of the famous theorist, led Oppen's second column through the Velp gate as Oppen's first column entered the town through the northern Jans gate. South of the fort, Colomb's troops moved along the Rhine, unlimbered their horse artillery, and blasted through Arnhem's barricaded Sabelpoort gate. After meeting little resistance, all three assault columns entered Arnhem around the same time. In fact, Charpentier never considered an attack on the Velp gate, which he only defended with a handful of skirmishers. The Prussians pursued the French to the closest of the two internal gates that led to the inner city and its bridge.

On the right wing, where Charpentier had thrown the majority of his troops into a forward-lying redoubt, the contest became fierce. After a short bombardment, the 1st Kolberg Battalion led the assault of Zglinitzki's column by scaling the breastwork. With three battalions following, the men of the 1st charged the enemy with bayonets fixed and pressed forward in the direction of the Rhine gate. At the same time, Schmidt's men scaled Arnhem's east wall despite being raked by case-shot from the opposite bank of the lower Rhine. In brutal hand-to-hand combat, the Prussians severely wounded both Charpentier and Marie, giving the latter three deep bayonet gashes. A barely conscious Charpentier managed to escape, but the Prussians captured Marie. Taking command of the chaotic situation, Amey ordered a retreat and led the remains of four battalions across the lower Rhine virtually unopposed except by Colomb's two guns that unlimbered on a dike parallel to the river.

After driving the French from the outer defenses on their side of Arnhem, Zastrow's two columns continued toward the barricaded Rhine gate, which three French battalions defended from the ramparts. According to Macdonald's after-action report, these three battalions could not follow the retreat because the gatekeeper charged with servicing the portal that led to the bridge had closed the gate and disappeared with the keys. Surrounded and knowing they would receive no quarter, the French infantry made a heroic stand. Zastrow's men attempted to scale the gate, but before they succeeded, the French withdrew into the inner city. Soon the gate opened from the inside: Colomb's men had smashed through the Rhine gate on their side of the city. In accordance with their instructions, they had proceeded to the closest gate. All five Prussian columns were now advancing through the city toward the Rhine bridge. Trapped, the French used whatever cover they could find to wage a bloody street fight. Overwhelmed by numbers, some French soldiers managed to escape, but the majority were killed or captured. Bülow's troops took 1,024 prisoners and fifteen guns; both sides lost approximately 700 men who were wounded and/or killed. Thümen's 4th Brigade alone lost twenty-three officers and 222 soldiers. This engagement reduced the French 2nd Brigade to four battalions as a result of the destruction of two battalions of the 112th Line; one officer and seventy-six men returned to Nijmegen. Charpentier's wounds were so severe that on 13 December, Napoleon ordered Brayer, the commandant of the 35th Division, to take command of the 31st in place of Charpentier. General Jean-Raymond-Charles Bourke, the governor of Wesel, assumed command of the 35th Division.[23]

The French sacrifice was not in vain. During the intense street fighting, the Prussian columns became disordered and intermingled. The time Bülow needed to reorganize afforded Amey a considerable head start on the road to Nijmegen. In addition, the French had ignited the Rhine bridge. After more time was lost while Prussian pioneers extinguished the flames and repaired the damage, Bülow finally dispatched Oppen with three cavalry regiments and one horse battery southwest along the highway to Nijmegen with orders to hunt down the French stragglers. At the village of Elst, approximately halfway to Nijmegen, the retreating French column united with Bigarré's 1st Brigade, which issued from Nijmegen after word arrived of Bülow's assault on Arnhem. Bigarré deployed his battalions and occupied the bridge over the small Linge River. Both sides exchanged artillery rounds until dusk, when

Oppen decided to break off the attack. The Brandenburg dragoons formed an outpost chain to observe the French position at Elst, while Oppen led the rest of his column to Elden; Bülow's corps passed the night in and around Arnhem.[24] That evening a confident Bülow informed his wife that "in a couple of days, I will virtually be master of Holland. In this war, I have administered several harmful blows to Napoleon; of them, the seizure of Holland may be the worst."[25]

Prior to crossing the Dutch frontier, Bülow learned that Benckendorff's Cossacks had slipped by the French posts and entered Amsterdam.[26] To assure the Prussians a presence in the Dutch capital, Bülow dispatched two cavalry regiments to Amsterdam. He also learned that William Frederick would arrive in Amsterdam on 1 December. To greet the prince and secure further aid, Bülow sent a delegation consisting of Major Karl von Royer, Prince Anton von Radziwill, and Captain Friedreich von Burgsdorf.[27] At Amsterdam the Prussians received William Frederick's acclaim along with his insistence that Bülow continue the campaign. William Frederick also promised that a British force possibly as large as 10,000 men under Graham would land in Holland within one week. He pledged that aid of all sorts would be provided for the Prussian and British troops. The three Prussians then accompanied William Frederick to the palace on Dam Square in Amersterdam.[28] Born in 1772, William Frederick was the oldest son of the last *stadtholder* of the Netherlands, William V. Rather than *stadtholder*, William Frederick was proclaimed King William I on 2 December 1813 by representatives of the provisional government headed by van Hogendorp.[29]

As for the French, Bülow's drive on Arnhem increased their difficulties but did not affect their strategy. Both Macdonald and Molitor had decided to abandon their respective positions at Arnhem and Utrecht. From the sheer standpoint of numbers, however, Charpentier's insubordination cost Macdonald considerably. After losing almost 1,500 men at Arnhem, the marshal also discovered that desertion continued to erode his units. A frustrated Macdonald scrapped his plan to occupy the Betuwe in favor of reforming his cordon. He posted the 1st Brigade of the 31st Division at Kranenburg, halfway between Nijmegen and Kleve; the 2nd Brigade remained at Nijmegen. Two divisions of the II Cavalry Corps observed the Waal between Nijmegen and Ft. St. Andries, and a third observed the Rhine between Wesel and Nijmegen. Molitor withdrew his 1,400 men across the Lek River and fortified its crossings at Nieuwpoort, Vianen, and Culemborg. He did not remain in this new position for long. Learning that the Cossacks had reached Vianen and crossed the Lek at other points, Molitor judged his position untenable. After reinforcing the garrison of Gorinchem and charging the recently arrived Rampon with its defense, he continued his retreat across the Waal to the region between that river and the Meuse: the Bommelerwaard. Covered by a large river, supported on the left by Ft. Loevenstein and on the right by Ft. St. Andries,

Molitor believed he could hold this position for some time. He retracted his posts in the night of 1–2 December and crossed the Waal on the morning of the 2nd. Molitor remained on the northern bank before crossing the river with the rearguard at dusk on 3 December.[30]

Macdonald sought to reestablish his cordon to hold the Prussians at the lower Rhine. From Nijmegen he explained his intentions to Berthier in a report dated 2 December. He temporarily established the 31st Division between Wesel and Nijmegen to maintain the link with Molitor's troops through Ft. St. Andries on the Waal or Hertogenbosch if the general had to withdraw south of the Meuse. Macdonald insisted that Molitor take a purely defensive position in the Bommelerwaard and occupy the line of the Waal as far as Nijmegen. He also complained to Berthier over the civil authorities. The provisioning of the fortresses proceeded slowly; Nijmegen received only a fraction of its requisitions. "I shudder at the idea of having to recross the Meuse," he reveals to Berthier, "it has no point to defend and the fortresses are neither provisioned nor garrisoned. Wesel has more than 6,000 men, but only 100 cavalry; the governor has sent back the rest as useless. Jülich has a garrison of only 1,400 or 1,500 dismounted cavalry, who I had previously sent to Wesel, and few or no gunners. I do not know the quantity of provisions: those of Wesel are almost complete for 6,000 men for six months; I requested a report on this subject from the governor. Grave and Venlo have nothing, and as garrisons have depots composed of invalids. What a dire situation if the enemy attempts a serious passage!"[31]

In accordance with his original plan, Bülow continued west to Utrecht rather than follow up his victory at Arnhem with a drive across the lower Rhine to Nijmegen. To enlist Dutch participation, Utrecht, the key city of the northern provinces, was his logical objective. He believed its fall would enable the insurrection to spread south, which in turn would hasten the collapse of French control. His decision to advance to Utrecht rather than pursue the French to Nijmegen later received criticism from both contemporaries and historians. Had Bülow advanced in this direction rather than Utrecht, his detractors claim that Nijmegen, Grave, Hertogenbosch, and the Bommelerwaard would have fallen much faster. With the fall of these positions, the remaining French garrisons also would have been forced to capitulate and Bülow would have attained mastery over Holland "upon a single stroke." Bülow's critics argue that he should not have attempted to secure a main position in the Dutch interior. Such views cannot be substantiated. It is doubtful the French garrisons would have fallen simultaneously. Moreover, Macdonald would have attempted to meet the Prussians in the field rather than permit Bülow to advance to Nijmegen unopposed. Strategic consumption presents another consideration that critics ignore. In addition to detaching one-quarter of his infantry to besiege Wesel, Bülow had to post garrisons in each fort his men captured.[32]

Bülow arrived in Utrecht on 2 December and established communication with Benckendorff's cavalry thirty miles southeast at Rotterdam. Oppen's vanguard issued from Utrecht in four flying columns that advanced in several directions. One arrived at the fortified town of Vianen. Uninformed of the Prussian advance, the French post left the gate open; the Prussians simply marched in. A second column marched through Meerkerk toward Gorinchem, but a French forward post at the Arkel dam halted its advance. The Prussians withdrew to Leerdam and Asperen after a few hours of inconsequential skirmishing. A third column reached the Waal to observe Zaltbommel. The fourth column secured a position outside of Nijmegen and dispatched patrols along the Waal.[33] Behind this screen of forward posts, Bülow remained at Utrecht, where he rested his infantry and planned the next step of his campaign.

By early December, Bülow had forced the lines of the Ijssel and the Lek. The Prussians controlled the Ijssel forts of Deventer, Doesburg, and Zutphen; Arnhem on the lower Rhine; and Utrecht. Allied forces had driven the French to the line of the Waal – the border of Brabant. Prussian units patrolled along the length of the northern bank of the lower Rhine. Of the Dutch departments, only the Bouches de l'Escaut remained occupied by French troops. Bülow understood that the myriad of lakes, rivers, canals, and ditches of southern and eastern Holland would hinder movement and impede operations. In addition to the numerous forts and redoubts found in this region, the nature of this difficult terrain along with the high dams that connected the various bodies of water afforded the French multiple defensive positions.[34]

Elsewhere a British supply convoy commanded by Major General Herbert Taylor arrived at Scheveningen with 20,000 muskets on 3 December. Taylor was neither greeted by the Dutch authorities nor did he find anyone authorized to receive the arms. In addition, no empty building could be found to store the muskets, nor had the Dutch organized any units to utilize the weapons. British historian John Fortescue laments that "there was much shouting of Orange boven, and nothing more."[35] Bülow eventually used the unclaimed muskets to arm the Westphalian Landwehr. Of greater importance, 8,000 British soldiers under Graham landed on the island of Tholen, sixty miles southeast of Utrecht, on the 4th. Bülow and Graham quickly established communication and reached an understanding that produced cooperation throughout the campaign. For the moment, however, Graham postponed joint operations by insisting that his men needed rest after the Channel crossing.

While the British rested, representatives from The Haag traveled to Utrecht to welcome Bülow as the liberator of Holland. They invited him to Amsterdam, where a great celebration would be held in his honor. He politely declined, explaining that his responsibilities required direct supervision and no time could be spared for festivities. Actually, Bülow had become increasingly annoyed with the Dutch for failing to field troops and took this opportunity to voice his impatience. He hoped Dutch forces would be able to occupy the captured forts, thus sparing his corps from further strategic consumption. This appeared impossible, and thus he had to summon the few completed units of the newly raised Westphalian Landwehr. His displeasure did indeed reach William Frederick, who promised to fulfill as many of Bülow's requests as possible. As a token of his goodwill, he sent his sixteen-year-old son, Frederick, to begin his military career under the tutelage of the Prussian commander.[36]

Although William Frederick had the authority to summon his people to arms, he refused to issue any decree that might upset his subjects. "I used to complain of the want of enthusiasm in Spain," explains James Stanhope, a British officer who served under Graham, "but the [Dutch] people are as dull and motionless as their canals. The country is full of young men – more than I ever saw in any country, but with the exception of some cries of Orange boven, some orange ribbons that begin to fade, and some triumphal arches that savor too strongly of French Prefecture and old drilling to Napoleon's victories, no travelers would know there was such a thing as war, much less that their independence was at stake."[37] Mobilization proceeded at an extremely slow pace and the Dutch experienced many problems. The Prussians found the resumption of trade to be more important to the Dutch than raising forces to fight for their freedom. A disappointed Bülow exclaimed to the members of his entourage that "the Dutch may brew a sharp gin, but they cannot shoot sharply."[38]

Notwithstanding the sluggish Dutch war effort, Bülow believed the mere report of a Dutch levée would unsettle the French. He instructed his officers to circulate a rumor that the entire Dutch population would rise against the French. The Prussian commander sought to break their spirit with the threat of widespread popular revolt. Maintaining the psychological pressure, he issued an inflammatory proclamation to the Belgians on 10 December urging them to cast off the chains of slavery (Appendix H). To further undermine French morale, Bülow raised the Prussian and Orange flags from the highest steeples of his outposts. Nevertheless, insufficient manpower restricted Bülow's plan to invade Belgium to a war of words.

Added to the difficulties of arming the Dutch was Bülow's failure to free Borstell's 5th Brigade from the siege of Wesel. Happy to exercise a degree of independent command, Borstell remained active and effective. On 2 December, he launched a surprise assault that almost captured Wesel. Despite the enmity between the French and Italian soldiers who constituted Wesel's garrison, the Prussians could not break through the city's defenses. On the same day, one of Borstell's detachments occupied Düsseldorf, while a second unit crossed the Rhine and raided Neuss on the left bank, taking a French pontoon train, considerable military supplies, the public chest, 100 prisoners, and the eagle of the 150th Line.[39]

These small operations caused Macdonald concern over his right flank and diverted his attention from Bülow's movements. More important for the Allies, Borstell's sudden appearance on the Rhine alarmed the French and decisively shattered their control over the peoples of this region of "new France." Situated on the left bank of the Rhine across from Düsseldorf, Neuss was approximately twenty-two miles north of Köln and forty-seven miles south of Kleve. Lasting for two days, the raid sent a wave of terror across the Roer Department. Carpenters and laborers stopped work on the fortifications at Maastricht and fled, while peasants hid their farm animals from imperial officials. Private contractors who hauled supplies for French authorities disappeared along with their draft animals. Politically, the raid on Neuss had enormous repercussions on French control. The Germans, Belgians, and Dutch no longer considered the territory of the empire inviolable, and panic overcame the French who resided in the departments of new France and propagated their flight to old France. According to historian Lefebvre de Béhaine: "The [Prussian] officers and soldiers ... committed all the excesses possible; their brutality, their intemperance, their taste for rapine plunged their compatriots on the left bank into amazement; for two days and two nights the town was the scene of pillage and orgie. The Prussians extracted an estimated 41,500 francs not counting the value of the merchandise and material. The confidence in the government, the respect for the army, the authority of the functionaries received blows from which they neither had the time nor the resources to recover."[40] Beauchamp adds:

> The rumor that the barrier of the Rhine had been forced reverberated in Paris and at the court of Napoleon, and a simple operation, magnified by the imagination of newsmongers, was transformed into the actual passage of an army of 60,000 men. Napoleon himself exaggerated the danger, dreaming from then on to nationalize a war that was undertaken for the sake of his own ambition. The reporters, regulators of *l'esprit public*, commanded by the minister of police [Jean-Mary René Savary], received the express injunction to arouse national honor and to stir the French from their numbness. The minister, in a kind of animated harangue, advised that the danger no longer be concealed and to call to arms all Frenchmen for the defense of the country.[41]

News of the Prussian occupation of Düsseldorf and Neuss soon reached Köln, where an ill Sébastiani could not even mount his horse. He judged the situation to be grave. "If I believe the police report," he wrote to Berthier that evening, "this is an operation whose goal is to capture Köln and ... begin an offensive operation against Belgium. We are so dispersed and weak all over that it is to fear that the majority of our posts will be destroyed piece-meal in succession, if the enemy does not force us to quit the left bank entirely, which will inevitably happen if his entire army crosses."[42] On the 4th, Albert entered Neuss after the Prussians had ended their sack of the town and withdrew. That same day Sébastiani informed Berthier that the operation to retake Neuss lacked energy from the moment the French first learned of the Prussian raid. He attributed this to the officers, who themselves complained about their tired and ill soldiers. Tired and ill himself, the general concluded his letter with words that no one in Paris wanted to hear: "A line as extensive as the one the V Corps occupies can hardly be defended by the 4,000 bayonets that form this force; the enemy can easily capture our posts and his forces are way out of proportion compared to ours. One cannot hide that our officers serve half-heartedly and that it is difficult for them to provide the energy that is needed in the actual circumstances."[43]

Notwithstanding the benefits of Borstell's activity, Bülow simply did not want his brigade of battle-hardened veterans wasted on auxiliary operations. He believed the Allies possessed enough units in the theater – particularly Wintzingerode's Russian corps – to assume the siege of Wesel and relieve Borstell. To his disbelief, the Russians remained east of the Rhine; Wintzingerode had his own reason to be discontent. Just as Bülow lost direct command over his 5th Brigade, the crown prince of Sweden had detached Vorontsov's infantry corps from Wintzingerode's command for his own use. Although Wintzingerode still had 18,000 men at his disposal, the offended Russian commander refused to budge for anyone. After establishing his headquarters at Bremen, he spread his units throughout north Germany. While some liberated Oldenburg, others such as Benckendorff invaded Ostfriesland and Holland, while still others established posts along the Rhine to open communications with Bülow. According to one eyewitness, Pavel Sukhtelen, "Wintzingerode's headquarters felt that these posts hardly sufficed to cover his extensive cantonments in addition to observing Wesel and the movements of the French corps at Kleve."[44] Despite Benckendorff's success, Wintzingerode "firmly" denied his request to cross the Ijssel on the grounds that his detachment was too weak to operate in the midst of Holland's numerous fortresses and on terrain completely inadequate for cavalry operations. "But I already had taken my first step," recalled Benckendorff, "all of Amsterdam was on the move, the inhabitants begged us to come.... Thus I decided to disobey orders."[45]

Bülow persistently requested support from both Wintzingerode and Bernadotte. He finally achieved a minor victory on 3 December when Bernadotte ordered Wintzingerode to proceed to Wesel but left it to the Russian to decide whether he should continue to Holland. According to the crown prince's instructions, Wintzingerode could advance to Holland if French operations warranted his presence. Bernadotte assured him that his 18,000 men would suffice "to insure Holland's independence." If he did cross the Ijssel, Bernadotte ordered him to Deventer.[46] In his letter to Bülow, also written on the 3rd, Bernadotte assured him that to maintain Dutch enthusiasm he had definitively "ordered Wintzingerode to march to Deventer with 15,000 men. He will cover your left flank and will link his operations with yours."[47]

Wintzingerode apparently thought a winter in the Rhineland would be much more comfortable than the cold, damp forts of Holland and thus did not feel the situation warranted his presence. He ignored Bülow's requests and delayed his own movements considerably. An outraged Bülow accused the Russian of insubordination and dispatched complaints to Bernadotte and Allied headquarters. Bernadotte's own duplicity and misleading letters complicated matters. On 9 December the crown prince informed Bülow that the entire region between the Elbe and the Weser had been liberated from French control. He maintained that "nothing now prevents Wintzingerode's movement... he will march on Ems and then either to the Ijssel, if you have need of support, or to the Rhine if necessary."[48] On the same day, Bernadotte assured Wintzingerode that according to his own reports, the situation in Holland did not require the Russians to support Bülow. "Now that Bülow has reached Utrecht," wrote the crown prince, "I think, like you, that he has more than enough troops to liberate this country from Napoleon's control. Therefore, you will remain in your position."[49] While assuring Bülow that Wintzingerode had orders to march to his support, Bernadotte allowed the Russian to remain east of the Rhine. Reports from Russian forces in Holland also influenced Wintzingerode. To clear his names, Benckendorff informed Wintzingerode that the Allies had secured Holland.[50]

Bülow's urging finally prompted Wintzingerode to quit Bremen and move closer to the Rhine. He transferred his headquarters to Münster, but moved no further. Although Sukhtelen claims that Wesel's garrison "did not cease to ravage the countryside," Wintzingerode's troops did not reach the fortress until the end of December.[51] In fact, Benckendorff experienced difficulties dealing with Wintzingerode. After reaching Rotterdam on 28 November, Benckendorff received unwanted news. "At the moment when I desperately needed all my troops, Wintzingerode recalled Naryschkin's three Cossack regiments and one of Balabin's five regiments. He knew I entered Holland against his will and although he had to praise my actions because of my success, he attempted to undermine me as much as possible. Now I had to surrender almost half of my cavalry."[52] Although the Allies needed additional manpower to expand their operations, as far as Wintzingerode was concerned Bülow and Benckendorff were on their own.

From Gorinchem to Köln Macdonald's "flimsy" cordon, as he described it to Berthier, began to collapse. On the evening of 3 December, the marshal received a report over the events at Neuss as well as the incredible claim that an Allied force of 10,000 men had crossed the Rhine at Düsseldorf. Macdonald immediately ordered the 31st Division and the II Cavalry Corps to concentrate at Kleve. He also instructed Molitor to march the majority of his 1,400 men to Nijmegen to replace the 31st Division and to provide an adequate garrison for Grave on the Meuse. Macdonald reached Kleve on the 4th only to be exasperated by conflicting reports. According to some, the Allies had evacuated Neuss and recrossed the Rhine. Others claimed the enemy continued to cross the Rhine in barges and had started work on a pontoon bridge at Düsseldorf.

When Macdonald penned his brief to Berthier at 10:00 P.M., he had yet to receive reports from Albert, Sébastiani, and Arrighi. The news he did receive was not good: Molitor reported that he could not extend his line to Nijmegen. The need to support Rampon at Gorinchem required Molitor to keep his handful of soldiers concentrated in the Bommelerwaard.[53] A stymied Macdonald realized the planned concentration at Kleve was out of the question. Uncertain whether an actual army corps crossed the Rhine in the Düsseldorf–Köln region, and, knowing that Bülow's troops would soon reach the Waal, Macdonald faced being encircled and crushed between the Meuse and the Rhine. "Oh my country," he wrote Molitor, "what gloomy and distressing omens! It is with weeping eyes that I write you, general. What future is there if the enemy actually has crossed in force. One stumbles around the Ijssel, at Arnhem and Utrecht, while France is exposed all along the Rhine."[54]

Searching for a solution to his mounting problems, the marshal decided to concentrate his "army" between Geldern and Krefeld, twenty-five miles south of Kleve. He planned to distribute a total of 400 men from the 31st Division among the Rhine crossings at Nijmegen, Kranenburg, and Emmerich. This reduced the eight battalions of the 31st Division to approximately 1,600 men, some of whom still could not be considered combat-ready. In his woeful report to Paris, the marshal stated that "200–300 [soldiers] are without weapons; they are accustomed to falling out, checking into the hospitals, or remaining in the rear."[55]

During the course of 5 December, Macdonald finally received some news. Reports arrived from Albert, Sébastiani, and Arrighi that clarified the situation, especially regarding the actual nature of the enemy operation at Neuss. This enabled Macdonald to hold his position at Nijmegen and countermand the ordered concentration further up the Rhine. Charpentier's 31st Division and Bordessoulle's II Cavalry Corps returned to Nijmegen which, incidentally, the emperor wanted held at all costs.[56] Regardless of the "good" news concerning Neuss, Macdonald could not be reconciled and drafted a searing yet truthful epistle to Berthier:

> The event that has just occurred demonstrates the enemy's audacity as well as how poorly we keep guard. It is the same all over: he becomes more enterprising and assembles more and more forces. I do not know where he will stop, and we cannot stop him with our weak resources on this line, which will be cut and difficult to hold; one dash across the Rhine will bring the enemy straight to the

Meuse. I have tried in vain to double the courage ... but this is like preaching in the desert. It is absolutely necessary that the emperor knows the truth, it is worth hearing. There is a great deal of discouragement, everyone is tired of war, the continuous marches and movements. Those who the emperor has showered with advancement and awards are the first who desire to enjoy them in tranquility and hope for nothing else. The officers lack everything, suffer, and are discontent; the soldiers, hardly well-groomed, discouraged by the talk they hear, do not fight and throw down their weapons. If one tells the emperor otherwise, one will only flatter and wrong him. His Majesty must not deceive himself, he only has men, not soldiers. The reward is worn out, it is necessary to put the fear of punishment into each who disregards his duty. Until now the emperor has been kind and lenient; it is necessary to show severity, without which all the resilience of this already exhausted army will shatter altogether.[57]

Purposely vague, Macdonald avoided launching accusations at individual officers in this letter. Instead he censured Albert, Arrighi, and Sébastiani in his private correspondence with each general. "I remained without news from Köln up until now," he wrote to Albert, commander of the V Corps's 1st Division, "and fell prey to all of the exaggerations that quickly spread ... I hope this lesson will lead to greater attention in the future." Macdonald reproached Arrighi for failing to send confirmed reports: "I have been in great perplexity by the exaggeration of the reports because no general officer took the trouble to go to the scene nor to send superior officers to ascertain the truth and the forces of the enemy." The marshal displayed leniency toward the ailing Sébastiani, recommending procedural improvements for observing and defending possible points of passage across the Rhine.[58] In a letter of 7 December, Berthier instructed Macdonald to investigate the conduct of the French officers at Neuss and conduct a military tribunal. In addition, he added that as commander in chief, it was Macdonald's responsibility to ensure the adherence to regulations and duties of all officers and to punish the negligent.

Two days later, Napoleon himself berated both Sébastiani and Arrighi for dereliction of duty and lack of vigor. Arrighi in particular earned the emperor's ire for failing to guard Neuss. Napoleon attributed this negligence to the fact that the wives of many French officers had taken advantage of what appeared to be a suspension of hostilities to join their husbands. Beginning with Arrighi's own wife, Napoleon demanded that the women depart immediately. "Order the duke of Padoue [Arrighi] to have his wife depart six hours after receiving your order," the emperor instructed Berthier. "You will tell him of my discontent and that he sets a bad example for the army." Napoleon's attention was soon absorbed by events of greater importance and Macdonald did nothing to punish the officers commanding the Neuss garrison.[59]

At Paris the emperor grew increasingly disgusted with the mistakes of his subordinates in the Netherlands. To him it appeared that both his civil and military officials simply gave up. A 2 December report from Clarke proposing the evacuation of the fortified Dutch port of Hellevoetsluis on the isle of Voorne particularly frustrated him.[60] That same day Napoleon named General Charles-Mathieu-Isidore Decaen commander in chief of all French forces in Belgium.[61] Napoleon hoped Decaen could organize the Army of the North with the troops of the 17th and 31st Military Districts, the I Corps, and the National Guard of Antwerp. At Antwerp itself Lebrun would organize the I Corps in part from Roguet's 3rd Young Guard Tirailleur Division and Lefebvre-Desnouettes 2nd Guard Cavalry Division. Regarding the National Guard of Antwerp, Napoleon expected Rampon to double its number to 6,000 Guardsmen.[62] With this paper tiger of 50,000 men, Decaen would cover Belgium and retake Holland by maneuvering between Utrecht, Gorinchem, Breda, Bergen-op-Zoom, and Antwerp. For the immediate task at hand, Napoleon directed him to Gorinchem to guard the line of the Waal in conjunction with Macdonald, whom Decaen would be subordinate to in all joint operations. The emperor wanted this line held in the expectation that French forces would soon resume the offensive. For this purpose, Decaen had to prepare the bridgehead over the Leck, which was formed by the works at Schoonhoven and Nieuwpoort on the northern and southern banks respectively. Finally, Napoleon ordered the isle of Voorn with the forts of Brielle and Hellevoetsluis, the isles of Goeree and Overflaekee, and the coast of the Bouches-de-la-Meuse Department with the fortress of Willemstad placed in a state of defense to prevent a British landing.[63]

Typically, the orders from Paris remained far behind events and Napoleon's expectations and estimations fell woefully short of the actual state of affairs. Arriving at Antwerp on 4 December, Decaen found it impossible to comply with the emperor's instructions. That same day, the British landed on the isle of Tholen; Lebrun already had evacuated Brielle and Hellevoetsluis. Rampon had moved to Gorinchem with the 1st and 2nd Regiments of the Antwerp National Guard, but Molitor already withdrew the troops of the 17th Military District from Nieuwpoort to the Bommelerwaard. The troops of the 31st Military District amounted to Ambert and his staff; the I Corps continued to slowly assemble in Antwerp. After surveying the situation, Decaen decided against a counteroffensive. He requested new instructions from Paris, concentrated his forces at Antwerp, and opted to hold the key fortresses in northern Brabant that guarded the roads to Belgium and particularly Antwerp: Breda, Gorinchem, Geertruidenberg, Bergen-op-Zoom, and Hertogenbosch.[64]

Decaen remained busy in Antwerp overseeing the arming and provisioning of the fortresses. He obtained from Admiral Edouard-Thomas de Missiessy several companies of native French marines and sailors to reinforce the garrisons of Breda and Bergen-op-Zoom. To maintain communication between Breda and Gorinchem, he formed under Ambert's command a flying column of 900 marines and conscripts supported by a half battery of artillery.[65] In a move perhaps designed to assist Decaen, Napoleon named Lebrun governor of Antwerp on 7 December. Although subordinate to Decaen, Lebrun's command extended over Breda, Bergen-op-Zoom, Willemstad, and the forts on the isles that guarded the mouth of the Scheldt, all of which the emperor considered to be part of greater Antwerp. Napoleon also placed 4,200 National Guardsmen from native French departments under his command for use in Belgium.[66]

The Allied presence on the Waal also convinced Napoleon that Macdonald needed considerable reinforcements. "Everything indicates the war has become serious on the side of Holland," he wrote on the 4th.[67] The emperor instructed Clarke to organize the equipment of the XI, V, and I Corps and have it join the respective corps at Nijmegen, Köln, and Gorinchem. He felt these three corps could reconquer Holland and restore the cordon along the lower Rhine.[68] Bonaparte also made arrangements to send more combat power to Macdonald. On 5 December, Berthier issued a myriad of orders designed to shift units to the lower Rhine. According to his letter to Macdonald, 5,000 reinforcements would be dispatched to Köln: 4,000 for the V Corps and 1,000 for the XI Corps.[69] The commandant of the 25th Military District, Merle, also received good news: three battalions from Morand's IV Corps as well as four additional battalions – a total of 2,020 men – would march to Maastricht shortly. To increase Maastricht's garrison further, Berthier authorizd Merle to summon all available men from the depots in Liège and Namur.[70] These measures did little to comfort Macdonald, who judged it necessary to direct Decaen's operations owing to the delay caused by the time required for information to pass to and from Paris. Coordinating operations along a line that stretched from Antwerp to Andernach on the Rhine taxed the weary marshal. Although Macdonald took on this responsibility, he requested that his command be divided in half.[71] On 12 December, Berthier shared the marshal's letter with Napoleon, who offered no response.[72]

Meanwhile the political situation in the Netherlands and the increasing Allied cooperation did not bode well for the French. On 6 December, Bülow and Boyen journeyed to The Haag to meet with William Frederick, Benckendorff, and Taylor. According to Boyen, the Prussians received a hero's welcome. "It is impossible for me to describe the tumultuous joy that now reigns over Holland," Boyen reported to Hardenberg, "we were lifted from our carriage, carried upon the streets, one touched our clothes as if they were sacred, miles of the country road were illuminated in the evening for the continuation of our journey and the inhabitants displayed an enthusiasm during the day that you could not attribute to the phlegmatic Dutch unless you had seen it personally." This reception soothed Bülow's despondence over the slack Dutch mobilization. In the meetings with his allies, he revealed his intention to invade Belgium as quickly as possible. Benckendorff, who had cordial relations with Bülow, agreed to take the French posts on Bülow's right flank that

extended across the Waal from Dordrecht and south beyond Breda. Frederick
William reiterated his promise to expedite the training of Dutch recruits so
that they could besiege the rearward lying French garrisons.[73] The British
also pledged to cover Bülow's right by advancing along the coast to assail
Missiessy's fleet at Antwerp. Bülow wanted to take advantage of this exceptional degree of cooperation and enthusiasm; no more time could be wasted,
he had to continue his operation.

Benckendorff wasted no time. On 7 December, he embarked his troops
at Dordrecht and sailed upstream the single body of water, the Merwede,
which was formed by the junction of the Waal and the Meuse. He drove
the French from the post at Werkendam, three miles from Gorinchem, and
landed on the left bank of the Waal on the next day, the 8th. Benckendorff
then turn south toward Breda, bypassing Geertruidenberg which, along with
Willemstad, he left to be observed by Dutch insurgents. The Russians cut
all communication between Gorinchem and Breda. Fearing for Antwerp,
Decaen authorized Ambert to evacuate Breda if the Allies arrived in force;
Colonel Antoine-Vincent-Jules-Louis Legrand received instructions to evacuate Willemstad. On 9 December, the Russians reached Breda. Ambert held
his position throughout the day, but concern over the mood of the inhabitants prompted him to retreat during the night. On the 10th, he continued to Brasschaat, fifteen miles south of Breda and eight miles northeast of
Antwerp. Legrand likewise evacuated Willemstad, leaving intact the artillery
and thirty-two gun boats. Colomb's Streifkorps joined Benckendorff at Breda
on the 12th. The Russian commander did not feel comfortable leading his
small force to Antwerp and thus decided to remain in Breda. Yet, Colomb
raided the region east of Antwerp from 14 to 20 December. The Prussian
made quite a nuisance of himself by stopping convoys, intercepting couriers, dispersing conscripts, sparking riots, and terrifying French authorities.
Elsewhere British troops reached Willemstad on the 13th, while the commandant of Geertruidenberg surrendered to the Russians on the condition
that his 100 conscripts be granted free passage to Antwerp.[74] On this day the
Russians, Prussians, and British gained control of Dutch Brabant, thus threatening Antwerp and flanking the French lines of defense on the Waal and Meuse
Rivers.[75]

Farther west, Bülow completed his plans for the crossing of the Waal on the
8th. Situated on the right bank of the river, the fortress of Gorinchem served
as the primary French base in this region. Purportedly occupied by 2,000
to 3,000 men, Napoleon valued its possession.[76] To envelope Gorinchem, the
Prussians had to seize the Bommelerwaard. According to Bülow's plan, Krafft
would invest Gorinchem with five battalions, while Oppen surprised the garrisons of the smaller forts in the Bommelerwaard. Reports indicated they were
either weakly held or had been abandoned. By taking the Bommelerwaard,
the Prussians could cross the Meuse and penetrate the heart of Belgium.

Although the moment had arrived to continue the offensive, Bülow's fire gave way to caution. He believed that strong French forces still occupied the forts in the Bommelerwaard.[77] Intercepted letters suggested otherwise, but Bülow remained wary. He feared a diversion against his left flank by Macdonald, whose forces remained between Wesel and Nijmegen. In view of Macdonald's position, he reconsidered a plan that would require him to divide his corps for operations against several small forts. Bülow also overestimated French troop strength and experienced difficulties ascertaining their positions and resources. He continued to hope that more time would allow the Dutch insurrection to spread south and facilitate his operations. With these considerations in mind, the Prussian commander postponed his offensive and waged a letter campaign. He demanded that Borstell be relieved from the siege of Wesel and that Wintzingerode accelerate his march. Bülow also suggested that the Allied units posted in central Germany cross the Rhine between Düsseldorf and Koblenz to threaten Macdonald.[78]

Bülow's hesitation allowed Molitor and Macdonald to regroup and somewhat coordinate a defense for the Bommelerwaard. Molitor informed the marshal that the Allies appeared to be preparing an offensive to complete the conquest of Holland and penetrate Belgium.[79] Concern over his left wing and the need to support Molitor's troops, whom he referred to as "brigands and assassins," prompted Macdonald to move one battalion nineteen miles west of Nijmegen to Wamel on the southern bank of the Waal.[80] To maintain communication with Molitor's units, Macdonald instructed the battalion commander to send a detachment of 100 men seven miles further west to occupy Ft. St. Andries on the road to Zaltbommel.[81] Three days later on 11 December, an alarmed Molitor warned Macdonald that Breda had fallen and the Allies appeared to be headed to Hertogenbosch, which the French garrison evacuated on the 12th after the inhabitants revolted.[82] At this point Molitor foolishly divided his forces. Leaving General Claude-Ursule Gency with 1,000 men in the Bommelerwaard, Molitor led 400 infantry and gendarmes to reoccupy Hertogenbosch. To support Molitor, Macdonald dispatched a column of 300 infantry, 100 cavalry, and two guns under General François-Isidore Wathiez to Hertogenbosch.[83] However, Wathiez abruptly stopped at Grave upon encountering the fugitive garrison coming from Hertogenbosch. Falling prey to the Allied campaign of misinformation, Wathiez feared continuing his mission and opted to remain at Grave until he received new orders from the marshal. In no mood to indulge his subordinate, Macdonald berated the general and ordered him to leave his infantry and artillery in Grave and join Molitor with his cavalry. Perhaps shaken by Macdonald's reproaches, Wathiez led his entire column to Hertogenbosch, where he joined Molitor. Apparently Macdonald did not reprimand him but instead approved a plan jointly submitted by Molitor and Wathiez to drive toward Breda.[84] Ever the realist, Macdonald could not bring himself to paint an optimistic picture of the situation even for the emperor's consumption: "Terror is spreading all over," he bemoans to Berthier on the 13th, "it is even amplified by the authorities and the customs agents who have abandoned their posts. Those on the Waal, from Nijmegen to Ft. St. Andries, have all fled."[85]

After twelve days passed without the arrival of any positive news regarding reinforcements, Bülow decided to continue the offensive by securing the Bommelerwaard. For 12 December Oppen received orders to divide his command into two columns. The first, five battalions, three cavalry regiments, and one battery commanded by Colonel von Sydow and accompanied by Oppen, would cross the Waal, secure Zaltbommel, then cross the Meuse and advance to Hertogenbosch. After detaching some units to invest Gorinchem, his second column under Krafft – five battalions and one cavalry regiment – would proceed to the Mervede. Once across the Mervede, Krafft would take the strongholds of Werkendam, Loevenstein, and Heusden. Krafft's column would thus envelop the Bommelerwaard and sever the French line of retreat to Breda and Antwerp. The Prussians also hoped to invest Gorinchem on both banks of the Waal. Thümen's 4th Brigade received orders to take Tiel on the right bank of the Waal, and the 3rd Brigade, temporarily commanded by Col. von Sjöholm II, would advance to the Lek and strike pontoon bridges at Vianen and Culemborg to support Sydow.[86]

Situated 700 to 800 yards from the left or southern bank of the Waal, Zaltbommel was small but formidable and could only be reached by boat. A solid rampart with seven bastions protected Zaltbommel's 600 houses from an attack by land, and an adequate wall enclosed the town along the riverbank. Although the French had either sailed off or sunk all craft in the vicinity, Oppen's scouts found an adequate number of vessels further upstream beyond the French-held Ft. St. Andries. Obtaining the boats proved to be fairly easy, yet they had to be sailed passed the fort. Located on a narrow spit of land, Ft. St. Andries commanded the eastern end of the Bommelerwaard. Little did the Prussians know that only thirty French soldiers occupied the fort rather than 100 as Macdonald had ordered. The fort itself was in such a state of disrepair that it could only be considered a post.[87] Regardless, Zglinitzki received the task of taking the position. Early on 13 December, he set sail from Varik with one Fusilier battalion and two Grenadier companies loaded in barges. A strong current carried them downstream the Waal, whose width on the eastern end of the Bommelerwaard averaged 700 to 800 yards. As the Prussians neared Ft. St. Andries, they lost control of the boats. Some moved too close to the fort, offering excellent targets for the small French post that did not hesitate to open fire. Under small-arms fire the Prussians labored to reach the safety of the opposite bank. After this inauspicious beginning, Zglinitzki postponed the attack, yet Bülow ordered him to make a second attempt on the following morning.

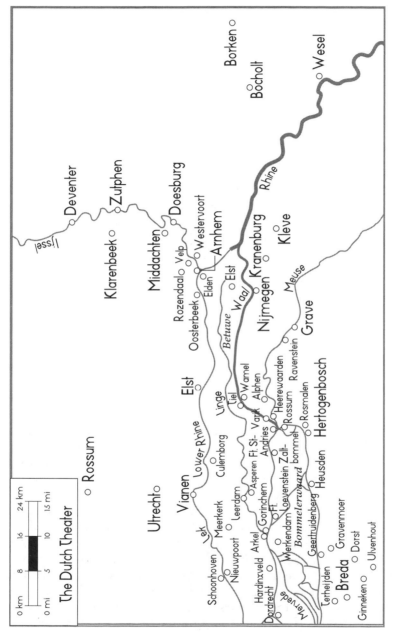

Map 4. The Dutch Theater.

171

No longer willing to delay his operations, particularly in view of Benck- endorff's success, Bülow ordered Oppen to attack Zaltbommel likewise on the 14th. Oppen's men found smaller boats further upstream the Waal and trans- ported them overland. To cover the assault on Zaltbommel, Bülow erected a massive battery of sixty guns on a dam facing the fort. In the cold hour just before dawn on 14 December, the lead boat slipped into the current with Oppen at its head. As the Prussian flotilla approached the opposite bank, Oppen sent ahead a small boat to reconnoiter the beach. Upon returning, his scouts reported that people lined the shore. Minutes slipped by as the Prussians worked to hold their boats steady against the current and Oppen contemplated his next move. He wasted too much time; dawn broke, and the surprised Prussians observed several boats approaching them. As the sky began to gray, the shouts of Orange boven sprang from both the shore and the approaching boats. To Oppen's relief, the long-awaited but thus far unseen Dutch insurgents stood along the shore and manned the approaching vessels. He learned that Gency's troops had evacuated Zaltbommel during the night. After the first wave of Prussians landed, the boats, assisted by the Dutch ves- sels, returned to the right bank and ferried the remaining troops, who were joined by Bülow.

Upriver Zglinitzki's detachment entered Ft. St. Andries after the French post withdrew to Wamel. The Prussians could not enjoy their success for long before Molitor's units, retreating eastward along the Bommelerwaard and seeking refuge in St. Andries, reached Rossum. Skirmishing broke out in the town, and the Prussians gradually retreated to the fort. Shortly after the fighting in Rossum began, the crackle of musket fire also could be heard from the direction of Heerewaarden. Coming from Nijmegen, General Nicolas- Marin Thiry, the commanding officer of the II Cavalry Corps's 2nd Division of Light Cavalry, arrived in Wamel with the 22nd Light Cavalry Regiment. Despite the fatigue of his horses, he launched a surprise attack on two of Zglinitzki's Grenadier companies as they attempted to establish a forward post near Heerewaarden. The appearance of French forces outside at Rossum forced Zglinitzki to abandon the grenadiers to their fate. Unfortunately for the grenadiers, the French managed to kill the majority of the officers at the beginning of the attack. Leaderless, the men of the Elbe Regiment, many of whom had seen service in the ranks of the French army, surrendered. Only one officer and fifty men escaped; the French killed or captured almost 300.

Inside Ft. St. Andries Zglinitzki received an unnerving communiqué from Bülow: the French units retreating east across the Bommelerwaard would probably reach the fort during the night. By 1:00 A.M. on the 15th the numer- ous bivouac fires around St. Andries led the anxious Prussians to believe that as many as five French battalions camped near the fort. With Thiry's cav- alry approaching from the east, Gency unlimbered his howitzers to lob shells into St. Andries starting at 8:00 in the morning. He halted his bombardment to summon the Prussians to surrender. Zglinitzki's refusal prompted the French to move their artillery closer. Discouraged by Zglinitzki's answer, which Gency interpreted as a sign that the Prussian expected reinforcements, the French general established a few cavalry posts and started to withdraw. Just as he disengaged, Bülow arrived from Zaltbommel with Oppen's vanguard. The appearance of this large enemy force prompted Gency to retreat all the way to Hertogenbosch, where he reunited with Molitor; Thiry returned to Wamel. Although the Allies had yet to sever communications between Hertogenbosch and Nijmegen, the loss of the Bommelerwaard opened the roads leading to the Belgian interior between Antwerp and the Meuse Valley.

Oppen led the main body of the advance guard across the Meuse on the 15th and pressed on toward Hertogenbosch. Garrisoned by Molitor's small force, the Prussians failed take the fort on the next day. Bülow also moved Sjöholm's 3rd Brigade closer to Gorinchem and Thümen's 4th Brigade east to Tiel, ten miles from Nijmegen. At Zaltbommel, where Bülow established his headquarters, Prussian engineers bridged the Waal, yet the river's strong current threatened to wreck the pontoons at any moment. On the opposite end of the Bommelerwaard, Krafft crossed the Mervede at Hardinxveld on 14 December, but a French sortie from Gorinchem delayed his advance until he could organize his battalions and repulse the attack. Following the action at Hardinxveld, Krafft continued to the forts at Werkendam, Loevenstein, and Heusden. Barely defended, he managed to disperse the small French detachments in succession and then proceeded toward Hertogenbosch from the northwest.[88]

Bülow's success multiplied the difficulties Macdonald could expect to encounter if he attempted to cooperate with the French generals in Belgium to defend Antwerp and to close the highways leading to old France. Macdonald's problems increased by the hour. After renouncing the planned operation on Breda, Molitor and Wathiez prepared to abandon Hertogenbosch and retreat to Grave, just a few miles southwest of Nijmegen.[89] On the 15th Molitor departed Hertogenbosch and led 1,000 men to Grave; the general himself went to Nijmegen.[90] Incredibly, the future marshal of France left behind 500 men to garrison Hertogenbosch's Papenbrill Citadel even though the available provisions could sustain the troops for only five days![91] With the Prussians approaching, these men were as good as lost. In light of his severe troop shortage, Macdonald could ill afford to have manpower wasted in such a thoughtless manner. Wanting to make one last effort to reestablish a foothold on the Bommelerwaard, Macdonald ordered Exelmans to retake Ft. St. Andries at any price. Learning from Thiry that considerable Prussian reinforcements already had reached the fort, Exelmans halted the operation on the 16th. Although Gency's retreat exposed Exelmans's left flank and provided the general with a degree of justification, Macdonald once again observed a subordinate's failure to execute his directives.

Figure 11. General Friedrich Wilhelm von Bülow (1755–1816). Commandant of the Prussian III Corps.

Mentally exhausted from weeks of enormous stress, the marshal's resolve began to crumble after the Prussians breached the Meuse. Trapped between this river and the Rhine, the positions of the XI and V Corps appeared untenable if not perilous. Withdrawing from the Rhine seemed his only recourse. From Kleve he instructed Sébastiani to deposit the infantry of the V Corps in Jülich and to lead the field artillery and the III Cavalry Corps either to Aachen or Koblenz to unite with the division of the VI Corps. Sébastiani, who had complained over the problems caused by disseminating the troops along the Rhine, now griped about having to coordinate the movements to assemble the infantry at Jülich and the cavalry at Aachen. "You tell me of your situation, but have you thought of mine?" responded Macdonald.[92]

With possession of Utrecht and the Bommelerwaard, the first and second phases of Bülow's invasion were marked by success, yet he remained discontent.[93] He forwarded requests to Frankfurt to hasten the relief of Borstell's brigade at Wesel.[94] Bülow insisted that his 5th Brigade had to rejoin the corps before he could cross the Belgian frontier and suggested that either Wintzingerode or General Johann Adolf Thielemann's Saxon division assume the siege of Wesel.[95] Bülow's success and initiative instigated complaints at Allied headquarters over Bernadotte's refusal to support the Prussian general. "It was strongly desired," notes Burghersh, "by many persons belonging to

Figure 12. General Ferdinand Fedorovich Wintzingerode (1770–1818). Russian corps commander.

the headquarters of Frankfurt, that the Russian, Prussian, and Hanoverian corps should be taken from his army: these councils, however, were not listened to."[96] Castlereagh became so tired of Bernadotte's indifference toward British interests in the Low Countries that he contemplated suspending Sweden's subsidy unless the crown prince directly participated in the campaign. "We are all in arms here against the prince-royal," he wrote Stewart on 24 December.[97]

Bülow's letter campaign caused enough controversy to induce Bernadotte to remind Wintzingerode on 18 December that "nothing now opposes your operations, therefore, place your corps in march on the road to Düsseldorf, and send a detachment to observe the garrison of Wesel. Inform Borstell of the day of your arrival. I have encouraged him to concentrate on your right and to reunite with Bülow." In an order to Borstell that same day, Bernadotte wrote: "Wintzingerode is on the march to Düsseldorf. As soon as he arrives, you will yield your positions to him and rejoin Bülow." The crown prince assured Borstell that the Russian corps would arrive no later than 26 December.[98] Disregarding Bernadotte's orders, the Russian continued to do nothing.

As the 200,000 men of the Bohemian army approached the Alsatian frontier, Napoleon's attention remained fixed on the Low Countries and the continued setbacks of his lieutenants. Making personnel changes, he still planned to assemble a significant force – the Army of the North – to deny the Allies any gains in Belgium and eventually drive them from Holland. On 21 December, the emperor recalled Decaen to Paris and appointed General Nicholas-Joseph Maison commander of all French forces in Belgium. Described as "already distinguished among the young generals destined to succeed the old marshals," Maison assumed command of the Army of the North, which consisted of only the I Corps.[99] He fortified the defensive positions that protected Antwerp, yet the squadron anchored in its port concerned Napoleon, who ordered the city to be extensively provisioned. Maison also received instructions to build an entrenched camp that could hold a corps of approximately 30,000 to 40,000 infantry and 6,000 cavalry of the Imperial Guard.[100] The reorganization of the Guard provided additional units for the emperor to send north to support French forces in Belgium and on the lower Meuse in particular. Napoleon planned to have a corps of 30,000 Guard in this camp by early January. The emperor appointed Marshal Oudinot to command this corps as soon as his health permitted. Although undesignated, the corps itself would consist of the 4th, 5th, and 6th Young Guard Divisions, which were already in Antwerp and together mustered 10,000 men.[101] On 17 December Mortier led the 4,800 men of the 1st Old Guard Division from Trier toward Namur, where he arrived on the 26th; the 2,400 troopers of the 1st Guard Cavalry Division likewise proceeded to Namur.[102]

Napoleon insisted that under no circumstances could the "Army of the North" be cut off from Antwerp.[103] He also termed the recapture of Breda the prerequisite for establishing an entrenched camp at Antwerp.[104] The emperor believed the Allies would attempt to take Antwerp, but could not gain an accurate assessment of their troop strength. "If we are superior to the enemy," he wrote Clarke on 25 December, "we will drive him across the Rhine; if we are inferior to him (and we are certainly inferior to him in cavalry if he moves large forces there), he will probably turn Antwerp by the right through the Kempen, threatening to reach Malines and Brussels, and place the army at Antwerp in a difficult position." To prevent this, Napoleon needed additional manpower to fill the ranks of the Guard and provide the forces for the entrenched camp at Antwerp. "I thus regard this camp as unassailable," he continues, "25,000 or 35,000 men will be protected there from an attack by an army 50,000 or 60,000 men."[105] Despite the clear indications that Schwarzenberg's massive army was preparing to drive across the Upper Rhine, the emperor allocated more forces in the opposite direction in the hopes of holding Belgium and retaking Holland.

From Paris also came demands to attack the Prussians and clear the Bommelerwaard of enemy forces. For this task Lefebvre-Desnouettes received instructions to move his 2nd Guard Cavalry Division to Gorinchem. The emperor also directed Roguet's 3rd Young Guard Tirailleur Division to retake Breda and restore communications with Gorinchem.[106] Although Roguet did not have enough experience for this mission, Napoleon attached "great importance to the recapture of Breda and the reestablishment of communications with Gorinchem."[107] "As for military operations," he notes, "the first objective is to retake Breda."[108]

On the evening of the 16th, the same day that a gloomy Macdonald ordered Sébastiani to withdraw the V Corps from the Rhine, the marshal received Berthier's 13 December letter that outlined these plans. According to the view from Paris, the Prussian concentration at Utrecht and the recently landed British corps posed too great of a threat to Antwerp. Typical of imperial headquarters and indicative of Napoleon's failure to attain accurate figures, Berthier considerably underestimated the size of the Allied forces operating in the Low Countries. Following the emperor's instructions, Berthier informed Macdonald that Bülow had only 8,000 to 9,000 men at Utrecht. He added the British could not have more than 4,000 troops, and made no mention of either the Russians or the Dutch insurgents, but commented that the Prussian IV Corps was well to the east at Magdeburg and Bernadotte's Swedes faced Hamburg. As always, imperial headquarters made sure to exaggerate the numbers of French troops involved in the operation: Roguet with 10,000 Guard infantry and Lefebvre-Desnouettes with 2,000 Guard cavalry would retake Breda. To support the counteroffensive, Berthier instructed Macdonald to unite the 31st Division and the II Cavalry Corps with Molitor's troops and advance west from Nijmegen to Hertogenbosch. "The moment of crisis has passed," concludes Berthier's attempt to reinvigorate Macdonald, adding that "80,000 uniformed, armed, and equipped conscripts are in march to reinforce the regiments of the various army corps; 300,000 other conscripts are heading to the regimental depots."[109]

Napoleon purposefully magnified the estimates of his own troops to mislead the enemy, encourage his corps commanders, and impress the public. Bonaparte's practice of waging a calculated campaign of misinformation has been criticized as proof that he remained out of touch with the actual situation and fell victim to his own deceptions. Such a charge fails to recognize the genius of Napoleon. His campaign of misinformation can be justified in light of pursuing the previously stated three short-term objectives. Napoleon's fault lies in the long-term negative effect this propaganda had on his subordinates. Although promised forces congruent to the stated figures, it always seemed that when reinforcements did arrive the numbers fell far short of those anticipated. This undermined the French command structure on all levels and, during the invasion of France in particular, increased the marshals' confusion.

For the 17th Macdonald instructed Molitor to reconnoiter toward Hertogenbosch with Wathiez's cavalry detachment.[110] Molitor patrolled as far as Rosmalen, three miles northeast of Hertogenbosch on the road to Nijmegen. It appeared the Prussians were regrouping in the Bommelerwaard. Infantry, cavalry, and artillery remained at Ft. St. Andries; detachments occupied Heusden and Breda.[111] Based on this information, Macdonald prepared to lead his troops personally to Hertogenbosch to support the Guard's counteroffensive against Breda. He assembled the few troops that he could spare for the mission: two regiments of the II Cavalry Corps, two battalions of the 31st Division, and one battery received orders to assemble at Grave on the 19th. Thiry, with Exelmans's remaining regiment and Bigarré with six battalions of the 31st Division, would guard the Waal and the Rhine from Ft. St. Andries to Wesel.[112] Sébastiani and Arrighi received orders to hold their positions on the Rhine from Wesel to Koblenz.[113] Although not yet broken in spirit, Macdonald perhaps described his own state of mind in a letter to Berthier on the eve of his operation: "the evil mood of the land and the alarming news that spreads with a surprising rapidity impedes and paralyzes my weak resources."[114]

As the French prepared their counteroffensive, Bülow ordered Oppen to assault Hertogenbosch on 19 December. Krafft dispatched a supporting force from Heusden. The lack of boats slowed the crossing of the Meuse, while the muddy roads hindered the approach march; Oppen did not reach the fortress until 11:30. Although Krafft's detachment had not arrived, he attacked around noon. Oppen pushed skirmishers along the dams and close to the gate, where the Prussians occupied the houses situated outside the walls. He positioned his artillery in the suburb of Orten and shelled the citadel. The Queen's Dragoons patrolled in the direction of Grave, searching for enemy reinforcements. Superb French artillery fire pinned the Prussians, yet an undaunted Oppen summoned the French to surrender the fort. Shortly after the commander rejected this ridiculous demand, Krafft arrived opposite Ft. Isabelle and likewise bombarded the fortress. The French immediately returned fire. After hearing Krafft's guns, Oppen ordered his Russian howitzers to resume shelling the citadel. As the artillery duel ensued, the Dragoons reported seeing Macdonald's forces assembling at Grave. This disturbing news prompted Oppen to withdraw.[115]

Conversely, Macdonald's patrols informed him on the 18th that the Prussians had made much progress in just twenty-four hours. Reconnaissance on the right bank of the Meuse stumbled upon the enemy at Alphen, seven miles east of Ft. St. Andries. On the left bank, a French patrol had to stop five miles west of Grave at Ravenstein, where a large Prussian force held the road to Hertogenbosch. These reports persuaded Macdonald to keep his forces at Grave rather than march to Hertogenbosch on the 19th. He suspected the Prussians were preparing to cross the Meuse at several points to envelop his position at Nijmegen. The marshal even returned to the idea that the Allies would cross the Rhine in an effort to completely surround him: "My situation is appalling, and it only takes one glance at a map to be convinced that I have good reason to be alarmed. The crisis is far from over and appears to be increasingly serious due to the rapid progress of the enemy, which will lead to the destruction of my debris of units." Macdonald did not want to risk fragmenting his scant manpower along the banks of the Meuse in a futile counteroffensive to relieve or recapture a fort. Instead, prudence demanded that he hold the region between the Meuse and the Rhine for as long as possible. For this purpose, he had to conserve his manpower rather than risk a defeat that would render him incapable of further operations. He hoped to contest every step of the enemy to gain time for the promised reinforcements to arrive.[116]

Macdonald's predicament offers insight into several issues that plagued the Napoleonic command structure during the invasion of the French empire. High on the list was Napoleon's inability to adequately explain his strategy to the marshals. He envisioned the counteroffensive in the Bommelerwaard as a means to reestablish French forces on the lower Meuse, stabilize Belgium, and initiate the conquest of Holland. Such objectives are typically discounted as obvious errors in judgment to be blamed on his haughty pride and obstinate refusal to surrender one league of territory. However, careful consideration shows that Napoleon acutely understood the degree to which his military success depended on his continued, maximum political control of the empire to its fullest extent. To maintain the administrative and bureaucratic machine that managed the conquered peoples and guaranteed the steady flow of manpower, revenue, and material to sustain the empire, he needed to hold as much territory as possible for as long as possible. Thus he had created the cordon system to hold the Allies along the Rhine from Switzerland through Germany to Holland and from there further north along the Ijssel to the North Sea.

Typically weak and ineffective, a cordon system cannot be viewed as the optimal strategy that the master of war willingly employed. Yet given the necessity of sheltering the departmental administrations that fed his war machine and filled his coffers, Bonaparte needed his decimated forces to gain time for him to mobilize a new army. To secure the smooth functioning of the imperial apparatus that would provide the resources to create this new army, his marshals had to hold the enemy as close to the frontier as possible once the invasion began. Any breech in the cordon had to be sealed, the lost territory retaken, the enemy pushed back, and the imperial bureaucracy restored. This meant that although plagued by manpower problems, the marshals could not trade land for time. Instead, they had to conduct tactical strikes and even strategic operations to force the Allies to retreat rather than conserve their forces for future use. The expenditure of the forces guarding the cordon was a risk Napoleon accepted as long as the result corresponded with his perception of the situation. His perception, to be sure, always underestimated the adversary's forces and resolve but overestimated the capabilities of his own.

Moreover, Napoleon failed to recognize the extent of his subordinates' inability to exercise independent command. He recognized their shortcomings and for this reason attempted to direct their actions from Paris, but the six days that it took for information to travel to and from the front meant that they often had to exercise their own judgment, which almost never corresponded with the emperor's views. Consequently, Napoleon sacrificed much by remaining in Paris during the invasion of France: he could not wage war from the Tuileries, St. Cloud, or Fountainebleau. Berthier conceded this fact in his letter to Macdonald on the 18th: "We are too far away to give you instructions; act according to circumstances."[117] Thus, Napoleon's ability to communicate his strategy became crucial. The frequent mistakes committed by the marshals and generals not only illustrate their shortcomings as independent commanders but also suggest that they could not fathom their master's intentions. For example, Napoleon desired a counteroffensive in the Bommelerwaard to reestablish the cordon along the lower Meuse and close the roads leading to the Belgian interior – roads that partisans such as Colomb did not hesitate to tread into to spread havoc behind French lines. Macdonald knew this and was well aware of the damage Colomb caused the French administration, yet he did nothing to stop the enemy Streifkorps. The disruption that this relatively tiny enemy unit caused to Napoleon's political and military control of Belgium cannot be underestimated. According to Lefebvre de Béhaine:

> What he [Colomb] did not know was the indescribable panic his passage caused, the strategic and political consequences were infinitely more serious than those of the Neuss Affair. Generals and prefects lost their heads. On 18 December Gen. [Jacques-Antoine] Chambarlhac de Laubespin in Brussels sent to Paris the news of the fall of Louvain to Prussian cavalry and included the most alarming information: enemy detachments were masters of the countryside, taking contributions meant for the French and freeing conscripts; communication with Macdonald was cut; it was no longer possible to organize the resistance because the Belgian conscripts already had deserted en masse. At Maastricht on the same day, Merle feared that Tirlemont and Brussels already had fallen to considerable enemy forces; he complained about not having anyone at hand as a result of the constant departure of reinforcements for the Grande Armée. On the 19th the prefect of the Meuse Inférieure complained that he had not received any couriers from Paris for ten days, the road to Brussels had been cut. The military units in Belgium were devastated by the desertion of Belgians, Dutch, and Germans.[118]

Napoleon viewed the recapture of Breda as a prerequisite for establishing an entrenched camp at Antwerp for the Imperial Guard. By January he calculated that he would have enough forces in Belgium to drive the Allies out of the Low Countries altogether. Consequently, the emperor planned for the future, while Macdonald and the other marshals understandably only saw and reacted to the present.

Another consideration in any evaluation of the French marshalate during the invasion must be their state of mind. As Macdonald himself stated, it is very easy to look at a map and judge; critics such as historians do this quite easily. Determining the state of mind and emotional stability of Macdonald and his fellow marshals and relating the influence of human nature on their actions and decisions is not as easy. In basic terms, the marshalate was mentally, physically, and emotionally exhausted by the end of 1813. Two consecutive years of hard campaigning in losing efforts across Russia and Germany had taken its toll on their fortitude, zeal, and ability to rationalize. Some like Macdonald chose the quill as means to express their depression: "What a fateful coincidence that the passage of Werkendam was not guarded by at least 100 men and artillery and that Breda was evacuated! Three-quarters of the 31st Division has been evacuated as sick; none have returned. What Providence will save us from the dreadful evil that threatens us? I see reinforcements only in a distant day and what kind of soldiers will they be?"[119] Such lamentations indicate Macdonald's predisposition to failure. "With the enemy on the banks of both the Waal and the Meuse," he explains to Sébastiani, "all he has to do is cross the Rhine at some point downstream of Wesel to trap me between these two rivers and sooner or later in Venlo. Do I take this step now, or wait until I am forced? I will likely retire on Venlo, falling back successively on Wesel and then Neuss."[120] Contemplating a retreat since the 17th, he finally chose this option three days later.

At his headquarters in Nijmegen, Macdonald received Molitor's alarm cry: the Prussians were marching on Grave from different directions! Prisoners, locals, and French scouts all confirmed the presence of considerable forces on the left bank of the Meuse.[121] From Maastricht Merle confirmed the presence of Prussian cavalry in Belgium; the Prussians cut all integral communication.[122] The marshal responded by ordering Molitor to garrison Grave with 1,300 men and move any remaining troops of the 17th Military District to Venlo.[123] With the 31st Division and the II Cavalry Corps, Macdonald intended to withdraw his left to Venlo, his center to Geldern, and his right to Wesel. In this way he could still escape across the Meuse if the Allies crossed the Rhine.[124] That same day, 20 December, Macdonald left Nijmegen and reached Kleve during the evening. On the following day, he received Berthier's 18 December letter that contained the emperor's views. Napoleon agreed the Allies were indeed audacious but reiterated that their numbers could not be as great as Macdonald believed. He repeated his instructions for Macdonald to drive west from Nijmegen to Hertogenbosch to facilitate the recapture of Breda.[125] As proof of the emperor's preoccupation with Breda, Berthier's dispatch to Macdonald on the 16th reiterated the 13 December instructions to support the operation to retake Breda, while the chief of staff's letter of 17 December demanded an account of the measures Macdonald would take to assist this mission. Macdonald received both letters when he arrived in Kleve on the night of 20 December. Berthier again attempted to lift the marshal's spirits and provide him with the proper motivation: "His Majesty has the greatest confidence in you; identify those who lack energy or who forget that they are French, make me aware of those who serve the emperor poorly."[126]

Berthier's encouragement only partially succeeded. The cantankerous Macdonald professed his loyalty to the emperor: "I can assure you without conceit that the emperor has not badly placed his confidence. Regarding the zeal and the devotion that animates me, I wish His Majesty had as many sensible officers in his service." On the other hand, he went on to explain that no amount of zeal could make up for his lack of manpower and equipment. "The cordon has been breached on my extreme left, where the enemy finds support from the water and the places that fate has placed in his hands. My theater is as narrow as it is extensive, and I have nothing to move even just to threaten my enemy who, not to contradict you, I find less audacious and more prudent because if he dared, we would suffer a disaster whose fate would leave us overwhelmed; we will persevere, I hope."

Such statements reveal Macdonald's frame of mind: he expected to be attacked by superior forces converging on Nijmegen from the Meuse, and he would not countermand his orders to retreat. That day his forward posts confirmed his suspicions: considerable enemy forces appeared to be moving up both banks of the Meuse. Nevertheless, the 21st passed, and no attack came. The considerable Allied forces turned out to be patrols conducting a general reconnaissance between the Waal and the Meuse. Of course Macdonald interpreted this as the quiet before the storm: perhaps the enemy was waiting for additional forces to cross the Rhine and surround him?[127] Despite the apocalyptic visions of a weary and stressed mind, Macdonald watched the next week pass without incident.

Around this time Macdonald did receive what appeared to be good news: another division, the new 36th, would be added to his command. Berthier wrote him on 25 December that the emperor instructed Clarke to make the arrangements for the 36th Division to assemble in Maastricht by combining seven battalions currently attached to the IV and VI Corps with nine battalions yet to be formed. Unfortunately for Macdonald, Napoleon's order to Clarke did not produce one additional soldier for the XI Corps. Blücher's crossing of the Rhine forced the IV Corps into Mainz and the VI Corps to retreat to Metz: neither one could send battalions to the XI Corps. In addition, nothing indicated when the nine new battalions being formed in the depots would be available. In early January, Macdonald sent Brayer to Maastricht with orders to complete the formation of the 36th Division. Later in the month this officer returned to Macdonald's headquarters: none of the battalions designated for the 36th Division ever arrived.[128]

Fortunately for Macdonald, Bülow occupied himself with invading Belgium and taking Antwerp rather than driving the marshal from his position between the Rhine and the Meuse. The Prussian commander knew that as soon as his countrymen led the Silesian Army across the Rhine between Mainz and Koblenz, Macdonald would be forced to retreat. On the 29th, Macdonald learned that the Bohemian Army had crossed the Rhine at Basel one week earlier. Although hundreds of miles away, Macdonald believed that his moment of reckoning had arrived. "My position here and on the line of the Waal exposes me to a catastrophe ... the enemy must be considering great projects and we hold an immense line without forces and without resistance."[129]

In the meantime, Roguet marched from Antwerp with 6,000 infantry, 800 cavalry, and thirty guns on the 19th. After driving Benckendorff's forward posts from Wustweezel, he besieged Breda and its Russian garrison on the following day. General Bertrand-Pierre Castex led the 3rd Guard Cavalry Division to Ginneken, halfway between Breda and Turnhout, to send patrols toward Hoogstraten and establish communication with Macdonald's troops. From all sides French guns pounded Breda during the night of 20–21 December. Breda's defenses consisted of thirteen bastions, an equal number of ravelins, several cavaliers, and five horn works.[130] The winter cold could freeze the moat at any moment, which would pose problems for the Russians to defend the entire circumference of the city of 10,000 inhabitants. Benckendorff's garrison consisted 1,100 cavalry and 400 infantry as well as 100 infantry of Colomb's Streifkorps, which he had left in Breda while the cavalry raided Belgium. At the first report of the French approach, Benckendorff placed 250 Russian jäger at the Antwerp gate. To defend the Ginneken gate, he reinforced the 100 Prussians with 150 Russian jäger, twenty dismounted Cossacks, and three guns. The rest of his cavalry, mostly Cossacks, remained in reserve.

During the six-hour bombardment, French skirmishers probed both gates. With eight light guns and limited ammunition, the Allies could do little in response. Roguet launched attacks on both of Breda's gates on the 21st but failed to penetrate. He ordered the bombardment to resume at 10:00 P.M.; the French guns did not stop firing until they exhausted their ammunition at 6:00 the following morning. Despite the French encirclement, the Allies managed to reinforce Breda. That night, Prince Gagarin, whose raiding party had returned from spreading terror as far as Brussels, drove a French post from Terheijden, just north of Breda. This enabled Gagarin to transport eighteen heavy guns with ammunition along the Mark Canal from Willemstad. In addition 500 Dutch soldiers arrived with the promise that 2,000 more would follow. On the 22nd, Benckendorff positioned his newly arrived artillery and answered Roguet's bombardment.

To break the stalemate at Breda, Bülow directed Krafft's brigade, which had just returned from the aborted operation against Hertogenbosch, southwest from Heusden to attack Roguet's left flank and rear. He also dispatched a letter to Benckendorff that urged the Russian to hold his position. Designed to fall into French hands, it contained Bülow's promise that he would arrive in two days with 15,000 men. The ploy worked. Lefebvre-Desnouettes reached Breda on 23 December just as news arrived of Krafft's approach from Heusden as well as the march of a British detachment from Willemstad. As the ranking officer, Lefebvre-Desnouettes assumed command and decided to raise the siege to save the only troops that could defend Antwerp.

Krafft's brigade reached Breda before the French departed. Skirmishing ensued throughout day, and the French managed to hold their position until they observed British troops advancing southeast through Zevenbergen. The appearance of this second Allied force convinced Lefebvre-Desnouettes to accelerate the retreat of his main body south to Minderhout, Hoogstraten, and Turnhout. Krafft pursued on the 24th, catching the French rearguard between Dorst and Ulvenhout. The Prussian 1st Leib Hussar Regiment routed the French Guard Chasseurs and took several prisoners. Heavy fog forced the Prussians to end the pursuit but enabled the French to reach Antwerp. Bülow reproached Krafft for not attacking with more intensity and for allowing the French division to escape.[131]

Notwithstanding the success at Breda, Bülow remained annoyed. A Prussian drive on Antwerp had to be postponed because of his perceived manpower shortage. Promises to release Borstell's brigade or provide other reinforcements remained unfulfilled. Bülow looked at the map and saw that simple Allied maneuvering could solve many of his problems. If Wintzingerode crossed the Rhine at Düsseldorf and took Jülich and Maastricht, Macdonald would be forced to abandon his positions at Grave, Nijmegen, and Kleve – the points that directly threatened Bülow's operations. With Macdonald removed, Bülow could move his entire corps against Antwerp and shatter French control of Belgium. He again pleaded with Wintzingerode to act responsibly.[132]

Continued Dutch incompetence also afforded Bülow little hope that their troops would soon be ready. "I have lost all patience for the laziness and idleness of the Dutch," he complains to his wife.[133] Dutch officials already had notified Bülow that their army would be placed under *British* command. Reports continued to claim that the Dutch lacked the necessary officers to train and organize the thousands of men who had volunteered for military service. The only action involving Dutch troops ended with their humiliation. An estimated 4,800 Dutch soldiers formed the garrison of Geertruidenberg.[134] On 22 December, the rumor of the enemy's approach prompted them to take flight; Bülow had to garrison the fort with his own troops. With French forces on the move, Bülow sought to shake the Dutch from their languor. He asked William Frederick to apply capital punishment to those responsible for the flight from Geertruidenberg. Bülow requested that all Dutch commanders be warned that future capitulations would be punishable by death. In addition, he wanted the forts of Heusden, Lowenstein, and St. Andries immediately placed in a state of defense. Lastly, he urged the Dutch to adopt Prussian conscription methods. These included confiscating the wealth of any Dutchman who shirked his military responsibility. The quintessence of the Dutch response to Prussian militarism was that they were doing what they could and that it was impossible to provide everything at once.[135]

Boyen maintained contact with the Prussian ambassador in London, Constanz Philipp Wilhelm von Jacobi-Klöst. He described the situation in

Holland and urged him to petition the British government to send more aid. Boyen forwarded the requests he and Bülow wanted submitted to the British government. "The bold decision of Gen. Bülow, the courage of the Prussian troops, and the successful exploitation of the agitated spirit of the Dutch has secured the independence of the prince of Orange for the moment," explains Boyen, "but it would be detrimental self-conceit if one attempted to conceal the difficulties that entail the further maintenance of this land, which is so important to all of Europe." According to his calculations, Bülow's 16,500 men had to hold Breda, Geertruidenberg, Heusden, Lowenstein, Grevenmoer, St. Andries, and Arnhem. In addition, the III Corps blockaded Gorinchem and Hertogenbosch and had to "show a bold front to the enemy in the field." Reports indicated that Macdonald's 11,000 troops remained at Kleve, while the garrison of Antwerp had been increased to 10,000 men; Brussels contained similar numbers. Boyen reminded Jacobi-Klöst that the crown prince of Sweden remained obsessed with securing his own objectives and that Dutch mobilization "lacks that energetic activity which will decide the fate of the state and guarantee the independence of its liberated people."

Boyen also outlined four points he hoped Jacobi-Klöst would present to the British. First, "It appears very important to me that England reinforce its troops in the Netherlands as much as possible so that we can advance in force on Belgium before France has finished its new mobilization, especially if the goal is to restore the European equilibrium." Second, he requested cannon, ammunition, flints, cartridges, and money for bribes to complete the Dutch mobilization and to arm any Belgian willing to participate in the insurrection. He encouraged Jacobi-Klöst to stress that "perhaps in the course of this war there has been nothing as risky an investment as this, but none so promising in returns." Boyen's third point touched on the complicated politics of the Low Countries. "The Dutch have found a rallying point in the prince of Orange and so blame is placed on the foreign yoke." This in turn allowed even those who had supported the French to make a new start and vindicate their actions. "The Belgians lack this bond," asserts Boyen, "and I do not know whether politics will allow it, but it would be extremely beneficial if one power promises to guarantee the Belgians and appoint a man who could serve in Belgium as a military leader or field-commander." He returned to the problems in Holland for his final point, making the bold suggestion that universal military service be introduced: "We understand that despite the sovereignty given to the prince of Orange, he has to contend with numerous considerations due to the new situation. However, it is infinitely important that one set as a condition to any alliance that every Dutchman is responsible for the defense of his land; this law is not in effect in Holland. Thus, the entire mobilization is based on money speculation that jeopardizes the independence of the country." Boyen concluded with a warning that he expected the Prussian envoy to communicate to the British: "Nobody can predict the outcome of the operation at

Basel. Political and natural stumbling blocks can paralyze the advance from there indefinitely, and woe be it to us and the good cause if an energetic defense of Holland has not been arranged, this [is] the key to continental freedom."[136]

To secure further aid, Bülow dispatched Auer on a second errand to London. He carried a letter from Bülow to the prince regent, which also clearly described the situation in Holland. It included a request for the immediate shipment of supplies through Rotterdam. Auer had been promised British aid on his first trip, but its form had mostly remained verbal. Other than the 20,000 muskets, only a slight amount of material actually reached the Prussians. His second mission proved more successful and the British approved Bülow's requests; supplies reached the Prussians as early as mid-January.[137] As a token of his esteem, the prince-regent ordered a golden sword to be forged for Bülow. On the other hand, Bülow continued to petition Bernadotte, Alexander, Hardenberg, and even Blücher for support. Frederick William wrote to Bernadotte on Bülow's behalf on 17 December. According to Burghersh, the tsar sent a similar letter on the 21st.[138] Stewart notes that the Prussian king hoped Bernadotte "would hasten to gather laurels in the Netherlands, as it was of the utmost importance not only to secure what was already gained in Holland, but also to push the advantages obtained there. His Majesty proposed that Borstell join Bülow, and be replaced by part of Wintzingerode's corps; and that the Saxon corps, and the remainder of Wintzingerode's, be ordered to advance to the Meuse and support the left wing of Bülow during his advance."[139]

In response to this pressure, Bernadotte – whose ability to direct the situation decreased as he continued his march north and away from his nominal subordinates – assured Bülow that the situation would improve shortly. "I believe the Saxons and Wintzingerode, who will be operating on the Rhine and the Meuse [respectively], will arrive in time to cover your left flank and will suffice to liberate [the remainder of] Holland," wrote the crown prince of Sweden – a master of rhetoric and empty promises.[140] Although Bernadotte's army exceeded 60,000 Swedes, Russians, Prussians, North Germans, and British troops, he simply refused to divert troops to Holland until the conclusion of his war with Denmark. A report from Stewart to Castlereagh reveals Bernadotte's self-serving politics:

> With regard to the military points, when I came to converse with the prince-royal on the absolute expediency of making every effort for Holland, I found him determinately set on taking no further steps. It was a vain struggle to persuade [him]. Indeed, he sealed my mouth with an entreaty to be silent, and Thornton assured me that it was quite vain to press him. I have endeavored to bring him to consider the question...of going to Holland himself. None of this, however, was heeded. *He thinks Austria has deceived him. He suspects Russia and Prussia have been privy to it, and even claims that Lord Aberdeen*

was acquainted with it. He declares that he may be deceived again, and that the Swedes have no one to look to but to him. He cannot waste their blood on the Rhine.[141]

Some Allied commanders had envisioned a rapid, simultaneous advance across the Rhine and through Holland. Blücher even predicted on 3 November that by executing such a plan, the Allies could win a "durable peace," yet any delay in crossing the Rhine would result in a "severe and bloody campaign."[142] The early-twentieth-century British historian F. L. Petre predicts that had the Allies followed this general outline, Napoleon would have fallen before the end of December.[143] Baron Fain recalls the consternation at imperial headquarters caused by Bülow's operation: "The Prussian forces of Gen. Bülow had just passed through Hanover and Hesse, and had destroyed the kingdom of Westphalia. This army ... was destined to take Holland, and afterwards to penetrate into Belgium. There was to be a general hurrah and a march to Paris."[144] Bülow's offensive in Holland also vindicated Gneisenau: "With his brave Pomeranians," he wrote, "Bülow has made a glorious campaign in Holland – a campaign which will live forever in the annals of military history. Timid advisers said that we had to avoid the fortresses; I said the opposite. ... What has happened in Holland justifies my claim."[145] Although the Allies could and should have achieved more results in the Low Countries before the end of the year, Bülow's operations fell victim to the general lethargy that set in after the Bohemian and Silesian Armies reached the Rhine. Wintzingerode should have crossed the Rhine at Düsseldorf to completely eliminate Macdonald's threat. Because of Wintzingerode's inactivity in December, Bülow had to devote most of January to securing Belgium rather than linking with Blücher's army on the Marne.

8

The Upper Rhine

To the units of the left wing that would wheel through Switzerland, all of which were composed exclusively of Austrian troops, Schwarzenberg issued the following proclamation from his headquarters at Lörrach on 21 December:

"Soldiers!" We enter Swiss territory as friends and liberators. Your conduct must be appropriate for this role. Show the Swiss how Austria's warriors are no less familiar with the duties that are expected of them during the passage through a friendly land and the careful treatment of the inhabitants as they are with the qualities that lead them to renown and victory on the day of battle. If the course of the war makes it necessary to expose you to arduous marches and exertions in the inclement time of year, forget not, soldiers, that it now depends on completing laudably what you have laudably started, that far greater difficulties and dangers than those which you will still encounter already have been defeated, and that from your bravery and steadfastness your Fatherland and the world expects a speedy, honorable and lasting peace.[1]

Despite Schwarzenberg's trepidation, the Basel operation proceeded smoothly. The Swiss withdrew their artillery from the Basel bridge during the night of 20–21 December. Swiss forces evacuated the city early on Tuesday, the 21st, without offering any resistance and leaving the bridge intact. At 8:00 A.M. Austrian troops occupied Basel's St. Paul suburb and gate. "An ugly old town," notes Wilson, "Basel seemed to frown on us all as unwelcome guests and I understand that when the troops entered there was no sign of goodwill."[2] At 9:30 A.M., French customs agents and gendarmes in nearby Bourglibre abandoned their posts and withdrew to Mulhouse. By 10:00, the Austrians severed communication between Huningue and Basel; the gates of the former were shut.[3] From Huningue's walls, the French observed masses of Austrian cavalry move through the small hamlet that separated the fortress from Basel. The commandant of the 3,000-man garrison, Colonel Théophile

Chancel, ordered 300 men of the garrison to raze the trees and garden fences and to burn the houses, barns, stables, sheds, and summerhouses that were too close to the fortifications.[4]

Throughout the 21st, the Austrian corps and light divisions marched into Switzerland after crossing the Rhine at Basel, Grenzach, Laufenberg, and Schaffhausen (Map 5). Gyulay's III Corps moved into Basel led by Crenneville's division, which continued to Huningue. Crossing the Rhine ahead of the army, an Austro–Bavarian Streifkorps of 700 cavalry under the Colonel Karl von Scheibler covered Schwarzenberg's right by dispatching patrols north and west through the Haut-Rhin Department toward Colmar and Nancy. By nightfall on the 21st, Scheibler's main body reached Bartenheim on the road to Mulhouse.[5]

North of Schwarzenberg's main body, Wittgenstein's Russian corps remained anchored on the right bank of the Rhine; his observation posts covered a 110-mile stretch of the river. General Andrey Ivanovich Gorchakov billeted the I Infantry Corps in and around Offenburg, where Wittgenstein transferred his headquarters on the 22nd. After relieving General Ludwig von Stockmayer's Württemberger brigade, Duke Eugene of Württemberg assumed the blockade of the Kehl bridgehead with the Russian II Infantry Corps. With cavalry to spare, Wittgenstein assigned a special task to General Alexander Nikitich Seslavin II, who commanded a small Streifkorps consisting of three Hussar squadrons and one Cossack regiment. His immediate objective was to find a passage across the Rhine upstream Strasbourg. After crossing the Rhine, Seslavin would operate against Victor's rear and gather intelligence on French movements. Furthermore, he was to establish communication between the Silesian Army to the north and Wrede's V Corps to the south.[6]

Schwarzenberg crowned his work on the 21st by issuing a declaration to the French that conformed with the Coalition's desire to win the hearts and minds of Napoleon's subjects:

Victory has led the Allied armies to your frontier; they will cross it. We do not make war on France, but we reject the yoke that your government forced upon our countries, which have the same right to independence and happiness as yours. Magistrates, proprietors, farmers, remain at ease: the maintenance of public law and order, the respect for private property, and the most severe discipline will mark the passage of the Allied armies. They are not animated by the hopeless spirit of vengeance; they only want to end the countless evils that for twenty years France has burdened on its neighbors and the most distant lands. Principles and views other than those that have driven your army home reside in the councils of the Allied monarchs. Their glory will be to bring the speediest end to Europe's misfortunes. The only conquest they desire is peace for France and a genuine state of repose for all of Europe. We hope to find this before we set foot on French territory; if not we will go there to find it.[7]

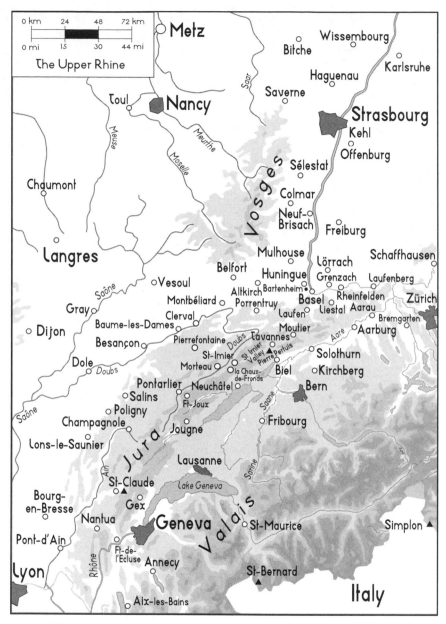

Map 5. The upper Rhine.

In his private correspondence, however, the commander in chief appeared less confident and more overwhelmed. "Here between Germany, Switzerland, and France I have established my headquarters," Schwarzenberg informed his wife two days later. "The entire Austrian army will assemble at Bern. I think that from there it will advance according to circumstances through Besançon and take a position at Langres by mid-month. In the meantime, the armies of Blücher and the crown prince [of Sweden] must be as active as the army in Holland [Bülow]. Any operation in France is beset with infinite difficulties but, in the current circumstances, the task must be executed. It has now begun; Switzerland and France, all lie burdensome upon me."[8]

As of yet, the burden was not too heavy, and Schwarzenberg's invasion of Switzerland proceeded according to plan. By the night of the 25th, the Austrian units on the Bohemian Army's left wing had made varying degrees of progress. The main body of Bubna's 1st Light Division moved through Solothurn toward Bern. After occupying this city on the 23rd, Bubna had orders to forward General Georg von Scheither's 1st Brigade to Pontarlier on the Doubs River. Alois von Liechtenstein's II Corps arrived in Solothurn on the 23rd and proceeded to Bern on the following day. Schwarzenberg likewise directed Liechtenstein to Pontarlier with the II Corps's 1st Division, which Liechtenstein himself commanded. From this position, both Liechtenstein and Scheither would cover the left flank of the columns advancing into Franche-Comté. During the 25th one of Liechtenstein's brigades reached Neuchâtel; its advance guard pressed on to Pontarlier – fairly rapid marching for the usually listless Austrians! In the meantime, Bubna led his 2nd Brigade and the 2nd Division of the II Corps through Fribourg toward Geneva.[9] Moritz von Liechtenstein's 2nd Light Division crossed the Rhine at Laufenberg and joined the Austrian Reserve after it passed the river at Schaffhausen. Except for the 1st and 2nd Infantry Divisions of the Austrian Reserve, both units proceeded through Aarburg and Bern to Neuchâtel.[10] Colloredo's I Corps conducted unimpressive, short marches to reach Kirchberg, just north of Bern.[11] Relieved by the Bavarians at Huningue on the 22nd, Crenneville's division united with General Friedrich von Bianchi's 1st Infantry Division of the Austrian Reserve at Laufen and proceeded to Solothurn on the 23rd. Two days later, the divisions continued through Moutier to Tavannes, north of Biel.[12] Gyulay's III Corps passed the night of the 22nd at Liestal and spent the next two days leisurely marching to Solothurn.[13] Finally, General Nicolaus von Weissenwolf's 2nd Infantry Division of the Austrian Reserve marched through Bremgarten to occupy Zurich on the 24th.[14]

While these columns trooped through Switzerland to execute Radetzky's grand wheeling movement, only the sixth column marched directly across the French frontier. The V Corps moved into Alsace to cover the right and rear of the Austrian units wheeling through Switzerland en route to Franche-Comté. Wrede received the task of driving through the French fortresses in

Upper Alsace to overwhelm Victor's forces. Rather than invest Huningue with one brigade, subsequent orders directed Wrede to assault Huningue with a full division to provide both a base and a pivot for the army's operations.[15] "The day after tomorrow we will turn up the heat on Huningue," exclaims Schwarzenberg to Metternich on the 22nd. Schwarzenberg also instructed Wrede to send a strong division forty miles west to Belfort to secure the pass through the Vosges at all costs.[16]

On 22 December, the Bavarian corps commander led his troops from Schliengen through Lörrach to Basel, crossed the Rhine in the afternoon, and struck the main highway to the French interior. Frimont's Austrians moved south from Müllheim to Schliengen. On the same day, the 22nd, six battalions from General Karl von Beckers's Bavarian 2nd Division reached Huningue, followed by Wrede himself, who established his headquarters at Hésingue. Far in front of the V Corps, General Joseph von Rechberg's Bavarian 1st Division continued west toward Belfort, followed by General Peter von Delamotte's Bavarian 3rd Division, whose main body halted at Altkirch, halfway between Basel and Belfort. North of Wrede's position at Huningue, Scheibler's Streifkorps established posts in Rixheim and Habsheim just east of Mulhouse. His patrols pushed north to Ensisheim and west to Cernay, encountering customs agents, gendarmes, and small army detachments attempting to reach Belfort and Huningue (Map 6).[17]

Panic swept the Haut-Rhin Department as word spread of the Allied invasion. Prefect Vieuville evacuated the public chest and archives from Colmar – *chef-lieu* of the Haut-Rhin – to St. Dié.[18] He also notified Victor of the Allied offensive and the events at Basel. The marshal received Vieuville's report on the morning of the 22nd and immediately directed the 3,500 troopers of Milhaud's V Cavalry Corps to proceed through Colmar toward Basel to obtain news of the enemy.[19] Throughout the day, additional information reached Victor's headquarters in Strasbourg. In both his summary of the day's events to Berthier and his formal report to the emperor, Victor estimated that the Allies had assembled 140,000 to 150,000 men with numerous artillery and bridging equipment in and around Basel. A reserve of 74,000 men appeared to be escorting Alexander and Francis from Darmstadt to Freiburg. Apparently, the Allies had divided their army between Wrede and Schwarzenberg. Although unsure of the objective of either enemy army, he believed the operation at Basel signaled the start of an Allied invasion. Victor expressed concern that he would soon be placed in a critical situation. "If they enter Alsace, I can oppose them with only 3,500 cavalry and 5,000 infantry. All I can do is delay their movement for a few days and lock myself in Strasbourg." He described the capital of Alsace as prepared, armed, and provisioned as best as possible in view of the scarcity of labor, material, and money.[20]

Additional intelligence that arrived on the 23rd helped Victor clarify the situation. After crossing the Rhine at Basel, the enemy columns evidently dispersed in three directions. One column took a southwest direction to Solothurn, a second moved west toward Altkirch, and the third to Colmar and Mulhouse. At 2:00 P.M., an Allied force of 600 cavalry followed by an infantry column and sixteen cannon reached Belfort. Victor received this news from the commandant of Belfort, Colonel Jean-Baptiste Legrand – it was the last communication he received from the fortress. "I am now preparing a column of 8,000–9,000 men and thirty-two cannons to support [Milhaud] if it is necessary," wrote Victor. The marshal concluded his report on the 23rd by expressing hope that he would receive positive information concerning the enemy's position within the next twenty-four hours.[21]

As soon as the Bavarians crossed the Basel bridge, Huningue's outworks reared before them. Both the bridge and the city of Basel were well within range of French heavy artillery, but the defenders did not fire one shot to impede Wrede's approach. After relieving Crenneville's posts, Beckers's troops besieged the fortress on the left bank of the Rhine, and six Würzburger battalions of the German VI Corps operated against the fortress on the right bank. Although the wounds he received at Hanau had not healed, Wrede, forced by the pain to dismount, reconnoitered Huningue on the 22nd. He selected battery positions and attempted to expedite the arrival of his siege train, which reached Lörrach, five miles from Basel, that same day.[22] That night Beckers's field guns fired several shells into Huningue but caused no significant damage. "Huningue is yet a virgin fortress," states Wilson's 22 December journal entry. "Vauban built it, and the site is excellent, but the works have been neglected. If the garrison, however, does its duty, it will be difficult for our 18-pounders to make any impression."[23]

On the 23rd, Wrede again surveyed the fortress from a dormer window at Petit-Huningue on the right bank of the Rhine. This second look convinced him that Huningue's works were virtually unassailable. In addition, Chancel definitively rejected a demand to surrender the fortress. Wrede could do nothing more than prepare for a formal siege. Returning to his headquarters in Hésingue, the frustrated corps commander probably regretted his failure to convince the Austrians during the councils of war in Frankfurt to attack the frontier fortresses before the French could place them in a state of defense. Regardless, Schwarzenberg, who personally reconnoitered Huningue on the 23rd, wanted the fortress bombarded in the hopes of destroying a magazine and demoralizing the garrison.[24] Covered by a bombardment, work began on the siege trenches on the 23rd. Wrede ordered the capture of the château of Machicoulis that stood upstream the Rhine and commanded his position. The Bavarians succeeded, but on the following day, the 24th, a French sortie supported by case-shot from an adjacent outwork drove out Wrede's troops. A Bavarian counterattack failed, which forced the engineers to move the first parallel further from Huningue.[25] In his 25 December diary entry, a sour Wilson, who continued to observe Wrede's operations, provides an interesting assessment of the Bavarians: "If the enemy can muster a force equal to Wrede's before the Russian Reserve is up to support him, I speculate upon Wrede being beaten. Although a most gallant officer, he is most unskilled. I do not feel confidence in any of his dispositions, nor much in the military conduct of the Bavarians."[26]

As Beckers's division commenced the siege of Huningue, the rest of Wrede's corps did not remain idle. The main body of Rechberg's 1st Division reached Belfort on the 24th and blockaded the fortress after Legrand refused to surrender.[27] Delamotte's division marched toward Porrentruy. On the evening of the 24th, a flying column from his division surprised and captured the fortified château of Lausanne, situated on a mountain in the Haut-Rhin Department, after a spirited defense by a handful of defenders claimed several Bavarian casualties.[28] A second unit repeated the feat on the morning of the 25th at Blamont, a fortified château located in the Doubs Department, whose defenders unbelievably neglected to raise the drawbridge. According to the Bavarian reports, a staff captain charged through the manor's open gate with one platoon of light cavalry and captured the bewildered French commandant.[29] Lausanne and Blamont provided the Bavarians with their first spoils of war: twenty-three guns and fully-stocked magazines. Behind the V Corps's front-line Bavarian divisions, Frimont's two Austrian divisions crossed the Basel bridge on the 24th and proceeded north to Mulhouse. Frimont established his headquarters at Rixheim, while the men billeted in and around the town.[30]

Despite the small victories at Lausanne and Blamont, the determination of the French defenders in Huningue and Belfort disturbed Schwarzenberg. Concern over the progress of the invasion turned to dismay when the generalissimo received a bundle of reports from Wrede detailing the operations on the 24th. In particular, the near destruction of Scheibler's Streifkorps stunned the commander in chief. On the 23rd, Scheibler had led his cavalry force of 250 Austrian and Bavarian troopers, reinforced by the 1st and 2nd Don Cossack Regiments, north through Mulhouse to Ensisheim on the road to Colmar. Outside Ensisheim, Allied scouts made contact with French pickets at daybreak. Scheibler forwarded a detachment of 200 troopers under the command of Captain von Schell who, after driving the French from Ensisheim, continued to Ste. Croix, five miles south of Colmar. Meeting no resistance at Ste. Croix, Schell made for Colmar. Near Andolsheim and not far from Colmar, Schell's detachment fell on a convoy of twelve ammunition caissons fleeing Colmar for Neuf-Brisach. Schell's advance guard of eighty troopers then entered Colmar, arrested the mayor, and demanded provisions. After learning that Milhaud's cavalry would reach Colmar on the 24th, Schell withdrew around 5:00 P.M. to Ste. Croix, forwarding this valuable information to Scheibler, who in turn informed Wrede.[31]

Map 6. Upper Alsace.

At 8:30 P.M. Milhaud's advance guard – 1,000 men of General Gabriel-Gaspard Montélégier's 2nd Dragoon Brigade – moved through Colmar to the southern or "Basel" suburb under the cover of darkness. Montélégier made contact with the commanding officer of a company of conscripts belonging to the 7th Light Infantry Regiment, which remained hidden in Colmar's eastern or "Breisach" suburb during Schell's soiree in Colmar. Milhaud himself arrived thirty minutes later. His 9:00 P.M. report to Victor confirmed that at least 100,000 men in several columns of 20,000 each had crossed the Rhine at Basel, where Schwarzenberg allegedly established his headquarters. The Allies occupied Mulhouse and invested Huningue; strong enemy columns covered the roads leading to Solothurn, Belfort, and Colmar. The advance guard of this last column reached Ste. Croix on the 23rd. Milhaud planned to continue south until he found the enemy.[32]

Ignoring Schell's warning about the approach of French cavalry, Scheibler wanted to unite the majority of his detachments at Ste. Croix and dive through Colmar with approximately 800 troopers. The Streifkorps departed Ensisheim at 7:00 on the morning of 24 December and reunited with Schell's detachment and the other patrols at Ste. Croix three hours later: light skirmishing between the Allied vedettes and the posts of the French 7th Light commenced at daybreak. After his subordinates assured the men that they would face only conscripts, Scheibler advanced. Schell's advance guard of 100 Hussars and Cossacks led the way to Colmar. As his scouts approached the Basel suburb, Montélégier's dragoons debouched. Schell fell back toward Ste. Croix hotly pursued by Montélégier. Scheibler moved up the Austrian cavalry and the 1st Don Cossack Regiment, leaving in Ste. Croix the Bavarian light cavalry and the 2nd Don Cossack Regiment under the orders of the Russian Colonel Korin. At a trot, Montélégier's troopers crossed a long defile formed by the bridge over the Thur and the large forest that marched alongside the river. His brigade emerged on the plain west of Ste. Croix with the 2nd Regiment in column by platoons on the road, the 6th and 11th Regiments in two lines on the left with the 6th in front. Satisfied with the deployment, Montélégier gave the order to charge. His 2nd and 6th Dragoons smashed through Scheibler's Austrian Hussars and Don Cossacks.

At Ste. Croix, Korin wanted to take part in the action and debouched from the village in time to engage Montélégier's first line, which had become disorganized during its charge. Korin managed to repulse the 2nd and 6th Dragoons, who withdrew to rally behind the 11th Dragoons. Montélégier signaled for the 11th Dragoons to charge; this blow overwhelmed the Allies. During this action, squadrons from General Jean-Antoine Collaert's 1st Dragoon Brigade moved east of Ste. Croix toward the road to Ensisheim and Scheibler's line of retreat, thus forcing the Austrian colonel to withdraw. Although he held Montélégier long enough to rally the German cavalry, most of the Cossacks attempted to flee. The French Dragoons took delight in finally cornering the elusive warriors, and most of the Russian horsemen did not escape. Upon returning to Ste. Croix, the Allies discovered the streets barricaded and defended by the inhabitants. The Austrian and Bavarian troopers had to cut their way through as Montélégier's men closed on their rear. Managing to escape from Ste. Croix, Scheibler's cavalry then had to charge through the two lead squadrons of Collaert's brigade. After receiving three wounds, Scheibler reached Ensisheim, but not before losing 200 men and nine officers killed and several others wounded or taken prisoner; the French lost eighty men killed. Montélégier pursued as far as Meyenheim, where the French recovered the dozen powder wagons pilfered by Schell's men the day before. Collaert's brigade moved into Ste. Croix, where it was joined by General Hippolyte-Marie-Guillaume Piré's 9th Light Cavalry Division; General Samuel-François Lhéritier's 6th Dragoon Division occupied Colmar.[33]

Despite is propaganda value, the combat of Ste. Croix does not rank among the epic battles of the Napoleonic period.[34] Yet the engagement's influence on Schwarzenberg's state of mind and the consequences it produced were nothing short of momentous. As an immediate result of Scheibler's setback, Wrede's headquarters simply instructed him to serve as the vanguard of Frimont's divisions around Mulhouse.[35] At Schwarzenberg's headquarters, however, the combat of Ste. Croix, like most bad news, took on tragic proportions. Thus far, the Austrian commander viewed the invasion as disappointing. The staffs of both the Bohemian and Silesian armies entertained exaggerated optimism regarding the demeanor of the German population along the left bank of the Rhine. Schwarzenberg hoped the Alsatians would welcome the Allies as liberators or, in the least, remain indifferent and not support the French in any way. News that peasants and townspeople were arming in self-defense stunned him. To his utter dismay, he learned that local resistance increasingly took the form of a guerilla war that could jeopardize his communications. In addition, he had believed the French fortresses would surrender at the mere sight of Allied troops, but Huningue and Belfort offered staunch resistance. "Even a dump like Lausanne," asserts Lefebvre de Béhaine, "did not capitulate until 25 December, after having inflicted on [Bavarian Colonel Friedrich von] Treuberg's detachment losses equal to the effectives of the garrison."[36] Finally, the generalissimo deemed his troops would encounter only conscripts and National Guard units, ready to flee at the first shot. Scheibler's thrashing by well-disciplined and well-led Line units caused panic at Schwarzenberg's headquarters.

To the Austrian General Staff, the encounter at Ste. Croix was not a mere coincidence. Instead, it was proof that large French forces were advancing south from Strasbourg. The Austrians labeled Milhaud's cavalry the vanguard of a French army assembling somewhere between Metz and Strasbourg. Anxious discussions centered on the belief that Napoleon himself had arrived at Strasbourg. Schwarzenberg expected to learn that a French corps had crossed the Rhine there and proceeded south to assail the Bohemian Army's right and rear, while the main French army in Strasbourg fell on its dispersed columns.[37] Fears of a national uprising and a French counteroffensive naturally raised the idea of withdrawing the army across the Rhine. Such a measure would force the men of the Bohemian Army to tighten their belts. Schwarzenberg counted on being able to feed his army at Langres. "I hope in this way to live at France's expense and to provide subsistence for some time at least"; he explains, "because of my numerous overeaters, this is an interminably great advantage."[38] Now, Schwarzenberg and Radetzky feared the army would starve to death on the right bank of the Rhine. On 30 December, Wilson noted in his journal: "Indeed Radetzky, as I was passing through Lörrach, entreated me to tell Aberdeen that the want of food was so great and the consequences so fatal, and the enemy's daily augmentation of force so considerable, that he expected an early and serious check; that the only way to avoid it, in his opinion, was to lose no time in negotiations *pro forma*, but to expedite peace on such preliminary arrangements as would enable the dislocation of the army on the principle of attention to subsistence. He thought that provisions could not be procured in time to sustain the military operations, even if the money was forthcoming."[39] In a letter to Metternich, Schwarzenberg revealed his deep concern over supply. "I worry for our magazines; with the little energy that we rightfully exert we will die of hunger if unfavorable circumstances force us to reestablish ourselves behind the Rhine ... the outlook is not good and I would not be surprised to see us impelled to conclude an armistice to save us from famine." Schwarzenberg concluded his letter with a shocking prediction: "You see that I feel the need to pour forth my heart to you ... for soon friends will do us more evil than the enemy, and regarding the salutary work of the peace, which the world generally feels the need, you will have more difficulty with friend than with foe."[40]

Fear of a crushing defeat, which perpetually haunted Schwarzenberg, led him to take measures to bilk this imaginary French counteroffensive and to maintain his foothold in Alsace without altering the operations of the Austrian corps moving through Switzerland. Wrede's corps would continue to operate on the left bank of the Rhine in Upper Alsace. Although the Bavarian divisions of the corps continued the sieges of Huningue and Belfort, Schwarzenberg wanted Frimont's Austrian divisions to play a greater role. Frimont received orders to move north from Mulhouse toward Colmar. By nightfall on the 25th, General Johann Antonn Leonhard von Hardegg's Austrian division reached Ensisheim with his advance guard spread between Meyenheim and Reguisheim on the road to Colmar. In second line, part of General Ignaz Spleny's Austrian division camped at Baldersheim and Battenheim, just north of Mulhouse. The rest of Spleny's command maintained communication with the Bavarian divisions at Huningue and Belfort. Specifically, strong detachments from Spleny's division covered Frimont's left by extending west on the road from Colmar to Cernay, linking with the Bavarians north of Belfort. Scheibler's Streifkorps covered the right by holding the road to Neuf-Brisach.[41] To support the V Corps, Schwarzenberg instructed the IV Corps to march rapidly from Offenburg to Freiburg and to select a point of passage between Huningue and Neuf-Breisach. Once across the Rhine, the Württembergers would take a position between the V Corps and the river to cover the siege of Huningue from the north.[42] Schwarzenberg ordered Wittgenstein's VI Corps to continue blockading Kehl and observing Strasbourg from its current position between the former and the hills of Offenburg. The generalissimo craved any detail of French movements that revealed the slightest possibility of enemy preparations to cross the Rhine in this region.[43]

The difference between the orders issued to Wittgenstein and Crown Prince Frederick William of Württemberg can only be described as baffling. Although Schwarzenberg encouraged both to accelerate their preparations to cross the Rhine, only Frederick William received specific instructions for this eventuality. Several advantages could have been gained by summoning Wittgenstein to cross the Rhine immediately and invade Lower Alsace. Victor could not prevent the Russian corps from crossing the river, and the French marshal certainly could not conduct any operations on the right bank against Wittgenstein. Victor's forces hardly sufficed to maintain communication between Strasbourg, Sélestat, and Saverne in central Alsace, where the main roads led to the passes through the Vosges at Ste. Marie, Saales, Donon, and Phalsbourg.[44] The combined troop strength of the V, IV, and VI Corps – Schwarzenberg's right wing – would have provided 75,000 combatants and almost 200 guns to contest Victor's 10,000 men. Most likely, the coordinated efforts of these three corps would have destroyed Victor's forces and delivered Alsace to the Allies before the end of the year. In the least, Russian operations in Lower Alsace would have eased the pressure that Schwarzenberg now anticipated would be placed on Wrede in Upper Alsace and also would have facilitated Blücher's invasion of Lorraine.

The reasons Schwarzenberg did not order Wittgenstein to cross the Rhine are not as clear as the advantages the Allies could have gained from such an operation. Rather than political conniving, his inherent, extreme caution in military matters offers the most plausible answer. He probably feared falling victim to Napoleon's famous *maneuver sur derrière*. Because of the wild scenarios that the combat of Ste. Croix conjured up in his headquarters, Schwarzenberg wanted Wittgenstein to remain on the right bank to warn him of any French attempt to cross the Rhine and fall on the rear of the Bohemian Army. Certain that Napoleon had concentrated a massive army between Metz and Strasbourg, he described Wittgenstein's corps of 25,000 men as too weak either to cross the Rhine or to prevent the French from crossing the river themselves. Such an attitude ruled out both an offensive and a defensive role for the VI Corps. If 25,000 men did not suffice to trouble Napoleon, what force would?

Blücher was the obvious yet bewildering answer. The same Blücher, recently promoted to field marshal, who the doves wanted to chain to Mainz while Metternich played peacemaker and Schwarzenberg maneuvered his army to win time for negotiations. A desperate Schwarzenberg appeared ready to sacrifice all of Metternich's meticulous work by summoning Blücher, Gneisenau, and the rest of the war-mongering Prussians across the Rhine. In a revealing letter to Blücher on 25 December, Schwarzenberg claimed that no significant French forces had concentrated in southern France. After subtracting the garrisons of Mainz, Metz, and Strasbourg, where Schwarzenberg believed "considerable masses have concentrated," he calculated that no more than 50,000 men could be posted along the Rhine to oppose the Allied advance. However, the cautious generalissimo expressed his unwarranted concern over the eighty-mile stretch between Strasbourg and Metz. He informed Blücher that Napoleon had assembled a large army at Metz, from where it could move along the left bank of the Rhine to threaten his right flank, or cross over to the right bank and operate against his rear. "Wittgenstein," he wrote, "is positioned at Kehl and has been instructed to ascertain the enemy's attentiveness especially on this point. However, he is too weak to cause the enemy serious concern and only your army can seriously occupy the enemy. I urgently request that you notify me as soon as possible of the necessary measures that should be taken under these conditions. Previously, you had decided to cross the Rhine, I agree with this.... It appears to me that ... an operation on your part against Nancy or Verdun would be most advantageous." In another symbolic concession to the Prussians, Schwarzenberg agreed that Wintzingerode and Thielemann should march to Holland to support Bülow.[45]

A second note dated 27 December soon followed with reconnaissance reports and Schwarzenberg's repeated request for Blücher to conduct an operation against Metz and Nancy. He reminded Blücher of the Trachenberg Plan and its great success during the German campaign. Ironically, the information that Schwarzenberg forwarded to Blücher indicated no immediate threat from the 30,000 to 40,000 men that supposedly stood at Metz. His intelligence claimed the majority of these troops consisted of raw conscripts armed with antiquated muskets. Moreover, disease reigned in Metz, Mainz, and Strasbourg.[46]

Blücher did not have to be asked twice to cross the Rhine. If Schwarzenberg was correct regarding a French counteroffensive, the logical operation for Blücher's smaller army would be to hang back and wait for Napoleon to move south against the Bohemian Army. Blücher would then have two options. He could honor the Trachenberg Plan by attacking the exposed flank of Napoleon's army as it marched south, or he could race across northern France, unite with Bülow coming from Holland, and proceed to Paris.

Fear that the peace party would gain the upper hand should Schwarzenberg suffer a defeat persuaded the Prussian field marshal to pay closer attention to the Bohemian Army's operations.[47] His reply of 29 December informed Schwarzenberg of his disposition for the Rhine passage, remarking that he already had made the necessary arrangements to move his forces southwest toward the Bohemian Army in order to reach Metz by 15 January. "I will command about 50,000 men for the advance to the Saar," wrote Blücher. "When I arrive there, I will deduct what I must for the blockades. I will establish communication with you on the left bank of the Rhine. To me it appears most expedient to direct myself toward Metz and it is likely I will encounter no great resistance on the way."[48]

"Since I already have initiated my offensive operations in the spirit of your plans," responds a grateful Schwarzenberg, "I have to express to you my complete appreciation for the preparations taken by your army for this union; what you have revealed promises the most brilliant results." The commander in chief also communicated the news that the Allied sovereigns had endorsed his decision to reinforce the Silesian Army with Kleist's corps. "You will see this, I hope, as new proof of how your glory, with which the good cause is so strongly attached, lies in the hearts of all; secondary objectives are always foreign to me and remain so."[49] An interesting comment from the Allied generalissimo whose front extended more than 200 miles from Kehl to Geneva! All of Schwarzenberg's operations sought to attain secondary objectives. Had he truly pursued a primary objective, his six corps already would have reached Langres.

As for the French, Victor worked diligently to prepare the infantry and artillery of the II Corps to march in support of Milhaud. On the morning of the 24th, one column of 3,000 men left Strasbourg for Colmar. On the following morning Victor planned to dispatch his reserve artillery escorted by a second column commanded by Jamin and consisting of the remaining battalions of the 1st Division, two batteries, and three or four march battalions formed from the men in Strasbourg's depot.[50] The marshal made sure Paris understood his manpower crisis: "At the moment, that is all I have at my disposal." According to Victor, the 2nd and 4th Battalions of his regiments still had not arrived, and the National Guard legions from the Meurthe and the Moselle were still en route from the 26th Military District.[51]

At Colmar Milhaud forwarded patrols south and west to procure news of the enemy throughout the 25th. Much to his chagrin, he learned that the check at Ste. Croix did not prevent the Austrians from creeping closer to Colmar. With Austrian troops at Ensisheim, Milhaud realized he could not hold Colmar without infantry support and so appealed to General François-Louis Forestier to move the 3,000 men and twelve guns of his brigade from Guémar to Colmar. Evacuating Colmar remained an option, but Milhaud did not fail to recognize the importance of the position. Colmar commanded the narrow Alsatian plain that stretched between the foothills of the Vosges and the left bank of the Rhine. By holding the town, Milhaud not only covered Strasbourg and the Bas-Rhin Department but also the roads leading through the Vosges to Remiremont and St. Dié. Pity for the inhabitants of Colmar also influenced Milhaud. "One could not abandon to excruciating reprisals the inhabitants, who, exasperated by the horrors committed by Scheibler's partisans, had taken part in the struggle," explains Lefebvre de Béhaine. "He [Milhaud] gave them time to send the women, children, cattle, and their most precious belongings to the Vosges." Much to the relief of the remaining inhabitants, Forestier's brigade marched into Colmar at noon on the 26th, bringing news that a second column under Jamin could arrive as early as the next day. This prospect helped ease Milhaud's growing anxiety over reports that the Austrians were concentrating to attack Colmar. That same evening, the emperor's aide-de-camp, Dejean, reached Colmar en route to Huningue with the special task of organizing the defense of the fortress. Unable to go any further, Dejean remained with Milhaud, sparking the rumor that Napoleon himself would soon arrive with an army to deliver Alsace.[52]

From Strasbourg Victor assured Berthier that if he had more combat power he would not hesitate to march on Basel, take the city, and then fall on the rear of the enemy. "But I have only 6,000–7,000 infantry at my disposal and 2,600 cavalry with which I must stop the enemy's movement in Alsace for as long as possible." Had Victor understood Schwarzenberg as Napoleon understood the Austrian commander, the victory at Ste. Croix would have been followed by a march on Huningue. As for increasing his combat power, Victor echoed Milhaud's report regarding the requests of locals to form partisan bands. "The inhabitants of the Haut-Rhin show much energy and good will. These people are naturally good horsemen." The men of Colmar even pledged to pay for their arms and ammunition.[53] Despite the brave enthusiasm of Colmar's inhabitants, the marshal did not take on the responsibility of arming the people.

Victor did little on the 26th other than write letters. His headquarters issued two reports to Berthier and a lengthy summary to Minister of War Clarke regarding the status of the Alsatian fortresses. His first letter to Berthier responded to Napoleon's "Orders" of 21 December to reorganize the II Corps into three divisions. Perhaps receiving instructions to restructure his command as opposed to definitive orders regarding strategy baffled the marshal. "I understand the extreme importance of the prompt organization of the II Corps," begins Victor's report with a tone of exasperation that foregoes the usual formalities such as "I have the honor to report to Your Excellency." As if hostilities had not commenced, he makes no mention of military operations. Yet these letters offer a glimpse of the resources available to Victor and, more important, the marshal's state of mind prior to his evacuation of Alsace. He informed Berthier that the reorganization of the II Corps could not be "made definitively" until the arrival of additional units. Victor complained over the shortage of manpower in his battalions, of the composition of the artillery, of the quality of his personnel and equipment, and of his lack of a full staff. Although the arsenal at Strasbourg "offers us all the material for the artillery that we could hope for," it lacked carriages to transport the guns.[54]

In his second report, Victor offered a summary of Milhaud's reconnaissance: between Huningue and Neuf-Brisach operated enemy light infantry and cavalry; a large enemy column moved through Porrentruy to besiege Belfort; the Bavarians had concentrated a considerable corps in front of Milhaud to attack him momentarily. "I await the news that I have requested from him regarding the offensive march that he supposes the enemy will make against him." At the moment, Milhaud's cavalry, Forestier's 3,000 men, twenty guns, and Jamin's column, which Victor had just finished forming in Strasbourg, was all the marshal had to hold Wrede. "With these means, we hope to stop the enemy while we await the arrival of the new forces that His Majesty will undoubtedly judge necessary to send us."[55]

Concerning the Alsatian fortresses, Victor explained to Clarke that since his arrival at Strasbourg, he had taken all possible measures to arm and provision the fortresses of the 5th Military District. Nevertheless, Belfort still lacked provisions as of the 21st. Victor's 10 December request to Vieuville to provision the fortress for sixty days had not been honored, and its warehouses stood empty. Belfort also lacked artillery crews. Sélestat, in central Alsace, likewise had no gunners, which prompted Victor to dispatch an artillery company from Strasbourg's garrison.[56] As for the other fortresses, Victor described the provisioning as sufficient but incomplete; the ammunition supply appeared satisfactory, but only three-fifths of the necessary powder was available. The garrisons of Huningue, Sélestat, and Neuf-Brisach neared their full complement but consisted mainly of National Guards who, although armed, lacked uniforms and equipment. The depots of the 63rd Line and 14th Chasseurs provided Belfort's garrison. The former numbered 838 men, of whom 600 were armed; the latter comprised 289 troopers without mounts. Belfort's Civic Guard of 506 unarmed men supported the Line troops. Sélestat, Huningue, and Neuf-Brisach possessed garrisons of approximately 3,000 men each.[57] Although Victor had not yet decided to abandon Alsace, he took no initiative. These letters suggest the marshal had already resigned himself to failure.

News that an Allied army of 160,000 men would cross the Rhine at Basel reached Paris late on the 24th in the form of a report dated 20 December from the French minister in Switzerland. Later that same night Berthier reiterated the emperor's instructions from the 21st for Marmont to establish his headquarters at Landau and to move the VI Infantry and the I Cavalry Corps up the Rhine; the divisions of the IV Corps would guard Mainz and cover Marmont's rear. "It is true that the enemy has taken Basel and will cross to the left bank there," confirmed Berthier in a letter to Marmont.[58] On 26 December,

Berthier sent Marmont another grave missive: the enemy had forced the bridge at Basel during the night of 20–21 December and reached Mulhouse on the 23rd. "You will march to support the duke of Bellune. His Majesty believes you have started your movement to Landau. It is of the utmost importance to support the duke of Bellune!" Berthier requested an update of Marmont's musters: the emperor wanted to know how many men the marshal could move into Upper Alsace. The hint of desperation in Berthier's letter reveals the importance Napoleon placed on Marmont's intervention. Incredibly, the emperor paid little heed to his most bitter foe, Blücher. Willing to denude the middle Rhine of the VI Infantry and I Cavalry Corps, the emperor willingly placed the defense of the 26th Military District solely in the hands of Morand and the IV Corps at Mainz. Despite the steady arrival of reinforcements, typhus consumed Morand's four divisions. Paris, however, did not take this into consideration. In fact, Berthier expressed hope that Morand soon would have enough troops to cede two of his divisions to Marmont. In no way would Morand's troop strength allow him to garrison Mainz and guard the frontier from Koblenz to Strasbourg – let alone relinquish half of his corps to Marmont.[59]

Dispatches took three days to pass to and from the Rhine frontier and Paris. Marmont still had not received the original letter of 24 December informing him of Basel's capitulation. On the 27th, in fact, Marmont succumbed to another panic attack before receiving either of Berthier's communiqués. His argument is long and interesting and offers insight into Marmont's perception of his role just a few days prior to the commencement of his retreat from the Rhine to the Marne. Informed by Victor of the events at Basel, Marmont reached the conclusion that he should withdraw from the middle Rhine with the precious cadres of seventy-two battalions. According to the most recent reports, Blücher's army still remained inactive around Höchst. In a letter to Berthier, he claims that "if, as everything appears, the principle enemy forces haven taken the direction on Belfort and from there will move into the interior, I suppose the emperor will want to employ some of the forces that are here." In this case, Marmont felt the need to inform the emperor of the horrible state of health of the IV and VI Corps, both of which had been ravaged by typhus. Although the IV Corps recently received 2,000 conscripts, it contained less than 11,000 combat-ready troops. The two divisions of the VI Corps numbered between 8,000 and 9,000 soldiers. After forming the garrison of Mainz, the marshal would have no mobile forces remaining at his disposal. As for this task, he objected to the emperor's notion that the garrison should consist of 20,000 men who, whether sick or healthy, would become trapped in Mainz if the Allies moved across the middle Rhine. From both corps, he suggested creating two divisions of twenty-four battalions to form the garrison of Mainz and to guard the banks of the Rhine for as long as possible along with some of the units of the I Cavalry Corps. Marmont himself would retreat to where the new army would be formed in the interior with the remainder of the IV and VI Corps, which he estimated could provide the cadres of seventy-two battalions. "It appears to me," speculates the marshal, "that in the current circumstances, the prompt creation of an army is necessary." In this case, the conscripts could not be delayed from reaching the depots by enemy partisans, which Marmont believed the Allies would dispatch in every direction. The force he planned to leave behind on the Rhine would presumably cover the retreat of his cadres to the interior and shield the depots from Allied raids.[60]

Marmont's proposal marks the beginning of a controversial disconnect between Napoleon and his front-line marshals. Both Victor and Marmont believed their main duty was to conserve their forces for the emperor's future use. Throughout the invasion, the two commanders traded land for time to protect their troops from inevitable destruction at the hands of a numerically superior adversary. On the contrary, Napoleon wanted to expend the remains of the Grande Armée far from the French interior. Bonaparte envisioned the Rhine as a buffer that would protect France while he mobilized the state's resources. Should the Allies cross the river, he expected his marshals to hold the enemy's forces as close to the eastern frontier as possible rather than conduct a precipitous retreat to the French interior that would disrupt the harvesting of manpower and material for the new army.

According to the estimates, the IV Corps would receive 4,600 reinforcements and the VI Corps 4,275 by 31 December. However, the emperor ordered Clarke to halt the reinforcements that were already en route. In fact, no conscript march battalions passed the frontier of old France; the furthest advanced units backtracked to Metz and Nancy, where they received new destinations.[61] Marmont correctly deemed the necessity to shield the formation of the new army and to protect the conscripts en route to the area of concentration. However, he misunderstood the emperor's material and political needs. As a monarch who based his popularity as well as his absolutism on his military exploits, trading land for time was not a viable option for Bonaparte. Popular support of his regime could steadily wane if the Allied invasion progressed. For his strapped economy and depleted budget, yielding the eastern departments to the Allies would deny him precious tax revenue. The increasing desertion of German, Dutch, and Belgian soldiers, whose homes now fell behind "enemy" lines, became a problem at the front. Napoleon could not afford to lose the manpower provided by his Rhenish departments. In short, the war could move no closer than the banks of the Rhine.

On the other side of the chess board, Schwarzenberg's columns continued to slither through Switzerland between 25 and 27 December as advance guard detachments crossed the French frontier along the entire front. Behind this screen, the army wheeled right, pivoting on Crenneville's division at Porrentruy and Bianchi's 1st Grenadier Division at Glovelier just east of the

Doubs River. As for the various corps, Colloredo's I reached Bern on the 27th, Liechtenstein moved his II Corps to Neuchâtel, and Gyulay halted at Biel. Northeast of the army, Barclay de Tolly received orders from the tsar himself to commence the movement of the Russo–Prussian Guard and Reserve toward Lörrach on the 28th.

On the verge of entering Franche-Comté, Schwarzenberg issued an army order regarding the entry of his army in France and the conduct of the troops.[62] He insisted that his corps commanders ensure the highest discipline of their troops as the only means to facilitate the provisioning of the army and to win the hearts and minds of the French people. The Allied commander in chief also sent one copy each of Friedrich Jacobs's *Deutschlands Gefahren und Hoffnungen: An Germaniens Jugend*, to Bubna, A. Liechtenstein, Colloredo, Gyulay, Wrede, Wittgenstein, Frederick William, Hesse-Homburg, Bianchi, and Barclay de Tolly. According to historian and German linguist Otto Johnston, this pamphlet, published in Basel that same year, was one of the few patriotic tracts that favored German nationalism and political unity over regionalism yet contained none of the telltale signs of Prussian literary collaboration. Schwarzenberg's cover letter further discussed the importance of winning the support of the peoples on the left bank of the Rhine.[63]

To fill the gap on his right caused by the deployment of the V Corps at Huningue and Belfort, Schwarzenberg instructed thirty-one-year-old Crown Prince Frederick William of Württemberg to proceed as quickly as possible through Freiburg to Märkt, where the IV Corps would cross the Rhine. On the 27th, Bavarian engineers at Märkt bridged the Rhine with pontoons as the IV Corps marched up the Rhine. That same day, Wittgenstein assembled his II Infantry Corps at Rastatt as part of the preparations to cross the Rhine at Plittersdorf, just a few miles west of Rastatt and opposite of Seltz.[64]

The 27th brought no relief to Milhaud, who persisted in believing he would be attacked by overwhelming forces. Neither he nor Victor knew of the inability of the Allied cavalry to ascertain an accurate estimate of French forces between Strasbourg and Colmar. Allied reconnaissance missions provided vague and contradictory details that grossly exaggerated the strength of Victor's troops along the upper Rhine.[65] Conversely, the aggressive French cavalry discerned Allied troop strengths and positions. Milhaud's cavalry conducted "strong" reconnaissance missions along the entire front. One patrol found a large Austrian bivouac near Cernay on the road to Belfort. A second detachment moved south from Colmar on the road to Mulhouse but stopped at Meyenheim after learning of the presence of an enemy division at Ensisheim. French troopers also drove Scheibler's post from Balgau on the road to Huningue. Based on the reports he received, Milhaud assumed that an Allied force of 15,000 to 20,000 men occupied the region between Belfort and Mulhouse. "With prudence and vigor I harass the flanks of the enemy," he reports to Berthier; "everyday my detachments of light cavalry and dragoons skirmish with enemy detachments; up until now these encounters have been to our advantage. I protect the communes from the requisitions of the enemy as much as my resources allow me." Milhaud likewise insisted on the élan of the Alsatians and their willingness to defend the land against "the enemies of the emperor and of France." The corps commander reiterated that the Alsatians were willing to defend their homes but needed weapons and direction. He requested the emperor's authorization to organize the inhabitants of the Haut-Rhin Department into a volunteer legion of both infantry and cavalry under General Berckheim, a zealous native Alsatian who lived in the department and enjoyed widespread popularity.[66]

Two days later the cavalry commander again urged Paris to take action: "Would it not be proper to answer the proclamations of the enemy, to employ all of the National Guardsmen of the region, to overwhelm the enemy's flanks in the forests and the mountains with Line detachments mixed with companies of volunteers, and to appeal to these loyal subjects of the emperor who love horses to participate in the defense of the frontiers?"[67] Milhaud did not exaggerate the state of affairs in Alsace. At the moment, Napoleon still maintained his prestige in Alsace, whose inhabitants feared the return of the archaic feudal regime of the German princes. Regardless, the emperor refused to resort to base revolutionary means to wage war and had yet to consider the idea of a *levée-en-masse* on par with that of the Revolution.[68]

An unconfirmed rumor that the Allies had crossed the Rhine at Koblenz and Spire reached Strasbourg on the morning of the 27th.[69] Victor also received the alarming news that another Allied corps (Wittgenstein's) had assembled at Rastatt. Unsure of the direction it would take, the marshal wondered if this corps would follow the Allied columns through Basel.[70] The other units of the Austrian army apparently remained in march to Porrentruy and Belfort. At 8:00 P.M. on the 27th Victor penned in his daily brief to Berthier and outlined his intentions. According to Milhaud's latest report, Wrede's corps faced him; the general expected to be attacked at any moment. Victor estimated the size of Wrede's corps to be 20,000 to 25,000 men. He planned to dispatch from Strasbourg the rest of the 1st Division along with two batteries to establish a second line behind Milhaud at Guémar. "I have chosen to await the enemy in this position because it is the narrowest in the valley and because it is suitable for the forces I have at my disposal. At the moment, they consist of 7,000 infantry, 3,500 cavalry, three light and two heavy batteries. Milhaud has been ordered to withdraw to Guémar if the enemy marches against him, but to cover and defend Colmar if he is able to do so without jeopardizing himself." Victor intended to move his headquarters to Guémar as soon as the enemy made "an offensive movement." The marshal concluded his report with an unbelievable revelation: No administrative services had been established to meet the needs of his troops. His men depended entirely on the goodwill of the inhabitants for their food. He feared the lack of organization would lead to requisitions and hardships for the Alsatians, who already appeared hard-pressed to provide provisions for the region's fortresses.[71] For the moment, however, the situation in Upper Alsace appeared to be improving. "The affair at Ste. Croix, near Colmar, has produced a very good result," states the 27 December report of a French agent, "and has reassured the inhabitants and the administration. The activity of the civil and military administrations to finish and complete the provisioning, exercising, and arming of those men who arrive is above all praiseworthy."[72]

North of Victor, Marmont's forces provided the only source of support that would enable the French to remain on the left bank of the upper Rhine. At Mainz on the night of the 27th, Marmont received Berthier's letter of the 24th directing the VI Infantry and I Cavalry Corps to Landau. The marshal issued the corresponding orders, but timing became an issue. Marmont could do nothing until the divisions of the IV Corps and 1st Honor Guard Regiment relieved the divisions of the VI Infantry and I Cavalry Corps along the left bank. General Pierre-François-Joseph Durutte's 32nd Division and the 1st Honor Guard Regiment were supposed to assume the posts that Ricard's 1st Division occupied between Koblenz and Bingen. According to Marmont's calculations, Ricard would have to remain at Koblenz until at least 30 December and could not reach Landau before 3 January. Upstream from Mainz, Lagrange's 3rd Division would relinquish its posts to General Jean-Baptiste-Pierre Semellé's 51st Division and the 2nd Honor Guard Regiment. Lagrange could commence his movement on the 29th and reach Neustadt the following day. Doumerc's I Cavalry Corps would assemble at Kreuznach on the 29th and arrive at Neustadt by 1 January. Marmont figured he needed at least eight days to assemble his corps at Landau and reach Strasbourg. The weakness of his battalions provided an even greater concern for the marshal.[73]

On the morning of the 29th, Marmont received the letter Berthier penned at 3:00 A.M. on the 26th containing the stirring cry: "It is of the utmost importance to support the duke of Bellune!" Marmont responded at 4:00 P.M. with an update regarding the movement of his units: The I Cavalry Corps and the 3rd Division were en route to Neustadt; the 1st Division would commence its march to Landau on the following morning. He also answered Berthier's query regarding troop strength. Because of a large sick list and the daily arrival of conscripts, Marmont could not provide an exact figure. He believed his infantry would not increase to more than 9,000 bayonets supported by 2,500 sabers and thirty-six cannons, including twelve guns that belonged to the IV Corps. "Voila, here is the force of the army corps that is marching, but I repeat – it is hardly combat-ready; almost all the battalions are extremely weak and each has no more than 150 men." As he concluded his letter to Berthier, reports reached Mainz of Allied preparations to cross the river at Philippsburg, across the Rhine from Landau. Returning to his original obsession, the marshal claimed patrols reported seeing numerous Allied troop formations marching to Mannheim. On the following day, the 30th, Marmont planned to reconnoiter the banks of the Rhine personally as he proceeded toward Strasbourg. Marmont informed Victor that relief was on the way, but no one knew if the VI Corps would arrive in time.[74]

One characteristic of an exceptional military leader is the ability to adjust to changing circumstances. Obviously Napoleon demanded flexibility from his corps commanders. Yet even his battle-hardened veteran officers had to contend with their emotions and their fatigue. The emperor continuously tested the limits of his lieutenants' perseverance, but in some cases the rational gave way to the absurd. In the situation that Victor and Marmont found themselves, utter despair could not have been far off. In the midst of receiving these urgent orders to move up the Rhine to support Victor, Berthier's letter of 25 December reached Mainz containing the instructions for the reorganization of the army. These tedious directives, coming in the immediate aftermath of the Allied invasion, called for Marmont to reorganize the two divisions of the VI Corps into three. To complete the reorganization of the VI Corps, Berthier promised Marmont that he would receive twenty-two battalions, which were currently forming in their depots. "Consequently," continues Berthier, "remove from Ricard's division [the 8th], which is now your 1st Division, the battalions of 9th and 16th Light and place them in your 2nd Division, which they will be part of henceforth. These battalions will form the 2nd Division with those from the 1st, 14th, 15th, 16th, 62nd, 70th and 121st Regiments of Lagrange's present division. The 3rd Division will be formed by the rest of the battalions of Lagrange's present division [the 20th]: the battalions of the 23rd and 37th Light, and the 1st, 3rd, and 4th Marine Regiments." In addition to the twenty-two new battalions, Marmont would receive the 2nd Battalion of 4th Light from the garrison of Antwerp and the 2nd Battalion of the 15th Line, currently at Landau. "You will note," concludes Berthier, "the new organization of the VI Corps will not include the 1st Battalion of the 28th Light, the 1st Battalion of the 22nd Line, the 2nd Battalion of the 59th Line, and the 3rd Battalion of the 69th Line. Hereafter, these four battalions must be considered part of the XI Corps. Prepare everything to make them march as soon as you have received the definitive order, which I will send you shortly."[75]

Victor, Macdonald, Morand, and Maison all received similar letters affecting their respective corps. Although originally formulated by Napoleon on the 21st – before he learned the Allies had crossed the Rhine at Basel – Berthier's follow-up letter reveals the emperor's determination to carry out this reorganization. We can only speculate what the marshals thought of this ludicrous task at such a critical period and how it affected their state of mind. No device exists to measure the mental strain, anxiety, depression, exhaustion, and frustration of these officers who felt the weighty burden of fighting for their nation's very survival. Their subsequent actions offer insight to the extent of their psychological collapse.

Although the Allied commander in chief was haunted by his own demons, he had 300,000 men at his disposal. On 28 December, Schwarzenberg finally took steps to honor a decision made during the councils of war in Frankfurt. Accordingly, the Allies agreed that numerous Streifkorps would precede the Bohemian Army into France. Headquarters issued instructions for the organization of six Streifkorps to cover the army's flanks.[76] "Schwarzenberg believes that upon entering France we must employ only bold and intrepid partisan commanders," wrote Toll to Volkonsky, "but above all officers who, through their ability to speak the language of the land, through their intelligence and their personal observations, can provide precise information of the enemy's movements."[77] The generalissimo hoped to employ the 5,000 horsemen of General Matvei Ivanovich Platov's Don Cossack Corps of the Russian Reserve. Toll, however, advised that the sixty-year-old Ataman did not fit Schwarzenberg's criteria, particularly regarding initiative. As a result, Barclay de Tolly detached four Cossack Regiments (1,064 men) from Platov's corps. Placed under General Nikolay Grigorievich Sherbatov II's command, the regiments departed for Lörrach on the 25th. These units were to augment the Cossacks and Allied light cavalry that already had crossed the Rhine. As for the rest of Platov's corps, Schwarzenberg requested that the tsar personally issue the orders for the Ataman's operations in the hope of motivating the Cossack commander.

According to Schwarzenberg's plans, the remains of Scheibler's command formed the first Streifkorps, which would follow the Rhine through Colmar toward Strasbourg. The instructions issued to the commander of the second Streifkorps, Lieutenant Colonel Thurn, initially directed him through the Moselle Valley to Nancy. Schwarzenberg modified this operation to place Thurn's Streifkorps on the point of the army's left wing. In accordance with this change, the third Streifkorps would proceed down the Moselle to Nancy. Sherbatov received this assignment when he arrived in Lörrach on 29 December with his four Cossack Regiments. After transferring one of his regiments to Thurn, Sherbatov crossed the Rhine and moved to Altkirch with approximately 800 men. "Your principal objective," states Schwarzenberg's orders, "will be to ascertain for me all the enemy's movements and to utilize favorable moments to deliver appreciable blows without risking an engagement with an enemy superior to you. During this march . . . you will forward detachments toward Langres and Vesoul. . . . I request that you send me daily reports in order to give me time to make the necessary arrangements concerning the movements of the army."[78] Schwarzenberg planned for a fourth Streifkorps to operate between the Saône and the Loire Rivers, but this never came to fruition. Major von Wöber received orders to lead the fifth Streifkorps through

Besançon to Bourges. Finally, Schwarzenberg planned to send Seslavin across France to Wellington's headquarters to deliver the Allied operations plan. Wittgenstein already employed Seslavin on the left bank to establish communication with both Blücher and Wrede, and so nothing came of this absurd idea. This proved to be the last word regarding the grand idea of having the Bohemian Army march west to link with the Anglo–Portuguese army.[79]

In the meantime, the rest of the Bohemian Army continued to move across the French frontier.[80] After reaching Biel on 30 December, Colloredo divided the I Corps into two columns. The first, composed of the 1st and 3rd Divisions and commanded by Colloredo himself, marched northwest to Baumeles-Dames on the Doubs River.[81] General Maximilian von Wimpffen's 2nd Division and Moritz von Liechtenstein's 2nd Light Division formed the second column, which received the task of blockading Besançon, *chef-lieu* of the Doubs Department.[82] Scheither, with the advance guard of the II Corps, by-passed Ft. Joux on the 29th and struck the road to Pontarlier. Behind him, the II Corps extended southwest along the French frontier from la Chaux-de-Fonds to Morteau on the highway to Pontarlier.[83] Gaining St. Imier on the 28th, Gyulay's III Corps marched north to support Bianchi, who occupied Porrentruy.[84] On the 30th, Bianchi received orders to relieve the Bavarians at Belfort. His division reached Montbéliard the following day. Far in front of the army, Crenneville's division stopped at Pierrefontaine and reconnoitered Besançon on the 29th.[85] As soon as Bianchi reached Belfort, Crenneville had orders to proceed to Vesoul.[86] Hesse-Homburg's Austrian Reserve reached Bern on the 29th and continued through Neuchâtel.[87] On New Year's Eve, a French force of 600 infantry and 300 cavalry led by the commandant of the 6th Military District, General Jacob-François Marulaz, attacked Wöber's Streifkorps at Baume-les-Dames on the Doubs, eighteen miles northeast of Besançon. Wöber's troopers had occupied this position – the halfway point between Besançon and Belfort – until Marulaz retook the town and obliged them to recross the Doubs at Clerval, leaving behind eighteen dead and 103 prisoners.[88]

On the extreme left wing of the army, Bubna continued his march, reaching Geneva on the 30th. On the same day, the French commandant of Geneva, General Nicolas-Louis Jordy, "struck as by a thunderbolt," fell unconscious in the midst of his staff after suffering a stroke that left him paralyzed from the waist down. The officer who replaced him, devoid of any instructions, only thought to capitulate. A white flag was hoisted and the French garrison of 1,500 poorly armed veterans surrendered. As Beauchamp laments, "the garrison and the French authorities abandoned Geneva and the bourgeoisie opened the gates to the Austrians, at the same moment when reinforcements arrived at Grenoble. The capture of Geneva, one of the gates to Napoleon's empire, opened to the Austrians the passes of Italy and the road to Lyon, and henceforth the direct communication between France and the plains of Piedmont and Lombardy." Irritated over the loss of Geneva, Napoleon dismissed Prefect Guillaume-Antoine-Benoît Capelle of the Léman Department for having abandoned the city. Although an investigating committee exonerated Capelle, Napoleon imprisoned him, claiming the civil official had forgotten that prefects were not simply the stewards of finances but were also the chief figures of law and order in their departments.[89]

Geneva's arsenal provided Bubna with 117 heavy guns, several howitzers, thirty field guns, fifteen munitions wagons, and enough small arms to outfit 1,000 infantry. After securing the city, Bubna dispatched several small detachments to secure the passes through the Jura and Alps.[90] One moved north through Gex to the pass at St. Claude, while a second marched west on the Geneva – Lyon highway toward the French-occupied Ft. de l'Ecluse. A third under Colonel Joseph Simbschen was en route from Lausanne to St. Maurice to sever French communications with Italy through the Simplon and St. Bernhard Passes. From this point, Bubna virtually operated as an independent commander in southern France. He left General Theophil Joseph von Zechmeister at Geneva with a small garrison. Here Schwarzenberg could have gained a great advantage from his eccentric wheeling movement by pushing Bubna south to Lyon and the Rhône Valley. Schwarzenberg's own operations journal states: "It is known that the middle of France is empty of troops and that one is only occupied with organizing forces at Lyon and Grenoble."[91] "One could have hindered the levée in the provinces of southeast France and provoked the agitation of the royalists," comments Clausewitz.[92] Bubna should have marched immediately to the Rhône Valley to occupy Lyon, the second city of France. With few troops and hardly any means to defend itself, Lyon would have fallen to Bubna's 5,000-man division. The loss of Lyon would have spread dismay as well as resentment toward the imperial administration throughout France. But instead of advancing south to Lyon, Schwarzenberg directed Bubna north to Dijon to cover the army's left wing as it proceeded to Langres.

The Allied operation on the upper Rhine persuaded Napoleon to take measures to secure Geneva. On 1 January, he instructed Berthier to work with Clarke in forming the Réserve de Genève between Geneva and Lyon. In his correspondence he noted Augereau would command the division assigned to defend Lyon. Over the next two days, this division was increased on paper to include the eighteen battalions of the Réserve de Genève, now commanded by Musnier, and designated a corps. After learning Allied forces occupied Geneva, Napoleon instructed Musnier to take a position between Geneva and Lyon, occupy Ft. de l'Ecluse, defend the Jura passes, and guard the crossings over the Rhône. Musnier soon discovered that manpower shortages did not allow him to comply with these ambitious orders. Until the mobilization was complete, he had to limit himself to occupying Lyon with 1,500 soldiers, Bourg-en-Bresse (*chef-lieu* of the Ain Department) with 500, and Nantua on the road from Bourg to Geneva with 300.[93]

On the Bohemian Army's right wing, a detachment from Rechberg's division entered Lure, halfway between Belfort and Vesoul, on the morning of the 27th. A wave of terror swept through the latter, which served as *chef-lieu* of the Haute-Saône Department. Although the Civic Guard had yet to be summoned and no measures were taken for the defense of Vesoul, Prefect Alexandre-André de Flavigny and the gendarmerie fled to Besançon that same night, leaving behind large magazines of forage as well as several sick soldiers.[94] On the 28th, the French launched a spirited sortie from Belfort that inflicted numerous casualties on Rechberg's division. As a result, Delamotte received orders to move the majority of his division to Belfort. At Huningue, the Bavarians constructed two batteries of four guns each and a battery of mortars facing Huningue's bridgehead on the 27th. The next day Wrede's troops opened the first parallel. On the night of 29–30 December, Wrede commenced the formal bombardment of Huningue with forty-four pieces of artillery; Rechberg likewise shelled Belfort.[95] "Last night the bombardment of Huningue commenced," states Wilson's journal entry of 30 December, "about fifty guns opened fire. I went into the trenches of the first parallel and remained there until almost 3:00 A.M., being ashamed to leave them, although I was very much vexed at seeing them so ill-constructed as to present scarcely any defense. The principal batteries of the besiegers were on the right bank of the Rhine, from whence they could not make any serious impression; and through the whole plan I never saw more unskillful arrangements. Huningue will never be taken by such means as are now used.... The whole operation is Bavarian."[96] Schwarzenberg, however, attributed the protracted siege of Huningue to an inadequate number of siege guns.[97]

The Bavarian guns failed to induce either French commandant to open his gates. At dawn on the 30th, an informant alerted Wrede to the approach of French forces to relieve *both* Huningue and Belfort. To meet this alleged threat, he modified the positions of his Bavarian divisions. Leaving only one of Rechberg's brigades at Belfort, he ordered the rest of the division east to Dannemarie. Wrede posted one of Delamotte's brigades near Altkirch; the other retraced its steps to Hegenheim to cover Beckers's division at Huningue more effectively. To shield the Bavarian divisions, Frimont's Austrians held the Mulhouse–Thann front with the main body between Thann and Cernay and a strong advance guard at Soultz.[98]

On the other side of the Rhine, the crown prince of Württemberg's IV Corps marched south through Baden in two columns. The Württemberger cavalry reached Märkt on the 29th, crossed the Rhine over a very sturdy pontoon bridge built by the Bavarians, and trooped through Ensisheim to Meyenheim. On the following day, the Württemberger troopers relieved Scheibler's posts. Commanded by General Christian Johann Gottgetreu von Koch, the right wing crossed the Rhine at Märkt and filed north along both sides of the Harth Forest. On the 31st, this column reached Balgau on the

Basel–Neuf-Brisach road. Franquemont led the left wing across the Rhine on New Year's Eve and proceeded to Mulhouse, where the crown prince established his headquarters.[99]

The approach of the IV Corps strengthened Wrede's desire to unfetter his divisions from the sieges and resume the offensive. Knowing that Blücher and Gneisenau were kindred spirits, he wanted to establish direct communication with the Prussians. On 30 December, one of his adjutants, Major August Maria Maximilian, the Prince of Thurn-Taxis, left Wrede's headquarters with the task of persuading Blücher to march south. The major reached Blücher's headquarters at Kreuznach on 3 January: The Silesian Army had just completed its passage of the middle Rhine. Gneisenau explained his intention to execute a concentric operation that would bring Blücher's army to Metz and move it closer to the Bohemian Army. A satisfied Thurn-Taxis departed the next day to deliver Blücher's formal response to Wrede.[100] "I have always felt the necessity to remain on your right and on the right of the Bohemian Army," wrote the field marshal, "and if Metz is not the point from which threatening operations can be launched against us, I believe that I will have to march on Nancy. Under the current circumstances I will seek the enemy's forces and this will greatly ease your operation."[101] Schwarzenberg was informed of this meeting as well as Blücher's plans to request support from Wittgenstein by the Austrian attaché in Blücher's headquarters, Major Wenzel Philipp Leopold von Mareschall. His letter of 4 January reached Schwarzenberg's headquarters on the 11th. The commander in chief did not react favorably to Wrede's initiative and Blücher's meddling in the internal affairs of his army.[102]

In the meantime, a tense Milhaud held the Colmar–Neuf-Brisach front but had nothing new to report to Victor other than the Allied camp at Cernay. With the front momentarily stabilized, the marshal passed his time in Strasbourg attempting to complete the frustrating chore of reorganizing the II Corps. Victor received letters dated the 21st, 23rd, 24th, and 25th relative to this assignment. Napoleon's instructions of the 23rd, which reached the marshal at 8:00 P.M. on the 26th, stated: "it is of the greatest importance to employ all possible means to complete the formation of the II Corps" by 1 January.[103] Receiving these letters as the crises in Alsace grew only perplexed the marshal. Several detachments of the Corps's 2nd Battalions did start arriving, but the troops lacked so much equipment and were so poorly uniformed that Victor could not use them in their current condition.

According to the instructions of the 21st, the artillery of the II Corps was to consist of eight batteries including one reserve and one horse. The 4th Division, which Napoleon's new order of battle designated as the 1st division of the II Corps, arrived in Strasbourg with one battery each of foot and horse; Victor had to form the remaining six batteries.[104] General François-Bernard Mongenet, the artillery commander of the II Corps, informed the marshal that he encountered "great obstacles" in his attempts to organize the remaining batteries because of the lack of personnel, horses, and equipment. The fact that Strasbourg's arsenal could provide enough guns for ten or twelve batteries within twenty-four hours only made the situation more depressing. Conscripts and remounts for the artillery barely trickled into Strasbourg. Conversely, requests for gunners, powder, and lead streamed into Strasbourg from the commandants of the Alsatian fortresses, whose own arsenals lacked sufficient quantities. Unable to meet these demands, Victor simply forwarded the requests to Berthier. He added his own concerns over the severe shortage of funds that prevented him from securing supplies for his troops: "The 4th [1st] Division and V Cavalry Corps are currently in the field and absolutely no measures have been taken to assure their subsidence." With no funds and no administrative services, the men continued to live off the land. The generosity of the Alsatians did have its limits. With each winter day, the region's food supply decreased; foraging soon gave way to pillaging in some areas. Victor expressed his vexation concerning the inhabitants' growing discontent over the conduct of his troops.[105]

More important for Victor, the 28th finally brought some directions from Paris. At 8:00 P.M. a courier delivered Berthier's response to Victor's 23 December report concerning the marshal's decision to dispatch Milhaud's corps and all available infantry to Colmar. Although the Allied invasion was in its sixth day, the emperor still did not comprehend its full magnitude. He approved Victor's measures as outlined in the marshal's letter of the 23rd and issued further directives. Reflective of Napoleon's superficial understanding of the gravity of the events along the Upper Rhine, the myriad of instructions that Berthier included in his letter to Victor lacked substance and can be described as general at best. Nevertheless, had Victor accurately interpreted the emperor's orders, he would have found sufficient reason to at least maintain his position in Upper Alsace. Berthier instructed Victor to sound the alarm and have the inhabitants *harass* the enemy; the emperor counted on the bravery and patriotism of the Alsatians to support the line troops. The chief of staff also informed Victor that Young Guard units would occupy the passes of the Vosges and that Marmont had received orders to move the VI Corps to Landau. With Marmont en route, Napoleon advised Victor to complete the arming and provisioning of Strasbourg and its citadel, confide the defense of the city to the National Guard, and join his troops in the field. "We are still too little informed of what the enemy intends to allow us to determine a general movement. But you must...not allow yourself to be cut off from Metz."[106] This simple statement probably cost the emperor Alsace.

Two roads ran from Strasbourg to Metz. The first passed though Saverne, Phalsbourg, and Château-Salins; the second crossed the Vosges at the Donon Pass and continued through Raon-l'Étape and Nancy. Because possession of Colmar was not vital for utilizing either route, Victor reached the conclusion that he no longer needed to hold the *chef-lieu*. He issued orders that same evening, the 28th, for his infantry to withdraw from the Haut-Rhin Department. On the next day, Forestier moved his brigade north from Colmar to a position between Guémar and Sélestat, while Jamin marched north from Guémar to echelon his brigade between Sélestat and Strasbourg. Even less comprehensible is the marshal's decision to leave Milhaud's cavalry isolated at Colmar.[107] Forestier's departure from Colmar on the 29th shattered the morale of the inhabitants and baffled Milhaud. The cavalry commander did not challenge Victor's order but did persuade Forestier to leave behind 400 men and three guns as a garrison.[108]

Victor's critical misunderstanding and misinterpretation of his role as outlined in Berthier's instructions cannot be underestimated. Like Marmont, he believed the emperor counted on him to conserve the troops under his command. This assumption is understandable owing to the amount of paperwork that flowed from Berthier's office regarding the reorganization of the II Corps as well as the emperor's personal interest in the subject. Moreover, Victor believed he commanded an observation corps and that his task was to monitor the enemy's movements but not engage his forces. In addition, he ignored a vital component of Berthier's letter: Marmont's advance to support him. Instead, Victor obsessed over the emperor's stern warning against being cut off from Metz.

Concern over the Russian concentration at Rastatt may have contributed to Victor's anxiety. Confirmed reports from inhabitants on the right bank of the Rhine indicated that the tsar had joined a corps of 40,000 men at Rastatt on the 28th; Marmont's brief on the 29th also confirmed the reports relative to the enemy's preparations to cross the river, but at Mannheim.[109] Because of the large amount of bridging equipment that accompanied the Allied troops, Victor believed "that the intention of this monarch is to immediately cross the Rhine at Seltz." In their correspondence with Paris, Victor and his subordinates constantly use the term "immediately" to describe Allied intentions to attack and, in this case, cross the Rhine. Paranoia appears to have eclipsed sound military judgment. If the Russians crossed at Seltz, Victor predicted that he would have no choice but to maneuver in the direction of Saverne to follow his line of retreat to Metz.[110] The marshal's correspondence does not reveal whether he believed Marmont could arrive in time to defend his left by preventing the Russians from crossing the Rhine. Although understandable in this light, the marshal's decision to evacuate Upper Alsace uncovered the southern passes through the Vosges – an error in judgment that cannot be excused.

While the French infantry marched downstream, the Allies increased their forces in Alsace. As noted, the IV Corps crossed the Rhine on the 29th and marched to Meyenheim. None of the French intelligence reports mention this corps, and Victor probably was not aware of its arrival. Wittgenstein's intentions also remained unclear. Victor could not determine whether the Russian would cross the Rhine at Seltz or further downstream near Strasbourg. As his desperation mounted, Victor suggested that the emperor sanction an insurrection and partisan war, particularly in the Vosges. Yet the marshal did nothing on his own other than to order the repair of a few hundred antiquated muskets found in Strasbourg's arsenal. Apparently, he knew the emperor's opinion regarding a people's war, yet stated for the record that a general insurrection, "as little as one wants to encourage and support it," would bolster the troops. But the moment had passed. With overwhelming Allied forces about to move into Upper Alsace, Victor soon would make the decision to retreat over the Vosges and yield the left bank of the Rhine to Schwarzenberg. By 30 December, the marshal's forlorn reports smacked of lost hope. His reports contained nothing more than the usual complaints and concerns over the organization of the II Corps and the lack of equipment, powder, ammunition, and food.[111]

Two letters that arrived in Paris on 30 December and furnished opposing views regarding the Allied invasion illustrate the difficulties Napoleon confronted in evaluating the strategic situation and formulating a response. The first, a communiqué dispatched from Strasbourg by a French agent, completely misjudged the state of affairs. The spy claimed "the enemy invasion of the Upper Rhine appears to have the procurement of food as its objective; it has started due to the depletion of the magazines in the Margraviate of Baden and to cover the enemy's march toward Italy by occupying the gorges of Porrentruy and cutting all communication with Switzerland."[112]

The second letter, written in Colmar by the emperor's aide-de-campe, Dejean, provided a frank and accurate overview of the situation. He insisted that all evidence suggested an Allied army of at least 100,000 men had crossed the Rhine. Dejean repeated that enemy columns had struck the roads to Belfort, Porrentruy, and Solothurn; rumors claimed that another was headed to Geneva. Like Milhaud, Dejean praised the élan of the inhabitants of the Haut-Rhin: "You have no loyaler subjects, and they will do whatever you want; you only have to give the order, arouse them with some proclamations, distribute some arms, place a chief in each canton, and you will raise all the heads that are already heavy and you will have as many soldiers as inhabitants; but you must give the order, because one does nothing without orders and nobody wants to take it upon himself to give any." On this note, Dejean did not hide his contempt for Victor and made several unfair and inaccurate charges. True, the marshal lacked initiative and energy; he was not the right man for the job. Yet Dejean criticized him for remaining in Strasbourg and not making plans, taking measures, or giving orders. He even claimed that Victor's mere presence paralyzed everyone. Dejean advised the emperor to replace him with a charismatic and energetic officer to organize the defense of Alsace. He wanted a man of action who would not hesitate to attack the flanks and rear of the enemy in order to slow his march.[113] Were any such men still to be found?

On 1 January 1814, Napoleon received the New Year's homage of his court for the last time. After a numerous crowd of imperial dignitaries, officials, and nobility assembled in the Tuileries, the emperor emerged from his inner apartments. "His manner was calm and grave," attests Madame Junot, "but on his brow there sat a cloud that denoted the approaching storm."[114] That same day Napoleon employed his superior organizational skills to formulate an extensive response to Schwarzenberg's invasion. Unaware of Blücher's offensive, the emperor decreed the formation of four "armies." He planned to create the first – the Army of Alsace – by concentrating at Colmar all mobile units stationed in Alsace to provide a force of 26,000 men under Marmont's command. The inactivity of the Silesian Army convinced the emperor that Blücher had no intention of conducting a winter offensive. Berthier issued orders on 2 January for Marmont to march to Colmar and cooperate with Victor to defend Alsace.[115] He informed the marshal to direct his VI Infantry and I Cavalry Corps to Colmar and assume command of the II Infantry and V Cavalry Corps. Victor, whose lack of initiative had been exposed by Dejean, would remain at Strasbourg to continue the organization of the II Corps. Napoleon redirected all remounts, artillery, equipment, and reinforcements in march for the I and V Cavalry and VI Infantry Corps to Phalsbourg, which would serve as the main depot for the Army of Alsace. In addition, he appointed Berckheim to organize the *levée-en-masse* in the Haut-Rhin and General Louis-Claude Chouard in the Bas-Rhin Departments.

Shielded by the Army of Alsace, the second army would be formed at Épinal, on the western side of the Vosges, sixty-six miles southwest of Strasbourg. The manpower for this army would be provided by the Imperial Guard. Napoleon ordered Curial to move the 1st Young Guard Voltigeur Division from Metz through Nancy to Épinal, while the 2nd Old Guard and 2nd Young Guard Voltigeur Divisions would likewise march to Épinal as soon as the batteries of both divisions were complete. Mortier, who had led the 1st Old Guard and 1st Guard Cavalry Divisions to Belgium, received orders to turn around and proceed to Langres. There, his 8,000 to 9,000 men would form the third army. The emperor instructed him to obtain enough supplies to support an army of 40,000 men. At Paris a reserve consisting of six battalions out of a projected eighteen was likewise placed under Mortier's orders to cover the Paris–Langres highway. Further south in Lyon, Marshal Augereau assumed command of the Réserve de Genève, whose cadres of eighteen battalions would serve as the core of the fourth army.

To support these armies, the emperor instructed Berthier to find suitable candidates to lead the insurrection in the departments situated in the Vosges, Champagne, Franche-Comté, Jura, Lyonnais, Savoy, and Dauphine. Moreover, he ordered the formation of four National Guard corps. The first,

30,000 men, would assemble at Meaux and Nogent. To support Marmont, the 10,000 men of the second corps would unite at Colmar. Napoleon estimated that 20,000 men could be raised in the 2nd, 3rd, and 4th Military Districts to provide the third corps, which would join Curial's troops at Épinal. The fourth corps, likewise 20,000 men, was designated for Augereau's army at Lyon. Supplies, arms, ammunition, and the backing of the people remained Napoleon's main concerns.[116] "The devastation of the Cossacks will arm the inhabitants and double our forces," he assured Caulaincourt. "If the nation supports me, the enemy will march to his loss. If fortune betrays me, my part is over, I cannot maintain the throne. I will debase neither the nation nor myself by accepting disgraceful conditions."[117]

As if Victor read Dejean's incriminating letter, he finally decided to take action in the final days of 1813. Oddly enough, this resolve came when the overwhelming number of enemy troops already in Upper Alsace or preparing to cross the Rhine would render a counteroffensive suicidal. Victor learned "that the enemy is projecting a new passage of the Rhine, which we must threaten to prevent him from effecting." Police Commissioner Charles Popp reported that Wittgenstein had concentrated his corps between Kehl and Rastatt after German contingents relieved his units at the former, thus freeing 30,000 Russians for operations in France.[118] Also, concern over the "enormity" of Allied requisitions, which would "soon lead to the desolation of the land," moved the marshal to at least make an attempt to save the people of Upper Alsace. "The forthcoming arrival of the duke of Raguse and the reinforcements that I have been promised places us in a position to achieve this important objective," wrote an optimistic Victor. If Wittgenstein crossed the river before Victor could move into position to stop him, Victor and Marmont planned to concentrate their forces on the road to Saverne to dispute the terrain step by step. Perhaps written simply to appease the emperor, Victor offered no details of how he would "achieve this important objective."[119] He apparently planned to remain in Strasbourg until Marmont arrived.

On the evening of the 31st, the lead regiments of Doumerc's I Cavalry Corps reached Neustadt, where Marmont established his headquarters. Lagrange remained en route from Kaiserslautern with the twenty-six battalions of his division. His muster did not exceed 4,000 men; 2,000 sick had to be left behind in the hospitals. At the time he penned his brief to Berthier at 8:00 P.M. on the 31st, Marmont still had not received any news of Ricard's approach from Koblenz. In addition, Marmont's report says nothing of cooperating with Victor to prevent the Allies from crossing the Rhine near Strasbourg. Poorly informed by his spies, Marmont continued to march up the Rhine with little concern for his own front. According to his intelligence, "the enemy has troops of all arms on the entire line of the Rhine...[but] reports of an enemy passage at Philippsburg [upstream of Mannheim] appear groundless." The marshal identified the Allied troops between Strasbourg and Koblenz as Blücher's army. "However," he adds, "I do not think he will attempt anything serious on this line during the current season." He hoped bad weather and drift ice would keep Blücher on the right bank. Marmont also forwarded to Berthier the incorrect news that Klenau's corps, which had conducted the siege of Dresden, already passed Heidelberg as it continued up the Rhine to Basel; he informed Victor of this as well.[120]

On the Allied side of the Alsatian front, the arrival of the IV Corps finally allowed Wrede to drive on Colmar. Because his cavalry failed to ascertain the size of the French force holding the *chef-lieu*, Wrede ordered a general reconnaissance along his front. Hardegg's Austrian 1st Division received the task of reconnoitering as far as Ste. Croix, while Scheibler probed Neuf-Brisach. Deserters informed Hardegg that Piré's 9th Light Cavalry Division held the advance posts south of Colmar with three regiments posted at Ste. Croix. At 2:00 A.M. on 31 December, Hardegg's light cavalry, infantry, and artillery advanced in three columns toward Ste. Croix. A dense fog allowed the Austrians to reach the village undetected. Hardegg's advance surprised the French post guarding the bridge leading to Ste. Croix's gate. Arriving in Ste. Croix at the same time as the fleeing French post, the Austrian cavalry stormed through the town at a gallop. Meanwhile, the other two columns enveloped both sides of Ste. Croix. The French managed to escape before the Austrian trap closed.

At 9:00 in the morning, Hardegg assembled his command in the vast plain north of Ste. Croix and continued on the road to Colmar. Although he did not encounter any resistance, the Austrian general cautiously advanced. Piré managed to reunite the majority of his squadrons and retreat north toward Colmar. He halted at the bridge over the Thur River after outpacing his adversary, who lost all contact with the French. Piré then seized the initiative, turned south, and smashed Hardegg's cavalry: the French troopers even drove the Austrians out of Ste. Croix. After the Austrian infantry and artillery arrived, Piré again evacuated Ste. Croix and retraced his steps to the bridge over the Thur. By this time, Milhaud arrived with the 1st Dragoon Division and proceeded south with all available squadrons. Judging his task complete, Hardegg withdrew from Ste. Croix. Milhaud returned to Colmar, leaving only one of Piré's squadrons at Ste. Croix and billeting the rest of the division in Sundhoffen, not far from Colmar.

To the east, Scheibler had a similar experience. His Streifkorps of 150 Cossacks and fifty Hussars surprised a French advance post and charged all the way to the walls of Neuf-Brisach before returning to its original position. Both sides lost no more than a handful of men and horses in either engagement. Although Wrede did not receive much information that could be considered new, the operation cleared the front of the IV Corps.[121]

Milhaud and Dejean recognized the meaning of Wrede's reconnaissance. Based on the statements of locals, they estimated that 30,000 Allied soldiers had taken positions between Huningue and Belfort on the 30th.[122] In addition, Prefect Vieuville's agents reported that an advance guard of 4,500 Württembergers entered Mulhouse, where the crown prince established his headquarters. Behind them the rest of the Allied army continued to pour over the Rhine. Others stated that 20,000 Austrians under Frimont's orders camped at Cernay. To the southwest, the main mass of Schwarzenberg's army invaded Franche-Comté. Exaggerated reports claimed the advance guard of a Russian army of 60,000 men had crossed through Basel on the 29th. The numbers of Allied troops cited by Milhaud in his 31 December report are staggering: 15,000 besieging Huningue, 20,000 at Belfort, 6,000 at Mulhouse, and 50,000 at Geneva.[123] Regardless of the inflated numbers, the two French generals bravely resolved to hold Colmar. Accepting Dejean's advice, Milhaud finally countermanded Victor's orders, recalling Forestier's brigade to Colmar and Jamin's brigade to Guémar.[124]

The new year started cold and calm. At Strasbourg Victor awaited Marmont and had second thoughts regarding his proposed counteroffensive. He expressed concern to Berthier over conserving the II Infantry and V Cavalry Corps. Moreover, with Marmont en route, Victor made the first of many pleas for Napoleon to name a commander in chief to avoid "an army where there are two chiefs."[125] Unfortunately for Victor, his fellow marshal never left Neustadt. Around noon Marmont learned that Allied forces had passed the Rhine at Mannheim that morning. Russian Cossacks swarmed the left bank, spreading the news that Blücher's army was crossing the Rhine. Throughout 1 January Marmont sought to confirm this rumor. He informed Berthier of his plans to repulse the Allied unit that had crossed the Rhine at Mannheim if it was only a strong raiding party. However, if the Allies had crossed in force, he planned to hold the roads to Metz and Nancy for as long as possible and defend the passes of the Vosges foot by foot. If forced, he would slowly withdraw to Neustadt, then Kaiserslautern and, if need be, to the Saar River.[126]

Time unquestionably favored the Allies during the protracted stalemate for control of the left bank of the upper Rhine. With a corps triple the size of Victor's, Wrede could have easily swept down the Rhine to Strasbourg. Perhaps cautious to a fault, Wrede had no incentive to conduct such an operation, which would have been opposed by Schwarzenberg. The Bavarian commander only had to wait for the IV and VI Corps to cross the Rhine and the French marshal would have been destroyed, driven across the Vosges, or trapped in Strasbourg. Victor, on the other hand, did not have the luxury of time. Although the marshal desperately needed to gain as many days as possible to allow Marmont to arrive, he languished in Strasbourg. The odds never favored the duke of Bellune, yet he could have taken measures to alleviate his situation. He should have utilized Milhaud's troopers to launch tactical strikes on an enemy whose inefficient cavalry failed to provide adequate intelligence. Any setback, such as the first combat of Ste. Croix, doubtlessly would have had a tremendous psychological impact on Schwarzenberg. Supported by the Alsatians, Milhaud could have operated more effectively against Allied communications, particularly prior to Frimont's arrival. After Frimont established his divisions north of Huningue to shield the Bavarians, Victor should have organized the defense of the thirteen-mile stretch between Colmar and Neuf-Brisach. He could have dammed the numerous watercourses that flowed between Colmar and Neuf-Brisach to partially flood the region, while the small villages lying between the two could have been entrenched to form a fortified line, such as the Prussians created south of Berlin earlier that year. Victor could have taken advantage of the patriotism of the Alsatians and employed peasant labor to construct the fortifications. Peasants likewise could have built abatis, tambours, and palisades to defend the principle passes through the Vosges.[127]

Sulking in Strasbourg, Victor took no such action and decided to retreat. He withdrew Forestier's and Jamin's brigades as a preliminary step to evacuating Upper Alsace. Not only did this leave the inhabitants of Colmar to their fate, but it demoralized both the troops and the rest of the Alsatians. News of Marmont's arrival sparked a brief glimmer of hope in Strasbourg that quickly faded. Victor had no way of knowing whether Marmont would arrive in time to support his troops once the Allies launched the inevitable offensive through Colmar. Marmont's troops consisted of veterans who had been idle for two months and raw conscripts unaccustomed to rigorous marching on empty bellies. With Marmont's men drudging along poor roads in the midst of winter, Victor expected to see Coalition forces reach Strasbourg long before the VI Corps. Perhaps Victor realized this disappointing fact, which served to strengthen his original preference to retreat. As for Marmont, his troubles had just begun: Blücher's entire army had crossed the Rhine.

9

The Middle Rhine

In mid-November, the Silesian Army moved into positions along the right bank of the Rhine that formerly had been occupied by Gyulay's III Corps. Yorck relieved the Austrian right wing at Kastel, Mainz's fortified suburb on the right bank of the Rhine. Sacken's corps assumed the left wing of the siege, and Langeron's troops billeted between Königsstein, Höchst, and Frankfurt. St. Priest's infantry corps marched from Kassel to the Lahn River. Gyulay already had complained over the shortage of provisions in the region. After the Austrians moved up the Rhine, the men of the Silesian Army found partially abandoned villages totally bare of food and fodder.[1] This made Blücher all the more resentful that Allied Headquarters rejected his plan to invade the Low Countries. "In Brabant and Holland there would have been time to recover; everything is in abundance there," groans Blücher to a relative on 29 November. "All we need could have been requisitioned, and we could have provided our brave people with warm clothing before winter. Here the shortages are so great that my own horse has had no fodder for two days. With this death increases."[2] To Tsar Alexander he wrote, "I thus found myself in the dreadful necessity of having the army live by plundering for eight days. Sacken informed me that these horrible means demoralize the soldiers, disgrace the army, and earns the hatred of the inhabitants. I alone am responsible for preventing Your Majesty's brave troops from starving to death."[3] Supply difficulties persisted despite Blücher's complaints. As late as 23 December, he notified Schwarzenberg that "the difficulty of provisioning the army continues, and I desire nothing more than for the operations of the Bohemian Army to continue soon so those of the Silesian can begin."[4]

News of Bülow's bold invasion of Holland breathed new life into Blücher and his staff, who had reached the limits of their patience over the absurd halt in operations. "Our troops already have conquered the majority of Holland," exclaims Blücher to his wife. "Amsterdam and Rotterdam are in our hands.

We stand here on the Rhine in order to recover, but we will soon cross the river and then . . . you will see that Herr Napoleon will be driven to dire straits if he is not saved by a dumb move on our part."[5]

In this atmosphere of unprecedented excitement, Blücher's headquarters issued orders for the Silesian army to cross the Rhine at three points. At daybreak on 1 January 1814, Yorck and Langeron would cross at Kaub between Mainz and Koblenz, Sacken at Mannheim, and St. Priest at Koblenz. If the passage succeeded, the X Infantry Corps of Langeron's army corps would invest Mainz along both banks of the Rhine. Sacken was instructed to build a bridgehead at Mannheim and strike a bridge. After its completion, he would send boats down the Rhine to Oppenheim, where they would be turned over to Langeron's men for the purpose of constructing a pontoon bridge in this area for Blücher's communication with Germany. At least one-third of the Silesian army's 75,000 men would remain behind to besiege Mainz and shield Blücher's right flank from Macdonald's forces on the lower Rhine. Blücher ordered Langeron and St. Priest to remain at Mainz and Koblenz, respectively; Olsufiew's IX Infantry Corps would march with the rest of the Silesian Army under Blücher's direct command. After crossing the Rhine, Sacken and Yorck were to maneuver to the Saar River. Blücher wanted both corps on line at Alzey and Kreuznach by 4 January (Map 7).[6]

According to information provided by partisans and spies, most of the French army succumbed to typhus after it had crossed the Rhine. The survivors lacked almost every necessity and the recruits left the depots without equipment. No troops were observed moving between Paris and Metz; the garrisons of Trier and Luxembourg had moved to the interior, and unreliable National Guard units occupied the strongholds of Metz and Longwy. Sympathetic locals helped keep the desertion rates high, particularly among the Dutch and Germans serving in the French army. The mayors of the towns along the left bank of the middle Rhine did not enforce Napoleon's conscription decrees out of fear of being murdered. Groups of deserters frequently escaped across the river. They confirmed that Marmont's 16,000 men occupied the Rhine between Koblenz and Speyer. Of this number, only Ricard's 4,000 infantry guarded the stretch between Mainz and Koblenz.[7] Sébastiani commanded 3,000 men at Köln, while 10,000 troops – mainly conscripts – occupied Mainz.[8]

To observe the left bank of the Rhine, a jäger detachment under Lieutenant Colonel Ernst von Klüx of Yorck's corps occupied the Pfalz island in the middle of the Rhine facing Kaub. With its tiny castle, the Pfalzgrafenstein, this island provided an excellent observation point. On 23 December, Klüx reported that for the past two days the French had been making extensive movements under the cover of darkness. The French posts at Bacharach and Bingen received infantry reinforcements and artillery. Blücher could not determine whether this meant the French were preparing to defend the very stretch of the Rhine he intended to cross. The Prussian commander fully understood that his operation had to be carefully prepared and executed quickly, or he could suffer an irreparable disaster.[9]

Two variables offered Blücher the best opportunity for success: if he caught the French by surprise or if Napoleon weakened his forces by dispersing them to the lower and upper Rhine. Blücher benefited from both. As for surprise, he wanted to give the impression that his army had taken winter quarters. On Christmas day the field marshal transferred his headquarters to Frankfurt, declaring that because he "now had to spend the winter as a lazy-bones, it will be at Frankfurt."[10] While he and his staff did their best to deceive the French spies operating on the right bank, secret preparations were underway for the army to the cross the Rhine on New Year's Day. As Blücher seemingly took comfortable winter quarters, his troops moved to the points selected for the Rhine passage: Sacken to Mannheim, St. Priest to Koblenz, and Yorck's corps with Langeron's remaining troops to Kaub.[11] "In two days our army will cross the Rhine in order to wish the French a Happy New Year," wrote Gneisenau.[12] Blücher summed up his thoughts in a letter to a kinsman on Wednesday, 29 December: "From here I go to France. With daybreak on 1 January I will cross the river with the entire army. With my brothers-in-arms I will wash off all enslavement in this proud river and as free Germans we will step onto the soil of the great nation. As victors, not as the vanquished, will we return. And when the honorable peace is attained our Fatherland shall greet us with gratitude."[13]

For 1 January Blücher instructed Yorck to have the infantry of his advance guard cross the Rhine at Kaub in boats. A pontoon bridge would be constructed to enable the rest of the corps to follow. For this purpose, Langeron's pontoon train would move to Nastätten on 30 December and Yorck would make the arrangements for it to be at Kaub by the 31st. As soon as the cavalry and artillery of Yorck's vanguard crossed, Blücher wanted the entire advance guard to march southwest through Rheinböllen and Stromberg. A detachment would proceed twenty miles southwest of Kaub to Simmern, the junction of the roads from Koblenz, Mainz, and Trier. After the I Corps crossed the Rhine, Yorck would move his main body into tight cantonments between Bacharach and Rheinböllen. Blücher instructed Langeron's two infantry corps, the IX and X, to reach Kaub on 1 January to follow Yorck's troops across the river.

Downstream from Kaub, the 5,000 men of St. Priest's VIII Infantry Corps would embark in boats at the mouth of the Lahn at dawn on the 1st. As soon as two heavy batteries destroyed the French redoubt that faced the mouth of the Lahn, the Russian infantry would cross and advance to Koblenz. The boats would then ferry the remainder of the infantry corps. Blücher also instructed St. Priest to send a detachment up the Rhine to eliminate the French posts between Koblenz and Mainz. After St. Priest's men secured Koblenz, the field marshal wanted the Russians to bridge the Rhine.[14]

Sacken's corps was slated to cross the Rhine at Mannheim, approximately sixty-five miles upstream of Kaub. This area allowed the Russians to conceal their boats and pontoons on the Neckar. Marmont's large redoubt at Friesenheim commanded both the mouth of the Neckar and the city of Mannheim. Surrounded by palisades, abatis, and a trench, the fortification held 500 men and six guns. Its artillery could easily prevent the Russians from bridging the Rhine, particularly because they had to float the pontoons down the Neckar and into the Rhine. The abutments of their bridge would have to be anchored within range of the French artillery.[15] Sacken informed Blücher that he would send thirty men across the Rhine to neutralize the sentries; 1,000 men would immediately follow to take the redoubt. By 28 December, the boats were positioned on the Neckar and the corps was ready to cross. "The bridge will be built last," wrote the Russian general. "Should this plan fail, a large battery will be erected on the isle at the mouth of the Neckar and the passage will be forced. Success is in God's hands."[16]

On Thursday, 30 December, Blücher issued the following proclamation to remind his army of their past feats as well as to insure that their conduct corresponded to the message the Coalition wanted to send to the peoples on the left bank:

> Brave Warriors of the Silesian Army!
> Your gallant progress from the Oder to the Rhine has torn provinces from the hands of the enemy. Now you will cross the Rhine to force peace on the enemy, who can ill-brook having lost in two campaigns his conquests of the past nineteen years. Soldiers! I need only to point out the path of glory to the victors of the Katzbach, Wartenburg, Möckern, and Leipzig to be sure of the result. But now it is incumbent on me to impose on you new responsibilities. The inhabitants of the left bank of the Rhine are not inimical to our cause. I have promised them safety and the protection of property; I have done so in *your* name. You must keep this promise sacred. Bravery confers honor on the soldier; but obedience and discipline provide his brightest decorations.[17]

On the next day, New Year's Eve, Yorck's corps left Wiesbaden and concentrated between Schwalbach and the Rhine.[18] His staff officers continued to Kaub to conduct preliminary reconnaissance. They reported that the crossing would be very difficult, impossible if the French resisted. On the opposite bank, the highway that ran parallel to the Rhine linked the French posts at Oberwesel, Bacharach, and Bingen. Yorck's officers quickly recognized the technical difficulties of their task, particularly if the French disputed the crossing. The Prussians had at their disposal a single narrow pass that descended into the Rhine Valley from the hills along the right bank. Running west from Weisel to Kaub, it was the only road that allowed the passage of artillery and cavalry. This narrow pass could be viewed from the opposite bank; its small, winding road could be shelled by expert gunners.

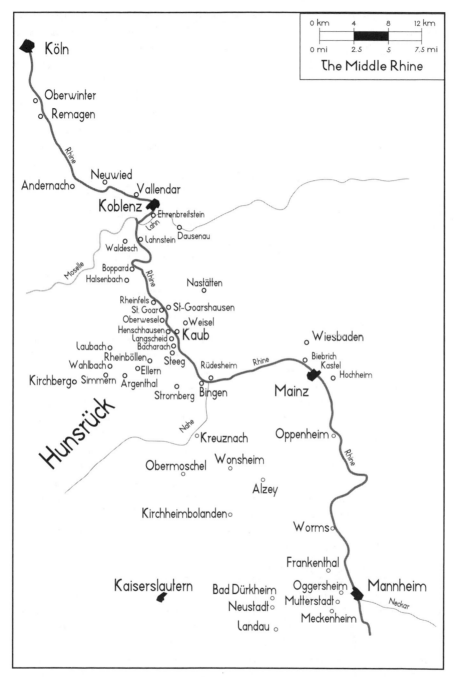

Map 7. The middle Rhine.

Kaub itself fell within range of French artillery positioned on the left bank. On a positive note, locals reported that the French units in Bacharach and Oberwesel, the towns closest to the left bank, consisted of a few hundred men, who apparently did not expect the Allies to cross the Rhine in this region.

General Karl Friedrich von Hünerbein's reinforced 8th Brigade (ten battalions, eleven squadrons, and sixteen guns) received the honor of forming Yorck's advance guard; it moved into Kaub with Blücher's and Yorck's headquarters. His men received strict instructions to avoid being seen on the riverbank. While the troops waited impatiently, Yorck's staff scoured the right bank to find a suitable place to build the bridge. Blocks of drift ice rode the Rhine's swift current like potential battering rams. The Prussians determined that the best point to strike a bridge was slightly upstream from Kaub, where the isle of Pfalz towered in the midst of the river.[19]

Yorck issued a detailed disposition for the crossing. He wanted one battery of heavy artillery brought up from Weisel and positioned on the right bank. A half-battery of 12-pounders would take a position by the ruins of the schloß of Guttenfels. These batteries were to sweep the left bank of the Rhine to silence any French artillery. As soon as the troops were ready to cross, two additional 12-pounders would unlimber on the bank downstream to fire on the bend in the highway that ran parallel to the left bank. One jäger company situated upstream at Rüdesheim would take position to fire across the river on the highway as it exited from Bingen. In the still of the night, the boats would sail downstream for Hünerbein's infantry to lead the invasion. After reaching the opposite bank, the Prussian battalions would execute multiple assignments: seize the ravines and heights, block the highway, and occupy Bacharach. His advance guard would march to Stromberg as soon as it completed the crossing. Once the Russians finished the pontoon bridge, Hünerbein's cavalry and artillery would cross, followed by the 1st, 2nd, and 7th Brigades, the Reserve Cavalry, and Reserve Artillery. Yorck instructed these units to assemble at Weisel and move in succession to Kaub. Behind the ridge and invisible to the French on the left bank, Weisel provided an ideal staging area. The corps commander insisted that not a single wagon be on the road until all of the troops had crossed. He wanted the crossing to begin at 12:00 A.M. on 1 January and expected the infantry of the 1st Brigade to cross seven hours later, even if the bridge was not ready.[20]

On the left bank opposite Kaub, the French sentries probably attributed the bright windows and loud noises across the river to New Year's Eve celebrations. Despite the noise caused by their own troops, the Prussians noticed nothing extraordinary on the left bank. A bright, starry night caused the temperature to drop and a sharp frost chilled the soldiers. Around midnight Yorck ordered Hünerbein's infantry to assemble on the riverbank; the cavalry and artillery of the advance guard lined the Kaub–Weisel road. Despite initial concerns, the Prussians managed to find enough boats for the crossing. Langeron's canvas pontoons also arrived around midnight and the Russian engineers began work on the bridge to the Pfalz, which was already occupied by East Prussian jäger companies. One 12-pounder battery unlimbered close to the bank, while the half battery moved into position at Guttenfels. Despite the unavoidable noise caused by the Prussian artillery, the left bank remained quiet. Around 2:30 A.M. 200 men of the Brandenburg Fusilier Battalion led by Maj. Friedrich Wilhelm, the count of Brandenburg, scrambled into the boats.[21] Yorck instructed this advance guard to land downstream of the toll house and disembark as quietly as possible. Despite the stillness of the opposite bank, the lights burning in the tollhouse made the Prussians uneasy and suspicious of French trickery.[22] According to Colonel Wilhelm Ludwig Henckel von Donnersmarck, "the night was clear and cold, but the narrow Rhine Valley seemed ominous."[23]

As they paddled across the great river, the Prussians strained to hear any indication of movement along the left bank. All remained quiet as they approached the tollhouse. After fifteen minutes, the boats ran aground on the shore. Against their orders, the fusiliers sprang forth and greeted the left bank with a loud "Hurrah." At that moment, shots rang out from the direction of the tollhouse, wounding a few men as well as a guide. Count Brandenburg's company then surged through the defile formed by the hills along the left bank to secure the high edge of the valley and envelop Bacharach. Shortly after, small French detachments moved up from Bacharach and Oberwesel to confront the Prussians. Totaling no more than sixty men each, they withdrew after a short firefight. As more infantry of the advance guard arrived, the Prussians constructed a crude bridge-head to defend the crossing of the cavalry and artillery.

Boats continued to ferry Hünerbein's infantry across the Rhine so that six battalions reached the left bank by 8:00 A.M. on 1 January, somewhat behind Yorck's schedule. Three battalions scaled the valley's edge to occupy Henschhausen and Langscheid; three others marched to Bacharach. A captured Frenchman revealed that an enemy detachment of sixty men and one gun was approaching on the highway, but only weak posts defended this stretch of the Rhine. Evidently, the Allied crossing caught the French completely by surprise. This French unit soon appeared on the road from Bacharach but consisted of 200 men instead of 60. The lone cannon fired between eight and nine ineffective rounds at the Prussian battalions on the highway. Once again the French retired after a brief skirmish. A detachment that pursued them found Bacharach abandoned; a second discovered Oberwesel likewise evacuated by French forces.

At 9:00 A.M. the Russians completed a bridge of twenty-seven pontoons at a length of 150 yards to the Pfalz island, which itself extended 120 yards across the Rhine. General Friedrich von Katzler, commanding the cavalry of the advance guard, led two horse guns and two Black Hussar squadrons across the bridge to the Pfalz. A makeshift ferry then transported the small unit to the left bank. After Hünerbein's troops completed the crossing, the boats started to ferry the infantry of the 1st Brigade, which had orders to march downstream to St. Goar, where a French depot supposedly contained a large quantity of powder, weapons, and food. The entire day of the 1st passed as the infantry crossed "amidst the great jubilation of the inhabitants, under continuous music making and rejoicing."[24] That evening, the jäger post at Rüdesheim reported the march of a 400-man French detachment from Bingen toward Bacharach and that stronger columns would be following. On account of this news, Yorck directed the 1st Brigade from St. Goar to Steeg near Bacharach to support Hünerbein. The exhausted, cold, and hungry men of the 1st Brigade arrived at Steeg late during the night of 1–2 January. Hünerbein's 8th Brigade camped at Bacharach, with forward posts on the roads to Rheinböllen and Bingen.

Although Yorck and Blücher calculated on having the entire pontoon bridge ready by 10:00 A.M. on 1 January, work on the stretch from the Pfalz to the left bank proceeded slowly because of drift ice and strong currents. Around 4:00 P.M., the Russians finished the second part of the pontoon bridge – forty-four pontoons covering 240 yards – but the powerful current tore the anchors and caused the bridge to drift into the middle of the river. Rejecting the advice of the Prussians, the Russian engineers refused to use heavy anchors. With construction on the bridge continuing into the cold and snowy night, the remainder of the I Corps bivouacked on the right bank between Weisel, St. Goarshausen, and Kaub, while Langeron's corps moved into Weisel.[25] According to the Journal of the Lithuanian Dragoon Regiment, the troops had no straw and little wood for fires.[26]

Blücher and his staff remained at Kaub throughout the 1st to oversee Yorck's operation. Excitement permeated army headquarters despite the delays. "Praise God, I have crossed the Rhine on New Year's Day, close to Kaub," wrote Blücher at 10:00 in the morning. "The enemy offers no serious resistance. At this moment 4,000 infantry are crossing in boats; the bridge will be ready around noon, then I will follow with the entire corps."[27] "Here I sit at a window under which the Silesian army is crossing the Rhine," reflects Gneisenau. "Sixteen battalions have already crossed by boat. The bridge is three-quarters complete. When it is finished, the artillery and cavalry will cross. The enemy has offered little resistance and fled after a few shots. The most superb spirit animates the troops; they vied over who would be first in the boats. Rejoicing, they took to the river and crossed with a cheer."[28]

Reports of Russian success added to the enthusiasm. Sacken's troops reached the mouth of the Neckar on New Year's Eve. Around 4:00 A.M. on 1 January the commander of the 10th Division of the XI Infantry Corps, General Alexander Pavlovich Zass II, led four battalions across the Rhine in boats.

General Fedor Ivanovich Talyzin III, commander of the 7th Division of the IV Infantry Corps, followed with the second wave. Altogether six jäger regiments crossed the river under the cover of a thick fog. A Badenese district magistrate who assisted Sacken during the entire operation placed himself and his son in the foremost boat. At 6:30 the redoubt opened fire, but the inaccurate salvos failed to prevent the Russians from landing. One hour later, they attacked the redoubt with the same intensity that characterized their conduct throughout the Napoleonic Wars. According to Müffling, "Sacken's men sprang into the trench and mounted the breastworks on each other's shoulders."[29] After thirty minutes and three failed attempts to take the redoubt by storm, all of the Russian light infantry reached the left bank and prepared for a final charge. In a general assault, the Russians overwhelmed the French, capturing five guns, two howitzers, seven officers, and 300 men. The rest of the French garrison was killed in brutal fighting that cost the Russians between 250 to 300 men; both Talyzin and Zass were wounded. Sometime after 2:00 P.M. General Akim Akimovich Karpov's Cossacks crossed the Rhine in barges followed by Biron's Streifkorps. Karpov moved to Mutterstadt and Biron proceeded to Alzey to link with Yorck's patrols.

After taking the redoubt, Austrian engineers attached to Sacken's corps started constructing the pontoon bridge, which they completed around 6:00 P.M. Despite the darkness of winter, the Russians crossed to the left bank of the Rhine that evening. The king of Prussia, who observed the combat, also crossed the Rhine and thanked the Russian soldiers. Sacken's main body continued west to Frankenthal, whose French post fled north to Worms after the fall of the redoubt. Russian detachments followed to Worms and pushed south to Speyer. On the following day, 2 January, the corps marched to Worms, the headquarters of General Henri-Jacques-Martin Lagarde's 1st Brigade of Semelé's 51st Division. The French brigadier had evacuated the city on the 1st, leaving behind more than 200 sick and 800 muskets; the Russians found a similar situation in Speyer.[30]

Downstream the Rhine at Koblenz, St. Priest's Russians caught the French in the midst of rotating their posts. As noted, Marmont's concentration of the VI Corps at Landau required the 2,000 men of Durutte's 32nd Division of the IV Corps to assume Ricard's posts in the Mainz–Koblenz sector of the cordon. Morand, the commander of the IV Corps, directed Durutte to echelon his division as well as General Cyrille-Simon Picquet's 1st Honor Guard Regiment between Mainz and Koblenz. An uneasy Durutte arrived at Koblenz on 30 December. He lacked the manpower to both guard a line of sixty miles and form a reserve. On 31 December, his 1st Brigade moved into positions from Koblenz to the redoubt facing Lahnstein, while his 2nd Brigade established posts between St. Goar and Bingen.

Conforming with Marmont's orders, Ricard left Koblenz on the 30th and reached Simmern that evening, en route to Kreuznach. The 3,000 men of his

1st Division were assembled in three columns; each commenced its march after being relieved by Durutte's units. On the 31st Ricard's advance guard, which consisted of the four battalions stationed between Mainz and Bingen as well as the Reserve Artillery, marched toward Alzey. The center column assembled in Stromberg and included the units stationed at Bacharach, St. Goar, and Boppard. Moving from Koblenz toward Laubach, the rearguard took in the troops posted between Boppard and Koblenz. Ricard apparently was not concerned over the distance between his columns nor their inability to support each other.[31]

Around 5:00 P.M. on 31 December, St. Priest assembled the two brigades of General Ivan Stepanovic Gurielov's 11th Division east of Ehrenbreitstein with the task of crossing the Rhine at Lahnstein. To expedite the passage and confuse the French, the four regiments of General Yegor Maksimovich Pillar's 17th Division would cross the river downstream of Koblenz at Neuwied and Vallendar. Around 9:00 P.M., eighty-two boats were in place, and St. Priest commenced his operation. Concealed by fog, Pillar's engineers hastily constructed a footbridge between the right bank and the Niederwerth island in the middle of the Rhine. From the island, 500 men supported by Cossacks crossed in boats to the opposite bank. Word soon reached Koblenz of the presence of Cossacks on the left bank. With only 350 men and four guns at his immediate disposal, Durutte sent a patrol north of the city to confirm the rumor; he took a position with the remainder of his men outside Koblenz. He received a very unnerving report: the officer charged with the reconnaissance claimed the amount of noise made by the Russians on the banks of the Rhine signaled the presence of a large force. After Durutte forwarded this information to Koblenz around 11:00 P.M., the Prefect of the Rhin-et-Moselle, Jean-Marie-Thérèse Doazan, evacuated the city, which served as the department's *chef-lieu*. Durutte hoped to be able to hold his position for at least another day.

Meanwhile, Gurielov led the brigades of Generals. Adam Ivanovich Bistrom II and Moisei Ivanovich Karpenko – a total of eight battalions – across the Rhine slightly upstream of Koblenz. Gurielov completely surprised the French. Not allowing their foes to fire one shot, the Russians took four guns and either bayoneted or captured the sole company of the 132nd Line that garrisoned the redoubt. Construction began on a bridge between Ehrenbreitstein and the left bank. Gurielov directed his men toward the Koblenz–Waldesch road: Durutte's only line of retreat. Around 2:00 A.M., the French general learned of this second enemy force and retreated just as the Russians closed in from both the north and south. The French conducted a fighting withdrawal through Waldesch to Halsenbach, where Durutte rallied the battalions posted in the St. Goar region.

St. Priest's Russians occupied Koblenz around 4:00 A.M. after sustaining only fifteen casualties. Advancing from Vallendar, General Ermolay

Fedorovich Kern secured the bridge over the Moselle with Pillar's 2nd Brigade. St. Priest directed Bistrom to pursue Durutte with the 33rd Jäger Regiment, Cossacks, and four pieces of horse artillery. As more cavalry crossed the Rhine, small detachments made their way west toward Trier and north to Bonn, capturing 250 men and seven guns in the process. After receiving St. Priest's after-action report, Blücher instructed him to garrison the city with between 1,000 and 1,500 men and proceed on 2 January toward Bacharach. Despite this promising start, drift ice on the Rhine eventually delayed the crossing of the remainder of St. Priest's cavalry and artillery, thus forcing the Russian commander to remain in Koblenz for several days before being relieved by General Dmitri Mikhailovich Juzefovich's detachment of three battalions, nine squadrons, and six guns from Köln. French losses at Koblenz and during Durutte's retreat amounted to 200 casualties in addition to the 1,200 soldiers left behind in Koblenz's hospital. In the city, the Russians liberated 500 prisoners of war and found a column honoring the capture of Moscow that featured the inscription, "To the Great Napoleon, in honor of the immortal campaign against the Russians in 1812." The new Russian commandant of the city left the monument standing, but added the words, "Seen and approved by Colonel Magdenko, the Russian commandant of Koblenz in 1814." That night, the inhabitants of Koblenz spontaneously illuminated the entire city. "Never have troops been received with a grander acclamation," reported Langeron to Barclay de Tolly. According to Langeron's journal, St. Priest's entire operation to take Koblenz cost the Russians only 165 casualties. Langeron claims the Russians took 500 prisoners, twelve guns, and a convoy of flour, clothing, and hospital supplies.[32]

Back in Kaub, construction on the second and longer section of the bridge continued into the morning of 2 January. According to the Journal of the Lithuanian Dragoon Regiment, the corps then "departed on the morning of the 2nd, crossing the river, which for so long had formed Germany's frontier, with song and music."[33] Even with the bridge fully operational by 9:00 A.M., the Prussians needed the entire day to move their material across the Rhine. The artillery and wagons had to be spread out to distribute the weight evenly, and thus the passage of Yorck's corps lasted into the night, meaning that Langeron could not cross until midnight on the 3rd.[34]

The crossing of the Rhine was a complete success despite the delays caused by drift ice, but Blücher now faced a difficult task. Marmont's three corps opposed his front, and Macdonald's four corps on the lower Rhine threatened his right. After Langeron's corps besieged Mainz, the Silesian Army would number only 50,000 men. With this force, Blücher had to cross the Saar, the Moselle, the Meurthe, and the Meuse. More important, he had to penetrate the center of the fortress belt that lined France's eastern frontier – namely, Saarlouis, Luxembourg, Longwy, Thionville, and Metz. Since early November, the Prussians had insisted that these fortresses were only weakly garrisoned, which indeed they were, yet Blücher and Gneisenau realized that these positions had to be observed or occupied by their detachments until German reinforcements arrived. With each step forward, strategic consumption would claim more manpower. Regardless, nothing could shake Blücher's confidence. He and his staff counted on surprise and speed – some of the same principles that launched young Bonaparte to fame almost two decades earlier in Italy.[35]

The additional time needed for the I Corps to cross the Rhine did not slow Yorck's units that already operated on the left bank. They advanced to attain objectives that Blücher's staff selected in accordance with the intelligence gleaned from intercepted French dispatches. Not only did Blücher and Gneisenau want to prevent Marmont from concentrating his divisions, but they envisioned a rapid pincer movement by Yorck and Sacken that would sever the marshal's line of retreat to Metz. The first step was to consolidate control of the left bank between Bacharach and Bingen, advance to Kreuznach, and forward detachments westward to disrupt Marmont's communications. Early on 2 January, Blücher's staff issued orders for Yorck's corps to march from Bacharach through Rheinböllen and Stromberg to Kreuznach. As soon the entire I Corps crossed the Rhine, Langeron would follow and strike the highway from Bacharach to Bingen. Blücher urged his commanders to keep the roads free of baggage. The field marshal expected to meet resistance, especially at Kreuznach.[36]

In his orders, Blücher reminded the troops of their prior accomplishments, stated the purpose of their current campaign, and encouraged them to observe the strictest military discipline. Continuing the Allied propaganda campaign, he issued a proclamation to the Rhinelanders:

> I have led the Silesian Army across the Rhine in order to attain peace and return freedom and independence to the nations. The Emperor Napoleon, who already has united Holland, a part of Germany, and Italy to the French monarchy, declared that he will not surrender one village of these conquests even if the enemy appears before Paris. Such declarations and such principles have brought all the states of Europe into the struggle. If you defend such principles, then remain in Napoleon's ranks and try your strength in the struggle against the good cause, which is protected by Providence. If you do not want this, then you can find protection with us. The inhabitants of the cities and villages should remain quietly in their homes; all officials should carry on their duties. With the Allied invasion ends any association of the inhabitants with the French government. Any who act against us will be viewed as traitors, brought before a military tribunal, and punished by death.[37]

On 1 January, customs agents fleeing the little town of Oggersheim opposite Mannheim informed Marmont that Russian forces had crossed the Rhine. He immediately pushed the cavalry of General Charles-Eugène Lalaing d'Audenarde's 1st Brigade from the 3rd Division of Doumerc's cavalry corps on the road to Mutterstadt and instructed the closest troops to follow. On arriving in the village of Meckenheim, six miles from Neustadt, the lead squadron of the 7th Dragoons encountered a detachment of 100 Cossacks. The French troopers cut through the Russians with ease and reached Mutterstadt but found a larger force of approximately 300 cavalry that withdrew as they approached. Marmont reached the village with Audenarde's main body at 3:00 P.M. According to the locals, the guns of the Friesenheim redoubt started firing around 6:30 A.M., and a fusillade erupted thirty minutes later. All firing ceased by 8:00; the French troops in Frankenthal moved to support the garrison in the redoubt but arrived too late. The inhabitants reported that the Russians claimed to have struck one bridge at Mannheim and that a second would be completed soon. With the winter sun setting, Marmont hoped to ascertain precise information before nightfall. He directed Audenarde to continue east of Mutterstadt to pursue the enemy. Less than one mile from Mutterstadt, Audenarde stumbled into Karpov's main body of 2,000 Cossacks. Unexpectedly confronted by double his own number, the French general had little time to deploy his eight squadrons. After losing 25 officers and 200 men – almost one-quarter of his effectives – Audenarde fell back to Mutterstadt.[38] Realizing he could not remain there, Marmont withdrew his cavalry four miles westward. That night he penned his thoughts to Berthier:

> Tomorrow morning I will learn what I face. If it is just a raiding party, I will drive through it. If it is the army that has crossed, I will retire on Neustadt and I will defend the gorges foot by foot, as much as my resources will allow. The 1st Division, en route from Koblenz, has not yet rejoined me. To accelerate its march, it has divided into three detachments. I have sent the proper instructions to each. If the enemy moves against me, I will retire on Kaiserslautern and from there to the Saar. If it is merely a raiding party, after forcing it to recross the Rhine, I will continue my movement to Kaiserslautern.[39]

Blücher struck when Marmont was most vulnerable. With two of the marshal's corps en route to Strasbourg, the Silesian Army found Marmont's units echelonned between Koblenz and Kaiserslautern. Lagrange's 3rd Division could not be reached by Allied forces, but little hope remained for Ricard's 1st Division, which was marching to Alzey in three isolated detachments. After relieving the posts of the I Cavalry Corps downstream of Mainz, the 1st Honor Guard Regiment was cut in half by the passage of Yorck's corps. Fortunately for the French, the majority of the squadrons escaped. One detachment of 180 troopers united with Ricard; a second retreated to the Saar.[40]

As much as Gneisenau complained over Schwarzenberg's seven-week delay, the operations on the lower and upper Rhine created diversions that immensely facilitated the Silesian Army's offensive. Napoleon's erroneous conviction that the Allies would cross the lower Rhine led him to shift manpower from Marmont's sector to Macdonald. Belatedly, he realized the danger to Upper Alsace, which he had considered threatened only by partisans. To bolster Victor, he attempted to move Marmont's VI Infantry and I Cavalry Corps south and cover the middle Rhine with the divisions of Morand's IV Corps. As late as 3 January, Berthier's correspondence urged Marmont to accelerate his march to Colmar in order to support Victor. "The emperor does not want you to be distracted by the fear that Blücher's army will cross the Rhine," wrote the chief of staff.[41] Clearly the master of war had been duped.

North of Marmont, Doazan delivered the news of the fall of Koblenz and the Allied passage of the Rhine near Bacharach to Ricard in Kreuznach around 7:00 A.M. on the 1st. The prefect added his belief that Durutte had been captured. Despite the verbal and written instructions Marmont issued throughout the previous two months to withdraw into Mainz or retreat to the Saar in the case of an Allied invasion, Ricard decided to turn around and march through the Hunsrück in the direction of Koblenz to support Durutte, who he learned had not been captured. "I did not hesitate one instant to recall all of my troops, forming around 3,000 bayonets, and to direct them on Koblenz," Ricard wrote to the assistant chief of staff of the army, Colonel-General Auguste-Daniel Belliard at army headquarters in Metz. Ricard summoned the center column, whose detachments had united at Stromberg. Colonel Jean-Philippe-Aimar d'Albignac's rearguard column, which had reached Laubach, likewise received orders to countermarch. "My rearguard soon will join Durutte, who is retreating on Simmern," adds the general. "With these reinforcements he can move forward and take a position at Halsenbach." Clearing Alzey on the 2nd, the advance guard column of four battalions and Ricard's Reserve Artillery continued its march south toward Marmont at Bad Dürkheim. While Albignac and Durutte united in Halsenbach, Ricard himself decided to halt at Laubach – eleven miles west of Bacharach and six miles north of Simmern. Ricard intended to rally the troops driven from Stromberg, St. Goar, and Rheinböllen as well as "to act in concert with Durutte according to circumstances."[42]

Marmont was not pleased with his subordinate's decision: "Ricard made an about-face to return to Koblenz," he later complained to Berthier, "where there was a rumor of an enemy passage. This general has not received my orders and is now separated from me by the crossing that the enemy effected at Bacharach [Kaub]. It is very troublesome that he did not continue his movement [toward Landau]. Several times this winter I have given both written and verbal instructions that indicate the plan of retreat for the corps, which is scattered, in the case of a sudden crossing of the Rhine by the enemy."[43] Although Ricard acknowledged both Marmont's instructions for just such a scenario as well as his obligation to execute the marshal's orders, he made the decision to countermarch, which risked having his division cut in half. In addition, his plans for a counteroffensive in unison with Durutte completely contradicted the marshal's directions and most likely would have led to a disaster. Fortunately for Ricard, the intelligence he received was wrong: The Prussians had yet to reach Rheinböllen or Stromberg. Consequently, the difficulties Yorck's corps encountered crossing the Rhine saved both Durutte and Ricard.

Nevertheless, the news Ricard received on 1 January did not paint a favorable picture. He learned of a second Allied crossing between St. Goar and Bacharach. After forcing the posts from these two towns, the enemy moved rapidly on Rheinböllen and Stromberg. "All the reports I have received," he wrote to Belliard, "confirm that the enemy forces that have crossed to the left bank are infinitely superior to those with which we can oppose him. He is master of all the debouches from the Rhine to the Hunsrück; he has strongly occupied Rheinböllen and Stromberg; the cavalry that debouched in the plain of Neuwied ascends, one has assured me, the left bank of the moselle." This news brought the troubling prospect that his four battalions and artillery coming from Alzey would be cut off and unable to unite with him. Direct communication with Mainz and Neustadt was cut. If Ricard and Durutte did not reach the crossroads at Simmern before the Allies, they risked being trapped on the plateau between the Rhine and the Moselle.

Upon learning the details of the Allied operation, Ricard convinced himself that Durutte's "400–500 men" combined with his own division could not stop the enemy advance.[44] After assuring the retreat of Doazan and the civil authorities with the public coffers, Ricard decided to retreat to Trier to guard the bridges over the Moselle. During the 2nd Albignac and the majority of Durutte's 32nd Division joined him in Laubach. From there Ricard led the divisions through Simmern and turned west on the highway to Trier. He passed the night of 2–3 January in Kirchberg, where Durutte joined him and agreed with the plan to retreat on Trier. Cut off from Marmont, they requested that Belliard inform the marshal of their intentions.[45]

Meanwhile, Marmont postponed making the difficult decision of abandoning Victor until confirmed reports arrived that Blücher's army had indeed crossed the Rhine. This conformation came during the night of 1–2 January. As a result, the marshal decided that he could not continue to Landau, despite the emperor's explicit orders. On the 2nd, he moved his headquarters further west to Bad Dürkheim on the Mannheim–Kaiserslautern road. During the day, he received news from Victor that the Russians had constructed a bridge near Ft. Vauban and "are crossing the river at this moment." An anxious Victor begged Marmont not to abandon him and suggested retreating and concentrating their forces at Saverne, twenty miles northwest of Strasbourg.[46] Knowing that his master expected more from him, Marmont ignored Victor's plea.

"We have taken several prisoners: Russians, Prussians, and Austrians," wrote Marmont regarding a reconnaissance he personally conducted with his cavalry on 2 January, "and I am almost certain that the majority of the Silesian

Army has debouched from Mannheim. I have just received news that the enemy has also crossed the Rhine at Koblenz; Gen. Ricard is retreating." He feared the Allies would trap Ricard's 1st Division as it marched to Landau. Marmont assumed the division stood between Alzey and Kreuznach, eche-lonned in three-weak detachments the enemy would destroy piecemeal. The concerned marshal dispatched a staff officer to hasten their march. This suc-ceeded in bringing Ricard's advance guard column safely to Bad Dürkheim on the 3rd, but the fate of the rest of the division remained unknown.[47] Dur-ing the 2nd Marmont posted Lagrange's 3rd Division east of Kaiserslautern with Doumerc's cavalry at Bad Dürkheim. He also composed a long expla-nation of the events to Morand, commander of the IV Corps and governor of Mainz. Not knowing that the units of the IV Corps (General Jacques-Robert Choisy's 2nd Brigade of Durutte's division and Semelé's 51st Division) and the Honor Guard squadrons that occupied the posts between Oppenheim and Bingen managed to escape to Mainz, he ordered the general to recall all his troops to the fortress and send the 1st and 2nd Honor Guard Regiments to him as soon as possible.[48] Marmont further requested that Morand forward to Ricard instructions to withdraw to the Saar. Morand complied with this latter request, but Yorck's Prussians captured his courier and the letter that revealed Marmont's intention to fall back to the Saar.[49]

The marshal established his headquarters at Bad Dürkheim for the night of 2–3 January. He advised Berthier of his critical situation. It appeared the Silesian Army had crossed the Rhine at several points between Koblenz and Mannheim. With his 4,500 infantry and 1,500 cavalry, Marmont intended to maintain his position and defend the gorges leading to Kaiserslautern until the Allies forced him to withdraw to that town, and from there to the Saar to defend the northeastern frontier of Lorraine.[50]

According to Blücher's general disposition, Langeron's corps was to invest Mainz on both banks of the Rhine. With its rear thus covered by Langeron, the Silesian Army would advance to the Saar. After crossing the Rhine, the march to the Saar through the rugged terrain of the Hunsrück became the main con-cern of Blücher's staff. Two main roads ran west through the Hunsrück: from Kreuznach to Merzig or from Kaiserslautern to Saarbrücken. Initial planning called for Yorck and Sacken to be on line by 4 January in the northern spurs of the Hunsrück with the former at Kreuznach and the latter in Alzey; Blücher wanted Russian forward posts at Neustadt, Bad Dürkheim, and Speyer.[51]

Yorck's operations on 2 January encountered harsh winter weather. Blücher ordered the I Corps to proceed through Rheinböllen and Stromberg to Kreuznach in order to cut off Ricard's division, which the Prussians believed would retreat through Simmern. Before dawn on the 2nd, the 8th Brigade emerged from the Rhine Valley at Bacharach and marched toward Rheinböllen, where the roads to Simmern and Kreuznach separated. While on the road, Hünerbein learned French forces still occupied Rheinböllen.

He assigned the task of clearing the town to Klüx with the lead units of the advance guard. Klüx led a Fusilier battalion into Rheinböllen and managed to drive out the small French post, taking fifty prisoners and suffering eleven casualties in the process.

After waiting for his cavalry and artillery to clear the left bank, Hünerbein continued the march to Stromberg, which the French evacuated. He arrived around 6:00 P.M. and received instructions to continue further south to secure Kreuznach. The lead units of the 8th Brigade occupied Kreuznach late in the evening. Patrols confirmed the statements of local villagers who claimed that between 800 and 1,000 men still held Waldalgesheim and Bingen east of the Prussians. These towns had to be cleared in order to open communication with Langeron. That same night, Lieutenant Colonel Hermann Otto von Stößel and the tired men of the Brandenburg Fusilier Battalion drove a French post from Waldalgesheim, whose 100 men melted into the darkness. Stößel learned that the 2nd Honor Guard Regiment and 1,000 infantry of Choisy's 2nd Brigade held Bingen. The Prussian officer forwarded this news to Langeron, whose men would deal with this French post on the following morning.[52]

Shielded by Hünerbein's advance guard, Yorck led his main body – the 1st and 7th Brigades, Reserve Cavalry and Artillery – toward Stromberg during the afternoon and evening of 2 January. A frost iced the roads, making the mountain paths through the Hunsrück treacherous. After two months of rest, the march exhausted Yorck's men, who had been on the move since 31 December. Between Hünerbein and Yorck's main body, Prince William of Prussia led the 2nd Brigade through Rheinböllen to Ellern, where he received orders to keep marching. After his scouts reported that French forces still held Argenthal and Wahlbach west of Ellern on the road to Simmern, the prince left one battalion and one squadron at Ellern to cover his march as he continued south to Stromberg.

In his original disposition, Blücher had emphasized the importance of Simmern, which stood at the junction of the roads to Koblenz, Trier, and Mainz. He had instructed Yorck to form a Streifkorps to take this town. The Streifkorps would march west through Rheinböllen, clear the French posts from Argenthal and Wahlbach, and proceed to Simmern.[53] Before crossing the Rhine and making for Bacharach, Yorck formed this Streifkorps with one battalion of light infantry, six Landwehr squadrons, and four pieces of horse artillery; all placed under Henckel's command. With the crossing delayed, Henckel received word to meet with Yorck at Bacharach. To get across the bridge, he and his adjutants had to go on foot due to "the great press of men and material." At Bacharach Yorck instructed him to advance through Rheinböllen to Simmern and to observe the roads leading to Kirchberg and Koblenz. By noon on 2 January, his units reached Bacharach and commenced the march westward. Throughout the day he received messages from Yorck indicating that Ricard's forward posts were withdrawing from the left bank to Simmern.[54] Arriving in Rheinböllen around 9:00 P.M., Henckel granted his men a short rest before continuing the march. That night, his forward units reached Argenthal and reported the French had evacuated the village fifteen minutes earlier. After conferring with his officers, Henckel opted for a night march to Simmern.[55]

Clouds now blanketed the stars that had guided the Prussians across the Rhine. In uncommonly raw weather in which frost and ice made the march through the hills of the Hunsrück exceedingly dangerous for cavalry, a captured French courier restrained by a rope guided Henckel's Streifkorps to Simmern. The skirmishers of the Fusilier battalion led the column followed by the rest of the battalion, the artillery, and the cavalry. Around 2:00 A.M. on 3 January the Prussians advanced to within 350 yards of Simmern. The highway in front of them descended through a narrow gorge; scouts informed Henckel that only weak posts guarded the approaches to Simmern. As the Prussians came up, French sentries called out several times. Receiving no response, they opened fire. After the shots rang out, the other posts rushed to Simmern's barricaded gate. A two-hour firefight ensued until Henckel's skirmishers scattered the enemy sentries but failed to break through the gate.

As the Prussians huddled around the gate, they received fire from all sides. Henckel called up the rest of the battalion and launched a general attack around 4:00 A.M. From a platform above the gate, the French discharged various material as if defending against a medieval siege. The Prussians could not smash the gates, so Henckel rode back toward Argenthal to speed the advance of his artillery. One gun finally arrived, but, inconceivably, the artillery officer disconnected the gun from its prolonge – a heavy rope with a hook and toggle used to pull the gun carriage. In the process of unlimbering, the gun slid into a ditch alongside the highway. Henckel directed a second cannon toward the gate, which unlimbered safely but shot too high. After adjusting his aim, the gunner finally hit the gate. The French withdrew from the shattered gate, allowing the Prussians to break through and enter Simmern. Henckel's skirmishers spread through the town in pursuit, while he followed with the battalion at the double-quick. By 4:30 A.M., the Prussians secured Simmern, severing Ricard's and Durutte's communications with Marmont. The brazen Henckel ordered all of Simmern to be illuminated. In this way French stragglers were hunted down as they attempted to follow their main body west to Kirchberg. From prisoners Henckel learned that his Streifkorps had defeated Ricard's rearguard. In two and a half hours of combat, the French lost eighty-two men, the Prussians sixteen. Prone to embellish his service record, Henckel claims that Ricard himself barely "escaped being taken prisoner by running through the garden." Reports arrived before dawn indicating the French also evacuated Kirchberg. Henckel allowed his men to rest before continuing there, which the Streifkorps reached around 3:00 P.M. on the 3rd.[56]

South of Yorck, Sacken's corps drove back Marmont's outpost from Bad Dürkheim on 2 January, and the Russian commander moved his headquarters to Worms. Biron, who had the task of establishing communication between Yorck and Sacken, learned the French evacuated Alzey sometime during the night of 1–2 January and proceeded to the town. Possession of Alzey severed Marmont's communications with Mainz. Continuing north toward Yorck's units, Biron used a thick fog to surprise and disperse a French detachment, capturing five officers, 120 men, sixty-five horses, and approximately 400 new muskets. Elsewhere, Karpov's 2,000 troopers rode southwest to ascertain Marmont's movements.[57]

To the north, St. Priest's Russians had one minor engagement on the 2nd. After crossing the Rhine downstream of Koblenz at Andernach, Pillar led his troops down the Rhine. Receiving news of a French column marching from Köln to Mainz, he forwarded a small detachment of 200 jäger, twenty-five Cossacks, and one gun to intercept the column. Langeron's journal states that the Russians overtook the convoy near Remagen, but the major who commanded the detachment imprudently advanced toward Bonn. Unexpectedly, the Russians ran into a large detachment from Sébastiani's V Corps led by Gens. Albert and Charles-Claude Jacquinot coming from Bonn. The Russian major paid for his imprudence. Wounded and captured, he watched the French route his detachment. Before taking a position at Remagen, the French drove the Russians to Andernach, inflicting 120 casualties and capturing the single gun – the first to be lost by the Silesian Army.[58]

Despite this minor check, Blücher burned with impatience, especially after Biron established communication between Yorck and Sacken. The Prussian field marshal knew that Morand's IV Corps remained behind to garrison the great fortress, but Marmont was retreating. He reluctantly delayed Yorck's operations on 3 January to wait for Langeron's corps to cross the Rhine and besiege Mainz. The majority of Yorck's corps received a day of rest; only the advance guard and Henckel's Streifkorps continued operations. Yorck utilized the day to make several personnel changes. Hünerbein, the commander of the 8th Brigade, had attempted to form an opposition party to Yorck's command in the corps. In late December when Yorck's staff commemorated the one-year anniversary of the signing of the Convention of Tauroggen, Hünerbein declared he would not celebrate "the Prussian capitulation," as he called the first act that some claimed made Prussia completely dependent on Russia. Such talk could be heard in certain military circles, and Metternich received the blame for propagating these views. On the 3rd, this situation diffused with Hünerbein's transfer to direct the mobilization in the former Prussian province of Berg. Yorck's chief of staff, Colonel Karl Heinrich von Zielinsky, likewise received a transfer to command a brigade in Bülow's III

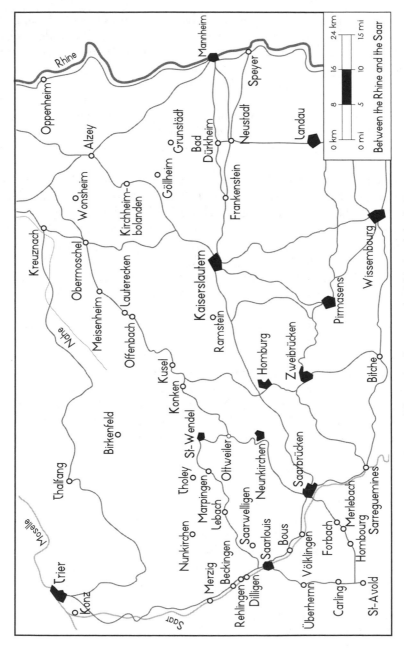

Map 8. The region between the Rhine and the Saar.

Between the Rhine and the Saar

| 0 km | 8 | 16 | 24 km |
| 0 mi | 5 | 10 | 15 mi |

Rhine

Oppenheim
Alzey
Wonsheim
Kirchheim-bolanden
Göllheim
Grunstädt
Bad Dürkheim
Neustadt
Mannheim
Speyer
Landau
Frankenstein
Kreuznach
Obermoschel
Meisenheim
Lauterecken
Offenbach
Kaiserslautern
Ramstein
Homburg
Zweibrücken
Pirmasens
Wissembourg
Bitche
Kusel
Konken
Birkenfeld
St-Wendel
Ottweiler
Neunkirchen
Saarbrücken
Tholey
Marpingen
Lebach
Nunkirchen
Thalfang
Trier
Konz
Merzig
Beckingen
Rehlingen
Dilligen
Saarlouis
Bous
Saarwellingen
Völklingen
Überhernn
Forbach
Merlebach
Homburg
Sarreguemines
Carling
St-Avold

Moselle
Nahe
Saar

Corps. It is not known how much Zielinsky supported Hünerbein, but the former derisively referred to the battles of the Katzbach, Wartenburg, and Möckern as "Yorck's sentimental journey."[59] Prince William, who temporarily commanded the 2nd Brigade for the wounded Prince Carl of Mecklenburg-Strelitz, assumed command of the 8th Brigade in Hünerbein's place. News that the Hohenzollern prince would permanently remain with the I Corps boosted morale. Until Prince Carl recovered, Colonel Friedrich Wilhelm von Warburg would command the 2nd Brigade. General Otto von Pirch, referred to as Pirch II to distinguish him from his brother Georg, who served in Kleist's corps, took command of the 1st Brigade. Georg Wilhelm von Valentini assumed the duties of Yorck's chief of staff. With these changes, Yorck created an affable environment in his headquarters. "We lived as a family; between us was frankness, cordiality, and mutual support," noted one of his staff officers. According to his nineteenth-century biographer, Johann Gustav Droysen, Yorck "felt completely comfortable in this circle; to him it was a pleasure to associate with these young men. They and the officers from the brigades visited his table daily."[60]

Although Yorck's corps did little on the 3rd, the Russians and Biron's Streifkorps made progress. After crossing the Rhine at Kaub, Langeron dispatched his adjutant, Captain von Schultz, with 50 Cossacks on the road to Bingen. An advance guard composed of the 10th, 12th, 22nd, and 38th Jäger Regiments, one large Cossack Regiment, and six guns all under the command of General Petr Yakovlevich Kornilov followed. Schultz drove small French posts from the various villages that he found along the length of the Rhine as he advanced toward Bingen, taking several prisoners while Kornilov continued to follow. After Stößel's dispatch regarding the French post at Bingen reached the Russians, Kornilov marched through the night to reach Bingen, which was somewhat fortified and situated in a defile. At dawn on 3 January, the majority of Kornilov's 15th Division assembled near Bingen. Like all the small towns in this region, which in earlier times had been a theater of constant war, Bingen was surrounded by a wall and a moat. The French had added several palisades. Langeron arrived and estimated the French force to be 800; only two pieces of artillery could be seen. "Field marshal Blücher ordered me to try to take Bingen," noted Langeron in his journal, "but not to sustain needless casualties if it resisted and to wait for Yorck's light cavalry to turn it by Kreuznach. . . ." Kornilov sent 200 skirmishers to probe the town; the French opened fire with three or four blasts of grape. The Russians skirmished with the 2nd Honor Guard Regiment and Choisy's 2nd Brigade for almost one hour. Arriving with the lead elements of the IX Infantry Corps, General Olsufiev advanced too close to the skirmishers and received a contusion in the arm from a musket ball. Learning that the French had withdrew their cannon, Kornilov ordered the 12th and 22nd Jäger Regiments to advance against the town. After a one-hour struggle, the French withdrew to Mainz and the Russians occupied Bingen. Although some estimates state that Choisy lost as many as 300 men, Langeron himself claims to have taken only fifty prisoners in addition to the 200 sick soldiers he found in Bingen's hospital. The Russian again placed his own losses at fifteen men. Langeron pursued the French from Bingen on the road to Mainz, pushing light cavalry all the way to the French-occupied suburbs of the fortress. The French cavalry became trapped in the fortress after Langeron commenced the siege; prompting Marmont to complain to Berthier that despite giving verbal orders to retreat in the case of a sudden enemy offensive across the Rhine, the 2nd Honor Guard Regiment was now cut off and useless.[61] Inhabitants from the neighboring villages reported that as many as 20,000 French soldiers remained in the disease-stricken city. Southwest of Bingen, Sacken's forward units fiercely attacked Marmont's rearguard at Neustadt, reducing the French force by three officers and fifty dragoons. Between Alzey and Kirchheim-bolanden, Biron's Streifkorps ambushed a supply convoy en route to Mainz and then took a position at Wonsheim.[62]

On the 3rd, Marmont received confirmed reports that Sacken's entire corps was bearing down on his left, center, and right. According to Marmont, "The enemy has posted considerable infantry forces at the head of the debouches of Grünstadt and has commenced moving through this defile while a numerous corps is in front of me, which places me in the situation of being trapped in the defile." With no other choice, the marshal evacuated Bad Dürkheim and Neustadt in the night of 3–4 January and marched west to Kaiserslautern, where he arrived on the afternoon of the 4th.

Both sides benefited from information provided by the inhabitants of the two middle Rhenish departments, Mont-Tonnerre and the Rhin-et-Moselle. The intelligence Marmont gleaned during the course of the 4th allowed him to form a fairly accurate view of the situation. In a comprehensive five-page brief to Berthier, the marshal attributed the success of the Allied operation "solely to the incapacity of our forces and the immensity of the enemy." He estimated the Silesian Army to be 60,000 men, supported by an Austrian division under General Johann Karl von Kolowrat. According to one peasant, 150 pieces of artillery passed through Mannheim, where the king of Prussia arrived on the day of the passage. More Austrian troops were en route; Klenau's troops reportedly reached Kassel. Worse, a Russian corps (Wittgenstein's) purportedly crossed the Rhine at Ft. Vauban. "It is remarkable," comments Marmont, "that on the same day and at the same hour the enemy crossed the Rhine simultaneously at Ft. Vauban, Mannheim, Bacharach, and the island of Niederwerth, without counting the crossings he already has made on the upper Rhine." Unable to stop what he described as a "major operation on the middle Rhine," he retreated to Kaiserslautern. Marmont predicted this position would soon become untenable as well. With Sacken's corps in pursuit, he feared an overwhelming frontal attack. Speculating on the direction the

Russians would take from Ft. Vauban, he expressed concern that this corps could move on Zweibrücken through either Pirmasens, Landau, or Bitche and compromise his line of retreat to the Saar. Of the three possible directions, it appeared the Russian corps would proceed through Bitche. The marshal had little to say of Morand's mobile troops; he hoped they escaped to Mainz or retreated beyond the enemy's reach. He still had no news of Ricard's division and hoped his subordinate was retreating to the Saar. "The speed with which the enemy has effected his operation and has flooded the countryside with very large forces is extraordinary," concludes the marshal's 4 January report.[63]

As for Ricard and Durutte, they initially planned to march from Kirchberg to the Moselle, cross the river at Bernkastel, and continue to Trier. Instead, on the 3rd the two divisions proceeded toward Saarbrücken to "approach Metz and to be able to cover the road from Metz to Mainz." The reason the generals changed their plans is not known, but Ricard hoped he would find news and orders at Saarbrücken. The two generals entertained different views regarding the Allied forces that had crossed the Rhine, illustrating their difficulties in piecing together the events since the 31st. Reaching Birkenfeld on the 4th, their reports only indicate that a small Prussian force of infantry and cavalry pursued them on the 2nd, fell behind, could not catch up, and purportedly stopped twenty miles east of Birkenfeld that same morning. Locals informed Ricard that this enemy force was not following them toward the Saar. Ricard correctly assigned this Prussian unit, Henckel's, "to the enemy corps that crossed at Bacharach [Kaub], which is composed of Prussian infantry and cavalry as well as Bavarian cavalry; a corps whose strength and composition are uncertain." Durutte, on the other hand, believed that three Russian divisions, one Prussian corps, and around 6,000 Saxons under St. Priest had driven him from Koblenz. The two generals received confusing information regarding the whereabouts of Marmont as well. "One claims that we have several troops in Offenbach," wrote Ricard. "One now claims that the enemy has appeared in the region of Kaiserslautern," adds Durutte.[64] Despite this confusion, the generals managed to escape what appeared to be a hopeless situation. Whether knowingly or not, their decision to retreat to the Saar rather than Trier complied precisely with Marmont's wishes.

By the night of 3 January, the staff of the Silesian Army knew for certain that Marmont had regrouped at Kaiserslautern – only the size of the force he commanded remained unclear. Blücher and Gneisenau planned to sever his line of retreat to the Saar and destroy his forces. While Sacken pinned the marshal at Kaiserslautern, Yorck would wheel southwest to the crossings over the Saar at Saarbrücken and Saarlouis. "By this maneuver," Blücher assured the tsar, "Marshal Marmont will be forced to retire in all haste." Blücher instructed St. Priest to modify his march to move the VIII Infantry Corps toward Macdonald's forces on the lower Rhine to cover Yorck's flanking movement. Upon reaching the Saar, Blücher planned to march directly to Metz in accordance with his promise to Schwarzenberg.[65] In a letter to Clausewitz, Gneisenau expressed the hope and growing optimism of Blücher's headquarters: "Marmont has retreated in front of us toward Neustadt. Provided that he does not withdraw over the Vosges in the following days, he shall not escape us." Gneisenau also revealed his intention to unite with Wittgenstein and Wrede. In conjunction with these two corps, he believed Blücher's army would suffice to seek battle with the French army that was presumably concentrating at Metz. "In a battle that turned out to be unfavorable," maintains Gneisenau, "our superior cavalry will allow us to prevent a disaster and give the Austrian army time to arrive. We therefore risk very little in order to win much, indeed everything, because should we win a victory, we will be able to march to Paris without encountering many obstacles."[66]

For 4 January, Blücher issued extensive instructions to Yorck's rested and reorganized corps. Prince William received orders to lead the 8th Brigade from Kreuznach to Kusel. From there it would proceed in two columns, the first to Saarlouis, the second to Saarbrücken. William had to achieve three main tasks. "First, prevent the enemy from establishing himself on the Saar; second, capture the fortress of Saarlouis if it does not appear to have a garrison and prevent it from being provisioned if it does; and third, cover the march of Yorck's corps." Just north of Yorck's main body, Blücher ordered Henckel's Streifkorps to continue west and, if possible, occupy Trier on the Moselle to secure the right flank of the army. As for Yorck's main body, it would march to a position between Kreuznach and Meisenheim.[67]

A sudden thaw reduced the roads to quagmires, preventing Prince William from reaching his march objective on the 4th. Katzler led William's advance guard to Offenbach, a few miles southwest of Lauterecken, where William's brigade camped. Yorck's main body reached Meisenheim; Yorck established his headquarters at Obermoschel and Blücher passed the night in Kreuznach. At Mainz Langeron continued his preparations to besiege the fortress along the left bank. Sacken pushed his forward units to Göllheim and Kirchheimbolanden, about nineteen miles northeast of Kaiserslautern. The majority of the Russian cavalry advanced to Neustadt and Bad Dürkheim to distract Marmont's attention from Yorck's flank march.[68]

The reports that arrived in Blücher's headquarters on the night of 4–5 January concerning Marmont's movements and Sacken's progress remained so unclear that the field marshal decided to grant Yorck's corps a day of rest on the 5th to allow time for the situation to be clarified. Only the advance guard and Henckel's Streifkorps continued the march to attain the objectives stated in their orders for 4 January. Katzler led the head of William's brigade to Konken, while the Hohenzollern prince reached Kusel with his main body. Blücher directed Langeron to complete the formal investment of Mainz and to summon the fortress to surrender. With Langeron's corps finally moving to Mainz, Sacken retracted the detachments he had pushed toward the fortress and redirected them south toward Landau. Biron received instructions to march through the mountains of Kirchheimbolanden toward Kaiserslautern in order to ascertain Marmont's position; if the enemy had evacuated Kaiserslautern, he would advance south to Pirmasens but still maintain communication with Yorck's advance guard. With Blücher's headquarters spending another day at Kreuznach, Gneisenau and Müffling had time to arrange the army's communications. They transferred the Austrian pontoon bridge used by Sacken's corps to Oppenheim to form the principal line of communication between the Silesian Army and Frankfurt. At Kaub the engineers dismantled the pontoon bridge, leaving a footbridge in its place.[69]

On 5 January, Katzler dispatched numerous patrols in all directions and sought communication with Henckel and Sacken. According to the exaggerated reports he received, an enemy corps of approximately 12,000 men had retreated through Kusel to St. Wendel in the direction of Saarlouis. Durutte purportedly stood at Birkenfeld north of St. Wendel with 5,000 to 6,000 men, while Marmont held Kaiserslautern with 15,000 to 20,000 men. All reports indicated the French possessed few pieces of artillery.[70]

On the right wing of the Silesian Army, Henckel made preparations to take Trier, which Ricard's troops held. The Prussian colonel arrived at Thalfang very late on 4 January because of the difficult journey through the Hunsrück. He dispatched two Landwehr squadrons and two infantry platoons in wagons toward Trier early on the 5th to conduct reconnaissance. His troops scattered the French outposts and took a position before the city. The appearance of the Prussians coupled with what the French commander of Trier, General Antoine Rigau, believed to be the sound of artillery coming from the direction of Luxembourg, caused him to retract all his forward posts. Skirmishing ensued between the Prussians and the weak French garrison throughout the day. Using this as cover, Rigau evacuated Trier's magazines to Grevenmachern. Thinking he had concluded the evacuation, Rigau himself left under the cover of darkness.[71]

Henckel reached the village of Nouvon on the evening of the 5th with his main body. Built on a hill, only one short mile separated Nouvon from the walls of Trier. To deceive the French, Henckel spread his companies and instructed the men to light numerous watch fires. He also made preparations to attack the two city gates on the right bank of the Moselle. Before long Trier's magistrate and a disguised French adjutant requested an audience. At his outpost, Henckel met the French deputation, which requested mercy for the city. Henckel granted the request on the condition that Trier surrender. The French agreed. "By the time I arrived at the gates the enemy had evacuated the city," recalls Henckel. "I must give Rigau credit for sparing the city and for conducting himself with honor. I led the cavalry right through the city and across the Moselle, whose beautiful old bridge had been left undamaged, and ordered the pursuit of the enemy, who withdrew to Luxembourg."

Rigau's evacuation was very incomplete; he left behind 600 to 800 sick and 1,500 conscripts, who Henckel sent back to their homes with passes. Henckel took possession of 1,500 muskets and a tobacco magazine worth an estimated 500,000 francs; he sent a portion of the booty to Yorck and Blücher.[72] In a local iron foundry, his men found 39,000 six-pound cannon balls and many accouterments for cavalry. For the sake of any French spies lingering in Trier, Henckel claimed to be the advance guard of Yorck's corps. He fondly recalled his stay in Trier: "the whole time I played the role of the great man, but used it as much as possible to acquire uniforms for the battalion and to outfit the Landwehr with all pieces of equipment. This was easy for me and it gave me a great reputation in the city since I purchased everything, which I could easily do since I had found the tobacco and sold it as confiscated imperial [French] property to cover these costs." Aside from providing his superiors with a coveted pleasure, Henckel's operation proved to be far more important to the Silesian Army. Not only did his Streifkorps capture Trier, but on the following day, the 6th, his men seized the stone bridge over the Saar at Konz, near the confluence with the Moselle.[73] One of only four permanent bridges that spanned the now swollen Saar, possession of the crossing at Konz enabled the Prussians to turn the extreme left of Marmont's position along the river.

On the 5th, Blücher received confirmed reports that Marmont still held Kaiserslautern and that Sacken's forward units reached Frankenstein, halfway between Bad Dürkheim and Kaiserslautern. With renewed hopes of being able to envelop Marmont, he ordered Sacken to concentrate his right wing in Kirchheimbolanden, his left in Göllheim, and the advance guard at Grünstadt. The corps would then advance in two columns against Kaiserslautern. Blücher instructed the Russian commander to pin the enemy until Yorck reached Ramstein in Marmont's rear. Should the marshal escape south on the road to Pirmasens in an attempt to reach the mountains and unite with Victor, Blücher's two corps would resume the original goal of blocking Marmont's road to Metz by stopping him at the Saar. In this case, Yorck would head for Saarlouis and Saarbrücken, while Sacken would adjust his march so his two columns would reach Sarreguemines and Bitche, pursuing the French through Pirmasens to the latter.[74]

Confidence remained high in Silesian Army Headquarters, as suggested by Müffling's 5 January letter to Knesebeck:

Today Sacken stands at Kirchheimbolanden, his cavalry is before Neustadt and Bad Dürkheim, both of which are occupied by Marmont, who appears to want to hold Kaiserslautern with 14,000 men. We will allow him this pleasure. Yorck remains on the march to the Saar and will cut-off Marmont from Metz. *If the enemy halts for one day we will make him a may-pole and have him dance a round-dance*. We take the first steps toward the Saar and will force the enemy to throw garrisons in Saarlouis, Thionville, and Luxembourg. *Then we will, if it is at all possible, pounce on him at Metz.* In our army is a most marvelous morale; that in the Russian corps is prickly, which could signal an end of their enthusiasm, at least militarily.[75]

Sacken's advance posed the immediate threat to Marmont, who pulled back Lagrange's division, the four battalions of Durutte's division, and Doumerc's I Cavalry Corps from Bad Dürkheim and Neustadt to Kaiserslautern during the night of 3–4 January. The French marshal soon realized that Blücher intended to fix his front with Sacken's corps, whereas Yorck either enveloped his left wing or reached the Saar before him. Marmont did not feel strong enough to make a stand at Kaiserslautern, nor could he risk losing his line of retreat to the Saar. After resting man and horse on the 4th, he decided to evacuate Kaiserslautern early on the 5th. Thanks to a sudden thaw, his men trooped along a horribly muddy road for twenty-three miles to Homburg, where the marshal arrived around 6:00 A.M. that same morning. Reports indicated that strong enemy cavalry detachments had passed through Kaiserslautern in pursuit. Despite the exhaustion of his troops and the poor condition of the road, Marmont continued the retreat to the Saar to reach Sarreguemines and Saarbrücken. In a fit of overambition, he also planned to escort a supply convoy to Bitche (eighteen miles east of Sarreguemines), because he believed the enemy would make an attempt to gain the fortress. The left bank of the Moselle concerned him as well. Although an officer had been dispatched to Trier, Marmont had not received any news from him. He turned to Belliard in Metz in the hope of obtaining news of the situation on his left.[76]

After leaving a cuirassier brigade at Homburg as rearguard, Marmont's soldiers marched another twenty-three miles to reach the Saar and evade Blücher's envelopment. On the morning of the 6th, Lagrange's 3rd Division, the four battalions of Ricard's division, and Doumerc's I Cavalry Corps crossed the river at Sarreguemines. According to reports, the Allied column that had crossed the Rhine at Bacharach (Yorck) would soon reach the Saar. The Prussian advance guard of this column, 700 to 800 troopers "of the Black and Blue Hussar Regiments" and 300 jäger, appeared at St. Wendel (seventeen miles northeast of Saarbrücken) but withdrew after a light skirmish with the 1st Honor Guard Regiment.

The marshal himself went to Saarbrücken to make all necessary preparations to defend the river "according to his resources," as he pointed out to Berthier. He dispatched cavalry and artillery to defend the fords downstream of Saarlouis and positioned his light cavalry and Lagrange's division at Sarreguemines to cover the provisioning of Bitche, to where he still planned to send a supply convoy that night. Doumerc received orders to transfer the

I Cavalry Corps's two heavy cavalry regiments to the château at Siersberg, downstream of Saarlouis, whose garrison would provide 600 infantry for support. Marmont instructed the cavalry to guard the fords of Pachten and Rehlingen, and to patrol the river as far as Merzig. Should Doumerc be forced to abandon his posts, the marshal directed him to retire directly on Metz.

Meanwhile, Ricard's and Durutte's divisions marched through St. Wendel on the 5th and likewise reached Saarbrücken. On the 6th, the two French generals reached Saarbrücken around the same time as Marmont, who assigned them the defense of the river between Saarlouis and Sarreguemines. Marmont instructed them to occupy the village of St. Johann on the right bank with a rearguard that would remain there throughout the day and during the night of 6–7 January to guard Saarbrücken's bridge while sappers mined the supporting arches. The marshal also wanted all barges firmly moored to the left bank. On the morning of the 7th, the rearguard would withdraw from St. Johann and destroy Saarbrücken's bridge. The main body of the 1st and 32nd Divisions would take position at Forbach, four miles west of Saarbrücken, with detachments guarding Saarbrücken and the fords upstream at Güdingen as well as downstream at Völklingen, Malstadt, and Wehrden. In all, Marmont possessed approximately 8,500 infantry, 2,500 cavalry, and thirty-six guns to defend the twenty-five-mile stretch of the Saar.[77]

For the moment, nature provided the best support for the defense of the river. Incessant showers and the sudden thaw caused the Saar to flood; its tributaries that flowed from the Vosges churned from melted snows. The floodwaters not only inundated the fords but also rendered bridge construction difficult. However, permanent bridges that could be accessed by embanked highways were located at Sarreguemines, Saarbrücken, Saarlouis, and Konz. Marmont wanted to place these points of passage in a state of defense but received little cooperation from the terrified populace and the stupefied local authorities. The day of the 6th passed quietly as the tired troops occupied their positions and built entrenchments for both infantry and artillery along the left bank to cover the fords. Marmont ordered all of the sick in Saarbrücken evacuated to Saarlouis; an escort of customs agents accompanied the patients from the hospital in Sarreguemines to Metz. The marshal returned from Saarbrücken and established his headquarters in Sarreguemines to observe the defensive preparations along the upper Saar. By rapidly moving to the Saar, Marmont frustrated Blücher's plans more than he imagined. Now at the Saar, he hoped to deceive the Prussian commander into believing he had received considerable reinforcements and would vigorously defend the left bank. However, provisioning the fortresses and evacuating the depots that had fled from the Rhine to the Saar remained his primary objective. The longer he held the river, the more time he would gain to place the fortresses of northern Lorraine in a state of defense and to cover the completion of the new battalions at Metz. "I am doing everything that is in my power to provision

Saarlouis," he reports to Berthier, "which we have not taken care of at all. The commanding officer at Saarlouis lost his head and I had to appoint another . . . I will increase its garrison, which is pretty badly composed . . . to make it 12,000 men and 400 National Guardsmen."[78]

In accordance with his orders, Sacken marched to Kaiserslautern on the 6th, which Biron had found vacated the night before. According to the locals, Marmont retreated southwest to Homburg on the road to Saarbrücken. This extremely important report, which did not reach Blücher's headquarters until the night of the 6th, would have changed the field marshal's plans had it been forwarded in a timely manner. What did arrive at Silesian Army Headquarters was the report of a staff officer who conducted reconnaissance south of Kaiserslautern, where the inhabitants informed him that the French still occupied the town. He forwarded this report without personally verifying the intelligence. As a result, the operation against Kaiserslautern continued. Thus, Blücher's first blow in the campaign of 1814 missed, and Marmont escaped.[79]

Nevertheless, the news that Marmont had indeed evacuated Kaiserslautern did not catch Blücher and Gneisenau wholly unprepared. Sacken's note regarding the withdrawal of the French posts from Neustadt and Bad Dürkheim to Kaiserslautern cast doubt on Marmont's intention to hold his ground. As a result, Blücher had issued additional orders to Yorck on the night of the 5th. "Since it is extremely important to cut off the enemy from the roads to Saarbrücken and Metz," wrote Blücher, "I thus request that you not only order Prince William to hasten his march to Saarbrücken, but also that you take every necessary measure to reach this objective as well."[80]

That same night, 5 January, Yorck's advance guard and Reserve Cavalry marched, but Marmont had too much of a head start and quickly covered the distance between Kaiserslautern and Saarbrücken. On 6 January, the pursuit continued, but the plan to cut off Marmont failed. While Marmont's men crossed the Saar, Katzler led the cavalry of the advance guard to Tholey and Marpingen. Katzler dispatched Colonel Leopold von Stutterheim with the Brandenburg Uhlan Regiment and one infantry battalion to Saarbrücken with the intention of executing a coup de main on the 7th if the fortress appeared to be weakly guarded. His detachment reached Ottweiler on the night of the 6th. The commander of the Reserve Cavalry, Colonel Ludwig von Jürgaß, led one dragoon brigade and four horse guns south from Kusel toward Homburg and Zweibrücken. With the main body of the advance guard, Prince William secured St. Wendel after the 1st Honor Guard Regiment withdrew. Yorck established his headquarters at Kusel with the main body of the I Corps; Blücher passed the night in Lauterecken. Sacken ordered General Sergei Nikolaevich Lanskoi to push his light cavalry southwest from Kaiserslautern to Pirmasens; Biron's Streifkorps secured Homburg. Sacken's Cossacks reached Zweibrücken and established communication with Yorck's corps.[81]

After confirming the news of Marmont's escape, Blücher and Gneisenau pursued. They had gained a fairly accurate view of the marshal's strength and knew that Yorck or Sacken alone outnumbered him. In the orders issued for 6 January, Blücher's staff included copies of an intercepted muster of Marmont's corps dated 1 December 1813, which placed the corps's strength at 13,278 men. In his report to the tsar on the following day, Blücher wrote: "the VI Corps under the orders of Marshal Marmont, and the I Cavalry Corps under the orders of Gen. Doumerc, a force of 15,000 to 16,000 men, have retired in front of me in forced marches to the Saar, where on the 5th a body of 4,000 men arrived from Metz." Because of the Silesian Army's numerical superiority, they elected to keep the two corps separated by twenty-five miles so that Yorck could cross the river downstream at Saarlouis and Sacken upstream at Sarreguemines. Should Marmont stand against one of the two, the other would sever his line of retreat to Metz. Reports arrived on the 7th claiming the French were building a pontoon bridge at Saarbrücken after they destroyed the stone bridge. Further intelligence stated that Marmont expected to have his forces concentrated on the Saar by 9 January. Regardless of Marmont's next move, Blücher decided to drive across the Saar and reach Metz by 15 January in accordance with his promise to Schwarzenberg.[82]

On 7 January, Katzler reached Saarlouis with instructions "to arrange everything to spread terror on the other side of the Saar and, if possible, to invest the fortress with detachments."[83] He distributed his troops in mixed units along the Saar from Dillingen to Völklingen. The French conceded the right bank but appeared ready to contest any Allied attempt to cross the river. Although Katzler's cavalry reconnoitered both downstream and upstream, the Prussians could not locate a suitable crossing point. His patrols reported that fieldworks and artillery positions defended the fords; several boats could be seen half-submerged or capsized in the Saar. On a positive note, locals claimed that Saarlouis's garrison consisted of mainly insufficiently supplied conscripts. Katzler shelled the fortress between 7:00 and 8:00 that night without effect. Elsewhere, Prince William initially wanted to proceed to Saarbrücken with his main body but changed his mind, turned toward Saarlouis, and established his headquarters slightly northeast at Lebach. East of his advance guard, Yorck's main body continued the march to the Saar in two columns on the 7th. Yorck led the first, consisting of the 1st and 2nd Brigades and Reserve Artillery, southwest from Kusel to St. Wendel, where also Silesian Army Headquarters arrived. General Heinrich Wilhelm von Horn moved the second column – his own 7th Brigade and Maj. von Bieberstein's Neumark Landwehr Cavalry Regiment of the Reserve Cavalry – due west to Birkenfeld.

Stutterheim proceeded to Saarbrücken with his detachment. On the night of the 7th, he united with Biron at St. Johann, on the right bank of the Saar across from Saarbrücken. The French had blasted two of the bridge's supports and, after receiving word that the Allies would soon arrive, burned their pontoon bridge. Some reports estimated the garrison to be as large as 6,000 men; others stated that the French had in fact withdrew. Stutterheim ordered a small detachment to cross the Saar by boat late on the 7th. Musket and artillery fire greeted the Prussians as they approached the left bank; they turned their boats around as quickly as they could.

During the course of the 7th, Sacken received Blücher's instructions to move to Sarreguemines. Biron's Streifkorps continued to maintain communication between the two corps, and Sacken sought to make contact with Wittgenstein by sending patrols through Bitche, Sarrewerden, and Sarrebourg. At the Rhine, General Friedrich Erhard von Röder arrived at Koblenz with a brigade of Kleist's Reserve Cavalry. There he received orders to reach Luxembourg on the 18th to observe the roads coming from Brussels because Blücher expected Napoleon to recall his Imperial Guard units from Belgium.[84]

Marmont reported to Berthier that an enemy advance guard of cavalry and infantry reached Saarbrücken on the 7th; he believed large Allied forces were converging on Zweibrücken as well. "I will do everything in my power to delay the enemy's crossing of the Saar," attests the marshal. "I have arranged the defense of the upper Saar, and tomorrow I will return to Saarbrücken." He took a central position at Forbach with his main force to be able to reinforce quickly the points of passage between Saarlouis and Saarbrücken. Also, the supply convoy departed for Bitche; he could only hope that it arrived in time because the fortress was "in very great need."[85]

Of 10,000 men, Marmont lost approximately 1,500 during his retreat from the Rhine to the Saar. Aside from combat losses, desertion was a growing problem. "What is happening here is very unfortunate for the good of His Majesty's service," states his report. Persuasive Allied propaganda induced German and Dutch soldiers to desert in larger numbers. Marmont informed Berthier that many men from the left bank departments of Mont-Tonnerre and Rhin-et-Moselle had deserted. For example, Ricard's battery had a mixed crew of German and French soldiers. All but three of the Germans deserted and the battery remained inoperative until twenty-five French gunners from the depot at Saarlouis joined the unit at Kirchberg. "All of the soldiers who are not from old France have deserted the flag," he laments. "All of the Dutchmen who enlisted have now left. The 11th Hussar Regiment, composed mainly of Dutchmen, dissolved instantly, and because the deserters were taking their horses with them, I was forced to put on foot those who were left and to give the horses to the most trusted soldiers." Between 6 and 13 January, his regiments lost 2,500 men to desertion; he eventually reached Metz with only 6,000 infantry.

In addition to the desertions, Marmont observed that French officials, both civil and military, as well as the gendarmes, abandoned their posts in an "alarming way." "The gendarmes left Zweibrücken four days ago," wrote

Marmont on the 7th, "the sub-prefect of Sarreguemines two days ago." With Allied forces approaching, French officials had little desire to linger. Their flight, which was observed by the army as indicated by Marmont, undermined the morale of the troops, hindered command and control, and signaled the general collapse of imperial authority beyond the borders of old France. This breakdown of imperial control hampered efforts to feed the army. As for supplying his men in a timely manner, Marmont insisted that "instead of providing order, the duke of Valmy [Kellermann] seems to make a mess of everything."[86]

French historian Beauchamp contends that the flight of French officials was applauded by the rural population, "because the people generally regarded the invasion as deliverance."[87] In every department along the Rhine where the French army cantoned in November after the evacuation of Germany, the retreating French troops had terrorized the local population with physical abuse or threats to life and property if victuals were not provided promptly. In the Department of the Roer, which extended along the length of the Rhine between Arnhem and Bonn, regional French authorities claimed this behavior stemmed from the general collapse of the army's discipline, morale, and supply. The inhabitants of the Rhin-et-Moselle and Mont-Tonnerre Departments, which neighbored the Roer to the south and formed Marmont's theater, received the same treatment if not worse.[88] Although not directly responsible for the army's excesses in November, French civil officials were unwilling to await retribution and so fled in January.

On the other side of the Saar, an impatient Blücher transferred his headquarters to Kusel on the 7th. Contrasting the optimism that had permeated his headquarters just two days earlier, the Prussian field marshal was frustrated. His staff lacked adequate maps, and his cavalry failed to provide precise information regarding the French forces on the opposite bank. He continued to receive conflicting reports over the mood of the population. Although Sacken's patrols made contact with Wittgenstein's Cossacks on the 6th, news of this had still not reached Silesian Army headquarters, and Blücher had absolutely no idea if his Russian ally had crossed the Rhine. To increase his own combat power directly, he ordered Kleist to reach Koblenz by 20 January and the German V Corps to relieve Langeron at Mainz. "The day after tomorrow I will assemble the corps of Sacken and Yorck on the Saar. If the enemy does not retreat I will cross this river and attack him immediately," reports the resolute field marshal to the tsar. "If I succeed in driving Marmont from the Saar, I will arrive on the 15th at Metz where, one claims, many conscripts have assembled."[89]

As noted, Wrede contacted Blücher. The Bavarian commander expressed his discontent over the irresolution that reigned in Schwarzenberg's headquarters and strangled Allied operations in Alsace. According to Wrede's aide-de-camp, the prince of Thurn-Taxis, the Bavarians desired to coordinate their movements with those of the Silesian Army. "Through the Prince of Thurn-Taxis you have expressed your desire to operate in unison against the enemy, for which I am fully prepared," Blücher wrote to Wrede on the 7th. "According to all reports the enemy finds himself in an extremely unfavorable situation, which invites a battle from our side since our cavalry, which is superior in number to that of the enemy, will prevent us from suffering the disadvantages of a dubious or unfortunate result, while the enemy risks everything. I have instructed Sacken to seek communication with Wittgenstein's corps by way of Bitche and Sarrewerden."[90] Blücher envisioned a grand, sweeping operation in unison with Schwarzenberg's right wing to crush the French before their reinforcements arrived. He hoped to achieve a victory that the numerically superior Allied cavalry could make decisive. To obtain the support of the V Corps for this operation, Blücher requested that Wrede reach Charmes by the 15th; on this day he planned to have the Silesian Army seventy miles north of Charmes at Thionville. "I have requested that Wittgenstein and Wrede coordinate their movements with mine and in a manner to be able to, if need be, attack the enemy in unison with me," he explained to the tsar to secure a strong voice in Allied headquarters to support his plans.[91]

On the 5th, Schwarzenberg received Blücher's 3 January report of the Silesian Army's crossing of the Rhine and its preparations to drive to the Saar.[92] Blücher's letter did nothing to induce the generalissimo to either accelerate the movement of the Bohemian Army in general, or the advance of Wittgenstein's VI Corps in particular. By forming Schwarzenberg's extreme right, Wittgenstein operated closest to Blücher. Instead, Schwarzenberg issued an evasive response that contained the seed that later sprouted Prussian accusations that the Austrians purposefully bled dry the Silesian Army for the sake of postwar leverage at the peace table. Schwarzenberg informed the Prussian field marshal of the Bohemian Army's movements since 30 December, communicated his views over the general situation, and expressed his belief that he could be master of Langres and Dijon before 20 January. Yet the investment of Belfort, Huningue, Neuf-Brisach, Besançon, and Auxonne, the detaching of Bubna to Geneva, and the observation of the garrisons of Strasbourg and Metz no longer allowed him "to make an eccentric advance from Langres." Schwarzenberg thus conceded that he had so stripped his center by pursuing geographic and secondary objectives that he would not be strong enough to advance from Langres to Paris. This was shocking news considering the Allied plan identified Langres as the Bohemian Army's objective – thus the army should reach it with maximum rather than minimum strength. Moreover, he expressed concern that Blücher would return to his original plan and move toward the Netherlands, forsaking the Bohemian Army. The Allied commander in chief also commented over reports that Napoleon was concentrating his main force at Paris rather than Metz. "If he does this, his intention is to deliver a decisive blow, which I would only consider accepting if I can coordinate my movements in unison with yours," wrote the Austrian. "This will be possible only if you move on Nancy, or at least Verdun. I do not believe you should continue moving right [northwest] in order to support the movements of the army in Holland. Otherwise, it would be better for me to turn south, since I proceed according to the principle that we either concentrate against the enemy's movement, or we must force him through our own expansive [and] likewise eccentric movements to accept the fact that our armies can quickly come together to exploit any obtained advantage, or to recover after any lost battle."[93]

In this way Schwarzenberg baited Blücher. Possessing an army three times the size of Blücher's, Schwarzenberg would use his own numerous corps to secure his flanks and pursue Austrian interests such as supporting Bubna's operations in southern France. He planned to push his weak center to Langres, while Blücher moved up in support. Schwarzenberg would accept battle only if he could execute his movements in unison with those of the Silesian Army. Thus, he requested that Blücher turn south to Nancy with his right going no further than Verdun. In this way the two armies could act concentrically, as at Leipzig. Should Napoleon arrive at Langres with a large army, then it would be Blücher whose head would be on the chopping block. With the Bohemian Army dispersed and Blücher's army reduced by strategic consumption, this supposed French army would enjoy numerical superiority according to Schwarzenberg's own estimates. Thus Napoleon and Blücher could maul each other, with the vast majority of Austrian troops far from the field of battle. The end result – dead Prussians, Russians, and French – would certainly strengthen Metternich's peace party. Although this did not become the case at Langres, this scenario came true on the 1 February 1814 Battle of la Rothière.

On the other hand, if Blücher could not change the axis of his march to make this cooperation possible, Schwarzenberg would be compelled to orient the Bohemian Army further south. This would force Napoleon either to divide his main force into two wings and make eccentric movements on his part, or lead the French army against Blücher. In the first case, the French emperor would not be in a position to reinforce either wing, exploit any advantage, or replenish battlefield losses. The second case would place Napoleon and an unsupported Blücher in a position to thrash each other.

Contrary to Schwarzenberg's intelligence concerning French troop strength at Metz, Blücher insisted Napoleon had concentrated between 40,000 and 80,000 men – mainly conscripts lacking training, equipment, and particularly muskets – in and around the fortress. "Metz right now is the principal organization point for all enemy forces," Blücher wrote to Schwarzenberg on the 8th.[94] On the following day, the 9th, Schwarzenberg's letter of 5 January reached Silesian Army Headquarters. Drafted on the same day, the Prussian response sought to meet Schwarzenberg halfway. After crossing the Saar,

Blücher would head for Nancy to be closer to the Bohemian Army. However, before turning south, he would force the French to either garrison the Moselle fortresses of Metz, Thionville, and Luxembourg, or he would launch an operation against one of the fortresses. The savvy Blücher added that "as long as the enemy remains in significant strength by Metz, or withdraws on the highway from Metz to Paris, I believe I will be proceeding in accordance with your intentions if I pursue him." The Prussian insinuated that he preferred to drive west and deeper into France, rather than unite with the Bohemian Army for the simple effect of impressing Napoleon, as Schwarzenberg suggested to be the reason to unite the two armies. Blücher also claimed he had to continue west to prevent the French forces at Metz from severing his own line of communication through Kaiserslautern to Mannheim, which he did not want to alter. He did attempt to sooth Schwarzenberg's anxiety by adding that he did not think it was necessary to support Bülow directly in the Low Countries. Yet he reminded the Austrian commander that their continued drive into France would indirectly help the situation in Holland by forcing Napoleon to recall more units from that secondary theater.[95] Schwarzenberg had sufficient reason to be satisfied with this response; he still had time to manipulate Blücher, and the slower the Bohemian Army marched, the better.

Although the headquarters of the two Allied armies appeared to be cooperating and Schwarzenberg even claimed to be working just as closely with Blücher as during the days of Leipzig, some significant differences in the two styles of command are apparent.[96] Schwarzenberg sought excuses to anchor his army to secondary objectives, whereas Blücher targeted the French army as the main Allied objective. Blücher and Gneisenau never abandoned the idea that the latter had argued so vehemently in Frankfurt: The Allies had to strike before Napoleon finished preparing his defenses and organizing his conscripts. Yet Schwarzenberg never believed he possessed enough combat power and thus sought Blücher's assistance. He based his strategy of caution on the exaggerated reports of French military preparations and his concern that Napoleon would exploit any separation of the Allied armies. The Austrian also possessed a healthy respect – if not fear – for the French emperor's martial abilities. Pragmatically, Austrian politics and military conservatism convinced him Napoleon would seek a negotiated peace as soon as the Bohemian Army controlled Langres and Dijon.[97]

Blücher granted his army a day of rest on the 8th in part to allow the rearward units to catch up. Jürgaß spread his Reserve Cavalry across a broad front to maintain communication between Saarbrücken and Saarlouis. Patrols also scouted the crossing at Merzig, north of Saarlouis. Hoping the inhabitants would induce the French to surrender, Katzler shelled Saarlouis with two howitzers between 4:00 and 5:00 on the morning of the 8th. His gunners fired several rounds that went unanswered. He also attempted to open negotiations, but the French greeted his adjutant with small-arms fire; the frustrated

Prussians returned to their billets in Saarwellingen shortly before daybreak. On the army's left wing, Sacken moved his headquarters to Homburg, fifteen miles northeast of Zweibrücken on the road to Sarreguemines. His advance guard under Lanskoi reached the upper Saar and found all the fords defended by French infantry and artillery. Sacken ordered his pontoons to move up and sent detachments southeast toward Bitche.[98]

On the right wing, Henckel entrenched himself at Trier. Yorck informed him on the evening of the 8th that "Trier is to be held as the center of the military excursions and small operations that you can execute with your detachment in order to deceive the enemy, to spread terror, and to frustrate the enemy's arrangements regarding requisitions, the calling-up of arms-bearing manpower, etc., and to report over the organization of the enemy, particularly how the arming and equipping of the conscripts is progressing."[99] Although he felt isolated and expected strong French forces to arrive at any moment to retake the city, the witty colonel managed to keep his sense of humor, reporting that his "fortified positions are now ready and it is said: *ou vaincre ou mourir* (victory or death). Today one has reported an envelopment, but our Landwehr will outflank everything, except taverns!" Henckel pushed a detachment of fifty troopers supported by some infantry transported in wagons toward Grevenmachern, which Rigau evacuated as he continued his inglorious retreat to Thionville. Henckel dispatched a patrol toward Malmédy to establish communication with Bülow's corps, supposedly en route to Brussels. In addition, he forwarded small units toward Luxembourg to prevent the provisioning of the fortress and to spread the rumor that an entire Prussian army corps would arrive soon. The deception succeeded; a Prussian patrol of twenty troopers put to flight a large French infantry unit that included two guns.

On the evening of the 8th, Lieutenant von der Chevallerie sped to Luxembourg with the marksmen of the Leib Fusilier Battalion in wagons to prevent the provisioning of the fortress. According to the statements of a captured French military musician, Luxembourg's garrison consisted of approximately 2,800 conscripts and one or two companies of Guard Artillery with few guns and insufficient supplies. The prisoner also reported that the majority of the garrison departed for Thionville the day before. On the 9th, a second report reached Henckel from a patrol of fifty Landwehr troopers that scoured the region around Luxembourg. The captain who commanded the mission informed Henckel of the departure of enemy cavalry to the French interior and that only about 1,000 men remained in the fortress. "All in all, Luxembourg will quickly fall into our hands if we could threaten it with a small corps; terror and desertion will be significant." Henckel forwarded this intelligence to Yorck, who received it on the 10th at 4:00 P.M. "If I was somewhat stronger," states the colonel's cover letter, "I would certainly make an attempt on Luxembourg because almost everyone has deserted; my patrols

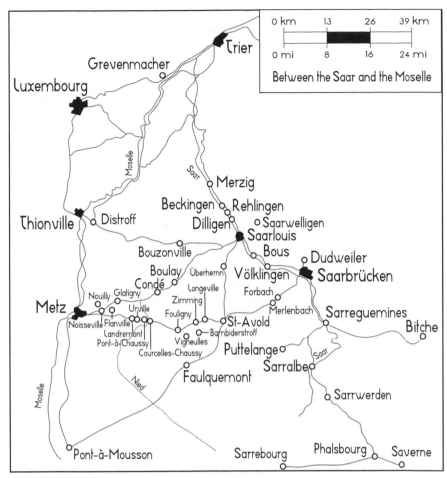

Map 9. The region between the Saar and the Maselle.

bring in fifty to sixty prisoners daily and my proclamations have had great results."[100] For the moment, Henckel remained at Trier, but his reports later influenced Blücher's planning considerably.

Marmont recognized the Allied preparations to cross the Saar. He inspected the river line on the morning of the 8th and withdrew his advance post from the right bank facing Sarreguemines. "Due to unimaginable negligence," all the barges his soldiers had anchored at Saarbrücken broke free of their moorings, descended the river, and fell into Prussian hands. Because the boats were large enough to transport 5,000 men, the marshal decided to have them destroyed. At 11:30 A.M., he ranged the canon to fire on a farmhouse west of St. Johann on the right bank that served as an outpost for

Stutterheim's detachment. Simultaneously a sixty-man detachment from the 9th Light Infantry would cross the Saar in boats and either retake or sink the barges. Around noon the guns of Saarbrücken suddenly unleashed their deadly salvos on the unsuspecting Prussians. At the same time, the crackle of small-arms fire erupted from the muskets of several French skirmishers posted along the left bank. Under oppressive fire, the Prussians hastily evacuated their post. The French detachment crossed the icy Saar, burned the farmhouse, and returned the barges to the left bank before Stutterheim could arrive with reinforcements. The French lieutenant who commanded the mission received the chevalier of the Legion of Honor in recognition of the operation's success.[101]

Regardless, the valor of the soldiers of the 9th Light could do nothing to stop the course of nature. The same waters that had provided Marmont with a defensive advantage now receded as winter refused to relinquish its hold over the Saarland. A bitter freeze returned, lowering the Saar by two feet in just twenty-four hours. At this rate, the Prussians would be able to utilize the Saar's many fords within another twenty-four hours. Reports indicated Allied forces threatened Marmont's left and right on the upper and lower Saar, respectively. "Without doubt I know the enemy [Henckel] is maneuvering on both banks of the Moselle," he informed Berthier. Henckel's Streifkorps, whose strength Marmont did not know, could soon jeopardize the retreat of Doumerc's squadrons that served as his left flank guard. On Marmont's right, Sacken's Cossacks crossed the Saar at several points and raided along the left bank. The marshal knew the troops facing Saarlouis belonged to Yorck and believed Sacken commanded the units to his right. Marmont planned to maintain all fords and crossings downstream of Saarlouis and upstream of Sarreguemines "as long as the enemy does not attack either of these points, or threaten my communications by marching on the upper Saar." Furthermore, a disconcerting rumor reached Marmont: Victor had retreated across the Vosges and was making for Nancy. Unsure of Victor's fate, he feared an enemy force could move north from Alsace through the Moselle Valley and sever his line of retreat to Metz. With the provisioning of Bitche and Saarlouis nearly complete, Marmont felt he had fulfilled his mission. At the end of the day, he transferred his headquarters to Forbach on the main highway to Metz.[102]

Marmont's commando operation against Stutterheim's post particularly demoralized Yorck, who had expected to find the French weak and disorganized. "I believe it is too risky to have troops cross to the left bank," states his report to the field marshal, "since the enemy is not merely observing the Saar, but shows intentions to defend it." Yorck did not think an operation against Saarlouis would succeed unless sufficient forces crossed the Saar to invest the fortress completely. He ordered Prince William to occupy Saarwellingen, to reconnoiter the points of passage, and observe the line, but to keep his main body concealed and avoid attracting attention.[103]

Unmoved by the events at Saarbrücken, Blücher issued a three-day disposition for the 9th, 10th, and 11th to envelop Marmont's forces. On 9 January, Blücher would position Yorck's main body between Merzig and Saarlouis, and Sacken's between Sarralbe and Saarbrücken. For 10 January, he ordered the cavalry and horse artillery of both corps to cross the Saar. The light cavalry and Cossacks would proceed toward St. Avold to block Marmont's retreat to Metz, while the line cavalry converged on Forbach. For the 11th, Blücher ordered the corps to converge on Forbach, pushing their advance guards to St. Avold. He informed his two subordinates that Marmont's troops intended to defend the Saar between Sarreguemines and Saarlouis; the field marshal urged his corps commanders to drive across the Saar and smash the enemy.[104]

With the resumption of offensive operations, Gneisenau shared his thoughts with Stein in a long letter no doubt meant to be read by Tsar Alexander himself. He begins by recounting the Silesian Army's accomplishments since crossing the Rhine: 2,500 prisoners and twenty guns. "Trier is ours," he boasted. "In a few days our cavalry will blockade Luxembourg." Gneisenau then explained how Marmont initially opposed Blücher. "We prepared to envelop him on the western slopes of the Vosges, but he escaped by making an eighteen-hour march." According to Gneisenau, Marmont already had abandoned the left bank of the Saar, destroyed the bridges over this river, and appeared headed for Metz. Blücher planned to pursue, but believed the marshal would retreat from there as well. After this progress report, the Prussian staff chief addressed the issues that had been haunting him since the councils of war in Frankfurt: "I shudder from the fear that one will allow himself to be deceived by the Emperor Napoleon's peace proposals–which will certainly happen–and detain us in our course of victory. Only in Paris can we dictate a peace. . . . If we do not use this moment, we do not deserve to see another, and two years from now we will be punished for our current weakness. We are now so close to the goal. . . . From here it is only sixteen short marches to Paris. The consternation, despondency, and confusion has reached all time highs in France. It has taken a long time to assemble the conscripts . . . weapons are lacking everywhere. The dragoons had to hand over their carbines. Such troops cannot resist our soldiers; their generals and soldiers have little will to do so."

The Prussians would stop at nothing to exploit this opportunity. Depending on the tsar to override a timid Schwarzenberg, Gneisenau revealed his intentions to Stein. "We, the Silesian Army, want Wrede and Wittgenstein to operate with us as we seek a battle. The highest military possibility exists that we will win such [a battle]. Fate could frown on us, but in such a case we would not be completely defeated, because our superior cavalry would provide the opportunity for us to withdraw and await the arrival of Prince Schwarzenberg with the great reserves. United with these, we can drive the enemy all the way back to Paris. The enemy cannot stop us." He concluded with an interesting observation, the spirit of which would later surface in the tsar's orders of 24 January: "The centralization of the government in Paris makes the loss of the French capital much more detrimental than the loss of the capitals of other states. Nevertheless, one does not need to go to Paris to conquer this city. The Aube, the Yonne, the Seine, and the Orleans Canal supply the foodstuffs of this city. Not far from Nemours is the confluence of these waters. If one went there, one could negotiate from a position of strength, because any prolongation of the negotiations would favor us." His final statement laid bear the hearts of the Prussian leadership of the Silesian Army: "National revenge must be taken and we must repay the visits of the French to our cities with visits to theirs. If this does not occur, revenge and victory are incomplete. Should the Silesian Army reach Paris first, I will have the bridges of Austerlitz and Jena destroyed, including Napoleon's victory monument." These last lines eventually echoed in Schwarzenberg's headquarters, thus earning Blücher and Gneisenau both the the biting critism of the Allied commander in chief as well as his deepest suspicions over the motives that drove their operations.[105]

An alarmed Marmont sent word to Paris at noon on 9 January that the Allied crossing had commenced – twenty-four hours before it actually started. According to exaggerated, overexcited, and incorrect reports, a corps of all arms had "forced the passage of the Saar at Rehlingen, downstream of Saarlouis, constructed a bridge, and crossed in force with infantry, cavalry, and artillery." On the opposite end of his line, messages from Sarreguemines indicated that Russian cavalry had massed on the right bank. Marmont also learned the enemy reached Saverne, twenty-eight miles southeast of Sarreguemines. Still without news of Victor, he feared another Allied trap. With his own supply problems beginning to mount, he decided to evacuate the line of the Saar and withdraw into northeastern Lorraine. On the following morning, the 10th, he planned to maneuver his troops to St. Avold and from there toward Metz according to circumstances.[106]

Additional and equally inaccurate reports arrived during the afternoon of the 9th that altered the situation. According to one, a large Russian cavalry corps crossed the river and proceeded to Sarralbe, from where its patrols scoured the entire front but mainly headed toward the junction of the Metz – Phalsbourg and Nancy – Sarreguemines roads at Puttelange (Map 9). "This movement," Marmont explains to Berthier, "cannot have any other objective than to reach the pass at St. Avold – my only line of retreat – before me." Twenty-five miles separated St. Avold from Metz, while the distance between Forbach and St. Avold and between Puttelange and St. Avold was the same: eleven miles. To beat the Russians to this important point, Marmont ordered his troops to march that same evening, the 9th, and to cover the eleven miles to St. Avold. Lagrange's 3rd Division departed Forbach at 6:30 followed by the Reserve Artillery and General Jean-Baptiste van Merlin's light cavalry brigade.

Durutte assembled his 32nd Division at Forbach and departed at 2:00 A.M. with Marmont's headquarters, and the 1st Honor Guard Regiment. Ricard's 1st Division and one cavalry brigade brought up the rear; Colonel Jean-Nicolas Curely's 10th Hussar Regiment remained at Forbach as rearguard. Marmont instructed Doumerc to transfer the regiments of the I Cavalry Corps from Siersberg to Saarlouis, collect his forward posts along the Saar, and proceed to rendezvous with the VI Corps on the 10th. The French post at Beckingen withdrew to Saarlouis; those at Völklingen and Bouss to Forbach. All troops had to be in battle order at St. Avold by 8:00 A.M. on the 10th.[107]

Several detachments of Prussian and Russian cavalry did indeed cross to the left bank on the 9th. Stutterheim dispatched patrols on the road to Metz, while Karpov's Cossacks crossed the Saar downstream of Sarreguemines and sent detachments toward Puttelange. In this first critical breakdown of his intelligence, Marmont mistook the movement of Allied patrols for that of corps and thus abandoned the Saar. Rather than defend the river or attack one of Blücher's corps as it crossed, Marmont chose to retreat. A pitched battle with the Silesian Army never crossed his mind – as well it should not have, considering the mission the marshal believed he had to complete and the numerical inferiority of his forces. Delivering his cadres to the haven of Metz remained Marmont's priority; this responsibility demanded that he trade land for time. Yet Napoleon's political needs and military preparations required Marmont to employ his soldiers as human shields. The marshals had to keep Coalition forces as far from the French interior as possible to maintain the emperor's administrative network and the precious tax revenues that it generated as well as to cover the march of the conscripts from the frontier departments to the depots that had been transferred deep within old France. Unfortunately for Napoleon, he failed to communicate this objective to Marmont and the other marshals in clear, irrefutable terms.

Coming at a time when Marmont's and Morand's corps were in a state of flux because of the emperor's orders for the former to move to Strasbourg to support Victor, the timing of Blücher's invasion could not have been better. By crossing the Rhine at this moment, Blücher ruled out any possibility that Marmont could hold him in the Rhine Valley or make a stand in the defiles of the Hunsrück. Consequently, the line of the Saar provided Marmont with the first feasible opportunity to slow the progress of the Silesian Army. Marmont would have served his master far better if he had contested the Saar and waged a war of attrition west of the Moselle rather than uncovering the border of old France. Napoleon's absence from the front and the time required for communications between the master and his lieutenants severely impeded the defense of the frontiers. How much territory would the marshals surrender before the emperor finally left Paris to take personal command of the army?

Blücher's headquarters issued the three-day disposition relatively late on the 9th and before the report arrived that Sacken's patrols had crossed the upper Saar. Yorck already instructed Prince William to position his brigade a few miles northeast of Saarlouis at Saarwellingen and to have Katzler's cavalry patrol the stretch of the Saar from Saarbrücken to Merzig. Katzler's troopers found the French still guarding the river crossings. Artillery and entrenched infantry defended the ford at Völklingen, while cavalry held the fords at Beckingen and Rehlingen. Farther north, Horn led his 7th Brigade to Merzig, while the 1st and 2nd Brigades turned south to Saarlouis. At 3:45 on the afternoon of the 9th, Blücher's disposition arrived in Yorck's headquarters at Lebach, eleven miles northeast of Rehlingen. Shortly after, the French started to withdraw their forward posts from the left bank, but a cautious Yorck did not exploit the opportunity, nor did he take advantage of the Saar's lower water level to utilize the fords. By the evening of the 9th, his I Corps stretched along the Saar from Merzig to Saarbrücken; Sacken's Russians extended from Sarreguemines to Sarralbe.

That night Blücher received a barrage of conflicting messages. Some claimed the French abandoned the river; others attributed movements along the left bank to the rotation of French posts. Believing the reports that fell in the category of the former, the salty Prussian directed his staff to amend the disposition for 10 and 11 January. As a result, Lanskoi forded the Saar upstream from Sarreguemines on the morning of the 10th with Sacken's advance guard and two Cossack Regiments. He advanced through Puttelange toward St. Avold; behind him Sacken moved his headquarters to Sarralbe. On the same day, Sacken's Cossacks linked with Wittgenstein's troops near Phalsbourg, twenty-five miles southeast of Sarreguemines. Biron, who at 7:00 A.M. notified Blücher of the French retreat and received the order to pursue, forded the Saar at the Güdingen and linked with Jürgaß's advance guard near Merlenbach. Patrolling south of St. Avold, Biron's detachments proceeded to within one hour of Metz without encountering the French.

For Yorck's corps to cross the Saar, Major Johann Ludwig Markhoff of the engineers received the task of constructing two bridges downstream of Saarlouis at Beckingen: a footbridge for infantry and a trestle bridge for artillery. Drift ice and a sharp frost complicated his work. Markhoff hoped to finish between 10:00 and 11:00 P.M. but did not complete the bridges until the morning of the 11th. Nevertheless, Prussian units began crossing on the 10th. Some infantry battalions crossed by boat, while Stößel, who had assumed command of the head of the advance guard for the sick Katzler, forded the Saar at Rehlingen with eight squadrons. He proceeded southwest through Bouzonville, arriving around 6:00 A.M. at Boulay, halfway between Saarlouis and Metz. Bieberstein with the 1st Neumark Landwehr Cavalry Regiment forded the river at Beckingen, invested Saarlouis on the left bank, and severed the fortress's communications with Metz, Thionville, and St. Avold. Upriver at Saarbrücken, Jürgaß learned the French had evacuated the fortress the previous night after being alarmed by the movement of Prussian cavalry between this point and Saarlouis. Moving to St. Johann on the 10th, he ordered his men to cross the river. French mines had destroyed two of the arches that supported Saarbrücken's stone bridge, thus forcing the Prussians to scramble to find materials for a makeshift pontoon bridge. By raising sunken barges, Jürgaß managed to move two dragoon regiments and a battery across the river. Stutterheim's detachment – the Fusilier Battalion of the 12th Reserve Regiment and the Brandenburg Uhlan Regiment – followed and occupied Saarbrücken. Reaching Forbach with his main body, Jürgaß pushed his advance guard to Merlebach, halfway between Saarbrücken and St. Avold, covered by patrols that reported the presence of French troops in the latter. He summoned Stutterheim's detachment from Saarbrücken in order to attack St. Avold on the next day.[108]

Early on the 10th, Marmont's units effected the retreat to St. Avold in good order. Informed on the previous day of the Russian advance on Puttelange and of the presence of Prussian cavalry at Boulay, he decided to continue the movement a few miles further west to Longeville, still on the road to Metz. Only one day's march east of the mighty fortress, he planned to make a stand and observe the enemy's approach without compromising his own security. In this position, the marshal could not retake the offensive but once again hoped to delay Blücher to win time to provision the fortresses of Lorraine, especially Metz. "The position itself is good enough to allow me to stay until I can force the enemy that marches against me to deploy all of his forces," he explains to Berthier. "I find myself covering Metz, which has many needs." Marmont also planned to defend the principal debouches from the Saar and, to cover from the north Victor's line of retreat, hold the road that ran south from Longeville through Falquemont and Château-Salins to Nancy. As for reinforcements, some of his units that escaped the Rhine had managed to reach Metz. Kellermann forwarded them as well as other detachments of uniformed and armed recruits to Marmont. To his utter disbelief, however, Kellermann directed them on roads already controlled by the Allies.[109]

Marmont's divisions executed the movement to Longeville under the protection of a rearguard that occupied St. Avold, with a strong post holding the defile of Moulin-Neuf, one mile east of St. Avold. Blücher himself arrived at Saarbrücken around the same time Marmont stopped at Longeville. Master of the line of the Saar, Lorraine and the heart of old France lay before the Prussian field marshal. Although the Silesian Army moved across the Saar as rapidly as possible, Marmont enjoyed a considerable head start. The Saar line had been breached, but the operations to envelop Marmont and destroy his forces failed: The French marshal escaped again.

In evaluating Blücher's invasion of "new" France, the main point to address is the boldness of the field marshal's decision to have 70,000 men cross a large river in three separate columns, exposed to the enemy, and with the French-occupied fortress of Mainz in their midst. Sixty-five miles separated

Kaub from Mannheim, and thirty miles divided Kaub and Koblenz. Thus, the points of passage did not allow any mutual support on the day of the crossing. Had the French attempted to stop the crossing at one of the three points, Blücher probably would have suffered an embarrassing setback. The defile that stretched from Weisel to Kaub could be easily seen and swept with fire from the hills on the left bank of the Rhine. French shells could have set fire to Kaub to prevent the Allies from reaching the riverbank. Once on the left bank, the difficult ascent up the river valley provided the French further opportunities to drive the Silesian Army across the river. Because few suitable crossing points could be found on the middle Rhine between Strasbourg and Köln, Blücher and Gneisenau accepted the separation of their columns as an inherent danger, but believed the element of surprise would counter this risk. Surprise did account for much of Blücher's success. Both Kaub and Mannheim were well suited to catch the French unprepared for an Allied crossing and offered Blücher some obvious advantages that the French should have realized. The former faced the Pfalz island in the middle of the Rhine, which facilitated bridge building. At the latter, the mouth of the Neckar likewise aided the crossing of the Rhine, and Mannheim's distance from Mainz made interference from the garrison unlikely. Blücher could have eliminated some of the riskier aspects of his plan only by sacrificing surprise. A point of passage that granted his columns mutual support would have required several days for the shifting of units, which in turn would have alerted French spies and ruined any chance of surprising Marmont. Also, Blücher and Gneisenau knew of Marmont's weakness. Blücher then benefited from Napoleon's decision to move Marmont toward Landau. As a result, St. Priest only faced one brigade of Durutte's division and Yorck found his stretch of the left bank held only by weak posts. Of course Marmont directly threatened Sacken's corps, but the marshal remained too distant from the Rhine to contest the crossing. In the end, the Silesian Army crossed the Rhine at three points without meeting any noteworthy resistance.

From the left bank of the Rhine to the Tuileries, no one in France expected the Silesian Army to cross the Rhine where and when it did. But why? Was Blücher's theatrics and propaganda so convincing that Napoleon actually believed the old Prussian would hibernate in Frankfurt while Schwarzenberg launched a winter offensive across the upper Rhine? Apparently so, but the emperor should have known better – perhaps the wish was the father of the thought. "That I moved my quarters to Frankfurt has saved the lives of many people since the French did not expect our crossing," wrote Blücher to Hardenberg, "they could have made endless difficulties for me if they had been ready."[110] Moreover, although Victor fell apart, it was Blücher's surprise and rapid advance against Marmont that provided the coup de grâce for the cordon system and the defense of the Rhine frontier. Marmont was in the process of moving south to support Victor when Blücher's army crossed the Rhine. With his own problems, Marmont had no other choice than to abandon Victor. At this stage of the campaign, the decision made by Silesian Army Headquarters to take advantage of the unfinished business of the Frankfurt councils of war opened the door to strategic and operational success for both Allied armies. Thanks in part to Gneisenau's tireless hand that produced suggestions and protests by the score, the Allies had never reached a final decision over the cooperation of the various armies. It was assumed that Blücher would remain on the right bank of the Rhine and protect Germany against a French invasion. If the Bohemian Army encountered resistance after its advance through Switzerland, the Silesian Army would support it by conducting diversions across the Rhine. On the night of 25 December 1813, Schwarzenberg penned his request for the Silesian Army to cross the Rhine, cover his right flank, and distract the enemy. The Prussian leadership of the Silesian Army interpreted this as an invitation to launch their own full-scale invasion.[111]

Several points surface when examining the military operations between the Rhine and the Saar. Blücher's plans after crossing the Rhine failed in execution. Durutte's and Ricard's divisions escaped, and the pincer movement to isolate and crush Marmont at Kaiserslautern likewise miscarried. The day of 5 January proved decisive for Marmont's escape. His corps covered the forty-five miles between Kaiserslautern and the Saar in twenty-four hours. As a result of this heroic march, fifty miles separated the main bodies of the opposing corps.[112] First and foremost among the causes of these failures was the delay in crossing the Rhine, which caused the fragmentation of Yorck's corps. Secondary factors include Yorck's slow progress on the left bank and the days of rest granted to his corps on the 3rd and 5th. Poor roads and bad weather account for the short marches; inadequate maps, insufficient news, and poor intelligence also hampered Allied operations. "I request that you provide me with news as often as possible," wrote Yorck to Henckel, "and I want you to send me French newspapers and pamphlets, and since it is probably easy to get maps in Trier, I request that you find me some, if possible in duplicate, and send them to me. It would great if you could find a copy of Cassini's map, or at least a departmental map."[113] Inadequate use of the cavalry and the poor performance of the officers who conducted reconnaissance attributed to the lack of accurate information. Throughout Blücher's advance, Allied cavalry failed to maintain steady contact with the retreating enemy due to the poor condition of the horses, the inability of the Landwehr cavalry to conduct reconnaissance, difficult roads, and the lack of maps. Sacken's cavalry should have been more diligent and efficient in reconnoitering Marmont's position at Kaiserslautern and should have detected the marshal's withdrawal. Moreover, a Prussian cavalry officer submitted an incorrect report because he accepted intelligence based on the statements of locals, rather than personally reconnoitering. Although Blücher reinforced his advance guard with cavalry and created Henckel's Streifkorps with units from Yorck's Reserve Cavalry, the remainder of the Prussian cavalry followed behind the main body of the I Corps. The field marshal utilized Langeron's cavalry to observe Mainz until the Russian infantry arrived to invest the fortress. Considering his army operated in the predominantly German regions of the French Empire, Blücher's cavalry should have been more effective in gathering intelligence.

Marmont withdrew from the Saar prematurely because he believed he was outnumbered and outflanked. In no position to prevent the Allies from crossing, he saved his troops for later use at the cost of a river line. His only alternative was to lock his men in Saarlouis, Saarbrücken, and Sarreguemines. Not knowing the strength of the Allies made this option appear to be a wasteful expenditure of a considerable portion of Napoleon's mobile forces, particularly because Blücher would probably mask the Saar fortresses, cross the river elsewhere, and continue toward the French interior. Macdonald's forces appeared to be paralyzed by Bülow's operations and did nothing to support Marmont or threaten Blücher's march as the emperor had envisioned. Napoleon's directives arrived too late to save the line of the Saar. Regardless, holding the left bank of the Saar with the forces Marmont had at his disposal would have gained two days at best before the impetuous Blücher willed his troops across the river.

10

Alsace and Franche-Comté

While the Silesian Army crossed the Rhine, the Austrian units on the left wing of the Bohemian Army continued the invasion of Franche-Comté. Marching south on the road to Pontarlier, Bubna's advance guard made contact with the French on 1 January at l'Hôpital-du-Grosbois, less than ten miles east of Besançon.[1] On the same day, Bianchi's and Crenneville's divisions marched into Montbéliard, forty miles northeast of Besançon.[2] After reaching Porrentruy on the 31st, Gyulay's III Corps entered French territory on New Year's Day at Delle, halfway between Belfort and Porrentruy. He posted his advance guard brigade at Blamont, while a second brigade received a double charge: support Wöber's Streifkorps after its check at Baume-les-Dames and take possession of the bridges over the Doubs at Clerval and Pont-de-Roide.[3] Liechtenstein's II Corps likewise crossed into Franche-Comté, halting at Morteau, forty miles south of Gyulay's position at Delle. Filling the gap between III and II Corps, Colloredo's I Corps moved to Porrentruy on the 2nd.[4]

On New Year's Day, Schwarzenberg assigned command of the II Corps and Moritz Liechtenstein's 2nd Light Division to Prince Friedrich of Hesse-Homburg, who received orders to besiege Besançon by 9 January with these units as well as his own Austrian Reserve Corps.[5] With such massive Allied forces approaching, Prefect Jean-Antoine-Joseph de Bry of the Doubs Department found Besançon's garrison composed only of newly arrived conscripts and poorly mounted cavalry hardly capable of resistance. To augment the garrison, Musnier, who took command of the fortress on the 28th, recalled to Besançon the customs agents who fled to Dole after learning of the Allied invasion. To hold Besançon, Bry staunchly placed all of the department's resources at Musnier's disposal.[6] Regardless, the fact that Schwarzenberg allocated the entire II Corps as well as the Austrian Reserve – two divisions each of elite grenadiers and cuirassier – to besiege Besançon illustrates his senseless prudence. Due at Pontarlier no later than 6 January, the Reserve

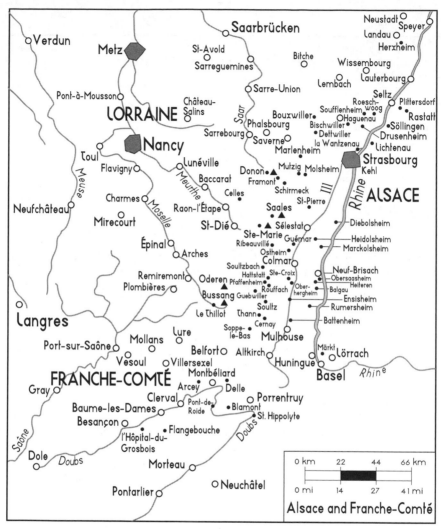

Map 10. Alsace and Franche–Comté.

casually trooped through Switzerland. By 1 January, Hesse-Homburg's
columns extended thirty miles between Neuchâtel and Berne.[7]

On the 3rd, Thurn led his Streifkorps north on the Besançon–Vesoul highway. He pushed detachments forward to skirmish with the French posts south
of Vesoul and to mask the westward movement of his main body. This enabled
him to execute a coup de main at Vesoul, the *chef-lieu* of the Haute-Saône
Department, from the west. His Cossacks collected 200 prisoners – mostly
sick and wounded left in the hospital. Although Vesoul served as an army

depot, Thurn found only large magazines of forage and tobacco.[8] Aside from arresting the war commissar, Thurn felt the main significance of securing the *chef-lieu* would be the disruptive effects its capture would have on implementing the *levée-en-masse*, which Napoleon issued on 4 January for the Bas-Rhin, Haut-Rhin, Vosges, Montblanc, Isère, Côte-d'Or, Jura, Doubs, and Haute-Saône Departments.[9] "The news from Paris signals great discontent among the population," he notes in his report to Schwarzenberg, "and leads one to believe in the eventual outbreak of serious disorder. According to the agent I have sent to Paris, the emperor will leave this city in six days."[10]

East of Vesoul, Bianchi relieved the Bavarians at Belfort and likewise failed in an attempt to convince Legrand to surrender the fortress. To support Bianchi, Gyulay's main body quartered at Montbéliard.[11] General Ignaz von Hardegg's light infantry division of Colloredo's I Corps relieved Gyulay's posts on the Doubs at St. Hippolyte, Pont-de-Roide, and Baume-les-Dames as the infantry of the III Corps moved to Montbéliard.[12] Southeast of Gyulay, Colloredo's main body remained idle at Porrentruy on the Franco-Swiss border throughout the 3rd, while the II Corps continued west toward Besançon; the head of the Austrian Reserve reached Pontarlier.[13]

On the extreme left wing of the Bohemian Army, Bubna's troops departed Geneva on the 2nd with the intention of crossing the narrow passes of the Juras on the 3rd and then turning northwest toward Dole. Bubna managed to honor this schedule. On the 3rd, his lead column reached Champagnole on the Ain River, twenty-five miles southwest of Pontarlier (see Map 14, Chapter 11). Ten miles south of Champagnole a second column escorted Bubna's headquarters to St. Laurent. With a detachment of 800 men, Simbschen moved into the Valais region, recruiting seven jäger companies from the hardy mountain folk. Assisted by these reinforcements, Simbschen blocked the roads to the Simplon and St. Bernard Passes on 3 January, thus severing the communications of the French army in Italy. Beauchamp maintains that "in the Valais all the inhabitants took up arms; they embraced the Allied cause with ardor, under the protection of Col. Baron Simschen. The occupation of the roads to the Simplon and the St. Bernard [Passes] opened the plains of Italy to them, and from Doma-Dossola to the gates of Milan no troops could be found other than a line of French customs agents."[14] Minor French counterattacks from Italy failed to reopen the passes. Elsewhere, Zechmeister forced the capitulation of the small French garrison at Ft. de l'Écluse, thus opening the Geneva–Lyon road.[15]

On the right wing of the Bohemian Army, Schwarzenberg tasked Wittgenstein with crossing the Rhine downstream of Strasbourg to prevent Victor from reinforcing Colmar. The Allied commander in chief directed the Russians to cross at Plittersdorf, across the Rhine from Seltz, the point chosen by the Austrians to invade France in 1793. In preparation, Gorchakov's I Infantry Corps received orders to relieve Duke Eugene of Württemberg's II Infantry Corps at Kehl, which would spearhead the VI Corps's invasion.

Wittgenstein encountered no obstacles moving the II Infantry Corps into position on the right bank of the Rhine but approached the entire operation with absurd, unwarranted caution. His concern was based on the incorrect information provided by Schwarzenberg regarding the presence of a 180,000-man French army between Nancy and Metz. Sharing the same anxiety first expressed by the generalissimo on 25 December, the Russian general feared this army would cross the Rhine at Strasbourg and sever his communications. He also recognized the threat to his own crossing posed by the 3,400-man garrison at Landau. Schwarzenberg finally issued firm orders for the VI Corps to attempt a passage at Plittersdorf.[16] On 27 December, in the midst of preparing his corps to cross the Rhine, Wittgenstein deemed the terrain too unfavorable and the current too violent to cross the river at this point.

Reconnaissance indicated a more favorable position at Söllingen, six miles upstream and twenty-two miles north of Strasbourg. Situated on the right bank, Söllingen faced an island upon which the French had built Ft. Vauban in 1688. On the left bank stood an outwork named Ft. d'Alsace. The Austrians had destroyed both in 1793; over the course of twenty years, the fortifications were only partially restored. Reports claimed the French paid little heed to either position, which could present formidable obstacles if sufficiently defended. Ft. Vauban's garrison consisted of forty sappers, eighty infantry, and one gun. In addition to the weakness of this unit, Ségur's 3rd Honor Guard Regiment, which patrolled the forty-mile stretch of the Rhine between Ft. Vauban and Germersheim, totaled only 1,550 troopers after losing 400 men to typhus and desertion.[17] Although Wittgenstein probably did not know these details, he decided to seize Ft. Vauban to provide his corps with a fortified bridgehead. From there, his troops could cross the secondary arm of the Rhine, called the Red Rhine, and take Ft.d' Alsace.[18] On 31 December, Wittgenstein moved Duke Eugene's II Infantry Corps and General Peter Petrovich Pahlen III's cavalry corps to the villages east of Söllingen. Eugene's 4th Division, commanded by General Dmitry Ilyich Pyshnitsky, received the honor of leading the Russian corps across the Rhine.

At 2:00 A.M. on 2 January, the Russian offensive finally began with a two-pronged landing attempt on the isle of Ft. Vauban. Six jäger companies clambered into twenty-four boats downstream of Söllingen with the objective of reaching the northeast side of the island. A smaller detachment of two jäger companies set sail in canoes upstream of Söllingen in the hope of disembarking on the southern tip of the island. Until that hour, the night had been clear and quiet, yet fog quickly blanketed the river after the moon set. Slightly disoriented by the fog, the boatmen lost control of their craft in the Rhine's swift current. As the boats separated, the Russian soldiers could feel the vessels gain speed. Some managed to muscle their way back to the right bank by way of frantic rowing, but the current slammed others onto the left bank: none of the boats reached the isle of Ft. Vauban. On the left bank, the jäger engaged the French posts guarding this stretch of the Rhine. Alerted by the crackle of musketry, Ft. Vauban's garrison took up arms and formed a line of skirmishers along a jetty.

French small-arms fire turned back a second Russian attempt to reach the isle by boat. Despite this setback, the engineers of the Austrian 10th Pontoon Company started work on the bridge. To protect the pontooners, Eugene directed some infantry and two guns to a sand bar. The artillery forced the French to withdraw from the jetty and allowed the Russians to make a third attempt to reach the island. After regrouping, the jäger who had managed to return to the right bank after the first attempt again headed across the icy water in a similar two-pronged operation. Both landings succeeded. One column converged on a redoubt that guarded the approach to Ft. Vauban, while the second turned the position and attacked the fort from the rear. Sometime after 10:00 A.M., the Russians entered Ft. Vauban, whose defenders fled across the Rhine to Drusenheim after losing eighteen men. One hour later, Russian troops reached the left bank and occupied Ft. d'Alsace; the entire operation cost Eugene forty casualties. Around 1:00 in the afternoon, the Austrian engineers completed the bridge to the island. Two Cossack regiments crossed, forded the Red Rhine, and struck the roads to Lauterbourg, Haguenau, and Strasbourg. Pyshnitsky's 4th Division followed the Cossacks, occupying the bridgehead and forwarding an advance guard to Roeschwoog to cut the road from Lauterbourg to Strasbourg.[19]

The commander of the 4th Honor Guard Regiment, General Raymond-Gaspard de Bonardi de St. Sulpice, learned of the attack on Ft. Vauban while en route to Roeschwoog from Haguenau. According to reports, a Russian advance guard of 3,000 cavalry occupied the village of Roeschwoog. Arriving in Drusenheim at noon, he assembled the fugitives from Ft. Vauban and established posts on the roads radiating from Ft. Vauban, especially the highway leading to Strasbourg. Equipped with few cartridges, the cavalry commander expected to be forced to retreat the next day and ordered the evacuation of the sick from Haguenau's hospital twenty miles west to Saverne. St. Sulpice hoped to receive support from Ségur's 3rd Honor Guard Regiment less than forty miles to the north at Landau. Although he had not been able to send word to Ségur of the events at Ft. Vauban, St. Sulpice trusted that information of the Russian crossing would reach Landau one way or another.[20]

News did indeed arrive at Landau of an enemy passage of the Rhine – but twenty-five miles to the northeast at Mannheim. After detecting the march of 5,000 to 6,000 men toward Neustadt, Ségur's patrols reported that his communication with Marmont had been severed. Around noon he mustered his regiment at Herxheim, six miles southeast of Landau, and dispatched patrols along a broad front extending from just south of Speyer to Lauterbourg. That evening Ségur went to Wissembourg, where he learned of the enemy crossing at Ft. Vauban. He instantly grasped the severity of his situation, being caught between Sacken's corps to the north and Wittgenstein's to the south. To escape this trap, Ségur ordered the 3rd Honor Guard Regiment to withdraw from the Rhine to the safety of the Vosges.[21]

Fear of an Allied operation downstream of Strasbourg had haunted Victor for some time. Consequently, when rumors reached him of Allied activity on 2 January, the marshal harbored little doubt over the nature of the enemy's intentions. Utilizing the French optical *télégraphique* system, the marshal managed to route a panicked message via Metz to the emperor: "An enemy corps is crossing the Rhine at Roppenheim between Ft. Vauban and Beinheim at this moment!" A confused Victor believed this corps belonged to the Silesian Army and mistook Crown Prince Frederick William's IV Corps for Wittgenstein's VI Corps. He thus reported that rather than the Württembergers, the Russians had crossed the Rhine at Basel and taken a position on the left bank at Blodelsheim between Huningue and Neuf-Brisach.[22] By the time he penned his brief to Berthier later that day, the marshal learned that the crossing actually occurred at Ft. Vauban. Knowing this report would be shared with Napoleon, he stated that unless the emperor placed an additional 30,000 men at his disposal by combining the Imperial Guard and the VI Corps with his II Corps, he would be forced to retreat to Saverne.[23] At this time, he also sent the urgent dispatch to Marmont requesting to unite their forces near Saverne. "This operation is undoubtedly in unison with that of the army on the upper Rhine and is designed to force us to evacuate Alsace," he explains to Marmont, not knowing that Blücher's army had just crossed the Rhine.[24]

Victor was not entirely wrong about Russian movements up the Rhine toward Basel. In accordance with the tsar's orders, Platov led the remaining regiments of his Cossack corps through Freiburg, crossed the Rhine at Basel on 1 January, and camped in Altkirch. On the 2nd, the Russians continued west, making for the passes of the Vosges. Barclay de Tolly's Russo–Prussian Guard and Reserve likewise filed through Freiburg en route for Basel.[25] Meanwhile, the Bavarians and Württembergers remained idle throughout the 1st. For some time Schwarzenberg held back Wrede from driving through Colmar to Strasbourg. Although committed to forcing the French from Alsace, the cautious Austrian commander first used the resistance Wrede encountered at Belfort and Huningue to delay an offensive. He then planned to wait until the IV and VI Corps could be utilized in conjunction with the V Corps to trap Victor. Days passed while headquarters waited for the right moment to commence the offensive in Alsace. While the rest of the army executed Radetzky's complicated maneuvers and turning movements, Schwarzenberg limited Wrede to conducting offensive reconnaissance. The generalissimo's prudence influenced his countryman, Frimont, who allowed his 15,000 men to be stopped in their tracks by Milhaud. Even with the arrival of the IV and VI Corps, the timid Schwarzenberg still did not believe he possessed enough combat power for offensive operations. Allied movements in Upper Alsace on

1 January amounted to Scheibler's small Streifkorps pushing west from Neuf-Brisach across Milhaud's front toward Guebwiller, twelve miles southeast of Colmar.[26]

To move closer to the operations, Schwarzenberg transferred his headquarters from Lörrach to Basel. He finally felt secure enough to begin the movement of his right wing on 2 January. To drive Milhaud's 3,000 troopers and four infantry battalions from Colmar, he instructed Wrede to maneuver the entire V Corps through Rouffach to Colmar, while the left wing of IV Corps advanced through Ensisheim on the Mulhouse–Colmar road. Simultaneously, the right wing would smash through any resistance to reach Neuf-Brisach, ten miles east of Colmar. Leaving only General Friedrich Johann von Zoller's 2nd Brigade of Beckers's division to continue the siege of Huningue, Wrede relocated his headquarters to Cernay. Throughout 2 January, he massed his divisions for the assault on Colmar. The Bavarian corps commander lined Hardegg's, Delamotte's, and Spleny's divisions from Rouffach to Cernay on the road to Colmar. As noted, Bianchi relieved Rechberg at Belfort, thus allowing this Bavarian division to reach Soppe-le-Bas on the road to Cernay. The crown prince of Württemberg concentrated Franquemont's left wing column on the Mulhouse–Colmar road between Ensisheim and Battenheim and echelonned Koch's right wing from Balgau to Rumersheim on the Huningue–Neuf-Brisach road.[27]

Wrede's concentration did not escape Milhaud. His advance posts extended in an east–west line from Heiteren, just south of Neuf-Brisach, through Ste. Croix to Pfaffenheim, on the Cernay–Colmar road. Reconnaissance led him to believe that at least 20,000 Austrians and Württembergers were in immediate contact with his forward units. In fact, Hardegg debouched from Rouffach to attack the post in Pfaffenheim with a strong detachment. He drove the French to Hattstatt, less than six miles from Colmar. Milhaud moved up Lhéritier's 4th Dragoon Division, but Hardegg's probe ended; the Austrians withdrew to Rouffach and the French reestablished their post at Pfaffenheim. From Colmar, Milhaud reported that the Württembergers had joined the Bavarians between the Rhine and Mulhouse on his left, while the Austrians remained at Cernay to his right. He expected to be attacked as soon as these superior forces covered the twenty miles that separated them from Colmar. Although the general expressed his intention to retreat once the Allies launched their offensive, he believed that Marmont, who was estimated to arrive in Strasbourg within the next two days, would provide enough reinforcements to launch a counteroffensive.[28]

The course of 2 January 1814 went from bad to worse for Marshal Victor. In the evening, word reached Strasbourg that aside from the Allied crossing at Ft. Vauban, the Silesian Army had crossed the Rhine at three points further downstream and severed his communication with Marmont. This shocking news brought the realization that he would not be able to unite with Marmont's forces which, consequently, would be hard pressed to reach Metz. "Marmont, who was at Neustadt on the 1st of this month, cannot join me and I can no longer correspond with him, communications are severed," bemoans Victor to Berthier. Faced with this prospect, Victor did not wait for the V Cavalry Corps to be attacked. Instead, he chose to completely evacuate Colmar and instructed Milhaud to retreat on Saverne. Early on the 3rd a staff officer arrived at Colmar with orders for Milhaud to proceed thirty-five miles north through Sélestat to Molsheim, where he would turn northwest to cover the additional fifteen miles to Saverne. Victor's justification for this retreat is strikingly similar to Marmont's views:

> In its actual state, the II Corps does not have enough strength to seriously confront the enemy, and another reason for prudence is the corps represents the cadres of thirty-six battalions, which cannot be compromised. . . . Thus it is necessary to proceed with caution. I do not share the opinion of many men who, without considering our resources, believe we can risk everything and not pay attention to the consequences that would result from poorly planned engagements; we are not in a position today as in other times to sustain appreciable losses. In my opinion we must carefully handle the resources that we possess until they have received the promised reinforcements. Until then, our operations are limited to maneuver and small combats to stop the enemy as much as possible. When all our forces are united, we will attempt more serious operations and we will try to drive the enemy from our territory.

The marshal expected Milhaud to reach Molsheim on the evening of the 3rd and the hills of Saverne on the following day but feared the enemy force advancing from Ft. Vauban would arrive there first. To secure the position, he ordered the commandant of Phalsbourg to dispatch every disposable man to Saverne. "I believe the troops of the II Infantry and V Cavalry Corps, which are in the valley of Colmar," states the marshal's brief to Berthier at 8:00 A.M. on the 3rd, "will unite today at Molsheim, and we should reach Saverne early tomorrow, where it will be possible to delay the enemy." Victor himself left Strasbourg on the 3rd to spend the day at Molsheim awaiting Milhaud and Jamin, who the marshal likewise ordered to retreat through Sélestat.[29] The II Infantry and V Cavalry Corps needed three days to cross the fifty miles between Colmar and Saverne, while Wittgenstein's Russians had a two-day march of thirty-five miles from Ft. Vauban to Saverne.[30] By choosing Molsheim as the point of assembly, Victor kept open the option of turning southwest to cross the Vosges through the Donon Pass and reach Raon-l'Étape rather than retreat northwest through Saverne to Phalsbourg.[31]

Early on the morning of 3 January, Schwarzenberg's much anticipated order to commence the operation against Colmar reached Wrede and Frederick William.[32] Shortly after, the commander in chief himself arrived in Wrede's camp to observe the operation – which the generalissimo privately labeled a reconnaissance – while his own staff established army headquarters at Altkirch.[33] At 9:00 A.M. Frimont led Hardegg's division toward Colmar followed by Delamotte, Spleny, and the Bavarian light cavalry. Rechberg's division marched to Soultz and formed the reserve. East of the V Corps, the two columns of the IV Corps commenced their movement at 8:00 A.M. Frederick William accompanied Franquemont's left wing during the march from Ensisheim through Ste. Croix to Colmar; Koch's right wing filed on the road toward Neuf-Brisach with the Rhine glittering to the right.[34] Scheibler's Streifkorps maintained communication between the V and IV Corps during the advance.

The distance between the Allied forward units and Colmar took less than six hours to cover. This provided ample time for Milhaud to retreat. That morning, his posts at Pfaffenheim, Ste. Croix, and Heiteren reported the advance of an Allied force twelve-times the size of the French troops holding Colmar. As his patrols returned to Colmar in the morning, Milhaud directed the cavalry to the plain north of the town in preparation for the retreat to Sélestat. A stupor seized the inhabitants of Colmar because of a false rumor that the Allies would take possession of the town at 2:00 P.M. as the result of a convention between Milhaud and Wrede. All shops were closed and the streets deserted because the terrified population expected the worse. "Officers and soldiers demanded to pillage, but Wrede limited himself to authorizing exorbitant requisitions and made his men respect the honor and the lives of the inhabitants, at least under his eyes because in the countryside the Germans gave a lesson in their bestial passions," howls Lefebvre de Béhaine. "The unfortunate surrounding villages were the theater of indescribable scenes: everything was stolen, befouled, smashed; all females: the elderly women, barely nubile girls or some at an even more tender age, suffered outrages of violence that brought about the death of several."[35] Although no agreement existed between the opposing commanders, Milhaud did depart at 2:00 P.M., thus abandoning the *chef-lieu* of the Haut-Rhin Department without firing a shot. To his credit, he did not lose a single man or horse during the retreat.

The Schwarzenberg Uhlan Regiment formed Frimont's advance guard. A scouting party of fifteen uhlans supported by ten Cossacks approached Colmar first. Finding the bridge over the Lauch barricaded and defended by a detachment from a French platoon – the last of Milhaud's troops at Colmar – the Allied cavalry charged forward. Breaking through, they pursued the French through the "Basel" gate to the town square, where the rest of the platoon stoically waited. The Allied troopers charged once again, and after some brief street fighting, the French broke, pursued by the Austrians and Russians to the "Sélestat" gate on the north side of Colmar. Upon exiting the town, the Allied troopers beheld all of Milhaud's cavalry drawn up for battle. The French 3rd Hussar Regiment charged: "one small fourteen-year-old bugler captured an Austrian corporal five feet, eight inches tall," relishes French historian Chuquet. In his proud and contemptuous Gascon manner, Milhaud conducted the retreat by echelons. At 3:00 Wrede entered Colmar just as the lead units of the IV Corps arrived from the east. The V Corps proceeded no further and billeted in the town.

The Württembergers backtracked from Colmar to camp at Ste. Croix and the surrounding villages; the crown prince established his headquarters at Oberhergheim. Meanwhile, Koch divided his right wing into two columns for the advance on Neuf-Brisach. His right column marched from Balgau and, after having lively skirmishes with French cavalry at Heiteren and Obersaasheim, occupied the suburbs of Neuf-Brisach to begin the investment of the fortress and its 3,000-man garrison. Following the country road that ran between the Mulhouse–Colmar and Huningue–Neuf-Brisach highways, Koch's left column proceeded north to a position on line with the Württemberger troops to the west at Ste. Croix and the east at Neuf-Brisach. With the mission of 3 January accomplished, the IV Corps moved into second line behind the V.

Although the Allied cavalry numbered sixty-four squadrons and forty-eight pieces of horse artillery to Milhaud's twenty-eight squadrons and twelve horse guns, only Scheibler's small Streifkorps followed the French. After learning respect for Milhaud's troopers at Ste. Croix on 24 December, he conducted a feeble pursuit before losing contact with the French altogether. Because Wrede believed Milhaud's task had been to keep open the passes through which the powerful French army at Metz would debouch into Alsace, this typical Allied failure to utilize cavalry properly is particularly glaring. Before going to his headquarters at Altkirch, Schwarzenberg accompanied Wrede's advance guard for one hour as it proceeded north toward Sélestat.[36] En route, he redirected Scheibler to Sélestat in the belief that Milhaud would reverse his march and withdraw on Strasbourg to unite with Victor. Frimont's cavalry crept forward to establish posts halfway to Sélestat along the Ribeauvillé–Guémar–Marckolsheim line, with Scheibler's men holding the last village.[37]

The V Cavalry Corps crossed the defile formed by the bridge over the Fecht River at Ostheim, where Milhaud reunited with a detachment of 200 dragoons and 100 infantry that had been east of Colmar observing Soultzbach. Its commander led the detachment along mountain paths to escape Frimont's drive to Colmar. Milhaud's regiments then crossed a second defile at Guémar and reached Sélestat, where they united with Forestier's brigade. "We maneuvered in the defiles and in the plain with the greatest of order," boasts Milhaud.[38] Thanks to Wrede's trepidation and unwarranted prudence, Milhaud brilliantly extracted his corps – arguably the best unit on the eastern front. Nevertheless, by lingering at Colmar until the early afternoon, the general only reached Sélestat rather than Molsheim as instructed by Victor.

Twenty miles separated Molsheim from Sélestat; Milhaud lost an entire day's march, meaning the V Cavalry Corps still faced the threat of being cut-off from Saverne by Wittgenstein and then crushed by the Allied IV, V, and VI Corps. In fact, unconfirmed reports reached Victor that the Russians were only one march from Saverne as of noon on the 3rd.[39]

A critical Lefebvre de Béhaine accuses Victor of making "a completely false account over the operations in front of Colmar" to explain Milhaud's failure to reach Molsheim on the 3rd, rather than accept responsibility for his own poor staff work. According to Victor's 6 January report to Berthier: "Milhaud was ready to start the movement with his cavalry and four infantry battalions when he was attacked by large forces and obliged to defend himself. The combat lasted all day to the advantage of our troops, but he realized that he would be prevented from reaching his destination (Molsheim) on the 3rd due to the circumstances; forced to hold the battlefield until night, he was only able to reach Sélestat." Lefebvre de Béhaine argues that "a simple examination of the map would have shown the duke or his chief of staff that the order given to Milhaud could not be executed because the infantry, if not the cavalry and artillery, could not cover in one day – above all in January and in presence of the enemy – the fifty-two kilometers [thirty-five miles] that separated Colmar and Molsheim."[40] The French historian's baseless accusation ignores the fact that the French army frequently executed such marches. Instead of an attempt to shield himself from criticism, Victor's report should be viewed as a fair attempt to protect a superb subordinate, whose momentary lapse of good judgment led him to tarry too long in Colmar to be able to reach Molsheim the same day.[41]

Sherbatov's Streifkorps likewise was active on the 3rd. The Russian commander led three small Cossack regiments (700 men) west on the road from Mulhouse, crossing the Vosges through the Bussang Pass and exploding into southern Lorraine. Sherbatov directed his troopers toward Remiremont, just south of Épinal, *chef-lieu* of the Vosges Department. After taking thirty-six prisoners in a short combat six miles from Remiremont, the Russians passed through the town around 1:00 P.M. and headed for Épinal. The commandant of the department, General Pierre Cassagne, assembled a handful of dragoons, chasseurs, and gendarmes to halt their advance. Although stopped by this motley force, the Cossacks intercepted a letter stating that 600 infantry were en route from Épinal to Remiremont followed by another cavalry troop of 500 sabers. Thus misinformed, Scheibler evacuated Remiremont and returned to Bussang. Despite this small French victory, both Cassagne and the prefect of the Vosges Department, Louis-Alexandre Himbert de Flegny, fled to Nancy, indicative of the poor performance of imperial authorities that so plagued Napoleon's cause during the Allied invasion.[42]

As for Wittgenstein, his lethargy rivaled that of Wintzingerode. During the night of 2–3 January, the Austrian pontooners completed work on the bridges over the Rhine, thus providing complete access to the left bank for artillery and trains. That same night, Pahlen led eleven Russian hussar and four Badenese dragoon squadrons supported by one horse battery across the river with specific orders to move on Haguenau and if possible to cut the Strasbourg–Nancy highway at Saverne. At dawn he linked with three Cossack squadrons between Ft. Vauban and Roeschwoog but dissipated half of his force to conduct general reconnaissance. Detachments thundered northwest toward Landau and Bitche; south toward Strasbourg and Sélestat, seeking Wrede's patrols; and north through Speyer to establish communication with Sacken. With nine squadrons remaining, Pahlen proceeded toward Haguenau but halted at Soufflenheim, less than four miles from Roeschwoog at the edge of the Haguenau Forest. Locals revealed the presence of the two Honor Guard Regiments to the north and south of the forest. In fact, St. Sulpice's lead squadrons stood in Bischwiller, only six miles southeast of Haguenau and less than ten southwest of Soufflenheim. After retreating through Wissembourg, Ségur reached Lembach, twelve miles north of Haguenau.[43] Pahlen hesitated to move any farther with two French regiments so close to Haguenau and in position to defend the road to Saverne. Only one Russian squadron continued to Haguenau but did not enter even though the French garrison had evacuated that morning. The proximity of the 4th Honor Guard Regiment also prevented Pahlen's detachment from moving no closer to Strasbourg than Drusenheim, twenty miles north of the Alsatian capital.

Pahlen's listless activity reflected the cautious attitude of Russian head-quarters at Rastatt, where Wittgenstein remained until 8 January. Current reports claimed Victor left Strasbourg to join his troops at Colmar. More-over, intelligence revealed the weakness of the French garrisons at Kehl and Strasbourg: 1,500 and 5,000 respectively. Other reports estimated the garrison of Landau to be 3,000 men and that of Bitche several hundred. All statements indicated that a large portion of the garrisons consisted of raw conscripts. Regardless, Wittgenstein persisted in his belief that 180,000 French soldiers between Nancy and Metz were poised to enter Alsace. Schwarzenberg could have done more to alleviate Wittgenstein of these fears. In his very accurate report to Schwarzenberg on 1 January, Thurn estimated the forces in and around Metz to be only 20,000 men. "The majority of the forces already assembled by the enemy have partially departed for Holland, partially con-centrated at Mainz," states Thurn's report.[44]

Because of Wittgenstein's anxiety, the ten battalions (5,400 men) and twenty-four guns of Gorchakov's I Infantry Corps continued to blockade Kehl, twenty-seven miles south of Rastatt. Pyshnitsky's 4th Division of Duke Eugene's II Infantry Corps and one Badenese infantry regiment occupied the bridgehead, Drusenheim, and Roeschwoog. Rather than send General Ivan Leontievich Shakhovsky's 3rd Division of the II Infantry Corps across the river, Wittgenstein moved it further up the right bank to Lichtenau, halfway between Rastatt and Kehl. At Lichtenau Shakhovsky served as a reserve for both Pyshnitsky on the left bank and Gorchakov at Kehl. Wittgenstein determined that Shakhovsky's nine battalions would remain on the right bank until Gorchakov took the redoubts protecting Kehl. [45]

Schwarzenberg allowed 4 January to pass without making much progress in Alsace or Franche-Comté. Excluding Bubna, the left wing made no appreciable gains: the II and III Corps remained at Flangebouche and Montbéliard respectively; the I Corps moved from Porrentruy to Delle, Hardegg's light infantry division maintained the bridges over the Doubs, and two divisions of the Austrian Reserve reached Pontarlier. Further south, Bubna's lead column marched eleven miles on the highway to Dole, stopping for the night at Poligny; Bubna led his second column to Champagnole. Less than twenty miles west of Champagnole, a detachment effected the end of imperial control of another department by occupying Lons-le-Saunier, *chef-lieu* of the Jura Department. [46]

On the right wing, the commander in chief failed to provide his subordinates with a clear objective after the capture of Colmar. He directed Wrede toward Sélestat, stating: "it would be quite agreeable if you attack the cavalry in front of you, overwhelm it, and spread a little terror from your side." [47] Equally at fault, Wrede and Wittgenstein remained idle except for the excursions of their cavalry. After Schwarzenberg redirected Scheibler on the 3rd, Wrede's patrols could not find the slightest trace of Milhaud, nor did the information provided by locals allow the Allies to draw any concrete conclusions.

Instead of advancing with his overwhelming numerical superiority, the Bavarian commander ordered three large reconnaissance missions that barely extended beyond the Ribeauvillé–Guémar–Marckolsheim line established the previous day; the rest of the V Corps remained completely idle on the 4th. Hugging the eastern spurs of the Vosges, the left detachment rode north through Guémar on the Colmar–Sélestat road; the center column proceeded northwest through Marckolsheim to Heidolsheim, less than halfway to Sélestat. Forming the right, Scheibler's Streifkorps scoured the region between the Ill River and the left bank of the Rhine. Still believing the French headed north for Strasbourg, Wrede did not consider the possibility that Milhaud would turn west to reach the Donon Pass through the Vosges. As a result, the left and center detachments only scouted to the south and southeast of Sélestat, while Scheibler, whose troopers covered one-third of the distance to Strasbourg before dismounting in Diebolsheim, patrolled to the east of the Sélestat–Strasbourg highway. None of the Allied patrols discovered any new tidings of the enemy. The information Wrede forwarded to Schwarzenberg amounted to the statements of a French deserter, who claimed that Milhaud's force was in fact the garrison of Strasbourg, which now sought to return to the city. [48]

After Württemberger patrols found the region around Neuf-Brisach clear of enemy forces on the morning of the 4th, the crown prince personally reconnoitered the fortress. Heavy fire met the Württembergers as they approached – a hearty greeting from their former allies. Aside from Koch having his horse shot out from under him, the prince and his entourage escaped unscathed. Locals informed the Württembergers that a garrison of approximately 4,000 men and 130 guns defended the amply supplied fortress.[49]

In Lower Alsace, Pahlen shed his fear of French cavalry and pushed his patrols through Haguenau to within ten miles of Saverne. Locals continued to inform him of the proximity of the French Honor Guard. Believing this to be Victor's rearguard, the Russian general remained wary because of the wide dispersal of his own squadrons. He assumed that both the 3rd and 4th Honor Guard Regiments were retreating toward Saverne. The rest of Wittgenstein's corps maintained the positions gained on the previous day (see Map 11).[50]

Throughout the day of 4 January the inhabitants of Alsace greeted the Allies well and appeared to be neutral. According to the reports made to the tsar by Wittgenstein and Barclay de Tolly, the entrance of the Russian uhlans in Haguenau caused no anxiety among the populace, who calmly went about their business – even the shops remained open.[51] This provided an exaggerated picture of the general mood of the Alsatians as the Allies mistook nervous obedience for friendly support. Conversely, French authorities began to suspect the collapse of morale. "Public spirit is dead, one cannot occupy himself with reviving it," wrote Belliard from Metz on the 3rd. "It seems that a wicked genie has scattered his poppies on France. The crisis is terrible, but we can emerge; the alarm must blare all over, the nation must be completely under arms, and only lay down its arms after chasing the foe from its territory, but the moment is pressing, and it is necessary that the wise measures ordered by the emperor be accelerated everywhere."[52]

Schwarzenberg's concern over the possibility of a popular insurrection increased after he received reports from Thurn and Prince Friedrich of Hesse-Homburg dated 1 and 2 January. Thurn, whose Streifkorps skirted Belfort en route to Vesoul, informed Schwarzenberg on the 1st that "the mood of the population surprises me and surpasses my hopes. Exhausted by a government that is held in contempt and detested, the inhabitants admit they impatiently await the hour of their deliverance. The proclamations we have distributed and the excellent conduct of our troops are contributing mightily to the development of these sentiments . . . serious problems have erupted in Lyon and in the Vendée. At Lyon the conscripts have refused to answer the summons of the government." On the 2nd, Thurn continued his assessment: "It appears the discipline and the conduct of our troops endear them to the population. My detachment has been received with joy. All seem to declare that the people, even inside the country, actually await our arrival with impatience."

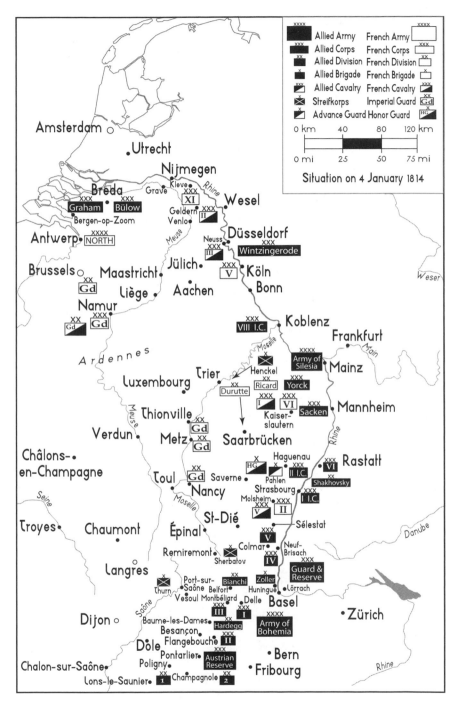

Map 11. Situation on 4 January 1814.

Aside from these encouraging statements, which Schwarzenberg had spent ten anxious days waiting to receive, Thurn added news that no Allied commander wanted to hear. Prefect Flavigny of the Haute-Saône Department had posted a decree in Vesoul for the *levée-en-masse*. The extraordinary-commissioner and senator Jean-Baptiste Valence arrived at Besançon to organize the levée as well as the resistance in Franche-Comté, which formed the 6th Military District.[53] Hesse-Homburg, who received the task of besieging Besançon, included with his 1 January report the actual proclamations from the commandant of the 6th Military District, General Marulaz, and Prefect Bry of the Doubs Department. Marulaz summoned the inhabitants of Besançon to take up arms in its defense, while Bry issued an appeal to the inhabitants to defend their department.[54] In a letter to Metternich, Schwarzenberg expressed his concern over this troubling development:

> Napoleon's response to a deputation from the Senate is one of the most curious documents that the history of this man has produced. He calls the French provinces by their ancient names: it is Bourgogne, Champagne, etc., that are appealed to in order to help Béarn, Alsace, Franche-Comté, etc. There is no talk of recovering the conquered [regions of the empire]. This response recalls a discussion I had with Tallyrand the previous spring: 'The moment has come when the emperor must become king of France'. Moreover, the prefects stir heaven and earth to organize the insurrection. I hope they will not succeed. It is essential that I attempt to take the debouches of the Vosges as soon as possible and that wise and calm individuals oversee the provisory government in the rear of the army. If Napoleon fails to convince the French he is willing to surrender all that is not French and that the Allies are attacking France herself, a general levée-en-masse will never succeed.[55]

An unsettled Schwarzenberg took proactive measures that seemingly contradicted his calls for an occupation reflecting the intentions of "wise and calm" men. Without first seeking the approval of the monarchs, the commander in chief imposed on the inhabitants of the occupied zones an oath of obedience and allegiance to the Allied sovereigns, Allied authority, and the Allied peoples. Inextricably linked to the oppression of foreign invasion and Allied might, this petty measure served to further aggravate a populace suffering from the inherent misery caused by the maltreatment of a conquering army.[56] At the same time, Schwarzenberg reiterated his call for strict military discipline. In a general order issued from Montbéliard on 8 January, Schwarzenberg wrote:

At this moment, when the army is advancing on French territory, I must remind the corps commanders of the orders that preceded this movement, and direct them to redouble their zeal in maintaining order and discipline. This falls under the most extensive responsibility of the commanders of the regiments, battalions, etc. The troops will make the plague of occupation weigh as little as possible on the inhabitants, and nowehere will they extend beyond the fixed march objective. The correct conduct and discipline of the soldier must fulfil the solemn pledge made to the French people in the declarations of the Allied monarchs; convince them that we do not make war against the French nation, that we come among them to win the peace and that we will share the blessings with them. In combining the strictest order with its much proven valor, the army will secure the admiration of its age and of future generations. The corps commanders will repeat the order to their troops that the most exemplary punishment will be administered to every offender as the honor of the army that is confided to me demands. Also spread the message everywhere, that any inhabitant who is captured bearing arms without a uniform will be regarded only as a malefactor or assassin, convicted as such without an appeal, and punished by death. Any city, town or village whose inhabitants resist us through hostile acts will be razed and reduced to ashes.[57]

Strategic concerns, fueled by confusing statements from agents operating in the French interior, sparked a flurry of activity at Schwarzenberg's headquarters on 4 January. Although he received no confirmed reports, the generalissimo still feared the presence of at least 40,000 conscripts at Metz. Thanks to Thurn's report of a French cavalry corps marching from Chaumont to Langres, he also began to suspect a French concentration between Besançon, Langres, and Épinal.[58] Arranging his army to meet the perceived threats from the Metz–Nancy and Besançon–Langres–Épinal regions became Schwarzenberg's immediate task.

On 4 January, his headquarters issued the "Disposition of 6–8 January 1814," which essentially created four army groups. Wrede's V and Wittgenstein's VI Corps formed "Army Group Alsace." The Bavarian corps commander received orders to invest Sélestat, relieve the Württembergers at Neuf-Brisach by 6 January, and establish communication with Wittgenstein. Schwarzenberg tasked Wittgenstein with occupying Lower Alsace and marching through Haguenau, Saverne, and Phalsbourg to invade Lorraine. "Army Group Vosges," which consisted of Sherbatov's detachment and the IV Corps reinforced by one Austrian heavy battery and the Archduke Ferdinand Hussar Regiment, received Épinal as its objective. Schwarzenberg instructed Frederick William to depart Ste. Croix on the 6th, march west, cross the Vosges through the Bussang Pass, and debouch on Remiremont in order to reach Épinal in the Moselle Valley by the 9th. Instead of directing the IV Corps through the closer Bonhomme Pass to Épinal, Schwarzenberg ordered it to make a retrograde movement through Thann and cross the Bussang Pass to Remiremont, from where the Württembergers would continue to Épinal. This direction lengthened the march by almost twenty-five miles and would force the troops to trudge through the most inhospitable region of the Vosges.

Thurn's Streifkorps, the I and III Corps including Crenneville's division, and Bianchi's 1st Grenadier Division of the Austrian Reserve formed Army Group Langres. As its objective, Schwarzenberg assigned Vesoul on the highway leading through Langres and Troyes to Paris. Gyulay's orders stated that he should leave Montbéliard on the 6th and march past Bianchi's division, which would continue the siege of Belfort. Schwarzenberg allotted Gyulay three days to cover the thirty-two miles between Montbéliard and Vesoul. At Belfort Bianchi's division was scheduled to be relieved on the 7th by General Nikolay Nikolayevich Rayevsky's grenadier corps of the Russian Reserve and then likewise follow to Vesoul. After Rayevsky relieved Bianchi at Belfort, Barclay de Tolly would post the remaining units of the Russo–Prussian Guard and Reserve between Altkirch and Belfort. Colloredo's I Corps would replace the III Corps at Montbéliard and post one division at Clerval to shield Crenneville's division as it marched northwest from the Doubs River to Vesoul. To add more sabers to Crenneville's thirteen squadrons, Schwarzenberg requested that Barclay de Tolly forward to Vesoul one cuirassier division from the Russian Reserve by 11 January.

Finally, Schwarzenberg tasked Army Group Franche-Comté with taking Besançon, which stood forty-two miles southwest of Montbéliard, twenty-seven miles south of Vesoul, and fifty-five miles southeast of Langres. Hesse-Homburg would continue his operation and begin the siege on 9 January with the II Corps, 2nd Light Division, and the Austrian Reserve. Wimpffen, with the 2nd Division of the I Corps, would likewise arrive at Besançon on the 9th to support Hesse-Homburg from the right bank of the Doubs. Bubna would cover the siege by leading his 1st Light Division as fast as possible to Lyon "to disrupt the assembly of conscripts in the southern and discontented part of France and through good order and discipline raise our credit. Then, when the merchants write from Lyon to all parts of France that the troops conduct themselves well, thus completely invalidating all of those fairy-tale statements issued by the government, our credit will be further increased."[59] Behind these troops Schwarzenberg planned to transfer his headquarters from Altkirch to Porrentruy.[60]

Designed to shuffle his units to provide more front-line combat power, the ill-conceived Disposition both stalled and dispersed the army when Schwarzenberg should have been striving to concentrate 150,000 men at Langres. In addition, the Disposition paralyzed operations in Alsace for almost five days. While the French escaped over the Vosges, Wrede once again found himself chained to a siege – Sélestat – and ordered to invest Neuf-Brisach. For the Württembergers, they, too, would have to remain idle until relieved by the Bavarians, thus delaying their march to Lorraine, which itself required a retrograde movement through Cernay and the Thur Valley. From there the Württembergers were to utilize the Bussang and Oderen Passes to cross the Vosges and reach the Moselle Valley. Schwarzenberg purposefully slowed operations in Alsace, ostensibly to provide time for Wittgenstein's VI Corps to establish a foothold on the left bank and fortify its bridgehead. Marches, countermarches, shifting, and realignment were inherent components of the orders issued by the Austrian General Staff, which rendered lip-service to a speedy and vigorous offensive but took measures that contradicted the principles of modern war.

The Disposition offers insight into Schwarzenberg's state of mind at a time when nothing stood in the way of his army. Allied spies revealed that southern France had been stripped of all military units; the new armies being formed at Lyon and Grenoble had to be created from scratch. This news should have induced Schwarzenberg to reduce the size of his forces operating on his left wing and in southern France to augment the main force marching on Langres. Instead, the Austrians assigned a huge mass of mainly elite troops who lacked siege guns to force Besançon to capitulate. Increasing his center with all available forces should have been Schwarzenberg's main concern in view of the threat posed by the alleged French concentration near Langres. Yet such a concentration would indicate Napoleon's desire to deliver a decisive battle. Schwarzenberg dreaded Napoleon's speed and thus saw himself in a very difficult position: the horrible memory of Ulm probably came to mind.

At this moment, when he placed Napoleon in the midst of tens of thousands of troops on the other side of the Vosges, Schwarzenberg again viewed Blücher as his salvation. Rather than the awful nightmare of Ulm, he naturally preferred to recall the glory Leipzig: only with Blücher's direct support would he accept battle. "Ah, my task is formidable," he confides to his wife. "If I am supported, the peace can and must be fought for, but if I am not accompanied in my procession by the Army of North Germany, by Wellington, by the Army of Italy, I will thus fall deeply. Of Blücher I am certain – just as at Leipzig we will not leave each other in the lurch, but that idle Bernadotte is a malicious fop adorned with strange feathers, who paralyzes many thousands at the decisive moment."[61]

Finally, the Disposition provides a glimpse of the primacy of Austrian politics in Schwarzenberg's strategy. After taking Alsace, crossing the extent of Switzerland, and penetrating Franche-Comté, he could not retreat to the right bank of the Rhine, nor could he justify halting operations for an extended period, especially because he believed the army would starve to death where it stood. Moreover, Tsar Alexander would never permit either. Yet as the Bohemian Army moved deeper into France, the chances increased that he could relive the horror of Ulm. More important, Austrian politics would not permit Schwarzenberg to denude his wings for a strong drive on Langres with his center. From the very beginning of the invasion, Schwarzenberg assigned the corps of the left or Austrian wing of the army controversial tasks that required them to move in bizarre directions. Although he arranged the three corps of the right wing in a logical manner, the Austrian commander strapped

Wrede's corps to Huningue and Belfort, wasted time bringing the IV and VI Corps across the Rhine, and then stalled the operations against Colmar. With his left wheeling through southern France and his right tied down in Alsace, Schwarzenberg had only the I and III Corps for the actual march to Langres – the stated operations goal of the Bohemian Army![62] The flank coverage for the march to Langres was thus the strength of armies. As the operations progressed, the flank commanders increasingly waited on the center to move forward, some in part due to their own assignments, others, such as Wittgenstein, allowed inertia to dictate their movements. The center of the army was too weak to execute its task, and the flank coverage did not keep up. With each step forward, the need for additional flank coverage increased. Schwarzenberg possessed no further reserves to expend on his flanks, and thus the logical solution was to prolong considerably the advance of the center, holding it back as much as possible. As a result, the march of Army Group Langres became extremely slow, even though nothing stood in its way. Conversely, the corps of the flank groups executed secondary operations or themselves hung back because of war weariness. Such a strategy completely corresponded to the goals of Austrian politics, which needed time to negotiate a peace with a Napoleonic France that retained its natural frontiers and dreaded a military decision that would lead to a draconian peace dictated in Paris by the tsar and his Prussian supporters.[63]

Regarding this last point and to Schwarzenberg's great relief, on 6 January, Caulaincourt penned a request from Lunéville for the commencement of negotiations. This letter reached the Allied sovereigns in Freiburg on the 7th. The French foreign minister expressed disappointment and confusion over the Coalition's failure to initiate the peace conference after Napoleon had accepted their terms in early January. Metternich responded that the peace conference would begin as soon as Castlereagh arrived from London. More important for the Austrians, Metternich believed Caulaincourt's letter signaled a pressing desire to negotiate that reflected Napoleon's growing inclination toward peace.[64] A negotiated peace seemed within reach. To attain the goal that had been so illusory just six months earlier during the Armistice of Pläswitz, the Austrian minister hastened to prevent Schwarzenberg's military operations from exerting any influence on the situation. To Metternich, the hour appeared favorable for the French emperor to make peace. In addition, the Austrian statesman believed he could both end the war and shape the future of Europe according to Vienna's interests. Of course the political situation brought Metternich into Schwarzenberg's war room. On 8 January, he advised Schwarzenberg to advance "cautiously" and "to utilize the common Frenchman's desire for peace by avoiding martial acts."[65] For the commander in chief, such advice amounted to an even more pronounced strategy of maneuver, which he preferred over Blücher's aggressive style. Admittedly, Blücher and his staff drew overly optimistic conclusions, but Silesian Army

Headquarters correctly interpreted the situation: the French marshals could not stop an energetic Allied offensive. Blücher ultimately failed to convince Schwarzenberg of this fundamental fact.

On the 4th, Grouchy and Dejean as well as the 7,000 men and forty-eight guns of the II Corps joined Victor at Molsheim; the 3,000 men of Milhaud's V Cavalry Corps rode to St. Pierre, nine miles south of Molsheim. Both Honor Guard Regiments continued to withdraw westward. From Lembach Ségur's 3rd Regiment covered much ground to reach Bouxwiller, halfway between Haguenau and Saverne, while St. Sulpice's 4th Regiment gained Dettwiller, just south of Ségur on a parallel road to Saverne. Victor knew the Russians had crossed the Rhine, but possessed few details over their operations in Lower Alsace. A rumor reached Molsheim of an enemy column en route to the pass of Ste. Marie to reach St. Dié on the western slopes of the Vosges. To verify this news, Grouchy ordered Milhaud to maintain his position at St. Pierre and dispatch patrols west and south. If the Allies caught up with Milhaud, he would continue his retreat to Molsheim, where Victor and Grouchy decided to remain until the enemy's intentions became clear.[66]

On the night of 4–5 January, Victor received news of Pahlen's patrols moving toward Saverne. Evidently, these reports confirmed the marshal's belief that Wittgenstein's corps was making for Saverne to sever his line of retreat. Other reports mistook Sherbatov's excursion to Épinal on the 3rd as the advance of Frimont's division to Remiremont. Based on this spotty information, Victor described a bleak situation to Berthier:

> On the 4th they [Milhaud's troops] continued their march on Molsheim; but on the same day the enemy's right column threatened Saverne and Milhaud was followed by the left, which had attacked him on the previous day. At the same time we learned of a third column commanded by Frimont taking the direction through St. Amarin to Remiremont. In this manner we can be attacked on both our flanks by quadruple forces and we face the loss of our communications. In moving on Saverne, I can encounter the enemy there (his advance guard is already at Hochfelden), but he has more forces than me, and I am being followed by the column that already attacked Milhaud. The forces that I possess are too disproportionate to those that I have to fight and I expose myself to losing all communication with the interior.

Claiming to have "examined all the disadvantages" and considering that Frimont could prevent him from reaching St. Dié, Victor decided to turn immediately west, cross the Vosges through the Donon Pass, and forsake Alsace. To prevent being cutoff from the French interior and believing he could better defend the mountain passes from the western slopes, Victor issued orders at 1:00 A.M. for the II Infantry and V Cavalry Corps to evacuate Alsace.[67]

Calling this letter an "extraordinary report," Lefebvre de Béhaine claims everything Victor stated was false. Once again, his accusation is unjustified. The historian argues that Wittgenstein's infantry was still at Ft. Vauban on the 4th, and had to advance thirty-five miles to reach Saverne. On the other hand, Victor had only seventeen miles to cover from Molsheim to Saverne. From Haguenau, Pahlen and his nine squadrons could not hope to stop the march of the II Corps and two Honor Guard regiments. Although true, Victor could not be sure of this and had no way of receiving confirmed reports because Cossacks controlled the roads. Victor only can be criticized for the confusion caused by Sherbatov's appearance at Remiremont and the inaccurate portrayal of Frimont's operations. In a broader analysis, which the French historian fails to conduct, Victor's decision to abandon Alsace reflects the ongoing confusion over his task – the same misunderstanding that afflicted Marmont and Macdonald. Victor clearly believed his mission was to save his skeletal corps and slow the enemy for as long as possible. What would the emperor have said if Victor knowingly marched his battalions into a trap at Saverne?[68]

The marshal thought only of escaping the trap that appeared to be closing around him ever since Wittgenstein's corps crossed the Rhine. Yet by saving his cadres, Victor's retreat opened the mountain passes and handed the initiative to his indolent adversaries. According to Napoleon's 1 January plans to create four armies, he clearly desired to maintain a military presence in Alsace. Although Blücher's offensive did more to damage the emperor's measures than Victor's retreat, Napoleon's political and material needs required Victor to remain as close to the Rhine as possible. Imagine Napoleon's frustration over Victor's conduct. Not only did the marshal abandon Alsace and the Vosges, he also retreated before Wrede, whom Napoleon hardly respected as a general; before the crown prince of Württemberg, barely thirty years of age; before the tired and languid Wittgenstein who, like many Russian officers, believed he had no vested interest in continuing the war; and finally, before Schwarzenberg, whose timidity could be exploited by a mere charge of French dragoons.

At 8:00 on the morning of 5 January, Grouchy issued directives for Milhaud to turn west from St. Pierre and ride to the Donon Pass to unite with the II Corps. Grouchy instructed him to post his two dragoon divisions at Framont, slightly south of the Donon, and Piré's light cavalry at Schirmeck, from where patrols would be dispatched to ascertain news of the enemy.[69] While Milhaud covered his flank, Victor led the II Corps on a grueling twenty-mile march that his column did not complete before nightfall. The head of the II Corps cleared the Donon and proceeded south toward Raon-l'Étape, passing the night at Celles in the Plaine Valley; the rear of the column straddled the pass.[70] Milhaud's cavalry established communication with Victor's rearguard during the night: neither French corps encountered the enemy during the course of the day.[71]

North of Molsheim neither St. Sulpice nor Ségur knew where to find Victor; they figured he was still at Strasbourg, possibly trapped. Evidently, the marshal evacuated Molsheim without issuing orders to either general. Assuming the Russians were already east of Haguenau, Ségur's 3rd Honor Guard Regiment executed a dangerous flank march southwest from Bouxwiller to reach Saverne, where the commander hoped to find Victor. Forming his squadrons into two columns, Ségur led the smaller unit, which served as a flank guard, south to Dettwiller; his main body of 1,000 troopers rode to Saverne. Still north of Dettwiller, he received word that 2,000 Russian cavalry under Seslavin occupied the village. Ségur advanced rapidly in an effort to surprise the enemy but found him formed for battle as his troopers approached. Fortunately the opposing sides recognized each other before combat began: Ségur's men faced the 600 troopers of the 4th Honor Guard Regiment, likewise retreating on Saverne. Both detachments passed the night at Dettwiller. An abundance of reports furnished by frightened locals painted a grim picture. Accordingly, all French troops had evacuated Alsace under Allied pressure. That night Victor's orders finally caught up with the two cavalry commanders: if pressed by the Russians, they would withdraw to Phalsbourg on the road to Nancy. Both regiments retreated to Saverne on 6th, crossed the Vosges, and reached Phalsbourg on the following day.[72]

For the Bohemian Army, 5 January represented no less of a wasted day than the 4th. Limiting himself to investing Sélestat – which opened a ferocious artillery barrage on Rechberg's troops – Wrede did little to reestablish contact with the French. However, he did discover that Milhaud had retreated west along the highway to Nancy on the previous day. To cover his left, Wrede forwarded General Franz Xaver von Deroy's 2nd Brigade of Delamotte's 3rd Division to observe the pass at Ste. Marie and the road that led to St. Dié in the Meurthe Valley. That same evening Deroy reported that nothing was moving in the forty-three-mile stretch between Ste. Marie and Nancy – quite a claim![73] General Nikolas von Maillot de la Traille's 2nd Brigade of Rechberg's 1st Division also started relieving the units of the IV Corps at Neuf-Brisach, but not before the garrison launched an aggressive sortie to cover a foraging mission.[74]

Although Wittgenstein's infantry remained idle, Pahlen dispatched patrols throughout Lower Alsace. The information reported to Pahlen provided a muddled view of the situation. A patrol sent north to Lauterbourg on the left bank of the Rhine claimed Marmont was retreating from Pirmasens toward Bitche, only twenty-three miles northwest of Haguenau. Another detachment rode northwest, ironically on the Haguenau–Bitche road, and learned of Ségur's movement to Saverne. The detachment that moved south toward Mutzig reached the Strasbourg–Saverne road where stragglers, whom they mistook to be Victor's advance guard, stopped them at Marlenheim. Finally, the Russian units sent southeast toward Strasbourg occupied the large town of la Wantzenau without combat and pursued the retreating French garrison (1,000 men and four guns) to the Alsatian capital. Based on this confusing information, Pahlen somehow managed to draw one correct conclusion – and an important one at that: it appeared Victor had not retreated northwest through Saverne to Phalsbourg, which meant the French marshal must be moving due west between Sélestat and Strasbourg.[75]

In the night of 4–5 January, Crown Prince Frederick William received the Disposition, which directed him to Remiremont to support Sherbatov and confront the French troops at Épinal.[76] Although Schwarzenberg instructed the IV Corps to begin its movement on the 6th, Frederick William's lead elements – one squadron and three infantry companies – reached the Bussang Pass on the 5th. This allowed Sherbatov to return to Remiremont; his advance guard continued north on the road to Épinal. About two hours south of the town, the vanguard encountered a French patrol that led the Russians to General Bernard-Etienne-Marie (Achille) Duvigneau's detachment of 400 cavalry and 100 infantry of the 4th Military District. Around 4:00 in the afternoon Sherbatov's Ural Cossack Regiment supported by 150 horsemen of the Tepter Regiment charged the French cavalry. A veteran of Napoleon's famous 1800 victory at Marengo, Duvigneau had retired that same year. Recalled to service, his first combat after a thirteen-year hiatus ended in a route. The Cossacks relentlessly pursued the enemy troopers to within two miles of Épinal, where the presence of French infantry forced the Russians to backtrack to Arches.[77] Among the twelve prisoners snared by the Cossacks, Sherbatov found two conscripts from Lyon, whom he sent home "so that they can tell all that the Allied troops do not come to make war on the French, but come to make peace for the happiness of the French nation." Sherbatov's comments on public opinion provided encouraging news: "Marshal Oudinot has been disgraced for having dared to say there are no resources to make war and that he cannot command a corps made up of weak and undisciplined children. The bourgeoisie are very discontent with the government and desire change. The prisoners that I have taken are, I believe, happy, for they claim they will serve no more."

From the rest of the prisoners as well as a Spanish lieutenant found by the Cossacks after he had escaped from Nancy, Sherbatov gleaned significant information that he dispatched directly to Schwarzenberg in a comprehensive report. Writing at midnight on 5–6 January, he claimed that only 4,000 infantry occupied Épinal, but three large bivouacs, including those of the Imperial Guard, covered the thirty-six miles between Épinal and Nancy. This grossly exaggerated report referred to General Claude-Marie Meunier's 1st Young Guard Voltigeur Division, whose 1st Brigade left Sarrelibre on the 31st, marched through Metz on 3 January, and reached Nancy on the 5th. On the following day, the 2nd Brigade arrived, pushing two battalions south to Flavigny and one to Charmes. This last battalion was to support Duvigneau's detachment in an operation against Sherbatov's Cossacks at Épinal.[78] According to Sherbatov, the French had assembled 30,000 conscripts at Metz before sending half this number to Brussels. Between the garrison and the conscripts, approximately 25,000 men remained at Metz, which served as both army and imperial headquarters, but the emperor had yet to arrive. Around 1,000 to 1,500 men occupied Nancy.[79]

Further unverified intelligence arrived from Thurn, who reported from Vesoul on the 6th. According to his spies, Kellermann held Metz with 8,000 men, almost all conscripts, and Napoleon had directed the majority of the French army to Brabant. In addition, 10,000 men of the Imperial Guard were marching to Paris and "another mass is moving to Strasbourg."[80]

Indicative of the sloppiness of Allied intelligence gathering, neither Sherbatov nor Thurn verified these claims and simply communicated the information en masse to the commander in chief. Most of the intelligence Schwarzenberg's forward units provided came from prisoners, deserters, agents, and spies. By not confirming their statements – either because of logistics or inertia – Allied intelligence did little to help Schwarzenberg avoid falling victim to Napoleon's campaign of misinformation. "The emperor neglected no means of intimidating the enemy during his advance," explains Baron Fain. "He knew well the extreme caution of the generals who opposed him, and he predicted their irresolution. Numerous military reviews took place in the courtyard of the Tuileries; the journals never failed to double or triple the real number of troops that had been reviewed. In less than one month, upwards of 100,000 men were stated to have marched through Paris to join the army."[81]

Operations gradually accelerated on the 6th for the rest of Schwarzenberg's corps with Army Group Vosges again being the most active. Sherbatov's main body occupied Arches; his reports to Russian headquarters in Basel regarding enemy forces at Épinal induced Barclay de Tolly to add Platov's Cossacks (2,000 men in five regiments) to Army Group Vosges. Platov was ordered to follow the Württembergers to Épinal, cooperate in driving the French from this position, and then slide thirty-seven miles northwest to Neufchâteau in the Meuse Valley to reconnoiter in front of the army's center. From Épinal Sherbatov would continue north with the task of patrolling the Moselle Valley toward Nancy and establishing communication with Blücher's left wing.[82] Crown Prince Frederick William reached Cernay in the morning; his advance guard moved to Thann.[83]

Behind the Württembergers, Army Group Alsace likewise stirred. General Anton von Volkmann's Austrian brigade repulsed a sortie by the garrison of Sélestat and completely invested the fortress, while one of Rechberg's brigades relieved the Württembergers at Neuf-Brisach. After the rest of Delamotte's division reached Ste. Marie, the Bavarians occupied the pass that led from Alsace to Lorraine. To the north, Wittgenstein's advance posts extended from Haguenau through Wissembourg to Speyer, where communication was established with Sacken's Cossacks. Frimont's cavalry linked at Molsheim with Wittgenstein's light troops; together their patrols finally produced an accurate view of French operations. Contrary to the report of the previous day, Wittgenstein's patrol learned that Marmont was not retreating on Bitche, whose garrison consisted only of invalids. Other patrols claimed National Guard units occupied Landau and that the two French Honor Guard regiments had retreated through Saverne toward Sarrebourg. The reports submitted by Wrede's patrols led the Bavarian corps commander to believe Victor had withdrew from Strasbourg through the Vosges toward Lunéville.[84] Based on this news, it appeared the French army had evacuated Alsace.

On the left wing of the Bohemian Army, Thurn executed a coup-de-main on the town of Port-sur-Saône, six miles west of Vesoul on the road to Langres, during the night of 5–6 January. To support the Streifkorps, Schwarzenberg wanted Army Group Langres to occupy Vesoul as quickly as possible. He demanded that Gyulay push his men to reach their march destinations one day earlier: Crenneville's division should reach Port-sur-Saône by 7 January and the head of the III Corps's main body should be at Vesoul on the 8th.[85] Strung out along the Doubs River between Arcey and Montbéliard, Army Group Franche-Comté did not make much progress on the 6th. Colloredo released Wimpffen's division for siege duty at Besançon. Liechtenstein's II Corps, serving as Hesse-Homburg's advance guard, reached l'Hôpital-du-Gros-Bois; the Austrian Reserve marched north from Pontarlier toward Besançon. The 2nd Light Division covered the Reserve's left.[86]

On the extreme left of Army Group Franche-Comté, Bubna united his division at Poligny on 5 January and forwarded one Hussar squadron to secure the bridge over the Doubs at Dole. After a two-hour affair, the Austrians drove the French post northwest toward Auxonne and secured the bridge. Receiving news of this on the 6th, Bubna ordered his detached units to reunite at Poligny and follow the division to Dijon.[87] That same day, the Disposition arrived from Schwarzenberg's headquarters, instructing him to turn around and march south through Bourg-en-Bresse to Lyon. After wasting precious time, it finally appeared Schwarzenberg would make an effort to obstruct French recruitment, disperse any troops already organized, and, if the circumstances permitted, take France's second city.

Owing to the news he received from his detachments, this new task provided no cause for celebration at Bubna's headquarters. From Lons-le-Saunier arrived a report that 1,500 troops under Musnier held Bourg-en-Bresse, *chef-lieu* of the Ain Department and halfway point between Lons and Lyon. Thirty miles west of Lons, General Claude-Juste-Alexandre Legrand guarded the bridge at Chalon-sur-Saône (see Map 14, Chapter 11). According to reports, both French generals were arming the population and organizing popular resistance.[88] Zechmeister's 4 January report from Geneva likewise did not sound promising. He informed Bubna that 5,000 men from Suchet's army had marched north through Grenoble en route to Chambéry: *chef-lieu* of the Mont-Blanc Department, historic capital of Savoy, and only forty miles south of Geneva. French infantry repulsed Zechmeister's patrols near Rumilly and Alby – the halfway points on the roads between Chambéry and Geneva. Another patrol encountered a post of 300 infantry at Nantua on the Geneva–Lyon road.[89] This news compounded rumors that General Joseph-Marie Dessaix had assembled between 3,000 and 6,000 men at Chambéry to retake Geneva.[90]

For the defense of the Isère and Savoie (Mont-Blanc) Departments, Napoleon appointed General Jean-Gabriel Marchand to command the *levée-en-masse* in the former and Dessaix in the latter on 4 January. Both officers assisted the commandant of the 7th Military Division, General Jean-Baptiste-Grégoire Delaroche, with summoning the National Guard and organizing the levée. The possibility of a rapid French counteroffensive against Geneva at a time when strategic consumption weakened his 5,000-man division troubled Bubna. Zechmeister's letter of 5 January hardly allayed his fears. "The enemy has been reinforced at Rumilly, Alby, and Aix-les-Bains, where Dessaix has 3,000 men," shrieks the Austrian commander. "As I already have informed you, he has 2,000 men at Chambéry." French infantry also advanced east of Nantua on the Geneva–Lyon road.[91] Bubna faced a difficult decision: return to Geneva and reinforce Zechmeister or comply with Schwarzenberg's orders and proceed to Lyon. He grudgingly chose the latter, but his orders would soon change again.

On the opposite end of Schwarzenberg's front, Victor evacuated Alsace by crossing the Donon Pass on 6 January. The duke of Bellune led the retreat of the demoralized II Infantry (7,000 men) and V Cavalry Corps (3,000 men) to Raon-l'Étape, where he arrived at noon. Posting a rearguard formed by the five battalions of Duhesme's 3rd Division, the eight squadrons of Piré's 9th Light Cavalry Division, and one battery of horse artillery, Victor's main body of ten battalions continued the demoralizing march to Baccarat in the Meurthe Valley, thirty miles southeast of Nancy. Victor's collapse shocked Grouchy, Dejean, Milhaud, and most of the general officers who accompanied him. Not pressured by the enemy and possessing adequate quantities of supplies and ammunition, the marshal simply appeared to have given up. Their complaints over Victor's conduct ranged from sensible to unjust, yet all illustrated the extreme despair that crept over the French officer corps during the twilight of the empire.

"Allow me," wrote Grouchy to Berthier, "to express my regret that we will not unite with the duke of Raguse. I also fear that if a central rendezvous point is not promptly assigned to the various corps, placed as they are between the enemy columns that appear ready to debouch and which probably are much stronger than each of these corps, they will find themselves paralyzed and damaged in a manner hardly advantageous to the interests of His Majesty."[92]

Figure 13. General Emmanuel Grouchy (1766–1847). French cavalry commander.

Taking absolutely no measures to defend the ridges and other passes through the Vosges baffled Milhaud. "What a misfortune," laments the cavalry commander, "not to be able to defend the entrance of the passes at Saverne, Mutzig, and Ste. Marie with a few battalions of light infantry. The inhabitants of the mountains need only to see one or two battalions defending the entrance of each pass and they will rise up to defend their homes."[93] Victor's staff failed to exert any influence on the marshal and evidently was too dumbfounded to make arrangements for food and lodging west of the Vosges.

Lefebvre de Béhaine calls Victor's abandonment of Alsace nothing less than a "sin." Relentless in his criticism of the marshal, the French historian unfairly asserts that Victor's decision to abandon Alsace "if not justifiable, would have been at least excusable if the enemy had showed some activity and pushed his advance guard on Saverne from one side, and on Molsheim or on Saales from the other. But in the first days of the invasion, Russians, Austrians, and Bavarians acted with excessive slowness and caution; the cavalry, which in the previous campaign had showed so much boldness, did not willingly move forward of the main columns and was stopped by the least obstacle." Victor realized the Allies had moved overwhelming forces into Alsace. After Wittgenstein and Sacken crossed the Rhine, the Bavarians and Württembergers moved north through Colmar on the 3rd; Russian cavalry reached Haguenau on the road to Saverne. In light of these movements, Victor acted with prudence; his failure to support the Alsatians and to coordinate a defense of the mountain passes with the inhabitants were his only faults. He could have defended the passes and launched tactical strikes against the flanks of the Allied columns to retard the progress of an already slow invasion. Moreover, his 7,000 men and 3,000 cavalry could have supported a guerilla war in Alsace, and in return the inhabitants could have served his needs. Rather than the marshal, blame for the failures on the eastern front falls squarely on Napoleon for not making the nature of his subordinates' tasks absolutely clear from the start; for misleading his marshals by inflating the number of recruits (600,000); and for not embracing a people's war.[94]

In his brief to Berthier that evening, Victor made a very logical argument in defense of his actions. This explanation is perfectly sound if his role was to save his corps for the emperor's use, which the marshal indeed believed was the case. Blücher's offensive caused him to renounce his original plan of retreating to Saverne, uniting with Marmont, and proceeding to Phalsbourg. Victor acknowledged that from Phalsbourg, he could continue to operate in Alsace and defend the roads to Nancy and Metz. However, his left and rear would be vulnerable to the Allied masses assembling in Upper Alsace, which he correctly estimated to be between 35,000 and 40,000 men. He expected these forces to move north and send detachments through the passes at Bussang, Ste. Marie, and Bonhomme to reach Remiremont and St. Dié in an attempt to sever his line of retreat. To the east and north, he had to contend with the Russians under Wittgenstein and Sacken, which he estimated to be only 20,000 men. Sacken appeared to be making for Kaiserslautern and Saarguemines, while Pahlen led Wittgenstein's advance guard toward Saverne and Phalsbourg. The marshal explained that a retreat to Baccarat maintained his communication with the interior and delayed Allied progress in the Meurthe Valley without jeopardizing his own line of retreat. At Baccarat and Phalsbourg, the two Honor Guard regiments covered his left, while the troops of the 4th Military District held the Moselle Valley to cover his right. Napoleon's campaign of misinformation backfired as the marshal again asked for the reinforcements promised by the emperor which, in lieu of the confident statements from Paris, were undoubtedly combat-ready by this time. According to his report, if the regiments of the II Corps received their 2nd and 4th Battalions to increase Victor's infantry to 12,000 men, the marshal believed he could maintain his position and perhaps even drive back the Allies. Conversely, unless these reinforcements arrived soon, he would not be able to hold the enemy for more than a few days. Victor continued to argue his case on the 9th by adding that on 4 January the Allied right wing was marching on Saverne, while another column pursued Milhaud, and a third under Frimont proceeded through St. Amarin toward Remiremont. Thus the marshal learned both of his flanks were threatened, his communications with

Saverne compromised, and Marmont could not unite with him. "As a result of the disproportion of forces and to prevent Frimont from debouching from Raon-l'Étape, I marched on the 5th through Mutzig to Raon-l'Étape," concludes his justification.[95]

As with Marmont, such arguments make sense only if the emperor wanted his marshals to trade land for time. A position east of the Vosges where Victor could have tied down the timid Allies would have served the emperor's political needs and military preparations far better than west of the mountains, with the departments of Lorraine exposed to Allied invasion. Victor's retreat triggered a panic among the civil officials that caused imperial authority to collapse completely, thus robbing Napoleon of manpower, revenue, and material. At Nancy Caulaincourt composed a disturbing report on 6 January:

> Here I found the prefect of Épinal with the sub-prefects of St. Dié and Remiremont. The sub-prefect of St. Dié fled well before the enemy appeared in his district. All three were escorted by gendarmes in such a manner that they have disorganized the means to rally the inhabitants to the defense. Their arrival in Nancy, at night and at the head of a civil force, has sounded the alarm; a great number of people seek only to save themselves. The flight of the authorities and the gendarmerie has destroyed the élan of the population, which was perfectly disposed. The prefect and the sub-prefects have promised to repair the damage and to conduct the levée-en-masse, which now will be difficult enough, owing to the terror that their flight has caused.[96]

On the 18th, Caulaincourt added: "It is quite necessary to prevent the civil authorities from being intimidated. The least disturbing rumor prompts them to flee, which spreads alarm throughout the land. This revives the enemy and accelerates his march, which a little bit of firmness would have delayed, if one had wanted, for quite a few days, ever since he crossed the Rhine and without compromising the slightest thing."[97] Beauchamp attributes the collapse of French control simply to the arrival of the Allies on French soil, "which produced such a spirited sensation in all the provinces of the left bank that the precariousness and turmoil did not allow the prefects, the generals, and the agents of the government to take decisive and uniform action."[98]

Unfortunately for Bonaparte, the marshals did not see the connection between their retreat and the collapse of imperial authority, nor did they recognize the extent of the damage to Napoleon's cause. Of the marshals employed to stop the invasion during December and January, only Ney demonstrated an understanding of these issues. Upon reaching Nancy on the 9th, he forced the subprefect who had fled from Mirecourt to return to his post.[99] "It is necessary to show a few troops on all points to end the disorder that is produced by the fear of the enemy, and to support the administration in the efforts that it makes to accelerate the raising of men, money, and material," he explains to Berthier on the 11th.[100] Yet Ney did not assume a command until 9 January. By this time, Victor, Marmont, and Macdonald had endured two months of mental strain and physical exhaustion. Like Caulaincourt, they simply fired complaints to Paris over the insubordinate conduct of the civil authorities without considering their own responsibility. Conversely, the conduct of the civil authorities did not go unnoticed by the troops.[101]

Equally at fault, the emperor attempted to implement from Paris a plan that required a confidence and a drive that his marshals had long lost. His demands required the marshals to exhibit an ardor and a diligence that quickly yielded to weariness, indifference, and despair.[102] Napoleon should have acknowledged this and assigned more authority to officers who still had reputations to gain such as Grouchy and Milhaud as opposed to the spent marshals, who increasingly felt they had nothing to gain and everything to lose. In the past, as with the case of Masséna following the final French campaign in Portugal, the emperor recognized the mental and physical exhaustion of this exceptional lieutenant and retired the marshal. Although the German campaign provided further proof of the marshalate's growing incapacity, the emperor did not feel compelled to turn over the reigns of the army to a new generation of untested commanders at such a critical time.

Regarding the emperor's intentions, a letter to Kellermann on 3 January explained his plans to assemble an army of 80,000 men at Langres, whose nucleus would be formed by Mortier's Old Guard infantry and cavalry divisions and five to six batteries en route from Namur and expected to reach Langres on the 10th. He planned to assemble troops gradually at Langres and proceed to Vesoul with three corps, which he judged sufficient to secure Besançon and to relieve Belfort and Huningue. Napoleon also reiterated his orders regarding the formation of a reserve at Épinal consisting of the 1st and 2nd Young Guard Voltigeur Divisions and the 2nd Old Guard Division. At Metz Kellermann had to complete the 3rd Battalions of both Young Guard Divisions – four battalions each for a total of 6,000 men – and forward these units to Épinal. Curial would command this force, which the emperor estimated to be 24,000 men and sixty-eight guns. Napoleon also planned to raise 20,000 recruits in the 2nd, 3rd, and 4th Military Districts as well as Alsace to form a reserve for Curial's reserve at Épinal.[103] Moreover, Napoleon's orders contained instructions regarding the reinforcements to be sent to Marmont and Victor – instructions that events rendered obsolete. Although he discussed the arming of Metz, Luxembourg, and Saarlouis, the emperor now urged Kellermann to hold back nothing that belonged to either marshal. Concern for the field army came first, yet Victor's retreat jeopardized all the emperor's arrangements.[104]

Reports from Milhaud, Dejean, and the civil officials reached Paris long before Victor's official explanations. On 6 January, the same day that Victor led his troops through the Donon, Napoleon learned from these earlier reports that Victor had opted to retreat toward Saverne. He wrote a sharp letter to

Berthier, instructing the chief of staff to write an equally sharp letter to the marshal: "Inform the duke of Bellune of my discontent over his movement from Colmar to the hills of Saverne, which abandons all of the Vosges and exposes Épinal . . . Nancy is completely exposed." The emperor felt it would have been better if Victor "had moved from Colmar to the [Bonhomme] pass at Épinal." Ironically, he drew the same conclusion as Victor regarding the pass at Saverne: Phalsbourg could guard the defile. Although Victor had not retreated to Saverne, and from his position at Baccarat he could cover the southern approaches to Nancy and reach Épinal in three days, the emperor did not learn of this until late on the 8th.[105]

From Napoleon's point of view on 6 January, Victor's retreat to Saverne opened the southern and central passes of the Vosges and jeopardized his plans for Curial's reserve at Épinal, possession of which provided the French a central position to stop the Allies at the Moselle. In fact, Belliard's 5 January telegraphic dispatch from Metz mistakenly claimed Allied cavalry had taken Épinal.[106] Napoleon held Victor responsible for the alleged loss of Épinal, the endpoint of one of the best roads through the Vosges and the gateway to Lorraine and Franche-Comté.[107] "If he is at Saverne today, order him to Nancy," barked the emperor. "Order Ney to depart this day for Nancy and take command of the Young Guard division there as well as all the troops there [Victor's included] in order to guard Nancy, retake Épinal . . . and contain the enemy." That same day Berthier relayed the pertinent order to Kellermann in Metz by way of the optical telegraph system. Kellermann attempted to forward this order to Victor, but Pahlen's Cossacks intercepted the courier on the night of 7–8 January. In a breakdown of communication that frequently plagued Allied operations, Wittgenstein's headquarters did not forward this letter to Schwarzenberg until 10 January; the Allied commander received it two days later.[108]

On 7 January, the emperor received shocking details describing the retreat of both Marmont and Victor. From Metz Kellermann informed the emperor via telegraphic dispatch that Ricard had reached Saarbrücken and Marmont Sarreguemines to defend the line of the Saar; Rigau had evacuated Trier on the Moselle to retire on Luxembourg. Victor crossed the Vosges and reunited with Milhaud at Raon-l'Étape.[109] Napoleon responded by ordering the formation of a division to serve as the "Reserve of Paris." Commanded by General Gérard, the division would consist of three brigades: two formed in Nogent and one in Troyes.[110] He also dispatched Ney from Paris this same day, the 7th; the marshal reached Nancy at 9:00 on the night of the 9th. The situation of his command changed as soon as he arrived. Rather than having the 1st and 2nd Young Guard Voltigeur and 2nd Old Guard Divisions at his disposal for the Épinal counteroffensive, he found only Meunier's 1st Young Guard Voltigeur Division at Nancy. Napoleon already had changed plans and ordered the 2nd Old Guard Division to Langres, where it would unite with Mortier's 1st Old

Guard Division. The 2nd Young Guard Voltigeur Division was directed to Châlons-en-Champagne.[111]

"The coffers of the II Corps do not contain more than a hundredth," complains Victor to Berthier, "I possess about the same to cover my own expenses."[112] Unable to provide for the needs of the troops, Victor granted his tired soldiers a day of rest of 7 January. Reports indicated that the Allies had yet to cross the Vosges in strength. Enemy detachments had been seen, particularly at St. Dié, only sixteen miles southeast of his headquarters at Baccarat, but they were few in number and Victor assumed they were foraging the bleak hills.[113] The largest force appeared to be a unit of 3,000 Bavarians at Ste. Marie. Dejean, the emperor's aide-de-camp, attempted to persuade Victor to advance fifteen miles south of Baccarat to St. Dié and drive the Allies from Ste. Marie. Victor flatly refused, claiming such an operation would compromise the corps. "I believe it is my duty to repeat to Your Majesty what I have already stated concerning the duke of Bellune: he is not the man of the hour and his command is a public calamity," howls Dejean. "Grouchy is of the absolute same opinion as me regarding all that has happened."[114] "Twenty Cossacks have seized each of the passes of the Vosges; one [Victor] has not even fired a musket," insists Caulaincourt. "Nothing proves that enemy infantry has already penetrated the Vosges."[115] Caulaincourt suggested that Napoleon either dispatch another senior officer or transfer command of the defense of Lorraine from Victor to the thirty-three-year-old Dejean: "If you do not send another commander, it would be useful to give the orders and instructions to Dejean, who has zeal and much good will. He electrifies the mayors and he will not find it difficult to assemble a good number of armed *montagnards* to defend the passes in conjunction with some Voltigeur companies."[116]

On the morning of 7 January, Pahlen's advance squadron entered Saverne shortly after Ségur's rearguard departed. Although the Russian horsemen could not catch up with the two Honor Guard regiments, patrols continued toward Phalsbourg and Sarrebourg. Five days after crossing the Rhine, Wittgenstein's infantry finally moved out of the Ft. d'Alsace bridgehead. One brigade from Pyshnitsky's 4th Division marched to Haguenau, while the other took post at Roeschwoog. Wittgenstein also permitted Shakhovsky's 3rd Division to cross the Rhine at Ft. Vauban and proceed toward Mutzig to link with Wrede's right.[117]

Because of Schwarzenberg's exaggerated concern over the garrison of Strasbourg as well as his lingering anxiety over an enemy counteroffensive in Alsace, Wrede's corps continued to stagnate in front of Sélestat and Neuf-Brisach; only his left wing at Ste. Marie remained active. Wrede informed Schwarzenberg that according to reports, Victor evacuated Strasbourg's garrison, and few troops remained in the city.[118] "I have ordered all of my commanders to at least dispatch patrols to obtain information," notes Wrede with a tone of disgust.[119] Deroy sent several patrols through the pass toward

St. Dié. Near the town, the Bavarians put to flight a French cavalry post esti-mated to be eighty troopers. The French retreated to Raon-l'Étape where, according to locals, Piré camped with 3,000 cavalry and infantry. Deroy's intelligence also found Victor: the marshal was purportedly in Baccarat with 12,000 men.[120]

South of the Bavarians, the Württembergers entered the Wesserling Valley, just west of the Bussang Pass. Platov's Cossacks passed the IV Corps, crossed into Lorraine, and headed north toward Épinal.[121] Leading Army Group Vosges, Sherbatov's Streifkorps continued its advance through the Moselle Valley toward the *chef-lieu* of the Vosges Department without encountering any French posts or patrols. In utter disbelief, he entered Épinal the same day. The inhabitants informed him the French had retreated fourteen miles northwest to Charmes.[122]

In a recurring theme, not much occurred on the left wing of the Bohemian Army during the 7th. Falling far short of its march goal of Port-sur-Saône, Crenneville's division reached Mollans, ten miles northeast of Vesoul. Gyu-lay's advance guard moved into Vesoul, while the main body marched less than six miles to camp east of Vesoul at Villersexel. Colloredo's I Corps spent another day enjoying the scenery around Montbéliard. The units of Army Group Franche-Comté continued their slow, methodical procession toward Besançon. Well behind the army, the columns of the Russo–Prussian Guard and Reserve stretched from Basel to Altkirch.

Bubna's 1st Light Division commenced a feeble march from Poligny to Lons-le-Saunier, needing two days to cover fourteen miles. Before departing Poligny, Bubna outlined his intentions to push cavalry west to the right bank of the Saône. He informed Schwarzenberg that only 1,800 unarmed conscripts guarded the bridge at Chalon-sur-Saône, thirty-three miles west of Lons. "I will make every effort to send cavalry to Chalon-sur-Saône and Mâcon in order to harass the enemy on the right bank of the Saône." Bubna's plan appears overambitious and perhaps served to provide Schwarzenberg with something to add in his reports to Kaiser Francis. "I calculate on turning on Bourg-en-Bresse and from there linking with Zechmeister," continues Bubna. "At the same time, I will proceed toward Lyon and hope to make myself master of the road to Chambéry." Although Bubna had no way of knowing it, on the same day that he penned this report, Schwarzenberg decided to change his march direction and again send him north through Auxonne to Dijon to cover the march on Langres. Bubna informed his commander in chief that small garrisons of unarmed conscripts held both Dijon and Auxonne and that all French forces in the region were marching to Metz.[123]

An epiphany occurred in Schwarzenberg's headquarters at Montbéliard on 7 January. The commander in chief finally gained a more accurate view of the situation in Alsace. Victor's forces had fled, and it did not appear that the French could launch a counteroffensive from Metz through Alsace to cross the Rhine at Strasbourg. Reports also confirmed the French army was not concentrating at Metz. Grossly exaggerated yet supposedly confirmed reports of French measures to defend Langres seemed more feasible than an operation to regain Alsace: Napoleon certainly would not fail to recognize the importance of this domineering plateau. These considerations finally prompted Austrian headquarters to accelerate slightly the pace of Army Group Alsace's operations, even though Wrede's reports over Victor's retreat should have provided sufficient cause for Schwarzenberg to implement a spirited offensive. According to the German General Staff historian Janson, who is just as critical of Schwarzenberg as Lefebvre de Béhaine is of Victor, in the course of the 7th "arrived 'definite and confirmed' reports that Napoleon had assembled 80,000 men at Langres."[124] Although not as disparaging as Janson, French historian Maurice Weil likewise states: "Worried by the rumor that claimed the imminent concentration on the plateau of Langres of an army of 80,000 men . . . Schwarzenberg was henceforth convinced that it would be necessary to take by force a strategic point as important as Langres and decided to shake free of the torpor that had seized him."[125] The statement regarding "definite and confirmed" reports cannot be verified by any evidence in the "Stärke, Eintheilung, und Tagesbegebenheiten der Hauptarmee im Monate Januar," nor in Schwarzenberg's private correspondence. Moreover, Knesebeck wrote Müffling on the 6th: "We know nothing for sure about the enemy. Victor, who occupied Strasbourg and Colmar with 14,000 men, must have departed, but one does not know where, probably for Metz. Our detachments have scoured the land as far as Épinal."[126] Two days later Schwarzenberg wrote his wife: "Up to this moment we still know nothing of a formal concentration of an army; I continue my movement in order to reach Langres and Dijon if possible. There, with the mountains behind me, my army can survive. Blücher can advance between Metz and Nancy so we can establish communication and, I think, the peace will then be concluded."[127] Conversely, in a 3 January letter to Kellermann, Napoleon ironically explained his preparations to assemble an army of 80,000 men at Langres, whose nucleus would be formed by Mortier's Old Guard infantry and cavalry divisions. No evidence can support the claim that the contents of this letter was known in Schwarzenberg's headquarters. Yet four days separated the day Napoleon dictated the letter on 3 January and the day that Schwarzenberg received "definite and confirmed" reports on 7 January – enough time for this information to travel from Paris or Metz to Montbéliard.[128]

With no significant enemy forces in the Rhine Valley or in Lower Alsace, Schwarzenberg instructed Wittgenstein to turn over the investment of Strasbourg and Kehl to Badenese troops as soon as possible; until they arrived, the Russians were to leave behind the necessary troops for the blockade. With the bulk of his corps, Wittgenstein was ordered to march west and form the right wing of the Bohemian Army. Wrede's V Corps received the order to advance on Remiremont but leave behind eleven battalions and six squadrons (8,000 men) to continue the sieges of Seléstat, Neuf-Brisach, and Huningue, whose combined garrisons Schwarzenberg estimated to be 8,000 to 10,000 men.[129] According to the Austrian staff's calculations, 30,000 men would remain at Wrede's disposal for field operations.

As for the other army groups, Schwarzenberg planned to dissolve Army Group Vosges after it cleared the mountains by directing Frederick William's IV Corps southwest to join Army Group Langres on the Vesoul–Langres road. Platov and Sherbatov would continue to patrol between the Moselle and the Meuse. Forming the center of Schwarzenberg's forces, the I and III Corps of Army Group Langres should clear Vesoul and reach the bridge over the Saône River thirty-six miles southeast of Langres by the 10th at the latest. For support, Barclay de Tolly agreed to echelon the Russo–Prussian Guard and Reserve between Vesoul and Besançon. After Rayevsky's Russian grenadier corps reached Belfort, Bianchi would march to Vesoul with two of his own brigades, leaving the third to continue the siege supported by the Russians. Schwarzenberg believed the bombardment would induce Legrand to yield the fortress and for this reason wanted Austrian troops to accept the surrender. If the bombardment failed to induce the French to capitulate, this final Austrian brigade would turn over the investment to the Russians and likewise depart. On the far left with Army Group Franche-Comté, only Bubna received a change of orders. As noted, thirty-six hours after receiving orders to march southwest to Lyon without delay, Schwarzenberg turned Bubna around and sent him northwest through Dole and Auxonne toward Dijon.

The orders issued by the Austrian staff on 7 January reflect the realization of one fact and the increasing concern caused by one rumor. Victor had evacuated the Rhine Valley, but fears that an extraordinary effort would be required to take Langres – virtually unoccupied by French forces – prompted Schwarzenberg to reinforce Army Group Langres with the 14,000 Württembergers of the IV Corps and to allow Bianchi to move two-thirds of his division to Vesoul after Rayevsky reached Belfort. Also, the generalissimo optimistically thought Barclay de Tolly's Russo–Prussian Guard and Reserve could be up in time to support the operation against Langres. Within these measures to consolidate his center, the primacy of Austrian politics can still be seen. Schwarzenberg augmented Army Group Langres with the Württemberger corps as well as the Russo–Prussian Guard and part of the Russian Reserve. For the moment, the Austrian contribution to this escalation was only two of Bianchi's brigades. The eccentric Austrian operation against Besançon in Franche-Comté by the II Corps, 2nd Light Division, the Austrian Reserve, and Wimpffen's 2nd Division from the I Corps remained unchanged with the exception that Bubna would move west to Dijon rather than south to Lyon. In the least, Schwarzenberg should have assigned Wrede and Wittgenstein objectives more congruent to the forces they possessed rather than leave them to languish before Huningue, Sélestat, Neuf-Brisach, Kehl, and Strasbourg. Despite the obvious effort to move away from the security of the Rhine, the Austrian commander ordered the construction of solid bridgeheads at Märkt and Rheinwiller – a retreat to the right bank was never far from his mind.[130]

Instead of the drive he had exhibited at the start of the fall campaign, Schwarzenberg again wasted an opportunity to conduct an operation that complemented the size of his army. Even by leaving his left wing to continue operations in Franche-Comté, he could have ordered a resolute advance by his center and right. Meeting only slight resistance, Wrede's V Corps could have pursued Victor into the Meurthe Valley through Baccarat to Lunéville and ultimately Nancy itself. By ordering Wittgenstein forward on 3 January, Schwarzenberg could have employed the VI Corps to occupy Nancy and to effect the union with the Silesian Army quickly, effortlessly, and without danger. Further west, Frederick William's IV Corps could have moved rapidly through the Moselle Valley from Épinal to the bridge at Pont-St. Vincent, just south of Nancy. In the meantime, the III and I Corps of Army Group Langres could have accelerated their march through Vesoul to Langres without encountering any resistance. Such an operation would have thoroughly disorganized Napoleon's countermeasures and opened the Marne, Aube, and Seine Rivers to the Allies. In the "Stärke, Eintheilung, und Tagesbegebenheiten der Hauptarmee im Monate Januar," Schwarzenberg's headquarters makes no attempt to explain the reasons behind the decision to employ the V and IV Corps to chase 3,000 French cavalry from Colmar; the loss of contact with Milhaud's cavalry; the sluggish operations of Wittgenstein's corps; or the allocation of the Austrian Reserve, II Corps, and 2nd Light Division to the siege of Besançon on the extreme left wing of the army. Austrian politics, Schwarzenberg's timidity, the lack of initiative on the part of some Allied corps commanders, and the general fear Napoleon still inspired in all but a few of the Allied generals account for the Coalition's failure to implement such a strategy. Weil claims that a "superstitious terror" haunted Schwarzenberg's headquarters from the moment he decided to tread on French soil.[131]

Instead of pushing his own army to effect the union with Blücher, the Allied commander in chief maintained his torpid, piecemeal advance – the Silesian Army would come to him, just as at Leipzig. He saw no reason to drive his columns forward and risk suffering a defeat in the Moselle, Meurthe, or Meuse Valleys. With a massive French army supposedly concentrating at Langres, a defeat could lead to a catastrophe. The principles of the Trachenberg Plan had worked best at Leipzig rather than Dresden; Schwarzenberg did not forget the lesson that had cost his army 35,000 men. "Believe me, Nani," he wrote to his wife on the 8th, "only through the greatest activity can we hope to force a peace, but my role in 100 ways is extremely difficult and dangerous – I count on the help of the Heavens."[132]

11

The Vosges and the Saône

On 7 January, fate granted Victor a relatively quiet day along his sector of the front. While his men recovered from the toils of crossing the Vosges, the marshal contemplated his next move and awaited the emperor's orders.[1] Having abandoned Alsace and with the Allied army preparing to storm into Lorraine, the duke of Bellune displayed absolutely no initiative. Evidently, Victor did not want to issue any orders until the courier arrived from Paris. Drafting his daily brief to Berthier at noon, he requested instructions and again petitioned Paris for the promised reinforcements, explaining that only additional combat power would enable him to halt Allied incursions at St. Dié and Ste. Marie. He also continued to bemoan the deplorable situation of his men. "The supply service has not been organized for the II Corps, which lacks everything . . . the troops are forced to depend on the generosity of the inhabitants."[2] "His Majesty orders you to make the masses pay for the troops," Berthier later replied.[3] Victor responded by writing the emperor directly: "the previous orders could hardly be executed; this one will have no more effect because so many people lack money."[4] His protests went unheeded.

Victor may have thought 7 January would end quietly; perhaps the Allies also would rest and leave him in peace until the emperor's directives arrived? Unfortunately for the tired marshal, the news that reached his headquarters promised no such respite. From Raon-l'Étape, Piré reported that Coalition forces had entered St. Dié, sixteen miles southeast of Baccarat.[5] Later in the day, Victor learned of the combat at Arches on the 6th. According to the initial report, an Allied detachment of 1,900 infantry and cavalry drove French forces from Arches. After being stopped at Épinal, the enemy returned to Arches. Still later, even more shocking news arrived: the Cossacks had taken Épinal earlier that same day. From there a detachment of 100 horsemen proceeded to Rambervillers, only ten miles southwest of Victor's headquarters at

Baccarat. The Russians arrived in the town at 9:00 P.M., helped themselves to the local cuisine, and departed two hours later with full bellies, taking a south-east direction toward St. Dié. Duhesme likewise made contact with Coalition forces. From his position at Raon-l'Étape, the general sent a foraging detachment further south to St. Dié. While the detachment collected food, its scouts proceeded on the road to Ste. Marie and encountered an Allied force of 200 to 300 infantry and 200 cavalry on the march to St. Dié.[6]

For the 8th, Victor only scheduled an early morning review of the II Corps's units by their respective generals. The marshal did not change these orders despite the increasing presence of Allied forces west of the Vosges.[7] For the second consecutive day Victor composed his brief to Berthier at noon. After explaining the events of the 6th and 7th at Arches, Épinal, and St. Dié, he proposed a counteroffensive that French historians either fail to mention or dismiss as insincere. Victor selected St. Dié as his objective and outlined a plan to attack the Allies while they remained dispersed in the mountain passes. Possession of St. Dié, which stood at the junction of the roads coming from Colmar and Sélestat, would allow him to "stop the enemy's incursions and be in position to force him to return to the Rhine," he explains to Kellermann. "Moreover, this operation appears to be very easy at this moment because the enemy divisions can be attacked separately in the defiles of the Vosges." If successful, Victor's counteroffensive could restore morale in soldier and civilian alike, unnerve Schwarzenberg, and perhaps close the mountain passes long enough for Ney to arrive with reinforcements.

Although a sound plan, caution tempered Victor's initiative. Certain that his own forces would not suffice, he sought reinforcements before launching his counteroffensive. A courier from Marmont's headquarters delivered the good news that the duke of Raguse currently held his position at Sarreguemines, forty-five miles north of Baccarat. Surprisingly, Victor made no effort to organize a joint operation with Marmont. Instead, he merely authorized Ségur at Phalsbourg to establish communication between the two marshals.[8] Rather than Marmont's troops, whose hands were full holding the Silesian Army at the Saar, Victor sought to augment the II Corps with "all available troops in the Meurthe and the Vosges Departments." Specifically, he requested that Kellermann forward the promised 2nd and 4th Battalions of his regiments.[9] Imagine Napoleon's frustration over the marshal's recalcitrance. Victor had the right idea: his best defense would be to launch tactical strikes against the dispersed Allied columns as they lumbered across the mountains. When would the marshal use the II Infantry and V Cavalry Corps – what was he waiting for? Had Victor not been with Bonaparte during the First Italian Campaign?

Events on the afternoon of the 8th finally stirred the languid marshal. As Victor had explained to Berthier, his men depended on the locals for food. However, this did not mean that French soldiers patiently waited to be served by patriotic inhabitants who were quite willing to open their dwindling pantries in the midst of winter. Instead, the army interpreted the "generosity of the inhabitants" as the people's ability to comply with enormous requisitions. On the 8th, Victor's commissars requisitioned 10,000 rations of meat and forage from Baccarat and 5,000 rations of bread from Raon-l'Étape. This added to the hardships of the region, which the Cossacks had been pillaging since the 5th. In fact, on the night of the 7th, the Cossacks seized the mayor of Rambervillers, Alexis Gérard, until the townspeople complied with their requisitions.[10]

To protest the requisitions and demand protection from the enemy, Gérard drafted a stirring letter to Victor at noon, just as 200 Cossacks started to sack the neighboring villages. "I have the honor to inform you that around noon today commissioners under your orders have come to this town to apportion among the communes of this vicinity supplies in victuals and forage for your army. Just as this allotment was completed, an order from Gen. Duhesme – which I respectfully attach – arrived requiring 5,000 rations of bread. I must tell you, it is quite impossible for the commune to provide requisitions for two armies at the same time." Gérard explained that he did not think it possible to provide even 1,000 rations of bread. Apparently, small town political rivalries played a role as well. The mayor of Baccarat had informed Victor that the villages around Rambervillers could supply his men. "The information given to you by the mayor of Baccarat would be best in any circumstance other than the present," continues Gérard. "He claims it is possible to find the victuals for your army in the communes near Rambervillers, but he undoubtedly did not know the enemy has made requisitions from Épinal. Among those towns that he has indicated are Badmenil, Deneuvre, and Zincourt, which have received orders and which already have provided more than they can; at this very moment the Cossacks are in the latter two making requisitions. The report that reaches me actually places their number at a couple of hundred and one tells me they make their visits at night." The good mayor concluded with a moving request: "In the name of people and in the interest of your army, post cavalry and infantry on the Rambervillers—Épinal road as means to end all of these enemy requisitions that exhaust your army's food supply." With Épinal only fourteen miles away, Gérard frankly informed the marshal that "if the enemy reaches Rambervillers, it will be impossible for Baccarat and Raon to provide the requisitions." According to the mayor's estimates, 4,000 Cossacks quartered at Épinal.[11]

An embarrassed Victor forwarded Gérard's note to Grouchy with a strong cover letter: "Gen. Grouchy will acquaint himself with this letter. He will see to the security of Rambervillers by transferring one dragoon division to Rambervillers to prevent the enemy from harassing the local villages. . . . This division will be covered by the other, which will be echelonned from Roville to Gerbéville. If necessary, this disposition can be supported by a few battalions. The division established at Rambervillers must attentively observe the roads from St. Dié and Épinal."[12] Deciphering this sharp and somewhat vague missive as best he could, Grouchy moved General Andrè Louis Elisabeth Marie Briche's 3rd Dragoon Division to Rambervillers and echelonned Lhéritier's 4th Dragoon Division according to the marshal's instructions. He alerted Milhaud's headquarters that Victor possibly would send Duhesme's infantry from Raon-l'Étape to Rambervillers. "This movement must be effected only in broad daylight," concludes Grouchy, to assure that both the inhabitants and the Cossacks felt the full effect of the arrival of two dragoon divisions.[13]

Victor did not receive any reinforcements for his own corps, yet additional forces finally reached the theater. Meunier assembled the 5,250 men of his 1st Young Guard Voltigeur Division at Nancy on the 6th. He echelonned three battalions from General Guillaume-Charles Rousseau's 1st Brigade south of Nancy between Flavigny and Charmes. Meunier ordered two of these battalions to support Cassagne's and Duvigneau's operation to drive the Cossacks from Épinal with 300 cavalry from the 4th Military District. On the evening of the 8th, Victor learned Cassagne had marched through Charmes with Rousseau's battalions and Duvigneau's cavalry to put an end to the Cossack menace.[14] Despite this news, Victor inexplicably allowed the 9th to pass without taking any action other than to plan an operation for the next day.

As Victor brooded at Baccarat, irrevocable damage was done to the emperor's political control. While still waiting to open negotiations with the Allies, Caulaincourt described for Napoleon the political and military situation in Lorraine on 8 January:

> Fifty Cossacks, who appeared at Épinal, have evacuated this town. They went as far as near Charmes.... They have retired, but the alarm has spread as far as Nancy. The countryside waits to be invaded, especially since people say the corps of the duke of Bellune is retreating. All of this produces the most deplorable effect. Requisitions are not being filled at all. The levée is not being conducted; discouragement spreads more and more. The language of the enemy is still much worse than his arms. This has the authorities quitting their posts prematurely and spreading alarm and discouragement all over the land. The sub-prefects and mayors lack instructions; they provide no news and I repeat: the generals here know about as much of what is happening around them as is happening in Russia. In the midst of an abundant land the troops lack supplies. One awaits the arrival tomorrow of 120 hundredweights of flour from Nancy to provide bread for the II Corps, which has none. This corps has many sick, several full carts arrive every day. Five have passed today. Typhus has decreased, but a large number of men are afflicted by the swelling of the legs, they find themselves weak and forced to fall out of the ranks. They appear discontent over retreating from the banks of the Rhine to behind the Vosges without having fired a musket. The duke of Bellune appears convinced the enemy debouches with considerable forces through Bitche and that the duke of Raguse is in full retreat.[15]

Rear-area security and communication became increasingly problematic for the French since the Cossacks prowled the roads. After receiving an optical telegraph dispatch from Berthier dated 6 January on that same day, Kellermann relayed the message – also via optical telegraph – from Metz to Pierre-Louis Roederer, extraordinary-commissioner of the 5th Military District, at Strasbourg along with the request that he forward the communiqué to Victor. Kellermann also included information regarding Marmont's movements as well as the defensive preparations being made in the Moselle Valley by the 1st Young Guard Voltigeur Division and the troops of the 4th Military District. Roederer received Kellermann's dispatch on the morning of the 7th and forwarded the brief to Victor, which Pahlen's Cossacks intercepted that same night. The letter that Roederer composed based on Kellermann's instructions states: "It is not on the hills of Saverne that the duke of Bellune must go, but to Épinal. If he is at Saverne today, order him to march to Nancy. Transmit this dispatch to the marshal and inform him that the 1st Young Guard Division and the troops of the 4th Division will unite between Nancy and Charmes with two batteries and be ready to turn on Épinal if the enemy cavalry in the Vosges is not supported by infantry. Today the duke of Raguse is at Homburg near Zweibrücken and Ricard is at Ottweiler with two divisions."[16]

Sherbatov's Cossacks added to the disruption of French communications by intercepting a letter from Nancy. According to this exaggerated dispatch: "The Young Guard goes to Épinal, Charmes, and Flavigny, and the 6th Cohort to Rambervillers, Raon-l'Étape, and St. Dié. Another cohort and other troops will be sent to the Vosges. An army of around 100,000 men commanded by the duke of Treviso [Mortier] and consisting of five corps of infantry and cavalry as well as all troops who were to go to Mainz to reinforce the corps of the duke of Raguse will be sent to the Meurthe and the Vosges Departments. Provisions must be furnished for 30,000 men on a line from Paris to Colmar."[17] Aside from the obvious misinformation contained in this latter dispatch, the intelligence provided the Allies with exact information over French movements. They could also count on Paris reiterating the instructions to Victor, who would subsequently make an attempt to retake Épinal and close the passes through the Vosges. This news could have been useful to Schwarzenberg, yet Sherbatov did not forward the letter until 13 January.[18]

At Baccarat the steady arrival of reports indicating the Allies had no more than 3,000 to 4,000 men at Épinal and 2,000 men at St. Dié finally moved Victor to take action.[19] On the morning of the 9th, his headquarters issued detailed orders that amounted to an extensive movement along his entire front from the Meurthe to the Moselle with the Lunéville–Rambervillers road forming the central axis of operations. From Charmes, Cassagne's troops of the 4th Military District would support the II Corps. In addition, Meunier's 1st Young Guard Voltigeur Division, echelonned between Nancy and Flavigny, would also participate. At dawn on the 10th Duhesme would advance to St. Dié with the 3rd Division and Piré's 9th Light Cavalry "to attack and drive the enemy from this town. The attack on St. Dié must be brisk and direct. If successful, Duhesme will leave his cavalry and two battalions to observe the pass, and take a position at St. Michel on the Rambervillers–St. Dié road with the rest of his division and artillery." If repulsed, Victor instructed Duhesme to withdraw all his troops to St. Michel or, if necessary, Rambervillers itself. Finally, should superior enemy forces attack Duhesme's advance guard on the road to St. Dié, the entire column would fall back to St. Michel. Victor wanted him to await support and defend St. Michel. If Duhesme could not hold this position, he would conduct a fighting withdrawal to Rambervillers, contesting each step the enemy attempted to make (See Map 13).[20]

As the 3rd Division and the 9th Light Cavalry marched from Raon-l'Étape to St. Dié, Jamin's 1st Division would move west from Baccarat to positions along the Lunéville–Rambervillers road. Victor and the 2nd Division would remain at Baccarat with advance posts on the road to Raon-l'Étape. Complying with Victor's response to Mayor Gérard's request, Grouchy had ordered Briche's 3rd Dragoon Division to Rambervillers where, according to Milhaud, the inhabitants "received the Dragoons with cries of 'Vive l'Empereur, Vive la France'. Such acclamations and cries really dignified the great French nation and electrified our warriors."[21] Victor instructed Grouchy to post Lhéritier's 4th Dragoon Division and the artillery of the V Cavalry Corps in the villages north of Rambervillers.[22] If Duhesme managed to take and hold St. Dié, Victor planned to move the rest of his forces to Épinal.[23]

Regarding Épinal, Victor advised Cassagne and Meunier that Briche's dragoon division would be in Rambervillers on the 9th. To secure his right, he asked Cassagne to establish communication with Briche. In addition, Victor planned to have Meunier's division unite with Cassagne at Charmes in the Moselle Valley and on the road to Épinal. After effecting their union, they would advance to Épinal, where they would encounter an enemy force of approximately 4,000 men according to Victor's estimate. Unfortunately for the marshal, Cossacks intercepted this letter; Victor's planned cooperation between his units and those in the Moselle Valley never materialized.[24]

Finally, Grouchy instructed Ségur and St. Sulpice to move the 3rd and 4th Honor Guard Regiments (1,100 and 450 men respectively) southwest from their position at Sarrebourg to Magnières, ten miles north of Rambervillers in the Mortagne Valley. A post of 200 men commanded by an "intelligent officer" would remain at Sarrebourg for as long as possible to maintain communication with the French garrison at Phalsbourg and to "observe everything."[25] Upon joining the II Corps, the 3rd and 4th Honor Guard Regiments would become part of General Jean-Marie-Antoine Defrance's cavalry division.[26] Transferring the Honor Guard from Sarrebourg to Rambervillers unwisely opened the road to Lunéville and Nancy to Wittgenstein's advance guard.

The afternoon of 9 January brought Victor a mixture of good and bad tidings. In accordance with Grouchy's orders from the 8th, Briche moved the 1,600 men of his 3rd Division to Rambervillers, where 200 Cossacks were ravaging the poor townspeople. As Montélégier's and General Denis-Eloi Ludot's brigades formed outside Rambervillers, the 2nd Dragoon Regiment skirted the town to gain the road to Épinal and sever the enemy's line of retreat. Upon receiving word that the 2nd Regiment reached its position, Montélégier's lead regiment, the 6th Dragoons, thundered into Rambervillers at a gallop. The French troopers completely overwhelmed the startled Russians. Yet the Cossacks mounted their steeds with incredible dexterity and managed to escape, but as soon as they cleared the town, the 2nd Regiment cut through them. "The enemy was chased and pursued with the sword in his back," states Grouchy's after-action report. When the dust cleared, Briche's men collected thirty prisoners; twenty others lay dead. Grouchy nominated his chief of staff, Théodore de Contamine, to receive the Officer of the Legion of Honor decoration for killing a Cossack, and Victor nominated a captain of the 6th Dragoon Regiment for the Cross of the Legion of Honor. Perhaps to somewhat exonerate himself, Victor described Briche's success at Rambervillers with painstaking detail in his 10 January report to Berthier which, as always, was meant for the emperor's consumption.[27]

Briche established his headquarters at Rambervillers, but a subsequent error marred his success. In a rare breakdown not only of initiative but also of procedure, he neglected to dispatch patrols toward Charmes or Épinal. As a result, Briche failed to establish communication with Rousseau's Young Guard battalions and Duvigneau's 300 cavalry of the 4th Military District as they proceeded from Charmes through the Moselle Valley toward Épinal.[28]

At Épinal Sherbatov's patrols informed him of the approach of a fairly large French column coming from Charmes. Desiring more information, the bold Russian commander moved his entire Streifkorps (700 men) up the road toward Charmes. Halfway there he encountered French troops, who easily repulsed his horsemen. The eager French soldiers then launched a stingy pursuit that drove the Russians south through Épinal and Arches to Pouxeux, halfway to Remiremont, where Platov's large Cossack force took in Sherbatov's harried warriors.[29] This success not only achieved one of the objectives Victor planned to attain the next day, it also covered his exposed right wing and minimized the damage caused by his courier's inability to reach Cassagne.

To offset this good news, Victor finally received a copy of Berthier's letter via Kellermann. Although the Cossacks intercepted the original communiqué from Roederer, Kellermann forwarded a written copy from Metz, which reached Victor's headquarters during the afternoon of the 9th. Victor took issue with the emperor's reproaches and accusations, particularly that he had abandoned the Vosges prematurely. In his rebuttal, Victor explained to

Berthier how his retrograde movement through the mountains corresponded precisely with Napoleon's demand that he conserve his line of retreat to Metz. If he had moved to the hills of Saverne, the enemy still would have crossed the Vosges and proceeded down the Moselle to the Meurthe, thus cutting his line of retreat to both Metz and Nancy. To counter imperial criticism, he stated his intention to attack St. Dié and Épinal on the next day. His letter ends with insight into the frustration all the marshals felt regarding Napoleon's failure to communicate his intentions: "It is very important that all the commanding generals are always aware of the general operations. Without this, it is very difficult not to make a mistake."[30] In his own eyes, the marshal had an opportunity to vindicate himself. Fate rarely offers second chances – would fortune smile on the bold?

In part because of Schwarzenberg's politically driven strategy and in part because of the lack of initiative of the field commanders, Army Group Alsace did little on 8 and 9 January. Although Pahlen was aware of the intelligence contained in the intercepted dispatch from Kellermann to Victor, he limited himself to occupying Saverne with Wittgenstein's advance guard.[31] Rather than drive west through Sarrebourg to Lunéville to sever Victor's line of retreat to Nancy and Metz, he probed the fortress of Phalsbourg. Sarrebourg was fifteen miles west of Saverne; from Sarrebourg the Russians would have had to cross another thirty miles to reach Lunéville – not overtaxing distances for Cossacks and light troops.[32] East of Pahlen, Duke Eugene of Württemberg moved the 4th Division to Haguenau. His 3rd Division crossed the Rhine, while the rest of the VI Corps remained idle on the right bank between Kehl and Rastatt.

Wrede, also aware of the information provided by the captured dispatch thanks to a note from Pahlen, was just as culpable as the Russian commanders. As of 7 January, the Bavarian corps commander had completely lost contact with the French.[33] Reconnaissance missions conducted on the 8th toward St. Dié and Raon-l'Étape rectified this situation and helped clarify the details contained in Kellermann's intercepted dispatch. Bavarian patrols ascertained that approximately 3,000 infantry and cavalry under Piré's orders held Raon-l'Étape as Victor's advance guard; the marshal himself quartered at Baccarat with around 12,000 men. Rather than push his divisions across the Vosges, Wrede ordered Deroy's 2nd Brigade to occupy Ste. Marie – twenty-five miles southeast of Raon-l'Étape by way of the mountain roads – as the advance guard of the V Corps. Southeast of Deroy, Rechberg's 1st Division moved to Kaysersberg to observe the Bonhomme Pass, even though French troops had evacuated this region of the Vosges. Behind these forward units, the sieges of Neuf-Brisach, Sélestat, Strasbourg, and Kehl continued.[34]

Thirty miles south of Ste. Marie, Crown Prince Frederick William's IV Corps began crossing the Vosges en route through Lorraine to join Army Group Langres. The Württembergers endured a grueling march on the 8th.

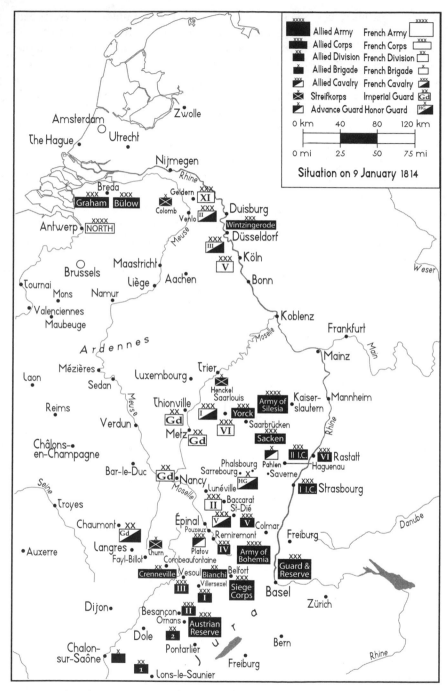

Map 12. Situation on 9 January 1814.

An unexpected change of weather produced a freeze the previous night, thus rendering the steep mountain paths treacherous for artillery and baggage. Frederick William's forward units occupied Remiremont, Stockmayer's advance guard and corps headquarters billeted at le Thillot, and the main body extended between St. Maurice and Bussang. Platov's Cossacks passed the night terrorizing the population of Eloyes, halfway between Remiremont and Épinal. Despite the increasing presence of French troops in the area, Sherbatov remained between Charmes and Épinal.[35]

In an interesting move to preempt Blücher, Schwarzenberg instructed Wittgenstein "to direct toward the southwest, by exiting from Saverne, in order to approach Wrede and to operate in concert with him against Langres. According to plans, when Blücher's army advances, it will be possible for you to move through Saverne with the majority of your corps in order to cover my right flank, link with Wrede, and move on Langres. It is my intention to concentrate the Bohemian Army between Dijon and Langres, and I believe Wrede's right flank cannot stretch much further than Langres. I thus request that you move left from Saverne as much as possible."[36] This directive, which arrived too late on the 9th to affect the operations of that day, did little to stir Wittgenstein, who remained idle on the right bank of the Rhine. He feared conducting a general advance without first gaining the keys of Phalsbourg as well as the dilapidated forts of la Petite-Pierre and Lichtenberg.[37] While Eugene moved his two divisions slightly west to Hochfelden and Haguenau respectively, Wittgenstein's headquarters remained anchored at Rastatt. On the 10th, five Badenese battalions with ten guns arrived to contend with Phalsbourg and la Petite-Pierre. The extent of the VI's Corps operations on this day amounted to blockading Landau and severing the lone duct that delivered fresh water to Phalsbourg. To give the appearance of doing something to support Wrede, Wittgenstein finally ordered Pahlen to move the advance guard to Lunéville.[38] Eugene's advance was intended to support Pahlen, but the distance his infantry had to cover reveals the superficial nature of this gesture. Incidentally, Pahlen's patrols reestablished communication with Sacken's left wing north of Phalsbourg.[39]

Allied headquarters also issued orders for Wrede to move west to Remiremont on the 9th and from there to Langres.[40] With the 2nd Division besieging the Alsatian fortresses, Deroy's 2nd Brigade led Delamotte's 3rd Division into the Vosges on the 9th, reaching Ste. Marie and pushing an advance guard to Ste. Marguerite, just east of St. Dié. Bavarian patrols proceeded as far west as Bruyères, fifteen miles east of Épinal, where they linked with Seslavin's detachment of Cossacks and hussars from Wittgenstein's corps. The effectives that Wrede had to leave behind in Alsace increased to include the garrison of Colmar. In all, eleven battalions and one company, eight squadrons, and three batteries remained in Alsace so that Wrede barely commanded 25,000 men. The Bavarian general became incensed over the reduction of his corps by one-third of its original strength.[41] He expressed his discontent to Schwarzenberg in offensive terms. The Allied commander in chief attempted to avoid open conflict by responding with a very tactful letter on the 13th.[42] Nevertheless, the corps commander's cheek offended the Austrian, as can be seen in his letter to Wrede on 15 January: "It remains not a slight difficulty for me to unite all the various views and interests, which are the unavoidable companions of any allied army."[43] Schwarzenberg had reason to be irritated with Wrede. In his reports to the Allied commander in chief, the corps commander never used the phrase "your obedient servant." Instead, he saw himself as Schwarzenberg's equal, and at most he added the empty phrase: "I have the honor to report."[44] Wrede would have gladly freed himself from Schwarzenberg's command to cooperate with Blücher. However, like so many of the individuals involved in this conflict, his demands to advance proved louder than his actions. No explanation other than concern over supply account for his sluggish movement across the Vosges.[45]

The IV Corps passed the day of the 9th trudging up the Moselle Valley deep in the Vosges. A small advance guard reached Remiremont, but Frederick William echelonned his main body in the mountains west of the Bussang Pass.[46] As noted, Platov reached Pouxeux, in front of the IV Corps. After taking in Sherbatov's battered Streifkorps, the unpredictable Platov hatched a scheme for Army Group Vosges to retake Épinal. According to Sherbatov, four strong columns of infantry supported by five squadrons and three guns had taken the town. Although the Ataman could not reconnoiter the enemy force, he planned to attack Épinal at 7:00 A.M. on the 10th as long as the crown prince of Württemberg supported him with three or four battalions.[47] Frederick William declined, reasoning that it would be better to wait until his entire corps could move up before attacking. Nevertheless, he encouraged the Russian to execute his operation on the 10th: "Indeed, I believe it is very important to drive the enemy from Épinal, and so if you do not succeed in your enterprise, I will attack on the 11th with all of my corps." In the meantime, the crown prince promised to position three battalions on the Pouxeux–Remiremont road for Platov "to fall back on if necessary."[48]

Frederick William feared the French force at Épinal formed the advance guard of a considerable enemy army charged with defending Lorraine and preventing the Allies from exiting the Vosges. For this reason, he preferred to wait twenty-four hours to concentrate his corps for a drive on Épinal. Unlike Schwarzenberg, Radetzky, Wrede, and Wittgenstein – the best that the Bohemian Army had to offer – Frederick William refused to take his turn on the alter of caution, pessimism, insecurity, and inaction. Although Schwarzenberg directed the IV Corps to advance as quickly as possible from Remiremont to Fayl-Billot to unite with Army Group Langres, the Württemberger did not hesitate to take the initiative and deviate from his mission to attack the French at Épinal.

In his report to Schwarzenberg on the evening of the 9th, the crown prince described the appearance of a French "corps" at Épinal that repulsed Sherbatov. French control of Épinal jeopardized his own communications both rearward and with Wrede to his right, and thus its capture was necessary for the IV to continue to Fayl-Billot. Despite his orders, Frederick William informed Schwarzenberg that if the French forced Platov from Pouxeux, he would march straight to Épinal on the 11th rather than lead the IV Corps toward Fayl-Billot. He justified his potential insubordination by stating that from Épinal, "the enemy can sever our communications with Remiremont and prevent Schaffer's brigade and the troops that are following from debouching." Frederick William hoped the French would considerably overestimate the size of his corps or perhaps even view it as the advance guard of a large army. By boldly striking, he counted on inducing the French to withdraw or at least halt their advance.[49] Initiative was a main tenet of Napoleon's system of warfare; few of his own lieutenants remembered this fundamental principle – would the youngest corps commander of either side employ it to effect the first significant Allied push into southern Lorraine?

According to Lefebvre de Béhaine, the circumstances "eminently" favored the French at this time: "Rousseau's and Duvigneau's troops were full of confidence; those of the II Infantry and V Cavalry Corps had completely shed the physical and moral depression caused by the evacuation of Alsace; their attitude during the days of the 9th, 10th, and 11th was energetic."[50] At dawn on the 10th Duhesme left Raon-l'Étape with the seven battalions (3,000 men) of his division and Piré's eight squadrons (1,000 men). Around the same time, Deroy's small advance guard of one infantry company, a half-squadron of light cavalry, and thirty Cossacks continued west from Ste. Marguerite and passed through St. Dié around 11:00 A.M. At noon, the French encountered the Bavarian vanguard. Piré's cavalry wasted no time pouncing on what appeared to be an isolated Allied patrol. The Bavarians and Cossacks fled as best they could in the direction of Ste. Marguerite. While Piré's cavalry and the two lead battalions pursued the enemy detachment, Duhesme moved the remaining five battalions and artillery into St. Dié. He instructed Piré to occupy Ste. Marguerite and close the roads coming from Ste. Marie and Saales. Encountering nothing but the brisk mountain air, Piré led his squadrons to Ste. Marguerite. Just after he entered the village, the cavalry commander observed "several fairly considerable columns, almost all infantry," approaching on the road from Ste. Marie. At the village of Coinches, less than two miles away, the enemy deployed for battle. It was Deroy marching west to secure the road through the Vosges to St. Dié with his main body of five battalions, two squadrons, and four guns. The Bavarians likewise spotted the French moving toward Ste. Marguerite. Deroy advanced to within a short distance of Ste. Marguerite and took measures to prevent the French from debouching. He wanted to capture the village before the French entrenched themselves and

Map 13. The region between the Meurthe and the Moselle.

any reinforcements arrived. The two support battalions had yet to catch up, and thus Piré realized his troopers could not hold the village against a "very superior force" of infantry. With no other option, he attempted to withdraw from Ste. Marguerite, but the Bavarians entered before his squadrons could clear the bridge over the Meurthe. After Deroy received a mortal wound in the ensuing melee, Col. Treuberg, the commander of the Bavarian 9th Line, assumed command and stormed the village. Shells from the Bavarian artillery prevented Piré's men from destroying the bridge and allowed Treuberg to pursue.

On the other side of the Meurthe, Piré reorganized his squadrons and kept the Bavarians at bay. "My cavalry took a position in the plain, while the infantry withdrew along the road," states Piré's after-action report, "the enemy was forced to make dispositions for the attack; he placed three guns at the head of the village [Ste. Marguerite], with which he fired grape and ball at me, but did not prevent me from executing my retreat with extreme slowness and in a manner that I wanted." One battalion and several guns issued from St. Dié to support Piré's column. Continuing his pursuit, Treuberg soon reached St. Dié. As Duhesme observed the increasing number of Bavarians – 5,000 to 6,000 infantry according to Piré's estimate – he concluded that St. Dié could not be held. Fortunately for him, Treuberg waited one full hour until his entire column arrived before attacking the French rearguard just east of St. Dié.

"I have the biggest commendation to make of the cavalry under my orders; it maneuvered with calm and sang-froid under the balls, bullets, and grape," wrote Piré. "I remained for one hour under the fire of the enemy artillery, which was placed at half-range and which was supported by the masses upon which I hardly dared to execute a charge, given the nature of the terrain." This one-hour interval allowed Duhesme to form a rearguard and evacuate his troops. The French rearguard met the Bavarians east of St. Dié and conducted a fighting withdrawal into the village, where a bitter street fight ensued between the former allies. Covered by this rearguard, Duhesme withdrew to St. Michel at the junction of the roads to Raon-l'Étape and Rambervillers.

"The countenance of the enemy force," continues Piré, "that marched on St. Dié and which I encountered leads me to believe that it is part of a considerable corps . . . the inhabitants have assured me that 500 Cossacks are at Corcieux and Bruyères." From Bruyères the Cossacks could move north along paths through the Rambervillers Forest and debouch on the St. Michel–Rambervillers road to sever Duhesme's communications with Victor. For these reasons, Duhesme did not believe he could hold the important junction at St. Michel. To comply with the marshal's orders, he intended to continue the retreat west to Rambervillers at 3:00 A.M. on the 11th. According to Victor's instructions of the previous day, Duhesme was to echelon his troops in the direction of Rambervillers and withdraw on this village. Moreover, Victor informed him at 3:00 on the afternoon of the 10th that the headquarters of the II Corps would be at Rambervillers on the morning of the 11th.[51]

West of Duhesme's infantry, Piré withdrew toward Rambervillers to link with the dragoon divisions of the V Cavalry Corps. He reached Nompatelize, where he composed his after-action report to Grouchy at 6:00 that evening. Treuberg, who received the Max-Joseph Military Order for his actions at St. Dié, broke off the pursuit but dispatched patrols on side roads to Lunéville, Rambervillers, and Raon-l'Étape. East of Trueberg, General Georg von Habermann's 1st Brigade moved into Ste. Marie; its advance guard of two battalions, two squadrons, and four guns reinforced Treuberg at St. Dié. The

Bavarians sustained ninety-two casualties; French losses amounted to 100 killed and wounded as well as 224 prisoners.[52]

Elsewhere on Victor's front, Milhaud's dragoon divisions conducted three strong reconnaissance missions from Rambervillers. At 3:00 P.M. on the 10th, Milhaud notified Grouchy of his findings: the news was not good.[53] Grouchy summarized Milhaud's report in a brief to Victor that smacked of resignation. His account of the operations on the 10th, written on the 11th to Berthier and thus meant for the emperor's eyes, likewise paints a hopeless picture: "The Allies have imposing cavalry forces at Bruyères and it is likely they will debouch in force on both Épinal and St. Dié."[54] A cavalry force of 1,000 Bavarians, Württembergers, and Cossacks held Bruyères, east of the Épinal–Rambervillers road. For this reason, none of Milhaud's three detachments could press beyond Grandvillers; one had not even returned by the time Grouchy composed his report. The Cossacks controlled the roads from Épinal to Rambervillers. "Cassagne occupied Épinal yesterday," wrote Grouchy to Victor, "but probably will be attacked there shortly. In this state of affairs, I beg you to come here [Rambervillers] early tomorrow, for Duhesme probably will be pursued and the day probably will not pass quietly."[55] Grouchy also informed Cassagne of the combat at St. Dié and Duhesme's retreat. Advising Cassagne that direct communication between Épinal and Rambervillers was cut, he encouraged the commandant to prepare for the inevitable Allied attack on Épinal. To prevent his letter from being intercepted, Grouchy directed the courier to cross the Moselle and proceed up the left bank to Épinal.[56]

From Baccarat Victor wrote Berthier at 5:00 in the evening. The last report he received from Duhesme delivered the news that the Bavarians had been ejected from St. Dié. Not yet knowing of Duhesme's setback, he reported the enemy had been driven from St. Dié to the hills of Ste. Marie, where he would undoubtedly regroup during the night. Careful to demonstrate his initiative, Victor informed Berthier he would move his headquarters to Rambervillers "to better direct the movements of the troops." He added that "the enemy spreads the rumor that their army is incessantly debouching on Épinal and St. Dié. I do not know if one can believe this news, but if it is true, it will be necessary to unite large forces on the Moselle, supposing those that are currently there are insufficient to maintain themselves." For this reason, he once again inquired over the status of the 2nd and 4th Battalions of his regiments.[57]

Just south of this action, Army Group Vosges provided a veritable wild-card for Allied operations in southern Lorraine. Should it succeed in taking Épinal on the 11th, the crown prince of Württemberg expected to find large French forces concentrated on the plains of Lorraine; French propaganda and Napoleon's campaign of misinformation worked diligently to spread such rumors. With less than 14,000 troops, Frederick William would need support if this proved true. Conversely, the crown prince planned to gamble and make his opponent fold by bluffing: an aggressive drive on Épinal surely would signal the approach of an Allied army. Further upping the ante, Sherbatov's patrols on the 10th discovered the French held a strong positions from Charmes through Rambervillers to Raon-l'Étape. Sherbatov also provided the information contained in the intercepted dispatch from Victor to Cassagne.[58] This meant that although Army Group Vosges outnumbered the French force at Épinal, Victor's II Infantry and V Cavalry Corps was massed at Rambervillers, only fifteen miles northeast of Épinal. The Russian Cossacks could not be counted on to confront French infantry, not to mention Milhaud's dragoons. Would Wrede continue his march through the Vosges to support the IV Corps? Who would be the first to yield in this game of nerves?

On the 10th, Frederick William concentrated his main body in and around Remiremont, with two detachments at Docelles and Xertigny, northeast and southwest of Pouxeux, respectively, to support Platov's Cossacks. For his part, Platov did not attack Épinal. Instead, he met with the crown prince to plan a concerted operation against the French position on the next day. The road from Remiremont to Epinal ran through the narrow Moselle Valley, which widened slightly in the vicinity of Épinal. On either side, steeply wooded hills blanketed the valley. Épinal itself stood on both sides of the river and, fortunately for the Allies, was not fortified. The nature of the terrain allowed for the separation of the army group into several columns that could converge on the enemy. After discussions with Platov, the crown prince decided on an extensive operation that called for a frontal assault as well as a double envelopment. According to his disposition, the Cossacks would proceed through the forest and envelop Épinal on both banks of the Moselle to sever the French line of retreat. Frederick William planned to divide his corps into three columns that would advance on Épinal at 8:00 A.M.[59]

After a hard frost, Franquemont assembled the main column of the IV Corps at Eloyes early on the 11th and, joined by Frederick William, commenced the march through the Moselle Valley. Franquemont's advance guard consisted of one jäger battalion, one squadron, and four guns of the 1st Horse Battery; his main body was composed the 2nd, 3rd, and 4th Infantry Regiments, the 2nd Battalion of the 6th Infantry Regiment, the 1st and 2nd Foot Batteries, and two squadrons. The munition wagons as well as the wagons that would be used to evacuate the wounded followed directly behind the main body. The rest of the baggage moved to Plombières, southwest of Remiremont, followed by the Austrian heavy battery escorted by one battalion. At the same time, General Peter Mateyevich Grekov VIII led two Cossack Regiments from Pouxeux around Épinal to Thaon, five miles to the north on the road to Charmes, which he occupied without being observed. Upon reaching Pouxeux, Franquemont detached the 2nd Infantry Regiment under General Christoph Friedrich David von Döring to the right bank of the Moselle with instructions to continue advancing close to the river through the village of

Archettes. Further up the road, the head of Franquemont's column reached
Arches, at which time Platov's main body commenced the turning movement to reach Thaon. Platov's task was to sever completely the French line of
retreat through a double envelopment. Because the road that ran east of Épinal
through Fontenay appeared poor, Platov abandoned the idea of enveloping the
French from the right and turned his entire force east to proceed through
the suburb of les Forges. "Ataman Count Platov thought obliged to extend
to the left [west] with his artillery and his cavalry and proceeded toward
Thaon, because the road to Charmes is better for the cavalry than the road
to Rambervillers," wrote Frederick William in his after-action report. The
tardy start and the additional time wasted by Platov's overextension to the
east combined with bad roads, marshy terrain, and the thick wood around les
Forges to ruin Frederick William's plans. "Platov," describes Weil, "one day
ambitious, the next day timid . . . gave the first proof of the insurmountable
malaise that he would show for the rest of the campaign, of the imaginary fear
that continuously paralyzed his operations and which hindered his Cossacks
from doing anything worthwhile up until the moment when the tsar, tired of
his faintheartedness that was made worse by the imprudence of his boasting,
relieved Platov of his command." According to Weil, had Platov merely succeeded in getting the light artillery of General Paisii Sergeyevich Kaisarov's
advance guard to Thaon, "Rousseau's column, taken between two fires, would
have been forced to lay down its arms."[60]

Franquemont's column continued to advance along the valley road. Just
south of Épinal, the Württembergers clashed with a strong French infantry
picket covered by a redoubt, whose brave resistance caused some delay. After
clearing this obstacle, Franquemont's troops skirmished with French infantry
posted in the gardens and thickets on the south side of Épinal. Rousseau's
Young Guard offered fierce yet brief resistance: the situation had become
hopeless in just a matter of minutes. General Karl August Maximillian von
Jett's left flank column – one battalion, five squadrons, and six guns – marched
due north from Xertigny straight to Épinal; Prince Adam of Württemberg
followed from Plombières with one cavalry regiment and four horse guns.
Crossing through St. Laurent, the head of Jett's column encountered a French
cavalry post near the junction of the roads leading from Xertigny and Pouxeux
to Épinal; the French did not oppose his march and withdrew to Épinal.
Observing Franquemont's main column engage the Young Guard, Jett moved
his infantry west to flank Épinal and enter the town from the north by way
of the road from Charmes. Franquemont detached the last battalion of his
column to support this movement. Meanwhile, the 7th Infantry Regiment
and one jäger battalion of Stockmayer's right flank column proceeded from
Docelles through la Baffe and the Épinal Forest to a concealed position facing
Épinal from the east with instructions to await Franquemont's attack. Several
Cossack detachments covered the right flank by taking position on the road

to Rambervillers. After seeing Döring's detachment attack a French post on the right bank of the Moselle not far from Épinal, Stockmayer gave the signal for his troops to advance. As Stockmayer moved west, Döring pursued the French into Épinal.

Rousseau commanded 4,000 men (two Imperial Guard regiments and infantry units of the 4th Military District), 600 cavalry, and four guns. Considering the élan of the Young Guard, his situation was not hopeless: the Württemberger soldiers were just as raw as the French when it came to combat experience, and the Cossacks would not challenge the bearskins in a street fight. Rousseau probably did not know or care that Frederick William commanded relatively green troops. Instead, appearances mattered. At the moment, superior enemy forces appeared to be approaching – probably a large Allied corps. To save his troops, he abandoned all thoughts of resistance and ordered an immediate retreat. Rousseau evacuated Épinal with such speed that by the time Franquemont positioned his artillery, the French had withdrawn from the gardens and moved out of range. He ordered his infantry and cavalry to drive into the town with all possible speed, but Rousseau's men escaped. Under these circumstances neither flank column contributed much to the combat. "The enemy did not await our attack on Épinal and agilely retreated on the road to Charmes," states Frederick William's report.

Rousseau's infantry retreated north toward Charmes in two groups: some through the Moselle Valley, others along the uneven terrain west of the river. Expecting Platov to bar the road and attack Rousseau's flanks, Frederick William halted at Épinal to regroup. After uniting his columns, he decided to leave two squadrons with his tired infantry at Épinal and pursue the French with ten squadrons and one horse battery. While making these arrangements, a would-be assassin fired on the prince at close range from a nearby house. Prefect Himbert de Flegny of the Vosges Department had summoned the inhabitants to arms three days earlier (Appendix I). Although the ball missed its target, the attempt infuriated the Allies, whose cavalry captured the prefect during the French retreat. The Cossacks forced the hapless official to strip naked and then looted his possessions.

Rousseau took a position on the hills north of Épinal but could not hold his ground for long. After learning that Cossacks held Thaon behind him, Rousseau continued his retreat. Grekov exited Thaon as soon as the head of the French column came into view. With great determination, his warriors charged the French cavalry, overwhelmed the enemy troopers and forced them to take shelter behind Rousseau's infantry after losing six officers and eighty men as prisoners and an undeterminable number of killed and wounded. With equal determination, the French infantry ploughed forward, forcing Grekov to evacuate Thaon and yield the road to the bearskins. Platov's delays and the rapid retreat of the French meant that the main body of his Cossack corps with its battery of heavy artillery could not reach Thaon before the

French infantry. Yet the Russian horsemen did have their way with the cavalry of the 4th Military District, attacking its flank and routing the unfortunate French troopers. From Thaon northward, the French infantry also suffered considerable losses from the fire of the Württemberger artillery, finally joined by the light artillery of Kaisarov's advance guard, which belatedly cleared the forest belt west of Épinal. Together, the Allied batteries hounded Rousseau's battalions with case shot until nightfall. Dead and wounded French soldiers littered the road along with arms and baggage jettisoned during the retreat.

Rousseau, who had two mounts shot out from under him and received the fifth wound of his career by way of a musket ball to the shoulder, withdrew to Charmes, before continuing the retreat to Flavigny on the 12th to join the Imperial Guard. That day Meunier posted the 1st and 2nd Voltigeur Regiments along with six companies of the 3rd Regiment in Flavigny on the Épinal–Nancy road to defend the bridge over the Moselle. The other two companies of the 3rd and the entire 4th Regiment remained at Nancy.[61]

While the Cossacks followed to Charmes, the crown prince halted his cavalry and artillery at Igney, two miles north of Thaon. To pass the night in security, the IV Corps reassembled at Épinal. Two strong advance detachments took posts north of Épinal on either side of the Moselle to guard the roads coming from Bruyères and Rambervillers on the right bank, and from Charmes on the left. The Württembergers maintained that their losses in the combat of Épinal amounted to ten soldiers. On the other hand, both they and the Russians claimed to have inflicted considerable casualties; dead and wounded Frenchmen along with muskets and haversacks purportedly covered the road from Thaon to Igney. In addition to a large quantity of weapons, more than 500 prisoners purportedly fell into Allied hands. "We pursued the enemy up to Charmes," wrote Sherbatov in his after-action report. "Nightfall protected his retreat and he halted in this village. The enemy lost many dead and even more prisoners. The number that retreated to Charmes cannot be more than 1,000. Among the prisoners taken today are commanders of the cuirassier, dragoons, hussars, and gendarmes. All of this cavalry has been reduced. The best prize is the prefect of the Vosges, M. Flegny, Baron of the Empire, a man not only detested by the inhabitants of Épinal, but by those of the entire region. It was he who attempted to stir and arm them. When I was at Épinal, one spoke much ill of him." Platov claimed twenty-five of his own as dead and wounded in addition to forty-two horses.[62]

Throughout the 12th, Frederick William expected to be attacked by Victor and hoped to receive support from Wrede. "If Wrede undertakes something against his flank, Victor will be very sorry," wrote the crown prince.[63] Victor did not attack and the IV Corps resumed its march to Langres on the 13th, thus dissolving Army Group Vosges. The young crown prince executed a bold and successful independent operation that secured the flank and rear of his corps for the march to Langres. Strategically, the combat of Épinal had a

profound effect on Marshal Victor. His reaction combined with Marmont's
retreat accelerated the fall of Lorraine. The Vosges were forced in every direction, and the army groups on Schwarzenberg's right wing occupied all of new
France.

Elsewhere on the Allied right wing, 11 January proved to be a trying day
for the V Corps. On the night of the 10th, Wrede, who remained at Colmar,
received a message from Seslavin regarding Sherbatov's defeat at Épinal and
the presence of French cavalry in Rambervillers on 9 January. The Russian
also included the intercepted dispatch from Victor to Cassagne, which outlined the former's plans to attack Coalition forces at St. Dié. Seslavin added
the discouraging news that a French army reached Nancy and would be supported by 40,000 men from Metz.[64] Wrede knew the Württembergers would
assault Épinal on the 11th. Seslavin's report now informed him of Victor's
intentions. Despite possessing this incredible information, the Bavarian commander continued to hesitate and hold back his troops. He did not alter his
disposition for the 11th, which his headquarters issued on the 9th, either to
support the IV Corps or to confirm Seslavin's report. Perhaps concern over
the French army rumored to be at Nancy recalled chilling memories of his
brush with death just a few months earlier at Hanau. The orders his headquarters issued for the 10th and 11th suggest Wrede feared the consequences
of having his dispersed columns debouch from the Vosges at different times.
Instead, he wanted the divisions of the V Corps to descend from the mountains simultaneously. According to his instructions, the entire V Corps would
begin a general advance to Rambervillers and Bruyères on the 13th.

On the 11th Deroy's brigade resumed the pursuit of Duhesme on the
road to Rambervillers but proceeded only to Nompatelize. Habermann's 1st
Brigade marched thirteen miles from Ste. Marie to St. Dié and forwarded
a detachment to Bruyères. En route to Ste. Marie, Frimont's division was
expected to clear the Vosges on the 13th; the same day Wrede designated for
Rechberg's Bavarian 1st Division to cross the Vosges. Poor weather hampered Wrede's units in the Vosges, where the Bavarians lost several wagons
and guns in the snow-covered ravines. Supplying ammunition and provisions
became troublesome; the men had to tighten their belts because the French had
exhausted the region around St. Dié.[65] As for the rest of Army Group Alsace, a
detachment from Scheibler's Streifkorps reached Raon-l'Étape; Wittgenstein's
VI Corps did not move on the 11th.

In the center of the army, Schwarzenberg had tasked the I and III Corps
of Army Group Langres with clearing Vesoul and reaching the bridge over
the Saône River at Port-sur-Saône southeast of Langres by the 10th. Far in
front of the army group, Thurn's Streifkorps pounded the road to Langres.
On the evening of the 8th, Thurn encountered a small French post at Cintrey,
three-quarters of the way to Langres on the highway from Vesoul. After
dispersing the French post, he pursued through Fayl-Billot toward Langres

before returning to Cintrey.[66] Southeast of Thurn, Crenneville's light division, which formed the advance guard of Gyulay's III Corps, reached Port-sur-Saône and pushed its forward units to Combeaufontaine. The main body of the III Corps passed the night in and around Vesoul. One Austrian squadron continued thirty miles southwest to the bridge over the Saône at Gray to sever communication between Langres and Besançon. Colloredo's I Corps remained on the road to Vesoul. While waiting to be relieved by the Russian Reserve, Bianchi bombarded Belfort. Of the Russians, Rayevsky led his 2nd Grenadier Division as well as the 2nd and 3rd Cuirassier Divisions to Altkirch, less than twenty miles east of Belfort.[67]

Gyulay's 8 January report to Schwarzenberg contained valuable news regarding the progress of the French *levée-en-masse* in the departments that the center and left wing of the Bohemian Army either occupied or would soon invade. Extraordinary-Commissioner to the 18th Military District and father of General Ségur of the Honor Guard, Senator Louis-Philippe Ségur, arrived at Dijon, the capital of Bourgogne, to organize the *levée-en-masse*. The inhabitants ignored him, and Dijon's mayor renounced all resistance, declaring that a levée in Bourgogne was impossible because of the lack of arms and shortage of men fit to serve. Ségur returned to Paris. Guylay also included news that probably brought great relief to Austrian headquarters: General Jean-Baptiste Valence likewise failed to organize the *levée-en-masse* in the Jura, Haute-Saône, and Doubs Departments. According to Guylay's informant, the wife of the receveur-général of the Haute-Saône Department, much unrest reigned in Paris. He also notified Schwarzenberg that the French posts in Gray, Dijon, and Langres had received orders to withdraw to Troyes as soon as the Allies approached. The Austrian corps commander added that Napoleon planned to concentrate a large number of troops at Troyes. Moreover, spies informed him that despite its large magazines, only poorly armed conscripts defended Auxonne.[68] All of the news Guylay provided helped to convince Schwarzenberg gradually that an operation against Langres and Dijon would not encounter significant French resistance.

On the 9th Gyulay rested his III Corps at Vesoul, while Colloredo's I Corps likewise remained idle at Villersexel. Finally relieved at Belfort by Rayevsky's Russians, Bianchi led two of his brigades toward Lure on the highway that ran through Vesoul to Langres.[69] In front of Army Group Langres, Thurn's Streifkorps brazenly advanced. Thinking Langres would fall just as easily as Vesoul, Thurn planned to take the town to ascertain the position and size of the French forces supposedly assembling in the region. Convinced he could capture Langres without firing a shot, Thurn led his advance guard of Austrian hussars into the suburb of Anges on the western side of the town. "The inhabitants invited us to enter; we were told they had been impatiently waiting a long time for us," states Thurn's after-action report. At dawn he sent a negotiator accompanied by a small escort of hussars to

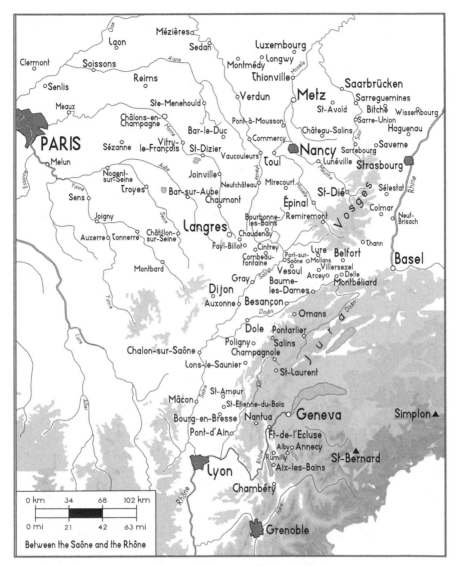

Map 14. The region between the Saône and the Rhône.

the "Dijon" gate with a request to confer with the mayor of Langres. The National Guard, which had assembled the day before after news arrived that the enemy reached Fayl-Billot, opened fire and drove off the Allied negotiator. At 5:00 P.M., Thurn sent an officer escorted by two hussars to Langres with a demand for the mayor and commandant to surrender the town. Once again the National Guard opened fire, killing one of the hussars and sending Thurn's officer back to Anges. Thurn then ordered his advance guard to enter Langres. Passing through the gates, it was met by the Imperial Guard: Mortier's vanguard had arrived. "The patrol at the head [of the column] had just passed some houses," reports Thurn, "when it was greeted by a general volley, by shots from the rooftops, and by the recruits of the levée and the Civic Guard supported by Line infantry."

Thurn immediately retreated. Attempting to return to Fayl-Billot, the Austrian hussars had to pass through the village of Chaudenay. Taking up arms, the villagers waylaid the Allied troopers, killing one officer and twelve men. "We had to clear a passage with the saber. We made the peasants suffer for their lack of judgment." Thurn regrouped at Fayl-Billot after one-quarter of his hussars sustained wounds. According to the statements of prisoners, the French planned to move in force against Fayl-Billot on the following day. Shaken by the events at Langres and Chaudenay, Thurn withdrew from Fayl-Billot and toward Crenneville's division at Combeaufontaine on the 10th.

On the Bohemian Army's left, Army Group Franche-Comté did even less than Army Group Langres on the 8th and 9th. The II Corps invested Besançon on the left bank of the Doubs, and the Austrian Reserve reached Ornans, ten miles southeast of Besançon. Bubna, who still had not received his new orders to turn north, continued through the southern region of Franche-Comté on the road to Lyon. On 8 January, his main body reached Lons-le-Saunier, while a flank guard of four squadrons, one battalion, and one horse battery marched toward Chalon-sur-Saône. These movements continued on the 9th and 10th. With his advance guard approaching Bourg-en-Bresse, Bubna's main body arrived at St. Amour, less than twenty miles north of Bourg.

On the 10th, eighty retired soldiers from Bourg took up arms to defend their town. With several gendarmes and an assortment of troops including 400 naval gunners sent from Lyon by Musnier, they surprised Bubna's forward post of 150 hussars at St. Etienne-du-Bois. The French troops drove the Austrians from St. Etienne into an ambush prepared by the pensioners north of the village. Many Austrians fell from their saddles killed or wounded; the French captured six of Bubna's troopers. East of Bourg, another surprise attack on an Austrian detachment near Nantua gained the French an additional eighteen prisoners to interrogate.

Bubna received Schwarzenberg's 7 January order to retrace his steps, but for several reasons decided to continue his movement as far as Bourg, *chef-lieu* of the Ain Department. By taking the departmental capital, he hoped to quell the growing insurrection and obstruct recruitment, both of which were supported by French troops in the region. From Bourg he also intended to support Zechmeister, whose reports from 4 and 5 January indicated a steady increase of French forces in the Mont-Blanc Department. Finally, possession of Bourg would allow Bubna access to the highway that ran along the Saône south to Lyon and north through Mâcon, Chalon-sur-Saône to Dijon and ultimately Langres. This route would allow his division greater mobility as opposed to the poor country roads that ran between Bourg, Dole, and Dijon.

On 10 January, Schwarzenberg traveled from his headquarters at Viller-sexel to reconnoiter Besançon. Convinced the fortress could be taken only through a formal siege, he instructed Alois von Liechtenstein to block-ade Besançon with his II Corps reinforced by one grenadier brigade and one cuirassier regiment from the Austrian Reserve. Schwarzenberg also released Prince Friedrich of Hesse-Homburg from the monotony of siege duty. He directed the prince to move Scheither's brigade, one brigade from Weissenwolf's division, and two cavalry divisions through Dole to Dijon, where he should arrive between the 15th and 16th. There he would be joined by Wimpffen's 2nd Division of Coloredo's I Corps coming from Gray. Now attached to Hesse-Homburg's command, Scheither's brigade of the 1st Light Division was replaced in Bubna's order of battle by the 2nd Brigade, 1st Division of Alois von Liechtenstein's II Corps.[70]

On the same day, Schwarzenberg received a letter from Metternich advising him to slow the advance and avoid "warlike acts," the Allied commander made the decision to direct Hesse-Homburg's formidable detachment southwest to Dijon. Such a movement needlessly and dangerously weakened Schwarzenberg's center and exposed it to a disaster if Mortier managed to assemble a large force at Langres. Although the reasons are unclear, by this time Schwarzenberg no longer believed Napoleon planned to concentrate his army at Langres. Of course this belief did not stop him from summoning the IV and V Corps to march to Langres rather than support the operations of the Silesian Army.

Each day Schwarzenberg's headquarters received at least two dozen reports over the progress of subordinates as well as the latest intelligence. The briefs that reached Schwarzenberg between 11 and 13 January offer an opportunity to evaluate the commander in chief's reactions to the fluid situation that he confronted. In a 9 January letter that Schwarzenberg received early on the 11th, Thurn submitted his after-action report describing his failed attempt to take Langres that same day. "I have taken several prisoners belonging to Italian regiments, who have confirmed that tomorrow, the 10th, Marshal Mortier will have 30,000 men at Langres and that other troops will arrive at Gray."[71] Moreover, on 10 January, Wrede forwarded to Schwarzenberg a 9 January dispatch from the Cossack commander Seslavin. "According to repeated reports," wrote the Russian, "an enemy army has rallied at Nancy and a corps of 40,000 men has concentrated at Metz."[72] On the 12th, Platov submitted his report regarding the pursuit of the French after the combat of Épinal: "The debris of the enemy infantry joined a small number of troops they found at Charmes and they were pursued today at 7:00 A.M. from Charmes by three Cossack regiments under the orders of Grekov, who will follow the road to Nancy until the enemy is completely destroyed or as long as circumstances allow, but not approach Nancy since, according to intelligence, a large enemy force is there under the orders of Marshal Ney."[73] Aside from Nancy, a new threat appeared to be forming 150 miles south of Langres at Lyon. Since 4 January, Bubna had been receiving disturbing reports concerning the arrival of French reinforcements from Suchet's army in Spain.[74]

In the midst of evaluating these reports, Schwarzenberg received Blücher's letter of 8 January on the 11th. According to the Prussian field marshal, after driving Marmont from the Saar, the Silesian Army would reach Metz on the 15th. Blücher informed the generalissimo of his requests to Wrede and Wittgenstein for support in a joint operation, which Schwarzenberg already was working to prevent.[75]

In view of this vast array of diverse information, the commander in chief and his staff had to decipher fact from fiction, the likely from the unlikely, and the possible from the impossible. Metternich did what he could to help Schwarzenberg and of course influence his decisions. "I do not know if you have received the latest news from Blücher," asks Metternich. "He wrote from Trier that he will move on Metz, claiming that he will be at Metz on the 15th. I believe this is much easier to say than to do."[76]

Doubting the most recent intelligence provided by Thurn, Schwarzenberg informed Kaiser Francis on the 11th that Mortier could not have 30,000 men at Langres. Instead, he accepted as fact Thurn's 8 January report that Napoleon was concentrating his conscripts sixty-five miles northwest of Langres at Troyes.[77] "The enemy has nothing at Langres," explains Schwarzenberg to Guylay on the 11th. "March to reach this town by the morning of the 13th."[78] Allied headquarters issued similar instructions to the I and IV Corps.

On 11 January, Schwarzenberg wrote an interesting reply to Metternich's note of 8 January." You wrote in your letter: 'Go, but prudently'. I will tell you that crossing the Rhine itself violated all rules of prudence, but it was dictated by the circumstances. This operation only can be conducted with the greatest energy; this must take the place of prudence. We must have the mountains to our backs and live in the fertile valley of the Saône; indeed this position is extended, but there is no other." It is curious to view Schwarzenberg employ the correct phrases regarding the needs of modern warfare. As opposed to the dramatic wording he employed in the letters to his wife, in this letter the Austrian general addresses his confidant and spiritual master, who had instructed him to proceed with caution, thus slowly. Without doubt, Schwarzenberg's letters to Metternich would be free of exaggerations. Thus, he must have truly believed his army was advancing "with the greatest energy." "Once my columns have arrived on these two points [Langres and Dijon], I must wait for some positive news on the direction of Blücher." Revealing his new and growing fear of the concentration of a French army at Lyon, Schwarzenberg adds: "If he [Blücher] believes he can go to Nancy or Verdun, my right will be consolidated to such an extent that I can issue forth with the grand mass of my left, in the supposition that the enemy wants to move the forces drawn from the south against it."[79]

Schwarzenberg realized the French could not prevent his army from advancing. "In glancing at the map," continues his letter to Metternich, "you will see that from Switzerland to Langres and Dijon there are no means to stop [us]." Regardless, Army Group Alsace received firm orders to accelerate its march to Langres rather than cooperate with Blücher. Schwarzenberg even dissolved Scheibler's Streifkorps and summoned its two Cossack regiments and Austrian hussar squadron to force march to Vesoul, explaining to Wrede that "the enemy appears to want to defend Langres and has repulsed Thurn's Streifkorps. The Haute-Marne Department agitates and has taken up arms. I have barely 500 cavalry on my front; this forces me to reinforce my cavalry."[80] If he no longer feared confronting Napoleon at Langres, why did the Allied commander in chief seek to be reinforced by the IV, V, and VI Corps?

Although a strategic explanation can be found in Schwarzenberg's concern over Lyon, an answer based on human nature lies in another of Tsar Alexander's absurd schemes. "I wait here with impatience for the [Russian] Reserve," wrote Schwarzenberg to his wife, "but why do you think it is not here? On the 13th, which is actually 1 January according to the Russian calendar, the tsar crossed the Niemen one year ago at the head of the Guard. For this reason he finds it completely necessary to cross the Rhine on 1 January of this year.... Thus, my Nani, must I command; if the Heavens do not protect me, or the war ends soon, an evil catastrophe will ultimately occur. At such an important, decisive time, when the fate of Europe will be decided, this puppet-show is really disgusting."[81] He also complained to Metternich: "I forgot to tell you that to amuse himself by crossing the Rhine on the Russian New Year, Tsar Alexander holds back the Guard, which forms the reserve of my army. As a result, Guylay will be at Langres on the 13th, while my reserve is still at Basel. He [Alexander] also had Volkonsky inform me he is stopping one cuirassier division, which I had march forward to support Guylay since I completely lack cavalry on this point. I still do not know if it will march. Admit it, my friend, it is a feat of strength and, I am tempted to say, of skill to command an army in this way."[82]

Despite the tsar's antics, denuding the right wing of the Bohemian Army appears even more puzzling considering the manner in which Schwarzenberg interpreted the intelligence that reached his headquarters:

> From captured dispatches I know all disposable troops are marching from Metz toward Nancy in order to unite with Victor, who will then proceed against my right which, without mishap, should easily resist. On the 4th Blücher was still at Kreuznach, I have asked him to drive quickly toward Nancy. This movement alone will force the enemy to quickly fall back; only

God knows if he [Blücher] will do this. All must work together, otherwise a disaster that will strike me first can easily occur. My calculations are correct, but when one holds back my reserve and if I am not supported in my flank, the plan will fail for sure.[83]

In this letter, Schwarzenberg's paranoia and illogical conclusions are obvious. Rather than direct the IV, V, and VI Corps against Nancy, he placed his hope in Blücher. He hardly acknowledged that the Prussian field marshal faced Marmont, who could wage a defensive struggle amid the fortresses of the Saar and Moselle, nor did he recognize that Macdonald threatened Blücher's right and rear. He complained of not having a reserve to employ at Langres, yet the generalissimo initially bound the elite troops of his Austrian Reserve to the siege of Besançon. Then, fear of the French concentration at Lyon prompted him to order Hesse-Homburg to march through Dole and Auxonne to Dijon, where he should arrive between the 15th and 16th to unite with Bubna. Forty miles south of Dole and 110 miles north of Lyon, the positioning of Army Group Franche-Comté at Dijon supposedly would cover the advance of his weak center to Langres. "There are so many who would be delighted if I become another victim of folly," Schwarzenberg divulges to his wife, "but to me the World's judgement is at most only secondary. My Nani, the affair is of such monstrous proportions that the head almost cannot comprehend everything, and then the restlessness: this makes for evil nights."[84]

After reaching these conclusions, shocking news arrived. "The main body of the enemy army has moved to Baccarat, Raon-l'Étape, and the surrounding areas," wrote Sherbatov to Schwarzenberg from Châtel, north of Épinal, on the night of the 11th. "One claims that a quantity of enemy troops has arrived at Nancy, where Marshal Ney and a senator have been sent to arm and stir up the people; but they have not had success. Having already sealed my report, I have learned from a gentleman from Chatel... that Napoleon will leave Paris to move on Langres and Besançon with 80,000 men."[85] Sherbatov's erroneous news induced Schwarzenberg to again change plans and realign his army groups. Immediately after ordering Guylay to attack Langres on the 13th, Schwarzenberg postponed the operation against Mortier's 12,000 men until the 18th. While Guylay wasted six days wandering around the outskirts of Langres, Schwarzenberg moved up the I and IV Corps as well as the Austrian Reserve. The commander in chief revealed his intimate thoughts in a 15 January letter to his wife:

I await a courier with the greatest impatience; Wrede should have attacked on the 13th, I still have no report; Bubna, who raids toward Lyon to cover my left flank, has reported nothing to me for a long time. This, my Nani, is not a sign of evil, yet the agonizing uncertainty is such that one can never breathe easy. My reserve is on the march; I think I will attack Langres on the 18th; a few days earlier 10,000 [French] Guards arrived there after a rapid march from Namur:

the consequence of the abject behavior of the villainous Bernadotte, who has not filled the gap to the right of Blücher. This lack of cooperation damages the general plan in a disturbing way. One claims Wellington has allowed several thousand French and Catalonians to escape who, united with conscripts and National Guardsmen, can considerably threaten my left wing. Louis Liechtenstein, who commands the blockades of Besançon, Ft. Joux, and Salins, reported that Ft. Joux will capitulate. Possession of this fort is extremely important to me, for it bars the road from Pontarlier, which is a main line for me in the case of a retreat.[86]

Although critical of the tsar, Schwarzenberg himself emerges as a theatrical, eccentric enigma, who vacillated between seeking victory and despondent anxiety.[87] Abrupt mood changes were indicative of his varying degrees of confidence. Painful indecision seized him during such mood swings. His opinion of his fellow army commanders likewise reflects the commander in chief's emotional highs and lows. Sleepless nights allowed his tired mind to conjure up bizarre scenarios. His correspondence of 10–12 January suggests that he sought to use Blücher's army to cover his own and counted on Blücher's impetuosity to secure his right flank. Yet after Blücher accomplished this task, the Austrian viewed him and Gneisenau as warmongers: "Blücher and still more Gneisenau – to whom the good old fellow must lend his name – drive on Paris with such a truly childish rage that they trample underfoot all principles of war . . . they only make plans to party in the Palais-Royal, which is so pitiful at this important time."[88] Despite knowing of Bernadotte's possible candidacy to replace Napoleon on the French throne, Schwarzenberg's anxiety led him to believe the former French marshal would defect from the Coalition to save his native land in its most desperate hour: "If the prince of Sweden makes a diversion to save Napoleon by paralyzing a large part of the forces of the Coalition armies and if Blücher finds himself forced to throw himself to his right, the great operation in France will become very perilous."[89]

His execution of the war corresponded to his unstable character. Schwarzenberg judged the crossing of the Rhine itself to be thoroughly imprudent and necessitated only by the inability to feed his troops on the river's right bank. After crossing the river, he slowly moved the Bohemian Army through Switzerland, southern Alsace, and northern Franche-Comté toward Langres and Dijon, while Bubna's 1st Light Division covered the left flank by marching on Geneva. With hardly any French forces opposing his army, Schwarzenberg only managed to capture a few fortresses. Nothing further than occupying the Plateau of Langres officially characterized his plans from the moment he left Frankfurt, although unofficially he intended to take any action necessary to secure Austrian interests and wage a war conducive to Metternich's efforts to secure a negotiated peace that favored Vienna. This proved far more difficult than Schwarzenberg imagined; he feared a disaster at every turn, reacted irrationally to rumors, and cared more about preserving his army rather than defeating the enemy. Yet as Clausewitz points out, his actual operations exposed his army to a crippling defeat that would have had a profound impact on the politics of the Coalition. "This 200,000-man army began its assault on France along four eccentric radii," explains Clausewitz, "not counting the detachment sent to Lyon, and extended itself 150 miles between Strasbourg and Dijon. Its reserves were in the middle of this immense circle, so the main force, by which the commanding general was found, was not stronger than 30,000 men (namely Gyulay's corps and the two divisions of Colloredo's corps at Vesoul). Indeed, if Victor with 14,000 men at Strasbourg and Mortier, who was on the march with 12,000 men from Reims to Langres, had been in position, this 200,000-man army would have been in peril."[90]

As the Bohemian Army moved into France, Schwarzenberg stripped his center of any sizeable forces to strengthen his wings. He reinforced the right wing to stop an imaginary French counteroffensive through Alsace to the right bank of the Rhine. The left wing was first used to establish Austrian influence in Switzerland and then to drive into southern France with no clear objective other than to destabilize Napoleonic control over the region of France that bordered French-controlled Italy. When Schwarzenberg perceived a French counteroffensive unfolding in Alsace, he summoned Blücher to cross the Rhine. Although the French withdrew from Alsace, new rumors of a French concentration of 80,000 men at Langres troubled the Allied commander. Realizing the weakness of his center, he shifted the units of his right wing to reinforce the army group that crawled toward the domineering plateau. He made few changes to the operations of the corps, light divisions, and reserves operating on his left wing. Instead, he again summoned Blücher to support the Bohemian Army. As the threat of serious French resistance at Langres passed, Schwarzenberg faced a perceived danger to both of his flanks – from Lyon and Nancy, respectively – as well as to his center from Troyes. Rather than direct his IV, V, and VI Corps to eliminate the alleged French concentration at Nancy by cooperating with the Silesian Army, he directed them to Langres.[91] Drawing the Silesian Army as close as possible to the Bohemian Army to cover its right flank became Schwarzenberg's new obsession. Thus secured by Blücher, he would assemble his main force on the Bohemian Army's left wing in anticipation of being attacked from Lyon to the south or Troyes to the northwest.

On the other hand, Metternich, by nature less apprehensive and less disturbed by nightmarish fantasies than Schwarzenberg, feared no serious military setback nor a general peoples war in France.[92] To secure Austrian objectives, Metternich opposed a bold advance as long as a negotiated peace still appeared possible. Schwarzenberg's cautious leadership, "which decided nothing and risked nothing," corresponded perfectly to Metternich's view of how the war should be conducted in Austria's interests.[93] Yet Metternich also succumbed to fits of desperation. After the first week of January the Austrian minister found himself forced to seek a rapprochement with Hardenberg. As Alexander's hand grew stronger, Metternich recognized the danger posed to his peace party. Having secured nothing beyond the French emperor's grudging acceptance of the controversial Frankfurt Proposals as the basis to open negotiations, Metternich had to come to terms with either Napoleon or Castlereagh, who was still in route from London. Because he could make no further progress with either for the moment, he turned to Hardenberg on 8 January – the same day he advised Schwarzenberg to advance cautiously and avoid "warlike acts" – and agreed to Prussia's annexation of Saxony.[94] Moreover, Metternich agreed to Prussia's acquisition of the whole of Saxony rather than just part of the state. Inherent in Metternich's offer was the condition that Prussia oppose the tsar's designs on Poland.[95] After his assistant, Humboldt, was snubbed during the discussions with St. Aignan, a grateful Hardenberg accepted Metternich's proposal. To show his appreciation, the Prussian chancellor started revising Prussia's stand on an array of issues, the sum of which amounted to major concessions to Metternich regarding Germany and Poland, as well as Hardenberg's admission that the central European powers needed union and alliance to counter Russia's growing strength. All was for naught. Hardenberg later had to renounce his agreements with Metternich after Frederick William strongly rebuked him for undermining the tsar.[96] Hardenberg's embarrassment mattered little to Metternich. By the time it occurred, he had a much larger fish to catch: Castlereagh had reached Allied Headquarters at Basel.

Two hundred and fifty-two miles from Basel, Napoleon could not form an accurate view of the war's progress. On 10 January, Berthier compiled Napoleon's response to Victor's report of 8 January. The letter illustrates the predicament in which the master of war found himself: "The distance and the circumstances do not allow us to give you precise instructions, but it is important to defend the passes of the Vosges, it is the best defense that we have. If you cannot attack the enemy, you must at least stop and delay his march."[97] Berthier addressed copies of this same letter to Ney, Marmont, and Kellermann; Pahlen's Cossacks intercepted Victor's on the night of the 12th. Regardless, it is doubtful that such a vague directive would have prompted Victor to act any different in Lorraine than he had in Alsace. The fundamental problem still existed: unlike Caulaincourt, Napoleon's marshals thought in military terms only; they did not understand that every mile yielded to the Allies weakened the emperor's political control and brought him one step closer to the fate that awaited him in April. In their defense, how could they understand the synergy of politics, war, and strategy? Napoleon's only solution would have been to leave Paris immediately and personally take command of the defense of Lorraine.

Such a solution becomes even more necessary when considering Berthier's 11 January response to Victor's report from the 9th. The chief of staff ordered

Victor to attack St. Dié, hold the passes through the Vosges and impose himself on the enemy. Berthier encouraged him to execute his movements with energy and stressed the importance of morale.[98] By the time this letter reached Victor, his men had abandoned St. Dié, and the marshal was in the process of evacuating the western slopes of the Vosges. This does not reflect poorly on Victor. He reacted as any prudent commander. Only the genius of the emperor could change the situation, yet here emerges Napoleon's conundrum. In his eyes, France needed Emperor Napoleon in Paris, yet the French army needed General Bonaparte in the field. This need became more acute with each passing day. Keeping in line with his foreign policy of rejecting the Coalition's philosophical demand that he transform himself from the Emperor of the French to the King of France, his domestic policy likewise catered to his imperial ego. Emperor Napoleon remained in Paris, while General Bonaparte languished in the opulent prison of the Tuileries.

"Our troops were in full retreat," recalls Baron Fain. "Napoleon did not flatter himself with the hope of stopping the Allied forces at the frontier for any length of time. Finding himself compelled to allow them to advance into the interior, he became intent on concerting a plan for our retrograde movements, which he wished to concentrate in order to cover Paris."[99] Indeed, Napoleon changed his plans considerably on 10 January. Instead of creating four small armies, he decided to assemble a reserve army of over 100,000 men at Paris. If the Allies bypassed his frontier fortresses to march directly on Paris, the emperor wanted Macdonald, Mortier, Marmont, Victor, and Ney to fall back on the capital. Although he considered an Allied advance on Paris to be highly unlikely, Bonaparte recognized the gravity of the situation. He believed Ney could coordinate the defense of Lorraine with the available resources including Victor's troops to slow the paranoid Schwarzenberg. However, more manpower would be needed to deal with the aggressive Blücher. Finally convinced the main Allied thrust would not come through the Low Countries and that Maison could contain the small Allied forces operating in Holland, Napoleon instructed Macdonald to garrison all of the fortresses on the Lower Rhine and proceed to the Meuse, maneuvering toward Maastricht and Namur to threaten Blücher's right.[100] On the same day, the 10th, Berthier directed Belliard to transfer army headquarters from Metz to Châlons-en-Champagne to be closer to the new reserve army.[101] As with all of Napoleon's calculations and estimates, time and space still remained the essential ingredient. His marshals had to keep the Allies as far away from Paris as possible for as long as possible. Yet with the emperor remaining at Paris, events in Lorraine were about to unravel for Victor, Ney, and Marmont. The impossible task of coordinating the operations of three marshals from Paris directly led to the premature evacuation of Nancy, the capital of Lorraine.[102]

After the operations on the 10th, Victor was inactive on the 11th. Accompanied by Caulaincourt, the marshal went to Rambervillers in the morning, but his orders for the day amounted to returning one battalion and two guns to Baccarat to cover his line of retreat to Lunéville, and to establishing a strong post to observe enemy movements around Raon-l'Étape.[103] Evidently, he intended to remain in Rambervillers for some time and ordered the advance posts to be relieved every twenty-four hours.[104] Duhesme continued his retreat toward Rambervillers but remained east of the town by nightfall.

Victor's subordinates provided a fairly accurate appraisal of the situation in the Vosges. He learned another "division" [brigade] had reached Ste. Marie on the evening of the 10th and would arrive at St. Dié that morning. In addition, his intelligence claimed the Württembergers had established an advance guard at Bruyères on the 10th. According to this information, he considered a counterattack on St. Dié unfeasible because of the "weak means" at his disposal. "One has assured me a third Allied column will arrive at Remiremont and continue marching on Épinal," states the marshal's brief to Berthier at 4:00 P.M. on the 11th. "This morning we heard cannon from this direction; we still do not know what happened there. The general opinion is the entire Allied army that crossed the Rhine will not delay crossing the Vosges and moving to the Moselle in a strength of 50,000–60,000 men." If this proved true, Victor planned to withdraw through Lunéville to Nancy but had yet to issue any instructions regarding this subject.[105]

To Ney he wrote: "Everything leads me to believe Wrede's army will not hesitate to march to the Moselle. In this case, I can oppose him with only weak resistance, having with me only 7,000 young infantry and 3,000 cavalry." He claimed that very considerable forces outflanked him on all sides and severed his communications. Victor's wish to escape the quagmire of independent command and settle into the more comfortable role of subordinate emerges in this letter, despite its sound premise: "It appears to me the emperor would do well to unite under your command all the troops found in the Moselle and the Vosges Departments in order to form an army capable of stopping the enemy. Their actual dissemination does not offer any means of defense and these troops can only be compromised if the enemy advances."[106] "I do not have any instructions to take command of troops other than those at Nancy," responded Ney.[107]

The Allied forces to the south actually concerned Victor more than the Bavarians to the east. "The advance guard under the orders of Duhesme will be compromised if the enemy marches in force from Bruyères to Rambervillers," he explains to Grouchy. "Therefore, Duhesme will retire tomorrow, two hours before dawn, on the village of Jeanménil." For 12 January, he decided to concentrate the II Infantry and V Cavalry Corps in a defensive position to block the advance of the Allied corps at Épinal.[108] The only definitive order in his disposition directed Grouchy to "attack and chase from Bruyères the enemy cavalry found there." After completing this mission, the marshal wanted Grouchy to deploy Briche's dragoon and Piré's light divisions, one battery, and the 24th Light Infantry Regiment in two lines. The first, consisting of the light infantry and cavalry, would extended west to east between Sercèur and Grandvillers on the Châtel–Bruyères road, two-thirds of the way to Épinal. Briche's 3rd Dragoons would form the second line with the artillery. Grouchy would position Lhéritier's 4th Dragoon Division and the rest of Milhaud's artillery "behind the second line so if needed it can move to support the two other cavalry divisions. The point of assembly in case the enemy attacks in force is the ridge north of Rambervillers on the right bank of the Montagne near the road to Lunéville." As for his infantry, Victor intended to maintain the 1st Division at Rambervillers, the 2nd in the villages four miles to the north, and the 3rd at Jeanménil, three miles east of Rambervillers. He planned to cover his left flank with two strong detachments of cavalry and infantry, while in the Moselle Valley Meunier's 1st Young Guard Voltigeur Division and Cassagne's troops of the 4th Military District shielded his right.[109]

"If the enemy marches, as all claim, I believe Your Majesty will not wait long before the II Corps retreats," wrote Caulaincourt, who returned to Lunéville on the evening of the 11th.[110] Caulaincourt's words proved prophetic. On the night of the 11th, Victor learned of Rousseau's defeat at Épinal. Frederick William's gamble singularly changed Victor's situation and the marshal issued orders to evacuate the line of the Vosges. Napoleon showed no mercy toward Victor in his criticism of the marshal's decision to abandon the Vosges. French historians such as Lefebvre de Béhaine follow the emperor's lead, claiming Victor could have held his position for several days.[111] Typically, the marshal is chided for not doing more to delay the march of the Allied columns through the Vosges, to block access to the Moselle Valley, and to threaten the communications of Schwarzenberg's troops in march on Vesoul and Langres.[112] In Napoleon's military and political situation, time was his most precious resource. Victor could have won time for his emperor if he had executed a bold counteroffensive on the 10th. But just how much time and at what cost remained the questions that clouded the marshal's judgment? Should he expend his forces when the imminent arrival of reinforcements and perhaps the emperor himself would change the situation? What if no reinforcements arrived, should Victor risk one of France's few remaining infantry corps and one of its best cavalry corps to be cut to pieces in the valleys of the Meurthe and the Moselle by forces three or four times superior in number? A successful operation on the 10th would have gained Victor perhaps two or three more days to defend the debouches of the mountains. In the end, Marmont's retreat from the Saar to the Moselle and Blücher's advance to Nancy would have forced Victor to retreat. What occurred next in Lorraine was a travesty for the French army as three marshals suffered lapses in judgment caused by mental, physical, and emotional fatigue that personified the exhausted state of the First French Empire in its twilight.

12

Lorraine

With the approach of Allied forces from the north, east, and south, Nancy bustled with a nervous energy reminiscent of Paris during the last foreign invasion almost twenty-two years earlier.Consequently, reports over morale in the provincial capital and its surrounding region vary considerably. "I have passed the day in all the anguish of uncertainty," commiserates Defrance, the newly appointed inspector general of the army's remounts. "All of Nancy is in consternation, each feels its affects."[1] "There is much despondency," comments Caulaincourt.[2] Napoleon's extraordinary-commissioner to the 4th Military District, Senator Jean-Victor Colchen, arrived at Nancy on the evening of 2 January and two days later briefed Minister of War Clarke over the situation. "The spirit of the inhabitants displays itself in such an advantageous manner, and the officials who direct it appear so full of zeal, that I believe the enemy will halt his plans once the duke of Valmy announces he will arrive with sufficient forces."[3] After reviewing the situation, Colchen issued proclamations on the 4th and 5th summoning the people to defend their homes.[4] These coincided with the 4 January imperial decree that enacted the *levée-en-masse* in some departments. "The excellent spirit that animates the inhabitants of this [military] division increasingly manifests itself," continues Colchen's report to Clarke. "The recruits, the horses, and requisitions of all kind flow in with ease and promptness. A great number of young men and veteran soldiers seek permission to form a corps and conduct a partisan war against the enemy."[5]

At Metz Kellermann became aware of the public's anxiety. He suggested the presence of line troops to calm the fear. Commenting on the march of Meunier's 1st Young Guard Voltigeur Division through Metz, he advised the emperor that "their presence produced the best effect. The citizens feel supported by the regular troops, who provide security."[6] It mattered little that these soldiers had never fired a musket; the mere sight of the bearskins sufficed to allay public consternation.[7]

As Alsace formed the 5th Military District, Lorraine composed the 4th, which contained the Departments of the Meurthe and the Vosges. A confusing array of military and civil authorities exercised varying degrees of jurisdiction throughout the military district. "No one seems to remember what they have said or what they have written," complains Caulaincourt. "Contradictory reports arrive from everywhere and one neither confirms nor verifies these reports because one claims to have no authority."[8] With the emperor at Paris, these regional officials had to compensate for the absence of his unrivaled stamina, genius, and charisma. None rivaled him in these categories; some had physical limitations, others suffered from the same malaise that paralyzed the Napoleonic regime during its most critical hour.

In addition to the numerous reports over public opinion, the French officials charged with the defense of Lorraine did not hesitate to comment on each other's performance. "Colchen appears to be animated by positive morale; everyone attests to his good intentions," notes Caulaincourt in his 6 January report to the emperor. Although Senator Colchen arrived in Nancy only two days earlier, the foreign minister unfairly criticized him, claiming "he still has done nothing."[9] The hero of the 1792 victory over the Prussians at Valmy, Marshal Kellermann, served as commander in chief of all troops stationed in the 2nd, 3rd, and 4th Military Districts. Entering his sixty-second year of military service, the seventy-eight-year old duke of Valmy zealously performed his duties, but with mixed results.[10] "He employs all his resources in the service of the emperor," attests Belliard; "he is truly an extraordinary man for his age."[11] On the other hand, a concerned Marmont commented on the aging marshal's organizational shortcomings: "I very much fear the hindrances that I will encounter in his vicinity."[12]

With Kellermann at Metz, much of the responsibility for defending the 4th Military District fell to the district's commander, the sixty-four-year old General Jean-Laurent-Justin Lacoste. Like Kellermann, Lacoste displayed both unquestionable loyalty to the regime as well as the ceaseless energy of a man half his age. Commandant of the 4th Military District since 19 April 1811, the unfortunate Lacoste suffered from asthma and rheumatism. These ailments, combined with his obsessive desire to execute each task personally, limited his efficiency.[13] "Lacoste is an extremely infirm, yet estimable old man," explains Colchen, "full of good will, activity, and devotion, but instead of supervising he wants to do everything himself and I fear the excess of work will render him unable to continue his functions."[14] Convinced that Lacoste was too old, Caulaincourt urged the emperor to appoint an officer to oversee the National Guard and the *levée-en-masse* "because one does not want to squander any of these resources, which could be useful, especially in the mountains."[15] The commandant of the Vosges Department, General Cassagne, assisted Lacoste

Figure 14. Marshal Michel Ney (1769–1815). French corps commander.

as best he could. Only fifty-one years old himself, Cassagne had been battling poor health since 1805. Victor likewise did not escape Caulaincourt's scrutiny:

> The precipitous retreat of the duke of Bellune, which resulted from false rumors, has thrust the region into panic. If he does not reoccupy the passes, it will be impossible to count on the levée of soldiers who, incidentally, are animated by the best spirit and only require leadership. All say the duke of Bellune does nothing to find out what passes in front of him, nor does he care to acquire this information. He does not even know if the enemy is four leagues from him in Lorraine or if he is in Russia. He imagines columns of 20,000 men where a handful of Cossacks and Hussars have passed. This corps needs a man who knows how to energize the authorities, who talks, who inspires confidence. Without the news I sent him this morning, he would still think the enemy occupies Épinal. If the marshal makes only a small movement forward, he will revive the spirit of the entire population. Alsace already has been lost because of lack of leadership; it soon will be the same for Lorraine unless the troops and the authorities of this region are electrified by a man who actually desires to serve you.[16]

Napoleon already had chosen this man: the fiery Marshal Ney. After Napoleon's first line of defense, the Rhine, had fallen so ingloriously, the emperor placed the defense of Lorraine in the hands of a native son, a warrior of France who, after the retreat from Russia in the final days of 1812, had gained a mythical aura. Despite Ney's recent setbacks in Germany, Bonaparte utilized this brave soldier to raise the esteem of the young recruits by giving them a marshal of France as their commander. On 3 January, Berthier asked Ney, who was convalescing in Paris from the wound he received at Leipzig, if he would accept a command. Receiving no response, Berthier repeated the question on the 4th. Providing more details, he explained that Ney would command one of the four armies being formed – the Army of the Center – which would assemble at Langres.[17] Ney accepted, requesting thirty-two pages of Cassini's map from Clarke, which he received on the 5th.[18]

Victor's evacuation of Alsace forced Napoleon to alter his plans. Acting on Belliard's erroneous message of 5 January that Allied cavalry had taken Épinal, Napoleon instructed Ney to go immediately to Nancy and retake Épinal. Berthier issued the pertinent instructions for Ney to depart on the 6th and take command of the 1st Young Guard Voltigeur Division "as well as all the troops available to defend Nancy, to retake Épinal, which is only occupied by cavalry, and to contain the enemy from this side. I have advised the duke of Valmy that command has been transferred to you; I have likewise alerted Curial and the commanding general of the 4th Military District."[19] Not having received his salary in five months, the marshal replied that he would execute this assignment only if he received the means to pay his expenses; the emperor offered no response.[20]

Born in Saarlouis eight months before Napoleon's birth on Corsica in 1769, Ney, the second son of a veteran of the Seven Years' War, became a civil servant after receiving an education at the Collège des Augustins. Leaving his position as an overseer of mines and forges, the eighteen year old enlisted as a hussar in Louis XVI's army. By the time France declared war on Austria in 1792, Ney had attained the rank of sergeant major and was noted for his courage and tactical ability. That same year, he earned a commission as a sublieutenant of the 5th Hussars on 29 October while serving in the Army of the North. In November 1794, he participated in the siege of Mainz, receiving a severe wound to his left shoulder. For the next two years, Ney commanded cavalry in the German theater. He attained the rank of general of brigade on 1 August 1796 for his role in the capture of Würzburg's citadel as well as his conduct in several combats that summer. As General Bonaparte concluded his brilliant First Italian Campaign hundreds of miles away, General Ney, commanding a hussar corps in the Army of the Sambre and Meuse, was captured by the Austrians at Giessen on 21 April 1797. Exchanged the following month, he resumed his position in the Army of the Sambre and Meuse for the rest of the year until receiving command of the reserve cavalry of the Army of Mainz in December. Six months later in May 1798, Ney found himself attached to the Army of England. After Napoleon decided to strike the British indirectly by invading Egypt, Ney bounced between the Army of Mainz and Bernadotte's

Army of the Lower Rhine, where he participated in the taking of Mannheim and received a promotion to general of division on 28 March 1799.

While Bonaparte's Army of the Orient waged the exotic Egyptian Campaign, Ney saw stints as a light cavalry commander in the Armies of Switzerland and the Danube. On 27 May, he received wounds to his thigh and wrist that forced him out of service for one month. After recovering he held two divisional commands until being transferred to Moreau's Army of the Rhine on 19 August. As new First Consul Bonaparte waged his Second Italian Campaign, Ney accumulated a stellar service record as well as two more wounds while serving under Moreau. On 3 December 1800, he played a decisive role in defeating the Austrians just east of Munich at Hohenlinden. With the dissolution of the Second Coalition and Bonaparte's ensuing peace initiative, Ney's next assignment came in September 1802, when he received command of the French army in Switzerland. As ministre plénipotentiaire en Suisse, Ney signed the Act of Mediation on 19 February 1803 that transformed Switzerland into a French satellite called the Helvetic Republic. Ney's early service to France climaxed when Napoleon awarded him a marshal's baton on 19 May 1804 – twelfth out of eighteen in order of seniority. His marriage to Aglaée-Louise-Auguiée, an intimate of Napoleon's first wife, Josephine, helped solidify Ney's relationship with the future emperor.

For the next ten years Ney played an integral part in the rise and fall of the First French Empire. His triumphs were accompanied by an equal number of mishaps, failures, and shortcomings that should have tempered the emperor's expectations of one of his favorite marshals. During Napoleon's preparations to invade Great Britain, he assigned Ney command of the VI Corps of the Grande Armée. Austria's decision to join the Third Coalition redirected Napoleon's gaze to central Europe. After the Grande Armée sped through Germany, Napoleon effected his brilliant maneuver to envelop the Austrian army at Ulm. During this operation, Ney pushed his VI Corps to the Danube, while the Austrians attempted to break out of the trap by driving along the north bank of the river. At 8:00 on the morning of 14 October, Ney closed the Austrian escape route by taking the town of Elchingen, where Napoleon accepted the Austrian commander's surrender six days later. Ney did not participate in the epic battle of Austerlitz later that year but instead invaded the Tyrol and drove Austrian forces from Innsbruck.

During the War of the Fourth Coalition, Ney's premature attack at Jena on 14 October 1806 earned him a gentle rebuke from the emperor. He returned to favor later in the campaign by occupying Erfurt and forcing the capitulation of Magdeburg, where 25,000 Prussians had regrouped after the French victories at Jena and Auerstädt. While the Grande Armée inundated Prussia, the remnant of Frederick William's army fled across the Vistula to link with the approaching Russians. Rather than pursue, Napoleon chose to place the army in winter quarters. Yet in the first week of January 1807, Ney moved his VI Corps sixty miles into East Prussia on a simple foraging mission. Not only was he repulsed by the Prussians, but the Russians believed the appearance of his corps marked the beginning of a French winter offensive and so themselves took the initiative to drive the enemy from the lower Vistula. Napoleon again frowned on Ney, whose actions seemingly provoked the Russian offensive. Ever the master of opportunity, Napoleon struck the exposed Russian wing at Eylau. The battle raged in horrible winter conditions on 7–8 February 1807. Ney's approach with the VI Corps encouraged the Russians to yield the battlefield after sustaining 25,000 casualties. Losing 10,000 soldiers himself, Napoleon suffered his first check since Egypt. Once the campaign resumed in the spring, the French emperor cornered the Russian army at Friedland. With their backs to a river, the Russians had no choice but to fight on 14 June 1807. Ney received the task of delivering the coup de grâce by driving the Russians into the river. Napoleon purportedly exclaimed, "That man is a lion" as Ney led the right wing against two Russian divisions. With the French victory at Friedland, the war of the Fourth Coalition ended. At the height of his triumph, the emperor did not forget his lieutenants. On 6 June 1808, he rewarded Ney with peerage under the title of the duke of Elchingen.

Ney's next assignment brought him and his VI Corps to Iberia for service in the French Armies of Spain and Portugal. Ney saw action in the Peninsular from August 1808 until his dismissal in March 1811. This inglorious period of his career exposed many of the problems that would later become acute. As one historian has stated: "He was to spend nearly two-and-one-half years in Spain and Portugal, a period of misfortune for the French and one that revealed Ney in a bad light: thoroughly insubordinate to any commander but the emperor himself, besides being unreasonably touchy, quarrelsome, and uncooperative."[21] Another adds: "His red hair indicated his hot and impolitic temper."[22] Very early in the campaign, Napoleon criticized the marshal for grossly exaggerating the size of the Spanish army. Moreover, Ney's failure to comply with Napoleon's orders allowed the Spanish army to escape a trap. Two years later, when Ney's corps was attached to Marshal Masséna's Army of Portugal, his command of the French rearguard during the retreat from Torres Vedras provided the only bright spot during a campaign that culminated with Masséna relieving Ney of his command on grounds of insubordination.

Ney next saw action during the monumental invasion of Russia. Commanding the III Corps of the Grande Armée, he figured prominently in the major actions of that campaign. On 17 August 1812, he received a wound to the neck during brutal combat at Smolensk. On 7 September, the marshal earned notable recognition as well as four more wounds while leading his III Corps against the Russian center at Borodino. Entrusted with command of the rearguard on 3 November, he covered one of the most famous retreats in the annals of history. Commanding only 2,000 men, Ney willed his way through the Russian forces that blocked his road, thus earning the emperor's acclaim of being "the bravest of the brave." Purportedly the last man of the Grande Armée to leave Russian soil, the emperor rewarded Ney for his service with a new title: prince of the Moskowa.[23] Regardless of his feats in Russia, Ney's conduct as an independent commander during the German campaign of 1813 was disastrous.[24]

In January 1814, Napoleon ordered Ney to take command of the Young Guard division at Nancy as well as all troops in the region. Implicitly, Victor would be subordinate to Ney's orders, and the prince's authority would supercede Kellermann's as well. Should Marmont move into Ney's area of operations, he, too, ostensibly would fall under Ney's jurisdiction. The bleak military situation could be salvaged if Ney provided unity of command, exploited his central position, and used interior lines to stop the advance of both Allied armies, keep them apart, and defeat them in detail. Yet the emperor never officially named him commander in chief nor did he notify the other marshals that Ney would exercise such authority. Although senior to Victor and Marmont, Ney still did not possess sufficient authority to subordinate the other marshals without the emperor's explicit orders. As Ney, Victor, and Marmont drew closer to each other, those who understood the intricacies of the marshalate foresaw the inevitable problems. "The two corps of the dukes of Bellune and Raguse approach," explains Belliard, "three marshals will find themselves united and it is quite urgent that one of them has the authority to avoid a conflict of command, which always undermines the interests of the emperor."[25] Upon reaching Châlons-en-Champagne on 14 January and believing Berthier was en route, Belliard issued another appeal: "Your arrival will do great good, I assure you; we await you with all impatience, you will centralize authority and all will be well because there is so little harmony in the movements of the army corps of the dukes of Raguse and Bellune, and the prince of the Moskowa, that one accomplishes nothing and will continue to do nothing unless you come or the emperor unites the three army corps under the command of a single chief."[26]

Ney reached Nancy on the evening of the 9th. He spent the next two days acquainting himself with the military situation and evaluating the threat posed by the fall of Épinal. The marshal found little infantry, hardly any cavalry to conduct reconnaissance, no general staff to dispatch and coordinate correspondence, and no authority over his colleagues.[27] If Ney hoped to execute the role assigned to him by the emperor, he had to rely on troops commanded by his fellow marshals. By the time he fully assessed the situation, no more thought could be wasted on a counteroffensive from Épinal or even an attempt to retake the town: both Marmont and Victor were in full retreat.

In the meantime, patrols informed Marmont on the 11th that Sacken's corps was pursuing the VI Infantry and I Cavalry Corps on the same road, while Yorck crossed the Saar at Rehlingen and struck the main highway from Saarlouis to Metz. Yorck's vanguard cleared the marshal's posts from Boulay on the 10th and reached Condé on the morning of the 11th. Sacken's advance units drove Marmont's rearguard from St. Avold after a short engagement. "According to all certainty," predicted the marshal, "tomorrow morning I will have Sacken's corps in front of me and the Prussian corps will be closer to Metz than I will be. I will leave tonight to get closer to that city, where I will arrive tomorrow evening, and I will hold a position behind the Moselle as long as I can." Desertion continued to plague Marmont – a problem he asked Napoleon to consider. One example was a detachment of 320 newly raised conscripts who left Metz on the 9th and reached Longeville two days later with only 210 men.[28]

With his army at the Saar, Blücher planned to march on Metz with 50,000 men. If the French managed to concentrate superior forces, the Silesian Army would maneuver until reinforcements arrived. He hoped to receive support from Wrede and Wittgenstein, not knowing the Allied generalissimo ordered Army Group Alsace southwest to Langres instead of northwest toward the Silesian Army. In a 8 January letter to Schwarzenberg, the Prussian commander hinted that perhaps "Wittgenstein and Wrede, maybe also Your Excellency, will appear on the enemy's right flank. Wittgenstein and Wrede are in communication with me. Since they have informed me that they are in position to support my offensive operations, I have notified them of my plan and the time of my arrival so we can act in unison."[29] That same day Blücher wrote Wittgenstein to coordinate their operations.[30] Long before he received Schwarzenberg's 13 January response, Blücher decided to continue his march to Metz, which had become his obsession. According to his intelligence, between 40,000 and 80,000 conscripts had assembled there. He still hoped to reach Metz by the 15th and intended to use his veteran army to disperse the French recruits. In the worst-case scenario, he could employ his stronger cavalry to extricate himself from an unfavorable situation.

Blücher had not received any instructions from Schwarzenberg since the commander in chief's letter of 5 January arrived on the 9th. After Sacken's patrols established communication with the VI Corps, Blücher did receive a note from Wittgenstein that promised Russian support in an operation against Metz. Wittgenstein informed Blücher that in addition to making an attempt to take Phalsbourg, his advance guard would move as far as possible toward Lunéville and Nancy. Furthermore, Eugene's II Infantry Corps would support Blücher with one division, while the other remained in reserve at Haguenau.[31] A few days later and much to Blücher's dismay, Wittgenstein, acting on Schwarzenberg's instructions, claimed he could not contribute anything to the operation against Metz and would not arrive at Saverne until the 21st. "Due to these circumstances," wrote the Russian, "the situation will perhaps persuade you against crossing the Saar with the bulk of your army until further notice."[32] Such was the spirit that dominated the Russian army, except for those units serving under the fiery Blücher. His hatred of Napoleon breathed new life into the tired Russian soldiers, many of whom had left their homes in the Urals or beyond to defend Mother Russia against the foreign invader in 1812; now they found themselves in the foreign invader's home.

Disregarding Wittgenstein's ridiculous advice, Blücher did not slow his advance. In a letter to Knesebeck, Müffling summarized the intentions of Blücher's headquarters: "From now until 20 January we will seek to divide the enemy's forces; we want to force him to garrison the fortresses of Saarlouis, Metz, Thionville, and Luxembourg."[33] These views found their first expression in Blücher's instructions to Yorck on 10 January. After clearing the enemy from the left bank of the Saar, he wanted Yorck to proceed as soon as possible to Saarbrücken and for a small detachment to invest Saarlouis. "As soon as you are certain the enemy has withdrawn to Metz," wrote Blücher, "order Horn to advance on the shortest road to Thionville. In general, his assignment is to spread terror and to force the enemy to garrison Thionville, and to make an attempt to capture this fortress if the possibility of success exists." The field marshal also ordered Yorck to have cavalry detachments raid along the Luxembourg–Thionville and Longwy–Thionville roads. Henckel received instructions to move from Trier to Thionville on the 15th to make room for Röder's cavalry brigade from Kleist's II Corps, which Blücher expected to arrive on the 16th.[34]

Based on these instructions, Yorck drafted his disposition for the 11th. Prince William would cross the Saar in two columns at Beckingen and Saarbrücken to reach Forbach by noon; from there he would continue to St. Avold. After crossing at either Merzig or Beckingen, Horn's 7th Brigade would advance to Thionville. The Reserve Cavalry and 1st and 2nd Brigades would cross at Saarbrücken and billet north of Forbach. For the sake of speed, the Reserve Artillery would remain on the right bank of the Saar. Yorck assigned the blockade of Saarlouis to the 1st Neumark Landwehr Cavalry Regiment and four Landwehr infantry battalions.

Nature slowed Yorck's advance on the 11th. The Saar's rising water and drift ice delayed Prince William's crossing until 3:00 P.M.; his brigade only reached Überherrn. After clearing the Saar at Beckingen, Horn's 7th Brigade formed the right wing and marched west to Bouzonville on the road to Thionville. This movement prompted the commandant of the fortress, General Joseph-Léopold-Sigisbert Hugo, the father of the famous nineteenth-century author, to inform Belliard that an enemy corps of 8,000 men would soon arrive.[35] At Saarbrücken, the 1st and 2nd Brigades utilized the pontoon bridge to cross the river and then trooped to Forbach, where Yorck established his headquarters; Blücher remained at Saarbrücken.[36]

Serving as Yorck's advance guard, Stutterheim's troops moved south along the same road as William's 8th Brigade but were farther ahead. His detachment found Marmont's troops holding the defile of Moulin-Neuf, one mile east of St. Avold. Choosing to attack across poor terrain, Stutterheim directed his fusilier battalion to proceed to the right of the highway and through the wooded hills north of St. Avold to assault the French position from the west. While the infantry took the French in the left flank, the Brandenburg Uhlans would charge the front of the French position. Supported by the jäger of Biron's Streifkorps, Stutterheim's small battalion of 230 fusiliers stormed the French position. Attacked in the front and the flank, the French withdrew to St. Avold. Granting their adversaries no time to recover, the Prussian fusiliers fixed bayonet and drove into St. Avold. By this time, Lanskoi arrived with the Russian light cavalry and one battery of horse artillery from Sacken's advance guard. To add to the mix, Jürgaß came up with Yorck's Reserve Cavalry. Behind these advance units, Sacken's VI Infantry Corps under General Aleksey Grigorievich Sherbatov reached Forbach. Faced by such overwhelming numbers, the French retreated west to Longeville with 600 infantry, 400 cavalry, and five guns. After securing St. Avold, Jürgaß, Stutterheim, Biron, and Lanskoi allowed their men to camp in the town; two West Prussian dragoon squadrons followed the French toward Metz.[37]

That same day, 11 January, Yorck's patrols pushed as far as the Moselle. One patrol of forty troopers rode close to Metz. Slightly northeast of the fortress, where the highways from Saarlouis and Saarbrücken intersect, the Prussians attacked a large column of trains, baggage, and fodder wagons with the intent of taking prisoners for interrogation. A captured sergeant-major claimed Marmont was marching from St. Avold to Metz with one infantry and one cavalry division. Thus forewarned, the Prussians managed to escape being cut off by the marshal's approaching forces. The captain commanding the team reported that Marmont was moving with approximately 15,000 men toward Metz but that consternation and confusion reigned in the city. The patrol also claimed that a large corps had marched to Châlons-en-Champagne on the previous night. In addition, French civilians in the villages surrounding Metz purportedly received the Prussians with courtesy. "If a strong detachment now advances to Metz," concludes the report, "something can certainly be achieved." Yorck forwarded this advice to Blücher at 3:00 P.M. on 12 January. Such news added to the growing conviction in Silesian Army Headquarters that an attempt to capture Metz – if not Thionville and Luxembourg as well – had to be made. Blücher and Gneisenau wanted to gain one of the strong fortresses to establish a depot for the Silesian Army. Bülow's success against the Dutch forts offered tantalizing hope that the same results could be achieved in Lorraine.[38] "If the enemy has thrown garrisons in all these fortresses, their supply must be very incomplete and their garrisons composed largely of conscripts," notes the perpetually optimistic field marshal.[39]

On 12 January, Blücher established his headquarters at St. Avold, while Yorck's corps continued moving across the ancient French frontier toward Metz. At St. Avold, Prince William turned west on the great highway that led to Metz and marched to Fouligny, some seventeen miles east of the fortress (see Map 9, Chapter 9). His forward units reached Glatigny, Flanville, and Urville. Between Noisseville and Flanville, Stutterheim's cavalry overtook three French squadrons conducting reconnaissance. The Prussians drove the French troopers west to Noisseville, inflicting forty casualties and taking thirty prisoners. Six squadrons and a few battalions debouched from Nouilly and forced the Prussians to retire on Glattigny. Pirch's 1st Brigade and War- burg's 2nd Brigade stretched between Vigneulles and Bambiderstroff, just west of St. Avold. Farther north, Horn's 7th Brigade remained on the road to Thionville, where it arrived on the night of the 12th. He made Distroff his headquarters and began the investment of the fortress. Excluding Horn's brigade, the I Corps was echelonned on the road from Saarbrücken to Metz along a front thirteen miles long and five miles wide; Yorck needed twenty- four hours to concentrate to be combat-ready. To the south, Sacken's infantry crossed the Saar and marched southwest to billets between Puttelange and Faulquemont. General Illarion Vasilievich Vasilchikov's cavalry advanced toward the Moselle and Lanskoi received instructions to proceed to the bridge at Pont-à-Mousson. Biron left the Saarbrücken–Metz road at St. Avold and turned south toward Nancy to establish communication with Wittgenstein, who Blücher assumed would be marching toward the provincial capital.[40]

After Yorck's forward patrols appeared on the road to Metz, a haggard Marmont decided to move closer to the fortress to protect his communica- tions. His outposts reported having "very strong engagements" during the night of 11–12 January with Prussian cavalry coming from the direction of Boulay and Courcelles-Chaussy; approximately 1,000 Allied troopers arrived from both directions. Writing to Belliard at 7:00 on the evening of the 11th, the marshal predicted he would be attacked by Sacken's corps and cut off from Metz by Yorck's corps on the following day. He assumed Yorck's cav- alry would reach Metz before him since it had less ground to cover along the direct route from Saarlouis to Metz.[41] During this nerve-wracking night, Marmont moved his troops into the eastern suburbs of Metz, thus abandoning the region between the Saar and the Moselle by the morning of 12 January. The marshal himself entered the fortress late on the evening of the 12th. As he penned his brief to Berthier at 11:00 P.M., Marmont concluded that on the 13th he would be faced by "strong advance guards" and "all the enemy's forces on the day after."[42]

Marmont immediately busied himself with preparations to defend Metz and Thionville. He forwarded to Châlons-en-Champagne all depots necessary for the army's reorganization but retained at Metz General Pierre Decouz's 2nd Young Guard Voltigeur Division (2,840 men), which had arrived on the 10th en route from Thionville to Nancy. He also assigned officers to expe- dite the organization of the conscripts. To reinforce the garrisons of Metz and Thionville, Marmont formed some battalions from cadres that had been designated for the IV and VI Corps, as well as Macdonald's XI Corps, which could proceed no further due to Blücher's proximity.[43]

Fifteen miles south of Metz, the 2nd Old Guard Division held the important bridge over the Moselle at Pont-à-Mousson. Upon learning the Guard had received orders to depart immediately for Langres, Marmont instructed Ricard to echelon his division between Pont-à-Mousson and Metz on the 13th to secure the bridge.[44] This movement prompted Allied scouts to report that the marshal was evacuating Metz. On the contrary, Marmont planned to hold his position for some time. The region west of the Moselle could provide men, horses, livestock, and commodities of all kind for both the army and the fortress. Regardless of his intentions, the marshal's arrangements depended on Victor's ability to hold Nancy in general, and the bridge over the Moselle at Frouard north of Nancy specifically. Ultimately, Marmont's fate was in Victor's hands.

For almost two weeks, Marmont retreated before an enemy seven times his own strength. He failed to coordinate his operations either with Macdonald in the Meuse Valley or with Victor in Alsace. Yet the situation appeared to be changing for the better. Macdonald was approaching Mézières on the road to old France, and, more important, Victor was withdrawing on Nancy. Marmont believed Victor would defend the Moselle and hoped he would not abandon this line without informing him. In normal times, the emperor would have provided the necessary unity of command for the two marshals to coordinate their operations across a span of only thirty miles. But with the emperor at Paris, the two commanders had to fill the void created by his absence. Given the exhausted and forlorn state of the French high command, this was simply too much to ask.[45]

Thick snow fell for three consecutive days. On the evening of the 11th, a warm front moved through, bringing heavy showers that transformed the ground into a sea of mud. Without a supply system to feed them, Victor's men quickly consumed the scant foodstuffs they found in neighboring villages. In this foreboding atmosphere, the demoralizing news reached Victor of the French defeat at Épinal earlier that day. Rousseau's retreat down the Moselle to guard the approaches to Nancy completely exposed Victor's right to the Coalition forces now at Épinal. All the valleys descending from the Grand Ballon toward the Meurthe were held by the Bavarians and those toward the Moselle by the Württembergers. To the French, it appeared the entire Allied army in Alsace had made one vast surge through the Vosges. Expecting to be enveloped by superior forces debouching in the Meurthe Valley (the Bavarians) and now the Moselle Valley (the Württembergers), Victor decided to fall back on his line of communication. That same night, 11 January, he issued extensive orders to extricate his two corps and withdraw eighteen miles down the small Mortagne – a tributary of the Meurthe – from Rambervillers to Lunéville.[46]

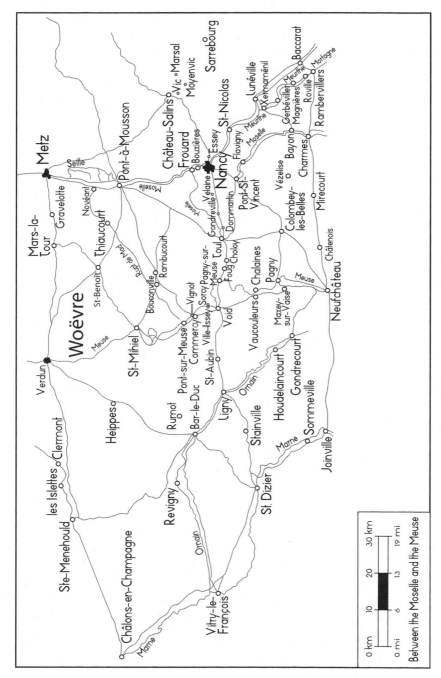

Map 15. The region between the Moselle and the Meuse.

Metz

Seille

Mars-la-Tour

Gravelotte

Novéant

Thiaucourt

St-Benoît

Rupt de Mad

Rambucourt

Bouconville

Pont-à-Mousson

Moselle

Château-Salins

Frouard

Bouxières

Vic

Marsal

Moyenvic

Sarrebourg

St-Nicolas

Lunéville

Gerbéviller

Meurthe

Xermaménil

Baccarat

Mortagne

Magnières

Roville

Rambervillers

Essey

Nancy

Velaine

Flavigny

Meurthe

Moselle

Bayon

Charmes

Gondreville

Dommartin

Toul

Pont-St-Vincent

Vézelise

Colombey-les-Belles

Mirecourt

Pagny-sur-Meuse

Sorcy

Foug

Choloy

Vignot

Ville-Issey

Void

Chalaines

Pagny

Meuse

Châtenois

Neufchâteau

Woëvre

Meuse

St-Mihiel

Verdun

Heippes

Rupt

Bar-le-Duc

Pont-sur-Meuse

Commercy

St-Aubin

Vaucouleurs

Mazey-sur-Vaise

Omain

Ligny

Stainville

Houdelaincourt

Gondrecourt

Sommeville

Joinville

Marne

Clermont

les Islettes

Revigny

Omain

St. Dizier

Ste-Menehould

Châlons-en-Champagne

Vitry-le-François

Marne

0 km   10   20   30 km

0 mi   6   13   19 mi

Between the Moselle and the Meuse

Ségur's Honor Guards arrived in Rambervillers around 7:00 P.M. on the evening of the 11th. Much to their dismay, they found neither lodging, food, nor forage. Ségur himself went to Victor's headquarters to request orders. He was told to wait with bridle in hand for the corps to depart, at which time his squadrons would join the rearguard. At 11:00 P.M. Victor summoned him to dinner. Ségur describes a pitiful scene. Sitting around a table in a poorly lit, damp room, the marshal shared a lugubrious, paltry meal with his somber guests. Victor discussed his situation in a low voice; bitter sarcasm permeated his words. "A true dinner of the defeated," notes Ségur, "which one had to finish hurriedly to escape during this same night, under a cold and battering rain, abandoning the unfortunate residents to the mercy of barbarians. This gloomy retreat was rendered even more distressful at daybreak, when a very strong east wind brought a freeze of ten degrees; the roads became mirrors of ice, the exhausted and famished men advanced with toil, the horses, especially those of the artillery, fell at every step."[47] In these trying conditions, Victor concentrated the II Infantry and V Cavalry Corps along the Rambervillers–Lunéville road early on the 12th.

Victor's situation became worse before the dawn of a new day. No new instructions arrived from Paris and Coalition forces were closing on his left, center, and right. The marshal spent the day of the 12th at Roville coordinating the retreat. There he received a morale-shattering letter from Ney dated 11:00 P.M. on the 11th containing valuable information provided by subprefect at Château-Salins, Pierre-Alexandre-Édouard Fleury de Chaboulon. According to the civil official, Marmont was retreating and Blücher's advance guard soon would reach Château-Salins, twenty-four miles north of Lunéville. Marmont failed to hold the Silesian Army at the Saar! "According to this report," speculates Ney, "it appears the duke of Raguse has been under the walls of Metz since yesterday; I have to suppose he has informed you of his retrograde movement, which is doubly evil since it exposes Nancy, where there are 3,000 men of the Young Guard . . . secondly, your army corps is exposed and risks losing its communications with Nancy. I believe the enemy has sent detachments to Mirecourt and Neufchâteau. I very much desire to hear from you."[48]

This news broke Victor's spirit; the marshal issued directives to continue the retreat immediately and to move as close as possible to Lunéville before nightfall on the 12th. He ordered his 1st, 2nd, and 3rd Divisions to camp on the Rambervillers–Lunéville road in Gerbéviller, Xermaménil, and Magnières respectively. After passing the night in these positions, all three divisions would depart at 4:00 A.M. on the 13th, march through Lunéville, and proceed to the bridge over the Meurthe at St. Nicolas, seven miles southeast of Nancy. As rearguard, Milhaud's dragoons would spend the night in Roville, while Piré's light cavalry along with the 24th Light Infantry Regiment occupied Baccarat to the east in the Meurthe Valley. They, too, would follow the infantry toward Nancy at 4:00 on the morning of the 13th.

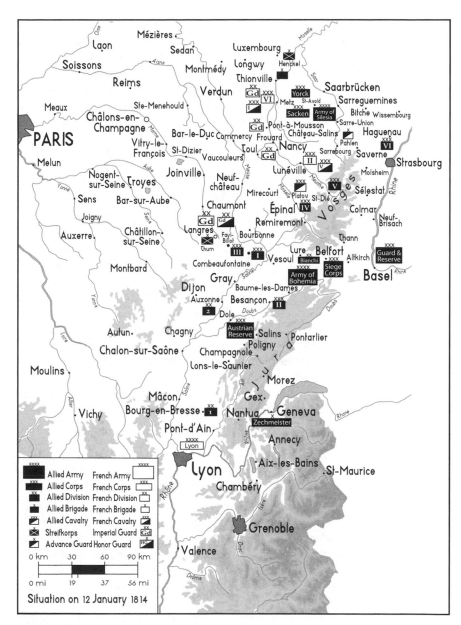

Map 16. Situation on 12 January 1814.

Victor's complicated orders for the cavalry directed the two dragoon divisions to Roville that same evening, from where they would depart at 4:00 A.M. on the 13th for St. Nicolas. The Honor Guard and 300 sabers of light cavalry were to remain on the road from St. Dié, while the 24th Light Infantry Regiment and one battery formed the extreme rearguard under Defrance; all would depart likewise at 4:00 and follow the general movement to Lunéville. Piré's light cavalry would withdraw along the parallel Lunéville–Baccarat road, uniting with Defrance's units at the former. After making this junction, Defrance would assume command of the Honor Guard, Piré's division, the battery, and the 24th Light Infantry Regiment to observe the enemy and cover Lunéville as much as possible. If need be, Defrance could fall back on St. Nicolas.[49]

At Nancy, Marshal Ney, "the bravest of the brave," felt the impending doom. His letter to Berthier on the 11th contains a litany of complaints – not the marshal's, but those he received from regional civil authorities. "The prefect at Épinal demands arms and ammunition to cultivate the good will of the inhabitants.[50] The subprefect at Sarrebourg fears being exposed to the incursions of the Cossacks, who already have appeared between this town and Phalsbourg because the retreat of the Honor Guard left the pass of Saverne defenseless." Of greater consequence was the information provided by Fleury de Chaboulon. The prefect forwarded a letter from the mayor of St. Avold, thirty-eight miles northeast of Nancy, announcing that Marmont's corps had arrived there on the 10th. In Ney's view, Marmont's retreat "uncovers the road from Sarreguemines to Nancy and exposes the Department of the Meurthe to the incursions of the enemy's light troops." The marshal did issue one complaint of his own regarding the excruciating shortage of funds. "The need of money is acute in all branches of the service. I ask you to inform His Majesty of this lack of resources, which paralyzes everything and is the reason and the excuse for all delays in the execution of measures that are ordered." Ney also informed Berthier that he would impress on Victor the need to cover Nancy but to avoid being outflanked on his right by the Allied forces moving toward Toul from Épinal: "a direction the enemy appears to want to take to reach Mirecourt or Neufchâteau [on the Meuse], where cavalry detachments already have appeared. An officer coming from the environs of Vesoul has confirmed seeing an enemy column marching on Langres between the 4th and the 7th; it will arrive there unless capable forces are prepared to stop the enemy from continuing his march."[51]

The situation at Nancy remained tense throughout the 12th. On a foggy morning, reports arrived around 7:00 that French troops had evacuated Sarrebourg and Baccarat.[52] The commandant of Phalsbourg informed Ney that on 9 January, a large Russian force of infantry, artillery, and cavalry reached Saverne and continued west toward Nancy. "Their cavalry is on this side of Sarrebourg," wrote Ney, "and their main communications are completely exposed."[53] To find news of Marmont, Ney sent a detachment of 100 dragoons to Château-Salins. During the day, he learned that a "column of 4,000 infantry with eight guns and light cavalry" had defeated Rousseau at Épinal on the previous day.[54] At 4:30 in the afternoon, the dull rumble of artillery could be heard from the direction of Flavigny, where the main body of Rousseau's 1st Brigade attempted to defend the bridge over the Moselle seven miles south of Nancy.[55] Ney again wrote Victor, urging him to cover the southern approaches of Nancy and Toul. Moreover, it appeared that Marmont's retreat toward Metz would expose the northern approaches of both cities. "He must not be left isolated if he is pressed by superior enemy forces and is in full march," Ney explains to Victor, who had nothing to send Marmont except his condolences.[56] During the day, a report from Kellermann at Metz confirmed Ney's assumptions regarding Marmont: "The duke of Raguse has retreated on Metz today."[57]

Victor left Roville around 3:00 on the afternoon of the 12th and rode further north to spend the night with his 1st Division in Gerbéviller. That evening he informed Ney that the "insignificant detachment which appeared at Épinal on the 11th" had dramatically increased in size. Victor believed that he was outflanked on his right by the Allied forces that passed the night of 11–12 January in Charmes and Châtel. Contrary to Ney's expectations, he had not received any news from Marmont. He planned to continue his retreat to St. Nicolas.[58] Responding to the mayor of Lunéville's request for instructions over the evacuation of the wounded, Victor allegedly stated: "It does not matter if they are taken here or elsewhere, we are finished."[59]

Dejean, who still accompanied Victor, composed a despondent report to Berthier that reflected the mood of the marshal's headquarters. The situation had grown worse from day to day; Victor, Ney, and Marmont lacked sufficient forces to operate independently. He urged the emperor to unite them without delay and form an army while there was still time. Reflecting Victor's concern over the Württembergers as opposed to the Bavarians, Dejean noted how the presence of enemy forces at Épinal considerably threatened the II Infantry and V Cavalry Corps. Although that day's forced march placed the French much closer to St. Nicholas than the Allied forces coming from Épinal, Dejean expressed concern the enemy would reach this town before Victor and seize the bridge over the Meurthe, thus severing the marshal's line of retreat to Nancy.[60] It did not matter that on the 13th the crown prince of Württemberg would march in the opposite direction, that Wrede would only emerge from the Vosges with one division, and that Wittgenstein would continue to snail westward; the mentally exhausted French commanders could only react to perceived threats – initiative was as absent as the emperor.

Thus aware of the dangers facing Nancy from the north, east, and south; of Marmont's and Victor's retreat; and of his own weak troop strength, Ney's frustration turned to panic. In this mind-set, he grasped the idea of conducting an orderly retreat rather than attempting a suicidal counteroffensive. From the moment Victor had concentrated the II Infantry and V Cavalry Corps around Rambervillers instead of moving closer to Nancy by withdrawing on Lunéville, Ney convinced himself that a successful defense of the provincial capital was unlikely. Around 5:00 in the evening, Ney informed Colchen that he still hoped Victor would reach Lunéville before the Allies could close his road. The marshal hinted he intended to defend Nancy by linking with Victor and Marmont. This proved to be little more than a smokescreen designed to shield Ney from imperial criticism. His hope that Victor would beat the Allies to Lunéville suggests he doubted his colleague could reach Lunéville ahead of the enemy. Moreover, Marmont's evacuation of German Lorraine and retreat to the Moselle made a joint operation with him impossible unless Ney abandoned Nancy. Finally, his own tiny force did not allow him to link the operations of the dukes of Raguse and Bellune.[61]

The fact that neither Ney nor Victor received direct communication from Marmont was more than just an irritant: it signaled that Allied cavalry probably kept pace with the marshal on parallel roads as he retreated from the Saar to the Moselle. "The enemy can thus arrive here easily and without the slightest hindrance," Ney reveals to Caulaincourt. "According to all likelihood, the enemy will attempt to debouch on Nancy and possibly Toul at the same time. The duke of Bellune has no time to lose to withdraw on Nancy or to attack the enemy in the flank as he debouches through Rambervillers." Ney also vented his frustration over the lack of information, which is somewhat debatable considering the amount of reports he received since reaching Nancy: "Perhaps you are better apprized of the enemy's movements," continues his note to Caulaincourt, "because I have learned nothing, absolutely nothing, since my arrival here although I have written to everyone."

In a second letter to Caulaincourt, Ney's anxiety becomes more pronounced: "According to all appearances, the enemy will attack the post at Flavigny and then I will be forced to abandon Nancy and echelon myself on Toul." Ney penned this letter before he received Victor's reply regarding his retreat to St. Nicolas. Once again the lack of communication between the marshals and the absence of a commander in chief took its toll. "The disposition of the troops of the duke de Bellune at Rambervillers appears inconceivable to me and very critical," concludes Ney's letter to Caulaincourt. "I have been informed that he has been outflanked by superior numbers. Why doesn't he take the initiative to attack the enemy at Charmes or, if it is too late, to withdraw on Nancy? I fear the enemy will not allow him this option, which will force him to take the direction through Lunéville to Pont-à-Mousson, thus abandoning the road to Toul."[62] Ney's daily report to Berthier reveals the full extent of the marshal's frustration over Victor as well as his growing determination to evacuate Nancy:

The duke of Bellune wrote me yesterday from Rambervillers; he informed me that he has very considerable forces in front of him, that he is outflanked on all sides, and that he is often without communication. I informed him of the evacuation of Épinal, and I have engaged him in several letters to depart and to not expose himself to having his line of retreat severed. The duke of Raguse was at Longeville yesterday, south of St. Avold, and I must presume that today he has been forced to retreat under the cannon of Metz. As a result, the city of Nancy and the retreat of the duke of Bellune are very compromised from this side [the north]; the road from Sarreguemines to Château-Salins remains absolutely defenseless. According to this state of affairs if, as everything leads me to believe, the enemy continues his march, it appears impossible to hold the city of Nancy. The duke of Bellune is not close enough to anything to hope for any important result from his efforts.[63]

Ney reached the conclusion that any further lingering in Nancy would be useless: the capital of Lorraine would be evacuated the next day. His headquarters issued orders for all troops, depots and the military administration in Nancy to leave for Toul at 5:00 A.M. on the 13th. All combat-ready soldiers would take post at Velaine, the halfway point along the thirteen miles that separated Nancy and Toul.[64] Ney ordered Meunier's division to hold Nancy until Victor's troops arrived. Approximately 1,500 men of the Young Guard took post at the city's various gates with the rest of Meunier's soldiers in reserve to maintain order; the cannon were turned to greet the invader.[65] Detachments of 150 dragoons each left Nancy to warily patrol the roads to Toul, Lunéville, and Château-Salins. The marshal advised Colchen to have the civil administration evacuate the city prior to the military's departure.[66]

At 10:00, an officer from Marmont's staff finally reached Nancy to deliver a verbal report. Marmont did not know the enemy's intentions but felt certain the Allies would advance either to Château-Salins or all the way to Nancy. Regarding the enemy, the report could not have been worse. The Allied army appeared considerably stronger and in good condition. This led Ney to believe the Allies would reach his own forward posts by the 13th. Although he still had not heard from Victor by 11:30 P.M. on the 12th, the prince of the Moskowa felt he could not change his time of departure on the following morning.[67]

The situation in the capital of Lorraine complimented the cold winter day of 13 January. Colchen, senator and extraordinary-commissioner to the 4th Military District, as well as Prefect Jean-Baptiste Maximilien Villot de Fréville of the Meurthe Department, left the city that morning. Taking Ney's advice, the secretary-general, bishop, and civil administration already had departed during the night.[68] Caulaincourt, who tarried in Nancy to observe the troops file out of the city, described the mood of the inhabitants in a letter to the emperor: "The roads are covered with fleeing people. One cannot hide the extreme consternation. The talk in the streets reveals the most black-hearted spirit. The military invasion – the invasion of a large part of our territory – has caused general dejection."[69] After learning that the head of Victor's column had arrived at St. Nicolas that morning, the foreign minister left Nancy around 9:00 A.M. and proceeded west to Void on the Meuse.

Ney himself remained at Nancy, hoping to meet with his fellow marshal sometime in the evening to gain a more accurate view of the threat from the south. He resolved not to evacuate the city completely until Victor's infantry arrived, at which time Meunier's division would withdraw to Toul.[70] While waiting for news from Victor himself, he received a letter from Kellermann penned at 4:00 A.M. on the 13th, stating that Marmont's headquarters had reached Metz and that his soldiers had moved into billets on the right bank of the Moselle. Moreover, Army Headquarters was being transferred from Metz to Châlons-en-Champagne.[71] After reading Kellermann's dispatch, he wrote Victor to share this information and encourage him to hasten his retreat. Ney also complained to his colleague that he had "indirectly" learned of the arrival of the II Corps at St. Nicolas, rather than receiving word from Victor himself. "I hope you have read my letter from yesterday evening," cautions Ney, "in which I express how pressing it is for you to accelerate your march on Toul. The enemy . . . marches by his left, probably on Toul . . . it appears the enemy is in full march on your flanks. . . . I sent an aide-de-camp to Paris to explain the state of affairs and to suggest a prompt concentration of troops at St. Dizier and Châlons in order to stop the progress of the enemy. I request news." Ney's statements over the enemy's march on Nancy and Toul probably did not surprise Victor. However, the prince's claim that Allied forces also were approaching the crossings over the Ornain River at Gondrecourt and the Marne River at Joinville provided sufficient motivation for Victor to increase the pace of his retreat.[72]

Much to Ney's surprise, the hours passed quietly and without Coalition forces attacking the men of the 4th Military District who guarded the bridges over the Moselle south of Nancy at Flavigny and Pont-St. Vincent. Reports from the countryside did claim that on the 12th a large Allied column with artillery crossed the Moselle between Remiremont and Épinal and headed west toward Mirecourt. Yet although the danger from the south appeared to have passed, the threat from the northeast drew closer. Coming from Château-Salins, Blücher's cavalry reached Nancy's eastern suburbs on the right bank of the Meurthe. The moment of reckoning had arrived, and Ney hoped to coordinate with Victor a defense of Nancy.

In his brief to Berthier, Ney outlined a strategy to hold the Allies until reinforcements arrived. He believed Nancy could be defended by maintaining a strong rearguard echelonned westward on the road to Toul. If the Allies forced the evacuation of Nancy's garrison, he planned to take a position between the Meuse and Toul at the town of Foug, which he wanted to defend as a bridgehead. The crossing over the Meuse at Vaucouleurs would be occupied by infantry, while cavalry patrolled the region between the Meuse and Moselle from Neufchâteau to Mirecourt. "The position of Foug is unique for defense," explained Ney, "the enemy can only force it if he crosses the Moselle at Pont-à-Mousson and proceeds to Bar-le-Duc, or crosses the Meuse at Vaucouleurs or Neufchâteau and proceeds to St. Dizier. By destroying these bridges, one can dispute the ground for a long time and await reinforcements, at least if the enemy does not swiftly gain Verdun and Langres." Although Ney's plans show initiative, his letter to Berthier provides further proof of the discomfort caused by the absence of a commander in chief as well as the abysmal state of communication between the French marshals: "I have no news from Metz or of the position of the troops that have been directed on Langres; it is essential that I know of their march in order to act in concert with their movements in a manner to slow the enemy and to be able to concentrate on a point that the emperor judges wise according to the actual circumstances."[73]

Many variables could unravel Ney's plan, but at least one marshal in Lorraine thought of stopping the Allies. Yet thought it remained, for later that evening Ney's resolve snapped under extreme anxiety. In his correspondence, the marshal did not reveal any particular detail that may have triggered his collapse. According to Caulaincourt, however, Ney feared the Allies would reach Toul before him and sever his line of retreat. "The prince of the Moskowa claims to have given you all the details of the affair at Épinal and all that has taken place in this region," wrote Caulaincourt to Napoleon. "He appears resolved to retire with the duke of Bellune on St. Dizier. One claims the enemy is at Langres. All reports announce he will debouch in the Department of the Meurthe in many columns. The prince fears very much that he will not be able to reach Toul ahead of him."[74]

That this fear finally mastered Ney and broke his spirit can be observed in two subsequent dispatches to Berthier, likewise composed on the evening of the 13th. The first served as a response to Berthier's general letter of 10 January to Victor, Ney, and Marmont, which stressed the importance of holding the defiles of the Vosges to slow the enemy's progress. "The enemy cannot be stopped in the gorges of the Vosges with the insufficient resources of the duke of Bellune, who is in full retreat on Toul," retorts Ney. "Headquarters is withdrawing from Metz to Châlons-en-Champagne; the former is closely invested by the enemy. The duke of Raguse has crossed the Moselle. The enemy's columns are in full march on Paris by the debouches of Langres, Nancy, Metz, and Verdun. It is still possible to promptly assemble forces either at St. Dizier or Châlons to momentarily stop his march. The forces of the enemy are considerable, one estimates them to be at least 200,000; never have the circumstances been more critical."

Perhaps aggravated by the extent Paris remained out of touch with the actual events at the front, Ney felt compelled to write the second letter to Berthier. "I received the dispatch you wrote me on the 10th in which you share with me the instructions you gave the duke of Bellune for the defense of the Vosges. My previous letters informed you that all the passes of these mountains have been in the enemy's hands since my arrival at Nancy. It is just a dream to be able stop the enemy on this side with the available resources. The duke of Bellune, who has very insignificant forces and who is outflanked on all sides, retreats on Toul." Whether for security reasons or to drive home his point, Ney repeated the same statements he made in his previous report regarding Army Headquarters, Marmont, the estimated size of the enemy army, and the possibility of concentrating at St. Dizier or Châlons. However, the marshal made the very interesting addition of Belgium to the list of regions from where the Allies were marching on Paris.[75]

Although at Nancy for less than four days, Marshal Ney was ready to extricate himself from the bleak situation. "The duke of Bellune has asked the prince of the Moskowa to take command of the two corps," notes Caulaincourt, "he does not want to increase his responsibility under these circumstances."[76] "Above all it is very important that several marshals do not find themselves united because they frustrate each other; it is necessary that only one has the command," warns Dejean, who observed the lack of cooperation between the marshals and their failure to appreciate Napoleon's military and political needs.[77] Without the presence of the emperor's energy and courage to drive his marshals they, like any humans in their circumstances, quickly succumbed to despondency.

As Ney evacuated Nancy and Marmont left Metz, Victor's II Infantry and V Cavalry Corps continued the retreat on the 13th. Before leaving Gerbéviller, he wrote Ney at 6:00 A.M. to request that the prince remain at Nancy.[78] By day's end Victor's units extended from Nancy's southeastern suburb to Lunéville, where the rearguard arrived around 11:00 P.M. Victor planned to maintain these positions and grant his tired men a day of rest on the 14th, but the panic that seized Ney did not spare him. During the evening of the 13th, Victor received Ney's letter informing him that a Prussian column from Château-Salins reached Nancy both to invest the city and link with the Württembergers, who were supposedly advancing down the Moselle. His note also alerted Victor to the advance of Coalition forces toward the valleys of the Ornain and Marne.[79] The existing correspondence does not reveal the source of these ridiculous stories, but both marshals were poorly served by their cavalry and intelligence-gathering services.

Regarding the Allies, only Platov's Cossacks operated between the Moselle and Meuse at this time. Army Group Alsace accomplished little on the 12th: Wittgenstein's VI Corps remained idle; Wrede's V Corps continued its trek through the Vosges. On the 13th, the Bavarians debouched from the mountains between St. Dié and Rambervillers. One battalion and two squadrons occupied Épinal following the departure of the Württembergers for Langres.[80] After receiving Blücher's 9 January report confirming that the Silesian Army would reach Metz on the 15th, Schwarzenberg's headquarters finally issued instructions for Wittgenstein to begin moving west toward Nancy to fill the gap between Schwarzenberg's right and Blücher's left.[81] Despite the actual circumstances, perceptions loomed larger than facts: to the demoralized warriors and terrified peasants of France, Cossack bands appeared to be army corps.

That evening Victor's headquarters issued orders for the retreat to continue at 5:00 on the morning of the 14th by marching through Nancy to Toul. "The enemy appears to be maneuvering on Toul. I advise that the movement commence precisely at 5:00 A.M." wrote the duke of Bellune.[82] Shortly after issuing these instructions to Grouchy, his fear that the Allies were on the verge of severing his line of retreat by seizing the bridges over the Meuse, Ornain, and Marne, induced Victor to move up the time of departure to 3:00 A.M. for the II Corps, 2:00 A.M. for the V Cavalry Corps, and 1:00 A.M. for the 24th Light Infantry Regiment, which served as the extreme rearguard.[83]

At Paris Napoleon wove together the incoming reports to produce a fairly accurate overview of the Allied invasion plan, but grossly underestimated the size of Schwarzenberg's army. In his "Note" of 12 January, the emperor concluded that the Allies had launched three main attacks. The first was against the Netherlands by the Army of North Germany. Napoleon estimated this Allied force to be no more than 20,000 men. He also speculated that Blücher's Silesian Army was marching toward Metz with no more than 45,000 men. Blücher's numbers would be further reduced by disease as well as the strategic consumption of observing Luxembourg, Saarlouis, and Metz. As for Schwarzenberg's army, Napoleon believed that according "to the most exaggerated calculations, this army has no more than 100,000 men," who have to besiege Huningue, Belfort, Strasbourg, Sélestat, Landau, and Besançon as well as occupy Geneva and hold Switzerland. Altogether he believed these three Allied armies could not exceed 180,000 men. Even this amount appeared to be too high. This number "must be quite exaggerated because the enemy himself, in his greatest claims, only states the number to be 200,000 men," concluded the master of war. To this total Napoleon added his estimates of the various Allied siege corps: approximately 100,000 men "on the right bank of the Rhine," as the emperor phrased it. He calculated that these 100,000 men, added to the 180,000 who had invaded France, provided the Allies with a total force of 280,000 to 300,000 men, exclusive of the Allied army in Italy. "We do not believe he can have more. Disease has been more devastating to his army than ours; their own reports concur that the battles have cost them many men."

Assuming Bülow and Graham together commanded around 20,000 men, Napoleon figured 4,000 would have to remain at Gorinchem, 2,000 at Bergen-op-Zoom, and 2,000 at Breda. Consequently, the Allies would have only 12,000 to 15,000 men, who would be needed to observe Antwerp. "I do not believe they will be a threat to us except to preach insurrection among some parties," states his "Note." As for Blücher, the Prussian field-marshal "could not have left fewer than 20,000 men at Mainz; Luxembourg, Saar-louis, and Thionville will occupy 10,000." Schwarzenberg would be forced to leave 10,000 men in Switzerland, 15,000 at Besançon, and 20,000 around the fortresses between Huningue and Landau, meaning that this army "could not march toward Langres and Nancy with more than 50,000 men. We suppose that 25,000 or 30,000 men of Blücher's army will unite with the 50,000 or 60,000 men of Prince Schwarzenberg; it does not appear they can march on Paris with more than 80,000 men. Although this operation would be crazy, we must consider it."[84]

To defend Paris, Napoleon continued to develop the plans he started draft-ing on 8 January. His "field armies," mainly the corps and divisions com-manded by Macdonald (10,000 men), Marmont (15,000 men), Victor (12,000 men), and Mortier (12,000 men), had escaped the Allied onslaught, but not without loss. Napoleon's "Note" divulges his plans for the marshals. Macdon-ald would "gather everything he could," and move to Liège and Charlemont to threaten Blücher's right flank. Although Napoleon's more immediate concern was Macdonald's ability to prevent Blücher from sending units to Belgium, if the Silesian Army marched on Paris, Macdonald had to reach the capital before the enemy.[85] He expected the other three marshals to delay the Allies by contesting their every step. If Paris appeared to be the Allied objective, then the marshals would unite with Macdonald in front of the capital, where Napoleon would join them with 60,000 men – a number the emperor believed he could triple if his marshals held the Allies for just one month.

The attention Napoleon devoted to the French capital in his "Note" sug-gests that he did not have confidence in the ability of his marshals to slow the Allied advance. "Never make plans to desert Paris," he insists, "and even bury ourselves under its ruins if necessary." He wanted to assemble a large num-ber of guns in Paris "in order to have a huge superiority in artillery over the enemy." His estimates called for between sixty and eighty pieces of artillery for the city's numerous barriers. He wanted the city wall repaired; palisades, tambours, and *chevaux de frise* were to be secretly prepared to obstruct the gates and the open areas before the capital. Officers of "discreet intelligence" would be placed in charge of occupying the hills of Paris as well as the bridges across the Seine and Marne with the Paris National Guard and sixty guns. Carriages would be built to hold fifty pieces of 24-pounder and 16-pounder cannon that would be positioned on the hills, at the bridges, and in redoubts. "An army of 120,000 men, which will increase daily," concludes Napoleon, "will cover the capital; perhaps it is a good idea for the suppliers to secretly provide Paris with 60,000 sacks of flour."

From these thoughts Napoleon drafted a thirteen-point program, eleven points of which dealt with Paris, the twelfth with fortifying Lyon in the same manner as the capital, and the final point concerning the creation of a com-mittee to study and evaluate defense plans before submitting a comprehensive draft for the emperor's approval. Napoleon's grasp of the task at hand is more than impressive. In summary, his thirteen points sought to assemble at Paris 1,000 pieces of artillery, 200,000 to 300,000 balls, and 8 to 10 million cartridges. Between 5,000 and 6,000 caissons and wagons would be brought in from as far away as Metz, Le Havre, and Cherbourg. He increased his demand for flour to between 80,000 and 100,000 sacks to ensure the capital's food supply for four to five months. Napoleon called for 40,000 to 50,000 tools as well as construction workers, supervisors "and all the resources to make Paris a fortress and arsenal." All conscripts and cadre battalions were to report to Paris. Lastly, as soon as the emperor accepted a general defense plan, he would inform the public "in order to give the impulse to the nation so that everyone will be convinced that we will do everything to defend Paris and Lyon."[86]

On the next day, 13 January, Napoleon condensed his thoughts and plans into uncomplicated, concise "General Instructions" for his field commanders: Maison, Macdonald, Marmont, Victor, Ney, and Mortier. Replete with words of encouragement, demands, estimates of Allied strength, and instructions for the marshals to employ propaganda, the master's "General Instructions" sought to provide unity of command in lieu of his absence. The orders contained his summary of the numbers and objectives of the three Allied forces that crossed the Rhine. He informed Maison that Bülow could not have more than 9,000 to 10,000 men: "Maison must hold him and defeat him." Napoleon further downgraded the size of Blücher's army to 30,000 men after it crossed the Rhine and left behind a siege corps of 20,000 to 25,000 men at Mainz. "He proceeds to the Saar and then will have to mask Saarlouis; if he proceeds to the Moselle, he will have to mask Luxembourg, Thionville, Marsal, and Metz. His army hardly suffices for all these operations." Marmont received orders to "observe, hold, maneuver among the fortresses, and if by chance this marshal has to cross the Moselle [retreat], he will place Durutte's division in Metz and harass the enemy on the road to Paris." He also explained how Marmont and Macdonald should work together against Blücher. If the Prussian marched on Paris, Macdonald would threaten Blücher's right, defend the Meuse, and cover the approaches to Paris. "On the contrary, if Blücher, after having reached the Saar, proceeds to the lower Meuse to threaten Belgium, the duke of Tarent [Macdonald] will defend the Meuse, and the duke of Raguse will follow the enemy's left in order to observe his movements, contain him, delay him, and hurt him as much as possible." As for Schwarzenberg, Napoleon did not provide a figure for the size of his army and only stated that the Austrian would be forced to detach 60,000 to 65,000 men for occupation and siege duties in Switzerland and Alsace. Regardless, he insisted that this army "must be held" by Mortier at Langres, Ney at Nancy and Épinal, and Victor at the passes through the Vosges. "These three marshals must communicate with each other; we must regain and secure the passes of the Vosges; if the enemy penetrates in force these three corps must block his path and always cover the road to the capital, where the emperor will assemble an army of 100,000 men." Perhaps the most interesting aspect of the "General Instructions" is Napoleon's advice on the use of propaganda: "The marshals can make some proclamations in order to counteract the invectives of the enemy generals. They must publicize that 200,000 men of the National Guard have formed in Brittany, Normandy, Picardie, and around Paris and are marching to Châlons, independent of a regular army of more than 100,000 men; peace has been concluded with King Ferdinand and the guerillas of Spain, our troops from Aragon and Catalogne are marching to Lyon, and those from Bayonne to Paris; finally, warn our enemies that the sacred territory they have violated will consume them."[87]

That same day, 13 January, Berthier forwarded duplicates of the "General Instructions" to the front-line commanders.[88] The efficient chief of staff also drafted cover letters for the marshals and Maison that contained details of certain aspects of the emperor's "Note" and "General Instructions." As a result of strategic consumption, Berthier assured Marmont "that the enemy does not appear to be in any position to further penetrate French territory." For the moment, Berthier's letters merely stated that Maison should be at Antwerp, Macdonald at the Meuse, Marmont at the Saar, Victor and Ney at the Vosges, and Mortier at Langres. The reserves forming in Paris, Troyes, and Châlons-en-Champagne would, after uniting with the marshals, form an army of 130,000 to 150,000 men, not counting the 50,000-man army forming at Lyon. Berthier portrayed the union of this reserve army and the marshals' mobile corps at Paris as an extremely unlikely scenario. "His Majesty thinks we are in a position to hold the enemy beyond the Vosges and not allow him to make progress beyond the Saar and the Meuse, and that if we can maintain things status quo for about twenty days we will be in a position to drive the enemy across the Rhine."[89]

French historian Campana correctly praises Bonaparte for providing "remarkable" instructions that "clearly define the role of the marshals, who commanded the *corps de couverture.*" "These corps," he continues, "had to dispute the ground step by step to slow the enemy for as long as possible. They must also, in their fighting retreat, always cover the roads to Paris" to provide time and space for the emperor to complete the Army of Reserve and because of the political situation. According to Campana, Napoleon predicted that if the Allies reached Paris, "there would be no more empire or emperor." "Unfortunately," concludes Campana, "after an initial resistance, the marshals all simply retired at the approach of the enemy." This evaluation is too easy on Napoleon and too harsh on the marshals. Campana fails to acknowledge that it took Napoleon almost four weeks after the Bohemian Army crossed the Rhine to issue these "remarkable instructions." Moreover, by the time the "General Instructions" reached the marshals, their erroneous understanding of their task had rendered the situation unsalvageable in view of their weak forces, the general demoralization of their troops, and their own mental exhaustion.[90]

By remaining at Paris, Napoleon placed himself in an impossible situation. In late December, he drafted a plan for the defense of Alsace after the province already had been invaded. On 13 January, he dictated another defense plan that sent Ney to Épinal and ordered Victor to reoccupy the Vosges. When planning the defense of Lorraine, the emperor had no way of knowing the Württembergers already had taken Épinal and the Bavarians had pushed across the Vosges, nor did he know Marmont had opened the northern frontier of the province to the Silesian Army. Unfortunately for Bonaparte, he remained several steps behind the flow of events. The lessons of Iberia and Germany went unheeded: Napoleon could not direct operations from hundreds of miles away. The French army desperately needed General Bonaparte in the field.

Napoleon issued few orders on 14 January, yet two are worthy of mention. The first instructed Bertrand, Napoleon's new grand marshal of the palace, to direct the emperor's horses to Châlons-en-Champagne.[91] The second consists of Napoleon's typical barrage of instructions to Berthier. Chief among his tasks for that day was to order Curial from Metz to Châlons, where he would assume command of all forces: Guard, Line, and artillery. Napoleon also authorized Berthier to sanction the *levée-en-masse* in the Departments of the Ardennes and the Marne as well as the prefecture of Châlons to "place everything in movement and under arms to defend the country." Finally, the diligent chief of staff had to instruct Clarke to accelerate the march of nineteen reserve battalions to Troyes.[92] All this indicated Napoleon had finally decided to leave Paris to assume command personally of his mobile corps, and he desperately sought more manpower.

Meanwhile, thirty-eight miles northeast of Nancy, Blücher moved his headquarters to St. Avold on the 12th and informed Schwarzenberg of his progress: "Today the Silesian Army arrived before Metz. Saarlouis and Landau are invested, Thionville and Luxembourg are burning." He stated that his next move would be determined by the enemy but politely added that he would direct his operations according to Schwarzenberg's wishes to maintain communication between the two armies. The field marshal also mentioned Bülow's problems with Wintzingerode, who demanded that a Prussian brigade support his crossing of the Rhine. Blücher complained to both Schwarzenberg and Frederick William, urging them to ask the tsar to reiterate his orders for Wintzingerode to assume the offensive and cooperate with Bülow.[93]

By 13 January, Blücher's confidence could not have been greater, as a letter to his kinsman suggests: "As long as the Rhine has been called the Rhine no army of 80,000 men has crossed it so easily, for I have thus captured thirteen cannon and taken 2,000 prisoners. I already have tightly invested Mainz and Saarlouis, and today I am eight hours away from Metz; I think

I will arrive before this fortress the day after tomorrow." Commenting on French preparations and the state of his own army, Blücher adds:

> Napoleon has now summoned the nation: all from twenty to sixty years of age will take up arms, but I believe they lack the weapons. The mortality is great here and the [French] nation is very tired. We have no shortages and our men are in the best spirit. As long as we do not make a dumb mistake everything is expected to go well. I have 50,000 Russians with me; they show me a confidence that is unequaled and have named me the 'German Suvarov'. The bravery of our troops is extraordinary and our Landwehr is in no way inferior to our veteran troops. For all of his suffering the king will be completely compensated since he will receive his entire monarchy back and still more. The noble Alexander is a friend of uncommon form.[94]

While Yorck's corps crossed the Saar and advanced toward Metz, Henckel launched reconnaissance missions from Trier. On the 9th, his units reached Luxembourg. The Prussians returned to Trier with prisoners and news that enemy cavalry left Luxembourg for the French interior. On the 10th, another scouting party rendered a favorable report over the possibility of taking Luxembourg. According to the inhabitants, the majority of French troops had departed, leaving behind a small garrison of 700 conscripts. Furthermore, Prussian scouts brought in a Spanish prisoner of war who was hiding in one of Luxembourg's suburbs after escaping the fortress. He insisted that 500 of his countrymen remained in Luxembourg, ready to revolt at the first opportunity. "The mood here is very favorable toward us," claims the Prussian lieutenant who commanded the mission. "The people are in a rage against the French.... Up to now two [Allied] proclamations have been posted; in general they spread the greatest joy because where a proclamation is posted, one believes it is impossible for the enemy to return. The confusion in the fortress is extreme."[95] Henckel informed Blücher that only 1,000 to 1,200 conscripts and at most 200 cavalry remained at Metz. He added that Napoleon appeared to be concentrating all available manpower at Châlons-en-Champagne. Blücher received Henckel's reports on the 14th: The intelligence had tremendous influence on the field marshal's plans.[96]

On the 13th, Prince William continued his march to Metz, where Prussian cavalry started the investment on the right bank of the Moselle. Jürgaß's Reserve Cavalry covered the roads leading to Metz, establishing communication with Lanskoi, who was en route to Pont-à-Mousson. The 1st and 2nd Brigades rested, and Yorck moved his headquarters to Longeville. All patrols mistook Ricard's march to Pont-à-Mousson as the retreat to Verdun by a considerable portion of Metz's garrison. Allied reports varied regarding the strength of the units that remained behind as well as those at Pont-à-Mousson and Nancy. In a letter to Blücher, Yorck summarized the various information he received from his forward troops: A strong garrison held Metz and a number of conscripts had moved from the fortress to the French interior. As a result, the majority of the garrison consisted of veteran troops. According to a preacher, the French had mined the ground around Metz and prepared entrenchments. Three-quarters of the inhabitants opposed a defense of the city; the remainder were tied to the French administration.[97]

Elsewhere along Blücher's front, Horn's 7th Brigade marched through a blizzard to reach Thionville late on 12 January. The brigadier wanted to sever all communication between Thionville and the neighboring fortresses but had no luck crossing the Moselle.[98] On the 13th, he moved his battalions to within 1,000 yards of the fortress. The mainly brick walls appeared to be in good condition, but no guns were seen on the ramparts. Locals revealed that the French lacked carriages for their artillery. Outposts could not be seen, so Horn rode undetected to within ten yards of the fortress. One Prussian squadron patrolled between Thionville and Metz but detected no French activity along the right bank of the Moselle. The Prussians did observe the departure of infantry and artillery from Thionville to Metz along the left bank; French cavalry rode off in the direction of Verdun. Horn could not cross the thin layer of ice that blanketed the Moselle and thus limited himself to investing the fortress on the right bank. The exhaustion of his cavalry and the dispersal of many detachments meant that he could only observe the fortress until reinforcements arrived.

Sacken's corps, which caught up with Yorck's, received a day of rest on 13 January, but patrols continued to pound the roads westward. To determine whether the French remained at Metz or had retreated to Verdun as reported, the Russians reached the Moselle. Vasilchikov led the Russian cavalry in the direction of Pont-à-Mousson. His light cavalry under Lanskoi investigated the condition of the bridges over the Meurthe at Bouxières and the Moselle at Frouard. In what proved to be the decisive blow to the French defense of Lorraine, the Russians found both bridges intact, crossed, and made for the bridges over the Meuse at Commercy and St. Mihiel. Patrols detected the march of French troops and artillery from Metz to Verdun. Vasilchikov himself reached Pont-à-Mousson and reported that French artillery and 7,000 infantry – about double the actual number – held the town and its bridge over the Moselle. The Russian commander failed to take Pont-à-Mousson; French skirmishers repulsed the Russians but limited themselves to maintaining posts outside the town walls.

Also on 13 January, Biron's advance troops made contact with French vedettes at Essey, one mile northeast of Nancy. Supported by one howitzer, French infantry defended the bridge over the Meurthe from the attacks of Biron's dismounted cavalry. Prisoners claimed that only 1,500 to 2,000 infantry, 150 dragoons, and eight guns held the city. With this encouraging news, Biron prepared to storm Nancy on the 14th but changed his mind after learning that French reinforcements – Victor's corps – had arrived. His luck changed yet again when the bulk of the garrison withdrew during the night followed by the rearguard in the afternoon. At 4:00 P.M. on 14 January Biron entered the capital of Lorraine without firing a shot; his cavalry pursued Victor's rearguard on the road to Toul, bringing back 150 stragglers.[99]

Fifteen miles southeast of Nancy two hussar squadrons from Wrede's advance guard occupied Lunéville, but the main body of the V Corps remained idle between Rambervillers and St. Dié. Wrede's Austrian divisions took advantage of this halt to move closer to Rambervillers. The Bavarian corps commander informed Schwarzenberg that Victor had evacuated Lunéville and taken either the Nancy–Langres road or the Toul–Paris road.[100]

Early on 14 January, Victor's demoralizing retreat continued along with the relentless snow. Before the Allied pincers could cut their line of retreat, the men of the II Infantry and V Cavalry Corps withdrew under a frigid north wind with empty stomachs. Around 8:00 A.M. the II Corps reached Nancy. At Victor's arrival, Ney met with him and Dejean to exchange intelligence. Ney informed Victor of his plans to move Meunier's 4,110 men to Toul that day and then to Pagny-sur-Meuse and Void on the 15th. He requested that Victor relieve the posts held by the troops of the 4th Military District on the Moselle at Flavigny and Pont-St. Vincent so these men could join his column. After naming General François-Xavier-Jacob Freytag the civil governor of Nancy, Ney departed at 10:00 A.M. for Void with Meunier's division and Cassagne's remaining troops.[101] The marshal left Nancy without removing or destroying the harnessing gear in the remount depots, the cartridge magazines, and a tobacco store valued at 6 million francs; Dejean had suggested distributing several pounds to each soldier and giving the rest to the population rather than leave it to the enemy. More important, Ney neglected to destroy the bridges at Frouard and Bouxières just north of Nancy.

By this time, the destitution of Victor's soldiers had become intolerable. Living for days on charity or plunder, the exhausted soldiers began yielding to the temptation to desert. "It is with the most acute chagrin," wrote Piré to Grouchy, "that I am forced to report that desertion has become routine in my division: ten hussars of the elite 3rd as well as the 11th and 27th Chasseurs have passed to the enemy; they were all first-rate veteran soldiers, they are Alsatian or from Lorraine; the troops themselves complain of low-pay, bad uniforms, etc."[102] "I am heartbroken over the desertion," Grouchy confessed to Defrance on the 15th.[103]

In addition to the plight of the soldier, the icy roads and lack of forage created a gruesome scene. Unable to provide their mounts with winter shoes, the French watched their undernourished steeds slip on the black ice and crash to the ground with blood-chilling screams. "I must say," continues Piré, "that due to the current state of the roads and the shoes, my cavalry . . . is more than at risk. I have traveled on foot since Nancy. You know the German cavalry is well-shod and although the Cossacks are not, their horses run famously on the ice. My presence here only compromises my division because, at the enemy's approach, I will be forced to retire as a simple large mass. My horses will suffer horribly and in a few days my division will no longer exist. Moreover, how am I to live? Gondreville has been ravished and there is not a wisp of straw to be found."[104] "The horses suffer much and many have died due to the lack of funds to maintain the shoeing," states Victor's report to Berthier.[105] Grouchy graphically summarized the suffering of man and horse in a brief likewise to the major-general:

> It is with extreme pain that I am forced to inform you of the considerable attrition the cavalry suffers from desertion; not only are the new effectives from the invaded departments abandoning the flag, but also veteran soldiers from these departments: each day is marked by the number of desertions. The causes of this evil, so troublesome by its increase, are the sufferings of the soldier, who has not been paid, who receives nothing, who is portrayed as evil and badly treaty by the inhabitants, [and] finally, who is tormented by the intrigues of the Coalition, which is seconded only by the unworthy Frenchmen we have encountered ever since we left Alsace. They speak so openly against the government that they weaken the army, which is always demoralized by any retrograde movement. On the other hand, the severe weather that has been typical since the cavalry recrossed the Vosges and the long marches has caused a large number of horses to die. The horses do not have shoes for ice and the regiments do not have the funds to allocate for this urgent expenditure. From Baccarat to Toul, the V Cavalry Corps, its artillery, and the two Honor Guard regiments have lost over 300 horses to broken legs.[106]

Normally each regiment received twelve francs per year for the shoeing of one horse. Alone this sum usually did not cover the cost, which could be as high as twenty francs. Owing to the government's current fiscal crisis, the army had absolutely no funds to cover these costs.[107] Overcome with grief from watching dozens of Milhaud's steeds euthanized because no money was available to pay for shoes, Victor and Grouchy remained in Nancy long enough to attempt to remedy this problem. On Milhaud's request, Grouchy submitted to Nancy's city council a letter signed by both Victor and Ney requisitioning 15,000 francs to cover the cost of shoeing the horses. The city council subscribed the sum and authorized the municipal tax collector to procure the necessary funds from Nancy's principal capitalists. Grouchy departed with Victor but instructed Ségur, whose 3rd and 4th Honor Guard Regiments formed the extreme rearguard, to collect the sum. Ségur reached Nancy around 1:00 in the afternoon and immediately went to city hall, where he demanded that the mayor deliver the sum in fifteen minutes! Ségur had little time to complete his mission: Biron's patrols had entered Nancy through the Château-Salins gate. The mayor, a reputed physician of a rare ethical authority acknowledged by all in Nancy, could not provide the money. After a long and stormy discussion, Ségur, acting on Grouchy's behalf, ordered his men to arrest the mayor along with two of his deputies. Around 2:00 P.M., Ségur's troopers led away the hostages on the road to Toul – a "rigorous measure that sadly had to be taken due to the critical position we are in," explains Grouchy. An appeal from the city council to Nancy's leading citizens produced a spontaneous subscription that managed to provide the full sum. At 3:00 P.M., two members of the city council – Nancy's justice of the peace and a businessman – departed to deliver the money to Ségur. However, the general insisted that the two citizens had to bring the money to Toul if they wanted the hostages released. Later in the day, after the two councilmen delivered the funds to Toul, where Grouchy, Victor, and Ney signed a receipt, the mayor and his deputies were released. The cash was distributed among the cavalry and artillery of Victor's two corps.[108]

Victor had departed Nancy as soon as he could. Like Ney, the duke of Bellune also overlooked the bridges at Frouard and Bouxières. Around 11:00 A.M. on the 14th, the II Corps filed through Nancy to commence the modest twelve-mile march to Toul. The 1st Division of the II Corps led the march to Toul; by late afternoon, all of Victor's units covered the short distance. His infantry occupied the city, which became overcrowded because of the arrival from Pont-à-Mousson of the 2nd Old Guard Division en route to Langres. Victor distributed his cavalry both east and west of Toul. Lhéritier's 4th Dragoon Division took positions west of the city at Foug and Choloy to link with Meunier's Young Guard division, which had one brigade holding the bridge at Pagny-sur-Meuse. Briche's 3rd Dragoon Division passed the night east of Toul at Dommartin to support Defrance's rearguard, which was formed by the Honor Guard and Piré's light cavalry. The marshal wanted Defrance to remain on the dominating hills west of Nancy with his center echelonned between Nancy and Toul, and his right extending to Pont-St. Vincent and Flavigny to defend the southern and eastern approaches to Toul. At nightfall Defrance was to withdraw all his forces to Gondreville just west of Toul.[109]

All remained quiet while the squadrons of the rearguard took their posts. Piré's division replaced Ségur's exhausted troopers as the extreme rearguard; the latter led his soldiers to Gondreville, where, for the first time since leaving Strasbourg, the men of the Honor Guard thought they would receive a full night of rest. But around 2:00 A.M. on the 15th Cossacks surprised the 4th Honor Guard Regiment in its billets – the Russian warriors killed, wounded, and captured several men. The negligence of both Ségur and Piré caused this unfortunate incident. Ségur failed to place barricades and posts at the entrances to Gondreville, and Piré preferred to pass the night in the warmth of the village of Velaine north of the Nancy–Toul road rather than bivouac on this cold highway. Finding the road to Toul open, the Cossacks charged into the midst of Victor's rearguard, further demoralizing the marshal's disheartened soldiers.[110]

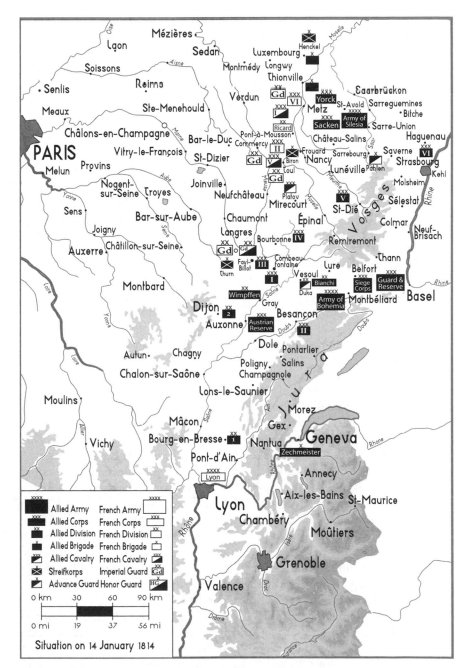

Map 17. Situation on 14 January 1814.

Victor planned to maintain his positions on the 15th but still labored under the erroneous belief fueled by Ney that the Allies had crossed the Meuse at Neufchâteau and were headed to the bridge over the Marne at Joinville. By this time Victor's headquarters knew the Allied forces operating in the Moselle Valley were not the Württembergers yet confused the Cossacks for Wrede's V Corps.[111] He also feared seeing his cavalry compromised in the long defile between Nancy and Toul formed by the Haye Forest. If it appeared the Allies would reach the Marne before him, Victor planned to lead the II Infantry and V Cavalry Corps further west to Vitry-le-François, thirty-one miles northwest of Joinville.[112] On the other hand, he hoped to hold Toul for as long as possible and to defend the Moselle jointly with Marmont, whom he assumed held the Thionville–Metz–Pont-à-Mousson line. Not knowing that Sacken's units had captured the bridge at Frouard, the marshal planned to utilize this crossing over the Moselle to link with Marmont. With this bridge in Allied hands, however, Sacken's cavalry could reach the crossings over the Meuse at St. Mihiel or Commercy before Victor.[113]

As for Marmont, the marshal took exception to the statements coming from Paris. Upon the receipt of Berthier's note of 11 January, which arrived on the 13th, he responded bitterly: "The movements I executed without battle were necessitated by the march on my flanks of superior forces, who threatened to secure before me the only points upon which I could retreat, and due to the fact that my troops are only cadres." Holding his ground and accepting battle before receiving reinforcements appeared suicidal until he retreated behind the Moselle, where he would "be supported at all places, and my retreat assured in all directions." Marmont asserted that the passes into Lorraine could not be defended without being occupied, "and to occupy all of them, more men are needed than those I have." He further argued that after garrisoning Metz, Saarlouis, and Thionville, his field units numbered only 6,000 infantry and 2,500 cavalry. "If I had 30,000 men here, I would completely change all the enemy's plans." Even with half that number, the marshal felt he could have accomplished much. It was easy for Napoleon to judge the situation from Paris, make estimations on paper, issue instructions, and then criticize his generals for not meeting his expectations. At the front, the Allied paper tiger that Napoleon portrayed in his instructions had little bearing on the realities the tired marshals faced. "I am preparing all possible means to make a good defense of the Moselle," concludes Marmont's report to Berthier, "as long as events at Nancy permit it."[114]

Ricard's division moved toward Pont-à-Mousson on the 13th to secure its bridge over the Moselle. Leaving Metz that morning, the unexpected flooding of the Moselle forced him to halt at Novéant on the river's left bank. Rather than proceed up the river, Ricard had to swing southwest to Thiaucourt and then east to Pont-à-Mousson. This movement did not escape the Prussians who, as noted, reported the enemy was retreating to Verdun. That same day

Ricard's advance guard reached Pont-à-Mousson, where it repulsed Sacken's forward cavalry units, estimated to be 500 to 600 troopers.[115]

Marmont feared this advance guard was in the process of "clearing the way to Nancy." The Allied threat to both Pont-à-Mousson and Nancy prompted him to order Ricard to observe the Moselle and reconnoiter the roads to Nancy and Toul during the 14th. Marmont gave Ricard precise instructions to investigate rumors concerning the fall of Nancy. The appearance of Allied forces at Pont-à-Mousson led the marshal to believe the enemy had changed plans. Rather than proceed against Thionville and Metz, he assumed Blücher had turned south to capture Nancy. In his note to Ricard, penned at 10:30 A.M. of the 14th, Marmont claimed he would probably march to support him on the 15th, depending on the news from Nancy.[116]

As the day progressed, Marmont developed a plan to save Nancy, link with Victor, and threaten the flank of any Allied forces marching on Toul. The confident marshal felt he could leave Metz and launch a counteroffensive. "Metz is in a very good state of defense," notes his report to Berthier. "The prefect has done much for its supplies, and it will have in troops, armed National Guard, artillery personnel, and military or civilian laborers a total of 12,000 men. I have sent almost all depots to Châlons-en-Champagne, and the last ones will leave tomorrow. The military equipment left this morning; all Guard Artillery also departed." After accusing General Mansuy-Dominique Roget de Belloguet, the commandant of the 3rd Military District and governor of Metz since 9 March 1809, of "absolute incompetence" and of doing "nothing to establish the security of the city," Marmont appointed Durutte the new commandant of Metz. The general's "efficiency and zeal" made him the logical choice. Moreover, Marmont judged Durutte's exhausted division to be "hardly in a condition to remain in the field." Approximately 100 guns were hauled up to the ramparts and grouped in batteries. Marmont also attempted to provision the city as best he could by securing large quantities of beef from the surrounding region.[117]

Whether Marmont truly intended to execute his counteroffensive or simply wished to please the critic in Paris will never be known – he abandoned the idea by 10:00 on the night of the 14th. "According to the news I received," he explains to Berthier, "the enemy must have entered this city [Nancy] this morning. I sent reconnaissance there. As soon as the enemy entered this city, my intention was to march, protected by the Moselle, against the corps facing me, in order to take in the flank the enemy's movement on Toul. But during the day the Moselle flooded the region between Metz and Pont-à-Mousson, rendering it completely impracticable for wagons." To add to the marshal's troubles, the Allied ring around Metz tightened. He received reports that Yorck's corps took a position between Metz and Thionville one mile from the right bank of the Moselle; Allied units also reached Thionville. He ended his report of 14 January by describing all he had accomplished in just two days to place Metz in a state of defense – obviously the marshal knew his days at the fortress and on the left bank of the Moselle were numbered.[118]

Although Marmont's impulse to cooperate with Victor to save Nancy is commendable, the marshal could have achieved much more by striking Blücher – much the same as if Victor had proceeded against Wrede in Upper Alsace earlier that month. The defensive-oriented orders issued to Yorck for the 14th indicate that Blücher's headquarters did not believe Marmont had evacuated Metz. Instead, the Prussians expected to be attacked by a large force debouching from the fortress. Yorck commanded only eighteen battalions to stop this anticipated counterattack; the rest of his battalions were maneuvering against Thionville and Luxembourg. Blücher had forwarded the ten battalions of the 1st Brigade to Thionville to relieve the nine battalions of the 7th Brigade, which he directed to Luxembourg to attempt a coup de main in unison with Henckel's Streifkorps coming from Trier. As a result of these detachments, Yorck at most had 10,000 men echelonned on the road to Metz and was in no position to repulse a French attack. Prince William's 8th Brigade, which served as Yorck's advance guard, occupied the defile formed by the mill of Landremont, the bridge at Pont-à-Chaussy over the small Neid river, and Courcelles-Chaussy on the right bank of the Neid (see Map 9, Chapter 9). William received instructions to hold his position for as long as possible, covered on his right flank by Stössel's squadrons on the road from Saarlouis and on his left by Jürgaß's Reserve Cavalry. Yorck assembled the 2nd Brigade west of Longeville between Fouligny and Zimming, holding the defile of the latter to receive the advance guard should it be repulsed.[119]

Late that same day, 14 January, Marmont's front started to unravel. Believing Allied forces were moving against his rear, Ricard decided to abandon Pont-à-Mousson and retreat to Thiacourt.[120] At 10:30 P.M. he withdrew without orders from Marmont, without notifying Victor or Ney, and most important, without destroying the bridge at Pont-à-Mousson. Around thirty minutes later, a courier who had passed through Pont-à-Mousson reached Metz and informed Marmont of Ricard's retreat. The disgusted marshal ordered his subordinate to halt, but it was too late. Marmont now feared being trapped in Metz. On account of this terrible news, the dispirited commander decided to depart Metz on 16 January with Lagrange's division, Decouz's 2nd Young Guard Voltigeur Division, and Doumerc's I Cavalry Corps.

At 11:30 P.M. on the 15th Marmont informed Berthier of his plans to leave the banks of the Moselle and move closer to the Meuse. Initially, the marshal attempted to conceal Ricard's mistake in this very short note to the chief of staff. Instead of criticizing his subordinate for evacuating Pont-à-Mousson, Marmont blamed Ney and Victor for Ricard's retreat. Informed of the enemy's arrival at Nancy and believing Coalition forces would soon reach Thiaucourt to block his line of retreat, Ricard decided to evacuate Pont-à-Mousson. Just as Ney's and Victor's retrograde movement on Toul forced Marmont to evacuate the Moselle and move closer to the Meuse, the marshal argued that these same movements forced Ricard to quit Pont-à-Mousson.[121] Marmont later realized this logic would not withstand his master's scrutiny and so partially recanted in another letter to Berthier on the 16th, placing blame squarely on Ricard. Yet he also took the opportunity to blast Ney for his negligence: "It is extremely unfortunate that the prince of the Moskowa did not order the destruction of the bridge over the Moselle at Frouard when he evacuated Nancy. Ricard likewise should have destroyed the one at Pont-à-Mousson, and he could have stayed on the banks of the Moselle without occupying Thiaucourt."[122] Regardless of who deserved the blame and to what degree, Marmont's reports of the 15th and 16th provided Paris with further proof of the lack of communication and cooperation between the three marshals.

Before noon on the 16th, a courier reached Metz with a letter from Victor. Marmont, who was still at the fortress, read the unwanted yet not unexpected news: Coalition forces occupied Nancy. Victor himself had withdrew to Toul; Ney's troops stood twenty-five miles west of him at Ligny and Void. As a result, Marmont decided to leave Metz immediately with Doumerc's cavalry and Lagrange's division, and proceed west to Gravelotte, the hub of the two roads leading from Metz to Verdun. Ricard's division would remain at Thiacourt to block the road from Pont-à-Mousson, while Decouz's division moved between Verdun and Void to the Meuse. Decouz's mission was vital: the young bearskins were to link with Ney's troops and guard the Meuse bridges to prevent the enemy from turning the VI Infantry and I Cavalry Corps.[123]

Marmont based his plan to hold Gravelotte and maintain communication with Metz on Victor's note, which convinced him that his colleague intended to defend Toul. "The letter from the duke of Bellune leads me to believe he intends to remain in this position [Toul] for some time," Marmont explains to Berthier. "I am taking a position at Gravelotte, two leagues from Metz, observing the Moselle, and having an advance garde facing Pont-à-Mousson." Marmont figured his main body could remain at Gravelotte as long as Victor held Toul and superior Coalition forces did not reach the bridge over the Meuse at St. Mihiel, which stood between their respective positions. Ricard would hold Thiacourt as long as possible, but Marmont himself could not move any closer to Nancy because enemy forces now controlled the vital bridge at Pont-à-Mousson. "I wanted to go to Pont-a-Mousson in order to link with the troops of the duke of Bellune, leaving Metz and Thionville to cover me against the Prussian corps.... This operation is no longer feasible since the enemy is master of the Pont-à-Mousson defile and the Frouard bridge."[124]

South of Marmont, apprehension permeated Victor's headquarters throughout the 14th and 15th. The tone of the correspondence that passed between the French generals was shrill. "At this moment, general, the II

Infantry and V Cavalry Corps cannot move tomorrow [the 15th]," Grouchy explains to Milhaud. "The enemy entered Nancy shortly after I left; I ask you to maintain extreme surveillance. At daybreak you must forward patrols on the roads to Vézelise and Vaucouleurs in order to obtain news from both directions."[125] "I have the honor to inform you," wrote Piré to Grouchy, "that I was forced to pass the day in a bivouac behind Gondreville with bridle in hand to avoid exposing my division to total loss because it is certain the enemy will come in considerable strength in order to force me back on Dommartin, which I will not have time to do ... if the enemy arrives on the road from Pont-St. Vincent to the right, which is very passable, according to what I hear."[126] Grouchy himself feared a large body of Allied cavalry was massing between Nancy and Toul. Even with Victor's rearguard just a few miles east of Toul at Gondreville, the French inconceivably could not gain an accurate view of the situation around Nancy. In fact, Grouchy believed Austrian Uhlans and Cossacks had driven Ségur's Honor Guards from Nancy.[127]

To obtain intelligence, the French resorted to the ploy of sending a negotiator toward enemy lines. Grouchy dispatched his chief of staff, Contamine, to Defrance's headquarters with an actual letter from Berthier to Schwarzenberg. "Perhaps the officer can proceed to Nancy or beyond," speculates Grouchy, "and this will provide the means to observe some of the Allied forces in this sector. It would be quite interesting to know if infantry is facing us; one is so uninformed that it is necessary to employ all possible means to gather news."[128] The officer commanding Biron's forward post at Velaine stopped Contamine, and demanded the letter, which he forwarded to Biron. Under the pretext that he could only receive communications exclusively addressed to Blücher, Biron returned the letter and identified himself as the commander of the advance guard of the Silesian Army's left wing. This allowed Victor and Grouchy to conclude that the Austro–Bavarian army (Wrede's V Corps) was further south. Grouchy then directed Contamine through Neufchâteau toward Mirecourt to locate the Austro–Bavarian army which, according to Ney's incorrect statements, had proceeded north from Épinal along the Moselle and then west toward the Meuse. Grouchy drew one positive conclusion from Biron's refusal to accept Berthier's letter to Schwarzenberg: "Perhaps it is permissible to induce that complete harmony does not exist between the Allies and to increase it, if this hypothesis is true," he wrote to Berthier.[129]

Victor himself took advantage of the lull to compose a brutally frank letter to the emperor describing his command's horrible internal state of affairs. Beginning with the issue of pay, he informed Napoleon that the instructions to make the masses foot the bill had produced nothing.[130] According to the marshal, "the suspension of payment after having been promised it would continue produces an effect all the more dangerous since the officers and troops experience privations too extreme to tolerate and, stirred against the government by their fellow citizens, they start to doubt they are still the soldiers of a great empire." Victor blamed this sentiment on the inability of Daru's Department of War Administration to fulfill its obligations:

> Your troops, Sire, are completely neglected, and all are always disposed to show themselves worthy of Your Majesty and the glory they have acquired over the past twenty years. But I must say the sentiments that constantly motivate them will be squashed if one does not pay more interest to their needs. Their misery has placed them at the mercy of public charity and, in general, the public attests to its disgust and even aversion to them. Your soldiers, Sire, acutely feel the predicament and humiliation by which this state of affairs has reduced them. I must confess that this cannot last much longer without the result being a catastrophe detrimental to Your Majesty. I am so certain of this that I can say for sure you will not have an army left if measures are not taken this very instant to meet the needs of the officers and soldiers who constitute it. We have a large number of desertions from all ranks. Misery and neglect cause desertion. For eight days we have lost many cavalry and artillery horses because of financial problems. In vain these two branches of the service requested funds to pay for the shoeing. Having no means to pay this expenditure, the horses without shoes can no longer serve and die by the hundreds from exertions on the icy roads. Your Majesty knows me well enough to know that I am not an alarmist. In my opinion it is time for you to think of the army and to consider that the salvation of the empire depends on the care the army requires. I have absolutely no instructions to regulate the movement of my troops. Until now I have acted according to assumptions, opinions, and love of the good cause. I must ask Your Majesty to inform me of the point where you will assemble your army to combat the enemy who appears determined to march on Paris.[131]

Despite the anxiety of their commanders, Victor's soldiers received a much-deserved rest on the 15th. The morning of the 16th dawned with the prospect of another quiet day. While the infantry rested, cavalry patrols cautiously sought to establish communication with Marmont's troops at Pont-à-Mousson. Their shocking reports reached Victor around 2:00 that afternoon: the VI Corps had evacuated Pont-à-Mousson and retreated to Metz! "I believe it is my duty to report that yesterday evening at 9:00 the post at Pont-à-Mousson was evacuated by the troops of Marshal Marmont without warning anyone," states Grouchy's report to Berthier. "I know of this only through the report of my reconnaissance. This evacuation forces us to abandon the line of the Moselle."[132]

Victor did not need to consult a map to see that Marmont's retrograde movement provided Blücher with a second bridge over the Moselle and widened the gap between the VI and II Corps. To make matters worse, the incorrect news arrived that Ney had continued his retreat from Void, but Victor had no idea where the prince of the Moskowa was marching. As with his letter to Napoleon on the previous day, Victor did little to conceal his aggravation when he drafted his daily report to Berthier at 6:00 that evening. "During the previous night, the duke of Raguse quit the position he had at Pont-à-Mousson without giving me any advance warning; I learned of this indirectly," complains the marshal. "The troops of the prince of the Moskowa, who were at Void, have left – to where I do not know and I have been informed of this in the same manner."[133]

Victor did not discover the error regarding Ney's supposed retreat until later that evening when Meunier's aide-de-camp arrived in Toul to discuss troop movements for the 17th.[134] Although Ney's Young Guard maintained its positions at Pagny-sur-Meuse and Void throughout the 16th, Victor did indeed react to the incorrect news. Before Meunier's aide-de-camp arrived, Victor issued orders for the evacuation of Toul to take place early on the 17th. Exposed on his left by Marmont's retreat, Ney's alleged withdrawal from the Meuse raised the prospect of another double envelopment, which terrified Victor. He feared having his road to the Ornain and Marne cut by the Allied forces that could now cross the Meuse before him. The marshal decided to withdraw to the Meuse and place his center at Void and Pagny-sur-Meuse, his right at Vaucouleurs, and his left at Commercy, linking with Marmont's right at St. Mihiel.

Victor's headquarters issued a myriad of orders that essentially organized the retreat in two columns. Milhaud received command of the first, consisting of the 1st Division, Lhéritier's 4th Dragoon Division, the 4th Honor Guard Regiment, and fourteen guns. According to Victor's order of the day, Milhaud would commence his march to Vaucouleurs at 6:00 A.M. on the 17th. Upon arriving at Vaucouleurs, he would organize the defense of the bridge over the Meuse by posting a battery of six guns supported by a strong infantry detachment on the left bank. Grouchy further instructed Milhaud to guard and observe the roads from Toul, Pont-St. Vincent, Neufchâteau, and "to find the position of the Austro-Bavarian army." Grouchy assumed Wrede had pushed an advance guard from Neufchâteau to Gondrecourt in the Ornain Valley, just southeast of Vaucouleurs on the road to Bar-le-Duc.

The second column, commanded by Briche and consisting of his own 3rd Dragoon Division, the 3rd Honor Guard Regiment, the artillery of the V Cavalry Corps, and the 2nd Division, would escort Victor's headquarters and the baggage to Void and Sorcy. Duhesme's 3rd Division received instructions to halt at Pagny-sur-Meuse, arrange the defense of the bridge, and only destroy it after the rearguard crossed to the right bank. Piré received command of this rearguard: his own 9th Light Cavalry Division as well as a single light infantry battalion and two guns. Grouchy instructed him to leave Gondreville between 7:00 and 8:00 A.M. and withdraw through Toul to Lay-St. Rémy with advance posts "under the walls of Toul and bent back successively to Foug." If forced to retreat, he would fall back on Duhesme's division at Pagny-sur-Meuse.[135]

Before leaving Toul, Victor organized a garrison by combining the National Guard with 400 invalids from the II Corps, of which only 193 were fit for service. With three bronze guns, one 12-pounder, and one iron gun, he formed a battery upstream the gates to cover the points of access, notably the bridge over the Moselle, which the French could not destroy due to a shortage of powder. Finally, Victor gave the obligatory order to the commandant, François-Louis Chaudron, a retired *chef de bataillon* who had lost one leg to the surgeon's saw, to hold the city for as long as possible.[136]

In the same report in which Victor vented his anger to Berthier over the lack of communication between the marshals, he depicted his retreat behind the Meuse as another negative result of Napoleon's absence from the front as well as the emperor's refusal to appoint a commander in chief:

> I have stated in my previous reports the motives that forced me to move away from the debouches of the Vosges. Today the same reasons force me to retire behind the Meuse. Unless His Majesty unites the II Corps as well as that of the prince de la Moskowa and the duke of Raguse under a single commander, the enemy may go as far as he wants and encounter no resistance. These parallel dispositions are detrimental. If one does not provide a remedy, the troops – exposed like mine are today – will be compromised. As I have stated, I am convinced that the three corps united under the command of a single marshal would be in a position to stop the progress of the enemy; divided as they are, their effectiveness is absolutely hopeless. I urgently request that you solicit this union from His Majesty. If the emperor agrees and His Majesty has in mind someone other than myself – as I must believe – to confide the command, I request to be assigned to an army where my services will be useful.[137]

Grouchy expressed similar sentiments in his brief to Berthier: "It is so disastrous to His Majesty's interests that the movements of the troops under the orders of the duke of Raguse and the prince of the Moskowa are not combined, which I cannot refrain from expressing my surprise."[138] Victor's statement regarding his belief Napoleon had someone in mind refers to the presence of Ney, whose poorly defined mission aroused the suspicions of Victor, Marmont, and Kellermann. It is worth mentioning that although Victor repeatedly called for Napoleon to appoint a commander in chief, he intimated his refusal to serve under Ney.[139]

Blücher knew of Marmont's retreat from the Moselle, but considered halting the direct pursuit, leaving Yorck before Metz and proceeding to Nancy with Sacken's corps. Yet the Prussian field-marshal set his sights on a goal larger than the capital of Lorraine. "The mass of the enemy is positioned at Metz" he wrote on the 14th. "But today I have received news they are marching on Verdun. *Therefore, the drive goes on to Paris.* As soon as all my troops are up I will follow, investing Metz in a few days. If the Bohemian Army advances far enough so a union with us can occur, I believe we will be strong enough to deliver a decisive blow that will decide everything. Napoleon can oppose us with a strong army, but it is filled with unwilling conscripts and disheartened people, who are poorly armed and uniformed."[140]

Blücher's internal communications lagged behind the flow of events during this decisive period. His headquarters did not learn that the Russians secured Pont-à-Mousson and that Biron entered Nancy until the 15th, a day in which the two corps of the Silesian Army largely remained idle. This news proved too irresistible and Blücher decided to go to Nancy himself. Sacken's corps would continue the advance, while Yorck's dealt with Lorraine's northern fortresses. "I believe it is necessary for me to turn on Nancy," wrote Blücher to Wrede, "in part to cover the right flank of the Bohemian Army, and in part to avoid the six strong fortresses located so close to one another north of Nancy. Tomorrow, 17 January, I will have around 30,000 men at Nancy; I have directed one column through Pont-à-Mousson on Commercy. The blockade troops [Yorck's corps] will assemble at St. Mihiel, and myself, with the majority of my forces, will march from Nancy through Toul to Ligny unless Prince Schwarzenberg desires that I execute another movement."[141] The Prussian also informed Schwarzenberg that Sacken's corps would be at Nancy on the 17th.[142]

Sacked received instructions for his infantry to occupy both Pont-à-Mousson and Nancy and for his cavalry to drive to the Meuse along the Nancy–Toul and Pont-à-Mousson–Commercy roads. "The iron is hot," exhorts Blücher to Hardenberg. "In a few months there must be peace or I will plant my war standard on Napoleon's thrown and drive him to Corsica."[143] Blücher believed his own army "could take everything up to Châlons-en-Champagne" but would need support in a decisive battle. By this time he had received Wittgenstein's negative response to his request for support. The Russian corps commander continued to move slowly, using as an excuse his concern over the French garrisons in Phalsbourg and Bitche as well as the small forts of la Petite-Pierre and Lichtenberg. Hardly venturing beyond Sarrebourg, the cavalry of VI Corps observed the Phalsbourg–Nancy road and forwarded patrols as far as Lunéville on 15 January.[144] With Wittgenstein anchored in Alsace, Blücher again turned to Wrede.[145]

On 14 January, Wrede transferred his headquarters from Colmar to St. Dié. His advance guard reached Bayon and pushed patrols to Lunéville, where the Bavarians met a detachment from Sacken's corps on the road to Nancy. Through this fortuitous encounter, Wrede learned of Sacken's arrival at Château-Salins, forty-three miles north of St. Dié. For the following day, the 15th, Wrede directed Delamotte's 3rd Division to Rambervillers and Rechberg's 1st Division to Bruyères. During this march, French fracteurs steadily harassed the troops. In fact, Wrede and his staff received small-arms fire at close range from bushes that lined the road. The staff escort drove off the marauders, who attempted to flee along the open road but were captured and flogged for the soldiers' amusement.[146]

On 13 January, Schwarzenberg instructed Wrede not to move any closer to Blücher but to consider himself an essential component of the Bohemian Army and to link with it as soon as possible.[147] Any plan to advance toward Blücher had to honor Schwarzenberg's order for the V Corps to form the right wing of the Bohemian Army, which was concentrating between Langres and Dijon. In addition, Wrede still had to cover his 2nd Division's siege operations in Alsace and keep open the passes through the Vosges, particularly Ste. Marie. In fact, Wrede's actual position did not allow him to support Blücher without blatantly disobeying Schwarzenberg. Nevertheless, he again dispatched his aide-de-camp to Blücher's headquarters. Thurn-Taxis carried a copy of Schwarzenberg's instructions regarding the V Corps as well as a letter from Wrede that announced his decision to march to Neufchâteau in order to support the Silesian Army. On 15 January, Wrede apprised Schwarzenberg of Victor's retreat. In this letter, the Bavarian corps commander revealed he had sent Thurn-Taxis to the Silesian Army headquarters yet claimed the purpose of the mission was to inform both Pahlen and Blücher of his operations.[148]

On the 16th, Wrede inched northward to Rambervillers. He reported to Schwarzenberg that Napoleon's *levée-en-masse* enjoyed even less success in the Meurthe Department compared to the other occupied territory. At Lunéville locals claimed that units of the Imperial Guard stood between Paris and Châlons-en-Champagne, where the emperor was assembling troops for a battle. From northern Lorraine, Wrede heard rumors that Marmont withdrew from Metz to Châlons. He also communicated to Schwarzenberg his intention to have his left wing at Mirecourt on the 18th, his right at Colombey-les-Belles, and to reach Châtenois just east of Neufchâteau on the 19th. "This moment," he wrote, "in which I will approach the right wing of the Bohemian Army, will allow me to participate in the battle you will deliver and to assure for you, in the case of a check or failure, the defense of the passes through the Vosges, which has been given to me as a primary responsibility."[149]

Thurn-Taxis reached Blücher's headquarters at St. Avold early on the 16th. That same day he accompanied the field marshal to Château-Salins, where he received a written response to Wrede's overtures. Blücher informed the Bavarian corps commander that according to the information he received, the French were concentrating around Châlons-en-Champagne; this news confirmed the reports Wrede received from Lunéville. "It is on this point that the corps of Marmont and Victor are withdrawing," wrote Blücher. "I do not believe I will need your support – support that I know through experience I can count on at the decisive moment – until I reach Châlons-en-Champagne." At this early stage of the campaign, Blücher and Gneisenau were reluctant to challenge openly Schwarzenberg's authority. In addition, they understood Wrede's predicament and did not want to add to his headaches. Blücher agreed with Wrede's plans to reach Neufchâteau, calling it "the most advantageous point for a movement of this manner. I request that you inform me of the direction you take in order for me to adjust my movements accordingly. Wittgenstein will not, according to the news I received today, reach Saverne until the 21st; it seems doubtful he will enter the line."[150]

Coincidentally, on the same day Blücher penned this response, Wrede received another letter from Schwarzenberg, dated the 15th. This curious dispatch temporarily granted Wrede greater freedom of action unless the French made a stand at Langres.[151] After Thurn-Taxis returned from Silesian Army headquarters on the 17th, Wrede assumed that by marching to Neufchâteau he could operate in complete accordance with Blücher's wishes and still honor Schwarzenberg's orders. Wrede informed the Prussian field-marshal that the headquarters of the V Corps would be at Charmes on the 17th, Mirecourt the 18th, and Neufchâteau the 19th. "All reports I have received lead me to believe the enemy will attempt to mass the few troops he has at Châlons-en-Champagne and Paris. Thus it will be a matter of pursuing as fast as possible, of delivering, when we unite, a battle which, in view of the precarious situation of his army, can only be decisive." Wrede requested that Blücher inform him of his movements and that he push south "in order to steadily approach the Bohemian Army's right and eventually completely link your army with that of Schwarzenberg's. I do not doubt Schwarzenberg will march against the enemy with all [of our] forces united and to attack the enemy everywhere he is found."[152]

In an attempt to embolden the Allied commander in chief, Wrede forwarded Blücher's letter of 16 January to Schwarzenberg. He also wanted to encourage Schwarzenberg by assuring him that no more than 15,000 French soldiers stood between Châlons-en-Champagne and Langres. He estimated Victor commanded 15,000 men, Marmont 10,000, and Napoleon 20,000 to 50,000 "cohorts" at most.[153]

Wrede's increased freedom of action and thus his ability to cooperate with Blücher proved fleeting. In a letter penned on the 16th and delivered to Wrede during the night of 17–18 January, Schwarzenberg informed Wrede of his agreement with the direction taken by the V Corps. "Nevertheless, from now on, I am of the opinion that you should move left [southwest] for the following reason. The enemy has force marched his Guard – 15,000 men – to Langres, which proves that he understands the importance of this point and that he has decided to direct himself against the Bohemian Army." Schwarzenberg also revealed his plans to attack Langres on the 18th with the I, III, and IV Corps. "This is the movement that you can and must support, because you will arrive too late to support Blücher, who attacked Metz on the 15th. The Silesian Army was either victorious or was defeated." If Blücher routed the French at Metz, Schwarzenberg assumed the enemy would retreat toward either Châlons-en-Champagne or Troyes. In this case, he suggested that Wrede seek the road from Troyes to Nancy by marching through Neufchâteau. Conversely, if Blücher suffered a setback at Metz, the Austrian commander believed the

Bohemian Army would be attacked next. It never crossed his mind that Army Group Alsace should attempt to aid Blücher. Instead, all Schwarzenberg could think of was the inevitable attack. "This will require your presence and the protection of my right flank," he reiterated to Wrede. "I have ordered the VI Corps to Nancy. Thus you can see how important it is to us for you to march to Mirecourt and Neufchâteau."[154]

On the 17th, the magnanimous Allied generalissimo responded to Blücher and issued another letter to remind Wrede of his obligations to the Bohemian Army. "I can gain an advantage if I am able to concentrate a large force on one point," he wrote Blücher. "Perhaps if the enemy falls on your army with superior numbers I will be in position to take him in the flank with the entire army and in this manner strongly support the Silesian Army."[155] These words implied that Blücher's smaller army either would be left on its own or used as bait to lure Napoleon away from Army Group Langres. In addition, Schwarzenberg gently reminded his Bavarian subordinate that the V Corps belonged to the Bohemian Army rather than Blücher's Silesian Army. He explained to Wrede that the Austro–Bavarian corps "constitutes the last echelon of my right wing. I have intentionally used the term 'the last echelon', because at present Wittgenstein cannot take an effective and direct part in the operations and his numerous cavalry will only be of use to maintain communication between the Bohemian and Silesian Armies."[156]

On 19 January, Schwarzenberg advised Wrede to seek communication with Blücher by forwarding detachments toward Toul and Joinville. He hoped Pahlen would soon arrive with Wittgenstein's advance guard to link Blücher's left with Wrede's right. Still concerned that Wrede would defy him and unite with Blücher, Schwarzenberg ordered the V Corps to move southwest as fast as possible.[157] Although the French evacuated Langres on the 17th, the Allied generalissimo feared a counterattack. "Napoleon understands the importance of the plateau of Langres; he has proven this by sending there his best troops from Namur," wrote Schwarzenberg to Wittgenstein. By moving Wrede southwest, he hoped Blücher would move closer to the Bohemian Army by proceeding west through Toul and Vaucouleurs.[158]

Wrede failed in his last attempt on 20 January to convince Schwarzenberg that Napoleon would be at Châlons-en-Champagne rather than Troyes. He advised the Austrian commander to move the left wing of the Bohemian Army closer to its right as well as the Silesian Army – the exact opposite of Schwarzenberg's plans.[159] Schwarzenberg refused. Consequently, a dispirited Wrede parked his corps between Neufchâteau and Clefmont until the end of the month. Gneisenau's letters to Hardenberg, Knesebeck, and Radetzky illustrate the frustration in Blücher's headquarters caused by Schwarzenberg's refusal to allow Wrede to cooperate with the Silesian Army: "We would soon arrive at Paris," wrote Gneisenau, "if we had the audacity to go there and the understanding of how to do the right thing!"[160] (Appendixes J and K).

Meanwhile, the head of Sacken's corps reached Château-Salins on 16 January. Russian infantry occupied Vic, Moyenvic, and Marsal on the Moyenvic – Puttelange–Sarreguemines road, which now formed the Silesian Army's main line of communication. Yorck's brigades continued to maneuver before the Moselle fortresses. That night Blücher quartered at Château-Salins, eighteen miles northeast of Nancy.[161] Twenty-eight miles southwest of Nancy, Platov reached Neufchâteau on the Meuse River. The French post that guarded the bridge withdrew without damaging the structure, thus enabling Cossack patrols to cross the river and head west toward the crossings over the Ornain and the French line of retreat to Châlons-en-Champagne. East of Platov, Sherbatov initially planned to lead his Streifkorps north to Toul on the morning of the 16th.[162] En route he learned from French deserters that Victor's 6,000-man rearguard still held the city. Moreover, fugitives from Nancy claimed that a strong cannonade could be heard from the direction of Pont-à-Mousson. On account of this news, Sherbatov decided to continue west in order to reach the crossing over the Meuse at Vaucouleurs on the 17th. From there he would strike the great east–west highway to Paris to investigate the rumor of large French forces assembling at Châlons-en-Champagne.[163]

On the next day, 17 January, Sacken's corps moved into cantonments along the road from Château-Salins to Nancy, with one infantry brigade in the city itself and Vasilchikov's cavalry at Pont-à-Mousson. Lanskoi's troopers pursued Ricard toward Commercy on the Meuse. Reinforcements also arrived, much to the field marshal's pleasure. Blücher instructed the portion of Langeron's corps that St. Priest had relieved at Mainz – General Olsufiev's IX Infantry Corps (5,595 men), General Nikolay Mikhailovich Borozdin II's 1st Dragoon Division (1,500 men), and eighteen guns – to separate at St. Avold on 17 January. From there Olsufiew and the artillery continued southwest to Nancy. Borozdin, however, proceeded due west to Metz to reinforce Prince William.[164]

Gneisenau believed Blücher should enter the capital of Lorraine with a degree of pomp and use the occasion to publish a proclamation to all of France. Karl von Nostitz of the Prussian General Staff accompanied the Russian advance guard into the city. The Prussian officer notified the mayor that he would officially receive Blücher and deliver a speech in German, which first had to be approved by the field marshal's headquarters. Nostitz returned with the mayor's speech. Gneisenau accepted the draft and composed the field marshal's response. On 17 January, Blücher and Sacked entered Nancy with their respective staffs. The intimidated mayor, city magistrates, and some of the inhabitants solemnly greeted the leadership of the Silesian Army at the gates. Blücher announced to the civic leaders "that the Allied army has invaded France only to liberate the French and Europe from the iron yoke of despotism."[165] At city hall, the mayor uttered what Müffling describes as "forced phrases" in which "his fear of Napoleon was unmistakable...on the other hand, our respectable Cossacks were very imposing, with their long, well-pointed *pencils* under their arm, indicating their skill in writing history." Blücher then delivered Gneisenau's carefully orchestrated speech in an attempt to win over the people of Lorraine. He promised to relieve them as much as possible from the burdens of war and to abolish the more odious taxes, specifically the *Douanes*, the *Droits Réunis*, and the salt tax.[166] "The people here are poor and under the cruelest weight of taxation," Blücher explains to his wife, "they bless me since I drive all customs officials, bureaucrats, and gendarmes to the devil and allow them free trade and commerce."[167] Blücher ordered his speech translated into French and circulated in the thousands.[168] "I am so fortunate," he wrote to Tsar Alexander, "to be able to lay the keys of Nancy, one of the good cities of old France – the first to be taken by Allied troops...at the feet of Your Imperial Majesty." The monarch answered: "I am delighted this honor was reserved for you."[169]

That evening the city held a dinner in Blücher's honor. After drinking too much, the old hussar made a toast to Nancy's prosperity. "Everything was proceeding beautifully," recalls Müffling, "when Sacked rose and said: 'I beg of you, gentlemen, to empty a glass with me to the prosperity of France, and to the peace and amity of this fine country with all the nations of Europe, who offer it the hand of friendship and expect it to be accepted. We come to bring you happiness and freedom; but you yourselves know this is only possible on one condition: death and destruction to the tyrant who for so long has been the scourge of the French nation and the plague of Europe'." The Allied officers emptied their glasses, while the civic leaders of Nancy watched with "downcast eyes and some uncompromising sighs."[170]

According to Lefebvre de Béhain, Victor's retreat from Rambervillers to Toul ended in a route. He bases this assessment on the worsening morale of the French soldiers. The marshals confronted the plague of desertion, not only by troops from the departments of new France, but from the regions of old France that now lay behind enemy lines as well. Both recruits and veterans from Alsace, Lorraine, and Franche-Comté left their units and returned to their homes. "As with the retreat from Moscow," notes the French historian, "one started to see isolated or small groups marching almost aimlessly on the roads." The mood of the local population grievously influenced the army's morale. No amount of propaganda could hide the collapse of imperial authority. The army's rapid retreat and the flight of the civil authorities ripped France's eastern departments from Napoleon's control faster than either he or the Allies ever imagined. Lorraine's population succumbed to panic, even welcoming the Allies since they could be no worse than the French generals and prefects. The idea soon spread that only a change in government would bring about lasting peace.[171]

Victor complained to Paris of being abandoned and forced to act according to conjectures. Napoleon responded by issuing his "General Instructions." Events at the front, however, rendered these instructions obsolete. Before the General Instructions reached the marshals, Frederick William's IV Corps captured Épinal, Gyulay's III Corps reached Langres, Wrede's V Corps crossed the Vosges, Wittgenstein's VI Corps needed only to execute a short march to reach the banks of the Moselle, and Blücher's patrols approached Nancy. Because the General Instructions provided no useful information or plan of action, the marshals were forced to react to the situation they faced.

Beaten back by Schwarzenberg's V Corps, threatened on one flank by the Silesian Army and on the other by the IV Corps, Victor logically retreated to Nancy in order to unite with Ney. He then withdrew to Nancy early on the 14th and continued the march to Toul on the same day to reach it before the Allies. In his haste, he neglected to destroy the bridges over the Meurthe at Nancy and Bouxières. Ney also withdrew from Nancy, likewise failing to destroy the crossings. Responsibility for these grievous mistakes falls squarely on the shoulders of the marshals and in no way can the absence of Napoleon or his dated "General Instructions" be blamed for such inexcusable oversights. With the lines of the Meurthe and Moselle successively breeched by Allied forces, Ney and Victor decided to retreat as far as the Marne to effect their junction with Mortier and support Marmont against the Silesian Army. Napoleon raged over the abandonment of the Meurthe and Moselle without a struggle. He vented all his anger on Victor, claiming the marshal's precipitous retreat opened the flood gates.[172] Of course Napoleon had placed himself in an impossible situation by deciding to remain at Paris and direct the war by way of dispatch. His attempts in 1812 and 1813 to subordinate his marshals to a commander in chief other than himself had failed miserably. In 1814, the emperor simply instructed his marshals to cooperate in order to avoid squabbling and jealousy. The results were nothing short of catastrophic.

In evaluating the French army's response to the Allied invasion, the most glaring issue that surfaces is the marshals' confusion over their role – what exactly was their task? Napoleon constantly preached his need of time. Be it in his December correspondence, which envisioned the creation a new Grand Armée in the hundreds of thousands, or his January correspondence, which discusses the formation of a modest 100,000-man Army of Reserve, Napoleon needed three months for the former and at least one month for the latter. Yet how should this time be bought and, after the Allied invasion began, what should be sacrificed in exchange? He dispersed his combat-ready units in a cordon hundreds of miles in length. With inadequate forces, Macdonald, Marmont, and Victor each had to defend a large stretch of the frontier. Admittedly, the cordon system worked well enough in Holland, where Maison and

Macdonald slowed Allied operations until the emperor could send reinforce-ments to Belgium. The difference in the Low Countries that temporarily vin-dicated the cordon system was that Allied lethargy, discord, and the fact that Bülow only commanded between 20,000 and 30,000 men all combined to delay operations rather than Macdonald, who almost froze himself into obscurity by not proceeding against either Bülow or Blücher.

Once the Allied invasion began along the upper and middle Rhine, Mar-mont and Victor first had to concentrate their respective units and then race to confront a numerically superior foe, who considerably outnumbered either marshal unless the two combined their forces. Consequently, the cordon sys-tem eliminated the first option: buying time by standing in the field and fighting. The time the marshals needed to concentrate their forces made this alternative impractical. On the other hand, if Marmont or Victor had man-aged to concentrate their forces to confront Blücher or Schwarzenberg on the Rhine, the consequences of a lost battle on the frontier would have been devastating.

A second option would have been for the marshals to throw their men into the frontier garrisons to await either disease or the arrival of Allied siege corps and starvation. In the German campaign, that Allies demon-strated they could adhere to the modern principles of war: after Coalition forces crossed the Rhine sieges of French-occupied fortresses in Poland and Germany were still underway. In 1813, fortresses and rear-area secu-rity issues did not slow the Allies in general and the Prussians in partic-ular, yet Napoleon gambled on these same factors in 1814 because of the tenuous extent of Allied communications. So the marshals did what they could, in part directed by the emperor, in part according to their own judg-ment, to garrison the fortresses with troops who for various reasons were not combat-ready and to extricate those units that could face the enemy in the field.

The third option, which both Marmont and Victor chose, was to preserve their combat forces by falling back, holding their positions until threatened, and then repeating the process. This is all the more understandable when considering the emperor's repeated calls for the marshals to ensure that the roads to Paris remained closed. Although Napoleon harshly scolded Vic-tor for not holding the Vosges, the marshal's conduct is not so perplexing when considering the actual options available to him and the other front-line marshals. Napoleon viewed the cordon system as a fluid shield or net that could contract and expand along the entire length of the Rhine and guarantee him the requisite time to build a new army around Paris. By inserting Mortier and Ney, he believed the cordon would slow the Allied march, which had forced the cordon to contract – thus his orders that cul-minated in the "General Instructions," for Maison, Marmont, and Victor to hold their ground and launch counteroffensives. His expectations of what the marshals could achieve reflect the same contempt for his opponent that had characterized his operations in Germany. In fact, Napoleon based his plan to hold the frontier more on his erroneous faith in the way his enemy would conduct the campaign rather than on a realistic assessment of what his own marshals could accomplish.[173] Were his "secret" preparations to fortify Paris prudence or a lack of confidence in his marshals' ability to stop the Allies?

13

The Saar and the Moselle

On 15 January, Blücher issued detailed orders for the operations of the I Corps against the Saar and Moselle fortresses. For the 16th, the field-marshal wanted Prince William's reinforced 8th Brigade to invest Metz on the right bank of the Moselle. Warburg's 2nd Brigade would move east on the Saarlouis–Metz highway to join William at Metz. On the following day, one of the two brigades would cross the Moselle to besiege Metz on the left bank. Blücher also wanted the investment of Thionville and Luxembourg completed on this day. In his cover letter to Yorck, the field marshal authorized the sieges of Metz, Thionville, Luxembourg, and Saarlouis from 17 January onward. "However, in no way is it my intention that this shall be a permanent post," he explains to his prickly subordinate. Regardless, Blücher emphasized the importance of gaining one of these fortresses as a base of operations for the Silesian Army. Because the majority of the garrisons consisted of conscripts, he believed at least one could be secured through negotiation or taken by storm: "even if we suffer the loss of 1,000 men or more." He instructed Yorck to have his officers evaluate the strength of each fortress. If any one appeared too strong, the field marshal insisted that Yorck first harass the garrison in order to test its preparedness. Should Yorck's mission fail, Röder's approaching cuirassier brigade would assume the investment of Luxembourg and Thionville until the rest of Kleist's II Corps arrived.[1] Borozdin's Russian cavalry, likewise en route, would assume the investment of Metz. Yorck would then lead the I Corps across the Meuse at St. Mihiel. "I do not know the state of the ammunition supply for your ten-pounder howitzers," adds Blücher, "but if you think a fortress can be compelled to surrender by a bombardment from the four howitzers then such an expenditure of ammunition would be acceptable. Nevertheless, we must spare ammunition for a battle."[2]

Receiving these instructions before 8:00 P.M. on the same day, 15 January, an enraged Yorck bitterly referred to his new assignment as "the

Champagne Disposition," inferring that Blücher and his staff must have been intoxicated when they drafted the orders. Later that day he received a second letter from the field-marshal further verifying the current intelligence: the Bohemian Army should arrive at Langres and Dijon that day; Châlons-en-Champagne appeared to be the primary point of concentration for the French army, Paris the secondary; Luxembourg had been reinforced by conscripts only. This second letter also specifically requested that Horn cooperate with the townspeople to make an attempt to capture Luxembourg. "Even if the operation does not succeed," wrote Blücher, "it will contribute to the enemy's confusion. In the aftermath, I want both detached brigades to take the closest roads to the Meuse to join you. Under the current circumstances, a march between the fortresses of Luxembourg, Longwy, Thionville, Metz, and Verdun can be undertaken without danger; it is also extremely important to prevent them from being provisioned."[3]

In the meantime, Henckel changed his mind concerning Luxembourg's strength. At 9:00 A.M. on 15 January, he informed Horn that "an earlier report from Lt. Chevallerie has led the field-marshal to believe that Luxembourg can be taken by storm, but it is absolutely impossible to execute this because 7,000–8,000 men are garrisoned there including a portion of the Guard. *The entire project was the suggestion of a young, impetuous officer who wants to distinguish himself, but has not calculated the means which are at his disposal.*"[4] Yorck's new chief of staff, Valentini, arrived at Horn's headquarters in Distroff near Thionville on 15 January to consult with the brigadier over the feasibility of a surprise attack on Luxembourg. Valentini read Henckel's report, which dismissed Chevallerie's initial findings as exaggerated. Moreover, the frequent sorties and harassment by the garrison convinced Valentini that a surprise attack was out of the question. Horn forwarded Henckel's letter to Yorck at 1:00 A.M. on the 16th, adding: "I am in agreement with Valentini that perhaps the march to Luxembourg cannot be continued since the circumstances have changed so much."[5] Valentini wrote Henckel: "I would gladly accept the trophy of Luxembourg, but I have a small suspicion that your Chevallerie is an Amadis who, with his twelve horses, would challenge 100,000. Gen. Horn has determined the same. You will hold your infantry at a respectful distance from Luxembourg and place yourself in a position to cover the important point of Trier if need be." Yorck's new chief of staff had recently served with Bülow in Holland and offered his perspective on the situation Yorck's corps now faced: "in Holland the capture of fortresses was easy. The enemy abandoned most as soon as we appeared. But this cannot be expected from 8,000 men at a place like Luxembourg."[6]

Horn's 7th Brigade had reached Thionville late on 12 January after marching through a blizzard. The brigade spent the next two days establishing posts around the fortress. Horn wanted to sever all communication between Thionville and the neighboring fortresses but had no luck crossing the Moselle.[7] His gunners fired twenty shells into the fortress from their two 7-pounder howitzers on the night of 14–15 January. After the French did not answer, the Prussians foraged several of the villages situated on the glacis. Further reconnaissance claimed that the only useable guns the French possessed were situated in the bridgehead on the right bank of the Moselle and that the garrison mainly consisted of 1,200 conscripts. Despite this positive information, Horn did not think his men would have success attacking one of Thionville's seven drawbridges on the right bank. An undertaking on the left bank appeared feasible if the frozen Moselle could support a crossing. Ironically, the temperature increased on this day, and the river began to thaw. Both Horn and Valentini informed Yorck that any chance for success at Thionville depended on the Moselle remaining frozen.[8] After receiving Blücher's orders, Horn commenced the march to Luxembourg. He first sent a detachment to Sierck to find a point of passage over the Moselle since a detour to the bridge at Trier would have delayed his march by twenty-four hours. In the afternoon, he learned that no crossing points could be located. On the 16th, the 7th Brigade conducted a short march to Sierck, where Horn decided to await further orders.

It became obvious to Yorck that his field commanders and his own chief of staff doubted the chances of success. After receiving the "Champagne-Disposition" and the two letters from Blücher on the 15th, he forwarded Henckel's and Horn's concerns to the field marshal on the 16th at 10:00 A.M., adding: "due to this situation, I can only rely on your judgement as to what should be done. I leave to your exalted judgement whether a place such as Luxembourg, which has a 7,000–8,000-man garrison, can be stormed by a brigade of 3,500 men. Concerning the investment of Thionville on the opposite bank as stated in the order, I must remark that the Moselle cannot be crossed in that region and Horn, as emerges from his letter, will be forced to march to Trier in order to pass the river. I await your instructions, which I will execute immediately. I have ordered the continuation of all troop movements."[9] Accordingly, an orderly arrived at Sierck around 10:00 P.M. on 16 January with Yorck's instructions for Horn to continue the march to Trier.[10]

Henckel again submitted new intelligence over the condition of Luxembourg. At noon on the 16th, he reported to Horn that a 75-year old greybeard commanded a garrison of only 2,000 conscripts. Moreover, approximately fifty old and unusable guns could be seen on the walls, the glacis could be easily undermined, and provisions would last for three days at most. Henckel now suggested an attack. Forwarded by Horn, this report reached Yorck at 10:00 A.M. on 17 January. One hour later, Yorck responded with a comment concerning his surprise over receiving three consecutive reports over Luxembourg that "contain such completely different content."[11] Yorck repeated his order for Horn to march to Luxembourg, reminding him of Blücher's specific instructions that "the loss of 1,000 or more men is not too high a price to pay to win a stronghold such as Luxembourg or one of the other fortresses in this region. After careful consideration of the prevailing circumstances, you will determine whether Luxembourg can fall into our hands through cunning, or through a formal attack. *If the possibility of success is present, if you believe that the blood of our troops would not be spilled in vain, then attack in the name of God."*[12]

Upon its arrival at Blücher's headquarters, Yorck's protest caused ill feelings to resurface, especially on the part of Gneisenau. In the margin of Yorck's letter, Gneisenau wrote: "Indeed you should not attack, but only make an attempt if the garrison is somewhat weak."[13] Blücher's reply, dated 1:45 A.M. on 17 January, reached Yorck's headquarters at 2:00 P.M. that afternoon. Most likely dictated by Gneisenau, the letter states that the new estimate of Luxembourg's garrison – 7,000 to 8,000 men – appeared too high, just as the estimate of Lieutenant Chevallerie was probably too low.[14] If Horn felt he could not achieve any success at Luxembourg, Blücher wanted him to proceed to St. Mihiel on the Meuse. Moreover, instead of having Pirch march all the way to Trier just to cross the Moselle, Blücher suggested that Yorck direct him south of Metz, where his brigade could pass the river at Jouy. Blücher only requested that a cavalry detachment remain on the right bank at Thionville to prevent a sortie from surprising Bieberstein at Saarlouis. Röder would assume the blockade of both Thionville and Luxembourg once he reached the latter.[15]

Yorck remained convinced that Blücher's desire to gain one of the fortresses had no chance of success. He thus waged his campaign against the French fortresses under protest. In the private circle of his entourage, the corps commander often contemptuously referred to the entire operation as the Champagne Disposition. Yorck, who feared his superior just as little as he feared his enemy, believed he had to provide a buffer to protect his men from the whimsical demands of Silesian Army Headquarters. Critical and negative from the start, he resolved only to execute the exact wording of the orders rather than the meaning. As for the exact wording, Yorck became increasingly preoccupied with the losses the field-marshal regarded as acceptable to capture one of the fortresses. Blücher's orders clearly state that an attack should be the last resort – after negotiations with the inhabitants failed – yet Yorck viewed the Champagne Disposition as a directive to storm one or more of the fortresses. However, it is also possible that Blücher authorized an attack to assume personal responsibility for the resulting heavy casualties and to relieve his subordinate of the onus of issuing such an order. In this sense, Blücher and Yorck were very similar: neither pushed any responsibility on their subordinates. For his current assignment, Yorck sought to relieve his subordinates of the responsibility of ordering their men to storm a fortress. In addition, concern that his impetuous brigade commanders would recklessly attack the fortresses probably troubled Yorck. Therefore, he decided to inspect the fortresses personally to make the decision to attack or not.

According to the reports Yorck received, a surprise attack on one of the fortresses appeared impossible and, in his opinion, he did not have time to conduct secret negotiations with the locals. Consequently, the only option left to his brigadiers was to assault the fortresses formally, a choice that certainly promised losses but did not guarantee success. After crossing the Rhine with 20,045 men on 1 January, Yorck already had lost more than 25 percent of his manpower without having participated in any noteworthy combat. Strategic consumption and illness reduced the muster to 550 officers and 14,986 men on 13 January. The arrival of the 1st East Prussian Regiment and replacement manpower increased the corps to 638 officers and 17,488 men by 25 January, yet the war remained far from over.[16] Many Prussians believed a bloody campaign still had to be waged in the French interior, which raised the question at Yorck's headquarters whether "1,000 men or more" should be wasted on operations that had no possibility of success. Yorck chose protest as a means to voice concern for his men and to protect them from what he perceived to be Blücher's excessive and shortsighted demands.

"I will employ everything," he assured Blücher in a letter dated 9:00 P.M. on 17 January, "that is in my power to execute the disposition given to me on the 15th." Yorck followed this obligatory opening by listing the obstacles he faced. "If all of the commanders of my corps," he continued, "who have been detached against four first-rate fortresses in such an expansive terrain, submit reports over the significant problems posed by their assignments, I thus see it as my duty to make you completely aware of it." Yorck explained how Jürgaß's Reserve Cavalry could not cross the Moselle near Metz on the 16th to pursue Marmont but instead had to ride to Pont-à-Mousson, which caused a considerable delay. Prince William, whose brigade should have invested Metz on the left bank of the Moselle on the 17th, likewise had to march to Pont-à-Mousson. As a result, the prince needed at least two more days to execute his assignment. Pirch, who should have invested Thionville on the left bank of the Moselle by the 17th, would first have to march almost thirty miles northeast to Trier, a round-trip of at least five marches! Horn likewise would probably be forced to advance to Trier to cross the Moselle and reach Luxembourg. "These are the difficulties that make it impossible to carry out the operations that you ordered in the disposition of the 15th," insists Yorck. Regardless of this sentiment, the corps commander informed Blücher that he issued orders for the continuation of the movements, drafted a march table, and provided his brigadiers with a new disposition based on their reports. "This disposition and the corresponding march table will convince you that despite all efforts I expect no positive results from these operations. All four fortresses are so solid in their construction, that even with the slight resistance by a weak garrison they are almost physically insurmountable due to their moats, revetment, and the quantity of difficult obstacles that the attacking infantry must overcome. I will personally go to Luxembourg, Thionville, and

Metz in order to leave no resource untapped to achieve the assigned task."
Knowing that Blücher eventually wanted the I Corps to reunite with Sacken's
Russians for a decisive battle, Yorck added that it would not be possible for
his corps to concentrate at St. Mihiel before 26 January.[17]

Yorck's march table designated 21 January as the deadline for concluding
the operations at Luxembourg.[18] Horn received instructions to march through
Trier, reach Luxembourg on the 19th, tightly invest the fortress with Henckel
on the 20th, and undertake the "attempt" on the 21st. If Luxembourg did
not fall, Horn would turn over the blockade to Röder's cavalry, return to
Thionville on the 22nd, and invest this fortress on the left bank of the Moselle.
After supporting Horn at Luxembourg, Henckel would lead his detachment
to Longwy on 22 January. If he determined the garrison to be weak, Yorck
wanted Henckel to attack but still be able to reach St. Mihiel by 26 January. In
the meantime, Pirch would bridge the Moselle and invest Thionville on both
banks. Once Horn arrived, the two brigades would undertake a joint attack
on the fortress. If this operation did not achieve success, both brigades would
proceed to Metz – Horn along the left bank of the Moselle and Pirch on the
right. As for Metz, Prince William should reach Pont-à-Mousson on the 18th,
cross the Moselle on the following day, and invest the fortress on the left bank
by 20 January, while Warburg operated on the right bank. With the Reserve
Artillery, 8th and 2nd Brigades, the prince would make an attempt to take
Metz. Yorck included no further details regarding Luxembourg and Thionville
mainly because he wanted to issue the orders himself after he arrived.[19]

One last influence on Yorck was a 17 January reply the corps commander
received from Colonel Johann Heinrich Otto von Schmidt, the commander of
his Reserve Artillery. Earlier Yorck asked the officer to determine "whether
enough ammunition is available to undertake something serious against the
fortresses of Metz, Thionville, Saarlouis, and Luxembourg without consum-
ing too much in the process and leaving the corps too short of ammunition
to deliver a battle."[20] The question mainly concerned the four 10-pounder
howitzers. Schmidt answered that the bombardment could not commence
for another two or three weeks because a total of only 200 shells remained
availble. He calculated that each howitzer required 60 for a general battle and
suggested the additional 40 be cast immediately from the available material.
Yorck's corps contained only one park column, and thus the extra powder
needed for siege operations had to be hauled to the front from the depot
at Gießen. Yorck accepted Schmidt's findings, but still complied with the
Champagne Disposition. He ordered Schmidt to assemble 190 shells for use
at Saarlouis and Metz, with 130 to 140 reserved for the latter, where Yorck
believed a bombardment would be more effective.[21]

At Silesian Army Headquarters, Gneisenau read Yorck's report and examined the accompanying march table. To the chief of staff it appeared that the
general's stubborn misunderstanding persisted, despite Blücher's attempt to

clarify the assignment. "It must be said to Yorck," wrote Gneisenau in the margin, "that the order for the capture of the fortresses is to be viewed as conditional and executed only if great weakness of the garrison invites an attack, a secret entry is found, or some type of agreement [with the inhabitants] is reached. All of this is up to the judgement of the generals."[22]

East of the corps, the siege of Saarlouis was the first operation to be scrapped. Bieberstein reported that the garrison consisted of approximately 1,800 men, including 600 veterans, 240 pensioners, and 60 cavalry.[23] According to locals, the French forced the townspeople to take up arms under the threat of death. Moreover, the fortress contained plenty of provisions. On 16 January, the garrison launched three sorties.[24] Schmidt began the bombardment of Saarlouis on 19 January with four 10-pounder and four 7-pounder howitzers. French deserters claimed the shells landed in the city and ignited three fires but caused little damage and no harm to the garrison. The Prussians failed to intimidate the garrison, which responded with more sorties. As a result, Schmidt limbered his artillery and departed for Metz.[25] Because success seemed unlikely, Yorck sought permission to move up the four battalions currently besieging Saarlouis "so the corps, which is already very weak, can move against the enemy on the day of battle with some hope of success."[26] Blücher partially approved the request, ordering Bieberstein to secure the roads between the Saar and the Moselle from a new base of operations at Hombourg.[27]

At Remich on the right bank of the Moselle, Horn managed to find two boats that enabled his brigade to start crossing the river at 10:00 A.M. on the 17th. The boats could carry 100 men, 10 horses, or one gun; hence, he needed at least eighteen hours to complete the crossing. After three guns crossed, drift ice and the rising level of the river made the transport of the remaining six pieces impossible. Horn had to direct the rest of his artillery train including the ammunition caissons to Trier, a delay of at least twenty-four hours. He moved his infantry and cavalry across the Moselle, but rather than continue the march, he had his men collect ladders and other materials needed for a siege. On 19 January, Horn and Henckel finally completed the investment of Luxembourg. After ejecting four French companies that attempted to hold the suburb of Hollerich, Henckel's men secured the west side of the city. Horn's brigade controlled the east side, while the small Alzette stream separated the two Prussian units.[28]

The Prussians tightened their ring around Luxembourg on the 20th. Reinforcements also arrived: Colonel Friedrich von Wrangel arrived from Grevenmacher with the Brandenburg Cuirassier Regiment and a half battery of horse artillery from Röder's Reserve Cavalry. According to Henckel, the French executed many sorties to gather wood and food. In fact, a sortie prevented him from holding a prearranged meeting with Yorck and Horn on the 20th. "We had an extremely difficult task," recalls Henckel, "since the enemy held us down the entire operation and many times we were in combat for whole days. When Gen. Röder wished to speak with me in Trier, I had the amusement of being arrested not far from Trier by the post of Col. Wrangel's brigade since I did know the password."[29]

On 21 January, Yorck ordered a general reconnaissance and personally inspected the fortress. Despite its extensive outworks, Luxembourg was a medium-sized city with approximately 10,000 to 12,000 inhabitants. Purportedly 4,000 to 5,000 men under General Joseph Christiani formed the garrison. To collect intelligence, Horn led his brigade in two columns from Roodt to Hamm in the midst of a snow storm. He found the French maintained very weak forward posts, but a previously undetected redoubt on a hill protected the approaches to the city along the Alzette. As for Yorck, with no escort other than a few marksmen, he made his way to the barricaded gate of the fortress's outworks. Quickly moving from the gate to an adjacent hill, the corps commander noted that only small posts occupied Luxembourg's outer defenses. Although confident his troops could overrun the outworks, the wide expanse of steep terrain that separated the outer defenses from the cannon on the walls of Luxembourg itself appeared daunting. While Horn and Yorck executed their respective tasks, Henckel spent the entire day engaged with the French on the western side of the Alzette. Apparently the French sought to dislodge the Prussian posts that threatened the approaches to the city. By day's end Henckel's soldiers had repulsed the sortie and maintained their positions.

Regardless of his personal reservations, Yorck complied with his orders and issued instructions for Luxembourg to be attacked on 22 January. At 1:00 P.M. Horn's brigade, reinforced by Wrangel's cavalry, would form two columns on the right bank of the Alzette in a concealed position close to the fortress. Fifty laborers with axes and other tools would follow the advance guard of each column. Yorck ordered Henckel, whose Leib Fusilier Battalion had repulsed another sortie earlier that morning and remained engaged with the French in the suburbs on the left bank of the Alzette, to attack at his own discretion. Before giving the order to commence the attack, Yorck decided to make one last round of inspections. Snow flurries allowed him to move very close to the fortress, and the moment seemed right for a surprise attack. Yorck, however, expressed concern over Luxembourg's main defenses and concluded that the brigade lacked the essential siege material. Moreover, he still did not know the dimensions of the trench despite his own inspections. He judged Horn's reconnaissance insufficient and persisted in his belief that the brigade lacked the proper equipment to attack. Yorck also feared the garrison's ability to repulse his assault and viewed the sortie against Henckel as a sign of French initiative. Regarding the supposed pro-Prussian or pro-Allied disposition of the inhabitants, he wanted to preserve these sentiments for Röder to cultivate. Instead of attacking, he ordered Horn's brigade to march halfway to Thionville.[30] Henckel likewise departed for Longwy and Röder's cavalry assumed the blockade of Luxembourg.[31]

Meanwhile, Pirch's forward units had relieved Horn at Thionville on 15 January. Pirch's reconnaissance added nothing new to the information that Horn's men had ascertained: the garrison consisted of some 4,000 men commanded by General Hugo. Further reports increased the estimate of the garrison's strength to 8,000 to 10,000 men, albeit mainly conscripts.[32] Frequent sorties soon convinced Pirch that his initial evaluation of Hugo's "slack" measures appeared to be incorrect. Around 1:00 P.M. on 17 January Hugo launched a sortie that bloodied Pirch's nose and drove back his forward posts. After the French withdrew, Hugo's heavy artillery opened fire on anything that could be spotted from the walls.

Pirch decided to cross the Moselle further downstream at Malling, where he assembled three battalions, three squadrons, three guns, and two howitzers on the night of 18 January to be ferried across the Moselle by boats sailing upstream from Trier. He instructed Colonel Heinrich von Losthin to take a position facing the French bridgehead on the right bank with the rest of the brigade – four Landwehr battalions, one squadron, and three guns. Nature, however, intervened to postpone the operation. Heavy showers that fell the previous day raised the water level of the already flooding Moselle and made the current too treacherous for the boats to leave Trier. On the 19th, Pirch met with Yorck, who was en route to Luxembourg. After evaluating the situation, the corps commander ordered the boats to remain at Trier due to the increased flooding, which postponed a crossing for the foreseeable future.

Nothing occurred at Thionville until Hugo launched another sortie at daybreak on 22 January. In an effort to gather firewood, a second and larger attack followed in which approximately 400 to 600 men and three guns attacked the Prussian post at Illange near the forest on the right bank of the Moselle. After six hours of combat with the 2nd and 3rd Battalions of the 5th Silesian Landwehr Infantry Regiment, the French withdrew. On the same day, two squadrons of Wrangel's Brandenburg Cuirassier Regiment arrived on the left bank. Horn's brigade followed on the 23rd and invested Thionville on the left bank of the Moselle. Yorck, who had returned to Pirch's headquarters at Distroff on the 22nd personally reconnoitered the right bank. He reported to Blücher that success at Thionville appeared doubtful. The garrison numbered 3,000 men and the moat was overflowing due to the flooding of the Moselle. Nevertheless, he ordered both Horn and Pirch to remain at Thionville, reevaluate the situation, use the 24th for a joint operation against the fortress, and depart one day later than scheduled.[33] Because communication between both banks still had to proceed via Trier, this order crossed in the post with Horn's 23 January report that Thionville could not be taken through a coup de main on the left bank. Yorck received this report during the afternoon of the 24th – another wasted day. On 25 January, the two brigades finally departed: Pirch marched to Metz, and Horn moved toward St. Mihiel. The remaining squadrons of the Brandenburg Cuirassier Regiment arrived to relieve Pirch's men.[34]

Meanwhile, the rest of Yorck's corps besieged Metz and its garrison of 12,700 men commanded by Durutte.[35] Drift ice on the flooding Moselle forced Prince William to lead his 8th Brigade to the bridge over the Moselle at Pont-à-Mousson, which the French had evacuated according to a report from Lanskoi. Between 16 and 18 January, he moved the 8th Brigade fifteen miles downstream to Pont-à-Mousson. His advance guard under Stutterheim crossed the river on the 18th and proceeded upstream to Vandières. William hoped to cross the river on the 19th with his main body, complete the investment of Metz on the left bank by the 20th, and attack the fortress on the following morning. "From each battalion," ordered the king's brother, "one officer and thirty volunteers will sneak up to the fortress, simultaneously attack all the gates, use tools to batter down the gates, and attempt to open the drawbridges. There must be much firing by the volunteers during the attack." If successful, battalion columns would advance to penetrate the fortress. William instructed the officers to withdraw if they encountered organized resistance. In this case, preparations would be made in the dark to storm the fortress that same night, beginning with a bombardment from both banks of the Moselle.

Prince William's plan of attack made little use of the element of surprise and thus made little sense, but his thought process deserves consideration. The volunteer squads would launch their "sneak attack" in broad daylight. By ordering the volunteers to fire many rounds, the Prussians would alert Durutte rather than surprise him. If their assault failed, then the fortress would be stormed – *after* the garrison had been forewarned. Only if the volunteer squads failed to break into Metz would preparations be made to storm the fortress. The attempt by the volunteers partially corresponded with the instructions that came from Silesian Army Headquarters, which called for reconnaissance prior to a general assault, as well as feints to evaluate enemy preparedness. Apparently, the prince had fallen into the same thought pattern as Yorck: to execute the orders contained in the Champagne Disposition reluctantly and literally without carefully considering the basic meaning of Blücher's instructions. According to the German General Staff historian Janson, this represents "a continuation of the negative, yet outwardly obedient disposition of Yorck's headquarters." He claims this sentiment "actually permeates the records included in the journal of the 8th Brigade, which reflects the same thought process as that of the corps." Hedemann, one of William's staff officers, enjoyed a close relationship with Valentini, Yorck's chief of staff. For his part, Valentini worked extremely well with the staff officers of Yorck's brigades. On the other hand, he had a very poor relationship with his own boss, Gneisenau. Valentini became actively involved in Yorck's opposition to Gneisenau. The corps commander took his chief of staff into confidence and often disclosed his thoughts to him. Valentini frequently shared Yorck's fundamental criticism and negative demeanor toward Silesian Army Head-quarters with brigade staff officers such as Hedemann. Valentini had served as Yorck's chief of staff before being transferred to Bülow's corps at the end of September. Valentini and Gneisenau had parted ways after the former crit-icized Gneisenau's actions in early September 1813. When Valentini returned to Yorck's corps on 7 January, he did not meet personally with Gneisenau because the I Corps operated at a distance from Silesian Army Headquar-ters. In early February, Valentini did seek to reconcile their differences, but Gneisenau's response is not known.

On 19 January, Stutterheim's advance guard moved north from Vandières to Bayonville, but floodwaters prevented his artillery from making any fur-ther progress. Leaving his battery behind, he continued the march. Stut-terheim reported to Prince William that the last of Marmont's troops had marched through Gorze and Mars-la-Tour toward Verdun on the 16th. He also reported that the water level appeared to be decreasing. William instructed Stutterheim to reach Metz on the following day, 20 January. The prince planned to follow, but the flooded terrain forced him to direct his artillery through Thiaucourt.

Contrary to Stutterheim's report, the water level continued to rise on the 20th. By noon all roads on the left bank of the Moselle were flooded, making communication possible only by boat. In fact, the highway to Metz remained under three feet of water for most of the day. Despite these difficulties, Stut-terheim managed to reach the suburb of Lorry and begin the investment on the left bank. Durutte maintained no forward posts outside of the fortress and many of the outworks were flooded; French posts could only been seen on the glacis. Across the river, reinforcements reached the right bank: Borozdin with one regiment each of Russian dragoons and Cossacks as well as the 1,700 men of the 1st East Prussian Infantry Regiment and 1,548 replacements. In addition, Schmidt arrived at Retonfey a few miles northeast of Metz with the four 10-pounder and four 7-pounder howitzers of the Reserve Artillery after the failed operation at Saarlouis. Durutte reminded the Prussians that Metz still remained in French hands by opening fire with his artillery; one ball decapitated a captain of the East Prussian National Cavalry Regiment.

On 22 January, the water level subsided and allowed William to reach Metz with his main body. The prince immediately went to the prominent hill by the suburb of Plappeville, which provided an overview of the fortress and the surrounding region. He observed that the main portion of both the city with its 40,000 inhabitants as well as the fortress stood on the right bank of the Moselle. A first-rate fortress, Metz was in superb condition compared with the neighboring strongholds. Its high citadel likewise faced the Saar from the right bank, where Ft. Belle Croix frowned on the highway from Saarlouis. On the left bank, the advantageous hills that lined the Moselle Valley rose up too far from the fortress to be utilized by the relatively small caliber and short range guns of the Prussian artillery. The river itself forked to form one large and one small arm as it flowed through the city; the smaller portion of the city on the left bank was actually built on the island formed by the split in the river. A large bridgehead containing several fronts and considerable redoubts protected the stone bridge that led to this island portion of the city. Should the bridge-head fall into enemy hands, a special enceinte protected the main part of the fortress. Yet country homes, vineyards, and structures of all types that would facilitate an investment extended along the approaches to Metz. St. Martin, a suburb on the left bank only 1,500 yards from the glacis, offered the best protection for the Prussians to move close to Metz. According to reports, the garrison consisted of 5,000 Line troops, 3,000 National Guard, and 200 cavalry; the Prussians could discern numerous guns on the walls and the reports said nothing about a shortage of ammunition. William had 6,000 men separated by the Moselle at his disposal; two small boats provided his only communication with Warburg on the right bank. He possessed fourteen pieces of siege artillery in addition to the two batteries of his and Warburg's brigade artillery – a total of sixteen 6-pounder field guns.[36]

Strong French sorties on the 23rd drove Stutterheim's posts from Lorry and Plappeville. Yorck arrived from Thionville at 11:30 P.M. and established his headquarters in the château at Pange, a few miles east of Metz. Because refugees had inundated Metz ahead of the Allied advance, he believed a bombardment could cause problems for Durutte. Nevertheless, the skeptical corps commander remained convinced that he did not possess enough shells to force a capitulation. In fact, the events at Saarlouis proved that a bombardment could actually stiffen the resolve of the garrison. Yorck reported to Blücher that a coup de main was out of the question. He thus planned to inspect the situation at Metz for himself on the 24th to determine "whether or not some circumstance exists that will favor an operation." By now, the reports of French sorties and stubborn resistance at Saarlouis, Luxembourg, Thionville, and Metz had convinced Yorck of not only the futileness of his assignment but more important, that these fortresses posed a dangerous threat to the further operations of the Silesian Army. Although Blücher wanted the I Corps to depart as soon as Yorck completed his task on the Moselle, the corps commander informed him that the intention to blockade the fortresses with cavalry after the I Corps marched off was imprudent. He claimed that the commandants of the four fortresses "have shown themselves through many sorties to be enterprising men" and that obviously the garrisons contained considerable strength. "I cannot refrain from expressing that the garrison of Metz in particular appears to be very dangerous to our communications. I now await your order regarding the departure of my corps from the blockade of the fortresses . . . and note that the corps cannot be concentrated at St. Mihiel until the 27th or 28th of this month."[37]

After Yorck's corps left to rejoin Sacken, Blücher's plan called for Röder's 700 troopers to invest Thionville and Luxembourg, whose combined garrisons numbered 7,000 men; Bieberstein's four Landwehr squadrons would invest Saarlouis; and Borozdin's 1,600 troopers would blockade Durutte's garrison of at least 8,000 men at Metz. Blücher's instructions made it very clear that although Yorck should take advantage of any opportunity that presented itself, the true nature of his mission was economy of force. Silesian Army headquarters wanted the fortresses invested by a minimal number of troops but still to have the I Corps available for a decisive battle as quickly as possible. Now, one week after receiving the Champagne Disposition, Yorck suggested chaining his corps to Metz to protect the army's communications. He knew Blücher and Gneisenau well enough to count on receiving the order to depart for St. Mihiel yet believed he had to express his opinion. "What worries us," states the field marshal's response, "is if the commandants cooperate and form a mobile corps of 8,000–10,000 men from the garrisons of the fortresses and march on our communications. The reinforcements from Langeron's corps that are gradually approaching will be assigned to prevent this." Blücher and Gneisenau did not ignore rear-area security but instead correctly assessed the threat and did not want unwarranted concern to paralyze their operations. They planned for the rearward echelons and detachments to assume the blockade of the fortresses as these units marched to the front. Gneisenau did not deceive himself over the disproportionate weakness of the troops that would invest Metz before being relieved by other newly arrived units. Rather, he believed that the need to concentrate as much force as possible for a decisive battle outweighed concerns over the rearward, enemy-occupied fortresses.[38]

As expected, Blücher instructed Yorck to begin the march to St. Mihiel immediately. "I find that all has proceeded that can according to the circumstances," adds the field-marshal. "The bombardment of Metz serves no purpose, as you have noted, and we will not expend any powder on it."[39] This response, penned on 25 January, had no impact on Yorck's operations over the next three days. Despite his critical evaluation of the task at hand, Yorck ordered his brigadiers to continue their operation on 24 January. At dawn Yorck conducted his reconnaissance along the right bank of the Moselle. What he found only strengthened his conviction that nothing could be achieved with his available resources.

William, who established his headquarters at St. Ruffine slightly upstream of Metz, contemplated firing thirty or forty shots from his two 7-pounder howitzers into Metz to give Durutte something to think about. Major von Huet of the artillery scouted the left bank for a position to place the artillery but could not locate suitable ground. The closest he could suggest was Longeville, 400 yards from a newly built redoubt and 1,800 yards from the city. On the right bank of the Moselle, Warburg pushed his first line to within musket shot of the fortress. Behind it the howitzers of the Reserve Artillery attempted to move into position. Schmidt, however, informed Warburg and Prince William that the 7-pounder howitzers could not move into effective range due to the forward lying outworks, particularly Ft. Belle Croix. He also encountered difficulties positioning the 10-pounder howitzers because of the flooding of the Moselle and its tributary, the Seille; he could only move to a vineyard within 1,800 to 2,000 yards of the fortress, opposite the bastions that protected the city's quays. Unlimbering in a vineyard presented its own difficulties and Schmidt expressed concern that a sortie would almost certainly lead to the loss of his guns.[40]

Blücher's response to Yorck's letter from the 23rd did not reach Yorck in time to affect his operations on either 24 or 25 January. However, on the morning of the 25th, he did receive the field-marshal's letter from 24 January, which contained the "March Table for the First Wave of the Silesian Army." According to this schedule, Sacken would march to Châlons-en-Champagne, while Yorck moved through Bar-le-Duc and St. Dizier to reach Vitry-le-François by 30 January. Should the French attempt to delay the Silesian Army's march by operating against its right flank, Blücher instructed Yorck to yield and withdraw south toward the Aube. More important, Blücher wanted him to "attentively observe Macdonald's march." He informed Yorck that Cossacks had followed Macdonald through Namur on 19 January, and it appeared certain the marshal was making for Châlons-en-Champagne.[41]

This order did not raise the morale of Yorck's headquarters. At the moment, the corps stood dispersed between Verdun and Saarlouis; it would be impossible to unite the brigades before the 28th to cross the Meuse at St. Mihiel, while Blücher himself would be at Brienne – sixty miles away! If Napoleon had indeed arrived at Châlons, Yorck expected the French emperor to drive between the corps of the Silesian Army, whose line of communication stretched from Champagne through Lorraine to the Rhine.[42] On a positive note, Yorck could at least bid farewell to the Moselle and the Champagne Disposition. Because of the forced marches and the siege duty which, in this time of year had uncommonly exhausted the men, Yorck granted a day of rest on the 25th, thus making the concentration of his corps at Vitry-le-François by 30 January impossible. During the course of the day, the Prussian corps commander received news that the French had evacuated St. Mihiel after destroying its bridge over the Moselle. That evening, he issued orders for his brigades to depart from the Moselle fortresses on the 26th. Yorck and Valentini drafted an extensive march disposition designed to move his units toward the Silesian Army as fast as possible. According to the timetable, Yorck's individual brigades and Reserve Artillery and Cavalry would reach Vitry between 31 January and 2 February.[43]

Blücher never intended for Yorck's corps to siege or invest formally any one of the fortresses.[44] In general, the purpose of the operation was to position a corps in this important region to cover Blücher's communications through the fortress belt and to secure the army's flank as it penetrated the French interior.[45] While executing this mission, Yorck had authorization to make an attempt to capture one of the fortresses, which Blücher desired to use as a base. The time frame would not permit extensive operations. Blücher expected Yorck to be relieved in a few days by the arrival of reinforcements. In this way, the I Corps would be able to participate in decisive operations against Napoleon, while only minimum forces blockaded the fortresses.[46] Basically, Blücher wanted to ensure that these fortresses could not threaten the operations of both his and Schwarzenberg's army. Initially, this would be accomplished by Yorck's corps followed by the Silesian Army's reinforcements. The desire to advance toward Schwarzenberg with all available forces as quickly as possible and meet Napoleon in a decisive battle prompted Blücher to drive into the French interior with Sacken's corps followed by Olsufiev's IX Infantry Corps. This required the blockade of the French fortresses that flanked the Russian march. In the least, the utilization of Yorck's corps for this task provides an example of economy of force.

The execution proved faulty for all concerned, with the exception that the French garrisons did not molest Blücher's advance. Nevertheless, not one French fortress fell into Yorck's hands despite the favorable situation and regardless of the fact that his corps was detached from the Silesian Army for this very purpose. The consequences of this operation was that Yorck's corps, delayed for one week in part by the flooding of the rivers, missed Blücher's first battles with Napoleon at Brienne on 29 January and la Rothière on 1 February. Gneisenau's intention to force Napoleon to provide his fortresses with considerable garrisons and thus prevent him from forming a large field army also influenced the thinking behind the Champagne Disposition and likewise failed. It appears there is blame enough for all involved in this operation.

Blücher's cover letter that accompanied the Champagne Disposition concludes with a very interesting statement: "Your Excellency will relinquish all differences of opinion in your corps toward these arrangements." Regardless of this warning, Yorck's headquarters derisively and habitually referred to the order as the "Champagne Disposition." However, based on Bülow's victories in Holland, Blücher's headquarters expected Yorck to succeed and the leadership of the Silesian Army certainly did not envision great deeds from the commandants of the French fortresses. After Yorck executed the so-called Champagne Disposition, Blücher's headquarters remained convinced that the general could have achieved more. "General Yorck," wrote Müffling on 25 January, "made a journey from one fortress to the other but was only committed to leaving his calling card before all and continuing his tour."[47]

Notorious for their opposition to Blücher and his staff, Yorck and his staff subjected all orders from Silesian Army Headquarters to "fundamental derogatory criticism."[48] From Yorck's point of view, the order appeared absurd. At this moment, his corps totaled approximately 19,000 men. In the midst of winter, four capital fortresses and two half-frozen rivers separated his brigades. Henckel and Horn blockaded and prepared to attack Luxembourg on both sides of the steep, rocky Alzette Valley. Prince William and Pirch received the task of capturing Metz and Thionville with their brigades, while a militia detachment besieged Saarlouis. Yorck's Reserve Artillery possessed *four* 10-pounder howitzers and 200 shells that had to be spared for battle.[49] To conduct these operations and invest Metz and Thionville on the left bank, the I Corps needed two crossings over the Moselle, preferably one near Metz, the other at Thionville or Sierck. However, no bridges were located between Metz and Thionville. Although Yorck needed pontoons, no bridging equipment had been assigned to his corps. The French had collected all of the vessels in the area and sailed them to Metz and Thionville. Even if Yorck had the means to build a bridge, the flooding and partly frozen Moselle would have made any attempt to cross the river virtually impossible. For this operation, Yorck had to divide his corps into five detachments none of which could be mutually supported. The Moselle overflowed its banks and limited communication on the highways and roads, thus complicating reconnaissance and causing a great loss of time.

The controversy over the Champagne Disposition offers an insightful example of the polarization that existed and grew increasingly worse between the Prussians of Blücher's staff and those of Yorck's. A larger issue that emerges from this conflict is the ideological division between the officers of the "Frederician" Prussian army and those of the post-Jena "Reformed" Prussian army. Although Yorck had agreed with the "reformers" concerning the implementation of light infantry tactics, in no way did he sympathize with their sociopolitical program. For this reason, he fell into the same category of the "Frederician" officers such as Bülow, Kleist, and Tauentzien, who, besides being reared in the army of Frederick II, believed that the only problem with the army Napoleon defeated in 1806 was weak and indecisive leadership. With new leaders, the army would be just as formidable as in the days of the great Frederick. Scharnhorst and his followers, who included Gneisenau, Müffling, Clausewitz, and Boyen, opposed this view and believed that Prussia had to be recreated not as an absolutist state – but as an enlightened constitutional monarchy that espoused the ideas of civic duty rather than feudal terror. Political views influenced the extent of the military reforms demanded by both camps and ultimately caused bitter divisions in the Prussian officer corps that spawned personal rivalries. For example, Bülow scornfully referred to Scharnhorst as "the schoolmaster." Clausewitz applied the same term to Valentini, who also became a prolific military theorist. These intense rivalries carried over into the campaigns of 1813–15 and often surfaced at the most inopportune moments. Yorck, who detested Gneisenau, knew the chief of staff exercised tremendous influence over Blücher and suspected that he actually ran the army instead of the old field-marshal.

The derisive phrases that emerged in army and corps headquarters for this operation – the Champagne Disposition and "General Yorck's Calling Card" – provide sufficient testimony of the acrid mood in both Prussian camps. Yorck's phrase, which indicates an ill-advised, imprudent, alcohol-induced decision on the part of Silesian Army Headquarters, particularly shows his contempt for Gneisenau. It would have been very easy to reprimand Yorck formally for his continued misunderstanding and opposition. Moreover, the army's high command could have accused him of insubordination, for not employing all available means to execute his orders, and for not taking advantage of the opportunities that arose. Although in a sarcastic guise, Müffling's comment clearly indicates that this feeling permeated Blücher's headquarters. Blücher and Gneisenau, however, did not allow thoughts of vengeance and petty emotions to master them. In fact, they even made excuses for this episode of insubordination, claiming that Yorck had been ill. Knowing he would never change and that they needed him as a corps commander, Blücher and Gneisenau even expressed their appreciation for his efforts. The continuing problems of Prussia's infant General Staff are also apparent during this episode. Although Blücher and Gneisenau represent the epitome of the military marriage envisioned by Scharnhorst and not matched again until Hindenburg and Ludendorff, the rejection of Gneisenau's authority and influence over the army by the senior corps commanders proved to be a problem that even the great Moltke had trouble overcoming in his time.[50]

14

Belgium

In late November, the Prussians invaded French-controlled Holland seeking to gain the credit and reward for liberating the Low Countries. Bülow, Boyen, and Gneisenau recognized the military and political advantages of driving through the Low Countries to threaten France's northern frontier and ultimately the flank of Napoleon's army. Yet strategic consumption and Bülow's entanglement among the Dutch forts fulfilled Napoleon's expectations. Inadequate manpower and harsh winter conditions impeded Bülow's progress. Desperate to secure assistance, the Prussian general looked to the other Allied units operating in the northern theater. With Wintzingerode's corps the closest, Bülow expected support, but the Russian commander refused. Fortunately for the Coalition, Bülow developed an excellent working relationship with Graham.[1] The cooperative attitude of the two Allied generals is noteworthy. Despite supply problems, inadequate combat power, and hostile weather, both commanders maintained a concerted, professional, and sensible approach to their related tasks, even if Graham's attitude reflected London's obsession with Antwerp.

Aside from the sluggish nature of Bülow's operations, his presence in the Low Countries created diplomatic opportunities for Prussia. The British had been interested in taking Antwerp since November. "The destruction of that arsenal is essential to our safety," wrote Castlereagh. "To leave it in the hands of France is little short of imposing upon Great Britain the charge of a perpetual war establishment."[2] Castlereagh informed Hardenberg that Prussia would earn London's full gratitude if Bülow's troops captured Antwerp. Thus Hardenberg encouraged Bülow to "acquire these new merits for the state."[3] Regardless, Bülow believed Macdonald's stand at Nijmegen and Borstell's deployment at Wesel did not permit him to extend his operations toward Antwerp. Moreover, Wintzingerode recalled Benckendorff's Streifkorps from Breda, thus forcing Bülow and Graham to each provide two battalions as a garrison for the fortress. In addition, Graham informed Bülow on 21 December that he needed additional time before all his units would be ready for joint operations. This news, along with Rouget's counteroffensive – a clear sign the French would not abandon Brabant – dashed Bülow's plans for a rapid strike into Belgium.

In an excellent example of the infant Prussian General Staff's evolution into an efficient tool of statecraft, Boyen, the chief of staff of the III Army Corps, maintained a lengthy three-way correspondence with both Gneisenau, Chief of the General Staff of the Prussian Army, and State Chancellor Hardenberg. The Prussians understood the importance of the Low Countries in Allied diplomacy. They hoped London's desire to create a bulwark in the Netherlands against France could be intertwined with Prussian interests. Hardenberg informed Boyen of the British government's approval of William Frederick's plan to reunite all of the Netherlands. The Prussians also heard rumors that the prince of Orange could emerge as the successor to the British throne. In the future, Boyen believed a prince of this house might cede Hanover to Prussia which, as Boyen explains to Hardenberg, "would be invaluable for the unity of a sensible military system in North Germany."[4] Situated between France and North Germany, the fate of the Low Countries figured prominently in Prussia's national security. A liberated and independent Holland could shield the states of North Germany – which Hardenberg hoped to unite in a Prussian-dominated confederation – from French aggression. In the least, a strong Holland would safeguard Prussia's Rhenish provinces and preserve Berlin's sphere of influence in North Germany. Gneisenau explained to Boyen that Holland had to be liberated from French rule and "raised to a mighty state" to safeguard Prussia's national security. He maintained that if a hostile France controlled Holland, an attack on Prussia could be flanked only by considerable forces posted on the North Sea coast. From a friendly Holland, however, the Prussians would be able to threaten the flank of a French invasion of North Germany. "After the conquest of Holland, Belgium must also be turned," advised Gneisenau. For defensive purposes – as well as an ominous portent for future offensives – the Prussians concurred that Holland and Belgium offered the opportunity to flank French defenses along the Rhine and launch a rapid strike against Paris.[5]

In general, the moment appeared right for an Allied invasion of Belgium. The need to defend Antwerp and the festering rebellious attitude of many Belgians deprived the French of military resources that could have been used to defend the frontier. Although ruled by the French for almost twenty years, the Belgians remained unsympathetic to Napoleon's cause. French authorities confronted the problem of harnessing Belgium's resources for the war effort in the face of growing internal agitation, mainly caused by years of heavy conscription. As early as October 1813, the French had reason to question Belgian loyalty. In complete disregard of a request from Paris, few Belgian municipal

councils published statements of devotion to Empress Marie Louise. With
unrest already apparent in Belgium, the Dutch revolt prompted Belgian conscripts to desert in the hundreds. Belgium's nine departments were slated to
provide 21,860 conscripts for the 9 October 1813 levée; a 75 percent desertion
and refractory rate produced less than half that number. Draft riots erupted in
several Belgian cities between 18 and 22 November. Insurgent bands roamed at
will in the Nord, Lys, and Pas-de-Calais Departments, and a general uprising
occurred in Ypres and Poperinge on 30 November. By mid-December insurgent bands operated in all Belgian departments – with some championing the
Bourbon cause.[6]

Although Borstell's brigade supposedly left Wesel, Bülow still requested
additional reinforcements to counter increasing French strength in Belgium.
Bülow's own morale deteriorated around this time. After the glory of the
German campaign, he perceived his career grind to a halt. "Here, it is like I
am on a deserted island – isolated from all and without support," he wrote.[7]
The general assumed Allied headquarters purposely ignored his needs. He
even accused his political opponents in the Prussian army of undermining
him. The apparent indifference of Allied headquarters convinced him that the
king no longer appreciated his services. To Bülow it appeared he received less
consideration than others, whose merits seemed less deserving than his own.
These feelings intensified, especially after Burgsdorf delivered the keys of
Breda, Zaltbommel, Grevenmoer, and St. Andries to Allied headquarters and
Bülow did not receive a much-anticipated promotion from Generalleutnant
to General der Infanterie. Instead, Frederick William awarded him the Order
of the Red Eagle – the same decoration the king lauded on his civil servants.
A sarcastic letter to his wife, Pauline, on 20 December exposes the full extent
of his disappointment:

> Tauentzien and Yorck are now Generals of Infantry, and Kleist and I are not?
> Now, without authorization, I have seized Holland from the enemy. In Europe
> there exists no other land that is so small, but has so many fortresses to conquer.
> For this I have received the Red Eagle First Class? Frederick II would have
> gladly promoted one to General of Infantry after his first victorious battle;
> and for the second, he would have made him a field-marshal. But these men
> have not continued his traditions; they claim his ideas are obsolete. Today one
> understands matters better, everything is exactly measured in order to award
> the credit of the Fatherland and so I have been sufficiently rewarded with the
> Red Eagle.[8]

Regardless of Bülow's private misgivings over his career, Burgsdorf's mis-
sion to Allied headquarters produced some success. During a meeting with
Tsar Alexander, the Prussian captain used a map to explain Bülow's operations.
Bülow's campaign purportedly impressed Alexander, who promised to have

Borstell's brigade relieved immediately. The tsar also assured the Prussians that both Wintzingerode and a Saxon contingent would march to Holland.[9]

Alexander's statements were encouraging, but Bülow needed immediate support to drive the French from Belgium. He hoped Wintzingerode, who was expected in Düsseldorf on 6 January, would cross the Rhine and quickly secure Jülich and Maastricht. In this way the Russians could threaten the right flank of any French reinforcements moving through Belgium toward Holland. According to Bülow's plan, Wintzingerode would advance to the Demmer River, establish communication with Graham, and support British operations against Antwerp. After taking Heusden, Geertruidenberg, and Breda, Bülow would begin operations on the lower Meuse against Antwerp, while detachments masked the weak garrisons at Hertogenbosch and Grave and observed Macdonald. As soon as Dutch troops garrisoned Breda, Benckendorff would depart to unite with Wintzingerode in an assault on Maastricht. Thus Bülow hoped to master the region between the Meuse, Scheldt, and Demmer and to be in a position to invade old France.[10]

Although Bülow's plan promised success, his adversary's increasing strength combined with his own strategic consumption to postpone the long-awaited invasion of Belgium. Thümen's 4th Brigade occupied the Bommelerwaard, while the 3rd Brigade held Gorinchem. Hertogenbosch had to be masked, and, as noted, Breda needed a garrison after Wintzingerode recalled Benckendorff before Dutch troops occupied the post. After manning the captured forts, few battalions remained available for Bülow's field operations. Maison's concentration at Antwerp threatened his dispersed brigades and reports indicated Macdonald remained between Nijmegen and Grave with no less than 7,000 men. Bülow knew this force had to be prevented from reaching Antwerp and uniting with Maison's 14,000 men. His anxiety intensified because of the effects of the harsh weather; drift ice on the Waal and Meuse threatened to crush his pontoon bridges at any moment. He eventually severed his own line of communication by dismantling the bridges to save them from the fury of winter. Without the collaboration of his allies, the Prussian corps commander could do little. Of Dutch troops, few were to be seen. Graham offered verbal assistance but committed his men to the siege of Bergen-op-Zoom. Only Wintzingerode's 8,000 infantry and 5,000 cavalry would enable Bülow to secure Holland and invade Belgium.

On 27 December, Bülow received some encouragement in the form of a letter from the tsar. Alexander again had become "extremely interested in the details" of Bülow's operations after reading the Prussian's reports from 6–18 December. The Russian monarch urged Bülow to push his operations south and attached "the greatest importance to the movements that will be executed in Belgium." Alexander promised the Saxons would accelerate their march to either Düsseldorf or Wesel to support Bülow.[11] However, as with Wittgenstein on the upper Rhine, the Russian monarch failed to motivate his own general to cross the lower Rhine. After masking Wesel and relieving Borstell on 26 December, Wintzingerode advanced upstream to Düsseldorf, but refused to go any further. Bülow implored him to cross the Rhine, assuring him that no enemy forces would threaten his passage.[12] Wintzingerode refused to move. Bülow requested Russian reinforcements, particularly General Alexander Ivanovich Chernishev's Cossacks. Wintzingerode refused to send any units, maintaining that drift ice threatened his communications across the Rhine. "The ice practically rendered immobile Wintzingerode's means of passage," notes Sukhtelen, "which consisted of boats in poor condition and several rafts." Moreover, the Russian claims that "two enemy redoubts facing Düsseldorf appeared to be occupied."[13]

Reaching Düsseldorf with Wintzingerode's advance guard, Chernishev nevertheless prepared to cross the Rhine. However, on 1 January Wintzingerode ordered him to postpone the crossing. Chernishev failed to convince the Russian commander that his advance guard would encounter no opposition. Regardless, Wintzingerode believed Macdonald could threaten the crossing from Nijmegen. Actually, Nijmegen was too far and Macdonald had greater concerns, such as garrisoning the numerous forts in the region. The marshal had to spread his XI Infantry (11,000 men) and II Cavalry Corps (2,241 men) between Nijmegen, Kleve, and Wesel. Molitor's division of 1,750 men held Venlo. The 7,372 men of Sébastiani's V Infantry and Arrighi's III Cavalry Corps guarded the region between Neuss and Köln. Altogether 20,000 men, these forces also had to garrison Wesel, Grave, Jülich, Venlo, and Maastricht, leaving Macdonald with a mobile corps of between 10,000 and 12,000 combatants. Essentially, only Sébastiani and Arrighi could oppose Wintzingerode's crossing. The situation became so absurd that even the crown prince of Sweden urged Wintzingerode to cross the Rhine. "By my letter of the 21st," wrote Bernadotte, "I requested that you focus your attention beyond the Rhine in order to facilitate Bülow's operations. I already notified you that Borstell's troops started the march to Holland. I received a report confirming that the French corps [Macdonald] . . . is not considerable."[14] Wintzingerode's hesitation eventually allowed Macdonald to withdraw unhindered from Kleve to Geldern and then Venlo.[15]

With his patience growing short, Bülow dispatched Major August von Reiche to Allied headquarters on 31 December to seek another audience with Alexander. While he waited for news from Reiche or the tsar himself, Bülow vented his anger to Pauline: "Only by great deeds and timely British assistance was the outcome [at Breda] not the complete opposite. I must remain content and do everything possible until reinforcements arrive. I have a very good understanding with the British Gen. Graham, who recently landed with many troops – he agrees with all that I wish. On the other hand, Wintzingerode belongs to those who quite literally do not care for the general cause; whether I would bring him over the Rhine with good will is another question."[16]

In the days following Reiche's departure, Bülow's situation unexpectedly worsened. To his amazement, he found himself placed under Wintzingerode's command. In mid-December, the tsar rewarded his officers for their success in the German campaign, and Wintzingerode received a promotion to General of Cavalry. Bülow, still a Generalleutnant, was now junior to the higher-ranked Russian. Bernadotte himself informed Wintzingerode on 22 December that the rank of "General of Cavalry gives you the right to temporarily replace me as commander in chief."[17] Aware of Wintzingerode's promotion, Bernadotte attempted to handle the situation with Bülow delicately:

> I have observed your need of reinforcements. The order was sent to Borstell to rejoin you. My letter of the 9th, sent to Wintzingerode at Ems, has started his march toward you. I ordered him to move along the Rhine between Wesel and Düsseldorf. If a strong enemy movement forces him to abandon that position, I advised him to cross the Ijssel and unite with you, leaving the majority of his cavalry between the Ijssel and Rhine. *If this should happen before I can join you, it is of the utmost importance for the unity of this operation that only one direct the movement and you will be able to judge who is the most senior.* I realize that according to the existing treaties between our sovereigns, I do not have the right to place you under any other's command without the authorization of your king. However, if the enemy is between us, and if circumstances force you to rejoin Wintzingerode before I can give you my dispositions, I count on your devotion to the general cause and above all to our military objectives, and on the belief that *the considerations that might influence ordinary men are inconsequential in the light of your noble actions.*[18]

Bernadotte's experience as a French minister of war and marshal had taught him the importance of unity of command. But to Bülow this was vintage Bernadotte: verbose and eloquent at the same time. He had suffered through the crown prince's theatrics during the German campaign, receiving similar notes on numerous occasions. He also knew how to handle the crown prince. Calling the letter absurd, he retorted that because Bernadotte could not place the Prussian corps under another commander's authority, he did not have to obey Wintzingerode unless King Frederick William explicitly instructed him to do so. Regardless of this loophole, Bülow could not conceal his rage and spoke of resigning. Boyen informed Hardenberg of this ill-conceived decision to subordinate Bülow to Wintzingerode. Believing the matter was political rather than a military concern, he urged Hardenberg to secure Bülow's permanent command of the Belgian offensive.[19]

Before Hardenberg could answer Boyen's letter, Reiche returned from Allied headquarters. He reported that although warmly received by Frederick William, the tsar's reception was cool. According to Reiche, Alexander reluctantly listened to the various complaints concerning Wintzingerode. In a surprising reversal of his previous disposition – a habit of Alexander's that kept Allied headquarters in a state of chaos – the tsar did not consider Bülow's requests justifiable. Unable to sway the monarch, Reiche was dismissed. The persistent officer managed to obtain a second meeting with Alexander. Similar to Burgsdorf a few weeks earlier, the Prussian used a map to display Bülow's exact positions and reacquaint the tsar with Bülow's situation. The tactic worked. Alexander reiterated his call for Wintzingerode to cross the Rhine immediately. He directed Bülow to commence the Belgian invasion and to count on Wintzingerode's cooperation.[20]

After receiving the tsar's orders, Wintzingerode announced that his corps would cross the Rhine at Düsseldorf on 5 January. He ordered Bülow to support the passage with a Cossack brigade that had been on loan to the Prussians since November. Bülow flatly refused this ludicrous request. Wintzingerode then sent a staff officer, Woldemar Hermann von Löwenstern, to Bülow's headquarters in early January to negotiate the return of the Cossacks. Löwenstern arrived armed with explicit instructions. "Hoping to succeed better than earlier efforts that had failed to return the brigade," recalls Löwenstern, "Wintzingerode advised me to handle the affair delicately, but not to return without the regiments."[21] Despite these instructions, Löwenstern also failed. Wintzingerode then turned to his higher rank and Bernadotte's mandate that required Bülow to obey the Russian. A disgusted Bülow sent neither a reply nor the Cossacks. In retaliation, Wintzingerode recalled all Russian troops west of the Rhine. Yet after receiving further orders from the tsar, he reluctantly assembled his units at Düsseldorf and eventually crossed the Rhine on 13 January.[22] Although Wintzingerode dropped the pointless dispute with Bülow, it serves as proof of the tenuous relations that sometimes existed between Allied commanders.

During this time, Macdonald finally realized that the Allied forces facing his 31st Division served as a mask to distract him. "The enemy marches unhindered toward Gorinchem and Breda," he wrote Berthier on 1 January. "In a few moments or in a few days there will be an invasion of Belgium; the Allies maneuver by their wings and distract us in the center. I repeat: the troops thus dispersed along this immense line will be destroyed without providing any use for the general defense. The barriers of the Rhine and Moselle are breeched, his person [Napoleon] and his capital are threatened!" Overwhelmed, Macdonald suggested evacuating all or at least part of new France, which he could not defend with his troops so widely disseminated:

> We approach a great crisis: would it not be sensible and prudent to make a great resolution? In these circumstances what purpose will be served by such distant fortresses; partly destitute and weakly garrisoned, they will succumb soon without providing the state any benefit. In the present crisis, at the moment when old France is threatened, is it not wise to dispense with the new and rally all of the scattered detachments, increasing them with the conscripts who are on the march and with men of national honor and French blood who

will triumph under the eagles of the emperor? I cannot hide it, all Frenchmen murmur; each wants to defend his country, which is not here, or fall with honor under the ruins of France.

The marshal concluded his report by proposing that he withdraw to the frontier of old France, rally the garrisons of the frontier fortresses, and collect all conscripts already in march from the depots.[23] Ironically, Marmont and Victor made the same suggestion at this time.

Knowing Wintzingerode's corps had reached Düsseldorf, only twenty miles north of Köln, Sébastiani's V Corps could no longer hold its seventy-mile stretch of the Rhine between Bonn and Wesel. At any moment, Allied columns could cross the Rhine north of Köln and sever his line of retreat. In addition, the fall of Koblenz to the Silesian Army on 1 January prompted Sébastiani's forward posts to withdraw thirty-five miles down the Rhine to Bonn. After receiving reports of the Allied crossing at Koblenz, Sébastiani sent what troops he could from Köln to Bonn: General Albert with a detachment of 400 infantry; only 471 combat-ready troops remained at Köln.

Albert arrived at Bonn on the morning of 2 January after a difficult night march – he found a tome of reports awaiting him. Rather than a mere raid, the Russian operation at Koblenz appeared to be part of a general offensive across the Rhine. Russian infantry occupied the city, while cavalry spread into the Moselle and Rhine valleys, severing all communication between Macdonald and Marmont. An advance guard reached Andernach, twenty-five miles upstream of Bonn. The Russians established their forward posts between Remagen and Mehlem in the Rhine Valley. Reinforced by the Bonn garrison and accompanied by Jacquinot, Albert moved against these forward posts with 700 infantry, 500 cavalry, and some cannon. He drove the Russians from Mehlem, reached Ober-Winter and, as noted, routed the detachment from Pillar's 17th Division coming from Andernach. Sébastiani arrived shortly after the action. Although pleased with the results, he returned to Köln and prepared for the retreat to Jülich. At 7:00 P.M. Albert's column departed for Bonn, where the tired troops arrived before midnight.[24]

Late on 2 January, Macdonald received Sébastiani's report concerning the Russian operation at Koblenz and the affair at Andernach. Like Sébastiani, the marshal recognized the profound implications of Blücher's passage of the Rhine. His daily brief to Berthier again emphasized his predicament:

Due to the occupation of Breda and the other fortresses, my position is not at all tenable without great risk, I have maintained this position only to hold as much ground as possible and to facilitate the provisioning [of the fortresses]. Once I leave it, the line of the lower Rhine will naturally fall ... and the fortresses of Grave, Wesel, Jülich, Venlo, and Maastricht will be left to their weak garrisons. In each fortress is only enough of a garrison to guard the bastions and close the gates because the conscripts have not arrived. If the peace is far off, we will lose both the fortresses and the garrisons.²⁵

The news Macdonald received on 3 January signaled the situation had taken a turn for the worse. A Russian corps had indeed crossed the Rhine in great strength near Koblenz, and a second now threatened to pass the river at Düsseldorf. Moreover, Prussian troops reached the left bank of the Meuse. As a result, Macdonald decided to transfer his headquarters twenty miles further south from Kleve to Geldern. He ordered Brayer's 31st Division to withdraw from Nijmegen in a manner that allowed it to unite with the left wing of the V Infantry and III Cavalry Corps. Macdonald's gloomy letters to Brayer, Maison, Merle, Sébastiani, and Berthier on 3 January reveal both the marshal's despair as well as his proclivity to view the situation in the worst light. "The latest reports from Sébastiani and the duke of Padua [Arrighi] announce the seriousness of the passages," states his report to Berthier. "Mouriez found the enemy in position with canon at Andernach . . . one claims that *Wittgenstein* is at Neuwied. Gens. Beauvais at Neuss and Ameil at Rheinberg report that at any moment a crossing will be effected at Düsseldorf and the confluence of the Ruhr, where a *Bavarian* division has arrived. Tomorrow I march to their support or to take them in. It is clear the Prussians are concentrating on the left bank of the Meuse; one believes they have several Russian units with them."²⁶ Berthier immediately forwarded this letter, which reached Paris on the 6th, to the emperor. Although Macdonald indicated his plan to retreat from the lower Rhine, Napoleon deferred to the marshal's judgment. "The circumstances are such that it is impossible to give precise orders," responds Berthier. "You must slow the march of the enemy as much as possible and cause him as much difficulty as circumstances will permit." Macdonald received this communiqué on the 9th.²⁷

From 4 to 8 January, French troops slowly evacuated the Bouches-du-Rhin Department. On 4 January, Exelmans and Bigarré withdrew their posts to Nijmegen, where they concentrated approximately 600 cavalry and 800 infantry. That same day, Brayer moved 600 infantry to Kleve; 200 cavalry followed the marshal to Geldern. During the day, Macdonald learned that two Russian divisions under St. Priest occupied Koblenz and that Bülow would soon commence an offensive in Brabant. From both east and west, Macdonald saw his line of retreat threatened by considerable Allied forces.²⁸ On the 5th, Exelmans and Bigarré left Nijmegen, moved their troops through Grave, and cantoned on the road to Venlo.²⁹ The retreat continued on the 6th along roads transformed into rivers of mud by a sudden thaw. Macdonald reported to Berthier that St. Priest was moving west in two columns in an attempt to envelop Sébastiani.³⁰

Macdonald's mood crumbled during the retreat. He requested information from Paris, Metz, and Mainz but received no response. The marshal freely expressed his concerns and discontent to his subordinates and peers. "No news from Paris," he howls to Maison on the 5th. "One leaves us with the impression that Bern, Franche-Comté, Alsace, and Brabant have been breeched."[31] He especially complained over knowing nothing about events along the middle and upper Rhine. On the 7th, he again vented his frustration to Maison: "Blücher does not hide the plans of the Allies, but we remain isolated and scattered, throwing into fortresses badly supplied armies that are so useful to defend our country; we will entomb ourselves under its ruins." In his letter to Marmont of the same day, which he addressed to Mainz thinking the marshal still quartered there, he stated that the garrisons would consume all the infantry of the V and XI Corps, leaving him with nothing but a few platoons of cavalry. "It is fatal to want to guard everything and thus disperse our forces," he warns. In addition, he notified Belliard that although the Allies menaced his army between Köln and Bonn, the concentration of Prussian, British, Russian, and Dutch troops in his rear was the true threat. "I do not know what passes near Andernach now that it is occupied by the enemy" he explained. "I do not know St. Priest's next move, one claims he was at Koblenz with 12,000 men on the 31st. We are again threatened between Köln and Bonn, but very disadvantaged by the situation in Brabant. It is a hell of a chore to guard everything, it is madness. I have woven a long web to contain the enemy, support Sébastiani or collect his troops.... Send me, if you will, news from the Moselle: I have sent to Luxembourg, but received nothing." The marshal informed Berthier that Prussian cavalry was approaching from the *west*, on the road from Antwerp, reconnoitering toward Grave and Venlo. To Sébastiani he wrote:

> Without question we must contract, we must concentrate. Such has been my plan for a long time, but I am deeply saddened to leave the fortresses badly reinforced, badly supplied, and weakly garrisoned. I have suggested the evacuation of all the fortresses: withdraw the garrisons, form a solid nucleus, unite it to the I Corps, which would form 30,000 men, including 6,000 cavalry. But I have not received any response and not a word on the events present and future. If in the next twenty-four hours nothing arrives concerning this and the circumstances allow us time, I will write you regarding our subsequent movements. But if it is ordered, our first line must be the Roer, then the Meuse; the points of junction, Jülich, Roermond, Maastricht, Aachen, and Liège. This is all the information I have; it is a fateful coincidence that we are in a situation where we cannot anticipate anything and nothing is in order.

Similar to this letter to Sébastiani, all of the communiqués issued on 7 January from Macdonald's headquarters at Geldern contained statements regarding the inevitable evacuation of the region between the Meuse and the Rhine.[32]

Macdonald hoped to keep open a line of retreat along the banks of the Meuse through Maastricht, Liège, and Namur to France. As for any hope of defending Belgium, possession of Maastricht offered his best chance.[33]

After analyzing intelligence, the marshal confirmed that St. Priest, Blücher, and Sacken had crossed the Rhine at various points, yet he had no idea what direction they would take. On 8 January, the marshal reported that Bülow had crossed the Meuse with the majority of his troops. Evidence also indicated Wintzingerode would cross the Rhine to join him in a joint invasion of Belgium. Sébastiani informed the marshal that St. Priest probably would move from Koblenz to either Bonn or Aachen – Macdonald believed the Russian would advance to support the Allied invasion of Belgium. Statements from travelers arriving at Kleve from the right bank of the Rhine confirmed that no Allied forces stood between Wesel and Nijmegen: all had marched to either Düsseldorf or Zaltbommel. Consequently, Macdonald assumed that Bülow from the west and Wintzingerode from the east would attempt to trap him in a double envelopment, while St. Priest's "divisions" attacked his rear. Moreover, he believed Bülow's advance guard could reach Namur ahead of him and sever his line of retreat. Macdonald incorrectly informed Berthier that Bülow had crossed the Meuse with his main body; he expected Wintzingerode to pass the Rhine at any moment. "Thus it is not without reason that I have made known the impending invasion of Belgium," he wrote. To avoid being trapped and to defend Belgium, he planned to place his cavalry on the Meuse and his infantry on the Roer "to gain two marches" and link with Maison.

To increase his combat forces, Macdonald again sought permission to withdraw the garrisons, in particular Wesel's 6,000 men, who the marshal wanted at Maastrict.[34] Hoping to receive the emperor's authorization, he waited as long as he possible before issuing any orders to this effect. Macdonald attempted to impress on both Berthier and Napoleon the need to reinforce and render the army mobile. "It is with profound pain," he explains to Berthier, "that I view the garrisons as insufficient – without mentioning their composition – uselessly abandoned in fortresses that can hold out only for a short time, while they would be so useful to us for the campaign."[35]

The marshal warned Sébastiani and Maison that "the enemy has concentrated on the left bank of the Meuse. The Rhine, from Wesel to the Waal and to the Meuse, is stripped of troops. There soon will be grave events. I must concentrate my weak resources in order to be in a position to combat the enemy." Macdonald intended to have the main body of the XI Infantry and II Cavalry Corps on the Roer between the 9th and 10th, in part to support the V Corps, which was still on the Rhine. A rearguard would maintain communication with Wesel for as long as possible.[36]

Regardless of Macdonald's plans, the vice continued to close on his army. On 9 January, an officer sent by Macdonald to Luxembourg returned with news from Belliard in Metz: Marmont was in full retreat to the Saar with Blücher's army in the midst of his columns. Blücher's forces reached Luxembourg, 135 miles south of Macdonald's headquarters at Geldern. Sébastiani warned that a considerable Allied force would cross the Rhine twenty-two miles downstream of Köln at Neuss. Patrols from the II Cavalry Corps reported the presence of Prussian forces at Eindhoven, thirty-three miles east of Breda and less than thirty miles west of Venlo. Thirteen miles west of Venlo at the village of Meijel, this Prussian force – the 170 troopers of Colomb's Streifkorps en route to the Meuse – surprised and destroyed a weak squadron from the 13th Hussars. On the next day, the 10th, Exelmans reported the march of an Allied corps of 10,000 men toward Maastricht and Liège to sever Macdonald's line of retreat up the Meuse to France.[37] This last piece of news, although untrue, left Macdonald no other option than to order a general retreat for the 11th.[38]

Macdonald established his headquarters at Venlo on the evening of 11 January with the intention of continuing twelve miles up the Meuse to Roermond the next day. The XI Corps would quarter at Venlo, while Sébastiani concentrated the V Infantry and III Cavalry Corps at either Jülich or Aachen. On the left bank of the Meuse, the II Cavalry Corps covered the army's retreat by proceeding south toward Maastricht.[39] The marshal claimed Colomb's movement toward Eindhoven prompted his retreat. "Tomorrow I will march to the Roer and withdraw my cavalry to Maastricht. As soon as we are reunited and rallied," he reported to Paris, "we will undertake something, and I assure you that I will do everything to warm up the men, who have been frozen by both the events and the season."[40] In a letter to Prefect Jean-Charles-François de Ladoucette of the Roer Department, the marshal attempted to justify his evacuation of new France: "It is with an army that one must defend provinces, but not the few troops I have at my disposal, spread along eighty leagues of terrain, bound until now to observe a part of the Rhine, while this river and the Meuse are crossed at several points, while the Allies have enveloped our wings and incessantly threaten my communication. My heart bleeds to abandon any ground, but I do not have the means do defend it."[41]

On the right bank of the Meuse, Macdonald arrived at Roermond on the 12th with the seven battalions that formed the main body of the 31st Division. Molitor guided the three battalions of the rearguard to Venlo, likewise on the right bank of the Meuse, but thirteen miles north of Roermond. West of the infantry and on the left bank, the II Cavalry Corps covered the movement up the river, which started to freeze as the temperature plummeted. As night fell on the 12th, the reports that reached Macdonald's headquarters offered some hope. From Maison came news of Bülow: The Prussian was proceeding southwest toward Antwerp rather than southeast toward Maastricht. Northeast of Macdonald's position, the Allied corps at Düsseldorf still had not crossed the Rhine. The remaining "threats" came from the southwest and southeast. From the former, Colomb's tiny Streifkorps continued toward the Meuse. On the other hand, a detachment of all arms from the Silesian Army had reached Malmédy, twenty-five miles southeast of Liège and the marshal's line of retreat to France. Macdonald planned to answer this threat by withdrawing further west and completely across the Meuse to cooperate with Maison between Maastricht and Antwerp in central Belgium. "I do not request reinforcements because I suppose one cannot provide them, being obliged to cover all the threatened points," concludes the marshal's brief to Berthier. "I do all that is humanly possible to cooperate with Maison, whose strength I do not know."[42]

On the left bank of the Meuse, the XI Corps could strike the flank of an enemy column moving against Maison's troops. Conversely, if the Anglo–Prussian force attacked the XI Corps, Maison could support the marshal. Macdonald's movement across the Meuse also would take care of Colomb's Streifkorps, which could not confront two French corps. That evening Macdonald's headquarters issued instructions for the two echelons of the 31st Division to unite at Maastricht by the 15th. Exelmans's cavalry would arrive on the 14th but send numerous detachments toward Antwerp. Sébastiani's V Corps would retire on Jülich and Aachen, with Arrighi's III Cavalry Corps securing the Aachen–Liège road for the V Corps. The marshal requested that all of his subordinates work to prevent the flight of French civil authorities.[43] The fatalistic details he included in a short letter to Maison indicated his sour mood: "The Rhine and the Meuse are taken. I will be at Maastricht on the 13th; my cavalry will be there on the 14th."[44] Events at Antwerp and Düsseldorf soon ruined Macdonald's plans.

Macdonald initially believed the appearance of Colomb's Streifkorps heralded the approach of Bülow's corps advancing eastward to drive him into the Rhine. However, the Prussian corps commander made plans to march in the opposite direction. Bülow's main body moved against the French lines between Turnhout and Hoogstraten. He sought to cut off from Antwerp the troops occupying the positions in front of the fortified port and at the same time force Macdonald to continue his retreat. Bülow then planned to take a defensive position until Wintzingerode arrived.[45] He met with Graham on 8 January to plan the Belgian offensive. Graham, a veteran of the Peninsular War, impressed Bülow, who informed his wife that the sixty-year-old British officer still displayed great stamina and "has solid intentions." The fact that the senior Graham waived his rank and declared his readiness to subordinate himself to the Prussian general in deference to the greater number of troops under Bülow's command certainly promoted good relations.[46] Bülow only regretted the small size of the British force – 5,000 infantry and 500 cavalry. Graham accepted Bülow's suggestion for the British to shield his right flank against a French operation from either Bergen-op-Zoom or the lower Scheldt while the Prussians opened the offensive by attacking Hoogstraten. Graham also would position a force south of Bülow to intercept the French retreat from Hoogstraten. After the fall of Hoogstraten, the Prussians planned to advance to Antwerp along secondary roads that ran east of Breda. They scheduled the joint operation to begin on 10 January.

The congenial discussions with Graham as well as the renewal of the offensive lifted Bülow's spirits and ended talk of his resignation. In addition, Borstell's 5th Brigade arrived from Wesel on 8 January. Bülow assembled the 18,000 men of his 4th, 5th, and 6th Brigades around Breda to begin the operation; the 3rd Brigade remained at Gorinchem and Hertogenbosch. On 9 January, he dispatched several light cavalry units across the Belgian frontier through Turnhout toward Venlo and Roermond to determine if Macdonald and Maison were attempting to unite. It appeared the marshal had evacuated Kleve and Nijmegen – the direct result of Blücher's 1 January crossing of the Rhine – but where exactly Macdonald proceeded remained unknown. Bülow also learned that drift ice had destroyed the pontoon bridge at Zaltbommel, thus severing his communication. Facing what he believed to be a superior foe, having no line of retreat, and with only 5,500 British troops for support, Bülow was in a precarious position. He decided to take the initiative and continue the operation before Maison could concentrate his forces.[47] "I have placed myself in an offensive posture," he explains to his wife, "but due to the limited means available to me, I must play the role of a braggart, and make people believe I am much stronger than I actually am."[48]

At Antwerp Maison correctly assumed the Prussian movement against Roermond and Venlo marked the beginning of an offensive. According to reports from Macdonald, Bülow was concentrating his forces toward Zaltbommel, facing Maison's right. Macdonald incorrectly informed him that Bülow would march southeast through Eindhoven to Maastricht. However, according to Maison's intelligence, the Prussian commander himself arrived at Breda with 10,000 men ready to invade Belgium. Maison did not think Bülow would drive on Antwerp and thus expose his own flank and rear to Macdonald. Instead, he assumed the Prussians would push through central Belgium to Liège, Huy, and Namur to sever Macdonald's line of retreat and prevent his junction with the I Corps.[49]

Bülow's advance guard of 400 cavalry and 300 infantry had moved to Zundert. On the 7th, Maison's troops drove out the Prussians, pursuing them almost to Breda. Nevertheless, the Prussians returned to Zundert on the next day. "If he was not supported, he would not have dared to do this," noted Maison. The French commander also learned the British recently received 3,000 reinforcements; as many as 2,000 British troops had taken a position at Roosendaal. "I have discovered the enemy has thrown four bridges across the Waal. According to this information, it appears Bülow will begin operations in Brabant; he boldly declares he will seize Belgium." In response, Maison concentrated Roguet's 6th Young Guard Division at Westmalle. Cavalry, supported by a few infantry companies, guarded Hoogstraten, Loenhout, and Wustweezel. He posted two battalions of the I Corps at Brasschaat and Donkmeer; the remaining three garrisoned Antwerp. Two battalions, 1,000 cavalry, and two guns at Turnhout formed his right wing. If Bülow drove

Map 18. The region between the Breda and Antwerp.

south from Breda, Maison planned to move General Pierre Barrois's 1st Young Guard Tirailleur Division from Brussels to Lier.[50]

A great opportunity presented itself to Maison if the Prussians proceeded according to his assumptions. A drive through central Belgium would expose Bülow's right flank to his counterattack. Yet the specific task of defending Antwerp – decreed by the emperor himself – hampered and frustrated Maison. "If it were not for this city of Antwerp," he wrote, "it would not be necessary to hesitate to march with all our means on the enemy, who dares to make a flank movement in front of us."[51]

In his "Note" of 12 January 1814, Napoleon estimated Allied strength in Holland at no more than 12,000–15,000 men." According to Napoleon's ridiculous estimates of his own forces, 29,400 men garrisoned the forts and main cities of Holland; 39,700 men were posted between the Meuse and Moselle; 33,700 men held the northern fortresses of Lille, Dunkirk, Maubeuge, Calais, and Ostend, with another 15,000 men at Brussels.[52] Fortunately for the Allies, Maison did not view the situation as optimistically. Instead, he saw himself outnumbered and chained to Antwerp. Without the emperor present,

Maison, like so many other French commanders, felt overwhelmed and simply gave up. Given Napoleon's instructions to defend Antwerp and maintain the link with Macdonald, Maison dismissed any notions of a counteroffensive and thought only of abandoning Belgium and retreating to old France. The following letter to Clarke shows the extent of Maison's confusion, indecision, and helplessness:

> If defended only by the Demer and the Nete [Rivers], Belgium will be conquered: we cannot hold anything other than this line and from there our fortresses on the old frontier. Had my corps been formed as fast as I thought, I perhaps could have stopped this invasion. But with what I possess I do not believe I can withdraw from Antwerp, for I must always leave a garrison in this place. I do not think concentrating all our troops below Antwerp will deter the enemy from advancing. On the other hand, if one does not guard the outside of this place, the enemy, through a bombardment, will burn the fleet and the dock yard. I ask you to inform me of His Majesty's intention regarding the number of troops to leave at Antwerp and the direction to take with the rest. If I am forced from here, I plan – at least until I receive contrary orders – to recross the Scheldt and gain Lille. I know this means renouncing Belgium, and uncovering Liège, Namur, and Huy, but the forces I have do not allow me to even think of doing something else.[53]

On 10 January, the invasion of Belgium began with Bülow's brigades issuing from Breda in three columns.[54] Bülow hoped a general advance against the enemy's front and left flank would prompt the French to abandon their positions which, five hours north of Antwerp, provided the great port's first line of defense. On the left wing, Borstell's 5th Brigade marched on the direct road from Breda to Hoogstraten. In the center, Thümen's 4th Brigade trooped through Zundert to Wuustwezel and Loenhout. On the right wing Oppen, commanding Krafft's 6th Brigade and the Reserve Cavalry, was supposed to advance through Kalmthout and then wheel into a position opposite Thümen at Wuustwezel. The British agreed to advance ahead of the Prussians through Roosendaal toward Antwerp. Graham's movement would cover Bülow's right by containing Antwerp's garrison. During the operation, Bülow's columns actually moved ahead of the British instead of behind them. Historian John Fortescue claims Bülow instructed Graham to remain at Roosendaal. Believing Graham should have pushed forward, the British historian states: "altogether, a promising operation was wrecked by Prussian imbecility."[55] Despite Fortescue's biting criticism, poor maps probably caused confusion at Bülow's headquarters, as is evident by the havoc that ensued as soon as the Prussian columns moved out of Breda. Bülow's staff had to spend much of 10 January reorganizing and redirecting the columns.[56]

At 8:00 A.M. on 11 January, Borstell began a frontal assault on the French positions around Hoogstraten just as Roguet was preparing to conduct reconnaissance from Minderhout with General Jean-François Flamand's 2nd

Young Guard Brigade. Borstell planned to pin the French at Minderhout with his main column, while Sydow led a detachment through Wortel to turn the French right. Advancing due east of Hoogstraten, Borstell attacked Minderhout. Supported by a swarm of skirmishers, the Pomeranian Fusiliers drove the French from Minderhout's outskirts and entered the town. The town church stood on a hill that mastered the surrounding terrain and formed the center of the French position. Borstell's Pomeranians stormed the churchyard and ejected the French after a short melee. Soon after the Prussians fortified this position, the French counterattacked. A murderous skirmish ensued until the French retired. Efficiently using terrain to keep the Prussians at bay, the French withdrew in good order toward Hoogstraten. Borstell pursued and the fighting continued for another three hours as the brigade commander waited for Sydow's column to arrive.

Meanwhile Sydow reached Wortel at 9:00 A.M. Shortly after, he received the report of a French force approaching from Turnhout. This was General Antoine Aymard's 1st Brigade of the 6th Young Guard Division, which Roguet summoned to Antwerp. Unsure of Aymard's intentions, Sydow halted his march and informed Borstell of the situation. The brigade commander dispatched three battalions to support Sydow in case Aymard stood his ground, but Aymard sought to avoid the Prussians. After receiving confirmation that the French column was moving southwest to Lier rather than northwest, Sydow turned west toward Hoogstraten. Arriving at noon, he made contact with Borstell, who ordered a general assault on Hoogstraten. Although attacked from two sides, the French stubbornly held their position. Bloody hand-to-hand combat claimed many lives on both sides until the French again withdrew in good order. With one Pomeranian squadron and the horse artillery leading the pursuit, Borstell made little progress as French skirmishers contested every step of the retreat toward Antwerp. Uneven land divided by thick hedges protected the French from Prussian cavalry and artillery. At Oostmalle Roguet received reinforcements and turned to face the Prussians north of the town. Borstell unlimbered his Russian twelve-pounder battery and one Prussian battery of 6-pounders – a total of sixteen guns. Under a thunderous bombardment Roguet withdrew into Oostmalle around 5:00 P.M.

Because his men had endured a full day of marching and fighting, Borstell decided to break off the combat. He posted pickets to observe Oostmalle and withdrew for the night. His troops captured sixteen officers and 200 men during the affair; Roguet lost approximately 600 dead and wounded. Prussian casualties amounted to eighteen officers and 465 men; Borstell himself was slightly wounded. "On the morning of the 11th," boasts Bülow to his wife, "I attacked the enemy and drove him back with considerable loss from all points; on the side where Borstell attacked was a stubborn combat, but the Pomeranians made the enemy suffer for it; the Pomeranian Grenadier Battalion massacred a couple of hundred without giving quarter."

Elsewhere, Thümen advanced from Zundert at 6:00 on the morning of the 11th. At Wernhout he observed French forces evacuating Wuustwezel and marching east toward Loenhout. The Prussians followed, attacking the front and flank of the French position. After a bloody stand around Loenhout's church, the French conceded the town and withdrew through Brecht to Westmalle; Thümen remained at Loenhout with the majority of his 4th Brigade.

Oppen's column encountered unexpected difficulties. Ice and snow rendered the country road that led to Wuustwezel impassable for cavalry and artillery. An alternate route through Roosendaal and Kalmthout delayed his march by five hours. To make matters worse, Oppen's forward patrols detected a body of troops moving in the distance. Oppen formed his battalions for battle and prepared to intercept the advancing foe, who also deployed for combat. After wasting more daylight, the Prussians learned too late that the supposed enemy column was actually Graham's men. The British mistakenly believed they, too, had stumbled on an enemy force. Although they discovered the error before either side opened fire, both lost what Bülow described as "very considerable and precious time." Indicative of the difficulty of maintaining communication, the near mishap also provides further proof that neither the Prussians nor the British possessed adequate maps. After the chaos of the previous day, Oppen's difficulties frustrated his commander. "This day would have been extremely successful if everything had unfolded according to orders," continues Bülow's letter to Pauline. "Oppen's column should have arrived directly in the rear of the enemy in order to completely cut him off from Antwerp. He should have attacked a predetermined point around 8:00 A.M., but unfortunately he did not arrive until 3:00 in the afternoon." Bülow ordered Krafft to remain at Wuustwezel with the infantry, while a portion of Oppen's tired cavalry cleared the French from Westmalle. Total losses sustained by the Prussians during the various engagements on the 11th exceeded 600 dead and wounded; the French lost approximately 1,000 casualties and 500 prisoners. Anglo–Prussian forces advanced ten miles south during this operation; Graham established his headquarters at Kalmthout and Bülow quartered at Loenhout.[57]

Roguet reached the formidable haven of Antwerp during the night of 11–12 January. On the 12th, he formed a forward position along the line of the Kleine Schijn brook. A few miles north, Flamand posted his brigade at Deurne, Wijnegem, and Schilde. To the west, Ambert, now commander of the 2nd Division of the I Corps, held Merxem. After summoning Barrois's division to leave Brussels on the 11th and force march twenty-five miles to reach Antwerp on the 12th, Maison directed Barrois to reinforce Aymard's brigade at Lier and cover the Breda–Lier–Brussels road. Despite Allied success on the 11th, Maison viewed the operation as a demonstration. Bülow's reconnaissance through Turnhout two days earlier had convinced the French commander

the Allies intended to advance to either Brussels or Liège, and then to the
frontier of old France. After reinforcing Antwerp with 3,000 men, Maison
did not feel his numbers sufficed to continue mobile operations. The rivers
that could have aided his defense of Belgium had froze and he feared being
outflanked and isolated by superior forces. As a result, the general requested
authorization from Paris to retreat either to the fortresses of old France or to
Liège in order to support Macdonald. Before he received the answer, Maison
expected to be forced to leave a substantial garrison in Antwerp, evacuate
Belgium, and withdraw to Lille on the French frontier. Anticipating the fall
of Brussels, he ordered General Jacques-Antoine Chambarlhac de Laubespin
to transfer the headquarters of the 24th Military District from the Belgian
capital to Valenciennes.[58]

The Allies continued their offensive on 12 January by advancing on a
broad front against Maison's forward positions. Bülow shuffled his brigades
for Thümen's 4th to form the right wing and move toward Brasschaat, while
Borstell's 5th advanced toward Lier on the left. Oppen, still in command
of the 6th Brigade and Reserve Cavalry, proceeded in the center to Massenhoven. Graham's troops linked with Bülow's right at Ekeren. The joint Anglo–
Prussian attack succeeded in driving Maison's forward troops behind the
Kleine Schijn brook. Some hundred men of the Young Guard drowned when
the frozen stream shattered as they attempted to escape across it. The Allies
captured another 500 prisoners.[59]

Granting the French no reprieve, Bülow decided to assault Wijnegem and
Merxem on the 13th. He believed the population of Antwerp would revolt
against the French if he made a strong demonstration in the field. By driving
toward the port itself, he hoped French resistance would crumble and his
troops could even enter Antwerp. Moreover, his operation had a more serious
yet less risky objective. He wanted to establish his corps in a better position
from where Prussian and British artillery could destroy the French squadron
on the Scheldt as he waited for Wintzingerode's corps to move closer.

Maison himself went to Lier on the morning of the 13th with 1,000 men
and three batteries to join Castex's and Barrois's Guard divisions as well as
Aymard's brigade, which had withdrew to Lier on the evening of the 11th. The
position at Lier allowed the I Corps to maneuver along the Demer and Nete
to defend western and central Belgium and to cooperate with Macdonald,
who covered the eastern portion.[60] Indicative of the problems of trying to
coordinate the war from Paris, Napoleon remained a step behind events. He
believed Maison could successfully end the affair with Bülow. "The enemy
is in three groups," he wrote Macdonald on the 13th. "It does not seem that
this group coming from Breda and commanded by Bülow can be more than
9,000 men. Maison is more than ready to fight him."[61]

Meanwhile, Bülow formed his corps into two columns with Borstell's
brigade in reserve and flanked on the right by the British. Early on the morning

of the 13th, the Prussian corps commander rode to Wijnegem and reconnoi-tered the French position. Wanting to test the defenses with a general assault, he instructed Oppen and Krafft to advance from Massenhoven against Wij-negem. Thümen received orders to attack the French position at Merxem in conjunction with Graham.

Around 8:00 A.M. on 13 January, Oppen led the left wing toward Wijnegem. He formed Krafft's brigade into two columns. The left wing, commanded by Zastrow, attacked Wijnegem, while Zglinitzki's right wing column marched to Deurne. French skirmishers and two guns stubbornly guarded the entrance to Wijnegem and initially stopped Zastrow's men in their tracks until Prus-sian skirmishers broke into the outlying houses and concentrated their fire against the enemy position. After the French withdrew into Wijnegem, the Prussians entered but encountered determined resistance in the barricaded streets since Roguet had moved up a fresh battalion and several guns. After a lull in the fighting, Oppen ordered a bayonet attack by the East Prussian Fusilier Battalion. The Prussians stormed the barricade and captured one gun. At that moment, French reinforcements in the form of 200 infantry and 100 cavalry arrived on the road from Lier and charged the disordered Prussian companies. Smashing into the enemy, the French regained their cannon and drove the Prussians from Wijnegem. After reorganizing the East Prussians, Zastrow ordered the Kolberg Fusilier Battalion to support them in a second assault. The two Prussian battalions slowly pushed the French toward the eastern exit of the village.

Meanwhile, as Zglinitzki's column approached Deurne, reports arrived of a French force advancing against Oppen's rear and flank from Schilde. Hearing artillery from the direction of Wijnegem, Flamand marched to the sound of the guns with all the troops he could assemble: one company of 100 men and some lancers. The French reached the rear of Zastrow's position before Borstell's reserve could move up. To buy time, many of the officers and orderlies who remained in the rear of the advancing column attacked the French; a musket-ball killed Zastrow's adjutant. Oppen likewise led his staff against the enemy lancers. Because of the small size of the enemy column, the Prussians slowed the French long enough to allow Zastrow to pull the Kolberg Fusiliers out of Wijnegem and force Flamand to veer toward Deurne. Reaching Deurne before Zglinitzki, Flamand united with the two French battalions posted there. Upon arriving, Oppen observed earthworks protecting the village and obstacles lining the road. Just at this moment, he received Bülow's order to break off the combat, observe the French position until dark, and then withdraw his main body.

On the Allied right, Thümen advanced from Brasschaat against Merxem with Graham's troops following in close support. Thümen's soldiers assaulted the village from the north, while the British reinforced by two Prus-sian battalions swept around the French position from the west. General

Antoine-Sylvain Avy held Merxem with five battalions from Ambert's division, which was composed entirely of conscripts about to experience battle for the first time. At 10:30 A.M. brisk skirmishing erupted on the Brasschaat–Merxem road. A half-battalion from the French 25th Line took cover behind *abatis* near a château located on the road to Merxem. Ambert moved up a part of his reserve to support these troops. The raw French troops repulsed the first attack of Bülow's veterans. Grapeshot from four Prussian guns then ripped gaping holes in the French line. "Our young soldiers were intimidated and broke as a result," states Ambert's after-action report, "but their officers reestablished them at their post. It was around noon: the firing on our left was still very brisk. I reinforced this point with three companies from the 58th and ordered the commander of the half-battalion of the 25th to follow the enemy's movement and cover the left of the village. Our troops held against a very brisk fire within pistol range until 1:00 P.M."

Learning that Allied reinforcements had arrived on his left, Ambert issued orders to retreat to Merxem. Unfortunately for the French, the retreat turned into a route after the young French soldiers believed they were outflanked. At Merxem's entrance, French artillery was positioned behind abatis. Seeing the flight of the infantry, the gunners "threw themselves pel-mel into the street of the village and made it impossible to make a stand," continues Ambert. "I immediately retired the artillery, which was found abandoned by a majority of the gunners and drivers. At the same time, a battalion of Scots debouched on the head of the village where I was with Gen. Avy and 150 men likewise fled through the village in disorder despite all our efforts." Enveloped, the Marie Louises broke, especially after witnessing Avy receive a mortal wound while fighting at the head of the 4th Light Infantry Regiment. "We found all the side-roads leading to the main road filled with enemy skirmishes," wrote Ambert. "I then asked Avy to go to the exit of the village to stop the column there and reform it, telling him that he would find there the detachment of the Guard Lancers. At that moment he was struck in the head by a ball and he fell dead at my side."[62] The French conceded the village and retreated in disorder to Antwerp. Thümen pursued through the suburbs and forced back into Antwerp a battalion that Governor Lebrun personally led forward to save Ambert's men. Moving to within 800 yards of the city, the Allies unlimbered their artillery. Although canon pounded the French troops assembling on the glacis, howitzers lobbed shells into the port. The Anglo–Prussian bombardment did not last long before Antwerp's guns forced the Allies to seek shelter or risk losing their artillery.

That evening Lebrun ordered Maison to launch a counterattack on Wijnegem, Westmalle, and Brasschaat. The Allied operation probably convinced Maison that both Napoleon and Lebrun grossly underestimated the enemy's strength. He refused to risk his men in a general counterattack and thus limited his operations to a small sortie in Oppen's sector. Advancing on the road to

Lier, 200 French dragoons penetrated the Prussian picket line and reached the enemy camp before the Prussians could react. The French troopers inflicted several casualties on the unsuspecting Prussians. As quickly as they appeared, the French melted into the darkness, but Maison's sortie achieved its purpose. Acknowledging the vulnerability of his brigades, Bülow postponed further operations.

Prussian losses between the 12th and 13th totaled forty officers and 600 men; those of the French exceeded 1,000. Bülow decided to maintain the gains of the 13th as forward posts and withdraw his main body to Breda, where it remained until the end of January. A strong vanguard under Borstell held Hoogstraten, Wuustwezel, and Loenhout. "The enemy stood directly across from me with considerable strength," explains Bülow. "In my left flank was the duke of Tarent [Macdonald], who at any moment could advance on my communications with 7,000 men. I had to make a quick decision in order to quit this region. Since I was not able to operate against Antwerp, which would not have been the case if Oppen executed his assignment on the 11th, I returned with the British to my cantonments and left my advance guard to face the enemy."[63]

Bülow instructed Thümen's 4th Brigade to camp at Merxem, one mile from Antwerp. The 4th Brigade drove the French from Merxem's outlying houses and Thümen reported that the French evacuated the suburb. Bülow then requested Graham to unite with Thümen. Upon reaching Merxem, however, the British were greeted by French musket fire. A negligent Thümen failed to secure the entire town, which allowed the French to regroup and counterattack. By the time Graham arrived, the Prussians had been driven out of Merxem and Thümen departed. Although Graham took Merxem by force, Bülow's withdrawal to Breda prompted the British to likewise abandon the town. Graham's vanguard remained at Roosendaal, while his main body moved to Oudenbosch. The British commander complained to Bülow over the incident. He had supposedly requested that Bülow delay his retreat to Breda until the British could join him. Fortescue maintains that Bülow refused because his columns were already marching. Given Bülow's dislike of creating confusion by countermanding his own orders, his reply to Graham does not seem out of character. Although both commanders continued to cooperate, Fortescue claims "the conduct of Bülow and his officers was characteristically Prussian – mean, tricky, selfish, dishonorable, and therefore necessarily carrying with it nervous apprehensions of reprisals alike from friend and foe."[64]

Ostensibly, Bülow attained his objective on 13 January: his forces reached Antwerp and bombarded both the fortress and the squadron. However, the Prussian commander actually gained relatively meager results compared to those he hoped to attain. The combats of 13 January proved Antwerp's garrison would defend its post. Moreover, the walls of the fortress were in good condition and sufficiently defended by large-caliber artillery. As of yet the inhabitants of Antwerp did not appear prepared to fight for their freedom. Antwerp would not fall to a coup de main and the Allies lacked the necessary equipment to besiege the city. Moreover, with the French position at Lier on his left and Antwerp's garrison on his right, Bülow felt a drive into central Belgium would be too risky. Graham agreed that their combined forces could not besiege Antwerp while Maison still operated in the field. In the end, the combats of 11, 12, and 13 January had no other result for Bülow than to secure possession of Hoogstraten, Wuustwezel, and Loenhout – points situated one days' march in front of his previous position at Breda.[65]

Although Maison had been on the verge of evacuating Belgium, his bold stand before Antwerp and the bravery of his men provided the only favorable news that reached Paris at this time. Yet the response from Paris remained far from complimentary. On the 18th, Napoleon informed his minister of war that he could not understand Maison's reports: "Why does he not know the enemy that he has in front of him and why has he been seized with dismay without reason? Tell him nothing should lead him to believe there are considerable forces; he should have united his resources at Antwerp; he should have driven the enemy from there to Breda. Instead of this he has alarmed Belgium and his timidity emboldens the enemy."[66] After receiving Maison's reports from the period of 12–17 January, the emperor berated him:

> His Majesty has viewed with pain the beautiful opportunity you missed to achieve an important victory over the enemy, to relieve Gorinchem, and to attain for yourself the 4,500 men who are in this fortress and who are now useless. You have disseminated your troops. If Roguet had been at Hoogstraten with Aymard's brigade and all of his division united on the 11th, there is no doubt he would have completely defeated the enemy. Then, on the 14th, since you summoned Barrois's division to you, you could have continued to pursue the enemy, who you would have completely defeated and forced to withdraw to Breda. *His Majesty does not approve of a line of twenty leagues; it is good for contraband, but this system of war has never succeeded.* Your plan to retreat on Lille and abandon all of Belgium is all the more fatal since the battalions that must compose your army have to be raised in this fortress. Your ideas regarding the enemy forces in the north are wrong. Bülow has only 12,000 men. In all of Holland there can be only 25,000 men including the British, thus 5,000 men before Bergen-op-Zoom, 5,000 before Gorinchem, Deventer and Naarden, some before the Helder, some in garrison at Breda. You have been attacked by no more than 10,000 men. You could have united 20,000, crushed the enemy, and won a brilliant victory. Instead of this, you have compromised the corps.[67]

This letter provides a classic example of the pressure Bonaparte placed on his field commanders. Napoleon's constant criticism sapped the zeal from his generals, increased their despondency, and made them loathe to show any initiative. Aside from the emperor's frustrating use of misinformation to over-estimate his own forces and underestimate those of the enemy, the psycho-logical impact of his rants is immeasurable. Napoleon's admonishments drip with his own utter frustration of being bound like Prometheus to the rock of Paris. Without doubt, his harsh words bit deep into his subordinate's psyche. After admonishing Maison, the emperor concluded by providing instructions:

> Thus, for the defense of Antwerp and Belgium, you have no other choice than to unite your troops at Antwerp as His Majesty already told you, to maintain strong advance guards, one on the road to Turnhout (Lier is too far in the rear) and the other on the road to Hoogstraten. In this situation, Belgium does not face any danger and your troops will always be concentrated. The enemy will never drive into Belgium as long as you can place yourself between him and Breda, and thus in a position to march on Gorinchem. This position, in front of Antwerp, occupied by the advance guard posted four or five leagues in front, is the only one that will assure Belgium against all the troops that can operate along the line of Willemstad, Breda, and Hertogenbosch. His Majesty's intention is that you immediately change your plan of battle, chose a good position one or two leagues from Antwerp, upon which you can pull back your advance guard and isolated corps, and deliver battle.[68]

Both the reproaches and the detailed instructions that commanders such as Maison received also reveal the shortcomings in Napoleon's system of war. France's military establishment, first rate in so many ways, had produced a system of warfare that demanded and rewarded individual initiative through-out the ranks. This had produced some of the finest soldiers – from private to general – in all of Europe. Yet, with few exceptions, at the army's highest lev-els, commanders became paralyzed by fear, seized by indecision, and reduced to mediocrity when the master was not present. Most of the marshals who remained active in 1813 and 1814 were good divisional generals and tacticians, but nothing more. Their ineffectiveness cannot be attributed to the simple explanation they had reputations to lose rather than gain. Napoleon assumed the subordinates whom he entrusted with independent command had gained sufficient knowledge for this awesome responsibility through experience. On many occasions, but particularly in 1813 and 1814, they proved him wrong. In the empire's hour of need Napoleon's commanders demonstrated they had little understanding of his strategic and operational principles of war. In order for the French empire to survive, Napoleon's generals needed the education, training, and skills to wage war on par with the great captain himself and remain one step ahead of France's enemies. In part because of his political insecurity, Napoleon did not want to see a new star rise on the merits of bat-tlefield exploits. He never established a formal system for training officers in the art of strategy and operations to prepare them properly for independent command. He placed his faith in them, still believing he could direct the war from Paris. Time and again their failures proved they had not been properly prepared for their tasks. Even a military genius like Napoleon could not direct the operations of multiple armies in multiple theaters from his throne.

On the Rhine, Sébastiani's sector remained quiet from 3–11 January. After the combat of Ober-Winter, St. Priest's Russians did not attempt to cross the Ahr – a tributary of the Rhine (Map 19). Regardless, St. Priest's inactivity did nothing to calm Sébastiani's fear of being enveloped by Allied forces crossing the Rhine between Koblenz and Düsseldorf. His resolve to hold his sector of the Rhine steadily eroded, particularly after he received word from Macdonald that Blücher's Prussians reached Trier. On the 10th, Sébastiani, still at Köln, disarmed the redoubt at Rheindorf and summoned the artillery to Köln. The next day, he learned that St. Priest's corps had followed the course of the Ahr to Blankenheim, the hub formed by the roads coming from Liège, Jülich, Aachen, and Bonn. Sébastiani responded by ordering the sick in Köln's hospital evacuated to Aachen. He dispatched two battalions with four pieces of heavy artillery to Bergheim on the road to Jülich to secure the bridge over the small Erft River. "The enemy's occupation of Trier places me in a critical situation," states his report to Berthier, "having the enemy on my front and on my two flanks, which are enveloped."[69]

On the 12th, the French general withdrew his posts from Remagen and Ober-Winter to Bonn, which he ordered evacuated by French civil officials. On the next day, Sébastiani's prediction proved correct: Wintzingerode finally authorized Chernishev to cross the Rhine at Düsseldorf. That evening French forces left Bonn; a rearguard remained until the morning of the 14th. Downstream and closer to Neuss, Albert's troops evacuated Köln on the evening of the 14th. Sébastiani led the V Corps and Arrighi's III Cavalry Corps to Jülich on the 15th. There he made the final arrangements for its defense by a garrison of 2,000 men and then continued his retreat through Aachen toward Liège. On the evening of the 13th, Macdonald ordered Sébastiani and Arrighi to leave the Rhine and reach Aachen by the 15th or 16th.[70] Macdonald then instructed both generals to be in front of Liège on the right bank of the Meuse by the 18th.[71]

Despite receiving news that an enemy force of less than 1,000 men opposed him and that elements of St. Priest's infantry corps had reached Bonn just thirty-seven miles south of Düsseldorf, Wintzingerode continued to loiter on the right bank of the Rhine.[72] Finally, the Russian corps commander reluctantly notified Chernishev that he could cross the Rhine, but warned he would hold him personally responsible should the operation fail. Following a heavy freeze that had blanketed the river with blocks of ice, Chernishev started moving the Russian advance guard of four battalions, one cavalry regiment, and one light battery across the Rhine on the night of 12–13 January. According to Sukhtelen's account, the Russians feared the supposedly pro-French locals would alert the enemy. Thus, to deceive the French, 200 to 300 Cossacks crossed the Rhine between Duisburg and Kaiserwerth to attack a French redoubt situated opposite the mouth of the Roer. A few hours later, Benckendorff led Chernishev's advance guard of 700 cavalry in boats across the Rhine further upstream near Düsseldorf under the protection of a thirty-six-gun battery on the right bank. More surprised than compromised, the French evacuated a small wood and the redoubts on the left bank, which Benckendorff's men immediately occupied. This advantage allowed him to defend the crossing against any French attempt to counter from Neuss. In addition, the strong position on the left bank allowed the rest of Chernishev's advance guard to cross the Rhine unchallenged in full daylight on 13 January.[73]

On the following day, the 14th, the Russians forced the evacuation of the 1,400-man French garrison at Neuss, across the Rhine from Düsseldorf. Reports indicated to Wintzingerode that his units would encounter minimal resistance along the left bank as Sébastiani and Arrighi retreated southwest to Jülich. Consequently, Wintzingerode's Cossacks entered Köln on 15 January.[74] Chernishev instructed his cavalry to pursue the French corps: he ordered Jülich invested and his cavalry to Aachen. On the 16th, Russian cavalry reached Aachen, less than twenty miles from Maastricht. "The enemy did not offer more than a feeble resistance," noted Sukhtelen, "and directed his retreat toward Maastricht and Roermond.[75]

Macdonald entered Maastricht on the 13th: the news he received over the next two days shattered what little remained of his morale. The marshal learned the Prussians had established posts only 800 yards from Antwerp and Maison decided against a defense of central Belgium.[76] The following morning, 14 January, a courier arrived from Paris with the emperor's instructions from 10 January. Napoleon's first sentence addresses Macdonald's question regarding the fortresses: "you must leave garrisons in all of the places," responded the emperor. This answer proves Napoleon learned little from the loss of thousands who had been left behind to garrison German and Polish fortresses the previous year. However, Macdonald could take satisfaction in the fact that his retreat corresponded with the emperor's intentions. Napoleon instructed him to reunite with Sébastiani, Arrighi, and Exelmans; move up the Meuse; and maneuver between Maastricht and Namur to threaten Blücher's right flank. Fortunately for the marshal, the letter indicated the Silesian Army was moving southwest toward the Saar rather than northwest into Belgium. At the moment, Marmont was withdrawing on Metz, Mortier held Langres, and both Ney and Victor were defending the debouches of the Vosges. According to the emperor's overall plan, he would concentrate a reserve army of more than 100,000 men in front of Paris. If the Allies chose to bypass the fortresses to march on Paris, the five marshals would unite with the reserve army to stop the enemy. "You must understand," lectured Napoleon, "how important it is to stop, or at least to slow the march of the enemy, and to present him every possible evil. Employ the foresters, the village police, and the National Guard to cause the enemy as much difficulty as possible."[77]

Later that day, Macdonald received two letters from Berthier dated 12 January. The first replied to Macdonald's 9 January proposal to withdraw Wesel's garrison, which consisted primarily of the 35th Division from his own XI Corps. Rejecting any notion of evacuating Wesel, Berthier explained the emperor's rationale for conserving the fortresses. Aside from their usefulness in the diplomatic posturing that would take place during the eventual negotiations, Napoleon still believed he would defeat his adversaries and the frontier fortresses thus served a purpose in his overall strategy. "In a short time," Berthier assured Macdonald, "we hope to drive the enemy from our territory. An enemy who finds himself having fortresses in his rear must naturally be very concerned in case of retreat." By maintaining the fortresses, the Allies would be forced to mask each with a force large enough to contain the garrison and guard their lines of communication. If the French evacuated the frontier fortresses, the Allies would not feel the bite of strategic consumption caused by rear-area security measures. Moreover, Napoleon could not risk the political repercussions of completely evacuating new France and the Rhine frontier. The tricolor flying from the ramparts of a mighty Vauban fortress provided a clear reminder of French military power as well as the glory of the empire and its ruler. An occupied fortress would offer a symbol of hope and resistance to pro-French inhabitants; collaborators would think twice before aiding the Allies for fear of retribution. Allied troops would be able to exploit the land much easier if the inhabitants interpreted the evacuation of a fortress as a sign the emperor no longer considered the region an integral part of the empire. Garrisons would consist of conscripts and National Guardsmen, who could be organized and trained within the safe confines of the fortress.[78]

Macdonald had suggested extracting the garrisons of the threatened fortresses in order to form a corps of 20,000 for use in France. Because of the emperor's demand for all strongholds to be maintained, he was forced to leave behind Wesel's garrison of 8,000 men as well as 1,300 men each in Grave and Venlo. Maastricht and Jülich likewise had to be garrisoned. In conjunction with the emperor's letter campaign, the minister of war issued a circular on 12 January to all military district commanders, all governors of fortresses, and all commandants of arms regarding the defense of fortresses and military posts. In this circular, Clarke called their attention to Articles 52 and 95 of the Imperial Decree of 24 December 1811 to remind these officers of the regulations they had to observe in a time of war. In short, the document intended to coerce commanders into maintaining their posts, especially during a siege.[79]

Berthier's second letter merely recapped Napoleon's "Note" of 12 January, which the major general sent to each field commander. Accordingly, the emperor instructed Macdonald to withdraw even further south to Liège to threaten Blücher's right flank and guard the Meuse. If the Allies marched on

Paris, Macdonald had to reach the capital before them. Napoleon estimated the marshal's mobile forces to consist of 10,000 men: approximately double their actual number. Conversely, he informed Macdonald that Blücher could not possess more than 30,000 men. All told, the emperor stated his belief that no more than 80,000 Allied soldiers would be available to march on Paris after Blücher and Schwarzenberg detached troops to mask the fortresses in Alsace and Lorraine.[80]

On account of the dispatches he received from Paris on the 14th, Macdonald, as noted, instructed Sébastiani and Arrighi to leave Aachen immediately and continue the retreat to Liège. "You will not say a word to anyone of what you will execute in front of Aachen so the enemy will know only that you have turned on the Meuse."[81] To Berthier he reported: "I have received your letter of the 10th. The orders have been executed. Accordingly, the XI Infantry and the II Cavalry Corps will unite tomorrow between Maastricht and Hasselt. The V Infantry and III Cavalry Corps will be at Aachen in a few days: from there they will march together. During this movement, Exelmans will maneuver ... against the enemy's flank."[82]

Macdonald's flight to Liège continued on the 15th. After garrisoning Maastricht with Swiss companies, Brayer led the main body of the 31st Division fifteen miles to Liège, followed by the Reserve Artillery, the XI Corps, and II Cavalry Corps; all billeted around Liège on the road to Namur. Molitor's rearguard marched through Maastricht and camped on the road to Liège. Exelmans covered the retreat and established communication with Maison's post at Lier, fifty-five miles northwest of Liège. Macdonald's headquarters remained at Maastricht until the 16th.[83]

Judging Liège untenable, Macdonald planned to move his army thirty-three miles further southwest to be concentrated at Namur by the 18th. On 16 January, Brayer's column reached Huy, twenty miles from Namur, while Molitor's rearguard entered Liège. On this day, the marshal received the emperor's "General Instructions" of 13 January that called for Macdonald and Marmont to cooperate against Blücher. Macdonald responded that the threat to his rear posed by Wintzingerode did not grant him such freedom to maneuver. According to his intelligence, the Allied corps that passed the Rhine at Düsseldorf had dispersed on the left bank in several columns. One column of approximately 4,000 troops appeared headed to Roermond, while a second invested Jülich. Macdonald again suggested a prompt retreat to the frontier of old France, claiming that neither he nor Maison had room to maneuver between Brussels and Liège. He believed his numbers would not permit him to make a stand against the Russians. After completing the garrison of Jülich, Sébastiani's V Corps contained 800 bayonets and Arrighi's III Cavalry Corps consisted of 1,200 troopers. Macdonald's own XI Corps had 1,400 to 1,500 men under arms, while the II cavalry corps mustered 1,800 to 1,900 men. Soldiers from the departments of new France whose homes were

Map 19. The Belgian theater.

or soon would be behind enemy lines deserted in droves. Only the native French soldiers remained loyal for the moment – what they would do as soon as they reached France remained another question. The Belgian population appeared so hostile that the French had to employ force to ensure lodging, food, and the means of transportation for both the military personnel and the civil functionaries fleeing to old France. Macdonald observed the complete collapse of the French administration: customs agents and the gendarmerie withdrew on Namur or Dinant in great haste.[84]

During the night of 16–17 January Macdonald received Maison's 15 January report that stated his decision to retreat on Leuven, forty miles northeast of Liège: the marshal did not object. Rather than attempt to direct the general's operations from afar, Macdonald simply informed him of his own plans. He suggested that Maison either lead the I Corps to the northern frontier fortresses of old France or unite with Macdonald's army at Namur. For the

17th, the marshal issued orders for Exelmans to push a brigade to Diest and link with Maison's troops. Brayer's column would continue to Namur and Molitor's to Huy: the two generals would conduct reconnaissance on both banks of the Meuse from a position that allowed mutual support. Molitor would leave a detachment in Liège to serve as rearguard. Macdonald advised both of his subordinates to guard the principal points of passages along the Meuse from Maastricht to Namur.[85] Just before leaving Maastricht, the marshal addressed a stirring proclamation to the soldiers of the 25th Military District, whom he left behind in the fortresses of new France (Appendix L).

The French retreat continued on the 17th along roads turned into bogs by a sudden thaw. Macdonald established his headquarters at Liège with the rearguard, while his columns moved to Namur. According to reports, a column from Blücher's army reached Arlon, sixty-six miles southwest of Namur. A frustrated Macdonald shared this news with Maison, adding: "I wish one would tell the truth about our forces. We are in a position to do nothing more than count those of the enemy. Victory or death must now be our battle cry."[86] On the 18th, the XI Corps united at Namur. Sébastiani joined Macdonald at Liège; the Russians had not pressed him on either bank of the Meuse. However, Brayer's patrols found Allied forces blocking the roads from Namur south to Metz and Luxembourg. This unit, the Falkenhausen Streifkorps, had detached from the Silesian Army with the task of disrupting conscription, inciting the Belgian peasants against the French, and gaining intelligence on French troop movements in the Meuse Valley. It reached Arlon on the 18th and, on the following day, Bastogne, forty-four miles south of Liège. Two days later, it chased the French post from Marche-en-Famène, only twenty-seven miles south of Liège. The small Allied raiding party lacked the numbers to threaten Macdonald's army, yet the marshal had no way of knowing this. The appearance of this Prussian detachment in the Ardennes troubled him. He feared it would attempt to debouch on his left between Namur and Givet to block the road through the Meuse Valley. Although the two squadrons of Silesian Landwehr cavalry that formed this Streifkorps hardly posed a threat, its continued presence caused Macdonald to post Exelmans's 600 sabers between Ciney and Dinant to cover the retreat.[87]

Macdonald planned to unite the XI Infantry and II Cavalry Corps at Namur on the 19th, while Sébastiani and Arrighi remained at Liège with the V Infantry and III Cavalry Corps. No longer concerned about the torpid Wintzingerode, the marshal now sought to close the roads through the Ardennes. He requested news from Marmont and Belliard to regulate his movements according to Napoleon's "General Instructions." His plan to continue south rather than seek a union with the I Corps to defend Belgium troubled Maison, who complained that the movement of the II Cavalry Corps south to Namur would force him to withdraw from Leuven and into Antwerp. Regardless, the marshal ignored his protest: "This cavalry is extremely useful to me for the implementation of this plan, otherwise the Ardennes will be open," he explains.[88]

Macdonald passed the morning of the 19th in Liège before departing and reaching Namur that evening. There he received Berthier's communiqué of 17 January that informed him of the emperor's intention to transfer his headquarters to Châlons-en-Champagne. As a result of this decision, Macdonald had to withdraw to the Argonne Forest, maneuver toward Châlons, and establish communication with Marmont.[89] On the 20th, he acknowledged receipt of the major-general's dispatch and provided a preliminary march itinerary. According to his plan, his column would march through Dinant, Givet, and Rocroi to reach Mézières by the 24th. The XI Corps would commence the movement toward the Upper Meuse on the 20th. As rearguard, Arrighi and Sébastiani would follow from Liège on the evening of the 21st to reach Mézières by the 27th. He informed Berthier that the French administrative machine had collapsed throughout the entire region.[90]

Macdonald's army followed the long defile formed by the Meuse Valley between Liège and Fumay accompanied by enormous convoys that also crept toward the French frontier. Some of the wagons belonged to French civil officials who sought to escape with their lives and precious possessions. Others carried material from the government's artillery foundry at Liège. An untimely warm front that thawed the frozen ground also brought showers that rendered the roads impracticable for wagons and barely passable for infantry and cavalry. The waters of the Meuse seemed to rise with each hour, rendering navigation perilous.[91]

As the XI Corps trudged along the riverbank to Dinant, the marshal himself remained at Namur on the 21st to ensure the departure of all French material. By now his mood had completely soured. Although he repeatedly suggested a retreat to old France, Macdonald never meant to abandon the French frontier without a fight. Responding to Maison's lamentations of 20 January, Macdonald disregarded all caution and criticized the emperor:

> One never should have separated us. Belgium and our frontiers, formerly so formidable, indeed deserve to be defended. Standing from Namur to Liège we can hold or withdraw together. But I have the order to withdraw on Châlons-en-Champagne, where one will unite all the pieces. What a dreadful situation! I repeat: what Providence will save us? One claims the mood of the capital is awful, as well as the majority of the large cities. What has become of the energy of the French? Each loses his head despite having the resources to save ourselves. It is as if one does not know how to put them in use. I have a broken heart and a torn soul.[92]

Macdonald arrived at Rocroi on the evening of the 23rd with Brayer's division but instructed Molitor to hold Dinant until the arrival of the V Infantry and the III Cavalry Corps. With the divisions of the XI Corps now separated by two marches, the concentration at Mézières on the 24th had to be postponed. Rumors of a Prussian column estimated between 5,000 and 6,000 troops that turned west from Arlon toward Dinant again troubled Macdonald. The intrepid activity of the Falkenhausen Streifkorps spawned such wild speculation. Small Prussian detachments pounded the roads to Sedan, Givet, and, in particular, Namur in the hope of establishing communication with Wintzingerode, who Blücher mistakenly believed had reached Liège. At this time, Macdonald learned Marmont was still at Verdun on the 20th. If Marmont maintained this position for a few more days, the V and XI Corps could advance through Mézières and cover the fifty miles to Verdun. Should Marmont withdraw on les Islettes, the V and the XI Corps could align with him to defend the defiles of the Argonne. Twenty-four hours later Macdonald arrived at Mézières with Brayer's division and the heavy cavalry of the II Cavalry Corps. On the following day, the rest of his army crawled out of the Meuse Valley and ascended the plateau of Rocroi. His patrols linked with Marmont's troops at les Islettes and guarding the debouches of the Argonne.[93] Although only fifty-five miles north of Châlons-en-Champagne, the marshal failed to rendezvous with the emperor before Napoleon marched in pursuit of Blücher's army at the end of the month.

As soon as Maison received news of Macdonald's retreat from the Rhine, he ordered Roguet to cover the approaches to Antwerp. Maison himself took a position at the crossroads of Leuven on the 16th with the 2,600 men of Barrois's 1st Young Guard Tirailleur Division and the eight squadrons of Castex's 3rd Guard Cavalry Division. From this position, he could cover Brussels, support Rouget at Antwerp, or march to Maastricht or Liège to unite with Macdonald. The future marshal of France recognized the Allied intention to conquer Belgium but misjudged Bülow's operation. Not knowing Coalition politics would detain Bülow at Breda longer than the Prussian expected, Maison assumed he would attempt to unite with Blücher's army, whose advance guard he mistakenly believed reached Malmédy. Although he had not received any news from the marshal for some time, he was determined to cooperate with Macdonald to stop Bülow at Leuven.

That same day, 16 January, Maison learned Bülow had withdrew to Breda. Again he attributed this new development to Blücher's supposed approach: Bülow would simply wait for the larger Silesian Army to clear out the I Corps. Maison maintained his position at Leuven until the reprimand arrived from Paris. Not daring to defy the emperor's order to concentrate at Antwerp despite how ludicrous this directive appeared given Macdonald's retreat, Maison reluctantly moved Barrois's 1st Young Guard Tirailleur Division to Antwerp on the 22nd. He also dispatched Castex with six squadrons, two battalions, and four guns west to Tienen, with orders to post an advance guard at St. Truiden to observe Wintzingerode's march to Liège. The news Macdonald would withdraw all the way to Châlons-en-Champagne flabbergasted

Maison, who clearly saw the implications such a movement would have on Belgium. "By cooperating with the duke of Tarent between the Meuse and the Scheldt," he assured Berthier, "we can perhaps still prevent the enemy from penetrating Belgium; but if one makes the marshal operate on Blücher's right, one cannot stop the enemy and I will be forced to evacuate Belgium."[94]

Despite the vacuum created by Macdonald's retreat, Wintzingerode's corps snailed forward; the Russian general did not complete the forty-five-mile march from Düsseldorf to Aachen until the 23rd. Even after he received Schwarzenberg's 19 January order to march on Reims, Wintzingerode, like his compatriot Wittgenstein, wasted several days before putting his main body on the road to old France.[95] Regardless of his commanding officer, Chernishev remained active. On 18 January the Russians stumbled on a French foraging mission, capturing 300 soldiers not far from the walls of Jülich. Six days later on 24 January, Russian light troops entered Liège, finding a large depot of arms and ammunition. Benckendorff led two Cossack regiments west in the direction of St. Truiden but soon encountered Castex's column, which Maison increased to 1,800 infantry and 800 cavalry. Benckendorff withdrew before the superior French force to the suburbs of Liège, where he launched tactical strikes to slow the enemy's advance. Resolving to hold Liège and its bridge over the Meuse, Chernishev charged forward to support Benckendorff. Russian reinforcements soon arrived as well as two Uhlan squadrons from the Lützow Freikorps, which had crossed the Rhine at Bonn on the 17th and reached Liège on the 24th. Attacked in the front by Benckendorff, the left by the Prussian Freikorps, the right by Chernishev's Hussars and Cossacks, the French cavalry fell back on the infantry, which formed two squares. "For a long time success appeared doubtful," recalled Sukhtelen, "but the effectiveness of the artillery and the countenance of the Cossacks settled the issue." Castex withdrew to St. Truiden after sustaining a large contusion from a blast of grape; he lost 170 men in the combat. Because of black ice and rugged terrain, the Russians could not pursue. Wintzingerode should have taken advantage of Castex's retreat to accelerate his march, but his movement from Liège to Namur – thirty-two miles – consumed six days although nothing opposed his columns. He did not transfer his headquarters to Namur until Bülow's corps arrived online with his own.[96] For this reason, Wintzingerode refused to continue his march until the German III Corps arrived in Belgium to free Bülow's corps to enter old France at the same time that he made his own grand entry.[97]

From Breda Bülow's troops observed the French positions around Antwerp and covered the operations at Gorinchem and Hertogenbosch; the French had retaken both. Of greater interest to Bülow was the approach of the duke of Weimar's German III Corps. Upon its arrival in Holland, Bülow had orders to march his entire corps to France. Like Wintzingerode, the duke moved at a snail's pace; by 18 January, he had reached only Münster. Impatient and eager to participate in the main theater after his own offensive had dragged on longer than anticipated, Bülow returned to his operations in Belgium. He ordered frequent assaults on Gorinchem and Hertogenbosch. At the former, the French repulsed the repeated attacks of his 3rd Brigade. On the other hand, the Prussians successfully stormed Hertogenbosch with the help of its inhabitants on the night of 25–26 January. Lacking food and with a hostile population, the French commander surrendered his garrison of 1,000 men, eighty guns, and large quantities of war material at noon on the 26th.[98] The fall of Hertogenbosch allowed Bülow to resume the general offensive. Outpost skirmishing ensued daily, and Allied raiding parties penetrated deeper into Belgium.[99] To secure his left, Bülow directed Borstell toward Lier and, if possible, as far as Mechelen, where he would occupy the banks of the Dijle and Demer. Borstell drove the French from Lier on the 31st.[100]

Graham remained focused on Antwerp and the French fleet anchored in its harbor. In this regard, Prince William Henry, the duke of Clarence, met with Bülow and repeated London's request for a joint attack on Antwerp. The prince bluntly stated that to receive future aid, the Prussians had to assist Graham. Convinced an assault would fail, Bülow only consented as a matter of honor and to maintain his supply line. The Allies decided that the Prussians would advance through Wijnegem to Antwerp, while the British proceeded through Merxem. Heavy artillery would be removed from the Dutch forts for use against Antwerp; the Anglo–Prussian force began its march south on 30 January.

On 29 January, Maison took a position on the Dijle between Mechelen and Leuven with 9,000 men. Although Wintzingerode had delayed Bülow's operations for weeks, even the Prussian had to admit his ally's approach ultimately proved decisive in the final push to take Belgium. With Bülow's renewed offensive against his front, the threat posed to his right by Wintzingerode, and Macdonald's retreat to Châlons-en-Champagne, Maison decided to withdraw to the French frontier. On 1 February, Maison evacuated Brussels, leading 4,133 infantry and 800 cavalry south toward Lille with the intention of establishing a defensive line along the French frontier. The cadres of fifty-five battalions, which originally were to form the I Corps, provided 8,000 men to support Roguet's division in the defense of Antwerp; several detachments remained in the Low Country's various forts and fortresses.

With Borstell and Wintzingerode covering his left, Bülow advanced from Breda toward Antwerp on 30 January; Graham moved in the same direction from Bergen-op-Zoom. The British arrived at Antwerp first and failed in an attempt to bribe the French commandant with one million gold francs. Allied scouts claimed the French still maintained strong forward posts along the Kleine Schijn, with infantry reserves in Wijnegem and Merxem. On 1 February, the Prussians assaulted Wijnegem, while Graham attacked Merxem. Thümen, who advanced from Schilde in three columns, found Wijnegem abandoned. Aymard withdrew and deployed his troops along the highway to Deurne; he then attacked the unsuspecting Prussians in the flank. Thümen committed his reserves and dispatched one battalion to flank Aymard's left wing. Although the French attack caught the Prussians completely by surprise, Thümen's men slowly regained their ground. After the flanking battalion arrived, the French abandoned their makeshift entrenchments and retreated toward Deurne. Taking 300 prisoners, the Prussians pursued. Lasting well into the night, the combat finally ended with the Prussians in possession of Deurne's outermost hamlets. On the same day, Krafft's brigade took the village of Schoten. Oppen, on the left, pushed toward Lier, while a unit of his cavalry moved toward Deurne. Graham, meanwhile, experienced difficulty moving his heavy guns and did not reach Merxem until late in the evening.

British operations around Antwerp continued on 2 February with the troops of Graham's 1st and 2nd Divisions taking Merxem after a lively firefight. They then pursued the French to within range of Antwerp's guns. As for the Prussians, Thümen's attempt to take Deurne through a double envelopment of the French position failed. Observing the contest from Wijnegem, Bülow ordered Thümen to launch a frontal assault. Prussian artillery and numerical superiority overwhelmed the French, who not only withdrew from Deurne but also abandoned their forward line along the Kleine Schijn, thus allowing Thümen's men to push across the brook and approach Antwerp. Although Antwerp's forward defenses had been breached, fighting at Deurne on 1–2 February cost the Prussians seventeen officers and 670 men.

Prussian and British artillery bombarded Antwerp during the night of 3–4 February. The shells ignited several fires in the city, but the flames caused minimal damage and were quickly extinguished. Intensifying on the 4th and 5th, the Allied bombardment still achieved little success. Graham admitted the attempt to bomb the French garrison into submission was fruitless and so postponed the operation. With a stalemate at Antwerp, Bülow received orders to march through Brussels to Laon in old France. On 6 February his brigades left their positions around Antwerp. On the same day the garrison in Gorinchem surrendered to Bülow's 3rd Brigade.[101]

Bülow assembled his corps at Brussels on the 8th. On 17 February, he informed Blücher that the III Corps would march through Laon and unite with the Silesian Army. Except for Borstell's 5th Brigade, which Bülow was forced to leave in Belgium to support the German III Corps, the Prussian III Corps began the march to France on the following day. Both the military situation and national security concerns warranted Bülow's arrival in France as soon as possible. To Bülow, the utilization of his 20,000 men in France eclipsed all other concerns. As he wrote to his wife, "Napoleon deceives himself into hoping we will not have enough energy to finish the war. I will try to contribute to giving him the coup de grâce."[102]

Notwithstanding Anglo–Prussian cooperation, Bülow and Graham lacked sufficient combat power to drive the French from the Low Countries until Blücher's army crossed the Rhine and changed the situation. Repeated calls for support in the Low Countries did not produce prompt results. Tsar Alexander's reaction to the operations in the Low Countries offers a glimpse of his erratic behavior. He often embraced and dismissed plans on a whim. Of the exalted entourage that made up Allied headquarters, not one career soldier or political dignitary could be certain what policy the tsar would pursue on a given day, thus his vacillation concerning the importance of Bülow's operations. This indifference was not a feeling endemic to Alexander, Bernadotte, or even Wintzingerode. Rather, it represented the divisive attitude that pervaded the Allies after Napoleon retreated across the Rhine. As the Allies pondered the next step of the war, opinions differed, partisan objectives eclipsed the goals of the war, and factional ambition dominated the Coalition. Allied operations slowed, but individual commanders such as Bülow remained energetic and focused. Although the Allied attempt to wrest the Low Countries from French control and sweep into northern France was strategically sound, insufficient manpower resulted in a protracted struggle that eliminated the possibility of quickly wheeling in force through the Low Countries.

"Allowing Bulow and Wintzingerode to advance to the lower Weser, from there to go to Holland, occurred without clear view of the circumstances, and probably at a time when the decision of whether to immediately invade France still had not been made, in which case no manpower could have been spared," opines Clausewitz. Looking ahead to the campaign in France, the philosopher of war asks whether the sending of Bülow to Holland was appropriate. "On the other hand, can one even ask what result Wintzingerode effected? From the battle of Leipzig up to the combats on the Marne in February these forces idly and pointlessly wandered from place to place." Clausewitz does not consider the strategic advantages Bülow's operation provided by inducing Napoleon to divert manpower to the Low Countries, nor does he take into account the political capital the Prussians hoped to pocket by liberating the Low Countries. Instead, he bases his conclusion on his own principle of the *Kulminationspunkte* needed to achieve total victory: the decisive defeat of the French army and the capture of Paris. In view of these twin objectives, he explains: "If one wants to decide everything in a principal battle against a field commander such as Bonaparte, a significant numerical superiority is a necessary precondition. Under these circumstances, one did not have 20,000–30,000 men to spare, and by sending them [to the Low Countries] the entire enterprise became dangerous."[103]

Napoleon's overall troop distribution in late 1813 and early 1814 seemingly reflects a continuation of the mistakes the emperor committed in the German campaign. Similar to the Prussian theater during the spring and fall campaigns of 1813, Napoleon attempted to sustain a campaign in Holland and Belgium, where events seemingly had no decisive influence on his fate. However, his concern for the Low Countries cannot be compared to his obsession with Berlin or his anxiety over Dresden during the German campaign. Berlin and Dresden were geographic objectives, but Holland and Belgium were organs of the French empire. Political necessity demanded that he hold as much of new France as possible. The situation was far more grave than simply pacifying public opinion in Paris. His administration machine in the Low Countries and along the left bank of the Rhine had to be keep functioning to provide the manpower, tax revenue, and material for the emperor's war machine. As he explained to Maison, the general could not evacuate Belgium because the recruits that were to form his corps had to be raised there. Napoleon allocated his dwindling resources to defend the Low Countries, but successive French commanders failed to drive the Allies out of Holland and Belgium. As with the German campaign, the inability of French commanders to lead successful independent operations severely undermined Napoleon's calculations.

15

The Marne

The Allied offensive across the middle Rhine caught Marmont in the midst of moving his two corps south to assist Victor in Alsace. Blücher's invasion separated the majority of Ricard's division from the rest of the VI Corps and shattered Marmont's command and control. For these reasons, his flight from the Rhine and his decision not to confront Blücher at Kaiserslautern are understandable, although Napoleon's political situation demanded that his marshals hold the Allies as close to the frontier as possible. Between the Rhine and the Saar, the marshal managed to slow Blücher's advance without engaging the Silesian Army and without suffering losses other than sickness and desertion. In this way he provided time for French authorities to complete the provisioning and garrisoning of Bitche, Saarlouis, Luxembourg, Thionville, and Metz. Conversely, the rapidity of his retreat did not allow French authorities to execute the *levée-en-masse* in either the countryside or the cities of the left bank.

Reaching the Saar, Marmont united with Ricard and Durutte, thus restoring command and control over his units. At this point, Marmont should have rallied his forces and contested every step of the Silesian Army. Instead, his mental and emotional fortitude started to crumble. Separated by the river, he faced the Silesian Army for two full days before the temptation to retreat overcame him. Rumors that Allied cavalry crossed the Saar induced the marshal to fall back on the Moselle and the fortress of Metz. In no way could the marshal blame Victor or Ney for his decision to retreat. After the Silesian Army crossed the Saar, he exhibited little proclivity to stop Blücher by bloodying the Prussian's nose. Marmont's retreat to Metz opened the roads to Nancy and the French interior; Blücher did not hesitate to march against the capital of Lorraine.

Coming on the heals of French defeats at St. Dié and Épinal, news of Marmont's retreat triggered the panicked flight of Ney and Victor from Nancy. All three marshals failed to secure or destroy the vital crossings over the Moselle at Pont-à-Mousson and Frouard. Blücher's Russians seized both bridges, crossed the river, and continued toward the Meuse. Still believing that Wrede and Frederick William threatened to envelop him from the south and learning that Blücher's army had breeched the line of the Moselle, Victor realized he could not remain at Toul and so continued his retreat to the Meuse. Marmont likewise withdrew to Verdun on the Meuse, chased only by Yorck's Reserve Cavalry. In his correspondence, Marmont attempts to protect his reputation and avoid the emperor's reproach. To curry favor with Napoleon, he portrayed himself as a master of maneuver. In so doing, he castigated Ney and criticized Victor. To conceal Ricard's mistake, he blamed Ney and Victor for his own successive retreats. Marmont claimed that after Ricard learned of the fall of Nancy, the general realized he had to evacuate Pont-à-Mousson. In short, Ricard withdrew as a result of the other marshals' retrograde movement to Toul. According to Marmont, this same movement forced his entire army group to quit the Moselle on the 16th and move closer to the Meuse. Rather than provide the emperor with a plausible excuse, Marmont simply exposed the full extent of the marshals' lack of communication and cooperation.[1]

For his part, Victor did not directly rebuke his fellow marshals until Napoleon harshly criticized his actions. "After my departure from Nancy," wrote Victor, "I maneuvered on Toul, where I spent a few days. I believed I could maintain this position to defend the Moselle, but all other crossings were abandoned to the enemy, which enabled him to head for the Meuse." To defend himself, he naturally attributed the loss of Nancy and Toul to Marmont's successive retreats to Metz and Verdun, as well as Ricard's failure to hold Pont-à-Mousson. Ney, the senior marshal, criticized both Victor and Marmont for not communicating with him. In their letters to Berthier, all three marshals blamed each other for the disgraceful retreat from one river line to the next. The invasion of France provides graphic testimony of one of the most important and fundamental principles of war: unity of command. Lack of unity caused the loss of Lorraine and the precipitous retreat of three marshals to Champagne.

Had Marmont, Victor, and Ney coordinated their operations, they could have stopped the Allies at the Moselle and provided crucial time for Napoleon to complete the organization of his reserve army. The actual situation in Lorraine offered the marshals plenty of opportunities. Charged with the complicated operation against Saarlouis, Metz, Thionville, and Luxembourg, Yorck divided his corps into no fewer than six detachments. Possessing neither bridging equipment, siege artillery, nor adequate ammunition, his task appeared impossible. The only reinforcements for Yorck's corps, which lost 3,000 men to disease after crossing the Rhine, reached Trier in the form of Röder's cavalry brigade from Kleist's Prussian II Corps. Despite their claim of being practitioners of modern war, the Prussian staff of the Silesian Army chose to haggle over four fortresses rather than make an attempt to destroy the enemy army. Escorting Blücher and army headquarters, Sacken's corps occupied Nancy, but the majority of his infantry remained echelonned on the Nancy–Château-Salins road. After crossing the Moselle, his cavalry made little progress; only Biron's Streifkorps moved on Gondreville and reconnoitered Toul. Farther to the east, Borozdin's cavalry reached St. Avold and Olsufiev's IX Infantry Corps moved into Forbach. Consequently, the Silesian Army required at least three marches to attack either Marmont or Victor. Stretched across a front of sixty-five miles, Blücher's army could not execute a serious operation against either marshal. Had unity of command existed among the marshals, Marmont and Victor could have operated in unison against Sacken with Ney's division serving as a central reserve.

Twenty miles south of Victor, Wrede's corps marched west from Charmes toward Neufchâteau on the Meuse. On the 17th, Delamotte's 3rd Division reached Mirecourt, Rechberg's 1st Division quartered at Charmes on the Moselle, and Frimont's Austrians passed the night slightly northeast at Bayon. Platov's Cossack corps cleared the way for the V Corps by occupying Neufchâteau. From this position, the Cossack commander also covered the right and front of the Bohemian Army, which occupied Langres on 17 January. Platov pushed a detachment north to the crossing over the Ornain at Houdelaincourt and sent a patrol toward Bar-le-Duc but could do nothing further because the crown prince of Württemberg instructed him to continue west to the Marne to intercept French communications along the Langres–Châlons-en-Champagne road.[2] Northeast of Platov, Sherbatov's Streifkorps of three Cossack regiments covered the front of Wrede's V Corps. On 17 January, Sherbatov proceeded to Colombey-les-Belles, approximately nine miles south of Toul. Elsewhere, Wittgenstein remained too far behind to offer any support: Eugene of Württemberg reached Saverne – fifty-five miles east of Nancy – on the 17th with his 4th Division and the Badenese 1st Dragoon Regiment, which did serve to free Pahlen's cavalry.[3]

Considering the positions of the Allied units, how did the experienced French marshals fail to recognize their adversary's imprudence and exploit the situation? Mental exhaustion provides one answer, the hoards of Cossacks and Allied cavalry another. The conduct of the marshals at the Moselle suggests they had reached the limits of rational decision making. Attributing the marshals' inability to coordinate their operations or even to communicate adequately with each other to personality conflict oversimplifies the complex psychological and physical challenges these commanders confronted on an hourly basis. Upon reaching the Moselle, both Victor and Marmont surrendered to their mental exhaustion and overburdened emotions. Ney, who never appeared to be committed to the 1814 campaign, continued his record of impotence in situations that required him to exercise independent command. In their laconic reports to Berthier, they sought to evade the emperor's criticism by blaming each other.

Covering the fronts of the Silesian Army and Army Group Alsace, the Cossacks moved with a rapidity and audacity that overwhelmed the French, terrified the inhabitants, and deprived the marshals of precious intelligence. By 17 January, approximately 16,400 Allied troopers were operating between the Moselle and the Meuse. Including Line, Landwehr, and Cossacks, Yorck's cavalry numbered 5,280 sabers; Sacken's 4,400; Wrede's, 6,120, and Sherbatov's 600. The available French cavalry numbered around 8,000 men and included the 1,900 men of Doumerc's I Cavalry Corps, the 915 troopers of Gen. Cyrille-Simon Picquet's brigade (1st Honor Guard Regiment and the 10th Hussars), the 3,704 sabers of Milhaud's V Cavalry Corps, and 750 men from Ségur's brigade (3rd and 4th Honor Guard Regiments).[4]

From Paris Napoleon continued to direct, encourage, and intimidate his marshals. On 15 January, he instructed Berthier to send Ney another note full of confidence, which perhaps the emperor hoped would fall into Allied hands. Receiving the communiqué on the 17th, Ney learned that Mortier had repulsed Schwarzenberg between Langres and Vesoul on the 13th, "so enemy forces are no longer between Langres and Vesoul. At Brussels we have learned the enemy has been defeated near Antwerp; the duke of Tarent has arrived at Liège." Berthier also claimed a portion of the Army of Spain would soon reach Paris and 40,000 National Guards from Normandy and Bretagne also would arrive at the capital. "The rest of the enemy's forces appear to be too disseminated to be able to seriously march on Paris.... The duke of Raguse defends the Moselle and is east of Metz on the roads from St. Avold, Sarreguemines, and Saarlouis. The duke of Valmy has gone to Verdun; he must, with the duke of Bellune, defend the Meurthe and the Moselle." Berthier emphasized the necessity to maintain these positions until 15 February, presumably the date the emperor's new army would be combat-ready.[5]

On the 16th, Napoleon took a deep draught from the bitter cup of regret. Following the evacuation of the Vosges and the loss of Épinal, he learned that Victor had evacuated Nancy; his irritation with the marshal reached new heights. Berthier sent a scathing letter to Victor informing him of Napoleon's "surprise and pain" over the loss of Nancy and the abandonment of the Meurthe without a fight, especially because Marmont's forces still held Metz and Pont-à-Mousson. Napoleon insisted that the Meurthe and Moselle formed a barrier Victor had to defend at all costs. "It is essential for you to delay the enemy's march as long as possible until at least 15 February, when we will again have a great army," states the major-general. "Communicate with the duke of Raguse."[6] It is worth noting that on this day, the 16th, the emperor also authorized Caulaincourt to seek an armistice. Napoleon addressed a savvy letter to Metternich (Appendix M) but dispatched the document to Caulaincourt with instructions to present it to the Austrian plenipotentiary after negotiations began. This transaction did not take place until 25 January.

On the next day, the 17th, Napoleon addressed a letter directly to Victor, further chastising the marshal: "The emperor disapproves of your abandonment of Nancy. His Majesty orders you not to quit the Moselle unless you are defeated. He has learned you have exhausted your troops through long marches and you have emboldened the enemy by retreating for no reason. This has forced the dukes of Raguse and Trevise to likewise make retrograde movements. Above all he is very troubled to see that you evacuated Nancy because of the arrival of [enemy] cavalry without awaiting the infantry."[7]

Berthier also advised Marmont regarding Napoleon's indignation over Victor's conduct: "I have informed the duke of Bellune of the emperor's surprise that he abandoned St. Nicolas and Nancy without being defeated and without defending the Meurthe, especially since your army corps is in front of Metz and occupying Pont-à-Mousson. Cooperate with the duke of Bellune and the prince of the Moskowa."[8] Rumors soon reached Paris, however, that Marmont had likewise evacuated the Moselle. "The emperor hopes you have not left Metz," wrote Berthier to Marmont at 11:00 on the night of the 17th, "because it is horrible how the duke of Bellune left Nancy for Toul; nothing is more ridiculous than the way this marshal is evacuating the countryside: I am sending him the order to remain at Toul." More important, Berthier announced that Napoleon planned to leave Paris and personally take command of the army at Châlons-en-Champagne.[9] On the 18th, the emperor reiterated his orders for Marmont to hold Metz for as long as possible. Napoleon also requested an assessment of the strength of Yorck and Sacken: "many inhabitants and military personnel must have seen them pass by and must have some idea about where they are and the size of their forces."[10] Such a request must have raised the question in Marmont's headquarters of how the emperor reached his estimates of Allied strength. Regardless, the flow of events rendered obsolete the order to hold Metz by the time the emperor's letter reached Marmont.

As the couriers carried Napoleon's directives from Paris to the respective commanders, Marmont, Victor, and Ney blindly continued their retreat. Marmont believed Sacken commanded 12,000 men, while Yorck had between 18,000 and 20,000 men at his disposal.[11] Although the latter's brigades were stalled at the Moselle, Marmont completed his preparations to fall back on Verdun. He remained at Metz on the 16th to assist Durutte with organizing the defenses, but his army group received orders to move out. At 8:30 A.M. the marshal directed Ricard to hold his position at Thiaucourt, destroy all bridges over the small Rupt-de-Mad, and delay for as long as possible the Allied columns that would attempt to move north from Pont-à-Mousson to intercept the Metz–Verdun road.[12] Marmont sent Lagrange's division and Doumerc's I Cavalry Corps to Gravelotte, while Decouz's 2nd Young Guard

Voltigeur Division continued further west to Mars-la-Tour. Throughout the afternoon of the 16th, the retreat proceeded smoothly without any sign of the enemy. Marmont heard nothing from Ricard but assumed the general had left Thiaucourt. That evening the chief of staff of the VI Corps, General Louis-Henri-René Meynadier, sent Ricard another copy of the orders issued that morning. He added Marmont's instructions to halt immediately, take a good position, and establish communication with the marshal.[13] Marmont also dispatched engineer officers to Verdun with the task of selecting suitable positions along the left bank of the Meuse and destroying the bridges along the sixteen-mile stretch of the river between Verdun and St. Mihiel. Before sunset the marshal departed Metz and joined his headquarters at Gravelotte.[14]

For some inexplicable reason, Berthier's courier took three days to reach Marmont with the "General Instructions" and the letter drafted on 13 January. Through these documents Marmont could vividly see the illusions entertained in Paris regarding the Coalition's forces and intentions. The emperor's inaccurate statements concerning the size of the Silesian Army amazed the marshal but did not leave him speechless. In his immediate response to Berthier, Marmont attempted to clarify the details concerning the Silesian Army, yet his rebuttal shows that he, too, failed to present a precise description of the opposing forces. Where the emperor underestimated, the marshal naturally overestimated. He confused detachments for corps, believing he faced an opponent far superior than the emperor realized. "To the details that your letter contains regarding the Army of Silesia, we must add Kleist's corps which, according to the reports I received last night, has just arrived. A Bavarian and Badenese corps of 7,000 to 8,000 men that was close to Bitche eight days ago appears to be ... proceeding to Metz; a considerable corps other than this one was seen the day before yesterday ... on the road from Strasbourg to Metz." The marshal added that Kleist had taken a position between Thionville and Metz.[15]

Although Marmont could not have known it at the time, the emperor was also incorrect regarding Blücher's intentions. Blücher did turn his attention to the fortresses of Lorraine, but not in the manner Napoleon had predicted. Against the fortresses Blücher only deployed Yorck's corps but retained Sacken's corps – behind which followed Olsufiev's infantry and Kleist's corps – for joint operations with Schwarzenberg. At that moment, Marmont could not carry out Napoleon's orders to stop the Allies on the great highway to Paris nor could he cover the capital by cooperating with his fellow marshals. After Ney and Victor evacuated the line of the Moselle, Marmont believed his position had been compromised and his line of retreat to the Meuse jeopardized.[16]

Conversely, Victor believed Marmont's collapse in the Saarland and retreat to the Moselle likewise rendered his position at Nancy untenable and threatened his line of retreat. Once again Napoleon's absence and his refusal to appoint a commander in chief led to the undoing of his marshals. Although placing blame on any one of the marshals is unfair, Marmont's actions warrant the least amount of criticism; the speed with which Ney evacuated Nancy followed by Victor's retreat rendered Marmont's position more critical and forced him to withdraw on Verdun. Blame for the inability of the three marshals to unite and coordinate their operations squarely falls on Napoleon who, despite all his contributions to the art of war, never developed a system of military education that would enable his field commanders, all able tacticians, to master warfare on the strategic and operational levels.

At daybreak on the 17th, Decouz's 2nd Young Guard Voltigeur Division departed Mars-la-Tour and covered the twenty-two miles to Verdun. East of Decouz, the VI Infantry and I Cavalry Corps spent the morning preparing to continue the retreat from Gravelotte. At 4:00 A.M. Meynadier directed Ricard to march northwest from Thiaucourt to Woël, leaving a rearguard at St. Benoît. Marmont also wanted Ricard to dispatch patrols due west to the crossing over the Meuse at St. Mihiel. The marshal himself planned to lead his main column to Harville on the road to Verdun, leaving a rearguard of cavalry at Mars-la-Tour.[17]

By 10:30 on the morning of 17 January, Marmont's headquarters still had not left Gravelotte. Around this time, an officer who routinely conducted reconnaissance arrived from St. Mihiel with the news that Allied forces had reached this town.[18] With only sixteen miles to cover from Woël to St. Mihiel, Ricard would be closer than Marmont to St. Mihiel and its precious bridge over the Meuse. Meynadier wrote a second note to Ricard instructing him to forward a detachment of 150 infantry and 100 cavalry to St. Mihiel immediately to confirm this report. If the enemy had yet to reach St. Mihiel in force, the detachment was to secure the bridge. If considerable Allied forces approached, Ricard's men would destroy the bridge and sail downstream to Verdun all the boats they could find.[19] The marshal wanted the rest of Ricard's division to unite with his main body, and thus Meynadier instructed Decouz's Young Guard to occupy St. Mihiel no later than dawn on the 18th.[20] Neither Ricard nor Decouz executed these orders. Ricard did not receive Meynadier's second letter until he arrived in Woël that evening and deemed it too late to dispatch a detachment that evidently had no chance of accomplishing its mission.[21] As for Decouz, he dragged his tired conscripts into Verdun after a rigorous forced march; he did not have the heart to ask his young soldiers to march an additional fifteen miles at night.[22]

From Harville Marmont drafted a short and unsettling brief to Berthier at 9:00 P.M. that illustrates the animosity between the marshals:

> Yesterday I sent some officers to prepare the defense of the Meuse and to blow the bridges from St. Mihiel to Verdun, but the *fatal imprudence* of the prince of the Moskowa who, in evacuating Nancy, did not destroy the bridge over the Moselle at Frouard, gave the enemy the means to reach the Meuse ahead

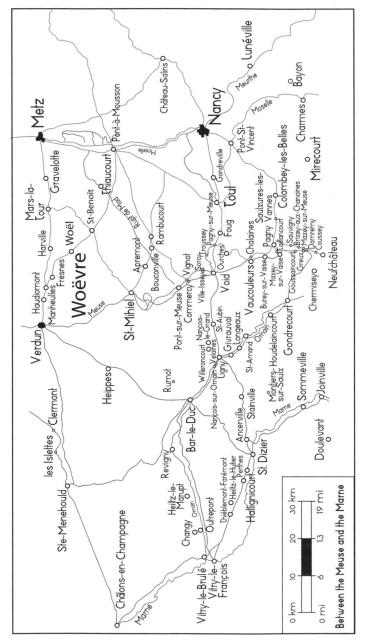

Map 20. The region between the Meuse and the Marne.

Les Islettes
Ste-Menehould
Châlons-en-Champagne
Clermont
Verdun
Haudiomont
Manheulles
Fresnes
Heippes
Rumot
Woël
Harville
Haudiomont
St-Benoit
Mars-la-Tour
Gravelotte
Metz
Thiaucourt
Pont-à-Mousson
Château-Salins
Nancy
Lunéville
Meurthe
Bayon
Charmes
Moselle
Mirecourt
Colombey-les-Belles
Pont-St-Vincent
Tool
Foug
Gondreville
Pagny-sur-Meuse
Saulxures-les-
Pagny Vannes
Chalaines
Vaucouleurs
Mazey-sur-Vaise
Taillancourt
Burey-sur-Vaise
Sauvigny
Goussaincourt
Brixey-aux-Chanoines
Greux Mazéy-sur-Meuse
Domremy
Coussey
Neufchâteau
Chermisey
Gondrecourt
Ourches
Void
Ville-Issey
Troussey
Soroy
Vignot
Commercy
Pont-sur-Meuse
Napois-le-Grand
St-Aubin
Givrauval
Longeaux
St-Amand
Ornain
Montiers-
sur-Saulx
Houdelaincourt
Sommeville
Joinville
Doulevant
Marne
Stainville
Ancerville
Napois-sur-Ornain
Ligny
Velaines
Willeroncourt
Bar-le-Duc
Revigny
Heiltz-le-Maupt
Changy
Ornain
Outrepont
Thiéblemont-Farémont
Heiltz-le-Hutier
Perthes
Hallignicourt
St. Dizier
Vitry-le-Brulé
Vitry-le-François
Marne
Woëvre
St-Mihiel
Meuse
Apremont
Bouconville
Rambucourt
Rupt de Mad
Moselle

Between the Meuse and the Marne

| 0 km | 10 | 20 | 30 km |
| 0 mi | 6 | 13 | 19 mi |

of me and prevented this task from being completed. Thus the maintenance of the bridge at Frouard has simultaneously prevented both the defense of the Moselle and that of the Meuse. If it had been destroyed, we could have probably defended the Moselle for four or five days and prepared the defense of the Meuse; we could have stopped the enemy for some time at least.

Marmont intended to defend the line of the Meuse, but in his opinion Ney's carelessness made this task impossible. According to the intelligence he received that morning, Marmont assumed Allied forces had crossed the Frouard bridge and penetrated the region between the Moselle and the Meuse called the Woëvre, which rendered useless any measures to defend the Moselle. In addition, it appeared that enemy troops had reached the Meuse before him and occupied St. Mihiel. He informed Berthier of his intention to continue to Verdun that night and "ascend the Meuse to reconnoiter the enemy and slow his march" as much as circumstances permitted.[23]

Thirty miles south of Marmont, Victor's two columns withdrew from Toul to the Meuse during the 17th. While riding to Void, the marshal learned that earlier in the morning 3,000 Cossacks left Nancy and appeared headed toward Vaucouleurs, just south of his line of retreat. In addition, reports claimed two regiments of Allied cavalry reached Vignot on the right bank of the Meuse facing Commercy, less than six miles north of Void. This news caused great concern in Victor's headquarters since Void sat on the crossroads formed by the north–south road from Verdun to Neufchâteau and the east–west road from Toul to Ligny, which provided the marshal's only escape route.

Once again, in a critical lapse of efficiency, none of the marshals thought either to destroy or to guard the bridge over the Meuse at Commercy. Reports claimed enemy cavalry wasted no time taking advantage of this golden opportunity. Allied patrols purportedly crossed the Meuse and dispersed along the left bank. Victor reacted as best he could by forwarding Briche's 3rd Dragoon Division to Commercy with orders to drive out the enemy and organize the defense of this position, which Victor hoped to utilize as the link between his left and Marmont's right. Briche's dragoons reached Commercy later in the day. After ejecting the Cossacks, the French secured the bridge and established a forward post at Vignot on the right bank of the Meuse.

Elsewhere, Victor's II Infantry and V Cavalry Corps extended east from Foug to Void and then five miles south to Vaucouleurs in the Meuse Valley along the Verdun–Neufchâteau road, where Milhaud's column arrived around noon. Vaucouleurs stood on a secondary arm of the river called the Haute-Meuse. Coming from Toul, the Allies would have to cross the main arm of the Meuse at the village of Chalaines and then proceed across a levy, commonly referred to as the Vaucouleurs's bridge, that spanned the Haute-Meuse to the town of Vaucouleurs. Although a seasoned veteran, Milhaud neglected to take any security measures other than posting 150 men at Chalaines. He

neither barricaded the bridge nor the levy. Defending the defile would have
been a simple task; the cresting Meuse inundated the valley. Perhaps this
natural defense deceived the French, or maybe they reached the point where
indifference eclipsed standard military procedure.

After the men of the 1st Division, 4th Dragoon Division, and 4th Honor
Guard Regiment dispersed to find food for their aching stomachs, Milhaud
and his officers settled down for lunch at an inn situated near the levy. After
looking forward to a moment of quiet, the French officers suddenly sprang
to their feet with sinking hearts. Outside the inn they could hear the savage
cries of the Cossacks. After surprising the post at Chalaines, a detachment
from Sherbatov's Streifkorps advanced across the levy to the entrance of Vaucouleurs. The Russians inflicted numerous casualties before departing with
several prisoners.[24]

In his 2:00 P.M. report to Berthier from Void, Victor skipped the usual formalities and immediately delved into his reasons for abandoning the Moselle.
"The line of the Moselle could have been defended for several days; the
position I held at Toul could have effectively contributed to this defense,"
wrote the marshal, echoing the exact sentiments penned by Marmont that
very same evening. "Yet this has become impossible because the bridges at
Pont-à-Mousson and Pont-St. Vincent were not guarded in strength. Pont-
à-Mousson was evacuated by the duc of Raguse during the night of 15/16
January; Pont-St. Vincent was not guarded at all." Victor explained that "these
two debouches provided the enemy with the means to march on Commercy
and Vaucouleurs," thus turning Toul from the north and the south, and reaching the Meuse ahead of him. Although Victor made a logical argument based
on this evidence, he made no mention of his own failure to destroy the bridge
at Frouard. Had Ricard maintained Pont-à-Mousson, Sacken's cavalry would
have crossed the Moselle at Frouard regardless and forced Ricard's isolated
division to yield Pont-à-Mousson as well. Rather than acknowledge his own
responsibility, Victor complained about Marmont. "I know nothing of the
duke of Raguse. According to the direction he took from Pont-à-Mousson,
I think he is headed to Verdun." After this statement, Victor returned to the
same plea for unity of command that he and almost all his colleagues submitted to Paris. "It is very much desired that the troops on the Meuse be
assembled under a single commander, because around 30,000 men, directed
by one marshal, can stop the enemy on this line, and give the emperor time
to assemble his reserves."[25]

The emperor's aide-de-camp, Dejean, scrutinized the deterioration of the
French position from the moment Victor evacuated Alsace. He recognized
the mistakes and the growing threat caused by the absence of a commander in
chief. Attempting to facilitate cooperation between Ney and Victor, Dejean
himself went to Ligny, but the prince of the Moskowa already had departed
for Bar-le-Duc. Aggravated and disheartened, he again warned the emperor

over the conduct of the marshals: "It is of the greatest urgency that a single person has the command here, because the marshals can not nor will not cooperate."[26]

West of Victor, Ney moved his headquarters and Meunier's 1st Brigade to Ligny on the Ornain River, while the 2nd Brigade continued to occupy Pagny-sur-Meuse and Void. On the evening of the 16th, Prefect Louis-Claire Beaupoil de St. Aulaire of the Meuse Department informed the marshal that strong Allied forces appeared to be marching toward the bridge over the Meuse at St. Mihiel. Ney dispatched an aide-de-camp to conduct reconnaissance. Through this officer, he again learned indirectly that Ricard had quit Pont-à-Mousson to retreat to Verdun with the rest of Marmont's corps. Locals also reported that the enemy appeared in force twenty-six miles south of Ligny at Neufchâteau. "One speaks of combats at Chaumont and Ligny without knowing the results," ends the marshal's 16 January report to Berthier. [27]

On the 17th, Ney moved to Bar-le-Duc with the 2nd Brigade of the 1st Young Guard Voltigeur Division; he kept Meunier's 1st Brigade at Ligny, where the roads from Commercy, Toul, and Neufchâteau converged. Ney had planned on remaining at Pagny-sur-Meuse and Void, but early on the 17th Meunier received a letter from Victor's chief of staff requesting that the Young Guard withdraw from these towns to make room for the II Infantry and V Cavalry Corps. Victor's retrograde movement surprised Ney, who griped to Berthier over his colleague's failure to communicate with him. Although Victor remained silent, reports provided by civil authorities, notably the prefect of the Meuse, led Ney to believe that 2,000 enemy cavalry had entered St. Mihiel that day and pushed a detachment to Commercy. Another report confirmed the presence of Allied cavalry and infantry at Neufchâteau. "Without doubt it is these demonstrations on the flanks of the II Corps that has caused the duke of Bellune to retreat," speculated Ney. "No doubt this marshal has given you extensive information, but he tells me nothing of what he does and what he intends to do. Since I do not get any news other than when his troops run into mine, I am limited to collecting reports from local civil authorities who have had contact with him. At this moment I am sending one of my aide-de-camps to locate the headquarters of the II Corps in order to have a meeting with the duke of Bellune, which I believe is necessary."[28]

In addition to Victor's retreat, the appearance of the Cossacks prompted the evacuation of the *chef-lieu* of another department. Beaupoil de St. Aulaire ordered the archives and public chest to leave Bar-le-Duc for Châlons-en-Champagne. Ney's arrival at the *chef-lieu* did nothing to calm the civil authorities nor the population, which was terrified by the approach of the Russian warriors and disenchanted with Napoleon.[29] "In the departments, in the army, one repeats that it is Your Majesty personally upon whom one makes war today," wrote Caulaincourt who, while waiting for Metternich to open peace negotiations, was forced to seek refuge at St. Dizier as a result of "the retrograde march of the duke of Bellune and the prince of the Moskowa. One separates the interests of the monarch from those of his people." Growing public unrest did not overly concern Napoleon, yet his marshals' successive failures undermined the emperor's popularity. Caulaincourt reminded him of the subtleties of negotiations and power politics. "Our situation has changed considerably since a few days ago. The rapid march of the enemy on all points, the invasion of a large portion of the empire, the discouragement that I have encountered almost everywhere I have gone renders the need of an armistice indisputable."[30]

The state of panic that engulfed Victor's headquarters did not abate on 18 January. That morning Grouchy's staff chief, Contamine, returned to Void and rendered an engaging account of his meeting with Platov. After being turned away at Nancy by Biron, Contamine, who bore Berthier's letter to Schwarzenberg, proceeded to Neufchâteau, where he presented his credentials to Platov's advance post. He initially encountered difficulties with the unrefined Cossacks, but the Russians eventually admitted Contamine into the town. Platov himself arranged an impressive reception for the French officer. "The Ataman had prepared three armchairs, as if to receive an ambassador," states Victor's report to Berthier. "He stood by the middle one, surrounded by officers of all ranks. The antechamber was filled by various officers charged with introducing my envoy. Contamine was well-received." The Russians then questioned Contamine over French politics. According to Grouchy, his chief of staff answered with "esprit and circumspection. All the [Russian] officers affirmed their desire for peace, which is the general view of the Allies, but all were concerned because they hear they will have to go to Paris to obtain it." Contamine assured his Russian hosts that peace remained the unanimous hope of the French but that going to Paris would be more difficult than the Allies believed. The French officer wove a tale that left the Russians with their mouths gaping and their eyes wide. He assured them their legions would have to fight 150,000 men coming from the Army of Spain, 200,000 newly raised Line troops, 200,000 National Guards, 80,000 men of the Imperial Guard, and 60,000 men of the Grande Armée. The Russians did not expect to encounter a force of even half this size. News regarding the end of the conflict in Spain particularly surprised them; all Platov could say in response was that Russia recently concluded a peace with Persia. Judging the moment had come, Contamine confided to Platov's care the letter from Berthier. Platov pledged to forward the letter to Schwarzenberg by way of extraordinary courier and authorized Contamine to return to Neufchâteau to receive the response. Before he departed, the Russians foolishly relaxed their guard. Forgetting they had a French officer in their midst, Platov's chief of staff escorted Contamine to his office, where Contamine caught a glimpse of a march itinerary that directed an infantry column through St. Thiébault to Langres, while Platov's Cossacks took a position between Neufchâteau and Gondrecourt to cover the column's movement.[31]

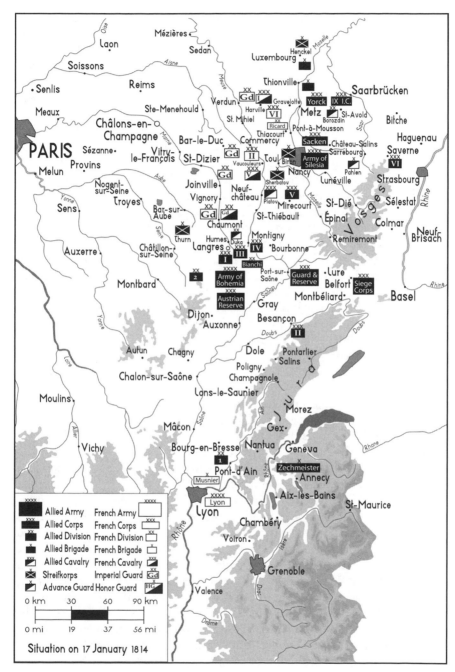

Map 21. Situation on 17 January 1814.

Victor did not need a map to understand the implications of Contamine's report. His headquarters at Void was less than sixty miles north-northeast of Langres. An Allied operation against Langres resurrected the marshal's fear of being enveloped from the south. From Neufchâteau the Allies could advance to either Vaucouleurs or Gondrecourt and Ligny, blocking the roads between the Meuse and the Ornain, and flanking Victor's corps. Immense numerical superiority would allow the Allies to execute both operations.[32] In addition, the intelligence he forwarded to Berthier suggests that neither his cavalry nor the locals provided correct details, yet enough information filtered in to paint a fairly accurate picture of the growing threat. The marshal believed Sacken's corps was pursuing Marmont toward Verdun; Yorck's corps had moved through Pont-à-Mousson to Nancy, taking a position facing Victor; and Kleist's corps appeared to be at Thionville. He communicated his position to Marmont and impressed on him the necessity of cooperating to hold the Allies at the Meuse to provide the emperor time to assemble the reserves. He asked Marmont to post Ricard's division at St. Mihiel.[33] Unfortunately for Victor, he did not receive any reply from Marmont. He ended his 18 January report to Berthier with yet another plea for the emperor to place Ney, Marmont, and himself under a single commander in chief.[34]

At Void the situation that confronted the II Infantry and V Cavalry Corps appeared grave. Blücher's right breeched the Moselle in pursuit of Marmont, while his left concentrated at Toul. To the south, Schwarzenberg's army acted like a wedge, driving apart Victor and Mortier. "General," wrote Grouchy to Defrance, "the emperor's orders are to slow the enemy's march for as long as possible and to hold everywhere we can. He intended for us to defend the line of the Moselle; since we were rejected from there to that of the Meuse, it is on this line that we must hold until the last extreme."[35]

Victor feared the Allies would attempt to gain the bridge at Commercy by advancing directly from Vignot or by moving up the left bank of the Meuse from St. Mihiel. The loss of Commercy would jeopardize his line of retreat through St. Aubin to Ligny. Yet nature and the movement of one infantry division offered some hope of holding the Meuse. Blizzard-like conditions slowly yielded to heavy rains that steadily raised the Meuse. Victor realized the river soon would flood the valley, cutting his communications along the Sorcy–Void and Sorcy–Commercy roads, and compromising Forestier's 2nd Division at Sorcy. The marshal developed a plan to defend his sector of the Meuse by uncovering his center to reinforce his left flank. Counting on the Meuse's swift waters to bar the road from Toul and secure his center, he directed Forestier to Commercy. "This division," explained Victor, "united with Briche's forces, will defend the bridge at Commercy to the last extreme. In case the bridge is forced, it will withdraw west in good order to St. Aubin on the road to Ligny, taking care to inform [me] quite promptly of this movement.

It will be arranged in battle order at St. Aubin and await the arrival of the rest of the II Infantry and V Cavalry Corps. Its strength will still permit it to have a detachment at St. Mihiel."[36] To defend the bridge at Sorcy, Grouchy posted half of Ségur's 4th Honor Guard Regiment in the village. The other half of the regiment occupied Ville-Issey on the left bank. For security, Grouchy instructed Briche to post a detachment of 300 dragoons between Commercy and St. Mihiel, with patrols advancing down both banks of the Meuse to the latter so "that they are constantly and promptly informed of what passes." Finally, Grouchy wanted Briche "to report every three hours and promptly report if an enemy column debouches on St. Mihiel or Bar-le-Duc."[37]

With the left wing and center thus covered, Grouchy ordered Defrance to Vaucouleurs, ostensibly to take command of the right wing as a response to Milhaud's lapse of judgment the previous day. Grouchy likewise instructed Defrance to hold Vaucouleurs to the last extreme. "In front of you at Neufchâteau is Platov's corps, which barely consists of 300 cavalry, but has artillery, which makes me regret that you have only four guns," wrote the future marshal. "Regardless, with your dragoons and Honor Guards, you must not fear Platov." The cresting Meuse made fording the river impossible, and so Grouchy felt certain Defrance could maintain his position simply by destroying the secondary bridges upstream and downstream of Vaucouleurs. To collect additional intelligence, Grouchy tasked Contamine with a second mission and requested that Defrance facilitate the staff officer's return to Neufchâteau. "Contamine will proceed this evening to Vaucouleurs, from there to Platov's headquarters," Grouchy instructs Defrance. "You will provide him a small, select detachment of Honor Guards and dragoons, with which he will proceed to Gondrecourt, where he will leave his detachment and proceed to Neufchâteau with only a herald. At Gondreville the officer commanding the detachment must record all information regarding the enemy's position, forces, and the direction he marches."[38]

During the day of the 18th, Sherbatov's Streifkorps rode northwest from Colombey-les-Belles to Chalaines with 1,200 to 1,500 Cossacks according to French estimates.[39] He drove the French post into Chalaines and gained the hills that dominated the village from the east. The Allied commander surveyed Defrance's preparations to defend Chalaines: barricades protected the entrances to the village, which was flanked by a battery on the left bank of the Meuse. Rather than challenge the daunting position, Sherbatov skirmished with Defrance's dragoons. A French charge compelled the Russians to withdraw for the night.[40] Both sides claimed to have inflicted numerous casualties. Under the cover of darkness, Defrance withdrew his troops from Chalaines to Vaucouleurs but failed to destroy completely the "Chalaines" bridge over the main arm of the Meuse. His efforts sufficed to weaken the structure so that a storm later that night caused the Meuse to further rise and collapse the bridge. The floodwaters also breeched the levy (or "Vaucouleurs" bridge) that spanned the Haute-Meuse and linked Vaucouleurs to the left bank of the Meuse.[41]

At 9:00 A.M. on 18 January, Marmont arrived in Verdun. Reports from the 17th led him to believe a strong enemy advance guard had occupied St. Mihiel; this news proved to be false. Early on the morning of the 18th, he learned that only Cossacks held St. Mihiel. The marshal scrambled to destroy the bridge before the Allies gained the crossing. He immediately forwarded his aide-de-campe, Colonel Charles-Nicolas Fabvier, to St. Mihiel with cavalry and infantry. According to Fabvier's estimates, he surprised and drove 500 Cossacks from the town, but not before more than 100 Russians reached the left bank and outdistanced their pursuers. After taking several prisoners, Fabvier secured the village and barricaded the bridge. At the end of the day, the 2,840 men and sixteen guns of Decouz's 2nd Young Guard Voltigeur Division arrived from Verdun to occupy the crossing. With orders to blow the bridge as soon as enemy forces approached, Fabvier mined the arches. His cavalry made contact with Briche's dragoons just south of St. Mihiel, finally establishing communication between Marmont and Victor.

Meanwhile the VI Corps assembled at Verdun on the 18th with a strong advance guard at Haudiomont, eleven miles east of the fortress. Marmont planned to defend the Meuse from Verdun to St. Mihiel as long as Victor held his sector, particularly the zone between St. Mihiel and Commercy.[42] Over the next twenty-four hours, Marmont's men destroyed all the bridges over the Meuse between Verdun and St. Mihiel.[43] Southwest of Marmont, Meunier's 1st Young Guard Voltigeur Division covered Victor's rearward communications and provided a general reserve at Ligny. Just as the possibility of actual cooperation between the marshals appeared, Ney wanted to withdraw Meunier's 1st Brigade from Ligny after he learned that Cossacks coming from St. Mihiel – the few who escaped Fabvier – reached Rumot, less than eight miles from the marshal's headquarters at Bar-le-Duc. Ney informed Marmont that "the enemy who crossed the Moselle at Pont-à-Mousson has occupied St. Mihiel with infantry, artillery, and cavalry."[44] The marshal did not know Marmont's units had secured St. Mihiel, thus reducing this Cossack band to nothing more than a handful of dangerous fugitives.

As the French withdrew to the Meuse, Allied cavalry raced to catch up. Biron, who continued his pursuit of Victor to Toul, found the city's gates barricaded and defended by infantry and artillery. Locals claimed that the garrison consisted of 600 to 700 men and four guns. He withdrew to await support from Sacken; in the evening, his patrols made contact with the Cossacks of the Bohemian Army to the south and with Lanskoi to the north. Lanskoi's patrols reported that a French rearguard of approximately 2,000 men and 800 cavalry held the bridge over the Meuse at Commercy as well as the large suburb of Vignot on the right bank. Because of the rising waters of the

Meuse, the Russians could not ford the river to reconnoiter the left bank. By the night of 18 January, Lanskoi's forward cavalry posts extended northwest from Rambucourt to St. Mihiel and southwest to Vignot. The Cossacks held every crossroad and nothing moved without attracting their ceaseless attention. On Lanskoi's right, his troopers made contact with Jürgaß's Reserve Cavalry near Verdun; to his left Sherbatov's Streifkorps occupied Chalaines after the French withdrew during the night of 18–19 January. On the morning of the 20th, Sherbatov turned over the position to the Cossack regiment that formed the advance guard of General Semen Davydovich Panchulidzev II's dragoon division of Sacken's corps. Sherbatov retired a few miles southeast to Saulxures to rest his exhausted men and horses.[45]

Behind this advance guard, Blücher and Sacken led one column of Russian infantry through Nancy toward Toul on the 19th. A second proceeded southwest from Nancy, crossed the Moselle at Pont-St. Vincent, and continued to Colombey-les-Belles. After learning that French forces remained at Toul, this second column marched northwest toward Void to assault Toul from the west on the 19th. Delays caused by rising flood waters, which made movement only possible on the highways, postponed the attack until 20 January. In fact, Blücher claimed his Russian infantry "advanced in water up to their stomachs."[46] Lieven's XI Infantry Corps moved east from Void on the 20th. His 10th Division took a position north of Toul, while Vasilchikov's cavalry made its way to the south side of the city. Russian gunners established a battery on the slopes of Mont St. Michel from where they could shell Toul's interior as well as its ramparts. This overwhelming threat induced Chaudron to capitulate. The Russians found an ammunition depot that included 2,000 cannon balls suitable for their artillery. Sacken's men also liberated 500 Spanish prisoners of war including one general and thirty officers, some of whom formed companies to garrison Toul and Nancy.[47] Sacken concluded his report to Blücher by including the statements of locals, who claimed French forces were massing at Châlons-en-Champagne to march on Langres. "The inhabitants are tired of war," he added. "The conscripts are untrained and the men between the ages of twenty and forty refuse to participate in the levée-en-masse."[48]

Elsewhere on Blücher's front, Jürgaß led the eight squadrons of Yorck's Reserve Cavalry across the Moselle on the 17th. His advance guard, which consisted of a mounted Lithuanian jäger detachment and two dragoon squadrons under the command of Maj. Friedrich von Woisky, reached Thiaucourt. After regaining Marmont's trail, the Prussian troopers continued the pursuit on the 18th. They learned Marmont's rearguard under Ricard was at St. Benoît, where the roads to Verdun and St. Mihiel separated. During the night of 18–19 January, Ricard withdrew toward Manheulles on the road to Verdun. Around 2:00 on the afternoon of the 19th, Woisky found the French vedettes near Fresnes and informed Jürgaß, whose cavalry had been riding since 1:00 A.M. on the road that ran northwest through St. Benoît to Verdun. The French withdrew to Manheulles, whose exits Colonel Curely barricaded, only leaving one narrow passage to receive his posts. The French colonel prepared an ambush by placing one infantry battalion just inside the entrance of Manheulles and behind a large trench the Prussian cavalry could not cross.

Jürgaß assembled his squadrons and attacked at sundown. Woisky's Lithuanian jäger and dragoon squadrons drove off the two squadrons that patrolled the eastern approaches to Manheulles. Distinguishing itself in the charge against the French cavalry, the Lithuanian jäger squadron burst into Manheulles. Just inside the village, the Prussian troopers received deadly fire at point-blank range from the French infantry posted behind the trench as well as artillery situated on a nearby hill; the Prussians withdrew as fast as they entered. Jürgaß advanced to support Woisky with the remaining squadrons of the 1st West Prussian Dragoon Regiment and two guns from his horse battery. After the two pieces of Prussian artillery opened fire on Manheulles, Curely opted to retreat instead of awaiting a second attack on the same village where his parents resided. Under the protection of the artillery that kept the Prussians at bay, the French infantry and 10th Hussars maneuvered and reformed on the road to Haudiomont.

The commander of the French rearguard, Picquet, believed that 1,200 cavalry, three battalions, and several guns drove Curely from Manheulles. Not wanting Curely's Hussars and infantry to be caught by the Allies in the open plain, he ordered the colonel to withdraw to Haudiomont, where Ricard's artillery and cavalry occupied a defile west of the town. The French maintained this position throughout the night before retreating to Verdun on the morning of the 20th. Prussian losses amounted to fifty killed and wounded – the majority being the Lithuanian jäger who had charged into Manheulles; Picquet claimed his losses amounted to eight men. The French also took several prisoners, who Marmont planned to personally interrogate. Yet by the time he wrote his report to Berthier at 9:00 P.M. on the 19th, the marshal had received news other than Picquet's exaggerated after-action report. Regarding the enemy force that attacked his posts, Marmont wrote: "We will say 800 horses and two guns, but no infantry . . . therefore I cannot say if this was an advance guard of an army corps. I will verify this tomorrow."[49]

That same evening Jürgaß established his quarters at the country town of Fresnes with the Lithuanian Dragoon Regiment. The 1st West Prussian Dragoon Regiment camped at Manheulles and the two squadrons of Woisky's advance guard bivouacked east of Haudiomont to maintain contact with the French posts. At daybreak Woisky's squadrons pursued, sending patrols on the road to Verdun. Jürgaß maintained his position before Verdun for the next eight days, during which time the French rejected his ridiculous demands to surrender the fortress.[50]

In the meantime, Marmont finally informed Ney at 4:00 on the morning of the 19th that his men still held St. Mihiel and were making preparations to destroy the bridges between there and Commercy. He suggested that Ney do the same to the bridges on the upper Meuse, "because only by the creation of obstacles can we stop or delay the enemy." Marmont reiterated his intention to defend the Meuse as long as the enemy did not outflank his forces. The marshal bluntly informed the prince of the Moskowa that his fear over the presence of Allied forces was exaggerated. "I calculate the enemy force of all arms you believe is at St. Mihiel to be 400 Cossacks," begins Marmont's letter. "Reports similar to those you received were presented to me and they appeared to be true, but I soon discovered the exaggerations. So I decided to send troops, who surprised the Cossacks, chased them out, and took some prisoners; I now occupy St. Mihiel with 9,000 men and six guns." Clearly an exaggeration of his own if not a blatant lie, Marmont's claim of having 9,000 men at St. Mihiel can only be explained as intentional misinformation designed to encourage Ney to support the defense of the Meuse. "I have sent 700 to 800 cavalry to reconnoiter the left bank of the Meuse from St. Mihiel to the positions held by the duke of Bellune," continues Marmont's letter. "I have destroyed all the bridges between Verdun and St. Mihiel. We will do the same between St. Mihiel and Commercy. Today the bridge at St. Mihiel will be mined and ready to blow at the slightest appearance of a serious enemy attack. Until now I see the enemy making demonstrations, but I do not see any serious operations on their part, and I am persuaded to believe his masses are still at the Moselle and the Meurthe."

Marmont also passed along to Ney the latest intelligence his headquarters had received. A traveler from Nancy erroneously claimed Allied forces had not entered the city as of the morning of 17 January. His own patrols informed him that Yorck's main body faced Metz, a strong Prussian detachment had marched up the Moselle toward Pont-à-Mousson, and Kleist appeared to be between Thionville and Metz. "I have a strong advance guard at Haudiomont with posts at Manheulles," continues Marmont's letter to Ney. "In this position, I can defend the Meuse and I will stay as long as the enemy does not cross the river before me." He also alerted Ney that perhaps 100 of the 500 Cossacks at St. Mihiel escaped along the left bank. "If I learn anything important, it will be my honor to inform you. I beg you to tell me what you learn."[51] This news arrived too late to placate Ney.

Marmont both encouraged and urged Victor to hold his sector of the Meuse: "After learning of your movement to the Meuse, I moved closer. I agree that you can defend the Meuse and, based on the knowledge of the region that I now occupy, I think I can succeed as long as you hold Commercy and Pagny-sur-Meuse."[52] He promised Victor cooperation and success, but Marmont's own situation did not allow much room for optimism. "On the day before yesterday [the 17th], several reports informed me that the enemy did not have infantry on the left bank of the Moselle," he wrote Berthier. On the 19th, however, Decouz informed him that 12,000 Allied bayonets reached Bouconville, fifteen miles east of St. Mihiel on the road from Pont-à-Mousson. Marmont could only order his subordinates to conduct more reconnaissance. The marshal could not determine whether the pursuing cavalry force that reached Manheulles belonged to the advance guard of an army corps or was merely a detachment, although Decouz's report indicated the former. He concluded his report to Berthier with an interesting request that speaks volumes of the difficulties caused by Napoleon's absence. Marmont suggested returning to the Moselle if the Allies did not continue their advance across this river within the next two days. "But, for this to be executed," he cautioned, "for us to arrive without danger and to hold the line, we would have to act methodically and with all troops under the same command. Without this, the distance of the troops that guard this line makes it too risky if they are not under the same commander. I think the troops should be positioned on the Moselle as follows: one division each at Pont-à-Mousson, Marbache and Pompey, Toul, Bernécourt and Thiaucourt, where headquarters would be established. A few posts would be enough to link Metz; *but I repeat: there must be only one commander to direct all of this.*"[53]

On Victor's front, the 19th brought more threats to his flanks, but the marshal felt confident. "At this moment our line from Verdun to Vaucouleurs appears to be well-guarded," he wrote Marmont at 5:00 P.M. "Except for the one at Pagny-sur-Meuse, the destruction of the bridges has been effected on this part of the line to below Commercy."[54] Victor's subordinates did not share his optimism. From Commercy Briche complained about the Cossacks preventing his patrols from obtaining reliable intelligence and hindering the flow of information from local civil authorities. A reconnaissance party of 300 dragoons sent north on the right bank to St. Mihiel reported that Allied infantry occupied Bouconville and Apremont. This news prompted Briche to reinforce his cavalry at Vignot with an infantry detachment and to form a bridgehead on the right bank. Although Briche passed the day in a state of panic, the Allies did not appear in his sector.[55]

In Victor's center, Duhesme's scouts reported the presence of strong enemy columns moving southwest through the Woëvre from Pont-à-Mousson. Concerned the Allies would attack Pagny-sur-Meuse, the general requested instructions. Instead of Pagny-sur-Meuse, Victor believed the enemy's advance guard would make an effort to cross the river just north of Commercy at Pont-sur-Meuse. Although the marshal did not think the Allies would attack before the 20th, he instructed Duhesme to "hold your troops ready to fight or march." If the enemy did advance on Pagny-sur-Meuse, Duhesme and Piré would cross to the left bank of the river and destroy the bridge. On the other hand, if the Allies marched on Commercy or St. Mihiel, Piré would maintain his position at Pagny-sur-Meuse to observe the road from Toul and destroy the bridge according to circumstances. Duhesme himself would reunite with the 2nd Division of the II Corps and Briche's dragoon division. Victor also charged Duhesme with destroying the bridges upstream at Ourches and downstream at Troussey.[56]

Despite the optimism Victor expressed in his letter to Marmont, the situation on the marshal's right appeared grave. Contamine proceeded south from Vaucouleurs along the road to Neufchâteau that ran parallel to the Meuse. Arriving at Goussaincourt around 5:00 A.M., the staff officer informed Defrance that Platov had moved north from Neufchâteau on the previous evening, turned northwest at Domremy, and appeared to be headed for the bridge over the Ornain at Gondrecourt, only nine miles southwest of Vaucouleurs. Additional reports indicated the Cossack commander struck the road to Joinville, whereas others claimed the Russians were headed for Bar-le-Duc.[57] At either Domremy or Neufchâteau, Platov's warriors could cross the Meuse before Defrance could contest their passage from Vaucouleurs. Such a movement would outflank Victor's right and wreck his plans to defend the Meuse. A vigilant Victor asked Ney to dispatch patrols toward Gondrecourt and pay close attention to Platov's possible movement on Bar-le-Duc or Joinville.[58]

Defrance, however, did not wait for verification of Contamine's report. Sensing the threat posed to his rear, he withdrew a few miles north on the road to Void. Repeating the same mistake that plagued French operations in Lorraine, Defrance unbelievably neglected to destroy Vaucouleurs's bridge, which spanned the secondary arm of the Meuse, the Haute-Meuse. While the generals and their staffs quartered in the comforts of a château, the men stood ready to continue the retreat, exposed to a frigid north wind without being able to light fires for eleven brutal hours.[59]

Just as Victor appeared to spring to life, a courier from Paris arrived at Void on the 19th to deliver the emperor's harsh reprimand for the evacuation of Nancy as well as his firm order to hold the Moselle and fight the enemy. Victor's four-page response, composed that same day, suggests that Napoleon's rebuke caught him by surprise and crushed his unstable spirit. To justify his successive retreats from the Meurthe to the Moselle and then to the Meuse, the marshal elected to let the facts speak for themselves, particularly in regard to the Coalition's overwhelming numeric superiority. At times his argument degenerates into a rambling list of complaints, yet nothing he wrote can be construed as false. His response to Berthier provides a sad synopsis of the crises the ill-prepared marshals of France confronted as they coped with independent command and the emperor's absence. Victor concluded his rebuttal with an ominous prediction:

> You have read the succinct report of my conduct. I hope it will convince you I could not have done anything else without compromising the interests of His Majesty. You will likewise see that three small corps under separate commanders charged with achieving a single objective cannot cooperate to

obtain this result and that the enemy always has the advantage as long as these small corps are not united and confided to the direction of a single chief, which I have suggested in my previous dispatches. I sense that if His Majesty does not decide to accept this suggestion, the same will take place on the Meuse as took place on the Meurthe and the Moselle. The enemy will maneuver through Neufchâteau or through St. Mihiel on Bar-le-Duc, since he has already displayed this intention, which will force me to withdraw unsupported on this town [Appendix N].[60]

Napoleon finally lost patience with Victor. On 19 January, the same day the marshal penned his defense, he ordered Berthier to go to the front and personally coordinate the defense of the Meuse. Bonaparte instructed his dutiful lieutenant to give command of Victor's troops as well as Meunier's Young Guard division to the best general and have Victor return to Paris. All of Victor's troops would be placed under Marmont's overall command and the emperor firmly instructed Berthier not to depart until "the duke of Raguse has taken all measures to defend the Meuse and fight." Berthier's orders said nothing regarding Ney's status. Apparently the marshal would remain on the eastern front but would not have troops under his orders. Napoleon knew that his pet, Marmont, felt Ney lacked both talent and character.[61]

After regaining his composure, Napoleon reassessed the situation. Ironically, his "Note" of 19 January maintains the command structure on the eastern front, despite the orders he issued to Berthier earlier in the day. Regarding the progress of the enemy, he knew Allied cavalry reached the Meuse and figured some had crossed. Regardless, he wanted the entire Allied front pushed back to the Moselle, but in case this failed, he decided on a fighting withdrawal from the Meuse to Châlons-en-Champagne. Assuming he could count on Marmont to contest each step from Verdun to Châlons, Napoleon hoped Victor and Ney would do the same. Realistically, he would be satisfied if the latter two marshals simply reached Vitry-le-François, where he planned to make them turn and face the enemy. At Châlons, Marmont would form the left, Ney and Victor the center, and Mortier with the Old Guard plus three additional battalions the right. Supporting forces included four battalions and sixteen guns at Arcis-sur-Aube. Curial had two battalions at Châlons itself; three more were en route from Meaux. General Henri Rottembourg's 2nd Young Guard Tirailleur Division likewise was marching to Châlons. Between these units Napoleon estimated a train of forty artillery pieces. As for Châlons itself, the emperor wanted the town on the Marne transformed into a bastion. Any breeches in the city's walls were to be repaired, tambours placed at the gates, batteries formed, and the town itself turned into a bridgehead.[62]

For the most part, Napoleon's portrayal of Allied progress was correct. As of 19 January, he predicted that the Allies could not reach the Meuse in considerable strength for several days. Besides being anchored to the fortresses of northern Lorraine, Yorck's four infantry brigades made little progress getting across the Moselle because of widespread flooding. Only Yorck's Reserve Cavalry crossed the Moselle and traversed the Woëvre to reach the suburbs of Verdun. Henckel's Streifkorps patrolled the roads west of Luxembourg, observing the retrograde movements of Macdonald's troops from Maastricht and Köln to Liège. Sacken took Toul, where he established his headquarters and directed Biron to Foug and Lanskoi's cavalry to Rambucourt on the road from Pont-à-Mousson to St. Mihiel. Blücher remained at Nancy, making outlandish plans to detach Lorraine from France by announcing the restoration of the duchy.[63]

South of the Silesian Army, Platov's main body of five Cossack regiments crossed the Meuse on the 19th and followed his detachments toward Joinville rather than Bar-le-Duc as Victor feared.[64] Wrede quartered at Neufchâteau with two Bavarian divisions, while Frimont's Austrians reached Colombey-les-Belles, fifteen miles northeast of Neufchâteau. Consequently, Wrede needed two days to concentrate for an attack on Victor's right. Although Schwarzenberg ordered Wittgenstein to immediately march to Joinville and support the V Corps, the Russian infantry would not reach the front line until February.[65] Pahlen, however, led Wittgenstein's advance guard of two cavalry regiments, four jäger battalions, Seslavin's Streifkorps, and four guns west at a furious pace to reach Lunéville on the 20th. There he established communication with Wrede and granted his exhausted men and horses a day of rest of the 21st. With Pahlen approaching to provide the link between the Bohemian Army's right and the Silesian Army's left, Schwarzenberg asked Wrede to continue approximately thirty miles west of Neufchâteau to Vignory on the Marne, halfway between Joinville and Chaumont, to sever Mortier's communication.[66] Typical of the Allied generalissimo, he feared for his own numerically superior forces that faced a single marshal. Thus he summoned Wrede to operate against Mortier's communications, rather than allow the Bavarian to cooperate with Blücher to crush Ney, Victor, and Marmont before they could reach Châlons, where the French emperor planned to make his stand.

Despite Napoleon's reprimand and his own stirring rebuttal, Allied progress on the 20th moved Victor to abandon the Meuse. Events between Vaucouleurs and Domremy proved more unsettling to the marshal than the emperor's scorn. After realizing his mistake, Defrance ordered Lhéritier's 4th Dragoon Division to return to Vaucouleurs with a detachment of sappers to destroy the levy (the Vaucouleurs's bridge) across the Haute-Meuse. Defrance also directed General Aguste-Etienne-Marie-Gourlez Lamotte's 1st Brigade of Lhéritier's division south to Maxey-sur-Vaise and Domremy to destroy their bridges and block the roads to Gondrecourt. Upon reaching Maxey-sur-Vaise – the halfway point between Vaucouleurs and Domremy – Lamotte forwarded patrols in several directions. Leaving the commander of the 18th Dragoon Regiment, Colonel François Dard, at Maxy-sur-Vaise with instructions to barricade the streets and question the locals, the brigadier proceeded to Taillancourt, where he would await the reports of his scouts.[67]

At 11:30 A.M., Lamotte wrote his superior, Lhéritier: "Dard has informed me that according to every statement made by the peasants, the enemy spent the entire night crossing the Meuse. He had 1,500 cavalry cross at Sauvigny, which is very close to Maxey-sur-Meuse. Reconnaissance on Sauvigny has been conducted; two prisoners confirmed that a large number of cavalry is there." Lamotte decided to summon Dard to rejoin him, but then countermanded the order and withdrew to Burey-en-Vaux after receiving even more disturbing news.[68] One lieutenant and twenty troopers of the 18th Dragoon Regiment had proceeded south to reconnoiter toward Domremy: only one trooper returned. At Greux the small detachment stumbled on 300 to 400 Russian cavalry already on the left bank; more were crossing by boat. Before being captured after a brief skirmish, the French dragoons observed two or three infantry columns on the right bank preparing to cross the river. The captured lieutenant revealed to Platov that Milhaud and Grouchy were advancing up the Meuse with Victor's advance guard and that infantry would soon occupy Vaucouleurs.[69]

While the Cossacks had their way with the nineteen French troopers, the lone soldier who escaped managed to return to Taillancourt, from where he continued to Vaucouleurs to deliver Lamotte's report to Lhéritier and render a verbal account of his patrol's fate. Around the same time the dragoon arrived with Lamotte's report, Lhéritier received a letter from the mayor of Chermisey – a town southwest of Domremy and northwest of Neufchâteau – announcing the departure of the Cossacks from the latter and the arrival of the Bavarians and Austrians. The Russians headed north to Coussey, while the Austro–Bavarian corps appeared to be directed south to St. Thiébault. After reading the mayor's letter and listening to the trooper's account, Lhéritier expressed his concerns to Grouchy at 1:00 P.M.: "If we remain in this position, I do not doubt we will be attacked tomorrow morning. If the enemy does not move on Gondrecourt, he will attempt to reach Ligny or St. Dizier before us. It is essential to be in position to avoid a debacle."[70]

Lhéritier shared the information with Defrance, who ordered Lamotte to remain at Burey-en-Vaux until Victor or Grouchy issued new instructions. Defrance wanted the brigadier to ascertain what Allied units were moving against him, but to avoid combat with superior forces. After reviewing the intelligence provided by the mayor and Lamotte, Defrance reported to Grouchy that the Allies were moving west to reach the Marne before them. Two Allied cavalry columns covered the march of the infantry. Defrance speculated that one column would proceed to Vaucouleurs, the other through Gondrecourt to Ligny. If forced from Vaucouleurs, he planned to retreat directly to Void. Defrance advised headquarters to alert the entire French line; he sent the sappers, the trains, and the majority of his infantry to Void. The evacuation of the Meuse had begun.

At Vaucouleurs itself, the situation improved before taking a turn for the worse. Russian artillery unlimbered on the hills of Chalaines to form a battery of seven guns. Sherbatov's crews opened fire, forcing the French post at the entrance of Vaucouleurs to seek cover. Defrance ordered his troopers to mount their steeds. He informed Grouchy that the forces in front of him appeared to be Cossack patrols covering the hills and scattering on the plain. "I do not think he can make us quit the post . . . the waters recede very slowly. I do not think he can cross the Meuse at any of the fords. My greatest concern is over the point Lamotte's brigade will occupy. If, as he has claimed, the enemy has taken the bridge at Maxey-sur-Meuse and we cannot destroy it, the enemy can effect a serious passage there."

Later that morning Sherbatov's Cossacks, as noted, left Chalaines, relieved by the Cossack regiment that formed the advance guard of Panchulidzev's dragoon division. Panchulidzev's troopers dismounted and maintained a lively skirmish with the French dragoons, likewise dismounted and positioned on the left bank behind abatis and barricades. At 4:30 P.M., a beleaguered Defrance dictated another letter to Grouchy. Eleven additional guns and twenty-one caissons arrived to augment the Russian battery on the hills of Chalaines. "I am certain there are at least 3,000 infantry behind the walls of Chalaines," he wrote. His trust in the protection of the Meuse's waters faded. Moreover, he no longer doubted that the Russians would attempt to force the passage, especially given that he failed to demolish Chalaines's collapsed bridge completely because of the waters that prevented the powder wagon from crossing the levy. Leaving a strong cavalry picket and one Voltigeur company at Vaucouleurs, Defrance ordered his artillery to retire north on the road to Void. He instructed Lamotte to rejoin him at Vaucouleurs. Defrance concluded his report to Grouchy by stating that Lamotte's brief had not been confirmed and that he could not verify if the enemy crossed the Meuse further upstream. "I am in position on the hills west of Vaucouleurs, my left on the road to Void and my right on the road to Neufchâteau. I await your orders."

Around 8:00 that night, 20 January, Defrance's penultimate report reached Victor's headquarters at Void. The dispatch contained news from Lamotte regarding Allied preparations to cross the Meuse at Burey-en-Vaux. "You can very easily see that he [Lamotte] does not have a moment to lose to make a retrograde movement. Without this, all that I command here will be extremely compromised." Defrance reiterated his fear of being cut off from the bridges over the Marne and expressed the urgent need to commence the retreat. His last brief arrived one hour later: Enemy scouts reached Joinville on the Marne, thirty-miles southwest of Vaucouleurs.[71]

Defrance's final two communiqués had little impact on Victor's decision to abandon the Meuse. Most likely the marshal had made up his mind earlier in the day. To Victor's credit, he did not become unnerved like his subordinates. His letter to Marmont, written at 5:00 P.M., offers insight into his calm state of mind: "A strong column of enemy cavalry crossed the Meuse last night between Vaucouleurs and Neufchâteau; it will probably be followed by Blücher's corps, which reached Nancy two days ago. Platov's Cossacks have gone in the direction of Langres via St. Thiebault. They were replaced yesterday at Neufchâteau by a Bavarian corps. We have another corps in front of us at Commercy; since yesterday it has made efforts to cross the Meuse, but our troops have opposed it." According to the marshal's opinion, the "combined Allied armies" maneuvered by their left to reach the Marne via Joinville and Langres, pushing a corps through Gondrecourt to Bar-le-Duc. "In this case, our position on the Meuse is untenable and possibly dangerous. I asked the prince of the Moskowa to maintain a post at Gondrecourt and to warn us in time of any movements the enemy may make on this road. I request that you be kind enough to instruct me."[72]

After receiving Defrance's final report, Victor started building his case for abandoning the Meuse in his daily brief to Berthier, who had joined army headquarters at Châlons-en-Champagne. He still maintained that after the Austro–Bavarian advance guard reached Neufchâteau, Platov led his Cossacks south through St. Thiebault toward Langres rather than to Joinville – Victor would change his mind in just a few hours. Another Allied corps, probably belonging to Blücher's army, would cross the Meuse that very night at Vaucouleurs. "I request that His Majesty make me aware of his intentions," asked the marshal, still despondent over Napoleon's criticism. At this time, Victor did not state his intention to fall back from the Meuse and closed his letter simply by stating that 800 of Defrance's dragoons would reconnoiter Burey-en-Vaux.[73]

At this critical period, the French sorely missed the fire displayed by Milhaud in Alsace. In part because of illness and mental strain, the commander of the V Cavalry Corps was eclipsed by Grouchy and Defrance. Had Milhaud led the French cavalry as he had three weeks earlier, the intrepid general would have pierced the screen of Cossacks and light cavalry that preceded the Coalition's main columns. Instead, the appearance of the Allied horsemen terrified the population to such an extent that the French military rarely received accurate reports. Like all good commanders, Victor attempted to form a general view of the situation by piecing together the information provided by his subordinates. Based on the news that reached his headquarters on the 20th, he knew his exhausted soldiers could not make a stand unless the emperor himself arrived to reinvigorate them. Victor also recognized the demoralizing effects the continuous retreat had on his subordinate commanders. Not

Grouchy, Defrance, or Milhaud dared to seek a battle. Falling back to ascertain the strength and direction of the enemy remained his only option.[74]

Victor did not wait for a response from Berthier, the emperor, or his fellow marshals. At 11:00 that same night, the 20th, two hours after concluding his letter to Berthier, Victor issued instructions for the retreat to the Ornain to commence on the 21st. "The enemy army has directed its movement on Gondrecourt," states the marshal's orders; "it is not clear whether he will march on Ligny or Joinville, but in either case the line of the Meuse is untenable since it has been turned; the troops that guard it run a risk if they remain there much longer considering they can be overtaken at Ligny by the Allied army." Duhesme's 3rd Division received instructions to depart Pagny-sur-Meuse precisely at 1:00 in the morning to lead the retreat through Void and St. Aubin to Ligny. Duhesme would take a position west of the town on the road to Bar-le-Duc followed by Forestier's 2nd Division. Victor ordered his 1st Division to depart from Commercy at 4:00 A.M. and proceed through St. Aubin to Ligny, where it would move into third line behind the two other infantry divisions. As for the V Cavalry Corps, Briche's 3rd Dragoon Division was to evacuate Commercy at 6:00 A.M. and follow the movement through St. Aubin to Ligny. Immediately after Duhesme's foot soldiers cleared the bridge at Pagny-sur-Meuse, Piré would destroy the structure and lead his light cavalry to Void. There, he would unite with Defrance's Honor Guard and Lhéritier's 4th Dragoon Division, which would completely evacuate Vaucouleurs at 4:00 A.M. Upon arriving at Void, Defrance would take command of the rearguard and withdraw to Ligny. After leaving a strong post at St. Aubin to patrol the Commercy–Void road, Defrance's cavalry would take a position east of Ligny. Victor wanted the first cavalry squadrons that reached Ligny to continue without rest on the road to Gondrecourt to collect intelligence.[75]

Just prior to leaving Ligny at 1:00 A.M. on the 21st, Victor penned his last report to Berthier from the Meuse. He informed the major-general that his troops were retreating to Ligny because the Allies had crossed the Meuse in force between Neufchâteau and Vaucouleurs during the night of 19–20 January and throughout the day of the 20th. Although all the bridges of this sector were supposed to have been rendered impassable, floodwaters prevented his men from destroying all of the structures. Because the marshal did not possess enough manpower to occupy adequately all points of passage along the length of his sector of the Meuse, Coalition forces gained the bridges as soon as the waters receded. He explained that on the 20th, he had to employ his troops at Commercy and Vaucouleurs "to repulse the enemy's efforts." Consequently, he could not defend the other points of passage. Ultimately, the enemy's apparent decision to move in force on Gondrecourt settled the issue for the marshal. Platov's advance from Neufchâteau to Joinville on the Marne proved to be the catalyst for Victor's retreat and the abandonment of the Meuse, even though he correctly assumed the Russians were headed south. To reach Joinville on the Langres–Châlons-en-Champagne road, Platov had to cross the Meuse at Domremy and take the road that ran northwest through Gondrecourt to Bar-le-Duc. Slightly northwest of Domremy, he would strike a country path that proceeded west to Joinville. Consequently, the first part of his march appeared to be directed through Gondrecourt toward Bar-le-Duc and Victor's line of retreat. "I do not know if from there he will go to Joinville or to Ligny, but it is clear that neither myself nor the duke of Raguse can remain on the line of the Meuse since the enemy has crossed this river. If we remain here any longer he will probably be several marches ahead of us toward Ligny or Joinville."[76] Victor forwarded copies of this letter to Ney and Marmont.

As Victor lost heart, Marmont regained some hope. At 12:00 A.M., on the 20th Meynadier issued orders that suggest Marmont planned to return to the Moselle. He instructed Picquet to withdraw from Haudiomont at 4:00 A.M. to a position at Haudainville on the hills east of Verdun. Lagrange and Ricard likewise would assemble their divisions on these hills and remain ready to march east.[77] The VI Corps spent the entire day of the 20th in this position awaiting the order to return to the Moselle. Although Marmont did not issue these orders, he wrote an encouraging report to Berthier at 9:00 on the night of the 20th. He identified the Allied force that attacked his rearguard at Haudiomont on the previous day as Yorck's advance guard and believed the main body of the corps was following. The marshal assured Berthier that he planned "to receive it well" at Verdun as long as the Allied corps was proportional in size to his own. Other reports indicated Sacken's corps was marching to St. Mihiel. Marmont also placed hope in the floodwaters of the Meuse which, according to his estimate, rendered a river crossing impossible. Moreover, he spoke favorably of Victor, claiming the marshal had made "good arrangements" along his sector of the Meuse.[78]

Berthier only went as far as Châlons-en-Champagne on the 20th and did not relieve Victor of his command. "In fact," fumes Lefebvre de Béhaine, "Berthier left [Paris] furnished with precise orders to make him master of the situation; for some reason he did not conform to these orders. The actual documents published or conserved in the various archives do not provide an exact answer. When he reached the army, instead of establishing unity of command, he left Victor at the head of the II Corps, Ney at the head of Meunier's division, and limited himself to coordinating extremely poorly the movements of the various army corps."[79] Perhaps the emperor's chief of staff felt sympathy for Victor because the situation did indeed grow worse by the hour, or Napoleon may have changed his mind and countermanded the order. Regardless, Berthier informed Victor of Napoleon's directive to defend the Meuse "and oppose the enemy, which the brave troops you command are so capable of doing."[80]

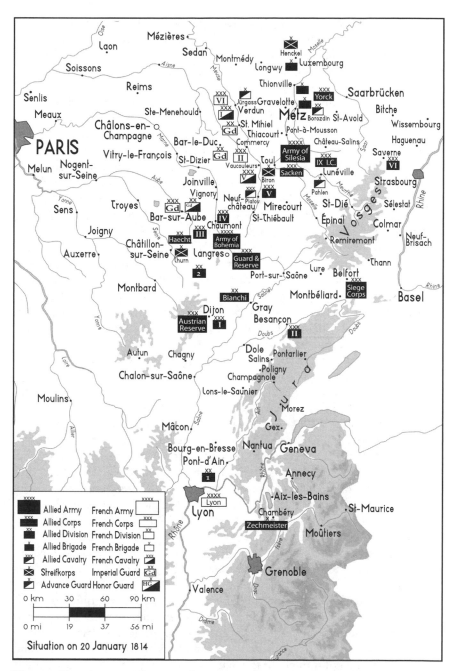

Map 22. Situation on 20 January 1814.

As for the duke of Raguse, Berthier expressed satisfaction with his measures. The major-general complimented Marmont's "excellent operation" to retake St. Mihiel. He informed the marshal that Victor would hold Commercy, Void, Vaucouleurs, and Houdelaincourt, yet Platov's "ten Cossack regiments" in Neufchâteau appeared to be preparing to harass Victor's right. Berthier wrote that he was immediately leaving Châlons to meet with Ney at Bar-le-Duc, and then Victor at Void. "I am sending to the emperor your letter of the 19th containing your plans to retake the line of the Moselle; I think we must pay attention to the duke of Bellune's right and the area between Gondrecourt and Chaumont. I am urging the duke of Bellune to defend himself at the Meuse. The duke of Trevise is at Chaumont with orders to maintain his position; Langres is in enemy hands."[81] The courier who carried Berthier's dispatch did not reach Marmont until the morning of the 21st after covering the fifty miles between Châlons-en-Champagne and Verdun.

By now Blücher and Gneisenau believed the concentration of enemy forces they expected to find at Metz would take place at Châlons-en-Champagne. Ney's sister lived in Nancy and confirmed Allied intelligence that claimed Napoleon planned to seek a decisive battle near Châlons. Regardless, the Prussians did not think Bonaparte would extend himself ninety miles east of Paris to fight at Châlons. Other than this error, Blücher's staff painted a fairly accurate picture of the situation. They knew the Silesian Army faced two marshals, each of whom commanded approximately 15,000 men. The first, Marmont, retreated from Metz to Verdun with the VI Infantry and I Cavalry Corps. The second, Victor, moved west from Nancy through Toul toward Void with the II Infantry and V Cavalry Corps. They also assumed Decouz's 5,000-man 2nd Young Guard Voltigeur Division was en route to Verdun. Moreover, Army Group Langres reached Chaumont, sixty miles southwest of Nancy and seventy miles southeast of Châlons-en-Champagne. At Neufchâteau, Wrede's corps filled the gap between the Silesian Army and Army Group Langres. Now that elements of Schwarzenberg's army were within supporting distance, Blücher wanted to test the French resolve to hold Châlons-en-Champagne. He planned to cross the Marne and proceed through Vitry-le-François to reach Arcis-sur-Aube no later than 30 January. By that time, he hoped Schwarzenberg's army would be in the triangle formed by Sens, Troyes, and Tonnerre. Sens, the apex of the triangle, stood sixty miles southeast of Paris.

On 19 January, Müffling summarized the thoughts of Blücher's staff regarding the French concentration at Châlons-en-Champagne: "In order to maneuver the enemy from his position and to keep the goal of Paris in mind, it appears most expedient if Schwarzenberg continues his march from Dijon and Langres with one column along the Seine, the other along the Yonne, and if Wrede marches from Neufchâteau to Bar-sur-Aube and Troyes. In this case, a part of the Silesian Army [Yorck] should take a position at Virty-le-François, while the rest marches through Joinville and Brienne to Arcis-sur-Aube." Müffling believed it would be highly unlikely for the French to launch a counteroffensive from Châlons – which was exactly what Napoleon planned to do.[82] Blücher described the situation in much simpler terms: "The Emperor Napoleon is now cooked well-done and can no longer resist."[83]

The salty Prussian forwarded Müffling's memo to Schwarzenberg, adding that Yorck would reach St. Mihiel on the 26th after testing the enemy's mettle at Luxembourg, Thionville, and Metz. With 40,000 men, Blücher himself would take "a concentric position" along a twenty-file-mile line between Vitry-le-François and Arcis-sur-Aube by 30 January. According to his calculations, Kleist's II Corps would arrive at Metz this same day. "I feel veritable satisfaction to learn you approve of my movements," wrote Blücher from Nancy, "and I think you know I have corresponded with Wrede, since you have pushed Wrede to the right in order to facilitate me and my army as we march to the Moselle. I have advised Wrede that I do not see the enemy opposing us on the Marne with serious resistance on account of his [Wrede's] advance to Neufchâteau. I hope you will approve my movement to Arcis. The enemy does not appear to want to defend the Meuse, where there is nothing more than a rearguard."[84]

On 20 January, Blücher received Schwarzenberg's progress report from Langres dated the 18th. Army Group Langres had cleared the French from the fortified city on the previous day and pursued toward Chaumont.[85] Detailed reports from Bülow regarding his operations and news that Wintzingerode started his march to Liège also arrived to keep the enthusiasm in Blücher's headquarters at a fever pitch. It appeared that all the pieces were falling into place for a decisive victory at Châlons-en-Champagne and then a glorious march to Paris. He informed Schwarzenberg that Sacken captured Toul and that "a man returned here [Nancy] yesterday and informed me he had found the army of Marshal Victor in march from Ligny to Châlons. The concentration of the enemy at Châlons can, in consequence, be completed by the 21st."[86] He offered no hint of his next step, but a letter to his wife reveals the Prussian's obsession: "The operations of the Silesian Army again have been very fortunate and it will probably be the first to see the gates of Paris."[87]

Wrede's Bavarian divisions remained at Neufchâteau on the 20th, while Spleny's Austrian division reached Colombey-les-Belles with Hardegg's division slightly to the east. One of Wrede's staff officers met with Platov at Greux to ensure that the Russians did not allow the French to blow the bridge. During this meeting, the Bavarian officer observed the capture of Lamotte's patrol. His account of this trivial affair led Wrede to link the French patrol at Greux with Napoleon's concentration at Châlons-en-Champagne. Although the logic did not make sense, Wrede reached the correct conclusion, prompting him to demand action from Schwarzenberg: "I have every reason to think Napoleon will move to Châlons rather than Troyes and I believe this is the movement the enemy will make because Blücher informed me of the duke of Raguse's retreat on Reims. Therefore, it appears the moment has arrived to march fast and direct against the enemy, even more so, because lacking cavalry, Napoleon will not want to fight on the plains of Châlons."[88] In addition, Sherbatov reported that all intercepted letters "announce that all [French] forces are moving on Châlons. The news from here is that Napoleon has informed the Senate he will deliver a decisive battle on the plains of Châlons."[89]

Despite the overwhelming evidence his headquarters received regarding a French concentration at Châlons-en-Champagne, Schwarzenberg acknowledged this scenario as only a possibility. Instead, he remained committed to directing Army Group Langres to Troyes, where he believed Napoleon was assembling his army. He informed Wrede that Army Group Langres would continue to Troyes, from where it would threaten Napoleon's right and render his position at Châlons untenable if indeed the French emperor appeared there. After forcing the French army to move, Schwarzenberg would attack from a position of his own choosing.[90]

Although Schwarzenberg proved unresponsive to Wrede's goading, Pahlen informed the Bavarian commander that Army Group Alsace soon would be partially reconstituted. The Russian general reported his arrival at Lunéville – forty miles east of Neufchâteau – with Wittgenstein's advance guard. As noted, he planned to rest his troops on the 21st and then force march to enter the line as soon as possible.[91] On the 21st, Schwarzenberg instructed Pahlen to move the VI Corps's advance guard to Joinville to fill the gap between Wrede and Blücher. He also attempted to accelerate Wittgenstein's march to Nancy.[92] After leaving the 5th Division at the sieges of Kehl and Strasbourg, two regiments of the 3rd Division to invest Landau, and two regiments of the 14th Division at Phalsbourg, Wittgenstein heeded Schwarzenberg's summons and ordered Eugene of Württemberg to lead the march of the VI Corps from Saverne to Nancy.[93]

During the night of 20–21 January Blücher and his staff made the arrangements to implement Müffling's plan "to concentrate the Silesian Army between Arcis-sur-Aube and Vitry-le-François by 30 July." At 9:00 on the morning of the 21st, Blücher informed Wrede that "today the Silesian Army marches to secure the bridges over the Meuse."[94] With the V Corps stalled at Neufchâteau and the VI Corps crawling westward from Saverne, the Prussians decided to press forward to Arcis-sur-Aube with the hope of dragging Schwarzenberg and his subordinates with them. For his part, the Allied generalissimo approved Blücher's plan to march on Arcis. Responding on the morning of the 22nd to Blücher's report of the 19th, Schwarzenberg added: "I believe it would be good of you to make a demonstration on Châlons by way of Vitry-le-François beforehand or at the same time." The Austrian also accepted Blücher's suggestion for the Bohemian Army to move north and promised to direct his III, IV, V, and VI Corps as well as the Russo–Prussian

Guard and Reserve to the crossroads at Troyes, only seventeen miles south of Arcis. "The direction given to the column of Dijon depends on the news that I expect to receive tomorrow," concluded the Allied commander. Schwarzenberg planned to unite Army Groups Langres and Alsace at Troyes – a questionable decision that required the V and VI Corps to march across Napoleon's front if indeed the emperor concentrated his army at Châlons. He encouraged Blücher to proceed with caution, warning the Prussian that if he appeared at Arcis too soon, the result may not be what he desired.[95]

Blücher believed the French marshals took positions west of the Meuse solely to cover the army's concentration at Châlons-en-Champagne. News that Macdonald abandoned the lower Moselle to likewise move to Châlons strengthened his conviction that this city rather than Troyes served as the French army's point of assembly. To disrupt Napoleon's concentration and forestall the forthcoming French offensive, Blücher decided to push to the Marne. He intended to drive Victor from Ligny to the Marne and then proceed as if he planned to attack Châlons. Instead, he would post an advance guard at Vitry-le-François to mask Châlons and proceed through Brienne to Arcis-sur-Aube.[96] "The question that remains," he wrote Sacken on the 21st, "is if the enemy has concentrated north at Châlons, will he accept battle there? I do not believe the enemy will oppose us at Châlons or elsewhere other than to cover his retreat."

Müffling and Gneisenau drafted a march table that divided Sacken's corps into an advance guard and two columns. According to the schedule, the advance guard would reach Vitry-le-François on 29 January, while the two columns united at Arcis-sur-Aube. Olsufiev's IX Infantry Corps would follow one day behind Sacken's second column, while Yorck's march table called for the I Corps to be at Bar-le-Duc by 27 January and Vitry-le-François four days later.[97] Although his correspondence with Schwarzenberg reveals nothing regarding Blücher's thoughts regarding where he would lead the Silesian Army after reaching Arcis-sur-Aube, there is little doubt the Prussians intended to cover the remaining eighty miles to the French capital.

On the other side of the front, Victor's divisions effected their retreat to the Ornain River in good order and without encountering Allied forces during the seventeen-mile march from the Meuse. By noon the three infantry divisions of his II Corps assembled west of Ligny; Duhesme received orders to defend the town. Defrance posted Lhéritier's dragoons northeast of Ligny on the plateau of St. Aubin facing the Void–Ligny road. Between St. Aubin and Ligny, Piré's light cavalry occupied Nançois-le-Grand and Willeroncourt to observe the gorges that led to the Ornain Valley. Briche's dragoon division took positions on the right, south of the Void–Ligny road, at Givrauval and Longeaux with a picket at St. Amand to guard the roads coming from Gondrecourt and Vaucouleurs. Despite all of Victor's foreboding, the Allies had not reached the Ornain before him.[98]

Yet as reports reached Victor, it appeared Coalition forces were not far behind. Late on the morning of the 21st Montélégier dispatched two communiqués from his post at Longeaux on the Gondrecourt–Ligny road. According to the first, locals claimed enemy infantry and cavalry commanded by an Austrian general entered Vaucouleurs that morning. Such news did not take Victor's headquarters by surprise. However, Montélégier's second dispatch provided unwelcome and unnerving details: Allied cavalry detachments had crossed the Ornain at Gondrecourt, Houdelaincourt, and Baudignécourt. A traveler who left Joinville on the Marne that same morning informed the brigadier that 1,500 Bavarian cavalry entered the town shortly after he departed.[99]

During the course of the day, uncommonly helpful locals assured Briche's patrols that the enemy remained at Vaucouleurs – the point that had so concerned Victor he had abandoned the Meuse.[100] This news somewhat alleviated the marshal's anxiety. In his 1:00 P.M. report to Berthier, he justified his decision to retreat. Using very pragmatic and frank terms, the marshal cited the weakness of his resources. Once the Allies crossed the Meuse between Neufchâteau and Vaucouleurs on the 20th, he feared the enemy would "gain several marches on me in the direction of Paris through either Châlons or Langres, rendering me useless on the Meuse, because according to all appearances the majority of Allied forces are headed to the upper Marne." Victor correctly assumed the Austrian "Grande Armée" intended to march on Langres and claimed two corps from Wrede's "army" would also proceed through Bourbonne-les-Baines to Langres. As for the Coalition forces immediately facing him, he believed a third corps had reached Neufchâteau to relieve Platov, who likewise marched to Langres and that "other Russian and Prussian troops appear to have Joinville as their objective." The marshal assumed the Silesian Army either would march to Gondrecourt or converge on the roads coming from Vaucouleurs and Neufchâteau to advance through Joinville or Ligny to Châlons-en-Champagne.

To threaten this movement, he emphasized the urgent need to conserve his communication with Ligny and suggested that Ney cover the road to Void if the II Infantry and V Cavalry Corps had to retreat to the Marne. To show a degree of offensive spirit, Victor proposed taking a position at Gondrecourt "to be able to engage and fight the enemy corps. From there, we will be able to obtain all the information we need to determine in a precise manner the direction taken by the majority of the Allied army, which would be very useful to the emperor." If the Allies marched on Ligny at the same time Victor moved to Gondrecourt, Ney would have had to block the enemy's march until Victor withdrew to Joinville or, if necessary, St. Dizier. He asked Berthier to judge the merits of his proposal.[101]

Victor did not have long to contemplate his next move. That same day, Sherbatov's Streifkorps crossed the Meuse at Sauvigny and proceeded across the Ornain at Gondrecourt; his detachments passed the night at Joinville to the west and Vaucouleurs to the east.[102] North of Sherbatov, Defrance's failure to destroy the bridge at Vaucouleurs enabled Blücher to continue his operations without delay. After learning of Victor's retreat, Vasilchikov led Sacken's cavalry across the Meuse at Vaucouleurs, proceeded north to Void, and then turned west toward St. Aubin. The mere approach of Vasilchikov's 4,900 men chased Lhéritier's dragoons from St. Aubin to a post halfway between that village and Ligny. To support the cavalry and bar the road to Ligny, Milhaud dispatched 200 infantry and two pieces of light artillery. Attempting to debouch from St. Aubin, Vasilchikov's advance guard of 200 troopers encountered Milhaud's infantry and fell back. Both sides unlimbered their artillery and commenced an ineffective cannonade that ensued for the remainder of the day.[103]

At Nançois-le-Grand, General Jacques-Gervais Subervie, one of Piré's brigadiers, watched eight to ten enemy squadrons move into St. Aubin, while a "fairly considerable column" of Russian cavalry maneuvered on its left. By nightfall, this large Russian force reached Nançois-le-Grand, prompting Subervie's brigade to retreat through Willeroncourt to Nançois-sur-Ornain, where the entire division rallied to stop the Russian advance. At 1:30 A.M. on the 22nd, Piré informed Grouchy that reconnaissance indicated the Russians had not occupied Nançois-le-Grand. One of Piré's patrol's took into custody an inhabitant of St. Aubin, who had been ordered by the mayor to deliver the Cossacks's orders for requisitions to the surrounding communes. The civilian informed Piré that 1,200 to 1,500 Russian cavalry occupied St. Aubin and the column Subervie observed had gone in search of one of the roads to St. Mihiel. This news minimized the threat that Piré faced and allowed his division to reoccupy the St. Aubin plateau on the 22nd.[104]

The reports from Victor's advance posts forced him to make a difficult decision. According to all probability, the marshal would not be able to hold Ligny. A semicircle of hills dominated Ligny, while numerous bridges and fords both upstream and downstream would facilitate the enemy's passage of the Ornain. Despite the emperor's demand to defend the Ornain, Victor's cavalry commanders helped undermine his will to fight by insisting the terrain offered no advantages. "It is very unfortunate all of our cavalry is forced to be in Ligny tonight," wrote Grouchy to Milhaud. "The enemy is under our nose and tomorrow morning he will make such a hurrah that he will take not only Ligny, but also Briche's division, and the flank of whatever he finds after crossing the Ornain."[105] Montélégier explained that the Ornain Valley formed a veritable trench 500 to 1,000 meters in width enclosed on the right by a craggy, vine-covered bank and on the left by the Ornain itself. "The little terrain in this narrow valley is flooded," he adds in his report to Grouchy. "There is absolutely no road." Although useful for infantry, such terrain rendered cavalry operations impossible. "If an entire division is forced to make a prompt retrograde movement in this long defile, its left will be completely sacrificed," warned Montélégier. Because the valley hardly favored cavalry operations, he suggested holding the hills of Givrauval with one battalion and a couple of guns.[106] The most compelling argument came from Piré's report to Grouchy. He claimed that if Victor's cavalry evacuated Nançois-sur-Ornain, enemy forces coming from Nançois-le-Grand and Willeroncourt would cut the road to Bar-le-Duc by crossing the Ornain via the bridges at Velaines or Nançois-sur-Ornain. On the other hand, Briche, who guarded the road from Gondrecourt, was not in a position to stop the enemy column that reportedly debouched from Vaucouleurs. Piré assumed that if this column did not attack Briche, it would drive through Joinville to St. Dizier, thus severing Victor's line of retreat to the Marne. Piré's letter offers a glimpse of the frustration felt by all of Victor's subordinates:

> It is my duty as a general of division and as commander of your advance guard to inform you that a very considerable enemy army is approaching you from all directions. All the information, all the reconnaissance, shows that the duke of Bellune's corps will be compromised if it continues to occupy Ligny, which is a bad position and a veritable grave. By glancing at the map it is easy to understand my reasoning. I challenge any serviceman who denies this possibility and potential. It is my responsibility to tell you that it will be a fatal disadvantage if we do not evacuate Ligny instantly. *Such is my opinion, such is that of all the general officers of the infantry and cavalry with whom I have spoken, and I do not fear if you submit this to either the duke of Bellune or to the major-general. The events will vindicate me.*[107]

Just as Victor's subordinates had failed to convince him to defend Alsace, they likewise failed to persuade him to abandon the Ornain. The marshal resolved to hold Ligny for as long as possible, despite the obvious disadvantages of the position. Even if forced to evacuate, he still intended to defend the Ornain and the road to the Marne. Issued on the 21st, his "Dispositions Défensives" for 22 January acknowledge that "the position at Ligny from the direction of St. Aubin is entirely to the enemy's advantage; it is possible that he will exploit it and establish himself on the hills that dominate this village and attack us. In this case, it is impossible to remain there if the following measures are not followed. Our line of operations will be on St. Dizier." To avoid a bottleneck at the bridge over the Ornain, Victor directed Defrance's Honor Guard to escort the baggage west to Stainville, half the distance to the Marne. Echelonned east of the trains would be the artillery of the 1st and 2nd Infantry Divisions. These divisions received instructions to leave their billets at 5:00 A.M. on the 22nd and take the road to St. Dizier. After crossing the Ornain, both divisions would form one column on the hills along the left bank of the Ornain a few miles west of Ligny. The artillery of the 3rd Infantry Division and V Cavalry Corps would follow but remain on the right bank just west of Ligny. Victor instructed his subordinates to have "the troops of the II Infantry and V Cavalry Corps echelonned on the road to St. Dizier in order to cause no embarrassment in case of a movement in this direction."

The marshal assigned the defense of Ligny and the advance posts to Duhesme's 3rd Division and Milhaud's V Cavalry Corps. To guard the town, where Victor planned to remain with his headquarters, he instructed Duhesme to position artillery and infantry at the gates, and outposts on the roads coming from Gondrecourt and St. Aubin. While Briche's division observed the road southeast to Gondrecourt, Piré's light cavalry division would serve as the advance guard on the plateau of St. Aubin, supported by a unit of 200 light infantry posted on the hills of Ligny. At dawn, Duhesme would send two battalions to reinforce this picket, "and only recall these battalions if he is certain the enemy is not present." Milhaud also received orders to dispatch the V Cavalry Corps's battery of horse artillery as well as 1,000 cavalry from Lhéritier's division to join Duhesme's two battalions on the hills of Ligny; "the rest of the cavalry will remain in battle order and ready to advance." In case the Allies debouched from St. Aubin, Duhesme and Milhaud would leave posts at Ligny and move all remaining troops onto the hills of Ligny.[108] Victor's "dispositions" remedied as much as possible the disadvantages of the Ornain Valley's terrain by echelonning the majority of his units along the road to St. Dizier on the left bank rather than bunching them on the right bank. Nevertheless, the retreat of Milhaud and Duhesme from the right bank would be difficult if pressed by the enemy.[109]

Victor's intentions conformed to Berthier's desperate pleas, which the chief of staff drafted at Bar-le-Duc at 9:00 on the night of the 21st. "Hold the position of Ligny tomorrow, hold the enemy as far as possible from you on the road to Void. Push strong patrols on the road to Gondrecourt to attain news of the enemy. Have the Honor Guard Regiment that is at Stainville push patrols in the direction of Joinville. If you have news of Marmont please share it with me. Guard the bridge over the Ornain at Tannois. You must understand the value and importance of the position at Ligny since it holds in check the enemy forces at Gondrecourt."[110]

Victor's preparations for the 22nd satisfied Berthier, yet to the north Marmont fumed over the duke of Bellune's decision to evacuate the Meuse. On the morning of the 21st, he received Victor's letter from 5:00 P.M. the previous day informing him that the Allies had breeched the Meuse and forced him to retreat to the Ornain. "It is deplorable that we neglected to destroy the bridges at Vaucouleurs," lamented Marmont, "because with surveillance and slight means we could have held the enemy at this line [the Meuse] for seven to eight days."[111]

Shortly after receiving Victor's letter, Berthier's affirmative response to Marmont's proposed counteroffensive to retake the line of the Moselle arrived.[112] However, Victor's retreat drastically changed the situation. The

Meuse had been breeched, and thus Marmont saw no justification "for remaining in position anywhere." Although he believed Yorck's 18,000 men had caught up with him at Verdun, Marmont could have remained in the fortress. Eventually, he would have discovered that only Yorck's Reserve Cavalry rather than the entire Prussian corps was demonstrating before the same fortress that would become infamous a century later. More pressing appeared to be Decouz's situation at St. Mihiel. Incorrectly assuming 12,000 men of Sacken's corps would attempt to take the crossing, he ordered Decouz to evacuate St. Mihiel, destroy the bridge, and take a position on the road from Verdun to Bar-le-Duc. Realizing he had to march southwest to support Victor and Ney, Marmont intended to move to Bar-le-Duc on the following day, the 22nd. His troops quietly passed the day of the 21st at Verdun.[113]

That night Marmont received a letter from Berthier penned earlier in the day. He learned that on the 21st Ney had one brigade at Bar-le-Duc and another at St. Dizier; the prince of the Moskawa would probably unite his division at the latter on the 23rd. According to Berthier, Victor, who had reached Ligny on the 21st, received orders to hold his ground on the 22nd but would probably retreat to Bar-le-Duc on the 23rd. Elsewhere, Mortier had reached Bar-sur-Aube, forty-two miles southwest of Bar-le-Duc. It appeared to Berthier that the Allied passage of the Meuse at Vaucouleurs and Neufchâteau indicated a great turning movement to envelop the French right wing. Based on this assumption, the chief of staff ordered a general retreat. He thus instructed Marmont to withdraw west to Ste. Menehould, arrange the defense of les Islettes, and then continue west to Châlons-en-Champagne. He would take a position north of Vitry-le-François to link his right with Victor's left. Both Ney and Victor were to withdraw as slowly as possible to Vitry-le-François: Victor covering the road to Châlons and Ney doing the same as he marched west from St. Dizier.[114]

On the 22nd, Marmont echelonned his troops on the road from Verdun to Bar-le-Duc once again without encountering the enemy. "Your movement toward us appears very good because everything leads me to believe the enemy is maneuvering by his left on Troyes," assumed Berthier. "By occupying les Islettes, two battalions can stop an army of 100,000 men. The forces you have in front of you are of no concern."[115] After arriving at Heippes that evening, Marmont departed at 8:00 P.M. to confer with Berthier at Bar-le-Duc per the latter's request.

On 22 January, Sherbatov's Streifkorps continued its advance through Houdelaincourt on the Vaucouleurs–Joinville road, while Platov reached Joinville en route to Bar-sur-Aube to sever Mortier's communications. Although these units of the Bohemian Army continued the advance, the V Corps remained idle along the Meuse from Neufchâteau upstream to Clefmont. Wittgenstein leisurely approached Nancy, which he eventually reached on the 25th. Pahlen crossed the Moselle at Flavigny and continued west to reach the Marne on the 25th.[116]

As for the Silesian Army, Sacken's advance guard reached the Meuse on the 21st. A Russian detachment moved into St. Mihiel but found the bridge destroyed. Victor's troops had likewise demolished the bridges at Vignot, Pagny-sur-Meuse, Sorcy, and Pont-sur-Meuse. In response to Russian demands, the frightened inhabitants of Vignot promised to restore the bridge in eight hours; Russian engineers started work to rebuild the bridges at Sorcy and Pont-sur-Meuse. Sacken's main body advanced to the Meuse in two columns on the 22nd. The Russian corps commander personally led the left wing column – Lieven's XI Infantry Corps – to Vaucouleurs. Following one day's march behind Sacken, Olsufiev's IX Infantry Corps escorted Blücher's headquarters to Toul. The 14,000 men of General-Lieut. Sherbatov's right wing column – his own VI Infantry Corps and Lanskoi's cavalry – headed straight for Ligny. Biron's Streifkorps maintained communication between the Russian columns.[117]

Most of the day of the 22nd passed quietly along Victor's narrow sector of the front. In his daily brief to Berthier, he resumed the tactic of listing complaints over the hardships of his troops. The countryside produced wine in abundance but little else. His soldiers lacked food and already exhausted the region's scant resources. To relieve the situation, Victor planned to send the cavalry and artillery to Bar-le-Duc or St. Dizier unless a supply convoy arrived by the 23rd.[118]

Berthier decided to make the short eight-mile ride from Bar-le-Duc to Ligny and personally inspect his colleague's position. He found Ligny in chaos: the Russians had arrived. That afternoon, Vasilchikov led the advance guard of Sherbatov's right wing column west from St. Aubin and encountered Piré's division not far from the village. French horse artillery immediately opened fire on the approaching Russians; Vasilchikov unlimbered his own guns to answer the French challenge. He then formed his cavalry and charged Piré's troopers. Duhesme's infantry did not arrive in time to support the French troopers, who retired to Ligny hotly pursued by the Russians. Vasilchikov soon reached Ligny but hesitated to attack until Sherbatov's infantry could support him. Around this time, Berthier arrived at Victor's headquarters. The senior marshal restored calm and ordered Milhaud to attack the Russian cavalry. Soon 2,000 French dragoons and light cavalry sortied from Ligny and drove the Russians back to St. Aubin. Horse artillery from both sides resumed an ineffective artillery duel. Sherbatov's main body eventually came up from Void, but the French returned to Ligny, and the onset of darkness ended the affair.

During the course of the day, Sherbatov had heard a rumor that both Ney and Berthier were at Ligny to meet with Victor. Only partially correct, Sherbatov's intelligence, which he promptly forwarded to Silesian Army

Headquarters, nevertheless excited Blücher. "On the morning of the 22nd," states his report to Schwarzenberg, "Berthier traveled from Paris to Ligny. After meeting there in a four-hour conference with Ney and Victor, he returned to Paris. The residents claim that during this conference one decided that Victor would hold Ligny and Bar-le-Duc until the 26th, the day of the arrival of the Young Guard from Antwerp." Blücher added that travelers who were present at Paris on the 12th and observed a military review claimed that at most 18,000 soldiers had paraded. "There is nothing to be seen between Paris and Châlons but two battalions of veterans of the Guard."[119] Ignoring the possible implications of the sudden presence of the emperor's own chief of staff at the front as well as two battalions of Napoleon's bodyguard, the desire to take Paris reached new heights at Blücher's headquarters.

Like so many times since the Allies crossed the Rhine, Victor's mental exhaustion, lack of fortitude, and discouragement allowed the invasion of France to progress. Despite Berthier's insistence that the emperor expected Victor to hold the line of the Ornain, the marshal prepared to withdraw soon after the chief of staff departed. Bad intelligence from panicked civil officials heightened the marshal's concern and induced him to prepare the evacuation of Ligny. According to reports he received throughout the course of the 22nd, the Allies would soon envelop his right and sever his line of retreat to the Marne. The mayor of St. Dizier claimed that Bavarian patrols followed by large numbers of Cossacks reached Joinville on the previous afternoon. In addition, the mayor of Montiers-sur-Saulx reported the presence of enemy detachments in the Marne Valley, specifically at Joinville and Sommeville. Later in the day, the magistrate informed Victor that Allied detachments passed near his own town of Montiers-sur-Saulx, which itself stood a few miles south of the Ligny–St. Dizier road.[120]

At first glance, Victor's "Placement des troupes pour le 23 Janvier," appears to indicate the marshal would indeed hold his ground at the Ornain. Victor planned to remain at Ligny with his headquarters. Moreover, Piré would continue to monitor the Russians at St. Aubin, while Duhesme's division defended Ligny itself. For support, the 2nd Infantry Division would recross the Ornain and occupy its former billets at Ligny. Behind this screen, however, the retreat would commence. Four-hundred dragoons from Briche's division supported by the 1st Infantry Division would occupy the villages on the left bank of the Ornain as far south as St. Amand to observe the road to Gondrecourt. The rest of Briche's division would canton between Ligny and Bar-le-Duc. Lhéritier received instructions to move his division to Stainville along with one battalion of the 2nd Division to escort the horse battery of the V Cavalry Corps and the three foot batteries of the II Infantry Corps. Defrance was to move his Honor Guard further west from Stainville to Ancerville, less than two miles from St. Dizier, to link the II Corps with Meunier's 1st Young Guard Voltigeur Division. All troops were to be under arms by daybreak.[121]

In a letter composed at 1:00 A.M. during a sleepless night, Victor informed the major-general that the foot batteries of the II Corps as well as part of the V Cavalry Corps would retire to Stainville. He cited the operations of the Bohemian Army as justification for the retrograde movement. The intelligence he received indicated that "the grand operations of the Allies are directed toward the upper Marne. It is clear the major part of their armies have taken the line from Langres to Joinville as the point of assembly to maneuver on Troyes. Their right column has crossed the Meuse between Neufchâteau and Vaucouleurs. If the enemy cavalry that proceeded through Montiers-sur-Saulz toward St. Dizier . . . takes this town . . . my line of operations cannot be on this point and it only remains for me to take the road to Bar-le-Duc." Recognizing St. Dizier's bridge across the Marne as the crucial gateway to Champagne, he suggested that Ney and Marmont unite with him there on the morning of the 24th to launch a counteroffensive against the Allied troops at Joinville. Evidently ignoring Blücher, Victor envisioned an operation against Schwarzenberg's flank and communications. He argued that success would breathe new life into the demoralized troops and allay the fears of the terrified population. An operation against Allied communications would stymie their plans for several days and place the French army in a much stronger position on the eve of the emperor's arrival.[122]

As Victor's letter made its way west, Berthier's courier was delivering a dispatch from the major-general to Ligny. After returning to Bar-le-Duc, Berthier wrote Victor at 2:00 A.M. on 23 January to firmly order the duke of Bellune to attack vigorously and hold his position at any cost on the 23rd. "If the enemy attacks you, it is necessary to repulse him. Do not disorganize your corps, do not send your artillery and cavalry to St. Dizier or Bar-le-Duc." He suggested the marshal make preparations to destroy the bridges over the Ornain in case the Allies forced him to withdraw to the left bank. Expressing concern over the Gondrecourt – Joinville sector, he instructed Victor to ascertain the enemy's movements.[123] One hour after drafting these orders, Berthier received Victor's 1:00 A.M. report that stated the marshal's intention to move his artillery and Lhéritier's cavalry division to Stainville. A miffed Berthier saw no justification for Victor's retreat. Marmont had reached Bar-le-Duc and Meunier held St. Dizier. Only the lack of communication between the marshals could account for Victor's behavior – which bordered on insubordination.

The irritated chief of staff fired off two letters in response, both dated 3:00 A.M. on 23 January. The first reiterated the order "to attack the enemy vigorously" since Marmont would be at Bar-le-Duc to support the II Corps. This note appears to have been an angry outburst over Victor's blatant disregard for Berthier's authority. He could easily see that Victor's decision to dispatch his artillery to Stainville greatly diminished the marshal's chances of holding Ligny. Berthier's second letter, although likewise dated 3:00 A.M., apparently was the product of some contemplation and self-doubt on Berthier's part. Unable to ignore completely Victor's claim that the Allies had reached the Marne, Berthier instructed the marshal to send an entire infantry brigade and "much" cavalry to Stainville to guard the road than ran from Montiers-sur-Saulx to Bar-le-Duc.[124]

Victor responded to Berthier's demand to fight vigorously and maintain Ligny at all costs by explaining that although the town could be defended by infantry and a few pieces of artillery, "the plateau [of St. Aubin] north of Ligny can neither be considered a defensive position nor a combat position, because on the side of the town [Ligny] is an extremely narrow defile that provides the sole line of communication." However, he believed his troops could occupy an almost impregnable position west of Ligny: the St. Dizier defile. To attack it, the enemy would be forced to negotiate a long gorge formed by the steep slopes of the hills on the right bank that encircled Ligny, the town's narrow streets, and the bridge over the Ornain. After clearing the town, the Allies would be able to attack only across a narrow front because of the difficult terrain. "Thus I have chosen to defend the defile of St. Dizier, whose hills are covered with infantry," concludes Victor's misleading rebuttal. "Several guns are in battery on the road."[125]

Hoping to find one or more of the French marshals still at Ligny, Sherbatov decided to attack on the 23rd. By 1:00 that afternoon, he had deployed the 6,000 men of his VI Infantry Corps along with Vasilchikov's cavalry on the plateau of St. Aubin. Arriving to reconnoiter the Russian position, Victor found his adversary ready for battle. Overestimating the Russian infantry by double its actual number, he decided to evacuate the plateau and ordered Piré's division to withdraw on Ligny. Piré's echelons executed the retreat in good order under the protection of Duhesme's skirmishers, hidden in vineyards and gardens. "My advance guard established itself on the hills," states Victor's after-action report. "Warned of the enemy's approach, I scouted him. His masses and his lines were already formed and I could very easily see that his force was 15,000–20,000 men, as I had claimed." During Piré's movement, Victor "ordered the cavalry to pass the defile of St. Dizier because it could not serve me on this terrain, which is narrow and cut by gullies. The infantry formed for battle on the hills of this defile. We awaited the enemy, who approached Ligny with a column of 2,000–3,000 men."

As the Russians approached Ligny, they observed that their road passed through a defile guarded by French infantry and artillery. Sherbatov formed two columns and immediately attacked. The first column, consisting of the Pskovskii and Sophia Infantry Regiments (two battalions), charged along the highway directly into the defile under the cover of artillery. His second column, the 11th and 36th Jäger Regiments (two battalions), attacked Ligny from the south side of the highway. After offering noteworthy resistance, the French withdrew into Ligny. A bloody bayonet charge enabled

Sherbatov's men to enter the town. Concealed in houses, French skirmishers greeted the charging Russians with deadly fire. After recovering from this initial shock, the Russians made steady progress and reached the town square. Duhesme withdrew from Ligny and moved his main body across the bridge over the Ornain. A strong rearguard remained west of Ligny on the right bank. Sherbatov's infantry made one attempt to debouch from Ligny, but Duhesme's men stopped them in their tracks. "Duhesme's battalions," continues Victor, "placed in the gardens, held until the town was evacuated, obstinately defending the entrance of the town and then retiring in good order. The enemy later attempted to attack our lines, but was stopped by *tirailleur* fire and a fairly sharp cannonade." By this time, night had fallen, and both sides bivouacked after losing approximately 200 men each.[126]

Around 10:00 P.M., the French advance posts reported that the enemy's bivouac fires had gradually decreased and that the rumbling of wagons could be heard on the road to Gondrecourt. Several officers attempted to conduct reconnaissance but did not venture far enough to gain an accurate view of the situation. Their reports incorrectly stated the majority of the Russian corps had departed for Gondrecourt and only a weak detachment held Ligny. Four hours later, at 2:00 A.M. on the 24th, a grateful Victor received a surprising order from Berthier. Issued from St. Dizier at 9:00 on the night of the 23rd, the chief of staff instructed Victor "to march as fast as possible with all your troops to St. Dizier" and to post a rearguard at Ancerville to guard the road from Ligny. He also ordered Victor to send a sapper detachment with an engineer officer ahead of the corps to prepare St. Dizier's Marne bridge for destruction. After the II Corps reached St. Dizier, Meunier's division would move further west to Vitry-le-François, where the army would concentrate on the 25th.[127] West of Victor, Ney reached St. Dizier on the 23rd and continued his retreat to Vitry on the following day.

Victor responded by immediately ordering the divisions of the II Corps to march. He planned to establish his headquarters at St. Dizier with the 1st and 2nd Divisions further west on the road to Vitry-le-François. Duhesme's 3rd Division would serve as rearguard and defend St. Dizier's eastern suburbs. At St. Dizier the troops would receive a much welcomed half-ration of bread as well as one ration each of meat, wine, and brandy.[128]

Elsewhere on the 23rd, Sacken reached Houdelaincourt with Lieven's XI Infantry Corps, while Blücher's headquarters moved to Vaucouleurs with Olsufiev's IX Infantry Corps. On the following day, Sacken continued the drive by reaching Joinville on the Marne, just fifteen miles south of St. Dizier. Olsufiev's IX Infantry Corps followed Sacken and arrived at Gondrecourt. Sherbatov's right wing column received orders to march northwest to Bar-le-Duc on the 24th and then turn southwest to reach St. Dizier on the 25th. Having learned en route that Ney was near Bar-le-Duc on the morning of the 24th with 8,000 men, the Russian general decided to keep his main body at

Ligny. Lanskoi led his cavalry to Stainville, while Karpov's Cossacks moved to Ancerville in close pursuit of Victor. Later in the day, patrols informed Sherbatov that the French had evacuated Bar-le-Duc. The Russians also established communication with Schwarzenberg's advance guard, which reached the region of Chaumont, twenty-one miles south of Joinville.[129]

Marmont continued his march to Bar-le-Duc on the 23rd. A detachment from Decouz's division occupied the town and relieved Meunier's brigade, which departed on the night of 23–24 January to rejoin the division at St. Dizier. That same night, Marmont transferred his headquarters to Bar-le-Duc.[130] For the 24th, he ordered Ricard to depart one hour before sunrise for les Islettes; the rest of the VI Infantry and I Cavalry Corps would move through Bar-le-Duc to Revigny.[131] Decouz's and Lagrange's divisions left their positions very early and marched through Bar-le-Duc on 24 January. To Marmont it appeared the Allies had moved a strong advance guard to Joinville and intended to isolate Mortier at Bar-sur-Aube. For this reason, Marmont decided to leave Bar-le-Duc and move closer to Victor. On the 24th, he covered half the distance to Vitry-le-François by reaching Heiltz-le-Marupt. His rearguard remained at Bar-le-Duc until 2:00 P.M., but no enemy forces appeared. This led the marshal to believe the Allies were marching on the same road as Victor and were headed to St. Dizier. Marmont described a grim situation to Macdonald: "The enemy's movement against our right has been declared. It seems there is no one, or almost no one, left behind the Meuse. I have no details of the situation. Toul surrendered without any resistance; we lost 500 men who the duke of Bellune had left behind. This, my dear marshal, is our current situation."[132]

At Paris, however, the situation did not seem so grim. On the 23rd, Napoleon informed Berthier he would reach Châlons-en-Champagne on the morning of the 25th. He counted on Lefebvre-Desnouettes and Rottembourg arriving at Vitry-le-François on the 25th with 8,000 infantry, 2,400 cavalry, and twenty-eight guns. At Châlons, this artillery train, according to the emperor's ever growing estimates, would be increased by seventy guns of the Guard Artillery. Finally, 5,000 men and eight guns under General Maurice-Etienne Gérard held Brienne, about forty miles south of Châlons. As for the marshals operating in the field, the emperor ordered Ney to unite Decouz's 2nd Young Guard Division with Meunier's 1st Young Guard Division to form a Voltigeur corps of 16,000 men and thirty-two guns. He estimated Mortier had 9,000 infantry, 2,400 cavalry, and sixty guns of the Old Guard at Bar-sur-Aube. Victor would provide 10,000 infantry and 5,000 cavalry, while Marmont would add 14,000 infantry, 4,000 cavalry, and sixty guns. "I will find myself with 50,000–60,000 infantry, 12,000–14,000 cavalry, 300 guns, thus with an army of 80,000 men," concludes the emperor. "All of this will need bread and bullets because on the 26th I will take the offensive and cause disorder in all the enemy's columns."[133]

Napoleon expressed his thoughts over the strategic situation to Belliard that same day: "I count on taking the offensive on the 26th. I suppose the duke of Bellune has maintained himself at Ligny or St. Dizier; the prince of the Moskowa is in the region with the 1st and 2nd Young Guard Divisions; Gérard is at Brienne, and the duke of Trevise at Bar-sur-Aube. I will unite these forces and I will fall on the first enemy corps that is within range. Make sure that upon my arrival at Châlons and Vitry I find information that tells me where the enemy infantry is so I can coordinate my movement and fall on him. In general, the duke of Raguse must be ready to return to the Meuse." Rather than publicize his approach in a campaign of misinformation, the emperor ordered Belliard to keep secret the news of his expected arrival. He planned to charge onto the scene, seek and defeat the closest enemy units, and exploit the success – all without a preconceived plan.[134]

As of the morning of 24 January, Berthier had not received any new instructions from the emperor. After finishing his business at St. Dizier, the major-general prepared to leave for Vitry-le-François. Before departing, he felt compelled to draft yet another letter to Victor at 10:00 A.M. to remind the marshal to destroy St. Dizier's bridge.[135] At Vitry-le-François later that day, Berthier received Napoleon's letter announcing his scheduled arrival on the 25th and the counteroffensive on the 26th. Between 4:00 and 5:00 P.M., Berthier's staff shared this information in dispatches to Victor, Marmont, and Ney. Because the emperor provided absolutely no details, the chief of staff had to guess the master of war's intentions. Consequently, destroying St. Dizier's bridge appeared useless and even detrimental to the emperor's operations. As a result, Berthier countermanded the order to Victor regarding the bridge's destruction and instructed him to depart for Vitry-le-François on the morning of the 25th, leaving a strong rearguard at St. Dizier.[136] As the senior marshal, Ney would determine the positions for the troops to occupy around Vitry-le-François, give the orders until the emperor assumed command, and receive all situation reports.[137] Berthier instructed Marmont to continue his march to Changy and Vitry-le-François.[138] Berthier had finally succeeded in coordinating the movements of all three marshals. Unfortunately for Napoleon, this cooperation came much too late and was not achieved until after his subordinates had retreated all the way to the Marne.

On the banks of the Marne, Marmont occupied Vitry-le-François with Decouz's Young Guard division and one cuirassier brigade on 25 January. Lagrange's division and the artillery took position at Vitry-le-Brulé with the light cavalry pushed to Outrepont and Changy.[139] Ricard remained at les Islettes with the main body of his division, posting at Clermont a rearguard composed of the 10th Hussars, three battalions, and two guns to ensure the flow of several convoys of sick and material, whose march had been slowed by the shortage of transports.[140] During the course of the day, Marmont's headquarters at Vitry-le-François issued instructions for Ricard to depart immediately and reach Vitry in two marches if possible. The emperor's imminent arrival and the anticipated counteroffensive account for this order.[141] With Meunier's division, Ney also moved into Vitry-le-François; his patrols sought Mortier's troops on the roads to Arcis-sur-Aube.[142]

Victor did not execute the eighteen-mile march from St. Dizier to Vitry-le-François in accordance with Berthier's orders. Instead, by 2:00 in the afternoon he had his divisions echelonned on the road leading to Vitry-le-François. The 1st Division camped at Thiéblemont-Farémont – the halfway point between St. Dizier and Vitry. *East* of this division, Defrance's Honor Guard halted at Heiltz-le-Hutin. Victor moved his headquarters and the 2nd Division to Perthes, less than five miles west of St. Dizier. Grouchy received orders to position the V Cavalry Corps between St. Dizier and Perthes to support the rearguard. Victor again called upon the 2,600 men of Duhesme's 3rd Division to serve as the rearguard along with a cavalry detachment under Subervie's command consisting of 600 cavalry and two batteries of light artillery. The marshal instructed Duhesme to hold St. Dizier for as long as possible, patrol the roads to Joinville, Ligny, and Bar-le-Duc, and hold enemy detachments as far back as possible. If the Allies threatened to attack St. Dizier in force, he would leave a detachment to defend the town, withdraw the majority of his troops, and conduct a fighting withdrawal west to Perthes.[143]

As early as 2:00 A.M. on the 25th, Duhesme reported that the Russians were approaching St. Dizier and he probably would be attacked sometime during the day.[144] He was right. Sherbatov's column moved north to Ancerville and Lanskoi's 11th and 36th Hussar Regiments supported by two jäger battalions and four pieces of horse artillery attacked St. Dizier. After a stubborn defense of the town, Duhesme withdrew around 4:30 P.M. to avoid being turned by the Russian cavalry. Covered by the V Cavalry Corps, he united with Victor and took a position east of Perthes at Hallignicourt.[145] Lanskoi's cavalry and Biron's Streifkorps pursued as far as the French outposts and then crossed to the left bank of the Marne to conduct reconnaissance to the southwest. Lanskoi secured St. Dizier with 800 dragoons and established posts to observe the road to Châlons-en-Champagne. Meanwhile, Sacken led his column over the Marne at Joinville – where Olsufiew's infantry corps also arrived with Silesian Army Headquarters – and camped in Doulevant.[146] Blücher crossed the Marne and the French marshals continued to fall back, but the time for retreating would soon end: Napoleon arrived at Châlons on 25 January according to plans. The invasion of France had ended, the war for France was about to begin.

Blücher could not have been happier. His army had covered 190 miles in twenty-five days, while the Bohemian Army marched 110 miles in approximately the same amount of time. By the end of January, the Allies controlled most of Holland, Belgium, Lorraine, Alsace, and Franche-Comté and had penetrated Champagne. Napoleon had hoped his marshals could stop the Allies at the Rhine during the initial invasion. After this failed, he implored them to hold the Allies at some point during the march to the French interior. Lack of cooperation between the marshals contributed to Blücher's success, as well as the limited and generally demoralized forces at their disposal. The French soldiers had not been paid for several months, and most were poorly clothed and hungry.

Blücher's army had poured across the Rhine with the tactical objective of enveloping Marmont and the strategic objective of reaching first Metz and then Châlons, from where the Prussian field-marshal would launch his coveted offensive against Paris – his general operational objective. The Prussian commander drove Marmont before him, but the marshal did his best under the circumstances and Blücher's virtual indifference to securing his tactical objective. Indeed, Blücher's invasion ended with the Rhine, Saar, Moselle, Meuse, and Marne breeched, but his successive attempts to crush the marshals through envelopments failed. The rising water level of the rivers and the inadequate preparations for their bridging contributed to this failure, yet Blücher's preoccupation with reaching Metz and then Châlons eclipsed his desire to destroy the marshals. In fact, Blücher was pleased that Marmont abandoned the Saar without a struggle.[147] With their outnumbered forces, the demoralized French marshals withdrew from one river line to the next, unaware of the rash mistakes being committed by Blücher – mistakes that the master of war would make the impetuous Prussians pay for dearly in February. Blücher and his staff failed to utilize the Silesian Army's numerical superiority, particularly in cavalry, which repeatedly failed to procure intelligence in a timely manner. Blücher's headquarters often hesitated and then allowed the French to retire on their own terms. Müffling and Gneisenau poorly regulated the marches, thus fatiguing man and horse. Paradoxically, the average daily march of less than eight miles resembled the pace of an eighteenth-century army during the Seven Years' War rather than a modern army.

The operations between the Rhine and the Marne offer a glimpse of the ideas and objectives that later mastered Blücher's headquarters. During the Allied councils of war at Frankfurt, Gneisenau pressed two interrelated themes: a decisive battle with Napoleon and the conquest of Paris. This meant that objectives such as Metz, Châlons-en-Champagne, Arcis-sur-Aube, and ultimately Paris received a higher priority from Blücher and Gneisenau than destroying the small forces commanded by the marshals. Consequently, the staff of the Silesian Army strove for a decisive battle with Napoleon himself and were not concerned that Marmont, Victor, and Ney slipped away. "In our particular case it comes down to a single battle in order to give us total victory," wrote Gneisenau to Knesebeck.

According to the correspondence of the Prussian leadership of the Silesian Army, only the concentration of overwhelming forces would ensure this victory. For this purpose, they moved closer to the Bohemian Army. After completing his mission against the Moselle fortresses, Yorck would reunite with Blücher; Kleist and Langeron would likewise join the Silesian Army as well as Bülow and Wintzingerode. Indifferent to the needs of rear-area security, the Prussians wanted to move up the siege corps to unite all Allied forces in a ruthless march on Paris. After crossing the rivers, the moment had come to concentrate and deliver this epic battle. Once the battle was fought and won, Paris would fall. If the French capital did not surrender, Gneisenau planned to starve the city into submission. "At Moret, between Montereau and Nemours," continues his letter to Knesebeck, "is a point where one can force Paris to capitulate in a bloodless manner in case the bloody way does not induce this capital to yield. This point is downstream the influx of the Yonne, Aube, Armançon, and the influx of the canals of Briaire and Orleans with the Seine, which bring the agricultural produce of the fertile lands to Paris and feeds this city."[148]

In comparison to the methodical siege warfare that Gneisenau refers to as the "orthodox" principles of war, the views of the Silesian Army were more analogous to Napoleonic or modern principles of war. However, Blücher's and Gneisenau's preference for operations that would lead to the defeat of an unseen enemy army either at Metz, Châlons, or Paris, rather than the French forces withdrawing before them, suggests that although they had learned much, their memory was selective, as the near destruction of the Silesian Army in February would prove. Numerous other factors can be found in the letters of Blücher, Gneisenau, and Müffling that reveal the belief in their ability to end the war with one decisive blow. Such factors include the open conflict between the emperor and the Legislative Corps, which the Prussians interpreted as dissension between Napoleon and the French nation. This led to numerous Allied proclamations that the Coalition was not fighting against the French nation but only to defend its own independence against Napoleon's hegemony. Müffling recalled that "the field-marshal wanted to make it appear that we were certain of our business, and considered the war as quite ended. All deserters who came to us were dismissed with passes to their homes; even the prisoners, if they wished, were publicly dismissed."[149] The positive reception Blücher's army received after crossing the Rhine led the Prussians to believe the new *levée-en-masse* Napoleon decreed for the provinces directly threatened by the Allied invasion was a complete failure. Not only did French males evade the mobilization, but not enough muskets could be found for those who did answer the call. Napoleon's factories could only produce limited quantities, and, as far as the Allies knew, he had not issued a general call for weapons. Thus the deeper the Allies advanced into France, the severely weakened state of Napoleon's military power became increasingly apparent. Conditions in France appeared much more favorable to the Allied cause than even Gneisenau had imagined in November. Together Blücher and Schwarzenberg commanded three times the number of forces compared to the French marshals, and a people's war had yet to materialize. Gneisenau concluded that the Allies had to march directly on Paris and end the war with one blow. He painstakingly rationalized this necessity in numerous letters to Stein, Knesebeck, Hardenberg, and Radetzky, the purpose of which were for these men to pass his ideas on to Alexander, Frederick William, and Schwarzenberg.[150]

The month of January illustrates the success of the Coalition's strategy to prevent a popular uprising. The rapid Allied advance and the lack of French resistance shattered the morale of first the German and then the French populace. Refugees streamed westward, and thousands flocked to Paris. Allied propaganda paid dividends. Pamphlets proclaiming that the Allied sovereigns were at war with Napoleon and not the French nation circulated throughout the countryside. Apathy quickly set in, and an increasing number of Napoleon's subjects remained indifferent to the outcome of the war. Bourbon sympathizers grew more vocal, especially in southern France. Nothing close to the rabid patriotism of the Revolutionary armies existed. A tired nation that no longer wanted to sacrifice its young grew anxious for peace. Moreover, the French had not experienced the brutal and material retribution of foreign occupation with its assortment of atrocities such as pillage, murder, arson, and rape. The Allied campaign to win hearts and minds combined with French war weariness to deny Napoleon a moral rallying ground that could be used to incite the people against the foreign invader. Yet all this would change in February, when supplying the Allied troops became extremely difficult. "The barbarous behavior of the Allies exasperated the population," notes French historian Houssaye, "reconciled the most hostile to Napoleon, and roused the most peaceful to resistance."[151]

Upon reaching the Moselle, Victor, Marmont, and Ney needed to coordinate their movements and operations more than ever to delay the invasion of the French heartland. Yet at this critical juncture, the marshals made the gravest of the mistakes they committed during the entire invasion. Inexcusable negligence handed the Allies the bridges at Frouard, Brouxières, Pont-à-Mousson, St. Mihiel, Commercy, Vaucouleurs, and St. Dizier. During the retreat from the Moselle to the Meuse, the marshals expended their dwindling emotional reserves in bitter yet legitimate complaints and recriminations against each other's conduct. Rather than work together, they sought only to escape the emperor's wrath by projecting blame on their fellow marshals for the mistakes they or their subordinates committed.

16

Bourgogne, the Rhône, and the Aube

Diplomatic posturing and increased political activity directly affected Schwarzenberg's operations during the second half of January. In addition to Russian and Prussian opposition, London's insistence on Holland's acquisition of Belgian territory and in particular Antwerp meant the Frankfurt Proposals no longer held prominence in Allied councils. Moreover, the future frontiers of France and "Germany" remained unclear.[1] "Therefore, to return to the principal question," Metternich explains to Schwarzenberg. "I will tell you peace must be concluded in less than fifteen days and at the very most in three weeks or indeed the Coalition must propose a new goal. That which had formed the basis of our previous arrangements has been achieved and nothing is worse for an alliance than ambiguity."[2]

To spare France a draconian peace that would cripple its ability to counter Russia, the Austrian minister hoped to end the war as soon as possible. A decisive victory over the French army in either Lorraine or Champagne that would embolden Alexander and the war party threatened his intricate plans. Metternich enjoyed a great advantage over Alexander in their expanding cold war. The war party could never be certain of Metternich's next move, yet the wily statesman effortlessly divined the tsar's actions and reactions. He understood that a major French defeat on the battlefield would increase the tsar's demands and make peace both more difficult to attain and less advantageous to Austrian interests.[3] Ever a grounded realist, Metternich recognized the growing possibility that the Allies eventually would have to take Paris and crush Napoleon to secure peace. "Since my arrival here," he wrote Schwarzenberg from Basel, "I have received very recent news from France that leaves no doubt that the mood there has not improved as a result of the levée-en-masse. It appears, according to the talk . . . that the best means to force the little man to peace is to do nothing for the war and that all and sundry will remain at home. Obtain what is desirable and useful without attempting to go to Paris or, indeed, go to Paris if you cannot obtain what you must. Here are my politics. Tsar Alexander has a different opinion, because he believes the Tuileries must suffer the same fate as Moscow."[4] Although the Allies could be forced to march on Paris to end the war, Metternich strove to prevent this expedient from becoming the Allied objective.

Alexander's wish to exact personal vengeance on Napoleon for the destruction of Moscow as well as his desire to humiliate France through a victorious invasion completely contradicted Metternich's designs. Aside from revanche, the tsar's plan to annex Poland required an energetic execution of the war, decisive victories, and the destruction of the French army. According to Alexander, the invasion of France "constitutes a mighty undertaking, having for its objective the annihilation of the enemy's resources, to deprive him of the means of forming an army, [and] to weaken his power. In short, to cause him all the harm possible in a time of war. I always have insisted on employing our forces in this manner, and on coordinating our actions with military considerations. It now only remains for us to carry this idea into execution with rapidity and judgement."[5] France had to be broken for the tsar to achieve his goals, particularly the cession of Alsace to Austria in exchange for Poland's acquisition of Galicia. Like Blücher and Gneisenau, Alexander openly stated his belief that the war only could end in Paris. The rhetoric of the former Prussian chancellor Stein, who never left the tsar's side, strengthened his conviction. Conversely, Schwarzenberg's lethargic advance through Franche-Comté to Champagne enraged the Russian monarch, who continuously urged the commander in chief to take bolder measures. To limit Alexander's influence on military operations, both Metternich and Francis conspired to keep the tsar as far as possible from Schwarzenberg's headquarters. This tactic largely succeeded in January, but Alexander always endeavored to overtake Schwarzenberg. "The kaiser will remain here for a few days," wrote Metternich from Basel, "and we will try to convince Tsar Alexander to do the same. We will have see what to do next because he will not stop for long."[6]

While in Basel, the tsar threw fresh fuel on the burning embers of Austro–Russian relations. Alexander pursued a twofold policy. On one hand, he maintained his position on the war: Peace with France was unattainable until the Allies physically eliminated French military power. Thus the war had to be continued and even accelerated. On the other hand, the tsar's latest diplomatic maneuvering alarmed Metternich and made the war's immediate termination all the more urgent in the eyes of the peace party. Feeling more confident than ever, the Russian monarch publicized his intention to replace Napoleon with none other than Bernadotte. The removal of Napoleon would indeed represent France's ultimate humiliation, which Metternich wanted to avoid for the sake of establishing a European equilibrium. Although no stooge, Bernadotte would indeed owe the tsar a debt of gratitude, which Metternich interpreted in the worst light: France would become a Russian satellite. In the least, with

Bernadotte on the French throne as a result of Alexander's patronage, the possibility remained of another Tilsit in which Russia and France divided Europe between them. Because Metternich already feared Prussia was a Russian satellite – or on its way to becoming one despite Hardenberg's efforts – this postwar arrangement did not bode well for Austria.[7]

Alexander also stated his intention to exclude the French from all postwar discussions except those pertaining to France's borders. This last issue proved particularly troublesome regarding the future of the Third Germany. Metternich needed a strong France to maintain an European equilibrium in general and to prevent Russian domination of the Third Germany specifically. "A Russian protectorate over the middle states was a possibility too real and too ominous to be ignored," notes Kraehe.[8] "The tsar thus proved that he was crafty, as well as mystical," explains Kissinger. "The exclusion of France from a voice in European affairs would have eliminated France from the balance of power by diplomatic means; while the installation of Bernadotte as king of France would, in effect, have reinstated the Franco–Russian alliance with Russia as the dominant party."[9]

"My friend, I write you at a moment of great importance," states Metternich's 16 January letter to Schwarzenberg. "We have reached the point where all must work for the good cause, where the salutary work that we have undertaken must find itself crowned or everything will crumble under our steps. It is not in our interest to sacrifice a single man to place Bernadotte on the throne of France. Do you believe I am mad? Well not quite, madness is the order of the day!"[10] Metternich feared Bernadotte would unchain the French Jacobins who in turn would again unleash revolution on all of Europe. "His previous life and career rendered him accessible to the revolutionary party," recalls Metternich in his memoirs.[11] Receiving this letter on the 18th, a flabbergasted Schwarzenberg replied: "I never imagined this of Bernadotte. . . . How? The universe has formed an alliance between the greatest sovereigns of Europe to achieve a result as scandalous as this! Impossible! I am counting on you!"[12] Metternich opposed Alexander on the general issue of dethroning Bonaparte because the Austrian minister believed peace was within reach. After attaining the goals of the Teplitz Accords and believing he could secure most of the Frankfurt Proposals, Metternich found no reason to drive Napoleon to acts of desperation to save his crown. This would certainly prolong the war, and a prolongation of the war would most likely lead to Napoleon's utter defeat and dethronement. Yet the crafty Austrian kept his options open: to maintain a strong France in the event of regime change, Metternich saw Louis XVIII as the only viable option. Neither Metternich nor the kaiser – Napoleon's own father-in-law – desired to maintain Bonaparte on the French throne for dynastic reasons.

Owing to the tsar's stated intention to remove Napoleon, Metternich naturally assumed the Russian monarch would refuse to conduct negotiations with

Caulaincourt. Although Metternich hoped Castlereagh's imminent arrival would diffuse the situation, he could not predict the British minister's disposition. Both Russian monarch and Austrian minister impatiently awaited Castlereagh's arrival. The two Allied factions strove to win British support and thus win the political chess match. For this reason, two sets of living quarters for Castlereagh were prepared in Basel: One in the Austrian section close to Metternich, the other in the Russian quarter near the tsar.[13] With the support of Castlereagh, Hardenberg, and Nesselrode, the Austrian statesman hoped to persuade Alexander to negotiate with Napoleon. Given the thorough success of the invasion, Metternich believed Bonaparte recognized the seriousness of his situation and would embrace an opportunity to make peace based on the fair terms contained in the Frankfurt Proposals. Should Bonaparte prove Metternich wrong and emerge as the true obstacle to peace, the Austrian would endorse regime change. Metternich would proceed toward this goal only after further discussions over the future goals and political intentions of the Coalition led to a new agreement among the Allied powers.

Alexander's ambitions had expanded considerably since the ponderous Allied councils of war at Frankfurt. Unlike Metternich, he wanted to achieve total victory and then reveal his intentions. It is unclear whether the tsar formulated his designs to remove Napoleon during those trying days at Frankfurt; he made no mention of this policy to his allies, who probably would not have supported regime change at the time. Alexander himself had assumed the war would be much more arduous than events actually proved. By mid-January, French resistance appeared to be collapsing on all fronts. Holland had fallen, and Belgium was invaded; neither Blücher nor Schwarzenberg encountered much opposition during their respective drives to the French interior. While Metternich believed peace was within his grasp, the tsar saw revenge within his. The poor performance of the French marshals led the Russian sovereign to believe Allied forces could take Paris with little effort and minimal loss. In view of these new circumstances, he publicized the prospect of crowing the Coalition's work by forcing Napoleon to abdicate.[14]

Metternich sensed the growing radicalization of the tsar's demands and shrewdly calculated his next move. Lesser statesmen would have yielded, yet Metternich refused to grant Alexander a free hand in determining Europe's future. "In four days you will be visited by Tsar Alexander," he warned Schwarzenberg. "We remain here [Basel] to await the arrival of Lord Castlereagh. The king of Prussia is with us. Lord Castlereagh, the chancellor [Hardenberg], and I will leave to find Alexander. I hope to conclude this business rather than submit to the Tsar of Russia. We must decide the political and military end of this first act or initiate a new political or military plan which, without doubt, will be the case if Napoleon refuses to make peace according to the terms we offered him. It appears he cannot refuse this opportunity. If he does, he is lost, but it will not be Bernadotte who replaces him."[15] In this atmosphere of uncertainty, military operations could hamper Metternich. Yet with an Austrian serving as Allied commander in chief, all the means necessary to direct Allied operations and strategy were at Metternich's fingertips.

Alexander saw through the Austrian smokescreen and refused to allow Schwarzenberg to slow the army's operations, particularly after the capture of Langres on 17 January. Just as Austrian politics required a rapid, negotiated peace to end the war with a Napoleonic France only moderately reduced in power, Alexander's politics demanded the vigorous persecution of the war, the utter destruction of French combat power, and Napoleon's abdication. A negotiated peace at this juncture would not provide the leverage he needed to secure his objectives. Forcing France to surrender Alsace to Austria as compensation for Vienna's cession of Galicia to Poland would not receive support from any party involved in the negotiations. Even the attainment of the tsar's own "minimal" program of incorporating Prussian Poland into his Polish state and compensating Berlin with Saxony appeared to be in doubt. Although Metternich acknowledged the need to revise the Frankfurt Proposals, Alexander realized that he could not depend on Austria to support any new and excessive Russian demands. At this point of the war, even Prussia's support of his objectives was questionable.[16] To impose exacting demands on France as well as his own allies, Alexander needed to strengthen his position at the bargaining table considerably.

After realizing his fear of French military capabilities were groundless, Alexander regretted another mistake he made at Frankfurt: his agreement to convene a peace conference on the condition of Napoleon's acceptance of the Frankfurt Proposals. He made this concession when the Allies still feared Napoleon's military prowess. By mid-January, however, Napoleon's impotence appeared to be more of a threat to the Coalition than French military might.[17] Alexander wanted to take advantage of his prostrate foe to maximize his stature in the Coalition and increase his demands for peace. The tsar had three options: renounce his designs on Poland; refuse to negotiate with the French and thus prevent peace from being concluded; or accelerate Allied military operations in an attempt to achieve a decisive victory that would destroy the French army. He immediately ruled out the first: Russian control of Poland had been his obsession since Napoleon created the Grand Duchy of Warsaw in 1807. The second option likewise was not feasible. Alexander could not risk jeopardizing Russia's great power status by boycotting the peace conference and allowing Metternich a free hand. All that remained was to pursue the simple policy that always had produced success for Napoleon: the destruction of the enemy's ability to wage war.

Such a decision required the Russian monarch to redirect considerably the Coalition's political and military policies. He knew Napoleon well enough to appreciate the French emperor's pride and delicate ego. Even if the tsar managed to generate support in the Allied camp for a draconian peace, the intransigent Bonaparte would reject any terms that required the surrender of large chunks of territory such as Alsace. True, the war would continue, and the tsar would receive the opportunity to secure peace on the battlefield as opposed to the negotiating table, but a Napoleonic France would remain stronger and more dangerous to Russia than a France ruled by another regime. Thus, the tsar reached the conclusion that the overthrow of Napoleon would considerably weaken France and provide him with a free hand to shape postwar Europe. With Napoleon removed from the throne and France impotent, Alexander would be less dependent on Austria and Prussia to secure his objectives. For this reason, the tsar publicly demanded Napoleon's abdication and hoped this political objective would be adopted by the Coalition. As for a new military policy, he would have to put an end to Schwarzenberg's listless parade through the French interior. If the Allied armies could achieve a decisive victory before peace negotiations commenced, Alexander hoped to secure British and Prussian support for regime change. With this plan in mind, the tsar departed in pursuit of Schwarzenberg.[18] On Stein's urging, he left in Basel a letter suggesting that Castlereagh join him and refuse to consult with any other diplomat until he met with the tsar. Stein himself wrote Stewart – Castlereagh's brother – to warn him of Metternich. Stewart informed Metternich of the letter, thus increasing the mutual dislike between Stein and the Austrian minister.[19] According to Stein, "Tsar Alexander was still embittered against Metternich, who dominated Nesselrode and Hardenberg. To prevent Castlereagh from falling under the same influence, I recommended [that] his brother, Sir Charles Stewart, with whom I had been on friendly terms since Dresden, warn him not to yield altogether to Metternich's influence, and so lose the tsar's confidence. . . . Stewart betrayed this confidential communication to Metternich, who spoke of it to the tsar and maliciously named me."[20] No friend of Metternich, Stein once warned Alexander that the Austrian possessed a "spirit of frivolity, conceit, and . . . lack of respect for truth and principle."[21]

Regardless of the political maneuvering, the contending forces converged on Langres. The slow advance of the Bohemian Army continued mainly due to the torpid movements of Schwarzenberg's lieutenants. Convinced the French did not have a large force at Langres, Schwarzenberg instructed Gyulay, Colloredo, and Crown Prince Frederick William on the 11th to accelerate their movements to reach Langres on the 13th.[22] On 14 January, Bohemian Army Headquarters issued orders for Gyulay, the crown prince, and Colloredo to attack Langres on the 18th.[23] French attempts to organize the *levée-en-masse* induced Schwarzenberg to have Gyulay force march to Langres to quell the agitation in the Haute-Marne Department.[24] "Napoleon moves heaven and earth to stir up a general insurrection," wrote Schwarzenberg. "In many places it will succeed, thus the country will suffer tremendously. Napoleon initially rejected such a measure, but now he embraces it."[25]

Reports over the *levée-en-masse* concerned Kaiser Francis, who instructed Metternich to order Schwarzenberg to "take strong measures to repress the spirit of opposition." Francis wanted Schwarzenberg to publish an *ordre du jour*, in which the Allied High Command declared "that any citizen captured with arms in hand will be treated as a serviceman and taken prisoner, that any town or village that defends itself will be treated as an armed place taken by assault or by brute force and handed over to pillage, that all houses whose residents fire at the troops will be razed. He has no doubt that such measures are necessary and urgent."[26] Although he had yet to receive this letter, Schwarzenberg ironically issued the following "Proclamation to the People of France":

> The name Charles Lequier, from the Igny commune, misled by the proclamations that honor and humanity disavow, arrested with arms in hand, appeared before a Military Tribunal in Vesoul on 13 January 1814. Convicted to death, he has obtained a pardon, accorded by the prayers of numerous and honest inhabitants and above all by the claim of being father to six infants, whose existence depends on his. The Military Tribunal will conduct itself henceforth at the scene where any criminal-assassin is arrested: there he will be judged and punished by death. His Highness, Marshal-Prince von Schwarzenberg has given this order to all commanders of the corps that compose the Allied army.[27]

In the meantime, Marshal Mortier's units started arriving at Langres on the 10th in the form of the chasseurs and grenadiers "à cheval" of General Louis-Marie Laferrière-Levêque's 1st Guard Cavalry Division (2,900 sabers). The entry of these magnificent veterans, none the worse after their grueling march from Belgium, reinvigorated the population, who feared that the French army had been destroyed. "The presence of the troops has produced a great effect on all the inhabitants of the region; the conduct of the National Guard also has been good," reported the marshal.[28] On the following day, Laferrière-Levêque's main body arrived followed by the eight battalions (4,800 bayonets) of General Louis Friant's 1st Old Guard Infantry Division. Artillery consisted of three horse and four foot companies servicing sixty guns. On the 12th, Mortier himself entered Langres.

Well over six feet, Mortier had a commanding presence that served to complement his friendly nature. Born in February 1768 to an English mother and a wealthy French cloth merchant and farmer, the young Mortier received an education from the English College at Douai. He saw his first military action at the very beginning of the war between Austria and France in April 1792. Serving as a company commander in the National Guard, the twenty-four-year-old captain fought in Belgium over the next two years, receiving a promotion to staff major in early September 1794. Although not fond of administrative duties, Mortier displayed an efficiency that led to the denial

Figure 15. Marshal Adolphe Edouard Casimir Joseph Mortier (1768–1835). French corps commander.

of his request for a transfer to the cavalry. The years 1795 and 1796 found Mortier serving in Germany as a colonel and divisional staff chief.

During the War of the Second Coalition, he fought with distinction against the Russians in Switzerland, earning a battlefield promotion to general of division after the second battle of Zurich. After the new regime took power, First Consul Bonaparte appointed him commander of Paris and the surrounding 17th Military District. Rather than join Bonaparte in Italy, Mortier applied his administrative talents to directing military business in the capital – a post he held from 1800 to 1803. When war with Great Britain resumed, Mortier received his first independent command. With less than 15,000 men and twenty guns, Napoleon tasked him with the important assignment of seizing Hanover. Foreshadowing the feat he would accomplish in early 1814, Mortier marched 145 miles in five days to cover the distance between the lower Rhine and the Weser. On 5 July 1803, he accepted the surrender of the 17,000-man Hanoverian army aboard a raft anchored in the Elbe River. Bonaparte rewarded Mortier with command of the artillery of the Consular Guard on 2 February 1804. Four months later, on 19 May, he received his baton with the creation of marshalate. Indicative of his loyalty to the emperor, Mortier named his first son Napoleon.

Mortier spent the opening round of the 1805 war as a staff officer, but after the Ulm Campaign, he received command of an ad hoc corps of 15,000 men and twenty-three guns. With only one division (5,000 men) at hand, he ran into 40,000 Russians along the north bank of the Danube River on 11 November. At the village of Durrenstein, the marshal held his troops together against these overwhelming numbers until reinforcements arrived. Although Mortier suffered 3,000 casualties, he estimated Russian losses at 6,000 men, five guns, two standards, and 700 to 800 prisoners. After seeing action at Durrenstein, Mortier returned to administrative duties, garrisoning Vienna from 19 November to 11 December. He missed the epic contest at Austerlitz yet received command of the V Corps during the final days of the War of the Third Coalition. Garrison duty in southern Germany followed until the Prussians decided to challenge Napoleon.

For the War of the Fourth Coalition, Mortier received command of the new VIII Corps. The destruction of the Prussian armies at Jena-Auerstädt on 14 October 1806 enabled the marshal to occupy the Electorate of Hesse-Cassel on 1 November with only 5,500 men and to disarm its army of 20,000 men. As French forces inundated North Germany, Mortier led his corps through Hanover to Mecklenburg-Schwerin. In January 1807, he received orders to take the Swedish territory of Stralsund, which he accomplished by mid-April. He fought under the emperor's gaze at Friedland, commanding the left wing as the Grande Armée ended the War of the Fourth Coalition by crushing the Russian army in June. For the next fourteen months, he administered Silesia and received his ducal title, the duke of Trevise, on 2 July 1808.

Two months later Mortier was in Spain commanding the V Corps. He remained in Iberia until 1811, seeing action at Somosierra and the sieges of Saragossa and Badajoz. Unlike the vast majority of the marshals who served in the Peninsular War, Mortier escaped with a sound reputation. Summoned to Paris to apply his administrative talents to the recruitment and organization of the Young Guard, Mortier assumed command of this 17,700-man unit during the invasion of Russia. He stood as a spectator with the Guard both Old and Young while the killing fields around Borodino consumed almost 80,000 men on 7 September 1812. Napoleon named Mortier governor of Moscow and ordered him to blow up the Kremlin when the retreat began. Although the marshal's sappers deposited 183,000 pounds of gunpowder under the Kremlin, rain-soaked fuses saved Moscow's historic district. Mortier left the city and rejoined the army with the 5,000 survivors of his Young Guard. By the time he covered the distance between Krasnöe and the Berezina River, the Young Guard had been reduced to 1,500 men. During the German Campaign of 1813, he again commanded the Young Guard, which helped deliver the coup de grâce at Lützen and Bautzen.

In 1814, Mortier received command of the Old Guard.[29] As noted, Napoleon originally directed Mortier to Belgium before ordering him to Langres. The return march was brutal. Crossing the Ardennes on atrocious roads in the midst of winter exhausted man and horse, yet Mortier's 1st Old Guard

Division marched 200 miles in fifteen days. The men had not rested since leaving Trier in December. Napoleon chose his most elite units to bar Schwarzenberg's path. Mortier and his men would not disappoint their emperor. For almost fifteen days the Imperial Guard delayed the invasion of Champagne and provided the French army the necessary time and space to concentrate at Châlons-en-Champagne. According to one historian: "Mortier was more than a good corps commander or an ideal subordinate. . . . Seldom given independent command for long or with many troops, he consistently showed his unfulfilled potential. . . . As a trainer, disciplinarian, administrator, and particularly caretaker of horses, he was ahead of most of his colleagues. As an honest and modest human being, Mortier surpassed them all."[30]

Laferrière-Levêque's cavalry established and maintained contact with Thurn's and Gyulay's forward troops. On the morning of the 12th, a strong French patrol found Crenneville's division west of Chaudenay on the main highway from Vesoul. After repulsing the French cavalry with his main body, Crenneville forwarded a detachment that pursued the enemy troopers until nightfall. This Austrian unit decided to pass the night by visiting the wine cellars of Chatenay-Vaudin. Mortier estimated the "Bavarian" post to number no more than 300 men with four pieces of artillery. Determined to bloody his adversary's nose, he dispatched Colonel Georges Albert at 10:00 P.M. with 300 men to greet the Austrians. Led by locals and marching in complete silence, Albert's men came within one mile of Chatenay-Vaudin when an Austrian picket hailed them with "Wer Da!" Receiving no response, the Austrians fired their carbines and fled to rally the troops at Chatenay-Vaudin. Fearing his mission had failed, the colonel boldly decided to make the best of what appeared to be a bad situation. Rather than retreat, he ordered the chasseurs and grenadiers of his detachment to cover the last mile to Chatenay-Vaudin quickly. The French arrived just as the staggering Austrians formed for battle. A calm and composed Albert divided his troops into three detachments: twenty-five *chasseurs-à-pied* attacked the village on the right, twenty-five grenadiers charged through the front gate, and the third group blocked the Austrians' line of retreat. Albert's assault succeeded brilliantly; every Austrian was killed except the commander, two officers, and twenty-five soldiers, all of whom surrendered. Albert held Chatenay-Vaudin until departing for Langres at dawn – Austrian patrols observed from a respectful distance.

Informed of Gyulay's advance on Langres, Thurn sought to facilitate the movement by distracting the French. On the morning of the 13th, he led his Streifkorps along the Dijon–Langres highway to Longeau. The Austrian commander expected to find a small French post of perhaps fifty men. Unfortunately for him, Mortier recognized the need to secure this town to cover the approach of supply convoys from Auxonne. On the evening of the 12th, the marshal posted two dragoon squadrons and 400 grenadiers at Longeau. At 7:00 A.M. on the 13th French skirmishers received Thurn's lead squadron

Map 23. The region between the Marne and the Aube.

with a brisk fusillade. Although surprised by the strength of the resistance that his men encountered, Thurn continued the skirmish until 11:00 A.M. Learning other French troops had reached Chalindrey to threaten his right, Thurn conceded the field and departed eastward in the direction of Fayl-Billot. In his report to Schwarzenberg, the cavalry commander stated his losses at thirteen killed, nineteen wounded, and eleven missing. Conversely, Mortier's brief to Berthier states the French assumed the odious task of interring forty-four mainly Bavarian corpses in the environs of Longeau, and the enemy had withdrawn toward Fayl-Billot with thirty wagons filled with wounded. French losses amounted to only three killed and twenty wounded. Elsewhere on the 13th, another French reconnaissance mission along the Langres–Vesoul road overran the Austrian post at Chaudenay and continued toward Fayl-Billot. Not far from Chaudenay, the chasseurs encountered three infantry posts and one squadron. After taking sixty prisoners including two officers, the French withdrew.[31]

On the 13th, the main body of the Austrian III Corps reached Fayl-Billot. Because of poor reconnaissance, Gyulay had no clear idea of the size of the French force that held Langres. Mortier's diligent harassment of the entire line of Austrian forward posts only made matters worse.[32] Through constant outpost skirmishing, Mortier intimidated his Austrian counterpart. Rather than conduct a general reconnaissance on the 13th, Gyulay chose to maintain his position ten miles east of Langres at Fayl-Billot until the I and IV Corps could support him. As for the Württembergers, Gyulay's patrols could not proceed beyond the Saône, which flooded its valley, and so found no sign of their approach. The main body of Colloredo's I Corps marched to Combeaufontaine, twenty miles east of Fayl-Billot, where it arrived that evening. Alois von Liechtenstein's II Corps assumed the blockade of Besançon on the 11th. Further west, Austrian forces flooded Bourgogne. Moritz von Liechtenstein's 2nd Light Division marched through Dole before turning northwest to reach Auxonne on the 13th, while the bulk of Hesse-Homburg's Austrian Reserve occupied Dole.[33]

The intelligence gleaned from prisoners provided Mortier with a general overview of an increasingly dangerous situation. He learned Gyulay's corps faced him, and the cavalry that had been repulsed on his right at Longeau consisted of Bavarian, Austrian, and Hungarian elements. Allied cavalry on his left threatened to sever his line of retreat by moving west through Bourbonne-les-Bains to Montigny-le-Roi and then enveloping Langres from the north. According to his 14 January report to Berthier, locals informed him of the march of 2,000 infantry, 1,200 cavalry, and four guns along the old Roman road to Chalindrey. French reconnaissance indicated the enemy appeared to be concentrating to attack the marshal's forward posts in the villages between Langres and Chalindrey. He moved up 200 infantry to support the cavalry, which maintained its positions. Concerned by the activity of Allied patrols twenty miles slightly northeast of Langres at Bourbonne-les-Bains, where the highway forked with one branch continuing to Langres and the other running to Chaumont, Mortier speculated that the enemy could be preparing to march to the latter to sever his line of retreat. An assortment of infantry, cavalry, and customs agents numbering less than 300 men formed the post at Bourbonne-les-Bains; they had orders to retreat on Langres or Chaumont if the Allies appeared in great number.

Mortier informed Paris that Langres lacked munitions, provisions, and forage. On his own initiative, he summoned an artillery convoy from the depot at Auxonne, which arrived on the 15th with four 12-pounder guns and 8,500 pounds of powder, but no cannon balls or gunners. He ordered the manufacture of 60,000 cartridges from the powder and lead that he found at Langres and purchased at his own expense. In view of the shortages the marshal discovered, he asked how the emperor could consider Langres an extremely important position? Mortier requested additional regular troops to place in his front line because the outpost skirmishing led to the loss of several brave men of the precious Old Guard, who in his opinion should be used as a reserve. Nevertheless, he assured Berthier that if the enemy attacked on the 15th, he would repulse him.[34]

On the 14th, Gyulay shook himself free of his malaise and launched a general reconnaissance with General Ferdinand Peter de Fresnel's division. Covered by a thick fog that engulfed the flat terrain of the region, the Austrian infantry advanced en masse and drove the semicircle of French posts that guarded the approaches to Langres all the way to the fortified city itself. In response, Mortier posted 8,000 men on the hills of the Sts. Geosmes suburb south of Langres. An ineffective cannonade ensued until Fresnel withdrew to Chalindrey for the night; the main body of the III Corps remained at Fayl-Billot. Gyulay believed he had encountered only three battalions and 600 cavalry.[35]

Mortier's intelligence indicated Allied troop strength had increased to between 7,000 and 8,000 infantry, which occupied the narrow space between the villages Balesmes and Chalindrey, less than two miles from Langres.[36] Once again the marshal requested more manpower – his men and horses were still exhausted after the taxing march from Belgium. Although Drouot informed him that General Claude-Etienne Michel's 2nd Old Guard Division, temporarily commanded by General Joseph Christiani, would arrive on the 16th, Mortier did not expect it until the 18th. "At this moment," he explains to Berthier, "it is very important to unite all resources to quickly secure Dijon and Chalon-sur-Saône, rescue Gray, occupy in force Bourbonne-les-Bains and Vesoul, and to reassure the unfortunate inhabitants of the regions invaded by the enemy, who have suffered the most from this war."[37]

Gyulay intended to follow up his operation of the 14th with an attack on the 15th. He concentrated his corps on the outskirts of Langres, where it remained throughout the day. At dusk after a long, fruitless day, the Austrian commander ordered his men to stand down. News of the approach of the IV Corps from the northeast probably accounted for Gyulay's decision to postpone the attack. Marching from Épinal on the 13th, the Württembergers struggled along treacherous, ice-covered roads that spanned the sixty-mile stretch of mainly hilly terrain between Épinal and Langres. Thirty-six hours later the corps reached Vauvillers, fifteen miles east of Bourbonne-les-Bains. The Württemberger cavalry continued southwest to Jussey, where they established communication with Gyulay's cavalry.[38] Learning the Saône's floodwaters had prevented the Austrians from completing a pontoon bridge at Jussey, Crown Prince Frederick William issued orders for the march to continue west toward Bourbonne-les-Bains on the 15th. Early that morning, Stockmayer led the three light battalions, 2nd Cavalry Regiment, and 1st Horse Battery of the Württemberger advance guard across the Saône at Jonvelle and covered half the distance to Bourbonne-les-Baines. Frederick William's main body passed the night at Jonvelle.[39] A courier from Vesoul reached Jonvelle with a letter from Schwarzenberg stating the attack on Langres would occur on the 18th. Strong French forces occupied Langres, and thus the commander in chief wanted the IV Corps to reach the battlefield no later than 1:00 P.M.[40] To avoid arriving too early, Frederick William slowed the pace of his march to rest man and horse. On the 16th, the main body of the IV Corps maintained its position, while the 7th Infantry Regiment, 4th Cavalry Regiment, and 2nd Horse Battery drove Mortier's post from Bourbonne-les-Bains, where the crown prince transferred his headquarters after his men secured the town.[41]

Elsewhere, the units of Army Groups Langres and Franche-Comté continued moving south and east of Gyulay. Colloredo's I Corps reached positions just east of Fayl-Billot.[42] General Ilya Mikhailovich Duka's Russian 3rd Cuirassier Division paraded through Vesoul to join Gyulay's cavalry on the 16th. Fifty-five miles east of Langres, the head of the Russo–Prussian Guard finally reached Vesoul on the 16th. Farther east, the French rejected Bianchi's 14 January demand to surrender Belfort.[43] Complying with his orders, Bianchi turned over the blockade to Rayevsky's Russians and directed his remaining brigade toward Vesoul with the intention of reaching Langres on the 18th with his entire division.[44]

Thurn's report on 14 January prompted Schwarzenberg to redirect elements of Army Group Franche-Comté to support the operation against Langres. According to Thurn, an informant claimed that more than 50,000 French troops stood between Dijon and Langres: "One tells the army Napoleon will arrive to take command, but this emissary assures me the field officers have affirmed that the emperor will not come." Unlike the inhabitants of the Haute-Saône Department, Thurn warned that the inhabitants of the Haute-Marne appeared decidedly hostile.[45] Consequently, Wimpffen, who was en route to Dijon with the 2nd Division of Colloredo's I Corps, was directed to cross the Saône thirty miles south of Langres at Gray. He informed Schwarzenberg of his intention to turn north to reach Langres on the 18th.[46] South of Wimpffen, Hesse-Homburg's Austrian Reserve reached Pesmes on the road to Dijon and then turned north to Gray, which it reached on the 16th.[47]

On Schwarzenberg's extreme left wing 150 miles south of Langres, Bubna's operation stalled. He did not execute Schwarzenberg's 7 January order to march through Dole and Auxonne to Dijon but instead continued toward Lyon. Believing Bourg-en-Bresse could not be held, the French Line troops who guarded the *chef-lieu* withdrew to Lyon on the 11th. Bubna easily drove the remaining National Guard units from Bourg that same day, thus establishing his division thirty-five miles north of Lyon. Austrian reinforcements also arrived in the region. East of Bourg, Prince Gustav of Hesse-Homburg moved up the 1st Brigade of Moritz von Liechtenstein's 2nd Light Division. That same day, the 11th, Bubna issued the following proclamation to the inhabitants of the Ain Department:

> Regarding the inhabitants of Bourg who dared to take up arms and fight the Allied troops under the walls of this town. Forced to abandon them, they have not escaped my discretion; their names are known to me. You know the laws of war; I can dispose of their lives and their property. But, deaf to any calls for vengeance, I will treat them with a restraint that will inspire in them regret over their conduct. I hear with great amazement that the villains have spread the rumor that I have burnt the town. If overly credulous inhabitants enter the walls of Bourg they will see calm and tranquility reign here and a provisional administration established. I appeal to the citizens of this town who have witnessed the generous manner in which I have stopped a combat that would have been disastrous to them. It is thus the way of the troops of the Allied armies. This moderate conduct proves to you how much they are faithful to the proclamations of their sovereigns.[48]

Meanwhile, Austrian cavalry pounded the roads leading to the Rhône and the Saône to confuse the French over Bubna's actual objective. His scouts pushed toward Mâcon and Chalon-sur-Saône, spreading alarm throughout the countryside. In response, French prefects and commissars worked to organize a defense of the Saône's bridges and fords in accordance with the emperor's 6 January orders. Napoleon issued instructions for all bridges over the Saône to be fortified with tambours and palisades and prepared for destruction if need be. He specified that National Guard units would perform the labor and guard all of the bridges along the 110-mile stretch of the river between Port-sur-Saône and Mâcon.[49] The regional officials responded by summoning all healthy men between the ages of twenty and fifty. Local units were to be immediately mobilized and formed into companies. Lacking muskets, the French authorities distributed hunting rifles, sabers, pikes, scythes, and any farm implements that could be used as weapons. One National Guard unit was to be formed in each canton to complete these measures. Drums would sound the warning at the mere rumor of the enemy's approach.[50]

After disobeying Schwarzenberg's direct order and despite the arrival of these additional forces, Bubna became timid. He spent the next three days covering his flanks, securing his communication with Zechmeister in Geneva, and waiting for Schwarzenberg's authorization to continue his operation. Although the main body of his division remained idle at Bourg-en-Bresse, one detachment of fifty hussars secured the bridge over the Saône twenty miles to the west at Mâcon after striking a deal with the municipal authorities to respect private property. A second Austrian unit occupied Nantua sixteen miles east of Bourg on the road to Geneva. On the other hand, the Chalonnais descended from their mountains, barricaded the bridges, and built redoubts. Protected by the National Guard of Autun and the inhabitants, Chalon-sur-Saône and its bridge escaped an Austrian coup de main, only to fall to Hesse-Homburg a few days later. Elsewhere, Simbschen entered Savoy and published an appeal to the Savoyards on the 14th. An Italian noble, the count de Sonnaz, repeated the proclamation in the name of Victor Emmanuel, king of Sardinia.[51]

Lyon had not escaped Napoleon's attention. On 23 December 1813, he named his former minister of the interior, Jean-Antoine Chaptal, extraordinary-commissioner to Lyon. After the Allied invasion was confirmed, Chaptal received "intense instructions, whose execution would be overseen by the government's secret agents," to organize the resistance.[52] In January, the emperor created the Army of Lyon and appointed Marshal Pierre François Augereau to command this paper tiger. Napoleon planned to form this army from the eighteen battalions of Musnier's Réserve de Genève and thirty-six National Guard battalions. Utilizing these forces, Augereau's mission included covering Lyon, retaking Geneva, and falling on the Allied line of operations in Franche-Comte.[53] On the 11th, the emperor notified Clarke that after French forces regained Geneva, Musnier would garrison the city with 5,000 to 6,000 men, thus implying that these troops were immediately available.[54] Three days later Napoleon issued orders for Suchet to transfer one division (8,000 to 10,000 men) and two-thirds of the cavalry from his Army of Catalogne to Lyon. Suchet would follow with the rest of his army as soon as the peace with Spain became official.[55] On the next day, 15 January, Bonaparte dictated lengthy orders concerning the organization of Augereau's army. He wanted Musnier's eighteen battalions infused with 20,000 conscripts. In addition, between five and six battalions at Marseille and Toulon were to depart for Lyon immediately. Finally, all available battalions (between ten and twelve) from the 7th, 8th, and 9th Military Districts likewise would converge on Lyon. He assured Berthier that these disparate units would "form a first rate army."[56]

Augereau arrived at Lyon on 14 January and met with Musnier to plan the defense of France's second city. Musnier reported having 1,200 men and 500 conscripts at hand; both French commanders realized this number would not suffice to hold Lyon. Knowing the Allies would not allow him the luxury to wait for Suchet's army to complete a march of almost 300 miles, Augereau believed the *levée-en-masse* had to be enforced to complete the mobilization of his army. Finding few resources for the defense of the city in Lyon itself, the marshal left on the following day. He rode fifty-five miles south along the Rhône to Valence in the 7th Military District to accelerate the mobilization of southern France. Musnier remained at Lyon with his 1,700 men. "The enemy," states Augereau's extremely pessimistic report to Berthier "can move on Lyon by both banks of the Rhône and the right bank of the Saône. As a result, Lyon is in great danger. He will probably attack tomorrow. The force we have in disposable Line troops is no more than 1,100 combatants, if one can call combatants men who, for the most part, received their arms yesterday and still do not know how to use them. Fear is painted on all their faces. You should regard Lyon as taken. . . . I shall do what I can to raise the mood of the public, if it can be, because it has fallen in a most distressing way."[57] "The rich families [of Lyon]," adds Beauchamp, "and the most affluent inhabitants hoped to escape a crisis whose result could repeat the catastrophe which, in the disastrous year of 1793, had caused the ruin of Lyon. They abandoned the city and fled to all parts of the Midi. . . . The goods, the merchandise were sent from Lyon to be hidden in the mountains of Beaujolais and Auvergne." According to Beauchamp, Extraordinary-Commissioner Chaptal and the chief municipal authorities also "were on the run."[58]

Concerned over the alleged French concentration in Savoy and unaware of the weakness of Lyon's garrison, Bubna remained idle at Bourg-en-Bresse on the 15th.[59] Although he had only twelve weak squadrons at his disposal, this cavalry should have provided adequate intelligence over the situation at Lyon. Rather than seize the initiative and execute a bold stroke that would have made up for lost time, Bubna continued to grope blindly the thirty-five miles of terrain that separated him from Lyon. On the 16th, he felt secure enough to make plans to leave Bourg on the 17th after wasting five days. Satisfied over the security of his communications with Zechmeister and somewhat convinced the situation in Savoy was not as bad as earlier reports indicated, Bubna planned a timid march ten miles *southeast* to Pont-d'Ain rather than southwest toward Lyon, ostensibly to "take post on the direct [line of] communication with Geneva." He also directed Zechmeister to drive into Savoy with a small detachment of five and one-half battalions, two squadrons, and one battery. "Since we have a major interest in occupying the capital of Savoy in order to encourage and support the uprising of the *Savoyens*, I have instructed Zechmeister to furnish the population with the means to take up arms and leave his main body at Chambéry because he has nothing to fear for Geneva for the moment and I plan to sever the enemy's communication with Italy through Mont-Cenis."[60]

On 16 January, Austrian patrols proceeded all the way to the walls of Lyon and exchanged small-arms fire with Musnier's men. Fearing his garrison would not hold, Musnier moved his forces north of the city to a position between the angle formed by the confluence of the Saône and Rhône Rivers on the 17th. Following a skirmish with Austrian hussars later that day, Musnier withdrew west across the Saône. That evening, Bubna learned the French had evacuated Lyon. An Austrian negotiator reached the city gates and demanded an interview with the mayor to deliver Bubna's summons to surrender. From his horse, he could see a hostile mob assembled on the wharf, the *place des Terreaux*. Jeers and insults rained upon him; some even shouted for his death: "A bas le parlementaire, à l'eau, en Saône!" Fearing for his life, he was brought to Musnier, who exploited the situation by exaggerating both his own forces and the exasperation of the Lyonnais. He concluded by advising the Austrian to avoid the rage of a frantic mob. Beauchamp maintains that it was the report of this negotiator that caused Bubna to hesitate and abort the operation to take Lyon.[61]

Unfortunately for the Austrians, some patriotic inhabitants of the Ain Department broke the dikes that reclaimed the swampy lowlands northeast of Lyon and thus flooded the roads around Pont-d'Ain. This forced Bubna to retrace his steps on the 18th to the direct road from Bourg-en-Bresse to Lyon. "Despite my desire to capture this city," continues Bubna's report to Schwarzenberg, "I did not think it would be wise to surrender myself to this temptation. Thus, for the 18th, I decided to reconnoiter Lyon and possibly enter it. But, during the night, I learned the enemy had cut the road on several points. He appeared to have decided to defend the city, which he had in fact re-occupied during the night of 17–18 January and the people took up arms to participate in the defense."

Bubna wasted the 18th maneuvering and reconnoitering but ultimately decided against an operation to capture Lyon. "Since I have at my disposal only few infantry, since I have many sick, since my five battalions provide at most 2,000 disposable and usable effectives, it appeared too risky for me to attempt a coup de main on Lyon in terrain that did not favor me and did not offer any advantageous position for my artillery. I limited myself to leaving my advance posts in front of this city to observe all that passes there." Events on the 19th caused Bubna to lose heart altogether: "It is clear to me that two parties exist in Lyon, the one, which is hostile to us, can only maintain itself with the aid and the support of the troops. One has confirmed that this group would have tore to pieces and killed one of our negotiators without the intervention of an officer of the gendarmes."

At sunset that evening, a sharp skirmish erupted between the Austrian and French posts around Lyon's St. Clair gate. The Austrians drove back the French and penetrated the suburb of la Guillotière. At 6:00 P.M., 1,200 reinforcements arrived from Valence, which Musnier immediately utilized for a counterattack. His troops drove the Austrians from Lyon's suburbs. Bubna withdrew all his posts northeast to Meximieux on the 20th and further to Point-d'Ain on the 21st. "Because I was too weak to occupy the city, I found it too dangerous to leave my advance posts before Lyon," concludes an overly propitious and truncated report of his operations. "Due to the actual circumstances, I did not think I could attempt to capture Lyon, but I have at least succeeded in attracting the enemy's attention to this place, fixing it, immobilizing his forces, and preventing him from making a movement against the Bohemian Army." Regardless of these self-serving comments, the French could not attempt any operation from Lyon against Schwarzenberg's left simply because they lacked troops.[62] Both Bubna and Schwarzenberg realized this. Yet instead of reprimanding Bubna for his lack of initiative, the cautious Schwarzenberg accepted his excuses.[63] While Bubna withdrew, 900 reinforcements with twenty guns reached Lyon on the 20th; Augereau himself returned on the next day with 200 light cavalry. Bubna squandered a golden opportunity to take this great city of southern France. "The capture of Chalon-sur-Saône," comments Beauchamp "could not compensate for the check before the second city of the empire; the moral effect, above all, was prodigiously in favor of Napoleon."[64]

Bubna's subordinate, Zechmeister, approached his task in Savoy with much more zeal than his commander exhibited at Lyon. Fifty-five miles east of Lyon, Zechmeister divided his brigade into three columns to advance against Rumilly and Annecy on the 18th. By 3:00 that afternoon, the Austrians secured both points. According to Zechmeister's estimates, Marchand, the newly appointed commandant of the 7th Military District, had held Rumilly with 500 men. Ten miles to the east, 600 men defended Annecy. Behind these forward posts, 400 additional troops stood at Alby and 500 at Albens. "Yet these troops all contained only conscripts and customs agents in their ranks," reported Zechmeister. For the 19th, he planned to unite his brigade at Albens and continue south to Aix-les-Bains, where locals claimed approximately 2,000 French troops had assembled. "It is impossible for me to say if I will proceed the day after tomorrow against Chambéry, where the enemy has three regimental depots and where, if he succeeds in rallying his troops, he can oppose me with 3,000 men, who likely will be nothing more than customs agents and conscripts. Everywhere the people have received me with cries of '*Vive le roi de Sardinia*'."[65]

At the approach of Zechmeister's advance guard, a French force of 1,600 men with three guns evacuated Aix-les-Bains late on 19 January. Darkness and heavy rains ended operations on the 19th, but Zechmeister succeeded in occupying Chambéry on the 20th after the French continued their retreat further south.[66] Thirty miles north of Grenoble and only ten miles from the

Isère Valley, Chambéry provided the Austrians a commanding position in Savoy and southeastern France. Thus, Bubna's patrols could inform him of all French activity between the Rhône and the Isère. Bubna did not fail to maximize Zechmeister's success in his reports to Schwarzenberg to mask his own failure at Lyon.[67] On the same day that Bubna withdrew to Pont-d'Ain, 21 January, Zechmeister moved south toward Grenoble. At Montmélian, the Austrians surprised Dessaix, forcing him to withdraw across the Isère to Chavanne before he could blow that town's vital bridge. Zechmeister's troops held Montmélian on the 22nd and 23rd, despite increasing French pressure.[68]

Bubna's lack of fortitude quickly unraveled the progress he had made and emboldened his adversary. After sending three weak companies to reinforce Zechmeister, the Austrian commander decided to continue his retreat to a position that would allow him to observe Lyon and cover both Geneva and Chambéry. Leaving a post of six squadrons and one battalion at Meximieux to patrol the environs of Lyon, Bubna withdrew first to Bourg-en-Bresse. There he posted six squadrons, two battalions, and one battery to maintain order in the Ain and Jura Departments. Meanwhile, French forces under Legrand drove the Austrians from the bridge over the Saône at Mâcon and fortified the position. Rather than make an attempt to recapture Mâcon, the timid Bubna continued his retrograde movement in the opposite direction. By 26 January, he was back at Geneva – an unbelievable turn of events that allowed Augereau to utilize Lyon as a rallying point for the mobilization of southern France. Had Augereau displayed the initiative Napoleon expected, he could have done much harm to the Allied war effort by severing Schwarzenberg's communication through Switzerland, a scenario the commander in chief solemnly feared.[69]

While Bubna conducted his unauthorized, lackluster campaign, the same demons that accompanied Schwarzenberg from Lörrach continued to haunt his headquarters at Vesoul. Intelligence provided little news over the French force at Langres. He believed 15,000 soldiers of the Old Guard held the fortified city. This convinced Schwarzenberg that Napoleon recognized the importance of the position. Moreover, the presence of the Old Guard indicated to Schwarzenberg that Napoleon himself would soon arrive at Langres.[70] He reiterated his instructions for Army Group Alsace to advance southwest rather than support Blücher, whom he figured was at Metz. To his credit, the generalissimo confirmed the directive for Army Group Langres to attack the fortified city on the 18th. According to his orders, the IV Corps would march west to Montigny-le-Roi, turn southwest, and assault Langres from the north. Gyulay's III Corps followed by Colloredo's I Corps – altogether 35,000 men and 120 guns – were to march due west on the road from Fayl-Billot. To operate on the left wing, Colloredo's 2nd Division under Wimpffen would advance northwest from Gray to Longeau, deploy on the Langres–Dijon road, and attack Langres from the south. Schwarzenberg ordered the

artillery of each assault column to lead the march and he wanted the men
to carry ladders to storm the city. Hesse-Homburg's Austrian Reserve was
instructed to provide flank and rear coverage against any French troops that
issued from Dijon, while the Russo–Prussian Guard would move up to Fayl-
Billot to form the general reserve. Schwarzenberg wanted everything to be in
place and the assault columns in front of Langres by 1:00 in the afternoon on
the 18th.[71] "At Langres we will have somewhat of a hard task, but we will
count on the protection of the Heavens," he confessed to his wife. "Perhaps
we approach the end?"[72]

Mortier sensed the inevitable attack as early as the 15th when his patrols
informed him that Allied forces reached Bourbonne-les-Bains. This news,
combined with Gyulay's resolute stand before Langres, indicated an imminent attack. After receiving Napoleon's "General Instructions," the marshal
deemed he had to withdraw from Langres to defend the road to Paris and
to avoid being outflanked.[73] He also felt the urgent need to preserve the Old
Guard for the emperor's use. "The dragoons and the chasseurs-à-cheval are
absolutely exhausted – it is impossible for me to say otherwise," he explained
to Berthier.[74] On the other hand, he was loathe to surrender Langres without a fight. Consequently, he decided to defend Langres, but to ensure his
line of retreat, he moved the grenadiers-à-cheval to positions on the road to
Chaumont. At Langres itself, the attitude of the townspeople changed as they
began to fear that the Guard's presence would prompt the enemy to attack: the
destruction of their homes and businesses would be the result. They glared
at Mortier's bearskins who labored to place the city in a state of defense.
Regardless, Mortier predicted that "the departure of the Imperial Guard will
place the inhabitants in the greatest consternation: our arrival had raised their
courage, once we depart, fear of the enemy will paralyze them."[75]

The news did not get any better. At Chaumont, Prefect Gabriel-Joseph de
Jerphanion of the Haute-Marne Department received on 15 January a letter
from François Roger, the mayor of Joinville, telling of the evacuation of Nancy
and Ney's retreat to Void. Although the Allies severed direct communication
along the Meuse between Langres and Toul, the marshal must have received
a copy of Roger's letter.[76] In both of Mortier's 16 January reports to Berthier,
his first sentence states he had received news of the fall of Nancy on the 13th.
He assumed Victor withdrew from the Moselle to the Meuse, and probably
Marmont had as well.

By noon on the 16th, Mortier had made his decision: the Guard would
evacuate Langres early on 17 January. That morning the marshal stated his
case to Berthier: "The enemy in front of me has been reinforced. One believes
a new column of 13,000 men coming from Épinal will turn toward Chaumont.
Dommartin is occupied and the enemy reached Montigny-le-Roi this morning. I am outflanked! One estimates I have 25,000 troops facing me; this number is probably exaggerated, but reinforcements have been steadily arriving

for four days . . . all villages in the region are occupied." The grenadiers-
à-cheval received orders to depart Rolampont at 4:00 A.M. on the 17th and
proceed to Chaumont, where Mortier planned to spend the night of 17–18
January. To prevent the 2nd Old Guard Division from marching into an
ambush, he ordered Christiani to unite with him at Chaumont. Reaching
Chaumont before the Allies became the key to Mortier's escape. If Coalition
forces gained Chaumont first, they could then cross the Marne and block the
Guard's retreat. In addition to securing Chaumont, Mortier instructed the
grenadiers-à-cheval to occupy Laville-aux-Bois in order to observe the road
from Montigny-le-Roi. Adding that he had not received any news from Ney,
the marshal informed Berthier of his plans to fall back on Troyes if the Allies
advanced from Nancy.

Because the total evacuation of Langres would "entail serious disadvantages," Mortier named Colonel Simon de la Mortière commandant and
ordered him to hold the city for as long as possible but to spare it from an
assault. To delay the enemy's entry into Langres by feigning a defense, Mortier
selected fifty of the "most fatigued" chasseurs and grenadiers-à-pied to form
the nucleus of the garrison. He hoped the presence of these bearskins would
reassure the inhabitants and encourage the 400 men of Langres's Civic Guard
as well as the twenty-five conscripts who had escorted the munitions convoy from Auxonne and now found themselves manning the ramparts. "I have
spoken with the sub-prefect, the mayor, and the commandant of the National
Guard," continues Mortier's account to Berthier, "they have promised to do
what they must and to defend themselves. They know through experience the
suffering of the unfortunate inhabitants in the regions invaded by the enemy;
their insidious and perfidious proclamations promise security and protection,
but as soon as the Allies (notably the Bavarians) are masters of a commune,
they [the inhabitants] will suffer the most revolting vexations." Much like
the lamentations of Milhaud and Grouchy during the evacuation of Colmar,
Mortier goes on to decry the army's inability to utilize the "good spirit that
animates the inhabitants of the countryside; they are exasperated, but without
means of defense. It is very unfortunate that one has disarmed the countryside;
if the enemy suffers a reverse, I hope we could have behind him numerous
vengeurs."[77]

In his last report from Langres, penned at noon on the 16th, Mortier
repeated much of what he had stated in his early briefs, but the tone was
more desperate. "The enemy is always in front of me in the same position; all
reports I have received indicate he has been reinforced. At this moment, one
has informed me that the post at Longeau has been attacked." He explained
to Berthier that although Langres's fortifications and thirteen guns sufficed
to defend the city against cavalry, in no way could it withstand the attack of
an army corps. The repair of the fortress works had hardly progressed due
to a shortage of labor and the frozen ground. "This garrison is completely

insufficient," he concluded.[78] With these final remarks, Marshal Mortier prepared to turn over the defense of Langres to Colonel Mortière and his assortment of invalids, National Guardsmen, conscripts, fifty veterans called out of
retirement, and three foresters.

Leaving the bivouac fires burning and a rearguard at Langres, the bearskins
filed out of the city around midnight. The rearguard followed at 6:00 A.M.
and took post at Vesaignes, halfway between Langres and Chaumont. That
evening Mortier quartered in Chaumont. On the left bank of the Marne,
one detachment occupied the hills of Marnay, which dominated the river
crossings between Vesaignes and Chaumont. Any Allied forces pursuing from
Langres would have to cross the defile of Marnay. On the right bank, a second
detachment of dragoons and infantry secured the town of Laville-aux-Bois on
the Montigny-le-Roi–Chaumont road. Patrols from this second detachment
detected Württemberger cavalry on this road less than ten miles southeast of
Chaumont at the town of Biesles.

By nightfall on the 17th, the Guard reached Chaumont. "One has assured
me the prince of the Moskowa is at Bar-sur-Ornain," states the marshal's
report from that evening. "I am in position to avoid being outflanked, thus
conforming to the emperor's orders. Unless he has other plans, I will remain at
Chaumont. If the prince of the Moskowa advances, I will reoccupy Langres."
He added that disease was spreading among his troops, who were extremely
exhausted, notably the dragoons and chasseurs-à-cheval, "who have not had
a moment of rest since our departure from Trier. The infantry is equally
fatigued." To support his tired soldiers, he summoned the three battalions
(1,800 men) of General Louis-Auguste-Victor de Bourmont's 113th Regiment to march fifty miles from Troyes to Chaumont. The whereabouts of
the 2nd Old Guard Division equally concerned Mortier. It was supposed to
reach Neufchâteau on the 16th, but Mortier had not received any news from
Christiani and feared he had been forced "to make a retrograde movement."[79]

On the Allied side of the front, the events at Langres proved once again
the ineptness of the Coalition's cavalry. The entire day of the 17th passed
without Gyulay's forward posts detecting the French retreat. Around 2:00,
one of Schwarzenberg's aide-de-camps escorted by two Russian staff officers
rode toward the city gates to open negotiations with Mortier. Encountering
no French posts or patrols, they continued into the suburbs and learned of
Mortier's retreat. Upon reaching the gates, they summoned the small garrison
to surrender, but Mortière refused. Although a stunned Gyulay wondered
how his forward posts could have missed the departure of two enemy divisions, he wasted little time. At 4:30 P.M. his advance guard deployed before
the "Dijon" gate and issued a summons for the city to surrender, backed by a
few rounds of artillery. "The townspeople of Langres conducted themselves
very poorly after my departure," moans Mortier. "They voluntarily opened
the gates to the enemy after several National Guardsmen threw down their

muskets." Indeed, Mortière's plans to defend the city encountered opposition from the mayor and the population of Langres in general. A mob warned Mortière's men not to resist the Allies, and the National Guard declared that it would not fight. In view of the internal dissent, Mortière signed the capitulation at 6:00, and Gyulay's troops entered Langres shortly after.[80]

Gyulay pushed his own cavalry, Duka's 3rd Cuirassier Division, and Crenneville's light infantry division through Langres to Humes on the road to Chaumont; the main body of the III Corps camped at Langres. Colloredo's I Corps moved into position between Langres and Longeau, where also Wimpffen's 2nd Division arrived on the road from Dijon.[81] In the excitement, Gyulay failed to inform the Württembergers of Mortier's retreat. In fact, Frederick William did not receive this surprising news until the early hours of 18 January. He spent the 17th leading the IV Corps from Bourbonne-les-Bains to Montigny-le-Roi in compliance with Schwarzenberg's instructions to reach Langres at 1:00 on the afternoon of the 18th.[82] Stockmayer led the advance guard to Frécourt on the road from Montigny-le-Roi to Langres; the main body of the IV Corps reached the former. At Montigny-le-Roi, Jett's cavalry brigade of eight squadrons and one horse battery turned on the road to Chaumont to cover the corps's right against a flank attack from this direction. Jett's vanguard of two squadrons patrolled toward Chaumont, stopping at Biesles. The officer commanding this detachment reported that French forces had evacuated Chaumont. Frederick William also instructed Platov to sever French communications along the Chaumont–Châlons-en-Champagne road. In his report to Schwarzenberg, Frederick William included the latest installment of Napoleon's campaign of misinformation, which, no doubt, added to the commander in chief's headaches: "You can see from the newspaper I send you that in Paris one is forming twelve legions of National Guard at whose head Napoleon and the dignitaries of his court have placed themselves."[83]

Nevertheless, Schwarzenberg was relieved by the bloodless capture of Langres. "We reached this important point with ease as I suspected, my Nani," he wrote his wife, "but I am convinced that storming it would have cost us much blood, in the least the capture of twelve new guns with a large supply of powder is never insignificant."[84] On the night of the 17th he issued new orders for the following day. Poorly served by Gyulay, whose cavalry lost all contact with the French, Schwarzenberg assumed Mortier retreated to Chaumont and kept going north. He expected his troops would take Chaumont just as easily as they had Langres. The Allied commander directed Frederick William's IV Corps and the three regiments of Duka's 3rd Cuirassier Division to advance on Chaumont. As the Württembergers marched on the right bank of the Marne along the Montigny-le-Roi–Chaumont road, the Russian heavy cavalry would follow the Langres–Chaumont road down the left bank to the defile at Marnay. Behind the Russians, Gyulay would concentrate his corps at Humes, while Colloredo remained between Longeau and Langres.

Farther south, Hesse-Homburg's Austrian Reserve and Liechtenstein's 2nd Light Division continued toward Dijon, which Schwarzenberg wanted in Austrian hands by the 19th.[85]

In the cold hour before dawn on the 18th, the Württembergers assembled. To form the advance guard, Frederick William reinforced Jett's brigade with one infantry regiment. Jett commenced the advance at 7:00 A.M. in a downpour. Stockmayer, who should have followed directly behind Jett, mistakenly set off for Langres. The time spent correcting Stockmayer delayed the march of the corps's main body, which brought up the rear of the column. The two squadrons that formed Jett's vanguard proceeded toward Chaumont on the road from Montigny-le-Roi. Passing through Biesles around noon, the Württemberger troopers clashed with French cavalry and infantry at Laville-aux-Bois. Frederick William, who joined the advance guard, rushed forward with the 4th Cavalry Regiment followed by the 2nd Cavalry Regiment and the horse artillery. Reaching Laville-aux-Bois, the crown prince charged the French left flank and threatened to envelop their position. The arrival of these superior numbers forced the French to yield the road, retreat through Laville-aux-Bois, and recross the Marne to Chaumont's suburb of Choignes. Two French battalions posted on the right bank covered the cavalry's passage of the river and halted the Württemberger pursuit.

Chaumont stood on a hill overlooking the left bank of the Marne. As for manmade defenses, crumbling ramparts and a trench extended across the city's eastern and southern sides. Nature, however, provided Chaumont's best protection. The city was situated on a peninsular surrounded by the Marne and Suize Rivers, which merged north of the city. The steep banks and considerable depth of both rivers posed difficult obstacles, particularly because the Marne was flooding. Two stone bridges spanned the Marne, one at Choignes, and the other further north, directly across from Chaumont. Heavy artillery covered the approaches to both crossings, which were guarded by strong infantry posts. A rearguard at Chamarandes held the road from Langres.

Mortier initially thought the Allies were conducting a strong reconnaissance and so moved three batteries – two horse and one heavy – to the left bank of the Marne to keep the Württembergers at a respectful distance. While the French positioned their batteries and unlimbered the guns, the Württemberger 3rd Cavalry Regiment came up followed by Jett's light infantry. The soldiers continued their advance on the Montigny-le-Roi–Chaumont road to the point where the lane leading to Choignes veered from the main road. Behind them the 7th Infantry Regiment continued along the main road to a hill facing the northern bridge directly across from Chaumont, where the regiment halted just out of range of Mortier's artillery. During this time, Franquemont gradually brought up the main body of the corps to support the advance guard. Seeing the Allied infantry arrive, Mortier pulled back his two battalions to the left bank.

To take Choignes, the 1st Battalion of the 9th Jäger Regiment moved through a gorge north of the lane that led to the bridge at Choignes. Two Württemberger horse batteries unlimbered across from Chaumont to answer the French artillery. Despite the fire of the French batteries, which Mortier claimed to have "great effect," the jäger reached Choignes's bridge, charged across, and entered the portion of the suburb on the left bank of the Marne. Once across the bridge, they received fire from the houses on both sides of the street. Unable to counterfire because the heavy rains soaked their cartridges, the jäger were forced to clear the French from house to house. Time hardly permitted this arduous and bloody task. Although the battalion managed to take the village for a moment, the grenadiers-à-pied of the Old Guard, the dreaded bearskins, advanced from Chaumont, fixed their bayonets, and charged into the disorganized Württembergers. Cold steel decided the affair. No match for the Imperial Guard, the Württemberger light infantry broke. The bearskins drove a good number of the Allied soldiers into the river, the violent current of which claimed many. According to Mortier's after-action report, Allied corpses littered both the village and the bridge. His grenadiers took sixty prisoners in the process, while purportedly suffering only five wounded.

Elsewhere, Duka had dispatched six squadrons along the old Roman road that ran along the left bank of the Suize to reach Chaumont through this river valley. Although the reasons are unclear, this mission did not succeed. With his remaining ten squadrons, Duka moved north on the main Langres–Chaumont road. Outside of Vesaignes, the Russian cavalry encountered enemy vedettes. The French conducted a slow, fighting withdrawal to Marnay's defile; infantry waited to ambush Duka's squadrons where the road narrowed between the hills of the left bank and the Marne. More accustomed to shock tactics than the duties of light cavalry, the cuirassiers imprudently charged into the tight, embanked valley. Greeted by a strong fusillade from the hills that dominated the defile, the Russians fell back on Rolampont after losing several men and horses. Recognizing that the terrain rendered his heavy cavalry useless, Duka requested the support of Austrian infantry. Gyulay complied that same night, sending one battalion, one half-battery, and one light cavalry squadron to open the road on the next day.

After waiting in vain for the anticipated Russian diversion, Frederick William postponed any further operations. His entire corps had arrived, but reconnaissance revealed the overall strength of Mortier's position. In view of the Guard's apparent commitment to a serious resistance, the crown prince refused to attempt another frontal assault until the III Corps advanced along the left bank of the Marne to assail Chaumont from the south. Although he had not received any word from Gyulay, the Württemberger hoped this advance would take place on the next day, the 19th. With this in mind, he sought to fix the French at Chaumont until the III Corps could assault Mortier's exposed right flank. For the remainder of the 18th, the French and Württemberger gunners engaged in an artillery duel that tested the mettle of the latter's horse batteries, which could barely stand against Mortier's heavier guns. The French made a few attempts to retake the portion of Choignes on the right bank of the Marne, but the charge across the bridge proved too costly. By dusk, flames engulfed the suburb and combat ended. Frederick William's headquarters passed the night at Biesles, with the main body of the corps withdrawing into tight quarters between this town and Laville-aux-Bois. Jett's advance guard maintained its position on the right bank of the Marne and spent a miserable winter night bivouacked in streaming rain and on ground so drenched that the men sunk into mud up to their shins.[86]

Prisoners revealed to Mortier the designations of the Allied units that faced him. He learned the corps that attacked Choignes was indeed the one that arrived from Épinal and consisted mainly of Württembergers commanded by their crown prince. He identified the Russian heavy cavalry that appeared at Marnay as being part of Gyulay's corps. The marshal estimated that at least two Allied corps still faced him. Interestingly, these details did not concern him as much as the operations of Victor, Marmont, and especially Ney. Similar to the days prior to the evacuation of Langres, Mortier tied his fate to that of Ney. "I would remain here tomorrow," he informed Berthier on the evening of the 18th, "but having learned the prince of the Moskowa passed St. Dizier yesterday on the way to Châlons-en-Champagne, I believe I must continue my movement on Troyes." Mortier's stout Guard divisions could have held Chaumont for perhaps another five days. With the flooding Marne separating him from the aggressive Württemberger crown prince, he could have harassed and intimidated Gyulay, and by extension Schwarzenberg. Nevertheless, Victor's collapse, Marmont's retreat, and Ney's impotence convinced Mortier to abandon the Marne and fall back across the Aube to the Seine. For the 19th, he planned to march twelve miles northwest to Colombey-les-deux-Églises. Unless the Allies pressed him, he would slowly fall back another fifty miles through Bar-sur-Aube to Troyes on the Seine, where he hoped to receive orders from Napoleon. The only good news for Mortier was that he finally established communication with Christiani's 2nd Old Guard Division. To his "great satisfaction," he learned the division would reach Brienne on the 19th. "Thus I will be in perfect position to unite with it either at Bar-sur-Aube or Troyes." To justify his retreat further, the marshal again impressed upon Berthier the "extremely exhausted" condition of his men as well as the growing problem of desertion.[87] Regardless of the reasons, another French marshal failed to recognize Napoleon's desperate need to treat every mile of French territory as vital to his political survival.

On the 18th, Schwarzenberg moved his headquarters to Langres: the goal that had played such a preponderant role in Allied war planning had been achieved. After spending more than one week maneuvering his corps to reinforce Army Group Langres, the effortless capture of the city caused another change in the commander's attitude. Although he suspected Napoleon was concentrating his army eighty-five miles north of Langres at Châlons-en-Champagne, Schwarzenberg again stripped units from his center.[88] Colloredo, who moved the I Corps to St. Maurice a few miles east of Langres, received orders to turn south and march forty miles to Dijon. Schwarzenberg instructed Hesse-Homburg's Austrian Reserve, which already had reached Mirebeau-sur-Bèze fifteen miles northeast of Dijon, to support Colloredo. To compensate partially for this reduction of combat power, Bianchi's division marched into Langres on the 18th. In the rear of Army Group Langres, the Russo–Prussian Guard reached Port-sur-Saône, with orders to cover the remaining thirty-five miles to Langres by the 20th. Schwarzenberg also made an attempt to move up Army Group Alsace by ordering Wittgenstein's VI Corps to advance as soon as possible between Commercy and Joinville to secure the Bohemian Army's right in unison with Wrede.[89]

In the current situation, all four French marshals were withdrawing along the eastern and southern fronts. The press of both the Silesian and Bohemian Armies constricted the entire French line to the seventy-two miles between Verdun and Chaumont. Schwarzenberg correctly assumed that Napoleon would concentrate his army at Châlons-en-Champagne. Rather than continue on his current course and repeat the strategic envelopment that had produced the great victory at Leipzig, Schwarzenberg decided to stall his drive and divert manpower away from the Verdun–Chaumont theater. He based his justification on the exhaustion of the troops – a disputable claim since his army had marched 125 miles in twenty-eight days, an average of less than five miles per day. To justify the routing of Army Group Franche-Comté to Dijon, the generalissimo claimed the handful of French troops who held the city demanded that he secure his left flank. Clausewitz maintains that the need to send Hesse-Homburg and Colloredo to Dijon is "difficult to understand." According to Clausewitz, Schwarzenberg's reasons – to maintain communication with Bubna and indirectly support him, to cover the blockades of the fortresses in Alsace and Franche-Comté, and to secure the left flank of his army – "obeyed the common rules of strategy, i.e. they are the dark ideas of habit. To indirectly support the operations of 12,000 men with a reserve of 40,000 is very poor economics."[90]

Indicative of the peace party's memory of Napoleon's Russian disaster and Schwarzenberg's own reluctance to campaign deep in hostile territory, anxiety over his army's line of retreat continued to haunt him. "Louis [Alois Liechtenstein], who commands the blockades of Besançon and Ft. Joux," wrote a relieved Schwarzenberg, "reported that [Colonel August Georg von] Leiningen received the capitulation of Ft. Joux on the 16th. Now the line of retreat through Pontarlier, which to me is extremely important, is completely free."[91] After wasting much time marching the long, circuitous route through

Switzerland and Franche-Comté to Champagne, Schwarzenberg again hesitated when he should have driven forward, united his separate columns, and effected the union of both Allied forces by supporting the march of the smaller Silesian Army.

In the strict sense of coalition warfare in which each member is required to subordinate its national interests to a "greater purpose," Schwarzenberg's decision to halt at Langres appears baffling, if not bizarre. Yet however contemptible Austrian actions may appear, they can be understood. Ever since Metternich rejected Hardenberg's January 1813 request to form an Austro–Prussian bloc to mediate between France and Russia, the Austrians had been striving to work outside the confines of a coalition. Forced by Napoleon's rejection of the Reichenbach Protocols to join the Sixth Coalition in August, Metternich gradually and covertly undermined the Anglo–Russian–Prussian war aims and steered the Coalition toward achieving Austria's national security objectives. The terms of both the Teplitz Accords and Frankfurt Proposals are glaring examples of his policy. Influenced by Metternich, the Allied commander in chief viewed Austria's objectives as more viable than those of the Coalition, which seemed to be growing increasingly unrealistic thanks to the Russian tsar. As for the general reasoning behind Schwarzenberg's decision to halt at Langres, Nicholson offers an excellent explanation that is rooted in the history of coalition warfare:

> In 1813 [and 1814], as in 1914 and 1939, that purpose was the defeat of a common enemy. Soon, however, as ultimate victory seems assured, the consciousness of separate interests tends to overshadow the sense of common purpose. The citizens of the several victorious countries seek rewards for their own sacrifices and compensations for their own suffering; they are apt to interpret these rewards and compensations in terms, not international, but of national requirements. And the jealousies, rivalries, and suspicions which in any protracted war arise between partners to an alliance generate poisons which war-wearied arteries are too inelastic to eliminate.[92]

Metternich's monumental letter of 16 January provides the specific and immediate motives that prompted Schwarzenberg to squat at Langres. "At the moment I cannot explain all that has passed with the detail that I desire," wrote Metternich, "but I tell you that Lord Castlereagh will arrive here tomorrow at the latest. The first hour of the discussion with him will decide the salvation of the good cause in the present course. If he digresses too much, it will be necessary for us to make other arrangements. In either case, it is extremely important that you do not extend your military movements beyond strict necessity." "To avoid exposing yourself to an *échec*," continues Metternich's letter to Schwarzenberg, "you will wait for new instructions – without saying anything to anyone – before undertaking new offensive operations, and these directions can be given only as a result of the political state of affairs."[93]

Metternich also hoped to stop Blücher by urging King Frederick William to issue orders for the Silesian Army to stop at Metz; this ploy failed.

Mortier's Guard divisions departed Chaumont at 6:00 A.M. on the 19th covered by a rearguard of 200 grenadiers-à-pied and 300 dragoons, who remained amid the smoldering ruins of Choignes. With no sign of Coalition forces either pursuing along the right bank of the Marne or keeping pace on the left bank, Mortier's column stopped for the night at Colombey-les-deux-Églises. Upon arriving, the marshal received Berthier's letter from 10:00 P.M. on 17 January. The detailed communiqué included the emperor's advice in case the enemy converged on Langres in force and Mortier could not hold his position. Again behind the flow of events, Napoleon instructed the marshal to transfer all artillery to Vitry-le-François and Troyes. Mortier himself would lead his troops to Châlons-en-Champagne "slowly and only if it is absolutely necessary." Indirectly the emperor made yet another plea to yet another marshal to hold his front. Berthier added that he should defend Langres or at least Chaumont to remain online with Victor. Including the 2nd Old Guard Division and the 113th Line, the major-general promised the arrival of reinforcements that would increase Mortier's corps to 25,000 men.[94]

"If I receive the reinforcements you promise me," responded the duke of Trevise, "I will be able to master the enemy who is at Langres, but instead of the 14,000 bayonets you claim, in reality I have only 4,500 and 2,200 cavalry, all excellent troops, but extremely tired." Mortier explained that he had ordered the 2nd Old Guard Division and the 113th Infantry Regiment to unite with him on the next day, the 20th, at Bar-sur-Aube, where he intended to make a stand. He again posed the question of whether the emperor truly wanted him to sacrifice the Old Guard in the position that he now found himself. Moreover, the fatigue, privations, weather, and discouragement did not spare his elite soldiers. "The 2nd Old Guard Division commanded by Christiani has less than 3,000 men under arms; I must tell you that it is being weakened daily by desertion." After informing Berthier of his retreat and intention to reach Bar-sur-Aube, he insisted that the poor state of defense in which he found Langres had convinced him to evacuate the fortified city. "If Langres had been placed in a state of defense, if one had been able to provide a suitable garrison, we would still be masters of this important point."

According to the reports he received, "the enemy is moving in two strong columns, the first is on the road to Troyes. The other, by that of Châlons, seeks to gain Paris." Knowing Victor and Ney had retreated, a retrograde movement to Bar-sur-Aube appeared to be Mortier's only means to escape an envelopment.[95] Unlike his normal rambling, conversational letters, he further developed this idea in a concise brief to Berthier from Bar-sur-Aube on the next day. "The column under the orders of the crown prince of Württemberg, whose march I have traced through Bourbonne-les-Bains and Montigny-le-Roi, and with whom I fought on the 18th, was detached from the Austrian army after the affair [at Épinal] with the duke of Bellune; it sought to arrive at Chaumont before me." Thus, Mortier concluded that Neufchâteau, only forty miles north-northeast of Langres, "already was occupied when I was at Langres."[96] And so the blame game continued. Had Victor or Ney held Neufchâteau, Mortier would still be at Langres. Such justification, however plausible, did little for the emperor's cause.

Mortier completed his retreat to Bar-sur-Aube on 20 January; a rearguard of four battalions, four squadrons, and six guns under General Louis-Michel Letort remained at Colombey-les-deux-Églises (Map 24). As planned, Christiani's 2nd Old Guard Division and Bourmont's 113th Line reached Bar late that afternoon. Reports indicated the enemy probably would move against Mortier's position with all available forces. The marshal wasted little time pushing Christiani's relatively fresh troops into forward positions to relieve Friant's weary warriors. Five miles east of Bar at Lignol on the highway to Chaumont he posted 200 infantry and 400 cavalry. Bourmont's troops secured the bridge over the Aube at Dolancourt, six miles west of Bar. A long defile that ran through the Clairvaux Forest and parallel to the Aube guarded the southern approaches to the French position. Behind these defenses Mortier's men rested in freezing temperatures after enduring six consecutive days of weather that the marshal described as "awful." This extreme cold came on the heels of the weather system that had produced heavy rain and a sudden thaw on the 16th.

Other than the arrival of Christiani and Bourmont, the only other positive news was the flooding of the Aube and its tributaries, which further protected Mortier's position by limiting the number of accessible points. On account of floodwaters and muddy terrain, only two highways could be used to reach Bar-sur-Aube, which itself stood on the right bank of the river. Coming from Chaumont and cut by several ridges, the first paralleled the right bank of the Aube at a healthy distance until approaching the river close to Bar itself. This road led to a long plateau that extends between Voigny and Bar, and thus provided a formidable barrier to protect the latter's eastern approaches. Washed-out country roads made turning this position difficult. The second highway ran north from Châtillon-sur-Seine along the left bank of the Aube. It snaked through the wooded hills and the riverbank between Clairvaux and Bayel before crossing the bridge at Boudelin and merging with the highway coming from Chaumont one mile east of Bar.[97] The strength of this position induced Mortier to include in his brief to Berthier the rough outline of a counteroffensive, although it is possible the marshal included this merely for the emperor's consumption.[98]

At Bar-sur-Aube Mortier received Berthier's most recent dispatch, dated 10:00 A.M. the 18th: 115 miles from Paris, couriers still required more than forty-eight hours to deliver the emperor's orders. Berthier reiterated the need to defend Langres or, if he had to retreat, to hold Chaumont at all cost. If

Mortier did retreat to Chaumont and Langres did not capitulate, the marshal should consider a counteroffensive to save the city. Berthier also requested intelligence concerning Allied movements between Besançon and Belfort because the emperor still did not know the details regarding the forces operating between Langres and Dijon.[99]

Around 8:00 on the morning of the 19th, Württemberger patrols found the left bank of the Marne abandoned and Chaumont evacuated. Just like his escape from Langres, Mortier's conscientious measures paid dividends. Frederick William's advance guard immediately occupied Chaumont, but Mortier's divisions had such a head start, the Württemberger pursuit could not catch up. At the head of the Bohemian Army, the IV Corps moved into billets in and around Chaumont, where Frederick William established his headquarters.[100] Schwarzenberg instructed him to maintain close contact with the French.[101] An advance guard took post at Jonchery, and patrols warily rode toward Colombey-les-deux-Églises. The Württembergers proceeded through Blaisy but observed French cavalry holding the road to Colombey-les-deux-Églises.

After masking Mortier, whose consecutive retreats indicated this marshal likewise had no desire to fight, a concerted push by Schwarzenberg could have brought the Bohemian Army to Joinville, St. Dizier, and even Bar-le-Duc. With Blücher advancing west from Nancy, Schwarzenberg could have reached the Marne ahead of Ney, Victor, and Marmont. The result would have been the utter destruction of French combat power. Instead, the III Corps moved to Foulain on the left bank of the Marne a few miles south of the IV Corps at Chaumont; the Russo–Prussian Guard and Reserve cantoned between Fayl-Billot and Combeaufontaine. Thirty-two miles northeast of the IV Corps, Wrede's V Corps held Neufchâteau on the Meuse. To the south, Hesse-Homburg's Austrian Reserve and Colloredo's I Corps entered Dijon – fifty miles south of Chaumont – on the 19th and 20th, respectively, to take possession of the capital of Bourgogne.[102] Bianchi's division also turned toward Dijon, reaching Gray on the 20th.[103] In these positions, all corps received orders to halt, except the Russo–Prussian Guard and Reserve, which was scheduled to reach Langres by the 21st. Rather than drive forward, Schwarzenberg wanted to gain time for the occupation of Langres to duly influence the political situation. In addition, he wanted to slow operations for Wittgenstein's VI Corps to fill the gap on Wrede's right.[104] As for assisting Blücher, once again Schwarzenberg preferred to see the impetuous Prussians and their Russian comrades bloodied as they cleared the front of the Bohemian Army. An opportunity to end the war in January was intentionally wasted.

In consequence, the Bohemian Army did little on 20 January. Following Thurn's Streifkorps, Gyulay's lead division, now commanded by General Joseph von Haecht in place of the sick Crenneville, crossed the Aube and marched to Courban as the III Corps extended west toward Châtillon-sur-Seine, where the peace talks would be held. Gyulay's main body moved west from the banks of the Marne to Arc-en-Barrois on the small Aujon River.[105] Colloredo, who marched his I Corps almost forty miles south from Langres to Dijon, received orders to turn around and troop another forty miles north-northwest to Châtillon-sur-Seine.

Schwarzenberg used the respite to again make pointless changes in his order of battle. Colloredo had to detach Wimpffen's division so the I Corps consisted only of Ignaz Hardegg's and Wied-Runkel's divisions. But to rein-force the I Corps and make an impression at Châtillon, Schwarzenberg attached Liechtenstein's 2nd Light Division, Bianchi's division, and one divi-sion each of grenadiers and cuirassiers from the Austrian Reserve. In turn, Hesse-Homburg received command of Wimpffen's division, which would assist the II Corps and the remaining units of the Austrian Reserve – one division each of grenadiers and cuirassiers – with blockading the fortresses in the army's rear and maintaining communications east to Switzerland and south to Bubna.[106]

Schwarzenberg wanted a more detailed picture of what lay before the front of his army than Blücher's reports provided. He thus directed Platov, who had reached the Marne, to proceed eighty miles southwest through Joinville and Bar-sur-Seine to Auxerre to cover the Bohemian Army's left. From Auxerre, the Cossacks would turn north between the Aube and Seine to terrorize Paris. Sherbatov would support this operation by moving between the Marne and Aube to cut French communications. To ensure the execution of these orders, Schwarzenberg requested that officers from Barclay's staff accompany Platov.[107] On the 21st, the commander in chief also issued orders for Pahlen to reach Joinville as soon as possible with the cavalry of Wittgenstein's VI Corps.[108]

Schwarzenberg either gave up his attempts to divine where Napoleon planned to concentrate his army or purposefully wanted to steer his own army in another direction. On the 21st, he informed Wrede of his intention to continue fifty miles west from Chaumont toward Troyes even though it appeared Napoleon would assemble his forces at Châlons-en-Champagne.[109] On the same day, he notified Blücher that the III, IV, V, and VI Corps as well as the Russo–Prussian Guard and Reserve would proceed to Troyes. For some reason, he did not feel inclined to reveal his plans for the reinforced I Corps and simply stated that its march depended on the news he expected to receive the following day.[110]

In the eighteenth century, Schwarzenberg's march on Troyes would have placed in check the French army at Châlons-en-Champagne, as the generalis-simo explained to Wrede: "when the Allied army arrives at Troyes, Napoleon, threatened on his right wing, will find it impossible to remain at Châlons. He will be forced to move forward, and can be attacked by the Allied army in a position it chooses in advance." However, the chess match of attrition that dominated the theories of warfare during the preceding century had given way to the bloodbath of annihilation that governed modern warfare. A score of battles from Austerlitz to Leipzig attest to this fundamental principle of Napoleonic warfare. Moreover, Napoleon proved far superior on the chessboard than any contemporary he faced. Whether Napoleon blundered, scrambled, or waged war in a manner that can be viewed as the military equivalent of realpolitik, the chances of outmaneuvering Bonaparte never favored an opposing commander. Perhaps realizing this basic fact, Schwarzenberg really intended to sit on the Chaumont–Langres–Dijon line hoping Metternich would end the war at the peace table.

In the meantime, the Württembergers maintained contact with Mortier's troops. On the 21st, Stockmayer led the advance guard further northwest to Juzennecourt on the Chaumont–Bar-sur-Aube road. Reports indicated the French still occupied Colombey-les-deux-Églises. Württemberger and French patrols clashed in the Dhuits Forest just south of Colombey. On this day, Thurn's Streifkorps and Haecht's division occupied Châtillon-sur-Seine, where Caulaincourt quietly awaited the opening of negotiations.[111] Typical of Austrian operations, Gyulay summoned Haecht's division to retrace its steps to Courban, turn north, and march to Laferté-sur-Aube to cover the advance of the III Corps, which Schwarzenberg ordered to march north toward Bar-sur-Aube rather than west to Châtillon-sur-Seine. Gyulay's main body resolutely moved north on the 22nd to reach Clairvaux and linked with Haecht's division on the 23rd. That same morning a French raid on Gyulay's forward post of light cavalry at Clairvaux snagged twelve Austrians before the main body of the III Corps started to arrive.[112] East of Gyulay, outpost skirmishing continued in the Dhuits Forest between the French and Württembergers, creating confusion among the latter regarding the strength of the French force that held Colombey. This unsettled Frederick William, who postponed a surprise attack on the French post scheduled for the 23rd. Instead, a staff officer conducted reconnaissance on the 23rd to clarify the situation. He encountered only French vedettes in the Dhuits Forest but confirmed earlier reports of a strong rearguard at Colombey. According to intelligence collected by patrols from both the III and IV Corps, Mortier's main force held Bar-sur-Aube.[113] In addition to the rearguard at Colombey, the French maintained posts at Baroville and Bayel on the opposite side of the Clairvaux Forest, which stretched before Mortier's position. On the basis of this information, Frederick William and Gyulay planned to attack Bar-sur-Aube jointly on the 24th; Schwarzenberg concurred.[114]

Tsar Alexander's arrival at Langres on 22 January explains the change in Gyulay's march direction and Schwarzenberg's approval of a plan to attack Bar-sur-Aube. Although Metternich warned him to be prepared for an encounter with the tsar, Alexander simply overwhelmed the Austrian commander. "Tsar Alexander has arrived," he wrote Metternich on the 22nd; "he thinks of nothing but mischief and fighting. Without openly contradicting him, I pointed out that the enemy's position is in truth very bad, but that I believe it is necessary to remain faithful to the principle of forcing a peace that corresponds to the outlook of the Coalition's sovereigns."[115] Tired of Schwarzenberg's languor, the Russian monarch openly charged him with sabotaging the war effort.[116] Alexander ordered Schwarzenberg to resume the offensive; the commander in chief countered that his men needed rest – a lame excuse that increased the tsar's suspicion.[117] The Austrians so infuriated him that he refused to conduct any negotiations with Napoleon. He expressed his intent to continue the offensive and dictate peace at Paris.

In Metternich's letter of 16 January, the Austrian minister explained to Schwarzenberg his strategy to bilk Alexander. His plan depended on the suspension of all military operations and the prevention of a decisive battle. He urged Schwarzenberg to postpone any offensive until Metternich clarified the political situation. Schwarzenberg received this letter on the 18th – the same day he achieved his operational goal, the capture of Langres. He agreed with Metternich and believed the easy capture of Langres would bring about the successful conclusion of the war by allowing Metternich to exploit the advantages of the Allied position during the upcoming peace negotiations. Moreover, Alexander's intention to place Bernadotte on the French throne appalled Schwarzenberg and strengthened his commitment to Metternich.[118] As a result, the commander in chief immediately suspended offensive operations to await new instructions from his liege. As for Metternich, his grasp of the situation began to loosen somewhat in the days just prior to Castlereagh's arrival at Basel. Unlike Schwarzenberg, Blücher had not received an order to halt.

After taking Chaumont, Schwarzenberg continued his methodical strategy of maneuver instead of crushing Mortier. Like Langres and Chaumont, the French marshal would eventually evacuate Bar-sur-Aube once he realized the growing threats to his flanks. In compliance with Metternich's advice, the generalissimo preferred to await the outcome of his current chess match with Mortier. However, in the presence of the tsar and without Metternich at hand, Schwarzenberg yielded. Alexander left Schwarzenberg few options. Out of political prudence, he decided to satisfy the tsar's demand to mark his arrival at the front with a bold stroke. The Austrian commander thus authorized the operation of the III and IV Corps against Bar-sur-Aube. Nevertheless, an indifferent Schwarzenberg allowed Gyulay and the crown prince of Württemberg to proceed according to their own plans. He had so little interest in the operation that he actually left Langres to meet with Hesse-Homburg in Dijon to discuss the occupation of Franche-Comté and Bourgogne.[119]

On 21 January, Mortier received a letter the emperor dictated on the 19th. Napoleon learned of the marshal's retrograde movement and expected him to be at Bar-sur-Aube. To bolster Mortier's resolve, Bonaparte revealed his plans to move toward the marshal. He included the news that Berthier left for Châlons-en-Champagne that same day, the 19th, and that he would soon follow. Mortier was instructed to reconnoiter the roads leading from Bar-sur-Aube west to Arcis-sur-Aube and north to Vitry-le-François. The marshal also learned that Dufour held the bridge at Arcis-sur-Aube on the road from Troyes to Châlons-en-Champagne with four battalions and sixteen guns.[120]

Knowing the emperor would soon reach the Marne relieved Mortier. In addition, his soldiers benefited from the relative quiet by receiving a few days of rest as well as provisions and ammunition. Yet the war granted them no reprieve. On the 23rd, Mortier became aware of Allied forces moving on his center, flanks and rear. The prisoners captured during the raid on the Austrian post at Clairvaux identified themselves as belonging to the advance guard of Haecht's division of the Austrian III Corps. Haecht purportedly reached Laferté-sur-Aube with his main body that morning. According to reports, the crown prince of Württemberg had established his headquarters at Juzennecourt, less than two miles from Mortier's rearguard at Colombey-les-deux-Églises. This led the marshal to believe his rearguard would be attacked on both banks of the Marne sometime that day. Just as alarming appeared the news that a large body of Cossacks – estimated to be 6,000 horsemen – had proceeded from Joinville to Doulevant, where it arrived at 9:00 that morning. Only fifteen miles northeast of Bar-sur-Aube, Mortier feared the Cossacks would converge on his position in conjunction with the Austrians and Württembergers. The Cossacks belonged to Platov, who had received Schwarzenberg's order to raid as far as the Seine, harass French communications, and cover the army's left. Although Mortier had no idea of the nature of Platov's mission, his concern arose from the realization that this Cossack corps could easily cut his road to Châlons-en-Champagne. To block Platov's road and ascertain his intentions, the marshal dispatched 500 infantry, 500 cavalry, and two guns to Trémilly, twelve miles north of Bar-sur-Aube. He also alerted Dufour and recommended he move southeast from Arcis-sur-Aube to occupy Brienne to close the road to Troyes. Despite these security measures, Mortier could not conceal his fear of being overwhelmed. "I count on being attacked tomorrow morning," concludes his report of 23 January. From his point of view, he could not hope to hold Bar-sur-Aube; he requested instructions on whether to retreat to Châlons-en-Champagne or Troyes.[121]

That evening Mortier learned that the detachment he sent to Trémilly arrived just in time to repulse Platov's Cossacks after a heated affair. At Trémilly his troops blocked the Joinville–Brienne road, but reconnaissance indicated the enemy occupied Montier-en-Der, halfway between Joinville and Brienne.[122] At 6:00 A.M. on the morning of the 24th, Mortier's troops took up arms and moved into position to await the imminent attack. To avoid having his forces on the right bank of the Aube cut off should the bridge at

Bar be taken by the enemy, the marshal instructed Bourmont's 1,200 men to occupy the bridge over the Aube at Dolancourt, where the road forked with one branch continuing west to Troyes, the other north to Brienne. Mortier positioned the grenadiers-à-cheval on the road between Dolancourt and Bar. To protect his line of retreat to Troyes, which an Austrian advance along the left bank of the Aube would threaten, he positioned one regiment and three guns to observe the plateau between Proverville and Spoy. Two battalions and the chasseurs held Fontaine and the hills of Ste. Germaine with detachments at Bayel and Baroville. Mortier placed his artillery in three groups. The first (twenty guns) unlimbered on the road to Chaumont. He posted the second (fourteen guns) on the right wing to cover the Boudelin bridge and shell both highways coming from Chaumont and Châtillon-sur-Seine. The third (seven guns) formed the reserve west of Bar and guarded the bridge over the Aube in that town. He arranged the rest of his troops, one battalion of the 1st Old Guard Division and nine of the 2nd, east of Bar on the road to Chaumont. At Colombey-les-deux-Églises Letort's rearguard of four battalions, four squadrons, and six guns continued to observe the road from Chaumont. Thus, Mortier's 13,000 men occupied the high ground on both sides of the Aube that mastered the terrain south of the French position along a front of eight miles. The marshal enjoyed the advantages of terrain and central position against an enemy whose operations would be separated by a river. Despite the strength of his position, he feared being overwhelmed by superior numbers and thus took every precaution to secure his line of retreat. Five hours later, around 11:00 A.M., the Allied columns debouched against him.[123]

According to an agreement between Gyulay and Frederick William, the III and IV Corps would simultaneously assault Colombey-les-deux-Églises and Bar-sur-Aube, respectively. Platov would advance south and support the Württembergers in an attempt to envelop Mortier's left. For the first phase of his attack, the crown prince intended to sever Letort's line of retreat from Colombey by hitting his front and rear at the same time. Stockmayer received command of the left wing column – three light battalions, four squadrons, and one horse battery. He assembled his troops at Juzennecourt around 9:00 A.M. on 24 January and marched due west to Montheries. From there he was to turn north, proceed through the Dhuits Forest, and emerge south of Lavilleneuve to attack Colombey from the west. The right column, commanded by Jett and consisting of two battalions, two cavalry regiments, and one horse battery, formed around 10:00 A.M. and marched on the highway from Chaumont to Colombey. Ostensibly, Jett would reach Colombey just as Stockmayer turned east from Lavilleneuve: both columns would then assault the French position. Frederick William followed Jett's column with a reserve consisting of two battalions, one cavalry regiment, and one foot battery. For reasons unknown, he left eight battalions, one foot battery, and one cavalry regiment at Chaumont – a critical mistake by the assiduous crown prince.

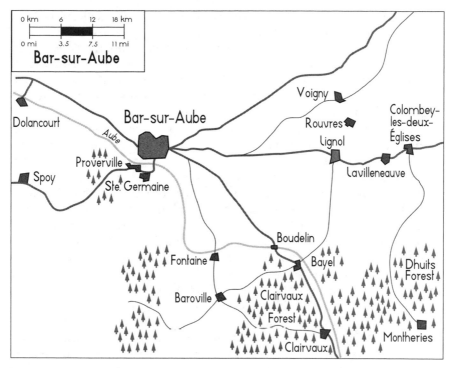

Map 24. Bar-sur-Aube.

The village of Colombey-les-deux-Églises stood at the edge of a high plateau that fell steeply to the southeast and offered the defenders an advantageous position. Although the dense Dhuits Forest concealed Stockmayer's advance, the thick undergrowth slowed his movement. To make matters worse, the Württemberger general failed to locate the path through the forest from Montheries to Villeneuve-aux-Fresnes. The staff officer who served as the guide left the head of the column at Montheries and, as the result of a misunderstanding, the lead units took the wrong road. Another thirty minutes were lost turning the head of the column. To avoid wasting further time, the Württembergers decided to strike the closest road to Colombey. This led Stockmayer's column to a point south of Colombey.

Although the crown prince's plan misfired, it mattered little by this time: Letort already had evacuated Colombey. As Jett's column approached the village, French artillery opened fire. After a few rounds, the shelling ceased, and Letort, guessing his adversary's intentions, withdrew west to Lignol. "Toward 11:00 the enemy debouched in two columns," recounted Mortier in his after-action report to Napoleon, "the first on the road from Chaumont, the second on that from Clairvaux. It was a real attack, and one could not mistake the depth of the columns they presented before us." Frederick William rode forward with the 2nd and 4th Cavalry Regiments and 2nd Horse Battery to cut Letort's line of retreat. The French general reached Lignol the same time as the Württemberger cavalry, but the arrival of infantry support stopped the Germans. Around this same time, a Württemberger hussar squadron made contact with Platov's posts at Bouzancourt, yet the Cossacks refused to participate in the battle, supposedly on account of the poor roads.

"Letort received the order to withdraw from Colombey-les-deux-Églises to Lignol, explains Mortier. "He was pursued by the corps of the crown prince of Württemberg and a swarm of Cossacks. He came online with us, his left in the direction of the plateau of Voigny, which I had occupied, and which we maintained despite the superiority of the forces that he had in front of him." From Lignol, Letort fell back on Mortier's main body between Bar and Voigny. The twenty-gun French battery halted the Württembergers in their tracks. With the majority of his artillery still in the rear, Frederick William could not attack this daunting position. To at least answer the French artillery, he unlimbered the 2nd Horse Battery south of Voigny. During the course of the day, the 1st Horse Battery followed by Austrian heavy battery moved into the battle line to conduct a brutal exchange with the French artillery. Württemberger shells silenced several French guns and blew up two ammunition wagons; numerous corpses littered the ground. The infantry of both columns halted at Lignol because the crown prince did not want to challenge the bearskins in their strong position until the III Corps appeared on the opposite bank. Consequently, the combat on the right bank of the Aube degenerated into an artillery contest that ended at dusk. Frederick William intended to resume the battle on the next day after the main body of his infantry – and he hoped Platov as well – arrived. The Württembergers passed the night at Lignol, Rouvres, and Lavilleneuve, with the crown prince establishing his headquarters at Colombey-les-deux-Églises.

On the left bank, Gyulay's troops conducted their operation with vigor. At 11:00 A.M., the III Corps advanced along the Aube in two columns. The right wing, General Ludwig Alois Joachim von Hohenlohe-Bartenstein's division, easily repulsed the French post at Bayel, which fell back on Christiani's infantry south of Fontaine. Gyulay's left wing column, Haecht's division, drove the French from Baroville. Both Austrian columns advanced toward Bar, becoming engaged in heavy, prolonged, and costly combats that focused on control of the Boudelin Bridge and the village of Fontaine. Hohenlohe-Bartenstein's division attempted to secure the Boudelin Bridge, while Haecht's men stormed Fontaine. Coming in range of the fourteen-gun French battery, the Austrians painfully felt the proficiency of the gunners who served in the Guard Artillery. Hohenlohe-Bartenstein's men failed to take the bridge after suffering numerous casualties. Haecht's men fared no better during a fierce struggle in Fontaine. From Bar, Christiani's battalions counterattacked

Fontaine three times to drive out the Austrians. "Strong masses of infantry from the column coming from Clairvaux attempted to capture the bridge upstream of Fontaine," continues Mortier's after-action report. "My artillery was elongated. Three times Fontaine was attacked with impetuosity, three times the enemy was repulsed."[124] "The affair was murderous," he wrote in a separate dispatch to Berthier, "and despite all his efforts the enemy could not seize Bar-sur-Aube."[125]

Believing he faced 12,000 men with fourteen guns, Gyulay decided to await the advance of the IV Corps along the right bank, but a French counterattack forced the Austrians to continue the struggle. "Having found that it was impossible to outflank this position without sacrificing many lives," states Schwarzenberg's report to the kaiser, "Gyulay decided to await the arrival of the IV Corps; but at noon, the enemy debouched from Bar-sur-Aube and attacked the III Corps. It rejected the enemy and pursued with cavalry up to his positions. The enemy repeated his attacks, which Gyulay successfully repulsed."[126] Around 6:00 P.M., the Austrians finally overpowered the French to win the Boudelin bridge. Despite this victory, a bitter Gyulay complained that the Württembergers made no effort to relieve the pressure on him through a diversion along the right bank of the Aube. He broke off the combat without attempting to sever Mortier's line of retreat by pushing his troops across the hills of Ste. Germaine toward the road from Bar to Dolancourt. Darkness brought an end to the day's combat. Mortier remained in possession of Bar-sur-Aube; the Austrians moved into tight quarters in their sector of the battlefield. Both Allied corps commanders planned to resume the attack on the following morning.[127] Each side presumably sustained around 1,000 casualties.[128]

After conserving his precious Guard units through successive withdrawals from Langres and Chaumont, Mortier did not hesitate to evacuate Bar-sur-Aube. In his report to the emperor at 11:00 that same night, 24 January, the marshal stated his case. According to the 100 Allied officers and soldiers captured during the combat around Bar, Gyulay's corps numbered 30,000 men exclusive of the crown prince of Württemberg's corps, which Mortier estimated to be between 12,000 and 15,000 men. Mortier pointed out that the Allies deployed sixty pieces of artillery including several batteries of 12-pounders. According to his estimates both sides fired a total of 15,000 rounds. "My position is no longer tenable," concluded the marshal. "Tomorrow I will proceed to Vendeuvre to cover the road to Paris. I will camp at the bridge of Guillotière, which offers me a good position and where I will again attempt the fate of battle before I withdraw to Troyes. Please tell me if you think I should march from Troyes to Arcis-sur-Aube. Platov is at Doulevant: His Cossacks flood the countryside."[129]

After writing the emperor and Berthier, Mortier issued orders for the retreat from Bar-sur-Aube to Vendeuvre, the halfway point between the former and Troyes. According to his plans, he would take a position on the right bank of the small Barse river and defend the bridge at la Guillotière "to gain time and cover Paris."[130] Before dawn, the French marched out of Bar-sur-Aube to cover the thirteen miles to Vendeuvre. Just like the evacuation of Langres and Chaumont, the Guard executed Mortier's measures with such perfection that neither the Austrians nor the Württembergers detected their movement. On the morning of the 25th, Allied patrols found Bar-sur-Aube and its surroundings completely clear of French forces. From the sick and severely wounded whom Mortier had to leave behind, the Allies learned the marshal had retreated in the direction of Troyes under the cover of darkness. Gyulay's troops occupied Bar that same morning but did not commence the pursuit until late in the day. West of Bar, his light troops and cavalry found Spoy's bridge over the small Landoin stream destroyed. The Austrians made no attempt to find another passage to extend the pursuit beyond Spoy. Another detachment followed the main road from Bar to Dolancourt but remained well behind the French. Instead of obtaining definite news of Mortier's whereabouts, Gyulay accepted the rumors and conjectures provided by locals and reported by his subordinates. He informed Schwarzenberg that the majority of Mortier's troops withdrew north from Bar toward Châlons-en-Champagne and only a garrison remained at Troyes.[131] Frederick William's Württembergers moved into extensive quarters north of the Aube in the angle formed by the roads that ran north from Chaumont to Joinville and Bar-sur-Aube, with headquarters remaining at Colombey-les-deux-Églises.[132]

After wasting almost an entire month meandering through Switzerland, Franche-Comté, and southern Champagne, Schwarzenberg spent from 13 until 24 January advancing through Langres and Chaumont to Bar-sur-Aube. Unlike Blücher, Schwarzenberg never understood that by accelerating his march he would achieve peace much faster than by slowing his operations to a virtual standstill. He unquestioningly accepted Metternich's guidance and advice. Unlike Blücher's understanding of the maxims of Napoleonic warfare, Schwarzenberg adhered to the principles of a statesman – albeit one of the greatest in history – rather than the lessons that Bonaparte's earlier campaigns provided. Consequently, he stopped exactly at the moment when an energetic offensive could have achieved decisive results. In his massive four-volume work of the 1814 campaign, French historian Weil adequately summarizes this point:

> Before an energetic adversary such as the emperor, it mattered above all to act briskly and determinedly. What would have happened if Napoleon had departed Paris, where his presence was unfortunately necessary, ten or twelve days earlier than he did? If he had been able to concentrate the corps of Mortier, Ney, and Victor, linking them with the troops he brought with him and pounced in succession on the separate columns of the Bohemian Army

echelonned, isolated, and too far apart from each other to offer mutual support? From the start the emperor had wanted to exploit the considerable advantages that existed due almost solely to Schwarzenberg's faulty dispositions. Fearing to risk exposing his army to imaginary danger, Schwarzenberg committed imprudence that Napoleon would have made him atone for if he had not been removed far from his army by necessities of all kind.[133]

With Blücher and Wrede moving to the Marne, Schwarzenberg should have pursued one of two options. He could have rapidly advanced through Langres to firmly establish his army on the Seine to threaten the French capital before Napoleon completed the organization of his scant forces. On the other hand, Schwarzenberg could have masked Mortier and closed on the French marshals in conjunction with Blücher to deliver a decisive pocket battle that would have eliminated the majority of Napoleon's available combat power. Instead, he allowed Austrian politics to master his operations; Mortier's bold operations provided great cover for Schwarzenberg's compliance with Metternich. The Austrian commander first allowed Mortier's relatively weak forces to freeze Gyulay's corps in front Langres for five days. In response to Mortier's demonstrations, Schwarzenberg altered the movement of his army groups and diverted Wrede and Platov from supporting Blücher against Victor, Ney, and Marmont. Although this exposed the Austrian commander to Tsar Alexander's wrath, help was on the way: Castlereagh reached Allied headquarters. In the antichamber, Metternich proceeded with the same speed that Napoleon displayed on the battlefield.

17

The Protocols of Langres

Schwarzenberg rejoined the tsar at Langres on the 24th, but the victory at Bar-sur-Aube did little to stem the growing antagonism. Alexander continued to press for a general offensive. That same day, the 24th, the impatient tsar instructed Toll to issue orders to Platov that captured the essence of the monarch's state of mind: "The tsar orders you to reach Bar-sur-Seine, from where you should continue to Auxon and Sens on the Yonne in order to position yourself on the road that runs...through Fountainebleau to Paris. Since foodstuffs of all kind flow from southern France to Paris...you will occupy with strong detachments Moret and Nemours – the places where all food transports must pass – in order to halt these transports, but do not destroy the foodstuffs, since our army can use it."[1] Such instructions correspond exactly with Gneisenau's belief that Moret should be one of Schwarzenberg's march objectives to master Paris by cutting off its food supply.

The extensive deployment of the Bohemian Army did little to alleviate Alexander's pressure on Schwarzenberg. In Bourgogne on the army's left wing, Colloredo echelonned his I Corps on the road from St. Seine to Châtillon-sur-Seine, Liechtenstein's light division continued toward Auxerre, and the Austrian Reserve occupied Dijon. Alois von Liechtenstein's II Corps remained chained to Besançon. Further south, Scheither's brigade held Chalon-sur-Saône and Mâcon to link Bubna's main body with the rest of the army. On the right wing, Wittgenstein's VI Corps finally reached Nancy, while Wrede's V remained idle on the Meuse between Neufchâteau and Clefmont. In the center, the Russo–Prussian Guard and Reserve loitered around Langres, thirty-five miles south of the head of the army – the III and IV Corps – at Bar-sur-Aube.[2]

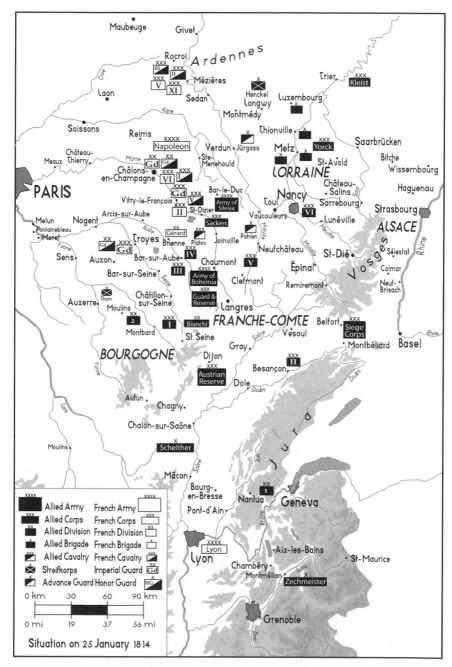

Map 25. Situation on 25 January 1814.

With the objective of Langres secured and questions over Schwarzenberg's next move looming large, a war of words soon engulfed Allied headquarters. Alexander's allies in the Silesian army resumed their paper bombardment of Schwarzenberg's staff. In a letter to Radetzky, Gneisenau urged the Austrians to continue their advance. He described a chance meeting with an old comrade, Count Valory of Louis XVI's Garde du Corps, who had escorted the king on his failed flight to Varennes in 1791 before the French noble left France for service in the Prussian army. Gneisenau described him as "a wise and experienced man of superb character." According to Gneisenau, Valory claimed that "French power is broken. The available troops are conscripts and only few veterans." Of the latter, many had fallen ill after crossing the Rhine and were now dead; the rest were wasting away in the hospitals. The majority of the new conscripts lacked arms and the army in general possessed little artillery. Gneisenau estimated Napoleon could assemble at most 100,000 men around Châlons-en-Champagne. According to Valory, the troops already at Châlons lacked provisions, weapons, and uniforms.

"One is extremely tired of this perpetual war and universally hates Napoleon's rule," Valory supposedly told the Prussian chief of staff. "People, soldiers, officers, and generals curse the emperor, especially those who most depend on him," states Gneisenau's letter Radetzky. "The aura of glory that surrounded his name is gone. With very few exceptions, all are tired of his rule." According to Valory, the French people would gladly bear the burden of the Allied invasion as long as they were "liberated from the monster." Touching on a topic that currently troubled the Coalition, Gneisenau declared that "if a Bourbon was present among our armies, he would be able to do great things in France. The people restrain themselves out of fear the Allied Powers might conclude peace with Napoleon, thus abandoning them to his vengeance. The people wish for nothing more than peace and quiet, and the opinion that such can only be achieved for good by a Bourbon is almost universal. Count Valory has told me this, but others have confirmed it." He also assured Radetzky that the officers charged with collecting intelligence on public opinion verified these statements.

According to the British military attaché, Lord Burghersh, "neither a feeling of national pride, nor the burden of a hostile army, without magazines, and subsisting entirely upon the inhabitants, engaged the people in any effort to assist the government in expelling the invaders from their country. In some places the Allies were received with acclamations. The spirit of the nation seemed broken; the contending armies moved in the midst of the inhabitants without aid or resistance from them; all was suffering and obedience."[3] Regarding a general rising in France, Madame Junot adds: "Doubtless this was naturally to be expected from the bravery and energy of the French people. But he [Napoleon] had worn out all their springs of action – they had lost their elasticity. The most determined and the most active required repose; a general desire for it prevailed from the cottage of the soldier to the palace of the marshal."[4]

As for the continuation of the war, a confident Gneisenau told Radetzky: "Should the French emperor take a position at Châlons, I consider him as good as lost. We, the Silesian Army, will detain him, as long as one supports us, while the other army advances on Paris." Still, Gneisenau did not believe Napoleon would accept battle at Châlons. Instead, the Prussians thought he would fall back to defend his capital. Gneisenau again explained to Radetzky that a battle before Paris "would neither be bloody nor risky. Then we can rest and dictate the peace with circumspection. So near to the goal, will we ever allow ourselves to reach it?"[5]

Such arguments had little effect on Schwarzenberg and the Austrians, who had neither political nor moral grounds to topple Napoleon. Radetzky, the best military mind in Schwarzenberg's headquarters, allowed his doubts over the internal state of the Austrian army to master his strategic thinking.[6] His superior, Schwarzenberg, held an advance on Paris as imprudent both militarily and politically. He also raised the important question of what then? In Schwarzenberg's opinion, taking Paris would not necessarily end the war and could prove to be just as much of a disaster for the Allies as Moscow had been for Napoleon. "Will we find peace there," he asks his wife, "or will we plunge into further chaos? I believe the latter."[7] Others in the Allied camp expressed similar reservations. According to the Russian historian Bogdanovich, Knesebeck argued that "Napoleon's advance from Smolensk to Moscow was his misfortune; it will be the same for us if we march to Paris."[8] A drive on Paris could prompt Napoleon to advance southeast to sever Allied communications with the Rhine – an operation that would be supported by the garrisons in the frontier fortresses still held by the French. "For example," lectures Knesebeck in a letter to Gneisenau, "let us assume Napoleon has assembled at Moulins[-en-Tonnerrois]. However, what if we believe he is at Paris and march in that direction, but he marches from Moulins through Besançon to Belfort – what will our situation be then?"[9] Should Napoleon execute his famous *manoeuvre sur les derrière*, he could cut Allied supply lines and communication in the midst of winter. This concern was never far from Schwarzenberg's thoughts: "I returned late last night from Chaumont," he explained to his wife in a letter of 21 January, "where I sought the crown prince [of Württemberg] and reconnoitered the point to build a bridgehead over the Marne for I never fail to secure my line of retreat."[10] To avoid such a disaster, Schwarzenberg concluded that Paris could not be the objective of an Allied offensive.

Knesebeck's quill likewise did not miss the opportunity to participate in the debate. On 22 January, he replied to Gneisenau's letter of the 15th, accepting the general's offer to put aside their differences "in order to work together for the great goal, which I believe we are so near." Yet the chasm that divided the systems of war propagated by the two Prussian officers could not be bridged by a few courteous words. "Nevertheless, I can honestly confess that I do not agree with your idea to move up all corps from the rear. Through this we would place our stakes on one battle and that is too high. Also it is very appropriate to remember that we do not make the mistakes of 1792 for a second time." One by one, he debunked Gneisenau's assumptions. Knesebeck countered that no one in the Allied camp knew for sure where Napoleon would concentrate and only assumed it would be near Paris. He feared the emperor would select a position such as Moulins and "assemble all of the conscripts, gendarmes, customs officials and a part of the Guard and repeat the maneuver of Kaluga as at Moscow. This scenario does not appear entirely unlikely to me because only the boldest move can rescue him." He further explained that because Napoleon could not hope to save Paris, he would look for a radical maneuver to prevent the impending disaster. "If he made such on Geneva or Basel or along the Rhine *he could establish himself with 200,000 men* on our communications and cut-off our ammunition." Before the Allies proceeded one step further, he advocated they first determine where Napoleon planned to concentrate his army. According to Knesebeck: "We have crossed the last hill chain that separates us from the plains of the Marne and the Seine, and we now possess all the great roads between the Rhine and Paris. From this position we must advance without delay – but first we must know where our enemy stands because any miscalculation from now on can be very dangerous." To Gneisenau's dismay, Knesebeck concluded "that the point has come where negotiations must begin; they must be conducted so they do not last for more than ten to fourteen days, and in these fourteen days we must determine where Napoleon has concentrated and direct our operations there. *Without knowing this for sure, I believe any further advance is too dangerous.* This is my opinion – I can be mistaken and beseech you to say so as your duty. If I am perhaps too cautious, you are perhaps too bold."[11] Thus the words of King Frederick William's closest advisor.

Two days later Knesebeck penned another rebuttal of Gneisenau's proposals. "No one knows where the enemy stands in a considerable mass. Should none exist, and instead the enemy has only Mortier, Victor, Marmont, Macdonald and 50,000 conscripts to face us, I will change my views and thus provide a significant voice for us."[12] On the 27th, Knesebeck addressed an exaggerated treatise on the value of the plateau of Langres to Gneisenau, calling it a "Rubicon which one cannot be allowed to cross."[13] Once again the adjutant-general made his position clear by siding with the Austrians. Yet Knesebeck's opinion was based on his own military perceptions, while Metternich directed Schwarzenberg according to politics.

As Knesebeck's friend, Müffling felt he had a better chance of persuading the king's adjutant-general than Gneisenau who, as Chief of the General Staff of the Prussian Army, was a natural rival to Knesebeck's influence over the monarch. Müffling, the quartermaster-general of the Silesian Army, also committed his thoughts to paper in an attempt to convince Knesebeck the time had come for a decisive operation:

> Despite all the rumors over French discontent with Napoleon, I assume their troops will fight and even have success if we make mistakes. But I am convinced that success depends on the speed of our operations. The Parisians have lost their heads, we cannot give them any time to recover . . . we must go forward! What do we fear? If one [Schwarzenberg] cannot decide to lead the entire army into battle, then one must allow the field-marshal [Blücher] to form the advance guard and attack the enemy. Come to us in a few days good Knesebeck, you will not regret it. I repeat: the French Empire is in our hands! If only Schwarzenberg would march straight to Paris and turn over the situation at Châlons to the field-marshal. If he reinforced him with Wrede's troops I guarantee success. According to the opinion of the nation and the troops, Napoleon has already fallen. Even French officers no longer admit he has any military abilities. One wrote from Paris that he sleeps for twelve hours every day![14]

Gneisenau did receive comforting words from his old friend and ally, Stein. The former Prussian minister assured Gneisenau that he shared all of his letters with Tsar Alexander, "who stands uniquely strong and points out the counsel of wretchedness and weakness. The empire of the tyrant will fall – and the cause of the just and of the free will be victorious."[15] This encouraged Gneisenau to respond to Knesebeck on 27 January: "If one wants a fourteen-day armistice, it must be purchased with at least the [surrender of] the fortresses of Strasbourg, Metz, Luxembourg, and Mainz, whereby the garrisons of these fortresses must be neutralized, otherwise they will increase the size of the French army while our own decreases."[16]

Gneisenau also replied to Stein: "Your assurances regarding the steadfast-ness of Tsar Alexander reinvigorate my hope. If the noble tsar proceeds in such a manner he will not only save Europe, as he already has done, but he will also become the benefactor of France. Why should he not drive the ogre from the throne?" He informed Stein of Knesebeck's arguments in favor of an armistice. "This is a risky thing and risky talk," he added, "I must advise against it." He continued his letter with a five-point enumeration of the sit-uation for Stein to show Alexander to undermine Knesebeck, whose ideas would be echoed by Frederick William. In an intriguing example of how the Prussians of the Silesian Army communicated their ideas to the tsar and thus circumvented their own cautious monarch, Gneisenau took his turn to refute Knesebeck's ideas. His first point attested to the weakness, poor composi-tion, and despondency of the French army. "All intelligence we have received from our informants, the royalists, and members of Bonaparte's own gov-ernment confirms this assessment." Even if Napoleon managed to assemble 100,000 to 120,000 men at Paris, "how could such an army defend itself against our troops? And with such troops should we conclude an armistice or even peace? Should our army come all the way from Moscow to be deceived by a despicable traitor a few marches from Paris?"

Gneisenau's second point focused on Napoleon himself and once again spoke of the advantages that could be gained if a Bourbon stepped forward. "One is tired of his tyranny and his overweening ambition. One no longer believes his lies." His third point contained a warning: "one should not allow himself to be deceived by the delusion that the enemy can move against our communications with the Rhine while we advance against Paris. The enemy has no forces for such an offensive." Should Napoleon produce an army and attempt such an offensive, the Prussian still insisted that the Allies advance to Paris. "In France, everything is centralized in the capital, [public] opinion, literature, government, and resources. What is eminent in France through birth, riches, quality, and talent dwells in the capital, and is not spread throughout the land. Conquering the French capital is thus much more significant than taking Vienna or Berlin. By taking the capital, we will paralyze the nerve center of the government and dictate the peace."

In his fourth point, Gneisenau expressed his belief that Napoleon would indeed "place himself immediately before Paris because the mood of Paris is very uncertain and only the presence of an army will insure the tranquility of the capital. There, the entire apparatus of government is in his hands: senators, privy councillors, secret police, and gendarmes." Finally, the Prussian general persisted:

> It is better to dictate the peace than to negotiate. The diplomats are an elite group; they cannot be assigned a definite period for diplomatic negotiations. If they conduct negotiations for an armistice, they will extend these [negotiations] beyond their charge and provide valuable time for Napoleon. *Strategy is the science of the use of time and space. I am less stingy regarding the latter than the former. Space we could always win back, but never lost time.* Providence has led us here. We may take revenge for so much suffering that was imposed on the peoples, for so much wantonness they had to endure, so that 'be warned: learn justice, do not offend the Gods' will stand the test. If we do not do this ... after two years of being idle we will again be threatened with the slave-whip. The noble Alexander will prevent such from happening, but I know certain people who always see phantoms.[17]

With these words, Gneisenau attempted to refute the arguments of Metternich's peace party. He insisted that French demoralization would enable the Coalition to end the war with either a victory over Napoleon's army or the capture of Paris. All was in vain; neither the Austrian camp nor the king of Prussia, under Knesebeck's influence, accepted Gneisenau's proposals. Frederick William's unimaginative nature increased his paranoia, and he was not inclined to attempt any eccentric operation that could possibly jeopardize everything the Coalition gained thus far. The Austrians firmly opposed a drive to Paris, believing it was nothing more than Blücher's desire to experience the refined pleasures of the French capital.[18] Thus, the Prussians of the Silesian Army placed their hopes in Tsar Alexander's ability to minimize the influence of the Austrian-dominated peace party, among whom their king and chancellor were counted.

Into this fray arrived Castlereagh, who had reached Basel on 18 January after leaving London on 28 December 1813. The tsar already had departed for Schwarzenberg's headquarters on the 16th, but left Stein to receive the British statesman on his behalf. Metternich, too, eagerly awaited Castlereagh's arrival. The Austrian perceived this golden opportunity and lost no time exploiting Alexander's absence. One historian even suggests Metternich attempted to convince Castlereagh that the tsar purposefully left Basel to snub the British minister. Regardless, Alexander left behind a letter addressed to Castlereagh that explained the situation and proposed a private meeting as soon as possible. Stein also warned Castlereagh to beware of the crafty Metternich.[19] Castlereagh had no intention of becoming a pawn of either Metternich or Alexander. Quite the contrary, Kissinger maintains that he possessed the power to "decide the fate of the Coalition and the result of the war."[20]

The British Foreign Minister arrived armed with a Cabinet Memorandum dated 26 December. Modeled on the Pitt plans of 1799 and 1805, the Memorandum specified London's national security objectives: maritime rights, the formation of a general alliance, France's dynastic future, and colonial concessions. In short, Castlereagh had to ensure that Aberdeen's imprudent forfeiture at Frankfurt of Great Britain's maritime rights never again surfaced and that the Allies understood London would not submit these issues to international arbitration. Second, Castlereagh would seek to establish a "common interest" of Allied objectives to provide a basis for a firm alliance among the members of the Coalition. Third, the British government would accept a peace with Napoleon remaining of the French throne as long as the terms limited France to its "ancient" frontiers as opposed to its "natural" frontiers. As much as public opinion in Great Britain and the personal wishes of the prince regent desired Napoleon's abdication and the restoration of the Bourbons, the British government did not take direct measures toward this objective. London planned to recognize Napoleon as long as the French themselves considered him their ruler; only if the French people dethroned him would the restoration of the Bourbons be pursued. Aside from maritime rights, the main goal of British policy was the creation of a strong kingdom in the Low Countries; the issue of the French throne remained secondary. London outlined its view of the Coalition's "common interests" in the following terms: no French presence on the Scheldt River; the guarantee of Dutch security through Holland's annexation of Belgium; the independence of Spain and Portugal; the restoration of the Italian states; and the continuation of the "Alliance" after the peace to provide collective security against future French aggression.[21] Should these conditions be met, London would agree to certain colonial concessions.

Castlereagh's memorandum was doomed from the moment the ink dried on the parchment. Representing a continuation of Great Britain's insular policy, the document failed to consider the points that most concerned Alexander and Metternich, and thus the Coalition itself, despite their need of the British pound. To the statesmen of the eastern empires, issues over Poland and Saxony, the future of Germany and Italy, and an equilibrium of power loomed more ominous than questions over the mouth of the Scheldt and, for that matter, colonies and islands the names of which were hardly known in Moscow and Vienna. "To be sure," notes Kissinger, "Britain spoke of common interests, but it meant the military defeat of France; it advocated a European equilibrium, but it was really thinking about Antwerp."[22] To save the situation, Castlereagh lost no time adjusting his policy, which he had been instructed to do to show that Great Britain could be a team player.

In several private discussions with Metternich, the British minister gained a new perspective of the Coalition, Austria's politics, and the war itself. He came to the Continent with many preconceived notions – several of which Metternich gleefully debunked. "I found Lord Castlereagh not quite thoroughly informed of the real state of affairs on the Continent," recalls the Austrian in his memoirs. Metternich strummed the right chords to court Castlereagh. Accordingly, Vienna had no interest in maritime rights and supported London's plans for Holland. Metternich also conceded to British demands to base any negotiations on France's ancient frontiers, although he realized this territorial solution would not establish lasting peace if Napoleon remained on the French throne. In his opinion, any peace that left Napoleon the ruler of a France limited to its ancient frontiers rather than its natural frontiers, "would have been a ridiculous armistice, and would have been immediately rejected by him."[23] Regarding the war, Castlereagh believed peace would be concluded very soon because Napoleon appeared beaten. Metternich promised that plenty of fighting remained to force the French emperor to accept terms. The Austrian statesman emphasized that not France's future but that of Poland would cause the most contention among the Allies. Castlereagh also learned that dynastic ties did not move the Austrian court to favor maintaining Napoleon on the French throne. Instead, Francis preferred a regency under Marie Louis, especially in view of the tsar's whimsical idea of placing Bernadotte on the throne, which Castlereagh could hardly believe.[24] Metternich explained that Austria saw only two alternatives: Napoleon or the Bourbons. Metternich based these options on the Revolution: Napoleon being "the man who had transcended the social revolution," or the Bourbons, "the dynasty which could exist only in opposition to it."[25] To spare both France and Europe future revolutions, the best solution according to Metternich would be to co-opt a Napoleonic France in the European order.[26] He also preferred a Napoleonic France to counter Russia but would negotiate with the Bourbons for the sake of British friendship and to prevent France from becoming a Russian satellite. Metternich claimed to be in complete agreement with the British government over the dynastic question, but insisted the Allies could not influence the issue by advancing into the French interior on behalf of the Bourbons as desired by British public opinion. He did not fail to inform Castlereagh of Alexander's plan regarding Bernadotte and the tsar's distaste for the Bourbons.[27] Metternich latter recalled in his memoirs:

> Thus there remained only three possibilities: the recall of the Bourbons; a regency until the majority of Napoleon's son; the nomination of a third person to the throne of France. Everything – just rights as well as reason, the interest of France as well as the general interest of Europe – spoke in favor of the first course. The Kaiser of Austria did not doubt this for a moment. The same thing cannot be said of His Majesty the Tsar of Russia. The revolutionary spirits who surrounded this monarch, and who at that time exercised a pernicious and only too decisive influence on the tendencies of his mind, had labored for a long time in a direction opposed to the legitimate claims of the Bourbon family. They did not cease to represent its return as a vain undertaking. The Tsar was convinced of this.[28]

During this courtship, Castlereagh likewise had many discussions with Hardenberg, who expressed his position in terms similar to those stated by Metternich. A delighted Castlereagh discovered that the two German powers supported Great Britain's interests and in principle did not oppose the restoration of the Bourbons. Castlereagh reciprocated by rejecting Stein's proposals for a federal reorganization of Germany. He also supported the notion that the Allies had to reassess and redefine the goals of the Coalition. Moreover, his concept of a balance of power resembled aspects of Metternich's own designs. Regarding Bernadotte, the three ministers agreed: The Swedish prince-royal would be struck from the list of possible contenders for the French throne.

Regardless of these agreements, Alexander's bizarre plans and Austria's opposition to them concerned the British statesman. From Metternich's diatribes he gathered the Austrians would not continue the march to Paris unless the tsar renounced his intentions to conduct the war without negotiations and to elevate Bernadotte to the French throne. Castlereagh feared these issues would bring the entire campaign to a standstill – a development the British public would not accept because Wellington continued to press the war on France's western frontier. Castlereagh even worried that the Coalition could dissolve and thus viewed the moment as nothing short of a crisis.[29]

Metternich emerged from these bilateral talks believing he had gained the advantage. Both he and Castlereagh feared that the tsar's refusal to identify objectives revealed his intent to use the war to push Russian influence deep into central Europe. He thought Castlereagh would never accept Alexander's plans and believed that he and his British counterpart would make a joint stand against the Russians. Moreover, Castlereagh's principles appeared to correspond with his own political views. In particular, because London did not oppose peace negotiations, Metternich inferred that the British would not object to concluding the war as quickly as possible. Moreover, Metternich had no interest in keeping Napoleon on the throne against the will of the French people. Privately, he already had accepted the idea of expanding Holland at the cost of France. In short, Metternich completely agreed with the British program.[30]

Although each minister expressed policies that pleased the other, convincing Castlereagh that the Russian colossus would emerge as the main threat to postwar Europe crowned Metternich's efforts. Castlereagh's 26 December Memorandum failed to recognize any threat to the balance of power other than Napoleonic France, but his time at Basel helped persuade him that Russian hegemony could replace French dominance.[31] Castlereagh's half-brother and the British envoy to the Army of North Germany, Charles Stewart, provides a British view of Russia's potential threat:

> If we consider the power of Russia, unassailable as she is in flank and rear, hovering over Europe with an immense front, mistress of the Caspian, the Euxine, and the Baltic, with forty million of hardy, docile, brave, enthusiastic, and submissive inhabitants, with immense armies, highly disciplined, excellently appointed; her innumerable hordes of desolating cavalry; her adoption of the French maxims of war. . . . When we further consider this power flushed with success, and disposed to consider treaties and engagements with her as a waste of paper if they stood in the way of any project of aggrandizement; and if we further contemplate her determined will to surmount every barrier which engagements have interposed in order to advance herself into the heart of Germany, to supplant on one side the ancient dominion of Prussia; on the other, to turn the northern flank of Austria on the Vistula, as she has turned the southern on the Danube; and demanding as it were by the fortresses of Thorn and Cracow the keys of Berlin and Vienna; *when we further reflect on the natural march of empires from north to south, from the regions of the frost, snow and famine to the climates of warmth, verdure, and fertility, and recollect the revolutions that have taken place in Europe, Asia, and Africa from the desolating invasions of northern hordes, what may we not fear and expect?*[32]

Castlereagh left Basel believing that Russia and perhaps Prussia as well had to be restrained. The *entente-cordiale* established between himself and Metternich created "an identity of thought and feeling" that lasted until the former committed suicide in 1822.[33] "It was here," recorded Metternich in his memoirs, "that a few hours of conversation sufficed to lay the foundation of a good feeling between this upright and enlightened statesman and myself, which the following eventful years cemented and enlarged."[34] "Lord Castlereagh is here and I am extremely content," Metternich wrote Schwarzenberg on the 21st.

"He has everything: affability, wisdom, moderation. He agrees with me in every way and I have the conviction from him to be equally well-suited. *We hold our own against the asininity of a certain personage, and I am no longer anxious over his plans. The love for Bernadotte is a sin that makes friends into enemies, but we will not fall into the trap.*"[35] With this fortuitous meeting, nothing appeared to hinder the restoration of the historic alliance between Great Britain and Austria.

Castlereagh's arrival came at a time when the likelihood of success posed more of a threat to the Coalition than the prospect of failure. The ease of the Allied advance into France conclusively exposed Napoleon's absolute weakness. Somewhat discredited by the rapid advance, the peace party could only continue to work on the minds of the weak. Now it appeared that Alexander alone could and would carry on the war against France. A member of no party other than the Austrian, Metternich brooded over his situation. Napoleon's weakness no longer afforded Austria the role of the pivotal power that could make or break the Coalition: Kaiser Francis's threat to withdraw from the Coalition could possibly fall on deaf ears. Consequently, not only did the perpetual Allied advance reveal Napoleon's impotence, it likewise weakened Austria's control over the Coalition and strengthened Russia's. Metternich watched as his war to reestablish Europe's equilibrium spiraled out of control with the increasing probability that Russia would simply take the place of France as the continental superpower.[36] With the unpleasant memory of the Swiss affair still fresh, a rapprochement between him and Alexander did not appear likely. To make matters worse, his calculations had failed. Metternich "had been confident that Napoleon could be brought to terms through a combination of psychological and military pressure," notes Kissinger, "through a war fought in the name of peace and peace offered with the threat of war."[37] Now Schwarzenberg stood at Langres, but Napoleon still insisted on the Frankfurt Proposals – terms that Austria's allies would no longer accept. In this contest between Alexander and Metternich, the latter turned to Castlereagh and managed to effect his own "diplomatic revolution," while Alexander remained obsessed with thoughts of a crushing victory.[38] Alexander's secretary, Mikhailovsky-Danilevsky, stated the substance of his sovereign's opinion:

> As long as this war continues, it is impossible to affirm that the objective of the Coalition has been achieved: victory must decide that. As long as a considerable part of Europe was occupied by French troops, we were obliged to proportion our demands to the amount of our force, and to express our objectives in general terms.... Such expressions do not infer the renunciation of those objectives, which Providence and our enormous sacrifices, allow us to hope for. This truth is established by the example of all wars, and even by our own acts. The conditions of peace which were unofficially discussed at Frankfurt, are not those we now desire.[39]

After five days at Basel, Metternich and Castlereagh departed for Langres on 23 January. Castlereagh immediately became aware of the tension in Allied headquarters. The sharp tone of Gneisenau's repeated demands for a march on Paris likewise unsettled the British diplomat.[40] Continued fear of the Coalition's dissolution fueled his passion for the establishment of a firm, general alliance. However, neither Metternich nor Alexander would yield their respective positions regarding Poland and sacrifice this vital objective in favor of "common interest."

An undaunted Castlereagh pressed on, presenting his plans for the future of France. London would consider negotiating with Napoleon if the French people retained him as their sovereign. Should Bonaparte be ousted from the throne, the British viewed a Bourbon restoration as the only alternative. In fact, Castlereagh preferred the Bourbons to prevent political upheaval in France, but he would negotiate with Napoleon to maintain Allied unity. Secretly, Metternich still hoped to negotiate a peace that would maintain Napoleon on the French throne, but publicly supported the British to frustrate Alexander. For his part, the tsar consented to London's preference for the "ancient" frontiers of France, the exclusion of the issue of maritime rights from any peace negotiations, as well as British plans for Holland.[41] Yet the Russian monarch remained noncommittal regarding France's ruling dynasty. "Soon after the arrival of the monarchs at Langres," recalled Metternich, "I was informed by the sagacious and far-seeing men of Tsar Alexander's cabinet that this monarch was much agitated at the necessity of coming to a conclusion with respect to the future form of government to be established in France, which indeed was the most important of all questions."[42] Alexander also pressed his demand that "all negotiations with her [France] must relate exclusively to her future frontiers."[43]

The multilateral talks at Langres came in the wake of Caulaincourt's repeated request for the opening of negotiations. As noted, the French minister had appeared personally at Schwarzenberg's outposts on 9 January seeking passage to Allied headquarters. He reiterated his master's intention to base the talks on the Frankfurt Proposals. The Allies replied that talks could not begin until Castlereagh arrived, at which time they would inform Caulaincourt if the Frankfurt Proposals were still on the table. With both Blücher and Schwarzenberg advancing, even the peace party found it difficult to justify offering these terms. Alexander simply refused and insisted that France's ancient frontiers form the basis of any territorial settlement.

Prior to the start of negotiations, Metternich wanted to induce the tsar to identify his war aims for the sake of Allied unity. A timely letter from Schwarzenberg to Kaiser Francis on 26 January aided his cause. In this memo, the Austrian commander stated his reservations over continuing the war. Although admitting the merits of continuing the advance, he belabored the risks involved: supply problems, a tenuous line of communication, overexposed flanks, and a growing sick list. As for politics, Schwarzenberg could not refrain from commenting that victory rather than defeat concerned him most. After Langres, the next stop was Paris. Schwarzenberg asked Francis whether the Bohemian Army "should descend onto the plain [of Langres and] begin a struggle of incalculable consequences" or remain in its current position to rest and resupply. His most powerful argument was that peace with Napoleon would be impossible if the Allies continued their advance to Paris.[44] "In thus posing the alternative between stability and chaos, both militarily and political," comments Kissinger," Schwarzenberg made clear the Austrian dilemma: beyond Langres lay victory, but victory would prove hollow."[45] With such concerns coming from his general, Francis authorized Metternich to meet with the tsar and press the Austrian position.

After securing the agreement of Hardenberg, Nesselrode, and Castlereagh, Metternich posed a series of policy questions to Alexander on the evenings of 26 and 27 January.[46] During the first night, the 26th, the recalcitrant sovereign remained evasive and militant. Metternich frankly informed Alexander that Austrian troops would not be squandered on a crusade to force Napoleon's abdication. Alexander defiantly claimed he would indeed continue the war alone or with Frederick William only.[47] The Russian monarch also refused to bind himself to any declaration of war aims, insisting that none should be identified until after the campaign. "We have increased our demands in proportion to our successes," the tsar bluntly stated. Moreover, the offensive would continue while the diplomats babbled. Alexander echoed Blücher and Gneisenau by lecturing Metternich that the surest means for success was to conduct military operations with the greatest possible speed and decisiveness. "I must direct the attention of the Allies to the enemy's forces," reasoned the tsar, "and to the necessity of crushing them, even during the course of the negotiations, in the event that all hope of peace disappears." Finally, he announced that all options regarding France's future dynasty should be considered to prevent the Allies from interfering in French politics. The Allies "have no right to canvass the opinion of the French on the subject of a ruling dynasty," he argued; "we are not waging war for that purpose; consequently it cannot become the subject of deliberation . . . our glory will be the greater, if, with the power in our hands, we show ourselves devoid of partiality."[48]

"He imparted to me," noted Metternich, "his particular wish . . . to learn on the very spot itself the true feeling of the French nation. 'If it is against the Bourbons', said the tsar to me, 'to bring them back to a throne they had failed to keep would expose France and eventually all of Europe to another revolution, of which no one can foretell the consequences'." Alexander went on to argue that choosing a new ruler would be a very difficult task for foreigners. He decreed "the operations against Paris must continue with vigor; we must take the city. On the eve of this event, which would crown the military success of the alliance, it will be necessary to issue a proclamation to the French people, declaring our determination to have nothing to do with their form of government or the selection of their ruler. At the same time, we must summon the original assemblies, and demand a proper number of deputies be sent to Paris to decide these points in the name of the nation."

Wanting the details of Alexander's scheme, Metternich baited him: "Bonaparte has mastered the Revolution; the plan of calling the nation to deliberate on questions concerning the foundation of the social edifice of France and thereby causing a second Convention would unchain the Revolution again and that can never be the objective of the alliance nor the meaning of its deliberations." Alexander countered by pointing to the obvious: Coalition armies flooded France and would thus restrain all "revolutionary evils." He insisted "the deputies of the nation will give their opinion on two questions – namely, the form of government and the selection of a ruler. The Republic is dead. It has fallen by its own excesses. The prince whom the nation will chose will have less difficulty establishing his authority. Napoleon's authority is broken and one will no longer have anything to do with it." Alexander planned to appoint La Harpe as president of this assembly to guarantee the suppression of any radical elements.

After the tsar unveiled the particulars of his plan, Metternich took the offensive. He insisted the kaiser would never accept it; if he did, Metternich promised to resign. He argued that such a plan "would cause France and the whole of Europe years of confusion and sorrow. If La Harpe thinks himself able to answer for the result, he is mistaken." The verbal joust then reached its climax: "What I am now going to say to you, Your Majesty, is what Kaiser Francis thinks. Napoleon's power is broken and will not rise again. This is the fate of the power of an usurper when a crisis arrives. When the overthrow of the empire comes, there will be only the Bourbons to take possession of their undying rights. They will do it by the power of events and the wish of the nation which, in my opinion, there can be no doubt. Kaiser Francis will never support any other dynasty." According to Metternich's account of the situation, Alexander dismissed him immediately after this statement. He returned to his quarters to find Nesselrode, the tsar's own foreign minister, eagerly waiting. After learning the details of the discussion, he purportedly begged Metternich to remain steadfast in his opposition to the Russian emperor.

During Metternich's meeting with the tsar on the evening of the 27th, Alexander asked for clarification of the kaiser's opinion. "I can only repeat what I said yesterday," replied the Austrian minister. "The kaiser is against any appeal to the nation – to a people who would be in the false position of deliberating in the face of 700,000 foreign bayonets. Moreover, the kaiser does not see what the subject of deliberation could be – the legitimate king is here." Metternich also held out the prospect of Austria concluding a separate peace with France; Francis had authorized him to threaten Alexander with the immediate withdrawal of Austrian troops from the war.[49] Yet at this point of the struggle, such threats from both sides were empty. Once the tsar insinuated he would wage war on his own, second thoughts besieged him. He realized Russia could not easily win without Austria. Conversely, Metternich understood that if Austria withdrew from the war, either a Russo–Prussian victory or defeat would be detrimental to Austria's interests. Consequently, Russo–Prussian dependence on both the Austrian army and British subsidies made a rupture unlikely at this stage of the war. Metternich thus concluded that he and Castlereagh could restrain the tsar only if the Anglo–Austrian partnership remained firm.[50]

Because coercion would not offset the tsar's current bout of optimism, Metternich made one last attempt to reach an understanding with him. Another intimate discussion on the 28th succeeded in reducing the tension. On the following day, the Allied ministers and envoys agreed to open negotiations with Caulaincourt at Châtillon-sur-Seine on 3 February. In part to expose Napoleon's intransigence, the Allies decided to offer France its 1792 frontiers as the basis of a peace settlement. Although the tsar clung to his own ideas, the Allied ministers agreed to allow the French people to decide the dynastic question. In return, France would be excluded from all negotiations regarding territory beyond its frontiers. Holland and Belgium would be united and maritime issues would be excluded from the discussions. While the diplomats negotiated at Châtillon, Schwarzenberg would continue the campaign, but in a manner that he saw fit. To provide a degree of formality to these decisions, the Allies signed the Protocols of Langres on 29 January 1814. In view of the unyielding attitude of the French and Russian monarchs, little could be expected from the peace talks. Regardless, Castlereagh and Metternich stabilized the Coalition for the moment. Despite having to abandon the Frankfurt Proposals, Metternich regained his leverage as the pivotal power thanks to Castlereagh. Alexander, whose own foreign minister collaborated with Metternich, found himself isolated. Although he wanted to avoid both negotiations with the French as well as a general discussion of Allied war aims, Alexander yielded.[51]

The course of operations now depended solely on Schwarzenberg: would he hearken to the calls of Blücher and Gneisenau or heed the advice of Knesebeck and Langenau? A letter to his wife on 26 January reveals his intimate hopes and fears:

> At this moment, when the most important work overwhelms me, the presence of the three sovereigns smothers me, all ministers benumb me, the most important questions must be decided.... My headquarters is already at Chaumont. Here we shall make peace; this is my advice. Any drive to Paris is in the highest degree *unmilitärisch*; our Kaiser, also Stadion, Metternich, and Castlereagh are in complete agreement with this opinion, but Tsar Alexander again has suffered one of the bouts of buffoonery that often seize him. This is the moment of the most crucial decisions, may the Heavens protect us in this

crisis. Caulaincourt has been at Châtillon-sur-Seine for five days and wants to negotiate; I hope one will finally present him the proposals tomorrow, but again one [Alexander] must state what he wants.... It may still come down to very heated scenes. As long as our struggle is just the Heavens will not fail to protect us, but my role is ever difficult, the sword incessantly hangs over my head.[52]

Metternich's urgent need to restrain "the exaggerated zeal of the Prussian generals" led to a council of war, convened at Langres on 27 January to debate the next phase of military operations.[53] For the meeting, Schwarzenberg asked the congenial Knesebeck to draft a detailed memo stating the case against a march on Paris. The drive through the French interior, wrote Knesebeck, "could be continued only if it really facilitated the attainment of peace, but not for mere glory and fame." Caution should be the ruling principle if the war continued. With each step further along an excessive line of communication, Allied forces would be reduced by combat losses, sickness, and strategic consumption. "Once one arrives on the other side of Troyes and Châlons-en-Champagne," Knesebeck warned, "where there are no attainable objectives, there will be no more halts, and one will have to advance to the gates of Paris, indeed through Paris and beyond, which would mean that everything will depend on the timely arrival of reinforcements." West of Langres all highways led to Paris. Communication would be difficult and flanking movements impossible because no north–south roads suitable for use in winter intersected these east–west highways. "For the enemy," states Knesebeck's memo, "all operations in the flank of an army that is advancing deeper into the French interior along these highways will become easier. Thus the enemy can envelop the Allies, while it would be impossible for us to strategically maneuver against him since the nature of the terrain only allows forward and backward movements." He also contended that the barren region of Champagne could not support the Allied armies for an extended period. "To the right," he concluded, "looms the French fortresses in the Netherlands, and in the rear, those of the Rhine, Lorraine, and Franche-Comté. If the Allies position weak reserves at Dijon, Langres, and Joinville, they will be harassed by the enemy in the rear, while in the front, Napoleon, driven to the extreme, will also defend himself to the extreme. The war, if it continues, will become a fanatical war of extermination." Despite the numerous and recognizable inaccuracies and exaggerations, the Austrians accepted this logic.[54]

A memorandum composed by Langenau and presented by Schwarzenberg contained similar points. Langenau's treatise began by praising the results of the operation that brought the Bohemian Army to Langres. He advocated speedy operations because the lowlands of the French interior were now exposed to Schwarzenberg's masses. From Langres, the Allies could freely move in any direction. According to his estimates, which placed the French army too high at 120,000 men and the Allies too low at 162,000 men, he came to the conclusion that victory completely favored the Coalition. To exploit this advantage, the Allies had to continue operations quickly to prevent Napoleon from completing his mobilization.

The tone of the memo then changed as Langenau extolled the advantages of remaining at Langres as well as the dangers of advancing. By halting at Langres, the Bohemian Army would be completely secure against a flanking movement. In addition, the Allies could sustain their troops at the enemy's expense. Langenau argued that a future advance had to be directed not at Napoleon's army but at the weakest point of any cordon the French formed to protect Paris. Moreover, by remaining at Langres, the Bohemian Army could still threaten the central departments.

After reiterating Knesebeck's warnings over the dangers of continuing the advance, Langenau's treatise reached a bizarre conclusion: at Paris the Allies would find themselves in a position similar to that of the French at Leipzig. He based this assumption on the same argument made by Knesebeck. By continuing the offensive, the Allies would move farther away from their base of operations and combat losses would inevitably increase, while unavoidable bivouacs and the difficulties of supply would contribute to the growing sick list. In the end, however, Langenau proved more aggressive than Knesebeck. He suggested the Bohemian Army maintain its current position and await the arrival of reserves and the flank corps. Although he provided no timetable for this, Langenau concluded that as soon as these reinforcements arrived, the Bohemian Army should descend onto the plain and resolve the war through battle. He assumed Napoleon would seek battle between Troyes and Châlons-en-Champagne.

In his oral presentation of Langenau's treatise, Schwarzenberg described every outcome, whether victory or defeat, as all equally fatal. Should the Allies defeat Napoleon, the French emperor would be driven to seek a desperate battle of annihilation to save his political existence. In such a battle, the Allies would suffer more losses than the approaching reinforcements could replace. A union with the Austro–Italian army could not be effected because of the distance between it and the Bohemian Army. Obviously choosing to ignore Wellington's army, the Austrians even expressed concern that Suchet would form a new army in southern France. Although Schwarzenberg's presentation clearly revealed his reluctance to resume the offensive, he concluded by offering no definite suggestion. Instead, Schwarzenberg relinquished to the Allied council whether the Bohemian Army should remain at Langres or seek a battle, whose outcome none could predict.[55]

On the following day, 28 January, when Metternich and Alexander reached their agreement to continue the war and open negotiations, Schwarzenberg received his answer. To satisfy the tsar, he decided to commence a cautious yet general advance on the following day. After confirming that a considerable

French force was indeed at Châlons-en-Champagne, his headquarters drafted orders for a march to Troyes in accordance with Radetzky's original invasion plan. Meant to threaten the right flank of the enemy army at Châlons, Schwarzenberg wanted to execute the march in three great columns that would unite at Troyes on 2 February. To cover this movement, Schwarzenberg planned to place Blücher on the Marne at Vitry-le-François. From there, the Prussian would send a column to Arcis-sur-Aube to cover the Bohemian Army's right flank and rearward communication.[56] Schwarzenberg still sought victory at the peace table rather than on the battlefield and deserves little credit for this initiative. After confirming the presence of a French army at Châlons-en-Champagne, he chose to conduct a flanking maneuver with the majority of his vast army. Troyes, a geographic objective, rather than the enemy army became the goal. "Do not abandon me, my dear friend," he wrote Metternich on the 29th. "At Frankfurt you promised me, if I committed myself to briskly push the military operations, to conduct the peace negotiations, I have kept my word, but alas, how far behind you remain!" Unfortunately history will never know the result of Schwarzenberg's maneuver on Troyes because events beyond his control forced him to abort the operation that same day.[57]

In conclusion, most of the dominant personalities at Allied headquarters considered the plateau of Langres to be the definitive goal of Allied operations. Nothing good could result from an advance beyond Langres – only inevitable danger awaited the Coalition. With the majority of eastern France occupied by Allied troops, the peace party believed Napoleon would seek terms. Fearing the preponderance of Russia and the rise of Prussia, Metternich hoped to use the Frankfurt Proposals as the basis of negotiations with France. He wanted Austria to be seen as granting France its natural frontiers of the Rhine, Alps, and Pyrenees. Metternich also planned to cede a portion of Italy to Napoleon's stepson, Eugène. In return, Austria and France would work together to counter Russia. Metternich employed all his skill to win the support of the other Allied dignitaries to negotiate a peace rather than continue the war. Although spellbound by Hardenberg and Knesebeck, both of whom convinced him that everything Prussia had thus far gained in the war could be lost if it continued, Frederick William declared his support for the Russian monarch.[58] Finally agreeing with Gneisenau on one point, the Prussian king reached the conclusion that no lasting peace could be attained as long as Napoleon wore the French crown. Probably aware that Frederick William was a lost cause, the Austrian minister nevertheless succeeded in convincing Castlereagh, Hardenberg, and Knesebeck that his plan would work. He encountered greater difficulties with Cathcart and Aberdeen but finally succeeded. Charles Stewart, Castlereagh's brother, was won over during the debates at Langres.[59] Nesselrode and several Russian generals also wanted to end the war through negotiation and thus inadvertently aided Metternich.

In addition to Stein, only the Hanoverian minister Count Münster and Karl Andreas Pozzo di Borgo of the tsar's entourage supported Alexander. Regardless of his postwar plans, Alexander believed Napoleon's rule over France was incompatible with peace. Gneisenau's friend, Münster, who arrived at Allied headquarters around the same time as Castlereagh, also favored continuing the war. Like Gneisenau, Münster supported a Bourbon restoration and believed that negotiating with Napoleon would weaken the influence of French royalists. Stein agreed with Alexander but also craved Napoleon's downfall as atonement for the suffering and indignities imposed on Germany by the French. As for the native Corsican Pozzo di Borgo, he simply hated Bonaparte.[60] Outside Allied headquarters, Blücher and Gneisenau easily found common ground with the Russian monarch when it came to Bonaparte: "The dog must go down," was Blücher's cry.[61]

Schwarzenberg and Radetzky certainly possessed enough military competence to reject Knesebeck's and Langenau's idiosyncratic arguments. Yet this is where Metternich's genius came into play. Since Frankfurt, hawks and doves sharply divided Allied councils. Behind the scenes, Metternich worked to attain his state's national interests, which bore little resemblance to the aims of either party except for pleasing the doves by ending the war as soon as possible. Although incongruous with his secret agenda, Metternich used the arguments drafted and supported by the peace party to win time for the Austrians to achieve their own objectives, which did not in the least support those of the Russian court. Like a master puppeteer, Metternich pulled the right strings. He probably chuckled with satisfaction in the privacy of his quarters after listening to Hardenberg urge an end to the war through negotiation, or Knesebeck predict disaster if the Bohemian Army crossed its Rubicon, or Nesselrode oppose his master. Few perceived how Metternich used the peace party as a shield behind which he worked to attain Austria's goals. Alexander, who hardly trusted Metternich, rejected his proposal to exchange offensive operations for negotiations. To the tsar, the results of the war depended on success on the battlefield rather than the peace table. Metternich, Castlereagh, and many others opposed his ideas, and thus Alexander finally declared that Russia alone would continue the war. This provoked Metternich to threaten a separate peace with Napoleon. The time for either course of action was premature; both Alexander and Metternich recognized this. Consequently, an uneasy truce emerged. With divided councils and secret agendas the Allies prepared for peace negotiations with the French. More important, these divided councils and secret agendas found their way to the battlefield.

On the military front, reaching Langres satisfied Schwarzenberg, who hoped to avoid a general battle with Napoleon. From the start, he rejected the idea of taking Paris. The commander in chief received indispensable support from Langenau, who still adhered to the methodical warfare of maneuver. Like most of his Austrian counterparts, the Saxon Langenau had been schooled in the principles of the Seven Years' War. He opposed a march on Paris and even argued that Prince Eugene of Savoy and the duke of Marlborough had not undertaken such an operation against Louis XIV.[62] Knesebeck agreed with the Austrians and proposed a two-week armistice to ascertain the extent of French preparations. In Blücher's impetuous desire to drive on Paris, Knesebeck saw a foolhardy gambler, who would risk everything on the cards but never thought of the consequences if he had to fold. Regarding Gneisenau's fervent quest to take Paris, Knesebeck perceived a vain desire to seek vengeance for Napoleon's entry in Berlin almost eight years earlier. Gneisenau's letters impressed Alexander, but not Metternich, Schwarzenberg, Radetzky, Knesebeck, Hardenberg, or Frederick William. Such men labeled Blücher, Gneisenau, and their supporters as "eccentric" and "overexcited." Schwarzenberg and Metternich firmly opposed the objectives of the war party, the former for military reasons, the latter political. Despite the successful invasion of France, Schwarzenberg rescinded command of the army to Metternich.[63] The war party and its tool, the Silesian Army, would pay dearly for this during the upcoming struggle for France.

Appendices

Appendix A

Clausewitz to Gneisenau

I am in great suspense over the operations that will soon occur at the Rhine; I do not doubt that Napoleon will withdraw across this river. The operations on the other side of the Rhine will be so difficult and under such different circumstances that I am almost convinced that one is stronger in the defensive than in the offensive. Nevertheless, I hold it as completely decisive that one must cross the Rhine and continue the operations without delay until the peace, going all the way to Paris. His army is almost destroyed; maybe he can field 80,000–100,000 men in the face of double and triple the strength which one can oppose him. Leave him no time to form a new army, or to make an orderly halt until he reaches Paris. What was organized for the defense of the land is for the most part marching off with the cohorts, the remainder lacks artillery and a thousand other things. Everything which one can say against an operation in France and [against] Paris in particular is incorrect and misguided. A conspiracy in Paris, a revolt by the army, rebellion in the provinces will meet us halfway and one will easily have the two cornerstones of a durable peace with the liberation of Holland and Switzerland. But if one makes a formal halt on the Rhine, he will rebuild his army during the winter, and by early next year he will again have a strength of 200,000–300,000 men on the Rhine. Although the Allies no doubt will be in a position to place twice the manpower against these forces, it is to be feared very much that the usual dissension will have time to produce an awful rupture. These thoughts haunt me day and night, ten times more than our situation here, and I confess, general, that I count on you only.

You had ended the standstill of the operations on the Elbe, without you one would still be standing there, you will probably effect similar results on the Rhine.[1]

APPENDIX B

"REGARDING EACH SUGGESTION OVER WHAT SHOULD BE DONE IF THE ENEMY CROSSES THE RHINE" 31 OCTOBER 1813, BY RADETZKY

At the current moment only two proposals can be considered: 1) The enemy will cross the Rhine and the Allied armies will move into winter posts and quarters on the Right Bank. 2) The enemy crosses the Rhine and the Allied army moves into winter quarters, while a portion will turn to the conquest of Holland and Italy.

1. The Rhine will be divided into three main sectors for observation: a) from Basel to Rastatt; b) from Rastatt to the Lahn; c) from the Lahn to Wesel; d) although separate, to this sector will be added the stretch from Wesel to the mouth of the Ems.

   a. The army of Gen. Wrede will cover from Basel to Rastatt. It will consist of: 35,000 Bavarians; 15,000 Württembergers and Badenese; 6,000 Hessen-Darmstadters, Würzburgers, and Frankfurters; 10,000 Austrians; total: 66,000 men. The headquarters of this sector will be at Freiburg-im-Breisgau. According to circumstances, the majority of the troops will be posted partly in the Breisgau and partly in the Black Forest.

   b. 60,000 Austrians will cover from Rastatt to the Lahn. The headquarters will be at Heidelberg. The Austrian Reserve will be established between the Neckar, Tauber, and Main in the line from Rothenburg-am-der-Tauber and Alsace.... The majority of the troops will be billeted in winter quarters between the Bergstraße and the Rhine, then up the Lahn.

   c. Field-Marshal Blücher will occupy from the Lahn to Wesel with 60,000 men. The headquarters will be established in Blankenberg or Solingen; the majority of troops will take winter quarters along the Western Forest and the Rhine.

d. The crown prince of Sweden, likewise with 60,000 men, will be assigned from Wesel to Emden. His sector extends from Wesel along the frontier of Holland to Lingen and from there along the right bank of the Ems to Emden. The majority of the troops will take winter quarters behind this line from Düsseldorf through Münster, Osnabrück to Ostfriesland. The headquarters will be established at Osnabrück....

Count Bennigsen will deal with the blockades of Dresden, Torgau, Wittenberg, and Magdeburg.

In the above-named stretch lie the bridge-heads of Huningue, Kehl, Kassel, Neuwied, and Wesel, which deserve careful consideration. Of these, Kehl and Kassel are the most important. The former will be the concern of Gen. Wrede. A single corps of 10,000 Austrians will be positioned at Hochheim facing the latter....

2. An operation against Holland can only be considered as feasible if in late winter all the canals and marshes are frozen and in this way the march through Holland, which may encounter great resistance, will be possible.

For this it is necessary that the army of the crown prince of Sweden be reinforced to at least 80,000 men. These reinforcements can only be provided by Blücher's army, whose detachments can in any case be replaced by Wittgenstein. The political negotiations that will be taking place in the meantime must decide the particulars of this operation, namely whether such an operation should be subordinated more to military success or should be subordinated solely to negotiations.

The situation may arise in which the forces on the upper Rhine must operate there in order to support the political measures of the Swiss and enter Switzerland.

Finally, if Dresden falls, it will thus probably be necessary to detach a portion of the Austrian forces to Italy to reinforce the army there.... The conquest of Italy will be based on the occupation of the region between the Adige and the Mincio as the first objective. Also included in this first objective is the conquest of the fortresses of Peschiera and Mantua, and if possible the citadel of Ferrara; through this the invasion through Bologna to Tuscany can be secured....

This position alone makes it possible for us to make the preparations to be able to ensure operations against Paris at the beginning of the new campaign.[2]

Appendix C

Gneisenau to Alexander:

Regarding the Great Question of the Day

Will one cross the Rhine in order to harvest all of the fruits of our victory and to further strike the enemy, who is dismayed by his setbacks, or will one remain on this side of the river and be satisfied with preparing for the defensive for the next campaign? This is the great question of the day.

The enemy lost an army of 400,000 men in the memorable campaign of 1812; in the last campaign he lost another 300,000 men. All of his troops that were able to escape over the Rhine cannot amount to more than 50,000. Only a few depots remain for him to build a new army.... A new conscription has been made in order to call up the conscripts of the class of 1815, i.e., in order to enlist young people fifteen years of age, and those who had been exempt from the conscriptions of 1802–1806 will now be affected by it. These two classes of conscripts, which will provide the French army with approximately 200,000 men, have thus far only been summoned; and the young conscripts cannot be adjusted and combat-ready before three months. Thus, for the defense of the eastern frontier of France, there remains at most 90,000 men, and until the creation of a new army we are free to undertake anything.

If we remain on this side of the Rhine, we will provide the enemy with invaluable time to rebuild his army in order for him to erase the misfortunes of the current campaign and to raise the morale. One will leave at his disposal the power over the population and over the means to control all the peoples of the left bank of the Rhine and of Holland; and finally one will give him the option of only equipping his fortresses in the first line, and of these only a few. In order to punish us for our languor, for allowing him time to prepare the means to undertake an offensive war with the opening of the campaign, he will drive through Holland, take our defensive positions on the Rhine in the flank, and force us to withdraw towards inner Germany. Any soldier knows that it is militarily impossible to remain on the Rhine as long as Holland is controlled by the enemy. Then we will have the pain of seeing Germany's fate once again placed in the outcome of a battle, and the favorable circumstances produced by the victory at Leipzig will hardly effect this one.

France is surrounded by 130–140 fortresses. In the previous wars, which were conducted far from its borders, these fortresses had no or very small garrisons. This has now changed. Under the current circumstances, these fortresses, once the bulwark of the Empire, have become a burden for France; the resources of the great Empire will not suffice to place all of these places in a defensible condition....

After carefully weighing all of these considerations, it is imperative for us to cross the Rhine as soon as possible and instead of avoiding these fortresses, as general military advice suggests, proceed in the midst of them in order to threaten several of them simultaneously. This would leave the enemy the choice, either to throw everything that he can assemble in a new levée in the fortresses and exhaust his resources to supply these places in which case he cannot build a new army capable of resisting us, or to avoid this, to surrender a portion of these places to us in order to save the rest, which would force him to relinquish some of his conquests and provide us with a sound operations base. If the Bohemian Army crosses the Rhine between Mainz and Strasbourg, it will simultaneously threaten these two strongholds including Landau and Huningue. Since these first two require strong garrisons, they will significantly reduce the army that the enemy can create from the survivors of his present army and the young conscripts from the depots. Our army, however, will then find itself in an excellent region that will provide all that is necessary for its supply, while it takes away the same from the enemy.

The Silesian Army must cross the Rhine as close as possible to Holland and take the direction on Maastricht. By going as far as Holland, it will attract enemy forces from there, oblige the enemy to dissipate his forces, and prevent the enemy from taking a middle position from which he can fall on one or the other of our armies should they remain too close to each other. If the Silesian Army takes the direction of Maastricht, it will be able to simultaneously threaten the fortresses in Holland, Brabant, Flanders and those of old France, and at the same time sever the first of these from old France and prevent any relief from reaching them. Under the protection of this army, one can attempt to bring Holland to insurrection.

To better support the operations of these two armies, one should send a force across the Rhine near Koblenz to the excellent position at Karthause. Should one take this position, he would sever the enemy's communications along the left bank of the Rhine and force him to maintain his communications through Trier with great difficulty. It is just as important for us to arrange ourselves at Trier in order to throw back the enemy's communications onto inner France. An invaluable advantage!

For the most rapid success it would be advantageous to separate Vorontsov and Bülow from the army of the crown prince of Sweden, since the Swedish corps and Wallmoden's corps will suffice to confront the Danes. Since it is nevertheless foreseeable that the crown prince by his tendency to take all liberties of the commander in chief will resist such a separation from his army, one should not calculate on this taking place. Otherwise, these two corps could march from Germany to Holland and occupy the Ijssel line. After the complete conquest of Holland, one has nothing further to fear for North Germany, for any enemy operation against the Ems and lower Weser would be taken in the flank by our army in Holland, which can receive support at any moment since this would be in our possession.

Should this plan of campaign be adopted and if one had more troops at his disposal and the Swiss declare for us, so would it be an advantageous consideration to send an army to Switzerland. This land is surrounded by mountains and easy to defend. From there one can threaten the interior districts of France and take all positions of the Vosges in the south. One can nevertheless not conceal that such a penetration would threaten the heart of France, provide the French government a great moral strength, and justify summoning the entire male population of the country to arms. But if one renounces this plan, the campaign plan suggested here will be adequate and can be accomplished according to the turn which the war has taken, namely: to oblige France to relinquish the conquests, which the lack of unity among the powers facing her had permitted.

I do not intend to discuss the war in Italy here. Undoubtedly, the condition of its fortresses will allow proceedings similar to those on the Rhine and in Holland and makes it imperative for us to place an army in the Piedmont and at the foot of the Alps.

Any other defense plan which allows the enemy control over the means of the conquered peoples, to create and deploy new forces, and to reanimate the crestfallen fortitude of the French soldiers should be condemned.[3]

APPENDIX D

GNEISENAU TO ALEXANDER, 24 NOVEMBER 1813

I. As long as Holland remains under enemy control there can be no security for North Germany and the army, which is assigned to either observe the Rhine or to cross it, will be driven back to inner Germany at the moment the enemy enjoys success elsewhere and is in the position to send an army to Holland and, supported by the strongholds of this land, invade Westphalia. On the other hand, if we take Holland, any offensive in North Germany will be taken in the flank by our army in Holland and this army can be supported instantaneously since we control the sea.

II. Belgian and Holland are the wealthiest states on the continent. If we do not attempt to wrest these states from the enemy he will thus be able to extract from them manpower, money, and military supplies. These resources can be ours if we do not delay to take them for ourselves.

III. France is surrounded by 100–140 fortresses. These places, once the bulwark of the Empire, have in the current circumstances become an immeasurable burden. All of these places in their current condition are depleted of manpower, munitions, and supplies of all kinds and to outfit them is a definite impossibility for France. Therefore, instead of fearing and avoiding these fortresses, we must place ourselves right in their midst and threaten them all. This will place the enemy in the grim necessity of choosing to either exhaust himself by provisioning all of these places and throw in them everything that he can amass in a new levée and therefore will have no army in the field to resist us, or to have only at his disposal an army in the field, relinquish a part of his fortresses to us which will then form a strong operations base for us.

IV. Leaving the conquest of Holland to depend on the good will of the crown prince of Sweden can be dangerous. Without a doubt he will find reasons to do nothing in this regard. Should a campaign plan assign the conquest of Brabant to the Silesian Army, this will forestall the crown prince of Sweden and circumvent Holland, so one can then appeal to the crown prince's vanity to undertake the easier and far-less dangerous conquest. Currently, if he does not see an army lead the way for him and deliver the first blow, he will find the operation too risky and the resources designated for him to carry out this conquest... will be wasted. This time the crown prince will provide powerful reasons in order to avoid the task appointed to him.

V. These negotiations with the crown prince, should they have the desired effect, will result in an irrevocable loss of time. The enemy, who is just as active as we, will use this time in order to make a new levée and to use any means necessary to prepare his defenses.

VI. If the negotiations with the crown prince fail and we must forgo the invasion of Brabant and the conquest of Holland, we would thus have the disadvantage of having given the enemy the freedom of leaving the fortresses of these states without garrisons and from the troops designated for them he can build a powerful army which can strongly hinder us in our operations from this side [of the Rhine].

VII. The invasion of France from Switzerland is a brilliant yet dangerous undertaking. One cannot deny that it will contribute to giving the French government a moral force and provide him an excuse to summon the entire people to arms. French national pride will thus be injured and... they will be compelled by their government [to act].

VIII. We need more than five weeks to move the Bohemian Army to the region of Geneva. This is time lost. During the march of this army, Blücher's army will be paralyzed. The enemy will be able to move wherever he wants.

IX. The line of communications of the Bohemian Army running from inner Germany with a large detour through Switzerland to Paris and with fortresses and good positions on its right must cause us concern because the enemy will lead as many new troop units against it as he can assemble since he will have the necessary time and will not be occupied elsewhere. This operation somewhat resembles Napoleon's on Moscow.[4]

APPENDIX E

MÜFFLING'S PRO MEMORIA OF 29 DECEMBER 1813

A movement from Switzerland and the upper Rhine into the French interior is not only possible and can be executed with speed, but it can also be very decisive. However, it does not represent a continuation of the march from Leipzig to the Rhine, and makes no use of the results of the battle of Leipzig. The enemy has been driven back on the single point of Mainz. It is therefore completely advisable to now chose a point of conquest where: 1) the combined [Allied] armies have shorter lines and 2) the provinces do not belong to France proper so that the dispositions of the subjects are not inherently loyal to France. As a result of the battle of Leipzig, Holland, the German provinces on the other side of the Rhine, and perhaps also Brabant can be conquered without bloodshed; but if the spirit of the Dutch nation and the Germans of the left bank is left in chains, if the fortresses are provisioned and garrisoned, the conquest of Holland will thus require the work of many years. According to the current position, the combined army will lose thirty days moving to the upper Rhine and Switzerland. This movement will further allow the enemy...to empty all of his Dutch fortresses in order to appear in the field with significant force, and both reasons taken together demand the assumption that this movement will allow the enemy sufficient time to free the forces needed for a battle on the Seine, a supposition which a movement on Holland completely rules out. This raises the question of which would bring peace faster: the fall of Holland and the Netherlands (exclusive of the fortresses) or a march of the combined army to Paris? Without doubt I believe that the fall of such significant provinces, causing such a great reduction of forces, will be more detrimental to Napoleon than a march on Paris, which would only be decisive if it caused a revolution, while Napoleon will certainly judge that such a large army with such a long and thin line of communications from the Rhine to Paris cannot long endure, all the more if it still has behind it twelve enemy-occupied fortresses.[5]

APPENDIX F

THE FRANKFURT DECLARATION

The Allied Powers do not wage war against France, but against the preponderance that has been so loudly proclaimed; that preponderance, which for the misfortune of Europe and France, the Emperor Napoleon has too long exercised beyond the limits of his empire. Victory led the Allied forces to the Rhine. The first step taken by their Imperial and Royal Majesties was to offer peace to his Majesty the Emperor of the French. These conditions are based on the independence of the French empire, as well as on the independence of the other states of Europe. The views of the Powers are just in their principle, generous and liberal in their application, satisfactory to all, and honorable to each. The Allied Sovereigns wish that France should be great, powerful, and happy. The Allied Powers guarantee to the French empire an extent of territory which France never possessed during the reigns of its kings. But the Allied Powers themselves also wish to be free, happy, and tranquil. They wish for a state of peace which, by a wise distribution of power and a just equilibrium, will henceforth protect the nations of Europe from the numerous calamities under which they have groaned for the last twenty years. The Allied Powers will not lay down arms until they have attained this great and salutary result, the noble object of their efforts. They will not lay down arms until the political state of Europe is reestablished; until solid principles have resumed the ascendency over vain pretensions; finally, until the sanctity of treaties has established a solid peace in Europe.[6]

APPENDIX G

BÜLOW'S PROCLAMATION TO THE DUTCH

Providence has crowned the arms of our monarchs with victory and the Great Alliance of the free people of Europe has destroyed the forces of the blood-thirsty oppressor, Napoleon, for the second time. Germany has completely thrown off the disgraceful chains under which it endured without welfare and prosperity.

Dutchmen! You, once before us, boldly opposed oppression. Earlier in history, you cast-off a servile destiny. The hour of deliverance from oppression now also rings for you. Through no fault of your own, you have been subjected to the same unfortunate fate as so many others. The Allied army, the successor of that of the great Gustavus Adolphus, which achieved victory in North Germany, now crosses your frontiers and urges you to follow the example that your friends and brothers in all of Germany have already provided. The Prussian corps under my orders, which forms a part of this army, is the first to offer you a hand to assist in your liberation and your welfare. When you are freed from oppression your flag will again fly on all of the seas, it will soon reappear and fly forever.

Have trust in us; once, long ago, we earned it from you; we also know how to respect your trust through the most strict military discipline and are only driven by your wish to be free. But we also stand with confidence in you, true-hearted and brave neighbors and friends. We also depend on your assistance in the successful completion of this great work, which, through the united effort of all powers, can no longer be doubted.

Show yourselves worthy of your forefathers, contribute to our cause as heartily as they, under the flags that wave for freedom and justice. In the age we live, the courage and the tenacity of the Batavian legions in a struggle for the just cause will long be honored.[7]

APPENDIX H

BÜLOW'S PROCLAMATION TO THE BELGIANS

The just punishment of the Heavens has reached the One who out of pride and insolence has devastated the world with a godless hand and destroyed everything that is sacred as soon as his devastating and bloody plan encountered any resistance. The army that he led was twice destroyed by the sword of revenge, and the time has now come when one need only say the name of Napoleon in order to provoke the curses of several millions of his subjects, whose fate he sacrificed without hesitation in his ruinous plans.

Belgians! By all that is dear to you, you are the only people who still carry the yoke of the madman, whose pride and insolence have devastated the world. The only people, whose brothers, sons, and relatives he can rip unopposed from your arms in order to lead them to the slaughter house and allow them to perish in disgrace and misery, wherein his foolish anger will inevitably overthrow him. You are the only people, whose hopes of regaining your former prosperity and the vested wealth of your economy under a just and paternal government have not wavered. Do you still want to bear the chains of slavery? Should the example of your neighbors and friends, who again enjoy all the advantages of the beauty and glory of past ages, not inflame you to noble emulation? Certainly the blood of your brave and noble-minded forefathers still flows in your veins! You are still the same heroic people that history gloriously mentions, worthy of the great alliances to which you belonged, and capable of freeing yourself through your own strength. Your deeds will break your shameful bonds.

Take courage! We are here for your protection and to assist in your liberation. We approach not to conquer, not to oppress, and not to consume. We only want to save brothers, who through the most sacred right deserve to be free and happy. For this reason, once more unite and act like a noble and independent people. Exterminate the hordes of the predatory foreigner that assailed your country's hearth. Eradicate the refuge where cowardice seeks to save itself. Through all danger, our flag will wave beside yours and, as always in such a holy and just cause, God will grant our army the victory.[8]

Appendix I

Himbert de Flegny to the mayors of the Vosges Department, 9 January 1814

I sent you my proclamation from the 8th of this month. First magistrates of the people, it is in you that they have placed their cherished interests. I arrive at the head of an armed force to deliver you. The common defense, the honor of the country is forever a duty that each must perform. This duty is imperious today. Surround yourselves with men of energy, men of courage, men who do not want their country to become a theater of outrages and misfortune. To arms! It is the only cry that one must hear; it is the battle cry of all Frenchmen. Set in the hand of all your fellow citizens the means of destruction with which one can oppose the enemy and recognize your superiority to him. Rally yourselves! Remember the very simple principle that unity provides strength! One talks of happiness, of a war of philosophy. No one allow themselves to mistake this shrewd language and of those who have heard it, there is no one who did not groan at its credulity. Again, to arms! The government deploys its forces, we must support them with all of our efforts and all of our resources.[9]

APPENDIX J

GNEISENAU TO RADETZKY

Nancy is ours! The enemy is incapable of resistance. His defensive system is worm-ridden. The inhabitants have greeted our troops with joy. Rebellion *en masse*, National Guards, and cohorts! Napoleon's misfortunes have made him hated by the same people who earlier had been blinded by his good fortune. We can reach Paris without great danger or exertions. Such a battle will be neither bloody nor dangerous. As true companions in arms we are ready to cooperate with anything that the Prince [Schwarzenberg] desires. *You can count on everything that lies in our power.* You know the principles of the art of war better than I, and I also know full-well that it often brings advantages to deviate from such. The time for this appears to have arrived. We have troops standing on the Rhine whose number taken together would make a formidable army. And for what purpose? In order to observe Mainz and Strasbourg? We have fourteen marches to Paris, eighteen days will suffice to complete these marches, deliver a battle, and dictate an armistice. In order to secure victory, why should we not move concentrically on Paris with everything that we have on the Rhine? I subject my ideas to your enlightened insight and long military experience. Many who are well-trained in the art of war will want to systematically conduct the war with orthodox sieges from the Rhine into the French interior, prolonging the war and thus increasing the chances of a setback; these people will pass the most condemning judgement over my audacity and view my ideas as eccentric. Such opinions would not change my views. But if a man such as you refutes my assertion with reasons that are drawn from a higher view of the situation, I will thus abandon my views. A temporary disadvantage, and one that is proportionately smaller, must be risked in order to secure a more enduring advantage. On the one hand is the sacrifice of some square miles, on the other is the dictation of a peace that will provide the people with peace and security for the throne.[10]

APPENDIX K

GNEISENAU TO KNESEBECK

Although I have a right to complain that you did not answer the letter that I wrote you while still in Frankfurt and that you also had refused to submit my memo to His Majesty the Tsar of Russia, I will nevertheless postpone everything that I have on my mind and once again offer to you the opportunity for true cooperation. Direct correspondence between us, I believe, will produce good results; we are so close to the goal, allow us to unite and proceed together.

What one did not believe of me in Frankfurt has happened. Holland is almost completely conquered because Bülow had the boldness to drive between the fortresses of this land. France has lost these fortresses because it does not have the resources to furnish them. All of Europe would not have the means for this. Had we immediately crossed the Rhine when we arrived at this river, we would have taken many of the most significant fortresses and we would now be in Paris. Confusion and despair now reign – even after the enemy has been allowed eight weeks to rest and recuperate. None of fortresses are sufficiently provisioned; there are no palisades; they are manned only by recruits; the majority of the veteran soldiers are sick or dying. Dissension rules the government. Encouraged by the mood of the people of Paris, the Legislative Corps sent its president to the emperor to demand an explanation – now it has been dissolved. Now or never is the time for us to march to Paris and dictate the type of peace that is demanded to satisfy the people and the security of the old royal families, then we may return home and enjoy our days in peace and quiet.

We must still deliver a battle; it will be neither difficult nor dangerous. Obviously one must carry the necessary ammunition for two battles. This is not much more than one usually carries. The II Corps discharged 5,000 rounds in the battle of Groß Görschen. The corps numbered 30,000 men at that time. The ammunition was transported in ten wagons. We now have in our army more 12-pounders than the II Corps had at that time. If we consider that due to the 12-pounders the ammunition requirement would be more than double and also that the battle would be twice as large as that of Groß Görschen, one can thus conclude that the ammunition for a second battle can be transported in thirty ammunition wagons for an army corps of 30,000 men; therefore the ammunition for 300,000 men on 300 wagons. What are 300 wagons compared to the enormous baggage train that we carry with us, and for the most part is superfluous? It is completely unnecessary to place in the rear of our army a corps let alone an actual army in order to escort the ammunition transports; the replacements and convalescents coming from Germany, if united in large masses, are sufficient to thwart all enemy attempts from the neighboring provinces.

The composition of the enemy troops is too poor. The entire system of our enemy is worm-ridden. You certainly agree with me over this. We sit here before Metz anxiously awaiting the news that we desire from Prince Schwarzenberg. In the meantime, we threaten Nancy, Thionville, and

Luxembourg; upon the latter perhaps we will make an attempt. We will probably take Nancy in a manner that will avoid bloodshed. On 26 January Kleist will reach Trier. In the meantime, Henckel, with a few people and much initiative struck terror and confusion in the French in the region of Trier, liberated conscripts, took prisoners in the range of over 3,000. Here over the past few days we have issued over 500 passes to deserters (enlisted soldiers). Chernishev, who reached Düsseldorf on the 6th, has written to me and seeks my opinion over which direction he should take? I answered that I believe it would be best for him to move in the direction of Liège. When he arrives there he will be in the land of the Walloons, a very militant people and well-disposed for an insurrection against the French government. He will also find there considerable French armories; by taking them he will became a very painful thorn. If he does this, I expect good results. As we know, there is a shortage of arms in the French army. The great factory near Strasbourg is now also no longer available to the enemy; that of Charleville by Mézières is insignificant; that of Versailles only produces sporting weapons; there is still a small one in the Rhône Department. We in Prussia have struggled through this school of experience and therefore know that what the French do not have ready in arms cannot be obtained in a few months. This condition alone must prompt us to concentrate and proceed to Paris. I also cannot ignore the thought, that in order to achieve this last, highest, and most decisive goal of our sensible quest, a goal, which we can reach in fourteen days if we want, it would be good for us to at least harass the French fortresses lying behind us, and to begin a mass migration on Paris with everything that we have on the Rhine. We can reinforce ourselves with a number of units that altogether can form a very considerable army and thus further guarantee our success. The worst that could come from such a decision is that the garrisons of Mainz and Strasbourg make excursions in the local vicinity and commit extortion. These excursions can achieving nothing more due to the nature and composition of the garrisons. This danger would be very short in duration because after some eighteen days, march and battle will be completed, and victory and peace earned. No one can dispute the certainty of success, because how can our enemy resist such superior forces since he now withdraws before us? Examine these unorthodox military ideas and share your opinion of them with me. I know how very much I deviate here from the principles of the art of war, but I also know that deviations from the principles of war are often beneficial. *And in the end what are the principles of war? Whether Schwarzenberg's army shall cover the rear standing at Strasbourg or at Châlons makes no difference as long as it prevents us from being enveloped.* Just now the news has arrived that the French evacuated Nancy and our troops have occupied this city! This only confirms everything I have just wrote. We can soon reach Paris – if we want it bad enough.[11]

APPENDIX L

MACDONALD'S PROCLAMATION TO THE SOLDIERS OF THE 25TH MILITARY DISTRICT

You have been summoned from your winter quarters; in a few moments you will be assembled, in a few days you will march to combat! Remember twenty years of glory, the innumerable feats of arms that they illustrate, and that the enemy still fears your valor and your intrepidity. Our frontiers are invaded, but the words of the Emperor have raised the Nation. Our country has appealed to its children. They have been called to arms; they march, advance; the Sovereign is at their head, showing in one hand the olive branch of peace and the deadly blade in the other. Soldiers, numerous battalions hasten to join your ranks; an army of reserve of 100,000 troops of the Line are in position behind you; it is supported by 200,000 National Guardsmen who are forming in Bretagne, Normandie, Picardie, and around the capital. These forces can be doubled and even tripled if necessary.

Soldiers! Our fortresses are armed, provisioned, and their defense is confided to you; woe to the enemy if he shows himself or if he dares to turn them! Reject with indignation his perfidious insinuations, his false promises; only remember the devastation, the pillage, and the death that mark all of the steps of these barbarian hordes.

Soldiers of the 25th Military Division! I tell you that peace is made with King Ferdinand of Spain. Our troops from Aragon and Catalogne are in march for Lyon; those from Bayonne for Paris. Frenchmen, it is for our country that we go fight, do not allow it to be invaded and ripped apart. The Emperor and France have their eyes on you. Victory or death must be our battle cry, and soon the foe who has crossed our frontiers will meet with shame and death; the sacred territory will consume all those who are spared by the blade.[12]

APPENDIX M

NAPOLEON TO METTERNICH, 16 JANUARY 1814

The delays that the negotiations experience are not attributable either to France or Austria, yet they will suffer the most from them. The Allied armies have already invaded several of our provinces: if they advance further, a battle will be inevitable, and surely the foresight of Austria must calculate and weigh the consequences that would attend such a battle, whether lost by the Allies or by France.

Writing to a minister as enlightened as you, it is not necessary that I should explain these consequences. I shall limit myself to merely hinting at them, being assured that they cannot escape your view.

The chances of war are growing greater each day. In proportion, as the Allies advance, their forces diminish, while the French armies are constantly receiving reinforcements. The Allied advance inspires with two-fold courage a nation that feels it has its greatest and dearest interests to defend. The consequences of a battle lost by the Allies, would not be so fatal to any as to Austria; she being both the chief of the Allies and one of the central powers of Europe.

Supposing Fortune should continue to favor the Allies, it is doubtlessly important for Austria to attentively consider the situation of Europe after a battle lost by the French in the heart of France, and whether such an event would not produce consequences diametrically opposite to the equilibrium that Austria seeks to establish, and at the same time hostile to her policy and the personal and family affections of Kaiser Francis.

Finally, Austria insists that she wishes for peace; but is she not likely to fall short of her goal, or perhaps to overreach it by continuing hostilities, when both parties wish to end them?

These considerations lead me to presume that in the present situation of the respective armies, and in this severe season of the year, a suspension of hostilities would be mutually advantageous to both parties.

This armistice may be concluded, either by a formal convention, or merely by an exchange of declarations between you and myself. It may be limited to a certain time, with the condition that hostilities shall not be resumed without an intimation to that effect, being made some days earlier.

The armistice seems to me to depend entirely on the will of Austria, since she directs the principal military affairs. And I believe that, in one case or the other, Austria's interests should be furthest advanced and pushed to the last extreme. This conviction induces me to address myself confidentially to you. If I am wrong, if these absolutely confidential suggestions have no effect, I request that you consider them as never having been made.

You have shown me so much personal confidence, and I have such a firm understanding of the views and sentiments that you have expressed in all circumstances, that I hope a letter thus dictated in confidence, should it fail to attain its goal, remain between you and me.[13]

APPENDIX N

VICTOR TO BERTHIER

According to your letters to me on the 16th and 17th, I did not defend as I should have the defiles of the Vosges nor the crossings of the Meurthe and the Moselle. This accusation is too serious for me to remain indifferent and I must believe that you will have the kindness to deliberate my defense or place it under the eyes of His Majesty.

I was before Colmar with 7,000 infantry and 3,000 cavalry when the enemy crossed the Rhine with an army of 60,000 men. This army moved behind me, at some days march, and I was in the presence of the army commanded by Gen. Wrede; not able to remain in Alsace in this situation, I had to withdraw. I was able to move through Saverne, according to the first instructions of the emperor; I was able to establish myself in the valley of St. Marie-aux-Mines and to defend this passage for some time, but none of the dispositions that I took could prevent the enemy from advancing on Nancy either through Saverne or through St. Dié. By defending one of the valleys of the Vosges, I would have had to open the roads to Metz and Nancy to the corps that came through Saverne. Wrede, for his part, marching on St. Dié through the valleys of Colmar and Remiremont, threatened my movement in the valley of St. Marie-aux-Mines. Moreover, the troops could not find any resources to live on. This movement had thus been useless and even dangerous because it would have been easy for the enemy to encircle me. If you like take the trouble to examine the positions and compare my forces to those that operated against me, I will be justified in this part of the accusation to which I am responding. Instead of engaging myself in one of the valleys of the Vosges, I presented myself at all of the debouches with the intention of engaging the first enemy column that appeared; I attempted this, but superior forces did not allow me to further pursue this project and I remained on the defensive until an enemy corps debouched on Épinal and advanced in two marches on Flavigny. After having fought the detachment making for Épinal, during which time Wrede, concentrated at St. Dié and prepared to attack me, the prince of the Moskowa informed me that a third enemy column coming from Château-Salins was at the gates of Nancy, and that if I did not want to compromise my troops, I had to march night and day to reach Toul. In view of this new situation should have I remained at the feet of the Vosges? In making this decision, I had to consider that the city of Nancy would fall to the enemy before I arrived since the prince was not in a position to maintain himself there. Moreover, the enemy was master of the bridges of the Moselle at Épinal, Charmes, Flavigny, and St. Vincent, and having on me Gen. Wrede, all of my communications were severed and I found myself enveloped and forced to draw the sword every day. Examining the places and the positions of the enemy in this circumstance will make you aware that the prince's fears regarding my affairs were grounded and that I have done what any other general would have in my place.

I then went to Nancy, believing to cooperate with the prince to defend this city. At the moment when I arrived the enemy column coming from Château-Salins was at the gates; that which came from Épinal was already before Flavigny and Pont-St. Vincent. The prince's troops had evacuated these two bridges as well as that of Nancy and were retiring on Ligny. This new situation was more embarrassing to me than the first two. I could not, without committing the greatest imprudence, engage my 7,000–8,000 men against all of the adversaries that surrounded me, a part of which was already maneuvering on my communications with Toul; I thus evacuated Nancy and if you still want to take the trouble to see the position where I found myself, you will sense that I was in the absolute necessity to withdraw on Toul.

I arrived in this city with the plan to defend myself there: all the necessary dispositions were made; I believed that the crossings of Pont-à-Mousson and Frouard were guarded by the duke of Ragusa's troops and turned all of my attention to Nancy and St. Vincent, but three days after my arrival in Toul I learned with distress that Pont-à-Mousson and Frouard had been abandoned, that the troops charged with defending them had retired on Thiaucourt, and that Commercy and St. Mihiel were uncovered by this movement. Again, the enemy was free to move behind me and to capture, if he wanted, the principal passages across the Meuse. I learned, in fact, that he was moving on them. Should I have remained at Toul to defend the passage of the Moselle when all the others were crossed by the enemy from Épinal up to Toul and from there to Pont-à-Mousson to run the risk of seeing myself cut off from the Meuse? I reported in this sense to His Majesty. Before leaving Toul, I left there a small garrison and appealed to the National Guard. I placed in a battery some pieces of cannon that were to remain in this city. I had designated the battalion chief Chaudron to be provisional commander and I had ordered him to defend himself for as long as he could. The enemy appeared before this city and was repulsed.

After having taken this position, I established myself at Commercy, Pagny-sur-Meuse, Void, and Vaucouleurs, leaving an advance guard at Foug. The enemy already had reached Commercy before us and was in march from another direction on Vaucouleurs. He drove our troops from these two towns. Yesterday Gen. Defrance sustained a combat at Vaucouleurs against 1,200–1,500 Allied cavalry that lasted all day; he repulsed them and they suffered losses; ours were not considerable.

You have read the succinct report of my conduct. I hope that it will convince you that I could not have done anything else without compromising the interests of His Majesty. You will likewise see that three small corps under separate commands charged with achieving a single objective cannot cooperate to obtain this result and that the enemy always has the advantage as long as these small corps are not united and confided to the direction of a single chief, in which I have had the honor to propose through my preceding dispatches. I sense that if His Majesty does not decide to accept this suggestion, there will occur on the Meuse the same that occurred on the Meurthe and the Moselle. The enemy will maneuver through Neufchâteau or through St. Mihiel on Bar-le-Duc, as he has already displayed the intention, which will force me to withdraw unsupported on this town.[14]

Bibliography

I. ARCHIVES

Germany

I. Geheimes Staatsarchiv Preußischer Kulturbesitz zu Berlin (GStA):
Rep. 15 A Preußischer Heeresarchiv und Heeresgeschichtliche Sammlung.
Rep. 92 Nachlaß Gneisenau.
Rep. 92 Nachlaß Albrecht.
Rep. 92 Nachlaß Gebhard Leberecht Fürst Blücher von Wahlstatt.
II. Bayerisch Hauptstaatsarchiv, Kriegsarchiv (BHStA, KA), B 545.
III. Ehemals Mitteilungen aus dem Gräflichen Bülow Familien-Archiv zu Grünhoff (BFA), Baden-Baden. Friedrich Wilhelm Graf Bülow von Dennewitz. Dokumentation in Briefen-Befehlen-Berichten. Gesammelt Übertragen und mit Anmerkungen Versehen von Joachim-Albrecht Graf Bülow von Dennewitz.

Austria

Österreichisches Staatsarchiv, Kriegsarchiv (ÖStA, KA):
Alte Feldakten, Kartons 1603–17.

France

I. Service Historique de l'Armée de Terre (SHAT):
Cartons C^2 160–73, 301–2, 316, 320, 322; C^{17} 182–3; MR 902.
II. Archives Nationales (AN):
Armand de Caulaincourt's Papers, 95 AP 14.
Michel Ney's Papers, 137 AP 5 and 15.

Russia

I. Rossiiskii Gosudarstvennyi Voenno-Istoricheskii (RGVIA):
Опись коллекции "Наполеоновские войны" 1805–1815 годы
Delo 3376, 4118–4210

II. PRIMARY WORKS

Beauchamp, A. *Histoire des campagnes de 1814 et de 1815, ou histoire politique et militaire des deux invasions de la France, de l'entreprise de Bounaparte au mois de mars, de la chute totale de sa paissance, et de la double restauration du trône, jusqu' à la seconde paix de Paris, inclusivement. Seconde partie, comprenantle récit de tous les événemens survenus en france en 1815. Rédigée sur des matériaux authentiques au inedits.* 3 vols. Paris, 1817.

Benoit, A. *Invasion de 1814 dans le département des Vosges. Correspondance inédite du général Cassagne.* Épinal, 1877.

Blücher, G. L. *Ausgewählte Briefe des Feldmarschalls Leberecht von Blücher.* Leipzig, n.d.

Blüchers Briefe. Ed. Wolfgang von Unger. Stuttgart, 1912.

Bonaparte, Napoléon. *La Correspondance de Napoléon Ier; publiée par ordre de l'empereur Napoléon III.* 32 vols. Paris, 1858–69.

Bourrienne, L. A. *Memoirs of Napoleon Bonaparte.* Ed. R. W. Phipps. 4 vols. London, 1895.

Boyen, H. *Erinnerungen aus dem Leben des General-Feldmarshalls Hermann von Boyen.* Ed. F. Nippold. 3 vols. Leipzig, 1889–90.

Erinnerungen aus dem Leben des General-Feldmarshalls Hermann von Boyen. Ed. D. Schmidt. 2 vols. Berlin, 1990.

Brett-James, A. *Europe against Napoleon: The Leipzig Campaign, 1813, from Eyewitness Accounts.* London, 1970.

Cathcart, G. *Commentaries on the War in Russia and Germany in 1812 and 1813.* London, 1850.

Caulaincourt, A. A. L. *Mémoires du general de Caulaincourt, duc de Vicence, Grand Écuyer de l'empereur.* Ed. J. Hanoteau. 3 vols. Paris, 1933.

No Peace with Napoleon: Concluding the Memoirs of General de Caulaincourt, Duke of Vicenza. New York, 1936.

Clausewitz, C. *Der Feldzug 1812 in Rußland und die Befreiungskriege von 1812–15.* Berlin, 1906.

Historical and Political Writings. Trans. and eds. P. Paret and D. Moran. Princeton, 1992.

"Übersichtdes Feldzuges von 1814 in Frankreich." Vol. 7 of *Hinterlassene Werke des Generals Carl von Clausewitz über Krieg und Kriegführung.* 10 vols. Berlin, 1832–37.

Damitz, K. *Geschichte des Feldzuges von 1814.* 4 vols. Berlin, 1843.

Donnersmarck, W. L. H. *Erinnerungen aus meinem Leben.* Leipzig, 1846.

Fabvier, C. N. *Journal des opérations du sizième corps pendant la campagne de 1814 en France.* Paris, 1819.

Fain, A. J. F. *Manuscrit de mil huit cent quatorze, trouvé dans les voitures impériales prises à Waterloo, contenant l'histoire des six derniers mois du regne de Napoléon.* 4th ed. Paris, 1830.

Fane, J. [Lord Burghersh]. *Memoir of the Operations of the Allied Armies under Prince Schwarzenberg and Marshal Blücher, during the later end of 1813, and the year 1814.* London, 1822; reprint ed., London, 1996.

Fezansac, R. *Souvenirs militaires de 1804 à 1814.* Paris, 1870.

Friccius, C. *Geschichte des Krieges in den Jahren 1813 und 1814 mit besonderer Rücksicht auf Ostpreußen und das Königsbergische Landwehrbattalion*. 2 vols. Berlin, 1848.

Girard, S. *Campagne de 1813–1814: Journal de marche d'un Garde d'Honneur*. Paris, 2002.

Giraud, P. F. F. J. *Campagne de Paris en 1814, précédée d'un coup-d'oeil sur celle de 1813, ou précis historique et impartial des événemens, depuis l'invasion de la France*. Paris, 1814.

Gneisenau, A. *The Life and Campaigns of Field-Marshal Prince Blücher*. London, 1815.

Griewank, K., ed. *Gneisenau: Ein Leben in Briefen*. Leipzig, 1939.

Grouchy, E. *Mémoires du maréchal de Grouchy, par le marquis de Grouchy*. Paris, 1873–74.

Hassenkamp, H. *General Graf Bülow von Dennewitz in den Feldzügen von 1814 und 1815*. Leipzig, 1843.

Hellwald, F. J. H. *Der k.k. österreichische Feldmarschall Graf Radetzky: eine biographische Skizze nach den eigenen Dictaten und der Correspondenz des Feldmarschalls von einem österreichischen Veteranen*. Stuttgart, 1858.

Hugo, J. L. S. *Journal historique du blocus de Thionville en 1814, et de Thionville, Sierck, et Rodemarck en 1815*. Blois, 1819.

Junot, L. A. C. *Memoirs of the Emperor Napoleon, from Ajaccio to Waterloo, as Soldier, Emperor, Husband*. 3 vols. Washington [D.C.], 1901.

Karl XIV, King of Sweden. *Recueil des ordres de mouvement proclamations et bulletins de S.A.R. le prince royal de suede, commandant en chef l'armée combinée du nord de l'Allemagne en 1813 et 1814*. Stockholm, 1838.

Klinkowström, A., ed. *Österreichs Theilnahme an den Befreiungskriegen. Ein Beitrag zur Geschichte der Jahres 1813 bis 1815 nach Aufzeichnungen von Friedrich von Gentz nebst einen Anhang: "Briefwechsel zwischen den Fürsten Schwarzenberg und Metternich."* Herausgegeben von Richard Fürst Metternich-Winneburg. Vienna, 1887.

Koch, F. *Mémoires pour servir à l'histoire de la campagne de 1814, accompagnés de plans, d'ordres de bataille et de situations*. Paris, 1819.

Löwenstern, W. *Mémoires du général-major russe Baron de Löwenstern, 1776–1858*. Ed. M. H. Weil. Paris, 1903.

Londonderry, Lieutenant-General Charles William Vane, Marquess [Sir Charles Stewart]. *Narrative of the War in Germany and France in 1813 and 1814*. London, 1830.

Macdonald, J.-É.-J.-A. *Souvenirs du maréchal Macdonald, duc de Tarente*. Ed. C. Rousset. 2 vols. London, 1892.

Marmont, A. *Mémoires du Duc de Raguse*. 9 vols. Paris, 1857.

Martens, F. F. *Recueil des traités et conventions conclus par la russie avec les puissances étrangéres*. 15 vols. St. Petersburg, 1874–1909.

Martens, G. F. *Recueil de traités d'alliance, de paix, de trêve, de neutralité, de commerce, de limites, déchange, etc., et plusieurs autres actes servant à la connoissance des relations étrangéres des puissances et états de l'Europe depuis 1761 jusqu' à présent*. 16 vols. Göttingen, 1817–42.

Méneval, C. F. *Memoirs of Napoleon Bonaparte, and the court of the First Empire, by Baron C. F. De Méneval, his private secretary.* 3 vols. New York, 1910.

Metternich, C. L. W. *Memoirs of Prince Metternich, 1773–1815.* 5 vols. Ed. R. Metternich. Trans. A. Napier. New York, 1970.

Mikhailovsky-Danilevsky, A. *History of the Campaign in France in the Year 1814.* London, 1840; reprint ed., Cambridge, 1992.

Müffling, F. K. *Aus meinem Leben.* Berlin, 1851.

   Passages from My Life; Together with Memoirs of the Campaign of 1813 and 1814. Trans. and ed. Philip Yorke, London, 1853.

Münster, E. *Political Sketches of the State of Europe, 1814–1867.* Edinburgh, 1868.

Pasquier, E. D. *Histoire de mon temps. Mémoires du chancelier Pasquier, publiés par M. Le duc d'Audiffret-Pasquier.* 6 vols. Paris, 1893–4.

Petiet, A. *Journal historique de la division de cavalerie légére au 5e corps de cavalerie pendant la campagne de 1814 en France.* Paris, 1821.

Philippart, J. *Campaign in Germany and France.* 2 vols. London, 1814.

   Memoirs and Campaigns of Charles Jean, Prince Royal of Sweden. Baltimore, 1815.

Pierer, H. A. *Der Feldzug des Corps des Generals Grafen Ludwig von Wallmoden-Gimborn an der Nieder-Elbe und in Belgien in den Jahren 1813 und 1814.* Altenburg, 1848.

Plotho, C. *Der Krieg in Deutschland und Frankreich in den Jahren 1813 und 1814.* 3 vols. Berlin, 1817.

Radetzky von Radetz. J. J. W. A. F. K. *Denkschriften militärisch-politischen Inhalts aus dem handschriftlichen Nachlaß des k.k. österreichischen Feldmarschalls Grafen Radetzky.* Stuttgart und Augsburg, 1858.

Recueil des traités de la France, publié sous les auspices du ministère des affairs étrangères. 23 vols. Paris, 1864–1907.

Reiche, L. *Memoiren des königlichen preußischen Generals der Infanterie Ludwig von Reiche.* Ed. L. Weltzien. Leipzig, 1857.

Savary, J. M. *Mémoires du duc de Rovigo.* 8 vols. Paris, 1828.

Schwarzenberg, K. *Briefe des Feldmarschalls Fürsten Schwarzenberg an Seine Frau, 1799–1816.* Leipzig, 1913.

Ségur, P. P. *Du Rhin à Fontainebleau: Mémoires du Général Comte de Ségur (Aide de camp de Napoléon) de l'Académie française.* Paris, n.d.

   Napoleon's Russian Campaign. Trans. J. D. Townsend. Alexandria, 1965.

Steffens, H. *Adventures on the Road to Paris, during the Campaigns of 1813/14.* London, 1848.

Stein, H. F. K. *Freiherr vom Stein: Briefwechsel, Denkschriften, unf Aufzeichnungen.* Ed. Erich Botzenhart. 7 vols. Berlin, 1931–37.

Stewart, R., Viscount Castlereagh. *The Correspondance, Despatches and other Papers of Viscount Castlereagh.* Ed. Charles William Vane. 12 vols. London, 1848–53.

Teissèdre, F., ed. *1814: Résistance et occupation des villes françaises.* Paris, 2001.

Temperley, H., and L. Penson. *Foundations of British Foreign Policy from Pitt to Salisbury on Documents, Old and New, Selected and Edited with Historical Introductions.* Cambridge, 1938.

Varnhagen von Ense, K. A. *Fürst Blücher von Wahlstadt.* Berlin, 1933.

   Das Leben der Generals Gräfen Bülow von Dennewitz. Berlin, 1853.

Vaudoncourt, G. *Histoire des campagnes de 1814 et 1815 en France.* 5 vols. Paris, 1826.

Venturini, C. *Rußlands und Deutschlands Befreiungskriege von der Franzosen-Herrschaft unter Napoleon Buonaparte in den Jahren 1812–1815.* 4 vols. Altenburg, 1816–18.

Webster, C. *British Diplomacy, 1813–1815; Select Documents Dealing with the Reconstruction of Europe.* London, 1921.

Wilson, R. *General Wilson's Journal, 1812–1814.* Ed. A. Brett-James. London, 1964.

   Private Diary of Travels, Personal Services, and Public Events: During the Mission Employed with the European Armies in the Campaigns of 1812, 1813, 1814. London, 1861.

III. SECONDARY WORKS

Arnold, J. "Le Beau Soleil," in *Napoleon's Marshals.* Ed. D. Chandler. New York, 1987.

Atteridge, A. H. *The Bravest of the Brave, Michel Ney, Marshal of France, Duke of Elchingen, Prince of the Moskowa 1769–1815.* London, 1912.

Balfour, F. *The Life of George, Fourth Earl of Aberdeen.* 2 vols. London, 1922.

Barton, D. P. *Bernadotte: Prince and King, 1810–1844.* London, 1925.

Benaerts, L. P. R. R. *Les Commissaires extraordinaires de Napoléon I en 1814 d'aprés leur correspondance inedited.* Paris, 1915.

Bercé, Yves-Marie. *La Fin de l'Europe napoléonienne, 1814: la vacance du pouvoir.* Paris, 1990.

Bergeron, L. *France under Napoleon.* Trans. R. R. Palmer. Princeton, 1981.

Bernhardi, T. *Denkwürdigkeiten aus dem Leben des Kaiserlich Russischen Generals von der Infanterie Carl Friedrich Grafen von Toll.* 4 vols. Leipzig, 1856–66.

Bertaud, Jean-Paul. *Guerre et société in France, de Louis XIV à Napolén I.* Paris, 1998.

   La France de Napoléon: 1799–1815. Paris, 1987.

Bertier de Sauvigny, G. de. *The Bourbon Restoration.* Trans. L. Case. Philadelphia, 1966.

   Metternich. Paris, 1986.

Bertin, G. *La Campagne de 1814, d'après des témoins oculaires.* Paris, 1897.

Bigelow, P. *The History of the German Struggle for Liberty.* 2 vols. New York, 1896–1903.

Billinger, R. *Metternich and the German Question: States' Rights and Federal Duties, 1820–1834.* Newark, 1991.

Black, Jeremy. *France From Louis XIV to Napoleon: The Fate of a Great Power.* London, 1999.

Blaison, L. M. *Un Défenseur alsacien en 1814. Le premier siège de Belfort et le commandant Legrand.* Paris, 1912.

Blanton, H. "Napoleon's Prefects and the Fall of the French Empire in 1813–1814." Ph.D. diss., Florida State University, 1999.

Bogdanovich, M. I. *Geschichte des Krieges 1814 in Frankreich und des Sturzes Napoleon's I., nach den zuverläßigsten Quellen.* Trans. G. Baumgarten. Leipzig, 1866.

Borrey, F. *L'Esprit public chez les prêtres francs-comtois pendant la crise de 1813 à 1815.* Paris, 1912.

Un Épisode de la campagne de France. Le blocus de Besançon par les Autrichiens (1814). Paris, 1909.

Bouvier, F. *Les premiers combats de 1814. Prologue de la campagne de France dans les Vosges.* Paris, 1895.

Brett-James, A. *General Graham, 1748–1844.* New York, 1959.

Bruun, G. *Europe and the French Imperium, 1799–1814.* New York, 1938.

Buckland, C. S. B. *Metternich and the British Government from 1809 to 1813.* London, 1932.

Caemmerer, R. *Die Befreiungskrieg, 1813–1815: Ein Strategischer Überblick.* Berlin, 1907.

Calmon-Maison, J. J. R. *Le général Maison et le 1er corps de la grande armée; campagne de Belgique décembre 1813 – avril 1814.* Paris, 1913.

Camon, H. *La Guerre naoléonienne. Précis de campagnes.* Paris, 1999.

Campana, I. R. *La Campagne de France 1814.* Paris, 1922.

Carrot, G. *Metz et Thion de 1811 à 1815.* Metz, 1971.

Chandler, D. *The Campaigns of Napoleon.* New York, 1966.

Dictionary of the Napoleonic Wars. New York, 1979.

Chardigny, Louis. *L' Homme Napoléon.* Paris, 1987.

Charras, J. B. A. *Histoire de la Guerre de 1813 en Allemagne. Derniers jours de la retraite, insurrection de l'Allemagne, armements, diplomatie, entrée en campagne.* 2nd ed. Paris, 1870.

Christophe, R. *Le Maréchal Marmont, duc de Raguse.* Paris, 1968.

Chuquet, A. *L'Alsace en 1814.* Paris, 1900.

Connelly, O. *Blundering to Glory: Napoleon's Military Campaigns.* Wilmington, 1987.

Cook, L. "Prince Schwarzenberg's Crisis in 1812: In the Service of Two Emperors.". *Consortium on Revolutionary, 1750–1850: Selected Papers* (1995): 351–8

"Prince Karl Philipp zu Schwarzenberg and Napoleon: Franco–Austrian Relations, 1800–1815." Ph.D. diss., Florida State University, 1999.

"Schwarzenberg at Dresden: Leadership and Command." *Consortium on Revolutionary, 1750–1850: Selected Papers* (1994): 642–51.

Coustumier, J. *Le Maréchal Victor: Claude Victor Perrin, 1764–1841.* Paris, 2004.

Craig, G. A. *Europe, 1815–1914.* 3rd ed. New York, 1989.

The Politics of the Prussian Army: 1640–1945. Oxford, 1956.

"Problems of Coalition Warfare: The Military Alliance against Napoleon, 1813–14," in *War, Politics, and Diplomacy: Selected Essays by Gordon Craig.* London, 1966.

Crusius, A. *Der Winterfeldzug in Holland, Brabant, und Flandern, eine Episode aus dem Befreiungskriege 1813 und 1814.* Luxembourg, 1865.

Droysen, J. *Das Leben des Feldmarshalls Grafen Yorck von Wartenburg.* 2 vols. Leipzig, 1851.

Du Casse, A. *Le Général Arrighi de Casanova, duc de Padoue.* 2 vols. Paris, 1866.

Précis historique des opérations de l'armée de Lyon en 1814. Paris, 1849.

Dupuy, T. N., C. Johnson, and D. L. Bongard. *The Harper Encyclopedia of Military Biography.* New York, 1992.

Englund, Steven. *Napoleon: A Political Life.* New York, 2003.

Fabry, G. J. *Souvenirs de la campagne de France.* Paris, 1914

Fisher, H. A. L. *Napoleonic Statesmanship in Germany.* Oxford, 1903.

Fleury, A. *Reims en 1814 pendant l'invasion*. Paris, 1902.

Fleury, É. *Histoire de l'invasion de 1814 dans les départments du nord-est de la France*. 2nd ed. Paris, 1858.

Floriet, L. *Marmont, maréchal d'empire: 1774–1852*. Marcilly-sur-Tille, 1996.

Ford, G. S. *Stein and the Era of Reform in Prussia, 1807–1815*. Princeton, 1922; reprint ed., Glouchester, 1965.

Fortescue, J. W. *British Statesmen of the Great War, 1793–1814*. Oxford, 1911.

Foster, J. T. *Napoleon's Marshal: The Life of Michel Ney*. New York, 1968.

Fournier, A. *Der Congress von Châtillon. Die Politik im Kriege von 1814*. Vienna and Prague, 1900.

Furet, F. *Revolutionary France, 1770–1880*. Trans. Antonia Nevil. Malden, Mass., 1999.

Friederich, R. *Die Befreiungskriege, 1813–1815*. 4 vols. Berlin, 1911–13.

Gallas, L. *Les invasions autrichiennes de 1814 et 1815 à Chalon-sur-Saône et en Bourgogne*. Chalon-sur-Saône, 1938–40.

Garros, L. *Ney: le brave des braves*. Paris, 1981.

Gates, D. *The Napoleonic Wars, 1803–1815*. London, 1997.

Geyl, Pieter. *Napoleon: For and Against*. Trans. O. Renier. New Haven, Conn, 1949.

Gill, J. *A Soldier for Napoleon: The Campaigns of Lieutenant Franz Joseph Hausmann, 7th Bavarian Infantry*. Trans. C. Hausmann. London, 1998.

Gray, R. "The Big Mortar," in *Napoleon's Marshals*. Ed. D. Chandler. New York, 1987.

Grimstead, Patricia Kennedy. *The Foreign Ministers of Alexander I: Political Attitudes and the Conduct of Russian Diplomacy, 1801–1825*. Berkeley, CA, 1969.

Grunwald, C. *The Life of Baron Stein: Napoleon's Nemesis*. Trans. C. F. Atkinson. New York, 1936.

Guerrini, M. *Napoleon and Paris: Thirty Years of History*. New York, 1967.

Hall, Christopher. *British Strategy in the Napoleonic War, 1803–1815*. Manchester, 1992.

Hartley, Janet. *Alexander I*. New York, 1994.

Hankinson, A. "His Outspokenness," in *Napoleon's Marshals*. Ed. D. Chandler. New York, 1987.

Haythornthwaite. P. *The Napoleonic Source Book*. New York, 1990.

Heilmann, J. *Feldmarschall Fürst Wrede*. Leipzig, 1881.

Henderson, E. *Blücher and the Uprising of Prussia Against Napoleon, 1806–1815*. London, 1911.

Hennequin, É. *Les opérations de 1814 dans l'Aube*. Troyes, 1921.

Hiller, F. *Geschichte des Feldzuges 1814 gegen Frankreich unter besonderer Berücksichtigung der Anteilnahme der Königlich württembergischen Truppen*. Leipzig, 1894.

Homan, G. "The Restoration of the House of Orange-Nassau in the Netherlands, 1813." *Consortium on Revolutionary, 1750–1850: Selected Papers* (1989): 402–410.

Horricks, R. *Marshal Ney: The Romance and the Real*. New York, 1982.

Horward, D. *Napoleon and Iberia: The Twin Sieges of Ciudad Rodrigo and Almeida, 1810*. Tallahassee, 1980.

Houssaye, H. *1814*. Paris, 1888; reprint ed., Paris, 1986.

Hulot, F. *Le Maréchal Ney*. Paris, 2000.

Janson, A. *Geschichte des Feldzuges 1814 in Frankreich.* 2 vols. Berlin, 1903–5, in *Geschichte der Befreiungskriege 1813–1815.* 9 vols. Berlin, 1903–9.

"Die Unternehmungen des Yorckschen Korps gegen die nordfranzösischen Festungen," *Militair-Wochenblatt* (1903): 1–66.

Jany, C. *Geschichte der königlichen preußischen Armee.* 4 vols. Berlin, 1929.

Johnston, O. W. *Der deutsche Nationalmythos.* Stuttgart, 1990.

Josselson, Michael and Dianna Josselson. *The Commander: A life of Barclay de Tolly.* New York, 1980.

Kerchnawe, H., and A. Veltze. *Feldmarschall Karl Fürst zu Schwarzenberg: der Führer der Verbündeten in den Befreiungskriegen.* Vienna, 1913.

Kissinger, H. *A World Restored: Metternich, Castlereagh and the Problems of Peace, 1812–22.* Boston, 1990.

Knoepfler, L. *Le blocus de Metz en 1814.* Paris, 1909.

Kraehe, E. *Metternich's German Policy.* 2 vols. Princeton, 1963.

La Force, Auguste de Caumont, duc de. *L'architrésorier Lebrun, gouverneur de la Hollande, 1810-1813.* Paris: 1907.

Lachouque, H. *Napoleon en 1814.* Paris, 1959.

Lefebvre, G. *Napoleon.* 2 vols. Trans. J. E. Anderson. New Yorck, 1969.

Lefebvre de Béhaine, F. *La Campagne de France.* 2 vols. Paris, 1913.

Leggiere, M. *Napoleon and Berlin: The Franco-Prussian War in North Germany, 1813.* Norman, 2002.

Lehmann, M. *Freiherr vom Stein.* 3 vols. Leipzig, 1902–05.

Lenoir, C. A. *Les Trois sièges d'Huningue (1796–1814–1815).* Paris, 1896.

Lentz, Thierry. *L'effondrement du système napoléonien, 1810–1814 vol. 2 of Nouvelle Histoire du Premier Empire.* Paris, 2004.

Levinger, M. *Enlightened Nationalism: The Transformation of Prussian Political Culture, 1806–1848.* Oxford, 2000.

Lobonov-Rostovsky, A. *Russia and Europe, 1789–1825.* Durham, 1947.

Lomier, E. *Historie des regiments de Gardes d'honneurs, 1813–1814.* Amiens, 1924.

Lucas-Dubreton, J. *Le maréchal Ney, 1769–1815.* Paris, 1941.

Mathieu, M. R. *Dernières victoires, 1814: la campagne de France aux alentours de Montmirail.* Paris, 1964.

Mauguin, G. *Ney et Blücher en Nancy en 1814.* Paris, 1930.

Maycock, F. W. O. *The Invasion of France, 1814.* London, 1914.

Meinecke, F. *Das Leben des Generalfeldmarschalls Hermann von Boyen.* 2 vols. Stuttgart, 1896–99.

Meynert, H. *Geschichte der k.k. österreichischen Armee.* 3 vols. Vienna, 1852–54.

Michel, M. *Metz en 1813 et 1814.* Metz, 1914.

Mikaberidze, A. *The Russian Officer Corps in the Revolutionary and Napoleonic Wars, 1792–1815.* New York, 2005.

Muir, R. *Britain and the Defeat of Napoleon, 1807–1815.* London, 1996.

Nerlinger, C. *Nicolas Wolff et la défense des Vosges, 1814–1815.* Strasbourg, 1897.

Nicholson, H. *The Congress of Vienna: A Study in Allied Unity.* New York, 1946.

Nipperdy, T. *Germany from Napoleon to Bismarck, 1800–1866.* Trans. D. Nolan. Princeton, 1996.

Oechscli, W. *Le Passage des Allies en Suisse, 1813–1814.* Trans. F. Borrey. Paris, 1912.

Oncken, W. *Österreich und Preußen im Befreiungskrieg.* 2 vols. Berlin, 1876–9.

Paret, P. *Clausewitz and the State.* Oxford, 1976.

Yorck and the Era of Prussian Reform, 1807–1815. Princeton, 1966.

Pawley, R. *Napoleon's Guards of Honor, 1813–1814*. Oxford, 2002.

Perrin, E. *Le Maréchal Ney*. Paris, 1993.

Pertz, G. H. *Das Leben des Ministers Freiherrn vom Stein*. 6 vols. Berlin, 1849–55.

and H. Delbrück. *Das Lebens des Feldmarshalls Grafen Neithardt von Gneisenau*. 5 vols. Berlin, 1864–80.

Petre, F. L. *Napoleon at Bay, 1814*. London, 1914; reprint ed., London, 1977.

Napoleon's Last Campaign in Germany, 1813. London, 1912; reprint ed., London, 1992.

Pfister, A. *Aus dem Lager des Rheinbundes 1812 und 1813*. Stuttgart, 1897.

Aus dem Lager der Verbündeten 1814 und 1815. Stuttgart, 1897.

König Friedrich von Württemberg und seine Zeit. Stuttgart, 1888.

Pflugk-Harttung, J. *Geschichte der Brefreiungskriege 1813–1815*. Stuttgart, 1913.

Pimlott, J. "Friendship's Choice," in *Napoleon's Marshals*. Ed. D. Chandler. New York, 1987.

Pingaud, L. *Bernadotte, Napoléon et les Bourbons, 1797–1844*. Paris, 1901.

Pougiat, F. E. *Invasion des armées étrangères dans le Départment de l'Aube*. Troyes, 1833.

Quennevat, Jean-Claud. *Atlas de la Grande Armée. Napoléon et ses campagnes: 1803–1814*. Paris, 1966.

Quintin, D., and B. Quintin. *Dictionnaire des colonels de Napoléon*. Paris, 1996.

Quistorp, B. *Geschichte der Nord-Armee im Jahre 1813*. 3 vols. Berlin, 1894.

Ranke, L. *Denkwürdigkeiten des Staatskanzlers Fürsten von Hardenberg vom Jahre 1806 bis zum Jahre 1813*. Leipzig, 1877.

Regele, O. *Feldmarschall Radetzky: Leben, Leistung, Erbe*. Vienna and Munich, 1957.

Régnault, J. C. L. *Le Maréchal Macdonald et la défense du Bas-Rhin, novembre-décembre 1813*. Nancy, 1931.

Regnier, G. J. *Great Britain and the Establishment of the Kingdom of the Netherlands, 1813–1815*. London, 1930.

Roloff, G. *Politik und Kriegführung während des Krieges von 1814*. Berlin, 1891.

Ross, S. *European Diplomatic History, 1789–1815: France against Europe*. New York, 1969.

Rössler, H. *Österreichs Kampf um Deutschlands Befreiung*. Hamburg, 1940.

Rothenberg, G. *Napoleon's Great Adversary: The Archduke Charles and the Austrian Army, 1792–1814*. Staplehurst, 1995.

Rougé, J. *Les Combats de Mâcon en 1814 et 1815*. Mâcon, 1918.

Roux, X. *L'Invasion de la Savoie et du Dauphiné par les Autrichiens en 1813 et 1814*. Grenoble, 1892.

Rowe, M. *From Reich to State: The Rhineland in the Revolutionary Age, 1780–1830*. Cambridge, 2003.

Sagnac, P. *Le Rhin française pendant la Révolution et l'Empire*. Paris, 1917.

Saint-marc, Pierre. *Le maréchal Marmont, duc de Raguse, 1774–1852*. Paris, 1957.

Schama, S. *Patriots and Liberators: Revolution in the Netherlands, 1780–1813*. New York, 1992.

Schneidawind, F. J. A. *Feldmarschall Graf Radetzky: sein kriegerisches Leben und seine Feldzüge vom Jahre 1784–1850*. Augsburg, 1851.

Schroeder, P. *The Transformation of European Politics, 1763–1848*. Oxford, 1994.

Scott, F. *Bernadotte and the Fall of Napoleon*. Cambridge, 1934.

Seeley, J. R. *Life and Times of Stein or Germany and Prussia in the Napoleonic Age.* 3 vols. New York, 1969.

Sheehan, James. *German History: 1770–1866.* Oxford, 1989.

Sherwig, J. *Guineas and Gunpoweder: British Foreign Aid in the Wars with France 1793–1815.* Cambridge, 1969.

Simms, B. "Political and Diplomatic Movements, 1800–1830: Napoleon, National Uprising, Restoration," in *Germany: 1800–1870.* Ed. J. Sperber. Oxford, 2004.

  The Struggle for Mastery in Germany, 1779–1850. Basingstoke, 1998.

Six, G. *Dictionnaire biographique des généraux et amiraux français de la révolution et de l'empire.* 2 vols. Paris, 1934.

Stamm-Kuhlmann, T. *König in Preußens grosser Zeit: Friedrich Wilhelm III, der Melancholiker auf dem Thron.* Berlin, 1992.

Steenackers, F. F. *L'Invasion de 1814 dans la Haute-Marne.* Paris, 1868.

Swederus, G. *Schwedens Politik und Kriege in den Jahren 1808 bis 1814 vorzüglich unter Leitung des Kronprinzen Carl Johan.* Translated to the German by C. F. Frisch. 2 vols. Leipzig, 1866.

Sweet, P. *Wilhelm von Humboldt: A Biography.* 2 vols. Columbus, 1980.

Thielen, M. F. *Der Feldzug der verbündeten Heere Europas 1814 in Frankreich unter dem Oberbefehle des k.k. Feldmarschalls Fürsten Karl zu Schwarzenberg.* Vienna, 1856.

Thiers, A. *History of the Consulate and Empire of France under Napoleon.* 12 vols. London, 1893–4.

Thiry, J. *La Campagne de France de* 1814. Paris, 1938.

Thiry, J. *La Chute de Napoléon I.* Paris, 1938.

  La Chute de Napoléon I. 2nd ed. Paris, 1949.

Tingsten, L. *Hunvuddragen av Sveriges Krig och Yttre Politik augusti 1813–januari 1814.* Stockholm, 1924.

Tranié, J., and J. C. Carmigniani. *Napoléon: 1814 La campagne de France.* Paris, 1989.

Tulard, J., ed. *Dictionnaire Napoléon.* Paris, 1987.

Tulard, Jean. *La France de la Révolution et de l'Empire.* Paris, 1995.

  Napoléon: ou, Le mythe du sauveur. Paris, 1977.

  Nouvelle bibliographie critique des mémoires sur l'époque napolénienne. Geneva, 1991.

  Paris et son administration: 1800–1830. Paris, 1976.

Vichier-Guerre, J. L. V. *1814: Opérations en Savoie et en Dauphiné*

Webster, C. *The Foreign Policy of Castlereagh, 1812–1815: Britain and the Reconstruction of Europe.* London, 1931.

Weil, M. *La Campagne de 1814.* 4 vols. Paris, 1892.

Weinzierl, J. "The Military and Political Career of Claude-Victor Perrin." Ph.D. diss., Florida State University, 1997.

White, C. *The Enlightened Soldier: Scharnhorst and the Militärische Gesellschaft in Berlin, 1801–1805.* Westport, 1989.

Young, P. "The Bravest of the Brave," in *Napoleon's Marshals.* Ed. D. Chandler. New York, 1987.

Notes

1. THE NEW CHARLEMAGNE

1. Nipperdey, *Germany from Napoleon to Bismarck*, 67.
2. Quoted in Roloff, *Politik und Kriegführung*, 2.
3. Kraehe, *Metternich's German Policy*, 1:155–6; Oncken, *Österreich und Preußen*, 1:54; Kissinger, *A World Restored*, 49, 52.
4. Cook, "Prince Schwarzenberg's Crisis in 1812," 357.
5. Nipperdey, *Germany from Napoleon to Bismarck*, 70.
6. Ibid., 67–8, 70–71; Roloff, *Politik und Kriegführung*, 3–4; Oncken, *Österreich und Preußen*, 2:318; Kraehe, *Metternich's German Policy*, 1:174; Nicolson, *The Congress of Vienna*, 53; Schroeder, *European Politics*, 460–1.
7. The Bohemian army consisted of 125,200 Austrians, 82,000 Russians, and 45,000 Prussians. Bernadotte's army included 80,000 Prussians, 30,000 Russians, 30,000 Swedes, and a combined corps of 10,000 Prussians and North Germans. Blücher's army numbered 48,500 Russians and 38,500 Prussians. Allied reserves and besieging forces provided an additional 110,000 men.
8. The full text of the treaty can be found in Martens, *Recueil des traités et conventions conclus par la russie*, 3:117–26.
9. Nipperdey, *Germany from Napoleon to Bismarck*, 71.
10. Schroeder, *European Politics*, 478. Schroeder argues that Russia maintained its leadership of the Coalition, whereas the older works of Kissinger, *A World Restored*, 82, 87–98, and Kraehe, *Metternich's German Policy*, 1:206–7, although differing in their interpretations of Metternich's motives, claim that leadership of the alliance securely belonged to the Austrian.
11. Petre, *Napoleon's Last Campaign*, 381.
12. Wilson, *Private Diary*, 2:184.
13. "Relation über die Ereignisse bei Hanau vom 29 Oktober bis 1 November 1813," Österreichisches Staatsarchiv Kriegsarchiv (ÖStA KA), FA 1539, 1.
14. Chandler, *Campaigns of Napoleon*, 938.
15. Marmont, *Mémoires*, 5:302–3.

16. "Relation über die Einnahme des verschantzen Postens von Hochheim-am-Main am 9 November 1813," ÖStA KA, FA 1539, 85.
17. Steffens, *Memoirs*, 123.
18. Gneisenau to Clausewitz, 22 October 1813, Geheimes Staatsarchiv Preußischer Kulturbesitz zu Berlin (GStA), Rep. 92, Nachlaß Gneisenau, Nr. 21. During this period, Clausewitz served as chief of staff of General Ludwig Georg von Wallmoden's corps in Bernadotte's army. During the invasion of France Wallmoden's corps blockaded Hamburg.
19. Thiers, *Consulate and the Empire*, 9:294.
20. Gneisenau to Frederick William, 31 October 1813, GStA, Rep. 92, Nachlaß Gneisenau, Nr. 16.
21. Gneisenau to Stewart, 31 October 1813, in Pertz, *Gneisenau*, 3:512–14.
22. Stewart to Gneisenau, 3 November 1813, GStA, Rep. 92, Nachlaß Gneisenau, Nr. 28.
23. Clausewitz, in *Hinterlassene Werk*, 363, 365, 367–8.
24. Radetzky von Radetz, *Denkschriften*, 225–30.
25. Quoted in Droysen, *Yorck*, 2:246. Italics mine.
26. Blücher to Frederick William, 3 November 1813, ÖStA KA, FA 1539, ad38.
27. Thiers, *Consulate and the Empire*, 9:294.
28. Müffling, *Passages*, 390.
29. Schwarzenberg to Maria Anna, 13 November 1813, Schwarzenberg, *Briefe*, Nr. 262, 353.
30. Wilson, *Private Diary*, 2:190.

2. BARBARIANS AT THE GATE

1. Metternich to Schwarzenberg, 2 November 1813, Klinkowström, *Österreichs Theilnahme*, No. 4, 772–3.
2. Wilson, *Private Diary*, 2:214, 217. "Sir Robert Wilson," states Charles Stewart, "had been acting since the Moscow campaign with the Russian, and subsequently with the Austrian, armies in the field, which gave him great insight into all that was planned, rejected, or adopted by the Allied sovereigns" (Stewart, *Narrative of the War*, 1:223).
3. Schwarzenberg to Maria Anna, 13 November 1813, Schwarzenberg, *Briefe*, No. 262, 353.
4. Stewart, *Narrative of the War*, 1:203–4.
5. Pertz, *Gneisenau*, 3:525.
6. Gneisenau to Clausewitz, 4 January 1814, GStA, Rep. 92, Nachlaß Gneisenau, Nr. 21.
7. Gneisenau to Clausewitz, 4 January 1814, GStA, Rep. 92, Nachlaß Gneisenau, Nr. 21; Roloff, *Politik und Kriegführung*, 12–13.
8. Knesebeck to Gneisenau, 22 January 1814, GStA, Rep. 92, Nachlaß Gneisenau, Nr. 23.
9. Bogdanovich, *Geschichte des Krieges*, 40; Janson, *Feldzuges 1814*, 1:6, 12. The early twentieth-century German General Staff historian, August von Janson, calls Knesebeck's plan "strange" and accuses Knesebeck of being "a pedantic, methodical

practitioner of the old school, who of course always claimed to be independent of systematic warfare." In regard to taking winter quarters, Janson remarks: "There it was again, as if one had not experienced the Napoleonic era at all." According to Russian historian Bogdanovich, in *Geschichte des Krieges*, 1:92, Knesebeck "held himself to be a great strategist because one attributed to him the drafting of the operations plan for the Russian Army in 1812." "I ought, here, to record for the honor of his country," insists Stewart, in *Narrative of the War*, 215–16, "the eminent services rendered in the Grand Allied General Staff, in all their councils and grand military combinations, by that highly-gifted Prussian officer Gen. Knesebeck. He was constantly attached to the king's person throughout the war; but his genius, commanding talents, and experience made him the most prominent adviser in every arrangement, and his ardor and skill in execution contributed toward every good result. *I can never forget his personal kindness to me.*" Italics mine.

10. This plan is reproduced in full in Radetzky von Radetz, *Denkshriften*, 231–9.
11. Wilson asserts that as early as 27 October Radetzky was "convinced that the enemy will be able to assemble means that will require the Allies to oppose 500,000 men in the spring." On the other hand, Radetzky himself wrote that Napoleon needed three months before he could field a formidable army. Wilson, *Private Diary*, 2:198; Pfister, *1814–1815*, 38–9; Rothenberg, *Napoleon's Great Adversary*, 240.
12. Radetzky von Radetz, *Denkschriften*, 278; Roloff, *Politik und Kriegführung*, 12; Friederich, *Die Befreiungskriege*, 3:9; Janson, *Feldzuges 1814*, 1:12–13, 26; Heilmann, *Wrede*, 322.
13. Beauchamp, *Histoire des campagnes*, 1:54–5.
14. Burghersh, *Operations of the Allied Armies*, 66. Well-placed to pass such judgments, Burghersh's comments can be considered insightful. According to Stewart, Burghersh "was immediately placed near Prince Schwarzenberg's person," winning "high favor" among the Austrians and "the friendship of their commander" (Stewart, *Narrative of the War*, 1:223).
15. Roloff, *Politik und Kriegführung*, 14.
16. Friederich, *Die Befreiungskriege*, 3:9; Janson, *Feldzuges 1814*, 1:13
17. Knesebeck to Gneisenau, 22 January 1814, GStA, Rep. 92, Nachlaß Gneisenau, Nr. 23.
18. Pertz, *Gneisenau*, 3:532.
19. Gneisenau to Clausewitz, 4 January 1814, GStA, Rep. 92, Nachlaß Gneisenau, Nr. 21; Stewart, *Narrative of the War*, 216; Pertz, *Gneisenau*, 3:532–3; Friederich, *Die Befreiungskriege*, 3:10.
20. Rossiiskii Gosudarstvennyi Voenno-Istoricheskii Archiv Moscow (RGVIA), delo 4122; Bernhardi, *Toll*, 4:18–22; Pertz, *Gneisenau*, 3:538–40; Bogdanovich, *Geschichte des Feldzuges*, 40; Janson, *Feldzuges 1814*, 1:14. Citing Gneisenau's correspondence, German historians such as Janson and Pertz claim that this plan was authored by Gneisenau and based on his treatise of 7 November, whereas the Russian Bogdanovich agrees with Bernhardi that the Austrian staff assisted with the drafting this proposal. Despite Bogdanovich's claim, the copy of the plan that can be found in the Russian state archives was drafted by Major von Rühle of the Prussian General Staff.

21. Gneisenau to Gibson, 17 December 1813, GStA, Rep. 92, Nachlaß Gneisenau, Nr. 21. Wilson, in *Private Diary*, 2:227, describes Bernadotte as "the greatest charlatan that ever appeared on the public stage." In *The Invasion of France, 1814*, 26, British historian Maycock states: "The crown prince of Sweden was so intensely vain, and his conduct was so entirely guided by self-interest, that his real views were always more or less of an enigma to his allies."

22. Gneisenau to Müffling, 10 November 1813, GStA, Rep. 92, Nachlaß Gneisenau, Nr. 18.

23. Wilson, *Private Diary*, 2:226.

24. Quoted in ibid., 2:229.

25. Stewart, *Narrative of the War*, 246.

26. Roloff, *Politik und Kriegführung*, 4.

27. Stewart, *Narrative of the War*, 208; Friederich, *Die Befreiungskriege*, 3:10.

28. Quoted in Droysen, *Yorck*, 2:254.

29. Quoted in Brett-James, *Europe against Napoleon*, 295–6.

30. Metternich, *Memoirs*, 1:213–14.

31. Schroeder, *Transformation of European Politics*, 492.

32. Schwarzenberg to Maria Anna, 12 December 1813, Schwarzenberg, *Briefe*, No. 265, 358.

33. Stewart, *Narrative of the War*, 1:221.

34. Metternich, *Memoirs*, 1:217–19; Bogdanovich, *Geschichte des Feldzuges*, 43–4; Schroeder, *European Politics*, 492–3.

35. Metternich to Schwarzenberg, n.d., 1813, Klinkowström, *Österreichs Theilnahme*, No. 6, 775.

36. Gneisenau to Alexander, 10 November 1813, in Pertz, *Gneisenau*, 3:536–7.

37. Quoted in Seeley, *Life and Times of Stein*, 3:190.

38. Bernhardi, *Toll*, 4:22–3; Bogdanovich, *Geschichte des Krieges*, 41; Friederich, *Die Befreiungskriege*, 3:12.

39. Burghersh, *Operations of the Allied Armies*, 63–4.

40. Gneisenau to Knesebeck, 13 November 1813, in Pertz, *Gneisenau*, 3:543.

41. Gneisenau to Caroline, 11 November 1813, GStA, Rep. 92, Nachlaß Gneisenau, Nr. 21.

42. Roloff, *Politik und Kriegführung*, 20–1.

43. This document is reproduced in full in Burghersh, *Operations of the Allied Armies*, 359–61.

44. On 19 November Radetzky first suggested occupying Langres by 16 January 1814. Radetzky von Radetz, *Denkschriften*, 272

45. Craig, "Problems of Coalition Warfare," 34.

46. Roloff, *Politik und Kriegführung*, 22.

47. Radetzky, *Denkschriften*, 253.

48. Schroeder, *European Politics*, 494.

49. Schwarzenberg to Maria Anna, 12 December 1813, Schwarzenberg, *Briefe*, No. 265, 358; Friederich, *Die Befreiungskriege*, 3:13; Cook, "Prince Karl Philip zu Schwarzenberg," 509.

50. Jomini to Alexander, 10 December 1813, RGVIA, delo 4122.

51. Maycock, *The Invasion of France 1814*, 29.

52. Stewart to Gneisenau, 4 December 1813, GStA, Rep. 92, Nachlaß Gneisenau, Nr. 28.
53. Gneisenau to Rüchel, 5 January 1814, in Delbrück, *Gneisenau*, 4:147–8.
54. Clausewitz, *Hinterlassene Werk*, 371, 389.
55. Maycock, *The Invasion of France 1814*, 36.
56. Gneisenau to Boyen, 4 January 1814, GStA, Rep. 92, Nachlaß Gneisenau, Nr. 23.
57. Gneisenau to Frederick William, 20 November 1813, GStA, Rep. 92, Nachlaß Gneisenau, Nr. 16. Italics mine.
58. Stewart, *Narrative of the War*, 206. Italics mine.
59. Clausewitz, *Hinterlassene Werk*, 371–3, 88–9.
60. Maycock, *The Invasion of France 1814*.
61. Campana, *La Campagne de France 1814*, 20.
62. Vaudoncourt, *Histoire des campagnes de 1814 et 1815*, 1:75, 82–3.
63. Friederich, *Die Befreiungskriege*, 3:14.
64. Janson, *Feldzuges 1814*, 1:18.
65. Ibid., 1:2.
66. Roloff, *Politik und Kriegführung*, 20.
67. Rothenberg, *Napoleon's Great Adversary*, 241.
68. Burghersh, *Operations of the Allied Armies*, 65–6.
69. Jomini to Alexander, 10 December 1813, RGVIA, delo 4122.
70. Mikhailovsky-Danilevsky, *History of the Campaign in France*, 10.
71. Burghersh, *Operations of the Allied Armies*, 55, 62.
72. Bogdanovich, *Geschichte des Krieges*, 39.

3. THE FRANKFURT PROPOSALS

1. Gneisenau to Münster, 4 December 1813, GStA, Rep. 92, Nachlaß Gneisenau, Nr. 20b.
2. Metternich to Schwarzenberg, 23 November 1813, Klinkowström, *Österreichs Theilnahme*, No. 7, 776.
3. Stein to his wife, 18 November 1813, Stein, *Briefwechsel*, No. 6446, 4:324.
4. Janson, *Feldzuges 1814*, 1:6–8.
5. Mikhailovsky-Danilevsky, in *History of the Campaign in France*, 14.
6. Seeley, *Life and Times of Stein*, 3:213–15.
7. Thiers, *Consulate and the Empire*, 9:323.
8. Nicolson, *The Congress of Vienna*, 52–3.
9. Schroeder, *European Politics*, 481–2.
10. Kraehe, *Metternich's German Policy*, 1:205, 207.
11. Sweet, *Humboldt*, 2:139.
12. The full text of the treaty can be found in Martens, *Nouveau recueil de traités de paix*, 1:610–14.
13. Schroeder, *European Politics*, 478–82; Nipperdey, *Germany from Napoleon to Bismarck*, 71.
14. Stein to Hardenberg, 30 October 1813, Stein, *Briefwechsel*, No. 405, 4:300.
15. Nipperdey, *Germany from Napoleon to Bismarck*, 72.
16. Stein, *Briefwechsel* No. 406, 4:300–1.

17. Pfister, *König Friedrich von Württemberg*, 290. The full text of the treaty of Fulda can be found in Martens, *Nouveau recueil de traités de paix*, 1:643–8.
18. Sheehan, *German History*, 321–2
19. Nipperdey, *Germany from Napoleon to Bismarck*, 71.
20. Wilson, *Private Diary*, 2:216, 239.
21. Sweet, *Humboldt*, 2:139, 148.
22. Kraehe, *Metternich's German Policy*, 1:193–4, 197–8, 212; Seeley, *Life and Times of Stein*, 3:192. For Stein's plans, see his memorandum dated 21 November in *Briefweschsel* No. 461, 4:332–3 as well as Stein to Stadion, 25 December 1813, *Briefweschsel*, No. 599, 4:394–6. See also Billinger, *Metternich and the German Question*, 18–19.
23. Nipperdey, *Germany from Napoleon to Bismarck*, 70.
24. Kraehe, *Metternich's German Policy*, 1:191.
25. Simms, *The Struggle for Mastery in Germany*, 100.
26. Nipperdey, *Germany from Napoleon to Bismarck*, 69; Nicolson, *The Congress of Vienna*, 58. See also Schroeder, *European Politics*, 453–6.
27. Simms, *The Struggle for Mastery in Germany*, 99.
28. One example was King Frederick of Württemberg–Alexander's maternal uncle. Kraehe, *Metternich's German Policy*, 1:195.
29. Billinger, *Metternich and the German Question*, 18.
30. Quoted in Sweet, *Humboldt*, 2:142.
31. Craig, *Europe, 1815–1914*, 14.
32. Kissinger, *A World Restored*, 90.
33. Ross, *European Diplomatic History*, 341.
34. Schwarzenberg to Metternich, n.d., December 1813, Klinkowström, *Österreichs Theilnahme*, No. 8, 777.
35. Metternich, *Memoirs*, 1:213.
36. Nipperdey, *Germany from Napoleon to Bismarck*, 69–70.
37. Craig, "Problems of Coalition Warfare," 33–4.
38. Webster, *The Foreign Policy of Castlereagh*, 1:170.
39. Ibid., 1:168.
40. Quoted in Balfour, *The Life of George*, 1:125.
41. Stewart, *Narrative of the War*, 218.
42. Kissinger, *A World Restored*, 100.
43. Muir, *Britain and the Defeat of Napoleon*, 294.
44. Schroeder, *European Politics*, 490.
45. Nicolson, *The Congress of Vienna*, 62.
46. Castlereagh to Aberdeen, 7 December 1813, Castlereagh, *Correspondence*, 9:89.
47. Thiry, *La chute de Napoléon I*, 32–4; Beauchamp, *Histoire des campagnes*, 1:38–40; Kissinger, *A World Restored*, 101; Ross, *European Diplomatic History*, 342; St. Aignan's report is reproduced in full in Burghersh, *Operations of the Allied Armies*, 354–6.
48. "Thanks to the ever-moderate tone of my discourse," contends Caulaincourt, "and to the fact that my pacific views were well known, I was regarded as *l'homme de la paix* at that time, during the overtures that were made to the emperor from Frankfurt by the Allied rulers" (Caulaincourt, *No Peace with Napoleon*, 4).

49. Metternich, *Memoirs*, 1:215; Roloff, *Politik und Kriegführung*, 5, 8.
50. Janson, *Feldzuges 1814*, 1:13.
51. Roloff, *Politik und Kriegführung*, 10–11.
52. Stewart, *Narrative of the War*, 251–2. Stewart was actually Great Britain's ambassador to Prussia. According to Muir, in *Britain and the Defeat of Napoleon*, 295, Stewart "was out of his depth dealing with Hardenberg and Humboldt, Metternich, and the tsar."
53. Quoted in Kissinger, *A World Restored*, 101.
54. In *Politik und Kriegführung*, 8, 10, Roloff describes the letter to Caulaincourt as a "diplomatic masterpiece; if it succeeded, Napoleon thus would be imbued with respect for the energy of the Allies and be moved to yield, then Metternich would have won the contest against Alexander."
55. Napoleon to Caulaincourt, 4 January 1814, *Correspondence*, No. 21062, 27:10.
56. Kissinger, *A World Restored*, 101.
57. Ranke, *Denkwürdigkeiten*, 4:425–6.
58. Fain, *Manuscrit de 1814*, 5–8.
59. Metternich, *Memoirs*, 1:225.
60. Sweet, *Humboldt*, 2:153.
61. Quoted in Thiers, *Consulate and the Empire*, 9:282–3. Napoleon's private secretary, Baron Claude-François de Méneval, describes the Frankfurt Proposals as "lying words of peace, dictated by a false semblance of moderation," (Méneval, *Memoirs*, 3:155). Both Thiers and Méneval have to be used with caution. Thiers does not indicate where he found this statement, and Méneval spews Napoleonic propaganda.
62. Ross, *European Diplomatic History*, 343.
63. Thiry, *La Chute de Napoléon I*, 69.
64. See Napoleon to Metternich, 16 January 1814, *Correspondance*, No. 21, 101, 27:42–4.
65. Muir, *Britain and the Defeat of Napoleon*, 256–7, 281, 294; Kraehe, *Metternich's German Policy*, 1:260; Nicolson, *The Congress of Vienna*, 42–3, 54–6, 58; Kissinger, *A World Restored*, 30; Nipperdey, *Germany from Napoleon to Bismarck*, 70.
66. Kraehe, *Metternich's German Policy*, 1:260–1.
67. Webster, *British Diplomacy*, 25–8, 35–8; Kraehe, *Metternich's German Policy*, 1:261. See Kissinger, *A World Restored*, 91–5, for an overview of the differences between Great Britain and Russia.
68. Quoted in Webster, *The Foreign Policy of Castlereagh*, 1:177.
69. Quoted in Sweet, *Humboldt*, 2:152–3.
70. Gneisenau to Münster, 4 December 1813, GStA, Rep. 92, Nachlaß Gneisenau, Nr. 20b.
71. Quoted in Webster, *The Foreign Policy of Castlereagh*, 1:168–9.
72. Stewart, *Narrative of the War*, 212, 249–50.
73. Wilson, *Private Diary*, 2:235; Fain, *Manuscrit de 1814*, 8.
74. The basis of this letter can be found in Caulaincourt to Metternich, 1 December 1813, *Correspondence*, No. 20, 956, 26:480.
75. Schroeder, *European Politics*, 491, 493.

76. Wilson, *Private Diary*, 2:236.
77. Kraehe, *Metternich's German Policy*, 1:257.
78. Castlereagh to Aberdeen, 13 November 1813, Castlereagh, *Correspondence*, 9:75; Webster, *The Foreign Policy of Castlereagh*, 1:179.
79. Wilson, *Private Diary*, 2:237; Webster, *The Foreign Policy of Castlereagh*, 1:177; Kraehe, *Metternich's German Policy*, 1:262–3; Schroeder, *European Politics*, 491.
80. Fain, *Manuscrit de 1814*, 9.
81. Thiers, in *Consulate and the Empire*, 9:283–4.
82. Caulaincourt, *No Peace with Napoleon*, 4.
83. Caulaincourt to Metternich, 1 December 1813, *Correspondence*, No. 20, 956, 26:480. This letter was dictated by Napoleon and specifically addressed Metternich's letter of 25 November.
84. "What moved the tsar to agree to such decisions is not known," claims Roloff in *Politik und Kriegführung*, 6. "Whether he was too weak to resist the charge of the diplomats or whether he was convinced of the hopelessness of the negotiations and expected the advantages of such a failure is impossible to say."
85. Bogdanovich, *Geschichte des Krieges*, 1:51; Roloff, *Politik und Kriegführung*, 23–5.
86. Caulaincourt to Napoleon, 8 January 1814, Archives Nationales, Paris, France (AN), 95 AP 14, No. 3.
87. Houssaye, *1814*, 17.
88. Beauchamp, *Histoire des campagnes*, 1:47.

4. NAPOLEON AND THE FRENCH

1. Fain, *Manuscrit de 1814*, 4.
2. Both Griois and Beugnot are quoted in Brett-James, *Europe against Napoleon*, 286–7.
3. Beauchamp, *Histoire des campagnes*, 1:35.
4. On 1 November, Charpentier, commander of the 31st Division of the XI Corps, was named temporary commander of the corps after Macdonald went to Köln to organize the defenses of the lower Rhine. On 7 November, Macdonald resumed command of the corps. Berthier to Macdonald and Charpentier, 1 and 7 November 1813, Service Historique de l'Armée de Terre, Paris (SHAT), C[17] 182.
5. Berthier to Bertrand, Macdonald, Victor, Albert, Marmont, Augereau, Kellermann, Drouot, Arrighi, Nansouty, Sébastiani, 1 November 1813, SHAT, C[17] 182; Lefebvre de Béhaine, *Campagne de 1814*, 2:3.
6. "Orders," 3 November 1813, SHAT, C[17] 182.
7. Lachouque, *Napoléon en 1814*, 65.
8. Lefebvre de Béhaine, *Campagne de 1814*, 2:1–2.
9. Berthier to Oudinot, Marmont, Durutte, Victor, Dombrowski, and Augereau, 1 November 1813; Berthier to Bertrand, Nansouty, Dombrowski, Drouot, and Kellermann, 2 November 1813; Berthier to Nansouty, Dombrowski, Marmont, Arrighi, Bertrand, Augereau, Durutte, 3 November 1813; Berthier to Mortier and Drouot, 4 November 1813, SHAT, C[17] 182; Napoleon to Berthier, 1 and 2 November 1813, *Correspondance*, Nos. 20,842 and 29,848, 26:391, 394; Marmont, *Mémoires*, 6:10–11; Lefebvre de Béhaine, *Campagne de 1814*, 2:2–5, 11–13.

10. Napoleon to Berthier, 3 November 1813, *Correspondance*, No. 20,858, 26:497; Berthier to Marmont, Macdonald, Victor, Clarke, and Kellermann, 5 November 1813, SHAT, C¹⁷ 182.

11. Berthier to Macdonald, 1, November 1813 and Orders, 7 November 1813, SHAT, C¹⁷ 182; Napoleon to Berthier, 1 and 6 November 1813, *Correspondance*, Nos. 20,845 and 20,869, 26:392–3, 411.

12. Berthier to Marmont, 5 November 1813, SHAT, C¹⁷ 182.

13. Berthier to Nansouty, Kellermann, Sorbier, and Clarke, 3 November 1813, SHAT, C¹⁷ 182; Marmont, *Mémoires*, 6:11; Napoleon to Berthier, 3 November 1813, *Correspondance*, No. 20,857, 26:406–7; Weinzierl, "Claude-Victor Perrin," 389.

14. Marmont, *Mémoires*, 6:9–10. Marmont wrote his self-serving memoirs in part to counter the allegations of treason at the end of the 1814 campaign.

15. Ségur, *Du Rhin a Fontainebleau*, 85.

16. Marmont, *Mémoires*, 6:7–9.

17. Thiers, *Consulate and the Empire*, 9:279–80.

18. Quoted in Fain, *Manuscrit de 1814*, 1–2.

19. Napoleon to Clarke, 10 November 1813, *Correspondance*, No. 20,874, 26:414–15.

20. Napoleon to Clarke, 10 November 1813, *Correspondance*, No. 20,874, 26:414–16; Thiry, *Rôle du Sénat de Napoléon*, 39–41; Lefebvre, *Napoleon*, 2:345; Koch, *Campagne de 1814*, 1:7–9; Thiry, *La Chute de Napoléon I*, 9–10; Lefebvre, *Napoleon*, 2:345; Houssaye, *1814*, 2n.1, 8; Damitz, *Geschichte des Feldzuges*, 1:61; Thiers, *Consulate and the Empire*, 9:286–7; Chandler, *The Campaigns of Napoleon*, 949; Blanton, "Napoleon's Prefects," 154.

21. Napoleon to Clarke, 10 November 1813, *Correspondance*, No. 20,874, 26:414–16.

22. Chandler, *The Campaigns of Napoleon*, 947.

23. Quoted in Savary, *Mémoires du duc de Rovigo*, 6:277.

24. Blanton, "Napoleon's Prefects," 154–6; Pertz, *Gneisenau*, 3:599; Houssaye, *1814*, 10.

25. Napoleon to Clarke, 10 January 1813, *Correspondance*, No. 21,078, 27:20.

26. Chandler, *The Campaigns of Napoleon*, 950.

27. In *La Chute de Napoléon I*, 8, Jean Thiry claims that Danzig, Modlin, Zamosc, Stettin, Küstrin, Glogau, Dresden, Torgau, Magdeburg, and Hamburg still contained 150,000 combatants. Eight months earlier, some of these fortresses had the following strengths: Stettin, 7,700 men; Küstrin, 3,400 men; Glogau, 4,500 men; Danzig, 27,300 men; Modlin, 4,300 men; Zamosc, 4,000 men. By November, illness probably claimed 25 percent of this manpower.

28. Berthier to Marmont, 18 November 1813, SHAT, C¹⁷ 180; Koch, *Campagne de 1814*, 1:46; Janson, *Feldzuges 1814*, 1:20.

29. The articles for the capitulations of Stettin and Zamosc are located in: ÖStA KA, FA 1540, 434 and 435, as well as SHAT, C² 166.

30. Stewart, *Narrative of the War in Germany and France*, 259; Burghersh, *Operations of the Allied Armies*, 52.

31. The articles for the capitulation of Dresden are located in: ÖStA KA, FA 1540, 433.

32. Thiry, *La Chute de Napoléon I*, 7, 78–81; Chandler, *The Campaigns of Napoleon*, 950; *Clausewitz, Hinterlassene Werke*, 363–4.

33. Blanton, "Napoleon's Prefects," 352–3; Houssaye, *1814*, 2n.1; Thiry, *La Chute de Napoléon* I, 10–11; Thiers, *Consulate and the Empire*, 9:296.

34. Napoleon to Marmont, 16 November 1813, *Correspondance*, No. 20,900, 26:433; Napoleon to Clarke, 5 February 1814, *Correspondance*, No. 21,185, 27:114–15.

35. Houssaye, *1814*, 10–12.

36. Beauchamp, *Histoire des campagnes*, 1:128.

37. Pasquier, *Histoire de mon temps*, 2:130.

38. Thiers, *Consulate and the Empire*, 9:296. See also Vaudoncourt, *Histoire des campagnes de 1814 et 1815*, 1:88.

39. Beauchamp, *Histoire des campagnes*, 1:114–15.

40. Pawley, *Napoleon's Guards of Honor*, 4–7.

41. Houssaye, *1814*, 8–9.

42. Thiers, *Consulate and the Empire*, 9:302; Thiry, *La Chute de Napoléon I*, 11; Lefebvre, *Napoleon*, 2:345.

43. Quoted in Savary, *Mémoires du duc de Rovigo*, 4:256.

44. Thiers, *Consulate and the Empire*, 9:302–3; Blanton, "Napoleon's Prefects," 156, 159; Thiry, *La Chute de Napoléon* I, 11–12; Houssaye, *1814*, 13.

45. Thiry, *La Chute de Napoléon I*, 11; Koch, *Campagne de 1814*, 1:119–20, 130; Thiers, *Consulate and the Empire*, 9:344.

46. Berthier to Marmont, 18 December 1813, SHAT, C¹⁷ 183.

47. See the discussion in Houssaye, *1814*, 4, 11–14.

48. Napoleon to Berthier, 1 January 1814, *Correspondance*, No. 21,055, 27:2; Berthier to Marmont, 3 January 1814, SHAT, C¹⁷ 183.

49. For a full list, see "Décret sur la levée-en-masse," 4 January 1814, *Correspondance*, No. 21,061, 27:9.

50. Quoted in Thiry, *La Chute de Napoléon I*, 66. "All over where these measures of desperation were proclaimed," asserts Beauchamp, "the people rejected them, not wanting to fulfil this measure of evil that entailed a useless resistance" (Beauchamp, *Histoire des campagnes*, 1:95–6).

51. Houssaye, *1814*, 2; Lefebvre, *Napoleon*, 2:345.

52. Houssaye, *1814*, 24–5.

53. Houssaye's extensive archival research produced the following figures regarding indirect taxes: registration fees produced 13,000,000 francs instead of 45,000,000; the post office yielded 17,000 instead of 2,750,000. A government report of 25 January stated that it had received 367,000 francs in one month as opposed to the 10,000,000 in would have normally obtained. Ibid., 25n.2.

54. Fain, *Manuscrit de 1814*, 2; Houssaye, *1814*, 2–3; Thiers, *Consulate and the Empire*, 9:288–89; Lefebvre, *Napoleon*, 2:345. For a complete overview of the empire's fiscal situation, see Thiry, *La Chute de Napoléon* I, 15–20.

55. Thiers, *Consulate and the Empire*, 9:280.

56. Thiry, *La Chute de Napoléon I*, 20; Lefebvre, *Napoleon*, 2:346.

57. Thiry, *La Chute de Napoléon I*, 21.

58. Maycock, *The Invasion of France 1814*, 2.

59. Lefebvre, *Napoleon*, 2:346.

60. Thiers, *Consulate and the Empire*, 9:280.
61. Houssaye, *1814*, 35; Guerrini, *Napoleon and Paris*, 309, 313.
62. Houssaye, *1814*, 7.
63. Wilson, *Private Journal*, 2:217–18.
64. Gates, *The Napoleonic Wars*, 256; Lefebvre, *Napoleon*, 2:345.
65. After claiming that Napoleon had died in Russia, General Claude-François de Malet attempted to form a republican government in Paris. Although many imperial officials believed him, the governor of Paris demanded proof. A deranged Malet, who had just escaped a private mental institution, shot the governor. Malet and his fellow conspirators were arrested, tried, and executed only six days after initiating the coup.
66. Thiers, *Consulate and the Empire*, 9:279.
67. Quoted in Guerrini, *Napoleon and Paris*, 303–4.
68. See the supplemental discussion in Fain, *Manuscrit de 1814*, 21–2.
69. Thiers, *Consulate and the Empire*, 9:281.
70. "Louis XVIII to the French," 1 January 1814, ÖStA KA, FA 1603, 28.
71. Mauguin, *Ney et Blücher à Nancy*, 4.
72. Lefebvre, *Napoleon*, 2:347.
73. Quoted in Bourrienne, *Memoirs of Napoleon Bonaparte*, 3:378.
74. Thiers, *Consulate and the Empire*, 9:281.
75. Méneval, *Memoirs of Napoleon Bonaparte*, 3:154–5. The objectivity of both Méneval and Bourrienne is questionable due to their personal attachment to Bonarparte. See: Tulard, *Nouvelle Bibliographie Critique*, 57–58, 204–5.
76. Vaudoncourt, *Histoire des campagnes* de 1814 et 1815, 1:85–6.
77. "He sought new support from public opinion," continues Beauchamp. "He had constantly defied it, and perhaps for the first time he strove to reclaim it through cunning declarations and hypocritical thought processes, which did not have much of an effect among a frivolous and credulous people" (*Histoire des campagnes de 1814 et de 1815*, 1:115–16).
78. Guerrini, *Napoleon and Paris*, 305–8.
79. Napoleon to Montalivet, 17 December 1813, *Correspondance*, No. 21,015, 26:515.
80. Quoted in Guerrini, *Napoleon and Paris*, 3141.
81. Ibid., 304.
82. Junot, *Memoirs of the Emperor Napoleon*, 3:346.
83. Beauchamp, *Histoire des campagnes*, 1:59–62; Vaudoncourt, *Histoire des campagnes de 1814 et 1815*, 1:51–4; Thiers, *Consulate and the Empire*, 9:290; Lachouque, *Napoléon en 1814*, 81; Thiry, *La Chute de Napoléon I*, 24–31.
84. This report is reproduced in its entirety in Beauchamp, *Histoire des campagnes*, 1:77–80.
85. Quoted in Fain, *Manuscrit de 1814*, 23–4.
86. Houssaye, *1814*, 7–8; Lefebvre, *Napoleon*, 2:346.
87. Quoted in Lachouque, *Napoléon en 1814*, 82. A full version of the address is reproduced in Bourrienne, *Memoirs of Napoleon*, 3:358–9.
88. Napoleon to Montalivet, 21 February 1814, *Correspondance*, No. 21,340, 27:222; Houssaye, *1814*, 19–20.
89. Quoted in Guerrini, *Napoleon and Paris*, 304.

90. Ibid; Lefebvre, *Napoleon*, 2:347; Thiers, *Consulate and the Empire*, 9:281–2. See also Pasquier, *Histoire de mon temps*, 2:139–47, and Thiry, *La Chute de Napoléon I*, 22–4, 81–4 for royalist subversion and domestic opposition to Napoleon.
91. Savary, *Mémoires du duc de Rovigo*, 4:307; Thiry, *La Chute de Napoléon I*, 81–2.
92. Koch, *Campagne de 1814*, 1:26–7.
93. Quoted in Marmont, *Mémoires*, 6:10.
94. Chandler, *The Campaigns of Napoleon*, 950.
95. Thiers, *History of the Consulate and the Empire*, 9:320. Thiers's monumental work of twenty volumes appeared between 1845 and 1862. According to Pieter Geyl, Thiers "accepted a certain reading of the figure [Napoleon] and of the aims which had been suggested by Napoleon's own propaganda. He is critical; but in all volumes, and especially the last, the dominant motif is admiration, and more than admiration – affection, love." (*Napoleon For and Against*, 55).

5. THE LEFT BLANK

1. Lefebvre de Béhaine, *Campagne de France*, 2:87.
2. For a description of the state of the French army, which Koch compares to the army that retreated from Russia, see Koch, *Campagne de 1814*, 1:26–8.
3. Napoleon to Clarke, 18 August 1813, *Correspondance*, No. 20,410, 26:93–5.
4. See also Napoleon to Cambacérès, 2 November 1813, *Correspondance*, No. 20,846, 26:393.
5. Marmont, *Mémoires*, 6:2.
6. Berthier to Marmont, 3, 5 and 10 November 1813, SHAT, C^{17} 182 and 183; Napoleon to Berthier, 7 November 1813, *Correspondance*, No. 20,871, 26:412–13.
7. Pimlott, "Friendship's Choice," 256–64; Chandler, *Dictionary of the Napoleonic Wars*, 272–4, 396–8; 462; Six, *Dictionnaire Biographique*, 2:158–9.
8. Ségur, *Russian Campaign*, 265; Petre, *Napoleon's Last Campaign*, 17.
9. Marmont, *Mémoires*, 6:12.
10. Schwarzenberg's disposition for the assault on Hochheim, 9 November 1813, ÖStA KA, FA 1539, 94.
11. Berthier to Marmont, 10 November 1813, SHAT, C^{17} 183; Napoleon to Marmont, 12 November 1813, *Correspondance*, No. 20,883, 26:423; Marmont, *Mémoires*, 6:12.
12. Berthier to Macdonald and Molitor, 1 November 1813, SHAT, C^{17} 183; Napoleon to Berthier, 1 November 1813, *Correspondance*, No. 20,845, 26:392–3.
13. Berthier to Macdonald, 7 November 1813, SHAT, C^{17} 183.
14. Beauchamp, *Histoire des campagnes*, 1:48.
15. The 15 November total for garrisons and depots stationed in the 25th Military District amounted to Wesel's 507 men; Maastrict's 2,607 men; Venlo's 539 men; Namur's 2,528 men; Jülich's 666 men; Liège's 975 men; Grave's 1,703 men; Hertogenbosch's (Bois-le-Duc) 412 men; Nijmegen's 97 men; Geldern's 456 men; and Alpen's: 94 men. Napoleon to Kellermann, 25 October 1813, *Correspondance*, No. 20,837, 26:384–5; Lefebvre de Béhaine, *Campagne de France*, 2:411–12, 418.
16. Quoted in Chuquet, *L'Alsace en 1814*, 2.

17. Hankinson, "His Outspokenness," 238–51; Chandler, *Dictionary of the Napoleonic Wars*, 259–60; Six, *Dictionnaire Biographique*, 2:137–8.
18. Berthier to Sébastiani and Arrighi, 6 November 1813 and Berthier to Charpentier and Albert, 7 November 1813, SHAT, C¹⁷ 182.
19. Napoleon to Berthier, 6 November 1813, *Correspondance*, No. 20,869, 26:411–12.
20. This figure includes the 800 troopers of the Jerome Napoleon Hussar Regiment, which was attached to the Corps, the detachments arriving from Westphalia, and two battalions each from the 51st and 55th Line Regiments.
21. Quoted in Lefebvre de Béhaine, *Campagne de France*, 2:404–5.
22. Napoleon to Berthier, 18 November 1813, *Correspondance*, No. 20,917, 26:445. Bordessoulle did not join the II Cavalry Corps until 2 December. Two days later Berthier reorganized the corps into one division of three regiments (3,042 officers and men with six pieces of horse artillery), commanded by General of Division Rémy-Joseph-Isidore Exelmans. Bourdessoulle remained commander of the II Cavalry Corps until 3 January, at which time Exelmans became the de facto corps commander.
23. "Order for the Reorganization of the Army," Mainz, 7 November 1814, SHAT, C¹⁷ 183. The emperor recalled Bertrand to Paris to serve as his new grand marshal of the palace – a curious personnel decision considering Napoleon could have better employed a corps commander with Bertrand's experience at the front. Napoleon to Berthier, 18 November 1813, *Correspondance*, No. 20,916, 26:445.
24. Napoleon to Marmont, 19 November 1813, *Correspondance*, No. 20,921, 26:448.
25. Napoleon to Clarke, 11 November 1813, *Correspondance*, No. 20,880, 26:420–1; Marmont, *Mémoires*, 6:11–12.
26. Napoleon to Marmont, 12 and 16 November 1813, *Correspondance*, Nos. 20,883 and 20,900, 26:423, 433.
27. Napoleon to Marmont, 16 November 1813, *Correspondance*, No. 20,900, 26:433; Chuquet, *L'Alsace en 1814*, 9.
28. Weinzierl, "Claude-Victor Perrin," 389.
29. Thiers, *Consulate and the Empire*, 294–5; Lefebvre de Béhaine, *Campagne de France*, 2:3; Damitz, *Geschichte des Feldzuges*, 1:61.
30. Napoleon to Clarke, 16 November 1813, *Correspondance*, No. 20,897, 26:430.
31. Napoleon to Marmont, 12 November 1813, *Correspondance*, No. 20,883, 26:423.
32. Berthier to Drouot, 6 November 1813, SHAT, C¹⁷ 182; Berthier to Mortier, 20 November, SHAT, C¹⁷ 183; Napoleon to Mortier, 22 November 1813, *Correspondance*, No. 20,934, 26:462–3; Koch, *Campagne de 1814*, 1:28–32.
33. Napoleon to Clarke, 16 November 1813, *Correspondance*, No. 20,897, 26:430; Napoleon to Marmont, 19 November 1813, *Correspondance*, No. 20,921, 26:448; Koch, *Campagne de 1814*, 1:28–32, 46; Bogdanovich, *Geschichte des Krieges*, 1:30–1.
34. Napoleon to Marmont, 19 November 1813, *Correspondance*, No. 20,921, 26:449.
35. Napoleon to Berthier, 18 November 1813, *Correspondance*, No. 20,869, 26:411. Napoleon to Marmont, 18 November 1813, in Marmont, *Mémoires*, 6:77–8.
36. Napoleon to Marmont, 25 November 1813, *Correspondance*, No. 20,946, 26:470.
37. Pertz, *Gneisenau*, 3:599; Thiers, *Consulate and the Empire*, 9:296.

38. Ségur, *Du Rhin à Fontainebleau*, 88–9.
39. Napoleon to Daru, 8 December 1813, *Correspondance*, No. 20,986, 26:497.
40. Marmont to Napoleon, 19 November 1813, AN, AF IV 1663[A] plaquette 2; Marmont, *Mémoires*, 6:3–5.
41. Marmont to Napoleon, 19 November 1813, AN, AF IV 1663[A] plaquette 2.
42. Marmont to Napoleon, 27 November 1813, AN, AF IV 1663[A] plaquette 2.
43. Marmont, *Mémoires*, 6:13.
44. Thiers, *Consulate and the Empire*, 9:296.
45. Marmont, *Mémoires*, 6:5–6.
46. Berthier to Marmont and Sorbier, 5 November 1813, SHAT, C[17] 182.
47. Marmont to Napoleon, 14 November 1813, AN, AF IV 1663[A] plaquette 2.
48. Coustumier, *Victor*, 189.
49. Quoted in ibid., 192.
50. Arnold, "Le Beau Soleil," 512–18; Chandler, *Dictionary of the Napoleonic Wars*, 462; Six, *Dictionnaire Biographique*, 2:549–50.
51. Victor to Berthier, 6 November 1813, SHAT, C[2] 301; Chuquet, *L'Alsace en 1814*, 15–19; Coustumier, *Victor*, 190.
52. Napoleon to Clarke, 11 November 1813, *Correspondance*, No. 20,878, 26:418.
53. Koch, *Campagne de 1814*, 1:54; Thiry, *La chute de Napoléon I*, 5; Lefebvre de Béhaine, *Campagne de France*, 2:426. See Crusius, *Der Winterfeldzug*, 16–18, for a detailed list listing of the French and Dutch garrison troops in November 1813.
54. Thiers, *Consulate and the Empire*, 9:326; Beauchamp, *Histoire des campagnes*, 1:48; Rovigo, *Mémoires*, 4:259.
55. Schama, *Patriots and Liberators*, 613, 623, 625–6.
56. Homan, "The Restoration of the House of Orange-Nassau," 404–6.
57. RGVIA, "Campagne de 1814 en France," par comte Pavel Petrovich Sukhtelen, delo 4118.
58. RGVIA, "Memories du comte Alexander Khristoforovich Benckendorff," delo 3376.
59. Lefebvre de Béhaine, *Campagne de France*, 2:425.
60. Fain, *Manuscrit de 1814*, 33–4. Russian light troops entered Düsseldorf on 12 November.
61. Schama, *Patriots and Liberators*, 636.
62. Lefebvre de Béhaine, *Campagne de France*, 2:438–9.
63. Macdonald to Berthier, 13 and 14 November 1813, SHAT, C[2] 160.
64. Berthier to Marmont, 12 November 1813, SHAT, C[17] 183.
65. Marmont to Napoleon, 14 November 1813, AN, AF IV 1663[A] plaquette 2.
66. Napoleon to Marmont, 16 November 1813, *Correspondance*, No. 20,900, 26:433.
67. Napoleon to Marmont, 18 November 1813, in Marmont, *Mémoires*, 6:77–8.
68. Berthier to Macdonald, 17, 18, and 20 November 1813, SHAT, C[17] 183.
69. Berthier to Sébastiani, Macdonald and Marmont, 18 November 1813, SHAT, C[17] 183; Napoleon to Marmont, 18 November 1813, in Marmont, *Mémoires*, 6:77–8; Napoleon to Berthier, 18 November 1813, *Correspondance*, No. 20,917, 26:445; Napoleon to Marmont, 19 and 20 November 1813, *Correspondance*, Nos. 20,921 and 20,927, 26:449, 451.
70. In the reorganization of the army, Albert's 10th Division became the 1st Division of the V Corps.

71. Marmont to Napoleon, 22 November 1813, AN, AF IV 1663^A plaquette 2.
72. Napoleon to Clarke, 25 November 1813, *Correspondance*, No. 20,943, 26:468–9.
73. Berthier to Macdonald and Marmont, 20 November 1813, SHAT, C^{17} 183.
74. Marmont to Napoleon, 27 November 1813, AN, AF IV 1663^A plaquette 2.
75. Marmont to Napoleon, 25 and 27 November 1813, AN, AF IV 1663^A plaquette 2.
76. Lefebvre de Béhaine, *Campagne de France*, 2:121–7.
77. Victor to Berthier, 11 November 1813, SHAT, C^2 301.
78. On 2 November 1813, General Jean-Baptiste Broussier was named commandant supérior of Strasbourg and Kehl, which were connected by a pontoon bridge. The French successively defended Kehl against Bavarian, Württemberger, Badenese, and finally Russian troops.
79. Chuquet, *L'Alsace en 1814*, 19.
80. Napoleon to Clarke, 11 and 18 November 1813, *Correspondance*, Nos. 20,879 and 20,912, 26:418–19, 441–2; Napoleon to D'Hastrel, 29 November 1813, *Correspondance*, No. 20,951, 26:476–7.
81. Chuquet, *L'Alsace en 1814*, 13–14.
82. Victor to Napoleon, 11 November 1813, AN, AF IV 1663^A plaquette 1^{II}.
83. Marmont to Napoleon, 19 and 20 November 1813, AN, AF IV 1663^A plaquette 2.
84. Napoleon to Marmont, 12 November 1813, *Correspondance*, No. 20,883, 26:423; Marmont, *Mémoires*, 6:13.
85. Marmont to Napoleon, 27 November 1813, AΓ, AN IV 1663^A plaquette 2.
86. Lefebvre de Béhaine, *Campagne de France*, 2:71.
87. Napoleon to Marmont, 16 November 1813, *Correspondance*, No. 20,900, 26:433.
88. Marmont to Napoleon, 19 November 1813, AN, AF IV 1663^A plaquette 2.
89. Lefebvre de Béhaine, *Campagne de France*, 2:91, 307.
90. Marmont to Napoleon, 15 November 1813, AN, AF IV 1663^A plaquette 2.
91. Marmont to Napoleon, 16 November 1813, AN, AF IV 1663^A plaquette 2.
92. Marmont to Napoleon, 19 November 1813, AN, AF IV 1663^A plaquette 2.
93. Marmont to Napoleon, 20 November 1813, AN, AF IV 1663^A plaquette 2.
94. Marmont to Napoleon, 24 November 1813, AN, AF IV 1663^A plaquette 2.
95. Napoleon to Marmont, 20 November 1813, *Correspondance*, No. 20,927, 26:451.
96. Victor to Napoleon, 14 November 1813, AN, AF IV 1663^A plaquette 1^{II}.
97. Lefebvre de Béhaine, *Campagne de France*, 2:309–11.
98. Napoleon to Marmont, 19 November 1813, *Correspondance*, No. 20,921, 26:449.
99. Marmont to Napoleon, 24 and 25 November 1813, AN, AF IV 1663^A plaquette 2.
100. Marmont to Napoleon, 27 November 1813, AN, AF IV 1663^A plaquette 2.
101. Lefebvre de Béhaine, *Campagne de France*, 2:94.
102. Macdonald to Berthier, 19 and 20 November 1813, SHAT, C^2 162.
103. Lefebvre de Béhaine, *Campagne de France*, 2:411–12.
104. Victor to Napoleon, 5 December 1813, AN, AF IV 1663^A plaquette 1^{II}; Lefebvre de Béhaine, *Campagne de France*, 2:314–15.
105. Lefebvre de Béhaine, *Campagne de France*, 2:94–5.
106. Marmont to Napoleon, 9 December 1813, AN, AF IV 1663^A plaquette 2.

107. Napoleon to Marmont, 20 November 1813, *Correspondance*, No. 20,927, 26:251.
108. Lefebvre de Béhaine, *Campagne de France*, 2:95–6.
109. Victor's letter states 40,000 men, but this appears excessive and is probably an error. Victor to Berthier, 9 December 1813, SHAT, C² 164.
110. Vieuville to Victor, 9 December 1813 and Victor to Napoleon, 10 December 1813, AN, AF IV 1663^A plaquette 1^II. Victor included Vieuville's letter with his report to Napoleon on the following day.
111. Victor to Berthier, 10 December 1813, SHAT, C² 164.
112. Victor to Napoleon, 12 December 1813, AN, AF IV 1663^A plaquette 1^II.
113. Victor to Berthier, 13 December 1813, SHAT, C² 164.
114. Lefebvre de Béhaine, *Campagne de France*, 2:318.
115. Victor to Berthier, 16 December 1813, SHAT, C² 165.
116. Chuquet, *L'Alsace en 1814*, 200–1.
117. Lefebvre de Béhaine, *Campagne de France*, 2:319.
118. Chuquet, *L'Alsace en 1814*, 214–15.
119. Victor to Berthier, 19 December 1813, SHAT, C² 165.
120. Victor to Berthier, 20 December 1813, SHAT, C² 165.
121. Berthier to Marmont, 7 December 1813, SHAT, C^17 183.
122. Berthier to Marmont, 7 and 12 December 1813, SHAT, C^17 183. On the 7th Berthier issued the order to General François-Marie Dufour, commander of the 4th Division. Serving as Napoleon's chief of staff since 1796 did not protect Berthier from the emperor's censure: "My cousin, I see from your daily report that you have addressed directly to Dufour the order to render to Strasbourg. It appears to me that you have made a great mistake. It is to the duke of Raguse that this order must be addressed because before this general leaves it is necessary that he be replaced . . . it is through such mistakes that the General Staff sometimes causes so much evil; I want to remedy this inconvenience." Such statements help explain Napoleon's aversion to establishing a General Staff to serve as the intellectual nerve center of his army. Napoleon to Berthier, 7 December 1813, No. 20,977, 26:491–2.
123. Marmont to Berthier, 10 December 1813, SHAT, C² 164.
124. Coustumier, *Victor*, 194.
125. Napoleon to Berthier, 5 December 1813, *Correspondence*, No. 20,969, 26:487.
126. Lefebvre de Béhaine, *Campagne de France*, 2:134.
127. Berthier to Marmont, 6 December 1813, SHAT, C^17 183.
128. Victor to Berthier, 20 and 22 December 1813, SHAT, C² 165.
129. Marmont to Napoleon, 30 November 1813, AN, AF IV 1663^A plaquette 2.
130. Berthier to Marmont, 17 December 1813, SHAT, C^17 183.
131. Napoleon to Mortier, 20 December 1813, *Correspondance*, No. 21,023, 26:520.
132. Victor to Berthier, 19 and 20 December 1813, SHAT, C² 165.
133. Berthier to Marmont, 21 December 1813, SHAT, C^17 183.
134. Grouchy's authority did not extend over the cavalry serving Marmont and Macdonald.
135. "Orders," 21 December 1813, *Correspondance*, No. 21,024, 26:520–3; Lefebvre de Béhaine, *Campagne de France*, 2:320.
136. Napoleon to Clarke, 21 December 1813, *Correspondance*, No. 21,026, 26:524.
137. Napoleon to Clarke, 14 November 1813, *Correspondance*, No. 20,891, 26:426–7.

138. Lefebvre de Béhaine, *Campagne de France*, 2:320.
139. "Orders," 21 December 1813, *Correspondance*, No. 21,024, 26:521; Berthier to Victor, 25 December 1813, SHAT, C¹⁷ 183.
140. Napoleon to Clarke, 23 December 1813, *Correspondance*, No. 21,028, 26:525–6.
141. Napoleon to Berthier, 23 December 1813, *Correspondance*, Nos. 21,030, 21,031, and 21,032, 26:526–8.
142. Lefebvre de Béhaine, *Campagne de France*, 2:322–3.
143. Ibid., 2:319.
144. Vaudoncourt, *Histoire des campagnes de 1814 et 1815*, 1:72.
145. Clausewitz, *Hinterlassene Werk*, 328.
146. Marmont, *Mémoires*, 6:7–8.
147. Lefebvre de Béhaine, *Campagne de France*, 2:128.
148. Chuquet, *L'Alsace en 1814*, 184.
149. According to the reorganization of the army, Ricard's and Lagrange's divisions were designated the 1st and 3rd Divisions, respectively. "Orders," 21 December 1813, *Correspondance*, No. 21,025, 26:523.
150. Lefebvre de Béhaine, *Campagne de France*, 2:432.
151. Piecing together an order of battle for the French army is difficult because of the steady influx of new units and the discrepancies between the divisions Napoleon ordered to be created and those actually fielded. For the order of battle, see "Orders," 21 December 1813; Napoleon to Berthier, 23 December 1813; Napoleon to Clarke, 24 December 1813; "Orders," 26 December 1813, *Correspondance*, Nos. 21,024, 21030, 21033, 21047, 26:520–3, 26–30, 43–4; Berthier to Sébastiani, Morand, Macdonald, and Marmont, 25 December 1813, SHAT, C¹⁷ 183; Campana, *La Campagne de France 1814*, 17; Janson, *Feldzuges 1814*, 1:appendix VI; Bogdanovich, *Geschichte des Krieges*, 1:28–30; Koch, *Campagne de 1814*, 1:47–8 and Situation Overview No. 14 of 15 December 1813; Damitz, *Geschichte des Feldzuges*, 1:56–8.
152. Marmont, *Mémoires*, 6:14–15.

6. THE RIGHT BLANK

1. Bogdanovich, *Geschichte des Krieges*, 1:26–8; Beauchamp, *Histoire des campagnes*, 1:100–1; Janson, *Feldzuges* 1814, 1:35–6.
2. See Rowe's *From Reich to State*, 213–40, for the Rhineland during the Allied occupation. See also Vaudoncourt, *Histoire des campagnes de 1814 et 1815*, 1:17–34, for a contemporary French view of the Allied mobilization of the Rheinbund.
3. Martens, *Recueil des traités d'alliance*, 12:622; Bogdanovich, *Geschichte des Krieges*, 1:34; Pertz, *Gneisenau*, 3:572; Seeley, *Life and Times of Stein*, 3:192, 206.
4. Gill, *A Soldier for Napoleon*, 203–4.
5. Pfister, *König Friedrich von Württemberg*, 287.
6. Kraehe, *Metternich's German Policy*, 1:280. Pfister adds that between the 24,000 men of the Württemberger corps and the reserves that were mobilizing, the kingdom was providing more than 2 percent of its total population for the Allied cause, which was more than any Württemberger contingent that had fought for the French emperor. Pfister, *König Friedrich von Württemberg*, 289.

7. Hiller, *Geschichte des Feldzuges 1814*, 6–10.

8. Stein to Hardenberg, 10 December 1813, Stein, *Briefwechsel*, No. 556, 4:375.

9. Quoted in Seeley, *Life and Times of Stein*, 3:206–7.

10. Janson, *Feldzuges 1814*, 1:16; Damitz, *Geschichte des Feldzuges*, 1:18–19.

11. Rothenberg, *Napoleon's Great Adversary*, 231–3.

12. This figure includes Ferdinand von Bubna's 1st Light Division (4,537 men and 14 guns); Moritz von Liechtenstein's 2nd Light Division (7,500 man and 18 guns); I Corps commanded by Hironimus von Colloredo (19,205 men and 48 guns); II Corps under Maximillian von Merveldt (12,939 men and 42 guns); Gyulay's III Corps (15,330 men and 40 guns); and Klenau's IV Corps (16,726 men and 48 guns). Prince Friedrich of Hesse-Homburg's Austrian Reserve Corps consisted of 15,900 men and 30 pieces of artillery.

13. Austrian losses consisted of 575 men from the 1st Light Division, 238 from the 2nd Light Division, 1,494 from the I Corps, 1,938 from the II Corps, 1,525 from the III Corps, 3,999 from the IV Corps, and 5,204 from the Reserve. The Russian units of the Bohemian Army lost 11,923 men, whereas the Prussian II Corps suffered 8,126 casualties.

14. Quistorp, *Geschichte der Nord-Armee*, 3:35–8, 155–63; Bogdanovich, *Geschichte des Krieges*, 2:380–2, 386–406. The 200,000 men were thus distributed: 140,600 infantry in 255 battalions; 35,000 cavalry in 304 squadrons, 8,000 Cossacks in 26 regiments, and 13,700 gunners and support personnel. French historian Lefebvre de Béhaine, in *Campagne de France*, 2:328, calculates the Bohemian Army to be 238 battalions, 309 squadrons, 684 guns, and 26 Cossack regiments for a total of 228,650 men.

15. Mikhailovsky-Danilevsky, *History of the Campaign in France*, 11–13.

16. GStA, Rep. 15 A Nr. 274.

17. RGVIA, "Journal des operations du Corps d' Armée Russe sous les orders du general d' Infanterie Comte de Langeron," delo 4140; Bogdanovich, in *Geschichte des Krieges*, 1:33.

18. Maycock, *The Invasion of France 1814*, 32.

19. RGVIA, "Journal des operations du Corps d" Armée Russe sous les orders du general d' Infanterie Comte de Langeron," delo 4140.

20. Janson, *Feldzuges 1814*, 1:Appendix 3; Damitz, in *Geschichte des Feldzuges*, 1:35, states 21,550 men and Bogdanovich, in *Geschichte des Krieges*, 1:34, places the total at 19,500.

21. Maycock, *The Invasion of France 1814*, 31.

22. RGVIA, "Journal des operations du Corps d'Armée Russe sous les orders du general d' Infanterie Comte de Langeron," delo 4140.

23. RGVIA, "Journal des operations du Corps d'Armée Russe sous les orders du general d'Infanterie Comte de Langeron," delo 4140.

24. RGVIA, "Journal des operations du Corps d'Armée Russe sous les orders du general d'Infanterie Comte de Langeron," delo 4140; Bogdanovich, *Geschichte des Krieges*, 1:408–10.

25. RGVIA, "Journal des operations du Corps d'Armée Russe sous les orders du general d' Infanterie Comte de Langeron," delo 4140.

26. Friederich, *Die Befreiungskriege* 3:18–22.

27. Mikhailovsky-Danilevsky, *History of the Campaign in France*, 10.

28. Quoted in Craig, "Problems of Coalition Warfare," 10.

29. Gneisenau to Stein, 9 January 1814, No. 157, GStA, Rep. 92, Nachlaß Gneisenau, Nr. 20b.

30. Muir, *Britain and the Defeat of Napoleon*, 292.

31. Gneisenau to Clausewitz, 4 January 1814, GStA, Rep. 92, Nachlaß Gneisenau, Nr. 21.

32. Gneisenau to Knesebeck, 15 January 1814, in Delbrück, *Gneisenau*, 4:156.

33. Gneisenau to Boyen, 13 January 1814, GStA, Rep. 92, Nachlaß Gneisenau, Nr. 23.

34. Schwarzenberg to Maria Anna, 1 and 9 December 1813, Schwarzenberg, *Briefe*, Nos. 263 and 264, 355–7.

35. Wilson, *Private Diary*, 2:225–6.

36. Blücher to Bonin, 29 November 1813, Unger, *Blüchers Briefe*, 201.

37. Gneisenau to Dörnberg, 4 December 1813, GStA, Rep. 92, Nachlaß Gneisenau, Nr. 23.

38. Gneisenau to Gibson, 17 December 1813, GStA, Rep. 92, Nachlaß Gneisenau, Nr. 21.

39. Gneisenau to Münster, 4 December 1813, GStA, Rep. 92, Nachlaß Gneisenau, Nr. 20b.

40. Boyen, *Erinnerungen*, ed. Dorothea Schmidt, 1:362–3; Varnhagen von Ense, *Blücher*, 84; Unger, *Blücher*, 1:338; Henderson, *Blücher*, 47–8; Chandler, *Dictionary of the Napoleonic Wars*, 58–9.

41. Maycock, *The Invasion of France*, 35; Weil, *Campagne de 1814*, 1:150.

42. Lefebvre de Béhaine, *Campagne de France*, 3:163.

43. Regele, *Feldmarshall Radetzsky*, 178; Cook, "Schwarzenberg at Dresden," 643; Kraehe, *Metternich's German Policy*, 1:187; Rothenberg, *Napoleon's Great Adversary*, 230; Craig, "Problems of Coalition Warfare," 28.

44. Kraehe, *Metternich's German Policy*, 1:187.

45. Maycock, *The Invasion of France*, 18–19.

46. Campana, *La Campagne de France 1814*, 19.

47. Janson in *Feldzuges 1814*, 1:4–5.

48. Rothenberg, *Napoleon's Great Adversary*, 229–30.

49. Schwarzenberg to Maria Anna, 5 September 1813, Schwarzenberg, *Briefe*, No. 247, 332.

50. Cook, "Prince Schwarzenberg's Crisis," 351–8; Chandler, *Dictionary of the Napoleonic Wars*, 405–6; Dupuy, *The Harper Encyclopedia of Military Biography*, 665–6.

51. Schwarzenberg to Francis, 12 December 1813, ÖStA KA, FA 1541, 125.

52. Schwarzenberg's General Disposition for 13–20 December, 13 December 1813, ÖStA KA, FA 1541, 135 and ad135.

53. Austrian political moves never remained far behind miliary operations as this passage from Metternich's memoirs suggests: "When he [Schwarzenberg] informed me that, in concert with the Swiss generals, he had made arrangements to cross the Rhine from Schaffhausen to Basel at all the necessary points, I presented myself to the Kaiser and departed without delay . . . authorized by His Majesty to make all arrangements for executing the operation with the commander in chief" (Metternich, *Memoirs*, 1:221).

54. Bogdanovich, in *Geschichte des Feldzuges*, 1:44–5; Koch, *Campagne de 1814*, 1:37–8; Bernhardi, *Toll*, 4:53–7; Friederich, *Die Befreiungskriege*, 3:17; Schroeder, *European Politics*, 494.

55. Metternich, *Memoirs*, 1:222–3.

56. Bernhardi, Toll, 4:63; Bogdanovich, *Geschichte des Krieges*, I:50.

57. Metternich, *Memoirs*, 1:218.

58. Schwarzenberg to Metternich, n.d. December 1813, Klinkowström, *Österreichs Theilnahme*, No. 8, 777.

59. Metternich to Schwarzenberg, n.d. December 1813, Klinkowström, *Österreichs Theilnahme*, No. 9, 778.

60. Metternich to Schwarzenberg, n.d. December 1813, Klinkowström, *Österreichs Theilnahme*, No. 10, 778–9.

61. Lefebvre de Béhaine, *Campagne de France*, 2:316–17.

62. Wilson, *Private Diary*, 2:274.

63. Wrede to Schwarzenberg, 18 December 1813, ÖStA KA, FA 1541, Nr. 202.

64. Report of 18 December 1813 and Schwarzenberg to Francis, Bellegarde, and Colloredo, 18 December 1813, ÖStA KA, FA 1541, Nrs. 211 and 223.

65. Schwarzenberg to Frederick William, 20 December 1813, ÖStA KA, FA 1541, Nr. 235.

66. Schwarzenberg's General Order, 20 December 1813, ÖStA KA, FA 1541, Nr. 233.

67. Schwarzenberg to Maria Anna, 20 December 1813, Schwarzenberg, *Briefe*, No. 265, 359.

7. THE LOWER RHINE

1. RGVIA, "Campagne de 1814 en France," par Comte Pavel Petrovich Sukhtelen, delo 4118.

2. Stewart, *Narrative of the War*, 205–6.

3. Boyen, *Erinnerungen*, ed. Friedrich Nippold, 3:203.

4. Bülow to Frederick William, 31 October and 7, 10, and 23 November 1813, GStA, Rep. 15 A Nr. 238. Meinecke, in *Boyen*, 349 (Vol. 1), maintains that from Bülow's reports to the king and his letters to Hardenberg on 7 and 22 November "it emerges with complete certainty that Bülow decided for the Dutch operation without definite orders."

5. Disposition of the 5th Brigade and March Table for the 5th Brigade, GStA, Rep. 15 A Nr. 2226; Damitz, *Geschichte des Feldzuges*, 1:90–1; Lefebvre de Béhaine, *Campagne de France*, 2:416–17.

6. Karl Johan to Bülow, 19 November 1813, *Recueil*, 469.

7. Friedrich Wilhelm to Bülow, 22 November 1813, GStA, Rep. 15 A Nr. 334.

8. Webster, *The Foreign Policy of Castlereagh*, 1:181; Crusius, *Der Winterfeldzug*, 37; Fortescue, *A History of the British Army*, 10:1–2.

9. Bülow to Frederick William, 20 November 1813, GStA, Rep. 15 A Nr. 238; Crusius, *Der Winterfeldzug*, 39–40.

10. Koch *Campagne de 1814*, 1:54.

11. Boyen to Hardenberg, 30 December 1813, GStA, Rep. 92, Nachlaß Albrecht, Nr. 44.

12. Bülow to Thile, 23 November 1813, in Meinecke, *Boyen*, 351.

13. Gneisenau to Boyen, 4 January 1814, in Delbrück, *Gneisenau*, 4:145–6.

14. March Table to the Ijssel, 25 to 30 November, issued in Münster on 24 November 1813, GStA, Rep. 15 A Nr. 226.

15. Crusius, *Der Winterfeldzug*, 10–11.

16. Lefebvre de Béhaine, *Campagne de France*, 2:413–14.

17. Meinecke, *Boyen*, 345–6.

18. Lefebvre de Béhaine, *Campagne de France*, 2:441. The French historian claims that Oppen did not know the Cossacks had been forced out of Doesburg and that the Prussians did not force their way into Doesburg but entered the fort through the Doetinchem gate after its fifty-man post, allegedly Prussians by birth, surrendered.

19. Bülow to William Frederick, 2 December 1813 and *Feldzeitung der Preußischen Armee*, 30, 26 November 1813, BFA, No. 117; Damitz, *Geschichte des Feldzuges*, 1:92–3; Hassenkamp, *Gen. Graf Bülow*, 247–8; Lefebvre de Béhaine, *Campagne de France*, 2:441–2; Varnhagen von Ense, *Bülow*, 299; Crusius, *Der Winterfeldzug*, 41–5.

20. Bülow to William Frederick, 3 December 1813 and *Feldzeitung der Preußischen Armee*, 30, 26 November 1813, BFA, No. 117; Damitz, *Geschichte des Feldzuges*, 1:94–5; Hassenkamp, *Gen. Graf Bülow*, 247–8; Lefebvre de Béhaine, *Campagne de France*, 2:442; Crusius, *Der Winterfeldzug*, 45–7.

21. "Situation en Hollande," Maison to Clarke, 21 December 1813, SHAT C² 316; Berthier to Macdonald, 22 November 1813, SHAT, C¹⁷ 183; Koch, *Campagne de 1814*, 1:54; Damitz, *Geschichte des Feldzuges*, 1:99; Pertz, *Gneisenau*, 3:601; Lefebvre de Béhaine, *Campagne de France*, 2:443–4.

22. Dislocation of the III Corps, 29 November 1813 and Dislocation of the 4th Brigade, 29 November 1813, GStA, Rep. 15 A Nr. 226; Macdonald to Berthier, 29 November 1813, SHAT, C² 162; Lefebvre de Béhaine, *Campagne de France*, 2:443–6.

23. Berthier to Macdonald, 13 December 1813, SHAT, C² 164; Crusius, *Der Winterfeldzug*, 70; Lefebvre de Béhaine, *Campagne de France*, 2:448.

24. Accounts for the operations at Arnhem between 25 and 30 November: Bülow to Frederick William, 30 November 1813, GStA, Rep. 15 A Nr. 238; Krafft to Boyen, 27 November 1813, GStA, Rep. 15 A Nr. 298; Dislocation of the III Corps, 30 November 1813 and Dislocation of the 4th Brigade, 30 November 1813 GStA, Rep. 15 A Nr. 226; Bülow to Pauline, 30 November 1813 and to William Frederick, 2 December 1813, BFA, Nos. 116 and 117; *Feldzeitung der Preußischen Armee*, Nos. 36, 37, and 39, 16 and 31 December 1813, BFA; Koch, *Campagne de 1814*, 1:55–7; Twenty-Sixth Bulletin, 6 December 1813, *Recueil*, 507; Damitz, *Geschichte des Feldzuges*, 1:99–111; Crusius, *Der Winterfeldzug*, 47–74; Lefebvre de Béhaine, *Campagne de France*, 2:447; Meinecke, *Boyen*, 355–6.

25. Bülow to Pauline, 30 November 1813, BFA, No. 116. Benckendorff described the capture of Arnhem as "the finest feat of arms in the war." RGVIA, "Mémoires du Comte Alexander Khristoforovich Benckendorff," delo 3376.

26. Bülow to Frederick William, 21 November 1813, GStA, Rep. 15 A Nr. 238.

27. Bülow to William Frederick, 2 December 1813, BFA, No. 117.

28. Bülow to Frederick William, 30 November and 31 December 1813, GStA, Rep. 15 A Nr. 238.

29. Homan, "The Restoration of the House of Orange-Nassau," 408–9.

30. Koch, *Campagne de 1814*, 1:57; Lefebvre de Béhaine, *Campagne de France*, 2:448–9.
31. Macdonald to Berthier, 2 and 4 December 1813, SHAT, C² 163.
32. Damitz, *Geschichte des Feldzuges*, 1:114; Meinecke, *Boyen*, 354.
33. Dislocation of the III Corps, 1 and 2 December, GStA, Rep. 15 A Nr. 226; Koch, *Campagne de 1814*, 1:57; *Feldzeitung der Preußischen Armee*, No. 34, 11 December 1813, BFA; Damitz, *Geschichte des Feldzuges*, 1:123–4.
34. Boyen to Hardenberg, 6 December 1813, GStA, Rep. 92, Nachlaß Albrecht, Nr. 44; Twenty-Sixth Bulletin, 6 December 1813, GStA, Rep. 92, Nachlaß Albrecht, Nr. 43; Koch, *Campagne de 1814*, 1:57; Hassenkamp, *General Graf Bülow*, 245–57; Philippart, *Memoirs and Campaigns*, 325–9; Reiche, *Memoiren*, 2:11–27.
35. Fortescue, *A History of the British Army*, 10:3.
36. Varnhagen von Ense, *Bülow*, 307–8.
37. Quoted in Brett-James, *Gen. Graham*, 288.
38. BFA, No. 118.
39. GStA, Rep. 15 A Nr. 226.
40. Lefebvre de Béhaine, *Campagne de France*, 2:451, 454, 463–4, 467; Blanton, "Napoleon's Prefects," 257–8.
41. Beauchamp, *Histoire des campagnes*, 1:56.
42. Sébastiani to Berthier, 2 December 1814, SHAT, C² 163.
43. Sébastiani to Berthier, 4 December 1814, SHAT, C² 163.
44. RGVIA, "Campagn de 1814 en France," par Comte Pavel Petrovich Sukhtelen, delo 4118.
45. RGVIA, "Mémoires du Comte Alexander Khristoforovich Benckendorff," delo 3376.
46. Karl Johan to Wintzingerode, 3 December 1813, *Recueil*, 494.
47. Karl Johan to Bülow, 3 December 1813, *Recueil*, 493.
48. Karl Johan to Bülow, 9 December 1813, *Recueil*, 521.
49. Karl Johan to Wintzingerode, 9 December 1813, *Recueil*, 517.
50. RGVIA, "Mémoires du Comte Alexander Khristoforovich Benckendorff," delo 3376.
51. RGVIA, "Campagne de 1814 en France," par Comte Pavel Petrovich Sukhtelen, delo 4118.
52. RGVIA, "Memories du Comte Alexander Khristoforovich Benckendorff," delo 3376.
53. Macdonald to Berthier, 3 December 1813, SHAT, C² 163.
54. Macdonald to Molitor, 4 December 1813, SHAT, C² 163.
55. Macdonald to Berthier, 4 December 1813, SHAT, C² 163; Lefebvre de Béhaine, *Campagne de France*, 2:458–60.
56. Napoleon to Berthier, 8 December 1813, *Correspondence*, No. 20,982, 26:493; Berthier to Macdonald, 8 December 1813, SHAT, C¹⁷ 183.
57. Macdonald to Berthier, 5 December 1813, SHAT, C² 163.
58. Macdonald to Albert, Sébastiani, and Arrighi, 5 December 1813, SHAT, C² 163.
59. Berthier to Macdonald, 7 December 1813, SHAT, C¹⁷ 183; Napoleon to Berthier, 9 December 1813, *Correspondence*, No. 20,991, 26:499.
60. Napoleon to Clarke, 3 December 1813, *Correspondence*, No. 20,959, 26:482.
61. Berthier to Macdonald, 7 December 1813, SHAT, C¹⁷ 183.

62. Napoleon to Lebrun, 7 December 1813, *Correspondence*, No. 20,981, 26:494–5; Napoleon to Clarke, 3 December 1813, *Correspondence*, No. 20,959, 26:482; Lefebvre de Béhaine, *Campagne de France*, 2:474.

63. Napoleon to Lebrun, 7 December 1813, *Correspondence*, No. 20,981, 26:494–5; Berthier to Macdonald, 7 December 1813, SHAT, C¹⁷ 183; Koch, *Campagne de 1814*, 1:58; Thiers, *Consulate and the Empire*, 9:298.

64. Decaen to Berthier, 6 December 1813, SHAT, C² 163.

65. Lefebvre de Béhaine, *Campagne de France*, 2:474.

66. Napoleon to Lebrun, 7 December 1813, *Correspondence*, No. 20,981, 26:494.

67. Napoleon to Clarke, 4 December 1813, *Correspondence*, No. 20,964, 26:485.

68. Napoleon to Clarke, 4 December 1813, *Correspondence*, No. 20,965, 26:485–6.

69. Berthier to Macdonald, 5 December 1813, SHAT, C¹⁷ 183.

70. Berthier to Merle, 6 December 1813, SHAT, C¹⁷ 183.

71. Macdonald to Berthier, 9 December 1813, SHAT, C² 164.

72. Lefebvre de Béhaine, *Campagne de France*, 2:479.

73. Boyen to Hardenberg, 6 December 1813, GStA, Rep. 92, Nachlaß Albrecht, Nr. 44.

74. Capitulation Articles for Geertruidenberg, 12 December 1813, SHAT, C² 164.

75. Lefebvre de Béhaine, *Campagne de France*, 2:475, 90.

76. Napoleon to Clarke, 11 and 14 November 1813, *Correspondence*, Nos. 20,878 and 20,889, 26:418, 426; Koch, *Campagne de 1814*, 1:58–60.

77. Bülow to William Frederick, 9 December, 1813 in Meinecke, *Boyen*, 357.

78. Bülow to Frederick William, 8 and 13 December 1813, GStA, Rep. 15 A Nr. 238; Boyen to Hardenberg, 6 December, 1813, GStA, Rep. 92, Nachlaß Albrecht, Nr. 44; Bülow to Bernadotte, 6 and 8 December 1813, in Meinecke, *Boyen*, 358.

79. Molitor to Macdonald, 7 December 1813, SHAT, C² 163.

80. According to Lefebvre de Béhaine, in *Campagne de France*, 2:494: "Almost everywhere they passed, the soldiers [of the 17th Military District] committed horrible excesses and the officers, without authority and without firmness, allowed it to go on."

81. Macdonald to Molitor and Berthier, 8 December 1813, SHAT, C² 163.

82. Molitor to Macdonald, 11 December 1813, SHAT, C² 164.

83. Macdonald to Molitor, 12 December 1813, SHAT, C² 164.

84. Macdonald to Wathiez, 11 and 12 December 1813; Molitor to Macdonald, 14 December 1813; Macdonald to Berthier, 14 (two) December 1813, SHAT, C² 164.

85. Macdonald to Berthier, 11, 12, and 13 December 1813, SHAT, C² 164; Lefebvre de Béhaine, *Campagne de France*, 2:482–3.

86. Dislocation of the III Corps," GStA, Rep. 15 A, Nr. 226; Damitz, *Geschichte des Feldzuges*, 1:126–8.

87. Lefebvre de Béhaine, *Campagne de France*, 2:481.

88. The account of the operations between 13–16 December has been compiled from: *Feldzeitung der Preußischen Armee*, Nos. 38 and 44, 30 December 1813 and 10 January 1814, BFA; Fain, *Manuscrit de 1814*, 34–5; Koch, *Campagne de 1814*, 1: 61–5; Damitz, *Geschichte des Feldzuges*, 1:127–41; Hassenkamp, *General Graf Bülow*, 270–71; Varnhagen von Ense, *Bülow*, 314–15.

89. Molitor to Macdonald, 14 December 1813, 10:00 P.M., SHAT, C² 164.

90. Molitor to Decaen, 15 December 1813, SHAT, C² 164.

91. Molitor to Macdonald, 16 December 1813, SHAT, C² 164. Molitor received his baton on 9 October 1823.
92. Macdonald to Sébastiani, 15 and 17 December 1813; Macdonald to Berthier, 15 (two) and 16 December 1813, Sébastiani to Macdonald, 16 December 1813, SHAT, C² 164 and 165.
93. Twenty-Ninth Bulletin, 21 December 1813, *Recueil*, 561; Philippart, *Memoirs and Campaigns*, 348–49; Reiche, *Memoiren*, 2:30–6.
94. Bülow to Schwarzenberg, 18 December 1813, ÖStA KA, FA 1542, Nr. 388.
95. Thielemann's advance guard was scheduled to arrive at Hildesheim on the 17th. Karl Johan to Thielemann, 14 December 1813, *Recueil*, 549.
96. Burghersh, *Operations of the Allied Armies*, 50.
97. Quoted in Webster, *Foreign Policy of Castlereagh*, 1:197–8.
98. Karl Johan to Wintzingerode and Borstell, 18 December 1813, *Recueil*, 555–6. According to Suchtelen, the crown prince's own operation in Schleswig resulted in orders for the cooperation by movements on the left bank of the Rhine. RGVIA, "Campagne de 1814 en France," par Comte Pavel Petrovich Sukhtelen, delo 4118.
99. Clarke to Maison, 21 December 1813, SHAT, C² 316; "Orders," 21 December 1813, *Correspondance*, No. 21,024, 26:607; Fain, *Manuscrit de 1814*, 41.
100. Napoleon planned to send considerable reinforcements to the Guard in the Low Countries and based the figure of 30,000–40,000 men on the following unit strengths he expected to achieve by 15 January, the actual musters as of 15 December are in parentheses: Guard Cavalry: 6,000 men (4,790); 1st Tirailleur Division: 9,600 men (600); 3rd Tirailleur Division: 8,000–9,000 men (650); 3rd Voltigeur Division: 6,000 men (294); 1st Old Guard Division: 6,000 men (4,800). Napoleon to Clarke, 24 December 1813, *Correspondance*, No. 21,033, 26:528.
101. Napoleon to Berthier, 14 December 1813, *Correspondance*, No. 21,005, 26:509; Berthier to Oudinot, 14 December 1814, SHAT, C¹⁷ 183.
102. Napoleon to Mortier, 20 December 1813, *Correspondance*, No. 21,023, 26:520.
103. Napoleon to Lebrun, 16 December 1813, *Correspondance*, No. 21,013, 26:513–14; Napoleon to Clarke, 24 December 1813, *Correspondance*, No. 21,033, 26:616–18.
104. "Mémoire des opérations du général Roguet," SHAT, MR 902; Koch, "Campagne de 1814," SHAT, MR 902; "Ordre de movement," 18 December 1813, Correspondance Roguet, SHAT, MR 902; Napoleon to Clarke, 24 December 1813, *Correspondance*, No. 21,033, 26:529.
105. Napoleon to Clarke, 24 December 1813, *Correspondance*, No. 21,035, 26:530–2.
106. Berthier to Roguet, 14 December 1813, SHAT, C¹⁷ 183.
107. "Mémoire des opérations du général Roguet," SHAT, MR 902; Koch, "Campagne de 1814," SHAT, MR 902.
108. Orders, 18 December 1813, Correspondance Roguet, SHAT, MR 902; Napoleon to Clarke, 24 December 1813, *Correspondance*, No. 21,033, 26:616–18.
109. Berthier to Macdonald, 13 December 1813, SHAT, C¹⁷ 183.
110. Macdonald to Molitor, 16 December 1813, SHAT, C² 164.
111. Molitor to Macdonald, 17 and 18 December 1813, SHAT, C² 165.
112. Macdonald to Berthier, 18 December 1813, SHAT, C² 165.
113. Macdonald to Sébastiani and Arrighi, 18 December 1813, SHAT, C² 165.
114. Macdonald to Berthier, 19 December 1813, SHAT, C² 165.

115. Maison to Clarke, 21 December 1813, SHAT, C² 316; Varnhagen von Ense, *Bülow*, 316.
116. Macdonald to Berthier, 19 December 1813, SHAT, C² 165.
117. Berthier to Macdonald, 18 December 1813, SHAT, C¹⁷ 183.
118. Lefebvre de Béhaine, *Campagne de France*, 2:490–1.
119. Macdonald to Berthier, 19 December 1813, SHAT, C² 165.
120. Macdonald to Sébastiani, 17 December 1813, SHAT, C² 165.
121. Molitor to Macdonald, 20 December 1813, SHAT, C² 165.
122. Lefebvre de Béhaine, *Campagne de France*, 2:493.
123. Macdonald to Molitor, 20 December 1813, SHAT, C² 165.
124. Macdonald to Berthier, 20 December 1813 from Nijmegen at 12:00 P.M. and from Kleve at 11:00 P.M., SHAT, C² 165.
125. Berthier to Macdonald, 16 and 17 December 1813, SHAT, C¹⁷ 183.
126. Berthier to Macdonald, 18 December 1813, SHAT, C¹⁷ 183.
127. Macdonald to Berthier, 21 December 1813, SHAT, C² 165.
128. Berthier to Macdonald, 25 December 1813, SHAT, C¹⁷ 183; Napoleon to Clarke, 24 December 1813, *Correspondance*, No. 21,033, 26:529; Lefebvre de Béhaine, *Campagne de France*, 2:496–7, 499–500.
129. Macdonald to Berthier, 29 December 1813, SHAT, C² 166.
130. Horward's glossary defines a ravelin, which was also called a demilune, as "a detached work composed of two faces forming a salient angle and raised before the counterscarp." According to Haythornthwaite's glossary, a hornwork is a "fortification consisting of a bastion front and two branches at the sides." A cavalier is a raised battery, usually contained inside a bastion. Horward, *Napoleon and Iberia*, 398, 403; Haythornthwaite, *Napoleonic Source Book*, 398, 401.
131. "Mémoires des opérations du général Roguet," and Roguet to Drouot, 19 and 24 December 1813 and Roguet to Lebrun, 21 December 1813, Correspondance Roguet, SHAT MR 902; Maison to Clarke, 21 December and 22 December 1813, SHAT, C² 316; Koch, "Campagne de 1814," SHAT, MR 902; Bülow to Pauline, 25 December 1813 and *Feldzeitung der Preußischen Armee*, 44, 10 January 1814, BFA, No. 122; Koch, *Campagne de 1814*, 1:68–9; Hassenkamp, *Gen. Graf Bülow*, 277; Damitz, *Geschichte des Feldzuges*, 1:145–50.
132. Bülow to Wintzingerode, 29 December 1813, RGVIA, delo 4124.
133. Bülow to Pauline, 20 December 1813, BFA, No. 119.
134. Crusius, *Der Winterfeldzug*, 11.
135. Bülow to William Frederick, 23 December 1813, in Meinecke, *Boyen*, 360.
136. Boyen to Jacobi-Klöst, 20 December 1813, in Pertz, *Gneisenau*, 3:596–8.
137. According to the unpublished memoirs of Bülow's sister-in-law, Friederike von Auer, Bülow sent her husband to London for a second time before Christmas 1813. Auer, "Erinnerungen aus der Jugendzeit für meine Kinder," and Bülow to Pauline, 20 December 1813, BFA, Nos. 115 and 119.
138. Burghersh, *Operations of the Allied Armies*, 50–1.
139. Stewart, *Narrative of the War*, 232.
140. Karl Johan to Bülow, 2 January 1814, *Recueil*, 584.
141. A copy of this letter is contained in Stewart to Castlereagh, 29 December 1813, GStA, Rep. 92, Nachlaß Albrecht, Nr. 44. Italics mine.
142. Blücher to Knesebeck, 3 November 1813, ÖStA KA, FA 1539, ad38.

143. Petre, *Napoleon at Bay*, 6–7.
144. Fain, *Manuscrit de 1814*, 15–16.
145. Gneisenau to Rüchel, 5 January 1814, in Delbrück, *Gneisenau*, 4:147–8.

8. THE UPPER RHINE

1. RGVIA, delo 4135
2. Wilson, *Private Diary*, 2:277.
3. Schwarzenberg to Francis, 21 December 1813, ÖStA KA, FA 1541, Nr. 251; Victor to Berthier, 22 December 1813, 10:00 A.M., SHAT, C², 165.
4. Blanchard, "Le journal du siège d'Huningue en 1814," reproduced in Teissedre, *1814*, 11.
5. Schwarzenberg to Francis, 21 and 22 December 1813 and Scheibler to Schwarzenberg, 21 December 1813, ÖStA KA, FA 1541, Nrs. 251, 254, and 252.
6. Wittgenstein to Schwarzenberg, 23 December 1814, ÖStA KA, FA 1542, Nr. 287; Weil, *Campagne de 1814*, 16, 22; Bogdanovich, *Geschichte des Krieges*, 2:65–6; Hiller, *Geschichte des Feldzuges 1814*, 24.
7. ÖStA KA, FA 1541, Nr. 248. That same day Schwarzenberg issued a proclamation to the Swiss, a copy can be found in RGVIA, delo 4135.
8. Schwarzenberg to Maria Anna, 23 December 1813, Schwarzenberg, *Briefe*, No. 266, 359–60.
9. Disposition for 23 December; Schwarzenberg to Bubna, 24 December 1813; and Bubna to Schwarzenberg, 23, 24, and 26 December 1813, ÖStA KA, FA 1542, Nrs. 276, 301, 277, 315, and 354.
10. Disposition for 23 December; Schwarzenberg to Liechtenstein, 24 December 1813; and Liechtenstein to Schwarzenberg, n.d. (probably 25 December 1813), ÖStA KA, FA 1542, Nrs. 276, 303, and ad345.
11. Disposition for 23 December; Colloredo to Schwarzenberg, 24 December 1813, ÖStA KA, FA 1542, Nrs. 276 and 312.
12. Bianchi to Schwarzenberg, 23, 24, and 25 December 1813 and Schwarzenberg to Bianchi, 24 December 1813, ÖStA KA, FA 1544, Nrs. 289, 311, 339, and 302.
13. Schwarzenberg to Gyulay, 24 December 1813 and Gyulay to Schwarzenberg, 22, 24, and 25 December 1813, ÖStA KA, FA 1542, Nrs. 304, 263, 310, and 340.
14. Schwarzenberg to Francis, 21 and 22 December 1813 and Disposition for 22 December 1813, ÖStA KA, FA 1541, Nrs. 251, 254, and 251b; Disposition for 23 December 1813; Schwarzenberg to Francis 24 and 25 December 1813, ÖStA KA, FA 1542, Nrs. 276, 308, and 334.
15. Schwarzenberg to Metternich, 22 December 1813, Klinkowström, *Österreichs Theilnahme*, No. 12, 777.
16. Schwarzenberg to Wrede, 21 December 1813 and Disposition for 22 December 1813, ÖStA KA, FA 1541, Nrs. 250 and 251b; Schwarzenberg to Wrede, 22 (two) December 1813 and Disposition for 23 December 1813, ÖStA KA, FA 1542, Nrs. 267, 270 and 276.
17. Wrede to Schwarzenberg, 22 December 1813, ÖStA KA, FA 1541, 259; Scheibler to Schwarzenberg, 22 December 1813, ÖStA KA, FA 1542, 272.

18. Lefebvre de Béhaine, *Campagne de France*, 2:330. "At the approach of the Allies," claims Beauchamp, in *Histoire des campagnes*, 1:72, "all French authorities evacuated the towns and cities, and abandoned the countryside, which the inhabitants refused to defend despite the efforts of the military commanders." Beauchamp's comments regarding the inhabitants are not supported by the reports of the "military commanders," which attest to the good will of the Alsatians and a strong desire to defend their homes.

19. Victor to Berthier, 22 December 1813, 10:00 A.M., SHAT, C² 165.

20. Victor to Napoleon, 22 December 1813, AN, AF IV 1663^A plaquette 1^II; Victor to Berthier, 22 December 1813, 4:00 P.M., SHAT, C² 165.

21. Victor to Berthier, 23 December 1813, SHAT, C² 165; Victor to Clarke, 26 December 1813, SHAT, C² 166.

22. Wrede's siege train consisted of both cannon and howitzers. In cannon, the Bavarians possessed four 24-pounders, eight 18-pounders, and twelve 12-pounders; howitzers: four 60-pounders, four 30-pounders, four 10-pounders, and two 7-pounders. Each gun had a supply of 300 rounds. Bogdanovich, *Geschichte des Krieges*, 40.

23. Wilson, *Private Diary*, 2:278.

24. Schwarzenberg to Maria Anna, 23 December 1813, Schwarzenberg, Briefe, No. 266, 359.

25. Wrede to Schwarzenberg, 23 and 24 December 1813, ÖStA KA, FA 1542, Nrs. 284 and 294; Blanchard, "Le journal du siège d'Huningue en 1814," reproduced in Teissedre, 1814, 11; Heilmann, *Wrede*, 321–3; Plotho, *Der Krieg*, 3:54–5; Bogdanovich, Geschichte des Feldzuges, 1:59.

26. Wilson, *Private Diary*, 2:280.

27. Rechberg to Legrand and Legrand to Rechberg, 25 December 1813; Rechberg to Wrede, 24 (two) and 25 December 1813, ÖStA KA, FA 1542, Nrs. 337b, 336a, 336b, and 337a; "Le siège de Belfort," reproduced in Teissedre, 1814, 23–5.

28. Delamotte to Wrede, 24 December 1813, Treuberg to Wrede, 25 December 1813, and "Capitulation of Lausanne," 24 December 1813, ÖStA KA, FA 1542, Nrs. 336b, 337e, and 337f.

29. Deroy to Wrede and "Capitulation of Blamont," 25 December 1813; Wrede to Schwarzenberg, 26 December 1813, ÖStA KA, FA 1542, Nrs. 344c, 344f, and 344.

30. Frimont to Wrede, 25 December 1813, ÖStA KA, FA 1542, Nr. 344a; Heilmann, *Wrede*, 323–24; Bogdanovich, *Geschichte des Feldzuges*, 1:59; Weil, Campagne de 1814, 1:17, 19; Beauchamp, *Histoire des campagnes*, 69–70.

31. Wrede to Schwarzenberg, 23 and 24 December 1813, ÖStA KA, FA 1542, Nrs. 284 and 294; Lefebvre de Béhaine, *Campagne de France*, 2:338; Weil, *Campagne de 1814*, 1:17–18.

32. Victor to Berthier, 24 December 1813, 3:00 P.M., SHAT, C² 165.

33. Sources for the combat at Ste. Croix: Scheibler to Wrede, ÖStA KA, FA 1542, 336d; Wrede to Schwarzenberg, 25 December 1813, ÖStA KA, FA 1542, Nr. 336; Milhaud to Berthier, 24 December 1813; Victor to Berthier, 25 December 1813; Grouchy to Berthier, 26 December 1813, SHAT, C² 166; Plotho, Der Krieg, 3:22–4; Chuquet, *L'Alsace en 1814*, 44–6; Lefebvre de Béhaine, *Campagne de France*, 2:340–1; Weil, *Campagne de 1814*, 1:17–19.

34. "The newspapers of Paris exaggerated the importance of this ephemeral success" (Beauchamp, *Histoire des campagnes*, 71).

35. Wrede to Schwarzenberg, 25 December 1813, ÖStA KA, FA 1542, Nrs. 336 and 337.

36. Lefebvre de Béhaine, *Campagne de France*, 2:344–5.

37. Bernhardi, *Toll*, 4:135; Weil, *Campagne de 1814*, 1:20.

38. Schwarzenberg to Maria Anna, 23 December 1813, Schwarzenberg, *Briefe*, No. 266, 359–60.

39. Wilson, *Private Diary*, 2:284.

40. Schwarzenberg to Metternich, 27 December 1813, Klinkowström, *Österreichs Theilnahme*, No. 17, 782.

41. Frimont to Wrede, 25 December 1813; Schwarzenberg to Wrede and Francis, 25 December 1813; and Wrede to Schwarzenberg, ÖStA KA, FA 1542, Nrs. 344a, 320, 333, and 344.

42. Schwarzenberg to Frederick William, 25 December 1813, ÖStA KA, FA 1542, Nr. 320.

43. Schwarzenberg to Wittgenstein, 25 December 1813, ÖStA KA, FA 1542, Nr. 322.

44. Lefebvre de Béhaine, *Campagne de France*, 2:346–7.

45. Schwarzenberg to Blücher, 25 December 1813, ÖStA KA, FA 1542, Nr. 324.

46. Schwarzenberg to Blücher, 27 December 1813, ÖStA KA, FA 1542, Nr. 363.

47. Müffling, *Passages*, 401.

48. Blücher to Schwarzenberg, 29 December 1813, ÖStA KA, FA 1542, Nr. 415.

49. Schwarzenberg to Blücher, 2 January 1814, ÖStA KA, FA 1603, Nrs. 32 and 34.

50. As of the 26th, this second column still had not left Strasbourg. Victor to Berthier, 26 December 1813, SHAT, C² 166.

51. Victor to Berthier, 24 December 1813, 3:00 P.M., SHAT, C² 165.

52. Lefebvre de Béhaine, *Campagne de France*, 2:347–9.

53. Victor to Berthier, 25 December 1813, SHAT, C² 165.

54. Victor to Berthier, 26 December 1813, SHAT, C² 166.

55. Victor's second report to Berthier, 26 December 1813, SHAT, C² 166.

56. "Le siège de Belfort," reproduced in Teissedre, *1814*, 18–19; Chuquet, *L'Alsace en 1814*, 263.

57. Victor to Clarke and Berthier, 26 December 1813, SHAT, C² 166; "Le siège de Belfort," reproduced in Teissedre, *1814*, 18–19.

58. Berthier to Marmont, 21 and 24 December 1813, SHAT, C¹⁷ 183.

59. Berthier to Marmont, 26 December 1813, SHAT, C¹⁷ 183.

60. Marmont to Berthier, 27 December 1813, SHAT, C² 166.

61. Lefebvre de Béhaine, *Campagne de France*, 2:193.

62. ÖStA KA, FA 1542: Bianchi and Gyulay to Schwarzenberg, 25 December 1813, Nrs. 339 and 340; Schwarzenberg to Bianchi, M. Liechtenstein, and Colloredo, 25 December 1813, Nrs. 325, 326, and 332; A. Liechtenstein to Schwarzenberg, 26 December 1813, Nr. ad345; Schwarzenberg to Francis, (two) 27 December 1813, Nrs. 347 and 352; Army Order, 27 December 1813, Nr. 358; Bianchi, Volkonsky, and Barclay de Tolly to Schwarzenberg, 27 December 1813, Nrs. 382, 384, 386.

63. ÖStA KA, FA 1542, Nr. 419. See Johnston, *Der deutsche Nationalmythos*, 227.

64. ÖStA KA, FA 1542: Wittgenstein to Schwarzenberg, 25 December 1813, Nr. 343; Schwarzenberg to Frederick William and Wittgenstein, 25 December 1813, Nrs. 320 and 322; Schwarzenberg to Frederick William, 26 December 1813, Nr. 348; Frederick William to Schwarzenberg (two) 27 December 1813, Nrs. 378 and 379; Wittgenstein to Schwarzenberg, (two) 27 December 1813, Nrs. 381 and 383.

65. Weil, *Campagne de 1814*, 1:24.

66. Milhaud to Berthier, 27 December 1813, SHAT, C² 166.

67. Milhaud to Berthier, 29 December 1813, SHAT, C² 166.

68. Lefebvre de Béhaine, *Campagne de France*, 2:356.

69. Letter of a French agent, 27 December 1813, SHAT, C² 166.

70. Lefebvre de Béhaine, in *Campagne de France*, 2:355, is too critical of Victor. The historian states that Victor believed Wittgenstein's corps would proceed to Basel, thus committing "a mistake even more serious by judging that the region north of Strasbourg was momentarily sheltered from enemy operations." In the actual letter, Victor poses the thought that Wittgenstein's corps could possibly march to Basel and ends his sentence with a question mark.

71. Victor to Berthier, 27 December 1813, SHAT, C² 166.

72. Letter of a French agent, 27 December 1813, SHAT, C² 166.

73. Marmont to Berthier, 28 December 1813, SHAT, C² 166.

74. Marmont to Berthier, 29 December 1813, SHAT, C² 166.

75. Berthier to Marmont, 25 December 1813, SHAT, C¹⁷ 183.

76. Schwarzenberg to Francis, 28 December 1813, ÖStA KA, FA 1542, Nr. 402.

77. Quoted in Bernhardi, *Toll*, 4:150–1.

78. Schwarzenberg to Sherbatov, 30 December 1813, ÖStA KA, FA 1542, Nr. 440.

79. Weil, *Campagne de 1814*, 1:27–8; Janson, *Feldzuges 1814*, 1:77–8.

80. A summary of the operations can be found in Schwarzenberg to Francis, 30 December 1813, ÖStA KA, FA 1542, Nr. 444.

81. Schwarzenberg to Colloredo, 27 and 31 December 1813, ÖStA KA, FA 1542, Nrs. 372 and 450.

82. Schwarzenberg to M. Liechtenstein, 27 and 28 December 1813; M. Liechtenstein to Schwarzenberg, 26 December 1813, ÖStA KA, FA 1542, Nrs. 370, 389, and ad389.

83. Schwarzenberg to A. Liechtenstein, 27 and 28 December 1813; A. Liechtenstein to Schwarzenberg, 29 December 1813, ÖStA KA, FA 1542, Nrs. 371, 398, and 427.

84. Schwarzenberg to Gyulay, 27, 28 and 30 December 1813; Gyulay to Schwarzenberg, 29 and 30 December 1813, ÖStA KA, FA 1542, Nrs. 375, 392, 442, 424, and 445.

85. Note of 29 December 1813, SHAT, C² 166.

86. Schwarzenberg to Bianchi, 27, 28, and 30 December 1813; Bianchi to Schwarzenberg, 27, 28, 29, and 30 December 1813, ÖStA KA, FA 1542, Nrs. 364, 391, 435, 382, 403, 426, and 448.

87. Schwarzenberg to Hesse-Homburg, 27 December 1813, ÖStA KA, FA 1542, Nr. 366; Hesse-Homburg to Schwarzenberg, 30 December 1813, ÖStA KA, FA 1603, Nr. 6.

88. Musnier to Berthier, 31 December 1813, SHAT, C² 166.

89. Beauchamp, *Histoire des campagnes*, 1:73–5; Thiry, *La Chute de Napoléon I*, 56; Six, *Dictionnaire biographique des généraux et amiraux français*, 1:385 and 604.
90. Bubna to Schwarzenberg, 28 and 30 December 1813, ÖStA KA, FA 1542, Nrs. 404 and 406, 449 and 449a; Reports from Geneva, 1 January 1814, SHAT, C² 169.
91. "Stärke, Eintheilung, und Tagesbegebenheiten der Hauptarmee im Monate Januar," ÖStA KA, FA 1603, Nr. 30. The "Stärke, Eintheilung, und Tagesbegebenheiten der Hauptarmee unter Feldmarschall Fürst Schwarzenberg im Monate Januar" is a mammoth handwritten journal that covers in detail the daily operations of each corps and detached division of the Bohemian Army. It provides summaries of both the orders issued by Schwarzenberg's headquarters as well as the reports received from the corps commanders in a manner that is very easy to read and understand. A journal exists for each month of the 1814 campaign and by far is the most valuable resource concerning the operations of the Bohemian Army in the Vienna Kriegsarchiv.
92. Clausewitz agrees in principle with Bubna's mission to capture Geneva: "The dispatching of Bubna to Geneva with 12,000 men had sufficient grounds if one wanted to make Switzerland a part of his base of operations, thus it was more than appropriate to take this seemingly important point, and 12,000 men would not be missed from among such numerous masses" (Clausewitz, *Hinterlassene Werke*, 390–1).
93. Napoleon to Berthier, 1 and 2 January 1814, *Correspondance*, Nos. 21,055 and 21,056, 27:2, 4; Weil, *Campagne de 1814*, 1:309–12.
94. Girbaud to Clarke, 27 December 1813, SHAT, C² 166; Beauchamp, *Histoire des campagnes*, 1:98.
95. "Le siège de Belfort," reproduced in Teissedre, *1814*, 13, 24, 30.
96. Wilson, *Private Diary*, 283.
97. Schwarzenberg to Maria Anna, 2 January 1814, Schwarzenberg, *Briefe*, No. 267, 361.
98. Wrede to Schwarzenberg, 28, 29, 30, and 31 December 1813; Frimont to Wrede, 28 and 29 December 1813; Beckers to Chancel, 30 December 1813; Chancel to Beckers, 30 December 1813; ÖStA KA, FA 1542, Nrs. 457, 407, 432, 461, 457a–c, ad432, 461b, and 461c.
99. The Austrian Colonel Theodor Count Baillet de la Tour joined the IV Corps as chief of staff on 1 January. Frederick William to Schwarzenberg, 29 December 1813 and Frederick William's report of operations between 21 and 31 December 1813, submitted to Schwarzenberg on 2 January 1814, ÖStA KA, FA 1542, Nr. ad434 and FA 1603, Nr. 42; Hiller, *Geschichte des Feldzuges 1814*, 29–30.
100. Heilmann, *Wrede*, 324–5.
101. Blücher to Wrede, 4 January 1814, Bayerisch Hauptstaatsarchiv, Kriegsarchiv (BHStA, KA), B 545.
102. Mareschall to Schwarzenberg, 4 January 1814, ÖStA KA, FA 1603, Nr. 74.
103. Berthier to Victor, 23 December 1813, SHAT, C² 302.
104. Berthier to Victor, 21 December 1813, SHAT, C² 302.
105. Victor to Berthier, 28 and 29 December 1813, SHAT, C² 166.
106. Berthier to Victor, 26 December 1813, SHAT, C¹⁷ 183.

107. Lefebvre de Béhaine, *Campagne de France*, 2:358.
108. Milhaud to Berthier, 29 December 1813, SHAT, C² 166.
109. Marmont to Berthier, 29 December 1813, SHAT, C² 166.
110. Victor to Berthier, 29 December 1813, SHAT, C² 166.
111. Victor to Napoleon, 30 December 1813, AN, AF IV 1663ᴬ plaquette 1ᴵᴵ; Victor to Berthier, 30 December 1813, SHAT, C² 166.
112. Letter from a French agent, 27 December 1813, SHAT, C² 166.
113. Dejean to Napoleon, 27 December 1813, AN, AF IV 1668 plaquette 1.
114. Junot, *Memoirs of the Emperor Napoleon*, 3:334.
115. Berthier to Marmont, 2 January 1814, SHAT, C¹⁷ 183.
116. Napoleon issued these orders on 1 January to Berthier, who then issued copies to the respective generals and administrators the next day. Napoleon to Berthier, 1 January 1814, *Correspondance*, No. 21, 055, 27:1–3; Berthier to Mortier, Kellermann, and Marmont, 2 January 1813, SHAT, C¹⁷ 183; Berthier to Marmont, 3 January 1813, SHAT, C¹⁷ 183. Napoleon then clarified his instructions in Orders, 2 January 1814, *Correspondance*, No. 21,056, 27:3–4.
117. Napoleon to Caulaincourt, 4 January 1814, *Correspondance*, No. 21,062, 27:10.
118. Lefebvre de Béhaine, *Campagne de France*, 2:369.
119. Victor to Berthier, 31 December 1813, SHAT, C² 166.
120. Marmont to Berthier, 31 December 1813, SHAT, C² 166.
121. Sources for the second combat of Ste. Croix: Frimont to Schwarzenberg and Wrede, 31 December 1813 and Wrede to Schwarzenberg, 1 January 1814, ÖStA KA, FA 1603, Nrs. 9, ad10, and 10; Piré to Berthier, 31 December 1813, SHAT, C² 166; Victor to Berthier, 1 January 1814, SHAT, C' 169; Lefebvre de Béhaine, *Campagne de France*, 2:367–9; Weil, *Campagne de 1814*, 1:31–2.
122. Milhaud to Grouchy, 30 December 1813, SHAT, C² 166.
123. Milhaud to Berthier, 31 December 1813, SHAT, C² 166.
124. Lefebvre de Béhaine, *Campagne de France*, 2:368–9.
125. Victor to Berthier, 1 January 1814, SHAT, C² 169.
126. Marmont to Berthier, 1 January 1814, SHAT, C² 169.
127. Lefebvre de Béhaine, *Campagne de France*, 2:353–4.

9. THE MIDDLE RHINE

1. RGVIA, "Journal des opérations du Corps d' Armée Russe sous les orders du general d' infanterie Comte de Langeron," delo 4120.
2. Blücher to Bonin, 29 November 1813, Unger, *Blüchers Briefe*, 201.
3. Blücher to Alexander, n.d., in Pertz, *Gneisenau*, 3:534–5.
4. Blücher to Schwarzenberg, 23 December 1813, ÖStA KA, FA 1542, Nr. ad363.
5. Blücher to Katharina, 23 November 1813, Unger, *Blüchers Briefe*, 200–1.
6. Disposition for 29 December 1813 to 1 January 1814, issued 26 December 1813, and Disposition for 1–4 January 1814, GStA, Rep. 92, Nachlaß Gneisenau, Nr. 18; Blücher to Schwarzenberg, 29 December 1813, ÖStA KA, FA 1542, Nrs. 415 and 415a.
7. Blücher to Schwarzenberg, 29 December 1813, ÖStA KA, FA 1542, Nr. 415; Pertz, *Gneisenau*, 3:598–99.

8. St. Priest to Blücher, 28 December 1813, ÖStA KA, FA 1542, Nr. 415b.

9. Janson, *Feldzuges 1814*, 1:40–1; Droysen, *Yorck*, 2:274–5.

10. Quoted in Bogdanovich, *Geschichte des Krieges*, 1:75; Damitz, *Geschichte des Feldzuges*, 1:243.

11. Varnhagen von Ense, *Blücher von Wahlstadt*, 261–70; Müffling, *Die Feldzuge der schlesischen Armee*, 125–9; Bogdanovich, *Geschichte des Krieges*, 1:75.

12. Gneisenau to Louis Radziwill, 29 December 1813, in Pertz, *Gneisenau*, 3:609.

13. Blücher to a relative, 29 December 1813, Unger, *Blüchers Briefe*, 209–10.

14. Disposition for 29 December 1813 to 1 January 1814, issued 26 December 1813, GStA, Rep. 92, Nachlaß Gneisenau, Nr. 18.

15. Mikhailovsky-Danilevsky, *History of the Campaign in France*, 25; Lefebvre de Béhaine, *Campagne de France*, 2:199.

16. Sacken to Blücher, 28 December 1813, in Janson, *Feldzuges 1814*, 1:48.

17. Quoted in Gneisenau, *Blücher*, 282–3.

18. Disposition for 29 December 1813 to 1 January 1814, issued 26 December 1813, GStA, Rep. 92, Nachlaß Gneisenau, Nr. 18.

19. Bogdanovich, *Geschichte des Krieges*, 1:77; Damitz, *Geschichte des Feldzuges*, 1:245; Droysen, *Yorck*, 2:276; Janson, *Feldzuges 1814*, 1:44.

20. Disposition for 29 December 1813 to 1 January 1814, issued 26 December 1813, GStA, Rep. 92, Nachlaß Gneisenau, Nr. 18; Janson, *Feldzuges 1814*, 1:44–5.

21. The count of Brandenburg (1792–1850) was the illegitimate son of King Frederick William II and Countess Sophia Dönhoff, his second morganatic wife. Stamm-Kuhlmann, *König in Preußens großer Zeit*, 62.

22. Damitz, *Geschichte des Feldzuges*, 1:250–1.

23. Henckel von Donnersmarck, *Erinnerungen*, 243.

24. Quoted in Droysen, *Yorck*, 2:278.

25. Sources for the crossing at Kaub: Blücher to Frederick William, 3 January 1814, GStA, Rep. 15, Nr. 18; Blücher to Alexander, 3 January 1814 and "Kriegstage-buch der Schlesischen Armee im Januar 1814," ÖStA KA, FA 1603, Nrs. ad52 and 31; "RGVIA, Journal des opérations du Corps d'Armée Russe sous les ordres du général d'Infanterie Comte de Langeron," delo 4140; Damitz, *Geschichte des Feldzuges*, 1:251–4; Bogdanovich, *Geschichte des Krieges*, 1:77–8; Droysen, *Yorck*, 2:277–8; Janson, *Feldzuges 1814*, 1:46; Weil, *Campagne de 1814*, 1:183–4; Beauchamp, *Histoire des campagnes*, 1:92–3. The "Kriegstagebuch der Schlesischen Armee im Januar 1814" is one of at least two handwritten journals that covers in detail the daily operations of the Silesian Army in January 1814. The German copy of this thirteen-page document was lost in the Second World War, but fortunately a copy is located in the Austrian Kriegsarchiv.

26. "Journal of the Lithuanian Dragoon Regiment," reproduced in Henckel von Donnersmarck, *Erinnerungen*, 454.

27. Blücher to L'Estocq, 1 January 1814, Unger, *Blüchers Briefe*, 213.

28. Gneisenau to Gruner, 1 January 1814, GStA, Rep. 92, Nachlaß Gneisenau, Nr. 20b.

29. Müffling, *Passages*, 405.

30. RGVIA, "Journal des opérations du Corps d'Armée Russe sous les ordres du général d'Infanterie Comte de Langeron," delo 4140; Blücher to Alexander, 3 January 1814 and "Kriegstagebuch der Schlesischen Armee im Januar 1814,"

ÖStA KA, FA 1603, Nrs. ad52 and 31; Marmont, *Mémoires*, 6:18; Mikhailovsky-Danilevsky, *History of the Campaign in France*, 25; Gneisenau, *Blücher*, 307; Bogdanovich, *Geschichte des Krieges*, 1:75–6; Damitz, *Geschichte des Feldzuges*, 1:246–7; Lefebvre de Béhaine, *Campagne de France*, 2:199–201; Beauchamp, *Histoire des campagnes*, 1:92–4.

31. Ricard to Belliard, 2 January 1814, SHAT, C² 169; Lefebvre de Béhaine, *Campagne de France*, 2:205–6.

32. Sources for the taking of Koblenz: Langeron to Barclay de Tolly, 13 January 1814, "RGVIA, delo 4120; Journal des opérations du Corps d'Armée Russe sous les ordres du général d'Infanterie Comte de Langeron," delo 4140; Blücher to Alexander, 3 January 1814 and "Kriegstagebuch der Schlesischen Armee im Januar 1814," ÖStA KA, FA 1603, Nrs. ad52 and 31; Durutte to Belliard, 2 January 1814, SHAT, C² 169; Lefebvre de Béhaine, *Campagne de France*, 2:206–8; Mikhailovsky-Danilevsky, *History of the Campaign in France*, 26; Gneisenau, *Blücher*, 306; Weil, *Campagne de 1814*, 1:185; Koch, *Campagne de 1814*, 1:107; Damitz, *Geschichte des Feldzuges*, 1:263; Beauchamp, *Histoire des campagnes*, 1:91; Friederich, *Die Befreiungskriege*, 3:61.

33. "Journal of the Lithuanian Dragoon Regiment," reproduced in Henckel von Donnersmarck, *Erinnerungen*, 454.

34. Damitz, *Geschichte des Feldzuges*, 1:255–6; Droysen, *Yorck*, 2:230–3; Plotho, *Der Krieg*, 3:48–52; Varnhagen von Ense, *Blücher von Wahlstadt*, 272.

35. Friederich, *Die Befreiungskriege*, 3:61–2.

36. Blücher to Schwarzenberg, 29 December 1813, ÖStA KA, FA 1542, Nr. 415; Disposition, 2 January 1814, GStA, Rep. 92, Nachlaß Gneisenau, Nr. 18.

37. Quoted in Gneisenau, *Blücher*, 286.

38. Langeron to Barclay de Tolly, 13 January 1814, RGVIA, delo 4120; Blücher to Alexander, 3 January 1814, ÖStA KA, FA 1603, Nr. ad52.

39. Marmont to Berthier, 1 January 1814, SHAT, C² 169.

40. Marmont to Berthier, 4 January 1814, SHAT, C² 169.

41. Berthier to Marmont, 3 January 1813, SHAT, C¹⁷ 183.

42. Ricard to Belliard, 2 January 1814, SHAT, C² 169.

43. Marmont to Berthier, 4 January 1814, SHAT, C² 169.

44. Ricard to Belliard, 2 January 1814, SHAT, C² 169. Ricard claimed that one of Durutte's aide-de-camps provided the figure of 400–500 men. According to Durutte to Belliard, 2 January 1814, SHAT, C² 169, Durutte actually managed to rally 1,100 men as well as six guns. Regardless, Durutte claimed that these six battalions "are nothing more than cadres" that could not be organized until they reached Metz.

45. Ricard and Durutte to Belliard, 2 January 1814, SHAT, C² 169.

46. Victor to Marmont, 2 January 1814, SHAT, C² 169.

47. Marmont to Berthier, 4 January 1814, SHAT, C² 169.

48. Marmont, *Mémoires*, 6:18.

49. Lefebvre de Béhaine, *Campagne de France*, 2:201–3.

50. Marmont to Berthier, 2 January 1814, SHAT, C² 169.

51. Disposition for 1–4 January 1814, GStA, Rep. 92, Nachlaß Gneisenau, Nr. 18 and ÖStA KA, FA 1542, Nr. 415a; Janson, *Feldzuges 1814*, 1:51.

52. Blücher to Alexander, 3 January 1814 and "Kriegstagebuch der Schlesischen Armee im Januar 1814," ÖStA KA, FA 1603, Nrs. ad52 and 31; Weil, *Campagne de 1814*, 1:189–90; Damitz, *Geschichte des Feldzuges*, 1:257–8, 260–1; Janson, *Feldzuges 1814*, 1:51.

53. Disposition for 29 December 1813 to 1 January 1814, issued 26 December 1813, GStA, Rep. 92, Nachlaß Gneisenau, Nr. 18; Weil, *Campagne de 1814*, 1:107; Damitz, *Geschichte des Feldzuges*, 1:258.

54. Yorck to Henckel, 2 January 1814, in Henckel von Donnersmarck, *Erinnerungen*, 557.

55. Blücher to Alexander, 3 January 1814 and "Kriegstagebuch der Schlesischen Armee im Januar 1814," ÖStA KA, FA 1603, Nrs. ad52 and 31; Henckel von Donnersmarck, *Erinnerungen*, 245; Damitz, *Geschichte des Feldzuges*, 1:258–9.

56. Henckel von Donnersmarck, *Erinnerungen*, 245–7.

57. Blücher to Alexander, 3 January 1814 and "Kriegstagebuch der Schlesischen Armee im Januar 1814," ÖStA KA, FA 1603, Nrs. ad52 and 31; Bogdanovich, *Geschichte des Krieges*, 1:76.

58. Langeron to Barclay de Tolly, 13 January 1814, RGVIA, delo 4120; "Journal des opérations du Corps d'Armée Russe sous les ordres du général d'Infanterie Comte de Langeron," delo 4140; Marmont to Berthier, 2 January 1814, SHAT, C² 169.

59. Droysen, *Yorck*, 2:262–3, 266–7.

60. Droysen, *Yorck*, 266–7, 272.

61. Langeron to Barclay de Tolly, 13 January 1814, RGVIA, delo 4120; Marmont to Berthier, 4 January 1814, SHAT, C² 169.

62. Zwölfter Bericht der Schlesischen Armee, 9 January 1814, ÖStA KA, FA 1604, Nr. 186; Langeron to Barclay de Tolly, 13 January 1814, RGVIA, delo 4120; Weil, *Campagne de 1814*, 1:191.

63. Marmont to Berthier, 4 January 1814, SHAT, C² 169.

64. Durutte and Ricard to Belliard, 4 January 1814, SHAT, C² 169.

65. Blücher to Alexander, 3 January 1814, ÖStA KA, FA 1603, Nr. ad52; Damitz, *Geschichte des Feldzuges*, 1:265; Friederich, *Die Befreiungskriege*, 3:62.

66. Gneisenau to Clausewitz, 4 January 1814, GStA, Rep. 92, Nachlaß Gneisenau, Nr. 21.

67. Disposition, 4 January 1814, GStA, Rep. 92, Nachlaß Gneisenau, Nr. 18.

68. Zwölfter Bericht der Schlesischen Armee, 9 January 1814, ÖStA KA, FA 1604, Nr. 186; "Kriegstagebuch der Schlesischen Armee im Januar 1814," ÖStA KA, FA 1603, Nr. 31.

69. Disposition for 5 January 1814, issued 4 January 1814, GStA, Rep. 92, Nachlaß Gneisenau, Nr. 18; Zwölfter Bericht der Schlesischen Armee, 9 January 1814, ÖStA KA, FA 1604, Nr. 186.

70. Weil, *Campagne de 1814*, 1:193; Janson, *Feldzuges 1814*, 1:57.

71. Rigau to Belliard, 6 January 1814, SHAT, C² 170.

72. Blücher to Alexander, 7 January 1814, ÖStA KA, FA 1604, Nr. 161a.

73. Henckel von Donnersmarck, *Erinnerungen*, 248–50; Damitz, *Geschichte des Feldzuges*, 1:274.

74. "Kriegstagebuch der Schlesischen Armee im Januar 1814," ÖStA KA, FA 1603, Nr. 31

75. Müffling to Knesebeck, 5 January 1814, in Droysen, *Yorck*, 2:279. Italics mine.

76. Marmont to Belliard, 6:30 A.M., 6 January 1814, SHAT, C² 170.
77. Durutte to Belliard, 5 January 1814, SHAT, C² 169; Marmont to Berthier, 10:30 P.M., 6 January 1814, SHAT, C² 170.
78. Marmont to Berthier, 8 January 1814, SHAT, C² 170; Lefebvre de Béhaine, *Campagne de France,* 3:148, 151.
79. Weil, *Campagne de 1814,* 1:194; Janson, *Feldzuges 1814,* 1:57.
80. Blücher to Yorck, 5 January 1814, GStA, Rep. 92, Nachlaß Gneisenau, Nr. 18.
81. Some accounts claim that Sacken's Cossacks helped themselves to Marshal Kellermann's baggage at Zweibrücken, but why his baggage would be there makes absolutely no sense and seems unlikely. Zwölfter Bericht der Schlesischen Armee, 9 January 1814, ÖStA KA, FA 1604, Nr. 186; "Journal of the Reserve Cavalry of the I Corps," reproduced in Henckel von Donnersmarck, *Erinnerungen,* 520–1; Damitz, *Geschichte des Feldzuges,* 1:269–70; Weil, *Campagne de 1814,* 1:196; Koch, *Campagne de 1814,* 1:109–10.
82. Blücher to Alexander, 7 January 1814, ÖStA KA, FA 1604, Nr. 161a.
83. Disposition for 7 January 1814, issued on 6 January 1814, GStA, Rep. 92, Nachlaß Gneisenau, Nr. 18.
84. "Kriegstagebuch der Schlesischen Armee im Januar 1814," ÖStA KA, FA 1603, Nr. 31; "Journal of the 1st West Prussian Dragoon Regiment," and "Journal of the Reserve Cavalry of the I Corps," reproduced in Henckel von Donnersmarck, *Erinnerungen,* 503, 521; Damitz, *Geschichte des Feldzuges,* 1:271–3; Weil, *Campagne de 1814,* 1:198–200, 213; Janson, *Feldzuges 1814,* 1:59–61.
85. Marmont to Berthier, 7 January 1814, SHAT, C² 170.
86. Marmont to Berthier, 7 and 9 January 1814, SHAT, C² 170; Marmont, *Mémoires,* 6:19, 115–16, 118–19; Janson, *Feldzuges 1814,* 1:70.
87. Beauchamp, *Histoire des campagnes,* 1:99.
88. Blanton, "Napoleon's Prefects," 298–9, 349.
89. Blücher to Alexander, 7 January 1814, ÖStA KA, FA 160, Nr. 161a.
90. Blücher to Wrede, 7 January 1814, ÖStA KA, FA 1605, Nr. 313a.
91. Blücher to Alexander, 7 January 1814, ÖStA KA, FA 160, Nr. 161a. Although addressed to the tsar, Schwarzenberg actually received this letter in Vesoul on the 11th.
92. Blücher to Schwarzenberg, 3 January 1814, ÖStA, KA, FA 1603, Nr. 52.
93. Schwarzenberg to Blücher, 5 January 1814, ÖStA, KA, FA 1603, Nr. 89.
94. Blücher to Schwarzenberg, 8 January 1814, ÖStA, KA, FA 1604, Nr. 161. Schwarzenberg received this letter in Vesoul on 11 January.
95. Blücher to Schwarzenberg, 9 January 1814, ÖStA, KA, FA 1603, Nr. 175.
96. "Blücher and I agree with each other as always, just as at Leipzig." Schwarzenberg to Metternich, 6 January 1814, Klinkowström, *Österreichs Theilnahme,* No. 20, 788.
97. Schwarzenberg to Marie Anna, 8 and 12 January 1814, Schwarzenberg, *Briefe,* Nos. 268 and 269, 363–4; Janson, *Feldzuges 1814,* 1:67, 84.
98. Marmont to Berthier, 8 January 1814, SHAT, C² 170; "Kriegstagebuch der Schlesischen Armee im Januar 1814," ÖStA KA, FA 1603, Nr. 31; "Journal of the 1st Lithuanian Dragoon Regiment," reproduced in Henckel von Donnersmarck, *Erinnerungen,* 455; Weil, *Campagne de 1814,* 1:199–200; Damitz, *Geschichte des Feldzuges,* 1:271–3; Janson, *Feldzuges 1814,* 1:62–4.

99. Yorck to Henckel, 8 January 1814, in Janson, *Feldzuges 1814*, 1:62.

100. Henckel to Yorck, 9 January 1814, in Janson, "Die Unternehmungen des Yorckschen Korps," 14–15, 55.

101. Marmont to Berthier, 8 January 1814, SHAT, C² 170; Lefebvre de Béhaine, *Campagne de France*, 3:155–6.

102. Marmont to Berthier, 8 January 1814, SHAT, C² 170.

103. Janson, *Feldzuges 1814*, 1:63.

104. Disposition for 9,10 and 11 January 1814, issued on 9 January 1814, GStA, Rep. 92, Nachlaß Gneisenau, Nr. 18; a copy can be found in ÖStA KA, FA 1604, Nr. 175b.

105. Gneisenau to Stein, 9 January 1814, Nr. 20b; GStA, Rep. 92, Nachlaß Gneisenau, copy can be found in: RGVIA, delo 4169.

106. Marmont to Berthier, noon, 9 January 1814, SHAT, C² 170.

107. General Orders for 10 January 1814, issued 9 January 1814 and Marmont to Berthier, 10 January 1814, SHAT, C² 170.

108. "Kriegstagebuch der Schlesischen Armee im Januar 1814," ÖStA KA, FA 1603, Nr. 31; Zwölfter Bericht der Schlesischen Armee, 9 January 1814, ÖStA KA, FA 1604, Nr. 186; "The Journal of the Lithuanian Dragoon Regiment," "The Journal of the 1st West Prussian Dragoon Regiment," "The Journal of the Reserve Cavalry of the I Army Corps," reproduced in Henckel von Donnersmarck, *Erinnerungen*, 455, 504, 521; Weil, *Campagne de 1814*, 1:204–5; Damitz, *Geschichte des Feldzuges*, 1:280–84; Lefebvre de Béhaine, *Campagne de France*, 3:162–4; Janson, *Feldzuges 1814*, 1:67–9; Janson, "Die Unternehmungen des Yorckschen Korps," 2; Droysen, *Yorck*, 2:279–80.

109. Marmont to Berthier, 10 January 1814, SHAT, C² 170.

110. Blücher to Hardenberg, 4 January 1814, Unger, *Blüchers Briefe*, 214.

111. Friederich, *Die Befreiungskriege*, 3:60–61; Janson, *Feldzuges 1814*, 1:49–50; Bogdanovich, *Geschichte des Krieges*, 1:77.

112. Lefebvre de Béhaine, *Campagne de France*, 3:151.

113. Yorck to Henckel, 7 January 1814, in Henkel von Donnersmarck, *Erinnerungen*, 560.

10. Alsace and Franche-Comté

1. Bubna to Schwarzenberg, 2 January 1814, ÖStA KA, FA 1603, Nr. 44.

2. Bianchi to Schwarzenberg, 1 January 1814, ÖStA KA, FA 1603, Nr. 22.

3. Gyulay to Schwarzenberg, 2 January 1814 and "Stärke, Eintheilung, und Tagesbegebenheiten der Hauptarmee im Monate Januar," ÖStA KA, FA 1603, Nrs. 40 and 30.

4. Colloredo to Schwarzenberg, 2 January 1814, ÖStA KA, FA 1603, Nr. ad53.

5. Schwarzenberg to Hesse-Homburg, 31 December 1813, ÖStA KA, FA 1542, Nr. 462.

6. Note of 29 December 1813, SHAT, C² 166.

7. Hesse-Homburg to Schwarzenberg, 1 January 1814, ÖStA KA, FA 1603, Nr. 23.

8. Beauchamp, *Histoire des campagnes*, 1:99.

9. Décret sur la levée-en-masse, 4 January 1814, *Correspondance*, No. 21,061, 27:9.

10. Thurn to Schwarzenberg, 4 January 1814, ÖStA KA, FA 1603, Nr. 73.

11. Bianchi to Schwarzenberg, 3 January 1814, ÖStA KA, FA 1603, Nr. 49.

12. Gyulay to Schwarzenberg, 3 January 1814, ÖStA KA, FA 1603, Nrs. 48 and 48a.

13. Hesse-Homburg to Schwarzenberg, 3 January 1814; A. Liechtenstein to Schwarzenberg, 4 January 1814," ÖStA KA, FA 1603, Nrs. 50 and 69.

14. Beauchamp, *Histoire des campagnes*, 1:105–6, 147–8,

15. Bubna to Schwarzenberg 1, 2 and 3 January 1814; Zechmeister to Bubna, 3 January 1814; Capitulation of Ft. l'Écluse, signed by Zechmeister on 3 January 1814; "Stärke, Eintheilung, und Tagesbegebenheiten der Hauptarmee im Monate Januar," ÖStA KA, FA 1603, Nrs. 25, 44, 103, 103a, 103c, and 30.

16. Schwarzenberg to Wittgenstein, 27 December 1813, ÖStA KA, FA 1542, Nr. 373; Bogdanovich, *Geschichte des Krieges*, 1:65–6.

17. Chuquet, *L'Alsace en 1814*, 57; Ségur, *Du Rhin à Fontainebleau*, 86–7, 89, 91.

18. The changes in Wittgenstein's plans are contained in four letters to Schwarzenberg, two written on the 27th and two on the 29th, and three letters from Schwarzenberg in response: Wittgenstein to Schwarzenberg, 27 and 29 December 1813; Schwarzenberg to Wittgenstein 28 and 31 December 1813, ÖStA KA, FA 1542, Nrs. 381, 383, 422, and 428; FA 1602, Nrs. 12:11, 12:14, and 12:15.

19. "Stärke, Eintheilung, und Tagesbegebenheiten der Hauptarmee im Monate Januar," 3 and Wittgenstein to Schwarzenberg, 2 and 3 January 1814, ÖStA KA, FA 1603, Nrs. 30, 43, and 84a; Bogdanovich, *Geschichte des Krieges*, 1:66; Janson, *Feldzuges 1814*, 1:74; Lefebvre de Béhaine, *Campagne de France*, 2:373–4; Beauchamp, *Histoire des campagnes*, 1:89–90.

20. St. Sulpice to Victor, 2 January 1814, SHAT, C² 169.

21. Ségur, *Du Rhin à Fontainebleau*, 92–94.

22. Victor to Napoleon, 2 January 1814, SHAT, C² 169.

23. Victor to Berthier, 2 January 1814, SHAT, C² 169.

24. Victor to Marmont, 2 January 1814, SHAT, C² 169.

25. "Stärke, Eintheilung, und Tagesbegebenheiten der Hauptarmee im Monate Januar," 2–3; Platov to Schwarzenberg, 31 December 1813; Barclay de Tolly to Schwarzenberg, 1 January 1814; and Schwarzenberg to Francis, 1 and 2 January 1814, ÖStA KA, FA 1603, Nrs. 30, 10, 21, 13, and 39.

26. Wrede to Schwarzenberg and Frederick William to Schwarzenberg, 1 January 1814; "Stärke, Eintheilung, und Tagesbegebenheiten der Hauptarmee im Monate Januar," 2, ÖSTA KA, FA 1603, Nrs. 10, 20, and 30.

27. Wrede to Schwarzenberg, 2 January 1814; Schwarzenberg to Wrede (two), 2 January 1814; Schwarzenberg to Francis, 1 and 2 January; "Stärke, Eintheilung, und Tagesbegebenheiten der Hauptarmee im Monate Januar," 3, ÖSTA KA, FA 1603, Nrs. 13, 39, 36b, 36, 37c, and 30.

28. Milhaud to Victor, 2 January 1814, SHAT, C² 169; "Stärke, Eintheilung, und Tagesbegebenheiten der Hauptarmee im Monate Januar," 3, ÖSTA KA, FA 1603, Nr. 30.

29. Victor to Berthier, 3 January 1814, SHAT, C² 169.

30. In his 1816 work, *Histoire des campagnes*, 1:90, Beauchamp attributes Victor's retreat to the passage of Wittgenstein's VI Corps.

31. Chuquet, *L'Alsace en 1814*, 64–5; Lefebvre de Béhaine, *Campagne de France*, 2:379–80.
32. Schwarzenberg to Wrede (two), 2 January 1814 and Disposition for 3 January, ÖSTA KA, FA 1603, Nrs. 36, 37a, and 47.
33. Schwarzenberg to Maria Anna, 2 January 1814, Schwarzenberg, *Briefe*, No. 267, 361.
34. Disposition of the IV Corps for 3 January 1814, ÖSTA KA, FA 1603, Nr. ad20.
35. Lefebvre de Béhaine, *Campagne de France*, 2:379–80.
36. Schwarzenberg to Maria Anna, 4 January 1814, Schwarzenberg, *Briefe*, No. 267, 361.
37. The account of the operation at Colmar has been taken from: Grouchy to Berthier, Victor to Berthier, and Milhaud to Berthier, 6 January 1814, SHAT, C² 170; "Stärke, Eintheilung, und Tagesbegebenheiten der Hauptarmee im Monate Januar," 3–4 and Schwarzenberg to Francis, 3 January 1814, ÖSTA KA, FA 1603, Nrs. 30 and 55; Lefebvre de Béhaine, *Campagne de France*, 2:381–4; Chuquet, *L'Alsace en 1814*, 65–7; Hiller, *Geschichte des Feldzuges 1814*, 31; Heilmann, *Wrede*, 325.
38. Milhaud to Berthier, 7 January 1814, SHAT, C² 170.
39. Victor to Milhaud, 3 January 1814, SHAT, C² 169.
40. Lefebvre de Béhaine, *Campagne de France*, 2:382.
41. Victor to Berthier, 6 January 1814, SHAT, C² 170.
42. Sherbatov to Schwarzenberg, 3 January 1814, ÖStA KA, FA 1603, Nr. 51; Cassagne to Lacoste, 3 January 1814, SHAT, C² 169.
43. Ségur, *Du Rhin à Fontainebleau*, 94.
44. Thurn to Schwarzenberg, 1 January 1814, ÖSTA KA, FA 1603, Nr. 31.
45. Wittgenstein to Schwarzenberg, 3 January 1814 and "Stärke, Eintheilung, und Tagesbegebenheiten der Hauptarmee im Monate Januar," ÖStA KA, FA 1603, Nrs. 84 and 30; Bogdanovich, *Geschichte des Krieges*, 1:67; Janson, *Feldzuges 1814*, 1:75–6.
46. Gyulay, Bianchi, and Liechtenstein to Schwarzenberg, 4 January 1814; Hesse-Homburg to Schwarzenberg, 5 January 1814; Bubna to Schwarzenberg, 6 January 1814; and "Stärke, Eintheilung, und Tagesbegebenheiten der Hauptarmee im Monate Januar," ÖStA KA, FA 1603, Nrs. 68, 70, 69, 101, 103, 119, and 30.
47. Schwarzenberg to Wrede, 4 January 1814, ÖStA KA, FA 1603, Nr. 66c.
48. Wrede to Schwarzenberg, 4 January 1814 and "Stärke, Eintheilung, und Tagesbegebenheiten der Hauptarmee im Monate Januar," ÖStA KA, FA 1603, Nrs. 72 and 30.
49. Frederick William to Schwarzenberg, 4 January 1814, ÖStA KA, FA 1603, Nr. ad82; Hiller, *Geschichte des Feldzuges 1814*, 31.
50. Wittgenstein to Schwarzenberg, 5 January 1814, ÖStA KA, FA 1603, Nr. 135.
51. Weil, *Campagne de 1814*, 1:39; Bogdanovich, *Geschichte des Krieges*, 1:67.
52. Belliard to Berthier, 3 January 1814, SHAT, C² 169.
53. Thurn to Schwarzenberg, 1 and 2 January 1814, ÖSTA KA, FA 1603, Nrs. 31 and 46.
54. Hesse-Homburg to Schwarzenberg, 1 January 1814, ÖSTA KA, FA 1603, Nrs. 23, 23a, and 23b.

55. Schwarzenberg to Metternich, 6 January 1814, Klinkowström, *Österreichs Theilnahme*, No. 20, 787.

56. Weil, *Campagne de 1814*, 1:39; Bogdanovich, *Geschichte des Krieges*, 1:67.

57. RGVIA, delo 4120.

58. Thurn to Schwarzenberg, 4 January 1814, ÖStA KA, FA 1603, Nr. 73.

59. Schwarzenberg to Maria Anna, 4 January 1814, Schwarzenberg, *Briefe*, No. 267, 361.

60. Disposition for 6–8 January 1814, 4 January 1814 and Schwarzenberg to Barclay de Tolly, Frederick William, Wrede, Gyulay, Bianchi, Colloredo, Bubna, and Hesse-Homburg, 4 January 1814, ÖStA KA, FA 1603, Nrs. 66, 66a, 66b, 66c, 66d, 66e, 66f, 63, and 64; Lefebvre de Béhaine, *Campagne de France*, 3:114.

61. Schwarzenberg to Maria Anna, 4 January 1814, Schwarzenberg, *Briefe*, No. 267, 361.

62. Radetzky added Bianchi's division to Army Group Langres but detached Wimpffen's division from the I Corps.

63. Janson, *Feldzuges 1814*, 1:29–30.

64. Roloff, *Politik und Kriegführung*, 31.

65. Metternich to Schwarzenberg, 8 January 1814, Klinkowström, *Österreichs Theilnahme*, No. 21, 788–9.

66. Grouchy to Milhaud, 4 January 1814 and Grouchy to Berthier, 5 January 1814, C² 169; Victor to Berthier, 6 January 1814, SHAT, C² 170. Lefebvre de Béhaine, in *Campagne de France*, 2:385–6, charges Victor with intentionally failing to report to Berthier on either 4 or 5 January so that he could present his decision to retreat as a faits accomplis in his report of the 6th. Although nothing can explain why Victor failed to report on the 4th or 5th and why his report of the 6th contains only a summary of the operations on these days, this charge appears ludicrous.

67. Victor to Berthier, 6 January 1814, SHAT, C² 170.

68. Lefebvre de Béhaine, *Campagne de France*, 2:389–90.

69. Grouchy to Milhaud, 5 January 1814, SHAT, C² 169.

70. Victor to Berthier, 6 January 1814, SHAT, C² 170.

71. Some accounts, including those considered authoritative such as Weil and Janson, mistakenly claim that Milhaud crossed the Vosges due west of Sélestat at Ste. Marie. This error arises from the fact that Schwarzenberg's headquarters believed this was the case and noted such in the "Stärke, Eintheilung, und Tagesbegebenheiten der Hauptarmee im Monate Januar."

72. Grouchy to Berthier, 6 January 1814, SHAT, C² 170; Ségur, *Du Rhin à Fontainebleau*, 96–8; Lefebvre de Béhaine, in *Campagne de France*, 2:391–2.

73. Deroy to Wrede, 5 January 1814, BHStA KA, B 545.

74. Wrede to Schwarzenberg and Frederick William to Schwarzenberg, 5 January 1814, ÖStA KA, FA 1603, Nrs. 100 and ad81.

75. Wittgenstein to Schwarzenberg, Schwarzenberg to Francis (two), 5 January 1814; "Stärke, Eintheilung, und Tagesbegebenheiten der Hauptarmee im Monate Januar," 5, ÖStA KA, FA 1603, Nrs. 84a, 97, 97a, and 30.

76. Frederick William to Schwarzenberg, 5 January 1814, ÖStA KA, FA 1603, Nr. ad81.

77. Victor to Berthier, 8 January 1814, SHAT, C² 170.
78. Mauguin, *Ney et Blücher à Nancy*, 6.
79. Sherbatov to Schwarzenberg, 6 January 1814, ÖStA KA, FA 1603, Nr. 118.
80. Thurn to Schwarzenberg, 6 January 1814, ÖStA KA, FA 1603, Nr. 117.
81. Fain, *Manuscrit de 1814*, 28–9.
82. Barclay de Tolly to Schwarzenberg, 6 January 1814, ÖStA KA, FA 1603, Nr. 113.
83. Frederick William to Schwarzenberg, 6 January 1814, ÖStA KA, FA 1603, Nr. 116.
84. Wrede to Schwarzenberg, 6 January 1814; Wittgenstein to Schwarzenberg, 7 January 1814; "Stärke, Eintheilung, und Tagesbegebenheiten der Hauptarmee im Monate Januar," ÖStA KA, FA 1603, Nrs. 115, 135, and 30.
85. Schwarzenberg to Gyulay and Bianchi, 6 January 1814, ÖStA KA, FA 1603, Nrs. 110 and ad110.
86. Hesse-Homburg to Schwarzenberg, 7 January 1814 and "Stärke, Eintheilung, und Tagesbegebenheiten der Hauptarmee im Monate Januar," ÖStA KA, FA 1603, Nrs. 141 and 30.
87. Bubna to Schwarzenberg, 6 January 1814, ÖStA KA, FA 1603, Nr. 119.
88. Weil, *Campagne de 1814*, 1:312–13.
89. Zechmeister to Bubna, 4 January 1814, ÖStA KA, FA 1603, Nr. 178f.
90. Beauchamp, *Histoire des campagnes*, 1:148.
91. Zechmeister to Bubna, 5 January 1814, ÖStA KA, FA 1603, Nr. 178v.
92. Grouchy to Berthier, 6 January 1814, SHAT, C² 170.
93. Milhaud to Berthier, 7 January 1814, SHAT, C² 170.
94. Lefebvre de Béhaine, *Campagne de France*, 2:392, 3:107.
95. Victor to Berthier, 6 and 9 January 1814, SHAT, C² 170.
96. Caulaincourt to Napoleon, 6 January 1814, AN, 95 AP 14, No. 1.
97. Caulaincourt to Napoleon, 18 January 1814, AN, 95 AP 14, No. 8.
98. Beauchamp, *Histoire des campagnes*, 1:89.
99. Ney to Berthier, 10 January 1814, SHAT, C² 170.
100. Ney to Berthier, 11 January 1814, SHAT, C² 171.
101. "The discouragement of the civil authorities spreads among the troops" (Caulaincourt to Napoleon, 7 January 1814, AN, 95 AP 14, No. 2).
102. Weil, *Campagne de 1814*, 1:44.
103. Orders, 2 January 1814, *Correspondance*, No. 21,056, 27:3–4.
104. Napoleon to Kellermann, 3 January 1814, *Correspondance*, No. 21,060, 27:8–9.
105. "I still do not know what the duke of Bellune is doing," wrote Napoleon earlier on the 8th. Napoleon to Kellermann, 8 January 1814, *Correspondance*, No. 21,073, 27:18.
106. Belliard to Napoleon, 5 January 1814, SHAT, C² 169.
107. Hiller, *Geschichte des Feldzuges 1814*, 34.
108. Napoleon to Berthier, 6 January 1814, *Correspondance*, No. 21,066, 27:15. Kellermann to Victor, 6 January 1814, ÖStA, KA, FA 1605, Nr. ad272; D'Auvrey to Schwarzenberg, 10 January 1814, ÖStA, KA, FA 1604, Nr. 205.
109. Kellermann to Napoleon, 7 January 1814, SHAT, C² 170.
110. Napoleon to Clarke, 7 January 1814, *Correspondance*, No. 21,068, 27:16.

111. In Napoleon to Kellermann, 8 January 1814, *Correspondance*, No. 21,072, 27:18, the emperor states that the 2nd Young Guard Voltigeur Division would proceed to Langres, but this is a mistake or misprint. In Napoleon to Mortier, 19 January 1814, *Correspondance*, No. 21,117, 27:55, he informs Mortier the 2nd Young Guard Division was due at Châlons that same day.

112. Victor to Berthier, 6 January 1814, SHAT, C² 170.

113. Victor to Berthier, 7 January 1814, SHAT, C² 170.

114. Dejean to Napoleon, 8 January 1814, AN, AF IV 1669[A] plaquette 2.

115. Caulaincourt to Napoleon, 6 January 1814, AN, 95 AP 14, No. 1.

116. Caulaincourt to Napoleon, 7 January 1814, AN, 95 AP 14, No. 2.

117. Wittgenstein to Schwarzenberg, 7 January 1814; "Stärke, Eintheilung, und Tagesbegebenheiten der Hauptarmee im Monate Januar," ÖStA, KA, FA 1603, Nrs. 135, and 30.

118. Roederer wrote Savary that Allied forces had pushed their way to within a half a league of the city on the previous day. He noted that "this situation has made a great change in the mood of the people." The talk "in the boutiques and cafes was that the city had been betrayed; that Victor had led away the garrison; that the city will surrender in less than three days. These rumors have spread terror among the masses. This terror arose from a good sentiment, but many of those who spread the alarm appear very suspicious to me." As a result, Roederer planned to issue a proclamation to reassure the people; order the arrest of the rabble-rousers; and take measures for the arrest of foreign "suspects" living in Strasbourg. The commissioner estimated that 8,000–9,000 Allied soldiers had crossed the Rhine at Ft. Vauban, but "spread throughout the countryside to link with the troops that crossed at Basel." This letter was intercepted by Cossacks. Roderer to Savary, 7 January 1814, RGVIA, delo 4119.

119. Wrede to Schwarzenberg, 8 January 1814, ÖStA KA, FA 1603, Nr. 165.

120. Deroy to Wrede, Delamotte to Wrede, Wrede to Schwarzenberg, 7 and 8 January 1814, ÖStA KA, FA 1604, Nrs. 144b, 144, 144, and 165.

121. Frederick William to Schwarzenberg, 7 January 1814, ÖStA KA, FA 1604, Nr. 137.

122. Sherbatov to Schwarzenberg, 7 January 1814," ÖStA KA, FA 1604, Nr. 166.

123. Bubna to Schwarzenberg, 7 January 1814, quoted in Weil, *Campagne de 1814*, 1:315.

124. Janson, *Feldzuges 1814*, 1:84.

125. Weil, *Campagne de 1814*, 1:67.

126. Knesebeck to Müffling, 6 January 1813, in Lefebvre de Béhaine, *Campagne de France*, 3:115.

127. Schwarzenberg to Maria Anna, 8 January 1814, Schwarzenberg, *Briefe*, No. 268, 363.

128. Napoleon to Kellermann, 3 January 1814, *Correspondance*, No. 21,060, 27:8–9.

129. "Stärke, Eintheilung, und Tagesbegebenheiten der Hauptarmee im Monate Januar," ÖStA KA, FA 1603, Nr. 30.

130. Schwarzenberg to Colloredo, Gyulay, Barclay de Tolly, Rayevsky, Bianchi, Frederick William, Wrede, Hesse-Homburg, and Francis, 7 January 1814; Schwarzenberg to Wittgenstein, 8 January 1814 and "Stärke, Eintheilung, und

Tagesbegebenheiten der Hauptarmee im Monate Januar," ÖStA KA, FA 1603, Nrs. 127, 127a, 127g, 127b, 127c, 127d, 127e, 127f, 130, 146, and 30; Weil, *Campagne de 1814*, 1:67.

131. Weil, *Campagne de 1814*, 1:44, 47–8.

132. Schwarzenberg to Maria Anna, 8 January 1814, Schwarzenberg, *Briefe*, No. 268, 363.

11. THE VOSGES AND THE SAÔNE

1. Victor to Kellermann, 7 January 1814, SHAT, C² 170.
2. Victor to Berthier, 7 January 1814, SHAT, C² 170.
3. Berthier to Victor, 11 January 1814, SHAT, C¹⁷ 183.
4. Victor to Napoleon, 15 January 1814, SHAT, C² 171.
5. Piré to Grouchy, 7 January 1814, SHAT, C² 170.
6. Victor to Berthier, 8 January 1814, SHAT, C² 170.
7. Order of the Day, 7 January 1814, SHAT, C² 170.
8. Phalsbourg was approximately twenty-six miles southeast of Sarreguemines and thirty miles northeast of Baccarat.
9. Victor to Kellermann, 7 January 1814, SHAT, C² 170.
10. Coustumier, *Victor*, 205.
11. Gérard to Victor, 8 January 1814, SHAT, C² 170.
12. Victor to Grouchy, 8 January 1814, SHAT, C² 170.
13. Grouchy to Chasseriau, 8 January 1814, SHAT, C² 170.
14. Cassagne to Victor, 8 January 1814, RGVIA, delo 4120. Wanting to make clear that Meunier's division was under his command, Victor frankly told Cassagne that because this division had been placed at his disposal by Kellermann, he had ordered Meunier to assemble all of his units at Charmes and to advance against the enemy in unison with the II Corps. This letter was intercepted by Cossacks.
15. Caulaincourt to Napoleon, 8 January 1814, AN, 95 AP 14, No. 3.
16. Kellermann to Victor, 6 January 1814, RGVIA, delo 4120.
17. Letter from the commissaire-ordonnateur at Nancy, 7 January 1814, ÖStA KA, FA 1605, Nr. ad283.
18. Sherbatov to Schwarzenberg, 13 January 1814, ÖStA KA, FA 1605, Nr. 283.
19. Victor to Berthier, 10 January 1814, SHAT, C² 170.
20. Victor to Duhesme, 9 January 1814, SHAT, C² 170.
21. Milhaud to Berthier, 10 January 1814, SHAT, C² 170.
22. Disposition for 10 January 1814, issued 9 January 1814, SHAT, C² 170.
23. Victor to Berthier, 9 January 1814, SHAT, C² 170.
24. Victor to Cassagne, 9 January 1814, RGVIA, delo 4120; Seslavin to Wrede, 9 January 1814, BHStA KA, B 545.
25. Grouchy to Ségur, 9 January 1814, SHAT, C² 170.
26. Defrance's division was to consist of all four Honor Guard Regiments. At this time, the 1st Honor Guard Regiment was operating with Marmont, and the majority of the 2nd was besieged in Mainz; 120 men of this latter unit did escape being trapped in Mainz and now rode with Ségur. Ségur to Defrance, 9 January 1814, SHAT, C² 170.

27. Grouchy to Berthier, and Victor to Berthier, 10 January 1814, SHAT, C² 170.
28. Lefebvre de Béhaine, *Campagne de France*, 3:124–5.
29. Ney to Berthier, 10 January 1814, SHAT, C² 170; Weil, *Campagne de 1814*, 1:81.
30. Victor to Berthier, 9 January 1814, SHAT, C² 170.
31. Pahlen to Wrede, 8 January 1814, BHStA KA, B 545.
32. "Stärke, Eintheilung, und Tagesbegebenheiten der Hauptarmee im Monate Januar," ÖStA KA, FA 1603, Nr. 30.
33. Wrede to Scheibler, 7 January 1814, BHStA KA, B 545.
34. Wrede to Frederick William, 8 January 1814, BHStA KA, B 545; Wrede to Schwarzenberg, 8 January 1814 and "Stärke, Eintheilung, und Tagesbegebenheiten der Hauptarmee im Monate Januar," ÖStA KA, FA 1604, Nr. 165 and FA 1603, Nr. 30.
35. Frederick William to Schwarzenberg, 9 January 1814 and "Stärke, Eintheilung, und Tagesbegebenheiten der Hauptarmee im Monate Januar," ÖStA KA, FA 1604, Nr. 171 and FA 1603, Nr. 30; Hiller, *Geschichte des Feldzuges 1814*, 33–4.
36. Schwarzenberg to Wittgenstein, 8 January 1814, ÖStA KA, FA 1604, Nr. 146.
37. Weil, *Campagne de 1814*, 1:90.
38. Wittgenstein to Schwarzenberg, 10 and 11 January 1814, ÖStA KA, FA 1602, Nrs. 1:25 and 1:28.
39. Lefebvre de Béhaine, *Campagne de France*, 3:131.
40. Schwarzenberg to Wrede, 8 January 1814, ÖStA KA, FA 1604, Nr. 144.
41. Wrede to Schwarzenberg, 9 January 1814, ÖStA KA, FA 1604, Nr. 169.
42. Schwarzenberg to Wrede, 13 January 1814, ÖStA KA, FA 1605, Nr. 298.
43. Schwarzenberg to Wrede, 15 January 1814, ÖStA KA, FA 1605, Nr. 350.
44. Heilmann, *Wrede*, 328.
45. Janson, *Feldzuges 1814*, 1:86–7.
46. "Stärke, Eintheilung, und Tagesbegebenheiten der Hauptarmee im Monate Januar," ÖStA KA, FA 1603, Nr. 30.
47. Platov to Frederick William, 9 January 1814, ÖStA KA, FA 1604, Nr. 173a.
48. Frederick William to Platov, 9 January 1814, ÖStA KA, FA 1604, Nr. 173b.
49. Frederick William to Schwarzenberg, 9 January 1814, ÖStA KA, FA 1604, Nr. 173; Hiller, *Geschichte des Feldzuges 1814*, 34–35.
50. Lefebvre de Béhaine, *Campagne de France*, 3:127.
51. Victor to Duhesme, 11 January 1814, SHAT, C² 170.
52. Sources for the combat of St. Dié: Piré to Grouchy, 10 January 1814; Grouchy to Berthier and Victor to Berthier, 11 January 1814, SHAT, C² 170 and C² 171; Wrede to Schwarzenberg, 10 January 1814; Wrede's Disposition for 10 and 11 January, 1814, issued 9 January 1814; Deroy to Wrede, 10 January 1814; Wrede to Schwarzenberg, 11 January 1814; Delamotte to Wrede, 10 January 1814; Deroy to Wrede, 10 January 1814; and "Stärke, Eintheilung, und Tagesbegebenheiten der Hauptarmee im Monate Januar," ÖStA KA, FA 1604, Nrs. 201, 201a, and 201m, FA 1605 Nrs. 222, 222d, and 222e, and FA 1603 Nr. 30; Beauchamp, *Histoire des campagnes*, 1:103–4; Heilmann, *Wrede*, 326–27; Lefebvre de Béhaine, *Campagne de France*, 3:127–9; Weil, *Campagne de 1814*, 1:91–2.
53. Milhaud to Grouchy, 10 January 1814, SHAT, C² 170.
54. Grouchy to Berthier, 11 January 1814, SHAT, C² 171.

55. Grouchy to Victor, 10 January 1814, SHAT, C^2 170.
56. Grouchy to Cassagne, 10 January 1814, SHAT, C^2 170.
57. Victor to Berthier, 10 January 1814, SHAT, C^2 170.
58. Sherbatov to Schwarzenberg, midnight 10–11 January 1814, ÖStA KA, FA 1604, Nr. 206.
59. Latour to Radetzky, 10 January 1814 and Disposition for the attack on Épinal on 11 January 1814, issued 10 January 1814, ÖStA KA, FA 1604, Nrs. 211 and ad211.
60. Weil, *Campagne de 1814*, 1:81, 102.
61. Meunier to Ney, 12 January 1814, AN, 137 AP 15.
62. Sources for the combat of Épinal: Platov to Schwarzenberg, 12 January 1814; "Stärke, Eintheilung, und Tagesbegebenheiten der Hauptarmee im Monate Januar"; Sherbatov to Schwarzenberg, 11 January 1814; Frederick William to Schwarzenberg, 12 January 1814, ÖStA KA, FA 1603, Nrs. 10 and 30; FA 1604, Nr. 225; and FA 1605, Nr. 254; "Armee-Nachrichten," Vesoul, 24 January 1814, RGVIA, delo 4135; Beauchamp, *Histoire des campagnes*, 1:104–5; Hiller, *Geschichte des Feldzuges 1814*, 36–40.
63. Frederick William to Schwarzenberg, 12 January 1814, ÖStA KA, FA 1605, Nr. 254.
64. Seslavin to Wrede, 9 January 1814, BHStA KA, B 545.
65. Wrede to Schwarzenberg, 10 January 1814; Disposition for 10 and 11 January 1814, issued 9 January 1814; Disposition for 13 and 14 January 1814, issued on 10 January 1814; Wrede to Schwarzenberg, 12 January 1814, Delamotte to Wrede and Deroy to Delamotte, 11 January 1814, ÖStA KA, FA 1604, Nrs. 201, 201a, 201k, 249, 249a, 249b.
66. Thurn to Gyulay, 9 January 1814, ÖStA KA, FA 1604, Nr. 168a-c.
67. "Stärke, Eintheilung, und Tagesbegebenheiten der Hauptarmee im Monate Januar," ÖStA KA, FA 1603, Nr. 30.
68. Gyulay to Schwarzenberg, 8 January 1814, ÖStA KA, FA 1604, Nr. 159.
69. "Stärke, Eintheilung, und Tagesbegebenheiten der Hauptarmee im Monate Januar," ÖStA KA, FA 1603, Nr. 30.
70. Ibid.; Thurn to Schwarzenberg, 9 January 1814, ÖStA KA, FA 1604, Nr. 170; Beauchamp, *Histoire des campagnes*, 1:106–7, 128–30; Weil, *Campagne de 1814*, 1:85–6, 316.
71. Thurn to Schwarzenberg, 9 January 1814, ÖStA KA, FA 1604, Nr. 170.
72. Seslavin to Wrede, 9 January 1814 and Wrede to Schwarzenberg, 10 January 1814; ÖStA KA, FA 1604, Nrs. 201t and 201.
73. Platov to Schwarzenberg, 12 January 1814, ÖStA KA, FA 1603, Nr. 10.
74. On 4 January Zechmeister informed Bubna of the arrival at Grenoble of 5,000 men from Suchet's army. Zechmeister to Bubna, 4 January 1814, ÖStA KA, FA 1603, Nr. 178f.
75. Blücher to Schwarzenberg, 8 January 1814, ÖStA KA, FA 1604, Nr. 161.
76. 78.Metternich to Schwarzenberg, 13 January 1814, Klinkowström, *Österreichs Theilnahme*, No. 25, 794.
77. Schwarzenberg to Francis, 11 January 1814, ÖStA KA, FA 1604, Nr. 238.
78. Schwarzenberg to Gyulay, 11 January 1814, ÖStA KA, FA 1604, Nr. 236. "The enemy has 1,000 men in Langres" (Schwarzenberg to Maria Anna, 12 January 1814, Schwarzenberg, *Briefe*, No. 269, 364).

79. Schwarzenberg to Metternich, 11 January 1814, ÖStA KA, FA 1605, Nr. 320a.

80. Schwarzenberg to Wrede, 11 January 1814, ÖStA KA, FA 1604, Nr. 231.

81. Schwarzenberg to Maria Anna, 12 January 1814, Schwarzenberg, *Briefe*, No. 269, 364–5. Schwarzenberg is referring to the Russo–Prussian Guard because the Russian Reserve itself had already crossed the Rhine.

82. Schwarzenberg to Metternich, 11 January 1814, 11 January 1814, ÖStA KA, FA 1605, Nr. 320a.

83. Schwarzenberg to Maria Anna, 12 January 1814, Schwarzenberg, *Briefe*, No. 269, 365.

84. Ibid.

85. Sherbatov to Schwarzenberg, 11 January 1814, ÖStA KA, FA 1604, Nr. 225.

86. Schwarzenberg to Maria Anna, 15 January 1814, Schwarzenberg, *Briefe*, No. 269, 366.

87. Roloff, *Politik und Kriegführung*, 27.

88. Schwarzenberg to Maria Anna, 29 January 1814, Schwarzenberg, *Briefe*, No. 271, 370.

89. Schwarzenberg to Metternich, 11 January 1814, ÖStA KA, FA 1605, Nr. 320a.

90. Clausewitz, *Hinterlassene Werke*, 330–1.

91. Ibid., 331. Clausewitz generally agrees with Schwarzenberg's decision to summon Army Group Alsace to Langres, calling its deployment on the right wing of the Bohemian Army "a dangerous dissipation of forces."

92. Metternich to Schwarzenberg, 8 January 1814, Klinkowström, *Österreichs Theilnahme*, No. 25, 794.

93. Roloff, *Politik und Kriegführung*, 27–8, 30.

94. Fournier, *Congress von Châtillon*, 51, 361; Kraehe, *Metternich's German Policy*, 1:280; Kissinger, *A World Restored*, 112.

95. Hardenberg to Alexander, 9 January 1814, in Martens, *Recueil de traités et conventions conclus par la russie*, 7:156.

96. Kraehe, *Metternich's German Policy*, 1:283.

97. Berthier to Victor, 10 January 1814, SHAT, C[17] 183.

98. Berthier to Victor, 11 January 1814, SHAT, C[17] 183.

99. Fain, *Manuscript of 1814*, 27.

100. Napoleon to Macdonald, 10 January 1814, *Correspondance*, No. 21,083, 27:23; Koch, *Campagne de 1814*, 1:111–12.

101. Berthier to Belliard, 10 January 1814, SHAT, C[17] 183.

102. Mauguin, *Ney et Blücher à Nancy*, 20.

103. Victor to Grouchy, 11 January 1814, SHAT, C[2] 171.

104. Lefebvre de Béhaine, *Campagne de France*, 3:132.

105. Victor to Berthier, 11 January 1814, SHAT, C[2] 171.

106. Victor to Ney, 11 January 1814, SHAT, C[2] 171 and AN, 137 AP 15.

107. Ney to Victor, 12 January 1814, AN, 137 AP 5.

108. Lefebvre de Béhaine, in *Campagne de France*, 3:132, claims that "Victor must have intended to move on Épinal, judging by the clear offensive character of the dispositions described for the 12th." Although Lefebvre de Béhaine is usually critical of Victor, this statement cannot be supported by the actual wording of the orders.

109. Victor to Grouchy, 11 January 1814 and Order of the Day for 12 January 1814, issued 11 January 1814, SHAT, C² 171.
110. Caulaincourt to Napoleon, 11 January 1814, AN, 95 AP 14, No. 5.
111. Lefebvre de Béhaine, *Campagne de France*, 3:134–5.
112. Weil, *Campagne de 1814*, 1:84.

12. LORRAINE

1. Defrance to Belliard, 3 January 1814, SHAT, C² 169.
2. Caulaincourt to Napoleon, 6 January 1814, AN, 95 AP 14, No. 1.
3. Colchen to Clarke, 4 January 1814, SHAT, C² 169.
4. SHAT, C² 169; RGVIA, delo 4135.
5. Colchen to Clarke, 6 January 1814, SHAT, C² 170.
6. Kellermann to Berthier, 5 January 1814, SHAT, C² 169.
7. Kellermann to Napoleon, 3 January 1814, AN, AF IV 1669^A plaquette 1.
8. Caulaincourt to Napoleon, 6 January 1814, AN, 95 AP 14, No. 1.
9. On 5 January Colchen issued a comprehensive, ten-article civil defense plan titled: "Dans la 4me Division Militaire, qui prescrit des Mesures de Défense contre les incursions de l'ennemi." RGVIA, delo 4135.
10. Lachouque, *Napoléon en 1814*, 85.
11. Belliard to Berthier, 8 January 1814, SHAT, C² 170.
12. Marmont to Berthier, 9 January 1814, SHAT, C² 170.
13. Mauguin, *Ney et Blücher à Nancy*, 7.
14. Colchen to Kellermann, 8 January 1814, SHAT, C² 170.
15. Caulaincourt to Napoleon, 6 January 1814, AN, 95 AP 14, No. 1.
16. Caulaincourt to Napoleon, 7 January 1814, AN, 95 AP 14, No. 2.
17. Berthier to Ney, 3 and 4 January 1814, SHAT, C¹⁷ 183.
18. Mauguin, *Ney et Blücher à Nancy*, 14–15.
19. Berthier to Ney, 6 January 1814, SHAT, C¹⁷ 183.
20. Mauguin, *Ney et Blücher à Nancy*, 16.
21. Young, "Ney: The Bravest of the Brave," 363.
22. Chandler, *Dictionary of the Napoleonic Wars*, 314.
23. Ibid., 313–15; Young, "Ney: The Bravest of the Brave," 360–7; Six, *Dictionnaire Biographique*, 2:253–5.
24. See Leggiere, *Napoleon and Berlin: The Franco-Prussian War in North Germany, 1813*.
25. Belliard to Berthier, 7 January 1814, SHAT, C² 170.
26. Belliard to Berthier, 14 January 1814, SHAT, C² 171.
27. Beauchamp, *Histoire des campagnes*, 1:135; Lefebvre de Béhaine, *Campagne de France*, 3:181.
28. Marmont to Berthier, 10 January 1814, SHAT, C² 170.
29. Blücher to Schwarzenberg, 8 January 1814, ÖStA KA, FA 1604, Nr. 161.
30. Blücher to Wittgenstein, 8 January 1814, ÖStA KA, FA 1602, Nr. 1:15.
31. Wittgenstein to Blücher, 10 January 1814, ÖStA KA, FA 1602, Nr. 1:24.
32. Wittgenstein to Blücher, 12 January 1814, ÖStA KA, FA 1602, Nr. 1:29.

33. Müffling to Knesebeck, 9 January 1814, in Janson, "Die Unternehmungen des Yorckschen Korps," 9.
34. Blücher to Yorck, 10 January 1814, in Damitz, *Geschichte des Feldzuges*, 1:282–3.
35. Hugo to Belliard, 11 January 1814, SHAT, C² 172.
36. "Disposition for 11 January," 10 January 1814, GStA, Rep. 92, Nachlaß Gneisenau, Nr. 18; "Kriegstagebuch der Schlesischen Armee im Januar 1814," ÖStA KA, FA 1603, Nr. 31.
37. "Kriegstagebuch der Schlesischen Armee im Januar 1814," ÖStA KA, FA 1603, Nr. 31; Weil, *Campagne de 1814*, 1:204–8; Damitz, *Geschichte des Feldzuges*, 1:286–7; Janson, *Feldzuges 1814*, 1:110.
38. Damitz, *Geschichte des Feldzuges*, 1:284–5, 296; Janson, "Die Unternehmungen des Yorckschen Korps," Appendix 8, 54.
39. Blücher to Wrede, 16 January 1814, ÖStA KA, FA 1605, Nr. ad392.
40. "Kriegstagebuch der Schlesischen Armee im Januar 1814," ÖStA KA, FA 1603, Nr. 31; "Journal of the Reserve Cavalry of the I Corps," reproduced in Henckel von Donnersmarck, *Erinnerungen*, 521; Weil, *Campagne de 1814*, 1:23; Damitz, *Geschichte des Feldzuges*, 1:288–90; Janson, *Feldzuges 1814*, 1:110; Lefebvre de Béhaine, *Campagne de France*, 3:168.
41. Marmont to Belliard, 11 January 1814, SHAT, C² 171.
42. Marmont to Berthier, 12 January 1814, SHAT, C² 171.
43. Marmont to Berthier, 13 January 1814, SHAT, C² 171.
44. Meynadier to Ricard, 12 January 1814, SHAT, C² 171.
45. Lefebvre de Béhaine, *Campagne de France*, 3:169–70.
46. Victor to Grouchy, 12 January 1814, SHAT, C² 171.
47. Ségur, *Du Rhin à Fontainebleau*, 105.
48. Ney to Victor, 11 January 1814, AN, 137 AP 5.
49. Victor to Grouchy, 12 January 1814, SHAT, C² 171.
50. By the time Ney penned this brief, the prefect he is referring to, Himbert de Flegny of the Vosges Department, was a guest of the Cossacks.
51. Ney to Berthier, 11 January 1814, SHAT, C² 171.
52. Mauguin, *Ney et Blücher à Nancy*, 24.
53. Ney to Berthier, 12 January 1814, SHAT, C² 171.
54. Ney to Caulaincourt, 12 January 1814, AN, 137 AP 5. It is interesting to note that by the time Ney composed his daily report to Berthier – the report the emperor would evaluate – the size of the Allied force that attacked Épinal had grown to "5,000–6,000 infantry and 4,000–5,000 cavalry" (Ney to Berthier, 12 January 1814, SHAT, C² 171).
55. Colchen to Ney, 12 January 1814, SHAT, C² 171.
56. Ney to Victor, 12 January 1814, AN, 137 AP 5.
57. Kellermann to Ney, 12 January 1814, AN, 137 AP 15.
58. Victor to Ney, 12 January 1814, AN, 137 AP 15.
59. Heilmann, *Wrede*, 327; Coustumier, *Victor*, 210.
60. Dejean to Berthier, 12 January 1814, SHAT, C² 171.
61. Ney to Colchen, 12 January 1814, SHAT, C² 171; Mauguin, *Ney et Blücher à Nancy*, 32.
62. Ney to Caulaincourt, 12 January 1814, AN, 137 AP 5.

63. Ney to Berthier, 12 January 1814, SHAT, C² 171.
64. Nancy and Toul were thirty and thirty-two miles south of Metz, respectively. Pont-à-Mousson lies halfway between Metz and Nancy.
65. Ney to Meunier and Lacoste, 12 January 1814, AN, 137 AP 5.
66. Colchen to Clarke, 14 January 1814, SHAT, C² 171.
67. Mauguin, *Ney et Blücher à Nancy*, 32–3.
68. Lefebvre de Béhaine, *Campagne de France*, 3:136.
69. Caulaincourt to Napoleon, 13 January 1814, AN, 95 AP 14, No. 6.
70. Ney to Meunier, 12 January 1814, AN, 137 AP 5.
71. Kellermann to Ney, 13 January 1814, AN, 137 AP 15.
72. Ney to Victor, 13 January 1814, AN, 137 AP 5.
73. Ney to Berthier, 13 January 1814, SHAT, C² 171.
74. Caulaincourt to Napoleon, 13 January 1814, AN, 95 AP 14, No. 6.
75. Ney to Berthier, 13 January 1814, SHAT, C² 171.
76. Caulaincourt to Napoleon, 13 January 1814, AN, 95 AP 14, No. 6.
77. Dejean to Napoleon, 14 January 1814, AN, AF IV 1669ᴬ plaquette 3.
78. Victor to Ney, 13 January 1814, AN, 137 AP 15.
79. Victor to Berthier, 14 January 1814, SHAT, C² 171.
80. Wrede's March Disposition for 13 January 1814, BHStA KA, B 545.
81. "Stärke, Eintheilung, und Tagesbegebenheiten der Hauptarmee im Monate Januar," ÖStA KA, FA 1603, Nr. 30.
82. Victor to Grouchy, 13 January 1814, SHAT, C² 171.
83. Grouchy to Defrance and Briche, 13 January 1814, SHAT, C² 171.
84. "Note sur la situation actuelle de la France," 12 January 1814, *Correspondance*, No. 21,089, 27:26–8. In Napoleon to Berthier, 13 January 1814, *Correspondance*, No. 21,090, 27:31–2, the emperor asked Berthier to send a new copy of "the situation of the enemy, because you will see in your report there were several mistakes." The above are the figures stated in Napoleon's published *Correspondance*, but when examining Berthier's unpublished order issued to Marmont on the following day, the numbers change slightly, and Napoleon assumes the Allies have an additional 100,000 soldiers in the hospitals. The following amended figures are found in Berthier to Marmont, 13 January 1814, SHAT, C¹⁷ 183: "That is, approximately 100,000 men on the right bank of the Rhine. This, added to the 160,000 men who are in our territory on the left bank, makes approximately 300,000 men. There must be around 100,000 men in the hospitals, sick or injured; this supposes 400,000 men exclusive of the army in Italy."
85. Napoleon to Berthier, 13 January 1814, *Correspondance*, No. 21,090, 27:31; Berthier to Marmont, 13 January 1814, SHAT, C¹⁷ 183.
86. "Note sur la situation actuelle de la France," 12 January 1814, *Correspondance*, No. 21,089, 27:29–31.
87. "General Instructions," 13 January 1814, *Correspondance*, No. 21,091, 27:32–3.
88. "General Instructions," 13 January 1814, SHAT, C¹⁷ 183.
89. Berthier to Marmont, 13 January 1814, SHAT, C¹⁷ 183.
90. Campana, *La campagne de France 1814*, 25.
91. Napoleon to Bertrand, 14 January 1814, *Correspondance*, No. 21,098, 27:39.
92. Napoleon to Berthier, 14 January 1814, *Correspondance*, No. 21,099, 27:39–40.

93. Blücher to Schwarzenberg, 12 January 1814, ÖStA KA, FA 1605, Nr. 252.

94. Blücher to Bonin, 13 January 1814, Unger, *Blücher's Briefe*, 217–18.

95. Chevallerie to Henckel, 10 January 1814, in Janson, "Die Unternehmungen des Yorckschen Korps," 55–6.

96. "Kriegstagebuch der Schlesischen Armee im Januar 1814," ÖStA KA, FA 1603, Nr. 31; Henckel von Donnersmarck, *Erinnerungen*, 254; Damitz, *Geschichte des Feldzuges*, 1:294–5.

97. "Kriegstagebuch der Schlesischen Armee im Januar 1814," ÖStA KA, FA 1603, Nr. 31; "Journal of the 1st Lithuanian Dragoon Regiment," reproduced in Henckel von Donnersmarck, *Erinnerungen*, 455–56; Weil, *Campagne de 1814*, 1:210–12.

98. Horn to Henckel, 13 January 1814, in Henckel von Donnersmarck, *Erinnerungen*, 568–9.

99. "Kriegstagebuch der Schlesischen Armee im Januar 1814," ÖStA KA, FA 1603, Nr. 31; Koch, *Campagne de 1814*, 1:117; Weil, *Campagne de 1814*, 1:213–15; Damitz, *Geschichte des Feldzuges*, 1:298–9; Janson, *Feldzuges 1814*, 1:112, 114–16; Bogdanovich, *Geschichte des Krieges*, 1:80; Janson, "Die Unternehmungen des Yorckschen Korps," 13–14, 17.

100. Wrede to Schwarzenberg, 14 January 1814, ÖStA KA, FA 1605, Nr. 313.

101. Ney to Berthier, 16 January 1814, SHAT, C² 172.

102. Piré to Grouchy, 15 January 1814, 9:00 A.M., SHAT, C² 171.

103. Grouchy to Defrance, 15 January 1814, SHAT, C² 171.

104. Piré to Grouchy, 15 January 1814, 2:00 P.M., SHAT, C² 171.

105. Victor to Berthier, 14 January 1814, SHAT, C² 171.

106. Grouchy to Berthier, 15 January 1814, SHAT, C² 171.

107. Coustumier, *Victor*, 211.

108. Grouchy to Berthier, 15 January 1814, SHAT, C² 171; Ségur, *Du Rhin à Fontainebleau*, 106–8; Mauguin, *Ney et Blücher à Nancy en 1814*, 42; Lefebvre de Béhaine, *Campagne de France*, 3:137–9; Coustumier, *Victor*, 209.

109. Victor to Grouchy and Victor to Berthier, 14 January 1814, SHAT, C² 171.

110. Piré to Grouchy, 15 January 1814, 9:00 A.M., SHAT, C² 171; Ségur, *Du Rhin à Fontainebleau*, 108–9; Lefebvre de Béhaine, *Campagne de France*, 3:139–40.

111. Grouchy to Berthier, 15 January 1814, SHAT, C² 171.

112. Victor to Berthier, 14 January 1814, SHAT, C² 171.

113. Lefebvre de Béhaine, *Campagne de France*, 3:139.

114. Marmont to Berthier, 13 January 1814, SHAT, C² 171.

115. Marmont to Berthier, 14 January 1814, SHAT, C² 171.

116. Marmont to Ricard, 14 January 1814, SHAT, C² 171.

117. Marmont to Berthier, 14 January 1814, SHAT, C² 171.

118. Marmont to Berthier, 14 January 1814, SHAT, C² 171.

119. "Kriegstagebuch der Schlesischen Armee im Januar 1814," ÖStA KA, FA 1603, Nr. 31; Lefebvre de Béhaine, *Campagne de France*, 3:172.

120. Koch, *Campagne de 1814*, 1:117.

121. Marmont to Berthier, 15 January 1814, SHAT, C² 171.

122. Marmont to Berthier, 16 January 1814, SHAT, C² 172.

123. Lefebvre de Béhaine, *Campagne de France*, 3:179.

124. Marmont to Berthier, 16 January 1814, SHAT, C² 172.

125. Grouchy to Milhaud, 14 January 1814, SHAT, C² 171.

126. Piré to Grouchy, 15 January 1814, 2:00 P.M., SHAT, C² 171.

127. Grouchy to Berthier, 15 January 1814, SHAT, C² 171.

128. Grouchy to Defrance, 15 January 1814, SHAT, C² 171.

129. Grouchy to Berthier, 16 January 1814, SHAT, C² 172.

130. Grouchy touched on the same subject in his daily brief to Berthier: "The order of 3 January prescribed the distribution of one month's pay to the army, but this order is unrealistic, since the money, which itself is non-existent, cannot be found. Please show this letter to His Majesty: it breaks the hearts of his faithful subjects" (Grouchy to Berthier, 15 January 1814, SHAT, C² 171).

131. Victor to Napoleon, 15 January 1814, SHAT, C² 171.

132. Grouchy to Berthier, 16 January 1814, SHAT, C² 172.

133. Victor to Berthier, 16 January 1814, SHAT, C² 172.

134. Ney to Berthier, 16 January 1814, SHAT, C² 172.

135. Victor's order of the day for 17 January 1814, issued on 16 January 1814, Victor to Duhesme, Grouchy to Milhaud, Grouchy to Piré, Grouchy to Lhéritier, 16 January 1814, SHAT, C² 172.

136. Victor to Berthier, 17 January 1814 and "Journal de la défense de Toul," par François-Louis Chaudron, SHAT, C² 172.

137. Victor to Berthier, 16 January 1814, SHAT, C² 172.

138. Grouchy to Berthier, 16 January 1814, SHAT, C² 172.

139. Lefebvre de Béhaine, *Campagne de France*, 3:142.

140. Blücher to Rüchel, 14 January 1814, Unger, *Blüchers Briefe*, 218. Italics mine.

141. Blücher to Wrede, 16 January 1814, ÖStA KA, FA 1605, Nr. ad392.

142. Blücher to Schwarzenberg, 15 January 1814, ÖStA KA, FA 1605, Nr. 346.

143. Blücher to Hardenberg, 15 January 1814, Unger, *Blüchers Briefe*, 220–1.

144. "Stärke, Eintheilung, und Tagesbegebenheiten der Hauptarmee im Monate Januar," ÖStA KA, FA 1603, Nr. 30; Weil, *Campagne de 1814*, 1:122.

145. Blücher to Wrede, 16 January 1814, ÖStA KA, FA 1605, Nr. ad392.

146. Heilmann, *Wrede*, 327.

147. Schwarzenberg to Wrede, 13 January 1814, BHStA KA, B 545.

148. Wrede to Schwarzenberg, 15 January 1814, ÖStA KA, FA 1605, Nr. 343.

149. Wrede to Schwarzenberg, 16 January 1814, ÖStA KA, FA 1605, Nr. 371.

150. Blücher to Wrede, 16 January 1814, ÖStA KA, FA 1605, Nr. ad392.

151. Schwarzenberg to Wrede, 15 January 1814, ÖStA KA, FA 1605, Nr. 350.

152. Wrede to Blücher, 17 January 1814, BHStA KA, B 545. A copy of Wrede's march disposition for 16 and 17 January can also be found in GStA, Rep. 92, Nachlaß Gneisenau, Nr. 18.

153. Wrede to Schwarzenberg, 17 January 1814, ÖStA KA, FA 1605, Nr. 392.

154. Schwarzenberg to Wrede, 16 January 1814, ÖStA KA, FA 1605, Nrs. 375 and 382.

155. Schwarzenberg to Blücher, 17 January 1814, ÖStA KA, FA 1606, Nr. 411.

156. Schwarzenberg to Wrede, 17 January 1814, ÖStA KA, FA 1606, Nr. 403.

157. Schwarzenberg to Wrede, 19 January 1814, ÖStA KA, FA 1606, Nr. 449.

158. Schwarzenberg to Wittgenstein, 19 January 1814, ÖStA KA, FA 1606, Nr. 452.

159. Wrede to Schwarzenberg, 20 January 1814, BHStA KA, B 545.
160. Gneisenau to Hardenberg, 15 January 1814, GStA, Rep. 92, Nachlaß Gneisenau, Nr. 20b.
161. "Kriegstagebuch der Schlesischen Armee im Januar 1814," ÖStA KA, FA 1603, Nr. 31.
162. Sherbatov to Schwarzenberg, 15 January 1814, ÖStA KA, FA 1605, Nr. 344.
163. Sherbatov to Schwarzenberg, 16 January 1814, ÖStA KA, FA 1605, Nr. 369.
164. "Disposition for 15 January," 14 January 1814, GStA, Rep. 92, Nachlaß Gneisenau, Nr. 18; "Kriegstagebuch der Schlesischen Armee im Januar 1814," ÖStA KA, FA 1603, Nr. 31; Damitz, *Geschichte des Feldzuges*, 1:303–4.
165. Quoted in Damitz, *Geschichte des Feldzuges*, 1:309.
166. Müffling, *Passages*, 408–9.
167. Blücher to Katharina, 18 January 1813, Unger, *Blüchers Briefe*, 222.
168. Müffling, *Aus meinem Leben*, 97–8; Varnhagen von Ense, *Blücher von Wahlstadt*, 274–9; Delbrück, *Gneisenau*, 4:26; Friederich, *Die Befreiungskriege*, 3:66.
169. Quoted in Bogdanovich, *Geschichte des Krieges*, 1:81.
170. Quoted in Müffling, *Aus meinem Leben*, 99–100.
171. Lefebvre de Béhaine, *Campagne de France*, 3:144–5.
172. Napoleon to Victor, 17 January 1814, *Correspondance*, No. 21,105, 27:47.
173. Somewhat of an apologist, Vaudoncourt offers an alternative explanation: "On the other hand, Napoleon, surprised by an invasion, which he thought would be delayed by the start of peace negotiations, was not able to draft any plan of campaign, since his army was still not united. All he could do, as soon as he learned of the crossing of the Rhine, was to name a point of concentration for the army corps located on the frontiers. They had been destined to form the advance guard of the army that he believed he would have time to assemble at Paris. The rapidity of events changed this, so that these same corps became the only army available. It was thus impossible for Napoleon to have the initiative in strategic operations. All he could do consisted of following Allied movements, harassing, and taking advantage of each mistake they made in order to delay their marches and to gain time to assemble the troops that he could unite from the rest of the empire" (Vaudoncourt, *Histoire des campagnes de 1814 et 1815*, 1:84–5).

13. THE SAAR AND THE MOSELLE

1. "Disposition for 16, 17, and 18 January," GStA, Rep. 92, Nachlaß Gneisenau, Nr. 18.
2. Blücher to Yorck, 15 January 1814, GStA, Rep. 92, Nachlaß Gneisenau, Nr. 18.
3. Blücher to Yorck, 15 January 1814, GStA, Rep. 92, Nachlaß Gneisenau, Nr. 18.
4. Henckel to Horn, 15 January 1814, in Henckel von Donnersmarck, *Erinnerungen*, 255. Italics mine.
5. Horn to Yorck, 16 January 1814, in Janson, "Die Unternehmungen des Yorckschen Korps," 19.
6. Valentini to Henckel, 16 January 1814, in Henckel von Donnersmarck, *Erinnerungen*, 570–1.

7. Horn to Henckel, 13 January 1814, in Henckel von Donnersmarck, *Erinnerungen*, 568–9.

8. Janson, "Die Unternehmungen des Yorckschen Korps," 18.

9. Yorck to Blücher, 16 January 1814, in Henckel von Donnersmarck, *Erinnerungen*, 256.

10. Janson, "Die Unternehmungen des Yorckschen Korps," 20.

11. Henckel notes that "the commanding general [Yorck] let me know his dissatisfaction" over the contradictions in this report" (Henckel von Donnersmarck, *Erinnerungen*, 268–9).

12. Yorck to Horn, 17 January 1814, in Janson, "Die Unternehmungen des Yorckschen Korps," 20–1. Italics mine.

13. Janson, "Die Unternehmungen des Yorckschen Korps," 20.

14. In his "Note" of 12 January, Napoleon states that the garrison consisted of 3,000 men ("Note," 12 January 1814, *Correspondance*, No. 21089, 27:28).

15. Blücher to Yorck, 17 January 1814, GStA, Rep. A 15 Nr. 269.

16. GStA, Rep. 15 A Nr. 274.

17. Yorck to Blücher, 17 January 1814, in Janson, "Die Unternehmungen des Yorckschen Korps," 21–3.

18. GStA, Rep. See note 16 for example. A Nr. 234.

19. Damitz, *Geschichte des Feldzuges von 1814*, 1:322–3.

20. Yorck to Schmidt, 16 January, in Janson, "Die Unternehmungen des Yorckschen Korps," 32.

21. Janson, "Die Unternehmungen des Yorckschen Korps," 32–3.

22. Ibid., 23–4.

23. According to Plotho, *Der Krieg*, 3:67, Saarlouis had a garrison of 1,500 men. In his "Note" of 12 January, Napoleon, who never underestimated his troop strength, claims that the garrison of Saarlouis consisted of 2,700 men ("Note," 12 January 1814, *Correspondance*, No. 21089, 27:28).

24. Yorck to Blücher, 17 January 1814, in Janson, "Die Unternehmungen des Yorckschen Korps," 22.

25. Janson, "Die Unternehmungen des Yorckschen Korps," 33.

26. Yorck to Blücher, 17 January 1814, in ibid., 22.

27. Blücher to Yorck, 25 January 1813, in Damitz, *Geschichte des Feldzuges von 1814*, 1:616.

28. Henckel von Donnersmarck, *Erinnerungen*, 257; Damitz, *Geschichte des Feldzuges von 1814*, 1:328; Janson, "Die Unternehmungen des Yorckschen Korps," 24.

29. Henckel von Donnersmarck, *Erinnerungen*, 257–8.

30. "The positioning of three seven-pounder howitzers, which I had at my disposal," states his report to Blücher, "had to be done in the open field, without cover from cross fire, if I wanted to bombard the fortress. Therefore, no success could be foreseen in an operation of 2,500 men against 4,000, whose losses could not be calculated and likewise would have compromised Prussian arms since the mood of the inhabitants would have been affected by the inevitable failure" (Yorck to Blücher, 23 January 1814, in Damitz, *Geschichte des Feldzuges von 1814*, 1:606–9).

31. Damitz, *Geschichte des Feldzuges von 1814*, 1:328–31; Weil, *Campagne de 1814*, 1:244–5; Janson, "Die Unternehmungen des Yorckschen Korps," 25–6.

32. According to Plotho, *Der Krieg in Deutschland und Frankreich*, appendix 13, 3:67, the garrison consisted of 4,000 men at the beginning of the campaign but by February had been reduced to three battalions, one squadron, and a half battery for a total of 2,500 men (3:494); Napoleon placed the garrison of Thionville at 1,800 men ("Note sur la situation actuelle de la France," 12 January 1814, *Correspondance*, No. 21089, 27:28).

33. Yorck to Horn, 23 January 1814, in Janson, "Die Unternehmungen des Yorckschen Korps," 27–8.

34. Damitz, *Geschichte des Feldzuges von 1814*, 1:328, 331–2; Janson, "Die Unternehmungen des Yorckschen Korps," 28.

35. "Note," 12 January 1814, *Correspondance*, No. 21089, 27:28.

36. Damitz, *Geschichte des Feldzuges von 1814*, 1:332–5; Weil, *Campagne de 1814*, 1:233–4.

37. Yorck to Blücher, 23 January 1814, in Damitz, *Geschichte des Feldzuges von 1814*, 1:606–9.

38. Janson, "Die Unternehmungen des Yorckschen Korps," 36.

39. Blücher to Yorck, 25 January, in Damitz, *Geschichte des Feldzuges von 1814*, 1:610.

40. Damitz, *Geschichte des Feldzuges von 1814*, 1:335–7; Janson, "Die Unternehmungen des Yorckschen Korps," 31–3.

41. Blücher to Yorck, 24 January 1814, in Damitz, *Geschichte des Feldzuges von 1814*, 1:610–11.

42. Droysen, *Yorck*, 2:287.

43. GStA, Rep. 15 A Nr. 274.

44. Blücher and Gneisenau should have shed all concern for the fortresses and maintained Yorck's corps in line with Sacken's Russians. A strong detachment could have been posted at Pont-à-Mousson and then St. Mihiel to guard against a sortie from Metz and Verdun, while the rest of Yorck's corps marched with Sacken. Admittedly, there is a degree of risk posed in this scenario because of the impassability of the Moselle meant the Prussians did not know for sure whether Marmont had remained at Metz or continued to withdraw west toward Verdun.

45. Janson, *Feldzuges 1814*, 1:119.

46. Regarding the reinforcements that were moving up, Kleist's II Corps reached Trier on 26 January and then moved through the fortress belt to join the Silesian Army. The Russian General Dmitri Mikhailovich Juzefovich left Koblenz on 14 January with his 3,700-man detachment; later that month, Kleist ordered him to Metz.

47. Quoted in Droysen, *Yorck*, 2:285.

48. Janson, "Die Unternehmungen des Yorckschen Korps," 53n.2.

49. As a point of reference, Yorck's howitzers had fired sixty shells at the battle of Möckern and seventy-two at the Katzbach (Yorck to Blücher, 17 January 1814, in ibid., 23).

50. See Wawro, *The Franco-Prussian War*, 108, for Moltke's problems with General Karl von Steinmetz in that conflict as well as the 1866 Austro-Prussian War.

14. BELGIUM

1. In his 6 February report to the British Secretary of War, Henry Bathurst, Graham praised Bülow's operations. A copy of this report is in Koch, "Campagne de 1814," SHAT, MR 902. Although Fortescue is critical of Bülow, the British historian claims Graham always spoke highly of him in his dispatches. Fortescue, *History of the British Army*, 10:10.
2. Castlereagh to Aberdeen, 30 November 1813, Castlereagh, *Correspondence*, 9:73–5.
3. Hardenberg to Bülow, 18 December 1813, in Meinecke, *Boyen*, 361.
4. Boyen to Hardenberg, 30 December 1813, GStA, Rep. 92, Nachlaß Albrecht, Nr. 44.
5. Gneisenau to Boyen, 15 December 1813, in Pertz, Gneisenau, 3:594; Boyen to Hardenberg, 30 December 1813, GStA, Rep. 92, Nr. 44.
6. Blanton, "Napoleon's Prefects," 251, 260–1, 288–9.
7. Bülow to Pauline, 20 December 1813, BFA, No. 119.
8. Bülow to Pauline, 20 December 1813, BFA, No. 119.
9. Bülow to Pauline, 25 December 1813, BFA, No. 122.
10. Bülow to Wintzingerode, 29 December 1813, RGVIA, delo 4124.
11. Alexander to Bülow, 27 December 1813, BFA, No. 121.
12. Bülow to Wintzingerode, 4 and 5 January 1814, RGVIA, delo 4124.
13. "RGVIA, Campagne de 1814 en France," par Comte Pavel Petrovich Sukhtelen, delo 4118.
14. Karl Johan to Wintzingerode, 22 December 1813, *Recueil*, 563.
15. Weil, *Campagne de 1814*, 1:273–4.
16. Bülow to Pauline, 3 January 1814, BFA, No. 123.
17. Karl Johan to Wintzingerode, 22 December 1813, *Recueil*, 566.
18. Karl Johan to Bülow, 22 December 1813, BFA, No. 120. Italics mine.
19. Boyen to Hardenberg, 30 December 1813, GStA, Rep. 92, Nachlaß Albrecht, Nr. 44.
20. Reiche, *Memoiren*, 2:39–43.
21. Löwenstern, *Mémoires*, 285–6.
22. Koch, *Campagne de 1814*, 1:127–8; Damitz, *Geschichte des Feldzuges*, 1:344–8; Varnhagen von Ense, *Bülow*, 329; Hassenkamp, *General Graf Bülow*, 289; Reiche, *Memoiren*, 2:49.
23. Macdonald to Berthier, 1 January 1814, SHAT, C² 169.
24. Sébastiani to Berthier, 2 January 1814, SHAT, C² 169; Lefebvre de Béhaine, *Campagne de France*, 2:518.
25. Macdonald to Berthier, 2 January 1814, SHAT, C² 169.
26. Macdonald to Berthier, 3 January 1814, SHAT, C² 169.
27. Berthier to Macdonald, 6 January 1814, SHAT, C¹⁷ 183.
28. Macdonald to Berthier and Sébastiani, 4 January 1814, SHAT, C² 169.
29. Macdonald to Berthier, Sébastiani, and Maison, 5 January 1814, SHAT, C² 170.
30. Macdonald to Berthier (two), Sébastiani, and Maison, 6 January 1814, SHAT, C² 170.
31. Macdonald to Maison, 5 January 1814, SHAT, C² 170.

32. Macdonald to Marmont, Belliard, Berthier, and Sébastiani, 7 January 1814, SHAT, C² 170.

33. Macdonald to Berthier and Sébastiani, 7 January 1814, SHAT, C² 170.

34. Macdonald to Bourke, 9 January 1814, SHAT, C² 170.

35. Macdonald to Berthier, 8 January 1814, SHAT, C² 170.

36. Macdonald to Sébastiani and Maison, 8 January 1814, SHAT, C² 170.

37. Macdonald to Berthier, Molitor, and Sébastiani, 9 January 1814; Macdonald to Maison, 10 January 1814, SHAT, C² 170; Macdonald to Berthier, 11 January 1814, SHAT, C² 171.

38. Order of the day for 11 January 1814, issued 10 January 1814, SHAT, C² 170

39. Macdonald to Sébastiani, Maison, and Arrighi, 11 January 1814, SHAT, C² 171.

40. Macdonald to Berthier, 11 January 1814, SHAT, C² 171.

41. Macdonald to Ladoucette, 11 January 1814, quoted in Lefebvre de Béhaine, *Campagne de France*, 2:507.

42. Macdonald to Berthier, 12 January 1814, SHAT, C² 171.

43. Macdonald to Berthier, Exelmans, Sébastiani, Arrighi, Brayer, Molitor, and Merle, 12 January 1814, SHAT, C² 171.

44. Macdonald to Maison, 12 January 1814, SHAT, C² 171.

45. Weil, *Campagne de 1814*, 1:277.

46. Fortescue, *History of the British Army*, 10:7.

47. Bülow to Frederick William, 9 January 1814, GStA, Rep. 15 A Nr. 238.

48. Bülow to Pauline, 9 January 1813, BFA, No. 124.

49. Rouget to Maison, 10 January 1814, Correspondance Rouget, SHAT, MR 902; Weil, *Campagne de 1814*, 1:276 7.

50. Maison to Clarke, 9 January 1814, SHAT, C² 316.

51. Maison to Rouget, 11 January 1814, Correspondance Rouget, SHAT, MR 902.

52. "Note sur la situation actuelle France," 12 January 1814, *Correspondance*, No. 21,089, 27:26–30.

53. Maison to Clarke, 9 January 1814, SHAT, C² 316.

54. *Feldzeitung der Preußischen Armee*, No. 51, 31 January 1814, BFA; Rouget to Maison and to Drouot, 10 January 1814, Correspondance Rouget, SHAT, MR 902.

55. Fortescue, *History of the British Army*, 10:7–8.

56. Bülow to Pauline, 16 January 1814, BFA, No. 125; Plotho, *Der Krieg*, 3:203; Damitz, *Geschichte des Feldzuges*, 1:357–8; Weil, *Campagne de 1814*, 1:277–80.

57. Sources for the operations on 11 January 1814: Bülow to Wintzingerode, 15 January 1814, RGVIA, delo 4124; "Rapport du 11, 12 et 13 janvier," Rouget to Drouot, 19 January 1814, Correspondance Rouget and "Mémoire des opérations du général Rouget," SHAT, MR 902; Bülow to Pauline, 16 January 1814, BFA, No. 125. Blanton, "Napoleon's Prefects," 313; Weil, *Campagne de 1814*, 1:279–82; Damitz, *Geschichte des Feldzuges*, 1:362–7; Hassenkamp, *General Graf Bülow*, 267–70; Fortescue, *History of the British Army*, 10:8; Beauchamp, *Histoire des campagnes*, 1:121–2; Varnhagen von Ense, *Bülow*, 332.

58. "Rapport du 11, 12 et 13 janvier," Rouget to Drouot, 19 January 1814, Correspondance Rouget and Koch, "Campagne de 1814," SHAT MR 902; Maison to Berthier, 12 and 13 January 1814, SHAT, C² 171; Maison to Clarke, 12 January

1814, SHAT, C² 316; "Journal de défense de la place d'Anvers, du 11 janvier au 27 mars 1814," SHAT, C² 322; Beauchamp, *Histoire des campagnes*, 122; Weil, *Campagne de 1814*, 1:282–3; Lefebvre de Béhaine, *Campagne de France*, 2:527.

59. Bülow to Wintzingerode, 15 January 1814, RGVIA, delo 4124; Bülow to Pauline, 16 January 1813, BFA, No. 125; Weil, *Campagne de 1814*, 1:283.

60. Weil, *Campagne de 1814*, 1:285–6.

61. Napoleon to Macdonald, 13 January 1814, *Correspondance*, No. 21,091, 27:37.

62. Ambert to Lebrun, 14 January 1814, quoted in Weil, *Campagne de 1814*, 1:287.

63. Bülow to Pauline, 16 January 1814, BFA, No. 125.

64. Fortescue, *History of the British Army*, 10:9.

65. Sources for the operations on 12, 13, and 14 January: Bülow to Wintzingerode, 15 January 1814, RGVIA, delo 4124; Bülow to Frederick William, 15 January 1814, GStA, Rep. 15 A Nr. 238; "Journal de défense de la place d'Anvers, du 11 janvier au 27 mars 1814," SHAT, C² 322; Maison to Clarke, 13 January 1814, SHAT, C² 316; Koch, "Campagne de 1814"; "Mémoire des opérations du général Rouget"; and "Rapport du 11, 12 et 13 janvier," Rouget to Drouot, 19 January 1814, Correspondance Rouget, SHAT, MR 902; Rouget to Berthier, 14 January 1814, SHAT C² 320; Bülow to Pauline, BFA, Brief No. 125; *Feldzeitung der Preußischen Armee*, No. 51, 31 January 1814; Plotho, *Der Krieg*, 3:206; Hassenkamp, *General Graf Bülow*, 271; Beauchamp, *Histoire des campagnes*, 122–3; Damitz, *Geschichte des Feldzuges*, 1:368–73; Weil, *Campagne de 1814*, 1: 286–90.

66. Napoleon to Clarke, 18 January 1814, *Correspondance*, No. 21,110, 27:50.

67. Napoleon to Maison, 20 January 1814, *Correspondance*, No. 21,120, 27:58. Italics mine.

68. Ibid., 58–9.

69. Sébastiani to Berthier, 11 January 1814, SHAT, C² 171.

70. Macdonald to Sébastiani, Arrighi, 13 January 1814, SHAT, C² 171.

71. Order of Movement for 17 January 1814, issued 16 January 1814, SHAT, C² 172; Beauchamp, *Histoire des campagnes*, 1:125; Lefebvre de Béhaine, *Campagne de France*, 2:519–20.

72. Report to Wintzingerode, 9 January 1814, RGVIA, delo 4125.

73. RGVIA, "Campagne de 1814 en France," par Comte Pavel Petrovich Sukhtelen, delo 4118.

74. Report to Wintzingerode, 14 and 15 January 1814, RGVIA, delo 4125.

75. RGVIA, "Campagne de 1814 en France," par Comte Pavel Petrovich Sukhtelen, delo 4118. Beauchamp, *Histoire des campagnes*, 1:124–5; Weil, *Campagne de 1814*, 1:294–5.

76. Macdonald to Berthier, 13 January 1814, SHAT, C² 171.

77. Napoleon to Macdonald, 10 January 1814, *Correspondance*, No. 21,083, 27:23.

78. Berthier to Macdonald, 12 January 1814, SHAT, C¹⁷ 183.

79. Circular of 12 January 1814, SHAT, C² 171.

80. Berthier to Macdonald, 12 January 1814, SHAT, C¹⁷ 183; "Note sur la situation actuelle de la France," 12 January 1814, *Correspondance*, No. 21,089, 27:29–31.

81. Macdonald to Sébastiani and Arrighi, 14 January 1814, SHAT, C² 171.

82. Macdonald to Berthier, 14 January 1814, SHAT, C² 171.

83. Order of movement for 15 January 1814, issued 14 January 1814; Macdonald to Maison, Brayer, Molitor, and Exelmans, 14 January 1814, SHAT, C² 171.

84. Macdonald to Berthier, 16 and 20 January 1814, SHAT, C² 172; Lefebvre de Béhaine, *Campagne de France*, 2:536 and 4:53.

85. Macdonald to Exelmans and Berthier, 17 January 1814 and Order of Movement for 17 January 1814, issued 16 January 1814, SHAT, C² 172.

86. Macdonald to Maison, 17 January 1814, SHAT, C² 172.

87. Beauchamp, *Histoire des campagnes*, 1:125; Lefebvre de Béhaine, *Campagne de France*, 4:53–4, 57.

88. Macdonald to Berthier, 18 January 1814, SHAT, C² 172.

89. Berthier to Macdonald, 17 January 1814, SHAT, C¹⁷ 183.

90. Macdonald to Berthier, 20 January 1814 and Order of Movement for 21 January 1814, issued 20 January 1814, SHAT, C² 172.

91. Lefebvre de Béhaine, *Campagne de France*, 4:54.

92. Macdonald to Maison, 21 January 1814, SHAT, C² 173.

93. Macdonald to Berthier, 23 and 25 January 1814, SHAT, C² 173.

94. Maison to Berthier, 21 January 1814, SHAT, C² 173; Weil, *Campagne de 1814*, 1:300–1.

95. Schwarzenberg to Wintzingerode, 19 January 1814, ÖStA KA, FA 1606, Nr. 452.

96. RGVIA, "Campagne de 1814 en France," par Comte Pavel Petrovich Sukhtelen, delo 4118.

97. Weil, *Campagne de 1814*, 1:302–6. "Despite Schwarzenberg's orders," notes Weil, "despite the retreat of the French, Wintzingerode persisted to believe that he was too weak to take the direction to Reims. . . . Despite the drift ice on the Rhine and the two affairs of Neuss and of Liège, his march had not encountered any obstacles, yet Wintzingerode advanced more slowly than the Army of Bohemia. He used more than three weeks to march from Düsseldorf and Köln to the region of Liège and Namur. Moreover, it is impossible to explain the reason for this apparently calculated slowness, except only excessive caution. Arriving at Namur, Wintzingerode subordinated his movement to the cooperation that he sought from Bülow, certain that this general was not able to immediately support him. From everything we can conclude, by waiting for a favorable moment to cross the Rhine, that in marching with such unnecessary caution and by compromising the III Corps, in exposing Bülow and forcing him to rely on his own forces during the first fifteen days of January when Maison and Macdonald were making offensive movements, the Russian general was conforming to the intentions of Schwarzenberg or at least serving the secret interests and ambitious projects of the crown prince of Sweden. Anyway he succeeded in concealing his own responsibility and waited for a formal order from his sovereign before taking his direction to the French interior." Although the facts are correct, Weil's conclusion smacks of conspiracy and is interesting speculation at best.

98. Bülow to Frederick William, 27 January 1814, GStA, Rep. 15 A Nr. 238; Maison to Berthier, 29 January 1814, SHAT, C² 316; *Feldzeitung der Preußischen Armee*, No. 57, 14 February 1814, BFA; Hassenkamp, *General Graf Bülow*, 290–4.

99. "Mémoire des opérations du général Rouget," and Rouget to Drouot, 22, 23, 26 and 31 January 1814, Correspondence Rouget," SHAT, MR 902.

100. Bülow to Wintzingerode, 3 February 1814, RGVIA, delo 4124.
101. Sources for the operations around Antwerp: Bülow to Wintzingerode, 3 February 1814, RGVIA, delo 4124; "Maison to Clarke, 2 February 1814, SHAT, C² 316; Journal de défense de la place d'Anvers, du 11 janvier au 27 mars 1814," SHAT, C² 322; "Mémoire des opérations du général Rouget"; Rouget to Drouot, 3 February 1814, "Correspondence Rouget"; and Koch, "Campagne de 1814," SHAT, MR 902; Plotho, *Der Krieg*, 3:208; Hassenkamp, *General Graf Bülow*, 296–9; Reiche, *Memoiren*, 2:56–9; Damitz, *Geschichte des Feldzuges*, 2:203–6; Brett-James, *Graham*, 291–3; Blanton, "Napoleon's Prefects," 315, 317.
102. Bülow to Pauline, 15 February 1814, BFA, No. 127.
103. Clausewitz, *Hinterlassene Werke*, 375–6, 90.

15. THE MARNE

1. Weil, *Campagne de 1814*, 1:219.
2. Frederick William to Schwarzenberg, 17 January 1814, ÖStA KA, FA 1605, Nr. 394.
3. "Stärke, Eintheilung, und Tagesbegebenheiten der Hauptarmee im Monate Januar," ÖStA KA, FA 1603, Nr. 30.
4. Lefebvre de Béhaine, *Campagne de France*, 3:182 and 4:2.
5. Berthier to Ney, 15 January 1814, SHAT, C¹⁷ 183.
6. Berthier to Victor, 16 January 1814, SHAT, C¹⁷ 183.
7. Napoleon to Victor, 17 January 1814, *Correspondance*, No. 21,105, 27:47.
8. Berthier to Marmont, 16 January 1814, SHAT, C¹⁷ 183.
9. Berthier to Marmont, 17 January 1814, SHAT, C¹⁷ 183.
10. Berthier to Marmont, 18 January 1814, SHAT, C¹⁷ 183.
11. Marmont to Berthier, 21 January 1814, SHAT, C² 173.
12. Meynadier to Ricard, 16 January 1814, 8:30 A.M., SHAT, C² 172.
13. Meynadier to Ricard, 16 January 1814, SHAT, C² 172.
14. Marmont to Berthier, 17 January 1814, SHAT, C² 172.
15. Marmont to Berthier, 16 January 1814, SHAT, C² 172.
16. Lefebvre de Béhaine, *Campagne de France*, 3:178.
17. Meynadier to Ricard, 17 January 1814, SHAT, C² 172.
18. Marmont to Berthier, 17 January 1814, SHAT, C² 172.
19. Meynadier to Ricard, 17 January 1814, 10:30 A.M., SHAT, C² 172.
20. Meynadier to Decouz, 17 January 1814, 10:30 A.M., SHAT, C² 172.
21. Lefebvre de Béhaine, *Campagne de France*, 3:180–1.
22. Marmont to Berthier, 17 January 1814, SHAT, C² 172.
23. Ibid.
24. Victor to Berthier, 17 and 18 January 1814, SHAT, C² 172; Lefebvre de Béhaine, *Campagne de France*, 4:3–5.
25. Victor to Berthier, 17 January 1814, SHAT, C² 172.
26. Dejean to Napoleon, 17 January 1814, AN, AF IV 1669ᴬ plaquette 2.
27. Ney to Berthier, 16 and 17 January 1814, SHAT, C² 172.
28. Ney to Berthier, 17 January 1814, SHAT, C² 172.
29. Lefebvre de Béhaine, *Campagne de France*, 4:6.

30. Caulaincourt to Napoleon, 17 January 1814, AN, AP 94, C^{14} No. 7.
31. Grouchy to Victor and Victor to Berthier, 18 January 1814, SHAT, C^{2} 172.
32. Lefebvre de Béhaine, *Campagne de France*, 4:10.
33. Victor to Monthion, 19 January 1814, SHAT, C^{2} 172.
34. Victor to Berthier, 18 January 1814, SHAT, C^{2} 172.
35. Grouchy to Defrance, 18 January 1814, SHAT, C^{2} 172.
36. Victor to Grouchy and Duhesme, 18 January 1814, SHAT, C^{2} 172.
37. Grouchy to Milhaud, 18 January 1814, SHAT, C^{2} 172.
38. Grouchy to Defrance, 18 January 1814, SHAT, C^{2} 172.
39. Victor to Marmont, 19 January 1814, SHAT, C^{2} 172.
40. Sherbatov to Schwarzenberg, 18 January 1814, ÖStA KA, FA 1606, Nr. 445.
41. Lefebvre de Béhaine, *Campagne de France*, 4:11.
42. Marmont to Berthier, 18 and 19 January 1814, SHAT, C^{2} 172.
43. Marmont to Ney, 19 January 1814, SHAT, C^{2} 172.
44. Ney to Marmont, 18 January 1814, SHAT, C^{2} 172.
45. "Kriegstagebuch der Schlesischen Armee im Januar 1814," ÖStA KA, FA 1603, Nr. 31; Koch, *Campagne de 1814*, 1:118, 120–1; Plotho, *Der Krieg*, 3:84; Janson, *Feldzuges 1814*, 1:123–4; Bogdanovich, *Geschichte des Krieges*, 1:81; Weil, *Campagne de 1814*, 1:226–7; Lefebvre de Béhaine, *Campagne de France*, 4:11.
46. Blücher to Hardenberg, 20 January 1814, Unger, *Blüchers Briefe*, 223.
47. "Kriegstagebuch der Schlesischen Armee im Januar 1814," ÖStA KA, FA 1603, Nr. 31; Beauchamp, *Histoire des campagnes*, 1:140; Koch, *Campagne de 1814*, 1:121; Damitz, *Geschichte des Feldzuges*, 1:313–14; Weil, *Campagne de 1814*, 1:228, 233, 236.
48. Sacken to Blücher, 20 January 1814, ÖStA KA, FA 1606, Nr. 466a.
49. Marmont to Berthier, 19 January 1814, SHAT, C^{2} 172.
50. "Kriegstagebuch der Schlesischen Armee im Januar 1814," ÖStA KA, FA 1603, Nr. 31; "Reports of the Battles and Combats of the Reserve Cavalry of the I Corps by Generalmajor von Jürgaß: The Combat of Manheulles by Verdun 19 January 1814"; "The Journal of the Reserve Cavalry of the I Army Corps," "The Journal of the 1st West Prussian Dragoon Regiment," "The Journal of the Lithuanian Dragoon Regiment," reproduced in Henckel von Donnersmarck, *Erinnerungen*, 456–7, 504–5, 521–2, 536–7; Damitz, *Geschichte des Feldzuges*, 1:32426; Weil, *Campagne de 1814*, 1:234; Lefebvre de Béhaine, *Campagne de France*, 4:42–3.
51. Marmont to Ney, 19 January 1814, SHAT, C^{2} 172.
52. Marmont to Victor, 19 January 1814, SHAT, C^{2} 172.
53. Marmont to Berthier, 19 January 1814, SHAT, C^{2} 172. Italics mine.
54. Victor to Marmont, 19 January 1814, SHAT, C^{2} 172.
55. Lefebvre de Béhaine, *Campagne de France*, 4:12.
56. Victor to Duhesme, 19 January 1814, SHAT, C^{2} 172.
57. Victor to Marmont, 19 January 1814, SHAT, C^{2} 172.
58. Victor to Ney, 19 January 1814, AN, 137 AP 15.
59. Defrance to Victor, 19 January 1814, SHAT, C^{2} 172; Lefebvre de Béhaine, *Campagne de France*, 4:12.
60. Victor to Berthier, 19 January 1814, SHAT, C^{2} 172.
61. Napoleon to Berthier, 19 January 1814, *Correspondance*, No. 21,115, 27:54.

62. "Note," 19 January 1814, *Correspondance*, No. 21,116, 27:54–5.

63. "Kriegstagebuch der Schlesischen Armee im Januar 1814," ÖStA KA, FA 1603, Nr. 31.

64. Platov to Schwarzenberg, 19 January 1814, ÖStA KA, FA 1606, Nr. 462.

65. Schwarzenberg to Wittgenstein, 18 January 1814 and Stärke, Eintheilung, und Tagesbegebenheiten der Hauptarmee im Monate Januar," ÖStA KA, FA 1606, Nr. 428 and FA 1603, Nr. 30. Two days later Schwarzenberg again urged the Russian to advance: "I will give the troops a day of rest in these positions in order for you, my right wing, to come in line with me as soon as possible. I count on you to continue your much to Nancy with all your troops and to establish communication with Blücher's advance guard" (Schwarzenberg to Wittgenstein, 20 January 1814, ÖStA KA, FA 1606, Nr. 470).

66. Schwarzenberg to Wrede, 19 January 1814, ÖStA KA, FA 1606, Nr. 462.

67. Confusion over Lamotte's exact position remains. Lamotte's correspondence preserved in SHAT consists of a June 1865 handwritten copy. The copy states that the original was written at Brixey-aux-Chanoines, slightly north of Greux, Domremy, and Maxey-sur-Meuse, and on the right bank of the Meuse. That Lamotte had ventured so far upstream does not seem likely owing to the presence of Allied forces at Sauvigny, downstream the river from Brixey and likewise on the right bank. From Allied correspondence, it emerges that Lamotte had stopped at Taillancourt and pushed a patrol of one officer and twenty dragoons to Greux. Greux stands opposite of both Maxey-sur-Meuse and Domremy. Slightly upstream of the Greux–Maxey bridge, the Meuse throws out several arms, and the river itself bends sharply west. On the southern bank is Domremy, whose bridge likewise exits at Greux.

68. Lamotte to Lhéritier, 20 January 1814, SHAT, C² 172.

69. Wrede to Schwarzenberg, 21 January 1814 and Schwarzenberg to Colloredo, 22 January 1814, ÖStA KA, FA 1606, Nrs. 492d and 518.

70. Lhéritier to Grouchy, 20 January 1814, SHAT, C² 172.

71. All five of Defrance's reports to Grouchy on 20 January 1814 are located in SHAT, C² 172.

72. Victor to Marmont, 20 January 1814, SHAT, C² 172.

73. Victor to Berthier, 20 January 1814, SHAT, C² 172.

74. Lefebvre de Béhaine, *Campagne de France*, 4:22.

75. Grouchy's orders of 11:30 P.M. on 20 January forming the rearguard under Defrance are located in SHAT, C² 172. Victor's "Order of Movement" for 21 January, issued at 11:00 P.M. on 20 January 1814, is in SHAT, C² 173.

76. Victor to Berthier, 21 January 1814, SHAT, C² 173.

77. General Order, issued midnight, 20 January 1813, SHAT, C² 172.

78. Marmont to Berthier, 20 January 1814, SHAT, C² 172.

79. Lefebvre de Béhaine, *Campagne de France*, 4:17.

80. Berthier to Victor, 20 January 1814, SHAT, C¹⁷ 183.

81. Berthier to Marmont, 20 January 1814, SHAT, C¹⁷ 183.

82. Müffling's Promemoria, 19 January 1814, ÖStA KA, FA 1606, Nr. 492b.

83. Blücher to Katharina, 18 January 1813, Unger, *Blüchers Briefe*, 221.

84. Blücher to Schwarzenberg, 19 January 1814, ÖStA KA, FA 1606, Nr. 492a.

85. Schwarzenberg to Blücher, 18 January 1814, ÖStA KA, FA 1606, Nr. 434.

86. Blücher to Schwarzenberg, 20 January 1814, ÖStA KA, FA 1606, Nr. 466. Schwarzenberg received this letter on the 22nd.

87. Blücher to Katharina, 18 January 1813, Unger, *Blüchers Briefe*, 222.

88. Wrede to Schwarzenberg, 21 January 1814, ÖStA KA, FA 1606, Nr. 492d.

89. Sherbatov to Schwarzenberg, 17 January 1814, ÖStA KA, FA 1605, Nr. ad369.

90. Schwarzenberg to Wrede, 21 January 1814, BHStA KA, B 545 and ÖStA KA, FA 1606, Nr. 492c.

91. Pahlen to Wrede, 20 January 1814, BHStA KA, B 545.

92. Schwarzenberg to Wittgenstein, 20 and 21 January 1814, ÖStA KA, FA 1606, Nrs. 470 and 466.

93. "Stärke, Eintheilung, und Tagesbegebenheiten der Hauptarmee im Monate Januar," ÖStA KA, FA 1603, Nr. 30; Weil, *Campagne de 1814*, 1:157.

94. Blücher to Wrede, 21 January 1814, BHStA KA, B 545.

95. Schwarzenberg to Blücher, 21 January 1814, ÖStA KA, FA 1606, Nr. 492.

96. Weil, *Campagne de 1814*, 1:240.

97. Blücher to Sacken, 21 January 1814, in Janson, *Feldzuges 1814*, 1:128.

98. Piré to Grouchy and Victor to Berthier, 21 January 1814, SHAT, C² 173.

99. Montélégier and Briche to Grouchy, 21 January 1814, SHAT, C² 173.

100. Laroche to Grouchy, 21 January 1814, SHAT, C² 173.

101. Victor to Berthier, 21 January 1814, SHAT, C² 173.

102. Sherbatov to Schwarzenberg, 22 January 1814, ÖStA KA, FA 1606, Nr. 512.

103. Milhaud to Grouchy, 21 January 1814, SHAT, C² 173.

104. Piré to Grouchy, 21 and 22 January 1814, SHAT, C² 173; Weil, *Campagne de 1814*, 1:241.

105. Grouchy to Milhaud, 21 January 1814, SHAT, C² 173.

106. Montélégier to Grouchy, 21 January 1814, SHAT, C² 173.

107. Piré to Grouchy, 21 January 1814, SHAT, C² 173. Italics mine.

108. Defensive Dispositions for 22 January 1814, issued 21 January 1814, SHAT, C² 173.

109. Lefebvre de Béhaine, *Campagne de France*, 4:27.

110. Berthier to Victor, 21 January 1814, SHAT, C¹⁷ 183.

111. Marmont to Berthier, 21 January 1814, SHAT, C² 173.

112. Berthier to Marmont, 20 January 1814, SHAT, C¹⁷ 183.

113. Marmont to Berthier, 21 January 1814, SHAT, C² 173.

114. Berthier to Marmont and Kellermann, 21 January 1814, SHAT, C¹⁷ 183. Berthier wrote Marmont and Kellermann on the 21st after he penned the letter to Victor imploring the marshal to hold Ligny. The letter to Victor says nothing about a slow retreat to Vitry-le-François. Berthier's actions become even more puzzling on the 22nd when he expressed the emperor's demand that Victor defend the Ornain.

115. Berthier to Marmont, 22 January 1814, SHAT, C¹⁷ 183.

116. "Stärke, Eintheilung, und Tagesbegebenheiten der Hauptarmee im Monate Januar," ÖStA KA, FA 1603, Nr. 30.

117. "Kriegstagebuch der Schlesischen Armee im Januar 1814," ÖStA KA, FA 1603, Nr. 31.

118. Victor to Berthier, 22 January 1814, SHAT, C² 173.
119. Blücher to Schwarzenberg, 24 January 1814, ÖStA KA, FA 1607, Nr. 550; "Kriegstagebuch der Schlesischen Armee im Januar 1814," ÖStA KA, FA 1603, Nr. 31; Weil, *Campagne de 1814*, 1:246–7.
120. Victor to Berthier, 23 January 1814, SHAT, C² 173; Lefebvre de Béhaine, *Campagne de France*, 4:29.
121. Victor to Grouchy, 22 January 1814, SHAT, C² 173. The handwritten copy at SHAT states "Placement des troupes pour le 22 Janvier," an obvious misprint.
122. Victor to Berthier, 23 January 1814, SHAT, C² 173.
123. Berthier to Victor, 23 January 1814, 2:00 A.M., SHAT, C¹⁷ 183.
124. Berthier to Victor, 23 January 1814, 3:00 A.M., SHAT, C¹⁷ 183.
125. Victor to Berthier, 23 January 1814, SHAT, C² 173.
126. Victor to Berthier, 24 January 1814, SHAT, C² 173; Blücher to Schwarzenberg, 22 January 1814, 24 January 1814, ÖStA KA, FA 1607, Nr. 550.
127. Berthier to Victor, 23 January 1814, SHAT, C¹⁷ 183.
128. SHAT, C² 173.
129. "Kriegstagebuch der Schlesischen Armee im Januar 1814," ÖStA KA, FA 1603, Nr. 31.
130. Marmont to Berthier, 23 January 1814, SHAT, C² 173.
131. Meynadier to Ricard, 23 January 1814, SHAT, C² 173.
132. Marmont to Macdonald, 24 January 1814, in Marmont, *Mémoires*, 6:154–5.
133. Napoleon to Berthier, 23 January 1814, *Correspondance*, No. 21,127, 27:63–4. Seemingly as a rule, Napoleon always overestimated his own troop strength and underestimated his adversary's numbers. For example, on 21 January, Marmont commanded 6,144 infantry, 2,620 cavalry, 970 gunners with fifty-two guns, and 300 sappers. Lefebvre de Béhaine, *Campagne de France*, 4:52.
134. Napoleon to Berthier, 23 January 1814, *Correspondance*, No. 21,131, 27:69.
135. Berthier to Victor, 24 January 1814, 10:00 A.M., SHAT, C¹⁷ 183.
136. Berthier to Victor, 24 January 1814, 4:00 P.M., SHAT, C¹⁷ 183.
137. Berthier to Ney, 24 January 1814, 5:00 P.M., SHAT, C¹⁷ 183.
138. Berthier to Marmont, 24 January 1814, 4:00 P.M., SHAT, C¹⁷ 183.
139. Marmont to Berthier, 25 January 1814, SHAT, C² 173.
140. .Marmont, *Mémoires*, 6:22; Koch, *Campagne de 1814*, 1:124–5; Lefebvre de Béhaine, *Campagne de France*, 4:50–1.
141. Meynadier to Ricard, 25 January 1814, SHAT, C² 173.
142. Ney to Berthier, 25 January 1814, SHAT, C² 173.
143. Victor to Grouchy, 25 January 1814, SHAT, C² 173.
144. Victor to Berthier, 25 January 1814, SHAT, C² 173.
145. Victor to Berthier, 25 January 1814, 6:00 P.M., SHAT, C² 173.
146. "Kriegstagebuch der Schlesischen Armee im Januar 1814," ÖStA KA, FA 1603, Nr. 31; Gneisenau, *Blücher*, 313–14; Weil, *Campagne de 1814*, 1:258–9; Damitz, *Geschichte des Feldzuges*, 1:319–20; Bogdanovich, *Geschichte des Krieges*, 1:82; Janson, *Feldzuges 1814*, 1:130–2.
147. Friederich, *Die Befreiunskriege*, 3:63.
148. Gneisenau to Knesebeck, 15 January 1814, GStA, Rep. 92, Nachlaß Gneisenau, Nr.23.

149. Müffling, *Aus meinem Leben*, 409.
150. Delbrück, *Gneisenau*, 4:26–7.
151. Houssaye, *1814*, 15, 54.

16. BOURGOGNE, THE RHÔNE, AND THE AUBE

1. Roloff, *Politik und Kriegführung*, 29; Webster, *The Foreign Policy of Castlereagh*, 1:202.
2. Metternich to Schwarzenberg, 16 January 1814, Klinkowström, *Österreichs Theilnahme*, No. 28, 798.
3. Roloff, *Politik und Kriegführung*, 29.
4. Metternich to Schwarzenberg, 13 January 1814, Klinkowström, *Österreichs Theilnahme*, No. 25, 794.
5. Quoted in Mikhailovsky-Danilevsky, *History of the Campaign in France*, 42.
6. Metternich to Schwarzenberg, 14 January 1814, Klinkowström, *Österreichs Theilnahme*, No. 26, 795.
7. Simms, *The Struggle for Mastery in Germany*, 99.
8. Kraehe, *Metternich's German Policy*, 1:279.
9. Kissinger, *A World Restored*, 112.
10. Metternich to Schwarzenberg, 16 January 1814, Klinkowström, *Österreichs Theilnahme*, No. 28, 797.
11. Metternich, *Memoirs*, 1:225.
12. Schwarzenberg to Metternich, 18 January 1814, Klinkowström, *Österreichs Theilnahme*, No. 30, 800.
13. Kissinger, *A World Restored*, 113.
14. Roloff, *Politik und Kriegführung*, 32–3, 35.
15. Metternich to Schwarzenberg, 16 January 1814, Klinkowström, *Österreichs Theilnahme*, No. 28, 798.
16. Schroeder, *European Politics*, 497; Kissinger, *A World Restored*, 113.
17. Kissinger, *A World Restored*, 113.
18. Roloff, *Politik und Kriegführung*, 33–4.
19. Webster, *The Foreign Policy of Castlereagh*, 1:200–1.
20. Quoted in Seeley, *Life and Times of Stein*, 3:222.
21. Stein to Alexander, 30 December 1813, Stein, *Briefwechsel*, No. 621, 4:406–7.
22. Schwarzenberg to Gyulay, Colloredo, and Frederick William, ÖStA KA, FA 1604, Nrs. 236, 239, and 232–4.
23. Disposition for the attack on Langres, issued on 14 January 1814; Schwarzenberg to Frederick William, Gyulay, Wimpffen, and Colloredo, 14 January 1814, ÖStA KA, FA 1606, Nrs. 431, 431a, 431b, 431c, and 431d.
24. Schwarzenberg to Gyulay, 11 January 1814, ÖStA KA, FA 1604, Nr. 236.
25. Schwarzenberg to Maria Anna, 13 January 1814, Schwarzenberg, *Briefe*, No. 269, 364–5.
26. Metternich to Schwarzenberg, 14 January 1814, Klinkowström, *Österreichs Theilnahme*, No. 26, 795.

27. "Proclamation to the People of France," 14 January 1814, ÖStA, KA, FA 1605, Nr. 327

28. Mortier to Berthier, 12 January 1814, SHAT, C² 171.

29. Chandler, *Dictionary of the Napoleonic Wars*, 290–1; Gray, "Mortier: The Big Mortar," 310–21; Six, *Dictionnaire biographique*, 232–4.

30. Gray, "Mortier: The Big Mortar," 325.

31. Sources for the combats at Chatenay-Vaudin and Longeau: Mortier to Berthier, 12, 13 and 16 January 1814, SHAT, C² 171 and C² 172; Thurn to Schwarzenberg, 13 January 1814, ÖStA KA, FA 1605, Nr. 282; Lefebvre de Béhaine, *Campagne de France*, 4:123–5.

32. Mortier to Napoleon, 13 January 1814, AN, AF IV 1669^A plaquette 3; Mortier to Berthier, 14 January 1814, SHAT, C² 171.

33. "Stärke, Eintheilung, und Tagesbegebenheiten der Hauptarmee im Monate Januar," and Gyulay to Schwarzenberg, 13 January 1814 ÖStA KA, FA 1603, Nr. 30 and 1605, Nr. 276.

34. Mortier to Berthier, 14 and 15 January 1814, SHAT, C² 171.

35. Gyulay to Schwarzenberg, 14 January 1814, ÖStA KA, FA 1605, Nr. 309.

36. Mortier to Berthier, 15 January 1814, 8:30 A.M., SHAT, C² 171.

37. Mortier to Berthier, 15 January 1814, SHAT, C² 171.

38. Frederick William to Schwarzenberg, 14 January 1814 and Disposition for 14 January 1814, ÖStA KA, FA 1605, Nrs. 311 and ad311.

39. Frederick William to Schwarzenberg, 15 January 1814 and Disposition for 15 January 1814, ÖStA KA, FA 1605, Nrs. 340 and ad340.

40. Schwarzenberg to Frederick William, 15 January 1814, ÖStA KA, FA 1605, Nr. 355.

41. Frederick William to Schwarzenberg, 16 January 1814, ÖStA KA, FA 1605, Nrs. 367 and 368.

42. Schwarzenberg to Colloredo, 13 and 14 January 1814; Colloredo to Schwarzenberg, 14 and 15 January 1814, ÖStA KA, FA 1605, Nrs. 288, 317, ad317, and 337b.

43. Bianchi to Schwarzenberg, 13 January 1814; Bianchi to Legrand and Legrand to Bianchi, 13 and 14 January 1814, ÖStA KA, FA 1605, Nrs. 289a, 289b, 289c, 339a, and 339b.

44. "Stärke, Eintheilung, und Tagesbegebenheiten der Hauptarmee im Monate Januar," ÖStA KA, FA 1603, Nr. 30.

45. Thurn to Schwarzenberg, 14 January 1814, ÖStA KA, FA 1605, Nr. 312.

46. Wimpffen to Schwarzenberg, 15 January 1814 and Disposition for 15–18 January 1814, ÖStA KA, FA 1605, Nrs. 342, 342a, 342b.

47. Schwarzenberg to Hesse-Homburg, 15 January 1814 and Hesse-Homburg to Schwarzenberg, 16 January 1814, ÖStA KA, FA 1605, Nrs. 356 and 365.

48. ÖStA KA, FA 1604, Nr. 242.

49. Napoleon to Clarke, 6 January 1814, *Correspondance*, No. 21,065, 27:14.

50. Beauchamp, *Histoire des campagnes*, 1:148–9.

51. Bubna to Schwarzenberg, 12, 13 (two) January 1814 and "Stärke, Eintheilung, und Tagesbegebenheiten der Hauptarmee im Monate Januar," ÖStA KA, FA 1604, Nr. 245, FA 1605, Nrs. 284 and 285, and FA 1603, Nr. 30; Beauchamp, *Histoire des campagnes*, 1:147–8.

52. Beauchamp, *Histoire des campagnes*, 1:150–51.

53. Weil, *Campagne de 1814*, 1:314.

54. Napoleon to Clarke, 11 January 1814, *Correspondance*, No. 21,086, 27:25.

55. Napoleon to Clarke, 14 January 1814, *Correspondance*, No. 21,097, 27:39. As of the 22nd, Suchet still had not released these troops, thus prompting the emperor to reissue the instructions in Napoleon to Clarke, 22 January 1814, *Correspondance*, No. 21,121, 27:61.

56. Napoleon to Berthier, 15 January 1814, *Correspondance*, No. 21,100, 27:40–1.

57. Augereau to Berthier, 15 January 1814, SHAT, C² 171.

58. Beauchamp, *Histoire des campagnes*, 1:151–2.

59. "Stärke, Eintheilung, und Tagesbegebenheiten der Hauptarmee im Monate Januar," ÖStA KA, FA 1603, Nr. 30. Weil, in *Campagne de 1814*, 1:319–22, claims that had Bubna known how to employ his cavalry judiciously, Lyon could have met the same fate as Nancy by falling to a platoon of Hussars. This is a gross exaggeration, yet there is little doubt that given the public's general despondency and the inexperience of Musnier's troops, Lyon would have fallen to the Austrians.

60. Bubna to Schwarzenberg, 21 January 1814, ÖStA KA, FA 1606, Nr. 488.

61. Beauchamp, *Histoire des campagnes*, 1:152.

62. Bubna to Schwarzenberg, 21 January 1814, ÖStA KA, FA 1606, Nr. 488; Weil, *Campagne de 1814*, 1:324–5, 332; Beauchamp, *Histoire des campagnes*, 1: 152–3.

63. Schwarzenberg to Francis, 24 January 1814, ÖStA KA, FA 1607, Nr. 567.

64. Beauchamp, *Histoire des campagnes*, 1:155.

65. Zechmeister to Bubna, 18 January 1814 and "Stärke, Eintheilung, und Tagesbegebenheiten der Hauptarmee im Monate Januar," ÖStA KA, FA 1606, Nr. 488a and FA 1603, Nr. 30.

66. Zechmeister to Bubna, 19 January 1814, ÖStA KA, FA 1606, Nr. 488b.

67. Bubna to Schwarzenberg, 21 and 22 January 1814, ÖStA KA, FA 1606, Nrs. 488 and 509.

68. Bubna to Schwarzenberg, 26 January 1814, ÖStA KA, FA 1607, Nr. 594.

69. Bubna to Schwarzenberg, 26 January 1814 and "Stärke, Eintheilung, und Tagesbegebenheiten der Hauptarmee im Monate Januar," ÖStA KA, FA 1607, Nr. 594 and FA 1603, Nr. 30; Weil, in *Campagne de 1814*, 1:330–4.

70. Schwarzenberg to Wrede, 16 January 1814, ÖStA KA, FA 1605, Nr. 375.

71. The original orders for the 18 January attack on Langres were issued from Vesoul on 14 January 1814, ÖStA KA, FA 1606, Nr. 431. The corresponding letters addressed to Frederick William, Gyulay, Wimpffen, and Colloredo are respectively numbered 431a–d. The confirmation orders on the 16th can be found in ÖStA KA, FA 1605 as follows: to Wimpffen, Nr. 376; to Hesse-Homburg, Nr. 379; to Frederick William, Nr. 380; to Colloredo, Nr. 381; and to Gyulay, Nr. 382.

72. Schwarzenberg to Maria Anna, 16 January 1814, Schwarzenberg, *Briefe*, No. 269, 367.

73. Mortier to Berthier, 16 January 1814, 12:00 P.M., SHAT, C² 172.

74. Mortier to Berthier, 15 January 1814, SHAT, C² 171.

75. Mortier to Berthier, 16 January 1814, 12:00 P.M., SHAT, C² 172.

76. Beauchamp, *Histoire des campagnes*, 1:131; Lefebvre de Béhaine, *Campagne de France*, 4:133–4.

77. Mortier to Berthier, 16 January 1814, SHAT, C² 172.

78. Mortier to Berthier, 16 January 1814, 12:00 P.M., SHAT, C² 172.

79. Mortier to Berthier, 17 January 1814, SHAT, C² 172.

80. Mortier to Berthier, 17 and 18 January 1814, SHAT, C² 172; Weil, *Campagne de 1814*, 1:135–6; Lefebvre de Béhaine, *Campagne de France*, 4:139.

81. Wimpffen to Schwarzenberg, Gyulay to Schwarzenberg, Schwarzenberg to Francis, 17 January 1814, ÖStA KA, FA 1605, Nr. 390 and FA 1606, Nrs. 409 and 415.

82. Disposition for 18 January 1814, issued 17 January 1814, ÖStA KA, FA 1606, Nr. ad394.

83. Frederick William to Schwarzenberg, 17 January 1814, ÖStA KA, FA 1605, Nr. 394.

84. Schwarzenberg to Maria Anna, 19 January 1814, Schwarzenberg, *Briefe*, No. 270, 368.

85. Schwarzenberg to Duka, Gyulay, Colloredo, Frederick William, and Wimpffen; "Stärke, Eintheilung, und Tagesbegebenheiten der Hauptarmee im Monate Januar," ÖStA KA, FA 1606, Nrs. 404, 408, 412, 413, 414 and FA 1603, Nr. 30.

86. Sources for the combat on the 18th: Mortier to Berthier, 18 January 1814, SHAT, C² 172; Hiller, *Geschichte des Feldzuges 1814*, 49–52; Weil, *Campagne de 1814*, 1:142–4; Lefebvre de Béhaine, *Campagne de France*, 4:164–6.

87. Mortier to Berthier, 18 January 1814, SHAT, C² 172;

88. Schwarzenberg to Metternich, 18 January 1814, Klinkowström, *Österreichs Theilnahme*, No. 30, 800.

89. Schwarzenberg to Colloredo, Hesse-Homburg, Barclay de Tolly, and Wittgenstein, 18 January 1814, ÖStA KA, FA 1606, Nrs. 433, 429, 430, and 428.

90. Clausewitz, *Hinterlassene Werk*, 391.

91. Schwarzenberg to Maria Anna, 19 January 1814, Schwarzenberg, *Briefe*, No. 270, 368.

92. Nicholson, *Congress of Vienna*, 51.

93. Metternich to Schwarzenberg, 16 January 1814, Klinkowström, *Österreichs Theilnahme*, No. 28, 797–8.

94. Napoleon to Berthier, 17 January 1814, *Correspondance*, No. 21,102, 27:44; Berthier to Mortier, 17 January 1814, SHAT, C¹⁷ 183.

95. Mortier to Berthier, 19 January 1814, SHAT, C² 172.

96. Mortier to Berthier, 20 January 1814, SHAT, C² 172.

97. Lefebvre de Béhaine, *Campagne de France*, 4:168, 178–9.

98. Mortier to Berthier, 20 January 1814, SHAT, C² 172.

99. Berthier to Mortier, 18 January 1814, SHAT, C¹⁷ 183.

100. Frederick William to Schwarzenberg, 19 January 1814, ÖStA KA, FA 1606, Nr. ad450.

101. Schwarzenberg to Frederick William, 19 January 1814, ÖStA KA, FA 1606, Nr. 450.

102. Disposition for 19 January, issued 18 January 1814, included in Hesse-Homburg to Schwarzenberg, 19 January 1814; ÖStA KA, FA 1606, Nrs. 444, 444a, 444b, and 465. Colloredo to Schwarzenberg, 19 January 1814, ÖStA KA, FA 1606, Nr. 457.

103. Bianchi to Schwarzenberg, 20 January 1814, ÖStA KA, FA 1606, Nr. 459. An embittered Beauchamp complained that unlike the Lyonnais, the Dijonais surrendered after an Austrian force of 2,000 cavalry, 500 infantry and twelve guns arrived before the gates of Dijon around noon on the 19th and gave assurances to respect the inhabitants and their property (Beauchamp, *Histoire des campagnes*, 1:159).

104. Schwarzenberg to Gyulay, Frederick William, Wrede, Wittgenstein, and Francis, 19 January 1814, ÖStA KA, FA 1606, Nrs. 448, 449, 450, 452, and 454; Schwarzenberg to Barclay de Tolly, 20 January 1814, ÖStA KA, FA 1606, Nr. 477; "Stärke, Eintheilung, und Tagesbegebenheiten der Hauptarmee im Monate Januar," ÖStA KA, FA 1603, Nr. 30; Weil, *Campagne de 1814*, 1:149–50.

105. Gyulay to Schwarzenberg, 20 January 1814, ÖStA KA, FA 1606, Nr. 461.

106. "Stärke, Eintheilung, und Tagesbegebenheiten der Hauptarmee im Monate Januar," ÖStA KA, FA 1603, Nr. 30.

107. Schwarzenberg to Hesse-Homburg, Colloredo, M. Liechtenstein, Barclay de Tolly, and Francis, ÖStA KA, FA 1606, Nrs. 472, 473, 475, 477, and 479.

108. Schwarzenberg to Wittgenstein, Francis, and Toll, 21 January 1814, ÖStA KA, FA 1606, Nrs. 466, 503, and 500.

109. Schwarzenberg to Wrede, 21 January 1814, BHStA KA, B 545 and ÖStA KA, FA 1606, Nr. 492c.

110. Schwarzenberg to Blücher, 21 January 1814, ÖStA KA, FA 1606, Nr. 492.

111. Thurn to Schwarzenberg, 21 January 1813, ÖStA KA, FA 1606, Nr. 485.

112. Mortier to Berthier, 23 January 1814, SHAT, C^2 173; Gyulay to Schwarzenberg, 21 (two), 22, and 23 January 1814, ÖStA KA, FA 1606, Nrs. 484, 486, 515b, and 525.

113. Frederick William to Schwarzenberg, 23 January 1814, ÖStA KA, FA 1607, Nr. 526.

114. Disposition for 24 January, issued 23 January 1814 and Schwarzenberg to Francis, 23 January 1814, ÖStA KA, FA 1607, Nrs. ad 526 and 540; "Stärke, Eintheilung, und Tagesbegebenheiten der Hauptarmee im Monate Januar," ÖStA KA, FA 1603, Nr. 30.

115. Schwarzenberg to Metternich, 22 January 1814, Klinkowström, *Österreichs Theilnahme*, No. 32, 801.

116. Caulaincourt's statements support the tsar's charges: "Austria, who long had boasted to me that she had made herself suspect among her allies by her feigned leaning toward us, and by the sloth and indecisiveness of her operations as well" (Caulaincourt, *No Peace with Napoleon*, 8).

117. Cook, "Schwarzenberg," 519.

118. Schwarzenberg to Metternich, 18 January 1814, Klinkowström, *Österreichs Theilnahme*, No. 30, 800.

119. Lefebvre de Béhaine, *Campagne de France*, 4:174. The Allies organized the occupied territories into four administrative districts: the Lower Rhine, the Middle Rhine, the Upper Rhine, and the Saône. The Lower Rhine consisted of the Roer, Ourthe, and Meuse-Inférieure Departments. The Middle Rhine contained the Mont-Tonnerre, Sarre, and Rhin-et-Moselle Departments. The Upper Rhine was formed by the Haut-Rhin and Bas-Rhin Departments. Finally, the

fourth administrative district was composed of territory detached from Switzerland as well as the Haute-Saône, Doubs, and Jura Departments. According to
Beauchamp, commerce and navigation resumed their course on the Rhine, and
"there prevailed in these provinces a tranquility that one could not believe possible in the midst of a general war" (Beauchamp, *Histoire des campagnes*, 1:141–2).

120. Napoleon to Mortier, 19 January 1814, *Correspondance*, No. 21,117, 27:55.
121. Mortier to Berthier, 23 January 1814, SHAT, C² 173.
122. Mortier to Belliard, 23 January 1814, 8:00 P.M., SHAT, C² 173.
123. Mortier to Napoleon, 24 January 1814, SHAT, C² 173; Janson, *Geschichte des Feldzuges in 1814*, 1:157; Lefebvre de Béhaine, *Campagne de France*, 4:179–80.
124. Mortier to Napoleon, 24 January 1814, SHAT, C² 173.
125. Mortier to Berthier, 24 January 1814, SHAT, C² 173.
126. Schwarzenberg to Francis, 25 January 1814, ÖStA KA, FA 1607, Nr. 582.
127. Sources for the battle of Bar-sur-Aube: Mortier to Napoleon and Berthier, 24 January 1814, SHAT, C² 173; Gyulay and Frederick William each wrote a "Relation
of the Affair at Bar-sur-Aube," 24 January 1814; Gyulay and Frederick William
to Schwarzenberg, 24 January 1814; Schwarzenberg to Francis, 25 January 1814,
ÖStA KA, FA 1607, Nrs. 547, 547b, 544, 546, and 582; Weil, *Campagne de 1814*,
1:165–7; Beauchamp, *Histoire des campagnes*, 1:161–4.
128. Casualty estimates vary between the German and French sources. Janson, in
Geschichte des Feldzuges in 1814, 1:158, claims the French lost 1,200 men including 190 prisoners, while Lefebvre de Béhaine, in *Campagne de France*, 4:181,
places Mortier's losses at a modest 500 killed and wounded. In *Geschichte des
Feldzuges 1814*, 60, Hiller's total of 1,500 French casualties appears exaggerated,
particularly when the German historian places Württemberger losses at thirteen
men. As for Allied losses, Janson estimates that of the 900 killed and wounded,
647 belonged to Gyulay's corps. According to Lefebvre de Béhaine the Allies lost
1,500 killed and wounded and 100 prisoners.
129. Mortier to Napoleon, 24 January 1814, SHAT, C² 173.
130. Mortier to Berthier, 24 January 1814, SHAT, C² 173.
131. Gyulay to Schwarzenberg, 25 January 1814, ÖStA KA, FA 1607, 575.
132. "Stärke, Eintheilung, und Tagesbegebenheiten der Hauptarmee im Monate Januar," ÖStA KA, FA 1603, Nr. 30.
133. Weil, *Campagne de 1814*, 1:141–2.

17. THE PROTOCOLS OF LANGRES

1. Quoted in Janson, *Geschichte des Feldzuges in 1814*, 1:150.
2. "Stärke, Eintheilung, und Tagesbegebenheiten der Hauptarmee im Monate Januar," ÖStA KA, FA 1603, Nr. 30.
3. Burghersh, *Operations of the Allied Armies*, 90.
4. Junot, *Memoirs of the Emperor Napoleon*, 3:346.
5. Gneisenau to Radetzky, 22 January 1814, ÖStA KA, FA 1606, Nr. 521.
6. Janson, *Geschichte des Feldzuges in 1814*, 1:3–4, 192.
7. Schwarzenberg to Marie Anna, 27 January 1814, Schwarzenberg, *Briefe*, No. 270,
370.
8. Bogdanovich, *Geschichte des Krieges*, 1:92.

9. Knesebeck to Gneisenau, 22 January 1814, GStA, Rep. 92, Nr. 23.

10. Schwarzenberg to Marie Anna, 21 January 1814, Schwarzenberg, *Briefe*, No. 270, 368.

11. Knesebeck to Gneisenau, 22 January 1814, GStA, Rep. 92, Nr. 23. Italics mine. Two drafts of this letter exist. The first, which was not sent to Gneisenau, stated that it would be a great mistake to grant Napoleon time to reorganize. Conversely, the second, which Gneisenau received, demanded negotiations to win time to ascertain Napoleon's military plans. No reason for this discrepancy exists. Delbrück suggests that Frederick William may have asked Knesebeck for revisions (Delbrück, *Gneisenau*, 4:35–6, 164–6).

12. Knesebeck to Gneisenau, 24 January 1814, GStA, Rep. 92, Nr. 23.

13. Knesebeck to Gneisenau, 27 January 1814, GStA, Rep. 92, Nr. 23.

14. Müffling to Knesebeck, 26 January 1814, in Janson, *Geschichte des Feldzuges in 1814*, appendix 54, 1:340–1.

15. Stein to Gneisenau, 24 January 1814, GStA, Rep. 92, Nr. 24a.

16. Gneisenau to Knesebeck, 27 January 1814, in Janson, *Geschichte des Feldzuges in 1814*, Appendix 54, 1:341–2.

17. Gneisenau to Stein, 27 January 1814, GStA, Rep. 92, Nr. 20b.

18. Schwarzenberg to Maria Anna, 29 January 1814, Schwarzenberg, *Briefe*, No. 279, 370–1.

19. Nicholson, *The Congress of Vienna*, 65–6.

20. Kissinger, *A World Restored*, 113.

21. Nicholson, *The Congress of Vienna*, 68; Ross, *European Diplomatic History*, 345; Roloff, *Politik und Kriegführung*, 36–7; Kissinger, *A World Restored*, 104.

22. Kissinger, *A World Restored*, 105.

23. Metternich, *Memoirs*, 1:223, 225.

24. Craig, "Problems of Coalition Warfare," 35; Nicholson, *The Congress of Vienna*, 70.

25. Kissinger, *A World Restored*, 113, 115.

26. Nipperdey, *Germany from Napoleon to Bismarck*, 70.

27. Roloff, *Politik und Kriegführung*, 37.

28. Metternich, *Memoirs*, 1:225.

29. Nicholson, *The Congress of Vienna*, 70; Roloff, *Politik und Kriegführung*, 37–8; Craig, "Problems of Coalition Warfare," 37.

30. Ross, *European Diplomatic History*, 345; Roloff, *Politik und Kriegführung*, 38–9.

31. Kissinger, *A World Restored*, 105.

32. Stewart, *Narrative of the War*, 255. Italics mine.

33. Nicholson, *The Congress of Vienna*, 70–1.

34. Metternich, *Memoirs*, 1:223.

35. Metternich to Schwarzenberg, 21 January 1814, Klinkowström, *Österreichs Theilnahme*, No. 31, 800. Italics mine.

36. Kissinger, *A World Restored*, 110.

37. Ibid., 109.

38. Kraehe, *Metternich's German Policy*, 1:284.

39. Mikhailovsky-Danilevsky, *History of the Campaign in France*, 42–3.

40. Craig, "Problems of Coalition Warfare," 35.

41. Kraehe, *Metternich's German Policy*, 1:284; Nicholson, *The Congress of Vienna*, 71–2; Kissinger, *A World Restored*, 115; Schroeder, *European Politics*, 497.
42. Metternich, *Memoirs*, 1:224.
43. Mikhailovsky-Danilevsky, *History of the Campaign in France*, 44.
44. Schwarzenberg to Francis, 26 January 1814, ÖStA KA, FA 1607, Nrs. 596 and 597.
45. Kissinger, *A World Restored*, 116.
46. Metternich, *Memoirs*, 1:224. According to Metternich, the principal questions were discussed between him and Alexander in private. Mikhailovsky-Danilevsky provides an abridged version of Metternich's questions in *History of the Campaign in France*, 40–1.
47. Bogdanovich, *Geschichte des Krieges*, 1:98; Craig, "Problems of Coalition Warfare," 37
48. Quoted in Mikhailovsky-Danilevsky, *History of the Campaign in France*, 43–4; Bogdanovich, *Geschichte des Krieges*, 1:97–8; Schroeder, *European Politics*, 497–8.
49. Metternich, *Memoirs*, 1:226–30; Kraehe, *Metternich's German Policy*, 1:288.
50. Craig, "Problems of Coalition Warfare," 37; Schroeder, *European Politics*, 497.
51. Fournier, *Congress von Châtillon, 306*; Ross, *European Diplomatic History*, 346; Craig, "Problems of Coalition Warfare," 37; Kraehe, *Metternich's German Policy*, 1:288–9.
52. Schwarzenberg to Marie Anna, 26 January 1814, Schwarzenberg, *Briefe*, No. 270, 369.
53. Metternich, *Memoirs*, 1:226.
54. Friederich, *Die Befreiungskriege*, 3:81–3.
55. Ibid.; Bogdanovich, *Geschichte des Krieges*, 1:96–7.
56. Friederich, *Die Befreiungskriege*, 3:87–8.
57. Schwarzenberg to Metternich, 29 January 1814, Klinkowström, *Österreichs Theilnahme*, No. 33, 803.
58. "The great personal friendship that existed between the monarchs aided this course of action," notes Stewart, in *Narrative of the War*, 250, "and Prussia acted in a degree of subordination to a bolder policy: she was forced to consider the mere view of her own safety. If she detached herself – unprepared and without arrangements – from Russia, to place herself as the advance guard of Europe against her, what could she expect from Russia other than resentment?"
59. Bogdanovich, *Geschichte des Krieges*, 1:92–3; Kissinger, *A World Restored*, 117.
60. Bogdanovich, *Geschichte des Krieges*, 1:93–4.
61. a Quoted in Beitzke, *Geschichte der deutschen Freiheitskriege*, 3:82–5.
62. Delbrück, *Gneisenau*, 4:28.
63. Friederich, *Die Befreiungskriege*, 3:81.

APPENDICES

1. Clausewitz to Gneisenau, n.d., GStA, Rep. 92, Nachlaß Gneisenau, Nr. 22.
2. Radetzky von Radetz, *Denkschriften*, 225–30.
3. Gneisenau to Alexander, 7 November 1813, in Pertz, *Gneisenau*, 3:527–31.
4. Gneisenau to Alexander, n.d., in Pertz, *Gneisenau*, 3:543–6.

5. Pro Memoria, 29 December 1813, ÖStA KA, FA 1603, 32b. Blücher forwarded this to Schwarzenberg on 1 January 1814, ÖSTA KA, FA 1603, 32a.

6. ÖStA KA, FA 1541, 6.

7. "Proclamation to the Dutch," 20 November 1813, BFA, No. 115.

8. "Proclamation to the Belgians," 10 December 1813, BFA, No. 118.

9. Le Préfet du Département des Vosges, Baron de l'Empire aux Maires du Département, 9 January 1814, ÖStA KA, FA 1605, Nr. ad254.

10. Gneisenau to Radetzky, 15 January 1814, ÖStA KA, FA 1605, 360.

11. Gneisenau to Knesebeck, 15 January 1814, in Delbrück, *Gneisenau*, 4:155–9.

12. Quoted in Lefebvre de Béhaine, *Campagne de France*, 2:538.

13. Napoleon to Metternich, 16 January 1814, *Correspondance*, No. 21,101, 27:42–4.

14. Victor to Berthier, 19 January 1814, SHAT, C² 172.

Index